Helen Hadley

CHAMBERS **HARRAP'S**

FRENCH
School
DICTIONARY

CHAMBERS
HARRAP

First published by Chambers Harrap Publishers Ltd 2005
7 Hopetoun Crescent
Edinburgh, EH7 4AY

ISBN 0550 10128 4

Designed and typeset by Chambers Harrap Publishers Ltd, Edinburgh
Printed in Italy by Legoprint

Contents

Contributors	iv
Preface	v
How to use your Dictionary	vi
Labels used in the Dictionary	xi
French-English side	1–302
French Verb Tables	303–326
English-French side	327–657

Contributors

Project Editor
Georges Pilard

Editors
Nadia Cornuau
Kate Nicholson
Anna Stevenson

Publishing Manager
Patrick White

Prepress Manager
Sharon McTeir

Prepress Controller
David Reid

Preface

The *Chambers Harrap's French School Dictionary* has been designed specifically for use by English-speaking learners of French aged 11 to 15; it contains over 12,000 entries which have been compiled with the target age group in mind and we have tried to make the book as simple and straightforward to use as possible.

We have deliberately avoided using confusing abbreviations in the text and instead have written all words in full. The text is clearly laid out and easy to find your way around, with headwords printed in blue, making them easy to locate. In addition, there are thousands of examples which show how the words are used.

Hundreds of notes on usage, grammatical difficulties, irregular plurals, French pronunciation and false friends also feature in the dictionary text. The notes are always given immediately after the relevant entries and have a blue background to make them stand out.

Feminine inflections of nouns and adjectives are always given both for headwords on the French-English side and for translations on the English-French side. Whenever possible, gender is indicated by an article (*la/la* or *un/une*) rather than by a *masculine/feminine* label as this makes it easier to memorize the gender of nouns.

French irregular verbs are clearly cross-referred to verb tables situated in the middle of the book. The verb tables are preceded by a short explanation of French tenses.

In order to stimulate pupils' curiosity about France and French life, there are several boxes on cultural topics such as *les délégués de classe*, *les colonies de vacances* and *le quatorze juillet* at the relevant entries.

Students should also be encouraged to take some time to go through the *How to use your Dictionary* section. This section explains the structure of a typical entry and shows how and where to find all the different types of information that the dictionary provides.

---

www

Photocopiable worksheets that accompany this dictionary can be downloaded from our website www.chambersharrap.co.uk

---

How to use your Dictionary

This dictionary has been designed:

1. to help you understand French words and phrases
2. to help you speak and write in French

This is why there are two parts to the dictionary:

The **first part**, which **goes from French into English**, will give you the translations of French words and phrases.

The **second part**, which **goes from English into French**, is to be used when you want to say or write something in French.

To check which part of dictionary you are in, look at the top of the page where it is marked *French-English* or *English-French*.

The top of the page will also tell you what the first and last words treated on that page are, so that you can locate the word you are looking for more easily.

As in an ordinary dictionary, words are listed alphabetically. They have been printed in blue to make them stand out.

1. The French-English side

This is the part of the dictionary you need to consult when you want to find out the meaning of a French word or phrase.

1. How do I know what type of word it is?

Each word is followed by a word in blue italics to help you identify what kind of word it is (for example a *noun*, a *verb*, an *adjective*, an *adverb* and so on). Next comes the translation and then, if necessary, some sentences showing different uses of the word:

LA **distance** *noun* distance; **à quelle distance sommes-nous de l'hôtel?** how far are we from the hotel?

accoucher *verb* to give birth; **elle a accouché d'une fille** she gave birth to a girl

discrètement *adverb* discreetly

2. How do I know if a noun is feminine or masculine?

Nouns are generally preceded by a definite article (*le* or *la*) so that you know if they are masculine or feminine (*le* for masculine and *la* for feminine).

LA **narine** *noun* nostril

When a noun starts with a vowel, an indefinite article (*un* or *une*) is given instead (this is because **L'** doesn't tell you if a noun is masculine or feminine).

UN **accessoire** *noun* accessory

However, there are types of words with which *un* or *une* would look very odd, so **L'** is given instead and there is a clear indication about whether the word is masculine or feminine:

L'**acier** *masculine noun* steel

L'**automne** *masculine noun* autumn

L'**Autriche** *feminine noun* Austria

3. How do I know what the feminine form of an adjective is?

The feminine form of an adjective is always given after the masculine form:

amical, amicale *adjective* friendly

amer, amère *adjective* bitter

Note that sometimes the masculine and the feminine forms of an adjective are the same (for example *facile, difficile, rouge, ridicule*).

4. What about plurals?

Irregular plurals (those which are not formed by adding an s) as well as plurals of hyphenated nouns (which are hard to predict) are always indicated in notes coming after the entry:

LE **râteau** *noun* rake

> The plural of *râteau* is *râteaux*.

LA **basse-cour** *noun* farmyard

> The plural of *basse-cour* is *basses-cours*.

5. Is there any help with conjugating verbs?

There are verb tables in the middle of the dictionary.

In the text, irregular verbs are accompanied by a note in a blue box that refers you to the relevant page of the verb tables.

dormir *verb* to sleep; **je dors bien dans ce lit** I sleep well in this bed

> See verb table p. 320.

When a verb is not accompanied by a note this means that it is a regular verb. The conjugation patterns of regular verbs are given at the beginning of the verb tables.

6. How do I choose the right translation?

First, **make sure you look up the right word**. Some words look the same but have completely different meanings. Here is an example:

UN **avocat¹** *noun* avocado

UN **avocat²**, UNE **avocate** *noun* lawyer

So if you need to translate the sentence *son père est avocat*, make sure you pick the second one.

In addition, try to work out what type of word you have to translate. For example, is it a noun, an adjective, a verb or a reflexive verb?

If you look up *reposer* to understand the sentence *le médecin a dit à ma mère de se reposer*, it is quite clear that the first translation won't work; it is the translation for the reflexive verb that you need to use:

reposer
1 *verb* to put back down
2 *reflexive verb* **se reposer** to rest, to have a rest

Note that the numbers in bold indicate that the word has various functions (for instance, it may be a noun as well as an adjective, or an ordinary verb as well a reflexive verb).

Remember: **the first translation you come across is not necessarily the one you are looking for,** so look at the others in the entry as well before making a decision. Think about the context in which the word is being used.

For instance, if you look up the word *bouchon* in order to understand the sentence *il est arrivé en retard parce qu'il y avait un bouchon sur la route*, then use your judgment...

LE **bouchon** *noun*
(**a**) top *(of a bottle)*
(**b**) cork
(**c**) traffic jam

Obviously, the correct translation can only be (c) as the other two would not make any sense in that sentence. Note that letters in brackets indicate different meanings.

7. What are all the notes for?

The notes in blue are there to give you additional help about many things, such as irregular plurals, pronunciation, spelling and also, very importantly, French words that look like English words but have a different meaning:

LA **cave** *noun* cellar

> Note that the English word *cave* is never a translation for the French word *cave*.

There are also some notes in boxes. These notes will tell you about various aspects of French life you might be unfamiliar with:

LE **TGV** *noun* high-speed train

> *TGV* is the abbreviation of *train à grande vitesse*. It does not change in the plural.

Le TGV
France has a network of high-speed trains that reach speeds of over 200 mph. TGVs have considerably reduced the travel times between many French cities.

2. The English-French side

This is the part of the dictionary you need to consult when you want to find out how to say or write something in French.

How do I go about translating something into French?

Make absolutely sure that you've got the right word before you translate anything, as some words look exactly the same but have different meanings.

For instance, if you want to translate the word *mug* in the "cup" sense, make sure you don't look up the word *mug* in the sense "to attack".

mug¹ *noun* *(for coffee, tea)* la grande tasse

mug² *verb* *(in the street)* agresser; **he was mugged on his way home yesterday** il s'est fait agresser hier en rentrant chez lui

Then make sure you look up the right section of the word. As on the French-English side, the numbers in bold placed just before the blue labels (such as *noun*, *verb*, *adjective* etc) mean that a word has various functions. For instance, it may be a noun as well as a verb or an adjective, as in the following example:

magic
1 *noun* la magie
2 *adjective* magique; **a magic wand** une baguette magique

So, before you translate the word *magic* into French, take a moment to decide if you want to use it as a noun or an adjective because the translation will be different in each case: **I'm interested in magic** = *je m'intéresse à la magie*, but **Jack has magic beans** = *Jack a des haricots magiques*.

Words can have several meanings even within the same function. The word *power*, for instance, will have different translations depending on whether it is used to mean *authority*, *strength*, *energy* or *electricity*. It is up to you to look carefully at the indications in brackets before you choose the translation you need:

> **power** *noun*
> (**a**) *(authority)* le pouvoir; **to be in power** être au pouvoir
> (**b**) *(strength)* la puissance; **military power** la puissance militaire
> (**c**) *(energy)* l'énergie *(feminine)*; **nuclear power** l'énergie nucléaire
> (**d**) *(electricity)* le courant électrique; **a power cut** une coupure de courant; **a power station** une centrale électrique

If you want to translate something into French but you can't find the English word you're looking for in the dictionary, try another word with a similar meaning. For instance, if you can't find the adjective *magnificent*, try *beautiful* instead.

Labels used in the Dictionary

adjective An adjective is a word which provides extra information about a noun, describing what something is like, eg *a small house*/une **petite** maison, *a red car*/une voiture **rouge**, *an interesting book*/un livre **intéressant**.

adverb An adverb is a word which gives a more precise meaning to a verb (eg *he eats slowly*/il mange **lentement**), an adjective (eg *the soup is* **very** *hot*/la soupe est **très** chaude) or another adverb (eg *he drives* **really** *fast*/il conduit **très** vite).

article An article is a word that accompanies a noun, eg *the cat*/ **le** chat, *a turtle*/ **une** tortue.

conjunction A conjunction is a word that joins sentences, phrases or words (such as *and*/ **et**, *but*/ **mais**, *or*/ **ou**).

exclamation An exclamation is a word or sentence used to express surprise or wonder, eg *what!*/ **quoi!**, *how lucky!*/ **quelle chance!**, *no way!*/ **pas question!**, *great!*/ **super!**

feminine In French, nouns and pronouns are either masculine or feminine. Feminine nouns are used with the articles *la* or *une*. Adjectives also have masculine and feminine forms, eg *mou*/ **molle**.

masculine In French, nouns and pronouns are either masculine or feminine. Masculine nouns are used with the articles *le* or *un*. Adjectives also have masculine and feminine forms, eg *beau*/ **belle**.

noun A noun is a word which refers to a living creature (eg *Paul*, *a girl*/une **fille**, *a fish*/un **poisson**), a thing (eg *a car*/une **voiture**, *a pen*/un **stylo**), a place (eg *Scotland*/l'**Écosse**, an *ocean*/un **océan**) or an idea (eg *freedom*/la **liberté**, *life*/la **vie**, *time*/le **temps**).

number In this dictionary all numbers – whether cardinal (eg *one*, *two*, *three*/ **un**, **deux**, **trois**) or ordinal (eg *first*, *second*, *third*/ **premier**, **deuxième**, **troisième**) – and fractions are labelled *number*.

plural noun This label is given when a word is always (or nearly always) used in the plural, eg *glasses*/les **lunettes**.

preposition   A preposition is a word placed before a noun or pronoun to show its relation to another word, eg ***through** the door/* **par** la porte, *she came **with** me/*elle est venue **avec** moi, *he's **at** the swimming pool/*il est **à** la piscine.

pronoun   A pronoun is a word that stands for a noun, eg *where's Anna? – **she's** in the kitchen/*où est Anna? – **elle** est dans la cuisine, *I like his parents, **they're** very kind/* j'aime bien ses parents, **ils** sont très gentils.

reflexive verb   In French, reflexive verbs are verbs which start with **se** in the infinitive, such as **se laver**, **se souvenir**, **se battre** etc.

verb   A verb is a word which describes an action, eg *to **sing**/* **chanter**, *to **work**/* **travailler**, *to **laugh**/* **rire** or a state or a situation, eg *to **be**/* **être**, *to **have**/* **avoir**, *to **hope**/* **espérer**, *to **remain**/* **rester**.

French-English

a *see* **avoir**
il a une voiture rouge he has a red car;
elle a mangé une glace she ate an ice
cream

A is a form of the verb *avoir* in the
present tense. See verb table p. 313.

à *preposition*
(**a**) to; **nous allons à Paris** we're going
to Paris; **de lundi à vendredi** from
Monday to Friday
(**b**) at, in; **il est à la piscine** he's at the
swimming pool; **la malle est au gre-
nier** the chest is in the attic
(**c**) in; **au vingtième siècle** in the
twentieth century; **au printemps** in
spring
(**d**) on; **il a des boutons au visage** he
has spots on his face; **il écrit au tableau** he's writing on the board; **au
troisième étage** on the third floor
(**e**) at; **il arrivera à midi** he'll be here at
noon
(**f**) with; **l'homme à la barbe blanche**
the man with the white beard
(**g**) to; **il apprend à lire** he's learning
to read; **j'ai des choses à faire** I've got
things to do; **il y a plein de choses à
voir dans cette région** there's lots to
see in that region
(**h**) from; **Orléans est à cent kilomètres de Paris** Orléans is a hundred
kilometres from Paris
(**i**) away; **c'est à trois kilomètres d'ici**
it's three kilometres away
(**j**) **il roulait à plus de cent à l'heure**
he was doing more than a hundred kilometres an hour; **il s'est acheté une
veste à mille euros** he bought a thou-
sand-euro jacket

(**k**) **à bicyclette** by bicycle; **à pied** on
foot; **je l'ai écrit au crayon** I wrote it
in pencil
(**l**) **ce livre est à elle** this book is hers;
à qui est ce livre? whose book is this?;
c'est à moi it's mine; **c'est à vous de
décider** it's up to you to decide; **c'est
à elle de jouer** it's her turn to play
(**m**) **à demain!** see you tomorrow!; **à
plus tard!** see you later!

Note that *à* + *le* is contracted to *au* (as
in *il est au cinéma*) and *à* + *les* to *aux*
(as in *aux États-Unis*). However, *à* +
la and *à* + *l'* do not change.

abandonner *verb*
(**a**) to abandon; **ils ont abandonné
leur chien** they abandoned their dog
(**b**) to give up; **j'en ai assez, j'abandonne** I've had enough, I give up

ᴜɴ **abat-jour** *noun* lampshade

The word *abat-jour* does not change
in the plural.

abattre *verb*
(**a**) to cut down *(a tree)*
(**b**) to knock down *(a wall)*
(**c**) to shoot dead *(a person)*
(**d**) to shoot down *(a plane)*

See verb table p. 320.

abattu, abattue *adjective*
(**a**) dejected
(**b**) exhausted

Abattu(e) is the past participle of the
verb *abattre*.

ᴜɴᴇ **abbaye** *noun* abbey

ᴜɴᴇ **abeille** *noun* bee

abîmer
1 *verb* to damage
2 *reflexive verb* **s'abîmer** to get damaged

UN **abonnement** *noun* subscription

s'abonner *reflexive verb* **s'abonner à un magazine** to take out a subscription to a magazine; **il est abonné au Times** he has a subscription to the Times

abord *noun* **d'abord** first; **d'abord je dois faire mes devoirs** first I have to do my homework

aborder *verb*
(**a**) to deal with *(a topic)*
(**b**) to reach land

aboutir *verb* **aboutir à quelque chose** to lead to something; **le chemin aboutit dans un champ** the path leads to a field; **les négociations n'ont abouti à rien** the negotiations came to nothing

aboyer *verb* to bark

UN **abri** *noun*
(**a**) shelter; **se mettre à l'abri** to take shelter; **mettons-nous à l'abri de la pluie sous cet arbre** let's shelter from the rain under this tree
(**b**) **être sans abri** to be homeless

UN **abricot** *noun* apricot

The *t* in *abricot* is not pronounced.

s'abriter *reflexive verb* to shelter, to take shelter; **ils se sont abrités de la pluie** they took shelter from the rain

abrutissant, abrutissante *adjective* mind-numbing

UNE **absence** *noun* absence; **quelqu'un a téléphoné pendant ton absence** somebody phoned while you were away

absent, absente
1 *adjective* absent
2 *noun* **un absent, une absente** an absent person; **il y avait cinq absents aujourd'hui en classe** five people were absent from school today

absolument *adverb* absolutely

absurde *adjective* ridiculous, absurd; **ce qu'il dit est absurde** what he says doesn't make any sense

abuser *verb*
(**a**) to go too far; **alors là, tu abuses!** now you're going too far!
(**b**) **abuser de quelque chose** to take advantage of something; **n'abuse pas de sa gentillesse** don't take advantage of his kindness
(**c**) **il ne faut pas abuser des médicaments** you mustn't take too much medicine

UNE **accalmie** *noun* lull

accélérer *verb* to accelerate, to speed up

UN **accent** *noun*
(**a**) *(way of pronouncing)* accent; **elle a l'accent allemand** she has a German accent
(**b**) *(on a letter)* **un accent aigu** an acute accent; **un accent grave** a grave accent; **un accent circonflexe** a circumflex accent

The *t* in *accent* is not pronounced.

accentuer *verb*
(**a**) to emphasize *(a point)*
(**b**) to stress *(a syllable)*

accepter *verb*
(**a**) to accept *(a gift, a situation)*
(**b**) **accepter de faire quelque chose** to agree to do something

UN **accessoire** *noun* accessory

UN **accident** *noun* accident; **un accident de la route** a road accident; **un accident d'avion** a plane crash

The *t* in *accident* is not pronounced.

accompagner *verb* to go with, to come with; **il m'a accompagné à la gare** he came to the station with me

accomplir *verb* to carry out, to accomplish

UN accord
1 *noun* agreement; **être d'accord avec quelqu'un** to agree with somebody; **se mettre d'accord avec quelqu'un** to come to an agreement with somebody
2 *adverb* **d'accord!** all right!

UN accordéon *noun* accordion

accorder *verb*
(**a**) to grant *(permission, an interview)*
(**b**) to tune *(a musical instrument)*

accoucher *verb* to give birth; **elle a accouché d'une fille** she gave birth to a girl

s'accoutumer *reflexive verb* **s'accoutumer à quelque chose** to get used to something

UN accrochage *noun* minor collision *(between vehicles)*

accrocher
1 *verb*
(**a**) to hang, to hang up *(a coat, a painting)*; **il a accroché sa veste au portemanteau** he hung his jacket on the coat rack
(**b**) to hitch up *(a trailer, a caravan)*; **nous avons accroché la remorque à la voiture** we hitched up the trailer to the car
2 *reflexive verb* **s'accrocher** to hang on; **s'accrocher à quelque chose** to hang on to something

s'accroupir *reflexive verb* to squat down; **elles étaient accroupies** they were squatting

L'accueil *masculine noun*
(**a**) welcome; **un accueil chaleureux** a warm welcome
(**b**) reception; **adressez-vous à l'accueil** ask at reception

accueillir *verb* to welcome *(a guest, a friend)*

See verb table p. 320.

accumuler
1 *verb* to accumulate
2 *reflexive verb* **s'accumuler** to pile up

accuser *verb* to accuse

UN achat *noun* purchase; **faire des achats** to do some shopping; **elle a fait l'achat d'un ordinateur** she bought a computer

acheter *verb* to buy

achever *verb* to finish, to finish off

Note that the English verb *to achieve* is never a translation for the French verb *achever*.

L'acier *masculine noun* steel

L'acné *feminine noun* acne

UN acte *noun* act

UN acteur *noun* actor; **il est acteur** he's an actor

UNE action *noun* action; **une bonne action** a good deed

UNE activité *noun* activity

UNE actrice *noun* actress; **elle est actrice** she's an actress

L'actualité *feminine noun* current affairs; **les actualités** the television news

actuel, actuelle *adjective* current, present

Note that the English word *actual* is never a translation for the French word *actuel*.

actuellement *adverb* currently

Note that the English word *actually* is never a translation for the French word *actuellement*.

UNE addition *noun*
(**a**) sum; **faire une addition** to do a sum
(**b**) bill *(at a restaurant)*

additionner *verb* to add up

UN adhérent, UNE adhérente *noun* member

adhérer *verb* **adhérer à un club** to join a club; **elle a décidé d'adhérer à un club de gym** she decided to join a gym

adieu *masculine noun* goodbye; **dire adieu à quelqu'un** to say goodbye to somebody

admettre *verb*
(a) to admit; **il a admis qu'il s'était trompé** he admitted that he'd made a mistake
(b) to allow; **je n'admets pas que tu me parles sur ce ton!** I won't have you speaking to me in that tone of voice!

See verb table p. 322.

admirer *verb* to admire

admis, admise *see* **admettre**
il a admis qu'il s'était trompé he admitted that he'd made a mistake

Admis (e) is the past participle of the verb *admettre*.

UN **adolescent**, UNE **adolescente** *noun* teenager

adorer *verb* to love, to adore

UNE **adresse** *noun* address; **une adresse électronique** an e-mail address

adresser
1 *verb*
(a) **adresser la parole à quelqu'un** to speak to somebody
(b) **adresser une lettre à quelqu'un** to send somebody a letter
2 *reflexive verb* **s'adresser**
(a) to go and speak to; **adressez-vous au patron** go and speak to the manager
(b) to go and ask; **adressez-vous à la réception** go and ask at reception
(c) to be aimed; **ce livre s'adresse aux adolescents** this book is aimed at teenagers

adroit, adroite *adjective*
(a) skilful
(b) clever

UN/UNE **adversaire** *noun* opponent

aérer *verb* to air; **il faut aérer ta chambre** you need to air your room

aérien, aérienne *adjective* air *(transport, attack)*; **une photo aérienne** an aerial photo; **une compagnie aérienne** an airline

UNE **aérogare** *noun* airport terminal

UN **aéroglisseur** *noun* hovercraft

UN **aéroport** *noun* airport

The *t* in *aéroport* is not pronounced.

UNE **affaire**
1 *noun*
(a) matter; **c'est une affaire très délicate** it's a very delicate matter
(b) case; **l'affaire des diamants volés** the case of the stolen diamonds
(c) bargain; **faire une bonne affaire** to get a bargain
2 *feminine plural noun* **les affaires**
(a) things, belongings; **prépare tes affaires pour demain** get your things ready for tomorrow
(b) business, concern; **occupe-toi de tes affaires** mind your own business
(c) business; **il est dans les affaires** he's in business

affamé, affamée *adjective* starving

affectueux, affectueuse *adjective* affectionate, loving

UNE **affiche** *noun* poster

afficher *verb*
(a) to put up, to hang up *(a poster, a notice)*
(b) to display

affreux, affreuse *adjective*
(a) horrible, awful
(b) ugly

affronter *verb* to face; **l'Angleterre affrontera l'Allemagne en finale** England will face Germany in the final; **affronter le mauvais temps** to brave the bad weather

afin
1 *preposition* **afin de faire quelque chose** in order to do something; **il a pris son portable afin de pouvoir me contacter** he took his mobile phone so that he'd be able to contact me

2 *conjunction* **afin que** so that; **il m'a envoyé un billet d'avion afin que je vienne le voir** he sent me a plane ticket so that I could go and visit him

UN **Africain,** UNE **Africaine** *noun (person)* African

africain, africaine *adjective* African

L'**Afrique** *feminine noun* Africa; **l'Afrique du Nord** North Africa; **l'Afrique du Sud** South Africa; **l'Afrique australe** southern Africa

agacer *verb* to irritate, to annoy; **il m'agace vraiment avec ses questions idiotes** he's really annoying me asking all those stupid questions

L'**âge** *masculine noun* age; **quel âge a-t-il?** how old is he?; **l'âge bête** the awkward age

âgé, âgée *adjective*
(a) old, elderly; **il a des parents âgés** he has elderly parents
(b) **un enfant âgé de huit ans** an eight-year-old child

UNE **agence** *noun*
(a) agency; **une agence de voyages** a travel agent's
(b) branch *(of a bank)*

UN **agenda** *noun* diary; **un agenda électronique** a personal organizer

Note that the English word *agenda* is never a translation for the French word *agenda*.

UN **agent** *noun* **un agent de police** a policeman/a policewoman; **un agent secret** a secret agent

The *t* in *agent* is not pronounced.

agir
1 *verb* to act; **il faut agir vite** we must act quickly
2 *reflexive verb* **s'agir**
(a) **s'agir de...** to be about...; **de quoi s'agit-il?** what is it about?; **il s'agit d'une famille de paysans qui part s'installer en Australie** it's about a

peasant family who emigrate to Australia
(b) **il s'agit de ne pas se tromper** we mustn't make any mistakes; **il s'agit de se dépêcher** we've got to hurry

agité, agitée *adjective*
(a) restless; **les enfants sont agités parce qu'ils ne sont pas sortis de la journée** the children are restless because they haven't been out all day
(b) rough; **la mer est agitée** the sea is rough

agiter
1 *verb*
(a) to shake *(a bottle)*
(b) to wave *(a flag, one's arms)*
2 *reflexive verb* **s'agiter**
(a) to fidget
(b) to become restless

UN **agneau** *noun* lamb

The plural of *agneau* is *agneaux*.

UNE **agrafe** *noun* staple

agrafer *verb* to staple

UNE **agrafeuse** *noun* stapler

agréable *adjective* pleasant, nice

agresser *verb* to attack

agricole *adjective* agricultural

UN **agriculteur,** UNE **agricultrice** *noun* farmer; **il est agriculteur** he's a farmer

ai *see* **avoir**
j'ai un téléphone portable I have a mobile phone; **j'ai fermé la porte** I closed the door

Ai is the form of the verb *avoir* used with *je* in the present tense. See verb table p. 313.

L'**aide** *feminine noun* help; **à l'aide!** help!; **il s'est fait une béquille à l'aide d'un bâton** he made a crutch out of a stick

aider *verb* to help; **il m'a aidé à faire mes devoirs** he helped me do my homework

aie, aies *see* avoir

ça m'étonnerait que j'aie le temps de le faire I don't expect I'll have time to do it; je ne pense pas que tu aies assez d'argent pour l'acheter I don't think you've got enough money to buy it

> *Aie* and *aies* are forms of the verb *avoir* in the subjunctive. See verb table p. 313.

aïe *exclamation* ouch

UN **aigle** *noun* eagle

aigre *adjective* sour

aigu, aiguë *adjective*
(a) sharp *(pain)*
(b) high-pitched
(c) un accent aigu an acute accent

UNE **aiguille** *noun*
(a) needle
(b) hand *(of a clock)*; dans le sens des aiguilles d'une montre clockwise; dans le sens inverse des aiguilles d'une montre anti-clockwise

L'**ail** *masculine noun* garlic; je n'aime pas l'ail I don't like garlic

UNE **aile** *noun* wing

aille, ailles *see* aller

il faut que j'aille chez le dentiste I need to go to the dentist; j'aimerais que tu ailles acheter du pain I would like you to go and buy some bread

> *Aille* and *ailles* are forms of the verb *aller* in the subjunctive. See verb table p. 312.

ailleurs *adverb*
(a) elsewhere, somewhere else
(b) d'ailleurs besides, anyway

aimable *adjective* kind

UN **aimant** *noun* magnet

aimer *verb*
(a) to love
(b) to like
(c) aimer mieux to prefer; j'aimerais mieux rester à la maison I'd rather stay at home

aîné, aînée
1 *adjective*
(a) elder
(b) eldest
2 *noun* un aîné, une aînée an eldest child; c'est elle l'aînée des enfants she is the eldest child

ainsi *adverb*
(a) in this way; c'est ainsi qu'il est devenu millionnaire that's how he became a millionaire
(b) ainsi que as well as; mon père ainsi que ma mère my father as well as my mother
(c) et ainsi de suite and so on

L'**air** *masculine noun*
(a) air; je vais prendre l'air I'm going to get some fresh air; ça manque d'air ici it's stuffy in here; un concert en plein air an open-air concert
(b) tune; j'aime bien cet air I like this tune
(c) expression, look; il avait l'air déçu he looked disappointed

L'**aise** *feminine noun* être à l'aise to be comfortable, to be at ease; être mal à l'aise to be uncomfortable, to be ill at ease; se mettre à l'aise to make oneself comfortable

UNE **aisselle** *noun* armpit

ait *see* avoir

j'ai peur qu'il ait oublié I'm afraid he might have forgotten

> *Ait* is a form of the verb *avoir* in the subjunctive. See verb table p. 313.

ajouter *verb* to add

UNE **alarme** *noun* alarm; une alarme de voiture a car alarm; donner l'alarme to raise the alarm

L'**alcool** *masculine noun* alcohol; elle ne boit pas d'alcool she doesn't drink alcohol; de l'alcool à 90° surgical spirit

LES **alentours** *masculine plural noun* dans les alentours in the area; aux alentours de midi around noon

L'**Algérie** *feminine noun* Algeria

UN **Algérien,** UNE **Algérienne** *noun (person)* Algerian

algérien, algérienne *adjective* Algerian

LES **algues** *feminine plural noun* seaweed; **il y a des algues sur la plage** there's seaweed on the beach

UN **aliment** *noun* food

L'**alimentation** *feminine noun*
(a) diet; **une alimentation saine** a healthy diet
(b) **un magasin d'alimentation** a grocer's (shop)

UNE **allée** *noun*
(a) path *(in a park, a garden)*
(b) drive *(leading to a house)*
(c) aisle *(in a cinema, a supermarket)*

L'**Allemagne** *feminine noun* Germany

UN **Allemand,** UNE **Allemande** *noun (person)* German

allemand, allemande
1 *adjective* German; **l'économie allemande** the German economy
2 *masculine noun* **l'allemand** *(language)* German; **il parle allemand** he speaks German

> In French, only the noun for the inhabitants of a country takes a capital letter, never the adjective or the noun for the language.

aller
1 *verb*
(a) to go; **allons-y!** let's go!; **je suis allé à la piscine hier** I went to the swimming pool yesterday; **allez, dépêche-toi!** come on, hurry up!
(b) **aller à quelqu'un** to suit somebody; **cette robe te va bien** that dress suits you
(c) **il va bien** he is well; **elle ne va pas bien** she is not well; **comment vas-tu?** how are you?; **tout va bien** everything's fine
(d) *(indicating the future tense)* to go; **je vais le prévenir** I'm going to warn

him; **il va partir** he's going to leave
2 *reflexive verb* **s'en aller** to go, to leave; **il s'en va demain** he's leaving tomorrow

> See verb table p. 312.

3 *masculine noun*
(a) outward journey
(b) single, single ticket; **un aller Paris, s'il vous plaît** a single to Paris, please

UNE **allergie** *noun* allergy; **une allergie aux cacahouètes** a peanut allergy

allô *exclamation* hello; **allô, pourrais-je parler à Pierre, s'il vous plaît?** hello, could I speak to Pierre, please?

> *Allô* is only used when making a phone call or answering the phone.

allonger
1 *verb* to stretch out; **allonge les jambes** stretch out your legs
2 *reflexive verb* **s'allonger** to lie down

allumer
1 *verb*
(a) to turn on, to switch on *(a light, the television, a heater)*
(b) to light *(a fire, a candle, a cigarette, a stove)*
2 *reflexive verb* **s'allumer** to light up, to come on; **un voyant s'allume quand le réservoir est presque vide** a light comes on when the tank is nearly empty

UNE **allumette** *noun* match; **une boîte d'allumettes** a box of matches

L'**allure** *feminine noun*
(a) speed, pace; **à toute allure** at top speed; **il faut accélérer l'allure sinon on va arriver en retard** we need to speed up or we'll be late
(b) look; **il a vraiment de l'allure dans son nouveau costume** he looks really stylish in his new suit; **il a une drôle d'allure avec ce chapeau** he looks funny in that hat

alors *adverb*
(a) then; **s'il ne peut pas venir me**

chercher, **alors je prendrai un taxi** if he can't come and pick me up, then I'll get a taxi

(**b**) so; **il pleuvait, alors j'ai pris mon parapluie** it was raining, so I took my umbrella

(**c**) **alors que** even though; **il est allé au cinéma alors qu'il avait promis de venir avec moi à la piscine** he went to the cinema even though he had promised to come swimming with me

(**d**) while; **elle dort alors que les autres travaillent** she's sleeping while the others are working

UNE **alouette** *noun* lark

LES **Alpes** *feminine plural noun* the Alps; **aller dans les Alpes** to go to the Alps

L'**alphabet** *masculine noun* alphabet

L'**alpinisme** *masculine noun* mountaineering; **il fait de l'alpinisme** he does mountaineering

L'**altitude** *feminine noun* height; **l'avion volait à 8000 mètres d'altitude** the plane was flying at an altitude of 8,000 metres; **le Mont Blanc fait 4807 mètres d'altitude** Mont Blanc is 4,807 metres high

UNE **amande** *noun* almond

UN **amateur** *noun*
(**a**) amateur
(**b**) enthusiast; **c'est un amateur de jazz** he's a jazz enthusiast

UNE **ambassade** *noun* embassy

L'**ambiance** *feminine noun* atmosphere; **il y a une bonne ambiance en classe** there's a good atmosphere in class; **il y avait de l'ambiance à la soirée** it was a lively party

UNE **âme** *noun* soul

UNE **amélioration** *noun* improvement

améliorer
1 *verb* to improve
2 *reflexive verb* **s'améliorer** to improve

UNE **amende** *noun* fine

amener *verb* to bring; **tu peux amener un copain si tu veux** you can bring a friend if you like

amer, amère *adjective* bitter

UN **Américain,** UNE **Américaine** *noun (person)* American

américain, américaine *adjective* American

In French, only the noun for the inhabitants of a country takes a capital letter, never the adjective.

L'**Amérique** *feminine noun* America; **l'Amérique du Nord** North America; **l'Amérique du Sud** South America; **l'Amérique latine** Latin America; **l'Amérique centrale** Central America

UN **ami,** UNE **amie** *noun*
(**a**) friend
(**b**) **un petit ami** a boyfriend; **une petite amie** a girlfriend; **c'est la petite amie de mon frère** she's my brother's girlfriend

amical, amicale *adjective* friendly

The masculine plural of *amical* is *amicaux*.

L'**amitié** *feminine noun*
(**a**) friendship
(**b**) **amitiés** *(at the end of a letter)* best wishes

L'**amour** *masculine noun* love

amoureux, amoureuse *adjective* **être amoureux de quelqu'un** to be in love with somebody; **tomber amoureux de quelqu'un** to fall in love with somebody

UNE **ampoule** *noun*
(**a**) light bulb; **changer une ampoule** to change a light bulb
(**b**) blister; **il a des ampoules aux pieds** he's got blisters on his feet

amusant, amusante *adjective* funny, amusing

amuser
1 *verb* to amuse, to entertain
2 *reflexive verb* **s'amuser**

(**a**) to have fun, to enjoy oneself
(**b**) to play

LES **amygdales** *feminine plural noun* tonsils

Amygdales is pronounced "amidal".

UN **an** *noun* year; **il a sept ans** he's seven years old

UNE **analyse** *noun*
(**a**) analysis
(**b**) test; **une analyse de sang** a blood test

UN **ananas** *noun* pineapple

UN **ancêtre** *noun* ancestor

UN **anchois** *noun* anchovy

ancien, ancienne *adjective*
(**a**) old; **mon ancienne voiture** my old car
(**b**) antique; **des meubles anciens** antique furniture
(**c**) former; **l'ancien Premier ministre** the former Prime Minister

UNE **ancre** *noun* anchor

UN **âne** *noun* donkey

UN **ange** *noun* angel

UNE **angine** *noun* throat infection

UN **Anglais**, UNE **Anglaise** *noun (person)* Englishman/Englishwoman

anglais, anglaise
1 *adjective* English
2 *masculine noun* **l'anglais** *(language)* English; **il parle anglais** he speaks English

In French, only the noun for the inhabitants of a country takes a capital letter, never the adjective or the noun for the language.

UN **angle** *noun* angle; **la maison qui fait l'angle** the house on the corner

L'**Angleterre** *feminine noun* England

UNE **anguille** *noun* eel

UN **animal** *noun* animal; **un animal domestique** a pet

The plural of *animal* is *animaux*.

UN **animateur**, UNE **animatrice** *noun*
(**a**) presenter *(on the radio, TV)*; **il est animateur** he's a presenter
(**b**) organizer, leader *(in an activity club)*

animé, animée *adjective*
(**a**) lively; **c'est une ville très animée** it's a very lively town
(**b**) **un dessin animé** *(film)* a cartoon

UN **anneau** *noun* ring

The plural of *anneau* is *anneaux*.

UNE **année** *noun* year; **bonne année!** happy new year!

UN **anniversaire** *noun*
(**a**) birthday; **joyeux anniversaire!** happy birthday!
(**b**) anniversary; **anniversaire de mariage** wedding anniversary

UNE **annonce** *noun*
(**a**) advertisement, ad; **les petites annonces** the small ads
(**b**) announcement

annoncer
1 *verb* to announce
2 *reflexive verb* **s'annoncer** **ça s'annonce bien** it looks promising

UN **annuaire** *noun* telephone directory

annuel, annuelle *adjective* annual, yearly

annuler *verb* to cancel

UNE **anse** *noun* handle

L'**Antarctique** *masculine noun* the Antarctic, Antarctica

UNE **antenne** *noun*
(**a**) aerial; **une antenne parabolique** a satellite dish
(**b**) feeler, antenna

UN **antibiotique** *noun* antibiotic; **il est sous antibiotiques** he's on antibiotics

UN **Antillais**, UNE **Antillaise** *noun (person)* West Indian

antillais, antillaise *adjective* West Indian

LES **Antilles** *feminine plural noun* the West Indies

antipathique *adjective* unfriendly, unpleasant

UNE **antiquité** *noun* antique; **un magasin d'antiquités** an antique shop

UN **antivol** *noun*
(a) lock
(b) antitheft device

anxieux, anxieuse *adjective* anxious

août *or masculine noun* August; **le premier août** the first of August; **le 15 août** the 15th of August

In French, the names of months are not written with a capital.

apaiser *verb*
(a) to calm down
(b) to soothe

apercevoir
1 *verb* to see
2 *reflexive verb* **s'apercevoir** s'apercevoir de quelque chose to realize something, to notice something; **il s'est aperçu que la porte était ouverte** he noticed that the door was open

See verb table p. 322.

UN **aphte** *noun* mouth ulcer

aplatir *verb* to flatten

UNE **apostrophe** *noun* apostrophe

apparaître *verb* to appear

See verb table p. 320.

UN **appareil** *noun*
(a) device; **un appareil photo** a camera; **les appareils ménagers** household appliances
(b) brace *(for teeth)*
(c) *(telephone)* **qui est à l'appareil?** who's speaking?; **Paul à l'appareil!** Paul speaking!; **on te demande à l'appareil** you're wanted on the phone
(d) aircraft; **l'appareil s'est écrasé au**

décollage the aircraft crashed on take-off

L'**apparence** *feminine noun* appearance

UN **appartement** *noun* flat

The *t* in *appartement* is not pronounced.

appartenir *verb* **appartenir à quelqu'un** to belong to somebody; **ce vélo ne m'appartient pas** this bike doesn't belong to me

See verb table p. 324.

apparu, apparue *see* **apparaître** **la fée est apparue** the fairy appeared

Apparu(e) is the past participle of the verb *apparaître*.

UN **appel** *noun*
(a) call, shout; **un appel au secours** a cry for help; **faire un appel de phares** to flash one's headlights
(b) phone call
(c) **faire l'appel** to call the register; **manquer à l'appel** to be absent

appeler
1 *verb*
(a) to call; **appeler au secours** to call for help
(b) to phone, to call
2 *reflexive verb* **s'appeler** to be called; **il s'appelle John** his name is John, he's called John

L'**appendicite** *feminine noun* appendicitis; **se faire opérer de l'appendicite** to have one's appendix out

L'**appétit** *masculine noun* appetite; **bon appétit!** enjoy your meal!

applaudir *verb* to clap, to applaud

LES **applaudissements** *masculine plural noun* applause

appliquer
1 *verb*
(a) to apply, to put on
(b) to enforce *(a law)*
2 *reflexive verb* **s'appliquer**

(a) to apply oneself *(to one's work)*
(b) to apply; **cette règle ne s'applique pas dans notre cas** this rule doesn't apply in our case

apporter *verb* to bring

apprécier *verb* to like, to appreciate

apprendre *verb*
(a) to learn
(b) to teach
(c) to hear *(news)*; **j'ai appris la nouvelle par mon frère** I heard the news from my brother
(d) to tell; **c'est mon frère qui m'a appris la nouvelle** my brother told me the news

See verb table p. 322.

L'**apprentissage** *masculine noun*
(a) training
(b) apprenticeship
(c) learning

apprivoiser *verb* to tame

approcher
1 *verb*
(a) to get closer; **approcher de quelqu'un** to get closer to somebody
(b) to move closer to; **approche ta chaise de la table** move your chair closer to the table
2 *reflexive verb* **s'approcher** to move closer; **approche-toi!** come closer!; **ne t'approche pas trop du bord!** don't go too close to the edge!; **ils se sont approchés de moi** they came up to me

approuver *verb* to approve of; **j'approuve ta décision** I approve of your decision; **mon frère a décidé de devenir acteur, mais mes parents ne l'approuvent pas** my brother has decided to become an actor, but my parents don't approve

appuyer
1 *verb*
(a) to rest, to lean; **il a appuyé l'échelle contre le mur** he leaned the ladder against the wall
(b) **appuyer sur quelque chose** to press something; **appuie sur le bouton** press the button
2 *reflexive verb* **s'appuyer** s'appuyer sur quelque chose to lean on something; **s'appuyer contre quelque chose** to lean against something; **il s'appuyait sur un bâton** he was leaning on a stick

après
1 *preposition* after; **après tout** after all; **d'après moi** in my opinion; **d'après lui** according to him
2 *adverb* after, afterwards; **je ferai ça après** I'll do that after; **il a pris le train d'après** he caught the next train

après-demain *adverb* the day after tomorrow

UN/UNE **après-midi** *noun* afternoon

The word *après-midi* can be masculine or feminine. It does not change in the plural.

UNE **aquarelle** *noun* watercolour (painting)

UN **aquarium** *noun*
(a) fish tank
(b) aquarium

UN/UNE **Arabe** *noun (person)* Arab

arabe
1 *adjective*
(a) Arab *(town, custom, tale)*
(b) Arabic *(word, dialect, writing)*
2 *masculine noun* **l'arabe** *(language)* Arabic; **il parle arabe** he speaks Arabic

In French, only the noun for the inhabitants of a country takes a capital letter, never the adjective or the noun for the language.

L'**Arabie saoudite** *feminine noun* Saudi Arabia

UNE **araignée** *noun* spider

UN **arbitre** *noun*
(a) referee
(b) umpire

UN **arbre** *noun* tree; **un arbre généalogique** a family tree

UN **arbuste** *noun* shrub

UN **arc** *noun* bow *(weapon)*

UN **arc-en-ciel** *noun* rainbow

> The plural of *arc-en-ciel* is *arcs-en-ciel*.

UNE **arche** *noun* arch

UN/UNE **archéologue** *noun* archaeologist; **il est archéologue** he's an archaeologist

UN/UNE **architecte** *noun* architect; **elle est architecte** she's an architect

L'**Arctique** *masculine noun* the Arctic

UNE **ardoise** *noun* slate

UNE **arête** *noun* fish bone

L'**argent** *masculine noun*
(**a**) money; **je n'ai plus d'argent** I have no money left
(**b**) silver

UN **Argentin**, UNE **Argentine** *noun* *(person)* Argentinian

argentin, argentine *adjective* Argentinian; **un tango argentin** an Argentinian tango

L'**Argentine** *feminine noun* Argentina

L'**argile** *feminine noun* clay; **un pot en argile** a clay pot

L'**argot** *masculine noun* slang; **il utilise beaucoup de mots d'argot** he uses a lot of slang words

UN **argument** *noun* argument *(reason)*

> Note that the French word *argument* never means *quarrel*.
> The *t* in *argument* is not pronounced.

UNE **arme** *noun* weapon

armé, armée[1] *adjective* **être armé** to be armed

UNE **armée**[2] *noun* army; **l'armée de terre** the army; **l'armée de l'air** the air force

UNE **armoire** *noun* wardrobe

UNE **armure** *noun* armour

arracher *verb*
(**a**) to pull out *(a tooth, somebody's hair)*
(**b**) to tear out *(a page)*
(**c**) to pull up *(a weed, a plant)*
(**d**) to snatch; **un voleur lui a arraché son sac à main** a thief snatched her handbag

arranger
1 *verb*
(**a**) to repair, to fix
(**b**) to tidy, to arrange *(one's hair, one's clothes)*
(**c**) to suit; **ça m'arrange** that suits me fine; **ça m'arrangerait que tu viennes demain** it would suit me if you could come tomorrow
2 *reflexive verb* **s'arranger**
(**a**) to manage; **ne vous inquiétez pas, je m'arrangerai** don't worry, I'll manage
(**b**) **arrangez-vous pour être là** make sure you're there; **il va falloir que je m'arrange pour trouver une baby-sitter** I'm going to have to organize a babysitter
(**c**) to work out, to turn out fine; **les choses ont fini par s'arranger** everything turned out all right in the end

UN **arrêt** *noun*
(**a**) stop; **un arrêt de bus** a bus stop
(**b**) **sans arrêt** constantly; **il se plaint sans arrêt** he's always complaining

arrêter
1 *verb*
(**a**) to stop; **arrête!** stop it!
(**b**) to switch off *(a machine)*
(**c**) to arrest *(a criminal)*
2 *reflexive verb* **s'arrêter** to stop

arrière
1 *masculine noun*
(**a**) back *(of a car, a building)*; **l'arrière de la voiture est abîmé** the back of the car is damaged; **je suis monté à l'arrière** I got in the back (seat)
(**b**) full back *(in football)*
2 *adverb* **en arrière** backwards; **il est tombé en arrière** he fell backwards

3 *adjective* back; **le siège arrière** the back seat; **les roues arrière** the back wheels; **les feux arrière de la voiture** the car's rear lights

The word *arrière* does not change in the plural when it is used as an adjective.

L'arrivée *feminine noun*
(**a**) arrival
(**b**) finish *(of a race)*

arriver *verb*
(**a**) to arrive; **je suis arrivé en retard à mon rendez-vous** I was late for my meeting
(**b**) to happen; **que vous est-il arrivé?** what happened to you?; **ça m'arrive d'aller à la piscine** I sometimes go to the swimming pool
(**c**) **arriver à faire quelque chose** to manage to do something; **Je ne peux pas y arriver tout seul** I can't manage by myself

In compound tenses this verb is conjugated with *être*, eg *je suis arrivé.*

arroser
1 *verb* to water *(a plant, the earth)*; **fais donc attention, tu m'arroses!** be careful, you're spraying me!
2 *reflexive verb* **s'arroser tu as eu ton permis de conduire? ça s'arrose!** so you've passed your driving test? that calls for a celebration!

UN **arrosoir** *noun* watering can

L'art *masculine noun* art

UN **artichaut** *noun* artichoke

UN **article** *noun*
(**a**) article
(**b**) item; **caisse de moins de dix articles** ten items or fewer checkout

artificiel, artificielle *adjective*
(**a**) artificial; **arôme artificiel** artificial flavouring
(**b**) man-made; **un lac artificiel** a man-made lake

UN/UNE **artiste** *noun* artist; **il est artiste** he's an artist

artistique *adjective* artistic

UN **as¹** *noun* ace; **l'as de carreau** the ace of diamonds

The *s* in *as* is pronounced.

as² *see* **avoir**
tu as de beaux yeux you have beautiful eyes; **tu as oublié d'acheter du lait** you forgot to buy milk

As is a form of the verb *avoir* in the present tense. See verb table p. 313. Note that the *s* in *as* is not pronounced.

UN **ascenseur** *noun* lift

L'Ascension *feminine noun* Ascension Day *(fortieth day after Easter, a public holiday in France)*

UNE **ascension** *noun* ascent; **faire l'ascension de l'Everest** to climb Everest

UN/UNE **Asiatique** *noun* *(person)* Asian

The word *Asiatique* usually refers to people from the Far East, not from the Indian subcontinent.

asiatique *adjective* Asian

L'Asie *feminine noun* Asia

L'aspect *masculine noun* appearance

The *c* and *t* in *aspect* are not pronounced.

UNE **asperge** *noun* **une asperge** a piece of asparagus; **j'aime les asperges** I like asparagus

UN **aspirateur** *noun* vacuum cleaner, hoover®; **passer l'aspirateur** to vacuum, to hoover

UNE **aspirine** *noun* aspirin; **un cachet d'aspirine** an aspirin

assaisonner *verb*
(**a**) to season *(a dish)*
(**b**) to dress *(a salad)*

UN **assassin** *noun*
(**a**) murderer
(**b**) assassin

UN **assassinat** *noun*
(**a**) murder
(**b**) assassination

assassiner *verb*
(**a**) to murder
(**b**) to assassinate

asseoir
1 *verb* to sit, to seat; **il a assis le bébé dans sa chaise** he sat the baby in its chair; **il était assis dans son fauteuil** he was sitting in his armchair
2 *reflexive verb* **s'asseoir** to sit down

See verb table p. 320.

assez *adverb*
(**a**) enough; **il ne fait pas assez chaud pour aller à la plage** it's not warm enough to go to the beach; **elle n'a pas assez d'argent pour aller au cinéma** she hasn't got enough money to go to the cinema
(**b**) fairly, quite; **il fait assez froid** it's quite cold

UNE **assiette** *noun* plate

assis, assise *adjective* sitting, sitting down; **être assis** to be sitting

Assis(e) is the past participle of the verb *asseoir*.

UN **assistant**, UNE **assistante** *noun* assistant; **une assistante sociale** a social worker

assister *verb* **assister à un cours** to attend a class; **assister à un accident** to witness an accident

UNE **association** *noun* association

assommer *verb* to knock out

s'assoupir *reflexive verb* to doze off

UNE **assurance** *noun*
(**a**) insurance; **assurance maladie** health insurance; **une assurance contre l'incendie** insurance against fire
(**b**) self-confidence; **il parle avec beaucoup d'assurance** he speaks very confidently
(**c**) assurance; **il m'a donné l'assurance que tout serait fini à temps** he assured me that everything would be finished in time

assurer
1 *verb*
(**a**) to assure; **il m'a assuré qu'il serait là à l'heure** he assured me he would be there on time; **je t'assure que c'est vrai** I assure you it's true
(**b**) to insure; **la maison est assurée contre l'incendie** the house is insured against fire
2 *reflexive verb* **s'assurer**
(**a**) to check, to make sure; **assure-toi que tu as bien fermé la fenêtre** make sure you shut the window
(**b**) to take out insurance

L'**asthme** *masculine noun* asthma; **il fait de l'asthme** he has asthma; **une crise d'asthme** an asthma attack

UN **asticot** *noun* maggot

UN/UNE **astronaute** *noun* astronaut; **il est astronaute** he's an astronaut

UN/UNE **astronome** *noun* astronomer; **elle est astronome** she's an astronomer

L'**astronomie** *feminine noun* astronomy; **il étudie l'astronomie** he studies astronomy

UN **atelier** *noun*
(**a**) workshop
(**b**) studio *(for an artist)*

Athènes *noun* Athens

UN/UNE **athlète** *noun* athlete

L'**athlétisme** *masculine noun* athletics; **j'adore l'athlétisme** I love athletics

L'**Atlantique** *masculine noun* the Atlantic

UN **atlas** *noun* atlas

L'**atmosphère** *feminine noun* atmosphere

UN **atout** *noun*
(**a**) asset; **cet employé est un atout pour notre société** this employee is an asset to our company

(**b**) trump; **atout trèfle** clubs are trumps

atroce *adjective* terrible, awful

attacher
1 *verb*
(**a**) to tie, to tie up; **il a attaché son chien à un poteau** he tied his dog to a post
(**b**) to fasten; **attache ta ceinture de sécurité** fasten your seatbelt
2 *reflexive verb* **s'attacher**
(**a**) to do up; **cette jupe s'attache par derrière** this skirt does up at the back
(**b**) **s'attacher à quelqu'un** to grow attached to somebody

UNE **attaque** *noun* attack

attaquer *verb* to attack

atteindre *verb* to reach

See verb table p. 320.

attendre *verb*
(**a**) to wait for; **ça fait une heure que je t'attends** I've been waiting for you for an hour
(**b**) to wait; **j'attends depuis midi** I've been waiting since midday
(**c**) to expect; **je l'attends à l'heure du dîner** I'm expecting him at dinner time
2 *reflexive verb* **s'attendre** to expect; **je ne m'attendais pas à ça** I wasn't expecting that; **il fallait s'y attendre** it was only to be expected

UN **attentat** *noun* attack; **un attentat à la bombe** a bombing; **un attentat à la voiture piégée** a car-bomb attack

L'**attente** *feminine noun* wait; **il y a trois heures d'attente** there's a three-hour wait

L'**attention** *feminine noun*
(**a**) attention; **c'est une tâche qui demande beaucoup d'attention** it's a task that requires a lot of attention; **fais bien attention à ce qu'il dit, c'est très important** pay attention to what he's saying, it's very important

(**b**) **fais attention, le trottoir est très glissant** be careful, the pavement is very slippery; **fais attention au chien, il mord** beware of the dog, he bites; **attention!** watch out!

atterrir *verb* to land

L'**atterrissage** *masculine noun* landing

attirer
1 *verb* to attract
2 *reflexive verb* **s'attirer** **s'attirer des ennuis** to get into trouble

UNE **attraction** *noun* attraction; **un parc d'attractions** an amusement park

attraper *verb* to catch

attrister *verb* to sadden

au *see* à
nous sommes allés au cinéma we went to the cinema; **la malle est au grenier** the trunk is in the attic

Au is the contraction of *à* + *le*.

L'**aube** *feminine noun* dawn; **à l'aube** at dawn

UNE **auberge** *noun* inn; **une auberge de jeunesse** a youth hostel

UNE **aubergine** *noun* aubergine

aucun, aucune
1 *adjective* no; **je n'en ai aucune idée** I have no idea; **je n'ai vu aucun livre sur la table** I didn't see any books on the table
2 *pronoun* none; **aucune de mes amies n'est venue** none of my friends came

au-delà de *preposition*
(**a**) beyond
(**b**) over

au-dessous *adverb*
(**a**) underneath, below
(**b**) downstairs; **il habite au-dessous** he lives downstairs
(**c**) **au-dessous de** below

au-dessus *adverb*
(**a**) above

(**b**) upstairs; **elle habite au-dessus** she lives upstairs
(**c**) **au-dessus de** above

UN **auditeur,** UNE **auditrice** *noun* listener

UNE **augmentation** *noun*
(**a**) increase
(**b**) pay rise

augmenter *verb* to increase

aujourd'hui *adverb* today

auparavant *adverb*
(**a**) before, beforehand
(**b**) first

auquel *see* **lequel**
ce n'est pas le film auquel je pensais it isn't the film I was thinking about

> *Auquel* is the contraction of *à* + *lequel*. Its feminine equivalent is *à laquelle*.

aura, aurai, aurons *see* **avoir**
j'aurai une grande maison quand je serai grand I'll have a big house when I'm grown up

> *Aura, aurai* etc are forms of the verb *avoir* in the future tense. See verb table p. 313.

aussi *adverb*
(**a**) too, also; **ton frère peut venir aussi** your brother can come too
(**b**) as; **je ne suis pas aussi grand que lui** I'm not as tall as he is

aussitôt *adverb*
(**a**) immediately; **il m'a prévenu aussitôt** he warned me immediately
(**b**) **aussitôt que** as soon as; **aussitôt qu'elle sera partie** as soon as she's left

L'**Australie** *feminine noun* Australia

UN **Australien,** UNE **Australienne** *noun* (*person*) Australian

australien, australienne *adjective* Australian

> In French, only the noun for the inhabitants of a country takes a capital letter, never the adjective.

autant *adverb*
(**a**) as much; **il a gagné autant d'argent que moi** he earned as much money as I did
(**b**) so much; **je n'ai jamais vu autant d'argent** I've never seen so much money; **il n'a jamais autant lu** he's never read so much
(**c**) as many; **elle a mangé autant de biscuits que toi** she ate as many biscuits as you did
(**d**) so many; **je n'ai jamais vu autant de monde** I've never seen so many people

UN **auteur** *noun* author

> The word *auteur* does not have a feminine but it can also refer to a woman.

UNE **auto** *noun* car; **les autos tamponneuses** the dodgems

UN **autobus** *noun* bus

UN **autocar** *noun* bus, coach

UN **autocollant** *noun* sticker

UNE **auto-école** *noun* driving school

> The plural of *auto-école* is *auto-écoles*.

L'**automne** *masculine noun* autumn; **en automne** in autumn

UNE **automobile** *noun* car

UN/UNE **automobiliste** *noun* motorist

UN **autoradio** *noun* car radio

autoriser *verb* **autoriser quelqu'un à faire quelque chose** to give somebody permission to do something

UNE **autoroute** *noun* motorway

UN **auto-stoppeur,** UNE **auto-stoppeuse** *noun* hitchhiker

autour *adverb* around; **autour de la ville** around the city

autre
1 *adjective*
(**a**) other; **l'autre jour** the other day; **tu veux une autre banane?** would

you like another banana?
(**b**) else; **autre chose** something else;
autre part somewhere else; **qui d'autre?** who else?; **quoi d'autre?** what
else?
2 *pronoun*
(**a**) **l'autre** the other one; **je veux l'autre** I want the other one
(**b**) **l'un l'autre, les uns les autres** each
other; **nous allons nous aider les uns
les autres** we'll help each other; **l'un
et l'autre** both of them; **l'un ou l'autre**
either of them; **ni l'un ni l'autre** neither of them

autrefois *adverb* in the past, in the
old days

autrement *adverb*
(**a**) otherwise
(**b**) in a different way; **si ça ne marche
pas, il faudra faire autrement** if
it doesn't work, we'll have to do it
differently; **autrement dit** in other
words

L'Autriche *feminine noun* Austria

UN Autrichien, UNE Autrichienne
noun (person) Austrian

autrichien, autrichienne *adjective* Austrian

> In French, only the noun for the in-
> habitants of a country takes a capital
> letter, never the adjective.

UNE autruche *noun* ostrich

aux *see* à
il est allé aux États-Unis he went to
the United States

> *Aux* is the contraction of *à + les*.

auxquels, auxquelles *see* lequel
ce sont les gens auxquels je pensais
they're the people I was thinking
about

> *Auxquels* is the contraction of *à +
> lesquels* and *auxquelles* is the
> contraction of *à + lesquelles*.

avais, avait *see* avoir
j'avais les cheveux longs quand

j'étais petite I had long hair when I
was little

> *Avais* and *avait* are forms of the verb
> *avoir* in the imperfect. See verb table
> p. 313.

UNE avalanche *noun* avalanche

avaler *verb* to swallow

L'avance *feminine noun*
(**a**) lead; **l'homme de tête a cinq minutes d'avance sur le peloton** the
man in front has a five-minute lead
over the rest of the pack
(**b**) advance *(money)*
(**c**) **en avance** early; **tu es en avance**
you're early
(**d**) **d'avance** in advance; **il faut payer
d'avance** you have to pay in advance
(**e**) in advance; **il faut réserver longtemps à l'avance pour avoir des
places** you have to book well in advance to get tickets

avancer
1 *verb*
(**a**) to move forward; **avance doucement** move forward slowly
(**b**) to bring forward; **ils ont décidé
d'avancer la réunion** they decided to
bring the meeting forward
(**c**) to be fast; **la pendule avance** the
clock is fast
(**d**) to lend; **est-ce que tu pourrais
m'avancer dix euros?** could you lend
me ten euros?
2 *reflexive verb* **s'avancer** to move
forward

avant
1 *masculine noun*
(**a**) front *(of a car, a plane)*; **l'avant de
la voiture est abîmé** the front of the
car is damaged; **je suis monté à
l'avant** I got in the front (seat)
(**b**) forward *(in football)*
2 *preposition* before; **passe me voir
avant sept heures** come and see me
before seven o'clock; **je mangerai
avant de me coucher** I'll eat before I
go to bed; **c'est le magasin juste avant**

la **poste** it's the shop just before the post office

3 *adverb*

(**a**) before; **un mois avant** a month before; **avant, il avait une moustache** he used to have a moustache; **le jour d'avant** the day before; **mon frère a pris le train d'avant** my brother caught the earlier train

(**b**) **en avant** forward; **il s'est penché en avant** he leaned forward; **en avant!** let's go!

4 *adjective* front; **les roues avant** the front wheels

The word *avant* does not change in the plural when it is used as an adjective.

ᴜɴ **avantage** *noun* advantage

avant-dernier, avant-dernière

1 *adjective* second-last; **l'avant-dernier jour** the second-last day

2 *noun* **l'avant-dernier, l'avant-dernière** the second last; **elle est arrivée avant-dernière** she came second last

The plural of *avant-dernier* is *avant-derniers* and the plural of *avant-dernière* is *avant-dernières*.

avant-hier *adverb* the day before yesterday

avare

1 *adjective* miserly

2 *noun* **un/une avare** a miser

avec *preposition* with; **nos ordinateurs sont assez lents, mais il faut faire avec** our computers are rather slow but we have to make do with them

ʟ'**avenir** *masculine noun* future; **dans un avenir proche** in the near future; **à l'avenir je voudrais que tu arrives à l'heure** in future I'd like you to arrive on time

ᴜɴᴇ **aventure** *noun* adventure

ᴜɴᴇ **averse** *noun* shower *(rain)*

avertir *verb* to warn

ᴜɴ **avertissement** *noun* warning

aveugle

1 *adjective* blind

2 *noun* **un aveugle** a blind man; **une aveugle** a blind woman; **les aveugles** the blind

avez *see* avoir

vous avez l'heure? have you got the time?; **vous avez gagné?** did you win?

Avez is a form of the verb *avoir* in the present tense. See verb table p. 313.

ᴜɴ **avion** *noun* plane

ᴜɴ **avis** *noun* opinion; **à mon avis** in my opinion; **la décision a été prise sans qu'on me demande mon avis** they made the decision without asking my opinion

ᴜɴ **avocat¹** *noun* avocado

ᴜɴ **avocat²**, ᴜɴᴇ **avocate** *noun* lawyer; **elle est avocate** she's a lawyer

ʟ'**avoine** *feminine noun* **de l'avoine** oats

avoir *verb*

(**a**) to have; **j'ai une grande maison** I have a big house

(**b**) to get; **j'ai eu un vélo pour mon anniversaire** I got a bike for my birthday

(**c**) to be; **j'ai douze ans** I'm twelve; **j'ai faim** I'm hungry; **j'ai trop chaud** I'm too hot; **elle a raison** she is right

(**d**) **qu'est-ce que tu as?** what's the matter with you?; **qu'est-ce qu'il y a?** what's the matter?

(**e**) to pass; **il a eu son permis de conduire** he passed his driving test

(**f**) **il y a** there is; *(in plural)* there are; **il y a un problème** there's a problem; **il y a des enfants dans le parc** there are children in the park; **il y a eu un accident** there was an accident; **il y avait beaucoup de bouteilles sur la table** there were a lot of bottles on the table

(**g**) **il y a** *(indicating time)* ago; **il y a trois jours** three days ago

(**h**) to have; **j'ai vu ce film** I have seen that film; **je n'ai pas encore vu ce film** I haven't seen that film yet; **j'ai vu ce**

film la semaine dernière I saw that film last week; **j'avais complètement oublié qu'il venait dîner ce soir** I had completely forgotten he was coming for dinner tonight

Avoir is used in compound tenses as an auxiliary with most verbs, as in the examples above.
See verb table p. 313.

avouer
1 *verb*
(**a**) to confess; **l'assassin a fini par avouer** the murderer confessed in the end
(**b**) to admit; **j'avoue que je ne suis pas très content** I admit I'm not very happy

2 *reflexive verb* **s'avouer** s'avouer **vaincu** to admit defeat

avril *masculine noun* April; **le premier avril** the first of April; **le 12 avril** the 12th of April

In French, the names of months are not written with a capital.

ayez, ayons *see* avoir
je ne pense pas que vous ayez assez d'argent pour ça I don't think you've got enough money for that

Ayez and *ayons* are forms of the verb *avoir* in the subjunctive. See verb table p. 313.

l'azote *masculine noun* nitrogen

LE **baby-foot** *noun* table football; **jouer au baby-foot** to play table football

LE **baby-sitting** *noun* babysitting; **elle fait du baby-sitting pour nous** she babysits for us

LE **bac** *noun* secondary school leaving certificate

> *Bac* is an informal word; it is the shortened form of *baccalauréat*. See note below.

LE **baccalauréat** *noun* secondary school leaving certificate

> ### Le Baccalauréat
> The *baccalauréat* or *bac* is a set of exams taken by pupils who have completed their final year of *lycée*, usually at age 17. It is more or less equivalent to English A levels, though it usually covers more subjects. People who have successfully passed the *baccalauréat* are allowed to go on to university. See also **lycée**.

bâcler *verb* to botch; **il a bâclé sa dissertation** he botched up his essay

bafouiller *verb* to stammer

LES **bagages** *masculine plural noun* luggage, baggage

LA **bagarre** *noun* fight

se bagarrer *reflexive verb* to fight

LA **bagnole** *noun* car

> This word is informal.

LA **bague** *noun* ring

LA **baguette** *noun*
  (**a**) baguette
  (**b**) drumstick *(for playing drums)*
  (**c**) chopstick
  (**d**) **une baguette magique** a magic wand

se baigner *reflexive verb* to go swimming

LE **baigneur,** LA **baigneuse** *noun* swimmer

LA **baignoire** *noun* bath, bathtub

bâiller *verb* to yawn

LE **bain** *noun* bath; **prendre un bain** to have a bath; **prendre un bain de soleil** to sunbathe

LE **baiser** *noun* kiss

LA **baisse** *noun* decrease, drop

baisser
  1 *verb*
  (**a**) to go down, to drop; **les prix ont baissé** prices have gone down
  (**b**) to turn down *(the heating, the sound)*
  (**c**) to lower *(blinds)*
  (**d**) **baisser la tête** to bend one's head
  2 *reflexive verb* **se baisser** to bend down

LE **bal** *noun* dance, ball

> The plural of *bal* is *bals*.

LA **balade** *noun*
  (**a**) walk
  (**b**) drive
  (**c**) ride *(on a bicycle, a horse)*

> This word is slightly informal.

se balader *reflexive verb*
  (**a**) to go for a walk
  (**b**) to go for a drive

(**c**) to go for a ride *(on a bicycle, a horse)*

This word is slightly informal.

LE **baladeur** *noun* personal stereo, walkman®

LE **balai** *noun* broom

LA **Balance** *noun* Libra; **elle est Balance** she's a Libra

LA **balance** *noun* scales; **une balance** a set of scales

se balancer *reflexive verb* to swing; **il n'arrête pas de se balancer sur sa chaise** he keeps swinging on his chair

LA **balançoire** *noun* swing

balayer *verb*
(**a**) to sweep
(**b**) to sweep up

LE **balcon** *noun* balcony

LA **baleine** *noun* whale

LA **balle** *noun*
(**a**) ball
(**b**) bullet

LE **ballon** *noun*
(**a**) balloon
(**b**) ball

banal, banale *adjective*
(**a**) ordinary
(**b**) common
(**c**) trite

The masculine plural of *banal* is *banals*.

LA **banane** *noun* banana

LE **banc** *noun* bench

The *c* in *banc* is not pronounced.

LA **bande** *noun*
(**a**) strip *(of land, paper)*
(**b**) bandage
(**c**) group *(of people)*
(**d**) **une bande magnétique** a tape *(for sound or video recording)*
(**e**) **une bande dessinée** a comic strip

Bande dessinée is often shortened to *BD*. See also the note at **BD**.

LE **bandeau** *noun*
(**a**) blindfold
(**b**) headband

The plural of *bandeau* is *bandeaux*.

LE **bandit** *noun* gangster

The *t* in *bandit* is not pronounced.

LA **banlieue** *noun* **la banlieue** the suburbs; **une banlieue** a suburb; **nous habitons en banlieue** we live in the suburbs; **un train de banlieue** a commuter train

LA **banque** *noun* bank

LA **banquette** *noun* seat *(in a car, a train)*

LE **banquier,** LA **banquière** *noun* banker; **il est banquier** he's a banker

LE **baptême** *noun* christening; **c'était mon baptême de l'air** it was my first flight

The *p* in *baptême* is not pronounced.

baptiser *verb*
(**a**) to baptize, to christen
(**b**) to name, to christen

The *p* in *baptiser* is not pronounced.

LE **bar** *noun* bar *(where people drink)*

LA **baraque** *noun*
(**a**) shack
(**b**) house

Sense (b) is an informal use of *baraque*.

LA **barbe** *noun*
(**a**) beard; **de la barbe à papa** candy-floss
(**b**) **quelle barbe!** *(informal phrase)* what a drag!

barboter *verb* to paddle

barbu
1 *adjective* bearded
2 *masculine noun* bearded man

LA **barque** *noun* small boat

LE **barrage** *noun*
(**a**) dam
(**b**) roadblock

LA **barre** *noun* bar *(of metal, chocolate)*

LE **barreau** *noun*
(**a**) rung
(**b**) bar *(of a window, a cage)*; **se retrouver derrière les barreaux** to end up behind bars

> The plural of *barreau* is *barreaux*.

barrer
1 *verb*
(**a**) to block *(a road)*
(**b**) to cross out *(a word, a sentence)*
2 *reflexive verb* **se barrer** to clear off

> The verb *se barrer* is informal.

LA **barrette** *noun* hair slide

LA **barrière** *noun*
(**a**) fence
(**b**) gate

LE **bas¹** *noun* stocking; **elle porte des bas** she wears stockings

bas², basse
1 *adjective* low; **ce travail ne m'intéresse pas, le salaire est trop bas** I'm not interested in that job, the salary's too low; **parler à voix basse** to speak in a low voice
2 *adverb* **bas**
(**a**) low; **le miroir est placé trop bas** the mirror is too low
(**b**) quietly; **ne parle pas si bas, je ne t'entends pas** don't speak so quietly, I can't hear you
(**c**) **à bas le président!** down with the president!
3 *adverb* **en bas**
(**a**) downstairs; **elle habite en bas** she lives downstairs
(**b**) at the bottom; **tout en bas** at the very bottom
(**c**) down below
(**d**) **la tête en bas** upside down
4 *masculine noun* **le bas** the bottom; **l'étagère du bas** the bottom shelf; **au**

bas de la page at the bottom of the page; **de bas en haut** upwards

basculer *verb* to topple over

LA **base** *noun* base

LE **basket** *noun* basketball

LES **baskets** *masculine plural noun* trainers *(shoes)*

basse *see* **bas²**

LA **basse-cour** *noun* farmyard

> The plural of *basse-cour* is *basses-cours*.

LE **bassin** *noun*
(**a**) pond
(**b**) pool

LA **bassine** *noun* bowl

LA **bataille** *noun* battle; **jouer à la bataille navale** to play battleships

LE **bateau** *noun* boat, ship

> The plural of *bateau* is *bateaux*.

LE **bâtiment** *noun*
(**a**) building
(**b**) ship

bâtir *verb* to build

LE **bâton** *noun* stick

LA **batterie** *noun*
(**a**) battery
(**b**) drums; **jouer de la batterie** to play the drums

battre
1 *verb*
(**a**) to beat
(**b**) to break *(a record)*
(**c**) to shuffle *(cards)*
(**d**) **l'oiseau bat des ailes** the bird is flapping its wings
2 *reflexive verb* **se battre** to fight

> See verb table p. 320.

bavard, bavarde *adjective* talkative

bavarder *verb* to chat

baver *verb* to dribble

LE **bavoir** *noun* bib

LE bazar *noun*
(a) general store
(b) mess

Sense (b) is an informal use of *bazar*.

LA BD *noun* comic strip; **il fait de la BD** he's a cartoonist

BD is an informal word; it is the shortened form of *bande dessinée*. It does not change in the plural.

La BD
Comic books are very popular in France among teenagers and adults alike. It is not uncommon for young people to own dozens of comic books. *Tintin*, *Astérix* and *Lucky Luke* are very famous examples. An annual festival of comic-book art is held in Angoulême in western France.

beau, belle
1 *adjective*
(a) beautiful
(b) good-looking, handsome
(c) lovely, fine, nice; **nous avons eu du beau temps** we had nice weather
2 *adverb* **beau**
(a) **il fait beau** the weather is nice
(b) **j'ai eu beau crier, personne n'est venu** however much I shouted, no one came; **elle avait beau chercher, elle ne trouvait rien** however hard she looked, she couldn't find anything

The plural of *beau* is *beaux*. *Beau* becomes *bel* in front of a vowel or a mute h, eg *un bel homme*. The plural is still *beaux*, eg *de beaux hommes*.

beaucoup *adverb*
(a) a lot; **il reste encore beaucoup à faire** there's still a lot to do
(b) much; **je n'ai pas beaucoup aimé le film** I didn't like the film much
(c) **beaucoup de** much, a lot of; **il n'a pas beaucoup d'argent** he hasn't got much money; **il faut mettre beaucoup de sucre** you have to put in a lot of sugar
(d) **beaucoup de** many, a lot of; **il a**

beaucoup de livres he has many books

LE beau-fils *noun* son-in-law

The plural of *beau-fils* is *beaux-fils*.

LE beau-frère *noun* brother-in-law

The plural of *beau-frère* is *beaux-frères*.

LE beau-père *noun*
(a) father-in-law
(b) stepfather

The plural of *beau-père* is *beaux-pères*.

LA beauté *noun* beauty

LES beaux-parents *masculine plural noun* parents-in-law

LE bébé *noun* baby

The word *bébé* does not have a feminine but it can also refer to a baby girl.

LE bec *noun* beak

LA bêche *noun* spade

bêcher *verb* to dig; **bêcher un jardin** to dig a garden

bégayer *verb* to stutter

beige
1 *adjective* beige; **une robe beige** a beige dress
2 *masculine noun* **le beige** beige; **le beige est ma couleur préférée** beige is my favourite colour

LE beignet *noun*
(a) fritter
(b) doughnut

bel *see* **beau**

LE/LA Belge *noun (person)* Belgian

belge *adjective* Belgian; **des chocolats belges** Belgian chocolates

In French, only the noun for the inhabitants of a country takes a capital letter, never the adjective.

LA Belgique *noun* Belgium

LE **Bélier** *noun* Aries; **il est Bélier** he's an Aries

LE **bélier** *noun* ram

belle *see* **beau**

LA **belle-fille** *noun*
(**a**) daughter-in-law
(**b**) stepdaughter

The plural of *belle-fille* is *belles-filles*.

LA **belle-mère** *noun*
(**a**) mother-in-law
(**b**) stepmother

The plural of *belle-mère* is *belles-mères*.

LA **belle-sœur** *noun* sister-in-law

The plural of *belle-sœur* is *belles-sœurs*.

LE **bénéfice** *noun* profit; **donner le bénéfice du doute à quelqu'un** to give somebody the benefit of the doubt

bénévole
1 *adjective* voluntary; **des travailleurs bénévoles** voluntary workers
2 *noun* **un/une bénévole** a volunteer, a voluntary worker

LA **béquille** *noun* crutch

LE **berceau** *noun* cradle

The plural of *berceau* is *berceaux*.

bercer *verb* to rock

LA **berceuse** *noun* lullaby

LE **berger,** LA **bergère** *noun* shepherd/shepherdess

LE **besoin** *noun* need; **avoir besoin de quelque chose** to need something

LE **bétail** *noun* livestock, cattle

LA **bête¹** *noun* animal

bête² *adjective* stupid

LA **bêtise** *noun*
(**a**) stupid thing
(**b**) stupidity

LE **béton** *noun* concrete

LA **betterave** *noun* beetroot

LE/LA **beur** *noun* North African born in France of immigrant parents

This word is informal.

LE **beurre** *noun* butter

beurrer *verb* to butter

LE **biberon** *noun* baby's bottle

LA **bible** *noun* bible

LE/LA **bibliothécaire** *noun* librarian; **elle est bibliothécaire** she's a librarian

LA **bibliothèque** *noun*
(**a**) library
(**b**) bookcase

LE **bic**® *noun* ballpoint (pen)

LA **bicyclette** *noun* bicycle

LE **bidon** *noun* can *(for petrol, oil, water)*

LE **bidonville** *noun* shanty town

bien
1 *adjective* good; **ce livre est très bien** this is a very good book; **ce sont des gens bien** they're nice people; **ce n'est pas bien de mentir** it's wrong to lie

Bien does not change in the feminine or in the plural.

2 *adverb*
(**a**) well; **il chante bien** he's a good singer
(**b**) very; **je suis bien content** I'm very pleased
(**c**) a lot; **il a bien grandi depuis l'an dernier** he's grown a lot since last year; **on a bien ri** we had a good laugh
(**d**) **bien sûr** of course
(**e**) **je te l'avais bien dit!** I told you so!; **je le savais bien!** I (just) knew it!
3 *exclamation* **bien! allons-y!** right! let's go!; **bien! je vous écoute!** OK, I'm listening!
4 *conjunction* **bien que** although, even though; **il est très généreux bien qu'il ne soit pas bien riche** he's very generous even though he hasn't got much money

5 *masculine noun*
(**a**) good; **bois ça, ça te fera du bien** drink this, it'll do you good; **c'est pour ton bien** it's for your own good; **le bien et le mal** good and evil
(**b**) possession; **il a vendu tous ses biens** he sold all his possessions

bientôt *adverb* soon; **à bientôt!** see you soon!

LE **bienvenu,** LA **bienvenue**
1 *noun* **soyez le bienvenu!** welcome!; **soyez les bienvenus!** welcome!; **votre fille peut venir dormir chez nous, elle est la bienvenue** your daughter is welcome to come and stay at our house
2 *feminine noun* **la bienvenue** welcome; **souhaiter la bienvenue à quelqu'un** to welcome somebody

LA **bière** *noun* beer

LE **bifteck** *noun* steak

LE **bigoudi** *noun* curler, roller

LE **bijou** *noun* jewel

The plural of *bijou* is *bijoux*.

LA **bijouterie** *noun* jeweller's (shop)

LE **bijoutier,** LA **bijoutière** *noun* jeweller; **il est bijoutier** he's a jeweller

LE **billard** *noun*
(**a**) billiards
(**b**) pool
(**c**) snooker

LA **bille** *noun* marble *(toy)*; **jouer aux billes** to play marbles

LE **billet** *noun*
(**a**) ticket
(**b**) (bank)note

LA **biologie** *noun* biology

LA **biscotte** *noun* piece of toasted bread sold in packets

LE **biscuit** *noun* biscuit

The *t* in *biscuit* is not pronounced.

LA **bise** *noun* kiss

LE **bisou** *noun* kiss; **bisous** *(at the end of a letter)* love

bissextile *adjective* **une année bissextile** a leap year

bizarre *adjective* odd, strange

LA **blague** *noun* joke; **faire une blague à quelqu'un** to play a trick on somebody; **sans blague!** no kidding!

blaguer *verb* to joke

LE **blaireau** *noun*
(**a**) badger
(**b**) shaving brush

The plural of *blaireau* is *blaireaux*.

UN **Blanc,** UNE **Blanche** *noun* white man/white woman; **les Blancs** white people

blanc, blanche
1 *adjective*
(**a**) white; **du vin blanc** white wine
(**b**) blank; **une page blanche** a blank page
2 *masculine noun* **le blanc**
(**a**) white; **le blanc est ma couleur préférée** white is my favourite colour; **il était habillé en blanc** he was dressed in white
(**b**) **un blanc d'œuf** an egg white
(**c**) **du blanc de poulet** a chicken breast

The *c* in *blanc* is not pronounced.

LA **blanchisserie** *noun* laundry

LE **blé** *noun* wheat

blême *adjective* very pale; **il était blême de peur** he was white with fear

blessé, blessée
1 *adjective*
(**a**) injured
(**b**) wounded
(**c**) hurt
2 *noun* **le blessé, la blessée**
(**a**) injured person; **les blessés** the injured
(**b**) wounded person; **les blessés** the wounded

blesser
1 *verb*
(**a**) to injure

(**b**) to wound
(**c**) to hurt
2 *reflexive verb* **se blesser** to hurt oneself

LA **blessure** *noun*
(**a**) injury
(**b**) wound

bleu, bleue
1 *adjective* blue
2 *masculine noun* **le bleu**
(**a**) blue; **le bleu est ma couleur préférée** blue is my favourite colour
(**b**) bruise; **ses bras sont couverts de bleus** his arms are covered in bruises

The plural of *bleu* is *bleus*.

LE **bloc** *noun*
(**a**) block
(**b**) **un bloc de papier à lettres** a writing pad; **un bloc de dessin** a sketch pad
(**c**) **un bloc opératoire** an operating theatre
(**d**) **à bloc** completely; **les pneus sont gonflés à bloc** the tyres are fully pumped up

LE **bloc-notes** *noun* notepad

The plural of *bloc-notes* is *blocs-notes*.

blond, blonde
1 *adjective* fair, blond; **du sable blond** golden sand
2 *noun* **un blond** a fair-haired man, a blond man; **une blonde** a fair-haired woman, a blonde

bloquer
1 *verb*
(**a**) to block *(a road, the traffic)*
(**b**) to jam *(a door, a mechanism)*
(**c**) to freeze *(salaries, prices)*
2 *reflexive verb* **se bloquer** to get stuck

LA **blouse** *noun* overall

LE **blouson** *noun* jacket; **un blouson de cuir** a leather jacket

LE **bœuf** *noun*
(**a**) ox
(**b**) beef

The *f* is pronounced in the singular but not in the plural; *bœufs* is pronounced "beu".

boire *verb* to drink; **elle ne boit jamais d'alcool** she never drinks alcohol; **il a bu un verre d'eau** he drank a glass of water

See verb table p. 320.

LE **bois¹** *noun*
(**a**) wood; **une chaise en bois** a wooden chair
(**b**) **un bois** a wood; **il est allé se promener dans les bois** he went for a walk in the woods
(**c**) **les bois d'un cerf** a stag's antlers

bois² *see* **boire**
tous les soirs, je bois un verre de lait every night I drink a glass of milk; **qu'est-ce que tu bois?** what would you like to drink?

Bois is a form of the verb *boire* in the present tense. See verb table p. 320.

LA **boisson** *noun* drink

LA **boîte** *noun*
(**a**) box
(**b**) can, tin
(**c**) **une boîte** *or* **une boîte de nuit** a nightclub

boiter *verb* to limp

LE **bol** *noun*
(**a**) bowl
(**b**) **prendre un bol d'air** to get a good breath of fresh air
(**c**) luck; **avoir du bol** to be lucky; **il n'a pas eu de bol** he was unlucky

Sense (c) is an informal use of *bol*.

bombarder *verb* to bomb

LA **bombe** *noun*
(**a**) bomb
(**b**) spray can; **une bombe insecticide** a can of fly spray

bon, bonne
1 *adjective*
(**a**) good; **c'est un très bon film** it's a

very good film; **viens te baigner, l'eau est bonne!** come for a swim, the water's lovely!

(**b**) right; **la bonne réponse** the right answer; **je n'ai pas pris la bonne clé** I didn't take the right key

(**c**) valid; **ce ticket n'est pas bon** this ticket is not valid; **ces yaourts sont-ils encore bons?** are the yoghurts still all right to eat?

(**d**) **bon anniversaire!** happy birthday!; **bonne année!** happy new year!; **bonne journée!** have a nice day!

(**e**) **bon marché** cheap; **des vêtements bon marché** cheap clothes

2 *exclamation* **bon bon! c'est l'heure!** OK, it's time!; **bon! qu'est-ce qu'on fait?** right then! what shall we do?; **bon! tu viens ou tu ne viens pas?** right! are you coming or not?; **ah bon?** really?

3 *adverb* **bon il fait bon aujourd'hui** it's nice and warm today; **ça sent bon** it smells nice

4 *masculine noun* **le bon**

(**a**) voucher; **un bon d'achat** a gift voucher

(**b**) coupon; **un bon de réduction** a money-off coupon

5 *feminine noun* **la bonne** maid

LE **bonbon** *noun* sweet

LE **bond** *noun* leap

> The *d* in *bond* is not pronounced.

bondé, bondée *adjective* crowded

bondir *verb* to leap

LE **bonheur** *noun* happiness

LE **bonhomme** *noun*

(**a**) chap, guy

> Sense (a) is an informal use of *bonhomme*.

(**b**) **un bonhomme de neige** a snowman

> The plural of *bonhomme* is *bonshommes*.

bonjour *exclamation*

(**a**) hello, good morning; **allez, dis bonjour à la dame!** come on, say hello to the lady!; **vous donnerez le bonjour à votre femme pour moi** please say hello to your wife for me

(**b**) hello, good afternoon

(**c**) **c'est simple comme bonjour** it's as easy as pie

bonne *see* **bon**

LE **bonnet** *noun* hat; **un bonnet de laine** a woolly hat; **un bonnet de bain** a bathing cap

> The *t* in *bonnet* is not pronounced.

bonsoir *exclamation*

(**a**) hello, good evening

(**b**) goodbye

LA **bonté** *noun* kindness

bord *noun*

(**a**) edge; **le bord de la table** the edge of the table; **il était au bord des larmes** he was on the verge of tears

(**b**) side; **elle s'est garée au bord de la route** she parked at the side of the road; **ils sont en vacances au bord de la mer** they're on holiday at the seaside; **ils ont pique-niqué au bord de la rivière** they had a picnic by the riverside

(**c**) rim *(of a glass, a cup)*

(**d**) **à bord** on board; **monter à bord** to go on board; **à bord d'un navire** on board a ship

LA **Bosnie** *noun* Bosnia; **la Bosnie-Herzégovine** Bosnia-Herzegovina

LA **bosse** *noun*

(**a**) bump

(**b**) hump *(of a camel)*

bosser *verb* to work

> This word is informal.

LA **botte** *noun* boot; **des bottes d'équitation** riding boots; **des bottes de caoutchouc** wellingtons

LE **bouc** *noun*

(**a**) billy goat

(**b**) goatee

LA **bouche** *noun* mouth; **une bouche de métro** a metro entrance

LA **bouchée** *noun* mouthful

boucher[1]
1 *verb*
(a) to fill in *(a hole)*
(b) to clog, to block up *(a sink, a pipe)*; **l'évier est bouché** the sink is blocked; **j'ai le nez bouché** my nose is blocked
(c) to cork *(a wine bottle)*
(d) to put the plug in *(a bathtub)*
2 *reflexive verb* **se boucher**
(a) to get blocked up
(b) **se boucher le nez** to hold one's nose; **se boucher les oreilles** to put one's fingers in one's ears

LE **boucher**[2], LA **bouchère** *noun* butcher; **il est boucher** he's a butcher; **aller chez le boucher** to go to the butcher's

LA **boucherie** *noun* butcher's (shop)

LE **bouchon** *noun*
(a) top *(of a bottle)*
(b) cork
(c) traffic jam

LA **boucle** *noun*
(a) curl *(of hair)*
(b) buckle *(of a belt)*
(c) **des boucles d'oreilles** earrings

bouclé, bouclée *adjective* curly

boucler *verb*
(a) to fasten
(b) to buckle

LE **bouclier** *noun* shield

LE/LA **bouddhiste** *noun* Buddhist

bouder *verb* to sulk

LA **boue** *noun* mud

LA **bouée** *noun*
(a) rubber ring
(b) **une bouée de sauvetage** a lifebelt
(c) buoy

boueux, boueuse *adjective* muddy

LA **bouffe** *noun* food

This word is informal.

LE **bougeoir** *noun* candlestick

bouger *verb* to move

LA **bougie** *noun*
(a) candle
(b) spark plug

bouillant, bouillante *adjective* boiling

bouillir *verb* to boil; **l'eau bout** the water is boiling; **il bouillait d'impatience** he was bursting with impatience

LA **bouilloire** *noun* kettle

LA **bouillotte** *noun* hot-water bottle

LE **boulanger**, LA **boulangère** *noun* baker; **il est boulanger** he's a baker; **aller chez le boulanger** to go to the baker's

LA **boulangerie** *noun* baker's (shop)

LA **boule** *noun*
(a) ball; **une boule de neige** a snowball
(b) bowl; **jouer aux boules** to play bowls
(c) **perdre la boule** *(informal phrase)* to be off one's head

LA **boulette** *noun* small ball; **des boulettes de viande** meatballs

bouleverser *verb*
(a) to upset greatly, to shatter
(b) to disrupt

LE **boulon** *noun* bolt

LE **boulot** *noun*
(a) work; **aller au boulot** to go to work
(b) job; **chercher du boulot** to look for a job

This word is informal.

boum
1 *feminine noun* **une boum** a party; **tu vas à la boum de Sandrine demain?** are you going to Sandrine's party tomorrow?
2 *exclamation* boom

LE **bouquet** *noun*
(a) **un bouquet** *or* **un bouquet de**

fleurs a bunch of flowers, a bouquet
(b) **c'est le bouquet!** *(informal phrase)* that takes the biscuit!

LE **bouquin** *noun* book

Both *bouquin* and *bouquiner* are informal.

bouquiner *verb* to read

bourdonner *verb* to buzz

LE **bourgeon** *noun* bud

bourrer *verb* to cram, to stuff; **la voiture était bourrée d'explosifs** the car was packed full of explosives

LA **Bourse** *noun* Stock Exchange; **la Bourse de Paris** the Paris Stock Exchange

LA **bourse** *noun*
(a) grant
(b) purse

bousculer *verb*
(a) to push
(b) to jostle
(c) to rush; **ne me bouscule pas, j'aime prendre mon temps!** don't rush me, I like to take my time!

LA **boussole** *noun*
(a) compass
(b) **perdre la boussole** *(informal phrase)* to be off one's head

LE **bout¹** *noun*
(a) end; **leur maison est au bout du chemin** their house is at the end of the path
(b) tip *(of a tongue, a finger, a cane)*
(c) bit, piece; **un bout de ficelle** a piece of string
(d) **au bout d'un mois** after a month; **au bout d'un moment** after a while
(e) **il est à bout** *or* **il est à bout de nerfs** he's at the end of his tether; **elle est à bout de forces** she's worn out; **j'étais à bout de souffle après avoir monté les escaliers** I was out of breath after climbing the stairs

bout² *see* **bouillir**
l'eau bout the water is boiling

Bout is a form of the verb *bouillir* in the present tense. See verb table p. 320.

LA **bouteille** *noun* bottle; **une bouteille de gaz** a gas cylinder

LA **boutique** *noun* shop

LE **bouton** *noun*
(a) pimple, spot
(b) button
(c) knob
(d) bud
(e) **un bouton d'or** a buttercup

boutonner *verb* to button up; **boutonne ta chemise!** button your shirt up!

LA **boxe** *noun* boxing

LE **boxeur** *noun* boxer; **il est boxeur** he's a boxer

LE **bracelet** *noun*
(a) bracelet
(b) **un bracelet de montre** a watch strap

LA **braguette** *noun* flies *(of trousers)*

LA **branche** *noun*
(a) branch
(b) field *(of activity)*

branché, branchée *adjective* cool, hip

This word is informal.

brancher *verb* to plug in *(a lamp, the television)*

LE **bras** *noun* arm; **c'est lui le bras droit du patron** he's the boss's right-hand man; **une partie de bras de fer** an arm-wrestling match

LA **brasse** *noun* breaststroke; **nager la brasse** to do the breaststroke

brave *adjective*
(a) nice; **de braves gens** nice people
(b) courageous, brave

bravo *exclamation* well done

LA **brebis** *noun* ewe

bref, brève
1 *adjective* short, brief; **la réunion a**

été très **brève** the meeting was very short

2 *adverb* **bref** in a word; **enfin bref, il n'était pas content du tout** well, basically, he wasn't at all happy

LE **Brésil** *noun* Brazil

LE **Brésilien,** LA **Brésilienne** *noun (person)* Brazilian

brésilien, brésilienne *adjective* Brazilian

> In French, only the noun for the inhabitants of a country takes a capital letter, never the adjective.

LA **Bretagne** *noun* Brittany

LA **bretelle** *noun*
(**a**) strap *(of a bra, a bag)*
(**b**) **une bretelle d'autoroute** a slip road
(**c**) **des bretelles** braces *(for trousers)*; **il portait des bretelles** he was wearing braces

UN **Breton,** UNE **Bretonne** *noun (person)* Breton

breton, bretonne
1 *adjective* Breton; **la musique bretonne** Breton music
2 *masculine noun* **le breton** *(language)* Breton; **il parle breton** he speaks Breton

brève *see* bref

LE **brevet** *noun*
(**a**) certificate; **il a un brevet de secouriste** he has a first-aid certificate; **il vient d'obtenir son brevet de pilote** he's just got his pilot's licence
(**b**) patent
(**c**) **le brevet des collèges** school exam taken at the age of 15

Le Brevet des Collèges

The *brevet des collèges* is a school exam taken by pupils who have completed their final year of *collège*, usually at age 15. It is more or less equivalent to English GCSEs. People who have successfully passed the *brevet* can go to a *lycée*. See also **collège** and **lycée**.

LE **bricolage** *noun* DIY; **mon père n'aime pas du tout le bricolage** my dad hates DIY

bricoler *verb*
(**a**) to do DIY; **elle aime bricoler** she likes doing DIY
(**b**) to make, to put together; **il a bricolé une armoire** he made a cupboard

brillant, brillante *adjective*
(**a**) shiny
(**b**) bright
(**c**) brilliant; **c'est une élève brillante** she's a brilliant student

> The *t* in *brillant* is not pronounced.

briller *verb* to shine

LE **brin** *noun* **un brin d'herbe** a blade of grass; **un brin de persil** a sprig of parsley; **un brin de muguet** a spray of lily of the valley

LA **brindille** *noun* twig

LA **brique** *noun*
(**a**) brick; **une maison en briques** a brick house
(**b**) carton; **une brique de lait** a carton of milk

LE **briquet** *noun* lighter

LA **brise** *noun* breeze

briser *verb* to break

LE/LA **Britannique** *noun* British man/ British woman, Briton

britannique *adjective* British; **l'économie britannique** the British economy; **les îles britanniques** the British Isles

LA **broche** *noun*
(**a**) brooch
(**b**) spit; **un poulet à la broche** a spit-roasted chicken

LA **brochure** *noun* brochure

LA **bronchite** *noun* bronchitis

LE **bronzage** *noun* suntan

bronzé, bronzée *adjective* suntanned

bronzer *verb* to get a suntan

LA **brosse** *noun* brush; **une brosse à cheveux** a hairbrush; **une brosse à dents** a toothbrush

brosser
1 *verb* to brush
2 *reflexive verb* **se brosser se brosser les dents** to brush one's teeth

LA **brouette** *noun* wheelbarrow

LE **brouillard** *noun* fog

brouillon, brouillonne
1 *adjective*
(a) disorganized
(b) untidy
2 *masculine noun* **un brouillon** a first draft

LES **broussailles** *feminine plural noun* undergrowth; **le chat se cachait dans les broussailles** the cat was hiding in the undergrowth

LE **bruit** *noun*
(a) noise
(b) rumour

brûlant, brûlante *adjective* boiling hot; **mon thé est brûlant** my tea is boiling hot

brûler
1 *verb* to burn
2 *reflexive verb* **se brûler** to burn oneself; **je me suis brûlé les doigts** I burnt my fingers

LA **brûlure** *noun* burn

LA **brume** *noun* mist

brun, brune
1 *adjective*
(a) dark-haired
(b) brown
2 *noun* **un brun** a dark-haired man; **une brune** a dark-haired woman, a brunette

LE **brushing**® *noun* blow-dry

brusque *adjective*
(a) sudden
(b) abrupt

brusquement *adverb*
(a) suddenly
(b) abruptly

brutal, brutale *adjective*
(a) brutal
(b) rough
(c) sudden

Bruxelles *noun* Brussels

bruyant, bruyante *adjective* noisy

bu, bue *see* **boire**
j'ai bu un verre d'eau I drank a glass of water

> *Bu(e)* is the past participle of the verb *boire*. See verb table p. 320.

LA **bûche** *noun* log

LE **bûcheron** *noun* woodcutter, lumberjack; **il est bûcheron** he's a woodcutter

LA **buée** *noun* condensation; **il y a plein de buée sur la vitre** there's lots of condensation on the windowpane

LE **buffet** *noun*
(a) sideboard
(b) buffet

LE **buisson** *noun* bush

buissonnière *feminine adjective* **faire l'école buissonnière** to play truant

LE/LA **Bulgare** *noun (person)* Bulgarian

bulgare
1 *adjective* Bulgarian; **l'économie bulgare** the Bulgarian economy
2 *masculine noun* **le bulgare** *(language)* Bulgarian; **elle parle bulgare** she speaks Bulgarian

> In French, only the noun for the inhabitants of a country takes a capital letter, never the adjective or the noun for the language.

LA **Bulgarie** *noun* Bulgaria

LA **bulle** *noun* bubble; **faire des bulles** to blow bubbles

LE **bulletin** *noun*
(a) **un bulletin** *or* **un bulletin scolaire** a school report
(b) **un bulletin de vote** a ballot paper

(**c**) un bulletin météorologique a weather report
(**d**) un bulletin d'informations a news bulletin

LE **bureau** *noun*
(**a**) desk
(**b**) office
(**c**) study

The plural of *bureau* is *bureaux*.

LE **bus** *noun* bus

LE **but** *noun*
(**a**) aim; **quel est le but du jeu?** what is the aim of the game?
(**b**) goal; **j'ai marqué trois buts** I scored three goals

buté, butée *adjective* stubborn

LE **butin** *noun* loot

LE **buvard** *noun* blotter

LA **buvette** *noun* refreshment bar

c' *pronoun* **c'est beau** it's beautiful

> *C'* is the contracted form of *ce* which is used in front of a vowel or a mute h. See also **ce¹**.

ça *pronoun*
(a) this, that; **c'est quoi, ça?** what's that?; **je n'aime pas ça** I don't like that
(b) it; **ça m'est égal** it's all the same to me; **ça ne fait rien** it doesn't matter; **c'est ça!** that's it!; **comment ça va?** how are you?, how's it going?
(c) **ça alors!** *(expressing amazement)* wow!, no way!
(d) **qui ça?** who?; **où ça?** where?

LA cabane *noun*
(a) shed
(b) hut, shack

LA cabine *noun*
(a) cabin
(b) **une cabine téléphonique** a phone box
(c) **une cabine d'essayage** a changing room

LE cabinet *noun*
(a) **un cabinet médical** a doctor's surgery
(b) **les cabinets** the toilet; **un cabinet de toilette** a small bathroom

LE câble *noun* cable; **est-ce que vous avez le câble?** have you got cable TV?

LA cacahouète *noun* peanut

LE cacao *noun* cocoa

LE cache-nez *noun* scarf

> The word *cache-nez* does not change in the plural.

cacher
1 *verb* to hide
2 *reflexive verb* **se cacher** to hide

LE cachet *noun* tablet; **un cachet d'aspirine** an aspirin; **il est blanc comme un cachet d'aspirine** he's as white as a sheet

LA cachette *noun* hiding place; **faire quelque chose en cachette** to do something in secret; **mon frère fume en cachette** my brother smokes in secret

LE cadavre *noun* dead body

LE caddie® *noun* shopping trolley

LE cadeau *noun* present, gift

> The plural of *cadeau* is *cadeaux*.

LE cadenas *noun* padlock

cadet, cadette
1 *adjective*
(a) younger
(b) youngest
2 *noun* **le cadet, la cadette** the youngest child; **le cadet de la famille** the youngest in the family *(a boy)*; **la cadette de la famille** the youngest in the family *(a girl)*

LE cadran *noun* dial; **un cadran solaire** a sundial

LE cadre *noun*
(a) frame
(b) setting, surroundings
(c) manager, executive

LE cafard *noun*
(a) cockroach
(b) **avoir le cafard** *(informal phrase)* to feel down

LE **café** *noun*
(**a**) coffee
(**b**) café

LA **cafetière** *noun*
(**a**) coffee pot
(**b**) coffee maker

LA **cage** *noun* cage

LE **cageot** *noun* crate

LA **cagoule** *noun* balaclava

> Note that the English word *cagoule* is never a translation for the French word *cagoule*.

LE **cahier** *noun* exercise book; **un cahier de brouillon** a rough (exercise) book; **un cahier de texte** a homework book

LE **caillou** *noun* stone

> The plural of *caillou* is *cailloux*.

LE **Caire** *noun* Cairo; **il habite au Caire** he lives in Cairo

LA **caisse** *noun*
(**a**) box, crate
(**b**) cash desk, checkout
(**c**) till, cash register
(**d**) **une caisse d'épargne** a savings bank

LE **caissier,** LA **caissière** *noun* cashier; **elle est caissière** she's a cashier

LE **calcul** *noun*
(**a**) calculation; **des calculs compliqués** complicated calculations
(**b**) **le calcul** arithmetic; **il est bon en calcul** he's good at arithmetic; **le calcul mental** mental arithmetic

LA **calculatrice** *noun* calculator

calculer *verb* to calculate, to work out

LA **calculette** *noun* pocket calculator

LE **caleçon** *noun*
(**a**) (pair of) boxer shorts; **où est mon caleçon?** where are my boxer shorts?
(**b**) (pair of) leggings; **elle porte un caleçon noir** she's wearing black leggings

LE **calendrier** *noun* calendar

LA **Californie** *noun* California

câlin, câline
1 *adjective* affectionate
2 *masculine noun* **un câlin** a cuddle; **faire un câlin à quelqu'un** to give somebody a cuddle

LE **calmant** *noun*
(**a**) sedative
(**b**) painkiller

calme
1 *adjective*
(**a**) quiet
(**b**) calm
2 *masculine noun* **le calme** peace and quiet; **j'ai besoin de calme pour réviser** I need some peace and quiet to revise; **du calme!** calm down!

calmer
1 *verb*
(**a**) to calm down
(**b**) to soothe
(**c**) to appease
2 *reflexive verb* **se calmer**
(**a**) to calm down
(**b**) to die down

LE/LA **camarade** *noun* friend

LE **Cambodge** *noun* Cambodia

LE **Cambodgien,** LA **Cambodgienne** *noun* (*person*) Cambodian

cambodgien, cambodgienne *adjective* Cambodian; **l'économie cambodgienne** the Cambodian economy

> In French, only the noun for the inhabitants of a country takes a capital letter, never the adjective.

LE **cambouis** *noun* grease (*for machinery*)

LE **cambriolage** *noun* burglary

cambrioler *verb* **cambrioler une maison** to burgle a house; **mon grand-père s'est fait cambrioler** my grandfather was burgled

LE **cambrioleur,** LA **cambrioleuse** *noun* burglar

LE **caméléon** *noun* chameleon

LA **caméra** *noun* TV camera, film camera

LE **caméscope**® *noun* camcorder

LE **camion** *noun* lorry

LE **camion-citerne** *noun* tanker

> The plural of *camion-citerne* is *camions-citernes*.

LA **camionnette** *noun* van

LE **camionneur,** LA **camionneuse** *noun* lorry driver; **il est camionneur** he's a lorry driver

LE **camp** *noun* camp; **un camp de vacances** a holiday camp

> The *p* in *camp* is not pronounced.

LA **campagne** *noun*
(a) country, countryside; **vivre à la campagne** to live in the country
(b) campaign

camper *verb* to camp

LE **campeur,** LA **campeuse** *noun* camper

LE **camping** *noun*
(a) camping; **je n'aime pas le camping** I don't like camping
(b) campsite; **un camping au bord de la mer** a campsite by the sea

LE **Canada** *noun* Canada

LE **Canadien,** LA **Canadienne** *noun* *(person)* Canadian

canadien, canadienne *adjective* Canadian

> In French, only the noun for the inhabitants of a country takes a capital letter, never the adjective.

LE **canal** *noun* canal

> The plural of *canal* is *canaux*.

LA **canalisation** *noun* pipe *(for water, gas)*

LE **canapé** *noun* sofa, couch

ᴸE **canard** *noun* duck

LE **canari** *noun* canary

LE **Cancer** *noun* Cancer; **elle est Cancer** she's a Cancer

LE **cancer** *noun* cancer; **il a un cancer** he's got cancer; **le cancer du poumon** lung cancer

LE **caniche** *noun* poodle

LA **canicule** *noun* heat wave

LE **canif** *noun* penknife

LE **caniveau** *noun* gutter

> The plural of *caniveau* is *caniveaux*.

LA **canne** *noun*
(a) walking stick
(b) **une canne à pêche** a fishing rod

LA **cannelle** *noun* cinnamon

LE **canoë** *noun*
(a) canoe
(b) canoeing

LE **canon** *noun*
(a) big gun
(b) cannon

LE **canot** *noun* dinghy; **un canot pneumatique** a rubber dinghy; **un canot de sauvetage** a lifeboat

> The *t* in *canot* is not pronounced.

LA **cantine** *noun* canteen

LE **caoutchouc** *noun* rubber; **des gants en caoutchouc** rubber gloves; **des bottes en caoutchouc** wellingtons

> The final *c* in *caoutchouc* is not pronounced.

LE **capitaine** *noun* captain; **il est capitaine** he's a captain

LA **capitale** *noun* capital, capital city; **quelle est la capitale du Paraguay?** what's the capital of Paraguay?

LE **capot** *noun* bonnet *(of car)*

> The *t* in *capot* is not pronounced.

LE **caprice** *noun*
(a) whim

(b) tantrum; **faire un caprice** to throw a tantrum

capricieux, capricieuse *adjective* temperamental

LE **Capricorne** *noun* Capricorn; **il est Capricorne** he's a Capricorn

LA **capsule** *noun* cap *(of a bottle)*

LA **capuche** *noun* hood *(of a coat, a sweater)*

LE **capuchon** *noun* cap *(of a pen)*

car[1] *conjunction* because; **je ne suis pas venu car j'avais du travail** I didn't come because I had work to do

LE **car**[2] *noun* bus, coach

> Note that the English word *car* is never a translation for the French word *car*.

LE **caractère** *noun*
(a) character, personality; **elle a bon caractère** she's good-natured; **il a mauvais caractère** he's bad-tempered
(b) character, letter; **un texte écrit en petits caractères** a text written in small print

LA **carafe** *noun* jug

LE **carambolage** *noun* pile-up *(of cars)*

LE **caramel** *noun*
(a) caramel
(b) toffee; **tu veux un caramel?** do you want a toffee?

LA **carapace** *noun* shell *(of a turtle)*

LA **caravane** *noun* caravan

LE **carburant** *noun* fuel

cardiaque *adjectif* **des problèmes cardiaques** heart problems; **une crise cardiaque** a heart attack; **il est cardiaque** he's got a heart condition

caresser *verb* to stroke

LA **cargaison** *noun* cargo

LA **carie** *noun* cavity; **vous avez deux caries** you have two cavities; **la carie dentaire** tooth decay

LE **carnaval** carnival

> The plural of *carnaval* is *carnavals*.

LE **carnet** *noun*
(a) notebook
(b) **un carnet de timbres** a book of stamps; **un carnet de chèques** a cheque book
(c) **un carnet de notes** a school report

carnivore *adjective* meat-eating, carnivorous

LA **carotte** *noun* carrot

carré, carrée
1 *adjective* square
2 *masculine noun* **un carré** a square

LE **carreau** *noun*
(a) window pane
(b) tile
(c) **une chemise à carreaux** a checked shirt
(d) diamonds *(in cards)*; **le dix de carreau** the ten of diamonds

> The plural of *carreau* is *carreaux*.

LE **carrefour** *noun* crossroads

LE **carrelage** *noun*
(a) tiles
(b) tiled floor

carrément *adverb*
(a) straight out; **je lui ai dit carrément ce que je pensais** I told him straight out what I thought
(b) completely; **la soupe était carrément froide** the soup was completely cold

LA **carrière** *noun*
(a) career
(b) quarry

LE **cartable** *noun* schoolbag

LA **carte** *noun*
(a) card; **une carte d'identité** an identity card; **une carte bleue**® a debit card; **une carte postale** a postcard; **une carte téléphonique** a phonecard; **une carte de vœux** a greetings card; **une carte de visite** a business card; **une carte orange** a

season ticket *(for the Paris transport network)*
(b) **une carte à jouer** a playing card; **jouer aux cartes** to play cards
(c) map
(d) menu

LE **carton** *noun*
(a) cardboard
(b) cardboard box

LA **cartouche** *noun* cartridge

LE **cas** *noun*
(a) case; **en tout cas** in any case; **dans ce cas** in that case; **beaucoup de gens croient qu'il est très riche mais ce n'est pas le cas** a lot of people think he's very rich, but that's not the case
(b) **en cas de** in the event of; **en cas d'accident** in the event of an accident; **en cas d'urgence** in case of an emergency
(c) **au cas où** in case, if; **au cas où elle tomberait** in case she falls *or* if she should fall; **prenez votre parapluie au cas où** take your umbrella just in case

LA **cascade** *noun* waterfall

LE **cascadeur,** LA **cascadeuse** *noun* stuntman/stuntwoman; **il est cascadeur** he's a stuntman

LA **case** *noun* box *(on a form)*

LA **caserne** *noun* barracks; **une caserne de pompiers** a fire station

LE **casque** *noun*
(a) helmet
(b) headphones

LA **casquette** *noun* cap *(hat)*

LE **casse-croûte** *noun* snack

> The word *casse-croûte* does not change in the plural.

LE **casse-noix** *noun* nutcracker

> The word *casse-noix* does not change in the plural.

casser
1 *verb* to break
2 *reflexive verb* **se casser** to break; **la**

branche **s'est cassée** the branch broke; **elle s'est cassé la jambe** she broke her leg

LA **casserole** *noun* saucepan

> Note that the English word *casserole* is never a translation for the French word *casserole*.

LA **cassette** *noun*
(a) tape, cassette
(b) **une cassette vidéo** a video, a video cassette

LE **cassis** *noun* blackcurrant

LE **castor** *noun* beaver

LA **catastrophe** *noun* disaster

LE **catch** *noun* wrestling

> Note that the English word *catch* is never a translation for the French word *catch*.

LE **cauchemar** *noun* nightmare; **il fait souvent des cauchemars** he often has nightmares

LA **cause** *noun*
(a) cause
(b) **à cause de** because of; **c'est à cause de toi qu'on est arrivé en retard** we arrived late because of you

causer *verb*
(a) to cause
(b) to chat

LA **cave** *noun* cellar

> Note that the English word *cave* is never a translation for the French word *cave*.

LA **caverne** *noun* cave

ce¹ *pronoun*
(a) it, that; **c'est amusant** it's funny; **qu'est-ce que c'est?** what is it?
(b) these; **ce sont mes lunettes** these are my glasses
(c) he, she, they; **c'est un écrivain français** he's a French writer; **c'est une musicienne célèbre** she's a famous musician; **ce sont des animaux dangereux** they're dangerous animals

(d) ce que, ce qui what; **je sais ce que tu veux** I know what you want; **c'est ce qui m'énerve** that's what I find irritating

(e) ce que, ce qui which; **elle est malade, ce que je ne savais pas** she's ill, which I didn't know; **il n'a pas encore téléphoné, ce qui m'inquiète** he hasn't phoned yet, which worries me

(f) ce qu'il est bête! he's so stupid!; **ce qu'il fait chaud!** it's so hot!

> *Ce* becomes *c'* in front of *e* and *é*, eg *c'est amusant*.

ce², cet, cette *adjective* this, that; **ce stylo m'appartient** this pen belongs to me; **ce livre-ci** this book; **cet homme-là** that man; **cet appareil photo ne coûte pas cher** this camera isn't expensive; **cette année nous allons en vacances en Normandie** this year we're going to Normandy on holiday

> *Ce* is used with masculine nouns and *cette* is used with feminine nouns. *Ce* becomes *cet* in front of a vowel or a mute h, eg *cet appareil*, *cet homme*. The plural of *ce*, *cet* and *cette* is *ces*. See also **ces**.

ceci *pronoun* this; **ceci est un mensonge** this is a lie

céder *verb* to give in

LA **cédille** *noun* cedilla

LA **ceinture** *noun* belt; **une ceinture de sécurité** a seatbelt

cela *pronoun* it, that; **cela ne vaut pas la peine** it isn't worth it

célèbre *adjective* famous

LE **céleri** *noun* celery; **une branche de céleri** a stick of celery

célibataire

1 *adjective* single; **ma sœur est célibataire** my sister is single

2 *noun* **un célibataire** a bachelor, a single man; **une célibataire** a single woman

celle *see* **celui**

celle-ci *see* **celui-ci**

celle-là *see* **celui-là**

celles-ci *see* **ceux-ci**

celles-là *see* **ceux-là**

LA **cellule** *noun* cell

celui, celle *pronoun* the one; **sur la photo, mon frère est celui qui fait une grimace** in the photo my brother's the one pulling a face; **des trois robes que j'ai essayées, c'est celle que je préfère** of the three dresses I tried on, this is the one I like best; **ce n'est pas ma chambre, c'est celle de ma sœur** this isn't my bedroom, it's my sister's

> *Celui* is a masculine pronoun and *celle* is a feminine pronoun. The plural of *celui* is *ceux* and the plural of *celle* is *celles*. See also **ceux**.

celui-ci, celle-ci *pronoun* this one; **celui-ci me plaît** I like this one; **celle-ci n'est pas assez grande** this one is not big enough

> *Celui-ci* is a masculine pronoun and *celle-ci* is a feminine pronoun. The plural of *celui-ci* is *ceux-ci* and the plural of *celle-ci* is *celles-ci*. See also **ceux-ci**.

celui-là, celle-là *pronoun* that one; **j'ai bien aimé ce livre-ci mais j'ai détesté celui-là** I liked this book but I hated that one; **celle-là est trop chère** that one is too expensive

> *Celui-là* is a masculine pronoun and *celle-là* is a feminine pronoun. The plural of *celui-là* is *ceux-là* and the plural of *celle-là* is *celles-là*. See also **ceux-là**.

LA **cendre** *noun* ash

LE **cendrier** *noun* ashtray

censé, censée *adjective* **être censé faire quelque chose** to be supposed to do something; **ce médicament est censé calmer la douleur** this medicine is supposed to relieve pain; **elle est censée venir me chercher** she is supposed to come and pick me up

censurer *verb* to censor

cent *number*

(**a**) a hundred; **cent personnes** a hundred people; **deux cents hommes** two hundred men

(**b**) **cinq pour cent** five percent

Cent is spelt with an s from deux cents onwards but there is no s after cent when another number follows, eg deux cent cinquante.

LA **centaine** *noun* about a hundred; **une centaine de personnes** about a hundred people; **des centaines de voitures** hundreds of cars

centième *number* hundredth

LE **centime** *noun* **un centime** a cent

LE **centimètre** *noun*

(**a**) centimetre

(**b**) tape measure

LA **centrale** *noun* **une centrale** *or* **une centrale électrique** a power station; **une centrale nucléaire** a nuclear power station

LE **centre** *noun* centre; **un centre commercial** a shopping centre

LE **centre-ville** *noun* city centre, town centre

The plural of centre-ville is centres-villes.

cependant *adverb* yet, however

LE **cercle** *noun* circle; **un cercle vicieux** a vicious circle

LE **cercueil** *noun* coffin

LA **céréale** *noun*

(**a**) **des céréales** cereal; **je mange des céréales au petit déjeuner** I eat cereal for breakfast

(**b**) cereal *(crop)*; **l'orge est une céréale** barley is a (type of) cereal

LA **cérémonie** *noun* ceremony

LE **cerf** *noun* stag

The f in cerf is not pronounced.

LE **cerf-volant** *noun* kite

The plural of cerf-volant is cerfs-volants.

LA **cerise** *noun* cherry

LE **cerisier** *noun* cherry tree

LE **cerne** *noun* ring *(under the eyes)*

cerner *verb*

(**a**) to surround; **nous sommes cernés** we're surrounded

(**b**) **j'ai du mal à le cerner** I can't figure him out

certain, certaine

1 *adjective*

(**a**) certain, sure; **je suis certain qu'il viendra** I'm sure he'll come; **ils vont gagner, c'est certain** they're certain to win

(**b**) some, certain; **c'est un sport qui demande une certaine adresse** it's a sport that requires a certain amount of skill; **un certain Paul a téléphoné pendant ton absence** someone called Paul phoned while you were away; **un certain temps** a while

2 *pronoun* **certains, certaines**

(**a**) some; **certains d'entre nous** some of us; **choisis bien les bananes car certaines sont pourries** choose the bananas carefully because some of them are rotten

(**b**) some people; **certains pensent qu'il ment** some people think he's lying

certainement *adverb* most probably; **certainement!** of course!; **certainement pas!** certainly not!

LE **cerveau** *noun* brain

The plural of cerveau is cerveaux.

ces *plural adjective* these, those; **à qui sont ces gants?** whose are these gloves?; **ces photos sont très belles** these photos are lovely

Ces is the plural of ce and cette.

cesse **sans cesse** constantly, all the time; **il pleut sans cesse depuis**

dimanche it's been raining non-stop since Sunday

cesser *verb* to stop

LE **cessez-le-feu** *noun* ceasefire

> The word *cessez-le-feu* does not change in the plural.

c'est-à-dire *conjunction*
(a) that is to say; **toute la famille, c'est-à-dire mes parents et mes sœurs** the whole family, that is to say, my parents and my sisters; **c'est-à-dire?** what do you mean?
(b) **c'est-à-dire que** actually; **est-ce que vous voulez venir avec nous? – c'est-à-dire que je suis un peu fatigué** do you want to come with us? – actually I'm a bit tired

cet, cette *see* ce²

ceux, celles *pronoun* the ones; **si tu as besoin de crayons de couleur, prends ceux qui sont sur mon bureau** if you need coloured pencils, take the ones on my desk; **ce ne sont pas mes lunettes, ce sont celles de mon frère** these aren't my glasses, they're my brother's

> *Ceux* is a masculine plural pronoun and *celles* is a feminine plural pronoun. *Ceux* is the plural of *celui* and *celles* is the plural of *celle*.

ceux-ci, celles-ci *pronoun* these ones; **ces ciseaux coupent mal, prends ceux-ci** those scissors don't cut very well, take these ones; **si tes chaussettes sont trop petites, essaie celles-ci** if your socks are too small, try these ones

> *Ceux-ci* is a masculine plural pronoun and *celles-ci* is a feminine plural pronoun. *Ceux-ci* is the plural of *celui-ci* and *celles-ci* is the plural of *celle-ci*.

ceux-là, celles-là *pronoun* those ones; **si ces gants sont trop petits, essaie ceux-là** if these gloves are too small, try those ones; **ces serviettes de table sont sales, prends celles-là** these napkins are dirty, take those ones

> *Ceux-là* is a masculine plural pronoun and *celles-là* is a feminine plural pronoun. *Ceux-là* is the plural of *celui-là* and *celles-là* is the plural of *celle-là*.

chacun, chacune *pronoun*
(a) each; **vous avez droit à une pomme chacun** you may have one apple each
(b) everyone; **chacun est libre de penser ce qu'il veut** everyone has the right to think what they want

LE **chagrin** *noun* grief; **avoir du chagrin** to be upset

LE **chahut** *noun* racket *(noise)*

LA **chaîne** *noun*
(a) chain; **une chaîne de vélo** a bicycle chain
(b) channel; **une chaîne de télévision** a television channel
(c) **une chaîne hi-fi** a hi-fi; **une chaîne laser** a CD system
(d) **une chaîne de montagnes** a mountain range

LA **chair** *noun* flesh; **avoir la chair de poule** to have goose bumps

LA **chaise** *noun* chair; **une chaise longue** a deckchair

LE **châle** *noun* shawl

LA **chaleur** *noun*
(a) heat
(b) warmth

chaleureux, chaleureuse *adjective* warm; **sa mère est quelqu'un de très chaleureux** his mother is a very warm person; **un accueil chaleureux** a warm welcome

LE **chalutier** *noun* trawler

se chamailler *reflexive verb* to squabble

LA **chambre** *noun* bedroom, room

LE **chameau** *noun* camel

The plural of *chameau* is *chameaux*.

LE **champ** *noun*
(**a**) field
(**b**) **faire quelque chose à tout bout de champ** *(informal phrase)* to do something all the time

The *p* in *champ* is not pronounced.

LE **champignon** *noun* mushroom

LE **champion**, LA **championne** *noun* champion; **le champion du monde** the world champion

LE **championnat** *noun* championship; **le championnat du monde** the world championship

LA **chance** *noun*
(**a**) luck; **tu as beaucoup de chance** you're very lucky; **bonne chance!** good luck!
(**b**) chance; **c'est sa dernière chance** it's his last chance; **elle a des chances de réussir** she has a chance of success

LE **chandelier** *noun* candlestick

Note that the English word *chandelier* is never a translation for the French word *chandelier*.

LE **changement** *noun* change

changer
1 *verb*
(**a**) to change; **il a beaucoup changé en deux ans** he changed a lot in two years; **il faut changer le bébé** the baby needs to be changed
(**b**) **changer d'avis** to change one's mind; **je vais changer de chaussures, celles-ci me font mal** I'm going to change my shoes, these ones are hurting me; **il faut changer de train à Londres** you need to change trains in London; **j'ai changé de voiture** I've changed my car; **changer de vitesse** to change gear; **changer de sujet** to change the subject
2 *reflexive verb* **se changer** to get changed, to change one's clothes

LA **chanson** *noun* song

LE **chant** *noun*
(**a**) singing
(**b**) **un chant de Noël** a Christmas carol

The *t* in *chant* is not pronounced.

LE **chantage** *noun* blackmail

chanter *verb*
(**a**) to sing
(**b**) **faire chanter quelqu'un** to blackmail somebody

LE **chanteur**, LA **chanteuse** *noun* singer; **elle est chanteuse** she's a singer

LE **chantier** *noun* building site

LE **chapeau** *noun*
(**a**) hat; **un chapeau melon** a bowler hat; **un chapeau de soleil** a sun hat
(**b**) **chapeau!** well done!

The plural of *chapeau* is *chapeaux*.

LA **chapelle** *noun* chapel

LE **chapitre** *noun* chapter

chaque *adjective* every, each

LE **char** *noun* tank *(military vehicle)*

LE **charbon** *noun* coal

LA **charcuterie** *noun*
(**a**) pork butcher's
(**b**) cold meats *(such as pâté, sausages, ham)*

LE **charcutier**, LA **charcutière** *noun* pork butcher; **il est charcutier** he's a pork butcher

LE **chardon** *noun* thistle

charger
1 *verb*
(**a**) to load, to load up; **il a chargé le camion** he loaded the lorry
(**b**) **charger quelqu'un de faire quelque chose** to tell somebody to do something
2 *reflexive verb* **se charger**
(**a**) **se charger de quelque chose** to take care of something; **occupe-toi de la nourriture, il se charge de la**

boisson you see to the food, he's taking care of the drinks
(**b**) **se charger de faire quelque chose** to take responsibility for doing something; **je me charge de les prévenir** I'll warn them, leave it to me

LE **chariot** *noun* trolley

The *t* in *chariot* is not pronounced.

charmant, charmante *adjective* charming

LE **charme** *noun* charm; **elle a beaucoup de charme** she's very charming

LE **charpentier** *noun* carpenter; **il est charpentier** he's a carpenter

LA **charrette** *noun* cart

LA **charrue** *noun* plough

LA **chasse** *noun*
(**a**) hunting; **je ne suis jamais allé à la chasse** I've never been hunting; **chasse au trésor** treasure hunt
(**b**) shooting; **la chasse au canard** duck shooting
(**c**) **chasse d'eau** flush *(of toilet)*; **tirer la chasse d'eau** to flush (the toilet)

LE **chasse-neige** *noun* snowplough

The word *chasse-neige* does not change in the plural.

chasser *verb*
(**a**) to hunt
(**b**) **chasser quelqu'un** to drive somebody away; **ils l'ont chassé du village** they drove him out of the village; **chasser les mouches** to brush the flies away; **chasser les odeurs** to get rid of bad smells

LE **chasseur**, LA **chasseuse** *noun* hunter

LE **chat** *noun* cat; **j'ai un chat dans la gorge** I have a frog in my throat; **il n'y a pas un chat** *(informal phrase)* there's not a soul about

LA **châtaigne** *noun* chestnut

LE **châtaignier** *noun* chestnut tree

châtain *adjective* brown; **elle a les** cheveux châtains she has brown hair

LE **château**
(**a**) castle
(**b**) palace

The plural of *château* is *châteaux*.

LE **chaton** *noun* kitten

chatouiller *verb* to tickle

chatouilleux, chatouilleuse *adjective* ticklish

LA **chatte** *noun* female cat

chaud, chaude
1 *adjective*
(**a**) hot; **baisse le chauffage si tu as trop chaud** turn the heating down if you're too hot
(**b**) warm; **tu as assez chaud?** are you warm enough?
(**c**) **on a eu chaud!** *(informal phrase)* we had a lucky escape!
2 *adverb* **chaud il fait chaud** it's hot, the weather's hot

LA **chaudière** *noun* boiler

LE **chauffage** *noun* heating

LE **chauffe-eau** *noun* water heater

The word *chauffe-eau* does not change in the plural.

chauffer *verb*
(**a**) to heat up, to heat; **la soupe est en train de chauffer** the soup's just heating up; **je vais faire chauffer de l'eau** I'm going to heat some water; **ça va chauffer!** *(informal phrase)* there's going to be trouble!
(**b**) to overheat

LE **chauffeur** *noun*
(**a**) driver; **un chauffeur routier** or **un chauffeur de camion** a lorry driver; **il est chauffeur de taxi** he's a taxi driver
(**b**) chauffeur

LA **chaussée** *noun* road

chausser *verb* **tu chausses du combien?** what's your shoe size?

LA **chaussette** *noun* sock

LE **chausson** *noun*
(a) slipper
(b) **un chausson aux pommes** an apple turnover

LA **chaussure** *noun*
(a) shoe; **des chaussures en cuir** leather shoes
(b) boot; **des chaussures de marche** walking boots; **des chaussures de ski** ski boots

chauve *adjective* bald

LA **chauve-souris** *noun* bat

> The plural of *chauve-souris* is *chauves-souris*.

chavirer *verb* to capsize

LE **chef** *noun*
(a) head; **un chef d'État** a head of state
(b) leader
(c) boss; **un chef d'entreprise** a company director
(d) **un chef d'orchestre** a conductor
(e) **un chef cuisinier** a chef

LE **chef-d'œuvre** *noun* masterpiece

> The plural of *chef-d'œuvre* is *chefs-d'œuvre*. Note that the *f* of *chef-d'œuvre* is not pronounced.

LE **chemin** *noun*
(a) road, path; **c'est un petit chemin bordé d'arbres** it's a little tree-lined path; **ne pas y aller par quatre chemins** *(informal phrase)* to get straight to the point
(b) way; **je connais un autre chemin pour y aller** I know another way to get there
(c) **les chemins de fer** the railways

LA **cheminée** *noun*
(a) chimney
(b) fireplace
(c) mantelpiece
(d) funnel

LA **chemise** *noun*
(a) shirt; **une chemise de nuit** a nightdress
(b) folder

LE **chemisier** *noun* blouse

LE **chêne** *noun* oak; **une table en chêne** an oak table

LA **chenille** *noun* caterpillar

LE **chèque** *noun* cheque; **un chèque sans provision** a bad cheque; **des chèques de voyage** traveller's cheques

LE **chéquier** *noun* cheque book

cher, chère *adjective*
(a) dear; **une amie très chère** a very dear friend; **cher Papa** *(at the beginning of a letter)* dear Dad
(b) expensive; **c'est trop cher** it's too expensive; **ça coûte très cher** it's very expensive

chercher *verb*
(a) to look for; **le prof cherche son sac** the teacher is looking for his bag
(b) **aller chercher quelque chose** to go and get something; **est-ce que tu pourrais aller chercher du lait, s'il te plaît?** could you go and get some milk, please?
(c) **aller chercher quelqu'un** to pick somebody up; **j'irai te chercher à la gare** I'll pick you up at the station

LE **chercheur,** LA **chercheuse** *noun* scientist; **il est chercheur** he's a scientist

chéri, chérie *noun* darling; **mon chéri, ma chérie** my darling

LE **cheval** *noun* horse; **un cheval de course** a racehorse; **faire du cheval** to go riding; **à cheval** on horseback

> The plural of *cheval* is *chevaux*.

LE **chevalier** *noun* knight

LE **cheveu** *noun* hair; **il y a un cheveu dans ma soupe** there's a hair in my soup; **les cheveux** hair; **elle a de beaux cheveux** she has beautiful hair; **elle a les cheveux blonds** she has blond hair

LA **cheville** *noun* ankle

LA **chèvre** *noun* goat

chez *preposition*

(a) at; **être chez quelqu'un** to be at somebody's house; **elle est chez Marie** she's at Marie's; **elle est chez le coiffeur** she's at the hairdresser's; **je suis chez moi** I'm at home
(b) to; **aller chez quelqu'un** to go to somebody's house; **elle va chez Marie** she's going to Marie's; **elle va chez le coiffeur** she's going to the hairdresser's; **je vais chez moi** I'm going home

chic *adjective*
(a) smart, elegant
(b) nice; **c'est chic de la part de Pierre de t'avoir invitée** it was nice of Pierre to invite you

> The word *chic* does not change in the plural or in the feminine, eg *des vêtements chic*.

LE **chien** *noun* dog; **il fait un temps de chien** *(informal phrase)* it's foul weather

LA **chienne** *noun* dog, bitch

LE **chiffon** *noun*
(a) rag
(b) duster

chiffonner *verb*
(a) to crumple
(b) to crease

LE **chiffre** *noun* figure, number

LE **chignon** *noun* bun; **ma grand-mère porte un chignon** my grandmother wears her hair in a bun

LE **Chili** *noun* Chile

LE **Chilien**, LA **Chilienne** *noun (person)* Chilean

chilien, chilienne *adjective* Chilean; **le gouvernement chilien** the Chilean government

LA **chimie** *noun* chemistry

chimique *adjective* chemical

LE **chimpanzé** *noun* chimpanzee

LA **Chine** *noun* China

LE **Chinois**, LA **Chinoise** *noun* Chinese man/Chinese woman; **les Chinois** the Chinese

chinois, chinoise
1 *adjective* Chinese; **l'économie chinoise** the Chinese economy
2 *masculine noun* **le chinois** *(language)* Chinese; **il parle chinois** he speaks Chinese

> In French, only the noun for the inhabitants of a country takes a capital letter, never the adjective or the noun for the language.

LE **chiot** *noun* puppy

> The *t* in *chiot* is not pronounced.

LES **chips** *feminine plural noun* crisps

> Note that the English word *chips* is never a translation for the French word *chips*.

LE **choc** *noun*
(a) impact; **le choc a été si violent que je suis tombé** the impact was so tremendous that I fell over
(b) shock; **ça m'a fait un choc d'apprendre ça** it was a shock to hear that

LE **chocolat** *noun* chocolate; **du chocolat au lait** milk chocolate; **du chocolat noir** dark chocolate; **un chocolat chaud** a hot chocolate

> The *t* in *chocolat* is not pronounced.

LE **chœur** *noun* choir

choisir *verb* to choose

LE **choix** *noun* choice

LE **chômage** *noun* unemployment

LE **chômeur**, LA **chômeuse** *noun* unemployed person; **les chômeurs** the unemployed

choquant, choquante *adjective* shocking

choquer *verb* to shock

LA **chorale** *noun* choir

LA **chose** *noun* thing

LE **chou** *noun*
(a) cabbage; **des choux de Bruxelles** Brussels sprouts; **des choux à la crème** cream puffs

(**b**) **mon petit chou** *(term of affection)* darling, honey

The plural of *chou* is *choux*.

LE **chouchou**, LA **chouchoute** *noun* teacher's pet

This word is informal.

LA **choucroute** *noun* sauerkraut

LA **chouette**[1] *noun* owl

chouette[2] *exclamation* great

LE **chou-fleur** *noun* cauliflower

The plural of *chou-fleur* is *choux-fleurs*.

chrétien, chrétienne
1 *adjective* Christian
2 *noun* **un chrétien, une chrétienne** a Christian

LE **chronomètre** *noun* stopwatch

chuchoter *verb* to whisper

chut *exclamation* sh, shush

LA **chute** *noun*
(**a**) fall; **faire une chute** to fall
(**b**) **une chute d'eau** a waterfall; **une chute de neige** a snowfall

Chypre *noun* Cyprus; **il vit à Chypre** he lives in Cyprus

LE **Chypriote**, LA **Chypriote** *noun* *(person)* Cypriot

chypriote *adjective* Cypriot; **la question chypriote** the Cypriot issue

-ci *adverb*
(**a**) **ces jours-ci** these days; **ces livres-ci** these books
(**b**) **par-ci par-là** here and there

LA **cible** *noun* target

LA **cicatrice** *noun* scar

cicatriser *verb* to heal

ci-dessous *adverb* below

ci-dessus *adverb* above

LE **cidre** *noun* cider

LE **ciel** *noun*
(**a**) sky

(**b**) heaven

LA **cigale** *noun* cicada

LE **cigare** *noun* cigar

LA **cigarette** *noun* cigarette

LA **cigogne** *noun* stork

LE **cil** *noun* eyelash

LE **ciment** *noun* cement

The *t* in *ciment* is not pronounced.

LE **cimetière** *noun* cemetery

LE **ciné** *noun* cinema

This word is informal.

LE **cinéma** *noun* cinema

cinglé, cinglée *adjective* mad, crazy

This word is informal.

cinq *number* five; **le cinq septembre** the fifth of September; **nous sommes le cinq avril** it's the fifth of April

LA **cinquantaine** *noun* about fifty; **une cinquantaine de personnes** about fifty people; **il a la cinquantaine** he's about fifty years old

cinquante *number* fifty; **cinquante et un** fifty-one; **cinquante-deux** fifty-two

cinquième
1 *number* fifth
2 *feminine noun* **la cinquième** the second year of secondary school (for pupils aged 12); **il est en cinquième** he's in his second year of secondary school

See also **collège**.

LE **cintre** *noun* coathanger

LE **cirage** *noun* shoe polish

circonflexe *adjective* **un accent circonflexe** a circumflex accent

LA **circonstance** *noun* circumstance; **étant donné les circonstances** given the circumstances

LE **circuit** *noun*
(**a**) circuit
(**b**) tour

The *t* in *circuit* is not pronounced.

LA **circulation** *noun*
(a) traffic; **il y a beaucoup de circulation** there's a lot of traffic
(b) circulation; **la circulation du sang** blood circulation

circuler *verb*
(a) to move; **circulez, il n'y a rien à voir** move along now, there's nothing to see
(b) to drive; **en Angleterre on circule à gauche** they drive on the left in England
(c) to run *(train, bus)*

LA **cire** *noun* wax

cirer *verb* to polish

LE **cirque** *noun*
(a) circus
(b) chaos; **c'est vraiment le cirque ici!** it's chaos in here!

Sense (b) is an informal use of *cirque*.

LES **ciseaux** *masculine plural noun* scissors; **une paire de ciseaux** a pair of scissors

LA **citation** *noun* quotation

LA **cité** *noun*
(a) housing estate
(b) city, town

citer *verb* to quote

LE **citoyen,** LA **citoyenne** *noun* citizen

LE **citron** *noun* lemon

LA **citrouille** *noun* pumpkin

LA **civière** *noun* stretcher

LE **civil,** LA **civile** *noun* civilian

clair, claire
1 *adjective*
(a) light; **cette pièce est très claire** this room is very light; **bleu clair** light blue; **en été, il fait clair très tôt** in summer it gets light very early
(b) clear; **l'eau est très claire** the water is very clear; **ses explications ne sont pas très claires** her explanations aren't very clear
2 *adverb* **clair voir clair** to see clearly

3 *masculine noun* **le clair de lune** moonlight

clairement *adverb* clearly

LA **clairière** *noun* clearing

claquer *noun*
(a) to slam; **claquer la porte** to slam the door
(b) to bang; **le vent fait claquer les volets** the wind makes the shutters bang
(c) **claquer des doigts** to snap one's fingers; **il claquait des dents** his teeth were chattering

LES **claquettes** *feminine plural noun* **faire des claquettes** to tap-dance

LA **clarinette** *noun* clarinet; **elle joue de la clarinette** she plays the clarinet

LA **classe** *noun*
(a) class; **elle est dans la classe de mon frère** she's in my brother's class; **il n'est pas allé en classe aujourd'hui** he didn't go to school today; **une classe de neige** a school skiing trip; **une classe de mer** a school trip to the seaside; **une classe verte** a nature study trip
(b) classroom

classer *verb*
(a) to file
(b) to arrange

LE **classeur** *noun* folder

LA **clavicule** *noun* collarbone

LE **clavier** *noun* keyboard

LA **clé** *noun* key; **fermer la porte à clé** to lock the door

LA **clef** *see* **clé**

The *f* in *clef* is not pronounced.

LE **client,** LA **cliente** *noun* customer, client

The *t* in *client* is not pronounced.

cligner *verb* **cligner des yeux** to blink

LE **clignotant** *noun* indicator; **n'oublie pas de mettre ton clignotant avant de tourner** don't forget to put your indicator on before you turn

clignoter *verb* to flash *(light)*

LE **climat** *noun* climate

The *t* in *climat* is not pronounced.

climatisé, climatisée *adjective* air-conditioned

LE **clin d'œil** *noun* wink; **faire un clin d'œil à quelqu'un** to wink at somebody; **faire quelque chose en un clin d'œil** to do something in the blink of an eye

LA **clinique** *noun* private clinic

cliquer *verb* to click *(with a computer mouse)*

LE **clochard**, LA **clocharde** *noun* tramp

LA **cloche** *noun* bell

cloche-pied *noun* **sauter à cloche-pied** to hop

LE **clocher** *noun* steeple

LA **clochette** *noun* small bell

LA **cloison** *noun* partition

LA **cloque** *noun* blister

LA **clôture** *noun* fence

LE **clou** *noun*
(a) nail
(b) **un clou de girofle** a clove

clouer *verb* to nail, to nail down

LE **clown** *noun* clown; **faire le clown** to clown around

LE **cobaye** *noun* guinea pig

LE **coca**® *noun* Coke®

LA **coccinelle** *noun* ladybird

LE **cochon** *noun* pig; **un cochon d'Inde** a guinea pig

LA **cochonnerie** *noun*
(a) rubbish; **il ne vend que de la cochonnerie** he only sells rubbish
(b) junk food; **il ne mange que des cochonneries** he only eats junk food
(c) **faire des cochonneries** to make a mess

(d) **dire des cochonneries** to say smutty things

This word is informal.

LE **coco** *noun* **une noix de coco** a coconut

LE **code** *noun* code; **le code de la route** the highway code; **un code postal** a postcode; **un code confidentiel** a PIN number

LE **cœur** *noun*
(a) heart; **avoir mal au cœur** to feel sick; **par cœur** by heart; **au cœur de la ville** in the heart of the town
(b) **avoir bon cœur** to be kind-hearted; **être sans cœur** to be heartless
(c) hearts *(in cards)*; **le sept de cœur** the seven of hearts

LE **coffre** *noun*
(a) chest *(piece of furniture)*
(b) boot *(of a car)*
(c) safe

LE **coffre-fort** *noun* safe

The plural of *coffre-fort* is *coffres-forts*.

cogner
1 *verb* to knock
2 *reflexive verb* **se cogner** **se cogner contre quelque chose** to bump into something; **je me suis cogné la tête** I banged my head

coiffé, coiffée *adjective* **elle est bien coiffée** her hair looks very nice

se coiffer *reflexive verb* to do one's hair

LE **coiffeur**, LA **coiffeuse** *noun* hairdresser; **elle est coiffeuse** she's a hairdresser

LA **coiffure** *noun* hairstyle

LE **coin** *noun*
(a) corner
(b) place, spot; **je connais un coin tranquille près d'ici** I know a quiet spot near here
(c) area; **je crois qu'il y a une banque**

dans le coin I think there is a bank in the area

coincer
1 *verb* to jam, to wedge
2 *reflexive verb* **se coincer** to get stuck; **ma fermeture éclair® s'est coincée** my zip got stuck; **elle s'est coincé le doigt dans le tiroir** she got her finger caught in the drawer

LE **col** *noun*
(a) collar
(b) pass *(of a mountain)*

LA **colère** *noun* anger; **être en colère contre quelqu'un** to be angry at somebody; **se mettre en colère** to get angry

LE **colis** *noun* parcel

collant¹, collante *adjective*
(a) sticky
(b) skin-tight

LE **collant²** *noun* (pair of) tights; **elle porte un collant noir** she's wearing black tights

LA **colle** *noun* glue

collectionner *verb* to collect; **il collectionne les timbres** he collects stamps

LE **collège** *noun* school *(for pupils between 11 and 15)*

Note that the English word *college* is never a translation for the French word *collège*.

Le Collège
Pupils in France leave primary school when they reach 11 to go to *collège*. The first year spent in collège is called *la sixième*, the second year *la cinquième*, the third year *la quatrième*, and the fourth and last year *la troisième*. Then pupils go on to *lycée* where they study for the *baccalauréat* exam. See also **baccalauréat** and **lycée**.

LE **collégien**, LA **collégienne** *noun* schoolboy/schoolgirl

LE/LA **collègue** *noun* colleague

coller *verb* to stick, to glue

LE **collier** *noun*
(a) necklace
(b) collar

LA **colline** *noun* hill

LA **colombe** *noun* dove

LA **colonie** *noun*
(a) colony; **ce pays est une ancienne colonie britannique** this country used to be a British colony
(b) **une colonie de vacances** a children's holiday camp

Les Colonies de Vacances
The *colonies de vacances*, or *colos*, are holiday camps for children, where they go for up to a month. They are usually reasonably priced and give children from all backgrounds an opportunity to go to the countryside, the seaside or the mountains, as well as to meet other children. The children's parents do not stay with them at the *colonie*. The children are supervised by *moniteurs* (group leaders), who organize games and activities.

LA **colonne** *noun*
(a) column
(b) **la colonne vertébrale** the spine

LE **colorant** *noun* artificial colouring

colorier *verb* to colour in, to colour

LE **coma** *noun* coma; **être dans le coma** to be in a coma

LE **combat** *noun*
(a) fight; **un combat de boxe** a boxing match
(b) **les combats ont repris** fighting has resumed

combattre *verb* to fight

See verb table p. 320.

combien
1 *adverb*
(a) how much; **combien d'argent est-ce que tu as?** how much money have you got?; **tu es resté combien de temps?** how long did you stay?
(b) how many; **tu as combien de frères et sœurs?** how many brothers

and sisters have you got?
2 *masculine noun* **on est le combien?** what's the date today?

LA **combinaison** *noun*
(**a**) combination; **quelle est la combinaison du coffre?** what's the combination for the safe?
(**b**) slip *(petticoat)*
(**c**) **une combinaison de plongée** a wetsuit; **une combinaison de ski** a ski suit

LA **comédie** *noun*
(**a**) comedy; **une comédie musicale** a musical
(**b**) act; **il n'est pas vraiment malade, c'est de la comédie** he's not really ill, it's all an act

LE **comédien**, LA **comédienne** *noun* actor/actress; **elle est comédienne** she's an actress

Note that the English word *comedian* is never a translation for the French word *comédien*.

comestible *adjective* edible

comique
1 *adjective* funny
2 *noun* **un/une comique** a comedian

LE **commandant** *noun* captain

LA **commande**
1 *noun* order *(for goods)*
2 *feminine plural noun* **les commandes** the controls; **être aux commandes** to be at the controls

commander *verb*
(**a**) to be in command; **c'est moi qui commande ici!** I'm the one giving the orders here!
(**b**) to order *(a meal, goods)*

comme
1 *adverb*
(**a**) like; **il est comme son frère** he's like his brother; **il criait comme un fou** he was yelling like a madman
(**b**) as; **elle travaille comme caissière au supermarché** she works as a supermarket cashier; **l'araignée était**

grande comme ma main the spider was as big as my hand; **comme toujours** as always; **il est excellent comme prof** he's an excellent teacher; **qu'est-ce que tu as eu comme cadeaux?** what presents did you get?
(**c**) **comme c'est beau!** it's so beautiful!; **comme je suis content!** I'm so happy!
(**d**) **comme ci comme ça** so-so
(**e**) **comme il faut** properly
2 *conjunction* since; **comme il n'était pas là, nous avons commencé sans lui** since he wasn't there, we started without him

LE **commencement** *noun* beginning, start

commencer *verb* to start, to begin

comment *adverb* how; **comment vas-tu?** how are you?; **comment?** what did you say?; **comment! il n'est pas encore rentré?** what? isn't he home yet?; **comment est-ce que tu as trouvé le film?** what did you think of the film?

LE **commentaire** *noun* commentary

LE **commerçant**, LA **commerçante** *noun* shopkeeper; **elle est commerçante** she's a shopkeeper

LE **commerce** *noun*
(**a**) trade
(**b**) business
(**c**) shop; **le petit commerce** small shops

commercial, commerciale *adjective* commercial; **un centre commercial** a shopping centre

The masculine plural of *commercial* is *commerciaux*.

commettre *verb* to commit

See verb table p. 322.

LE **commissariat** *noun* police station

LES **commissions** *feminine plural noun* shopping; **faire les commissions** to go shopping

commode¹ *adjective* handy, convenient

LA **commode²** *noun* chest of drawers

commun, commune *adjective*
(a) common; **une espèce commune** a common species; **un nom peu commun** an unusual name
(b) shared; **les deux maisons ont un jardin commun** the two houses have a shared garden
(c) **un ami commun** a mutual friend
(d) **en commun** in common; **nous n'avons rien en commun** we have nothing in common; **les transports en commun** public transport

LA **communauté** *noun* community

LA **communication** *noun*
(a) communication
(b) **une communication téléphonique** a telephone call

communiquer *verb* to communicate

LA **compagne** *noun*
(a) companion
(b) partner

LA **compagnie** *noun* company; **une compagnie aérienne** an airline; **je suis allé la voir en compagnie de mon frère** I went to see her with my brother

LE **compagnon** *noun*
(a) companion
(b) partner

LA **comparaison** *noun* comparison

comparer *verb* to compare

LE **compartiment** *noun* compartment

LE **compas** *noun* compasses, pair of compasses

The *s* in *compas* is not pronounced.

LA **compétition** *noun*
(a) competition
(b) sporting event

complet, complète *adjective*
(a) complete
(b) full

complètement *adverb* completely

compléter *verb*
(a) to complete
(b) to fill in

LE **complice** *noun* accomplice

LE **compliment** *noun* compliment; **faire des compliments à quelqu'un** to compliment somebody

The *t* in *compliment* is not pronounced.

compliqué, compliquée *adjective* complicated

LE **complot** *noun* plot, conspiracy

The *t* in *complot* is not pronounced.

LE **comportement** *noun* behaviour

comporter
1 *verb*
(a) to consist of
(b) to include, to involve; **cela comporte des difficultés** there are some difficulties involved
2 *reflexive verb* **se comporter** to behave

composer
1 *verb*
(a) to compose; **qui a composé ce morceau?** who composed this piece of music?
(b) to dial; **composer un numéro** to dial a number
(c) to make up; **quels sont les ingrédients qui composent le plat?** what's this dish made up of?
2 *reflexive verb* **se composer** se composer de to consist of, to be made up of

LE **compositeur,** LA **compositrice** *noun* composer; **il est compositeur** he's a composer

composter *verb* to punch, to validate *(a train or a bus ticket)*

LA **compote** *noun* stewed fruit, compote; **de la compote de pommes** stewed apples

comprendre
1 *verb*

(a) to understand; **il n'a toujours pas compris** he still hasn't understood
(b) to include; **le prix comprend le petit déjeuner** the price includes breakfast
2 *reflexive verb* **se comprendre**
(a) to understand each other
(b) to be understandable

See verb table p. 322.

LE **comprimé** *noun* tablet

compris, comprise *adjective*
(a) included; **le petit déjeuner n'est pas compris** breakfast isn't included
(b) **y compris** including; **ils sont tous partis, y compris ma sœur** they've all left, including my sister

Compris(e) is the past participle of the verb *comprendre*.

LE/LA **comptable** *noun* accountant; **elle est comptable** she's an accountant

The *p* in *comptable* is not pronounced.

LE **compte** *noun*
(a) account; **un compte en banque** a bank account
(b) calculation; **je ne sais pas combien de gâteaux on a vendu, je n'ai pas fait le compte** I don't know how many cakes we sold, I haven't counted; **le compte à rebours** the countdown
(c) **tenir compte de quelque chose** to take something into account
(d) **se rendre compte de quelque chose** to realize something
(e) **en fin de compte** *or* **tout compte fait** all things considered

The *p* in *compte* is not pronounced.

compter *verb*
(a) to count
(b) to intend; **je compte y aller** I intend to go
(c) **compter sur quelqu'un** to rely on somebody, to count on somebody

The *p* in *compter* is not pronounced.

LE **compteur** *noun* meter *(for gas, electricity)*; **le compteur de vitesse** the speedometer

The *p* in *compteur* is not pronounced.

LE **comptoir** *noun*
(a) bar *(in a café, a pub)*
(b) counter

The *p* in *comptoir* is not pronounced.

se concentrer *reflexive verb* to concentrate

concerner *verb*
(a) to concern
(b) to affect

LE **concert** *noun* concert

The *t* in *concert* is not pronounced.

LE/LA **concierge** *noun* caretaker; **elle est concierge** she's a caretaker

conclure *verb* to conclude

See verb table p. 320.

LE **concombre** *noun* cucumber

LE **concours** *noun*
(a) competition, contest
(b) competitive examination

LA **concurrence** *noun* competition *(in business)*

LE **concurrent,** LA **concurrente** *noun* competitor

condamner *verb*
(a) to sentence
(b) to condemn
(c) to block up *(a window, a door)*

The *m* in *condamner* is not pronounced.

LA **condition** *noun*
(a) condition
(b) **on ira à condition que ton père soit d'accord** we'll go as long as your dad agrees; **on arrivera peut-être à avoir le train, à condition de se dépêcher** we might make the train if we hurry up

LE **conducteur,** LA **conductrice** *noun* driver; **il est conducteur de bus** he's a bus driver

> Note that the English word *conductor* is never a translation for the French word *conducteur*.

conduire
1 *verb*
(a) to drive
(b) to lead; **ce chemin conduit à la mer** this path leads to the sea
2 *reflexive verb* **se conduire** to behave

> See verb table p. 320.

LA **conduite** *noun* behaviour

LA **confiance** *noun*
(a) trust; **faire confiance à quelqu'un** to trust somebody
(b) **la confiance en soi** self-confidence

confier *verb*
(a) to entrust; **est-ce que je peux te confier mon portefeuille?** can I entrust you with my wallet?
(b) to tell; **confier un secret à quelqu'un** to tell somebody a secret
2 *reflexive verb* **se confier** se confier à quelqu'un to confide in somebody

LA **confiserie** *noun* sweet shop

confisquer *verb* to confiscate

LA **confiture** *noun* jam

confondre *verb*
(a) to mix up; **je confonds toujours Slovénie et Slovaquie** I always mix up Slovenia and Slovakia
(b) **je la confonds toujours avec sa sœur** I always mistake her for her sister

LE **confort** *noun* comfort

> The *t* in *confort* is not pronounced.

confortable *adjective* comfortable

confus, confuse *adjective*
(a) confused
(b) embarrassed

LA **confusion** *noun*
(a) confusion
(b) embarrassment

LE **congé** *noun* holiday; **il a pris une semaine de congé** he took a week off; **congé de maladie** sick leave; **congé de maternité** maternity leave

LE **congélateur** *noun* freezer

congeler *verb* to freeze *(food)*

LA **conjugaison** *noun* conjugation

conjuguer *verb* to conjugate

LA **connaissance** *noun*
(a) knowledge
(b) acquaintance
(c) consciousness; **perdre connaissance** to lose consciousness; **reprendre connaissance** to regain consciousness

connaître *verb*
(a) to know
(b) to meet; **ils se sont connus au lycée** they met at secondary school
(c) **s'y connaître en quelque chose** to know a lot about something; **il s'y connaît en informatique** he knows a lot about computers

> See verb table p. 320.

connu, connue *adjective* well-known

consacrer
1 *verb* to devote; **il consacre tout son temps à ses études** he devotes all his time to his studies
2 *reflexive verb* **se consacrer** se consacrer à quelque chose to devote oneself to something; **elle se consacre entièrement à sa famille** she's completely devoted to her family

consciencieux, consciencieuse *adjective* conscientious

LE **conseil** *noun*
(a) **un conseil** a piece of advice; **des conseils** advice; **donner des conseils à quelqu'un** to give somebody some advice
(b) council; **le conseil municipal** the town council

(**c**) **un conseil de classe** a school staff meeting *(held every term to discuss the progress of the pupils)*

conseiller¹ *verb*
(**a**) **conseiller à quelqu'un de faire quelque chose** to advise somebody to do something; **je lui ai conseillé de ne pas y aller** I advised him not to go; **être mal conseillé** to be badly advised
(**b**) **conseiller quelque chose à quelqu'un** to recommend something to somebody

LE **conseiller²,** LA **conseillère** *noun*
(**a**) adviser, consultant; **il est conseiller** he's a consultant; **un conseiller d'orientation** a careers adviser
(**b**) councillor; **un conseiller municipal** a town councillor

LE **conservatoire** *noun* school *(of music, drama)*

Note that the English word *conservatory* is never a translation for the French word *conservatoire*.

LA **conserve** *noun* **une conserve** *or* **une boîte de conserve** a tin; **des conserves** tinned food; **des petits pois en conserve** tinned peas

conserver
1 *verb* to keep
2 *reflexive verb* **se conserver** to keep; **ce pain se conserve plusieurs jours** this bread keeps for several days

LA **consigne** *noun*
(**a**) left-luggage office
(**b**) deposit *(for bottles)*
(**c**) instructions; **est-ce que tu lui as donné la consigne?** did you give him the instructions?

consoler *verb* to console, to comfort

LE **consommateur,** LA **consommatrice** *noun*
(**a**) consumer
(**b**) customer *(in a café)*

LA **consommation** *noun*
(**a**) consumption
(**b**) drink *(in a café)*

consommer *verb* to consume; **ma voiture consomme beaucoup** my car uses a lot of petrol

LA **consonne** *noun* consonant

constamment *adverb* constantly

constater *verb* to notice

LA **construction** *noun*
(**a**) building *(house, office etc)*
(**b**) construction, building *(industry)*

construire *verb* to build

See verb table p. 320.

consulter *verb* to consult; **consulter un médecin** to see a doctor

LE **contact** *noun*
(**a**) contact; **prendre contact avec quelqu'un** to get in touch with somebody
(**b**) ignition *(in a car)*

contagieux, contagieuse *adjective* contagious

LE **conte** *noun* tale; **un conte de fées** a fairy tale

contenir
1 *verb*
(**a**) to contain
(**b**) to hold
2 *reflexive verb* **se contenir** to control oneself

See verb table p. 324.

content, contente *adjective* pleased, happy; **j'étais content de le revoir** I was happy to see him again

The final *t* in *content* is not pronounced.

contenter
1 *verb* to please
2 *reflexive verb* **se contenter** se contenter de quelque chose to make do with something

LE **continent** *noun* continent

The final *t* in *continent* is not pronounced.

continu, continue *adjective* continuous

continuer *verb* to carry on, to continue

LE **contraire** *noun* opposite; **au contraire** on the contrary

contrairement *adverb* contrairement à contrary to; **contrairement à ce que je t'avais dit, il n'est pas anglais** contrary to what I told you, he isn't English

contrarier *verb*
(**a**) to annoy
(**b**) to upset

LE **contrat** *noun* contract

> The final *t* in *contrat* is not pronounced.

LA **contravention** *noun* fine

contre *preposition*
(**a**) against
(**b**) for; **échanger une chose contre une autre** to exchange one thing for another
(**c**) **par contre** on the other hand

LA **contrebasse** *noun* double bass

LE **contreplaqué** *noun* plywood

LE **contrôle** *noun*
(**a**) check, inspection
(**b**) control
(**c**) test; **un contrôle de maths** a maths test

contrôler *verb* to check, to inspect

LE **contrôleur,** LA **contrôleuse** *noun* ticket inspector; **il est contrôleur** he's a ticket inspector

convaincre *verb*
(**a**) to convince
(**b**) to persuade; **il m'a convaincu de venir** he persuaded me to come

> See verb table p. 324.

convaincu, convaincue *adjective* convinced; **je suis convaincu de son innocence** I'm convinced that he is innocent

> *Convaincu(e)* is the past participle of the verb *convaincre*.

convenir *verb* convenir à quelqu'un to suit somebody; **si ça vous convient** if that suits you

> See verb table p. 324.

convertir *verb* to convert; **convertir des livres en euros** to convert pounds into euros

convoquer *verb* to summon

LE **copain** *noun*
(**a**) friend
(**b**) boyfriend

Copenhague *noun* Copenhagen

LA **copie** *noun*
(**a**) copy
(**b**) paper; **le prof va bientôt ramasser les copies** the teacher will soon collect the papers

copier *verb* to copy

copieux, copieuse *adjective*
(**a**) large *(meal)*
(**b**) generous *(portion)*

LA **copine** *noun*
(**a**) friend
(**b**) girlfriend

LE **coq** *noun* rooster, cock

LA **coque** *noun*
(**a**) shell *(of a nut, an egg)*
(**b**) **un œuf à la coque** a soft-boiled egg
(**c**) hull *(of a ship)*

LE **coquelicot** *noun* poppy

LE **coquetier** *noun* egg-cup

LE **coquillage** *noun*
(**a**) shellfish
(**b**) (sea)shell

LA **coquille** *noun* shell; **une coquille d'œuf** an eggshell; **une coquille Saint-Jacques** a scallop

LE **corbeau** *noun* crow

> The plural of *corbeau* is *corbeaux*.

LA **corbeille** *noun* basket; **une corbeille à papier** a wastepaper basket

LE **corbillard** *noun* hearse

LA **corde** *noun*
(a) rope
(b) string *(of a musical instrument, a racket)*

LE **cordonnier**, LA **cordonnière** *noun* shoe repairer, cobbler; **il est cordonnier** he's a shoe repairer

coriace *adjective* tough

LA **corne** *noun* horn

LA **cornemuse** *noun* bagpipes; **jouer de la cornemuse** to play the bagpipes

LE **cornet** *noun*
(a) cone
(b) cornet

LE **cornichon** *noun* gherkin

LE **corps** *noun* body

The *p* and the *s* of *corps* are not pronounced.

correct, correcte *adjective*
(a) correct
(b) proper
(c) acceptable, reasonable

correctement *adverb*
(a) correctly
(b) properly
(c) reasonably

LA **correspondance** *noun*
(a) correspondence; **être en correspondance avec quelqu'un** to correspond with somebody
(b) connection; **nous avons raté notre correspondance** we missed our connection

LE **correspondant**, LA **correspondante** *noun* pen friend

correspondre *verb* to correspond

corriger *verb*
(a) to correct
(b) to mark; **le prof n'a pas encore corrigé nos dissertations** the teacher hasn't marked our essays yet

LE/LA **Corse**
1 *noun (person)* Corsican man/Corsican woman
2 *feminine noun* **la Corse** Corsica

corse
1 *adjective* Corsican; **l'économie corse** the Corsican economy
2 *masculine noun* **le corse** *(language)* Corsican; **elle parle corse** she speaks Corsican

LA **corvée** *noun* chore

LE **costume** *noun*
(a) suit
(b) costume; **un costume de pirate** a pirate costume

LA **côte** *noun*
(a) coastline; **la Côte d'Azur** the French Riviera
(b) rib; **il s'est cassé une côte** he broke a rib
(c) chop; **une côte de porc** a pork chop
(d) hill; **il est descendu de vélo dans la côte** he got off his bike on the hill
(e) **côte à côte** side by side

LE **côté**
1 *noun*
(a) side; **un carré a quatre côtés** a square has four sides
(b) way; **de quel côté se trouve la poste, s'il vous plaît?** which way is the post office, please?
(c) **à côté** nearby; **nous habitons à côté** we live next door
(d) **d'un côté** on the one hand; **d'un autre côté** on the other hand
2 *preposition* **à côté de**
(a) next to; **assieds-toi à côté de moi** sit down next to me
(b) compared to; **à côté de moi il est très riche** compared to me he's very rich

LA **côtelette** *noun* chop; **une côtelette d'agneau** a lamb chop

LE **coton** *noun*
(a) cotton; **une chemise en coton** a cotton shirt
(b) **du coton hydrophile** cotton wool

LE **cou** *noun* neck; **je me suis fait mal au cou** I hurt my neck; **elle a sauté**

au cou de son grand-père she threw her arms around her grandfather's neck

LA **couche** *noun*
(a) layer
(b) coat *(of paint)*
(c) nappy

couché, couchée *adjective*
(a) in bed; **quand je suis rentré elle était déjà couchée** when I got back she was already in bed
(b) lying down; **il était couché sur le canapé** he was lying on the sofa

coucher
1 *verb*
(a) to sleep; **je couche dans la même chambre que mon frère** I sleep in the same room as my brother
(b) to put to bed; **il est tard, il faut coucher les enfants** it's late, it's time to put the children to bed
2 *reflexive verb* **se coucher**
(a) to go to bed
(b) to lie down
(c) to set; **le soleil se couche tôt en hiver** the sun sets early in winter
3 *masculine noun* **le coucher du soleil** sunset; **au coucher du soleil** at sunset; **on a vu un magnifique coucher de soleil hier** we saw a beautiful sunset yesterday

LA **couchette** *noun*
(a) couchette, berth
(b) bunk

LE **coude** *noun* elbow; **elle s'est fait mal au coude** she hurt her elbow; **il faut se serrer les coudes** we've got to stick together

coudre *verb* to sew; **j'ai cousu un bouton à ma chemise** I've sewn a button on my shirt

See verb table p. 320.

LA **couette** *noun*
(a) duvet
(b) **des couettes** bunches *(hairstyle)*; **elle porte des couettes** she wears her hair in bunches

couler *verb*
(a) to flow
(b) to run; **faire couler un bain** to run a bath; **il a le nez qui coule** he's got a runny nose
(c) to sink; **un bateau a coulé pendant la tempête** a boat sank during the storm

LA **couleur** *noun* colour

LA **couleuvre** *noun* grass snake

LE **couloir** *noun*
(a) corridor
(b) **un couloir d'autobus** a bus lane

LE **coup** *noun*
(a) blow, knock; **il m'a donné un coup sur la tête** he hit me on the head; **un coup de marteau** a blow with a hammer; **un coup de poing** a punch; **un coup de pied** a kick
(b) **un coup de feu** a shot; **un coup de sifflet** a whistle; **un coup de sonnette** a ring; **un coup de téléphone** a telephone call
(c) shock, blow; **ça m'a fait un coup d'apprendre qu'il était mort** it came as a shock when I heard that he was dead
(d) **donne un coup de brosse à ton manteau** give your coat a brush; **donne-toi un coup de peigne** give your hair a comb
(e) **après coup** afterwards
(f) **du coup** as a result; **du coup j'y suis allé tout seul** as a result I went on my own
(g) **tout à coup** *or* **tout d'un coup** suddenly
(h) **d'un seul coup** in one go
(i) **sur le coup** at first; **sur le coup j'ai cru qu'il s'était trompé** at first, I thought he'd made a mistake; **il est mort sur le coup** he died instantly
(j) **du premier coup** first time; **il a réussi son examen du premier coup** he passed his exam first time
(k) **un coup d'œil** a quick look; **jeter un coup d'œil à quelque chose** to have a quick look at something

(l) un coup de soleil sunburn
(m) donner un coup de main à quelqu'un to give somebody a hand
(n) un coup franc *(in football)* a free kick

The *p* in *coup* is not pronounced.

coupable *adjective* guilty

LA **coupe** *noun*
(a) cup *(trophy)*; **la coupe du monde** the World Cup
(b) bowl; **une coupe de glace** a bowl of ice-cream
(c) glass; **une coupe de champagne** a glass of champagne
(d) **une coupe de cheveux** a haircut

LE **coupe-papier** *noun* letter opener

The word *coupe-papier* does not change in the plural.

couper
1 *verb*
(a) to cut
(b) to cut off
2 *reflexive verb* **se couper** to cut oneself; **elle s'est coupé le doigt** she cut her finger

LE **couple** *noun* couple; **ils vivent en couple** they live together *(as a couple)*

LE **couplet** *noun* verse

LA **coupure** *noun*
(a) cut
(b) **une coupure de courant** a power cut

LA **cour** *noun*
(a) yard, courtyard
(b) playground
(c) court *(of a king or queen)*

LE **courage** *noun* courage

courageux, courageuse *adjective* brave

couramment *adverb*
(a) fluently; **elle parle anglais couramment** she speaks English fluently
(b) frequently

courant¹, courante *adjective* common

Note that the English word *current* is never a translation for the French adjective *courant*.

LE **courant²** *noun*
(a) current; **on ne peut pas traverser la rivière ici, le courant est trop fort** we can't cross the river here, the current is too strong
(b) **un courant d'air** a draught
(c) **être au courant de quelque chose** to know about something; **mettre quelqu'un au courant de quelque chose** to tell somebody about something; **je suis au courant** I know about it
(d) **dans le courant de la semaine prochaine** during the course of next week

LE **coureur** *noun*
(a) **un coureur** *or* **un coureur à pied** a runner
(b) **un coureur cycliste** a racing cyclist
(c) **un coureur automobile** a racing driver

courir *verb*
(a) to run; **descendre les escaliers en courant** to run down the stairs
(b) to race
(c) **courir un risque** to run a risk

See verb table p. 320.

LA **couronne** *noun*
(a) crown
(b) wreath

LE **courrier** *noun*
(a) mail, post; **est-ce qu'il y avait du courrier ce matin?** was there any post this morning?
(b) **le courrier électronique** e-mail

LE **cours** *noun*
(a) lesson, class; **un cours particulier** a private lesson
(b) **au cours de** during; **au cours du voyage** during the journey
(c) **en cours de route** on the way; **on s'est arrêté en cours de route** we stopped on the way
(d) **un cours d'eau** a stream, a river

LA **course**
1 *noun*
(a) race; **la course à pied** running; **la course cycliste** cycle racing; **la course automobile** motor racing
(b) errand; **il est sorti faire une course** he went out on an errand
2 *feminine plural noun* **les courses** the shopping; **faire les courses** to do the shopping

LE **coursier,** LA **coursière** *noun* courier; **il est coursier** he's a courier

court¹, courte *adjective* short

LE **court²** *noun* **un court de tennis** a tennis court

LE **cousin,** LA **cousine** *noun* cousin

LE **coussin** *noun* cushion

LE **coût** *noun* cost

LE **couteau** *noun* knife

The plural of *couteau* is *couteaux*.

coûter *verb* to cost; **combien ça coûte?** how much is it?; **ça coûte cher** it's expensive

LA **coutume** *noun* custom

LA **couture** *noun*
(a) sewing
(b) seam; **la couture de mon sac s'est défaite** the seam of my bag split

LA **couturière** *noun* dressmaker; **elle est couturière** she's a dressmaker

LE **couvent** *noun* convent

LE **couvercle** *noun*
(a) lid
(b) top *(of a tube)*

couvert¹, couverte *adjective*
(a) covered; **couvert de poussière** covered in dust
(b) overcast

Couvert(e) is the past participle of the verb *couvrir*. See verb table p. 320.

LE **couvert²** *noun* **mettre le couvert** to lay the table; **les couverts** the knives and forks

LA **couverture** *noun*
(a) blanket
(b) cover

LA **couveuse** *noun* incubator

LE **couvre-lit** *noun* bedspread

The plural of *couvre-lit* is *couvre-lits*.

couvrir
1 *verb* to cover; **il avait couvert le mur de posters** he'd covered the wall with posters
2 *reflexive verb* **se couvrir**
(a) to cloud over; **le ciel se couvre** the sky is clouding over
(b) to wrap up; **couvre-toi bien, il fait froid dehors** wrap up warm, it's cold outside

See verb table p. 320.

LE **crabe** *noun* crab

cracher *verb* to spit

LE **crachin** *noun* drizzle

LA **craie** *noun* chalk

craindre *verb*
(a) to be afraid of, to fear; **il n'a rien à craindre** he's got nothing to fear
(b) **ces plantes craignent le gel** these plants don't like frost

See verb table p. 320.

LA **crainte** *noun* fear

LA **crampe** *noun* cramp

LE **crâne** *noun* skull

LE **crapaud** *noun* toad

craquer *verb*
(a) to split, to rip; **mon sac a craqué et tout est tombé par terre** my bag split and everything fell on the ground
(b) to break, to snap; **la branche a craqué** the branch snapped
(c) to creak; **le plancher craque** the floor creaks
(d) to crack up; **je vais craquer si je ne prends pas de vacances bientôt** I'm going to crack up if I don't take a holiday soon

LA **cravate** *noun* tie

LE **crayon** *noun* pencil; **un crayon de couleur** a coloured pencil; **un crayon à bille** a ballpoint pen; **un crayon feutre** a felt-tip pen

LA **crèche** *noun*
(a) nursery, day nursery
(b) nativity scene

LE **crédit** *noun* credit; **acheter quelque chose à crédit** to buy something on credit; **faire crédit à quelqu'un** to give somebody credit

> The *t* in *crédit* is not pronounced.

créer *verb*
(a) to create
(b) to set up; **il a créé un club d'échecs dans son école** he set up a chess club at his school

LA **crème** *noun* cream; **la crème Chantilly** whipped cream

LA **crêpe** *noun* pancake

LE **crépuscule** *noun* dusk

creuser
1 *verb* to dig
2 *reflexive verb* **se creuser** se creuser **la cervelle** *(informal phrase)* to rack one's brains

creux, creuse *adjective* hollow

LA **crevaison** *noun* puncture

crevé, crevée *adjective*
(a) worn out, exhausted

> Sense (a) is an informal use of *crevé*.

(b) punctured

crever *verb*
(a) to burst
(b) to have a puncture
(c) to die

> Sense (c) is an informal use of *crever* when the subject is a person, but not when it is an animal or a plant.

(d) *(informal phrases)* **crever de faim** to be starving; **crever de froid** to be freezing; **crever de chaleur** to be boiling

LA **crevette** *noun* **une crevette (rose)** a prawn; **une crevette grise** a shrimp

LE **cri** *noun*
(a) shout, cry
(b) scream; **pousser un cri** to scream
(c) call, cry

crier *verb*
(a) to shout, to cry out
(b) to scream

LE **crime** *noun*
(a) crime
(b) murder

LE **criminel,** LA **criminelle** *noun*
(a) criminal
(b) murderer

LA **crinière** *noun* mane

LA **crise** *noun*
(a) crisis; **la crise économique** the economic crisis
(b) attack; **une crise cardiaque** a heart attack; **une crise d'asthme** an asthma attack
(c) fit; **avoir une crise de fou rire** to have a fit of the giggles; **piquer une crise** *(informal phrase)* to have a fit

LA **critique** *noun*
(a) criticism; **le prof nous fait toujours plein de critiques** the teacher is always criticizing us
(b) review; **ce film a reçu de bonnes critiques** this film has had good reviews

critiquer *verb* to criticize

LA **Croatie** *noun* Croatia

LE **croche-pied** *noun* **faire un croche-pied à quelqu'un** to trip somebody up

> The plural of *croche-pied* is *croche-pieds*.

LE **crochet** *noun*
(a) hook
(b) detour; **on a fait un crochet par Paris au retour** we made a detour via Paris on the way back

croire
1 *verb*
(a) to believe; **je la crois** I believe her;

je n'ai pas cru ce qu'elle m'a dit I didn't believe what she told me; **je crois en Dieu** I believe in God
(**b**) to think, to believe; **je crois que oui** I think so; **je ne crois pas qu'il viendra** I don't think he'll come
2 *reflexive verb* **se croire il se croit plus intelligent que les autres** he thinks he's cleverer than anyone else

See verb table p. 320.

LE **croisement** *noun* intersection, crossroads

croiser
1 *verb*
(**a**) to cross; **croiser les bras** to fold one's arms; **croiser les jambes** to cross one's legs
(**b**) **croiser quelqu'un** (*without stopping*) to pass somebody; (*meet*) to bump into somebody; **je l'ai croisé dans la rue hier mais il ne m'a pas vu** I passed him in the street yesterday but he didn't see me; **j'ai croisé ton frère dans la rue et on est allé boire un café** I bumped into your brother in the street and we went for a coffee
2 *reflexive verb* **se croiser**
(**a**) to cross, to intersect
(**b**) to pass each other; **on s'est croisés dans l'escalier** we passed each other on the stairs
(**c**) to meet briefly

LA **croisière** *noun* cruise; **ils ont fait une croisière** they went on a cruise

LE **croissant** *noun*
(**a**) croissant
(**b**) crescent

LA **croix** *noun* cross; **la Croix-Rouge** the Red Cross

croquer *verb* to munch, to crunch

LE **croquis** *noun* sketch

LA **crotte** *noun* dog dirt

croustillant, croustillante *adjective*
(**a**) crusty
(**b**) crispy

LA **croûte** *noun*
(**a**) crust
(**b**) rind
(**c**) scab

cru¹, crue¹ *see* **croire**
je ne l'ai pas cru I didn't believe him; **j'ai cru qu'il s'était trompé** I thought he had made a mistake

Cru(e) is the past participle of the verb *croire*. See verb table p. 320.

cru², crue² *adjective* raw; **de la viande crue** raw meat

LA **cruauté** *noun* cruelty

LA **cruche** *noun* jug

LES **crudités** *feminine plural noun* assorted raw vegetables, crudités

cruel, cruelle *adjective* cruel

Cuba *noun* Cuba; **il est allé à Cuba** he went to Cuba

LE **Cubain**, LA **Cubaine** *noun* (*person*) Cuban

cubain, cubaine *adjective* Cuban

In French, only the noun for the inhabitants of a country takes a capital letter, never the adjective.

cueillir *verb* to pick (*a flower, fruit*)

See verb table p. 320.

LA **cuillère** *noun* spoon

LA **cuillerée** *noun* spoonful

LE **cuir** *noun* leather; **un blouson en cuir** a leather jacket

cuire *verb*
(**a**) to cook; **j'ai fait cuire des légumes** I cooked some vegetables; **les légumes sont en train de cuire** the vegetables are cooking
(**b**) to bake; **le gâteau doit cuire une heure** the cake has to bake for an hour

See verb table p. 320.

LA **cuisine** *noun*
(**a**) kitchen; **on a mangé dans la cuisine** we ate in the kitchen

(b) cooking; **c'est toujours elle qui fait la cuisine** it's always her who does the cooking; **il fait très bien la cuisine** he's a very good cook

LE **cuisinier,** LA **cuisinière¹** *noun* cook; **elle est très bonne cuisinière** she's a very good cook

LA **cuisinière²** *noun* cooker, stove

LA **cuisse** *noun*
(a) thigh
(b) **une cuisse de poulet** a chicken leg

cuit, cuite *adjective* cooked; **bien cuit** well done

> *Cuit(e)* is the past participle of the verb *cuire*.

LE **cuivre** *noun* copper

LE **culot** *noun* cheek, nerve

> The *t* in *culot* is not pronounced.

LA **culotte** *noun* pants

cultivé, cultivée *adjective*
(a) cultured
(b) cultivated

cultiver *verb*
(a) to grow *(plants, vegetables)*
(b) to farm *(the land)*

(c) to cultivate *(fields)*

LA **culture** *noun*
(a) growing; **la culture du maïs nécessite beaucoup d'eau** growing corn requires a lot of water
(b) **les cultures** crops; **il pleut, c'est bon pour les cultures** it's raining, that's good for the crops
(c) culture; **la culture générale** general knowledge

LE **curé** *noun* parish priest

LE **cure-dents** *noun* toothpick

> The word *cure-dents* does not change in the plural.

curieux, curieuse *adjective*
(a) inquisitive, curious
(b) strange; **c'est curieux qu'il ne soit pas encore arrivé** it's strange that he hasn't arrived yet

LA **cuvette** *noun* basin, bowl

LE **cybercafé** *noun* Internet café

LE/LA **cycliste** *noun* cyclist

LE **cyclomoteur** *noun* moped

LE **cygne** *noun* swan

d' *see* **de**

> *D'* is the contracted form of *de* which is used in front of a vowel or a mute h.

d'abord *see* **abord**

d'accord *see* **accord**

d'ailleurs *see* **ailleurs**

LE **daim** *noun*
  (**a**) deer
  (**b**) suede; **une veste en daim** a suede jacket

LA **dame** *noun*
  (**a**) lady
  (**b**) queen *(in chess, cards)*; **la dame de cœur** the queen of hearts
  (**c**) **les dames** *or* **le jeu de dames** draughts; **est-ce que tu veux jouer aux dames?** do you want to play draughts?

LE **Danemark** *noun* Denmark

LE **danger** *noun* danger; **il est en danger** he's in danger

dangereux, dangereuse *adjective* dangerous; **c'est dangereux pour la santé** it's bad for your health

LE **Danois,** LA **Danoise** *noun (person)* Dane

danois, danoise
  1 *adjective* Danish; **le Premier ministre danois** the Danish Prime Minister
  2 *masculine noun* **le danois** *(language)* Danish; **il parle danois** he speaks Danish

> In French, only the noun for the inhabitants of a country takes a capital letter, never the adjective or the noun for the language.

dans *preposition*
  (**a**) in; **ils ont cherché partout dans la maison** they looked everywhere in the house; **l'avion atterrit dans dix minutes** the plane lands in ten minutes
  (**b**) into; **elle est entrée dans la classe** she went into the classroom
  (**c**) on; **il est dans le bus** he's on the bus
  (**d**) out of, from; **j'ai pris l'argent dans le tiroir** I took the money from the drawer
  (**e**) through; **nous sommes passés dans un tunnel** we went through a tunnel
  (**f**) **dans les** around, about; **ça coûtera dans les vingt euros** it'll cost around twenty euros; **il doit avoir dans les cinquante ans** he must be about fifty

LA **danse** *noun* dancing; **elle aime la danse** she likes dancing; **je fais de la danse classique** I do ballet; **une danse espagnole** a Spanish dance

danser *verb* to dance; **il danse bien la salsa** he's a good salsa dancer

LE **danseur,** LA **danseuse** *noun* dancer; **elle est danseuse** she's a dancer

LA **date** *noun* date; **date de naissance** date of birth; **date limite** deadline; **la date limite pour rendre vos dissertations est le 19 novembre** the deadline for returning your essays is 19 November; **date limite de consommation** best-before date

dater *verb* **dater de** to date from, to go back to; **un livre qui date du XVIIe siècle** a book dating back to the 17th century; **de quand date votre**

dernière visite? when was your last
visite?

LA **datte** *noun* date *(fruit)*

LE **dauphin** *noun* dolphin

davantage *adverb*
(a) more; **tu devrais étudier davantage** you should study more; **il faut
qu'il consacre davantage de temps
à la lecture** he needs to spend more
time reading
(b) longer; **je n'attendrai pas davantage** I won't wait any longer

de
1 *preposition*
(a) of; **le toit de la maison** the roof of
the house; **une bouteille d'eau** a
bottle of water; **les clés de la voiture**
the car keys; **le frère de Stéphane** Stéphane's brother
(b) from; **il vient de Paris** he comes
from Paris; **c'est un cadeau de mon
oncle** it's a present from my uncle; **de
Noël à Pâques** from Christmas to
Easter
(c) by; **un livre de Victor Hugo** a book
by Victor Hugo; **accompagné de ses
amis** accompanied by his friends
(d) in; **le plus jeune de la classe** the
youngest pupil in the class; **trois
heures de l'après-midi** three o'clock
in the afternoon
(e) with; **de toutes ses forces** with all
his strength; **trembler de froid** to
shiver with cold
(f) about; **parler de quelque chose** to
speak about something
(g) to; **il a décidé de partir** he decided
to leave; **je suis content d'être ici** I'm
happy to be here
(h) than; **j'ai attendu plus de trois
heures** I waited for more than three
hours
2 *article*
(a) some; **j'ai acheté de la viande** I
bought some meat; **elle a des amis**
she's got some friends; **il a de bonnes
idées** he's got some good ideas
(b) any; **il n'y a pas de place** there isn't

any room; **avez-vous du lait?** do you
have any milk?; **sans faire de fautes**
without making any mistakes

Note that *de* becomes *d'* in front of a
vowel or a mute h and that *de + le* is
contracted to *du* (as in *la porte du garage*) and *de + les* to *des* (as in *le professeur des élèves*). However, *de + la*
and *de + l'* do not change.

LE **dé** *noun*
(a) dice; **jeter les dés** *or* **lancer les dés**
to throw the dice
(b) thimble

déballer *verb* to unpack; **aide-moi à
déballer les livres** help me unpack
the books

débarquer *verb*
(a) to unload
(b) to disembark *(from a boat, a plane)*
(c) to turn up; **il a débarqué chez moi
à minuit** he turned up at my place at
midnight

Sense (c) is an informal use of *débarquer*.

débarrasser
1 *verb* to clear; **c'est à ton tour de débarrasser (la table)** it's your turn to
clear the table
2 *reflexive verb* **se débarrasser** se
débarrasser de quelque chose to get
rid of something; **je me suis débar-
rassé de mes vieux livres** I got rid of
my old books

LE **débat** *noun* debate

The *t* in *débat* is not pronounced.

se débattre *reflexive verb* to struggle; **il s'est débattu contre les agents
de police** he struggled with the police
officers

See verb table p. 320.

déborder *verb*
(a) to overflow; **la baignoire a débordé** the bath overflowed; **la rivière
a débordé** the river has burst its banks
(b) to boil over

(c) **je suis débordé de travail** I'm up to my eyes in work; **elle déborde d'énergie** she's bursting with energy; **elle déborde d'imagination** she has a vivid imagination

déboucher *verb*
(a) to open *(a bottle)*
(b) to unblock *(a sink)*
(c) **déboucher sur** to lead to; **ce chemin débouche sur la mer** this path leads to the sea

debout *adverb*
(a) standing, standing up; **nous avons mangé debout** we ate standing up; **il était debout sur la table** he was standing on the table; **elle préfère rester debout** she'd rather stand; **se mettre debout** to stand up; **il s'est mis debout** he stood up
(b) up; **il faut être debout à cinq heures** we need to be up at five o'clock; **debout!** get up!
(c) **votre histoire ne tient pas debout** your story doesn't make sense

Debout does not change in the feminine or in the plural, eg *une fille debout, deux personnes debout.*

débrancher *verb* to unplug *(the TV, a lamp)*

LES débris *masculine plural noun*
(a) broken pieces, fragments; **des débris de verre** bits of broken glass
(b) wreckage

se débrouiller *reflexive verb*
(a) to manage; **débrouille-toi!** you'll have to manage by yourself!; **je me suis débrouillé pour avoir des places** I managed to get some tickets
(b) to get by; **je me débrouille en anglais** I get by in English

LE début *noun*
(a) beginning, start; **je n'ai pas aimé le début du film** I didn't like the beginning of the film; **j'y suis allé au début de l'année** I went at the beginning of the year; **début mars** at the beginning of March

(b) **au début** at first; **au début je l'ai cru** at first I believed him
(c) **dès le début** *or* **depuis le début** from the very start; **je le savais depuis le début** I knew all along

LE débutant, LA débutante *noun* beginner

débuter *verb* to begin, to start

LE décalage horaire *noun*
(a) time difference; **il y a un décalage horaire de six heures** there's a six-hour time difference
(b) jet lag; **je suis encore sous le coup du décalage horaire** I'm still suffering from jet lag

décaler
1 *verb*
(a) to shift; **décaler quelque chose vers la gauche** to shift something to the left
(b) to reschedule; **le cours a été décalé d'une heure** *(earlier)* the class was brought forward an hour; *(later)* the class was moved back an hour
2 *reflexive verb* **se décaler** to move

décembre *masculine noun* December; **le premier décembre** the first of December; **le 25 décembre** the 25th of December

In French, the names of months are not written with a capital.

LA décennie *noun* decade

LA déception *noun* disappointment

Note that the English word *deception* is never a translation for the French word *déception*.

LE décès *noun* death

décevant, décevante *adjective* disappointing

décevoir *verb* to disappoint; **tu me déçois** I'm disappointed in you; **je suis très déçu par ses résultats** I'm very disappointed with his results

Note that the English verb *to deceive* is never a translation for the French verb *décevoir*. See verb table p. 322.

se déchaîner *reflexive verb*
(a) to go wild; **la foule s'est déchaînée** the crowd went wild
(b) to rage; **la mer se déchaîne** the sea is raging

décharger *verb* to unload

LES déchets *masculine plural noun* waste; **des déchets toxiques** toxic waste

déchiffrer *verb* to decipher, to decode; **je n'arrive pas à déchiffrer son écriture** I can't make out her handwriting

déchirer
1 *verb*
(a) to tear, to tear up
(b) to tear out
2 *reflexive verb* **se déchirer** to tear; **mon gant s'est déchiré** my glove got torn

décidé, décidée *adjective*
(a) determined; **être décidé à faire quelque chose** to be determined to do something
(b) settled; **c'est décidé!** that's settled!

décider
1 *verb*
(a) to decide
(b) to convince; **décider quelqu'un à faire quelque chose** to convince somebody to do something
2 *reflexive verb* **se décider** to make up one's mind

déclarer
1 *verb* to declare, to announce; **le principal a déclaré que l'école serait fermée** the headmaster announced that the school would be closed; **ils ont déclaré la guerre à l'Irak** they declared war on Iraq
2 *reflexive verb* **se déclarer** to break out *(fire)*

décoiffer *verb* to mess up *(somebody's hair)*; **arrête, tu vas me décoiffer!** stop it, you'll mess up my hair!; **elle est toute décoiffée** her hair's all messed up

LE décollage *noun* take-off *(of a plane)*

décoller
1 *verb*
(a) to peel off *(a label, wallpaper)*
(b) *(plane)* to take off
2 *reflexive verb* **se décoller** to come off

décolleté, décolletée
1 *adjective* low-cut *(top, dress)*
2 *masculine noun* **un décolleté** a low neckline

déconcentrer
1 *verb* **déconcentrer quelqu'un** to distract somebody; **le bruit m'a déconcentré** the noise distracted me
2 *reflexive verb* **se déconcentrer** to lose one's concentration

décontracté, décontractée *adjective*
(a) relaxed
(b) casual; **en tenue décontractée** casually dressed

LE décor *noun*
(a) decor, decoration
(b) set *(of a film, a play)*

décorer *verb* to decorate

découper *verb*
(a) to cut, to cut up; **il a découpé le gâteau en parts égales** he cut the cake into equal pieces
(b) to cut out; **il a découpé des photos dans le journal** he cut out pictures from the paper
(c) to carve *(meat)*

décourager
1 *verb* to discourage
2 *reflexive verb* **se décourager** to get discouraged, to lose heart

LA découverte *noun* discovery

découvrir *verb* to discover; **ils ont découvert un passage secret** they discovered a secret passage

See verb table p. 320.

décrire *verb* to describe

See verb table p. 322.

décrocher *verb*
(**a**) to take down; **peux-tu m'aider à décrocher les rideaux?** can you help me take the curtains down?
(**b**) **décrocher le téléphone** to pick up the phone
(**c**) to get; **elle a décroché le premier prix** she got first prize

Sense (c) is a slightly informal use of *décrocher*.

déçu, déçue *see* **décevoir**
elle l'a beaucoup déçu he was very disappointed in her

Déçu(e) is the past participle of the verb *décevoir*.

dedans *preposition* inside

déduire *verb*
(**a**) to deduct; **il a déduit dix euros du prix** he deducted ten euros from the price
(**b**) to deduce

See verb table p. 320.

défaire
1 *verb*
(**a**) to undo *(clothes, a knot)*
(**b**) to unpack; **je n'ai pas encore défait ma valise** I haven't unpacked my suitcase yet
2 *reflexive verb* **se défaire** to come undone *(clothes, a knot)*

See verb table p. 317.

LA défaite *noun* defeat

LE défaut *noun*
(**a**) fault *(of a person)*
(**b**) flaw, defect *(of an object)*

défavorable *adjective* unfavourable

défendre
1 *verb*
(**a**) to defend
(**b**) to forbid; **c'est défendu** it's forbidden; **son père lui défend de sortir le soir** his father doesn't allow him to go out at night

2 *reflexive verb* **se défendre** to defend oneself

LA défense *noun*
(**a**) defence; **prendre la défense de quelqu'un** to defend somebody, to stand up for somebody
(**b**) **défense de fumer** no smoking; **défense d'entrer** no entry
(**c**) tusk

LE défenseur *noun* defender

LE défi *noun* challenge; **lancer un défi à quelqu'un** to challenge somebody; **relever un défi** to take up a challenge

LE défilé *noun* procession; **un défilé militaire** a military parade; **un défilé de mode** a fashion show

défiler *verb* to march

définir *verb* to define

définitivement *adverb* for good; **ils se sont installés définitivement dans le pays** they've settled in the country for good

Note that the English word *definitely* is never a translation for the French word *définitivement*.

défoncer *verb* to break down, to smash in *(a door)*

dégagé, dégagée *adjective* clear *(sky, road)*

dégager *verb*
(**a**) to clear *(a road, a room)*
(**b**) to free; **il a fallu deux heures pour le dégager de la voiture** it took two hours to free him from the car

LES dégâts *masculine plural noun* damage; **les chenilles ont fait des dégâts dans le jardin** the caterpillars have caused damage in the garden

dégeler *verb*
(**a**) to thaw
(**b**) to defrost

dégénérer *verb* to degenerate, to get worse

dégonfler
1 *verb*

(a) to deflate, to let the air out of; **ils ont dégonflé le ballon** they let the air out of the balloon
(b) to become less swollen; **sa cheville a dégonflé** his ankle is less swollen
2 *reflexive verb* **se dégonfler**
(a) to go down, to deflate
(b) to chicken out

Sense (b) is an informal use of *se dégonfler*.

dégoûtant, dégoûtante *adjective* disgusting

dégoûter *verb*
(a) to disgust
(b) to put off; **ça m'a dégoûté de la viande** that put me off meat

se dégrader *reflexive verb* to deteriorate, to get worse

LE **degré** *noun* degree; **il fait vingt degrés** it's twenty degrees

LE **déguisement** *noun*
(a) costume
(b) disguise

se déguiser *reflexive verb*
(a) to dress up; **il s'est déguisé en pirate** he dressed up as a pirate
(b) to disguise oneself; **elle s'est déguisée en vieille dame pour échapper à la police** she disguised herself as an old lady to escape from the police

dehors *adverb*
(a) outside; **ne reste pas dehors** don't stay outside; **en dehors du pays** outside the country; **mettre quelqu'un dehors** to throw somebody out
(b) **en dehors de mes amis** apart from my friends

déjà *adverb*
(a) already; **je vous l'ai déjà dit** I've told you already; **il est déjà quatre heures** it's already four o'clock
(b) yet; **est-ce qu'il est déjà parti?** has he left yet?
(c) ever; **vous êtes déjà allé au Canada?** have you ever been to Canada?

déjeuner
1 *verb*
(a) to have lunch
(b) to have breakfast
2 *masculine noun* **le déjeuner** lunch; **le petit déjeuner** breakfast

LE **délai** *noun*
(a) extension; **j'ai demandé un délai pour ma dissertation** I asked for an extension for my essay
(b) time limit, deadline; **nous devons respecter les délais** we have to meet the deadlines; **vous devez rendre vos devoirs vendredi, dernier délai** you have to hand in your homework on Friday at the latest; **dans un délai de dix jours** within ten days

Note that the English word *delay* is never a translation for the French word *délai*.

LE **délégué, LA déléguée** *noun* representative; **un délégué de classe** a class representative

Le Délégué de Classe
In French secondary schools (*collège* and *lycée*), each class elects two representatives who act as a link between the teachers or school administration and their fellow students. These students also represent each of their classmates at the *conseil de classe*, a staff meeting held at the end of every term where teachers discuss pupils' progress. At the last *conseil de classe* of the school year, it is decided whether anyone needs to repeat the year or change options.

délicat, délicate *adjective*
(a) delicate
(b) tricky
(c) thoughtful

délicieux, délicieuse *adjective* delicious

LE **délit** *noun* criminal offence

délivrer *verb* to release, to set free

LE **deltaplane**® *noun*
(a) hang-glider

(b) hang-gliding; **faire du delta-plane®** to go hang-gliding

demain *adverb* tomorrow; **à demain!** see you tomorrow!

LA **demande** *noun*
(a) request; **une demande d'argent** a request for money
(b) proposal; **une demande en mariage** a marriage proposal
(c) application; **une demande d'emploi** a job application; **faire une demande de bourse** to apply for a grant
(d) demand

demander
1 *verb*
(a) to ask; **elle a demandé à Marie si elle était d'accord** she asked Marie if she agreed; **il m'a demandé de lui prêter mon vélo** he asked me to lend him my bike
(b) to ask for; **demander quelque chose à quelqu'un** to ask somebody for something; **demander la permission** to ask for permission
(c) to need, to require; **ce travail demande toute votre attention** the work requires all your attention
2 *reflexive verb* **se demander** to wonder; **je me demande ce que je vais dire** I'm wondering what to say; **je me demande bien pourquoi** I wonder why

Note that the English verb *demand* is rarely a translation for the French verb *demander*.

LA **démangeaison** *noun* itch; **j'ai des démangeaisons dans les jambes** my legs are itchy

démanger *verb* to itch; **ce pull me démange** this sweater's making me itch

se démaquiller *reflexive verb* to remove one's make-up

LA **démarche** *noun*
(a) walk *(way of walking)*
(b) step; **faire les démarches nécessaires** to take all the necessary steps

démarrer *verb*
(a) to start; **je n'arrive pas à faire démarrer la voiture** I can't get the car to start
(b) to drive off

démêler *verb* to untangle

LE **déménagement** *noun*
(a) move; **c'est mon quatrième déménagement** it's the fourth time I've moved house
(b) removal; **un camion de déménagement** a removal van

déménager *verb* to move house

demeurer *verb*
(a) to remain
(b) to live

demi, demie
1 *adjective* half; **une demi-pomme** half an apple; **quinze mètres et demi** fifteen and a half metres; **ça dure deux heures et demie** it lasts two and a half hours; **être à demi convaincu** to be half-convinced

The adjective *demi* does not change when it is in front of a feminine noun and is followed by a hyphen; the form will always be masculine: *une demi-pomme*.

2 *feminine noun* **la demie** half past; **on va attendre la demie** we'll wait till half past

LA **demi-douzaine** *noun* half a dozen; **une demi-douzaine d'œufs** half a dozen eggs

The plural of *demi-douzaine* is *demi-douzaines*.

LA **demi-finale** *noun* semi-final

The plural of *demi-finale* is *demi-finales*.

LE **demi-frère** *noun* half-brother

The plural of *demi-frère* is *demi-frères*.

LA **demi-heure** *noun* half an hour, half-hour; **il a attendu une demi-**

heure he waited for half an hour

> The plural of *demi-heure* is *demi-heures*.

LA **demi-journée** *noun* half a day, half-day; **j'ai une demi-journée de congé** I have a half-day

> The plural of *demi-journée* is *demi-journées*.

LA **demi-pension** *noun*
(a) half-board
(b) **être en demi-pension** *(at school)* to have school dinners

LE/LA **demi-pensionnaire** *noun* pupil who has school dinners

> The plural of *demi-pensionnaire* is *demi-pensionnaires*.

LA **demi-sœur** *noun* half-sister

> The plural of *demi-sœur* is *demi-sœurs*.

démissionner *verb* to resign

LE **demi-tarif** *noun* half-price; **un billet demi-tarif** a half-price ticket

> The plural of *demi-tarif* is *demi-tarifs*.

LE **demi-tour** *noun* U-turn; **faire demi-tour** to turn back

> The plural of *demi-tour* is *demi-tours*.

LA **démocratie** *noun* democracy

> The t of *démocratie* is pronounced like an *s*.

démodé, démodée *adjective* old-fashioned

LA **demoiselle** *noun*
(a) young lady
(b) **une demoiselle d'honneur** a bridesmaid

démolir *verb* to demolish, to knock down

LA **démonstration** *noun* demonstration

> Note that the French word *démonstration* never means *protest*.

démonter *verb*
(a) to dismantle, to take apart *(an engine, a clock)*
(b) to take down *(a tent)*

démontrer *verb* to demonstrate

se démoraliser *reflexive verb* to become demoralized, to lose heart

dénoncer
1 *verb*
(a) to denounce; **dénoncer quelqu'un à la police** to report somebody to the police
(b) to tell on; **ne me dénonce pas** don't tell on me
2 *reflexive verb* **se dénoncer**
(a) to give oneself up
(b) to own up

LA **dent** *noun* tooth; **une dent de lait** a milk tooth; **une dent de sagesse** a wisdom tooth; **j'ai mal aux dents** I have toothache

LA **dentelle** *noun* lace

LE **dentifrice** *noun* toothpaste

LE/LA **dentiste** *noun* dentist; **elle est dentiste** she's a dentist

dépanner *verb*
(a) to repair, to fix
(b) to help out; **est-ce que tu peux me dépanner?** can you help me out?

> Sense (b) is an informal use of *dépanner*.

LE **départ** *noun*
(a) departure
(b) start
(c) **au départ** at first

départager *verb* **il a posé une dernière question pour départager les ex æquo** he asked a tie-breaker question

LE **département** *noun*
(a) department
(b) chief administrative division of France

Le Département

A *département* is an administrative division. France is divided into *régions*, which are themselves divided into *départements*. There are 96 *départements* in mainland France and 4 overseas (see also **DOM-TOM**). The number of the *département* corresponds to the first two figures in a postcode and the last two of a car registration number. For example, Paris is *département* 75, so its postcodes all begin with 75 and its car registrations end with 75.

dépasser *verb*
(a) to overtake
(b) to pass, to go past; **fais demi-tour, nous avons dépassé l'hôtel** turn around, we've gone past the hotel
(c) to exceed
(d) to be taller than; **il me dépasse d'une tête** he's a head taller than me
(e) to be ahead of, to be better than; **elle me dépasse en maths** she's better at maths than me
(f) to stick out; **un cahier dépassait de son sac** a notebook was sticking out of his bag

se dépêcher *reflexive verb* to hurry up, to hurry; **dépêche-toi, tu vas être en retard** hurry up, you're going to be late; **dépêchez-vous de rentrer** hurry up and come home

dépendre *verb* to depend; **ça dépend de sa décision** it depends on his decision

ʟᴀ **dépense** *noun* expense; **faire de grosses dépenses** to spend a lot of money

dépenser *verb* to spend *(money)*

déplacer
1 *verb* to move, to shift
2 *reflexive verb* **se déplacer**
(a) to move about
(b) to travel

déplaire *verb* **déplaire à quelqu'un** to put somebody off; **son attitude m'a déplu** I didn't like his attitude

See verb table p. 322.

ʟᴇ **dépliant** *noun* brochure, leaflet

déplier *verb* to unfold, to open out

déposer *verb*
(a) to put down; **tu peux déposer tes livres ici** you can put your books down here
(b) to leave; **quelqu'un a déposé une lettre pour vous** somebody left a letter for you
(c) to drop off; **ils m'ont déposé à la gare** they dropped me off at the station
(d) to deposit *(money)*

ʟᴀ **dépression** *noun* depression; **une dépression nerveuse** a nervous breakdown

déprimer *verb*
(a) to depress; **son histoire m'a déprimé** his story depressed me
(b) to be depressed; **je déprime en ce moment** I'm a bit depressed at the moment

depuis
1 *preposition*
(a) since; **il est là depuis hier** he's been here since yesterday; **je ne l'ai pas vu depuis son spectacle** I haven't seen him since his show; **je ne l'ai pas revu depuis qu'il s'est marié** I haven't seen him again since he got married
(b) for; **depuis dix ans** for ten years; **depuis longtemps** for a long time
(c) from; **depuis ma fenêtre** from my window
2 *adverb* since, since then; **j'ai reçu deux lettres en janvier et rien depuis** I received two letters in January and nothing since then

ʟᴇ **député**, ʟᴀ **députée** *noun* Member of Parliament, MP

déranger
1 *verb* to disturb, to bother; **excusez-moi de vous déranger** I'm sorry to bother you; **ça vous dérange si je laisse la porte ouverte?** do you mind if I leave the door open?

2 *reflexive verb* **se déranger**
(a) to bother; **ne te dérange pas, je te l'apporte** don't bother, I'll bring it to you
(b) to come, to come out; **le plombier a refusé de se déranger** the plumber wouldn't come out
(c) to go; **je refuse de me déranger** I refuse to go

déraper *verb* to skid

dernier, dernière
1 *adjective*
(a) last; **la semaine dernière** last week
(b) latest; **son dernier album** his latest album
2 *noun* **le dernier, la dernière** the last one; **arriver le dernier** *or* **arriver en dernier** to arrive last; **elle est la dernière de la classe** she's at the bottom of the class

dérouler
1 *verb* to unroll, to unwind
2 *reflexive verb* **se dérouler** to take place

derrière
1 *preposition* behind; **derrière l'arbre** behind the tree
2 *adverb*
(a) behind
(b) at the back; **mettez les plus grands de la classe derrière** put the tallest pupils at the back
3 *masculine noun*
(a) back; **le derrière de la maison** the back of the house; **la porte de derrière** the back door
(b) backside

des *see* **de**
le toit des maisons the roofs of the houses; **il vient des États-Unis** he comes from the United States; **nous avons parlé des problèmes actuels** we talked about current issues; **est-ce que tu veux des biscuits?** would you like some biscuits?

Des is the contraction of *de + les.*

dès *preposition*
(a) from; **dès le début** from the beginning
(b) **dès son retour** as soon as he comes back; **dès qu'elle viendra** as soon as she comes

LE désaccord *noun* disagreement

désagréable *adjective* unpleasant

désapprouver *verb*
(a) to disapprove of
(b) to object to

LE désastre *noun* disaster

LE désavantage *noun* disadvantage

descendre *verb*
(a) to go down, to come down; **je suis descendu à la cave** I went down to the cellar; **j'ai descendu les escaliers** I went down the stairs
(b) to go downstairs, to come downstairs
(c) to get off; **je suis descendu du train** I got off the train
(d) to take down, to bring down; **il a descendu les poubelles** he took the rubbish down

LA descente *noun*
(a) slope
(b) **à ma descente de l'avion** when I got off the plane
(c) **une descente de police** a police raid
(d) downhill event *(in skiing)*

désert¹, déserte *adjective* deserted

LE désert² *noun* desert

The *t* in *désert* is not pronounced.

désespéré, désespérée *adjective*
(a) desperate
(b) hopeless; **c'est un cas désespéré** it's a hopeless case

désespérer *verb* to despair, to give up hope

déshabiller
1 *verb* to undress *(somebody)*
2 *reflexive verb* **se déshabiller** to undress, to get undressed; **déshabille-**

toi et mets ton pyjama get undressed and put your pyjamas on

désigner *verb*
(a) to refer to
(b) to point at; **il m'a désigné du doigt** he pointed at me
(c) to appoint; **il a été désigné délégué de classe** he was appointed class representative
2 *reflexive verb* **se désigner** to volunteer

LE **désir** *noun* wish

désirer *verb* to want; **je désire aller voir mon père** I want to go and see my father

désobéir *verb* to disobey; **désobéir à quelqu'un** to disobey somebody; **il a désobéi à son professeur** he disobeyed his teacher

désobéissant, désobéissante *adjective* disobedient

désolé, désolée *adjective* sorry; **je suis désolé d'avoir oublié ton anniversaire** I'm sorry I forgot your birthday

LE **désordre** *noun* mess; **quel désordre là-dedans!** it's such a mess in here!; **il a mis le désordre dans mes affaires** he messed up my things; **une chambre en désordre** an untidy room

désormais *adverb* from now on

desquels, desquelles *see* **lequel**
les vacances au cours desquelles j'ai fait de la plongée the holidays during which I went diving

> *Desquels* is the contraction of *de* + *lesquels* and *desquelles* is the contraction of *de* + *lesquelles*.

desserrer *verb* to loosen

LE **dessert** *noun* dessert

> The *t* in *dessert* is not pronounced.

LE **dessin** *noun*
(a) drawing
(b) **un dessin animé** a cartoon *(film, TV programme)*

LE **dessinateur,** LA **dessinatrice** *noun*
(a) draughtsman/draughtswoman
(b) designer
(c) cartoonist

dessiner *verb* to draw; **il dessine bien** he's good at drawing

dessous
1 *adverb*
(a) underneath; **les prix sont marqués dessous** the prices are marked underneath
(b) **en dessous** underneath
2 *preposition* **en dessous de** below; **en dessous de zéro** below zero
3 *masculine noun*
(a) bottom; **le dessous de l'assiette** the bottom of the plate
(b) underneath
(c) **les gens du dessous** the people downstairs

> See also **au-dessous**.

dessus
1 *adverb*
(a) on top; **un gâteau avec du chocolat dessus** a cake with chocolate on top; **monte dessus, tu verras mieux** climb on top, you'll have a better view
(b) on it; **écrivez l'adresse dessus** write the address on it
2 *masculine noun*
(a) top; **prends le livre du dessus** take the top book
(b) **les gens du dessus** the people upstairs
(c) **avoir le dessus** to have the upper hand

> See also **au-dessus**.

LE **destin** *noun* fate

LA **destination** *noun* destination; **le train à destination de Paris** the train to Paris

détacher
1 *verb*
(a) to untie
(b) to unfasten

(**c**) to take off; **elle a détaché l'affiche du mur** she took the poster off the wall

2 *reflexive verb* **se détacher**

(**a**) to untie oneself

(**b**) to come undone

(**c**) to come off

(**d**) **elle s'est détaché les cheveux** she took her hair down

LE **détail** *noun* detail; **il a raconté l'histoire en détail** he told the story in detail

déteindre *verb*

(**a**) to fade; **mon jean a déteint** my jeans have faded

(**b**) to run; **le noir va déteindre sur le rouge** the black will run into the red

See verb table p. 320.

détendre

1 *verb* to relax; **le yoga me détend** yoga relaxes me

2 *reflexive verb* **se détendre**

(**a**) to relax; **détends-toi!** relax!

(**b**) to become more relaxed *(atmosphere)*

(**c**) to slacken *(rope)*

(**d**) to lose its shape; **ce vieux pull s'est détendu** this old sweater has lost its shape

détendu, détendue *adjective*

(**a**) relaxed

(**b**) slack *(rope)*

LA **détente** *noun*

(**a**) relaxation

(**b**) trigger *(of a gun)*

se détériorer *reflexive verb* to deteriorate, to get worse

déterminé, déterminée *adj* determined

détester *verb* to hate; **elle déteste se lever tôt** she hates getting up early

détruire *verb* to destroy

See verb table p. 320.

LA **dette** *noun* debt

LE **deuil** *noun* **être en deuil** to be in mourning

deux *number* two; **le deux janvier** the

second of January; **nous sommes le deux aôut** it's the second of August; **les deux** both

deuxième *number* second

dévaliser *verb* to rob

devant

1 *preposition* in front of; **devant l'arbre** in front of the tree

2 *adverb* in front; **mettez les plus petits élèves devant** put the smallest pupils in front

3 *noun* **le devant de la maison** the front of the house; **les dents de devant** the front teeth

LE **développement** *noun*

(**a**) development

(**b**) developing *(of photos)*

The *t* in *développement* is not pronounced.

développer

1 *verb* to develop

2 *reflexive verb* **se développer** to develop

devenir *verb* to become; **il est devenu professeur** he became a teacher

See verb table p. 324.

deviner *verb* to guess

LA **devinette** *noun* riddle; **il m'a posé une devinette** he asked me a riddle

LA **devise** *noun*

(**a**) motto

(**b**) currency

dévisser *verb* to unscrew

devoir¹ *verb*

(**a**) *(obligation)* must, have to; **je dois partir** I have to go; **j'ai dû refuser** I had to refuse

(**b**) *(possibility)* must; **il doit être fatigué** he must be tired; **elle a dû oublier** she must have forgotten

(**c**) should; **vous devriez rester** you should stay; **tu ne devrais pas boire** you shouldn't drink; **il aurait dû venir** he should have come

(**d**) to be supposed to, to be due to; **elle**

doit arriver à midi she's due to arrive at noon; **il devait venir mais je ne l'ai pas vu** he was supposed to come but I didn't see him
(e) to owe; **tu me dois cinq euros** you owe me five euros; **je te dois des excuses** I owe you an apology

> Note that the past participle of *devoir* is *dû/due*. See verb table p. 314.

LE **devoir²** *noun*
(a) duty
(b) exercise, test; **j'ai un devoir de maths à rendre pour lundi** I've got a maths exercise to hand in by Monday; **un devoir sur table** a written class test
(c) **les devoirs** homework; **faire ses devoirs** to do one's homework

dévorer *verb* to devour

dévoué, dévouée *adjective* devoted, dedicated

se dévouer *reflexive verb* to volunteer

LE **diable** *noun* devil

LE **diamant** *noun* diamond; **un collier de diamants** a diamond necklace

LA **diapositive** *noun* slide *(photo)*

LA **dictée** *noun* dictation

LE **dictionnaire** *noun* dictionary

LE **dieu** *noun* god; **croire en Dieu** to believe in God; **oh mon Dieu!** oh my God!

> The plural of *dieu* is *dieux*.

LA **différence** *noun* difference; **à la différence des autres élèves** unlike the other pupils

différent, différente *adjective*
(a) different; **le film est différent du livre** the film is different from the book
(b) *(in plural)* various; **différentes personnes l'ont vu** various people saw him

> The *t* in *différent* is not pronounced.

difficile *adjective* difficult

LA **difficulté** *noun* difficulty; **il a des difficultés en maths** he has difficulty with maths

diffuser *verb*
(a) to broadcast
(b) to spread *(disease, news)*

digérer *verb* to digest

LE **dimanche** *noun* Sunday; **elle est venue dimanche** she came on Sunday; **il travaille parfois le dimanche** he sometimes works on Sundays; **tous les dimanches** every Sunday

> In French, the names of days are not written with a capital.

diminuer *verb*
(a) to decrease; **le nombre d'étudiants a diminué de 5%** the number of students has decreased by 5%
(b) to reduce; **ils ont diminué les prix** they've reduced their prices

LE **diminutif** *noun* diminutive; **Greg est le diminutif de Gregory** Greg is short for Gregory

LA **diminution** *noun*
(a) decrease; **une diminution du nombre d'élèves** a decrease in the number of pupils
(b) reduction

LA **dinde** *noun* turkey

dîner
1 *verb* to have dinner
2 *masculine noun* dinner

LE **diplôme** *noun* diploma, certificate

diplômé, diplômée
1 *adjective*
(a) graduate
(b) qualified
2 *noun* **un diplômé, une diplômée** a graduate

dire
1 *verb*
(a) to say; **qu'est-ce que tu as dit?** what did you say?
(b) to tell; **dis-moi la vérité** tell me the truth; **il m'a dit que tu n'étais pas là** he told me you weren't there

(**c**) to think; **que dis-tu de ma robe?** what do you think of my dress?; **et dire que j'étais si maigre avant!** to think that I used to be so thin!

(**d**) **on dirait un château** it looks like a castle; **on dirait qu'il va pleuvoir** it looks like it's going to rain; **on dirait du poulet** it tastes like chicken

2 *reflexive verb* **se dire**

(**a**) to be said; **comment se dit "bonsoir" en japonais?** what's the Japanese for "bonsoir"?; **cela ne se dit pas devant les enfants** such things shouldn't be said in front of the children

(**b**) to think; **maintenant, je me dis que j'aurais dû accepter** now I think I should have accepted

See verb table p. 315.

direct, directe *adjective*
(**a**) direct
(**b**) **en direct** live; **une émission en direct** a live broadcast

directement *adverb*
(**a**) directly
(**b**) straight; **vas-y directement!** go straight there!

LE directeur, LA directrice *noun*
(**a**) headmaster/headmistress
(**b**) manager, director

LA direction *noun*
(**a**) direction, way; **tu vas dans quelle direction?** which way are you going?; **vous êtes dans la mauvaise direction** you're going the wrong way
(**b**) management

directrice *see* **directeur**

LE dirigeant, LA dirigeante *noun*
(**a**) manager
(**b**) leader

diriger
1 *verb*
(**a**) to run, to manage
(**b**) to lead *(a team)*
(**c**) to aim *(a weapon)*
2 *reflexive verb* **se diriger**
(**a**) to make one's way; **il se sont dirigés vers la sortie** they made their

way to the exit *or* they headed for the exit
(**b**) to find one's way; **les chats peuvent se diriger dans le noir** cats can find their way in the dark

dis *see* **dire**
je dis la vérité I'm telling the truth; **tu dis des bêtises** you're talking nonsense; **dis-moi ce que tu en penses** tell me what you think

Dis is a form of the verb *dire* in the present tense and in the imperative. See verb table p. 315.

LA discipline *noun*
(**a**) discipline
(**b**) subject; **quelle est ta discipline préférée?** what's your favourite subject?

LA discothèque *noun*
(**a**) disco, nightclub
(**b**) music library

LE discours *noun* speech

discret, discrète *adjective*
(**a**) discreet
(**b**) subtle

discrètement *adverb* discreetly

LA discussion *noun*
(**a**) discussion, conversation
(**b**) argument; **pas de discussion!** no argument!

discuter *verb*
(**a**) to talk; **on discute du match d'hier soir** we're talking about last night's match
(**b**) to argue; **cesse de discuter!** don't argue!

disent, disons *see* **dire**
ils disent des bêtises they're talking nonsense; **nous disons la vérité** we're telling the truth

Disent and *disons* are forms of the verb *dire* in the present tense. See verb table p. 315.

disparaître *verb*
(**a**) to disappear; **mes livres ont disparu** my books have disappeared; **faire**

disparaître quelque chose to remove something, to get rid of something
(**b**) to die

See verb table p. 320.

LA **disparition** *noun* disappearance

disparu, disparue *adjective*
(**a**) missing
(**b**) dead

dispenser *verb* **dispenser quelqu'un de quelque chose** to excuse somebody from something; **je suis dispensé de gymnastique** I'm excused from gym

se disperser *reflexive verb (crowd)* to break up, to scatter

disponible *adjective* available

disposé, disposée *adjective* **être disposé à faire quelque chose** to be prepared to do something

disposer *verb*
(**a**) to arrange *(objects)*
(**b**) **disposer de quelque chose** to have something

LA **disposition** *noun*
(**a**) layout, arrangement
(**b**) **je suis à ta disposition** I'm at your service; **mon ordinateur est à ta disposition** feel free to use my computer

LA **dispute** *noun* quarrel, argument

se disputer *reflexive verb* to quarrel, to argue; **elle s'est disputée avec sa meilleure amie** she had an argument with her best friend

disqualifier *verb* to disqualify; **l'équipe s'est fait disqualifier** the team was disqualified

LE **disque** *noun*
(**a**) record; **mettre un disque** to put a record on; **un disque compact** a compact disc
(**b**) disk *(of a computer)*
(**c**) **le lancer du disque** the discus *(sport)*

LA **disquette** *noun* floppy disk

LA **dissertation** *noun* essay

dissipé, dissipée *adjective* unruly, rowdy

LA **distance** *noun* distance; **à quelle distance sommes-nous de l'hôtel?** how far are we from the hotel?

distinctement *adverb* clearly

distinguer *verb*
(**a**) to distinguish, to make out
(**b**) **distinguer quelque chose de quelque chose** to tell something from something; **ils n'arrivent pas à distinguer le bien du mal** they can't tell good from evil

LA **distraction** *noun*
(**a**) entertainment
(**b**) absent-mindedness

distraire
1 *verb*
(**a**) to distract
(**b**) to entertain
2 *reflexive verb* **se distraire**
(**a**) to have fun
(**b**) to relax; **j'ai besoin de me distraire** I need to relax *or* I need to take my mind off things

distrait, distraite *adjective* absent-minded

Note that the English word *distracted* is never a translation for the French word *distrait*.

distribuer *verb*
(**a**) to distribute, to give; **il nous a distribué les copies** he handed us out the papers
(**b**) to assign *(tasks)*
(**c**) to deal *(cards)*
(**d**) to deliver *(mail)*

LE **distributeur** *noun* **un distributeur automatique** *or* **un distributeur de billets** a cash machine; **un distributeur de boissons** a vending machine

dit¹, dite *see* **dire**
qu'est-ce que tu as dit? what did you say?

Dit(e) is the past participle of the verb *dire*. See verb table p. 315.

dit² *see* **dire**
elle dit la vérité she's telling the truth

Dit is a form of the verb *dire* in the present tense. See verb table p. 315.

dites *see* **dire**
qu'est-ce que vous dites? what are you saying?

Dites is a form of the verb *dire* in the present tense. See verb table p. 315.

LE **divan** *noun* sofa, couch

divers, diverses *adjective*
(a) various; **pour diverses raisons** for various reasons
(b) varied
(c) miscellaneous

se divertir *reflexive verb*
(a) to entertain oneself
(b) to have fun

LE **divertissement** *noun* entertainment

diviser *verb*
(a) to divide; **divisez 9 par 3** divide 9 by 3
(b) to divide up; **la classe est divisée en trois groupes** the class is divided up into three groups

LA **division** *noun* division; **j'ai des divisions à faire** I've got some division to do

divorcé, divorcée
1 *adjective* divorced
2 *noun* **un divorcé, une divorcée** a divorcee

divorcer *verb* to get divorced

dix *number* ten; **le dix mai** the tenth of May; **nous sommes le dix juin** it's the tenth of June

Dix is pronounced "di" in front of a consonant, "diz" in front of a vowel or a mute h and "dis" on its own.

dix-huit *number* eighteen; **le dix-huit février** the eighteenth of February; **nous sommes le dix-huit novembre** it's the eighteenth of November; **à dix-**huit heures at six o'clock in the evening

dixième *number* tenth

dix-neuf *number* nineteen; **le dix-neuf mars** the nineteenth of March; **nous sommes le dix-neuf juillet** it's the nineteenth of July; **à dix-neuf heures** at seven o'clock in the evening

dix-sept *number* seventeen; **le dix-sept avril** the seventeenth of April; **nous sommes le dix-sept août** it's the seventeenth of August; **à dix-sept heures** at five o'clock in the afternoon

LA **dizaine** *noun* about ten; **une dizaine de personnes** about ten people

LE **docteur** *noun* doctor; **elle est docteur** she's a doctor

LE **documentaire** *noun* documentary

LE/LA **documentaliste** *noun* librarian; **elle est documentaliste** she's a librarian

LA **documentation** *noun* information

se documenter *reflexive verb* to do some research, to gather information

LE **doigt** *noun*
(a) finger; **Pierre a levé le doigt** Pierre put his hand up
(b) **un doigt de pied** a toe

The *g* and *t* of *doigt* are not pronounced.

dois, doit, doivent *see* **devoir¹**
tu dois te tromper you must be mistaken; **elles doivent faire leurs devoirs** they have to do their homework

Dois, *doit* and *doivent* are forms of the verb *devoir* in the present tense. See verb table p. 314.

LE **domaine** *noun*
(a) property; **vous êtes sur mon domaine** you're on my property
(b) field; **dans tous les domaines scientifiques** in every scientific field

domestique
1 *adjective*
(a) household
(b) **un animal domestique** a pet
2 *noun* **un/une domestique** a servant

LE **domicile** *noun*
(a) home; **ma mère travaille à domicile** my mother works from home; **un match à domicile** a home game
(b) home address

dominer *verb*
(a) to dominate
(b) to outclass
(c) to control *(one's emotions)*
(d) to tower above

dommage *masculine noun*
(a) **quel dommage!** what a shame!; **c'est dommage qu'elle ne soit pas venue** it's a pity she didn't come
(b) **les dommages** damage; **l'accident a causé des dommages** the accident caused some damage

LES **DOM-TOM** *masculine plural noun* French overseas départements and territories

Les Dom-Tom
This is the name given to all the overseas areas which belong to France. These are divided into *Départements d'Outre-Mer* (*DOM*) and *Territoires d'Outre-Mer* (*TOM*). The inhabitants of the four *départements* (Guadeloupe, Martinique, French Guiana and La Réunion) are French citizens, whereas the *territoires* (which include various South Pacific islands such as French Polynesia) are independent, though supervised by a French government representative.

LE **don** *noun* gift; **avoir un don** to have a gift; **faire don de quelque chose** to give something as a gift

donc *conjunction*
(a) so; **elle est tombée malade et elle a donc annulé son voyage** she fell ill, and so she cancelled her trip
(b) *(to insist)* **asseyez-vous donc!** will you sit down!

donné, donnée
1 *adjective*
(a) given
(b) specific; **à un moment donné** *(in the past)* at one point; *(in the future)* at some point
(c) cheap; **ce n'est pas donné!** it's hardly what you'd call cheap!
(d) **étant donné que** seeing that
2 *feminine noun* **une donnée** a piece of data, a piece of information; **des données** data

donner *verb*
(a) to give
(b) to make; **ça donne soif** it makes you thirsty
(c) **donner sur** to overlook; **la chambre donne sur le jardin** the room overlooks the garden

dont *pronoun*
(a) of whom; **il y a 95 candidats, dont 33 Canadiens** there are 95 candidates, of whom 33 are Canadians
(b) of which; **le club dont je suis membre** the club of which I'm a member, the club I'm a member of; **des livres dont la plupart ne valent rien** books, most of which are worthless
(c) which; **la famille dont je viens** the family (which) I come from; **le garçon dont tu as peur** the boy (whom) you are afraid of; **les gens dont tu parles ne m'intéressent pas** I'm not interested in the people you're talking about; **l'enfant dont elle s'occupe n'est pas le sien** the child she's looking after is not hers
(d) whose; **cette femme, dont le mari est journaliste** this woman, whose husband is a journalist

Note, with this last example, that the noun which follows *dont* is used with the definite article *(le, la, les, l')*.

doré, dorée *adjective* golden

dorénavant *adverb* from now on

dormir *verb* to sleep; **je dors bien dans ce lit** I sleep well in this bed

See verb table p. 320.

LE **dortoir** *noun* dormitory

LE **dos** *noun*
(a) back; **j'ai mal au dos** I've got backache; **au dos de la page** on the back of the page; **j'étais dos à la fenêtre** I had my back to the window; **tourner le dos à quelqu'un** to stand with one's back to somebody
(b) de dos from behind; **je ne l'ai vu que de dos** I only saw him from behind

LE **dossier** *noun*
(a) back *(of a chair)*
(b) project *(at school)*; **on nous a demandé de faire un dossier sur les mammifères** we were asked to do a project on mammals
(c) record; **un dossier scolaire** a school record; **un dossier médical** a medical record
(d) file; **ils ont un dossier sur chaque client** they have a file on each client

LA **douane** *noun* customs

double
1 *adjective* double; **une chambre double** a double room; **j'ai fermé à double tour** I double-locked the door
2 *masculine noun*
(a) twice as much, double; **j'ai payé le double** I paid double
(b) doubles; **jouer en double** to play doubles
(c) **j'ai une photo en double** I've got two of the same photograph
(d) copy; **j'ai fait un double de la lettre** I made a copy of the letter
(e) duplicate; **j'ai fait faire un double de la clé** I had a duplicate key made

doubler *verb*
(a) to double
(b) to overtake

douce *see* doux

doucement *adverb*
(a) gently

(b) softly
(c) slowly

LA **douche** *noun* shower

se doucher *reflexive verb* to have a shower

doué, douée *adjective* talented, gifted; **cet artiste est très doué** he's a very talented artist; **il est doué en dessin** he has a gift for drawing

LA **douleur** *noun* pain

douloureux, douloureuse *adjective* painful

LE **doute** *noun*
(a) doubt; **j'ai des doutes** I have my doubts; **il n'y a aucun doute, c'est lui** it's him, there's no doubt about it
(b) **sans doute** probably

douter
1 *verb* to doubt; **douter de quelque chose** to doubt something; **je doute de ses sentiments** I have doubts about his feelings; **je doute qu'il soit d'accord** I doubt that he agrees
2 *reflexive verb* **se douter de quelque chose** to suspect something; **il ne se doute de rien** he doesn't suspect anything; **je m'en doute!** no wonder!

doux, douce *adjective*
(a) soft
(b) gentle
(c) mild

LA **douzaine** *noun*
(a) dozen; **une douzaine d'œufs** a dozen eggs
(b) about twelve; **il y avait une douzaine de personnes** there were about twelve people

douze *number* twelve; **le douze octobre** the twelfth of October; **nous sommes le douze avril** it's the twelfth of April

douzième *number* twelfth

LE **drame** *noun*
(a) drama
(b) tragedy

LE **drap** *noun* sheet *(for a bed)*

LE **drapeau** *noun* flag

> The plural of *drapeau* is *drapeaux*.

dresser
1 *verb*
(**a**) to train *(an animal)*
(**b**) to put up *(a tent, a statue)*
(**c**) to raise *(one's head)*
(**d**) to prick up *(one's ears)*
2 *reflexive verb* **se dresser** to stand, to stand up

LA **drogue** *noun* drugs; **la lutte contre la drogue** the fight against drugs; **c'est une drogue très dangereuse** it's a very dangerous drug

LE **drogué,** LA **droguée** *noun* drug addict

se droguer *reflexive verb* to take drugs

LE **droit¹** *noun*
(**a**) right; **avoir le droit de faire quelque chose** to have the right to do something, to be allowed to do something; **donner à quelqu'un le droit de faire quelque chose** to give somebody the right to do something, to allow somebody to do something
(**b**) law; **un étudiant en droit** a law student

droit², droite
1 *adjective*
(**a**) right; **ma main droite** my right hand; **le côté droit** the right-hand side
(**b**) straight
2 *adverb* **droit** straight; **allez tout droit** go straight ahead
3 *feminine noun* **la droite** the right; **le tiroir de droite** the right-hand drawer; **tourner à droite** to turn right; **rouler à droite** to drive on the right-hand side; **c'est à droite** it's on the right; **c'est à droite du fauteuil** it's to the right of the armchair

droitier, droitière *adjective* right-handed

drôle *adjective*
(**a**) funny
(**b**) strange

du *see* **de**
le toit du gymnase the roof of the gym; **l'homme le plus riche du monde** the richest man in the world; **nous avons parlé du film** we talked about the film; **j'ai acheté du lait** I bought some milk

> *Du* is the contraction of *de + le*.

dû, due *see* **devoir¹**
il a dû se tromper he must have made a mistake

> *Dû/due* is the past participle of the verb *devoir*. See verb table p. 314.

duquel *see* **lequel**
le bâtiment à côté duquel je suis passé the building that I walked past

> *Duquel* is the contraction of *de + lequel*. Its feminine equivalent is *de laquelle*.

dur, dure
1 *adjective*
(**a**) hard; **un matelas dur** a hard mattress; **c'est un exercice très dur** it's a very hard exercise
(**b**) harsh
(**c**) tough; **elle est dure, elle ne se plaint jamais** she's tough, she never complains
2 *adverb* **dur** **travailler dur** to work hard

durant *preposition* during, for

LA **durée** *noun* length, duration; **quelle est la durée du film?** how long is the film?; **un séjour de courte durée** a short stay

durement *adverb* harshly

durer *verb*
(**a**) to last
(**b**) to go on; **ça dure depuis un mois** it's been going on for a month

LE **duvet** *noun*
(**a**) down *(soft hair or soft feathers)*
(**b**) sleeping bag

> Note that the English word *duvet* is never a translation for the French word *duvet*.

E

L'eau *feminine noun* water; **de l'eau gazeuse** sparkling water, fizzy water; **de l'eau plate** still water; **de l'eau potable** drinking water; **de l'eau du robinet** tap water; **de l'eau de source** spring water

The plural of *eau* is *eaux*.

éblouir *verb* to dazzle

UN éboueur *noun* dustman; **il est éboueur** he's a dustman

écarlate *adjective* scarlet; **devenir écarlate** *(blush)* to go bright red

UN écart *noun*
(a) difference
(b) gap; **ils ont huit ans d'écart** there's an eight-year gap between them
(c) **faire un écart** to swerve
(d) **faire le grand écart** to do the splits
(e) **à l'écart du village** away from the village; **nous vivons à l'écart** we live in a remote spot

écarter
1 *verb*
(a) to open *(curtains, arms)*
(b) to spread; **écarte les doigts** spread your fingers
(c) to move away; **écarte la table du mur** move the table away from the wall
2 *reflexive verb* **s'écarter**
(a) to move apart
(b) to move out of the way
(c) to stray; **il s'est écarté du sujet** he strayed from the subject

UN échange *noun* exchange; **ils ont fait l'échange de leurs vélos** they swapped bikes; **en échange de ce service** in return for this favour

échanger *verb* to exchange, to swap; **je t'échange ce CD contre celui-là** I'll swap you this CD for that one

échapper
1 *verb*
(a) to escape; **il a échappé à la police** he escaped from the police
(b) to slip out; **ça m'a échappé des mains** it slipped out of my hands **je n'aurais pas dû le dire mais ça m'a échappé** I shouldn't have said it but it just slipped out
2 *reflexive verb* **s'échapper** to escape; **il s'est échappé de prison** he escaped from prison

UNE écharde *noun* splinter *(in one's finger)*

UNE écharpe *noun* scarf

UN échauffement *noun* warm-up; **des exercices d'échauffement** warm-up exercises

s'échauffer *reflexive verb* to warm up

UN échec
1 *noun* failure
2 *masculine plural noun* **les échecs** chess

UNE échelle *noun*
(a) ladder
(b) scale
(c) **faire la courte échelle à quelqu'un** to give somebody a leg up

échouer
1 *verb* to fail; **il a échoué à l'examen** he failed the exam
2 *reflexive verb* **s'échouer** to run aground

éclabousser *verb* to splash, to spatter

UN éclair *noun*
(a) flash of lightning; **les éclairs me font peur** I'm scared of lightning
(b) **un éclair au chocolat** a chocolate eclair

L'éclairage *masculine noun* lighting

éclaircir
1 *verb* to lighten
2 *reflexive verb* **s'éclaircir**
(a) *(sky)* to clear up
(b) *(situation)* to become clearer
(c) **s'éclaircir les cheveux** to lighten one's hair

éclairer
1 *verb*
(a) to light; **une bougie éclairait la pièce** the room was lit by a candle
(b) to brighten up
(c) **éclairer une situation** to make a situation clearer
2 *reflexive verb* **s'éclairer**
(a) to light up
(b) to get clearer

UN éclat *noun*
(a) brightness
(b) splinter *(of wood, glass)*; **des éclats de verre** pieces of broken glass; **la lampe a volé en éclats** the lamp was smashed to pieces
(c) burst; **un éclat de rire** a burst of laughter; **rire aux éclats** to burst out laughing

éclater
1 *verb*
(a) to burst *(a balloon)*; **on a éclaté de rire** we burst out laughing; **elle a éclaté en sanglots** she burst into tears
(b) to explode
(c) *(war)* to break out
2 *reflexive verb* **s'éclater** to have a great time

The verb *s'éclater* is informal.

écœurant, écœurante *adjective*
(a) nauseating
(b) disgusting

écœurer *verb* **écœurer quelqu'un** to make somebody feel sick; **ce gâteau**

m'écœure this cake is making me feel sick

UNE école *noun* school; **l'école maternelle** nursery school; **l'école primaire** primary school; **une école publique** a state school; **une école privée** a public school, a private school; **faire l'école buissonnière** to play truant

L'École
State schools in France are known as *laïques*, which means that they are independent of the Church and have no religious instruction or ceremonies (though these may be offered in private schools). Students in state schools are not allowed to wear any religious symbols such as Muslim headscarves, Jewish skullcaps or large Catholic crosses. Unlike in Britain, French students do not wear school uniform; they can wear their own clothes to school.

L'École Primaire
L'école primaire provides five years' teaching after *l'école maternelle* and before *le collège*. It is for pupils between 6 and 11. The first year is known as *le CP* (*cours préparatoire*) in which pupils learn to read. The second year is called *le CE1* (*cours élémentaire 1ère année*), the third year *le CE2* (*cours élémentaire 2ème année*), the fourth year *le CM1* (*cours moyen 1ère année*) and the fifth and last year *le CM2* (*cours moyen 2ème*). See also **maternelle**, **collège** and **lycée**.

UN écolier, UNE écolière *noun* schoolboy/schoolgirl

écologique *adjective* environmental

L'économie
1 *feminine noun*
(a) economy
(b) economics
2 *feminine plural noun* **les économies** savings; **faire des économies** to save money

économique *adjective*
(a) economic
(b) economical, cheap

économiser *verb* to save *(money, energy)*

L'**écorce** *feminine noun*
(a) bark *(of a tree)*
(b) peel *(of an orange)*

s'**écorcher** *reflexive verb* to graze oneself

UN **Écossais**, UNE **Écossaise** *noun* *(person)* Scot, Scotsman/Scotswoman; **les Écossais** Scottish people, the Scots

écossais, écossaise *adjective* Scottish

> In French, only the noun for the inhabitants of a country takes a capital letter, never the adjective.

L'**Écosse** *feminine noun* Scotland

s'**écouler** *reflexive verb*
(a) to flow
(b) to go by

écouter *verb* to listen to; **j'écoute le professeur** I'm listening to the teacher; **écoutez-moi!** listen to me!

UN **écran** *noun* screen

écraser
1 *verb*
(a) to crush
(b) to run over; **j'ai failli me faire écraser** I nearly got run over
2 *reflexive verb* **s'écraser** to crash

écrémé, écrémée *adjective* skimmed

s'**écrier** *reflexive verb* to shout, to exclaim

écrire
1 *verb* to write; **elle a écrit à son oncle** she wrote to her uncle
2 *reflexive verb* **s'écrire**
(a) to be spelled; **ça s'écrit comment?** how do you spell it?
(b) to write to each other

> See verb table p. 322.

UN **écrit** *noun*
(a) written exam; **il a échoué à l'écrit**
he failed the written exam
(b) **par écrit** in writing

L'**écriture** *feminine noun*
(a) writing
(b) handwriting

UN **écrivain** *noun* writer; **elle est écrivain** she's a writer

> The word *écrivain* does not have a feminine but it can also refer to a woman.

UN **écrou** *noun* nut; **des écrous et des boulons** nuts and bolts

s'**écrouler** *reflexive verb* to collapse

UN **écureuil** *noun* squirrel

UNE **écurie** *noun* stable

UN **édifice** *noun* building

Édimbourg *noun* Edinburgh

UN **éducateur**, UNE **éducatrice** *noun* youth leader; **elle est éducatrice** she's a youth leader; **un éducateur spécialisé, une éducatrice spécialisée** a special needs teacher

L'**éducation** *feminine noun*
(a) education; **l'éducation physique** physical education, PE
(b) upbringing
(c) good manners

éducatrice *see* **éducateur**

éduquer *verb*
(a) to educate
(b) to bring up; **un enfant bien éduqué** a well-brought-up child

effacer *verb*
(a) to erase
(b) to wipe *(blackboard)*
(c) to delete

effectivement *adverb*
(a) actually
(b) indeed

> Note that the English word *effectively* is never a translation for the French word *effectivement*.

effectuer *verb* to make

UN **effet** *noun*
(a) effect; **tes somnifères ne m'ont fait aucun effet** your sleeping pills had no effect on me
(b) impression; **faire bon effet** to make a good impression
(c) **en effet** indeed

efficace *adjective*
(a) effective
(b) efficient

s'effondrer *reflexive verb* to collapse

UN **effort** *noun* effort; **tu dois encore faire des efforts** you still need to make an effort

> The *t* in *effort* is not pronounced.

effrayant, effrayante *adjective* frightening

effrayer *verb* to frighten, to scare

égal, égale *adjective*
(a) equal; **il faut le partager en parts égales** we need to divide it up into equal parts; **3 est égal à 2 plus 1** 3 is equal to 2 plus 1
(b) **ça m'est égal** I don't mind

> The masculine plural of *égal* is *égaux*.

également *adverb* also, as well

égaler *verb* to equal

égaliser *verb* to equalize, to tie

L'**égalité** *feminine noun*
(a) equality; **l'égalité des droits** equal rights
(b) **les deux équipes sont à égalité** the two teams are level (with each other)

égarer
1 *verb* to lose
2 *reflexive verb* **s'égarer** to get lost

UNE **église** *noun* church

égoïste *adjective* selfish

UNE **égratignure** *noun* scratch

L'**Égypte** *feminine noun* Egypt

UN **Égyptien**, UNE **Égyptienne** *noun* *(person)* Egyptian

égyptien, égyptienne *adjective* Egyptian; **les pyramides égyptiennes** the Egyptian pyramids

eh *exclamation* hey; **eh vous, là-bas!** hey you, over there!; **eh bien, je crois que vous avez raison** well, I think you're right; **eh non** well, no; **eh oui** well, yes

UN **élan** *noun*
(a) elk, moose
(b) run-up; **prendre son élan** to take a run-up
(c) momentum

s'élancer *reflexive verb*
(a) to rush; **il s'est élancé vers moi** he rushed towards me
(b) to take a run-up

élargir
1 *verb*
(a) to widen
(b) to broaden
2 *reflexive verb* **s'élargir**
(a) to widen
(b) to stretch; **mes chaussures se sont élargies** my shoes have stretched

UN **élastique** *noun* elastic band

UN **électeur**, UNE **électrice** *noun* voter

UN **électricien**, UNE **électricienne** *noun* electrician; **il est électricien** he's an electrician

UN **élément** *noun*
(a) element
(b) component

UN **éléphant** *noun* elephant; **un éléphant d'Asie** an Indian elephant; **un éléphant d'Afrique** an African elephant

> The *t* in *éléphant* is not pronounced.

L'**élevage** *masculine noun*
(a) breeding; **faire de l'élevage** to breed animals; **l'élevage industriel** factory farming
(b) farm

élevé, élevée *adjective*
(**a**) high
(**b**) **un enfant bien élevé** a well-brought-up child; **un enfant mal élevé** a badly brought-up child

UN/UNE **élève** *noun* pupil, student

élever
1 *verb*
(**a**) to bring up
(**b**) to breed
(**c**) to raise; **élever la voix** to raise one's voice
2 *reflexive verb* **s'élever**
(**a**) to rise
(**b**) **s'élever à** to come to; **les réparations s'élèvent à 50 euros** the repairs come to 50 euros

UN **éleveur,** UNE **éleveuse** *noun* breeder; **un éleveur de chiens** a dog breeder

éliminer *verb*
(**a**) to eliminate
(**b**) to get rid of

élire *verb* to elect; **j'ai été élu délégué** I've been elected as representative

See verb table p. 322.

elle *pronoun*
(**a**) she; **elle est ici** she's here; **c'est elle qui prend les décisions** she's the one who takes the decisions
(**b**) it; **j'ai jeté la lampe car elle était cassée** I threw the lamp away because it was broken
(**c**) her; **c'est à cause d'elle** it's because of her; **il travaille mieux qu'elle** he works better than her; **un ami à elle** a friend of hers; **ce livre n'est pas à elle** this book is not hers
(**d**) herself; **elle était fière d'elle** she was proud of herself

Elle only refers to feminine nouns.

elle-même *pronoun* herself; **elle l'a écrit elle-même** she wrote it herself

Elle-même only refers to feminine nouns.

elles *pronoun*
(**a**) they; **elles sont ici** they're here; **ce sont elles qui sont parties en premier** they left first
(**b**) them; **c'est à cause d'elles** it's because of them; **ils travaillent mieux qu'elles** they work better than them; **un ami à elles** a friend of theirs; **ces livres ne sont pas à elles** these books aren't theirs
(**c**) themselves; **elles étaient contentes d'elles** they were pleased with themselves

Elles is the plural of *elle*. It only refers to feminine plural nouns.

elles-mêmes *pronoun* themselves; **elles l'ont fait elles-mêmes** they did it themselves

Elles-mêmes is the plural of *elle-même*. It only refers to feminine plural nouns.

éloigné, éloignée *adjective*
(**a**) far away; **ce n'est pas très éloigné de l'aéroport** it's not very far away from the airport
(**b**) distant; **nos cousins éloignés** our distant cousins

éloigner
1 *verb*
(**a**) to move away; **éloigne la table du mur** move the table away from the wall
(**b**) to keep away; **mes parents veulent m'éloigner de toi** my parents want to keep me away from you
2 *reflexive verb* **s'éloigner** to move away; **éloignez-vous du bord** move away from the edge

UN **emballage** *noun* packaging; **du papier d'emballage** wrapping paper

emballer *verb* to wrap up

embarquer
1 *verb*
(**a**) to load
(**b**) to board
(**c**) to walk away with; **n'embarque pas ma veste!** don't walk away with

my jacket!; **les voleurs ont tout embarqué** the burglars walked away with everything there was

Sense (c) is an informal use of *embarquer*.

2 *reflexive verb* **s'embarquer**
(**a**) to board
(**b**) to embark; **je me suis embarqué dans une aventure risquée** I embarked on a risky venture

embarrasser
1 *verb*
(**a**) to embarrass; **ça m'embarrasse de lui demander** I'm embarrassed to ask him
(**b**) to clutter up
2 *reflexive verb* **s'embarrasser** s'embarrasser de quelque chose to burden oneself with something

embaucher *verb* to hire *(somebody)*

embêtant, embêtante *adjective* annoying

embêter
1 *verb*
(**a**) to annoy; **arrête de m'embêter!** stop annoying me!; **ça t'embête si j'ouvre la fenêtre?** do you mind if I open the window?
(**b**) to bore
2 *reflexive verb* **s'embêter** to be bored

UN **embouteillage** *noun* traffic jam

embrasser
1 *verb* to kiss
2 *reflexive verb* **s'embrasser** to kiss; **ils se sont embrassés** they kissed

embrouiller
1 *verb*
(**a**) to tangle up
(**b**) to complicate
2 *reflexive verb* **s'embrouiller** to get muddled up

s'émerveiller *reflexive verb* s'émerveiller devant quelque chose to marvel at something

UNE **émeute** *noun* riot

UN **émigré,** UNE **émigrée** *noun* emigrant

émigrer *verb* to emigrate

UNE **émission** *noun* programme *(on TV, radio)*

emmêler
1 *verb* to tangle up
2 *reflexive verb* **s'emmêler**
(**a**) to be tangled up
(**b**) to get mixed up

emménager *verb* to move in *(to a new house)*

emmener *verb* to take

UNE **émotion** *noun*
(**a**) feeling
(**b**) emotion
(**c**) shock; **quelle émotion de l'avoir revu!** seeing him again was quite a shock!

émouvant, émouvante *adjective* moving, touching

émouvoir
1 *verb* to move, to touch; **ému jusqu'aux larmes** moved to tears
2 *reflexive verb* **s'émouvoir** to be moved, to be touched

The past participle of *émouvoir* is *ému(e)*.

UN **empêchement** *noun* difficulty, hold-up; **si tu as un empêchement, téléphone** if you get held up, give me a call

empêcher
1 *verb* to prevent, to stop
2 *reflexive verb* **s'empêcher** je ne peux pas m'en empêcher I can't help it; **je ne pouvais pas m'empêcher de rire** I couldn't help laughing

empiler *verb* to pile up

empirer *verb* to get worse

L' **emploi** *masculine noun*
(**a**) job
(**b**) employment
(**c**) **un emploi du temps** a timetable
(**d**) use; **les différents emplois d'un**

verbe the different uses of a verb

UN **employé,** UNE **employée** *noun* employee, worker; **elle est employée de bureau** she's an office worker

employer
1 *verb*
(**a**) to employ
(**b**) to use
2 *reflexive verb* **s'employer** to be used

empoisonner *verb* to poison

emporter
1 *verb*
(**a**) to take; **emporte ton maillot de bain** take your swimming costume; **plats à emporter** take-away food
(**b**) to blow off; **l'ouragan a emporté les toits des maisons** the hurricane blew the roofs off the houses
(**c**) to carry away; **le courant a emporté le radeau au large** the current carried the raft out to sea
(**d**) to win; **l'équipe parisienne l'a emporté par deux buts à zéro** the Paris team won by two goals to nil
2 *reflexive verb* **s'emporter** to lose one's temper

UNE **empreinte** *noun* footprint; **les empreintes digitales** fingerprints

emprunter *verb*
(**a**) to borrow; **emprunter de l'argent** to borrow money; **j'ai emprunté ce livre à Sébastien** I borrowed this book from Sébastien
(**b**) to take *(a road, a passage)*

ému, émue *adjective*
(**a**) moved, overcome with emotion
(**b**) upset

Ému(e) is the past participle of the verb *émouvoir*.

en
1 *preposition*
(**a**) in; **en 2006** in 2006; **en janvier** in January; **en hiver** in winter; **je l'ai lu en quatre heures** I read it in four hours; **il est en réunion** he's in a meeting; **j'habite en France** I live in France; **j'habite en ville** I live in town
(**b**) to; **je vais en Espagne** I'm going to Spain; **je vais en ville** I'm going to town
(**c**) by; **en voiture** by car; **en avion** by plane
(**d**) at, in; **il est bon en maths** he's good at maths; **il a eu une bonne note en histoire** he got a good mark in history
(**e**) as a; **je l'ai eu en cadeau** I was given it as a present; **je suis venu en ami** I came as a friend
(**f**) **une table en bois** a wooden table; **elle est en bois** it's made out of wood; **un bracelet en or** a gold bracelet; **il est en or** it's gold; **je la préfère en vert** I prefer it in green
(**g**) **il est en colère** he's angry; **il est en forme** he's on form; **il est en sueur** he's sweaty
(**h**) while, when; **il est tombé en courant** he fell while he was running; **c'est en le voyant que j'ai compris** when I saw him I understood

En is used with the present participle (verb form which ends in *-ant*) to describe a continuous action which is taking place when something else suddenly happens, as shown in the above examples.

(**i**) **il est parti en courant** he ran off; **il marche en boitant** he walks with a limp

En can also be used with the present participle to describe the way an action is performed, as shown in the above examples.

2 *pronoun*
(**a**) from there; **il faudra que tu ailles à la poste – j'en viens** you'll have to go to the post office – I've just got back from there
(**b**) it; **je m'en souviens** I remember it; **il en est content** he's pleased with it; **est-ce que tu veux en parler?** would you like to talk about it?; **on peut en**

mourir you can die of it; **elle en a cinq** she's got five of them
(**c**) some; **voilà des fraises, prends-en** here are some strawberries, take some
(**d**) any; **si tu n'aimes pas les olives, n'en mange pas** if you don't like olives, don't eat any

encadrer *verb*
(**a**) to frame
(**b**) to supervise

enceinte
1 *feminine adjective* pregnant; **elle est enceinte de son premier enfant** she's expecting her first child; **elle est enceinte de trois mois** she's three months pregnant
2 *feminine noun*
(**a**) surrounding wall, fence; **dans l'enceinte de** within; **dans l'enceinte de l'école** on school premises
(**b**) speaker *(of a stereo)*

enchanté, enchantée *adjective* delighted, pleased; **elle était enchantée de son voyage** she really enjoyed her trip; **enchanté!** *or* **enchanté de faire votre connaissance!** how do you do?, pleased to meet you!

encombrant, encombrante *adjective* bulky

UN encombrement *noun* traffic jam

encombrer *verb*
(**a**) to clutter up
(**b**) to block *(a road)*
(**c**) to burden

encore *adverb*
(**a**) still; **il travaillait encore à minuit** he was still working at midnight
(**b**) **pas encore** not yet; **je n'ai pas encore fini** I haven't finished yet
(**c**) again; **il est encore venu la voir** he came to see her again; **encore une fois** once again
(**d**) more; **vous en voulez encore?** would you like some more?; **encore un café** another coffee; **encore du pain** some more bread
(**e**) even; **il est encore plus gentil que je n'imaginais** he is even nicer than I'd imagined; **encore pire** even worse

encourager *verb* to encourage

L'encre *feminine noun* ink; **écrire à l'encre** to write in ink

endommager *verb* to damage

endormi, endormie *adjective*
(**a**) asleep
(**b**) sleepy

endormir
1 *verb*
(**a**) to send to sleep
(**b**) to put to sleep *(to operate on a person or an animal)*
2 *reflexive verb* **s'endormir** to fall asleep, to go to sleep

See verb table p. 320.

UN endroit *noun*
(**a**) place; **ce n'est pas au bon endroit** it's not in the right place; **un endroit tranquille** a quiet place; **par endroits** in places
(**b**) **ton pull n'est pas à l'endroit** your sweater's on the wrong way round; **remets la bouteille à l'endroit** turn the bottle the right way up

L'énergie *feminine noun* energy; **il manque d'énergie** he lacks energy; **l'énergie solaire** solar energy

énergique *adjective*
(**a**) energetic, with plenty of drive *(person)*
(**b**) strong *(measures, speech, treatment)*

énervant, énervante *adjective* annoying

énervé, énervée *adjective*
(**a**) annoyed
(**b**) edgy
(**c**) agitated

énerver
1 *verb*
(**a**) to annoy; **cette musique m'énerve** this music is getting on my nerves
(**b**) to excite; **n'énerve pas les enfants** don't excite the children

2 *reflexive verb* **s'énerver** to get worked up

L'**enfance** *feminine noun* childhood; **dans mon enfance** when I was a child; **des souvenirs d'enfance** childhood memories

UN/UNE **enfant** *noun* child

> Note that the English word *infant* is never a translation for the French word *enfant*. *Enfant* can refer to children of all ages and not just babies.

L'**enfer** *masculine noun* hell; **un bruit d'enfer** a deafening racket

enfermer
1 *verb*
(**a**) to shut up
(**b**) to lock up *(a criminal)*
(**c**) to coop up; **je me sens enfermé** I feel cooped up
2 *reflexive verb* **s'enfermer**
(**a**) to lock oneself in
(**b**) to shut oneself away; **elle s'enferme à la bibliothèque toute la journée** she spends all day shut up in the library

enfiler *verb*
(**a**) to thread *(a needle)*
(**b**) to slip on *(a ring, tights)*
(**c**) to put on *(a coat, a jumper, gloves)*

enfin *adverb*
(**a**) at last
(**b**) finally
(**c**) still; **ce sera difficile, enfin, on peut essayer** it'll be difficult, still we can try
(**d**) well; **elle est blonde, enfin châtain clair** she's got blond hair, well, light brown

enflé, enflée *adjective* swollen *(ankle, cheek)*

enfler *verb* to swell

enfoncer
1 *verb*
(**a**) to push in, to drive in, to stick in
(**b**) to break down *(a door)*
2 *reflexive verb* **s'enfoncer**

(**a**) to sink; **je m'enfonçais dans la boue** I was sinking into the mud
(**b**) to make matters worse; **plus tu t'excuses, plus tu t'enfonces** you're only making matters worse for yourself by apologizing so much

s'enfuir *reflexive verb*
(**a**) to run away; **elle s'est enfuie de chez elle** she ran away from home
(**b**) to escape; **il s'est enfui de prison** he escaped from jail
(**c**) to flee; **il s'est enfui en Suisse** he fled to Switzerland

See verb table p. 322.

UNE **énigme** *noun* riddle

enlever
1 *verb*
(**a**) to take away, to remove
(**b**) to take off; **enlève ton manteau** take off your coat
2 *reflexive verb* **s'enlever** to come off

UN **ennemi** *noun* enemy

UN **ennui** *noun*
(**a**) problem; **des ennuis de santé** health problems; **tu vas avoir des ennuis** you're going to get into trouble
(**b**) **l'ennui** boredom

ennuyer
1 *verb*
(**a**) to bother; **ça t'ennuie si j'ouvre la fenêtre?** do you mind if I open the window?
(**b**) to bore
2 *reflexive verb* **s'ennuyer** to be bored

ennuyeux, ennuyeuse *adjective*
(**a**) boring
(**b**) annoying

énorme *adjective* enormous, huge

énormément *adverb*
(**a**) enormously, tremendously
(**b**) **énormément de** a huge amount of; **il y avait énormément de monde** there was a huge number of people

UNE **enquête** *noun*
(**a**) investigation, inquiry; **la police**

fait une enquête sur le meurtre the police are conducting an investigation into the murder
(**b**) survey

enquêter _verb_ to investigate; **ils enquêtent sur un meurtre** they're investigating a murder

ᴜɴ **enregistrement** _noun_
(**a**) recording
(**b**) **l'enregistrement des bagages** baggage check-in

enregistrer _verb_
(**a**) to record _(a song, a film)_
(**b**) to check in _(one's baggage)_

enrhumé, enrhumée _adjective_ **être enrhumé** to have a cold

s'enrhumer _reflexive verb_ to catch a cold

s'enrichir _reflexive verb_ to become rich

enrouler
1 _verb_
(**a**) to wind up _(a rope, wire)_
(**b**) to roll up _(a map, a carpet)_
(**c**) to wrap
2 _reflexive verb_ **s'enrouler**
(**a**) to wind; **le papier s'enroule autour de ce cylindre** the paper winds round this cylinder
(**b**) to wrap oneself up

ᴜɴ **enseignant,** ᴜɴᴇ **enseignante** _noun_ teacher; **il est enseignant** he's a teacher

ʟ'**enseignement** _masculine noun_
(**a**) education; **l'enseignement privé** private education; **l'enseignement public** state education; **l'enseignement supérieur** higher education
(**b**) teaching; **une méthode d'enseignement** a teaching method; **il est entré dans l'enseignement** he went into teaching

enseigner _verb_ to teach

ensemble
1 _adverb_
(**a**) together; **ces couleurs vont bien ensemble** these colours go well together
(**b**) at once, at the same time
2 _masculine noun_
(**a**) set _(of objects)_
(**b**) suit, outfit
(**c**) whole; **l'ensemble de la classe** the whole class; **l'ensemble des joueurs** all the players; **dans l'ensemble** on the whole

ensoleillé, ensoleillée _adjective_ sunny

ensuite _adverb_ then, next

entasser _verb_
(**a**) to pile up
(**b**) to cram in

entendre
1 _verb_
(**a**) to hear; **je n'ai jamais entendu parler d'une chose pareille** I've never heard of such a thing; **j'ai entendu parler de ce film** I've heard about this film; **j'ai entendu dire qu'il était parti** I heard that he had left
(**b**) to mean; **qu'entendez-vous par là?** what do you mean by that?
2 _reflexive verb_ **s'entendre** to get on; **elle s'entend très bien avec lui** she gets on very well with him; **ils ne s'entendent pas** they don't get on

entendu, entendue _adjective_
(**a**) **entendu!** agreed!; **c'est entendu, je viendrai** all right, I'll come
(**b**) **bien entendu** of course

ᴜɴ **enterrement** _noun_
(**a**) burial
(**b**) funeral

enterrer _verb_ to bury

entêté, entêtée _adjective_ obstinate, stubborn

s'entêter _reflexive verb_ to persist; **s'entêter à faire quelque chose** to persist in doing something

enthousiasmer
1 _verb_ to fill with enthusiasm; **ça n'a pas l'air de t'enthousiasmer** you don't seem very enthusiastic about it

2 *reflexive verb* **s'enthousiasmer** to get enthusiastic

entier, entière
1 *adjective* whole, entire; **une semaine entière** a whole week; **il a mangé le gâteau tout entier** he ate the whole cake
2 *adverb* **en entier** completely; **il a mangé le gâteau en entier** he ate the whole cake; **je l'ai lu en entier** I read all of it

entièrement *adverb* entirely, completely

UNE **entorse** *noun* sprain; **je me suis fait une entorse à la cheville** I sprained my ankle

entourer *verb*
(**a**) to surround; **le jardin est entouré d'un mur** the garden is surrounded by a wall
(**b**) to circle *(a word)*

UN **entracte** *noun* interval *(of a play)*

L'**entraînement** *masculine noun*
(**a**) training; **il s'est blessé à l'entraînement** he hurt himself during a training session; **un terrain d'entraînement** a training ground
(**b**) practice; **il me faut juste un peu d'entraînement** I just need a bit of practice

entraîner
1 *verb*
(**a**) to sweep along; **entraîné par la foule** swept along by the crowd
(**b**) to drag; **c'est lui qui m'a entraîné dans cette affaire** he's the one who dragged me into this mess
(**c**) to lead to
(**d**) to coach
2 *reflexive verb* **s'entraîner**
(**a**) to train; **il s'entraîne pour les jeux Olympiques** he's training for the Olympics
(**b**) to practise

UN **entraîneur**, UNE **entraîneuse** *noun* coach; **il est entraîneur** he's a coach

entre *preposition*
(**a**) between; **la distance entre ces deux villes** the distance between these two towns; **entre nous, il n'a pas tort** between you and me, he's right
(**b**) among; **une soirée entre amis** an evening among friends; **l'un d'entre vous** one of you; **certains d'entre eux** some of them; **entre autres** among other things

UNE **entrée** *noun*
(**a**) starter, first course
(**b**) entrance; **à l'entrée de l'école** at the entrance to the school
(**c**) hall, hallway
(**d**) entry
(**e**) admission; **entrée gratuite** or **entrée libre** free admission
(**f**) ticket; **j'ai deux entrées pour la pièce** I've got two tickets for the play

UNE **entreprise** *noun* company, business

entrer *verb*
(**a**) to go in; **je suis entré dans sa chambre** I went into his bedroom
(**b**) to come in; **entrez!** come in!
(**c**) to enter; **le navire est entré dans le port** the ship entered the harbour
(**d**) to get in; **la clé est trop grosse pour entrer dans la serrure** the key is too big to get in the keyhole
(**e**) to join; **il est entré dans l'entreprise il y a deux ans** he joined the company two years ago
(**f**) **j'entre en sixième l'année prochaine** I'm starting first year next year

entre-temps *adverb* meanwhile, in the meantime

entretenir
1 *verb*
(**a**) to look after *(a house, a park)*; **un jardin bien entretenu** a well-kept garden
(**b**) to maintain *(a car, equipment)*
2 *reflexive verb* **s'entretenir** **s'entretenir avec quelqu'un** to speak to somebody

Note that the English verb *to enter-tain* is never a translation for the French verb *entretenir*. See verb table p. 324.

UN entretien *noun*
(a) interview
(b) maintenance; **l'entretien de la voiture** car maintenance

envahir *verb*
(a) to invade
(b) to overrun; **un grenier envahi par les souris** an attic overrun with mice

UNE enveloppe *noun* envelope; **une enveloppe affranchie** a stamped addressed envelope; **mettez-le sous enveloppe** put it in an envelope

envelopper *verb* to wrap up, to wrap

envers
1 *preposition* to, towards; **il est cruel envers moi** he's cruel to me
2 *masculine noun* **il a mis ses chaussettes à l'envers** he put his socks on inside out; **la carte est à l'envers** the map is upside down; **sa casquette est à l'envers** his cap is back to front

L'envie *feminine noun*
(a) **j'ai envie d'un bonbon** I want a sweet; **elle a envie de savoir** she wants to know; **j'avais envie de pleurer** I felt like crying; **j'ai envie de dormir** I feel sleepy; **j'ai envie de vomir** I feel sick
(b) craving; **j'ai une envie de chocolat** I have a craving for chocolate
(c) urge
(d) envy

environ *adverb* about, around

L'environnement *masculine noun*
(a) environment; **c'est mauvais pour l'environnement** it's bad for the environment
(b) background; **son environnement familial** his family background

LES environs *masculine plural noun*
(a) surrounding area; **dans les environs de Nantes** *or* **aux environs de Nantes** near Nantes

(b) **aux environs de midi** around noon

envisager *verb* to consider; **j'envisage de partir** I'm considering leaving

s'envoler *reflexive verb*
(a) to fly away
(b) to take off
(c) to blow off, to blow away

envoyer *verb*
(a) to send
(b) to throw; **envoie-moi la balle** throw me the ball

See verb table p. 322.

épais, épaisse *adjective* thick; **une planche épaisse de dix centimètres** a board ten centimetres thick; **peu épais** thin

L'épaisseur *feminine noun*
(a) thickness; **un mur d'une épaisseur de vingt centimètres** *or* **un mur de vingt centimètres d'épaisseur** a wall twenty centimetres thick
(b) layer; **plusieurs épaisseurs de vêtements** several layers of clothes

UNE épaule *noun* shoulder

UNE épée *noun* sword

épeler *verb* to spell

UNE épice *noun* spice

épicé, épicée *adjective* spicy

UNE épicerie *noun* grocer's (shop)

UNE épicier, UNE épicière *noun* grocer; **il est épicier** he's a grocer

UNE épidémie *noun* epidemic

LES épinards *masculine plural noun* spinach

UNE épine *noun* thorn, prickle

UNE épingle *noun* pin; **une épingle à cheveux** a hairpin; **une épingle à linge** a clothes peg; **une épingle à nourrice** a safety pin

éplucher *verb* to peel *(vegetables)*

UNE éponge *noun* sponge

UNE **époque** *noun*
(a) time; **à cette époque-là** at that time; **à l'époque, elle était très connue** at the time she was very well-known; **à l'époque où j'étais étudiant** when I was a student
(b) age, era

L'**épouse** *feminine noun* wife

épouser *verb* to marry

épouvantable *adjective*
(a) awful, terrible
(b) frightening

UN **épouvantail** *noun* scarecrow

L'**époux** *masculine noun* husband

UNE **épreuve** *noun*
(a) test; **une épreuve écrite** a written test; **une épreuve orale** an oral test; **corriger des épreuves** to mark exam papers
(b) event *(in sports)*

éprouver *verb*
(a) to feel; **les sentiments qu'il éprouve pour moi** the feelings that he has for me
(b) to experience; **elle a éprouvé une grande déception** she experienced great disappointment
(c) to try; **son divorce l'a beaucoup éprouvée** her divorce was a very trying experience for her

L'**EPS** *feminine noun* PE

EPS is the abbreviation of *éducation physique et sportive*.

épuisé, épuisée *adjective*
(a) exhausted
(b) sold out; *(book)* out of print

L'**équateur** *masculine noun* equator; **sous l'équateur** at the equator

UNE **équation** *noun* equation

UNE **équerre** *noun* set square

équestre *adjective* horseriding; **le sport équestre** horseriding; **un centre équestre** a riding school

L'**équilibre** *masculine noun* balance; **j'ai perdu l'équilibre** I lost my balance;

le verre était en équilibre au bord de la table the glass was balanced on the edge of the table

UN **équipage** *noun* crew *(on a plane, a ship)*

UNE **équipe** *noun*
(a) team; **un sport d'équipe** a team game; **un travail d'équipe** teamwork; **faire équipe avec quelqu'un** to team up with somebody
(b) crew *(in rowing, film-making)*

UN **équipement** *noun*
(a) equipment
(b) gear
(c) **les équipements** facilities; **des équipements sportifs** sports facilities

équiper *verb*
(a) to equip; **une cuisine tout équipée** a fully-equipped kitchen
(b) to fit out

L'**équitation** *feminine noun* horseriding; **je fais de l'équitation** I go horseriding; **une école d'équitation** a riding school

UNE **erreur** *noun*
(a) mistake; **par erreur** by mistake
(b) error

es *see* **être**
tu es de mauvaise humeur aujourd'hui you're in a bad mood today

Es is a form of the verb *être* in the present tense. See verb table p. 316.

L'**escalade** *feminine noun* rock climbing; **je fais de l'escalade** I go rock climbing; **un mur d'escalade** a climbing wall

escalader *verb* to climb

UNE **escale** *noun* stopover, call; **l'avion a fait escale à Rio** the plane made a stopover at Rio; **le bateau a fait escale à Marseille** the boat called at Marseilles; **un voyage sans escale** a direct trip

UN **escalier** *noun*
(a) stairs; **les escaliers** the stairs;

monter l'escalier *or* **monter les escaliers** to go up the stairs
(**b**) staircase

UN **escargot** *noun* snail

UN/UNE **esclave** *noun* slave

L'**escrime** *feminine noun* fencing; **je fais de l'escrime** I do fencing

UN **escroc** *noun* swindler, crook

> The final *c* in *escroc* is not pronounced.

L'**espace** *masculine noun*
(**a**) gap
(**b**) space; **voyager dans l'espace** to travel through space; **as-tu assez d'espace?** do you have enough space?; **il a été malade cinq fois en l'espace d'un mois** he's been ill five times within the space of a month
(**c**) **un espace vert** a park

L'**Espagne** *feminine noun* Spain

UN **Espagnol**, UNE **Espagnole** *noun* (*person*) Spaniard; **les Espagnols** the Spanish

espagnol, espagnole
1 *adjective* Spanish; **une danse espagnole** a Spanish dance
2 *masculine noun* **l'espagnol** (*language*) Spanish; **il parle espagnol** he speaks Spanish

> In French, only the noun for the inhabitants of a country takes a capital letter, never the adjective or the noun for the language.

UNE **espèce**
1 *noun*
(**a**) kind, sort; **il y a plusieurs espèces de café** there are various sorts of coffee
(**b**) species; **une espèce en voie de disparition** *or* **une espèce menacée** an endangered species
(**c**) **espèce d'idiot!** (*informal phrase*) you idiot!
2 *feminine plural noun* **les espèces** cash; **payer en espèces** to pay in cash

espérer *verb*
(**a**) to hope
(**b**) to expect

UN **espion**, UNE **espionne** *noun* spy

L'**espionnage** *masculine noun*
(**a**) spying; **un roman d'espionnage** a spy novel
(**b**) espionage; **l'espionnage industriel** industrial espionage

espionner *verb* to spy on

L'**espoir** *masculine noun* hope; **sans espoir** hopeless

L'**esprit** *masculine noun*
(**a**) spirit; **l'esprit d'équipe** team spirit
(**b**) mind; **avoir l'esprit critique** to have a critical mind; **ça m'a traversé l'esprit** it crossed my mind
(**c**) wit
(**d**) ghost

> The *t* in *esprit* is not pronounced.

UN **essai** *noun*
(**a**) attempt
(**b**) test; **un essai nucléaire** a nuclear test
(**c**) try (*in rugby*)
(**d**) essay (*in literature*)

UN **essaim** *noun* swarm

essayer *verb*
(**a**) to try
(**b**) to test
(**c**) to try on (*clothes*)

L'**essence** *feminine noun* petrol

essentiel, essentielle
1 *adjective*
(**a**) essential
(**b**) main
2 *masculine noun* **l'essentiel**
(**a**) bare essentials; **n'apportez que l'essentiel** bring only the bare essentials
(**b**) the most important thing, the main thing; **l'essentiel, c'est que tu comprennes** the most important thing is that you understand
(**c**) most; **elle passe l'essentiel de son temps au téléphone** she spends most

of her time on the phone

essoufflé, essoufflée *adjective*
breathless, out of breath

UN **essuie-glace** *noun* windscreen
wiper

> The plural of *essuie-glace* is *essuie-glaces.*

essuyer
1 *verb*
(**a**) to wipe
(**b**) to dry *(the dishes)*
2 *reflexive verb* **s'essuyer** to dry oneself; **essuie-toi les mains** dry your
hands

est¹
1 *masculine noun* **l'est** the east; **il habite dans l'est de Paris** he lives in the
east of Paris; **Strasbourg est à l'est
de Paris** Strasbourg is to the east of
Paris; **les gens de l'est** people from the
east; **un vent d'est** an easterly wind;
l'Europe de l'Est Eastern Europe; **les
pays de l'Est** Eastern European countries
2 *adjective* east, eastern; **la côte est**
the east coast; **il habite dans la banlieue est de la ville** he lives in the eastern suburbs of the city

est²
(**a**) *see* **être**
elle est au téléphone she's on the
phone; **mon frère est malade** my brother is ill

> *Est* is a form of the verb *être* in the
> present tense. See verb table p. 316.

(**b**) *see* **c'est-à-dire**
(**c**) *see* **n'est-ce pas**

est-ce que *adverb*
(**a**) **est-ce que tu aimes ce film?** do
you like this film?; **est-ce que tu l'as
acheté?** did you buy it?; **est-ce que tu
iras?** will you go?; **est-ce qu'elle est
là?** is she there?; **est-ce qu'elle était
là?** was she there?; **est-ce que tu as
une enveloppe?** have you got an envelope?; **est-ce que tu vas lui télé-**

phoner? are you going to phone him?;
est-ce que je peux ouvrir la fenêtre?
can I open the window?
(**b**) *(after a pronoun or another adverb)*
qui est-ce que tu as vu? who did you
see?; **qu'est-ce que tu as dit?** what did
you say?; **quand est-ce qu'il arrive?**
when does he arrive?; **où est-ce que
tu vas?** where are you going?; **pourquoi est-ce que tu ris?** why are you
laughing?

> This expression is one way of form-
> ing questions in French. In front of a
> vowel or a mute h *est-ce que* becomes
> *est-ce qu'.*

L'**estomac** *masculine noun* stomach;
j'ai mal à l'estomac I have stomach
ache

> The *c* in *estomac* is not pronounced.

L'**Estonie** *feminine noun* Estonia

UN **Estonien**, UNE **Estonienne** *noun*
(person) Estonian

estonien, estonienne
1 *adjective* Estonian; **l'économie estonienne** the Estonian economy
2 *masculine noun* **l'estonien** *(language)* Estonian; **il parle estonien** he
speaks Estonian

UNE **estrade** *noun* platform

et *conjunction* and; **j'ai bien aimé ce
film, et toi?** I really liked the film,
what about you?; **et voilà!** there you
are!, there you go!

établir
1 *verb*
(**a**) to establish
(**b**) to set up
(**c**) to draw up *(a list)*
2 *reflexive verb* **s'établir**
(**a**) to settle, to live
(**b**) to set oneself up

UN **établissement** *noun*
(**a**) **un établissement scolaire** a school
(**b**) business, firm

UN **étage** *noun* floor; **au deuxième
étage** on the second floor; **au dernier**

étage on the top floor; **à l'étage** upstairs

UNE **étagère** *noun* shelf

étaient, étais, était *see* être

ils étaient en vacances quand ça s'est passé they were on holidays when this happened; **elle était très contente** she was very pleased

Étaient, étais and *était* are forms of the verb *être* in the past tense. See verb table p. 316.

étaler
1 *verb*
(a) to spread, to spread out
(b) to show off; **étaler ses connaissances** to show off one's knowledge
(c) to display *(goods)*
2 *reflexive verb* **s'étaler**
(a) to spread out
(b) to spread over; **les vacances s'étalent sur trois mois** the holidays are spread over three months
(c) to fall over

Sense (c) is an informal use of *s'étaler*.

UN **étang** *noun* pond

The *g* in *étang* is not pronounced.

étant
(a) **étant donné** because of; **nous avons dû annuler la réunion étant donné les circonstances** we had to cancel the meeting because of the circumstances
(b) **étant donné que** since, as; **étant donné qu'il pleut, nous devons tout annuler** as it's raining, we have to cancel everything

UNE **étape** *noun*
(a) stop, stopover
(b) stage; **un voyage en deux étapes** a trip in two stages; **les différentes étapes de la vie** the different stages of life; **étape par étape** stage by stage, step by step

UN **État** *noun* state

Unlike English, this word has a capital letter in French when it refers to a country or part of a country. When there is no capital letter, the meaning is different (see word below).

UN **état** *noun*
(a) state, condition; **être en bon état** to be in good condition; **être en mauvais état** to be in poor condition
(b) **elle est dans tous ses états** *(informal phrase)* she's beside herself with anxiety

LES **États-Unis** *masculine plural noun* the United States; **les États-Unis sont un grand pays** the United States is a big country

L'**été**¹ *masculine noun* summer; **en été** in summer; **les vacances d'été** the summer holiday

été² *see* être
il a été malade he's been ill

Été is the past participle of the verb *être*. See verb table p. 316.

éteindre
1 *verb*
(a) to turn off, to switch off *(a light, the television, a heater)*
(b) to put out *(a fire, a candle, a cigarette)*
2 *reflexive verb* **s'éteindre** to go out; **les lumières se sont éteintes** the lights went out

See verb table p. 320.

étendre
1 *verb*
(a) to spread, to spread out *(a tablecloth)*
(b) to stretch out *(one's arm, a person)*
(c) to hang up, to hang out; **j'ai étendu le linge dehors** I hung out the washing
(d) to extend
2 *reflexive verb* **s'étendre**
(a) to stretch, to extend
(b) to spread
(c) to lie down, to stretch out

étendu, étendue
1 *adjective*
(a) wide, vast

(**b**) outstretched, stretched out
2 *feminine noun* **l'étendue**
(**a**) extent; **l'étendue des dégâts** the extent of the damage; **l'étendue de son vocabulaire** the extent of his vocabulary
(**b**) area, stretch; **une étendue d'eau** a stretch of water

L'**éternité** *feminine noun* eternity; **il y avait une éternité que je ne l'avais pas vu** I hadn't seen him for ages

éternuer *verb* to sneeze

êtes *see* **être**
vous êtes vraiment énervants you are really annoying

Êtes is a form of the verb *être* in the present tense. See verb table p. 316.

UNE **étincelle** *noun* spark

UNE **étiquette** *noun* label

s'étirer *reflexive verb* to stretch, to stretch out

UNE **étoile** *noun* star; **dormir à la belle étoile** to sleep out in the open

étonnant, étonnante *adjective*
(**a**) surprising, amazing
(**b**) remarkable

étonner
1 *verb* to surprise, to amaze; **je suis étonné de ses progrès** I'm amazed at the progress he's made
2 *reflexive verb* **s'étonner** to be surprised; **ne t'étonne pas si elle te met une mauvaise note** don't be surprised if she gives you a bad mark

étouffer
1 *verb*
(**a**) to suffocate
(**b**) to stifle; **on étouffe ici!** it's stifling here!
2 *reflexive verb* **s'étouffer** to choke

UNE **étourderie** *noun* careless mistake; **une faute d'étourderie** a foolish mistake

étourdi, étourdie
1 *adjective* careless

2 *noun* **un étourdi, une étourdie** a scatterbrain

étrange *adjective* strange, odd

étranger, étrangère
1 *adjective*
(**a**) foreign
(**b**) unknown
2 *noun* **un étranger, une étrangère**
(**a**) foreigner; **il y a une étrangère dans notre classe** there's a foreign girl in our class
(**b**) stranger; **ne parle pas aux étrangers** don't talk to strangers
3 *masculine noun* **l'étranger** foreign countries; **ça vient de l'étranger** it comes from abroad; **aller vivre à l'étranger** to go and live abroad; **des voyages à l'étranger** foreign travel

étrangler
1 *verb* to strangle
2 *reflexive verb* **s'étrangler** to choke

être
1 *verb*
(**a**) to be; **je suis grand** I'm tall; **tu es gentil** you're nice; **elle est dentiste** she's a dentist; **c'est facile** it's easy; **vous êtes en retard** you're late; **nous sommes contents** we are happy; **ils sont jeunes** they're young
(**b**) to go; **j'ai été à Paris l'an dernier** I went to Paris last year
(**c**) **quel jour sommes-nous?** what day is it today?; **nous sommes le huit** today is the 8th; **on est jeudi** today is Thursday; **il est cinq heures** it's five o'clock
(**d**) **être à** to belong to; **le dictionnaire est à elle** the dictionary belongs to her *or* the dictionary is hers
(**e**) **être de** to come from; **je suis de la Martinique** I come from Martinique
(**f**) to have; **il est venu** he has come; **il était parti** he had left; **il serait resté** he would have stayed; **je suis allé au cinéma** I went to the cinema

Être is used in compound tenses as an auxiliary with some verbs, as in the examples above. See verb table p. 316.

2 *masculine noun*
(**a**) being; **un être humain** a human being
(**b**) person; **c'est un être cruel** he's a cruel person

LES **étrennes** *feminine plural noun*
(**a**) New Year's Day present
(**b**) Christmas box; **les étrennes du facteur** the postman's Christmas box

étroit, étroite *adjective*
(**a**) narrow
(**b**) tight *(clothes)*
(**c**) cramped *(room, flat)*; **on est un peu à l'étroit ici** it's rather cramped in here
(**d**) close; **sous étroite surveillance** under close surveillance

UNE **étude** *noun*
(**a**) study; **une étude de cas** a case study; **une étude de texte** a textual analysis
(**b**) *(a room in a school)* study room, prep room; *(a period)* study-time
(**c**) **les études** studies; **faire des études de droit** to study law; **il a fait ses études à Eton** he went to Eton; **les études secondaires** secondary education; **les études supérieures** higher education

UN **étudiant**, UNE **étudiante** *noun*
student; **elle est étudiante** she's a student; **un étudiant en médecine** a medical student

étudier *verb*
(**a**) to study
(**b**) to learn
(**c**) to consider *(an offer)*

UN **étui** *noun* case; **un étui à lunettes** a glasses case

eu, eue *see* **avoir**
j'ai eu peur I was scared

Eu(e) is the past participle of the verb *avoir*. See verb table p. 313.

UN **euro** *noun* euro

L'**Europe** *feminine noun* Europe; **l'Europe centrale** Central Europe; **l'Europe de l'Est** Eastern Europe; **l'Europe du Nord** Northern Europe; **l'Europe du Sud** Southern Europe; **l'Europe de l'Ouest** *or* **l'Europe occidentale** Western Europe

UN **Européen**, UNE **Européenne** *noun (person)* European

européen, européenne *adjective* European; **les élections européennes** the European elections

eux *pronoun*
(**a**) them; **c'est à cause d'eux** it's because of them; **elles travaillent mieux qu'eux** they work better than them; **un ami à eux** a friend of theirs; **ces livres ne sont pas à eux** these books aren't theirs
(**b**) they; **si eux refusent, nous n'y pouvons rien** if *they* refuse, there's nothing we can do; **ils le savent bien, eux** *they* know it all right; **ce sont eux qui sont partis en premier** they left first
(**c**) themselves; **ils étaient contents d'eux** they were pleased with themselves

Eux is the plural of *lui*. It only refers to masculine plural nouns.

eux-mêmes *pronoun* themselves; **ils l'ont fait eux-mêmes** they did it themselves

Eux-mêmes is the plural of *lui-même*. It only refers to masculine plural nouns.

évacuer *verb* to evacuate

s'évader *reflexive verb* to escape; **il s'est évadé de prison** he escaped from prison

Note that the English verb *to evade* is never a translation for the French verb *s'évader*.

UNE **évaluation** *noun*
(**a**) assessment

(**b**) appraisal
(**c**) estimation

évaluer *verb*
(**a**) to assess
(**b**) to appraise
(**c**) to estimate

s'évanouir *reflexive verb* to faint, to pass out

UNE **évasion** *noun* escape

> Note that the English word *evasion* is never a translation for the French word *évasion*.

éveillé, éveillée *adjective*
(**a**) awake
(**b**) sharp *(intelligent)*

UN **événement** *noun* event; **un événement sportif** a sporting event

UN **éventail** *noun* fan *(held in hand)*

éventuel, éventuelle *adjective* possible; **un éventuel changement** a possible change

> Note that the English word *eventual* is never a translation for the French word *éventuel*.

éventuellement *adverb* possibly, maybe

> Note that the English word *eventually* is never a translation for the French word *éventuellement*.

évidemment *adverb* of course, obviously

> The middle *e* of *évidemment* is pronounced like the *a* in *cat*.

L'**évidence** *feminine noun* obvious fact; **se rendre à l'évidence** to face facts; **nier l'évidence** to deny the obvious; **c'est l'évidence même!** it's quite obvious!; **de toute évidence** evidently, obviously; **j'ai laissé le message bien en évidence sur la table** I left the message on the table in a place where it couldn't be missed

> Note that the English word *evidence* is never a translation for the French

word *évidence*.

évident, évidente *adjective*
(**a**) obvious
(**b**) easy; **cet exercice n'est pas évident** this exercise is not that easy

UN **évier** *noun* sink *(in a kitchen)*

éviter *verb*
(**a**) to avoid
(**b**) to save; **cela lui évitera d'avoir à sortir** that'll save him having to go out

évoluer *verb*
(**a**) to develop
(**b**) to evolve
(**c**) to change
(**d**) to mature *(for a person)*

exact, exacte *adjective*
(**a**) correct
(**b**) exact
(**c**) right

exactement *adverb* exactly

ex æquo *adjective* placed equal; **ils sont ex æquo** they are placed equal

> The word *ex æquo* does not change in the plural.

exagérer *verb*
(**a**) to exaggerate
(**b**) **cette fois ils exagèrent, j'appelle la police!** this time they've really gone too far, I'm calling the police!

UN **examen** *noun*
(**a**) exam; **passer un examen** to sit an exam; **réussir un examen** to pass an exam; **un examen blanc** a mock exam
(**b**) examination; **un examen médical** a medical examination

examiner *verb* to examine

excepté *preposition* except, apart from

UNE **exception** *noun* exception; **à l'exception de Vincent** apart from Vincent

exceptionnel, exceptionnelle *adjective*
(**a**) exceptional
(**b**) special

exciter
1 *verb*
(a) to excite
(b) to arouse *(curiosity)*
2 *reflexive verb* **s'exciter**
(a) to get carried away
(b) to get worked up

> Sense (b) is an informal use of *s'exciter*.

UNE **exclamation** *noun*
(a) cry
(b) exclamation; **un point d'exclamation** an exclamation mark

s'exclamer *reflexive verb* to exclaim, to cry out

exclure *verb*
(a) to expel; **elle a été exclue de l'école** she was expelled from school
(b) to exclude; **le mois d'août jusqu'au 31 exclu** the month of August excluding the 31st
(c) to rule out; **l'hypothèse d'un meurtre n'est pas exclue** murder hasn't been ruled out

> See verb table p. 320.

UNE **excursion** *noun* trip; **une excursion en car** a coach trip; **une excursion en mer** a boat trip

UNE **excuse** *noun*
(a) excuse
(b) **des excuses** an apology; **faire des excuses à quelqu'un** to apologize to somebody

excuser
1 *verb* to excuse, to forgive; **excusez-moi, pourriez-vous m'aider?** excuse me, could you help me?; **oh, excusez-moi, je vous ai fait mal?** oh, sorry, did I hurt you?; **excusez-moi de vous déranger** I'm sorry to disturb you
2 *reflexive verb* **s'excuser** to apologize; **je m'excuse!** sorry!, excuse me!

UN **exemplaire** *noun* copy *(of a document)*

UN **exemple** *noun* example; **par exemple** for example; **donner l'exemple** to set an example; **suivre l'exemple de quelqu'un** to follow somebody's example; **prends exemple sur ta sœur!** let your sister be an example to you!

exercer
1 *verb* to exercise; **quel métier exercez-vous?** what's your job?; **il exerce la médecine** he practises medicine
2 *reflexive verb* **s'exercer** to practise; **j'ai besoin de m'exercer** I need to practise

UN **exercice** *noun* exercise; **des exercices d'échauffement** warm-up exercises; **des exercices de grammaire** grammar exercises

exiger *verb*
(a) to demand
(b) to require

L'**existence** *feminine noun*
(a) existence
(b) life

exister *verb*
(a) to exist
(b) **il existe** there is; *(in plural)* there are; **il n'existe pas de meilleure explication** there is no better explanation; **il existe des appareils pour ça** there are machines for that

L'**expérience** *feminine noun*
(a) experience; **il a beaucoup d'expérience** he's very experienced; **il manque d'expérience** he's inexperienced
(b) experiment; **une expérience de chimie** a chemistry experiment

UNE **explication** *noun*
(a) explanation
(b) **une explication de texte** a critical analysis of a text
(c) discussion, argument

expliquer
1 *verb*
(a) to explain
(b) to analyse, to comment on *(a text)*
2 *reflexive verb* **s'expliquer**
(a) to be explained; **il y a des choses qui ne s'expliquent pas** some things

can't be explained; **tout s'explique!** that explains it!
(**b**) to explain oneself
(**c**) **expliquez-vous une bonne fois pour toutes** get it sorted out once and for all

UN **exploit** *noun* feat, achievement

exploser *verb*
(**a**) to explode; **il a fait exploser la bombe** he set off the bomb; **ils ont fait exploser la maison** they blew up the house
(**b**) **il a explosé de rire** *(informal phrase)* he burst out laughing

exporter *verb* to export

UN **exposé** *noun (oral)* talk, presentation; *(written)* essay, report; **nous avons fait un exposé en cours d'histoire** we did a presentation in history

exposer *verb*
(**a**) to exhibit
(**b**) to display
(**c**) to expose
(**d**) to explain

UNE **exposition** *noun* exhibition

exprès *adverb*
(**a**) on purpose; **je ne l'ai pas fait exprès** I didn't do it on purpose
(**b**) specially

The *s* of *exprès* is not pronounced.

UNE **expression** *noun*
(**a**) expression
(**b**) look; **si tu avais vu ton expression!** if only you'd seen the look on your face!

exprimer
1 *verb* to express
2 *reflexive verb* **s'exprimer**
(**a**) to express oneself
(**b**) to speak

expulser *verb*
(**a**) to evict
(**b**) to expel
(**c**) to send off; **elle a été expulsée du terrain** she was sent off the field

extérieur, extérieure
1 *adjective*
(**a**) outside
(**b**) outer
(**c**) external
(**d**) foreign
2 *masculine noun* **l'extérieur**
(**a**) outside; **à l'extérieur de la maison** outside the house
(**b**) exterior
(**c**) **jouer à l'extérieur** *(in sport)* to play away

externe
1 *adjective*
(**a**) external
(**b**) outer
2 *noun* **un/une externe**
(**a**) non-resident medical student *(in a hospital)*
(**b**) day pupil, non-boarder

extraordinaire *adjective*
(**a**) extraordinary
(**b**) amazing
(**c**) special; **des pouvoirs extraordinaires** special powers; **le repas n'avait rien d'extraordinaire** there was nothing special about the meal
(**d**) outstanding

UN/UNE **extraterrestre** *noun* alien, extraterrestrial

extrême *adjective* extreme; **un parti politique d'extrême droite** a far-right political party

extrêmement *adverb* extremely

L'**Extrême-Orient** *masculine noun* the Far East

LA **fabrication** *noun* manufacture, production; **des produits de fabrication artisanale** handmade products

fabriquer *verb*
(a) to make; **fabriqué à la main** handmade; **une histoire fabriquée de toutes pièces** a made-up story
(b) to do; **mais qu'est-ce qu'il fabrique?** what's he up to?

> Sense (b) is an informal use of *fabriquer*.

LA **fac** *noun* university

> *Fac* is an informal word; it is the shortened form of *faculté*.

LA **façade** *noun* façade, front

LA **face** *noun*
(a) side
(b) face; **j'ai le soleil en face** I have the sun in my face; **je lui ai dit la vérité en face** I told him the truth to his face
(c) **en face de** opposite; **les maisons en face de l'école** the houses opposite the school; **juste en face de moi** right in front of me; **nous habitons en face** we live across the road; **la maison d'en face** the house opposite

fâché, fâchée *adjective* angry; **elle est fâchée contre moi** she's angry with me

se fâcher *reflexive verb*
(a) to get angry; **elle s'est fâchée contre moi** she got angry with me
(b) to quarrel

facile *adjective* easy; **c'est facile à comprendre** it's easy to understand

facilement *adverb* easily

LA **façon** *noun*
(a) way; **sa façon de parler** his way of talking; **la façon dont le français est enseigné** the way French is taught
(b) **de toute façon** anyway

LE **facteur,** LA **factrice** *noun* postman/postwoman; **il est facteur** he's a postman

LA **facture** *noun* bill, invoice

facultatif, facultative *adjective* optional

LA **faculté** *noun*
(a) university, faculty; **il entre en faculté** he's going to university; **la faculté des sciences** the science faculty
(b) ability; **il a la faculté de comprendre les enfants** he has the ability to understand children
(c) **les facultés intellectuelles** intellectual faculties

faible *adjective* weak

LA **faiblesse** *noun* weakness

faille *see* falloir
j'ai peur qu'il faille recommencer I'm afraid we'll have to start again

> *Faille* is a form of the verb *falloir* in the subjunctive. See verb table p. 322.

faillir *verb* **il a failli tomber** he almost fell; **j'ai failli ne pas venir** I nearly didn't come

> The French verb *faillir* is usually translated by using the English adverbs *nearly* or *almost*. See verb table p. 322.

LA **faillite** *noun* bankruptcy; **l'entreprise a fait faillite** the company went bankrupt

LA **faim** *noun* hunger; **j'ai faim** I'm hungry

fainéant, fainéante
1 *adjective* lazy
2 *noun* **un fainéant, une fainéante** a layabout

faire
1 *verb*
(**a**) to do; **que fais-tu dans la vie?** what do you do for a living?; **qu'est-ce que vous faites?** what are you doing?; **est-ce que tu as fait tes devoirs?** have you done your homework?; **je fais mes maths** I'm doing my maths homework; **qu'est-ce que j'ai fait de mes clés?** what have I done with my keys?
(**b**) to make *(a noise, a cake, a mistake)*; **je vais faire du café** I'm going to make some coffee; **il a fait un nouveau film** he made a new film
(**c**) **il m'a fait pleurer** he made me cry; **il m'a fait rire** he made me laugh
(**d**) to be; **il fait chaud** it's hot; **il fait froid** it's cold; **il fait nuit** it's dark
(**e**) to have; **faire une promenade** to have a walk; **faire la sieste** to have a nap
(**f**) **faire faire quelque chose** to have something done; **ils ont fait construire une maison** they had a house built
(**g**) to play *(an instrument, a sport)*; to do *(an activity)*; **il fait du tennis** he plays tennis; **il fait du piano** he plays the piano; **elle fait de la danse** she goes to dance classes; **il fait de l'équitation** he goes horseriding; **je fais du théâtre** I do drama
(**h**) *(with numbers and measurements)* **le bateau fait neuf mètres de long** the boat is nine metres long; **je fais 1 m 90** I'm 1 m 90 tall; **je fais du 38** I take size 5; **je fais 60 kilos** I weigh 60 kilos; **ça fait combien?** how much is it?; **ça fait cinq euros** it's five euros
(**i**) *(with periods of time)* **ça fait deux jours qu'il n'a pas mangé** he hasn't eaten for two days; **ça faisait deux ans que je ne l'avais pas vu** I hadn't seen him for two years
(**j**) to clean *(a room, the windows)*
(**k**) to say; **"non," fit-elle** "no," she said; **elle a fait oui de la tête** she nodded
(**l**) to search through; **j'ai fait tous mes tiroirs mais je ne l'ai pas trouvé** I searched through all my drawers but I couldn't find it
(**m**) to look; **ça fait bizarre** it looks strange; **elle ne fait pas son âge** she doesn't look her age
(**n**) **ne fais pas l'idiot** don't be stupid; **ne fais pas l'innocent** don't play the innocent; **elle a fait l'étonnée** she pretended to be surprised; **arrête de faire ton intéressant!** stop showing off!
(**o**) **faire avec** to make do; **faire sans** to make do without; **je n'ai que ce stylo alors il faudra faire avec** I've only got this pen so I'll have to make do with that; **il faudra faire sans** we'll just have to make do without it
(**p**) **ça ne fait rien** it doesn't matter; **si cela ne vous fait rien** if you don't mind
(**q**) *(other phrases)* **je fais mes études à Paris** I study in Paris; **je vais faire la cuisine** I'll cook; **je vais faire le ménage** I'll do the housework; **il m'a fait peur** he frightened me; **il m'a fait de la peine** he upset me; **il m'a fait un bisou** he gave me a kiss; **il m'a fait une grimace** he made a face at me; **il fait la tête** *(informal phrase)* he's sulking
2 *reflexive verb* **se faire**
(**a**) to make; **il s'est fait des amis** he made friends
(**b**) to make oneself; **elle s'est fait vomir** she made herself vomit
(**c**) to get, to have; **il s'est fait tuer** he got killed; **il s'est fait prendre en photo** he had his picture taken; **je me suis fait opérer** I had an operation; **je me suis fait couper les cheveux** I had my hair cut

(d) **ça ne se fait pas de manger avec les doigts** it's rude to eat with your fingers

(e) **comment se fait-il que tu sois là?** how come you're here?

(f) **s'en faire** to worry; **je ne m'en fais pas pour lui** I'm not worried about him; **ne t'en fais pas!** don't worry!

See verb table p. 317.

fais, faisais, faisait *see* **faire**
je fais mes devoirs I'm doing my homework; **tu faisais la vaisselle** you were doing the washing-up; **il faisait froid** it was cold

Fais is a form of the verb *faire* in the present tense. *Faisais* and *faisait* are forms of the verb *faire* in the imperfect. See verb table p. 317.

LE **faisan** *noun* pheasant

faisons *see* **faire**
nous faisons la vaisselle we're doing the washing-up

Faisons is a form of the verb *faire* in the present tense. See verb table p. 317.

fait¹ *see* **faire**
il fait la cuisine he's doing the cooking; **elle fait son lit** she's making her bed

Fait is a form of the verb *faire* in the present tense. See verb table p. 317.

fait², faite *see* **faire**
j'ai fait une erreur I've made a mistake

Fait(e) is the past participle of the verb *faire*. See verb table p. 317.

LE **fait³** *noun*
(a) act; **le fait de boire** the act of drinking
(b) fact; **c'est un fait** it's a fact
(c) point; **venons-en au fait** let's get to the point
(d) **faits divers** *(in a newspaper)* news in brief

(e) **au fait** by the way
(f) **en fait** actually, in fact

faites *see* **faire**
qu'est-ce que vous faites ce soir? what are you doing tonight?

Faites is a form of the verb *faire* in the present tense. See verb table p. 317.

LA **falaise** *noun* cliff

falloir *verb*
(a) to have to; **il faut travailler** we have to work; **il faut que je travaille** I have to work; **il a fallu que je lui dise** I had to tell him; **s'il le faut** if necessary
(b) to need; **il faut encore du pain** we need more bread; **il me faut un stylo** I need a pen
(c) to take; **il faut deux heures pour y aller** it takes two hours to get there
(d) **il faudrait qu'elle parte** she ought to leave; **il faudrait que tu lui parles** you ought to talk to him

See verb table p. 322.

fameux, fameuse *adjective* famous

familial, familiale *adjective* family; **la vie familiale** family life; **cet élève a des problèmes familiaux** this pupil has problems at home

The masculine plural of *familial* is *familiaux*.

familier, familière *adjective*
(a) familiar
(b) friendly
(c) usual
(d) **un animal familier** a pet

LA **famille** *noun*
(a) family; **c'est une famille nombreuse** it's a large family; **je passe Noël en famille** I'm spending Christmas with my family
(b) relatives; **j'ai de la famille à Paris** I have relatives in Paris; **nous sommes de la même famille** we're related

faner
1 *verb* to wither, to fade; **des fleurs fanées** faded flowers

2 *reflexive verb* **se faner** to wither, to fade

LA **fanfare** *noun*
(**a**) brass band
(**b**) military band

LA **fantaisie** *noun*
(**a**) imagination
(**b**) whim
(**c**) fantasy *(in literature)*
(**d**) **des bijoux de fantaisie** costume jewellery

fantastique *adjective*
(**a**) fantastic
(**b**) fantasy; **un film fantastique** a fantasy film

LE **fantôme** *noun* ghost

LA **farce** *noun*
(**a**) practical joke; **faire une farce à quelqu'un** to play a trick on somebody
(**b**) stuffing

LE **farceur**, LA **farceuse** *noun* joker

farcir *verb* to stuff; **des tomates farcies** stuffed tomatoes

LA **farine** *noun* flour

farouche *adjective*
(**a**) fierce *(character)*
(**b**) wild *(animal)*
(**c**) shy *(person)*
(**d**) savage *(fight)*

fasse, fassent, fasses *see* **faire**
il faut que je fasse mes devoirs I need to do my homework; **Maman voudrait que tu fasses ton lit** Mum wants you to make your bed

Fasse, fassent and *fasses* are forms of the verb *faire* in the subjunctive. See verb table p. 317.

fatigant, fatigante *adjective*
(**a**) tiring;
(**b**) annoying

LA **fatigue** *noun* tiredness; **je suis mort de fatigue** I'm dead on my feet; **il tombe de fatigue** he's fit to drop

fatigué, fatiguée *adjective* tired

fatiguer
1 *verb*
(**a**) to tire; **ce voyage m'a fatigué** this trip has tired me out
(**b**) to annoy; **tu me fatigues avec tes questions!** you're really annoying me with your questions!
2 *reflexive verb* **se fatiguer**
(**a**) to get tired
(**b**) to tire oneself out

LE **faucon** *noun* hawk

faudra, faudrait *see* **falloir**
il faudra que je sorte pour acheter le journal I'll have to go out to buy the paper; **il faudrait donner à manger au chien** somebody should feed the dog

Faudra is a form of the verb *falloir* in the future tense. *Faudrait* is a form of the verb *falloir* in the conditional. See verb table p. 322.

se faufiler *reflexive verb*
(**a**) to weave one's way; **le cycliste se faufilait entre les voitures** the cyclist was weaving his way between the cars
(**b**) to sneak in

fausse *see* **faux**

faut *see* **falloir**
il faut toujours dire la vérité you should always tell the truth; **il faut qu'on aille faire les courses** we have to go shopping

Faut is a form of the verb *falloir* in the present tense. See verb table p. 322.

LA **faute** *noun*
(**a**) mistake; **une faute d'étourderie** a careless mistake; **une faute d'orthographe** a spelling mistake
(**b**) fault; **c'est ma faute** *or* **c'est de ma faute** it's my fault
(**c**) foul; *(in tennis)* fault

LE **fauteuil** *noun*
(**a**) armchair
(**b**) **un fauteuil roulant** a wheelchair

LE **fauve** *noun* big cat

faux, fausse
1 *adjective*
(**a**) wrong
(**b**) false
(**c**) untrue
(**d**) fake, forged
2 *adverb* **faux** out of tune; **je chante faux** I sing out of tune

LA **faveur** *noun*
(**a**) favour; **faites-moi une faveur** do me a favour
(**b**) **ils sont en faveur d'une élection** they're in favour of an election

favori, favorite *adjective* favourite

favoriser *verb* to favour

faxer *verb* to fax

LA **fée** *noun* fairy

feignant, feignante
1 *adjective* lazy
2 *noun* **un feignant, une feignante** a layabout

LA **feinte** *noun*
(**a**) ruse
(**b**) feint *(in boxing)*; dummy *(in football, rugby)*

fêler
1 *verb* to crack
2 *reflexive verb* **se fêler** to crack; **l'assiette s'est fêlée** the plate cracked

LES **félicitations** *feminine plural noun* congratulations; **félicitations pour ton nouveau travail** congratulations on your new job

féliciter *verb* to congratulate; **je l'ai félicité d'avoir réussi son examen** I congratulated him on having passed his exam

LA **femelle** *noun* female *(for animals)*

féminin, féminine *adjective*
(**a**) feminine
(**b**) female
(**c**) women's; **le tennis féminin** women's tennis

LA **femme** *noun*
(**a**) woman; **une femme d'affaires** a businesswoman

(**b**) lady; **une veste pour femme** a lady's jacket; **une femme de ménage** a cleaning lady
(**c**) wife

> This word is pronounced "fam".

fendre
1 *verb* to split *(wood)*
2 *reflexive verb* **se fendre** to crack; **l'assiette s'est fendue** the plate cracked

LA **fenêtre** *noun* window; **regarder par la fenêtre** to look out of the window

LA **fente** *noun*
(**a**) cleft *(in wood)*
(**b**) crack *(in a wall)*
(**c**) slit *(of a skirt)*
(**d**) slot *(for coins)*

LE **fer** *noun*
(**a**) iron; **du fer forgé** wrought iron; **un fer** *or* **un fer à repasser** an iron *(for clothes)*; **un fer à friser** curling tongs; **un fer à souder** a soldering iron
(**b**) **un fer à cheval** a horseshoe

fera, ferai *see* **faire**
il fera beau demain the weather will be nice tomorrow; **je ferai la vaisselle plus tard** I will do the washing-up later

> *Fera* and *ferai* are forms of the verb *faire* in the future tense. See verb table p. 317.

ferais, ferait *see* **faire**
tu ferais mieux de rentrer chez toi you'd better go home; **tu crois qu'il ferait ça pour moi?** do you think he would do that for me?

> *Ferais* and *ferait* are forms of the verb *faire* in the conditional. See verb table p. 317.

férié, fériée *adjective* **un jour férié** a public holiday

LA **ferme¹** *noun* farm

ferme² *adjective*
(**a**) firm
(**b**) steady

fermer *verb*
(a) to close; **fermez vos cahiers** close your exercise books; **ferme les yeux** close your eyes; **ferme la porte à clé** lock the door
(b) to turn off; **le radiateur est fermé** the heater is off

LA **fermeture** *noun*
(a) closing; **au moment de la fermeture** at closing time
(b) closure
(c) **une fermeture éclair**® a zip

LE **fermier**, LA **fermière** *noun* farmer; **elle est fermière** she's a farmer

féroce *adjective*
(a) fierce, ferocious *(animal)*
(b) cruel *(person, humour)*

ferons, feront *see* **faire**
nous ferons nos devoirs demain we'll do our homework tomorrow; **Paul et Claire feront la cuisine** Paul and Claire will do the cooking

Ferons and *feront* are forms of the verb *faire* in the future tense. See verb table p. 317.

ferroviaire *adjective* rail, railway

LA **fesse** *noun* buttock; **les fesses** the bottom

LA **fessée** *noun* spanking; **recevoir une fessée** to get spanked; **donner une fessée à quelqu'un** to spank somebody

LA **fête** *noun*
(a) party; **faire une fête** to have a party
(b) fair, festival; **la fête de la Musique** French music festival held on 21st June
(c) saint's day, name day; **il m'a souhaité ma fête** he wished me a happy saint's day

See also the note at the word **saint**.

(d) holiday; **un jour de fête** a public holiday; **la fête nationale** the national holiday; *(in France)* Bastille Day; **les fêtes de fin d'année** the Christmas and New Year holidays; **la fête des Mères** Mother's Day; **la fête des Pères** Father's Day; **la fête du Travail** Labour Day

La Fête de la Musique

La fête de la Musique is an annual music festival that takes place on the first day of summer (21st June). It was created in 1982 to develop musical arts and encourage amateur musicians. Amateur and professional bands play free in every French town and city, and big concerts are organized in large cities. There is a lively atmosphere and people wander through the streets to listen to all types of music, from choirs to rock.

fêter *verb* to celebrate

LE **feu** *noun*
(a) fire; **ils ont mis le feu à la voiture** they set the car on fire; **une maison en feu** a house on fire; **j'ai la bouche en feu** my mouth is burning
(b) **un feu d'artifice** fireworks
(c) **faire feu** to fire; **ouvrir le feu** to open fire
(d) heat; **à feu doux** on a slow heat; **à feu vif** on a high heat; **j'ai quelque chose sur le feu** I'm in the middle of cooking something
(e) light *(of a car)*; **les feux arrière** the tail-lights
(f) traffic lights; **un feu rouge** a red light; **un feu orange** an amber light; **un feu vert** a green light
(g) **tu as du feu?** do you have a light?

The plural of *feu* is *feux*.

LA **feuille** *noun*
(a) leaf
(b) sheet *(paper)*
(c) form

feuilleter *verb* to flick through

LE **feuilleton** *noun* series *(on TV)*

LE **feutre** *noun* felt-tip pen

février *masculine noun* February; **le premier février** the first of February; **le 28 février** the 28th of February

In French, the names of months are not written with a capital.

LES fiançailles *feminine plural noun* engagement

LE fiancé, LA fiancée *noun* fiancé/fiancée

se fiancer *reflexive verb* to get engaged; **elle s'est fiancée avec Ludovic** she got engaged to Ludovic

LA ficelle *noun* string; **une ficelle** a piece of string

LA fiche *noun*
(a) index card
(b) form

ficher
1 *verb*
(a) to chuck; **fiche ça dans le placard** chuck it in the closet; **il l'a fichu à la porte** he chucked him out
(b) to do; **qu'est-ce que tu fiches ici?** what on earth are you doing here?; **je n'ai rien fichu aujourd'hui** I haven't done a thing today
(c) **fiche-moi la paix!** leave me alone!
2 *reflexive verb* **se ficher**
(a) **se ficher de quelqu'un** to make fun of somebody
(b) **se ficher de quelque chose** not to care about something
(c) **il s'est fichu en colère** he lost his rag

This word is informal.

LE fichier *noun* file

fichu, fichue *adjective*
(a) **ma jupe est fichue** my skirt's had it; **sa voiture est fichue** his car's a write-off; **pour samedi soir, c'est fichu** Saturday evening's up the spout
(b) **quel fichu temps!** what horrible weather!
(c) **il n'est même pas fichu d'attraper la balle** he can't even catch the ball
(d) **il est mal fichu** he's a bit under the weather

This word is informal.

fidèle *adjective* faithful

fier, fière *adjective* proud

LA fierté *noun* pride

LA fièvre *noun* temperature, fever; **j'ai de la fièvre** I have a fever; **il a 40 de fièvre** his temperature is up to 40°

LA figue *noun* fig

LA figure *noun* face

Note that the French word *figure* never means *number*.

figurer
1 *verb* to appear
2 *reflexive verb* **se figurer** to believe; **figure-toi qu'il n'a même pas appelé!** he didn't even call, can you believe it!

LE fil *noun*
(a) thread
(b) wire; **un fil électrique** an electric wire; **un fil de fer** a wire; **du fil de fer barbelé** barbed wire
(c) **un coup de fil** a phone call; **passer un coup de fil à quelqu'un** to call somebody; **au bout du fil** on the phone

Sense (c) is an informal use of *fil*.

LA file *noun*
(a) line; **une file d'attente** a queue
(b) lane; **la file de droite** the right-hand lane; **il est garé en double file** he's double-parked

filer *verb*
(a) to dash; **je dois filer** I must dash; **la voiture filait à toute vitesse** the car was speeding along

Sense (a) is an informal use of *filer*.

(b) to give; **file-moi un coup de main** give me a hand

Sense (b) is an informal use of *filer*.

(c) to shadow *(somebody)*
(d) to spin *(wool)*
(e) to ladder *(tights, stocking)*

LE filet *noun*
(a) net
(b) fillet *(of meat, fish)*
(c) **un filet d'eau** a trickle of water; **ur**

filet de bave a dribble of saliva

LA **filière** *noun*
(**a**) network *(of criminals)*
(**b**) **cet élève a choisi la filière scientifique** this student has chosen science subjects

> ### La Filière
> *Une filière* is a specific education path chosen by pupils at age 15. In French secondary schools, the three main ones are the *filière littéraire* (arts subjects), the *filière scientifique* (sciences) and the *filière économique et sociale* (economics and social studies). They all lead to the *baccalauréat* exam (see also **baccalauréat**). Students can also take *une filière technique* which provides them with a more technical and vocational education.

LA **fille** *noun*
(**a**) girl
(**b**) daughter

LA **fillette** *noun* little girl

LE **filleul,** LA **filleule** *noun* godson/goddaughter, godchild

LE **film** *noun* film; **un film de guerre** a war film; **un film policier** a detective film; **un film de science-fiction** a sci-fi film

filmer *verb* to film, to shoot

LE **fils** *noun* son

> The pronounciation of *fils* is "fis": the *s* is pronounced but not the *l*. This word does not change in the plural.

LA **fin¹** *noun* end; **on se reverra fin novembre** we'll meet again at the end of November; **le glossaire est à la fin du livre** the glossary is at the back of the book; **en fin d'année** at the end of the year; **en fin de soirée** towards the end of the evening; **en fin de compte** in the end, after all

fin², fine *adjective*
(**a**) fine
(**b**) thin
(**c**) slender

(**d**) delicate
(**e**) clever

final, finale
1 *adjective* final
2 *feminine noun* **la finale** the final

> The masculine plural of *final* is *finals* or *finaux*.

finalement *adverb* in the end

finir *verb*
(**a**) to finish; **il a fini de travailler** he finished working
(**b**) to end; **finir par faire quelque chose** to end up doing something; **tu vas finir par le faire pleurer** you're going to end up making him cry

LE **Finlandais,** LA **Finlandaise** *noun* *(person)* Finn

finlandais, finlandaise
1 *adjective* Finnish
2 *masculine noun* **le finlandais** *(language)* Finnish; **il parle finlandais** he speaks Finnish

> In French, only the noun for the inhabitants of a country takes a capital letter, never the adjective or the noun for the language.

LA **Finlande** *noun* Finland

finnois, finnoise
1 *adjective* Finnish
2 *masculine noun* **le finnois** *(language)* Finnish; **il parle finnois** he speaks Finnish

LA **fissure** *noun* crack *(in a wall)*

fixe *adjective*
(**a**) fixed
(**b**) set; **à heure fixe** at a set time
(**c**) permanent

fixer
1 *verb*
(**a**) to fix; **il a fixé un miroir au mur** he hung a mirror on the wall
(**b**) to set *(a time, a date)*
(**c**) to stare at; **il m'a fixé du regard** he stared at me
2 *reflexive verb* **se fixer**

(a) to settle, to settle down
(b) **se fixer rendez-vous** to arrange to meet
(c) **vous vous êtes fixé un délai très court** you've set yourself a very short deadline

LE **Flamand**, LA **Flamande** *noun* *(person)* Flemish man/Flemish woman; **les Flamands** the Flemish

flamand, flamande
1 *adjective* Flemish; **une ville flamande** a Flemish town
2 *masculine noun* **le flamand** *(language)* Flemish; **il parle flamand** he speaks Flemish

LE **flamant** *noun* flamingo; **un flamant rose** a pink flamingo

LA **flamme** *noun* flame; **une maison en flammes** a burning house

flanquer *verb*
(a) to chuck; **il a flanqué les livres par terre** he chucked the books on the floor; **il l'a flanqué dehors** he kicked him out
(b) **il m'a flanqué une gifle** he slapped me; **il m'a flanqué un coup de poing** he punched me; **il m'a flanqué un coup de pied** he kicked me

This word is informal.

LA **flaque** *noun* **une flaque d'eau** a puddle; **une flaque d'huile** a pool of oil

LA **flèche** *noun* arrow

LA **fléchette** *noun* dart; **il joue aux fléchettes** he plays darts

LA **flemme** *noun* laziness; **j'ai la flemme d'y aller** I can't be bothered to go

This word is informal.

LA **fleur** *noun* flower

fleurir *verb* to flower, to bloom

LE/LA **fleuriste** *noun* florist; **elle est fleuriste** she's a florist

LE **fleuve** *noun* river

LE **flipper** *noun* pinball; **il joue au flipper** he's playing pinball

LE **flocon** *noun* flake; **des flocons de neige** snowflakes

flotter *verb*
(a) to float
(b) **elle flotte dans sa robe** her dress is drowning her

flou, floue *adjective* blurred

LA **flûte** *noun* flute; **une flûte traversière** a flute; **une flûte à bec** a recorder

LA **foi** *noun* faith

LE **foie** *noun* liver

LE **foin** *noun* hay

LA **foire** *noun*
(a) trade fair
(b) funfair

LA **fois** *noun*
(a) time; **cette fois, je gagnerai** this time, I'll win; **chaque fois que j'essaie, je rate** every time I try, I fail; **trois fois quatre font douze** three times four is twelve; **c'est trois fois plus grand** it's three times as big
(b) **une fois** once; **pour une fois** for once; **une fois qu'il sera arrivé** once he's arrived
(c) **deux fois** twice
(d) **à la fois** at a time, at the same time; **les deux à la fois** both of them

fol *see* **fou**

LA **folie** *noun* madness

folle *see* **fou**

foncé, foncée *adjective* dark *(colour)*

foncer *verb*
(a) to charge, to rush; **il a foncé sur son adversaire** he rushed at his opponent
(b) to speed along

Sense (b) is an informal use of *foncer*.

LA **fonction** *noun*
(a) function, role

(**b**) post, job
(**c**) facility *(on a computer)*
(**d**) **la fonction publique** civil service
(**e**) **en fonction de** according to

LE/LA **fonctionnaire** *noun* civil servant; **il est fonctionnaire** he's a civil servant

LE **fonctionnement** *noun* running, working *(of a machine)*

fonctionner *verb* to run, to work; **je n'arrive pas à faire fonctionner la machine à laver** I can't get the washing machine to work

LE **fond** *noun*
(**a**) bottom; **au fond de la rivière** at the bottom of the river; **je vous remercie du fond du cœur** I thank you from the bottom of my heart
(**b**) back; **elle est restée au fond de la salle** she stayed at the back of the room
(**c**) far end; **c'est au fond du couloir** it's at the far end of the corridor
(**d**) background
(**e**) **enfoncer un clou à fond** to drive a nail all the way in; **respirer à fond** to breathe deeply; **elle a fait le ménage à fond dans la maison** she cleaned the house thoroughly; **la radio était à fond** the radio was on full blast
(**f**) **une course de fond** a long-distance race; **le ski de fond** cross-country skiing
(**g**) **du fond de teint** foundation *(make-up)*

The *d* in *fond* is not pronounced.

fonder
1 *verb* to found; **fonder une famille** to start a family
2 *reflexive verb* **se fonder se fonder sur quelque chose** *(theory)* to be based on something

fondre
1 *verb*
(**a**) to melt
(**b**) to dissolve; **faire fondre du sucre** to dissolve sugar; **elle a fondu en larmes** she burst into tears

2 *reflexive verb* **se fondre se fondre dans la foule** to blend into the crowd

font *see* **faire**
ils font la vaisselle they're doing the washing-up

Font is a form of the verb *faire* in the present tense. See verb table p. 317.

LA **fontaine** *noun* fountain

LE **footing** *noun* jogging; **elle sont parties faire un footing** they went jogging

LA **force** *noun*
(**a**) strength; **ça va me donner des forces** it will give me strength
(**b**) force; **pas besoin d'utiliser la force** no need to use force; **de force** by force
(**c**) **à force de crier** by shouting so much; **à force de répéter** by constant repetition; **à force de travailler** by sheer hard work

forcément *adverb* obviously; **elle sera forcément déçue** she's bound to be disappointed; **pas forcément** not necessarily

forcer
1 *verb*
(**a**) to force; **ma mère m'a forcé à lui dire** my mother forced me to tell him
(**b**) to force open *(a safe, a door)*
(**c**) to strain; **forcer sa voix** to strain one's voice; **sans forcer** without straining
(**d**) **j'ai forcé sur le poivre** I've put too much pepper in
2 *reflexive verb* **se forcer** to force oneself

LA **forêt** *noun* forest

LE **forfait** *noun*
(**a**) season ticket
(**b**) ski pass
(**c**) withdrawal *(in sports)*; **l'équipe a déclaré forfait** the team withdrew; **gagner par forfait** to win by default

LE **format** *noun*
(**a**) size
(**b**) format

LA **formation** *noun*
(a) training
(b) formation

LA **forme** *noun*
(a) shape
(b) form; **être en pleine forme** to be on top form

former *verb*
(a) to shape
(b) to form
(c) to train

formidable *adjective* great

> Note that the English word *formidable* is never a translation for the French word *formidable*.

LE **formulaire** *noun* form *(document)*

LA **formule** *noun*
(a) phrase
(b) formula *(in maths)*
(c) way, method

fort, forte
1 *adjective*
(a) strong
(b) loud
(c) good; **elle est forte en langues** she's good at languages
(d) spicy
(e) large; **une forte augmentation** a large increase
(f) great; **une forte douleur** a great pain
(g) **le prix fort** the full price
(h) powerful *(film, argument)*
(i) **c'est plus fort que moi** I can't help it
2 *adverb* **fort**
(a) hard
(b) loudly; **parle plus fort!** speak up!
(c) **ça sent fort** it has a strong smell
3 *masculine noun* **un fort** a fort

LA **fortune** *noun* wealth, fortune; **il est venu à Paris pour faire fortune** he came to Paris to make his fortune

LE **fossé** *noun*
(a) ditch
(b) gap; **le fossé des générations** the generation gap

LA **fossette** *noun* dimple *(in somebody's cheek)*

fou, folle
1 *adjective*
(a) mad, crazy; **devenir fou** to go mad; **ça me rend fou** it drives me mad; **être fou de joie** to be beside oneself with joy; **être fou d'inquiétude** to be mad with worry; **être fou amoureux de quelqu'un** to be madly in love with somebody; **il est fou d'elle** he's mad about her
(b) huge; **il y avait un monde fou** there was a huge crowd; **ce film a eu un succès fou** this film was a huge success; **ça a mis un temps fou** it took ages

> Sense (b) is an informal use of *fou*.

(c) incredible *(story)*
(d) **avoir le fou rire** to have a fit of the giggles
2 *noun* **un fou** a madman; **une folle** a madwoman; **il n'arrête pas de courir comme un fou** he keeps running around like a madman
3 *masculine noun* **un fou** a bishop *(in chess)*

> The masculine plural of *fou* is *fous*, the feminine plural is *folles*. *Fol* is used instead of *fou* in front of masculine singular nouns beginning with a vowel (*un fol espoir*) or in front of a mute h.

LA **foudre** *noun*
(a) lightning
(b) **le coup de foudre** love at first sight

LE **fouet** *noun*
(a) whip; **un coup de fouet** a lash
(b) whisk

fouetter *verb*
(a) to whip
(b) to whisk

LA **fougère** *noun* fern, bracken

LA **fouille**
1 *noun* search

2 *feminine plural noun* **les fouilles** excavations; **faire des fouilles** to carry out excavations

fouiller *verb*
(**a**) to search
(**b**) to go through; **ils ont fouillé sa valise** *or* **ils ont fouillé dans sa valise** they went through his suitcase

LE **fouillis** *noun* mess; **quel fouillis!** what a mess!

LE **foulard** *noun* scarf, headscarf

LA **foule** *noun* crowd

se fouler *reflexive verb*
(**a**) to sprain; **il s'est foulé la cheville** he sprained his ankle
(**b**) to strain oneself; **il ne s'est pas foulé** he didn't exactly strain himself

Sense (b) is an informal use of *se fouler*.

LE **four** *noun* oven; **un four à micro-ondes** a microwave (oven)

LA **fourche** *noun* fork *(for gardening)*

LA **fourchette** *noun* fork *(for eating)*

LE **fourgon** *noun* van

LA **fourmi** *noun*
(**a**) ant
(**b**) **j'ai des fourmis dans les pieds** I have pins and needles in my feet

LE **fourneau** *noun* stove

The plural of *fourneau* is *fourneaux*.

fournir *verb*
(**a**) to supply; **son entreprise fournit les restaurants de la région en vin** his company supplies local restaurants with wine
(**b**) to provide; **l'école fournit les manuels scolaires aux élèves** the school provides pupils with textbooks

LES **fournitures** *feminine plural noun* **les fournitures de bureau** office supplies; **les fournitures scolaires** school stationery

fourrer
1 *verb*

(**a**) **des gants fourrés** fur-lined gloves
(**b**) **un gâteau fourré à la confiture** a cake filled with jam
(**c**) to stick, to put; **je les ai fourrés dans le coin** I stuck them in the corner; **où as-tu fourré ce dossier?** where have you put that file?; **il est toujours fourré chez ses parents** he's always at his parents' place

Sense (c) is an informal use of *fourrer*.

2 *reflexive verb* **se fourrer** to get; **se fourrer une idée dans la tête** to get an idea into one's head; **il s'est fourré dans une sale affaire** he got mixed up in a nasty business

The verb *se fourrer* is informal.

LA **fourrure** *noun* fur; **un manteau de fourrure** a fur coat

LE **foyer** *noun*
(**a**) hearth
(**b**) home; **le foyer conjugal** the marital home; **une femme au foyer** *or* **une mère au foyer** a housewife
(**c**) hall; *(in a school)* common room; **un foyer d'étudiants** a students' hall of residence
(**d**) hostel *(for homeless people)*

fragile *adjective*
(**a**) fragile
(**b**) frail
(**c**) delicate

fraîche *see* **frais²**

LA **fraîcheur** *noun*
(**a**) coolness
(**b**) freshness

LES **frais¹** *masculine plural noun* expenses, costs

frais², fraîche
1 *adjective*
(**a**) cool
(**b**) fresh *(food)*
(**c**) **peinture fraîche** wet paint
2 *adverb* **frais il fait frais** it's cool, the weather's cool; **servir frais** serve chilled

3 *masculine noun* **le frais**
(**a**) fresh air; **je vais prendre le frais** I'm going out for some fresh air
(**b**) cool place; **mets la bouteille au frais** put the bottle in a cool place

LA **fraise** *noun* strawberry

LA **framboise** *noun* raspberry

LE **franc**[1] *noun* franc *(old French money)*

franc[2], **franche** *adjective*
(**a**) frank, honest
(**b**) open; **un rire franc** an open laugh; **un regard franc** an open look

LE **Français, LA Française** *noun (person)* Frenchman/Frenchwoman; **les Français** French people, the French

français, française
1 *adjective* French; **un mot français** a French word
2 *masculine noun* **le français** *(language)* French; **est-ce que tu parles français?** do you speak French?

> In French, only the noun for the inhabitants of a country takes a capital letter, never the adjective or the noun for the language.

LA **France** *noun* France

Francfort *noun* Frankfurt

franchement *adverb*
(**a**) frankly, honestly
(**b**) really

franchir *verb*
(**a**) to get over *(a fence, a wall)*
(**b**) to cross; **il a franchi la ligne d'arrivée** he crossed the finishing line
(**c**) to pass through

LA **frange** *noun* fringe

frapper *verb*
(**a**) to hit
(**b**) to strike
(**c**) to knock; **frapper à la porte** to knock on the door

fredonner *verb* to hum

LE **freezer** *noun* freezer (compartment)

LE **frein** *noun* brake; **le frein à main** the handbrake; **donner un coup de frein** to brake

freiner *verb*
(**a**) to brake
(**b**) to slow down
(**c**) to curb

LA **fréquentation** *noun*
(**a**) acquaintance; **elle a de mauvaises fréquentations** she keeps bad company
(**b**) **la fréquentation des théâtres a baissé** theatre-going has decreased

fréquenter *verb*
(**a**) to frequent, to visit regularly; **un endroit peu fréquenté** a place hardly anyone ever goes to; **c'est très fréquenté** it's very popular; **c'est bien fréquenté** it's got a good reputation
(**b**) to associate with, to see regularly; **je fréquente peu ce genre de personnes** I don't associate much with people like that

LE **frère** *noun* brother; **mon grand frère** my big brother; **mon petit frère** my little brother

LA **friandise** *noun* sweet thing; **j'aime les friandises** I have a sweet tooth

LE **frigidaire**® *noun* fridge

LE **frigo** *noun* fridge

> This word is informal.

frileux, frileuse *adjective* sensitive to the cold; **elle est très frileuse** she really feels the cold

frire *verb* to fry; **faire frire du poisson** to fry fish

> See verb table p. 324.

frisé, frisée *adjective*
(**a**) curly
(**b**) curly-haired

LE **frisson** *noun* shiver; **j'ai des frissons** I'm shivering

frit, frite[1] *adjective* fried; **du poisson frit** fried fish

LA **frite**[2] *noun* chip; **on a mangé des frites** we ate chips

froid, froide
1 *adjective* cold
2 *adverb* **froid il fait froid** it's cold, the weather's cold
3 *masculine noun* **le froid** cold weather, the cold; **j'ai froid** I'm cold; **j'ai froid aux mains** my hands are cold

froisser
1 *verb* to crease, to crumple
2 *reflexive verb* **se froisser**
(**a**) to crease
(**b**) to take offence, to be offended
(**c**) **se froisser un muscle** to strain a muscle

frôler
1 *verb*
(**a**) to brush against, to touch lightly; **la branche lui a frôlé les cheveux** the branch brushed against his hair
(**b**) to come within a hair's breadth of *(death, disaster)*
2 *reflexive verb* **se frôler** to brush against each other

LE **fromage** *noun* cheese; **du fromage de chèvre** goat's cheese; **du fromage blanc** fromage frais

froncer *verb* **froncer les sourcils** to frown

LE **front** *noun*
(**a**) forehead
(**b**) front

LA **frontière** *noun* border; **à la frontière entre la France et l'Espagne** on the border between France and Spain

frotter
1 *verb* to rub
2 *reflexive verb* **se frotter** to rub oneself; **arrête de te frotter les yeux** stop rubbing your eyes

LE **fruit** *noun*
(**a**) fruit, piece of fruit; **les fruits** fruit
(**b**) **les fruits de mer** seafood

The *t* in *fruit* is not pronounced.

LA **fugue** *noun* **faire une fugue** to run away from home

fuir *verb*
(**a**) to run away
(**b**) to flee; **elle a fui le pays** she fled the country
(**c**) to avoid; **il me fuit** he's avoiding me
(**d**) to leak; **ça fuit** it's leaking; **un stylo qui fuit** a leaky pen

See verb table p. 322.

LA **fuite** *noun*
(**a**) escape, flight; **le prisonnier a pris la fuite** the prisoner escaped; **il est en fuite** he's on the run
(**b**) leak; **une fuite de gaz** a gas leak

LA **fumée** *noun* smoke

fumer *verb* to smoke; **du jambon fumé** smoked ham

LE **fumeur,** LA **fumeuse** *noun* smoker

furieux, furieuse *adjective* furious; **elle était furieuse contre moi** she was furious with me

LE **fuseau** *noun* **un fuseau horaire** a time zone

The plural of *fuseau* is *fuseaux*.

LA **fusée** *noun* rocket

LE **fusible** *noun* fuse; **un fusible a grillé** a fuse blew

LE **fusil** *noun* rifle, gun; **un fusil de chasse** a shotgun

The *l* of *fusil* is not pronounced.

fusiller *verb*
(**a**) to shoot *(by a firing squad)*
(**b**) **il m'a fusillé du regard** he looked daggers at me

futur, future
1 *adjective*
(**a**) future
(**b**) **une future mère** a mother-to-be; **mon futur mari** my husband-to-be; **la future mariée** the bride-to-be
2 *masculine noun* **le futur** the future

gâcher *verb*
(**a**) to waste
(**b**) to spoil

LA **gaffe** *noun*
(**a**) blunder; **j'ai fait une gaffe** I put my foot in it
(**b**) **fais gaffe, c'est chaud!** careful, it's hot!; **fais gaffe à ce que tu dis!** watch what you say!

> This word is informal.

LE **gagnant**, LA **gagnante** *noun* winner

gagner *verb*
(**a**) to win
(**b**) to earn; **gagner sa vie** to earn one's living
(**c**) to gain
(**d**) to save; **gagner du temps** to save time

gai, gaie *adjective* cheerful, happy

LA **galerie**
(**a**) gallery
(**b**) **une galerie marchande** a shopping centre
(**c**) roof rack
(**d**) **amuser la galerie** to play for laughs

LE **galet** *noun* pebble

LA **galette** *noun*
(**a**) pancake
(**b**) biscuit
(**c**) **la galette des Rois** pastry traditionally eaten on Twelfth Night in France

> ### La Galette des Rois
> The French traditionally celebrate Twelfth Night with a round, almond-flavoured pastry (*la galette des Rois*) containing a small porcelain figurine (*la fève* - originally a dried bean). The pastry is shared out and the person who finds the *fève* is appointed "king" or "queen" and given a cardboard crown to wear. This tradition is called *tirer les Rois*. Although Twelfth Night is on 6th January, people can buy a *galette* a few days before and after this date.

Galles le pays de Galles Wales

LE **Gallois**, LA **Galloise** *noun (person)* Welshman/Welshwoman; **les Gallois** Welsh people, the Welsh

gallois, galloise
1 *adjective* Welsh
2 *masculine noun* **le gallois** *(language)* Welsh; **elle parle gallois** she speaks Welsh

galoper *verb*
(**a**) to gallop
(**b**) to rush around

> Sense (b) is a slightly informal use of *galoper*.

LE **gamin**, LA **gamine** *noun* kid, child

> This word is informal.

LA **gamme** *noun*
(**a**) scale *(in music)*
(**b**) range *(of products, colours)*; **un ordinateur bas de gamme** a bottom-of-the-range computer; **un ordinateur haut de gamme** a top-of-the-range computer

LE **gant** *noun* glove; **mets tes gants** put your gloves on; **un gant de boxe** a boxing glove; **un gant de toilette** a flannel

LE **garage** *noun*
(a) garage
(b) shed

LE/LA **garagiste** *noun* garage mechanic; **il est garagiste** he's a garage mechanic

LA **garantie** *noun* guarantee, warranty

LE **garçon** *noun*
(a) boy
(b) son
(c) **un garçon de café** a waiter
(d) **un garçon d'honneur** a best man

garde
1 *feminine noun*
(a) care; **je confierai la garde des enfants à ma tante** I'll leave the children in the care of my aunt
(b) custody; **en garde à vue** in police custody
(c) guard; **monter la garde** to stand guard; **être sur ses gardes** to be on one's guard
(d) **mettre quelqu'un en garde** to warn somebody
(e) **être de garde** to be on duty; **un médecin de garde** a doctor on call
(f) **une garde d'enfants** a childminder
2 *masculine noun*
(a) guard; **un garde du corps** a bodyguard
(b) warden; **un garde forestier** a forest ranger

garder *verb*
(a) to keep
(b) to look after *(a child, a suitcase)*
(c) to guard *(a palace, a prisoner)*

LA **garderie** *noun*
(a) day nursery
(b) childminding service

LE **gardien**, LA **gardienne** *noun*
(a) caretaker
(b) security guard; **un gardien de prison** a prison officer; **un gardien de la paix** a police officer
(c) keeper *(of a zoo)*; **un gardien de but** a goalkeeper
(d) attendant *(of a museum, a car park)*

(e) **une gardienne d'enfants** a childminder

gare
1 *feminine noun* a train station; **une gare routière** a bus station; **le hall de la gare** the station concourse
2 *exclamation* **gare à toi!** you just watch it!; **gare à tes doigts avec ce couteau** watch your fingers with that knife

garer
1 *verb* to park; **il est garé en doublefile** he's double-parked
2 *reflexive verb* **se garer** to park; **c'est difficile de trouver à se garer ici** it's hard to find a parking space here

LE **gars** *noun* lad, guy; **salut les gars!** hi guys!

> This word is informal.

LE **gaspillage** *noun* waste; **quel gaspillage d'argent!** what a waste of money!

gaspiller *verb* to waste

LE **gâteau** *noun*
(a) cake; **un gâteau d'anniversaire** a birthday cake
(b) biscuit; **des petits gâteaux** biscuits; **des gâteaux apéritif** savoury biscuits

> The plural of *gâteau* is *gâteaux*.

gâter
1 *verb* to spoil; **cet enfant est gâté** this child is spoiled
2 *reflexive verb* **se gâter**
(a) to go bad, to go off
(b) to take a turn for the worse; **le temps se gâte** the weather's changing for the worse

gauche
1 *adjective*
(a) left; **ma main gauche** my left hand; **le côté gauche** the left-hand side
(b) awkward
2 *feminine noun* **la gauche** the left; **le tiroir de gauche** the left-hand drawer; **tourner à gauche** to turn left; **rouler à**

gauche to drive on the left-hand side; **c'est à gauche** it's on the left; **c'est à gauche du fauteuil** it's to the left of the armchair

gaucher, gauchère *adjective* left-handed

LA **gaufre** *noun* waffle

se gaver *reflexive verb* to stuff oneself; **ils se sont gavés de fraises** they stuffed themselves with strawberries

LE **gaz** *noun*
(a) gas; **cuisiner au gaz** to cook with gas; **le gaz carbonique** carbon dioxide; **le gaz lacrymogène** tear gas
(b) **les gaz d'échappement** exhaust fumes
(c) **avoir des gaz** to have wind

> The word *gaz* does not change in the plural.

gazeux, gazeuse *adjective*
(a) fizzy, sparkling; **les boissons gazeuses** fizzy drinks; **de l'eau gazeuse** fizzy water, sparkling water
(b) gaseous

LE **gazon** *noun*
(a) turf
(b) lawn

géant, géante *adjective* giant, huge

LE **gel** *noun*
(a) frost
(b) gel

gelé, gelée
1 *adjective* frozen
2 *feminine noun* **la gelée**
(a) frost
(b) jelly

geler *verb* to freeze; **on gèle ici** it's freezing in here

LES **Gémeaux** *masculine plural noun* Gemini; **elle est Gémeaux** she's a Gemini

gémir *verb*
(a) to groan
(b) to moan

gênant, gênante *adjective*
(a) annoying
(b) embarrassing, awkward

LA **gencive** *noun* gum

LE **gendarme** *noun* policeman; **il est gendarme** he's a policeman; **une femme gendarme** a policewoman; **jouer aux gendarmes et aux voleurs** to play cops and robbers

LA **gendarmerie** *noun*
(a) police station
(b) police force

LE **gendre** *noun* son-in-law

gêner
1 *verb*
(a) to bother; **le bruit me gêne** the noise is bothering me; **ça vous gêne si j'ouvre la fenêtre?** do you mind if I open the window?
(b) to embarrass; **j'étais gêné** I was embarrassed
(c) to be in the way of; **ma valise vous gêne-t-elle?** is my case in your way?
2 *reflexive verb* **se gêner je ne me suis pas gêné pour le lui dire** I didn't hesitate to tell him so

général, générale
1 *adjective* general
2 *adverb* **en général** generally, in general
3 *masculine noun* **un général** a general

> The plural of the masculine adjective and noun *général* is *généraux*.

généralement *adverb* generally

généreux, généreuse *adjective*
(a) generous
(b) noble *(gesture, feelings)*

LE **générique** *noun* credits *(of a film)*

Genève *noun* Geneva

génial, géniale *adjective* brilliant, great; **ces sont des idées géniales** they're brilliant ideas; **c'est génial!** that's great!

> The masculine plural of *génial* is *géniaux*.

LE **génie** *noun* genius; **une idée de génie** a brilliant idea

LE **genou** *noun* knee; **viens t'asseoir sur mes genoux** come and sit on my lap; **il s'est mis à genoux** he knelt down

The plural of *genou* is *genoux*.

LE **genre** *noun*
(**a**) kind, type; **c'est quel genre de film?** what kind of film is it?
(**b**) gender *(in grammar)*
(**c**) genre; **le genre policier** the detective genre

LES **gens** *masculine plural noun* people; **peu de gens le savent** few people know that

gentil, gentille *adjective*
(**a**) nice, kind; **ils sont gentils avec moi** they're nice to me; **c'est gentil de m'aider** it's nice of you to help me; **c'est gentil de votre part** it's kind of you
(**b**) good; **il a été gentil aujourd'hui?** was he good today?; **sois gentil!** be a good boy!

Note that the English words *gentle* and *genteel* are never translations for the French word *gentil*. Note also that the final *l* of *gentil* is not pronounced in French.

LA **gentillesse** *noun* kindness

gentiment *adverb* kindly, nicely

LA **géographie** *noun* geography

gérer *verb* to manage *(a company)*

LE **geste** *noun*
(**a**) movement; **ses gestes sont précis** his movements are precise; **faire un geste de la main** to wave
(**b**) gesture; **un beau geste** a nice gesture

LA **gifle** *noun* slap in the face; **elle lui a donné une gifle** she slapped his face

gifler *verb* to slap in the face; **elle l'a giflé** she slapped his face

gigantesque *adjective* gigantic

LE **gigot** *noun* **un gigot d'agneau** a leg of lamb

LE **gilet** *noun*
(**a**) cardigan
(**b**) waistcoat
(**c**) **un gilet de sauvetage** a life jacket

LE **gitan,** LA **gitane** *noun* gypsy

LE **givre** *noun* frost

LA **glace** *noun*
(**a**) ice
(**b**) ice-cream
(**c**) mirror
(**d**) window

glacé, glacée *adjective*
(**a**) frozen
(**b**) freezing, ice-cold
(**c**) iced; **du thé glacé** iced tea

glacial, glaciale *adjective*
(**a**) icy, freezing
(**b**) frosty *(atmosphere, smile)*
(**c**) cold *(person)*

The masculine plural of *glacial* is *glaciaux* or *glacials*.

LA **glacière** *noun* cool box

LE **glaçon** *noun* ice cube

glissant, glissante *adjective* slippery

glisser
1 *verb*
(**a**) to slip; **ça m'a glissé des mains** it slipped out of my hands
(**b**) to slide
(**c**) to be slippery; **attention, ça glisse** watch out, it's slippery
(**d**) **faire glisser** to drag *(with a computer mouse)*
2 *reflexive verb* **se glisser** to slip; **il s'est glissé dans son lit** he slipped into bed; **elle s'est glissée au premier rang** she slipped into the front row

LA **gloire** *noun*
(**a**) fame
(**b**) glory

LE **gobelet** *noun* tumbler; **un gobelet en plastique** a plastic cup

LA **gomme** *noun* eraser, rubber

gommer *verb* to erase, to rub out

gonfler *verb*
(**a**) to blow up, to inflate *(a balloon, a tyre)*
(**b**) to swell; **un abcès lui gonflait la joue** his cheek was swollen with an abscess; **des yeux gonflés** swollen eyes

LA **gorge** *noun* throat; **j'ai mal à la gorge** I have a sore throat

LA **gorgée** *noun*
(**a**) sip; **à petites gorgées** in little sips
(**b**) gulp; **d'une seule gorgée** in one gulp
(**c**) mouthful

LE/LA **gosse** *noun* kid; **ce n'est qu'un gosse** he's just a kid

This word is informal.

LE **goudron** *noun* tar

LE **goulot** *noun* neck *(of a bottle)*

LA **gourde** *noun*
(**a**) flask *(for water)*
(**b**) fool

Sense (b) is an informal use of *gourde.*

gourmand, gourmande *adjective* greedy *(for food)*; **je suis très gourmand** *(for food in general)* I'm very fond of good food; *(for sweet things)* I have a very sweet tooth

LA **gourmandise** *noun*
(**a**) greed *(for food)*
(**b**) sweet delicacy; **j'aime les gourmandises** I have a sweet tooth

LA **gousse** *noun* pod; **une gousse de vanille** a vanilla pod; **une gousse d'ail** a clove of garlic

LE **goût** *noun* taste; **ça a un drôle de goût** it tastes funny; **quel goût ça a?** what does it taste like?; **il faut leur donner le goût des maths** we've got to give them a taste for maths

goûter
1 *verb*
(**a**) to taste, to try; **voulez-vous goûter ma sauce?** would you like to try my sauce?
(**b**) to have an afternoon snack
2 *masculine noun* **le goûter** the afternoon snack; **un goûter d'anniversaire** a children's birthday party

LA **goutte** *noun* drop; **des gouttes pour les yeux** eye drops; **goutte à goutte** drop by drop; **il tombe des gouttes** it's spitting with rain

LA **gouttière** *noun* gutter *(on a roof)*

LE **gouvernail** *noun* rudder *(of a boat)*

LE **gouvernement** *noun* government

grâce
1 *feminine noun*
(**a**) grace; **elle a beaucoup de grâce** she's very graceful
(**b**) **je vous fais grâce des détails** I'll spare you the details
2 *preposition* **grâce à** thanks to; **j'ai réussi grâce à vous** I succeeded thanks to you; **c'est grâce à ton aide** it's thanks to your help

LES **gradins** *masculine plural noun*
(**a**) stepped rows of seats *(in a theatre)*
(**b**) terraces *(in a stadium)*

LE **grain** *noun*
(**a**) grain
(**b**) **un grain de beauté** a mole, a beauty spot

LA **graine** *noun* seed

LA **graisse** *noun*
(**a**) fat
(**b**) grease

LA **grammaire** *noun* grammar; **les règles de grammaire** grammatical rules

LE **gramme** *noun* gram, gramme

grand, grande
1 *adjective*
(**a**) tall; **son frère est très grand** his brother is very tall
(**b**) big; **c'est mon grand frère** he's my

big brother; **quand je serai grand** when I grow up
(**c**) large *(family, organization)*
(**d**) long *(journey)*
(**e**) great; **ils ont fait une grande découverte** they made a great discovery; **il a fait de grands progrès** he has made great progress
2 *adverb* wide; **la porte est grande ouverte** the door is wide open; **il a les yeux grand ouverts** he has his eyes wide open
3 *noun* **un grand** a big boy; **une grande** a big girl; **je me débrouillerai toute seule, comme une grande** I'll manage on my own, like a big girl; **les grands** grown-ups

grand-chose *pronoun* **pas grand-chose** not much; **je n'ai pas grand-chose à faire** I don't have much to do; **il n'y a plus grand-chose à manger** there's not much left to eat

LA **Grande-Bretagne** *noun* Great Britain

grandir *verb*
(**a**) to grow; **elle a grandi** she has grown; **son inquiétude grandit** she's growing more anxious
(**b**) to grow up

LA **grand-mère** *noun* grandmother

> The plural of *grand-mère* is *grands-mères.*

LE **grand-père** *noun* grandfather

> The plural of *grand-père* is *grands-pères.*

LES **grands-parents** *masculine plural noun* grandparents

LA **grange** *noun* barn

LA **grappe** *noun*
(**a**) bunch *(of fruit)*; **une grappe de raisin** a bunch of grapes
(**b**) cluster *(of flowers)*

> Note that the English word *grape* is never a translation for the French word *grappe.*

gras, grasse
1 *adjective*
(**a**) fatty, full of fat
(**b**) plump
(**c**) greasy
(**d**) bold; **un mot écrit en caractères gras** a word written in bold
(**e**) **faire la grasse matinée** to have a lie-in
2 *masculine noun* **le gras**
(**a**) fat; **le gras du jambon** the fat off the ham
(**b**) **le gras** grease; **une tache de gras** a grease stain

LE **gratte-ciel** *noun* skyscraper

> The word *gratte-ciel* does not change in the plural.

gratter
1 *verb*
(**a**) to scratch, to scratch out
(**b**) to scrape, to scrape off
(**c**) to itch; **ça me gratte** it's itchy
2 *reflexive verb* **se gratter** to scratch oneself; **arrête de te gratter la tête!** stop scratching your head!

gratuit, gratuite *adjective* free

gratuitement *adverb* free, for free

grave *adjective*
(**a**) serious *(error, disease)*
(**b**) **ce n'est pas grave!** it doesn't matter!
(**c**) solemn
(**d**) low, bass *(music note)*
(**e**) deep *(voice)*
(**f**) **un accent grave** a grave accent

gravement *adverb*
(**a**) seriously
(**b**) solemnly

graver *verb*
(**a**) to carve, to engrave
(**b**) to burn, to write *(a CD)*

LE **graveur, LA graveuse**
1 *noun* carver, engraver
2 *masculine noun* **un graveur de CD** a CD burner

LE **gravier** *noun* gravel

LE **gravillon** *noun* grit, fine gravel

LE **Grec,** LA **Grecque** *noun (person)* Greek

grec, grecque
1 *adjective* Greek; **une ville grecque** a Greek town
2 *masculine noun* **le grec** *(language)* Greek; **il parle grec** he speaks Greek; **le grec ancien** ancient Greek

> In French, only the noun for the inhabitants of a country takes a capital letter, never the adjective or the noun for the language.

LA **Grèce** *noun* Greece

grecque *see* **grec**

LA **grêle** *noun* hail

grêler *verb* to hail; **il grêle** it's hailing

grelotter *verb* to shiver; **elle grelottait de froid** she was shivering with cold

LE **grenier** *noun* attic, loft

LA **grenouille** *noun* frog; **des cuisses de grenouille** frogs' legs

LA **grève** *noun* strike; **faire grève** or **être en grève** to be on strike

LA **griffe** *noun* claw; **le chat fait ses griffes** the cat is sharpening its claws

griffer *verb* to scratch; **elle m'a griffé la joue** she scratched me on the cheek

grignoter *verb* to nibble

LE **grillage** *noun*
(**a**) wire netting
(**b**) wire fence
(**c**) wire screen *(of a window)*

LA **grille** *noun*
(**a**) gate
(**b**) railings
(**c**) grid

LE **grille-pain** *noun* toaster

> The word *grille-pain* does not change in the plural.

griller *verb*
(**a**) to toast; **tu peux faire griller du**

pain? can you make some toast?; **une tartine grillée** a piece of toast
(**b**) to grill; **du poulet grillé** grilled chicken
(**c**) to scorch; **de l'herbe grillée** scorched grass
(**d**) to blow; **l'ampoule a grillé** the bulb has blown
(**e**) **griller un feu rouge** to go through a red light

LE **grillon** *noun* cricket *(insect)*

LA **grimace** *noun* funny face; **faire des grimaces** to make faces; **quand il a vu le prix, il a fait la grimace** when he saw the price he winced

grimper *verb*
(**a**) to climb
(**b**) to soar *(temperature, prices)*

grincer *verb*
(**a**) to creak
(**b**) to squeal
(**c**) to squeak
(**d**) **grincer des dents** to grind one's teeth

grincheux, grincheuse *adjective* grumpy

LA **grippe** *noun* flu; **j'ai attrapé la grippe** I've got (the) flu

gris, grise *adjective*
(**a**) grey
(**b**) overcast
(**c**) dull

grogner *verb*
(**a**) to growl
(**b**) to grunt
(**c**) to grumble

gronder *verb*
(**a**) to tell off; **je me suis fait gronder** I got told off
(**b**) to rumble, to roar

gros, grosse *adjective*
(**a**) big, large
(**b**) fat
(**c**) heavy

LA **groseille** *noun* redcurrant

grosse *see* **gros**

grossier, grossière *adjective*
  (**a**) rude; **il est grossier avec moi** he's rude to me
  (**b**) coarse
  (**c**) rough; **un dessin grossier** a rough sketch
  (**d**) gross *(error)*

grossir *verb*
  (**a**) to put on weight; **j'ai grossi de cinq kilos** I've put on five kilos
  (**b**) to get bigger
  (**c**) to swell
  (**d**) to exaggerate

LA **grotte** *noun* cave

LE **groupe** *noun*
  (**a**) group; **mettez-vous par groupes de trois** get into groups of three; **un groupe de rock** a rock band; **beaucoup de groupes scolaires visitent le château** many school parties visit the castle
  (**b**) complex; **un groupe hospitalier** a hospital complex; **un groupe scolaire** a school complex

grouper
  1 *verb* to put together, to group together
  2 *reflexive verb* **se grouper** to gather

LA **grue** *noun* crane

LE **guépard** *noun* cheetah

LA **guêpe** *noun* wasp

guérir *verb*
  (**a**) to cure
  (**b**) to heal
  (**c**) to recover

LA **guerre** *noun* war; **ils sont en guerre contre ce pays** they're at war with this country; **ils sont entrés en guerre** they went to war; **ils ont déclaré la guerre** they declared war

guetter *verb*
  (**a**) to watch; **il me guette** he's watching me
  (**b**) to watch out for; **le chat guette la souris** the cat is watching out for the mouse

LA **gueule** *noun*
  (**a**) mouth *(of an animal)*
  (**b**) gob *(of a person)*

This word is informal when referring to a person.

LE **gui** *noun* mistletoe

LE **guichet** *noun*
  (**a**) ticket office
  (**b**) counter, window *(of a bank, a post office)*
  (**c**) **un guichet automatique** a cash dispenser

LE **guide** *noun*
  (**a**) guide *(person)*; **il est guide** he's a guide
  (**b**) guide, guidebook; **mon guide d'Écosse a de très belles photos à l'intérieur** my guidebook to Scotland has lovely photos in it

guider *verb* to guide

LE **guidon** *noun* handlebars

LE **guignol** *noun*
  (**a**) glove puppet
  (**b**) puppet show

LE **guillemet** *noun* inverted comma; **entre guillemets** in inverted commas

LA **guimauve** *noun* marshmallow

LA **guirlande** *noun*
  (**a**) tinsel; **on a mis les guirlandes de Noël** we hung up the Christmas decorations; **une guirlande électrique** fairy lights
  (**b**) garland

LA **guitare** *noun* guitar; **il joue de la guitare sèche** he plays acoustic guitar

LA **gym** *noun*
  (**a**) gym; **faire de la gym** to work out
  (**b**) PE; **il est professeur de gym** he's a PE teacher

LE **gymnase** *noun* gymnasium

LA **gymnastique** *noun*
  (**a**) gymnastics; **faire de la gymnastique** to work out
  (**b**) physical education; **il est professeur de gymnastique** he's a PE teacher

H

habile *adjective*
(a) skilful
(b) clever

habiller
1 *verb* to dress; **il est toujours habillé en noir** he's always dressed in black
2 *reflexive verb* **s'habiller**
(a) to get dressed; **habille-toi vite!** hurry up and get dressed!
(b) **il faut bien s'habiller pour cette soirée** you need to dress up for this party *(to wear formal clothes)*
(c) **il s'est habillé en clown** he dressed up as a clown

UN **habit**
1 *noun* outfit; **un habit de sorcière** a witch's outfit; **un habit de soirée** evening dress
2 *masculine plural noun* **les habits** clothes; **il porte des habits noirs** he's wearing black clothes

> Note that the English word *habit* is never a translation for the French word *habit*. Note also that the final *t* is not pronounced in French.

UN **habitant**, UNE **habitante** *noun* inhabitant

habiter *verb* to live, to live in; **où habitez-vous** where do you live?; **il habite à Paris** he lives in Paris; **ils habitent une très belle maison** they live in a very nice house

UNE **habitude** *noun*
(a) habit; **ce sont de mauvaises habitudes** those are bad habits
(b) **avoir l'habitude de quelque chose** to be used to something

(c) **d'habitude** usually; **comme d'habitude** as usual

habituel, habituelle *adjective* usual

habituer
1 *verb* **il faut habituer les enfants à manger un peu de tout** you should get children used to eating a little bit of everything; **elle est habituée à rester seule** she's used to being alone
2 *reflexive verb* **s'habituer s'habituer à quelque chose** to get used to something; **elle a fini par s'habituer à notre petite ville** she eventually got used to our little town

LA **hache** *noun* axe; **abattre un arbre à la hache** to chop down a tree

hacher *verb*
(a) to chop
(b) to mince; **de la viande hachée** mince; **un steak haché** a beefburger

LA **haie** *noun* hedge

LA **haine** *noun* hatred

haïr
1 *verb* to hate; **il me hait** he hates me
2 *reflexive verb* **se haïr** to hate each other; **nous nous haïssons** we hate each other

See verb table p. 322.

L'**haleine** *feminine noun* breath; **hors d'haleine** out of breath; **il a mauvaise haleine** he has bad breath

LES **halles** *feminine plural noun* covered market

LA **halte** *noun*
(a) stop; **faire halte** to stop
(b) stopping place

LE hamac *noun* hammock

UN hameçon *noun* fish hook

LA hanche *noun* hip

handicapé, handicapée
1 *adjective* disabled, handicapped
2 *noun* **un handicapé, une handicapée** a disabled person, a handicapped person

LE hangar *noun* shed

harceler *verb* to harass; **il me harcelait de questions** he was pestering me with questions

LE haricot *noun* bean; **les haricots verts** French beans; **les haricots blancs** white beans

LE hasard *noun*
(a) coincidence
(b) chance; **par hasard** by chance; **au hasard** at random

Note that the English word *hazard* is never a translation for the French word *hasard*.

LA hâte *noun* hurry, rush; **avoir hâte de faire quelque chose** to be looking forward to doing something; **j'ai hâte que vous veniez** I can't wait for you to come; **il a fait ses devoirs à la hâte** he did his homework in a rush

LA hausse *noun* rise, increase; **une hausse du nombre de touristes** an increase in the number of tourists; **les prix sont en hausse** prices are rising

hausser *verb* to raise; **hausser les sourcils** to raise one's eyebrows; **hausser les épaules** to shrug (one's shoulders); **il a haussé les épaules** he shrugged his shoulders

haut, haute
1 *adjective*
(a) high
(b) tall
(c) **je l'ai lu à haute voix** I read it aloud
2 *adverb* **haut**
(a) high; **voler haut** to fly high
(b) **tout haut** aloud; **je l'ai lu tout haut** I read it aloud

3 *adverb* **en haut**
(a) upstairs; **elle habite en haut** she lives upstairs
(b) at the top; **tout en haut** at the very top
(c) up in the air
4 *masculine noun* **le haut**
(a) top; **le haut de la page** the top of the page
(b) **j'ai acheté un nouveau haut** I bought a new top
(c) **en haut de** at the top of; **il est en haut de la tour Eiffel** he's at the top of the Eiffel Tower
(d) **il fait trois mètres de haut** it's three metres high

LE hautbois *noun* oboe

LA hauteur *noun* height; **trois mètres de hauteur** three metres high; **le saut en hauteur** the high jump

LE haut-parleur *noun* loudspeaker

The plural of *haut-parleur* is *haut-parleurs*.

LA Havane *noun* Havana

LA Haye *noun* The Hague

hebdomadaire
1 *adjective* weekly
2 *masculine noun* **un hebdomadaire** a weekly

l'hébergement *masculine noun* accommodation

héberger *verb* to put up; **tu peux m'héberger cette nuit?** can you put me up for the night?

hein *exclamation*
(a) **hein?** what?, eh?
(b) **c'est drôle, hein?** it's funny, isn't it?; **tu ne vas pas le répéter, hein?** you won't tell anyone, will you?

hélas *exclamation* unfortunately

UNE hélice *noun* propeller

UN hélicoptère *noun* helicopter

l'herbe *feminine noun*
(a) grass
(b) **une mauvaise herbe** a weed

(c) **les fines herbes** herbs

LE **hérisson** *noun* hedgehog

UN **héritage** *noun* inheritance

hériter *verb* to inherit; **elle a hérité de tout l'argent de son père** she inherited all her father's money

UN **héritier,** UNE **héritière** *noun* heir/heiress

LE **héros,** L'**héroïne** *noun* hero/heroine

hésiter *verb* to hesitate; **n'hésitez pas à m'appeler** don't hesitate to call me

LE **hêtre** *noun* beech (tree)

UNE **heure** *noun*
(a) hour; **toutes les heures** every hour; **à 45 km à l'heure** *or* **à 45 km heure** at 45 km an hour; **c'est payé à l'heure** it's paid by the hour; **15 euros de l'heure** *or* **15 euros par heure** 15 euros per hour
(b) time; **quelle heure est-il?** what time is it?; **vous avez l'heure?** do you have the time?; **c'est l'heure de partir** it's time to go; **c'est l'heure!** time's up!
(c) o'clock; **il est deux heures** it's two o'clock; **il est cinq heures moins dix** it's ten to five
(d) period, class; **une heure d'histoire** a history period
(e) **de bonne heure** early
(f) **tout à l'heure** *(in the future)* later; *(in the past)* a little while ago; **à tout à l'heure!** see you later!

heureusement *adverb* fortunately

heureux, heureuse *adjective* happy

heurter *verb* to hit *(a wall, a car)*

LE **hibou** *noun* owl

The plural of *hibou* is *hiboux*.

hier *adverb* yesterday

UNE **hirondelle** *noun* swallow *(bird)*

L'**histoire** *feminine noun*
(a) history; **un livre d'histoire** a history book
(b) story; **c'est une belle histoire** it's a nice story
(c) tall story; **raconter des histoires** to tell tall stories; **allez, tu me racontes des histoires!** come on, you're pulling my leg!
(d) trouble; **tu vas nous attirer des histoires** you'll get us into trouble
(e) fuss; **faire des histoires** to make a fuss; **elle en a fait toute une histoire** she kicked up a huge fuss about it

L'**hiver** *masculine noun* winter; **l'hiver dernier** last winter; **elle part en vacances l'hiver** *or* **elle part en vacances en hiver** she goes on holiday in winter

LE **HLM** *noun* council flat

HLM is the abbreviation of *habitation à loyer modéré*. It does not change in the plural.

hocher *verb* **hocher la tête** to nod

LE **Hollandais,** LA **Hollandaise** *noun* *(person)* Dutchman/Dutchwoman; **les Hollandais** Dutch people, the Dutch

hollandais, hollandaise
1 *adjective* Dutch; **le paysage hollandais** the Dutch landscape
2 *masculine noun* **le hollandais** *(language)* Dutch; **il parle hollandais** he speaks Dutch

In French, only the noun for the inhabitants of a country takes a capital letter, never the adjective or the noun for the language.

LA **Hollande** *noun* Holland

LE **homard** *noun* lobster

UN **hommage** *noun* tribute, homage; **rendre hommage à quelqu'un** to pay tribute to somebody

UN **homme** *noun* man; **sors si t'es un homme!** step outside if you're man enough!; **l'homme descend du singe** man is descended from the apes; **un homme d'affaires** a businessman; **un homme des cavernes** a caveman; **un homme politique** a politician

LA **Hongrie** *noun* Hungary

LE **Hongrois**, LA **Hongroise** *noun* (person) Hungarian

hongrois, hongroise
  1 *adjective* Hungarian; **l'économie hongroise** the Hungarian economy
  2 *masculine noun* **le hongrois** (language) Hungarian; **il parle hongrois** he speaks Hungarian

> In French, only the noun for the inhabitants of a country takes a capital letter, never the adjective or the noun for the language.

honnête *adjective*
  (a) honest
  (b) respectable
  (c) reasonable (price)

honnêtement *adverb* honestly

L'**honnêteté** *feminine noun* honesty; **il est d'une grande honnêteté** he's very honest; **répondez en toute honnêteté** give an honest answer; **en toute honnêteté, je ne l'aime pas beaucoup** to tell you the truth, I don't really like him

L'**honneur** *masculine noun* honour; **j'ai l'honneur de vous présenter votre nouveau professeur** it's a great pleasure for me to introduce your new teacher

LA **honte** *noun*
  (a) shame; **avoir honte de quelque chose** to be ashamed of something; **j'ai honte de lui dire** I'm ashamed to tell him; **tu me fais honte!** I'm ashamed of you!; **j'avais la honte** (informal phrase) I was mortified
  (b) disgrace; **il est la honte de sa famille** he's a disgrace to his family

honteux, honteuse *adjective*
  (a) shameful
  (b) disgraceful; **c'est honteux!** it's a disgrace!
  (c) ashamed

UN **hôpital** *noun* hospital

> The plural of *hôpital* is *hôpitaux*.

LE **hoquet** *noun* hiccups; **j'ai le hoquet** I have hiccups

UN **horaire** *noun* timetable; **les horaires de bus** the bus timetable; **les horaires de travail** the working hours

UNE **horloge** *noun* clock

L'**horreur** *feminine noun* horror; **un film d'horreur** a horror film; **j'ai horreur des araignées** I hate spiders; **c'est une horreur** (informal phrase) it's hideous; **quelle horreur!** that's awful!

horrible *adjective* horrible

hors *preposition*
  (a) **hors d'atteinte** out of reach; **hors service** out of order; **hors d'haleine** out of breath; **c'est hors de question** it's out of the question; **hors de la ville** out of town
  (b) **hors antenne** off the air; **hors jeu** offside; **faire du hors piste** to ski off piste; **hors sujet** off the subject, irrelevant
  (c) **être hors de danger** to be safe
  (d) **être hors de prix** to be ridiculously expensive
  (e) **il était hors de lui** he was beside himself

UN **hors-d'œuvre** *noun* starter (of a meal)

> The word *hors-d'œuvre* does not change in the plural.

UN **hôte**, UNE **hôtesse**
  1 *noun* host/hostess
  2 *masculine noun* **un hôte** guest; **nos hôtes sont arrivés** our guests have arrived
  3 *feminine noun* **une hôtesse d'accueil** a receptionist; **une hôtesse de l'air** an air hostess; **elle est hôtesse de l'air** she's an air hostess

> Only the context can indicate if the French word *hôte* refers to the person who is inviting (host) or the person who is invited (guest).

UN **hôtel** *noun* hotel; **un hôtel quatre étoiles** a four-star hotel; **un hôtel particulier** a mansion, a town house; **l'hôtel de ville** the town hall

hôtesse *see* hôte

LA **housse** *noun* cover; **une housse de couette** a duvet cover

LE **houx** *noun* holly

> The word *houx* does not change in the plural. The *x* is not pronounced.

LE **hublot** *noun*
(**a**) window *(of a plane)*
(**b**) porthole *(of a boat)*

huer *verb* to boo

L'**huile** *feminine noun* oil; **l'huile d'olive** olive oil; **l'huile de tournesol** sunflower oil; **l'huile de moteur** engine oil

huit *number* eight; **le huit octobre** the 8th of October; **nous sommes le huit novembre** it's the 8th of November; **dans huit jours** in a week, a week today

> The final *t* in *huit* is not pronounced in front of a consonant.

huitième *number* eighth

UNE **huître** *noun* oyster

humain, humaine
1 *adjective* human; **un être humain** a human being
2 *masculine noun* **un humain** a

human; **les humains** mankind, human beings

L'**humeur** *feminine noun* mood; **il est de bonne humeur** he's in a good mood; **il est de mauvaise humeur** he's in a bad mood

humide *adjective* damp

humilier *verb* to humiliate

L'**humour** *masculine noun* humour; **un livre plein d'humour** a humorous book

LE **hurlement** *noun*
(**a**) yell, shout *(of a person)*
(**b**) howl *(of an animal)*

hurler *verb*
(**a**) to shout, to scream; **il a hurlé de joie** he shouted with joy; **il a hurlé de rire** he screamed with laughter
(**b**) to howl *(for an animal)*

UN **hydravion** *noun* seaplane

hygiénique *adjective* hygienic; **du papier hygiénique** toilet paper; **une serviette hygiénique** a sanitary towel

UN **hymne** *noun* **un hymne national** a national anthem

> Note that the English word *hymn* is never a translation for the French word *hymne*.

hypocrite
1 *adjective* hypocritical
2 *noun* **un/une hypocrite** a hypocrite

I

ici *adverb*
(**a**) here; **ici même** in this very place; **c'est à cinq minutes d'ici** it's five minutes from here; **venez par ici** come this way
(**b**) **d'ici demain** by tomorrow; **d'ici là** by then; **d'ici peu** before long

UNE **icône** *noun* icon

UNE **idée** *noun* idea; **bonne idée!** good idea!; **se faire des idées** to imagine things

identifier *verb* to identify

identique *adjective* identical; **sa coiffure est identique à celle de Lucie** her hairstyle is identical to Lucie's

L'**identité** *feminine noun* identity; **une carte d'identité** an ID card; **un contrôle d'identité** an identity check; **avez-vous une pièce d'identité?** do you have any ID?

idiot, idiote
1 *adjective* silly, stupid; **c'est idiot!** it's stupid!
2 *noun* **un idiot, une idiote** an idiot; **arrête de faire l'idiot!** stop fooling around!

The *t* in *idiot* is not pronounced.

ignorer *verb*
(**a**) not to know, to be unaware of; **j'ignore où il est** I don't know where he is
(**b**) to ignore *(a person)*

Note that the English verb *to ignore* is never a translation for the French verb *ignorer* when it refers to sense (a).

il *pronoun*
(**a**) he; **il est ici** he's here
(**b**) it; **j'ai jeté le verre car il était cassé** I threw the glass away because it was broken; **je suis allé au zoo pour voir le tigre mais il n'était pas là** I went to the zoo to see the tiger but it wasn't there

Note that in senses (a) and (b) *il* only refers to masculine nouns.

(**c**) it *(impersonal)*; **il pleut** it's raining; **il est tard** it's late
(**d**) **il y a** there is; *(in plural)* there are; **il y a un problème** there's a problem; **il y avait des enfants dans cette voiture** there were children in that car; **il y a eu un accident** there was an accident; **qu'est-ce qu'il y a?** what's the matter?
(**e**) **il y a** *(indicating time)* ago; **il y a trois ans** three years ago; **il y a une heure qu'il travaille** he's been working for an hour

UNE **île** *noun* island

illisible *adjective* illegible

UNE **illusion** *noun* illusion; **se faire des illusions** to delude oneself

illustrer *verb* to illustrate

ils *pronoun* they; **ils sont ici** they're here

Ils is the plural of *il*. It only refers to masculine plural nouns.

il y a *see* **il**

UNE **image** *noun*
(**a**) picture
(**b**) image

imaginer

1 *verb*
(**a**) to imagine
(**b**) to suppose; **imagine qu'il refuse** suppose he refuses
2 *reflexive verb* **s'imaginer**
(**a**) to picture oneself; **essaye de t'imaginer à cinquante ans** try to picture yourself at fifty
(**b**) to imagine; **imaginez-vous une plage de sable fin** imagine a beach of white sand
(**c**) to think; **il s'imagine qu'il peut réussir sans travailler** he thinks he can succeed without working

UN/UNE **imbécile** *noun* idiot; **arrête de faire l'imbécile!** stop fooling around!

imiter *verb* to imitate

immédiat, immédiate

1 *adjective* immediate; **une réponse immédiate** an immediate answer
2 *masculine noun* **dans l'immédiat** for the time being

immédiatement *adverb* immediately

immense *adjective*
(**a**) huge
(**b**) immense
(**c**) great; **un immense plaisir** a great pleasure

UN **immeuble** *noun*
(**a**) building
(**b**) block of flats

UN **immigré**, UNE **immigrée** immigrant

immigrer *verb* to immigrate

immobile *adjective* still; **gardez votre bras immobile** keep your arm still

impair, impaire *adjective* **un nombre impair** an odd number

impardonnable *adjective* unforgivable

UNE **impasse** *noun* dead end

s'impatienter *reflexive verb* to grow impatient, to lose one's patience

impératif, impérative

1 *adjective* imperative
2 *masculine noun* **l'impératif** the imperative; **un verbe à l'impératif** a verb in the imperative

imperméable

1 *adjective* waterproof
2 *masculine noun* **un imperméable** a raincoat

impliquer *verb* to involve

impoli, impolie *adjective* rude, impolite

L'**importance** *feminine noun*
(**a**) importance
(**b**) size, extent; **l'importance des dégâts** the extent of the damage

important, importante *adjective*
(**a**) important; **un homme important** an important man
(**b**) large; **une somme importante** a large amount

> The final *t* in *important* is not pronounced.

importer *verb*
(**a**) to import; **un produit importé des États-Unis** a product imported from the United States
(**b**) to matter; **peu importe** it doesn't matter; **ce qui importe, c'est que tu sois heureuse** what matters is your happiness
(**c**) *see* **n'importe**

imposer

1 *verb* to impose
2 *reflexive verb* **s'imposer**
(**a**) to impose oneself
(**b**) to win *(in sports)*
(**c**) to be necessary; **des excuses s'imposent** apologies are due

UN **impôt** *noun* tax; **l'impôt sur le revenu** income tax

UNE **impression** *noun*
(**a**) impression; **elle m'a fait bonne impression** she made a good impression on me
(**b**) feeling; **j'ai l'impression qu'elle ne**

viendra pas I have a feeling that she won't come

impressionnant, impressionnante *adjective* impressive

impressionner *verb* to impress

UNE **imprimante** *noun* printer *(for a computer)*

imprimer *verb* to print

improviste *noun* à l'improviste unexpectedly, without warning; **il est arrivé à l'improviste** he turned up without warning

imprudent, imprudente *adjective* careless

inadmissible *adjective* unacceptable

inattendu, inattendue *adjective* unexpected

L'**inattention** *feminine noun* lack of attention, lack of concentration; **une faute d'inattention** a careless mistake

incapable
1 *adjective* incapable; **elle est incapable de tricher** she's incapable of cheating; **elle était incapable de répondre** she couldn't answer
2 *noun* **un/une incapable** an incompetent

UN **incendie** *noun* fire; **un incendie de forêt** a forest fire; **un incendie criminel** arson

UN **incident** *noun*
(**a**) incident
(**b**) hitch

> The *t* in *incident* is not pronounced.

inciter *verb* to encourage; **inciter quelqu'un à faire quelque chose** to encourage somebody to do something

inclure *verb*
(**a**) to include; **le service est inclus** service is included; **jusqu'au dimanche inclus** up to and including Sunday
(**b**) to enclose

> See verb table p. 320.

inconnu, inconnue
1 *adjective* unknown
2 *noun* **un inconnu, une inconnue**
(**a**) stranger; **ne parle pas aux inconnus** don't talk to strangers
(**b**) unknown person; **c'est un inconnu qui a gagné** the winner was unknown

UN **inconvénient** *noun* disadvantage, drawback; **les avantages et les inconvénients** the advantages and disadvantages, the pros and cons; **je n'y vois pas d'inconvénient** I can't see why not, I have no objections

> The *t* in *inconvénient* is not pronounced.

incorrect, incorrecte *adjective*
(**a**) incorrect
(**b**) rude
(**c**) improper

incroyable *adjective* incredible

L'**Inde** *feminine noun* India

indépendant, indépendante *adjective*
(**a**) independent
(**b**) separate; **avec salle de bains indépendante** with separate bathroom

> The *t* in *indépendant* is not pronounced. Do not confuse the spellings of the French *indépendant* and English *independent*.

UN **index** *noun*
(**a**) index
(**b**) index finger, forefinger

> The word *index* does not change in the plural.

UNE **indication** *noun*
(**a**) indication
(**b**) instruction; **suivez les indications** follow the instructions

UN **indice** *noun*
(**a**) clue
(**b**) sign

(**c**) index; **l'indice des prix** the price index

UNE **Indien,** UNE **Indienne** *noun*
(**a**) Indian *(from India)*
(**b**) American Indian, Native American

indien, indienne *adjective*
(**a**) Indian *(from India)*; **la nourriture indienne** Indian food
(**b**) American Indian, Native American
(**c**) **mettez-vous en file indienne** line up in single file

In French, only the noun for the inhabitants of a country takes a capital letter, never the adjective.

indiquer *verb*
(**a**) to show
(**b**) to indicate
(**c**) to write
(**d**) to tell; **pouvez-vous m'indiquer la gare?** could you tell me where the station is?
(**e**) to recommend

indiscipliné, indisciplinée *adjective* unruly

indiscret, indiscrète *adjective*
(**a**) inquisitive
(**b**) indiscreet

indispensable *adjective* essential

UN **individu** *noun* individual; **c'est un drôle d'individu** he's a strange character

individuel, individuelle *adjective*
(**a**) individual
(**b**) personal
(**c**) private; **un compartiment individuel** a private compartment; **une chambre individuelle** a single room

UNE **industrie** *noun* industry; **l'industrie automobile** the car industry

industriel, industrielle
1 *adjective*
(**a**) industrial
(**b**) mass-produced
2 *masculine noun* **un industriel** a manufacturer, an industrialist

inexact, inexacte *adjective*
(**a**) incorrect, wrong
(**b**) inaccurate

infect, infecte *adjective*
(**a**) disgusting *(food)*
(**b**) foul *(smell)*
(**c**) awful *(person)*

s'infecter *reflexive verb* to get infected

inférieur, inférieure *adjective*
(**a**) lower; **la lèvre inférieure** the lower lip *or* the bottom lip
(**b**) below; **à l'étage inférieur** on the floor below; **inférieur à la moyenne** below average
(**c**) inferior; **il s'est toujours senti inférieur à son frère** he always felt inferior to his brother
(**d**) **X est inférieur ou égal à 3** X is less than or equal to 3

infirme
1 *adjective* disabled
2 *noun* **un/une infirme** a disabled person

UNE **infirmerie** *noun* sickbay, infirmary

UN **infirmier,** UNE **infirmière** *noun* nurse; **elle est infirmière** she's a nurse

influencer *verb* to influence; **ne te laisse pas influencer** don't let yourself be influenced

UN **informaticien,** UNE **informaticienne** *noun* computer scientist; **il est informaticien** he's a computer scientist

UNE **information** *noun*
(**a**) piece of information; **on manque d'informations sur les causes de l'accident** we lack information about the cause of the accident; **pour ton information** for your information
(**b**) piece of news; **voici une information de dernière minute** here is some news just in; **j'ai regardé les informations** I watched the news; **c'est passé aux informations** it was on the news

informatique
1 *adjective* computer; **un système informatique** a computer system
2 *feminine noun* **l'informatique** computer science; **il travaille dans l'informatique** he works in computing

informer
1 *verb* to inform
2 *reflexive verb* **s'informer**
(a) to ask, to inquire
(b) to keep oneself informed

ᴜɴ **ingénieur** *noun* engineer; **elle est ingénieur** she's an engineer

ᴜɴᴇ **initiale** *noun* initial; **mets tes initiales sur la feuille** put your initials on the sheet

ʟ'**initiation** *feminine noun* introduction; **une initiation au russe** an introduction to Russian

ᴜɴᴇ **injure** *noun* insult

> Note that the English word *injury* is never a translation for the French word *injure*.

injurier *verb* to insult

> Note that the English verb *to injure* is never a translation for the French verb *injurier*.

injuste *adjective* unfair

innocent, innocente
1 *adjective* innocent; **il a été déclaré innocent** he was found innocent
2 *noun* **un innocent, une innocente** an innocent person; **ne fais pas l'innocent!** don't play the innocent with me!

> The *t* in *innocent* is not pronounced.

ᴜɴᴇ **inondation** *noun* flood, flooding

inonder *verb* to flood; **ma maison est inondée** my house is flooded

inquiet, inquiète *adjective* worried

inquiétant, inquiétante *adjective* worrying

inquiéter
1 *verb* to worry

2 *reflexive verb* **s'inquiéter** to worry, to be worried; **ne t'inquiète pas pour elle!** don't worry about her!

ʟ'**inquiétude** *feminine noun* worry, concern

ᴜɴᴇ **inscription** *noun*
(a) writing
(b) registration, enrolment

inscrire
1 *verb*
(a) to write down
(b) to register, to enrol *(somebody)*
2 *reflexive verb* **s'inscrire**
(a) to register, to enrol
(b) to put one's name down
(c) to appear; **le numéro de téléphone va s'inscrire sur vos écrans** the phone number will appear on your screens

> See verb table p. 322.

ᴜɴ **insecte** *noun* insect

insinuer *verb* to imply; **tu insinues que je mens?** are you implying that I'm lying?

insister *verb*
(a) to insist; **elle a insisté pour que nous dormions chez elle** she insisted that we stay the night at her place
(b) to emphasize; **il a insisté sur ce problème** he emphasized the importance of this problem

ᴜɴᴇ **insolation** *noun* sunstroke

insolent, insolente *adjective* insolent, cheeky; **ne sois pas insolent avec moi!** don't be cheeky!

ʟ'**insomnie** *feminine noun* insomnia; **avoir des insomnies** to have insomnia

ʟ'**insouciance** *feminine noun* careless attitude, lack of concern

insouciant, insouciante *adjective* carefree, unconcerned

inspecter *verb* to inspect

ᴜɴ **inspecteur,** ᴜɴᴇ **inspectrice** *noun* inspector; **un inspecteur des impôts** a tax inspector; **un inspecteur**

pédagogique a schools inspector; **un inspecteur de police** a detective sergeant

inspirer
1 *verb*
(**a**) to breathe in
(**b**) to inspire; **le sujet de dissertation ne m'inspire pas du tout** the essay topic doesn't inspire me at all; **cet homme ne m'inspire pas confiance** this man doesn't inspire confidence
2 *reflexive verb* **s'inspirer s'inspirer de quelque chose** to be inspired by something

L'**installation** *feminine noun*
(**a**) installation
(**b**) setting up
(**c**) **des installations sportives** sports facilities

installer
1 *verb*
(**a**) to install
(**b**) to put in *(machine, central heating)*
(**c**) to put up *(shelves)*
(**d**) to set up
2 *reflexive verb* **s'installer**
(**a**) to settle *(in a country)*
(**b**) to settle down
(**c**) to sit
(**d**) to set up; **je me suis installé à mon compte** I set up my own business

UN **instant** *noun* moment; **il s'arrêta un instant** he stopped for a moment; **je suis rentré à l'instant** I've just come in; **pour l'instant** for the moment; **il peut arriver d'un instant à l'autre** he could arrive any minute now

The final *t* in *instant* is not pronounced.

UN **institut** *noun* institute; **un institut de recherches** a research institute; **un institut de beauté** a beauty salon

The final *t* in *institut* is not pronounced.

UN **instituteur,** UNE **institutrice** *noun* teacher *(in a primary school)*;

elle est institutrice she's a primary school teacher

L'**instruction** *feminine noun*
(**a**) education
(**b**) **l'instruction civique** civics
(**c**) instruction; **il nous a donné des instructions** he gave us instructions

instruit, instruite *adjective* educated

UN **instrument** *noun* instrument; **un instrument de musique** a musical instrument; **un instrument de travail** a tool

The final *t* in *instrument* is not pronounced.

insulter *verb* to insult

insupportable *adjective*
(**a**) unbearable
(**b**) impossible; **tu es insupportable!** you're being impossible!

intégrer
1 *verb*
(**a**) to integrate
(**b**) to include
(**c**) to enter *(a school, a company)*
2 *reflexive verb* **s'intégrer** to integrate, to become integrated

intelligent, intelligente *adjective* intelligent, clever

The final *t* in *intelligent* is not pronounced.

intense *adjective*
(**a**) intense
(**b**) bright *(light, colour)*
(**c**) heavy *(traffic, bombing)*

UNE **intention** *noun* intention; **je n'ai pas l'intention de l'acheter** I have no intention of buying it; **un film à l'intention des enfants** a film aimed at children

UNE **interdiction** *noun* ban, banning

interdire *verb*
(**a**) to forbid; **ma mère m'a interdit de sortir** my mother won't allow me to go out; **il est interdit de fumer dans**

l'école smoking is forbidden in the school
(**b**) *(by law)* to prohibit, to ban

> See verb table p. 322.

interdit, interdite *adjective* forbidden; **baignade interdite** no swimming; **stationnement interdit** no parking

> *Interdit (e)* is the past participle of the verb *interdire*.

intéressant, intéressante *adjective*
(**a**) interesting
(**b**) worthwhile; *(price)* attractive

intéressé, intéressée *adjective*
(**a**) self-interested
(**b**) interested; **elle semble intéressée par la proposition** she seems interested in the offer

intéresser
1 *verb* to interest
2 *reflexive verb* **s'intéresser** s'intéresser à quelque chose to be interested in something; **elle ne s'intéresse à rien** she's not interested in anything

UN **intérêt** *noun*
(**a**) interest; **manifester de l'intérêt pour quelque chose** to show an interest in something; **sans intérêt** uninteresting, of no interest; **que disais-tu? – c'est sans intérêt** what were you saying? – it's not important
(**b**) point; **quel est l'intérêt?** what's the point?
(**c**) **on a intérêt à réserver si on veut avoir des places** we'd better book if we want seats

intérieur, intérieure
1 *adjective*
(**a**) inside; **dans ma poche intérieure** in my inside pocket
(**b**) inner
(**c**) domestic; **les vols intérieurs** domestic flights
2 *masculine noun* **l'intérieur**
(**a**) inside; **à l'intérieur de la boîte**

inside the box
(**b**) interior

intermédiaire
1 *adjective* intermediate
2 *noun* **un/une intermédiaire** an intermediary; **je l'ai appris par l'intermédiaire de Cécile** I heard it from Cécile

interminable *adjective* never-ending, endless

UN **internat** *noun* boarding school

UN/UNE **internaute** *noun* Internet user

interne
1 *adjective*
(**a**) internal
(**b**) inner
(**c**) in-house
2 *noun* **un/une interne**
(**a**) junior doctor
(**b**) boarder; **elle est interne** she's at boarding school

UN **interphone**® *noun*
(**a**) intercom
(**b**) entryphone

UN/UNE **interprète** *noun*
(**a**) performer, player; **les interprètes du film** the cast of the film
(**b**) interpreter; **elle est interprète** she's an interpreter

interpréter *verb*
(**a**) to perform, to play; **interpréter un rôle** to play a part
(**b**) to interpret

L'**interrogation** *feminine noun*
(**a**) interrogation, questioning
(**b**) test; **une interrogation écrite** a written test; **une interrogation orale** an oral test
(**c**) question; **un point d'interrogation** a question mark

UN **interrogatoire** *noun* interrogation, questioning *(by the police)*

interroger *verb*
(**a**) to question
(**b**) to interview
(**c**) to test; **on a été interrogés en géographie** we were tested in geography

interrompre
1 *verb*
(**a**) to interrupt
(**b**) to stop; **elle a interrompu sa lecture** she stopped reading
2 *reflexive verb* **s'interrompre** to stop, to break off

See verb table p. 324.

UN **interrupteur** *noun* switch *(for light)*

UNE **interruption** *noun*
(**a**) breaking off; **sans interruption** continously, without stopping
(**b**) break; **une brève interruption** a short break
(**c**) interruption

UN **intervalle** *noun*
(**a**) interval; **ils se sont retrouvés à trois mois d'intervalle** they met again after an interval of three months
(**b**) gap, space

intervenir *verb*
(**a**) to intervene
(**b**) to speak; **il n'est pas intervenu au cours de la discussion** he didn't speak during the discussion

See verb table p. 324.

interviewer *verb* to interview

intime *adjective*
(**a**) close; **un ami intime** a close friend
(**b**) intimate; **des détails intimes** intimate details
(**c**) personal, private; **une conversation intime** a private conversation
(**d**) quiet; **une soirée intime** a quiet dinner

intimider *verb* to intimidate

intituler
1 *verb* to call
2 *reflexive verb* **s'intituler** to be called, to be entitled

UNE **intoxication** *noun* poisoning; **une intoxication alimentaire** food poisoning

UNE **intrigue** *noun* plot

introduire
1 *verb*
(**a**) to insert
(**b**) to introduce
2 *reflexive verb* **s'introduire**
(**a**) **s'introduire dans une pièce** to enter a room; **le cambrioleur s'est introduit dans la maison** the burglar got into the house
(**b**) **l'eau s'introduit dans la cave** the water is seeping into the cellar

See verb table p. 320.

introuvable *adjective* nowhere to be found

inutile *adjective*
(**a**) useless
(**b**) pointless
(**c**) needless; **c'est inutile de lire le livre en entier** you don't need to read the whole book

invalide
1 *adjective*
(**a**) disabled
(**b**) invalid; **mot de passe invalide** invalid password
2 *noun* **un/une invalide** a disabled person

inventer *verb*
(**a**) to invent
(**b**) to make up

UN **inventeur**, UNE **inventrice** *noun* inventor

inverse
1 *adjective* opposite, reverse; **les voitures qui viennent en sens inverse** cars coming from the opposite direction; **dans l'ordre inverse** in reverse order, the other way around; **dans le sens inverse des aiguilles d'une montre** anticlockwise
2 *masculine noun* **l'inverse** the opposite, the reverse; **à l'inverse** conversely; **à l'inverse de mon collègue** contrary to my colleague

UN **invité**, UNE **invitée** *noun* guest

inviter *verb* to invite

invraisemblable *adjective*
(a) unlikely
(b) incredible

ira, irai *see* **aller**
mon frère ira au Japon l'année pro-chaine my brother will go to Japan next year; **je n'irai pas à la fête de Pierre** I won't go to Pierre's party

> *Ira* and *irai* are forms of the verb *aller* in the future tense. See verb table p. 312.

L'Irak *masculine noun* Iraq

L'Iran *masculine noun* Iran

UN Irlandais, **UNE Irlandaise** *noun* *(person)* Irishman/Irishwoman; **les Irlandais** Irish people, the Irish

irlandais, irlandaise
1 *adjective* Irish; **une étudiante irlandaise** an Irish student
2 *masculine noun* **l'irlandais** *(language)* Irish; **il parle irlandais** he speaks Irish

> In French, only the noun for the inhabitants of a country takes a capital letter, never the adjective or the noun for the language.

L'Irlande *feminine noun* Ireland

irons, iront *see* **aller**
nous n'irons pas au cinéma ce soir we won't go to the cinema tonight; **mes amis iront à la plage cet après-midi** my friends will go to the beach this afternoon

> *Irons* and *iront* are forms of the verb *aller* in the future tense. See verb table p. 312.

irréparable *adjective* beyond repair

irréprochable *adjective*
(a) irreproachable *(person)*
(b) impeccable *(work)*

irriter *verb*
(a) to annoy; **il est irrité contre moi** he's annoyed with me
(b) to irritate; **la peau est irritée** the skin is irritated

islamique *adjective* Islamic

L'Islande *feminine noun* Iceland

UN Islandais, **UNE Islandaise** *noun* *(person)* Icelandic man/Icelandic woman, Icelander

islandais, islandaise
1 *adjective* Icelandic
2 *masculine noun* **l'islandais** *(language)* Icelandic; **elle parle islandais** she speaks Icelandic

isolé, isolée *adjective* isolated

Israël *masculine noun* Israel

UN Israélien, **UNE Israélienne** *noun* *(person)* Israeli

israélien, israélienne *adjective* Israeli; **le peuple israélien** the Israeli people

UNE issue *noun*
(a) exit; **une issue de secours** an emergency exit; **une ruelle sans issue** a dead end
(b) solution
(c) **à l'issue du match** at the end of the game

> Note that the English word *issue* is never a translation for the French word *issue*.

L'Italie *feminine noun* Italy

UN Italien, **UNE Italienne** *noun (person)* Italian

italien, italienne
1 *adjective* Italian; **un restaurant italien** an Italian restaurant
2 *masculine noun* **l'italien** *(language)* Italian; **il parle italien** he speaks Italian

L'italique *masculine noun* italics; **un mot écrit en italique** a word written in italics

UN itinéraire *noun* route; **un itinéraire touristique** a tourist route

L'ivoire *masculine noun* ivory

ivre *adjective* drunk

LA jalousie *noun* jealousy

jaloux, jalouse *adjective* jealous

jamais *adverb*
(**a**) never; **il n'est jamais trop tard** it's never too late

> In French, the negation using *jamais* is expressed with two words: *ne* (or *n'* in front of a vowel or a mute h) and *jamais*. *Ne* goes in front of the verb or auxiliary, and *jamais* goes after the verb in simple tenses (as in *il ne comprend jamais*), and between the auxiliary and the past participle in compound tenses (as in *il n'a jamais compris*).

(**b**) ever; **si jamais il revenait** if he ever came back; **on s'amuse plus que jamais** we're having more fun than ever; **il y a renoncé à jamais** *or* **à tout jamais** he's given it up forever

LA jambe *noun* leg

LE jambon *noun* ham; **du jambon blanc** cooked ham; **du jambon fumé** smoked ham

janvier *masculine noun* January; **le premier janvier** the first of January; **le 2 janvier** the 2nd of January

> In French, the names of months are not written with a capital.

LE Japon *noun* Japan

LE Japonais, LA Japonaise *noun* (person) Japanese; **les Japonais** Japanese people, the Japanese

japonais, japonaise
1 *adjective* Japanese; **une tradition japonaise** a Japanese tradition

2 *masculine noun* **le japonais** *(language)* Japanese; **il parle japonais** he speaks Japanese

> In French, only the noun for the inhabitants of a country takes a capital letter, never the adjective or the noun for the language.

LE jardin *noun*
(**a**) garden; **un jardin potager** a vegetable garden; **un jardin public** a park
(**b**) **un jardin d'enfants** a nursery (school)

LE jardinage *noun* gardening

LE jardinier, LA jardinière *noun* gardener; **il est jardinier** he's a gardener

jaune
1 *adjective* yellow; **une robe jaune** a yellow dress; **jaune citron** lemon yellow
2 *masculine noun*
(**a**) **le jaune** yellow; **le jaune est ma couleur préférée** yellow is my favourite colour
(**b**) **un jaune d'œuf** an egg yolk

LA Javel *noun* **de la Javel** *or* **de l'eau de Javel** bleach

LE javelot *noun* javelin; **le lancer du javelot** the javelin

je *pronoun* I; **je ne comprends pas** I don't understand; **j'y vais demain** I'm going there tomorrow; **puis-je ouvrir la fenêtre?** may I open the window?

> *Je* becomes *j'* in front of a vowel or a mute h.

LE jean *noun*
(**a**) denim; **une veste en jean** a denim jacket

(**b**) jeans; **j'ai acheté un nouveau jean** I bought a new pair of jeans

jetable *adjective* disposable *(nappy, lighter, camera)*

jeter
1 *verb*
(**a**) to throw; **il a jeté un os au chien** he threw the dog a bone; **ils ont jeté Olivier à l'eau** they threw Olivier in the water
(**b**) to throw away *(rubbish)*; **jette-le à la poubelle** throw it away
(**c**) **jeter un coup d'œil à quelqu'un** to glance at somebody
2 *reflexive verb* **se jeter**
(**a**) to throw oneself, to leap; **les enfants se sont jetés à l'eau** the children leaped into the water
(**b**) **ils se sont tous jetés sur moi** they all set upon me

LE **jeton** *noun*
(**a**) token *(for a machine, a telephone)*
(**b**) counter *(for board games)*

LE **jeu** *noun*
(**a**) game; **un jeu d'équipe** a team game; **un jeu de hasard** a game of chance; **un jeu de société** a board game; **un jeu télévisé** a game show, a quiz show; **jeu, set et match** *(in tennis)* game, set and match; **les jeux Olympiques** the Olympic Games
(**b**) gambling; **il aime le jeu** he likes gambling
(**c**) hand *(in cards)*; **il avait du jeu** *or* **il avait un bon jeu** he had a good hand
(**d**) set; **un jeu d'échecs** a chess set; **un jeu de 52 cartes** a pack of 52 cards
(**e**) **un jeu de mots** a play on words, a pun
(**f**) **mettre quelque chose en jeu** to put something at stake

The plural of *jeu* is *jeux*.

LE **jeudi** *noun* Thursday; **elle est venue jeudi** she came on Thursday; **il fait du tennis le jeudi** he plays tennis on Thursdays; **tous les jeudis** every Thursday

In French, the names of days are not written with a capital.

jeun
1 *adverb* **à jeun** on an empty stomach; **trois comprimés à prendre à jeun** three tablets to be taken on an empty stomach
2 *adjective* **il est à jeun** he hasn't eaten anything

jeune
1 *adjective* young; **un jeune homme** a young man; **une jeune femme** a young woman; **une jeune fille** a young girl; **il fait plus jeune que son âge** he looks younger than he is
2 *noun* **un jeune** a young man; **une jeune** a young girl; **les jeunes** young people

LA **jeunesse** *noun* youth; **dans ma jeunesse** when I was young

LE **jogging** *noun*
(**a**) jogging; **faire du jogging** to go jogging
(**b**) track suit

LA **joie** *noun*
(**a**) joy; **il a sauté de joie** he jumped for joy
(**b**) pleasure; **avec joie!** with great pleasure!; **je me faisais une joie de les revoir** I was delighted at the idea of seeing them again

joindre
1 *verb*
(**a**) to join
(**b**) to contact; **joindre quelqu'un par téléphone** to contact somebody by phone
(**c**) to enclose *(in a letter)*; to attach *(to an e-mail)*
2 *reflexive verb* **se joindre** **tu veux te joindre à nous?** would you like to join us?

See verb table p. 324.

joint, jointe *adjective*
(**a**) **une pièce jointe** an enclosure *(in a letter)*; an attachment *(to an e-mail)*

(**b**) **sauter à pieds joints** to jump with one's feet together

joli, jolie *adjective*
(**a**) pretty
(**b**) handsome
(**c**) nice; **un joli mariage** a nice wedding; **ce n'est pas joli de mentir** it's not nice to tell lies

Note that the English word *jolly* is never a translation for the French word *joli*.

jongler *verb* to juggle

LA **jonquille** *noun* daffodil

LA **Jordanie** *noun* Jordan

LA **joue** *noun* cheek

jouer
1 *verb*
(**a**) to play; **il joue du violon** he plays the violin; **jouer aux cartes** to play cards; **c'est à toi de jouer** it's your turn
(**b**) to act *(in a film, a play)*
(**c**) to gamble *(in a casino)*
(**d**) to bet; **jouer aux courses** to bet on the horses
(**e**) **jouer une pièce de théâtre** to put on a play
2 *reflexive verb* **se jouer** to be played; **le match se jouera la semaine prochaine** the match will be played next week

LE **jouet** *noun* toy

LE **joueur**, LA **joueuse** *noun*
(**a**) player; **un joueur de basket** a basketball player; **il est mauvais joueur** he's a bad loser
(**b**) gambler

LE **jour** *noun*
(**a**) day; **il travaille sept heures par jour** he works seven hours a day; **tous les jours** every day; **dans huit jours** in a week; **dans quinze jours** in a fortnight; **le jour de l'An** New Year's Day
(**b**) light, daylight; **le jour se lève** it's getting light; **il fait encore jour** it's still light
(**c**) **de nos jours** nowadays

(**d**) **mettre quelque chose à jour** to update something

LE **journal** *noun*
(**a**) paper, newspaper
(**b**) **le journal télévisé** the television news
(**c**) **un journal intime** a diary

The plural of *journal* is *journaux*.

LE/LA **journaliste** *noun* journalist; **il est journaliste sportif** he's a sports journalist

LA **journée** *noun* day; **dans la journée** during the day; **en début de journée** early in the day; **bonne journée!** have a good day!; **une journée de travail** a day's work; **une journée portes ouvertes** an open day

Note that the English word *journey* is never a translation for the French word *journée*.

joyeux, joyeuse *adjective* happy; **Joyeux anniversaire!** Happy birthday!; **Joyeux Noël!** Merry Christmas!

jubiler *verb*
(**a**) to be jubilant, to rejoice
(**b**) to gloat; **il jubilait de me voir humilié** he was gloating at my humiliation

LE **judo** *noun* judo; **je fais du judo** I do judo

LE/LA **juge** *noun*
(**a**) judge; **il est juge** he's a judge
(**b**) **un juge de touche** a linesman *(in football)*; a touch judge *(in rugby)*; **un juge de chaise** an umpire *(in tennis)*

LE **jugement** *noun*
(**a**) trial
(**b**) sentence; **la Cour suprême a rendu son jugement** the Supreme Court has passed sentence
(**c**) judgment; **porter un jugement sur quelqu'un** to pass judgment on somebody; **une erreur de jugement** an error of judgment

The *t* in *jugement* is not pronounced.

juger *verb*
(a) to try; **il a été jugé pour vol** he was tried for theft
(b) to judge; **juger par soi-même** to judge for oneself
(c) to consider; **elle a jugé qu'il était nécessaire d'intervenir** she considered it necessary to intervene

juif, juive
1 *adjective* Jewish
2 *noun* **un juif, une juive** a Jew

> French, unlike English, does not use capital letters for religions.

juillet *masculine noun* July; **le premier juillet** the first of July; **le 3 juillet** the 3rd of July; **le 14 juillet** Bastille Day

> In French, the names of months are not written with a capital.

La Fête du 14 Juillet
The celebrations to mark the anniversary of the storming of the Bastille begin on the 13th July with outdoor public dances (*les bals du quatorze juillet*) and firework displays, and continue on the 14th with a military parade in the morning. Firework displays are also held in the evening of Bastille Day.

---

juin *masculine noun* June; **le premier juin** the first of June; **le 22 juin** the 22nd of June

> In French, the names of months are not written with a capital.

jumeau, jumelle
1 *adjective* twin; **des frères jumeaux** twin brothers; **des sœurs jumelles** twin sisters
2 *noun* **un jumeau, une jumelle** a twin; **de vrais jumeaux** identical twins; **de faux jumeaux** non-identical twins

> The plural of *jumeau* is *jumeaux*.

jumelé, jumelée *adjective* **des villes jumelées** twin towns

jumelle *see* **jumeau**

LES jumelles *feminine plural noun* binoculars

LA jument *noun* mare

LA jupe *noun* skirt

jurer *verb* to swear; **je te jure que c'est vrai** I swear it's true

LE jury *noun*
(a) jury
(b) board of examiners

LE jus *noun* juice; **un jus d'orange** an orange juice; **du jus de viande** gravy

> The *s* in *jus* is not pronounced.

jusque *preposition*
(a) **jusqu'où?** how far?; **jusqu'à Marseille** as far as Marseille; **je suis monté jusqu'en haut de la tour** I climbed right to the top of the tower
(b) **jusqu'au 17 juillet** until the 17th of July; **jusqu'en avril** until April; **tout allait bien jusqu'à ce qu'il arrive** everything was going fine until he turned up
(c) **jusqu'à un certain point** up to a certain point
(d) **jusqu'ici** *or* **jusque-là** *(in space)* up to here, as far as here; **approchez-vous jusqu'ici** come as far as here; **on avait de l'eau jusque-là** the water was up to here
(e) **jusqu'ici, rien de grave** nothing serious so far; **jusque-là, tout va bien** so far so good; **tout s'était bien passé jusque-là** everything had gone well up to then

> *Jusque* becomes *jusqu'* in front of a vowel.

juste
1 *adjective*
(a) fair; **ce n'est pas juste!** it's not fair!
(b) right; **la réponse juste** the right answer
(c) tight *(garment, shoes)*
(d) **trois bouteilles pour sept personnes, c'est un peu juste!** three bottles won't really be enough for seven people!; **une heure pour aller à**

l'aéroport, c'est trop juste an hour to get to the airport is cutting it a bit fine

2 *adverb*

(**a**) in tune; **elle chante juste** she sings in tune

(**b**) right; **tu as deviné juste** you guessed right

(**c**) just; **il est arrivé juste à l'heure** he arrived just in time; **j'ai bu juste une gorgée pour goûter** I just drank a mouthful to taste it

(**d**) exactly; **il est deux heures juste** it's exactly two o'clock; **qu'est-ce que ça veut dire au juste?** what does that mean exactly?

justement *adverb*

(**a**) exactly; **j'ai justement ce qu'il vous faut** I've got exactly what you need; **tu ne vas pas partir sans lui dire au revoir? – si, justement!** you're not going without saying good-bye to him? – that's exactly what I'm doing!

(**b**) **voilà justement Paul** talking of Paul, here he is

(**c**) rightly

LA **justesse** *noun*

(**a**) accuracy

(**b**) **de justesse** just, narrowly; **il a gagné de justesse** he won by a narrow margin; **on a eu le train de justesse** we only just caught the train

LA **justice** *noun*

(**a**) fairness

(**b**) justice

(**c**) **la justice** the law; **aller en justice** to go to court

justifier

1 *verb*

(**a**) to justify

(**b**) to prove

2 *reflexive verb* **se justifier** to justify oneself

LE **kangourou** *noun* kangaroo

LE **karaté** *noun* karate; **je fais du karaté** I do karate

LE **kayak** *noun*
(**a**) kayak
(**b**) kayaking; **je fais du kayak** I go kayaking

LA **kermesse** *noun* charity fête; **la kermesse de l'école** the school fête

kidnapper *verb* to kidnap; **il s'est fait kidnapper** he got kidnapped

LE **kilo** *noun* kilo; **il pèse soixante kilos** he weighs sixty kilos

LE **kilomètre** *noun* kilometre; **cent kilomètres à l'heure** *or* **cent kilomètres-heure** a hundred kilometres an hour; **un kilomètre carré** a square kilometre

LE **kiosque** *noun* kiosk; **un kiosque à journaux** a news-stand; **un kiosque à musique** a bandstand

LE **klaxon**® *noun* horn *(of a car)*

klaxonner *verb* to sound one's horn, to hoot; **il m'a klaxonné** he hooted at me

K.-O. *adjective*
(**a**) **mettre quelqu'un K.-O.** to knock somebody out; **le boxeur était K.-O.** the boxer was out for the count
(**b**) dead beat, shattered

Sense (b) is an informal use of *K.-O.*.

LE **k-way**® *noun* cagoule, waterproof jacket; **un pantalon de k-way**® waterproof trousers

L*l*

l'

1 *article*

(**a**) the; **l'ordinateur** the computeur; **l'ambiance** the atmosphere; **l'arbitre** the referee; **l'honneur** honour; **l'Espagne** Spain

(**b**) *(with body parts)* one's, my, your, his, her, our, their; **se gratter l'oreille** to scratch one's ear; **je me suis fait mal à l'épaule** I hurt my shoulder; **il s'est cogné l'orteil contre le lit** he stubbed his toe on the bed

(**c**) a, per; **dix euros l'heure** ten euros an hour

2 *pronoun*

(**a**) him; **le nouvel élève est arrivé, je l'ai vu** the new student has arrived, I've seen him

(**b**) her; **la nouvelle directrice est arrivée, je l'ai vue** the new headmistress has arrived, I've seen her

(**c**) it; **il y avait un écureuil là-bas, tu l'as vu?** there was a squirrel over there, did you see it?

> *L'* is the contracted form of *le* ou *la* which is used in front of a vowel or a mute h. It is an article when it comes in front of a noun and a pronoun when it stands for a noun. The plural of *l'* is *les*. See also **la**, **le** and **les**.

la

1 *article*

(**a**) the; **la lampe** the lamp; **la fille** the girl; **la joie** joy; **la France** France

(**b**) *(with body parts)* one's, my, your, his, her, our, their; **se casser la jambe** to break one's leg; **je me suis brûlé la langue** I burnt my tongue; **il a levé la tête** he raised his head

(**c**) a, per; **un euro la douzaine** one euro a dozen

2 *pronoun*

(**a**) her; **la nouvelle directrice est là-bas, tu la vois?** the new headmistress is over there, can you see her?

(**b**) it; **voici ma valise, tu peux la garder?** here's my suitcase, can you look after it?; **tu vois la girafe là-bas? – oui, je la vois** can you see the giraffe over there? – yes, I can see it

> *La* is feminine. It is an article when it comes before a feminine noun and a pronoun when it stands for a feminine noun. *La* becomes *l'* in front of a vowel or a mute h. The plural of *la* is *les*. See also **l'** and **les**.

là *adverb*

(**a**) there; **de là je me suis dirigée vers l'église** from there I headed towards the church; **c'est par là** it's over there

(**b**) here; **vous n'êtes pas là pour bavarder** you're not here to chat; **viens là!** come here!

(**c**) where; **elle habite à Paris maintenant, c'est là qu'elle a trouvé du travail** she lives in Paris now, that's where she found work; **restez là où vous êtes** stay where you are; **c'est là le problème** that's where the problem lies

(**d**) then, when; **d'ici là** between now and then; **c'est là que j'ai paniqué** that's when I panicked

(**e**) *(with a hyphen)* that, those; **cette femme-là** that woman; **ce stylo-là** that pen; **dans ces endroits-là** in those places; **je veux celui-là** I want that one; **en ce temps-là** at that time

Note that the adverb *là* is written with an accent to distinguish it from the article and pronoun.

là-bas *adverb*
(**a**) there, over there
(**b**) down there; **là-bas dans la vallée** down there in the valley

LE **laboratoire** *noun* laboratory; **un laboratoire de langues** a language laboratory; **un laboratoire de photo** a photo-processing laboratory

labourer *verb* to plough

LE **lac** *noun* lake

LE **lacet** *noun*
(**a**) lace *(of a shoe)*
(**b**) **une route en lacets** a winding road

lâche
1 *adjective*
(**a**) cowardly
(**b**) loose *(garment, knot)*
2 *noun* **un/une lâche** a coward

lâcher *verb*
(**a**) to let go of; **lâche-moi!** let go of me!
(**b**) to drop; **elle a lâché la pile d'assiettes** she dropped the pile of plates
(**c**) to snap; **la corde a lâché** the rope snapped

là-dedans *adverb* in there, in it

là-dessous *adverb* under there, under it

là-dessus *adverb*
(**a**) on there, on it; **ne t'appuie pas là-dessus!** don't lean on it!
(**b**) about it; **je n'en sais pas plus que toi là-dessus** I don't know any more about it than you

là-haut *adverb*
(**a**) up there
(**b**) upstairs

laid, laide *adjective* ugly

LA **laideur** *noun* ugliness

LA **laine** *noun* wool; **un pull en laine** a woollen sweater

LA **laisse** *noun* leash; **les chiens doivent être tenus en laisse** dogs must be kept on a leash

laisser
1 *verb*
(**a**) to leave; **laisse-leur quelques fruits** leave them some fruit; **j'ai laissé mon sac à la maison** I left my bag at home; **laisse, je vais le faire** leave it, I'll do it myself
(**b**) to let; **je les laisse jouer dans la cour** I let them play in the yard; **laisse-le dormir** let him sleep; **laissez-moi passer** let me past; **laisse-moi voir la lettre** let me see the letter
(**c**) **laisser tomber quelque chose** to drop something
2 *reflexive verb* **se laisser** il s'est laissé aller he let himself go; **ne te laisse pas faire!** stand up for yourself!

LE **lait** *noun* milk; **du lait demi-écrémé** semi-skimmed milk; **du lait écrémé** skimmed milk; **du lait entier** whole milk; **du chocolat au lait** milk chocolate; **un café au lait** a white coffee; **du lait démaquillant** cleansing milk

laitier, laitière
1 *adjective* dairy; **des produits laitiers** dairy produce; **une vache laitière** a dairy cow
2 *noun* **le laitier, la laitière**
(**a**) milkman/milkwoman
(**b**) dairyman/dairywoman

LA **laitue** *noun* lettuce

LA **lame** *noun* blade *(of a knife, a razor, a tool)*

lamentable *adjective*
(**a**) appalling; **des résultats lamentables** appalling results
(**b**) terrible; **il est dans un état lamentable** he's in a terrible state
(**c**) pitiful

se lamenter *reflexive verb* to whine, to complain; **cela ne sert à rien de se lamenter sur son sort** it's no use complaining about your situation

LE **lampadaire** *noun*
(a) street light
(b) standard lamp

LA **lampe** *noun* lamp; **une lampe de bureau** a desk lamp; **une lampe de chevet** a bedside lamp; **une lampe de poche** a torch

LE **lance-pierre** *noun* catapult *(for children)*

> The plural of *lance-pierre* is *lance-pierres*. The singular can also be found with an *s*: *un lance-pierres*.

lancer
1 *verb*
(a) to throw; **lance-moi la balle** throw me the ball
(b) to drop *(a bomb)*
(c) to launch *(a rocket, a campaign, a new product)*
(d) **ils ont lancé un appel à la radio** they broadcast an appeal on the radio
2 *reflexive verb* **se lancer**
(a) **ils se lançaient des pierres** they were throwing stones at each other
(b) **se lancer à la poursuite de quelqu'un** to set off in pursuit of somebody
(c) to take the plunge; **allez, lance-toi et demande-lui** go on, take the plunge and ask him
(d) to embark on *(an adventure, an explanation)*
(e) **il s'est lancé dans les affaires** he launched himself into the world of business; **il s'est lancé dans la politique** he went into politics
3 *masculine noun*
(a) throw; **un lancer franc** a free throw *(in basketball)*
(b) **le lancer du disque** the discus; **le lancer du javelot** the javelin; **le lancer du poids** the shotput

LE **landau** *noun* pram

> The plural of *landau* is *landaus*. It is not a plural in *-aux* like most French words ending with *-au*.

LE **langage** *noun* language; **le langage familier** informal language

LA **langue** *noun*
(a) tongue
(b) **je donne ma langue au chat!** I give up!
(c) language; **les langues étrangères** foreign languages; **les langues vivantes** modern languages

LE **lapin** *noun* rabbit

LA **laque** *noun*
(a) hair spray
(b) lacquer
(c) gloss paint

laquelle *pronoun*
(a) which; **une réaction à laquelle je ne m'attendais pas** a reaction which I wasn't expecting
(b) which one; **laquelle de ces jupes préférez-vous?** which one of these skirts do you prefer?
(c) who; **il était avec sa sœur, laquelle m'a reconnu** he was with his sister, who recognized me
(d) whom; **la personne à laquelle je parlais** the person I was talking to *or* the person to whom I was talking

> This pronoun is feminine. For the masculine form, see also **lequel**. For the plural form, see also **lesquels**.

LE **lard** *noun* bacon

> Note that the English word *lard* is never a translation for the French word *lard*.
> The *d* in *lard* is not pronounced.

LE **lardon** *noun* piece of diced bacon, lardon

large
1 *adjective* wide
2 *masculine noun*
(a) **il fait six mètres de large** it's six metres wide
(b) **le large** the open sea; **un vent du large** an offshore wind; **le bateau a coulé au large de Hong Kong** the boat sank off the coast of Hong Kong

Note that the English word *large* is rarely a translation for the French word *large*.

largement *adverb*
(a) **tu auras largement le temps** you'll have more than enough time; **il y en a largement assez** there's more than enough; **elle a largement 60 ans** she's well over 60
(b) easily; **il gagne largement le double** he easily earns twice that

Note that the English word *largely* is never a translation for the French word *largement*.

LA **largeur** *noun* width; **trois mètres de largeur** three metres wide

LA **larme** *noun* tear; **elle était en larmes** she was in tears; **il a les larmes aux yeux** he has tears in his eyes; **il a fondu en larmes** he burst into tears

lassant, lassante *adjective* tedious

se lasser *reflexive verb* to get tired; **elle se lassera vite de lui** she'll soon get tired of him; **je ne me lasse pas d'écouter du Mozart** I never get tired of listening to Mozart

LE **latin** *noun* Latin

French, unlike English, does not use capital letters for languages.

LE **laurier** *noun*
(a) laurel
(b) **une feuille de laurier** a bay leaf

LE **lavabo** *noun* washbasin, sink

LE **lavage** *noun* washing; **ma chemise a rétréci au lavage** my shirt has shrunk in the wash

LA **lavande** *noun* lavender

LA **lave** *noun* lava

LE **lave-linge** *noun* washing machine

The word *lave-linge* does not change in the plural.

laver
1 *verb* to wash; **laver la vaisselle** to do the washing-up
2 *reflexive verb* **se laver** to have a wash; **se laver les mains** to wash one's hands; **va te laver les dents** go and brush your teeth

LA **laverie** *noun* **une laverie automatique** a launderette

LE **lave-vaisselle** *noun* dishwasher

The word *lave-vaisselle* does not change in the plural.

le
1 *article*
(a) the; **le ballon** the ball; **le garçon** the boy; **le bonheur** happiness; **le Japon** Japan
(b) *(with body parts)* one's, my, your, his, her, our, their; **se gratter le dos** to scratch one's back; **je me suis cassé le poignet** I broke my wrist; **il a levé le bras** he raised his arm
(c) a, per; **un euro le kilo** one euro a kilo
2 *pronoun*
(a) him; **le nouveau directeur est là-bas, tu le vois?** the new headmaster is over there, can you see him?
(b) it; **voici mon sac, tu peux le garder?** here's my bag, can you look after it?; **tu vois l'éléphant là-bas? – oui, je le vois** can you see the elephant over there? – yes, I can see it

Le is masculine. It is an article when it comes before a masculine noun and a pronoun when it stands for a masculine noun. *Le* becomes *l'* in front of a vowel or a mute h. The plural of *le* is *les*. See also **l'** and **les**.

lécher *verb* to lick

LA **leçon** *noun*
(a) lesson; **des leçons de français** French lessons
(b) homework; **as-tu appris tes leçons?** have you done your homework?
(c) **tu n'as pas besoin de me faire la leçon** you don't need to tell me what to do

LE **lecteur**, LA **lectrice**
1 *noun*
(a) reader
(b) foreign language assistant *(at university)*
2 *masculine noun* **le lecteur**
(a) **un lecteur de CD** a CD player; **un lecteur de DVD** a DVD player
(b) drive; **un lecteur de disquettes** a disk drive

LA **lecture** *noun*
(a) reading; **une leçon de lecture** a reading lesson
(b) something to read; **est-ce que vous voulez de la lecture?** would you like something to read?

> Note that the English word *lecture* is never a translation for the French word *lecture*.

LA **légende** *noun*
(a) legend
(b) caption *(under a photograph, an illustration)*
(c) key *(on a map)*

léger, légère *adjective*
(a) light; **léger comme une plume** as light as a feather
(b) slight *(noise, pain, difference, error)*; **un blessé léger** a slightly injured person
(c) weak *(tea, coffee)*

légèrement *adverb* slightly; **il boite légèrement** he has a slight limp; **elle était habillée légèrement** she was wearing light clothes

LE **légume** *noun* vegetable

LE **lendemain** *noun* the next day; **il est venu le lendemain** he came the next day; **le lendemain de la fête** the day after the party; **le lendemain matin** the next morning

lent, lente *adjective* slow

lentement *adverb* slowly

LA **lentille** *noun*
(a) contact lens
(b) lentil

lequel *pronoun*
(a) which; **le bureau dans lequel elle travaille** the office in which she works
(b) which one; **lequel veux-tu?** which one do you want?
(c) who; **elle était avec son frère, lequel m'a reconnu** she was with her brother, who recognized me
(d) whom; **un ami avec lequel il sort souvent** a friend he often goes out with *or* a friend with whom he often goes out

> This pronoun is masculine. For the feminine form, see also **laquelle**. For the plural form, see **lesquels**. *Lequel* contracts with *à* to form *auquel* and with *de* to form *duquel*. See also **auquel** and **duquel**.

les
1 *article*
(a) the; **les livres que j'ai achetés** the books I bought; **j'aime les livres** I like books; **les Pays-Bas** the Netherlands
(b) *(with body parts)* one's, my, your, his, her, our, their; **se brosser les dents** to brush one's teeth; **je me suis sali les mains** I got my hands dirty; **il a levé les bras** he raised his arms; **elle s'est lavé les cheveux** she washed her hair
2 *pronoun* them; **les nouveaux élèves sont là-bas, tu les vois?** the new students are over there, can you see them?; **voici mes sacs, tu peux les garder?** here are my bags, can you look after them?

> *Les* is the plural form of *la*, *le* and *l'*. It is an article when it comes before a plural noun and a pronoun when it stands for a plural noun. See also **l'**, **la** and **le**.

lesquels, lesquelles *pronoun*
(a) which; **les vacances durant lesquelles j'ai fait de la plongée** the holidays during which I went diving
(b) which ones; **lesquels veux-tu?** which ones do you want?; **lesquelles de ces jupes préférez-vous?** which

ones of these skirts do you prefer?
(**c**) who; **elle était avec ses parents, lesquels m'ont reconnu** she was with her parents, who recognized me
(**d**) whom; **les amis sans lesquels je n'aurais pas réussi** the friends without whom I wouldn't have succeeded; **il y avait beaucoup de gens, parmi lesquels le président lui-même** there were a lot of people there, including the President himself

These pronouns are plural. For the singular form, see also **lequel**. *Lequels* and *lesquelles* contract with *à* to form *auquels* and *auxquelles*, and with *de* to form *duquels* and *desquelles*. See also **auxquels** and **desquels**.

ʟᴀ **lessive** *noun*
(**a**) washing powder
(**b**) washing, laundry; **je vais faire la lessive** I'm going to do the laundry; **va étendre la lessive** go and hang out the washing

ʟᴇ **Letton**, ʟᴀ **Lettonne** *noun (person)* Latvian

letton, lettonne
1 *adjective* Latvian; **l'économie lettonne** the Latvian economy
2 *noun* **le letton** *(language)* Latvian; **il parle letton** he speaks Latvian

In French, only the noun for the inhabitants of a country takes a capital letter, never the adjective or the noun for the language.

ʟᴀ **Lettonie** *noun* Latvia

ʟᴀ **lettre**
1 *noun*
(**a**) letter; **un mot de neuf lettres** a nine-letter word; **une lettre majuscule** a capital letter; **une lettre minuscule** a small letter; **écrivez votre nom en toutes lettres** write your name in full
(**b**) **une lettre d'amour** a love letter
2 *feminine plural noun* **les lettres** arts subjects; **un étudiant en lettres** an arts student; **il enseigne les lettres clas-**

siques he teaches Latin and Greek; **les lettres modernes** modern literature

leur
1 *adjective* their; **leur chien** their dog; **leur école** their school; **leurs amis** their friends

Note that *leur* is in plural when the noun which follows is in plural.

2 *pronoun*
(**a**) them, to them; **je leur ai donné la lettre** I gave them the letter; **elle leur en a parlé** she spoke to them about it; **donnez-le-leur** give it to them; **je leur ai serré la main** I shook their hands
(**b**) **le leur, la leur, les leurs** theirs; **c'est notre problème, pas le leur** it's our problem, not theirs; **ils ont pris une valise qui n'était pas la leur** they took a suitcase that wasn't theirs; **mes enfants et les leurs** my children and theirs

In French, possessive pronouns have the same gender and the same number as the nouns they stand for, eg the corresponding pronoun for *leurs enfants* is *les leurs* because the word *enfants* is plural.

levé, levée *adjective*
(**a**) **être levé** to be up; **tu es déjà levé?** are you up already?
(**b**) **voter à main levée** to vote by a show of hands

lever
1 *verb*
(**a**) to raise; **lève la main avant de prendre la parole** raise your hand before speaking; **il leva les yeux** he looked up
(**b**) to lift *(a barrier, an embargo)*
2 *reflexive verb* **se lever**
(**a**) to get up; **lève-toi!** get up!; **je n'arrive pas à me lever le matin** I can't get up in the morning; **il s'est levé du pied gauche** he got out of the wrong side of the bed
(**b**) to stand up; **levez-vous quand le proviseur entre** stand up when the

headmaster comes in
(**c**) to rise; **le soleil se lève tôt en été** the sun rises early in the summer; **le jour se lève** it's getting light
3 *noun* **le lever du soleil** sunrise; **le lever du jour** daybreak

LA **lèvre** *noun* lip; **elle avait le sourire aux lèvres** she had a smile on her lips

LE **lézard** *noun* lizard

> The *d* in *lézard* is not pronounced.

LE **Liban** *noun* Lebanon

libérer
1 *verb*
(**a**) to free *(a prisoner)*
(**b**) to let go; **il a libéré les élèves avant l'heure** he let the students go early
(**c**) to vacate *(a hotel room)*
(**d**) to clear; **libérez le passage** clear the way
2 *reflexive verb* **se libérer**
(**a**) to free oneself
(**b**) **je ne pourrai pas me libérer avant 17 heures** I won't be able to get away before 5 o'clock; **essaie de te libérer pour demain** try to make some time tomorrow

LA **liberté** *noun*
(**a**) freedom; **la liberté d'expression** freedom of speech
(**b**) liberty; **la statue de la Liberté** the Statue of Liberty; **Liberté, Égalité, Fraternité** Liberty, Equality, Fraternity *(motto of the French Revolution and, today, of France)*
(**c**) free time
(**d**) **être en liberté** to be free; **remettre quelqu'un en liberté** to set somebody free

LE/LA **libraire** *noun* bookseller; **il est libraire** he's a bookseller

> Note that the English word *librarian* is never a translation for the French word *libraire*.

LA **librairie** *noun* bookshop

> Note that the English word *library* is never a translation for the French word *librairie*.

LIBRE **libre** *adjective* free *(person, room)*; **tu es libre ce soir?** are you free tonight?; **tu as un moment de libre?** have you got a minute to spare?

LE **libre-service** *noun* self-service; **une laverie en libre-service** a self-service launderette

> The plural of *libre-service* is *libres-services*.

LA **licence** *noun*
(**a**) degree; **une licence d'économie** a degree in economics; **une licence de droit** a law degree
(**b**) licence

licencier *verb*
(**a**) to lay off, to make redundant; **vingt personnes ont été licenciées** twenty people were laid off
(**b**) to dismiss; **il s'est fait licencié pour faute professionnelle** he was dismissed for professional misconduct

LE **liège** *noun* cork *(substance)*; **les semelles de ces chaussures sont en liège** the soles of these shoes are made of cork; **un bouchon de liège** a cork

LE **lien** *noun*
(**a**) connection
(**b**) link; **un lien hypertexte** a hypertext link
(**c**) tie; **des liens de parenté** *or* **des liens familiaux** family ties

LE **lierre** *noun* ivy

LE **lieu**
1 *noun*
(**a**) place; **votre lieu de naissance** your place of birth; **un lieu de rendez-vous** a meeting place

> The plural of *lieu* is *lieux*.

(**b**) **avoir lieu** to take place; **la réunion aura lieu à Paris** the meeting will take place in Paris

(c) **j'ai tout lieu de croire qu'il ne viendra pas** I have every reason to believe that he won't come; **il n'y a pas lieu de s'affoler** there's no reason to panic
(d) **donner lieu à quelque chose** to cause something
(e) **au lieu de** instead of
2 *masculine plural noun* **les lieux**
(a) premises
(b) scene; **les lieux du crime** the scene of the crime

LE **lièvre** *noun* hare

LA **ligne** *noun*
(a) line; **une ligne de métro** an underground line; **une ligne de téléphone** a phone line; **se mettre en ligne** to line up
(b) figure *(of a person)*; **elle surveille sa ligne** she's watching her figure
(c) fishing line

LE **lilas** *noun* lilac

LA **limace** *noun* slug *(animal)*

LA **lime** *noun* file; **une lime à ongles** a nail file

LA **limitation** *noun* restriction; **la limitation de vitesse** the speed limit

limite
1 *feminine noun*
(a) limit
(b) boundary
(c) deadline; **c'est pour lundi dernière limite** Monday is the absolute deadline
(d) **à la limite** if necessary; **à la limite, on peut toujours dormir dans la voiture** if necessary, we can always sleep in the car
2 *adjective* maximum; **l'âge limite** the maximum age; **la vitesse limite** the maximum speed

limiter
1 *verb* to limit
2 *reflexive verb* **se limiter** to limit oneself; **je me limite à un dessert par jour** I limit myself to one dessert a day

LA **limonade** *noun* lemonade

LE **linge** *noun*
(a) linen; **le linge de table** table linen
(b) washing; **étendre le linge** to hang out the washing; **repasser le linge** to do the ironing

LE **Lion** *noun* Leo; **je suis Lion** I'm a Leo

LE **lion** *noun* lion

liquide
1 *masculine noun*
(a) **un liquide** a liquid; **du liquide vaisselle** washing-up liquid
(b) cash; **payer en liquide** to pay in cash; **je n'ai pas de liquide** I haven't got any cash
2 *adjective*
(a) liquid
(b) watery; **une soupe liquide** a watery soup
(c) **de l'argent liquide** cash

lire *verb* to read; **je lis tous les soirs** I read every night; **je l'ai lu dans le journal** I read it in the paper

See verb table p. 322.

lis *see* **lire**
qu'est-ce que tu lis? what are you reading?; **tous les soirs, je lis dans mon lit** every night, I read in bed

Lis is a form of the verb *lire* in the present tense. See verb table p. 322.

Lisbonne *noun* Lisbon

lisse *adjective* smooth

LA **liste** *noun*
(a) list; **une liste d'attente** a waiting list
(b) **il est inscrit sur les listes électorales** he's on the electoral roll
(c) **elle est sur liste rouge** she's ex-directory

lit¹ *see* **lire**
il lit un roman he's reading a novel

Lit is a form of the verb *lire* in the present tense. See verb table p. 322.

LE **lit²** *noun* bed; **va au lit!** go to bed!; **un lit à une place** *or* **un lit d'une personne** a single bed; **un lit à deux places** *or* **un lit de deux personnes** a double bed; **des lits jumeaux** twin beds; **des lits superposés** bunk beds

LE **litre** *noun* litre; **une bouteille de deux litres** a two-litre bottle

littéraire *adjective* literary; **il fera des études littéraires** he's going to study literature

LA **littérature** *noun* literature

LA **Lituanie** *noun* Lithuania

LE **Lituanien**, LA **Lituanienne** *noun* *(person)* Lithuanian

lituanien, lituanienne
1 *adjective* Lithuanian; **la cuisine lituanienne** Lithuanian food
2 *masculine noun* **le lituanien** *(language)* Lithuanian; **elle parle lituanien** she speaks Lithuanian

> In French, only the noun for the inhabitants of a country takes a capital letter, never the adjective or the noun for the language.

LA **livraison** *noun* delivery; **livraison à domicile** home delivery

livre
1 *masculine noun* book; **un livre d'histoire** a history book; **un livre scolaire** a schoolbook, a textbook; **un livre de cuisine** a cookery book; **un livre de poche** a paperback
2 *feminine noun*
(a) pound *(money)*; **ça coûte trois livres** it costs three pounds; **la livre sterling** the pound (sterling)
(b) pound *(weight)*; **une livre de tomates** a pound of tomatoes

livrer
1 *verb*
(a) to deliver *(goods, the newspaper)*
(b) to hand over *(a person)*
2 *reflexive verb* **se livrer** to give oneself up

LE **livret** *noun*
(a) notebook
(b) **un livret scolaire** a school report
(c) bank book; **un livret de caisse d'épargne** a savings book, a passbook

local, locale
1 *adjective* local; **la radio locale** local radio
2 *masculine noun* premises; **je cherche un local pour le club de foot** I'm looking for premises for the football club

> The masculine plural of *local* is *locaux*.

LE/LA **locataire** *noun*
(a) tenant
(b) lodger

LA **location** *noun*
(a) *(by the owner)* renting, letting *(of a flat)*; rental, hiring *(of a machine)*; **il a mis la maison en location** he's rented out the house; **location de voitures** car hire
(b) *(by the tenant)* renting *(of a flat)*; hiring *(of a machine)*; **je suis en location** I'm renting
(c) rented accommodation; **location meublée** furnished accommodation

> Note that the English word *location* is never a translation for the French word *location*.

LA **locomotive** *noun* railway engine, locomotive

LE **logement** *noun*
(a) accommodation; **je cherche un logement** I'm looking for accommodation
(b) flat
(c) house
(d) housing; **la crise du logement** the housing shortage

loger
1 *verb*
(a) to live; **elle loge chez sa tante** she lives with her aunt; **pour l'instant je loge chez lui** I'm staying at his place at the moment

(**b**) to put up; **nous pouvons vous loger pour une nuit** we can put you up for a night

(**c**) to accommodate; **l'école peut loger cinq cents élèves** the school can accommodate five hundred pupils

(**d**) to put; **j'ai réussi à loger ton sac entre les deux valises** I managed to squeeze your bag between the two cases

2 *reflexive verb* **se loger**

(**a**) to find accommodation, to find somewhere to live

(**b**) to lodge itself; **un éclat de verre s'est logé dans son œil** a splinter of glass lodged itself in his eye

LE **logiciel** *noun* software; **un logiciel** a software package

logique

1 *adjective* logical

2 *feminine noun* **la logique** logic

LA **loi** *noun* law; **il faut respecter la loi** you must obey the law

loin *adverb*

(**a**) far; **est-ce que c'est loin?** is it far?; **ce n'est pas loin d'ici** it's not far from here; **l'école est plus loin que la poste** the school is farther than the post office; **l'hôtel est moins loin que la gare** the hotel is not as far as the train station; **de loin** from a distance

(**b**) a long way off; **Noël n'est plus très loin** *(in the future)* Christmas isn't a long way off now; **c'est loin tout ça!** *(in the past)* that seems a long way off now!

(**c**) **il est de loin le plus compétent** he's by far the most competent

(**d**) **elle est loin d'être bête** she is far from stupid; **je suis encore loin d'avoir fini** I'm still far from finished

(**e**) **il n'est pas loin de midi** it's nearly midday

lointain, lointaine *adjective* distant, far-off; **un cousin lointain** a distant cousin

LE **loisir** *noun*

(**a**) spare time; **comment occupez-vous vos heures de loisir?** what do you do in your spare time?

(**b**) **les loisirs** hobbies; **quels sont vos loisirs?** what are your hobbies?

Londres *noun* London

long, longue

1 *adjective* long

2 *masculine noun*

(**a**) **ce mur fait dix mètres de long** this wall is ten metres long

(**b**) **le long de** along; **le long de la rivière** along the river

(**c**) **tout au long de l'année** throughout the year

(**d**) **marcher de long en large** to walk back and forth

longtemps *adverb* a long time; **elle a mis longtemps** she took a long time; **je n'en ai pas pour longtemps** I won't be long; **j'ai attendu longtemps avant d'entrer** I waited for a long time before going in; **il n'y a pas longtemps** not long ago; **cela fait longtemps que je l'ai lu** it's been a long time since I read it

LA **longueur** *noun*

(**a**) length; **trois mètres de longueur** three metres long; **le saut en longueur** the long jump

(**b**) **à longueur d'année** all year long; **il se plaint à longueur de temps** he complains all the time

lors de *preposition*

(**a**) during; **lors du déjeuner** during lunch

(**b**) at the time of; **lors de sa mort** at the time of his death

lorsque *conjunction* when; **j'allais partir lorsqu'on a sonné** I was about to leave when the doorbell rang

Lorsque becomes *lorsqu'* in front of a vowel or a mute h.

LE **losange** *noun* diamond *(shape)*; **en forme de losange** diamond-shaped

LE **lot** *noun*

(**a**) prize; **un lot de consolation** a consolation prize; **il a gagné le gros**

lot he won the jackpot
(**b**) set; **des torchons vendus par lots** tea towels sold in sets
(**c**) pack; **un lot d'éponges** a pack of sponges

The *t* in *lot* is not pronounced.

LA **loterie** *noun* lottery; **gagner à la loterie** to win the lottery

LE **lotissement** *noun* housing estate

LE **loto** *noun*
(**a**) bingo
(**b**) **le Loto** the French lottery; **il a gagné au Loto** he won the lottery
(**c**) **le Loto sportif** the football pools

louche¹ *adjective* dodgy *(person, place)*

LA **louche²** *noun* ladle

loucher *verb* to have a squint

louer *verb*
(**a**) to rent; **il va louer son appartement au lieu de le vendre** he's going to rent his flat out instead of selling it; **nous avons loué la villa de Philippe pour le mois de juillet** we've rented Philippe's villa for the month of July
(**b**) **chambre à louer** room to let
(**c**) **voitures à louer** cars for hire

LE **loup** *noun*
(**a**) wolf
(**b**) **avoir une faim de loup** to be starving

The *p* in *loup* is not pronounced.

LA **loupe** *noun* magnifying glass

lourd, lourde
1 *adjective*
(**a**) heavy
(**b**) clumsy *(writing style)*
2 *adverb* **lourd il fait très lourd aujourd'hui** it's very close today

LE **loyer** *noun* rent *(for a house, a flat)*

lu, lue *see* lire
j'ai lu ce livre l'année dernière I read this book last year

Lu(e) is the past participle of the verb *lire*. See verb table p. 322.

LA **luge** *noun* sledge; **faire de la luge** to go sledging

lui *pronoun*
(**a**) him, to him; **qui le lui a dit?** who told him?; **je lui ai parlé** I spoke to him; **donne-le-lui** give it to him; **c'est à cause de lui** it's because of him; **elle travaille mieux que lui** she works better than him; **un ami à lui** a friend of his; **ce livre n'est pas à lui** this book is not his
(**b**) he; **elle aime le cinéma, lui non** she likes the cinema, he doesn't; **il le sait bien, lui** *he* knows it all right; **c'est lui qui est parti en premier** he's the one who left first
(**c**) himself; **il était content de lui** he was pleased with himself
(**d**) her, to her; **qui le lui a dit?** who told her?; **je lui ai parlé** I spoke to her; **donne-le-lui** give it to her
(**e**) it, to it; **ce chien a l'air méchant, fais attention à lui** watch out for the dog, it looks dangerous

Note that when it is used as an indirect object *lui* can refer to a male, a female, an animal or an object. However, when it is used after a preposition, *lui* usually refers to a male.

lui-même *pronoun* himself; **il l'a écrit lui-même** he wrote it himself

Lui-même only refers to masculine nouns.

LA **lumière** *noun* light; **la lumière du jour** daylight; **allume la lumière** turn on the light; **éteins la lumière** turn off the light

LE **lundi** *noun* Monday; **elle est venue lundi** she came on Monday; **il fait du tennis le lundi** he plays tennis on Mondays; **tous les lundis** every Monday

In French, the names of days are not written with a capital.

LA **lune** *noun*
(**a**) moon; **c'est la pleine lune** there's a

full moon; **c'est leur lune de miel** it's their honeymoon
(b) être dans la lune to have one's head in the clouds; **pardon, j'étais dans la lune** sorry, I was miles away

LES **lunettes** *feminine plural noun* glasses; **il porte des lunettes** he wears glasses

LA **lutte** *noun*
(**a**) fight
(**b**) struggle; **la lutte pour l'indépendance du pays** the country's struggle for independence
(**c**) wrestling; **faire de la lutte** to wrestle

lutter *verb*
(**a**) to fight; **lutter contre les injustices** to fight against injustice
(**b**) to struggle
(**c**) to wrestle

LE **luxe** *noun* luxury; **un hôtel de luxe** a luxury hotel

LE **Luxembourg** *noun* Luxembourg

LE **Luxembourgeois**, LA **Luxembourgeoise** *noun (person)* Luxembourger, person from Luxembourg

luxembourgeois, luxembourgeoise *adjective* from Luxembourg

luxueux, luxueuse *adjective* luxurious

LE **lycée** *noun* secondary school; **un lycée d'enseignement général** a secondary school; **un lycée professionnel** a vocational secondary school

---

Although it ends in -*ée*, this word is masculine.

LE LYCÉE

The *lycée* provides three years' teaching after *collège* and is for pupils between 15 and 18. The first year in the *lycée* is called *la seconde*, the second *la première* and the last *la terminale*. It prepares students for the *baccalauréat* examination, also called informally *le bac*. This final examination allows them to go to university. French pupils may also go to a *lycée professionnel* (a vocational secondary school) where they learn technical and professional skills and study for various types of vocational diploma; the most common of these are *le CAP*, *le BEP* and *le bac professionnel*. See also **baccalauréat**, **collège** and **filière**.

LE **lycéen**, LA **lycéenne** *noun* secondary school pupil

M m

M. Mr

M. is the abbreviation of *Monsieur*.

m' *pronoun* **il m'aime** he loves me; **je m'améliore** I'm improving; **je m'en vais demain** I'm leaving tomorrow

M' is the contracted form of *me* which is used in front of a vowel or a mute h. See also **me**.

ma *adjective* my; **ma mère** my mother; **ma valise** my suitcase

Ma is used in front of feminine nouns. The plural of *ma* is *mes*. *Ma* becomes *mon* before a feminine noun starting with a vowel or a mute h, as in *mon école, mon histoire*. See also **mes** and **mon**.

mâcher *verb*
(**a**) to chew
(**b**) **il ne mâche pas ses mots** he doesn't mince his words

LE **machin** *noun* thing, thingy; **ça sert à quoi, ce machin?** what's this thing for?

This word is informal.

LA **machine** *noun*
(**a**) machine; **une machine à coudre** a sewing machine; **une machine à écrire** a typewriter; **une machine à laver** a washing machine
(**b**) engine; **une machine à vapeur** a steam engine

LA **mâchoire** *noun* jaw

LE **maçon** *noun* builder; **il est maçon** he's a builder

Madame *feminine noun*
(**a**) Madam; **bonjour Madame!** good morning, Madam!; **merci, Madame!** thank you!
(**b**) Mrs; **allez voir Madame Duval** go and see Mrs Duval
(**c**) *(at school)* Miss; **Madame, j'ai fini mon addition!** Miss, I've finished my sums!

The plural of *Madame* is *Mesdames*. Note that the word *Madame* is very commonly used in French when addressing strangers and will not always need a translation in English: *je peux vous aider, Madame?* can I help you?

Mademoiselle *feminine noun* Miss; **bonjour Mademoiselle!** good morning, Miss!; **merci Mademoiselle!** thank you!; **allez voir Mademoiselle Duval** go and see Miss Duval

The plural of *Mademoiselle* is *Mesdemoiselles*. Note that the word *Mademoiselle* is very commonly used in French when addressing strangers and will not always need a translation in English: *je peux vous aider, Mademoiselle?* can I help you?

LE **magasin** *noun*
(**a**) shop; **faire les magasins** to go shopping; **un magasin d'alimentation** a food shop; **un grand magasin** a department store
(**b**) warehouse *(of a factory)*; storeroom *(of a shop)*; **nous ne l'avons pas en magasin** we don't have it in stock

LE **magicien**, LA **magicienne** *noun* magician

LA **magie** *noun* magic; **il fait de la magie** he does magic

magique *adjective*
(a) magic; **une baguette magique** a magic wand
(b) magical

LE **magnétophone** *noun* tape recorder

LE **magnétoscope** *noun* video recorder

magnifique *adjective*
(a) gorgeous; **elle était magnifique dans sa robe de mariée** she looked gorgeous in her wedding dress
(b) wonderful; **il y a une vue magnifique** there is a wonderful view

mai *masculine noun* May; **le premier mai** the first of May; **le 11 mai** the 11th of May

In French, the names of months are not written with a capital.

maigre *adjective*
(a) thin; **un homme grand et maigre** a tall, thin man
(b) small; **de maigres économies** small savings

maigrir *verb* to lose weight

LE **maillot** *noun*
(a) shirt *(of a footballer, a cyclist)*
(b) **un maillot de bain** *(for women)* swimsuit, swimming costume; *(for men)* swimming trunks
(c) **un maillot de corps** vest *(for men)*

LA **main** *noun* hand; **il m'a donné la main** he held my hand; **faire un signe de la main** to wave; **donner un coup de main à quelqu'un** to lend somebody a hand; **je lui ai donné en mains propres** I gave it to him in person; **gagner haut la main** to win hands down; **est-ce que tu as un stylo sous la main?** have you got a pen handy?; **j'en mettrais ma main au feu** *or* **j'en mettrais ma main à couper** I'd swear to it

LA **main-d'œuvre** *noun* workforce, labour; **la main-d'œuvre étrangère** foreign labour

The plural of *main-d'œuvre* is *mains-d'œuvre*.

maintenant *adverb* now

maintenir *verb*
(a) to keep; **maintenir au frais** keep in a cool place
(b) to hold in position
(c) to maintain *(an opinion, peace, order)*

See verb table p. 324.

LE **maire** *noun* mayor

LA **mairie** *noun*
(a) town hall
(b) town council, city council

mais *conjunction*
(a) but; **ces chaussures sont jolies mais trop chères** these shoes are nice, but they're too expensive; **ce n'est pas bleu, mais vert** it's not blue, it's green
(b) *(to insist)* **mais oui!** oh yes!; **mais non!** oh no!; **mais vous êtes fou!** you're mad!; **mais ça suffit maintenant!** that's enough now!; **non mais tu plaisantes?** you must be joking!; **mais tu saignes!** you're bleeding!

LE **maïs** *noun*
(a) maize
(b) sweetcorn

This word is pronounced as two syllables: "ma-ees".

LA **maison** *noun*
(a) house
(b) home; **je rentre à la maison** I'm going home; **un dessert fait maison** a home-made dessert; **une maison de retraite** an old people's home
(c) company; **une maison d'édition** a publishing company; **la maison mère** the parent company

LE **maître** *noun*
(a) master
(b) teacher *(in primary school)*
(c) **le maître de maison** the host

(d) un maître de conférence a lecturer; **un maître de recherches** a research director

(e) un maître chanteur a blackmailer

(f) un maître d'hôtel *(in a restaurant)* a head waiter; *(in a house)* a butler

(g) un maître nageur a swimming instructor

The word *maître* does not have a feminine in senses (d) to (g) but it can also refer to a woman: *elle est maître de conférence.*

LA **maîtresse** *noun*

(a) mistress

(b) teacher *(in primary school)*; **Maîtresse, j'ai trouvé!** Miss, I've found the answer!

(c) la maîtresse de maison the hostess

maîtriser

1 *verb*

(a) to control *(a person, an animal, an emotion)*

(b) to bring under control *(a situation, a fire)*

(c) to master; **il ne maîtrise pas la langue** he hasn't mastered the language; **il n'arrive pas à maîtriser sa peur de l'avion** he can't get over his fear of flying

2 *reflexive verb* **se maîtriser** to control oneself

majeur, majeure

1 *adjective*

(a) major; **la majeure partie de son temps** the major part of his time

(b) être majeur to be of age

2 *masculine noun* **le majeur** the middle finger

LA **majorité** *noun*

(a) majority; **la majorité des spectateurs étaient choqués par la pièce** the majority of the audience was shocked by the play

(b) atteindre sa majorité to come of age

majuscule

1 *adjective* capital; **B majuscule** capital B; **en lettres majuscules** in capital letters

2 *feminine noun* **une majuscule** a capital; **écrivez votre nom en majuscules** write your name in capitals

mal

1 *adverb*

(a) badly; **il l'a mal pris** he took it badly; **il est mal habillé** he's badly dressed

(b) not properly; **la porte est mal fermée** the door isn't closed properly; **c'est mal fait** it hasn't been done properly

(c) not well; **il va très mal** he's not at all well; **j'entends mal** I can't hear very well; **il mange mal** he doesn't eat well

(d) wrong; **tout va mal** everything's going wrong

(e) pas mal de *(informal phrase)* quite a lot of; **elle a pas mal d'argent** she's got quite a lot of money

2 *adjective*

(a) wrong; **c'est mal de tricher** it's wrong to cheat; **je n'ai rien dit de mal** I haven't said anything wrong

(b) bad; **ce n'était pas si mal** it wasn't that bad; **ce n'était pas mal du tout** it wasn't bad at all

(c) être mal à l'aise to be uncomfortable, to be ill at ease

Note that the adjective *mal* does not change in the plural or in the feminine.

3 *masculine noun*

(a) ache, pain; **un mal de dents** toothache; **des maux de tête** headaches; **j'ai mal à la gorge** I have a sore throat

The plural of the noun *mal* is *maux.*

(b) sickness; **le mal du pays** homesickness; **le mal de l'air** airsickness; **le mal de mer** seasickness; **avoir le mal de mer** to be seasick

(c) harm; **bois du lait, ça ne peut pas te faire de mal** drink some milk, it can't do you any harm

(d) faire mal à quelqu'un to hurt

somebody; **se faire mal** to hurt oneself; **mes chaussures me font mal** my shoes are hurting me; **aïe, ça fait mal!** ouch, that hurts!
(**e**) trouble, difficulty; **avoir du mal à faire quelque chose** to have trouble doing something
(**f**) evil; **le bien et le mal** good and evil

malade
1 *adjective*
(**a**) ill; **tomber malade** to fall ill
(**b**) sick; **je suis malade en avion** I get sick on planes; **j'étais malade de peur** I was sick with fear
(**c**) crazy; **ne hurle pas comme ça, tu es malade ou quoi?** stop yelling like that, are you crazy?

Sense (c) is an informal use of *malade.*

2 *noun* **le/la malade**
(**a**) sick person, ill person
(**b**) patient
(**c**) maniac; **il conduit comme un malade** he drives like a maniac; **on a travaillé comme des malades pour finir à temps** we worked like mad to finish on time

Sense (c) is an informal use of *malade.*

LA **maladie** *noun*
(**a**) illness; **une longue maladie** a long illness
(**b**) disease; **la maladie de la vache folle** mad cow disease
(**c**) **être en congé maladie** to be on sick leave

maladroit, maladroite *adjective* clumsy

LE **malaise** *noun*
(**a**) faintness; **il a été pris d'un malaise** he fainted; **mon grand-père a eu un malaise** my grandpa had a dizzy spell
(**b**) discontent; **il y a un malaise croissant chez les professeurs** there's mounting discontent among teachers
(**c**) embarrassment; **la remarque a**

créé un malaise the remark caused a moment of embarrassment

LA **malchance** *noun* bad luck

mâle
1 *adjective*
(**a**) male; **un ours mâle** a male bear
(**b**) manly *(voice, face, behaviour)*
2 *masculine noun* **un mâle** a male *(for animals)*

LE **malentendu** *noun* misunderstanding

malgré *preposition* in spite of; **il est sorti malgré la pluie** he went out in spite of the rain; **malgré tout** all the same

LE **malheur** *noun*
(**a**) misfortune
(**b**) bad luck; **arrête, ça porte malheur!** stop it, that's bad luck!

malheureusement *adverb* unfortunately

malheureux, malheureuse *adjective*
(**a**) unhappy
(**b**) unfortunate

malhonnête *adjective* dishonest

LA **malhonnêteté** *noun* dishonesty

LA **malice** *noun* mischief

Note that the English word *malice* is not a translation for the French word *malice.*

malicieux, malicieuse *adjective* mischievous

Note that the English word *malicious* is not a translation for the French word *malicieux.*

malin, maligne *adjective*
(**a**) cunning
(**b**) clever

LA **malle** *noun* trunk *(suitcase)*

LA **mallette** *noun* briefcase

malpoli, malpolie *adjective* rude, impolite

LE Maltais, LA Maltaise *noun (person)* Maltese; **les Maltais** Maltese People, the Maltese

maltais, maltaise *adjective* Maltese; **l'économie maltaise** the Maltese economy

In French, only the noun for the inhabitants of a country takes a capital letter, never the adjective.

Malte *noun* Malta; **à Malte** in Malta; **il est allé à Malte** he went to Malta

LA maman *noun* mum

LA mamie *noun*
(a) grandma, granny
(b) old lady

LE mammifère *noun* mammal

LA Manche *noun* the English Channel

manche
1 *feminine noun*
(a) sleeve; **une chemise à manches courtes** a short-sleeved shirt; **une chemise à manches longues** a long-sleeved shirt
(b) round *(of a game)*; **gagner la première manche** to win the first round
(c) set *(in tennis)*
(d) **faire la manche** *(informal phrase)* to beg
2 *masculine noun* **un manche** a handle *(of a knife, a tool)*; **un manche à balai** a broomstick

LA mandarine *noun* tangerine

LE manège *noun*
(a) fairground ride
(b) riding school
(c) riding exercises
(d) little game; **tu copies sur ton frère, j'ai bien vu ton manège** you've been copying from your brother's work, I'm on to your little game

manger *verb* to eat; **qu'est-ce que tu veux manger?** what would you like to eat?; **est-ce que tu as donné à manger au chien?** did you feed the dog?

manier *verb* to handle *(an object, a tool)*

LA manière *noun*
(a) way; **la manière dont elle s'habille** the way she dresses
(b) **de toute manière** anyway, in any case
(c) **de manière générale** on the whole, generally
(d) **de manière à faire quelque chose** so as to do something
(e) **les manières** manners; **avoir de bonnes manières** to have good manners

LE manifestant, LA manifestante *noun* demonstrator, protester

LA manifestation *noun*
(a) demonstration; **une manifestation contre la guerre** an anti-war demonstration
(b) event; **une manifestation sportive** a sporting event
(c) expression; **des manifestations de joie** expressions of joy

manifester
1 *verb*
(a) to demonstrate; **les professeurs manifestent dans la rue** teachers are demonstrating in the streets
(b) to show, to express; **manifester son mécontentement** to express one's dissatisfaction
2 *reflexive verb* **se manifester** to come forward; **le gagnant ne s'est pas manifesté** the winner didn't come forward

LE mannequin *noun*
(a) model; **elle est mannequin** she's a model

The word *mannequin* is masculine but it refers to both men and women.

(b) dummy, mannequin *(in a shop window)*

LE manque *noun* lack; **le manque de sommeil** lack of sleep

manquer *verb*
(a) to miss *(a train, a ball, a target)*
(b) to be missing; **le bouton qui manque à ma veste** the button that's

missing from my jacket; **il manque un bouton** there's a button missing

(**c**) to lack, to be short; **tu manques de confiance** you lack confidence; **il nous manque trois joueurs** we're three players short; **nous manquons d'argent** we're short of money; **ça manque de sel** there isn't enough salt

(**d**) **tu me manques** I miss you; **ses enfants lui manquent** he misses his children

LE **manteau** *noun*
(**a**) coat *(garment)*
(**b**) blanket; **le jardin était recouvert d'un manteau de neige** the garden was covered with a blanket of snow

> The plural of *manteau* is *manteaux*.

LE **maquillage** *noun* make-up

maquiller
1 *verb* to make up; **elle est bien maquillée** she's nicely made-up
2 *reflexive verb* **se maquiller** to put on one's make-up; **se maquiller les yeux** to put one's eye make-up on

LE **marais** *noun* marsh

LE **marbre** *noun* marble *(stone, sculpture)*

LE **marchand,** LA **marchande** *noun*
(**a**) shopkeeper; **il est marchand** he's a shopkeeper
(**b**) stallholder
(**c**) dealer *(of furniture)*
(**d**) merchant *(of wine, cheese)*

marchander *verb* to haggle, to bargain

LA **marchandise** *noun* goods; **on lui a volé toute sa marchandise** all his goods were stolen; **des marchandises de qualité** quality goods

LA **marche** *noun*
(**a**) step; **attention à la marche!** mind the step!; **monter les marches** to go up the stairs
(**b**) walking; **elle fait de la marche** she goes walking

(**c**) walk; **une marche de cinq kilomètres** a five-kilometre walk
(**d**) march
(**e**) working, running; **en bon état de marche** in good working order; **la machine est en marche** the machine is running
(**f**) **mettre en marche** to start *(a machine, an engine)*; **un véhicule en marche** a moving vehicle
(**g**) **faire marche arrière** to reverse *(in a car)*

LE **marché** *noun*
(**a**) market
(**b**) deal; **conclure un marché avec quelqu'un** to make a deal with somebody; **marché conclu!** it's a deal!
(**c**) **bon marché** cheap; **meilleur marché** cheaper; **des chaussures bon marché** cheap shoes

> The phrases *bon marché* and *meilleur marché* do not change in the plural or in the feminine.

marcher *verb*
(**a**) to walk
(**b**) to step *(in a puddle, on somebody's feet)*
(**c**) to work; **ça ne marche pas** it's not working
(**d**) to be going well; **les affaires marchent** business is going well
(**e**) to fall for it; **elle a marché** she fell for it; **faire marcher quelqu'un** to pull somebody's leg, to wind somebody up; **tu me fais marcher?** are you winding me up?

> Sense (e) is an informal use of *marcher*.

LE **mardi** *noun* Tuesday; **elle est venue mardi** she came on Tuesday; **il fait du tennis le mardi** he plays tennis on Tuesdays; **tous les mardis** every Tuesday; **Mardi gras** Shrove Tuesday, Pancake Day

> In French, the names of days are not written with a capital.

Mardi Gras

This is a very popular festival in France, falling on the eve of Ash Wednesday. On this day, *crêpes* are prepared and eaten, and children dress up at school.

LA **mare** *noun* pond

LA **marée** *noun*
(a) tide
(b) **une marée noire** an oil slick

LA **marge** *noun* margin

LE **mari** *noun* husband

LE **mariage** *noun*
(a) marriage
(b) wedding

marié, mariée
1 *adjective* married
2 *noun* **le marié** the groom; **la mariée** the bride; **les mariés** the bride and groom

marier
1 *verb* to marry; **le curé du village les a mariés** the local vicar married them
2 *reflexive verb* **se marier**
(a) to get married; **elle s'est mariée avec Pascal** she got married to Pascal
(b) **ces couleurs se marient bien** these colours go well together

marin, marine
1 *adjective* sea; **l'air marin** the sea air
2 *masculine noun* **un marin** a sailor; **il est marin** he's a sailor; **un marin pêcheur** a deep-sea fisherman
3 *feminine noun* **la marine** the navy; **bleu marine** navy blue

Note that the phrase *bleu marine* does not change in the plural: *des chaussettes bleu marine.*

LA **marionnette** *noun* puppet

LA **marmite** *noun* cooking pot

LE **Maroc** *noun* Morocco

LE **Marocain**, LA **Marocaine** *noun* (*person*) Moroccan

marocain, marocaine *adjective* Moroccan; **la cuisine marocaine** Moroccan food

In French, only the noun for the inhabitants of a country takes a capital letter, never the adjective.

LA **marque** *noun*
(a) mark; **une marque au crayon** a pencil mark; **on voit encore la marque du coup qu'il a reçu** you can still see where he was hit
(b) brand (*of a product*); make (*of a car*)
(c) **à vos marques! prêts! partez!** ready! steady! go!

marquer *verb*
(a) to mark; **est-ce que je la marque absente?** shall I mark her absent?
(b) to write; **marquez votre nom en haut à gauche** write your name in the top left-hand corner
(c) to score; **marquer un but** to score a goal; **marquer un point** to score a point
(d) to affect, to make an impression on; **ce film m'a beaucoup marqué** that film made a big impression on me

LA **marraine** *noun* godmother

marrant, marrante *adjective* funny

This word is informal.

marre *adverb* **en avoir marre** to be fed up; **ils en ont marre de travailler** they're fed up working; **il en a marre des études** he's fed up with studying; **j'en ai marre de l'école** I'm fed up with school; **j'en ai marre!** I've had enough!

This word is informal.

marron
1 *adjective* brown

Note that the adjective *marron* does not change in the plural or in the feminine: *des chaussures marron, une jupe marron.*

2 *masculine noun*
(a) **un marron** a chestnut; **des marrons chauds** roasted chestnuts
(b) **le marron** brown; **le marron est**

ma couleur préférée brown is my favourite colour

LE **marronnier** *noun* (horse) chestnut tree

mars *masculine noun* March; **le premier mars** the first of March; **le 6 mars** the 6th of March

> In French, the names of months are not written with a capital.

LE **marteau** *noun* hammer

> The plural of *marteau* is *marteaux*.

masculin, masculine *adjective*
(a) masculine
(b) male
(c) men's; **le tennis masculin** men's tennis

LE **masque** *noun* mask; **un masque de plongée** a diving mask

LA **masse** *noun*
(a) mass; **une masse de cheveux** a mass of hair
(b) **des masses** *(informal phrase)* masses, lots; **il y avait des masses de livres** there were masses of books; **des amis, il n'en a pas des masses** he hasn't got that many friends

masser *verb* to massage; **se faire masser** to be massaged

mat, mate *adjective*
(a) matt *(paint, photo)*
(b) olive *(skin, complexion)*
(c) **le roi est mat** the king has been checkmated; **échec et mat!** checkmate!

LE **mât** *noun*
(a) mast *(on a ship)*
(b) flagpole

> The *t* in *mât* is not pronounced.

LE **matelas** *noun* mattress; **un matelas pneumatique** an air mattress, an air bed

matériel, matérielle
1 *adjective* material
2 *masculine noun* **le matériel**
(a) equipment; **le matériel agricole** agricultural equipment; **le matériel de bureau** office equipment
(b) material; **le matériel pédagogique** teaching materials
(c) hardware; **le matériel informatique** computer hardware

maternel, maternelle
1 *adjective*
(a) maternal; **mon grand-père maternel** my maternal grandfather, my grandfather on my mother's side
(b) motherly
2 *feminine noun* **la maternelle** nursery school

> **La Maternelle**
> Nursery education for children from 2 to 6 years old is provided by the state and is available to all families in France. Although it is not compulsory, the vast majority of children go there and are thus well-prepared for entry into primary school.

LES **mathématiques** *feminine plural noun* mathematics

LA **matière** *noun*
(a) subject *(at school)*
(b) material; **les matières premières** raw materials; **la matière plastique** plastic
(c) matter; **il n'y a pas là matière à rire** this is no laughing matter
(d) **les matières grasses** fat; **il y a beaucoup de matières grasses dans les frites** chips are high in fat

LE **matin** *noun* morning; **ce matin** this morning; **à huit heures du matin** at eight o'clock in the morning

LA **matinée** *noun* morning; **dans la matinée** in the morning; **en fin de matinée** at the end of the morning

LA **matraque** *noun* truncheon

mauvais, mauvaise
1 *adjective*
(a) bad; **je suis mauvais en maths** I'm bad at maths; **mauvaise nouvelle, elle ne vient plus** I've got bad news, she's

not coming any more; **elle a mauvaise haleine** she has bad breath; **il a une mauvaise vue** he's got bad eyesight

(**b**) poor; **il est en mauvaise santé** he's in poor health; **un produit de mauvaise qualité** a poor-quality product

(**c**) nasty; **il a l'air mauvais** he looks nasty; **il a attrapé un mauvais rhume** he caught a nasty cold

(**d**) wrong; **une mauvaise réponse** a wrong answer; **tu vas dans la mauvaise direction** you're going the wrong way

(**e**) **la balle est mauvaise** *(in sport)* the ball is out

2 *adverb* **mauvais** bad; **ça sent mauvais** it smells bad; **il fait mauvais** the weather's bad

LES maux *masculine plural noun* **des maux de tête** headaches; **des maux de ventre** stomach pains

Maux is the plural of *mal.*

maximum

1 *adjective* maximum; **la vitesse maximum** the maximum speed, the top speed

2 *masculine noun*

(**a**) maximum; **on a mis le chauffage au maximum** we turned the heating on full

(**b**) utmost; **je ferai le maximum pour finir à temps** I'll do my utmost to finish on time

(**c**) **au maximum** at the most; **deux jours au maximum** two days at the most; **au grand maximum** at the very most

me *pronoun*

(**a**) me; **il me connaît** he knows me; **il m'aime** he loves me

(**b**) to me; **il me l'a donné** he gave it to me

(**c**) myself; **je me suis brûlé** I burned myself

(**d**) **je me lave les mains** I'm washing my hands; **je me suis cassé le bras** I broke my arm

Me becomes *m'* in front of a vowel or a mute h. Note that there are many cases when *me* is simply not translated in English, as in *je me souviens* (I remember), *je me rase* (I shave) and *je me lève* (I get up).

LE mécanicien, LA mécanicienne *noun* mechanic; **il est mécanicien** he's a mechanic

mécanique

1 *adjective*

(**a**) mechanical

(**b**) wind-up *(toy, watch)*

2 *feminine noun* **la mécanique** mechanics

Note that the English word *mechanic* is never a translation for the French word *mécanique.*

LE mécanisme *noun* mechanism

LA méchanceté *noun*

(**a**) nastiness, malice

(**b**) nasty thing; **il m'a dit des méchancetés** he said nasty things to me

méchant, méchante

1 *adjective*

(**a**) nasty; **elle est méchante avec son petit frère** she's nasty to her little brother

(**b**) wicked; **il n'est pas méchant** he's harmless

(**c**) naughty *(child)*

(**d**) vicious *(animal)*; **attention chien méchant** beware of the dog

2 *noun* **un méchant, une méchante** a baddy *(in a story)*

LA mèche *noun*

(**a**) lock, strand *(of hair)*

(**b**) wick *(of a candle)*

(**c**) fuse *(of a bomb)*

mécontent, mécontente *adjective* dissatisfied, unhappy

LA Mecque *noun* Mecca

LA médaille *noun* medal

LE médecin *noun* doctor; **elle est médecin** she's a doctor

The word *médecin* does not have a feminine but it can also refer to a woman.

LA **médecine** *noun* medicine *(science)*; **un étudiant en médecine** a medical student

Note that the French word *médecine* is never used to refer to tablets or other medical drugs.

LE **médicament** *noun* medicine *(drug)*

médiocre *adjective* poor, second-rate

LA **Méditerranée** *noun* the Mediterranean

LA **méduse** *noun* jellyfish

méfiant, méfiante *adjective* distrustful, suspicious

se méfier *reflexive verb*
(a) to be careful
(b) **se méfier de quelqu'un** to distrust somebody, to be suspicious of somebody; **méfie-toi de lui** don't trust him

LE **mégot** *noun* cigarette butt

meilleur, meilleure
1 *adjective*
(a) better; **elle est meilleure que lui** she is better than him
(b) best; **c'est le meilleur élève de la classe** he's the best student in the class; **ma meilleure amie** my best friend
2 *noun* **le meilleur, la meilleure** the best one; **j'ai choisi les meilleurs** I chose the best ones; **tu es le meilleur!** you're the best!

LE **mélange** *noun* mixture

mélanger
1 *verb*
(a) to mix *(ingredients)*
(b) to shuffle *(cards)*
(c) to mix up; **ne mélange pas tout** don't get everything mixed up
2 *reflexive verb* **se mélanger**
(a) to mix; **l'eau et l'huile ne se mélangent pas bien** water and oil don't mix well
(b) to get mixed up

LA **mêlée** *noun* scrum, scrummage

mêler
1 *verb*
(a) to mix, to combine
(b) **mêler quelqu'un à la conversation** to bring somebody into the conversation
(c) **être mêlé à un scandale** to be involved in a scandal
2 *reflexive verb* **se mêler**
(a) **se mêler de quelque chose** to interfere in something; **mêle-toi de tes affaires!** *(informal phrase)* mind your own business!
(b) **se mêler à la foule** to mingle with the crowd
(c) **se mêler à la conversation** to take part in the conversation

LE **membre** *noun*
(a) member
(b) limb *(of the body)*

même
1 *adjective*
(a) same; **elles sont nées le même jour** they were born on the same day; **il a le même âge que moi** he's the same age as me; **faire de même** to do the same, to do likewise
(b) very; **ils sont repartis le soir même** they left that very evening; **il habite ici même** he lives in this very place
(c) **moi-même** myself; **toi-même** yourself; **lui-même** himself, itself; **elle-même** herself, itself; **soi-même** oneself; **nous-mêmes** ourselves; **vous-même** yourself; **vous-mêmes** yourselves; **eux-mêmes, elles-mêmes** themselves
2 *pronoun* **le même, la même** the same one; **ce sont toujours les mêmes qui gagnent** it's always the same ones who win
3 *adverb* even; **même Paul est d'accord** even Paul agrees; **je ne sais même pas l'heure qu'il est** I don't even know what time it is; **même s'il pleut** even if it rains

LA mémé *noun*
(**a**) grandma, granny
(**b**) old lady

This word is informal.

mémoire
1 *feminine noun* **la mémoire** memory
2 *masculine noun*
(**a**) **un mémoire** a thesis, a dissertation *(at university)*
(**b**) **des mémoires** memoirs *(in literature)*

LA menace *noun* threat

menacer *verb* to threaten

LE ménage *noun*
(**a**) housework, cleaning
(**b**) couple; **être heureux en ménage** to be happily married; **ils se sont mis en ménage** they've moved in together

ménager, ménagère
1 *adjective* household; **les appareils ménagers** household appliances
2 *feminine noun* **une ménagère** a housewife

LE mendiant, LA mendiante *noun* beggar

mendier *verb* to beg

mener *verb*
(**a**) to lead *(a race, a team)*; **cette porte mène à la cave** this door leads to the cellar; **elle mène une vie heureuse** she leads a happy life; **l'équipe locale mène par 3 buts à 0** the local team is leading by 3 goals to nil
(**b**) to conduct *(a campaign, an inquiry, negotiations)*
(**c**) **mener à bien un projet** to carry out a plan

LES menottes *feminine plural noun* handcuffs; **passer les menottes à quelqu'un** to handcuff somebody

LE mensonge *noun* lie; **elle dit des mensonges** she's telling lies

mensuel, mensuelle *adjective* monthly

LE menteur, LA menteuse *noun* liar

LA menthe *noun* mint; **des bonbons à la menthe** mints; **une menthe à l'eau** a glass of mint cordial

mentir *verb* to lie; **tu mens!** you're lying!

See verb table p. 322.

LE menton *noun* chin

menu¹, menue *adjective*
(**a**) slim *(person)*
(**b**) small *(person, object)*

LE menu² *noun*
(**a**) menu *(in a restaurant, on a computer)*
(**b**) set meal

LE menuisier *noun* joiner, carpenter; **il est menuisier** he's a joiner

LE mépris *noun* contempt, scorn

mépriser *verb* to look down on, to despise

LA mer *noun*
(**a**) sea; **ils sont partis en mer** they've gone out to sea; **la mer Méditerranée** the Mediterranean Sea; **la mer du Nord** the North Sea
(**b**) seaside; **aller à la mer** to go to the seaside; **au bord de la mer** at the seaside

merci *exclamation* thank you; **merci pour votre lettre** thanks for your letter; **merci d'avoir répondu** thanks for answering; **merci beaucoup** thank you very much, thanks a lot

LE mercredi *noun* Wednesday; **elle est venue mercredi** she came on Wednesday; **il fait du tennis le mercredi** he plays tennis on Wednesdays; **tous les mercredis** every Wednesday

In French, the names of days are not written with a capital.

LA mère *noun* mother

mériter *verb* to deserve

LE merle *noun* blackbird

LA merveille *noun*
(**a**) marvel, wonder; **les merveilles de**

la **technologie** the wonders of technology; **faire des merveilles** to work wonders
(**b**) **à merveille** marvellously, wonderfully; **ils s'entendent à merveille** they get on like a house on fire

merveilleux, merveilleuse *adjective*
(**a**) wonderful, marvellous
(**b**) magical; **une histoire merveilleuse** a magical story

mes *adjective* my; **mes parents** my parents; **mes livres** my books; **mes valises** my suitcases

> *Mes* is used in front of plural nouns. It is the plural of *ma* and *mon*. See also **ma** and **mon**.

Mesdames *feminine plural noun*
(**a**) ladies; **bonjour Mesdames!** good morning, ladies!; **Mesdames, Mesdemoiselles, Messieurs!** ladies and gentlemen!
(**b**) **Mesdames Duval et Lamiel** Mrs Duval and Mrs Lamiel

> *Mesdames* is the plural of *Madame*. Note that the word *Mesdames* is very commonly used in French when addressing strangers and will not always need a translation in English: *je peux vous aider, Mesdames?* can I help you?

Mesdemoiselles *feminine plural noun*
(**a**) ladies; **bonjour Mesdemoiselles!** good morning, ladies!; **Mesdemoiselles, un peu de silence, s'il vous plaît!** ladies, would you please be quiet!
(**b**) Misses; **Mesdemoiselles Duval** the Misses Duval; **Mesdemoiselles Duval et Jonville** Miss Duval and Miss Jonville

> *Mesdemoiselles* is the plural of *Mademoiselle*. Note that the word *Mesdemoiselles* is very commonly used in French when addressing strangers and will not always need a translation in English: *je peux vous aider, Mesdemoiselles?* can I help you?

LA **messagerie** *noun*
(**a**) **une messagerie électronique** an e-mail; **la messagerie vocale** voice mail
(**b**) **les messageries** the parcels service

LA **messe** *noun*
(**a**) Mass; **aller à la messe** to go to Mass
(**b**) **faire des messes basses** to whisper

messieurs *masculine plural noun*
(**a**) Sirs; **Messieurs** *(in a letter)* Dear Sirs
(**b**) Messrs; **Messieurs Thon et Lamiel** Messrs Thon and Lamiel
(**c**) gentlemen; **bonjour Messieurs!** good morning, gentlemen!; **Mesdames, Mesdemoiselles, Messieurs!** ladies and gentlemen!

> *Messieurs* is pronounced "méssieu". *Messieurs* is the plural of *Monsieur*. Note that *Messieurs* is very commonly used in French when addressing strangers and will not always need a translation in English: *je peux vous aider, Messieurs?* can I help you?

LA **mesure** *noun*
(**a**) measurement; **prendre les mesures de quelque chose** to take the measurements of something
(**b**) measure; **une mesure d'urgence** an emergency measure; **par mesure de sécurité** as a safety precaution; **nous avons pris des mesures** we took action
(**c**) **un costume sur mesure** a made-to-measure suit
(**d**) extent; **dans une certaine mesure** to some extent
(**e**) time *(in music)*; **battre la mesure** to beat time
(**f**) **elle a un adversaire à sa mesure** she's got an opponent who is a match for her
(**g**) **à mesure que** as; **à mesure que le temps passe** as time goes by

mesurer
1 *verb*
(a) to measure
(b) **combien mesures-tu?** how tall are you?; **il mesure presque deux mètres** he's almost two metres tall
(c) **mesure tes paroles** be careful what you say
(d) **il ne mesure pas sa force** he doesn't know his own strength
2 *reflexive verb* **se mesurer** se mesurer à quelqu'un to have a confrontation with somebody, to pit oneself against somebody

LE **métal** *noun* metal

The plural of *métal* is *métaux*.

LA **météo** *noun* weather forecast

LA **méthode** *noun*
(a) method
(b) manual, book; **une méthode d'anglais** an English course book

LE **métier** *noun* job

LE **mètre** *noun*
(a) metre; **un mètre carré** a square metre; **un mètre cube** a cubic metre; **le 400 mètres** the 400 metres, the 400-metre race
(b) metre rule; **un mètre pliant** a folding rule; **un mètre à ruban** a tape measure

LE **métro** *noun* underground *(railway)*

Le Métro
The *métro* is the underground system in Paris and other big cities. Most of the stations are entirely underground, and their entrances are known as *bouches de métro*. People refer to the lines in Paris mainly by their number and not by their name. The last stop indicates the direction of travel. For example, line 6 goes from *Charles de Gaulle Étoile* station to *Nation* station. A French speaker would say for example *je prends la 6 direction Nation*.

mets *see* mettre
je mets le couvert I'm laying the table; **tu mets quelle robe pour le mariage?** which dress are you wearing for the wedding?

Mets is a form of the verb *mettre* in the present tense. See verb table p. 322.

mettre
1 *verb*
(a) to put
(b) to put on *(clothes, the heating, music)*
(c) to take; **il a mis trois heures à faire ses devoirs** he took three hours to do his homework
(d) to give; **le prof d'histoire m'a mis une bonne note** the history teacher gave me a good mark
(e) **mettre le couvert** to lay the table
2 *reflexive verb* **se mettre**
(a) to go; **où se mettent les tasses?** where do the cups go?
(b) to stand; **se mettre debout** to stand up; **il s'est mis juste devant moi** he came and stood right in front of me
(c) to sit; **mets-toi sur cette chaise** sit on that chair; **se mettre à table** to sit down at the table
(d) **se mettre sur le dos** to lie down on one's back; **se mettre sur le ventre** to lie down on one's stomach
(e) to put on; **se mettre du parfum** to put on some perfume; **se mettre en pantalon** to put on a pair of trousers; **elle se met toujours en jupe** she always wears a skirt
(f) **se mettre avec quelqu'un** to team up with somebody
(g) **se mettre à faire quelque chose** to start doing something; **il s'est mis à rire** he started laughing; **on s'est mis au travail** we set to work

The past participle of *mettre* is *mis(e)*. See verb table p. 322.

LE **meuble** *noun* piece of furniture; **des meubles** furniture; **un meuble de salon** a piece of living-room furniture

meubler *verb*
(**a**) to furnish *(a room)*; **un apparte-ment meublé** *or* **un meublé** a fur-nished flat
(**b**) **meubler la conversation** to make conversation

LA meule *noun* stack; **une meule de foin** a haystack

LE meurtre *noun* murder

meurtrier, meurtrière
1 *adjective* deadly, murderous; **un at-tentat meurtrier** a murderous attack; **une route meurtrière** a very danger-ous road
2 *noun* **le meurtrier** the murderer; **la meurtrière** the murderess

Mexico *noun* Mexico City

LE Mexique *noun* Mexico

miauler *verb* to miaow, to mew

LE micro *noun* mike

LE microbe *noun* germ; **j'ai attrapé un microbe** I caught a bug

LE micro-ondes *noun* microwave

The word *micro-ondes* does not change in the plural.

midi *masculine noun*
(**a**) lunchtime; **je joue au badminton à midi** I play badminton at lunchtime; **il mange des pâtes tous les midis** he has pasta for lunch every day
(**b**) midday, twelve o'clock, noon; **il est midi** it's midday, it's twelve o'clock; **midi et quart** a quarter past twelve; **midi et demi** half-past twelve; **midi vingt** twenty past twelve; **midi moins vingt** twenty to twelve
(**c**) south; **exposé au midi** south-facing; **le Midi de la France** the South of France; **l'accent du Midi** the south-ern French accent

LA mie *noun* soft part of the bread *(as opposed to the crust)*

LE miel *noun* honey

mien, mienne *pronoun* **le mien, la mienne, les miens, les miennes** mine;

ce crayon, c'est le mien this pencil is mine; **ce n'est pas votre place, c'est la mienne** it's not your seat, it's mine; **ses parents et les miens** his parents and mine

In French, possessive pronouns have the same gender and the same num-ber as the nouns they stand for, eg the corresponding pronoun for *mes pa-rents* is *les miens* because the word *parents* is masculine plural.

LA miette *noun*
(**a**) crumb; **des miettes de pain** bread-crumbs
(**b**) **une miette de quelque chose** a little bit of something
(**c**) **mettre quelque chose en miettes** to smash something to pieces

mieux
1 *adverb*
(**a**) better; **elle va mieux** she's better; **elle travaille de mieux en mieux** she's working better and better; **elle a changé en mieux** she changed for the better; **moins je le vois, mieux je me porte!** the less I see of him, the better I feel!
(**b**) **le mieux, la mieux, les mieux** the best; **c'est elle qui chante le mieux** she sings the best; **ce sont eux les mieux payés** they are the best paid
2 *adjective* **ce livre est mieux que celui-là** this book is better than that one; **c'est mieux que rien** it's better than nothing; **tu n'as rien de mieux à faire?** have you got nothing better to do?
3 *masculine noun*
(**a**) **il y a du mieux** there's some im-provement
(**b**) **le mieux, c'est de partir un peu plus tôt** it's best to leave a bit earlier; **je fais de mon mieux** I do my best; **fais pour le mieux!** do what's best!
(**c**) **je m'attendais à mieux** I was ex-pecting better
(**d**) **il est au mieux de sa forme** he's on top form

mignon, mignonne *adjective*
(**a**) cute
(**b**) pretty
(**c**) lovely; **il est mignon, ton apparte-ment** you've got a lovely little flat
(**d**) sweet; **il m'a apporté des fleurs, c'était mignon comme tout** he brought me flowers, it was so sweet of him

LE **milieu** *noun*
(**a**) middle; **la table du milieu** the middle table; **au milieu de la pièce** in the middle of the room; **au milieu de la nuit** in the middle of the night
(**b**) medium; **le juste milieu** a happy medium
(**c**) environment; **le milieu familial** the home environment

> The plural of *milieu* is *milieux*.

militaire
1 *adjective* military, service; **tous les personnels militaires** all service personnel
2 *masculine noun* **un militaire** a soldier, a serviceman; **il est militaire** he's a soldier

mille
1 *adjective*
(**a**) a thousand; **mille hommes** a thousand men; **dix mille** ten thousand; **cent mille** a hundred thousand; **l'an deux mille** the year two thousand
(**b**) many; **mille mercis** many thanks
(**c**) **casser quelque chose en mille morceaux** to smash something to pieces
2 *masculine noun*
(**a**) a thousand; **une chance sur mille** a one-in-a-thousand chance
(**b**) bull's eye; **en plein dans le mille!** bull's eye!
(**c**) nautical mile

> *Mille* does not change in the plural, except when it is a unit of measure as in 2 (c).

LE **milliard** *noun* billion

LE **millier** *noun* thousand; **un millier de personnes** about a thousand people; **des milliers de papillons** thousands of butterflies; **ils sont arrivés par milliers** they arrived in their thousands

LE **millimètre** *noun* millimetre

LE **million** *noun* million; **un million de personnes** a million people; **deux millions** two million

mince
1 *adjective*
(**a**) thin *(layer, slice)*
(**b**) slim *(person)*
2 *exclamation*
(**a**) *(surprise)* **mince!** *or* **mince alors!** wow!, blimey!
(**b**) *(annoyance)* **mince! j'ai perdu mes clés** damn! I've lost my keys

LA **mine** *noun*
(**a**) lead *(of a pencil)*
(**b**) mine; **une mine de charbon** a coal mine; **une mine d'or** a gold mine
(**c**) look, expression; **une mine boudeuse** a sulky expression; **avoir bonne mine** to look well; **il a mauvaise mine** he doesn't look very well
(**d**) **ne fais pas mine de ne pas comprendre** don't pretend you don't understand; **elle a fait mine de raccrocher** she made as if to hang up

mineur, mineure
1 *adjective*
(**a**) minor; **un incident mineur** a minor incident
(**b**) **être mineur** to be under age
2 *noun* **un mineur, une mineure** a minor; **cet établissement est interdit aux mineurs** people under 18 are not allowed in this establishment
3 *masculine noun* **un mineur** a miner; **il est mineur** he's a miner

minimum
1 *adjective* minimum; **le poids minimum** the minimum weight
2 *masculine noun*
(**a**) minimum; **mets le chauffage au minimum** turn the heating down as low as it'll go
(**b**) least; **c'est vraiment le minimum**

que tu puisses faire pour elle it's the least you can do for her
(**c**) **au minimum** at the least; **deux jours au minimum** at least two days

LE/LA **ministre** *noun* minister; **le Premier ministre** the Prime Minister

LE **minitel**® *noun* minitel®

Le Minitel

This service run by *France Télécom* (the French equivalent of BT) allows subscribers to view all kinds of information at home. Using a monitor and keyboard provided free by *France Télécom*, subscribers dial a four-digit number (typically 3615), followed by a code word to access a particular service. Some *Minitel* services are purely informative (the weather, road conditions, news etc), while others are interactive (enabling users to carry out bank transactions or book travel tickets, for example). The *Minitel* also serves as an electronic telephone directory. Nowadays, most *Minitel* services are available on the Internet.

---

minuit *masculine noun* midnight, twelve o'clock; **il est minuit** it's midnight, it's twelve o'clock; **minuit et quart** a quarter past midnight; **minuit et demi** half-past midnight; **minuit vingt** twenty past midnight; **minuit moins vingt** twenty to midnight

minuscule
1 *adjective*
(**a**) tiny, minute
(**b**) small; **un b minuscule** a small b; **en lettres minuscules** in small letters
2 *feminine noun* **une minuscule** a small letter

LA **minute** *noun* minute

LA **minuterie** *noun*
(**a**) timer *(of a cooker)*
(**b**) time switch; **il y a une minuterie dans l'escalier** the stair light is on a time switch

minutieux, minutieuse *adjective*
(**a**) meticulous *(person)*
(**b**) thorough, detailed *(work)*

LE **miroir** *noun* mirror

mis, mise¹ *see* **mettre**
ne cherche pas la cafetière, je l'ai mise dans le placard don't look for the coffee pot, I put it in the cupboard

Mis (e) is the past participle of the verb *mettre*. See verb table p. 322.

LA **mise²** *noun*
(**a**) stake *(in gambling)*
(**b**) **mise à feu** firing *(of a missile)*; launch *(of a rocket)*
(**c**) **mise à jour** update, updating
(**d**) **mise en marche** *or* **mise en route** starting up
(**e**) **mise en page** layout *(of a book)*; editing *(of text on a computer)*
(**f**) **mise en place** setting up
(**g**) **mise au point** clarification; *(of a document)* finalizing; *(of a machine)* tuning; *(of a camera)* focusing
(**h**) **mise en scène** production *(of a play, a film)*
(**i**) **mise en vente** sale; *(of a product)* launch

miser *verb*
(**a**) to bet; **j'ai misé sur ce cheval** I bet on that horse; **il a misé vingt euros** he bet twenty euros
(**b**) **elle mise sur le succès de son livre pour s'acheter une maison** she's counting on her book being a success so she can buy a house

LA **misère** *noun*
(**a**) poverty; **être dans la misère** to be poverty-stricken
(**b**) pittance; **il gagne une misère** he earns a pittance
(**c**) **des misères** trifles, minor irritations; **faire des misères à quelqu'un** to torment somebody

Note that the English word *misery* is never a translation for the French word *misère*.

mi-temps
1 *feminine noun*
(**a**) half *(in sport)*; **la première mi-temps** the first half; **la seconde**

mi-temps the second half
(**b**) half-time *(in sport)*; **le score est de 0 à 0 à la mi-temps** the half-time score is nil nil
2 *adverb* **à mi-temps** part-time; **un travail à mi-temps** a part-time job; **travailler à mi-temps** to work part-time

LA **mitraillette** *noun* submachine gun

LA **mitrailleuse** *noun* machine gun

mixte *adjective* mixed; **une équipe mixte** a mixed team

Mlle Miss

Mlle is the abbreviation of *Mademoiselle*.

Mme Mrs

Mme is the abbreviation of *Madame*.

LE **mobilier** *noun* furniture

LA **mobylette**® *noun* moped; **il y va en mobylette**® he goes there on his moped

moche *adjective*
(**a**) ugly
(**b**) rotten; **c'est moche ce qui lui est arrivé** it was rotten what happened to him

This word is informal.

mode
1 *feminine noun* **la mode** fashion; **c'est passé de mode** it's out of fashion; **ce sont des gens à la mode** they're very fashionable
2 *masculine noun*
(**a**) mode
(**b**) instructions; **un mode d'emploi** directions for use
(**c**) **un mode de paiement** method of payment
(**d**) **un mode de vie** a lifestyle

LE **modèle** *noun*
(**a**) model *(example)*
(**b**) pattern
(**c**) design; **une voiture dernier modèle** a car of the latest design

(**d**) **un modèle réduit** a small-scale model

moderne *adjective* modern

modeste *adjective* modest

LA **moelle** *noun* (bone) marrow; **la moelle épinière** the spinal cord

Moelle is pronounced "moual".

moelleux, moelleuse *adjective*
(**a**) soft; **des coussins moelleux** soft cushions
(**b**) tender *(meat)*
(**c**) moist *(cake)*
(**d**) smooth *(cheese)*

Moelleux is pronounced "moualeu" and *moelleuse* is pronounced "moualeuz".

moi *pronoun*
(**a**) me, to me; **appelle-moi ce soir** call me tonight; **donne-le-moi** give it to me; **c'est à cause de moi** it's because of me; **elle travaille mieux que moi** she works better than me; **un ami à moi** a friend of mine; **ce livre n'est pas à moi** this book is not mine
(**b**) I; **il aime le cinéma, moi non** he likes the cinema, I don't; **moi, je comprends très bien** I understand perfectly; **c'est moi qui lui ai dit de venir** I was the one who told him to come
(**c**) myself; **j'étais content de moi** I was pleased with myself

moi-même *pronoun* myself; **je l'ai écrit moi-même** I wrote it myself

moindre *adjective*
(**a**) lesser; **de moindre importance** of lesser importance
(**b**) **le moindre, la moindre** the least, the slightest; **je n'ai pas la moindre chance** I haven't got the slightest chance; **je n'en ai pas la moindre idée** I haven't the faintest idea; **dis merci, c'est la moindre des choses!** the least you could do is say thank you!

LE **moine** *noun* monk

LE **moineau** *noun* sparrow

The plural of *moineau* is *moineaux*.

moins
1 *adverb*
(**a**) less; **il travaille moins que sa sœur** he works less than his sister; **je suis moins patient que toi** I'm less patient than you are; **c'est moins bien que l'an dernier** it's not as good as last year; **tu as moins de livres que moi** you have fewer books than me; **moins de temps** less time; **moins de gens** fewer people; **moins d'un kilo** less than a kilo; **un de moins** one less; **deux heures de moins** two hours less; **j'ai trois ans de moins que vous** I'm three years younger than you; **de moins en moins** less and less; **en moins d'une heure** in less than an hour
(**b**) the less; **moins on mange, moins on grossit** the less you eat, the less weight you put on
(**c**) **le moins, la moins, les moins** the least; **c'est elle la moins riche des trois** she's the least wealthy of the three; **les moins chers** the least expensive ones; **le moins possible** as little as possible; **c'est celui que j'aime le moins** it's the one I like the least; **c'est lui qui fait le moins de bruit** he makes the least noise
(**d**) **au moins** at least
(**e**) **de moins** *or* **en moins** missing; **il y a une chaise de moins** *or* **en moins** there's one chair missing
(**f**) **à moins que** unless; **à moins qu'elle ne parte** unless she leaves
2 *preposition*
(**a**) minus; **10 moins 8 égalent 2** 10 minus 8 makes 2
(**b**) to; **il est dix heures moins vingt** it's twenty to ten

LE **mois** *noun* month; **au mois de mars** in March; **tous les mois** every month

LA **moisson** *noun* harvest

moite *adjective*
(**a**) muggy *(air)*
(**b**) clammy *(hands)*

LA **moitié** *noun* half; **la moitié des élèves** half the pupils; **une moitié de poulet** half a chicken; **réduire quelque chose de moitié** to reduce something by half; **à moitié endormi** half-asleep

LA **molaire** *noun* molar

molle *see* **mou**

LE **mollet** *noun* calf *(part of the leg)*

LE **moment** *noun*
(**a**) moment; **il a eu un moment d'hésitation** he hesitated for a moment; **au moment de son départ** when he was leaving; **juste au moment où le téléphone a sonné** just when the phone rang
(**b**) time; **arriver au bon moment** to come at the right time; **nous avons eu de bons moments** we had some good times
(**c**) **il va arriver d'un moment à l'autre** he's going to arrive any minute now

The *t* in *moment* is not pronounced.

mon *adjective* my; **mon père** my father; **mon livre** my book; **mon amie** my friend

Mon is used in front of masculine nouns, as well as before feminine nouns starting with a vowel or a mute h, as in *mon école, mon histoire*. The plural of *mon* is *mes* and the feminine is *ma*. See also **ma** and **mes**.

LE **monde** *noun*
(**a**) world; **le monde entier** the whole world; **le plus célèbre du monde** the most famous in the world; **le monde des affaires** the business world; **le monde du spectacle** the world of showbusiness
(**b**) people; **tu attends du monde?** are you expecting people?; **beaucoup de monde** a lot of people; **pas grand monde** not many people
(**c**) **tout le monde** everybody

mondial, mondiale
1 *adjective* worldwide, world; **la population mondiale** the world population

2 *masculine noun* **le Mondial** *(in football)* the World Cup

The masculine plural of *mondial* is *mondiaux*.

LA **mondialisation** *noun* globalization

LA **monnaie** *noun*
(**a**) currency
(**b**) change *(money)*; **faire de la monnaie** to get some change; **il m'a rendu la monnaie sur dix euros** he gave me the change from ten euros

Note that the English word *money* is never a translation for the French word *monnaie*.

Monsieur *masculine noun*
(**a**) Sir; **Monsieur** *(in a letter)* Dear Sir; **et voilà, Monsieur, le plat du jour!** here you are, Sir, today's special!
(**b**) Mr; **bonjour Monsieur Leroy!** good morning, Mr Leroy!
(**c**) **un monsieur** a man, a gentleman; **un monsieur vous a demandé** a man was asking for you

Monsieur is pronounced "meussieu". The plural of *Monsieur* is *Messieurs*. Note that *Monsieur* is very commonly used in French when addressing strangers and will not always need a translation in English: *je peux vous aider, Monsieur?* can I help you?

LE **monstre** *noun* monster

monstrueux, monstrueuse *adjective* monstrous

LE **montage** *noun*
(**a**) assembly *(of furniture)*
(**b**) installation *(of a machine)*
(**c**) editing *(of a film)*

LA **montagne** *noun*
(**a**) mountain; **aller à la montagne** to go to the mountains
(**b**) **les montagnes russes** the big dipper
(**c**) **il en a fait toute une montagne** he made a big song and dance about it

montant, montante
1 *adjective*
(**a**) rising
(**b**) **un col montant** a high neck *(of a jumper)*; **des chaussures montantes** ankle boots
2 *masculine noun* **le montant**
(**a**) amount, sum; **écrivez le montant sur le chèque** write the amount on the cheque
(**b**) **le montant de la porte** the door jamb

LA **montée** *noun*
(**a**) uphill slope; **en haut de la montée** at the top of the hill
(**b**) climb; **la montée jusqu'au chalet** the climb up to the chalet
(**c**) rise; **la montée des prix** the rise in prices; **la montée des eaux** the rise in the water level

monter
1 *verb*
(**a**) to go up, to come up; **je suis monté au grenier** I went up to the attic; **j'ai monté les escaliers** I went up the stairs
(**b**) to go upstairs, to come upstairs
(**c**) to rise; **les prix montent** prices are rising
(**d**) to climb; **monter à un arbre** to climb a tree
(**e**) to get on; **je suis monté dans le train** I got on the train; **il est monté sur le vélo** he got on the bike
(**f**) **monter à cheval** to ride a horse
(**g**) to take up, to bring up; **je vais monter les valises** I'll take the suitcases up; **monte-moi mes lunettes** bring my glasses up for me
(**h**) to assemble; **monter une tente** to put up a tent
(**i**) **monter une entreprise** to set up a business; **monter une pièce de théâtre** to put on a play
2 *reflexive verb* **se monter**
(**a**) **se monter à** to come to; **la facture se monte à deux cents euros** the bill comes to two hundred euros
(**b**) **cette bibliothèque se monte**

facilement these bookshelves are easy to assemble

LA **montre** *noun* watch; **il est six heures à ma montre** it's six o'clock by my watch

montrer
1 *verb*
(**a**) to show
(**b**) **montrer quelqu'un du doigt** to point at somebody
(**c**) **montrer l'exemple** to set an example
2 *reflexive verb* **se montrer**
(**a**) to show oneself, to be seen
(**b**) **il s'est montré très courageux** he was very courageous

LA **monture** *noun* frame, rim *(of glasses)*

LE **monument** *noun*
(**a**) building
(**b**) monument
(**c**) **un monument aux morts** a war memorial

> The *t* in *monument* is not pronounced.

se moquer *reflexive verb*
(**a**) **les gens vont se moquer d'elle** people will laugh at her
(**b**) **je me moque de ce que les gens pensent** I don't care what people think; **je m'en moque!** I couldn't care less!
(**c**) **je crois bien qu'on s'est moqué de toi** I think you've been taken for a ride

LA **moquette** *noun* carpet

moral, morale
1 *adjective* moral

> The masculine plural of *moral* is *moraux*.

2 *masculine noun* **le moral** morale, spirits; **j'ai le moral** I'm in good spirits; **il n'a pas le moral en ce moment** he's a bit depressed at the moment; **allez, il faut garder le moral!** come on, keep your spirits up!; **je vais te remonter le moral** I'll cheer you up
3 *feminine noun* **la morale**

(**a**) morality; **c'est contraire à la morale** it's not moral
(**b**) moral *(of a story)*
(**c**) **faire la morale à quelqu'un** to lecture somebody

LE **morceau** *noun*
(**a**) piece; **des morceaux de verre** pieces of glass; **mettre en morceaux** *(an object)* to smash to pieces; *(a sheet of paper)* to tear up; **un morceau de piano** a piece for piano
(**b**) lump; **un morceau de sucre** a lump of sugar, a sugar lump
(**c**) passage *(of a text)*; **un recueil de morceaux choisis** a collection of selected passages

> The plural of *morceau* is *morceaux*.

mordre *verb* to bite; **il s'est fait mordre à la main** he was bitten on the hand; **le chien l'a mordu à la jambe** the dog bit him on the leg

LA **morsure** *noun* bite *(of an animal)*

mort, morte
1 *adjective*
(**a**) dead
(**b**) **mort de peur** scared to death; **elle était morte de fatigue** she was dead tired; **j'étais mort de rire** *(informal phrase)* I was killing myself laughing

> *Mort(e)* is the past participle of *mourir*. See verb table p. 322.

2 *noun* **un mort** a dead man; **une morte** a dead woman; **les morts** the dead; **l'accident a fait trois morts** three people died in the accident
3 *feminine noun* **la mort** death; **à la mort de leur père** on their father's death

mortel, mortelle *adjective*
(**a**) fatal *(accident)*
(**b**) deadly *(poison)*
(**c**) mortal; **tous les hommes sont mortels** all men are mortal

LA **morue** *noun* cod

Moscou *noun* Moscow

LA **mosquée** *noun* mosque

LE **mot** *noun* word

LE **moteur** *noun* engine, motor

LE **motif** *noun*
(a) reason; **quel est le motif de votre visite?** what's the reason for your visit?
(b) pattern; **un motif à fleurs** a floral pattern

motiver *verb* to motivate; **je n'arrive pas à motiver mes élèves** I can't motivate my pupils

LA **moto** *noun* motorbike; **il fait de la moto** he rides a motorbike

mou, molle *adjective*
(a) soft *(pillow, bed)*
(b) limp *(handshake, movement)*; **j'ai les jambes toutes molles** my legs feel all weak
(c) lethargic

LA **mouche** *noun* fly *(insect)*

LE **moucheron** *noun* midge

se moucher *reflexive verb* to blow one's nose

LE **mouchoir** *noun* handkerchief; **un mouchoir en papier** a tissue

moudre *verb* to grind *(coffee)*; **il a moulu du café** he ground some coffee

See verb table p. 322.

LA **mouette** *noun* seagull

LA **moufle** *noun* mitten

mouillé, mouillée *adjective* wet

mouiller
1 *verb* **mouiller quelque chose** to get something wet
2 *reflexive verb* **se mouiller** to wet, to get wet; **se mouiller les cheveux** to wet one's hair

moule
1 *masculine noun* **un moule** a mould; **un moule à gâteau** a cake tin; **un moule à tarte** pie dish; **un moule à gaufres** a waffle iron
2 *feminine noun* **une moule** a mussel

LE **moulin** *noun*
(a) mill; **un moulin à vent** a windmill

(b) **un moulin à café** a coffee grinder
(c) **un moulin à poivre** a peppermill

moulu, moulue *adjective* ground *(coffee)*

Moulu(e) is the past participle of the verb *moudre*.

mourant, mourante *adjective* dying; **il est mourant** he's dying

mourir *verb* to die; **mourir sur le coup** to die instantly; **il est mort de vieillesse** he died of old age; **je meurs de soif** I'm dying of thirst

The past participle of *mourir* is *mort(e)*. To say that somebody has died, you must use the verb in the present perfect – not the past – using *être* as the auxiliary, eg *Victor Hugo est mort en 1885*. See verb table p. 322.

LA **mousse** *noun*
(a) moss
(b) mousse; **une mousse au chocolat** a chocolate mousse
(c) foam; **de la mousse à raser** shaving foam
(d) bubbles *(in a bath, champagne)*
(e) froth *(of beer)*

mousser *verb*
(a) to bubble
(b) to froth
(c) to lather

mousseux, mousseuse
1 *adjective*
(a) sparkling *(wine)*
(b) frothy *(beer, hot chocolate)*
2 *masculine noun* **un mousseux** a sparkling wine

LA **moustache** *noun*
(a) moustache
(b) **les moustaches** whiskers

LE **moustique** *noun* mosquito

LA **moutarde** *noun* mustard

LE **mouton** *noun*
(a) sheep
(b) mutton

LE **mouvement** *noun* movement; **se mettre en mouvement** to start moving

> The *t* in *movement* is not pronounced.

moyen, moyenne
1 *adjective*
(a) medium, medium-sized
(b) average; **il est moyen en maths** he's average at maths
(c) **le Moyen Âge** the Middle Ages
2 *masculine noun* **le moyen**
(a) way, means; **nous devons trouver un moyen** we have to find a way; **moyen de transport** means of transport
(b) **au moyen de** with
(c) **il a les moyens** he's well-off; **je n'ai pas les moyens de l'acheter** I can't afford it
3 *feminine noun* **la moyenne**
(a) average; **faire la moyenne** to work out the average; **la moyenne d'âge** the average age; **en moyenne** on average
(b) pass mark

LE **Moyen-Orient** *noun* the Middle East

muet, muette *adjective*
(a) dumb *(unable to speak)*
(b) silent *(film, vowel)*

LE **muguet** *noun* lily of the valley

> **Le Muguet**
> On May Day in France, bunches of lily of the valley are sold in the streets and given as presents. The flowers are supposed to bring good luck.

multiplier
1 *verb*
(a) to multiply; **2 multiplié par 3** 2 multiplied by 3
(b) to increase
2 *reflexive verb* **se multiplier**
(a) to multiply *(to reproduce)*
(b) to increase; **les attentats se multiplient** attacks are on the increase

LA **multitude** *noun* **une multitude de livres** a great many books; **une multitude de gens** crowds of people

LES **munitions** *feminine plural noun* ammunition

LE **mur** *noun* wall; **un mur d'escalade** a climbing wall

mûr, mûre[1] *adjective*
(a) ripe *(fruit, vegetable)*
(b) mature *(person)*

LA **mûre**[2] *noun* blackberry

murmurer *verb*
(a) to murmur
(b) to mutter

LE **museau** *noun* muzzle, snout *(of an animal)*

> The plural of *museau* is *museaux*.

LE **musée** *noun* museum, art gallery

> Although it ends in -*ée*, this word is masculine.

LE **musicien**, LA **musicienne** *noun* musician

LA **musique** *noun*
(a) music; **je fais de la musique** I play an instrument
(b) theme tune *(of a film)*; **il veut acheter la musique du film** he wants to buy the soundtrack

musulman, musulmane
1 *adjective* Muslim; **la foi musulmane** the Muslim faith
2 *noun* **un musulman, une musulmane** a Muslim

> French, unlike English, does not use capital letters for religions.

myope *adjective* short-sighted

LA **myrtille** *noun* blueberry

LE **mystère** *noun* mystery

mystérieux, mystérieuse *adjective* mysterious

n' *adverb* **il n'a pas compris** he didn't understand; **il n'habite pas là** he doesn't live here

> *N'* is the contracted form of *ne* which is used in front of a vowel or a mute h. See also **ne.**

LA **nage** *noun*
(**a**) (swimming) stroke; **le crawl est la nage la plus rapide** the crawl is the fastest stroke; **elle a traversé la rivière à la nage** she swam across the river; **nage libre** freestyle
(**b**) **il est en nage** he's dripping with sweat

LA **nageoire** *noun* fin, flipper

nager *verb*
(**a**) to swim; **est-ce que tu sais nager?** can you swim?; **je ne sais pas nager** I can't swim; **nager le crawl** to do the crawl; **elle nage très bien** she's a very good swimmer
(**b**) **il nage complètement en chimie** he's completely lost in chemistry

> Sense (b) is an informal use of *nager.*

(**c**) **je nage dans le pull de mon frère** my brother's jumper is far too big for me

> Sense (c) is an informal use of *nager.*

LE **nageur,** LA **nageuse** *noun* swimmer

naïf, naïve *adjective* naive

LE **nain,** LA **naine** *noun* dwarf

LA **naissance** *noun* birth; **date de naissance** date of birth; **elle a donné naissance à des jumeaux** she gave birth to twins; **il est aveugle de naissance** he was born blind

naître *verb* to be born; **je suis né en 1992** I was born in 1992; **l'enfant devrait naître bientôt** the baby is due soon; **elle n'est pas née de la dernière pluie** she wasn't born yesterday

> The past participle of *naître* is *né(e).* When you refer to somebody having been born, you must use the verb in the present perfect – not the past – using *être* as the auxiliary, eg *Victor Hugo est né en 1802.* See verb table p. 322.

naïve *see* **naïf**

LA **nappe** *noun*
(**a**) tablecloth
(**b**) **une nappe de brouillard** a blanket of fog; **une nappe de pétrole** *(underground)* a layer of oil; *(on water)* an oil slick

LA **narine** *noun* nostril

natal, natale *adjective* native; **mon village natal** the village where I was born

LA **natalité** *noun* birth rate

LA **natation** *noun* swimming; **je fais de la natation** I swim

LA **nation** *noun* nation; **les Nations unies** the United Nations

national, nationale
1 *adjective* national

> The masculine plural of *national* is *nationaux.*

2 *feminine noun* **une nationale** a main

road, an A road; **l'autoroute est fer-mée, nous devons prendre la natio-nale** the motorway is closed, we have to take the main road

LA **nationalité** *noun* nationality

LA **natte** *noun* plait; **elle porte des nattes** she wears her hair in plaits

naturaliser *verb* **il s'est fait naturali-ser français** he was granted French citizenship

nature
1 *feminine noun*
(**a**) nature; **la protection de la nature** (nature) conservation
(**b**) country, countryside; **il aime se promener dans la nature** he likes go-ing for walks in the countryside; **en pleine nature** in the middle of the country
(**c**) **ce n'est pas dans sa nature de mentir** it's not in his nature to lie
(**d**) *(in painting)* **une nature morte** a still life
2 *adjective* **une omelette nature** a plain omelette; **un thé nature** a cup of black tea

The word *nature* does not change in the plural when it is used as an adjec-tive: *des yaourts nature* plain yog-hurts.

naturel, naturelle
1 *adjective* natural; **c'est naturel qu'il ne soit pas content** it's only natural that he should be unhappy
2 *masculine noun* **le naturel** nature, character; **il est d'un naturel enjoué** he has a lively nature

naturellement *adverb*
(**a**) of course; **naturellement, il est ar-rivé en retard** of course, he arrived late
(**b**) naturally; **ce fruit est naturelle-ment sucré** this fruit is naturally sweet

LE **naufrage** *noun* shipwreck; **le na-vire a fait naufrage** the ship was wrecked; **le marin a fait naufrage** the sailor was shipwrecked

LE **naufragé**, LA **naufragée** *noun* shipwrecked person, castaway

LA **nausée** *noun* nausea, sickness; **j'ai la nausée** I feel sick

LE **navet** *noun* turnip

LA **navette** *noun* shuttle; **il y a une navette pour aller de la gare à l'aéro-port** there is a shuttle (bus) service from the station to the airport; **il fait la navette entre Paris et Lille tous les jours de la semaine** he commutes between Paris and Lille every week-day; **une navette spatiale** a space shuttle

LE **navigateur**, LA **navigatrice**
1 *noun* navigator; **un navigateur soli-taire** a lone yachtsman
2 *masculine noun* **un navigateur In-ternet** an Internet browser

naviguer *verb*
(**a**) to sail
(**b**) **naviguer sur Internet** to surf the Net

LE **navire** *noun* ship

navré, navrée *adjective* sorry; **je suis navré** I'm terribly sorry

ne *adverb*
(**a**) **ne... pas** not; **je ne sais pas** I don't know
(**b**) **ne... plus** not... any more; **je ne les vois plus** I don't see them any more
(**c**) **ne... rien** not... anything; **il n'a rien compris** he didn't understand any-thing
(**d**) **ne... personne** not... anyone; **je n'ai vu personne** I didn't see anyone
(**e**) **ne... jamais** never; **elle ne sort ja-mais** she never goes out
(**f**) **ne... que** only; **je n'ai que cinq euros** I've only got five euros

In French, *not* is expressed with two words: *ne* and *pas*. *Ne* goes in front of the verb or auxiliary, and *pas* goes after the verb in simple tenses (as in *je ne comprends pas*), and between the auxiliary and the past participle in compound tenses (as in *je n'ai pas compris*). In front of a vowel or a mute h *ne* becomes *n'*.

né, née *see* **naître**
je suis né en 1992 I was born in 1992

Né (e) is the past participle of the verb *naître*. See verb table p. 322.

néanmoins *adverb* nevertheless

nécessaire
1 *adjective* necessary
2 *masculine noun*
(a) **le nécessaire** the bare necessities, the bare essentials; **n'emportez que le strict nécessaire** just take what's absolutely necessary
(b) **nous ferons le nécessaire** we will do what has to be done
(c) **un nécessaire de toilette** a toilet bag; **un nécessaire de couture** a sewing kit

nécessiter *verb* to require, to necessitate; **ce travail nécessite beaucoup de patience** this job requires a lot of patience

LE Néerlandais, LA Néerlandaise *noun (person)* Dutchman/Dutchwoman; **les Néerlandais** Dutch people, the Dutch

néerlandais, néerlandaise
1 *adjective* Dutch; **l'économie néerlandaise** the Dutch economy
2 *noun* **le néerlandais** *(language)* Dutch; **il parle néerlandais** he speaks Dutch

In French, only the noun for the inhabitants of a country takes a capital letter, never the adjective or the noun for the language.

négatif, négative
1 *adjective* negative
2 *masculine noun* **un négatif** a negative

négligé, négligée *adjective* scruffy, untidy

négligent, négligente *adjective* careless

négliger
1 *verb* to neglect; **il néglige son travail** he neglects his work
2 *reflexive verb* **se négliger** il se néglige depuis quelques temps he hasn't been looking after himself lately

LA négociation *noun* negotiation

négocier *verb* to negotiate

LA neige *noun* snow; **il y a de la neige sur le trottoir** there's snow on the pavement; **aller à la neige** to go skiing

neiger *verb* to snow; **il neige** it's snowing

LE nénuphar *noun* water lily

LE Néo-Zélandais, LA Néo-Zélandaise *noun (person)* New Zealander

néo-zélandais, néo-zélandaise *adjective* from New Zealand; **la campagne néo-zélandaise** the New Zealand countryside

In French, only the noun for the inhabitants of a country takes a capital letter, never the adjective.

LE nerf *noun* nerve; **il me tape sur les nerfs** *(informal phrase)* he gets on my nerves; **je suis à bout de nerfs** I'm at the end of my tether; **elle est sur les nerfs** she's on edge

The *f* in *nerf* is not pronounced.

nerveux, nerveuse *adjective* nervous

LA nervosité *noun* nervousness

n'est-ce pas *adverb* **n'est-ce pas?** isn't he?, don't you?, won't they? *etc*; **tu viendras, n'est-ce pas?** you'll come, won't you?; **il fait beau, n'est-ce pas?** the weather's nice, isn't it?

LE Net *noun* the Net; **sur le Net** on the Net

net, nette
1 *adjective*
(a) net; **le montant net** the net amount
(b) clear; **une image nette** a clear

picture; **une réponse nette** a clear answer

(c) clean; **tes ongles ne sont pas très nets** your nails aren't very clean

2 *adverb* **net la branche s'est cassée net** the branch snapped; **il a refusé net** he flatly refused; **il s'est arrêté net** he stopped dead

nettement *adverb*

(a) much, a lot; **il va nettement mieux** he's much better

(b) clearly; **on voit nettement la fracture sur la radio** you can see the fracture clearly on the X-ray

LE **nettoyage** *noun* cleaning; **nettoyage à sec** dry cleaning

nettoyer

1 *verb* to clean

2 *reflexive verb* **se nettoyer tu devrais te nettoyer les oreilles** you should clean your ears

neuf¹ *number* nine; **le neuf septembre** the ninth of September; **nous sommes le neuf janvier** it's the ninth of January

Neuf is pronounced "neuve" in front of a vowel or a mute h.

neuf², neuve *adjective* new; **il a une voiture toute neuve** he's got a brand new car; **alors, quoi de neuf?** what's new?

neutre *adjective* neutral

neuve *see* neuf²

neuvième *number* ninth

LE **neveu** *noun* nephew

The plural of *neveu* is *neveux*.

LE **nez** *noun*

(a) nose

(b) **je me suis retrouvé nez à nez avec lui** I found myself face to face with him; **rire au nez de quelqu'un** to laugh in somebody's face

ni *conjunction* **ni... ni...** neither... nor...; **ni Pierre ni Paul ne sont venus** neither Pierre nor Paul came; **il n'a ni faim ni soif** he's neither hungry nor thirsty; **sans manger ni boire** without eating or drinking; **ni l'un ni l'autre** neither (of them)

LA **niche** *noun* kennel

LE **nid** *noun* nest

The *d* in *nid* is not pronounced.

LA **nièce** *noun* niece

nier *verb* to deny

n'importe *adverb*

(a) it doesn't matter; **quel pull mets-tu? – n'importe** which sweater are you going to wear? – it doesn't matter

(b) **n'importe comment** any old how, anyhow

(c) **n'importe lequel, n'importe laquelle** any of them; **ces écharpes sont toutes au même prix, tu peux choisir n'importe laquelle** these scarves are all the same price, you can choose any of them

(d) **n'importe où** anywhere

(e) **n'importe quand** anytime, whenever

(f) **n'importe quel, n'importe quelle** any; **prends n'importe quelle robe** take any dress

(g) **n'importe qui** anybody

(h) **n'importe quoi** anything; **tu dis vraiment n'importe quoi!** you're talking absolute nonsense!

LE **niveau** *noun*

(a) level; **au niveau de la mer** at sea level; **elle a un très bon niveau en ski** she's a very good skier; **il n'est pas au niveau en physique** he's not up to scratch in physics

(b) **au niveau technologique, le pays est plutôt en retard** the country is quite backward as far as technology is concerned

(c) **le niveau de vie** the standard of living

The plural of *niveau* is *niveaux*.

LA **noce** *noun* wedding; **les noces d'argent** silver wedding anniversary; **les**

noces d'or golden wedding anniversary

Noël *masculine noun* Christmas; **joyeux Noël!** merry Christmas!; **le père Noël** Father Christmas, Santa Claus

> **Noël**
>
> Christmas is the main holiday in France. Presents are put at the foot of the Christmas tree and are often opened on Christmas Eve, during the *réveillon*, which is the long dinner that people enjoy on that night. *Réveillon* often consists of oysters for the starter, followed by turkey, and then Yule log for dessert, with people often drinking champagne. The French tend not to send lots of Christmas cards as people do in Britain and they don't pull Christmas crackers. They do sometimes sing Christmas carols but less so than British people. Many people attend Midnight Mass on Christmas Eve.

LE **nœud** *noun*
(a) knot; **faire un nœud** to tie a knot
(b) bow; **un nœud papillon** a bow tie

LE **Noir,** LA **Noire** *noun* black man/black woman; **les Noirs** black people

noir, noire
1 *adjective*
(a) black; **une voiture noire** a black car
(b) dark; **il fait noir** it's dark
2 *masculine noun* **le noir**
(a) black; **elle était tout en noir** she was dressed all in black; **il voit toujours tout en noir** he always sees the worst in everything
(b) dark; **elle a peur du noir** she's afraid of the dark

noisette
1 *adjective* hazel; **elle a les yeux noisette** she has hazel eyes

> The word *noisette* does not change in the plural when it is used as an adjective.

2 *feminine noun*
(a) hazelnut

(b) small piece; **une noisette de beurre** a knob of butter

LA **noix** *noun*
(a) walnut

> When the word *noix* is used on its own it always refers to a walnut.

(b) **une noix de coco** a coconut; **une noix de cajou** a cashew nut
(c) small piece; **une noix de beurre** a knob of butter
(d) **à la noix** *(informal phrase)* lousy, rubbish; **encore une de ses excuses à la noix!** another of his lame excuses!

LE **nom** *noun*
(a) name; **nom de famille** surname; **nom de jeune fille** maiden name; **je le connais de nom** I know him by name
(b) noun; **un nom commun** a common noun; **un nom propre** a proper noun
(c) **au nom de quelqu'un** on somebody's behalf; **je parle au nom de l'équipe** I'm speaking for the whole team; **au nom de notre amitié** for the sake of our friendship

LE **nombre** *noun* number; **un nombre pair** an even number; **un nombre impair** an odd number; **j'ai trouvé un certain nombre d'erreurs** I found some mistakes; **un grand nombre d'erreurs** a lot of mistakes

nombreux, nombreuse *adjective*
(a) many; **de nombreuses erreurs** many mistakes; **les manifestants étaient peu nombreux** there weren't many demonstrators; **vous étiez nombreux?** were there many of you?
(b) large; **une famille nombreuse** a large family

LE **nombril** *noun* navel

> There are two ways of pronouncing *nombril*: with or without the *l*. Both pronunciations are equally acceptable.

nommer

1 *verb*

(**a**) to name, to call; **ils ont nommé leurs fils Victor** they named their son Victor

(**b**) to name; **nommez la capitale de la Slovénie** name the capital of Slovenia

(**c**) to appoint; **il a été nommé directeur** he was appointed manager

2 *reflexive verb* **se nommer** to be named, to be called; **il se nomme Luc Gros** his name is Luc Gros

non *adverb*

(**a**) no; **non merci** no, thanks

(**b**) not; **il s'appelle Ben, et non Bill** he's called Ben, not Bill; **je ne sais pas si tu as aimé la fête, mais moi non** I don't know if you liked the party, but I didn't; **je crois que non** I don't think so; **je n'ai pas pris de parapluie – moi non plus** I didn't bring an umbrella – neither did I; **je n'y suis pas allé non plus** I didn't go either; **non seulement** not only

(**c**) **c'est une bonne idée, non?** it's a good idea, isn't it?

nonante *number* ninety; **dans les années nonante** in the nineties

Nonante is only used in Belgium and Switzerland. In France people say *quatre-vingt-dix.*

LE non-voyant, LA non-voyante *noun* blind person

nord

1 *masculine noun* **le nord** the north; **c'est une ville située dans le nord du pays** it's a town in the north of the country; **Lille est au nord de Paris** Lille is to the north of Paris; **les gens du nord** people from the north; **un vent du nord** a northerly wind; **l'Amérique du Nord** North America; **l'Europe du Nord** Northern Europe

2 *adjective* north, northern; **la côte nord** the north coast; **il habite dans la banlieue nord de la ville** he lives in the northern suburbs of the city

LE nord-est *noun* northeast

LE nord-ouest *noun* northwest

normal, normale *adjective*

(**a**) normal, ordinary; **en temps normal** in normal circumstances, normally

(**b**) **c'est normal qu'il ne soit pas content** it's quite understandable that he should be unhappy; **ce n'est pas normal qu'il ne soit pas encore arrivé** it's strange he hasn't arrived yet

The masculine plural of *normal* is *normaux.*

normalement *adverb*

(**a**) normally; **la machine fonctionne normalement** the machine is working normally

(**b**) usually; **normalement il vient le mercredi** he usually comes on Wednesdays

(**c**) if all goes well, if nothing goes wrong; **normalement elle devrait arriver demain** if all goes well she should arrive tomorrow

LE Normand, LA Normande *noun (person)* Norman

normand, normande *adjective* from Normandy; **je suis normand** I'm from Normandy

LA Normandie *noun* Normandy

LA Norvège *noun* Norway

LE Norvégien, LA Norvégienne *noun (person)* Norwegian

norvégien, norvégienne

1 *adjective* Norwegian; **la cuisine norvégienne** Norwegian cooking

2 *noun* **le norvégien** *(language)* Norwegian; **il parle norvégien** he speaks Norwegian

In French, only the noun for the inhabitants of a country takes a capital letter, never the adjective or the noun for the language.

nos *adjective* our; **nos amis** our friends; **nos valises** our suitcases

Nos is used in front of plural nouns. It is the plural of *notre*. See also **notre**.

notamment *adverb* especially, notably

LA **note** *noun*
(a) note; **prendre des notes** to take notes
(b) mark; **elle a eu la meilleure note en français** she had the best mark in French
(c) *(in music)* note; **faire une fausse note** to play a wrong note
(d) bill; **la note, s'il vous plaît** can we have the bill, please?

noter *verb*
(a) to note down, to write down
(b) to mark *(a paper, an essay)*

LA **notice** *noun* instructions; **lis bien la notice** read the instructions carefully

Note that the English word *notice* is never a translation for the French word *notice*.

LA **notion** *noun* **il a quelques notions de russe** he has some knowledge of Russian

notre *adjective* our; **notre professeur** our teacher; **notre école** our school

nôtre *pronoun* **le nôtre, la nôtre, les nôtres** ours; **ce n'est pas votre table, c'est la nôtre** it isn't your table, it's ours; **leurs enfants et les nôtres** their children and ours

In French, possessive pronouns have the same gender and the same number as the nouns they stand for, eg the corresponding pronoun for *nos enfants* is *les nôtres* because the word *enfants* is plural.

nouer *verb* to tie, to tie up

LA **nouille** *noun* **des nouilles** pasta, noodles; **tu as fait tomber une nouille** you dropped a piece of pasta

LA **nourrice** *noun* childminder

nourrir
1 *verb* to feed
2 *reflexive verb* **se nourrir** to eat; **cet animal se nourrit d'insectes** this animal feeds on insects

LE **nourrisson** *noun* infant

The word *nourrisson* does not have a feminine but it can also refer to a baby girl.

LA **nourriture** *noun* food

nous *pronoun*
(a) we; **nous sommes ici** we are here; **c'est nous qui prenons la décision** *we* are making the decision
(b) us, to us; **il nous connaît** he knows us; **elle nous en a parlé** she spoke to us about it; **lisez-le-nous** read it to us; **c'est pour nous** it's for us; **un ami à nous** a friend of ours; **ces livres ne sont pas à nous** these books aren't ours
(c) ourselves; **nous étions contents de nous** we were pleased with ourselves
(d) each other, to each other; **nous nous connaissons** we know each other; **nous nous détestons** we hate each other; **nous nous écrivons** we write to each other
(e) **nous nous sommes lavé les mains** we washed our hands; **nous nous sommes habillés en vitesse** we got dressed quickly; **allons-nous en** let's go

Note that there are many cases when *nous* is simply not translated in English, as in *nous nous souvenons* (we remember), *nous nous rasons* (we shave) and *nous nous levons* (we get up).

nous-mêmes *pronoun* ourselves; **nous l'avons écrit nous-mêmes** we wrote it ourselves

nouveau, nouvelle[1]
1 *adjective* new; **un nouveau livre** a new book; **une nouvelle amie** a new friend; **un nouvel appartement** a

new flat; **un nouvel hôtel** a new hotel; **le Nouvel An** the New Year

2 *noun (at school)* **un nouveau** a new boy; **une nouvelle** a new girl

3 *adverb* **de nouveau, à nouveau** again; **elle l'a de nouveau oublié** she forgot it again

> The masculine plural of *nouveau* is *nouveaux*, the feminine plural is *nouvelles*. *Nouvel* is used instead of *nouveau* before masculine singular nouns beginning with a vowel or a mute h. The plural of *nouvel* is still *nouveaux: de nouveaux appartements*.

LE **nouveau-né**, LA **nouveau-née** *noun* newborn baby

> The masculine plural of *nouveau-né* is *nouveau-nés*, the feminine plural is *nouveau-nées*.

nouvel *see* **nouveau**

LA **nouvelle²** *noun*
(**a**) piece of news; **une nouvelle très intéressante** a very interesting piece of news; **c'est une bonne nouvelle** this is good news; **les nouvelles sont bonnes** the news is good
(**b**) **Paul m'a demandé de tes nouvelles** Paul was asking after you; **j'ai eu des nouvelles de Marie** I've had news from Marie, I've heard from Marie
(**c**) short story

LA **Nouvelle-Orléans** *noun* New Orleans

LA **Nouvelle-Zélande** *noun* New Zealand

novembre *masculine noun* November; **le premier novembre** the first of November; **le 12 novembre** the 12th of November

> In French, the names of months are not written with a capital.

LE **noyau** *noun* stone *(of a fruit)*

> The plural of *noyau* is *noyaux*.

LE **noyé**, LA **noyée** *noun* drowned person

noyer¹
1 *verb* to drown
2 *reflexive verb* **se noyer** to drown; **il s'est noyé dans la rivière** he drowned in the river

LE **noyer²** *noun* walnut tree

nu, nue *adjective*
(**a**) naked; **elle était toute nue** she was completely naked
(**b**) bare; **marcher pieds nus** to walk barefoot; **les murs de la pièce étaient nus** the room had bare walls

LE **nuage** *noun* cloud; **être dans les nuages** to have one's head in the clouds, to be daydreaming

nuageux, nuageuse *adjective* cloudy

LA **nuance** *noun*
(**a**) shade; **des nuances de rouge** shades of red
(**b**) nuance, difference; **je ne saisis pas la nuance** I don't quite see the difference

nucléaire
1 *adjective* nuclear
2 *masculine noun* **le nucléaire** nuclear energy

nuire *verb* **nuire à quelqu'un** to harm somebody

> See verb table p. 320.

nuisible *adjective* harmful

LA **nuit** *noun*
(**a**) night; **en pleine nuit** in the middle of the night; **il aime travailler la nuit** he likes working at night; **bonne nuit!** good night!; **cette nuit** *(yesterday)* last night; *(today)* tonight
(**b**) dark, darkness; **il fait nuit** it's dark; **il fait nuit noire** it's pitch-black

nul, nulle
1 *adjective*
(**a**) bad, rubbish; **ce livre est vraiment nul** this book is really bad

> Sense (a) is an informal use of *nul*.

(**b**) hopeless, useless; **il est nul en géographie** he's hopeless at geography

---

Sense (b) is an informal use of *nul*.

(**c**) **match nul** draw; **il ont fait match nul** they drew
(**d**) no; **sans nul doute** without any doubt; **nul homme n'est parfait** nobody's perfect
2 *masculine pronoun* **nul** no one; **nul n'a le droit de faire ça** no one has the right to do that

nulle part *adverb* nowhere; **nulle part ailleurs** nowhere else

numérique *adjective* digital; **un appareil photo numérique** a digital camera

LE **numéro** *noun*
(**a**) number; **un numéro de téléphone** a telephone number
(**b**) issue *(of a magazine)*
(**c**) act *(at the circus)*

numéroter *verb* to number

LA **nuque** *noun* back of the neck, nape

obéir *verb* to obey; **ils obéissent à leur professeur** they obey their teacher; **tu dois obéir aux ordres** you must obey orders

obéissant, obéissante *adjective* obedient

objectif, objective
1 *adjective* objective
2 *masculine noun* **un objectif**
(**a**) objective; **atteindre un objectif** to reach an objective
(**b**) target; **un objectif de vente** a sales target
(**c**) lens *(of a camera)*; **regarder l'objectif** to look at the camera

UN **objet** *noun*
(**a**) object
(**b**) subject *(of a discussion)*
(**c**) aim; **l'objet de l'émission est de divertir** the aim of the programme is to entertain
(**d**) target; **il fait l'objet de vives critiques** he's the target of sharp criticism
(**e**) reason; **quel est l'objet de votre visite?** what's the reason for your visit?

obligatoire *adjective* compulsory

obliger *verb* to oblige, to force; **obliger quelqu'un à faire quelque chose** to force somebody to do something; **je suis obligé de le faire** I have to do it

obscur, obscure *adjective*
(**a**) dark; **une pièce obscure** a dark room
(**b**) obscure

obscurité *feminine noun* dark, dark-

ness; **dans l'obscurité** in darkness

observer *verb*
(**a**) to observe
(**b**) to watch
(**c**) to respect *(the law, the rules)*
(**d**) to notice

UN **obstacle** *noun*
(**a**) obstacle
(**b**) fence *(in horseracing)*; **une course d'obstacles** a steeplechase

s'obstiner *reflexive verb* to persist, to insist; **elle s'obstine à vouloir partir** she insists on leaving

obtenir *verb* to get, to obtain; **j'ai obtenu un bon résultat** I got a good result; **en divisant par deux on obtient 24** if you divide by two you get 24

See verb table p. 324.

UN **obus** *noun* shell *(missile)*

UNE **occasion** *noun*
(**a**) chance, opportunity; **profiter de l'occasion pour faire quelque chose** to take the opportunity to do something; **sauter sur l'occasion** to jump at the chance
(**b**) occasion; **pour les grandes occasions** for special occasions
(**c**) bargain; **c'est une occasion!** it's a real bargain!
(**d**) **une voiture d'occasion** a second-hand car, a used car; **je l'ai acheté d'occasion** I bought it second-hand

L'**Occident** *masculine noun* the West

occidental, occidentale *adjective*
(**a**) west; **la côte occidentale** the west coast

(b) Western; **l'Europe occidentale** Western Europe; **les pays occidentaux** Western countries

The masculine plural of *occidental* is *occidentaux*.

occupé, occupée *adjective*
(a) busy *(person)*
(b) taken *(seat)*
(c) engaged *(telephone, toilet)*

occuper
1 *verb*
(a) **occuper quelqu'un** to keep somebody busy; **ça m'occupe** it keeps me busy
(b) to occupy *(a house, a country)*
(c) to take up; **le bar occupe trop de place** the bar takes up too much space; **la réunion a occupé la matinée** the meeting took up the whole morning
2 *reflexive verb* **s'occuper**
(a) to keep oneself busy
(b) **s'occuper d'un enfant** to take care of a child
(c) **s'occuper d'un problème** to deal with a problem
(d) **ne t'occupe pas de moi!** don't mind me!; **occupe-toi de tes affaires!** *(informal phrase)* mind your own business!

UN océan *noun* ocean; **l'océan Atlantique** the Atlantic Ocean; **l'océan Pacifique** the Pacific Ocean

octante *number* eighty

Octante is only used in Belgium and Switzerland. In France people say *quatre-vingt*.

octobre *masculine noun* October; **le premier octobre** the first of October; **le 13 octobre** the 13th of October

In French, the names of months are not written with a capital.

UNE odeur *noun* smell *(of food, flowers)*

odieux, odieuse *adjective*
(a) hateful *(person)*
(b) atrocious *(crime, behaviour)*

L'odorat *masculine noun* sense of smell; **il n'a pas d'odorat** he has no sense of smell

UN œil *noun*
(a) eye; **un œil au beurre noir** a black eye; **je t'ai à l'œil!** I've got my eye on you!
(b) look; **il m'a regardé d'un œil furieux** he gave me a furious look; **regarder quelque chose d'un œil critique** to look critically at something; **un coup d'œil** a look, a glance; **jeter un coup d'œil à quelque chose** to have a quick look at something; **ça vaut le coup d'œil** it's worth seeing

The plural of *œil* is *yeux*.

UN œuf *noun* egg; **un œuf sur le plat** a fried egg; **un œuf à la coque** a boiled egg; **un œuf dur** a hard-boiled egg

The *f* is pronounced in the singular but not in the plural; *des œufs* is pronounced "dézeu".

UNE œuvre *noun*
(a) work; **une œuvre d'art** a work of art; **les œuvres complètes de Shakespeare** the complete works of Shakespeare
(b) **se mettre à l'œuvre** to get down to work
(c) **mettre tout en œuvre pour faire quelque chose** to do everything in one's power to do something
(d) **une œuvre de bienfaisance** a charitable organization

UN office *noun*
(a) service *(in a church)*
(b) **un office du tourisme** a tourist office
(c) **faire office de président** to act as president
(d) **d'office** automatically

UN officier *noun* officer

UNE offre *noun*
(a) offer; **une offre d'emploi** a job offer
(b) bid

(c) supply; **l'offre et la demande** supply and demand

offrir

1 *verb*

(a) to offer; **il m'a offert son aide** he offered to help me; **ils lui ont offert le travail** they offered him the job

(b) to give *(as a present)*

(c) to buy; **je vous offre un verre?** can I buy you a drink?

2 *reflexive verb* **s'offrir** to treat oneself to; **je me suis offert un manteau neuf** I treated myself to a new coat

See verb table p. 320.

un OGM *noun* genetically modified organism, GMO

OGM is the abbreviation of *organisme génétiquement modifié*. It does not change in the plural.

une oie *noun*

(a) goose

(b) **le jeu de l'oie** snakes and ladders

un oignon *noun*

(a) onion

(b) **mêle-toi de tes oignons!** *(informal phrase)* mind your own business!

un oiseau *noun* bird; **un oiseau de proie** a bird of prey

The plural of *oiseau* is *oiseaux*.

un olivier *noun* olive tree

l'ombre *feminine noun*

(a) shade; **reste à l'ombre** stay in the shade

(b) shadow

l'ombrelle *feminine noun* parasol

Note that the English word *umbrella* is never a translation for the French word *ombrelle*.

on *pronoun*

(a) they, people; **en Espagne, on mange plus tard** in Spain they eat later

(b) we; **on est allés au cinema** we went to the cinema; **on y va** let's go;

on est dix there are ten of us

(c) you; **on n'a pas le droit de fumer ici** you can't smoke in here; **on ne sait jamais** you never know

(d) somebody; **on m'a volé mon sac** somebody's stolen my bag; **on frappe à la porte** somebody's knocking at the door

The article *l'* can be found before *on* in a formal context.

un oncle *noun* uncle

une onde *noun* wave *(of heat, light, sound)*; **les ondes radio** radio waves; **une onde de choc** a shockwave

un ongle *noun* nail, fingernail

ont *see* avoir

ils ont une voiture rouge they have a red car; **elles ont mangé un gâteau** they ate a cake

Ont is a form of the verb *avoir* in the present tense. See verb table p. 313.

l'ONU *feminine noun* the UN

ONU is the abbreviation of *Organisation des Nations unies*.

onze *number* eleven; **le onze septembre** the eleventh of September; **nous sommes le onze février** it's the eleventh of February

onzième *number* eleventh

une opération *noun*

(a) operation; **j'ai eu une opération** I had an operation; **une opération de sauvetage** a rescue operation

(b) sums; **je n'ai pas fini mes devoirs, il me reste des opérations à faire** I haven't finished my homework, I still have some sums to do

(c) transaction; **une opération bancaire** a bank transaction

opérer *verb* **opérer quelqu'un** to operate on somebody; **se faire opérer** to have an operation; **il s'est fait opérer des yeux** he had an eye operation

une opinion *noun*

(a) opinion; **j'avais une mauvaise**

opinion de lui I had a bad opinion of him
(b) mind; **changer d'opinion** to change one's mind; **se faire une opinion sur quelque chose** to make up one's mind about something

opposé, opposée
1 *adjective*
(a) opposite; **sur le mur opposé** on the opposite wall; **nous avons des goûts opposés** we have completely different tastes
(b) opposed; **être opposé à quelque chose** to be opposed to something
2 *masculine noun* **l'opposé** the opposite; **la gare est à l'opposé** the station is in the opposite direction

opposer
1 *verb*
(a) to bring into conflict; **deux guerres ont opposé nos pays** two wars have brought our countries into conflict
(b) **la finale opposera le joueur français au joueur américain** the final will pit the French player against the American
2 *reflexive verb* **s'opposer** s'opposer **à quelque chose** to be opposed to something

UN **opticien,** UNE **opticienne** *noun* optician; **elle est opticienne** she's an optician

optimiste
1 *adjective* optimistic
2 *noun* **un/une optimiste** an optimist

or¹ *masculine noun*
(a) gold; **une bague en or** a gold ring
(b) **une affaire en or** a real bargain; **une occasion en or** a golden opportunity

or² *conjunction*
(a) now; **or, pour revenir à ce que nous disions** now, to come back to what we were saying
(b) well, yet; **avant de le lire, je pensais que le livre était bon – or, il ne l'était pas** before I read it, I thought the book was good – well, it wasn't

(c) but; **je devais y aller, or je n'ai pas pu** I was supposed to go, but I couldn't

> Note that the French word *or* is never a translation for the English word *or*.

UN **orage** *noun*
(a) thunderstorm; **un temps d'orage** stormy weather
(b) **il y a de l'orage dans l'air** there's trouble brewing

orageux, orageuse *adjective* stormy, thundery

orange
1 *adjective* orange

> Note that the adjective *orange* does not change in the plural: *des chaussures orange.*

2 *masculine noun* **l'orange** orange; **l'orange est ma couleur préférée** orange is my favourite colour
3 *feminine noun* **une orange** an orange; **une orange pressée** a glass of freshly squeezed orange juice

UN **oranger** *noun* orange tree

UN **orchestre** *noun*
(a) orchestra
(b) band; **un orchestre de cuivres** a brass band

ordinaire *adjective*
(a) ordinary; **des gens ordinaires** ordinary people
(b) usual; **elle parlait avec son arrogance ordinaire** she was talking with her usual arrogance; **en temps ordinaire** usually

UN **ordinateur** *noun* computer; **un ordinateur portable** a laptop

UNE **ordonnance** *noun* prescription *(from the doctor)*

ordonné, ordonnée *adjective*
(a) tidy *(person, room)*
(b) orderly *(lifestyle, routine, system)*

ordonner *verb*
(a) to order; **ordonner à quelqu'un de faire quelque chose** to order somebody to do something

(b) to put in order *(documents, ideas)*

L'**ordre** *masculine noun*
(a) order *(command)*
(b) **cet élève s'est fait rappeler à l'ordre** this pupil got told off
(c) tidiness; **sa chambre est en ordre** his bedroom is tidy; **je dois mettre de l'ordre dans mes papiers** I need to sort out my papers
(d) **par ordre alphabétique** in alphabetical order; **par ordre croissant** in ascending order; **par ordre décroissant** in descending order
(e) **des problèmes d'ordre professionnel** problems of a professional nature
(f) **un chèque à mon ordre** a cheque payable to me
(g) **l'ordre du jour** the agenda *(of a meeting)*

LES **ordures** *feminine plural noun* rubbish; **ramasser les ordures** to collect the rubbish

UNE **oreille** *noun*
(a) ear; **j'ai mal aux oreilles** I've got earache; **ouvrez bien vos oreilles!** listen very carefully!; **tu vas te faire tirer les oreilles** you'll get told off
(b) sense of hearing; **avoir l'oreille fine** to have excellent hearing

UN **oreiller** *noun* pillow

LES **oreillons** *masculine plural noun* mumps; **avoir les oreillons** to have mumps

UN **organe** *noun* organ *(of the body)*

L'**organisation** *feminine noun* organization; **une organisation internationale** an international organization

organiser
1 *verb* to organize
2 *reflexive verb* **s'organiser**
(a) to get oneself organized
(b) to be planned; **un voyage, ça s'organise longtemps à l'avance** trips have to be planned well in advance

UN **orgue** *noun* organ *(musical instrument)*

L'**orgueil** *masculine noun* pride; **il a trop d'orgueil pour faire des excuses** he's too proud to apologize

orgueilleux, orgueilleuse *adjective*
(a) arrogant
(b) proud

L'**Orient** *masculine noun* the East; **un tapis d'Orient** an oriental rug

oriental, orientale *adjective*
(a) east, eastern; **la côte orientale** the east coast; **l'Afrique orientale** East Africa
(b) oriental *(art, food, language)*

> The masculine plural of *oriental* is *orientaux*.

originaire *adjective* **être originaire de** to be a native of; **ma mère est originaire de Paris** my mother comes from Paris

original, originale
1 *adjective*
(a) original
(b) eccentric
2 *masculine noun* **un original** an original *(painting, book, document)*; **il ne possède que des originaux** he owns only original works of art

> The masculine plural of *original* is *originaux*.

UNE **origine** *noun*
(a) origin; **à l'origine** originally; **il est d'origine espagnole** he's of Spanish origin
(b) **ma voiture a encore son moteur d'origine** my car has still got its original engine

UN **orphelin**, UNE **orpheline** *noun* orphan

UN **orphelinat** *noun* orphanage

UN **orteil** *noun* toe; **le gros orteil** the big toe

L'**orthographe** *feminine noun* spelling; **il y a deux orthographes possibles** there are two possible spellings; **je ne connais pas l'orthographe de**

ce mot I don't know how to spell this word

UNE **ortie** *noun* nettle

UN **os** *noun*
(a) bone
(b) **tomber sur un os** *(informal phrase)* to hit a snag

> The *s* is pronounced in the singular but not in the plural.

oser *verb*
(a) to dare; **comment oses-tu!** how dare you!
(b) to risk *(an answer)*
(c) **si j'ose dire** if I may say so; **j'ose espérer qu'il viendra** I hope he'll come

L'**osier** *masculine noun* wicker; **une chaise en osier** a wicker chair

UN **otage** *noun* hostage

L'**OTAN** *feminine noun* NATO

> *OTAN* is the abbreviation of *Organisation du traité de l'Atlantique Nord.*

ôter *verb*
(a) to take off *(a hat, a coat)*
(b) to take away; **ôter quelque chose à quelqu'un** to take something away from somebody
(c) to remove

UNE **otite** *noun* ear infection

ou *conjunction*
(a) or; **tu viens ou quoi?** are you coming or not?
(b) **ou... ou** *or* **ou bien... ou bien** either... or; **ou c'est lui ou c'est moi!** it's either him or me!; **ou bien tu viens et tu es aimable, ou bien tu restes chez toi!** either you come along and be nice, or you stay at home!

où
1 *pronoun*
(a) where; **la maison où j'habite** the house where I live
(b) **à l'époque où je travaillais** in the days when I was working; **le jour où je suis venu** the day I came
(c) **au cas où il viendrait** in case he comes
2 *adverb*
(a) where; **où vas-tu?** where are you going?; **d'où viens-tu en Angleterre?** whereabouts are you from in England?
(b) **d'où mon étonnement** hence my surprise

L'**ouate** *feminine noun*
(a) cotton wool
(b) padding *(for clothes)*

oublier *verb*
(a) to forget
(b) to leave; **j'ai oublié mes lunettes chez moi** I've left my glasses at home

ouest
1 *masculine noun* **l'ouest** the west; **il habite dans l'ouest de Paris** he lives in the west of Paris; **Caen est à l'ouest de Paris** Caen is to the west of Paris; **les gens de l'ouest** people from the west; **un vent d'ouest** a westerly wind; **l'Europe de l'Ouest** Western Europe
2 *adjective* west, western; **la côte ouest** the west coast; **il habite dans la banlieue ouest de la ville** he lives in the western suburbs of the city

oui *adverb*
(a) yes; **il a dit oui** he said yes
(b) so; **elle vient aussi? si oui, je reste** will she be there too? if so I'll stay; **je crois que oui** I think so
(c) **tu viens, oui ou non?** are you coming or not?; **tu me réponds, oui?** will you answer me?

L'**ouïe** *feminine noun*
(a) sense of hearing; **avoir l'ouïe fine** to have excellent hearing
(b) gill *(of fish)*

UN **ouragan** *noun* hurricane

UN **ourlet** *noun* hem

UN **ours** *noun* bear; **un ours en peluche** a teddy bear

UN **oursin** *noun* sea urchin

UN **outil** *noun* tool; **une boîte à outils** a tool box; **une cabane à outils** a tool shed

The *l* at the end of *outil* is not pronounced.

outre-mer *adverb* overseas

ouvert, ouverte *adjective*
(**a**) open; **la porte est grande ouverte** the door is wide open
(**b**) on; **le robinet est ouvert** the tap is on
(**c**) cut open; **elle a eu la lèvre ouverte** her lip was split

Ouvert(e) is the past participle of the verb *ouvrir*. See verb table p. 320.

UNE **ouverture** *noun* opening; **les heures d'ouverture** opening hours

UN **ouvrage** *noun*
(**a**) work; **se mettre à l'ouvrage** to get down to work; **le gros de l'ouvrage** the bulk of the work
(**b**) book, work; **un ouvrage de philosophie** a philosophy book

UN **ouvre-boîte** *masculine noun* tin opener

The plural of *ouvre-boîte* is *ouvre-boîtes*. The singular can also be found with an *s*: *un ouvre-boîtes*.

UN **ouvre-bouteille** *masculine noun* bottle opener

The plural of *ouvre-bouteille* is *ouvre-bouteilles*. The singular can also be found with an *s*: *un ouvre-bouteilles*.

ouvrier, ouvrière
1 *adjective*
(**a**) working-class; **un quartier ouvrier** a working-class neighbourhood;

la classe ouvrière the working class
(**b**) **une abeille ouvrière** a worker bee
2 *noun* **un ouvrier, une ouvrière** a worker; **un ouvrier agricole** an agricultural worker

ouvrir
1 *verb*
(**a**) to open; **ouvrez vos cahiers** open your exercise books; **ouvre les yeux** open your eyes
(**b**) to open the door; **c'est moi, ouvre** it's me, open the door; **va ouvrir** go and answer the door
(**c**) to turn on *(a tap)*
2 *reflexive verb* **s'ouvrir**
(**a**) to open; **la porte s'ouvre mal** the door doesn't open properly
(**b**) to open up; **il a besoin de s'ouvrir** he needs to open up; **s'ouvrir à des cultures nouvelles** to open one's mind to new cultures
(**c**) to cut; **il s'est ouvert le pied** he's cut his foot open
(**d**) **s'ouvrir à quelqu'un** to confide in somebody; **il éprouvait le besoin de s'ouvrir** he felt the need to talk to somebody

See verb table p. 320.

UN **ovni** *noun* UFO

Ovni is the abbreviation of *objet volant non identifié*.

L'**oxygène** *masculine noun* oxygen; **une bouteille d'oxygène** an oxygen cylinder

L'**ozone** *masculine noun* ozone; **la couche d'ozone** the ozone layer

LE Pacifique *noun* the Pacific

pacifique *adjective* peaceful

LA pagaille *noun*
(a) mess; **ma chambre est en pagaille** my room's a mess; **arrête de mettre la pagaille dans mes affaires** stop messing up my things
(b) chaos; **c'est la pagaille dans les rues de Paris** the streets of Paris are in absolute chaos; **semer la pagaille** to cause trouble

> This word is informal.

LA page *noun*
(a) page; **une page blanche** a blank page; **une page d'accueil** a home page
(b) **une page de publicité** a commercial break
(c) **mettre en page** to design
(d) **tourner la page** to make a fresh start

LA paie *noun* pay; **c'est le jour de paie** it's payday

LE paiement *noun* payment

LE paillasson *noun* doormat

LA paille *noun*
(a) straw; **un chapeau de paille** a straw hat
(b) drinking straw; **boire quelque chose avec une paille** to drink something through a straw

LE pain *noun*
(a) bread; **du pain de mie** sandwich bread; **du pain grillé** toast; **du pain d'épice** gingerbread
(b) loaf; **un pain de campagne** a farmhouse loaf

(c) **un pain au chocolat** pastry with chocolate filling; **un pain au lait** sweet finger roll made with milk
(d) **avoir du pain sur la planche** to have one's work cut out

pair, paire
1 *adjective* even; **un nombre pair** an even number
2 *feminine noun* **une paire** a pair; **j'ai une nouvelle paire de chaussures** I have a new pair of shoes

LA paix *noun*
(a) peace; **faire la paix** to make peace
(b) **est-ce qu'on peut avoir la paix, s'il vous plaît?** can we have some peace and quiet, please?; **fiche-moi la paix!** *(informal phrase)* clear off!, leave me alone!

> The *x* in *paix* is not pronounced.

LE palace *noun* luxury hotel

> Note that the English word *palace* is never a translation for the French word *palace*.

LE palais *noun*
(a) palace
(b) **un palais des congrès** a conference centre; **un palais des sports** a stadium; **un Palais de justice** a law court
(c) palate

> The *s* in *palais* is not pronounced.

pâle *adjective* pale

LE palier *noun* landing *(on a staircase)*

LA palme *noun*
(a) palm *(award)*; **la Palme d'Or**

trophy awarded for best film at the Cannes film festival; **remporter la palme** to win
(**b**) flipper *(for swimming)*
(**c**) palm leaf

LE **palmier** *noun* palm tree

LE **pamplemousse** *noun* grapefruit

LE **panaché** *noun* shandy

LA **pancarte** *noun*
(**a**) sign
(**b**) placard

pané, panée *adjective* breaded; **du poisson pané** fish in breadcrumbs, breaded fish

LE **panier** *noun*
(**a**) basket; **un panier à linge** a linen basket
(**b**) **marquer un panier** to score a basket *(in basketball)*

LA **panique** *noun* panic; **pris de panique** panic-stricken

paniquer *verb* to panic

LA **panne** *noun*
(**a**) breakdown; **tomber en panne** to break down; **en panne** out of order
(**b**) **je suis en panne d'essence** I've run out of petrol
(**c**) **une panne de courant** *or* **une panne d'électricité** a power cut

LE **panneau** *noun*
(**a**) sign; **un panneau de signalisation** a road sign
(**b**) board; **un panneau d'affichage** a notice board; **un panneau publicitaire** a hoarding
(**c**) panel *(of wood, glass)*; **un panneau solaire** a solar panel

The plural of *panneau* is *panneaux*.

LA **panoplie** *noun*
(**a**) complete set, kit; **une panoplie de bricoleur** a do-it-yourself kit
(**b**) outfit; **une panoplie de Spiderman** a Spiderman outfit
(**c**) array, collection

LE **pansement** *noun*
(**a**) dressing; **il lui a fait un pansement à la jambe** he put a dressing on her leg
(**b**) plaster; **mon pansement s'est décollé** my plaster's come off

LE **pantalon** *noun* pair of trousers; **mon pantalon** my trousers

LA **pantoufle** *noun* slipper

LE **paon** *noun* peacock

Paon rhymes with "blanc".

LE **papa** *noun* dad

LE **pape** *noun* pope

LE **papi** *noun* granddad, grandpa

LE **papier** *noun*
(**a**) paper; **du papier calque** tracing paper; **du papier à lettres** writing paper; **du papier cadeau** wrapping paper; **du papier hygiénique** *or* **du papier toilette** toilet paper; **du papier peint** wallpaper
(**b**) piece of paper; **as-tu un papier et un crayon?** do you have a piece of paper and a pencil?
(**c**) **les papiers d'identité** identity papers

LE **papillon** *noun*
(**a**) butterfly; **un papillon de nuit** a moth
(**b**) butterfly stroke; **nager le papillon** to swim the butterfly

LE **papy** *noun* granddad, grandpa

LE **paquebot** *noun* liner *(ship)*

LA **pâquerette** *noun* daisy

Pâques *masculine noun* Easter; **j'irai la voir à Pâques** I'll go and see her at Easter; **un œuf de Pâques** an Easter egg; **le dimanche de Pâques** Easter Sunday; **Joyeuses Pâques!** Happy Easter!

Pâques becomes feminine in plural, hence *joyeuses* in the phrase *Joyeuses Pâques*.

Pâques

In France, Easter is traditionally symbolized not only by eggs but also by bells; according to legend, church bells fly to Rome at Easter. At this time of year, people give each other chocolate eggs, bells, fish or hens.

LE **paquet** *noun*
(**a**) parcel
(**b**) packet; **un paquet de gâteaux** a packet of biscuits
(**c**) pack; **un paquet familial** a family-size pack
(**d**) bag
(**e**) bundle *(of papers)*
(**f**) **il y a un paquet d'erreurs** *(informal phrase)* there are loads of mistakes

par *preposition*
(**a**) by; **prends le couteau par le manche** take the knife by the handle; **voyager par avion** to travel by plane; **la maison a été achetée par des étrangers** the house has been bought by foreigners
(**b**) through; **faut-il passer par Paris?** do we have to go through Paris?; **je l'ai appris par un ami** I heard it through a friend
(**c**) out of; **il l'a jeté par la fenêtre** he thew it out of the window; **faire quelque chose par habitude** to do something out of habit; **par amour** out of love
(**d**) from; **je le sais par expérience** I know from experience
(**e**) on; **elle est assise par terre** she's sitting on the ground *or* she's sitting on the floor; **par un beau jour d'été** on a fine summer's day
(**f**) in; **par endroits** in places
(**g**) **des livres traînaient par-ci par-là** books were lying around here and there
(**h**) a, per; **une heure par jour** one hour a day *or* one hour per day; **une fois par an** once a year
(**i**) **il a fini par avouer** he eventually owned up; **ça finira par arriver** it will happen in the end

LE **parachute** *noun* parachute

LE/LA **parachutiste** *noun*
(**a**) parachutist
(**b**) paratrooper

LE **paradis** *noun* heaven

The *s* in *paradis* is not pronounced.

LES **parages** *masculine plural noun* surroundings; **il habite dans les parages** he lives around here somewhere; **ils sont dans les parages** they're around somewhere

paraître *verb*
(**a**) to seem; **elle paraît très gentille** she seems very nice
(**b**) to look; **il paraissait furieux** he looked furious
(**c**) to show; **laisser paraître son émotion** to let one's emotion show
(**d**) to be published; **un livre paru en 1963** a book published in 1963
(**e**) **paraît-il** *or* **à ce qu'il paraît** apparently; **tu as retrouvé du travail, paraît-il** I hear you've got a new job; **il paraît qu'il a trois enfants** apparently he's got three children

See verb table p. 320.

LE **parapente** *noun*
(**a**) paragliding; **faire du parapente** to go paragliding
(**b**) paraglider

LE **parapluie** *noun* umbrella

LE **parc** *noun*
(**a**) park; **un parc animalier** a safari park; **un parc aquatique** a water park; **un parc d'attractions** an amusement park; **un parc naturel** a nature reserve
(**b**) grounds *(around a house)*
(**c**) **un parc d'expositions** an exhibition centre
(**d**) playpen

parce que *conjunction* because; **elle n'est pas venue parce qu'elle se sentait fatiguée** she didn't come because she was feeling tired

Parce que becomes *parce qu'* in front of a vowel or a mute h.

LE **parcmètre** *noun* parking meter

parcourir *verb*
(a) to cover *(a distance)*
(b) to travel through; **ils ont parcouru toute l'Amérique** they've travelled the length and breadth of America; **je parcourais la ville à la recherche d'un emploi** I was looking all over town for a job
(c) to skim through, to scan *(a book, an article)*
(d) to run through; **un frisson me parcourut le corps** a shiver ran through my body

See verb table p. 320.

LE **parcours** *noun*
(a) way *(distance)*
(b) journey; **il a effectué le parcours en deux heures** he did the journey in two hours
(c) route *(of a demonstration, a race)*
(d) course *(in athletics, golf)*
(e) circuit *(in motor racing)*
(f) career, path; **mon parcours professionnel** my career; **mon parcours scolaire** my school record

par-derrière *preposition*
(a) behind, round the back of; **passe par-derrière la maison** go round the back of the house
(b) **il me critique par-derrière** he criticizes me behind my back

par-dessous *preposition* under, underneath; **passe par-dessous la barrière** go under the fence

LE **pardessus** *noun* overcoat

par-dessus *preposition*
(a) over; **passe par-dessus la barrière** go over the fence
(b) **par-dessus tout** most of all; **ce que j'aime par-dessus tout, c'est son humour** what I love most of all is his sense of humour

pardon *masculine noun*
(a) sorry; **oh pardon, je ne vous avais pas vu** oh sorry, I didn't see you
(b) pardon, sorry; **pardon? je ne vous**

ai pas bien entendu pardon? *or* sorry? I didn't hear you properly
(c) excuse me; **pardon, auriez-vous un crayon?** excuse me, do you have a pencil?
(d) forgiveness; **demander pardon à quelqu'un** to ask for somebody's forgiveness, to apologize to somebody

pardonner *verb* to forgive

LE **pare-brise** *noun* windscreen

The word *pare-brise* does not change in the plural.

LE **pare-chocs** *noun* bumper

The word *pare-chocs* does not change in the plural.

pareil, pareille
1 *adjective*
(a) the same; **ta jupe est pareille que la mienne** your skirt's the same as mine; **comment vas-tu? – toujours pareil!** how are you? – same as ever!
(b) such; **mais je n'ai jamais dit une chose pareille!** but I never said any such thing!
2 *adverb* **pareil ils sont habillés pareil** they're dressed the same

LE **parent,** LA **parente**
1 *noun* relative, relation; **un parent proche** a close relative; **un parent éloigné** a distant relative
2 *masculine plural noun* **les parents** parents; **une réunion de parents d'élèves** a parents' evening

The *t* in *parent* is not pronounced.

LA **parenthèse** *noun*
(a) bracket; **mettre un mot entre parenthèses** to put a word in brackets
(b) **entre parenthèses, elle n'était pas très intelligente** incidentally, she wasn't very bright

parents *see* parent

paresseux, paresseuse *adjective* lazy

parfait, parfaite *adjective* perfect

parfaitement *adverb*
(**a**) perfectly
(**b**) certainly; **c'est vrai? – parfaitement!** is that true? – it certainly is!

parfois *adverb* sometimes

LE **parfum** *noun*
(**a**) perfume
(**b**) smell *(of flowers, fruit)*
(**c**) flavour *(of ice-cream, yoghurt)*

parfumer
1 *verb*
(**a**) to perfume *(a room)*
(**b**) to flavour; **un yaourt parfumé à la mangue** a mango-flavoured yoghurt
2 *reflexive verb* **se parfumer** to put on perfume; **je ne me parfume jamais** I never wear perfume

LA **parfumerie** *noun* perfumery

LE **pari** *noun* bet; **faire un pari** to bet; **il a gagné son pari** he won his bet

parier *verb* to bet

Paris *noun* Paris; **je travaille sur Paris** I work in Paris

The *s* in *Paris* is not pronounced.

parisien, parisienne *adjective* Paris, Parisian; **la banlieue parisienne** the Paris suburbs

LE **parking** *noun* car park

LE **parlement** *noun* parliament

parler
1 *verb*
(**a**) to speak; **parler à voix basse** to speak softly; **parler à voix haute** to speak loudly; **parle plus fort** speak up; **il parle espagnol** he speaks Spanish
(**b**) to talk; **ne me parle pas sur ce ton!** don't talk to me like that!; **tout le monde en parle** everybody's talking about it; **elle parle de déménager** she's talking about moving house
(**c**) to mention; **n'en parlons plus** let's not mention it again; **sans parler de** not to mention
2 *reflexive verb* **se parler** to talk to each other

parmi *preposition* among

LA **paroi** *noun*
(**a**) wall *(indoors)*
(**b**) **une paroi rocheuse** a rock face

LA **parole**
1 *noun*
(**a**) speech; **perdre l'usage de la parole** to lose the power of speech
(**b**) **elle a demandé la parole** she asked to speak; **prendre la parole** to speak; **adresser la parole à quelqu'un** to speak to somebody; **couper la parole à quelqu'un** to interrupt somebody; **laisser la parole à quelqu'un** to hand over to somebody
(**c**) word; **des paroles blessantes** hurtful words; **ce sont ses propres paroles** those are his very own words; **c'est votre parole contre la sienne** it's your word against his; **donner sa parole d'honneur à quelqu'un** to give somebody one's word of honour; **tenir parole** to keep one's word
2 *feminine plural noun* **les paroles** the lyrics

LE **parrain** *noun* godfather

LA **part** *noun*
(**a**) piece
(**b**) portion
(**c**) share *(of work, profits)*
(**d**) part; **couper quelque chose en parts égales** to cut something into equal parts; **prendre part à** to take part in *(an activity, a conversation)*
(**e**) side; **de toutes parts** from all sides; **de part et d'autre** on both sides; **prendre quelqu'un à part** to take somebody to one side
(**f**) **faire part de quelque chose à quelqu'un** to inform somebody of something
(**g**) **de la part de** from; **un cadeau de la part de ton père** a present from your father; **c'est très généreux de ta part** that's very generous of you; **dis-lui au revoir de ma part** say goodbye to him for me; **je vous appelle de la part de Jacques** I'm calling on behalf

of Jacques; **c'est de la part de qui?** *(on the phone)* who shall I say is calling? **(h) d'une part... d'autre part...** on the one hand..., on the other hand... **(i) à part** except for, apart from; **à part toi, personne ne le sait** nobody knows apart from you **(j) j'ai un compte à part** I've got a separate account; **faites cuire la viande à part** cook the meat separately

> The *t* in *part* is not pronounced.

LE **partage** *noun*
(a) sharing out *(of money, tasks)*
(b) slicing *(of a cake)*

partager
1 *verb*
(a) to share; **je partage son avis** I share his opinion
(b) to divide up; **elle partage son temps entre deux occupations** she divides her time between two jobs
2 *reflexive verb* **se partager**
(a) to share; **ils se sont partagé l'argent** they shared the money
(b) to divide; **le groupe s'est partagé en deux** the group divided into two

LE/LA **partenaire** *noun* partner

LE **parti** *noun*
(a) party; **un parti politique** a political party
(b) **prendre parti pour quelqu'un** to side with somebody; **prendre parti pour quelque chose** to declare oneself in favour of something; **je n'ai aucun parti pris** I'm not biased
(c) **tirer parti de la situation** to take advantage of the situation

LE **participant,** LA **participante** *noun*
(a) participant
(b) competitor *(in sports)*

> The *t* in *participant* is not pronounced.

participer *verb*
(a) to take part; **participer à un jeu** to take part in a game

(b) to contribute; **participer à un cadeau** to contribute to a present; **tu ne participes pas assez en classe** you don't contribute enough in class
(c) to share; **participer à la joie de quelqu'un** to share in somebody's joy; **participer aux bénéfices** to share in the profits

particulier, particulière
1 *adjective*
(a) particular
(b) peculiar *(style, humour, smell)*
(c) private; **des cours particuliers** private lessons
2 *adverb* **en particulier**
(a) in particular; **les Français en général et les Parisiens en particulier** French people in general and Parisians in particular
(b) in private; **puis-je vous parler en particulier?** may I have a private word with you?

particulièrement *adverb* particularly

LA **partie** *noun*
(a) part; **les parties du corps** the parts of the body; **faire partie d'un club** to belong to a club; **faire partie des victimes** to be among the casualites; **ça fait partie du jeu** it's part of the game; **en partie** partly
(b) game *(of cards, chess, tennis)*; **on fait une partie?** shall we have a game?

partir *verb*
(a) to leave; **le train part à 8h36** the train leaves at 8.36
(b) to go; **elle est partie se promener** she's gone for a walk; **partir en vacances** to go on holiday
(c) to set off; **il est parti en courant** he set off at a run *or* he ran off; **partir en voiture** to drive off
(d) to start; **le match est bien parti pour notre équipe** the match has started well for our team
(e) to come off; **la tache ne part pas** the stain won't come off; **je n'arrive pas à faire partir les traces de doigts**

I can't get the finger marks off
(**f**) **à partir de** from; **à partir d'aujourd'hui** from today onwards; **la deuxième à partir de la droite** the second one from the right; **c'est fait à partir de restes** it's made from leftovers

See verb table p. 322.

LA **partition** *noun*
(**a**) score *(musical composition)*
(**b**) partition *(of a country)*

Note that the English word *partition* is rarely a translation for the French word *partition*, unless it refers to the splitting of a country.

partout *adverb*
(**a**) everywhere; **je l'ai cherché partout** I've looked everywhere for it
(**b**) all over; **j'ai mal partout** I ache all over; **il laisse toujours traîner ses affaires partout** he always leaves his things lying all over the place
(**c**) all; **trois buts partout** three goals all

paru, parue *see* **paraître**
elle m'a paru très gentille she seemed very nice

Paru(e) is the past participle of the verb *paraître*.

pas¹ *adverb*
(**a**) not; **je ne sais pas** I don't know; **elle ne viendra pas** she won't come; **fatigué ou pas, tu viens avec nous** tired or not, you're coming with us; **pas du tout** *or* **absolument pas** not at all; **pas un mot!** not a word!; **pas un n'est arrivé à l'heure** not a single one got there on time
(**b**) **pas de** no; **pas de dessert pour moi, merci** no dessert for me, thank you
(**c**) **pas mal** *(informal phrase)* not bad; **ce n'était pas si mal** it wasn't that bad; **ce n'était pas mal du tout** it wasn't bad at all; **pas mal de** *(informal phrase)* quite a lot of; **elle a pas mal d'argent** she's got quite a lot of money

In French, *not* is expressed with two words: *ne* (or *n'*) and *pas*. *Ne* goes in front of the verb or auxiliary, and *pas* goes after the verb in simple tenses (as in *je ne comprends pas*), and between the auxiliary and the past participle in compound tenses (as in *je n'ai pas compris*). The use of *pas* without *ne* is common but informal (eg *je sais pas* instead of *je ne sais pas*).

LE **pas²** *noun*
(**a**) step; **revenir sur ses pas** to retrace one's steps; **faire un pas en arrière** to step back; **marcher à grands pas** to stride along; **pas à pas** step by step
(**b**) pace; **ralentir le pas** to slow one's pace
(**c**) tread; **marcher d'un pas léger** to walk with a light tread
(**d**) footstep; **j'entends des pas** I hear footsteps
(**e**) footprint
(**f**) **au pas** at a walk; **au pas de course** at a run
(**g**) **le pas de la porte** the doorstep
(**h**) **l'enquête avance à grands pas** the investigation is making great progress
(**i**) strait; **le pas de Calais** the Straits of Dover

passable *adjective* average *(mark, result)*

LE **passage** *noun*
(**a**) passage *(of a book, a film)*
(**b**) **ils attendaient le passage des coureurs** they were waiting for the runners to go by
(**c**) way; **enlève ton sac du passage** move your bag out of the way; **céder le passage** to give way
(**d**) crossing; **un passage clouté** *or* **un passage piétons** a pedestrian crossing; **un passage à niveau** a level crossing; **un passage souterrain** an underground passage
(**e**) change; **le passage de l'hiver au printemps** the change from winter to spring; **le passage à l'euro** the changeover to the euro

(**f**) traffic; **il y a beaucoup de passage dans notre rue** there's a lot of traffic in our street

(**g**) **de passage** visiting, passing through; **je suis de passage à Paris** I'm in Paris for a few days

(**h**) **au passage** by the way; **tiens, au passage, je te signale trois fautes page 32** by the way, there are three mistakes on page 32

passager, passagère
1 *adjective*
(**a**) short-lived
(**b**) busy *(street)*
2 *noun* **un passager, une passagère** a passenger; **les passagers à destination d'Athènes** passengers for Athens; **un passager clandestin** a stowaway

LE **passant**, LA **passante** *noun* passer-by

passé, passée
1 *adjective* **il est cinq heures passées** it's after five
2 *masculine noun* **le passé**
(**a**) past; **dans le passé** in the past
(**b**) past tense; **le passé composé** the perfect, the present perfect; **le passé simple** the past historic

LE **passeport** *noun* passport

> The *t* in *passeport* is not pronounced.

passer
1 *verb*
(**a**) to go, to go past; **il regarde passer les coureurs** he's watching the runners go past; **où est-il passé?** where's he gone?; **un avion passait dans le ciel** a plane was flying past
(**b**) to go through; **laissez-les passer!** let them through!; **il a passé la porte** he went through the door; **il est passé au rouge** he went through a red light; **on passera par Paris** we'll go through Paris; **je suis passé par des moments difficiles** I've been through difficult times
(**c**) to come; **le facteur n'est pas encore passé** the postman hasn't come

yet; **je passerai te chercher** I'll come and fetch you

(**d**) to go round; **passer chez quelqu'un** to go round to somebody's house

(**e**) to pass, to give; **passe-moi le sel** pass the salt; **il a passé sa grippe à tout le monde** he gave his flu to everybody

(**f**) **pourriez-vous me passer M. Pilon, s'il vous plaît?** could you put me through to Mr Pilon, please?; **je te passe Julien** I'll hand you over to Julien

(**g**) to spend *(time)*; **j'ai passé deux semaines en Espagne** I spent two weeks in Spain; **il passe son temps à dormir** he spends his time sleeping

(**h**) to go by; **à mesure que les jours passaient** as the days went by

(**i**) to disappear, to die out; **la mode est passée** the fashion has died out

(**j**) to put; **il passa son doigt à travers le grillage** he put a finger through the wire netting; **passez la viande au four** put the meat in the oven

(**k**) to put on *(a film, a dress, a cream)*

(**l**) to be on; **passer à la télévision** to be on TV

(**m**) to move up; **passer dans la classe supérieure** to move up to the next form; **passer en seconde** to move up to the fifth form

(**n**) **passer l'aspirateur** to hoover; **passer le balai** to sweep up

(**o**) **passer un examen** to take an exam

(**p**) **passer un accord** to enter into an agreement

(**q**) **passer la commande** to order *(in a restaurant)*

(**r**) **passer les vitesses** to change gear

(**s**) **passons sur les détails** let's skip the details

(**t**) **je vais passer pour un idiot** people will take me for an idiot; **se faire passer pour quelqu'un** to pass oneself off as somebody

2 *reflexive verb* **se passer**
(**a**) to happen; **ça s'est passé ce matin** it happened this morning; **qu'est-ce**

qui se passe? what's happening?
(**b**) to take place; **l'histoire se passe à Paris** the story takes place in Paris
(**c**) to go; **ça s'est bien passé** it went well
(**d**) to put; **se passer de la crème sur les mains** to put some hand cream on
(**e**) **se passer de quelque chose** to do without something
(**f**) to pass off, to be over

LA **passerelle** *noun*
(**a**) footbridge
(**b**) gangway

LE **passe-temps** *noun*   pastime, hobby

The word *passe-temps* does not change in the plural.

passionnant, passionnante *adjective* fascinating

passionné, passionnée
1 *adjective*
(**a**) passionate
(**b**) avid; **un lecteur passionné** an avid reader; **être passionné de quelque chose** to be mad about something
2 *noun* **un passionné, une passionnée** an enthusiast; **c'est une passionnée de moto** she's a motorbike enthusiast

LA **passoire** *noun*
(**a**) sieve
(**b**) colander

LA **pastille** *noun*
(**a**) lozenge; **une pastille pour la gorge** a throat lozenge
(**b**) **une pastille de menthe** a mint

LA **patate** *noun* potato, spud

This word is slightly informal.

patauger *verb*
(**a**) to paddle about *(in water)*
(**b**) to squelch about *(in mud)*
(**c**) to get bogged down

LA **pâte**
1 *noun*
(**a**) dough *(for bread)*; batter *(for pancakes)*; pastry *(for tarts)*; **de la pâte**

brisée shortcrust pastry; **de la pâte feuilletée** puff pastry
(**b**) **la pâte d'amandes** marzipan
(**c**) **une pâte de fruits** a fruit jelly
(**d**) **la pâte à papier** paper pulp
(**e**) **la pâte à modeler** plasticine®
2 *feminine plural noun* **les pâtes** pasta; **les pâtes sont trop cuites** the pasta's overcooked

LE **pâté** *noun*
(**a**) pâté
(**b**) **un pâté de sable** a sand pie
(**c**) **un pâté de maisons** a block *(an area of land with houses)*

LA **pâtée** *noun* pet food

paternel, paternelle *adjective*
(**a**) paternal; **ma grand-mère paternelle** my paternal grandmother, my grandmother on my father's side
(**b**) fatherly

LA **patience** *noun* patience

patient, patiente
1 *adjective* patient
2 *noun* **un patient, une patiente** a patient

The final *t* in *patient* is not pronounced.

patienter *verb* to wait

LE **patin** *noun* skate; **faire du patin à glace** to go ice-skating; **faire du patin à roulettes** to go roller-skating

LE **patinage** *noun* skating; **du patinage artistique** figure skating

LA **patinoire** *noun* ice rink

LA **pâtisserie** *noun*
(**a**) cake
(**b**) cake-making; **faire de la pâtisserie** to bake cakes
(**c**) cake shop

LE **pâtissier**, LA **pâtissière** *noun* pastry chef; **il est pâtissier** he's a pastry chef

LA **patrie** *noun* native country

LE **patron**, LA **patronne** *noun*
(**a**) boss, manager

(**b**) owner *(of a company, a bar, a restaurant)*
(**c**) patron saint

> Note that the English word *patron* is never a translation for the French word *patron*.

LA **patte** *noun*
(**a**) paw
(**b**) leg *(of an animal)*; **les pattes de devant** the forelegs; **les pattes de derrière** the hind legs
(**c**) **se mettre à quatre pattes** to go down on all fours

LA **paume** *noun* palm *(of the hand)*

LA **paupière** *noun* eyelid

LA **pause** *noun*
(**a**) break; **la pause de midi** the lunch break; **faire une pause** to have a break
(**b**) pause *(in a conversation)*; **marquer une pause** to pause
(**c**) rest *(in music)*
(**d**) half-time *(in sport)*

pauvre *adjective* poor

LA **pauvreté** *noun* poverty

pavé, pavée
1 *adjective* cobbled
2 *masculine noun* **un pavé** a cobblestone

LE **pavillon** *noun*
(**a**) detached house
(**b**) lodge *(for hunters, on an estate)*
(**c**) flag *(on a ship)*

payant, payante *adjective* **les boissons sont payantes** you have to pay for your drinks; **l'entrée est payante** there is an admission charge

LA **paye** *noun* pay; **c'est le jour de paye** it's payday

> *Paye* is pronounced "peille".

payer *verb*
(**a**) to pay
(**b**) to buy, to pay for; **payer à boire à quelqu'un** to buy somebody a drink; **je lui ai payé le repas** I paid for his meal

(**c**) **faire payer quelqu'un** to charge somebody; **faire payer quelque chose à quelqu'un** to charge somebody for something

LE **pays** *noun*
(**a**) country; **un pays étranger** a foreign country; **un pays en voie de développement** a developing country
(**b**) region; **des produits du pays** local produce
(**c**) **le pays de Galles** Wales

LE **paysage** *noun*
(**a**) landscape; **un paysage montagneux** a mountain landscape
(**b**) scenery; **un beau paysage** beautiful scenery

paysan, paysanne
1 *adjective*
(**a**) rural; **la population paysanne** the rural population; **le monde paysan** the farming world
(**b**) rustic *(house, style, food)*
2 *noun* **un paysan, une paysanne** a farmer

LES **Pays-Bas** *masculine plural noun* the Netherlands

LE **péage** *noun* toll *(on a bridge, a road)*

LA **peau** *noun*
(**a**) skin; **elle a la peau douce** she has soft skin; **une peau de banane** a banana skin
(**b**) peel *(of orange, lemon, apple)*
(**c**) leather, hide
(**d**) **être bien dans sa peau** to feel good about oneself; **être mal dans sa peau** to feel bad about oneself

> The plural of *peau* is *peaux*.

LE **péché** *noun* sin

LA **pêche** *noun*
(**a**) peach; **avoir la pêche** *(informal phrase)* to be full of beans
(**b**) fishing; **aller à la pêche** to go fishing

pêcher *verb*
(**a**) to fish

(b) to catch; **j'ai pêché trois truites** I caught three trout

LE **pêcheur,** LA **pêcheuse** *noun* fisherman/fisherwoman; **il est pêcheur** he's a fisherman; **un pêcheur à la ligne** an angler

LA **pédale** *noun* pedal

IF **pédalo**® *noun* pedalo, pedal boat

LE **peigne** *noun* comb

peigner
1 *verb* **peigner quelqu'un** to comb somebody's hair
2 *reflexive verb* **se peigner** to comb one's hair

LE **peignoir** *noun*
(a) bathrobe
(b) dressing gown

peindre *verb* to paint; **j'ai peint la porte en bleu** I painted the door blue

See verb table p. 320.

LA **peine** *noun*
(a) sentence; **une peine de prison** a prison sentence; **la peine de mort** the death penalty
(b) sadness; **il a de la peine** he's sad; **faire de la peine à quelqu'un** to upset somebody
(c) trouble; **il a de la peine à marcher** he has trouble walking; **prendre la peine de faire quelque chose** to go to the trouble of doing something
(d) **ça vaut la peine d'essayer** it's worth trying; **ça ne vaut pas la peine** *or* **ce n'est pas la peine** it's not worth it; **ce n'est pas la peine de tout récrire** there's no point writing it all out again
(e) **à peine** hardly, barely; **elle sait à peine lire** she can hardly read; **il y a à peine une semaine** barely a week ago; **à peine guérie, elle a repris le travail** no sooner had she recovered than she went back to work

LE **peintre** *noun* painter; **elle est peintre** she's a painter

The word *peintre* does not have a feminine but it can also refer to a woman.

LA **peinture** *noun*
(a) paint; **de la peinture à l'huile** oil paint; **peinture fraîche** wet paint
(b) painting; **la peinture abstraite** abstract painting; **faire de la peinture** to paint; **il y a de magnifiques peintures dans ce musée** there are some lovely paintings in this gallery

peler *verb* to peel

LA **pelle** *noun*
(a) shovel, spade
(b) **une pelle à tarte** a cake slice

LA **pellicule**
1 *noun*
(a) film *(for a camera)*
(b) skin *(on milk, sauce)*
2 *feminine plural noun* dandruff; **il a des pellicules** he has dandruff

LA **pelote** *noun* **une pelote de laine** a ball of wool

LE **peloton** *noun*
(a) pack *(of runners, cyclists)*
(b) squad; **un peloton d'exécution** a firing squad

LA **pelouse** *noun* lawn, grass; **tondre la pelouse** to mow the lawn

LA **peluche** *noun*
(a) soft toy, cuddly toy; **un chien en peluche** a cuddly toy dog
(b) **mon pull a des peluches** my jumper has gone all bobbly

penché, penchée *adjective*
(a) leaning
(b) slanting

pencher
1 *verb*
(a) to lean; **le mur penche vers la droite** the wall leans to the right
(b) to slope
(c) to tilt; **il a penché la bouteille** he tilted the bottle
(d) **pencher pour quelque chose** to favour something
2 *reflexive verb* **se pencher**
(a) to lean, to bend; **se pencher par la fenêtre** to lean out of the window; **elle se pencha sur le berceau** she

bent over the cradle
(**b**) **se pencher sur un problème** to look into a problem

pendant *preposition*
(**a**) during; **pendant l'hiver** during the winter
(**b**) for; **pendant une heure** for an hour
(**c**) **pendant que** while

> Note that the French word *pendant* is never a translation for the English word *pendant*.

LE **pendentif** *noun* pendant *(necklace)*

LA **penderie** *noun* wardrobe

pendre
1 *verb* to hang; **il a été condamné à être pendu** he was sentenced to be hanged; **il restait là, les bras pendants** he stood there with his arms hanging at his sides
2 *reflexive verb* **se pendre** to hang oneself

LA **pendule** *noun* clock

pénible *adjective*
(**a**) hard, difficult
(**b**) painful, upsetting
(**c**) annoying; **tu es vraiment pénible!** you're a real pain in the neck!

péniblement *adverb* with difficulty

LA **péniche** *noun* barge

LA **pensée** *noun* thought

penser *verb*
(**a**) to think; **je pense à l'avenir** I'm thinking about the future; **elle ne pense qu'à elle** she only thinks of herself
(**b**) to remember; **pense à lui envoyer une carte** remember to send him a postcard; **cela me fait penser à mon frère** it reminds me of my brother; **n'y pense plus!** forget all about it!

LA **pension** *noun*
(**a**) boarding school; **être en pension** to be at boarding school
(**b**) board and lodging *(in a hotel,*

somebody's house)
(**c**) pension

LE/LA **pensionnaire** *noun*
(**a**) boarder
(**b**) guest *(in a hotel)*
(**c**) resident *(in an old people's home)*

LE **pensionnat** *noun* boarding school

LA **pente** *noun* slope; **en pente** sloping

LA **Pentecôte** *noun* Whitsun; **le dimanche de Pentecôte** Whit Sunday

LA **pénurie** *noun* shortage; **une pénurie d'eau** a water shortage

LE **pépé** *noun*
(**a**) granddad, grandpa
(**b**) old man

> This word is informal.

LE **pépin** *noun*
(**a**) pip *(in fruit)*
(**b**) hitch; **il y a un petit pépin** there's a slight hitch; **j'ai un pépin** I have a problem

> Sense (b) is an informal use of *pépin*.

percer *verb*
(**a**) to pierce; **elle a les oreilles percées** she has pierced ears
(**b**) to drill
(**c**) to become famous

LA **perceuse** *noun* drill *(tool)*

LA **perche** *noun* pole; **le saut à la perche** pole vaulting

percuter *verb* to crash into

LE **perdant**, LA **perdante** *noun* loser

perdre
1 *verb*
(**a**) to lose; **il a perdu** he lost; **j'ai perdu mes lunettes** I've lost my glasses
(**b**) to waste; **perdre du temps** to waste time
(**c**) **perdre connaissance** to lose consciousness
(**d**) **perdre la tête** to go mad
2 *reflexive verb* **se perdre**
(**a**) to get lost; **je me suis perdu** I got lost

(**b**) to die out; **ce sont des métiers qui se perdent** these trades are dying out

perdu, perdue *adjective*
(**a**) lost
(**b**) wasted; **c'est du temps perdu!** it's a waste of time!
(**c**) spare; **faire quelque chose à temps perdu** to do something in a spare moment
(**d**) **une balle perdue** a stray bullet

LE **père** *noun*
(**a**) father
(**b**) **le père Noël** Father Christmas, Santa Claus

perfectionné, perfectionnée *adjective* sophisticated *(machine, techniques)*

perfectionner
1 *verb* to improve
2 *reflexive verb* **se perfectionner** to improve; **se perfectionner en français** to improve one's French

périmé, périmée *adjective*
(**a**) expired, out-of-date *(passport, ticket)*
(**b**) past its sell-by date; **ce yaourt est périmé** this yoghurt's past its sell-by date

LA **période** *noun*
(**a**) period *(of time)*
(**b**) time; **pendant la période électorale** during election time; **pendant la période des fêtes** over the festive season

LE **périphérique** *noun* ring road

LA **perle** *noun*
(**a**) pearl
(**b**) drop *(of dew)*
(**c**) bead *(of sweat)*
(**d**) gem; **sa femme est une perle!** his wife is a real gem!

LA **permanence** *noun*
(**a**) **en permanence** permanently
(**b**) duty; **je suis de permanence** I'm on duty; **le professeur d'anglais assure une permanence le mercredi matin** the English teacher is available

to see students every Wednesday morning
(**c**) study room *(at school)*; **il est en permanence** he's in the study room; **j'ai deux heures de permanence** I have a two-hour study period

permettre
1 *verb* to allow; **il m'a permis d'aller la voir** he allowed me to go and see her; **permettez-moi de vous présenter mon frère** let me introduce my brother
2 *reflexive verb* **se permettre**
(**a**) to allow oneself
(**b**) to be able to afford; **je ne peux pas me le permettre** I can't afford it
(**c**) **se permettre de faire quelque chose** to take the liberty of doing something; **si je peux me permettre** if I may say so

The past participle of *permettre* is *permis(e)*. See verb table p. 322.

permis, permise
1 *adjective* allowed; **les dictionnaires ne sont pas permis** dictionaries are not allowed
2 *masculine noun* **un permis de conduire** a driving licence

LA **permission** *noun*
(**a**) permission; **demander la permission** to ask permission
(**b**) leave; **ces militaires sont en permission** these soldiers are on leave

LE **Pérou** *noun* Peru

LE **perroquet** *noun* parrot

LA **perruche** *noun* budgerigar, budgie

LA **perruque** *noun* wig

LE **persil** *noun* parsley

LE **personnage** *noun*
(**a**) character *(in a book, a film)*
(**b**) important figure; **un personnage connu** a celebrity

LA **personnalité** *noun* personality

personne
1 *pronoun*
(**a**) nobody; **personne n'a compris** nobody understood; **il n'y a personne**

there's nobody there
(**b**) anybody; **je ne connais personne**
I don't know anybody

In French, the negation using *personne* is expressed with two words: *ne* (or *n'* in front of a vowel or a mute h) and *personne*. *Ne* always goes in front of the verb or auxiliary but *personne* can go before or after the verb depending on whether it is the subject of the sentence or not.

2 *feminine noun*
(**a**) **une personne** a person; **il est venu en personne** he came in person; **à la première personne du singulier** in the first person singular
(**b**) **plusieurs personnes** several people; **quelques personnes** a few people; **les personnes âgées** the elderly; **les grandes personnes** grown-ups

Even though the word *personne* is feminine it can refer to a male as well as to a female.

personnel, personnelle
1 *adjective* personal
2 *masculine noun* **le personnel** the staff

persuader *verb* to persuade, to convince; **je suis persuadé qu'il a raison** I'm convinced he's right; **je n'en suis pas persuadé** I'm not convinced

LA **perte** *noun*
(**a**) loss; **la perte de poids** weight loss
(**b**) waste; **quelle perte de temps!** what a waste of time!
(**c**) **à perte de vue** as far as the eye can see

perturber *verb*
(**a**) to disrupt
(**b**) to upset; **des enfants perturbés** children with behavioural problems

LE **Péruvien,** LA **Péruvienne** *noun* (*person*) Peruvian

péruvien, péruvienne *adjective* Peruvian; **l'économie péruvienne** the Peruvian economy

In French, only the noun for the inhabitants of a country takes a capital letter, never the adjective or the noun for the language.

LE **pèse-personne** *noun* (bathroom) scales

The plural of *pèse-personne* can be *pèse-personne* or *pèse-personnes*.

peser
1 *verb*
(**a**) to weigh; **ça pèse lourd** it weighs a lot *or* it's heavy
(**b**) **une menace qui pèse sur nous** a threat that is hanging over us
(**c**) **mes notes vont peser sur leur décision** my marks will influence their decision
(**d**) **la solitude me pèse** loneliness gets me down
2 *reflexive verb* **se peser** to weigh oneself

pessimiste
1 *adjective* pessimistic
2 *noun* **un/une pessimiste** a pessimist

LE **pétale** *noun* petal

LA **pétanque** *noun* game of bowls

La Pétanque
Originally invented in the south of France, where it has become a local institution, this bowling game is equally popular with tourists. The game, which requires two teams, is played outdoors on a flat sandy or earth surface. Each team consists of two to three players, each of whom has three steel *boules*. Each player tosses or rolls their *boule* so that it ends up as near as possible to the *cochonnet* (a small wooden ball). Players take turns, and whoever ends up closest to the *cochonnet* when all balls are played, wins the points.

LE **pétard** *noun* firecracker

The *d* in *pétard* is not pronounced.

péter *verb*
(**a**) to fart

(b) to blow up
(c) to break, to bust
(d) **péter les plombs** to hit the roof;
péter la forme to be full of beans

This word is informal.

pétillant, pétillante *adjective*
(a) sparkling *(water, wine)*
(b) **elle a le regard pétillant** her eyes
sparkle

petit, petite
1 *adjective*
(a) small
(b) short
(c) little; **petit à petit** little by little
(d) young; **il est encore trop petit** he's
still too young
2 *noun* **le petit** the little boy; **la petite**
the little girl; **c'est pour les petits**
that's for children
3 *masculine noun* **un petit** a baby *(of
an animal)*; **ma chatte a eu des petits**
my cat has had kittens

ʟᴇ **petit-déjeuner** *noun* breakfast;
prendre le petit-déjeuner to have
breakfast

The plural of *petit-déjeuner* is *petits-
déjeuners.*

ʟᴀ **petite-fille** *noun* granddaughter

The plural of *petite-fille* is *petites-
filles.*

ʟᴇ **petit-fils** *noun* grandson

The plural of *petit-fils* is *petits-fils.*

ʟᴇs **petits-enfants** *masculine plural
noun* grandchildren

ʟᴇ **pétrole** *noun* oil; **un puits de pétrole** an oil well; **une lampe à pétrole**
an oil lamp

Note that the English word *petrol* is
never a translation for the French
word *pétrole*.

pétrolier, pétrolière
1 *adjective* oil; **une compagnie pétrolière** an oil company; **un pays pétrolier** an oil-producing country

2 *masculine noun* **un pétrolier** an oil
tanker

peu *adverb*
(a) not much; **il travaille peu** he
doesn't work much
(b) not very; **c'est peu intéressant** it's
not very interesting
(c) not long; **peu avant** not long before; **peu après** not long after; **je travaille ici depuis peu** I haven't been
working here long
(d) **peu de** not much, little; **il reste
peu de temps** there's not much time
left; **très peu de temps** very little
time; **le peu d'expérience que j'avais**
what little experience I had
(e) **peu de** not many, few; **il y avait
peu de gens** there were not many people
(f) **un peu** a bit, a little; **elle a mangé
un peu** she ate a bit; **un peu fatigué** a
bit tired, a little tired; **un peu de fromage** a bit of cheese, a little cheese;
un petit peu a little bit
(g) **à peu près** about, roughly; **il est à
peu près cinq heures** it's about five
o'clock
(h) **peu à peu** little by little

ʟᴇ **peuple** *noun* people; **le peuple
francais** the French people; **les différents peuples d'Europe** the various
peoples of Europe

ʟᴇ **peuplier** *noun* poplar tree

ʟᴀ **peur** *noun* fear; **avoir peur** to be
scared, to be afraid; **j'ai très peur** I'm
very scared; **faire peur à quelqu'un**
to frighten somebody; **un film qui fait
peur** a scary film

peut, peuvent, peux *see* **pouvoir**
est-ce qu'il peut venir ce soir? can
he come tonight?; **ils peuvent venir
me chercher à la gare** they can pick
me up at the station; **tu peux sortir si
tu veux** you can go out if you want to

Peut, peuvent and *peux* are forms of
the verb *pouvoir* in the present tense.
See verb table p. 318.

peut-être *adverb* perhaps, maybe; **ils sont peut-être sortis** maybe they've gone out; **peut-être qu'il est malade** maybe he's ill

LE **phare** *noun*
(**a**) headlight
(**b**) lighthouse

LA **pharmacie** *noun* chemist's, pharmacy

LE **pharmacien,** LA **pharmacienne** *noun* chemist, pharmacist; **elle est pharmacienne** she's a chemist

LE/LA **philosophe** *noun* philosopher

LE **phoque** *noun* seal *(animal)*

LA **photo** *noun*
(**a**) photo; **prendre quelqu'un en photo** to take somebody's photo; **avez-vous pris des photos?** did you take any photos?; **une photo d'identité** a passport photo
(**b**) photography

LA **photocopie** *noun* photocopy

LA **photocopieuse** *noun* photocopier

LE/LA **photographe** *noun*
(**a**) photographer; **il est photographe** he's a photographer
(**b**) photo shop

> Note that the English word *photograph* is never a translation for the French word *photographe*.

LA **photographie** *noun*
(**a**) photography
(**b**) photograph; **prendre une photographie** to take a photograph

photographier *verb* to take a photo of, to photograph; **se faire photographier** to have one's photo taken

LE **photomaton**® *noun* photo booth

LA **phrase** *noun* sentence; **une phrase toute faite** a set phrase

physique
1 *adjective* physical; **l'éducation physique** physical education, PE
2 *masculine noun* **le physique** physi-cal appearance; **il a un beau physique** he's got a nice body
3 *feminine noun* **la physique** physics; **un cours de physique** a physics lesson

LE **piano** *noun* piano; **il fait du piano** he plays the piano; **un piano à queue** a grand piano

LE **pic** *noun*
(**a**) peak *(of a mountain)*
(**b**) pickaxe
(**c**) woodpecker
(**d**) **une falaise à pic** a sheer cliff; **le bateau a coulé à pic** the boat sank straight to the bottom
(**e**) **tu tombes à pic!** *(informal phrase)* you've come at just the right moment!

LE **pichet** *noun* jug

LA **pièce** *noun*
(**a**) room *(in a house)*
(**b**) piece; **les pièces d'un puzzle** the pieces of a jigsaw puzzle; **j'ai retrouvé son jouet en pièces** I found his toy in pieces
(**c**) **une pièce de monnaie** *or* **une pièce** a coin
(**d**) **une pièce de théâtre** a play
(**e**) **une pièce d'identité** ID
(**f**) **une pièce jointe** enclosure *(in a letter)*; attachment *(to an e-mail)*

LE **pied** *noun*
(**a**) foot; **je suis pieds nus** I'm bare-foot; **à pied** on foot; **on ira au stade à pied** we'll walk to the stadium; **au pied de la tour Eiffel** at the foot of the Eiffel Tower
(**b**) **un coup de pied** a kick; **donner un coup de pied à quelqu'un** to kick somebody
(**c**) leg *(of a table, a chair)*
(**d**) base *(of a lamp)*

LE **piège** *noun* trap; **tendre un piège à quelqu'un** to set a trap for somebody

LA **pierre** *noun* stone; **une pierre précieuse** a precious stone

piétiner *verb*
(**a**) to shuffle about, to shuffle along
(**b**) to trample on

(**c**) **piétiner de rage** to stamp one's feet in rage

(**d**) **l'enquête piétine** the enquiry is getting nowhere

LE **piéton,** LA **piétonne** *noun* pedestrian

LA **pieuvre** *noun* octopus

pile

1 *feminine noun*

(**a**) battery

(**b**) pile; **une pile de livres** a pile of books

(**c**) **pile ou face?** heads or tails?; **jouer à pile ou face** to toss a coin

2 *adverb* right; **pile au milieu** right in the middle; **ça commence à huit heures pile** it begins at eight o'clock sharp

LE **pilier** *noun* pillar

LE **pilote** *noun*

(**a**) pilot

(**b**) **un pilote de course** a racing driver

LA **pilule** *noun* pill

LE **piment** *noun* chilli

LE **pin** *noun* pine tree; **une aiguille de pin** a pine needle; **une pomme de pin** a pine cone; **un meuble en pin** a piece of pine furniture

LA **pince** *noun*

(**a**) pliers

(**b**) claw *(of a crab)*

(**c**) **une pince à cheveux** a hair clip

(**d**) **une pince à épiler** tweezers

(**e**) **une pince à linge** a clothes peg

(**f**) **une pince à sucre** sugar tongs

LE **pinceau** *noun* paintbrush, brush

The plural of *pinceau* is *pinceaux*.

pincer

1 *verb*

(**a**) to pinch; **son grand-père lui a pincé la joue** his grandfather pinched his cheek

(**b**) **il en pince pour elle** *(informal phrase)* he's crazy about her

2 *reflexive verb* **se pincer**

(**a**) to pinch oneself

(**b**) to catch; **je me suis pincé le doigt dans le tiroir** I caught my finger in the drawer

LE **pingouin** *noun* penguin

LA **pioche** *noun*

(**a**) pickaxe

(**b**) pile *(in card games)*

piocher *verb*

(**a**) to dig

(**b**) to draw from the pile *(in card games)*; **pioche!** take a card!

LE **pion,** LA **pionne**

1 *masculine noun* **un pion** a piece *(for board games)*; a pawn *(in chess)*

2 *noun* supervisor *(at school)*

> **Les Pions**
>
> In French secondary schools, the *pions* (officially called *surveillants*) are responsible for supervising pupils outside class hours – during breaks and at lunch time. They are often university students who do the job to make a little extra money.

pipi *noun* **faire pipi** to pee; **aller faire pipi** to go to the loo; **faire pipi au lit** to wet the bed

This word is informal.

piquant, piquante *adjective*

(**a**) thorny, prickly

(**b**) hot *(sauce, mustard)*

pique *noun* spades *(in cards)*; **le dix de pique** the ten of spades

LE **pique-nique** *noun* picnic; **faire un pique-nique** to have a picnic

The plural of *pique-nique* is *pique-niques*.

pique-niquer *verb* to have a picnic

piquer

1 *verb*

(**a**) to prick; **elle m'a piqué avec une épingle** she pricked me with a pin

(**b**) to bite; **se faire piquer par un moustique** to get bitten by a mosquito

(**c**) to sting; **se faire piquer par une abeille** to get stung by a bee

(**d**) to burn *(tongue, eyes)*; **une moutarde qui pique** hot mustard
(**e**) to dive *(for a plane)*; **piquer du nez** *(for a plane)* to nosedive; *(for a person)* to nod off; **piquer une tête dans l'eau** *(informal phrase)* to dive into the water
(**f**) to nick; **je me suis fait piquer mon vélo** my bike's been nicked

Sense (f) is an informal use of *piquer*.

(**g**) *(informal phrases)* **piquer une colère** to go ballistic; **piquer une crise** to get hysterical; **piquer un somme** to take a nap
2 *reflexive verb* **se piquer** to prick oneself

LE **piquet** *noun*
(**a**) post, stake; **un piquet de tente** a tent peg
(**b**) **mettre un enfant au piquet** to send a child to stand in the corner

LA **piqûre** *noun*
(**a**) injection; **ils m'ont fait une piqûre** they gave me an injection
(**b**) prick *(of a pin, a thorn)*
(**c**) bite *(of a mosquito)*
(**d**) sting *(of a bee, a nettle)*

LE **pirate** *noun*
(**a**) pirate
(**b**) **un pirate de l'air** a hijacker
(**c**) **un pirate informatique** a hacker

pire
1 *adjective*
(**a**) worse; **c'est encore pire** it's even worse; **c'est de pire en pire** it's getting worse and worse; **elle est pire que lui** she is worse than him
(**b**) worst; **mon pire ennemi** my worst enemy; **c'est la pire chose qui pouvait lui arriver** it's the worst thing that could happen to him; **il fait les pires bêtises** he does the stupidest things
2 *noun* **le pire, la pire** the worst one; **ce sont eux les pires** they are the worst
3 *masculine noun*
(**a**) **il y a pire** there's worse
(**b**) **je crains le pire** I fear the worst; **je m'attends au pire** I'm expecting the worst

LA **piscine** *noun* swimming pool

LA **pistache** *noun* pistachio (nut)

LA **piste** *noun*
(**a**) trail; **les policiers sont sur sa piste** the police are on his trail; **un jeu de piste** a treasure hunt
(**b**) lead; **la police cherche une piste** the police are looking for leads
(**c**) track *(in sport)*; **une piste de course à pied** a running track; **une piste cyclable** a cycle path; **être sur la bonne piste** to be on the right track; **être sur la mauvaise piste** to be on the wrong track
(**d**) ski run
(**e**) runway; **une piste d'atterrissage** a landing strip
(**f**) **une piste de danse** a dancefloor

LE **pistolet** *noun* gun, pistol

LA **pitié** *noun*
(**a**) pity; **avoir pitié de quelqu'un** to feel pity for somebody; **cela faisait pitié à voir** it was pitiful to see
(**b**) mercy; **ils sont sans pitié** they are merciless

pittoresque *adjective* picturesque

LE **placard** *noun* cupboard

Note that the English word *placard* is never a translation for the French word *placard*.

LA **place** *noun*
(**a**) room; **ne prends pas toute la place** don't take up so much room
(**b**) space; **une place de parking** a parking space
(**c**) place; **tout est à sa place** everything's in its place
(**d**) seat *(on a plane, at the theatre)*
(**e**) ticket; **j'ai trois places de concert** I have three tickets for the concert
(**f**) square; **la place du village** the village square
(**g**) rank *(in a competition)*
(**h**) **à la place** instead; **emmenez-moi à sa place** take me instead (of him); **on a vu un documentaire à la place du film** we watched a documentary

instead of the film
(i) **sur place** there; **ils sont déjà sur place** they're already there
(j) **mettre en place** to set up

placer *verb*
(a) to place *(an object)*
(b) to seat *(a person)*
(c) to invest *(money)*
(d) **je n'ai pas pu placer un mot** I couldn't get a word in edgeways

LE **plafond** *noun* ceiling

LA **plage** *noun*
(a) beach; **une serviette de plage** a beach towel; **aller en vacances à la plage** to go on holiday to the seaside
(b) **la plage arrière** the parcel shelf *(of a car)*

LA **plaie** *noun* wound; **quelle plaie!** *(informal phrase)* what a nuisance!

plaindre
1 *verb* to feel sorry for; **je la plains** I feel sorry for her
2 *reflexive verb* **se plaindre** to complain; **arrête de te plaindre** stop complaining

See verb table p. 320.

LA **plainte** *noun*
(a) moan *(sound)*
(b) complaint; **il a porté plainte à la police** he made an official complaint to the police

plaire
1 *verb*
(a) **elle lui plaît** he likes her; **ça me plaît** I like it; **le film m'a plu** I liked the film
(b) to be attractive; **il plaît aux femmes** women find him attractive
2 *reflexive verb* **se plaire je me plais bien dans ma nouvelle maison** I like it in my new house; **alors, vous vous plaisez à Paris?** so, how do you like living in Paris?

The past participle of *plaire* is *plu(e)*. See verb table p. 322.

plaisanter *verb* to joke; **tu plaisantes!**

you've got to be joking!

LA **plaisanterie** *noun* joke; **c'est une mauvaise plaisanterie** it's a cruel joke

LE **plaisir** *noun* pleasure; **faire plaisir à quelqu'un** to please somebody; **ça va lui faire plaisir** he'll be pleased

plaît *see* plaire, s'il te plaît, s'il vous plaît

LE **plan** *noun*
(a) map; **un plan du métro** an underground map
(b) plan; **un plan d'action** a plan of action; **un plan d'épargne** a savings plan
(c) shot *(in cinema)*
(d) **au premier plan** in the foreground
(e) **sur le plan personnel** on a personal level

LA **planche** *noun*
(a) plank
(b) board; **une planche à découper** a chopping board; **une planche à repasser** an ironing board; **une planche de surf** a surfboard
(c) **une planche à voile** a sailboard; **faire de la planche à voile** to go windsurfing
(d) **faire la planche** to float on one's back
(e) **monter sur les planches** to tread the boards

LE **plancher** *noun* floor; **refaire le plancher d'une pièce** to lay a new floor in a room

planer *verb*
(a) to glide *(for a plane)*
(b) to soar *(for a bird)*
(c) to have one's head in the clouds

Sense (c) is an informal use of the *planer.*

LA **planète** *noun* planet

LE **planeur** *noun* glider; **faire du planeur** to go gliding

LA **plante** *noun*
(a) plant
(b) **la plante du pied** the sole of the foot

planter
1 *verb*
(**a**) to plant *(a flower)*
(**b**) to hammer in *(a nail)*
(**c**) to stick in *(a knife)*
(**d**) to put up *(a tent)*
(**e**) to crash *(for a computer)*
2 *reflexive verb* **se planter**
(**a**) to get it wrong
(**b**) to fail *(an exam)*
(**c**) to have a crash *(in a car)*

The verb *se planter* is informal.

LA **plaque** *noun*
(**a**) plate *(made of metal)*; **une plaque d'immatriculation** a number plate; **une plaque de cuisson** *or* **une plaque chauffante** a hot plate; **une plaque de four** a baking tray
(**b**) **une plaque de beurre** a block of butter
(**c**) **une plaque de verglas** an icy patch

LE **plastique** *noun* plastic

plat, plate
1 *adjective*
(**a**) flat; **un pneu à plat** a flat tyre
(**b**) still *(water)*
(**c**) **à plat ventre** face downwards; **être couché à plat ventre** to be lying face downwards
2 *masculine noun* **le plat**
(**a**) flat part; **le plat de la main** the flat of the hand
(**b**) dish; **c'est mon plat préféré** it's my favourite dish
(**c**) course; **le plat de résistance** the main course; **le plat du jour** today's special

LE **plateau** *noun*
(**a**) tray
(**b**) **un plateau de fromages** a cheeseboard
(**c**) stage, set *(in theatre, cinema, television)*
(**d**) plate *(of scales)*
(**e**) turntable *(in a microwave)*
(**f**) plateau

The plural of *plateau* is *plateaux*.

LA **plate-forme** *noun*
(**a**) platform
(**b**) rig; **une plate-forme pétrolière** an oil rig

The plural of *plate-forme* is *plates-formes*.

LA **platine laser** *noun* CD player

LE **plâtre** *noun* plaster; **il a un bras dans le plâtre** he has an arm in plaster

plein, pleine
1 *adjective*
(**a**) full; **c'est la pleine lune** there's a full moon; **un travail à plein temps** a full-time job; **une pièce pleine de livres** a room full of books
(**b**) **plein de** lots of; **il y avait plein de livres** there were lots of books; **j'en ai plein** I've got lots
(**c**) **une piscine en plein air** an outdoor pool; **en pleine nuit** in the middle of the night; **en plein jour** in broad daylight; **en pleine mer** out in the open sea; **en plein milieu** right in the middle; **j'ai mis le pied en plein dans une flaque** I stepped right in the middle of a puddle
(**d**) **être en pleine forme** to be on top form
2 *preposition* **plein** all over; **il a de la boue plein son pantalon** he's got mud all over his trousers
3 *masculine noun* **le plein** full tank *(of petrol)*; **faire le plein** to fill up with petrol

pleurer *verb* to cry

pleut *see* **pleuvoir**
il pleut depuis trois jours it's been raining for three days

Pleut is a form of the verb *pleuvoir* in the present tense. See verb table p. 322.

pleuvoir *verb* to rain; **il pleut** it's raining; **il a plu toute la journée** it's been raining all day

The past participle of *pleuvoir* is *plu*. See verb table p. 322.

LE **pli** *noun*
(a) fold, crease; **le drap fait des plis** the sheet is creased
(b) habit; **c'est un pli à prendre** you've just got to get into the habit
(c) trick *(in card games)*; **faire un pli** to take a trick
(d) envelope; **sous pli cacheté** in a sealed envelope

plier
1 *verb*
(a) to fold *(a newspaper, clothes)*
(b) to fold up *(a chair, an umbrella)*; **une chaise pliante** a folding chair
(c) to bend; **plier les jambes** to bend one's legs
2 *reflexive verb* **se plier**
(a) to fold up *(for a chair, an umbrella)*
(b) to bend; **se plier en deux** to bend double

LE **plomb** *noun*
(a) lead *(metal)*
(b) shot *(shotgun pellets)*
(c) fuse; **un plomb a sauté** a fuse has blown
(d) **péter les plombs** *(informal phrase)* to hit the roof

> The *b* in *plomb* is not pronounced.

LE **plombage** *noun* filling *(in a tooth)*

LE **plombier** *noun* plumber; **il est plombier** he's a plumber

LA **plongée** *noun* diving; **faire de la plongée** to go diving; **la plongée sous-marine** scuba diving

LE **plongeoir** *noun* diving board

LE **plongeon** *noun* dive; **faire un plongeon** to dive

plonger
1 *verb*
(a) to dive
(b) to plunge; **la pièce était plongée dans l'obscurité** the room was plunged into darkness
(c) **être plongé dans ses pensées** to be deep in thought
2 *reflexive verb* **se plonger** se plonger **dans un livre** to bury oneself in a book

LE **plongeur,** LA **plongeuse** *noun*
(a) diver; **un plongeur sous-marin** a scuba diver
(b) washer-up, dishwasher *(in a restaurant)*

plu *see* **plaire, pleuvoir**
(a) **ça m'a beaucoup plu** I liked it very much
(b) **il a plu hier** it rained yesterday

> *Plu* is the past participle of the verbs *plaire* and *pleuvoir*. See verb tables p. 322.

LA **pluie** *noun*
(a) rain
(b) shower *(of confetti, meteors)*

LA **plume** *noun*
(a) feather
(b) quill
(c) nib *(of a fountain pen)*

plumer *verb* to pluck *(a chicken)*

LA **plupart** *noun* **la plupart du temps** most of the time; **la plupart d'entre eux** most of them; **dans la plupart des cas** in most cases; **pour la plupart** for the most part

LE **pluriel** *noun* plural

plus
1 *adverb*
(a) more; **plus intéressant** more interesting; **plus tard** later; **tu es plus patient que moi** you're more patient than I am; **tu as plus de livres que moi** you have more books than me; **un de plus** one more; **deux heures de plus** two hours more; **j'ai quatre ans de plus que vous** I'm four years older than you; **de plus en plus** more and more; **c'était bien, sans plus** it was nice, but no more than that
(b) the more; **plus je réfléchis, plus je me dis qu'il a raison** the more I think about it, the more I think he's right
(c) **le plus, la plus, les plus** the most; **les plus beaux** the most attractive; **l'homme le plus riche du monde** the richest man in the world; **la montagne la plus haute** the highest mountain;

c'est moi qui travaille le plus I'm the one who works the most; **c'est moi qui ai le plus de livres** I have the most books

(**d**) **de plus** or **en plus** moreover, what's more; **de plus** or **en plus, il m'a menti** what's more, he lied to me

(**e**) **de plus** or **en plus** extra; **mets deux couverts de plus** or **en plus** lay two extra places; **as-tu un ticket en plus?** do you have a spare ticket?

(**f**) **en plus de** in addition to

(**g**) **ne... plus** not... any more; **elle n'est plus très jeune** she isn't very young any more; **il n'a plus de pain** he doesn't have any more bread; **il n'y a plus rien** there's nothing left

---

In French, the negation using *plus* is expressed with two words: *ne* (or *n'* in front of a vowel or a mute h) and *plus*. *Ne* goes in front of the verb or auxiliary, and *plus* goes after the verb (as in *il ne comprend plus*) or the auxiliary.

(**h**) **plus un mot!** not another word!

(**i**) **non plus** neither, not... either; **je n'ai pas pris de parapluie – moi non plus** I didn't bring an umbrella – neither did I; **je n'y suis pas allé non plus** I didn't go either

2 *conjunction* plus; **le transport, plus le logement, plus la nourriture, ça revient cher** travel, plus accommodation, plus food: it all works out quite expensive; **3 plus 3 égalent 6** 3 plus 3 makes 6

The final *s* is only pronounced when *plus* is a conjunction (see 2 above). *Plus* is pronounced "plu" when it is an adverb (see 1 above).

---

plusieurs
1 *adjective* several; **plusieurs élèves** several pupils
2 *pronoun* several people; **nous serons plusieurs à la réunion** there will be several of us at the meeting

plutôt *adverb*
(**a**) rather; **elle est plutôt jolie** she's rather pretty

(**b**) instead; **n'y va pas en voiture, prends plutôt le train** don't go by car, take the train instead; **prenez le rouge plutôt que le vert** take the red one instead of the green

LE **pneu** *noun* tyre; **j'ai deux pneus crevés** I have two flat tyres

LA **poche** *noun*
(**a**) pocket
(**b**) **un livre de poche** a paperback

LA **pochette** *noun*
(**a**) pocket handkerchief
(**b**) plastic document holder
(**c**) **une pochette de disque** a record sleeve

poêle
1 *feminine noun* **une poêle** a frying pan
2 *masculine noun* **un poêle** a stove *(for heating)*

Poêle is pronounced like *poil*.

LE **poème** *noun* poem

LA **poésie** *noun*
(**a**) poetry
(**b**) poem

LE **poète** *noun* poet

LE **poids** *noun*
(**a**) weight; **prendre du poids** to put on weight
(**b**) shot *(in athletics)*; **le lancer du poids** the shotput
(**c**) **un poids lourd** a lorry

LE **poignard** *noun* dagger; **il lui a donné un coup de poignard** he stabbed him

poignarder *verb* to stab

LA **poignée** *noun*
(**a**) handle *(of a door, a suitcase)*
(**b**) handful; **une poignée de bonbons** a handful of sweets
(**c**) **une poignée de main** a handshake

LE **poignet** *noun* wrist

LE **poil** *noun*
(**a**) hair

(**b**) bristle *(of a brush)*
(**c**) **à poil** *(informal phrase)* starkers

poilu, poilue *adjective* hairy

poinçonner *verb* to punch *(a ticket)*

LE **poing** *noun* fist

LE **point** *noun*
(**a**) point; **mon point de vue** my point of view; **un point fort** a strong point; **un point faible** a weak point
(**b**) dot
(**c**) place, point; **le point de départ** the starting point
(**d**) mark; **c'est quatre points en moins pour une faute d'orthographe** four marks are taken off for each spelling mistake
(**e**) **marquer un point** to score a point
(**f**) stitch *(in sewing)*; **un point de suture** a stitch *(in a wound)*
(**g**) **un point de côté** a stitch *(pain)*
(**h**) **un point de repère** *(in space)* a landmark; *(in time)* a reference point
(**i**) **un point** *or* **un point final** a full stop; **un point d'exclamation** an exclamation mark; **un point d'interrogation** a question mark; **un point virgule** a semicolon; **deux-points** colon; **des points de suspension** suspension points
(**j**) **ils ont des points communs** they have things in common
(**k**) **être sur le point de faire quelque chose** to be about to do something
(**l**) **faire le point** to take stock of the situation
(**m**) **mettre au point** to focus *(a camera)*; to finalize *(a speech, a project)*; **mettons les choses au point** let's get things straight; **la machine n'est pas encore au point** the machine still needs some working on
(**n**) **ton travail est dur à ce point?** is your job that hard?; **elle est déprimée, à tel point qu'elle ne veut plus voir personne** she's so depressed that she won't see anyone any more; **au point où j'en suis, autant continuer** having

got this far, I might as well carry on
(**o**) **à point** medium *(meat)*
(**p**) **la voiture est au point mort** the car is in neutral

The *t* in *point* is not pronounced.

LA **pointe** *noun*
(**a**) point *(of a knife, a needle)*
(**b**) tip; **sur la pointe des pieds** on tip-toe
(**c**) nail *(pin)*
(**d**) **une pointe de vitesse** a burst of speed; **la vitesse de pointe** the top speed
(**e**) **l'heure de pointe** rush hour
(**f**) **un secteur de pointe** a high-tech sector; **une technologie de pointe** cutting-edge technology
(**g**) trace *(of irony, jealousy)*

LE **pointillé** *noun* dotted line

pointu, pointue *adjective* sharp *(knife, pencil)*

LA **pointure** *noun* size *(of shoes)*; **quelle est ta pointure?** what size do you take?

LA **poire** *noun* pear

LE **poireau** *noun* leek

The plural of *poireau* is *poireaux*.

LE **poirier** *noun*
(**a**) pear tree
(**b**) **faire le poirier** to do a headstand

LE **pois** *noun*
(**a**) pea; **les petits pois** peas; **un pois cassé** a split pea; **un pois chiche** a chickpea
(**b**) dot, spot; **un chemisier à pois blancs** a blouse with white spots

LES **Poissons** *masculine plural noun* Pisces; **elle est Poissons** she's a Pisces

LE **poisson** *noun*
(**a**) fish; **un poisson rouge** a goldfish
(**b**) **faire une queue de poisson à quelqu'un** to cut in front of somebody *(when driving)*
(**c**) **poisson d'avril!** April fool!

Poisson d'Avril

In France and other French-speaking countries, on the first of April children cut fish shapes out of paper and stick them on their unsuspecting classmates' backs, and people play practical jokes on one another before shouting *Poisson d'avril!* (April fool!).

LA **poissonnerie** *noun* fishmonger's

LA **poitrine** *noun* chest *(part of the body)*

LE **poivre** *noun* pepper *(spice)*

poivrer *verb* to put pepper on/in; **la soupe est trop poivrée** there's too much pepper in the soup

LE **poivron** *noun* pepper *(vegetable)*; **un poivron rouge** a red pepper; **un poivron vert** a green pepper

polaire
1 *adjective*
(a) polar; **une expédition polaire** a polar expedition
(b) **la laine polaire** fleecy material, fleece
2 *feminine noun* **une polaire** a fleece

LE **pôle** *noun* pole; **le pôle Nord** the North Pole; **le pôle Sud** the South Pole

poli, polie *adjective*
(a) polite; **elle est très polie avec moi** she's very polite to me; **ce n'est pas poli de répondre!** it's rude to answer back!
(b) polished

LA **police** *noun*
(a) police
(b) **une police d'assurance** an insurance policy
(c) **une police de caractères** a font *(in word processing)*

policier, policière
1 *adjective*
(a) police; **une enquête policière** a police investigation
(b) detective *(novel, film)*
2 *masculine noun* **un policier** a police-man, a police officer; **il est policier** he's a policeman; **une femme policier** a policewoman

LA **politesse** *noun* politeness; **il est toujours d'une grande politesse** he's always very polite; **par politesse** out of politeness

politique
1 *adjective* political; **un prisonnier politique** a political prisoner; **un homme politique, une femme politique** a politician
2 *feminine noun*
(a) politics; **faire de la politique** to be involved in politics
(b) policy; **la politique extérieure** foreign policy

polluer *verb* to pollute; **un produit qui pollue** *or* **un produit polluant** a pollutant

LA **Pologne** *noun* Poland

LE **Polonais,** LA **Polonaise** *noun* *(person)* Pole

polonais, polonaise
1 *adjective* Polish; **une danse polonaise** a Polish dance
2 *masculine noun* **le polonais** *(language)* Polish; **il parle polonais** he speaks Polish

In French, only the noun for the inhabitants of a country takes a capital letter, never the adjective or the noun for the language.

LA **pommade** *noun* ointment

LA **pomme** *noun*
(a) apple; **une tarte aux pommes** an apple tart
(b) **une pomme de terre** a potato; **des pommes frites** chips; **des pommes vapeur** steamed potatoes; **des pommes de terre à l'eau** boiled potatoes
(c) **une pomme de pin** a pine cone
(d) **une pomme de douche** a shower head; **une pomme d'arrosoir** a rose *(of a watering can)*

LE **pommier** *noun* apple tree

LA **pompe** *noun*
(a) pump; **une pompe à essence** a petrol pump
(b) **faire des pompes** to do press-ups
(c) **les pompes funèbres** funeral parlour, undertaker's

LE **pompier** *noun* fireman, fire fighter; **il est pompier** he's a fireman; **les pomplers** the fire brigade

pondre *verb* to lay *(an egg)*

LE **poney** *noun* pony

LE **pont** *noun*
(a) bridge
(b) deck *(on a ship)*
(c) day off between a national holiday and a weekend; **le 14 juillet tombe un jeudi, je vais faire le pont** the 14th of July is on a Thursday, so I'll take Friday off and make a long weekend of it

populaire *adjective*
(a) popular
(b) working-class; **un quartier populaire** a working-class area
(c) folk; **les traditions populaires** folk traditions

LE **porc** *noun*
(a) pig
(b) pork

> The *c* in *porc* is not pronounced.

LA **porcelaine** *noun* china, porcelain

LE **port** *noun*
(a) port, harbour; **un port de pêche** a fishing port; **un port de plaisance** a marina
(b) **à bon port** safely; **nous sommes arrivés à bon port** we got there safe and sound
(c) postage; **port et emballage** postage and packing
(d) **le port du casque est obligatoire** it is compulsory to wear a helmet
(e) carrying *(of a weapon)*

> The *t* in *port* is not pronounced.

portable
1 *adjective*
(a) portable

(b) mobile *(phone)*
(c) laptop *(computer)*
2 *masculine noun* **un portable** a mobile *(phone)*

LE **portail** *noun* gate

LA **porte** *noun*
(a) door; **la porte d'entrée** the front door
(b) gate; **la porte d'embarquement** the departure gate
(c) **mettre quelqu'un à la porte** to throw somebody out

LE **porte-bagages** *noun* carrier *(on a bike)*

> The word *porte-bagages* does not change in the plural.

LE **porte-bonheur** *noun* lucky charm

> The word *porte-bonheur* does not change in the plural.

LE **porte-clefs** *noun* keyring

> The word *porte-clefs* does not change in the plural.

porte-clés *see* **porte-clefs**

LA **porte-fenêtre** *noun* French window

> The plural of *porte-fenêtre* is *portes-fenêtres*.

LE **portefeuille** *noun* wallet

LE **portemanteau** *noun*
(a) coat stand, coat rack
(b) coathanger

> The plural of *portemanteau* is *porte-manteaux*.

LE **porte-monnaie** *noun* purse

> The word *porte-monnaie* does not change in the plural.

porter
1 *verb*
(a) to carry
(b) to wear; **elle porte des lunettes** she wears glasses
(c) to bear; **la lettre porte sa signa-**

ture the letter bears her signature
(**d**) to take; **porte-lui ce colis** take him this parcel
(**e**) to bring; **ça porte bonheur** it brings good luck; **ça porte malheur** it brings bad luck
(**f**) **porter sur** to be about; **ce chapitre porte sur la nourriture italienne** this chapter is about Italian food
2 *reflexive verb* **se porter**
(**a**) to be; **se porter bien** to be well; **se porter mal** to be ill; **comment vous portez-vous?** how are you?
(**b**) **se porter volontaire** to volunteer; **se porter candidat** to stand as a candidate

LE **porteur,** LA **porteuse** *noun*
(**a**) porter *(of luggage)*
(**b**) bearer *(of a coffin, a letter)*

LE **portier,** LA **portière**
1 *noun* doorman/doorwoman *(of a hotel)*
2 *feminine noun* **la portière** the door *(of a vehicle)*

LE **portillon** *noun* gate, barrier

LA **portion** *noun*
(**a**) portion *(of food)*
(**b**) share *(of money)*
(**c**) stretch *(of a road)*

LE **portrait** *noun*
(**a**) portrait
(**b**) portrayal, description
(**c**) **c'est son portrait vivant** he's the spitting image of him

The *t* in *portrait* is not pronounced.

LE **Portugais,** LA **Portugaise** *noun* *(person)* Portuguese man/Portuguese woman; **les Portugais** the Portuguese

portugais, portugaise
1 *adjective* Portuguese; **un plat portugais** a Portuguese dish
2 *masculine noun* **le portugais** *(language)* Portuguese; **il parle portugais** he speaks Portuguese

In French, only the noun for the inhabitants of a country takes a capital letter, never the adjective or the noun for the language.

LE **Portugal** *noun* Portugal

poser
1 *verb*
(**a**) to put; **poser ses coudes sur la table** to put one's elbows on the table
(**b**) to put down; **posez vos stylos et rendez vos copies** put down your pens and hand in your papers
(**c**) to put in *(a window)*; to put up *(wallpaper)*; to lay *(carpet)*
(**d**) to pose *(for a photo)*
(**e**) **poser une question à quelqu'un** to ask somebody a question; **ça me pose un problème** that poses a problem for me
(**f**) **poser une opération** to set out a sum
2 *reflexive verb* **se poser**
(**a**) *(plane)* to land
(**b**) to come up; **ce problème ne s'est jamais posé** that problem has never come up

LA **position** *noun*
(**a**) position; **vous me mettez dans une position délicate** you're putting me in a difficult position
(**b**) posture
(**c**) **arriver en première position** *(for an athlete)* to come first; *(for a candidate)* to come top
(**d**) **prendre position** to take a stand; **prendre position contre quelque chose** to take a stand against something; **rester sur ses positions** to stick to one's guns

posséder *verb*
(**a**) to own
(**b**) to have; **je possède des preuves** I have proof
(**c**) to possess

LA **possibilité** *noun*
(**a**) possibility
(**b**) opportunity; **mon travail me donne la possibilité de voyager** my job gives me the opportunity of travelling

possible *adjective*
(a) possible; **rendre quelque chose possible** to make something possible
(b) **au possible** extremely; **elle a été désagréable au possible** she couldn't have been more unpleasant

poste
1 *feminine noun*
(a) post, mail; **envoyer quelque chose par la poste** to send something by post
(b) post office; **il travaille à la poste** he works for the post office
2 *masculine noun*
(a) post, job; **il a obtenu le poste de directeur financier** he was given the post of financial director
(b) set; **un poste de télévision** a television (set); **un poste de radio** a radio
(c) extension *(telephone number)*
(d) **un poste de police** a police station

poster *verb* to post *(a letter)*

LE **postier,** LA **postière** *noun* post office worker; **il est postier** he's a post office worker

postillonner *verb* to splutter; **il nous postillonnait dessus** he spluttered all over us

LE **pot** *noun*
(a) jar; **un pot de confiture** a jar of jam; **un petit pot** a jar of baby food
(b) pot; **un pot de fleurs** a plant pot
(c) potty
(d) **un pot d'échappement** an exhaust pipe
(e) drink; **allons prendre un pot** let's go for a drink; **un pot de départ** a leaving drink

Sense (e) is an informal use of *pot*.

(f) luck; **avoir du pot** to be lucky; **ne pas avoir de pot** to be unlucky

Sense (f) is an informal use of *pot*. Note that the *t* in *pot* is not pronounced in French.

potable *adjective*
(a) **de l'eau potable** drinking water

(b) reasonable *(work, film)*

Sense (b) is an informal use of *potable*.

LE **potage** *noun* soup

LE **pot-au-feu** *noun* beef stew with vegetables

The word *pot-au-feu* does not change in the plural.

LE **pot-de-vin** *noun* bribe; **verser des pots-de-vin à quelqu'un** to bribe somebody

The plural of *pot-de-vin* is *pots-de-vin*.

LE **poteau** *noun*
(a) post; **le poteau d'arrivée** the winning post; **un poteau électrique** a telegraph pole
(b) goalpost

The plural of *poteau* is *poteaux*.

LA **poterie** *noun* pottery; **faire de la poterie** to make pottery

LE **potiron** *noun* pumpkin

LE **pou** *noun* louse; **il a des poux** he's got lice

The plural of *pou* is *poux*.

LA **poubelle** *noun* dustbin, bin

LE **pouce** *noun*
(a) thumb
(b) inch

LA **poudre** *noun* powder; **du lait en poudre** powdered milk

LE **poulain** *noun* foal

LA **poule** *noun*
(a) hen
(b) **quand les poules auront des dents!** when pigs fly!
(c) group, pool *(in sport)*

LE **poulet** *noun* chicken *(meat)*; **un poulet rôti** a roast chicken

LE **pouls** *noun* pulse; **il m'a pris le pouls** he took my pulse

The final letters *l* and *s* are not pronounced.

LE **poumon** *noun* lung

LA **poupée** *noun* doll; **jouer à la pou-pée** to play with dolls

pour *preposition*
(a) for; **il est parti pour l'Italie** he left for Italy; **pour la première fois** for the first time; **elle est absente pour deux semaines** she's away for two weeks; **merci pour ton aide** thanks for your help; **j'ai beaucoup d'admiration pour lui** I've got a lot of admiration for him; **pour quoi faire?** what for?
(b) to, in order to; **pour faire quelque chose** to do something; **je travaille pour vivre** I work to live; **pour mieux comprendre** in order to understand better; **pour ne pas tomber** so as not to fall
(c) **pour que** so that; **pour que tu le saches** so that you know
(d) in favour of; **qui est pour?** who's in favour?
(e) per; **dix pour cent** ten percent

LE **pourboire** *noun* tip *(for a waiter)*

pourquoi *adverb* why; **pourquoi pars-tu?** *or* **pourquoi est-ce que tu pars?** why are you going?; **pourquoi pas?** why not?; **je ne sais pas pourquoi tu dis ça** I don't know why you're saying that

pourra, pourrai *see* **pouvoir¹**
est-ce que ta sœur pourra venir me chercher à la gare? will your sister be able to pick me up at the station?; **je ne sais pas si je pourrai venir à ta soirée** I don't know if I'll be able to come to your party

Pourra and *pourrai* are forms of the verb *pouvoir* in the future tense. See verb table p. 318.

pourrais, pourrait *see* **pouvoir¹**
est-ce que je pourrais partir plus tôt aujourd'hui? could I leave earlier today?; **tu crois qu'il pourrait me prê-ter son ordinateur?** do you think he could lend me his computer?

Pourrais and *pourrait* are forms of the verb *pouvoir* in the conditional. See verb table p. 318.

pourri, pourrie *adjective*
(a) rotten *(food, wood, weather)*
(b) spoilt *(child)*

pourrir *verb*
(a) to rot, to go rotten
(b) to spoil *(a child)*

LA **poursuite** *noun*
(a) chase; **il est à la poursuite du vo-leur** he's chasing the thief
(b) continuation; **la poursuite de la grève** the continuation of the strike
(c) **les poursuites judiciaires** legal proceedings; **engager des poursuites judiciaires contre quelqu'un** to take legal action against somebody

poursuivre *verb*
(a) to chase; **il poursuit le voleur** he's chasing the thief
(b) to carry on *(one's work, one's jour-ney)*
(c) **ils ont poursuivi leur voisin en justice** they sued their neighbour

See verb table p. 324.

pourtant *adverb*
(a) yet; **elle est pourtant très gentille** and yet she's very nice
(b) *(used in exlamations)* **c'est pour-tant simple!** but it's quite simple!; **ce n'est pourtant pas compliqué!** it's not exactly complicated!; **je t'avais pourtant prévenu!** I did warn you!

pourvu que *conjunction*
(a) let's hope; **pourvu qu'il vienne!** let's hope he's coming!; **pourvu qu'il ne pleuve pas!** let's hope it doesn't rain!
(b) so long as, provided that; **tout ira bien pourvu que vous soyez à l'heure** everything will be fine so long as you're on time

pousser
1 *verb*
(a) to push

(**b**) to encourage; **pousser quelqu'un à la dépense** to encourage somebody to spend more money; **mes parents ne m'ont jamais poussé à faire des études** my parents never encouraged me to study

(**c**) to grow; **il fait pousser des laitues** he's growing lettuces; **elle a laissé pousser ses cheveux** she's let her hair grow

(**d**) **pousser un cri** to cry out; **pousser un soupir** to sigh, to heave a sigh

(**e**) **il a poussé la plaisanterie un peu loin** he took the joke a bit too far

2 *reflexive verb* **se pousser** to move; **tu peux te pousser un peu?** could you move over a bit?; **pousse-toi!** move!, budge!

LA **poussette** *noun* pushchair

LA **poussière** *noun*
(**a**) dust; **faire la poussière** *or* **faire les poussières** to dust; **prendre la poussière** to collect dust
(**b**) **réduire quelque chose en poussière** to smash something to pieces

poussiéreux, poussiéreuse *adjective* dusty

LE **poussin** *noun* chick

LA **poutre** *noun* beam

pouvoir¹
1 *verb*
(**a**) can; **il peut le faire** he can do it; **nous ne pouvons pas venir** we can't come; **est-ce que tu peux m'aider?** can you help me?; **on n'y peut rien** it can't be helped
(**b**) could; **s'il pouvait venir** if he could come; **j'aurais pu gagner** I could have won; **est-ce que tu pourrais m'aider?** could you help me?; **pourriez-vous ouvrir la fenêtre?** could you open the window?; **tu peux toujours essayer de lui téléphoner** you could always try phoning him
(**c**) to manage, to be able to; **avez-vous pu entrer en contact avec lui?** did you manage to contact him?
(**d**) may; **vous pouvez vous asseoir**

you may sit down; **si je peux m'exprimer ainsi** if I may say so
(**e**) might; **ça peut exploser à tout moment** it might explode at any moment; **c'est plus facile qu'on ne pourrait le croire** it's easier than you might think; **j'ai pu me tromper** I might have got it wrong
(**f**) **je n'en peux plus** *(physically)* I'm exhausted; *(emotionally)* I can't stand it any longer; *(after a meal)* I'm full
2 *reflexive verb* **se pouvoir** ça se peut it's possible; **il va pleuvoir – ça se pourrait bien!** it's going to rain – that's quite possible!; **il se peut que je vienne** I might come; **il se peut qu'elle soit malade** she might be ill

The past participle of *pouvoir* is *pu.* See verb table p. 318.

LE **pouvoir²** *noun* power; **ils sont au pouvoir** they're in power

LA **prairie** *noun* meadow

pratique
1 *adjective*
(**a**) practical; **il a l'esprit pratique** he's practically minded
(**b**) convenient, handy; **il faut changer de bus trois fois, ce n'est pas pratique!** you have to change buses three times, it's not very convenient!
2 *feminine noun* **la pratique** practice; **mettre en pratique** to put into practice

pratiquement *adverb* practically; **il n'y avait pratiquement personne** there was hardly anybody there

pratiquer *verb*
(**a**) to practise *(a language, a profession)*
(**b**) to do *(a sport)*; **tu pratiques quel sport?** what sport do you do?; **elle pratique la natation** she swims
(**c**) to make; **pratiquer une incision** to make an incision; **pratiquer une intervention chirurgicale** to perform surgery
(**d**) to be a churchgoer; **il est catholique, mais il ne pratique pas** he is

not a practising Catholic

LE pré *noun* meadow

LA précaution *noun*
(a) precaution; **j'ai pris mes précautions** I took precautions; **par mesure de précaution** as a precaution
(b) caution, care; **avec précaution** cautiously; **sans précaution** carelessly

précédent, précédente *adjective* previous; **la semaine précédente** the previous week

précieux, précieuse *adjective*
(a) precious
(b) invaluable *(help)*

se précipiter *reflexive verb*
(a) to rush; **il s'est précipité dans l'ascenseur** he rushed into the lift
(b) to hurl oneself; **il s'est précipité dans le vide** he hurled himself into the air

précis, précise *adjective*
(a) precise, accurate *(work, description)*
(b) particular, specific; **sans raison précise** for no particular reason

préciser
1 *verb*
(a) to make clearer
(b) to specify; **l'invitation ne précise pas l'heure** the invitation doesn't specify a time; **pourriez-vous préciser?** could you be more specific?
2 *reflexive verb* **se préciser** to become clearer

LA précision *noun*
(a) precision, accuracy *(of work, description)*
(b) detail; **demander des précisions sur quelque chose** to ask for more details about something

prédire *verb* to predict
See verb table p. 315.

préféré, préférée *adjective* favourite

LA préférence *noun* preference; **de préférence** preferably

préférer *verb* to prefer; **ils préfèrent les échecs aux cartes** they prefer chess to playing cards

LE préjugé *noun* prejudice

premier, première
1 *adjective*
(a) first; **la première fois** the first time
(b) front; **en première page du journal** on the front page of the newspaper; **au premier rang** in the front row
(c) leading; **le premier pays producteur de vin au monde** the world's leading wine-producing country
(d) **le Premier ministre** the Prime Minister
2 *noun* **le premier, la première** the first one; **arriver le premier** *or* **arriver en premier** to arrive first; **elle est la première de la classe** she's top of the class
3 *masculine noun* **le premier**
(a) first floor; **j'habite au premier** I live on the first floor
(b) **le premier juin** the first of June; **le premier de l'an** New Year's Day
4 *feminine noun* **la première**
(a) sixth year of secondary school (for pupils aged 16); **il est en première** he's in his sixth year of secondary school

See also **lycée** and **filière**.

(b) first class *(in a train)*; **il a voyagé en première** he travelled first class; **un billet de première** a first-class ticket
(c) première, opening night *(of a film, a play)*

premièrement *adverb*
(a) first; **premièrement il faut de l'argent, deuxièmement il faut du temps** first you need the money, then you need the time
(b) to start with; **premièrement, ça ne te regarde pas!** to start with, it's none of your business!

prendre
1 *verb*
(a) to take; **il a pris mon stylo** he took my pen; **prendre une photo** to take a picture

(**b**) to get; **prendre des renseignements** to get some information

(**c**) to have; **je vais prendre le plat du jour** I'll have today's special; **allons prendre un verre** let's go for a drink

(**d**) to catch *(a fish, a thief)*

(**e**) **pour qui tu me prends?** who do you think I am?; **on me prend souvent pour ma sœur** I'm often mistaken for my sister

(**f**) **prendre une décision** to make a decision

(**g**) **passer prendre quelqu'un** to pick somebody up

(**h**) **prendre à gauche** to turn left

(**i**) **qu'est-ce qui te prend?** what's wrong with you?

2 *reflexive verb* **se prendre**

(**a**) to get caught; **mon manteau s'est pris dans la porte** my coat got caught in the door

(**b**) to consider oneself; **elle se prend pour une artiste** she thinks she's an artist

(**c**) **s'en prendre à quelqu'un** to have a go at somebody

(**d**) **tu t'y prends mal** you're doing it wrong; **elle s'y prend bien avec les enfants** she's good with children

See verb table p. 322.

LE **prénom** *noun* first name

préoccuper

1 *verb*

(**a**) to worry; **il a l'air préoccupé** he looks worried

(**b**) **le foot est tout ce qui le préoccupe** football is all he thinks about

2 *reflexive verb* **se préoccuper de** to concern oneself with; **ne te préoccupe donc pas de ça!** don't bother about that!

préparer

1 *verb* to prepare

2 *reflexive verb* **se préparer**

(**a**) to get ready

(**b**) to train *(for an athlete)*

(**c**) **il se prépare un café** he's making himself a coffee

(**d**) **un orage se prépare** there's a storm brewing

(**e**) **nous nous préparions à partir** we were about to leave

près *adverb*

(**a**) near; **j'habite tout près** I live very near; **près de la gare** near the station; **près d'ici** near here

(**b**) soon; **Noël, c'est tout près maintenant** Christmas will be here very soon now; **il doit être près de la retraite** he must be about to retire

(**c**) **de près** at close range; **je vois mal de près** I can't see very well close up; **surveiller quelqu'un de près** to keep a close eye on somebody

(**d**) **il est près de midi** it's nearly midday; **cela fait près de deux ans** it's been nearly two years

(**e**) **à peu près** about; **on était à peu près cinquante** there were about fifty of us; **à peu de choses près** more or less

(**f**) **c'est parfait, à un détail près** it's perfect but for one thing; **j'ai raté mon train à quelques secondes près** I missed my train by a few seconds

LA **présence** *noun*

(**a**) presence

(**b**) attendance *(at school, a meeting)*

présent, présente

1 *adjective* present *(in a place, at an event)*

2 *masculine noun* **le présent**

(**a**) present; **à présent** now, at present

(**b**) present tense; **le présent du subjonctif** the present subjunctive

Note that the *t* in *présent* is not pronounced.

LE **présentateur,** LA **présentatrice** *noun*

(**a**) presenter, host

(**b**) newsreader

LA **présentation** *noun*

(**a**) introduction; **je vais faire les présentations** I'll do the introductions

(**b**) presentation

(**c**) display *(in a shop)*
(**d**) layout *(of a letter)*

présenter
1 *verb*
(**a**) to introduce; **je te présente ma sœur Aurore** let me introduce my sister Aurore
(**b**) to show; **nous devons présenter notre passeport** we have to show our passports
(**c**) to present, to host *(a TV programme)*; **il présente le journal télévisé** he reads the news on TV
(**d**) to display *(objects)*
2 *reflexive verb* **se présenter**
(**a**) to introduce oneself
(**b**) **se présenter à un entretien** to attend an interview; **se présenter à un examen** to take an exam; **aucun témoin ne s'est encore présenté** no witness has come forward as yet
(**c**) to arise; **si l'occasion se présente** if the occasion arises
(**d**) **les choses se présentent mal** things aren't looking good

LE **préservatif** *noun* condom

> Note that the English word *preservative* is never a translation for the French word *préservatif*.

LE **président**, LA **présidente** *noun*
(**a**) president; **le président de la République française** the French President
(**b**) chairman/chairwoman

> Note that the *t* in *président* is not pronounced.

LA **presqu'île** *noun* peninsula

presque *adverb*
(**a**) almost; **il est presque minuit** it's almost midnight
(**b**) **presque pas** hardly; **ils ne se sont presque pas parlé** they hardly spoke to each other

LA **presse** *noun* press; **la presse nationale** the national press; **la presse féminine** women's magazines

pressé, pressée *adjective*
(**a**) in a hurry; **je suis pressé** I'm in a hurry
(**b**) urgent; **cette réparation, c'est pressé?** is this repair urgent?
(**c**) **une orange pressée** a glass of freshly squeezed orange juice

presser
1 *verb*
(**a**) to squeeze
(**b**) to rush; **rien ne presse** there's no rush
2 *reflexive verb* **se presser**
(**a**) to hurry
(**b**) to crowd; **les photographes se pressaient à sa porte** photographers crowded round his door

LE **pressing** *noun* dry cleaner's

LA **pression** *noun*
(**a**) pressure; **faire pression sur quelqu'un** to put pressure on somebody
(**b**) draught beer

LE **prestidigitateur**, LA **prestidigitatrice** *noun* conjuror, magician

LE **prêt**[1] *noun* loan

prêt[2], **prête** *adjective* ready; **elle est prête à partir** she's ready to go

prétendre *verb* to claim; **il prétend qu'il peut rester dix minutes sans respirer** he claims he can go for ten minutes without breathing

> Note that the English *to pretend* is rarely a translation for the French word *prétendre*.

prétentieux, prétentieuse
1 *adjective* pretentious
2 *noun* **un prétentieux, une prétentieuse** a self-important person

prêter *verb*
(**a**) to lend; **je lui ai prêté mon vélo** I lent him my bike
(**b**) **prêter de l'importance à quelque chose** to attach importance to something
(**c**) **prêter attention à quelque chose** to pay attention to something

(d) **prêter serment** to take an oath
(e) **le texte prête à confusion** the text could cause confusion

LE **prétexte** *noun*
(a) excuse
(b) **sous aucun prétexte** on no account

LE **prêtre** *noun* priest; **il est prêtre** he's a priest

LA **preuve** *noun*
(a) proof
(b) evidence

prévenir *verb*
(a) to warn; **je te préviens, si tu recommences tu seras puni!** I'm warning you, if you do that again you'll be punished!
(b) **prévenir quelqu'un** to let somebody know; **je vais le prévenir que vous êtes ici** I'll tell him you're here; **préviens-moi s'il y a du nouveau** let me know if anything new comes up

See verb table p. 324.

LA **prévision** *noun*
(a) expectation; **le coût de la maison a dépassé nos prévisions** the house cost more than we expected
(b) forecast; **les prévisions météo** the weather forecast

prévoir *verb*
(a) to plan; **on a dîné plus tôt que prévu** we had dinner earlier than planned
(b) to allow; **il faut prévoir une heure pour la correspondance** you should allow an hour for the connection
(c) to anticipate; **je n'avais pas prévu sa réaction** I hadn't anticipated his reaction
(d) to forecast; **ils prévoient de la pluie pour le week-end** they're forecasting rain for the weekend
(e) to bring; **prévoyez des vêtements chauds** make sure you bring some warm clothes

See verb table p. 324.

prier *verb*
(a) to pray
(b) **prier quelqu'un de faire quelque chose** to ask somebody to do something; **vous êtes priés d'arriver à l'heure** please arrive on time
(c) **je vous en prie** *(after being thanked)* you're welcome; *(when answering a question)* please do; **je vous remercie d'être venu – je vous en prie** thank you for coming – you're welcome; **puis-je entrer? – je vous en prie** may I come in? – please do

LA **prière** *noun*
(a) prayer; **faire une prière** to say a prayer
(b) plea
(c) *(written on signs)* **prière de fermer la porte** please close the door; **prière de ne pas fumer** no smoking

primaire *adjective* primary; **une école primaire** a primary school; **les couleurs primaires** the primary colours

See also **école** for more information on the French *écoles primaires*.

LA **prime** *noun*
(a) bonus
(b) **une prime de licenciement** a redundancy payment
(c) **une prime d'assurance** an insurance premium

principal, principale
1 *adjective* main; **la proposition principale** the main clause *(in grammar)*
2 *masculine noun* **le principal**
(a) headmaster
(b) **le principal, c'est que tu ne sois pas blessé** the main thing is that you're not hurt

The masculine plural of *principal* is *principaux*.

LE **principe** *noun*
(a) principle; **par principe** on principle
(b) **en principe, je devrais pouvoir venir** in theory, I should be able to come

(c) **en principe, il arrive à huit heures** all being well, he'll arrive at eight o'clock

LE **printemps** *noun* spring; **elle part en vacances au printemps** she goes on holiday in the spring

LA **priorité** *noun*
(a) right of way *(on the road)*
(b) priority

pris, prise
1 *adjective*
(a) taken *(seat)*
(b) busy *(person)*
(c) **pris de peur** stricken by fear; **pris de panique** panic-stricken

Pris(e) is the past participle of the verb *prendre*. See verb table p. 322.

2 *feminine noun* **la prise**
(a) **une prise** *or* **une prise de courant** *(in the wall)* a socket; *(on an appliance)* a plug
(b) hold *(in rock climbing, judo)*
(c) taking; **la prise d'otages** hostage-taking; **la prise de notes** note-taking; **une prise de sang** a blood test; **la prise de décision** decision-making; **la prise de conscience** realization *(awareness)*

LA **prison** *noun* prison, jail

prisonnier, prisonnière
1 *adjective* captive
2 *noun* **un prisonnier, une prisonnière** a prisoner

privé, privée
1 *adjective* private
2 *masculine noun* **le privé** the private sector; **il enseigne dans le privé** he teaches in a private school

priver
1 *verb* to deprive; **être privé de quelque chose** to be deprived of something; **il a été privé de sortie** he wasn't allowed to go out; **tu seras privé de télévision** no television for you
2 *reflexive verb* **se priver**
(a) **il n'aime pas se priver** he hates denying himself anything

(b) **je ne vais pas me priver de le lui dire!** I won't hesitate to tell him!

privilégié, privilégiée *adjective*
(a) privileged
(b) favoured

LE **prix** *noun*
(a) price; **à moitié prix** half price
(b) prize; **un prix littéraire** a literary prize
(c) award; **un prix d'interprétation** an award for best actor
(d) **à tout prix** at all costs; **tu dois être rentré à minuit à tout prix** you must be home by midnight at all costs

probable *adjective* likely, probable; **il est peu probable qu'il réussisse** there is little chance of his succeeding

probablement *adverb* probably

LE **problème** *noun*
(a) problem; **un problème de maths** a maths problem; **nous avons un gros problème** we have a major problem
(b) issue; **soulever un problème** to raise an issue

LE **procès** *noun* trial; **intenter un procès à quelqu'un** to take somebody to court

The word *procès* does not change in the plural. Note that the *s* in *procès* is not pronounced.

prochain, prochaine *adjective*
(a) next; **la semaine prochaine** next week; **à samedi prochain!** see you next Saturday!; **à la prochaine!** *(informal phrase)* see you!
(b) **un jour prochain** one day soon

prochainement *adverb* shortly, soon

proche *adjective*
(a) near; **dans un avenir proche** in the near future
(b) close; **elle est très proche de sa sœur** she's very close to her sister; **la famille proche** close relatives
(c) similar; **nos goûts sont très proches** we have very similar tastes

procurer
1 *verb*
(a) to get; **procurer des renseignements à quelqu'un** to get information for somebody; **je lui ai procuré un emploi** I found him a job
(b) to bring; **la lecture me procure beaucoup de plaisir** reading brings me great pleasure
2 *reflexive verb* **se procurer** to get, to obtain

producteur, productrice
1 *adjective* producing; **les pays producteurs de pétrole** oil-producing countries
2 *noun* **un producteur, une productrice** a producer

LA **production** *noun*
(a) production
(b) output *(in industry)*; **la production a augmenté** output has risen
(c) yield *(in agriculture)*

produire
1 *verb*
(a) to produce; **l'usine produit cent voitures par jour** the factory produces a hundred cars a day
(b) to create
2 *reflexive verb* **se produire**
(a) to happen, to take place; **l'accident s'est produit hier** the accident happened yesterday
(b) to give a performance; **se produire sur scène** to appear on stage

See verb table p. 320.

LE **produit** *noun*
(a) product; **le produit national brut** the gross national product; **les produits d'entretien** cleaning products; **les produits chimiques** chemicals
(b) produce; **les produits laitiers** dairy produce; **les produits de la ferme** farm produce; **les produits alimentaires** foodstuffs

LE/LA **prof** *noun*
(a) teacher; **elle est prof** she's a teacher; **ma prof de maths** my maths teacher

(b) lecturer; **elle est prof de fac** she's a lecturer

Prof is an informal word; it is the shortened form of *professeur*. It can be either masculine or feminine, unlike the word *professeur* (see below).

LE **professeur** *noun*
(a) teacher; **elle est professeur des écoles** she's a primary school teacher; **un professeur principal** a form tutor
(b) lecturer, professor

The word *professeur* does not have a feminine but it can also refer to a woman.

LA **profession** *noun*
(a) job; **quelle est votre profession?** what do you do for a living?; **sans profession** unemployed
(b) profession
(c) trade *(craft)*

professionnel, professionnelle
adjective
(a) occupational, work; **il a des soucis professionnels** he's got problems at work; **comment va ta vie professionnelle?** how's your job going?
(b) vocational; **l'enseignement professionnel** vocational education; **une école professionnelle** a technical college
(c) professional; **des compétences professionnelles** professional skills

LE **profil** *noun*
(a) profile; **être de profil** to be in profile; **se mettre de profil** to turn to the side
(b) **il a le profil de l'emploi** he fits the job description

LE **profit** *noun*
(a) profit *(money)*
(b) advantage; **tirer profit d'une situation** to take advantage of a situation
(c) **au profit de** in aid of; **une collecte au profit des sans-abri** a collection in aid of the homeless

Note that the *t* in *profit* is not pronounced.

profiter *verb*
(**a**) **profiter de quelque chose** to take advantage of something; **il faut profiter du soleil** we have to make the most of the sunshine; **profiter de l'occasion** to seize the opportunity; **profiter de la vie** to enjoy life; **il profite de sa retraite** he's making the most of his retirement
(**b**) **profiter de quelqu'un** to exploit somebody, to use somebody
(**c**) **profiter à quelqu'un** to benefit somebody

profond, profonde *adjective* deep; **peu profond** shallow

LA **profondeur** *noun* depth; **trois mètres de profondeur** three metres deep; **une étude en profondeur** an in-depth study; **des changements en profondeur** fundamental changes

LE **programme** *noun*
(**a**) programme *(of events)*
(**b**) listings *(of films, TV programmes)*
(**c**) schedule; **nous avons un programme chargé cette semaine** we have a busy schedule this week
(**d**) plans; **quel est ton programme pour les vacances?** what are your plans for the holidays?
(**e**) syllabus
(**f**) program *(on computer)*
(**g**) **le programme du gouvernement** the government manifesto

programmer *verb*
(**a**) to set *(a video recorder)*
(**b**) to plan; **j'ai programmé tout le week-end** I planned the entire weekend
(**c**) to program *(on computer)*

LE **progrès** *noun* progress; **cet élève a fait des progrès** this pupil has made a lot of progress

Note that the *s* in *progrès* is not pronounced.

progresser *verb*
(**a**) to improve; **vous avez bien progressé cette année** you've improved a lot this year
(**b**) to make progress; **l'enquête progresse** the investigation is making progress
(**c**) to spread *(for a disease)*
(**d**) to advance *(for an enemy)*

progressivement *adverb* progressively, gradually

LA **proie** *noun* prey

LE **projecteur** *noun*
(**a**) spotlight
(**b**) projector *(for films)*; **un projecteur de diapositives** a slide projector

LE **projet** *noun*
(**a**) plan; **faire des projets d'avenir** to make plans for the future
(**b**) project *(at school, work)*

projeter *verb*
(**a**) to plan; **j'ai projeté un voyage pour cet été** I've planned a trip for this summer
(**b**) to throw; **elle a été projetée hors de la voiture** she was thrown out of the car
(**c**) to project *(a light)*
(**d**) to show, to screen *(a film)*

prolonger
1 *verb* to extend *(a road, a holiday)*
2 *reflexive verb* **se prolonger** to go on

LA **promenade** *noun* walk; **allons faire une promenade** let's go for a walk; **une promenade en voiture** a drive; **une promenade en vélo** a bike ride

promener
1 *verb* to take out for a walk; **promener le chien** to walk the dog
2 *reflexive verb* **se promener** to go for a walk; **ils sont partis se promener en vélo** they went for a bike ride

LA **promesse** *noun* promise; **tenir sa promesse** to keep one's promise

promettre *verb* to promise; **elle lui a**

promis she promised him; **je te rembourserai, c'est promis** *or* **je te promets** I'll pay you back, I promise

See verb table p. 322.

LA **promotion** *noun*
(a) promotion; **j'ai eu une promotion** I've been promoted
(b) special offer
(c) year *(at university)*; **il est premier de sa promotion** he's first in his year

LE **pronom** *noun* pronoun

prononcer
1 *verb*
(a) to say; **il a prononcé quelques mots à l'enterrement** he said a few words at the funeral; **ne prononce plus jamais son nom** never mention his name again
(b) to pronounce *(a word)*
(c) to deliver *(a speech)*
2 *reflexive verb* **se prononcer**
(a) to be pronounced; **comment ça se prononce?** how is it pronounced?
(b) to give one's opinion

LA **prononciation** *noun* pronunciation

propager
1 *verb* to spread; **le vent a propagé l'incendie** the wind spread the fire
2 *reflexive verb* **se propager** to spread

LE **propos** *noun*
(a) **à ce propos, que penses-tu de ma suggestion?** which reminds me, what do you think of my suggestion?; **à propos, as-tu reçu ma carte?** by the way, did you get my postcard?; **il faut que je te parle à propos des vacances** I need to talk to you about the holidays; **c'est à quel propos?** what's it about?
(b) **des propos** words, talk; **il a tenu des propos choquants** he made some shocking remarks

proposer
1 *verb*
(a) to suggest; **je propose qu'on regarde un film** I suggest we watch a film; **je vous propose de rester dîner** I suggest you stay for dinner
(b) to offer; **il a proposé sa place à la vieille dame** he offered the old lady his seat
2 *reflexive verb* **se proposer** to offer one's services; **je me suis proposé pour le faire** I volunteered to do it

LA **proposition** *noun*
(a) suggestion, proposal
(b) offer; **j'ai refusé sa proposition** I turned down his offer
(c) clause *(in grammar)*; **une proposition principale** a main clause

propre *adjective*
(a) clean
(b) neat; **il a rendu un travail très propre** he handed in a very neat piece of work; **mettre quelque chose au propre** to copy something out neatly
(c) own; **de mes propres yeux** with my own eyes; **pour des raisons qui lui sont propres** for reasons of his own
(d) **un nom propre** a proper noun

Note that the English word *proper* is rarely a translation for the French word *propre*.

proprement *adverb*
(a) neatly; **écrire proprement** to write neatly; **mange proprement!** eat properly!
(b) **à proprement parler** strictly speaking
(c) **proprement dit** actual; **la maison proprement dite** the actual house

Note that the English word *properly* is rarely a translation for the French word *proprement*.

LE/LA **propriétaire** *noun*
(a) owner
(b) landlord/landlady

LA **propriété** *noun*
(a) property; **une propriété** a property
(b) ownership

LE **prospectus** *noun* leaflet, brochure

protéger
1 *verb* to protect
2 *reflexive verb* **se protéger** to protect oneself; **se protéger du froid** to protect oneself from the cold

protester *verb* to protest

prouver *verb* to prove; **la police n'a rien pu prouver** the police couldn't prove anything; **cela prouve bien que j'avais raison** that proves that I was right

LA **provenance** *noun*
(**a**) origin; **des produits de provenance inconnue** goods of unknown origin
(**b**) **en provenance de** coming from; **le train en provenance de Paris** the train from Paris

provenir *verb* **provenir de** to come from; **d'où provient ce produit?** where does this product come from?

See verb table p. 324.

LE **proverbe** *noun* proverb, saying

LA **province** *noun*
(**a**) provincial France *(not Paris)*; **elle habite en province** she lives in the provinces; **un week-end en province** a weekend out of town

Do no confuse *la province* with *la Provence* (the south of France).

(**b**) province

LE **proviseur** *noun* head teacher

LA **provision** *noun*
(**a**) stock, supply; **une provision de pommes de terre** a stock of potatoes; **j'ai fait des provisions de chocolat** I stocked up on chocolate
(**b**) **faire des provisions** to go shopping *(for food)*; **je suis allé faire des provisions hier** I went shopping yesterday

provisoire *adjective* temporary

provoquer *verb*
(**a**) to cause *(an accident, a fire)*
(**b**) to provoke *(a person)*

LA **proximité** *noun* closeness; **ses parents habitent à proximité** his parents live nearby; **la maison est à proximité de la mer** the house is close to the sea; **les commerces de proximité** local shops

prudemment *adverb* carefully

The middle *e* of *prudemment* is pronounced like the *a* in *cat*.

LA **prudence** *noun* caution; **avec prudence** carefully; **par mesure de prudence** as a precaution

prudent, prudente *adjective*
(**a**) careful *(person)*
(**b**) sensible *(decision)*

Note that the *t* in *prudent* is not pronounced.

LA **prune** *noun* plum

Note that the English word *prune* is never a translation for the French word *prune*.

LE **pruneau** prune

The plural of *pruneau* is *pruneaux*.

LE **prunier** *noun* plum tree

LE/LA **psychiatre** *noun* psychiatrist; **elle est psychiatre** she's a psychiatrist

The letter *p* is pronounced in French.

LE/LA **psychologue** *noun* psychologist; **il est psychologue** he's a psychologist

The letter *p* is pronounced in French.

pu *see* **pouvoir**[1]
je n'ai pas pu venir I couldn't come; **ils ont pu s'acheter une voiture** they were able to buy a car

Pu is the past participle of the verb *pouvoir*. See verb table p. 318.

LA **pub** *noun*
(**a**) advertising
(**b**) ad, commercial
(**c**) publicity

Pub is an informal word; it is the shortened form of *publicité*.

public, publique
1 *adjective* public
2 *masculine noun* **le public**
(**a**) public; **le grand public** the general public
(**b**) audience *(of a show)*
(**c**) spectators *(of a sporting event)*
(**d**) public sector; **il enseigne dans le public** he teaches in a state school

LA **publicité** *noun*
(**a**) advertising
(**b**) advertisement; **une publicité télévisée** a television advertisement
(**c**) publicity

publier *verb* to publish

LA **puce**
1 *noun*
(**a**) flea
(**b**) chip *(in a computer, an electronic appliance)*
(**c**) bullet (point); **une liste à puces** a bulleted list
(**d**) **ma puce** *(term of affection)* sweetie; **tu veux quelque chose, ma puce?** do you want something, sweetie?
2 *feminine plural noun*
(**a**) flea market; **ils sont allés aux puces** they went to the flea market
(**b**) **le jeu de puces** tiddlywinks

puer *verb* to stink; **il pue le vin** he stinks of wine; **ça pue ici!** it stinks in here!

LA **puéricultrice** *noun* nursery nurse; **elle est puéricultrice** she's a nursery nurse

puis *adverb*
(**a**) then; **tournez à gauche puis à droite** turn left then right; **et puis qu'est-ce qui s'est passé?** then what happened?
(**b**) **il y avait ses parents, ses frères et puis aussi ses cousins** there were his parents, his brothers and also his cousins
(**c**) **je n'ai pas envie de sortir, et puis il fait trop froid** I don't feel like going out, and anyway it's too cold

puisque *conjunction*
(**a**) since; **je viendrai dîner, puisque vous insistez** I will come to dinner, since you insist
(**b**) **mais puisque je te dis que je ne veux pas!** but I'm telling you that I don't want to!

LA **puissance** *noun* power; **six puissance cinq** six to the power of five

puissant, puissante *adjective* powerful

puisse, puissent *see* **pouvoir¹**
j'aimerais qu'il puisse venir avec moi à cette soirée I'd like him to be able to come with me to this party; **donne-leur ton numéro pour qu'ils puissent te joindre** give them your number so they can get in touch with you

Puisse and *puissent* are forms of the verb *pouvoir* in the subjunctive. See verb table p. 318.

LE **puits** *noun* well; **un puits de pétrole** an oil well

LE **pull** *noun* sweater, jumper

LE **pull-over** *noun* sweater, jumper

The plural of *pull-over* is *pull-overs*.

LA **punaise** *noun*
(**a**) drawing pin
(**b**) bed bug

punir *verb* to punish

LA **punition** *noun* punishment

pur, pure *adjective*
(**a**) pure
(**b**) straight, neat *(spirits)*
(**c**) sheer; **par pure méchanceté** out of sheer malice

LA **purée** *noun*
(**a**) mashed potatoes; **la purée mousseline**® instant mashed potato
(**b**) puree *(of fruit, vegetables)*

LE **puzzle** *noun* jigsaw puzzle

LE **PV** *noun*
(**a**) speeding ticket

(**b**) parking ticket

> *PV* is an informal word; it is the shortened form of *procès-verbal*. It does not change in the plural.

LE **pyjama** *noun* pyjamas; **je suis en pyjama** I'm in my pyjamas

LA **pyramide** *noun* pyramid

LES **Pyrénées** *feminine plural noun* the Pyrenees; **aller dans les Pyrénées** to go to the Pyrenees

qu' *see* **que, qu'est-ce que, qu'est-ce qui**

> *Qu'* is the contracted form of *que* which is used in front of a vowel or a mute h.

LE **quai** *noun*
(**a**) platform *(of a railway station)*
(**b**) quay
(**c**) bank, embankment

qualifié, qualifiée *adjective* qualified

se qualifier *reflexive verb* to qualify; **il s'est qualifié pour la finale** he qualified for the final

LA **qualité** *noun* quality

quand *adverb*
(**a**) when; **téléphone-moi quand tu arriveras** phone me when you arrive
(**b**) **quand même** all the same; **il n'était pas invité mais il est venu quand même** he wasn't invited but he came all the same; **quand même! il aurait pu nous prévenir!** he really could have warned us!

quant à *preposition* as for; **quant à Pierre, j'irai le chercher en voiture** as for Pierre, I'll pick him up in the car

LA **quantité** *noun* quantity, amount; **cela pose des quantités de problèmes** that raises a great number of problems

LA **quarantaine** *noun* about forty; **une quarantaine de personnes** about forty people; **il a la quarantaine** he's about forty years old

quarante *number* forty; **quarante et un** forty-one; **quarante-deux** forty-two

LE **quart** *noun* quarter; **un quart d'heure** a quarter of an hour; **une heure et quart** an hour and a quarter; **il est une heure et quart** it's a quarter past one; **une heure moins le quart** a quarter to one

> The *t* in *quart* is not pronounced.

LE **quartier** *noun*
(**a**) area, neighbourhood; **les beaux quartiers** the fashionable areas
(**b**) piece; **un quartier d'orange** an orange segment

quasiment *adverb* nearly, almost

quatorze *number* fourteen; **le quatorze septembre** the fourteenth of September; **nous sommes le quatorze juin** it's the fourteenth of June; **à quatorze heures** at two o'clock in the afternoon

Le Quatorze Juillet

The 14th of July is France's national holiday, known in English as Bastille Day. It celebrates the storming of the Bastille on the 14th of July 1789, during the French revolution (the Bastille was a prison for the king's enemies). Celebrations begin on the 13th of July with outdoor public dances and firework displays, and continue on the 14th with a military parade in Paris in the morning. Firework displays are also held in the evening of Bastille Day.

quatre *number* four; **le quatre avril** the fourth of April; **nous sommes le quatre décembre** it's the fourth of

December; **descendre les escaliers quatre à quatre** to rush down the stairs; **un de ces quatre** *(informal phrase)* one of these days; **il mange comme quatre** he eats like a horse

quatre-vingt(s) *number* eighty; **quatre-vingts livres** eighty pounds; **les années quatre-vingts** the eighties; **quatre-vingt-un** eighty-one; **quatre-vingt-deux** eighty-two; **quatre-vingt-dix** ninety; **quatre-vingt-onze** ninety-one; **quatre-vingt-douze** ninety-two; **les années quatre-vingt-dix** the nineties

---

Quatre-vingts takes an *s* when it is used on its own or when it is followed by a noun, eg *quatre-vingts ans.* When it is followed by another number it is spelled without an *s*, eg *quatre-vingt-deux.*

---

quatrième
1 *number* fourth
2 *feminine noun* **la quatrième** the third year of secondary school (for pupils aged 13); **il est en quatrième** he's in his third year of secondary school

---

See also **collège**.

---

que
1 *conjunction*
(**a**) that; **je sais que tu ne dis pas la vérité** I know (that) you're not telling the truth; **j'aimerais que tu viennes** I would like you to come; **qu'il s'en aille!** let him leave!
(**b**) **ne... que** only; **je n'ai qu'un euro** I only have one euro; **ce n'est que le début** it's only the beginning
(**c**) than; **il est plus grand que moi** he is taller than me
(**d**) as; **elle n'est pas aussi belle que toi** she's not as pretty as you
2 *pronoun*
(**a**) that, which; **où est le CD que je t'ai prêté?** where's the CD (that) I lent you?; **c'est le film que je suis allé voir dimanche** that's the film (that) I went to see on Sunday

(**b**) that, whom; **c'est la fille que je t'ai présentée hier** that's the girl I introduced you to yesterday
(**c**) what; **que fais-tu?** what are you doing?; **que veux-tu manger?** what do you want to eat?
3 *adverb* **que c'est beau!** it's really lovely!; **qu'il est bête!** he's so stupid!

Que becomes *qu'* in front of a vowel or a mute h, eg *je veux qu'il vienne.* See also **qu'est-ce que** and **qu'est-ce qui**.

---

quel, quelle
1 *adjective*
(**a**) what, which; **quel manteau vas-tu mettre?** which coat are you going to wear?; **quelle heure est-il?** what time is it?
(**b**) what; **quelle belle journée!** what a beautiful day!; **quel idiot!** what a fool!
(**d**) who; **quel est ton prof préféré?** who is your favourite teacher?
(**e**) **quel que soit** *(for a thing)* whatever; *(for a person)* whoever; **nous irons nous promener, quel que soit le temps** we'll go for a walk, whatever the weather may be; **quelles que soient ses raisons, elle n'aurait jamais dû faire ça** whatever reasons she had, she still should never have done that; **j'espère qu'ils arrêteront le meurtrier, quel qu'il soit** I hope they arrest the murderer, whoever he is
2 *pronoun* which, which one; **des trois films, quel est ton préféré?** out of the three films, which one do you like best?

The plural of *quel* is *quels*, the plural of *quelle* is *quelles*.

---

quelconque *adjective*
(**a**) any; **si pour une raison quelconque tu ne peux pas venir, téléphone-moi** if for any reason you can't come, phone me
(**b**) average; **le repas était quelconque** the meal was average

quelque chose *pronoun*
(**a**) something; **il faut que tu manges**

quelque chose you need to eat something

(**b**) anything; **est-ce que tu as besoin de quelque chose?** do you need anything?

quelquefois *adverb* sometimes

quelque part *adverb*
(**a**) somewhere; **je suis sûr de l'avoir déjà vu quelque part** I'm sure I've seen him somewhere before
(**b**) anywhere; **tu veux aller quelque part ce week-end?** do you want to go anywhere this weekend?

quelque *adjective*
(**a**) some; **depuis quelque temps** for some time
(**b**) **quelques** some, a few; **quelques jours** a few days; **j'ai dépensé les quelques euros qui me restaient** I spent the last few euros I had left

quelques-uns, quelques-unes *pronoun* some, a few

quelqu'un *pronoun*
(**a**) somebody; **quelqu'un a cassé un carreau** somebody broke a window
(**b**) anyone; **est-ce que quelqu'un connaît son numéro de téléphone?** does anyone know his phone number?

qu'est-ce que *pronoun* what; **qu'est-ce que ça veut dire?** what does it mean?; **qu'est-ce que tu veux manger?** what do you want to eat?; **qu'est-ce qu'il t'a dit?** what did he say to you?

qu'est-ce qui *pronoun* what; **qu'est-ce qui ne va pas?** what's wrong?; **qu'est-ce qui fait ce bruit?** what's making that noise?

LA **question** *noun*
(**a**) question; **poser une question à quelqu'un** to ask somebody a question
(**b**) matter; **c'est une question de principe** it's a matter of principle
(**c**) **il a été question du racisme au cours du débat** they talked about racism during the debate
(**d**) **il n'en est pas question** *or* **c'est**

hors de question it's out of the question; **pas question!** no way!

LA **quête** *noun* collection; **faire la quête** to take the collection

LA **queue** *noun*
(**a**) tail
(**b**) queue; **faire la queue** to queue
(**c**) **monter en queue de train** to get in the rear of the train

LA **queue-de-cheval** *noun* ponytail; **elle porte une queue-de-cheval** she has a ponytail

The plural of *queue-de-cheval* is *queues-de-cheval*.

qui *pronoun*
(**a**) who; **qui a cassé le vase?** who broke the vase?; **c'est le garçon à qui tu parlais** that's the boy you were talking to; **à qui appartient ce sac?** whose bag is this?
(**b**) which, that; **voici un livre qui pourrait t'intéresser** here is a book which might interest you
(**c**) who, that; **c'est la fille qui m'a invité à son anniversaire** she's the girl who invited me to her birthday party

LA **quille** *noun* skittle; **jouer aux quilles** to play skittles

LA **quincaillerie** *noun* ironmonger's, hardware shop

LA **quinzaine** *noun* about fifteen; **une quinzaine de personnes** about fifteen people; **une quinzaine de jours** a fortnight

quinze *number* fifteen; **quinze jours** a fortnight; **le quinze juillet** the fifteenth of July; **nous sommes le quinze décembre** it's the fifteenth of December; **à quinze heures** at three o'clock in the afternoon

quinzième *number* fifteenth

quitter
1 *verb*
(**a**) to leave
(**b**) **ne quittez pas!** hold the line!
2 *reflexive verb* **se quitter** to part

quoi *pronoun*

(**a**) what; **je ne sais pas quoi faire** I don't know what to do; **à quoi penses-tu?** what are you thinking about?

(**b**) **quoi que** whatever; **quoi qu'il arrive** whatever happens

(**c**) **merci! – il n'y a pas de quoi!** thank you! – don't mention it!

(**d**) **il n'y pas de quoi te mettre en colère** there's no reason to get angry

(**e**) **je n'ai pas de quoi m'acheter une planche à roulettes** I can't afford to buy myself a skateboard

quotidien, quotidienne

1 *adjective* daily

2 *masculine noun* **un quotidien** a daily newspaper

rabâcher *verb* rabâcher quelque chose to repeat something over and over

LE **rabais** *noun* discount, reduction; **il m'a fait un rabais** he gave me a discount

raccommoder *verb* to mend *(a garment)*

raccompagner *verb* raccompagner quelqu'un to take somebody back home

LE **raccourci** *noun* shortcut

raccourcir *verb*
(**a**) to shorten
(**b**) to get shorter

raccrocher *verb* to hang up; **elle m'a raccroché au nez** she hung up on me

LA **race** *noun*
(**a**) race; **la race humaine** the human race
(**b**) breed; **mon chien est d'une race très commune** my dog is a very common breed

racheter
1 *verb*
(**a**) to buy another; **j'ai perdu ma montre, il va falloir que j'en rachète une** I lost my watch, I'll have to buy another one
(**b**) to buy some more; **rachète du lait si tu sors** buy some more milk if you go out
(**c**) to buy over; **la société a été rachetée par une entreprise étrangère** the firm was bought over by a foreign company
2 *reflexive verb* **se racheter** to make amends

LA **racine** *noun*
(**a**) root *(of a plant, a tooth)*
(**b**) **racine carrée** square root; **quelle est la racine carrée de 81?** what is the square root of 81?

raconter *verb*
(**a**) to tell; **quand j'étais petit mon père me racontait des histoires** when I was little my dad used to tell me stories; **il nous a raconté ses vacances** he told us about his holidays
(**b**) **mais qu'est-ce que tu racontes?** what are you going on about?

LE **radiateur** *noun*
(**a**) heater
(**b**) radiator

radin, radine *adjective* stingy, mean

This word is informal.

LA **radio** *noun*
(**a**) radio; **c'est une chanson qui passe souvent à la radio** you hear that song on the radio a lot
(**b**) X-ray; **une radio des poumons** a lung X-ray; **passer une radio** to have an X-ray

LE **radio-réveil** *noun* clock radio

The plural of *radio-réveil* is *radios-réveils*.

LE **radis** *noun* radish

se radoucir *reflexive verb* to turn milder; **le temps s'est radouci** the weather's milder

LA **rafale** *noun*
(**a**) **une rafale de vent** a gust of wind
(**b**) **une rafale de mitraillette** a burst of machine-gun fire

rafraîchir
1 *verb*
(**a**) to cool down
(**b**) to refresh *(web page)*
2 *reflexive verb* **se rafraîchir**
(**a**) to get cooler; **le temps se rafraî-chit** it's getting cooler
(**b**) to freshen up
(**c**) to have a drink

LA **rage** *noun*
(**a**) rage; **elle était folle de rage** she was absolutely furious; **une rage de dents** severe toothache
(**b**) rabies

LE **ragoût** *noun* stew

raide *adjective*
(**a**) steep; **une pente très raide** a very steep slope
(**b**) stiff; **le col de ma chemise est raide** my shirt collar is stiff
(**c**) straight; **elle a les cheveux raides** she has straight hair

LA **raie** *noun*
(**a**) stripe
(**b**) parting *(in hair)*; **il se fait la raie au milieu** he parts his hair in the middle
(**c**) skate *(fish)*

LE **raisin** *noun*
(**a**) grapes; **j'aime le raisin** I like grapes; **un grain de raisin** a grape
(**b**) **un raisin sec** a raisin

Note that the English word *raisin* is only a translation for the French *raisin sec*.

LA **raison** *noun*
(**a**) reason
(**b**) **avoir raison** to be right

raisonnable *adjective*
(**a**) reasonable
(**b**) sensible

LE **raisonnement** *noun*
(**a**) argument *(to prove a point)*; **ton raisonnement ne tient pas debout** your argument doesn't hold up
(**b**) reasoning

rajouter *verb* to add

LE **ralenti** *noun* slow motion; **ils ont re-passé le but au ralenti** they replayed the goal in slow motion

ralentir *verb* to slow down

LE **ralentisseur** *noun* speed bump

râler *verb* to moan; **mon père est tou-jours en train de râler** my dad is always moaning

This word is informal.

LA **rallonge** *noun*
(**a**) extension lead
(**b**) extension *(of a table)*

rallonger *verb*
(**a**) to lengthen
(**b**) to extend
(**c**) to get longer

LE **ramassage** *noun* **le ramassage scolaire** the school bus service; **le ra-massage des ordures** rubbish collection

ramasser *verb*
(**a**) to pick up; **ramasse le papier que tu viens de faire tomber** pick up that piece of paper you've just dropped
(**b**) to collect; **j'aime bien ramasser des coquillages sur la plage** I like collecting shells on the beach

LA **rame** *noun*
(**a**) oar
(**b**) **une rame de métro** an underground train

ramener *verb*
(**a**) to bring back; **il ramène toujours quelque chose pour ses enfants** he always brings something back for his children
(**b**) to take back; **un bus les ramène à l'école après la séance de piscine** a bus takes them back to school after they've been swimming
(**c**) to take home; **mon père peut te ramener si tu veux** my dad can take you home if you like

ramer *verb* to row

LA **rampe** *noun*
(**a**) banister
(**b**) ramp *(for wheelchair access)*

ramper *verb* to crawl

LA **rançon** *noun* ransom

LA **rancune** *noun*
(**a**) spite; **sans rancune!** no hard feelings!
(**b**) grudge; **une vieille rancune** an old grudge

LA **randonnée** *noun*
(**a**) hike; **on a fait une randonnée** we went on a hike
(**b**) hiking; **elle fait de la randonnée tous les dimanches** she goes hiking every Sunday
(**c**) **une randonnée à vélo** a ride

LE **rang** *noun*
(**a**) row *(line)*; **on était au premier rang** we were in the front row; **se mettre en rangs** to line up
(**b**) rank

The *g* in *rang* is not pronounced.

LA **rangée** *noun* row, line; **une rangée de chaises** a row of chairs

ranger *verb*
(**a**) to put away; **il ne range jamais ses jouets** he never puts his toys away
(**b**) to tidy, to tidy up; **ma mère m'a dit de ranger ma chambre** my mum told me to tidy (up) my room

LE **rapace** *noun* bird of prey

râpé, râpée *adjective* grated; **du fromage râpé** grated cheese; **des carottes râpées** grated carrot

rapide
1 *adjective* fast, quick
2 *masculine noun* **un rapide** an express train

rapidement *adverb* fast, quickly

LE **rappel** *noun*
(**a**) reminder
(**b**) booster *(vaccination)*

rappeler
1 *verb*

(**a**) to call back; **elle a demandé à ce que tu la rappelles** she asked for you to call her back; **rappelle dans une heure, il sera rentré** call back in an hour, he'll be back by then
(**b**) to remind; **ça me rappelle mes vacances** that reminds me of my holidays; **rappelle-moi qu'il faut que je passe à la poste** remind me that I have to go by the post office
2 *reflexive verb* **se rappeler** se rappeler quelque chose to remember something

LE **rapport** *noun*
(**a**) connection; **je ne vois pas le rapport entre les deux** I don't see the connection between the two
(**b**) report; **rédiger un rapport** to write a report
(**c**) **des rapports** relations; **il a de bons rapports avec ses camarades de classe** he gets on well with his classmates; **des rapports sexuels** sexual intercourse, sex

The *t* in *rapport* is not pronounced.

rapporter *verb*
(**a**) to bring back
(**b**) to take back

LE **rapporteur,** LA **rapporteuse** *noun* tell-tale

rapprocher
1 *verb*
(**a**) to bring closer; **rapproche ta chaise de la table** bring your chair closer to the table
(**b**) to bring together; **cette expérience les a rapprochés** the experience brought them closer together
2 *reflexive verb* **se rapprocher** to move closer

LA **raquette** *noun*
(**a**) racket
(**b**) bat
(**c**) snowshoe

rare *adjective*
(**a**) rare
(**b**) scarce

rarement *adverb* rarely, seldom

ras, rase
1 *adjective*
(a) short; **il a les cheveux ras** he has close-cropped hair
(b) **il a rempli mon verre à ras bord** he filled my glass to the brim
2 *adverb* **ras j'en ai ras le bol** *(informal phrase)* I'm fed up

raser
1 *verb*
(a) to shave; **il a demandé au coiffeur de le raser** he asked the barber to give him a shave
(b) to shave off; **il s'est rasé la barbe** he shaved his beard off
(c) to graze; **la voiture a rasé le cycliste** the car grazed the cyclist; **la balle a rasé le filet** the ball skimmed over the net
(d) to raze; **l'aviation ennemie a rasé la ville** enemy aircraft razed the city to the ground
(e) to bore; **son grand-père nous rase avec ses histoires de jeunesse!** his grandpa bores us to tears with his stories about when he was young!

Sense (e) is an informal use of *raser*.

2 *reflexive verb* **se raser** to shave; **elle se rase les jambes** she shaves her legs

LE **rasoir** *noun*
(a) razor
(b) shaver

rassembler
1 *verb*
(a) to gather
(b) to bring together
2 *reflexive verb* **se rassembler**
(a) to gather
(b) to get together

se rasseoir *reflexive verb* to sit down again, to sit back down

See verb table p. 320.

rassis, rassise *adjective* **du pain rassis** stale bread

rassurer *verb* **rassurer quelqu'un** to put somebody's mind at rest; **rassure-toi!** don't worry!

LE **rat** *noun* rat

The *t* in *rat* is not pronounced.

LE **râteau** *noun* rake

The plural of *râteau* is *râteaux*.

rater *verb*
(a) to miss
(b) to fail

rattraper
1 *verb*
(a) to catch up with; **il faut qu'on se dépêche si on veut les rattraper** we have to hurry if we're going to catch them up
(b) to make up for; **rattraper le temps perdu** to make up for lost time
(c) to recapture; **ils n'ont toujours pas rattrapé le prisonnier qui s'est évadé** they still haven't caught the escaped prisoner
2 *reflexive verb* **se rattraper je me suis rattrapé au bras de mon père** I grabbed hold of my dad's arm to stop myself falling

raturer *verb* to cross out

rauque *adjective* hoarse

ravi, ravie *adjective* delighted; **je suis ravi de faire votre connaissance** I'm very pleased to meet you

LE **ravin** *noun* ravine

rayé, rayée *adjective*
(a) striped
(b) scratched

rayer *verb*
(a) to scratch; **quelqu'un lui a rayé sa voiture** someone has scratched his car
(b) to cross out; **il a rayé le mot** he crossed out the word; **ton nom a été rayé de la liste** your name has been crossed off the list

LE **rayon** *noun*
(a) ray, beam; **un rayon de soleil** a sunbeam; **un rayon laser** a laser beam

(**b**) department *(in a shop)*; **où se trouve le rayon jouets, s'il vous plaît?** where's the toy department, please?
(**c**) spoke *(of a wheel)*
(**d**) radius; **le cercle fait trois centimètres de rayon** the circle has a radius of three centimetres
(**e**) shelf; **le livre est sur le rayon du haut** the book is on the top shelf

LA **rayure** *noun*
(**a**) stripe
(**b**) scratch

LA **réaction** *noun*
(**a**) reaction; **il a eu une réaction bizarre** he reacted strangely
(**b**) **un avion à réaction** a jet plane

réagir *verb* to react

LE **réalisateur**, LA **réalisatrice** *noun* film director; **elle est réalisatrice** she's a film director

réaliser
1 *verb*
(**a**) to carry out *(a plan)*
(**b**) to fulfil *(a dream)*
(**c**) to make, to direct *(a film)*
(**d**) to realize
2 *reflexive verb* **se réaliser** to come true

réaliste *adjective* realistic

LA **réalité** *noun* reality; **en réalité** in fact

rebondir *verb* to bounce; **faire rebondir quelque chose** to bounce something

LE **rebord** *noun* edge; **le rebord de la fenêtre** the window sill

récemment *adverb* recently

The middle *e* in *récemment* is pronounced like the *a* in *cat*.

récent, récente *adjective* recent

The *t* in *récent* is not pronounced.

LA **réception** *noun*
(**a**) reception (desk); **demandez à la réception** ask at reception

(**b**) reception; **ils ont organisé une grande réception** they organized a big reception

LA **recette** *noun* recipe

recevoir *verb*
(**a**) to receive
(**b**) to get; **il a reçu une gifle** he got a slap
(**c**) to see; **les profs reçoivent les parents d'élèves ce soir** the teachers are seeing the pupils' parents this evening
(**d**) to have round; **mes parents reçoivent des amis ce soir** my parents are having friends round this evening; **nous avons été très bien reçus** we were made to feel very welcome
(**e**) **être reçu à un examen** to pass an exam

See verb table p. 322.

rechange *masculine noun* **de rechange** spare; **des piles de rechange** spare batteries

LE **réchaud** *noun* portable stove

réchauffer
1 *verb*
(**a**) to reheat; **je vais faire réchauffer le café** I'm going to reheat the coffee
(**b**) to warm up; **bois ça, ça te réchauffera** drink this, it'll warm you up
2 *reflexive verb* **se réchauffer**
(**a**) to get warmer; **le temps se réchauffe** the weather's getting warmer
(**b**) **il se réchauffe les mains** he's warming his hands; **entrez vous réchauffer, il fait froid dehors** come in and get warm, it's cold outside

LA **recherche** *noun*
(**a**) research
(**b**) search; **il est à la recherche d'un emploi** he's looking for a job; **les sauveteurs ont abandonné les recherches** the rescuers have abandoned the search

rechercher *verb* to search for, to look for

LE **récif** *noun* reef; **un récif de corail** a coral reef

LE **récipient** *noun* container

Note that the English word *recipient* is never a translation for the French word *récipient*.

réciproque *adjective* mutual

LE **récit** *noun* story; **il m'a fait le récit de ses aventures** he told me about his adventures

réciter *verb* to recite

LA **réclamation** *noun* complaint

réclamer *verb*
(**a**) to ask for; **il réclame une augmentation** he's asking for a pay rise
(**b**) to complain

LA **récolte** *noun* harvest

récolter *verb* to harvest

recommandé, recommandée
1 *adjective*
(**a**) advisable
(**b**) **par courrier recommandé** by recorded delivery
2 *masculine noun* **un recommandé** a recorded-delivery item; **envoyer une lettre en recommandé** to send a letter by recorded delivery

recommander *verb*
(**a**) to recommend; **je te recommande ce film, il est génial** I can recommend that film, it's great
(**b**) to advise; **le prof nous a recommandé de bien réviser avant l'interrogation** the teacher advised us to do plenty of revision before the test

recommencer *verb*
(**a**) to start again
(**b**) to do again

LA **récompense** *noun* reward

récompenser *verb* to reward

se réconcilier *reflexive verb* **se réconcilier avec quelqu'un** to make up with somebody

réconforter *verb* to comfort

reconnaissant, reconnaissante *adjective* grateful

reconnaître *verb*
(**a**) to recognize; **je ne l'ai pas reconnu** I didn't recognize him
(**b**) to admit; **je reconnais que ce n'est pas facile** I admit it's not easy

See verb table p. 320.

reconstruire *verb* to rebuild

recopier *verb* to copy out

LE **record** *noun* record; **battre un record** to break a record

The *d* in *record* is not pronounced.

se recoucher *reflexive verb* to go back to bed

recoudre *verb*
(**a**) to sew back on; **j'ai recousu le bouton** I sewed the button back on
(**b**) to stitch up

See verb table p. 320.

recouvrir *verb* to cover

See verb table p. 320.

LA **récré** *noun* break *(at school)*

Récré is an informal word; it is the shortened form of *récréation*.

LA **récréation** *noun* break *(at school)*

LE **reçu**[1] *noun* receipt

reçu[2]**, reçue** *see* **recevoir**
j'ai reçu une carte postale I received a postcard

Reçu(e) is the past participle of the verb *recevoir*. See verb table p. 322.

LE **recueil** *noun* collection; **un recueil de nouvelles** a collection of short stories

reculer *verb*
(**a**) to move back, to step back
(**b**) to reverse; **recule encore d'un mètre** reverse another metre
(**c**) to put back, to postpone; **ils ont reculé la date de l'examen** they've postponed the exam

reculons *noun* **à reculons** backwards;

marcher à reculons to walk backwards

récupérer verb
(a) to get back; **tu auras du mal à récupérer l'argent que tu lui as prêté** you'll have trouble getting back the money you lent him
(b) to collect; **je passerai chez toi pour récupérer mes affaires** I'll come by yours to collect my things
(c) to recover; **il lui faudra du temps pour récupérer après sa maladie** it'll take him a while to recover from his illness

recycler verb to recycle

LA **rédaction** noun
(a) essay; **on a une rédaction à faire pour lundi** we have an essay to do for Monday
(b) writing; **la rédaction de son livre lui a pris trois ans** it took him three years to write his book

redescendre verb
(a) to go back down, to come back down; **je suis redescendu à la cave** I went back down to the cellar
(b) to take back down, to bring back down; **il a redescendu ma valise** he brought my suitcase back down

rédiger verb to write

redire verb
(a) to repeat
(b) **trouver à redire à quelque chose** to find fault with something

See verb table p. 315.

redonner verb
(a) to give back; **tu me redonnes mon stylo s'il te plaît?** could you give me my pen back, please?
(b) **redonne-moi un peu de soupe** give me some more soup
(c) **cela m'a redonné espoir** it gave me fresh hope

LE **redoublant**, LA **redoublante** noun pupil repeating a year

redoubler verb to repeat a year

LA **réduction** noun
(a) reduction
(b) discount

réduire verb to cut, to reduce

See verb table p. 320.

réel, réelle verb real

refaire verb
(a) to do again, to redo (exercise, work)
(b) to do up (a room, a house)
(c) to make again (a mistake)
(d) to do up (one's laces)

See verb table p. 317.

LE **réfectoire** noun refectory, dining hall

refermer verb to close, to shut

réfléchir verb
(a) to think
(b) to reflect

LE **reflet** noun reflection

refléter verb to reflect

LA **réflexion** noun
(a) thought
(b) remark

LE **refrain** noun
(a) chorus
(b) **c'est toujours le même refrain** it's always the same old story

LE **réfrigérateur** noun refrigerator

refroidir
1 verb to cool down
2 reflexive verb **se refroidir** to get colder

LE **refuge** noun
(a) refuge; **chercher refuge** to seek refuge
(b) mountain hut

LA **réfugié**, LA **réfugiée** noun refugee

se réfugier reflexive verb
(a) to take shelter
(b) to take refuge

LE **refus** noun refusal

refuser *verb*
(a) to refuse; **le patron a refusé de lui donner une augmentation** the boss refused to give him a pay rise
(b) to turn down; **il a refusé mon offre** he turned down my offer

se régaler *reflexive verb* **on s'est bien régalés au restaurant** we had a really good meal at the restaurant

LE regard *noun*
(a) look; **un regard plein de haine** a look of hatred
(b) eyes; **elle a un très beau regard** she has beautiful eyes

> Note that the English word *regard* is never a translation for the French word *regard*.
> The *d* in *regard* is not pronounced.

regarder *verb*
(a) to look at; **il regardait un tableau** he was looking at a painting
(b) to watch; **regarder la télévision** to watch television
(c) to concern; **cette question nous regarde tous** this matter concerns us all; **cela ne te regarde pas** it's got nothing to do with you

> Note that the English verb *to regard* is never a translation for the French verb *regarder*.

LE régime *noun*
(a) diet; **être au régime** to be on a diet
(b) regime; **un régime fasciste** a fascist regime

LA région *noun* region, area

LA règle *noun*
(a) rule; **est-ce que tu connais les règles du jeu d'échecs?** do you know the rules of chess?; **en règle générale** as a general rule
(b) ruler; **sers-toi d'une règle pour tracer le trait** use a ruler to draw the line
(c) **avoir ses règles** to have one's period

LE règlement *noun* rules; **le règlement du lycée** the school rules

régler *verb*
(a) to settle *(a problem, an argument)*
(b) to adjust *(a seat, the heating)*
(c) to pay *(a bill, a debt)*

LE/LA réglisse *noun* liquorice; **he doesn't like liquorice** il n'aime pas le réglisse *or* la réglisse

LE règne *noun*
(a) reign
(b) **le règne animal** the animal kingdom

régner *verb*
(a) to reign
(b) **il régnait un grand désordre dans la pièce** the room was in a complete mess

LE regret *noun* regret; **je n'ai pas de regrets** I have no regrets

> The *t* in *regret* is not pronounced.

regretter *verb*
(a) to be sorry; **je regrette de t'avoir crié dessus** I'm sorry I shouted at you
(b) to regret; **je ne regrette pas d'y être allé** I don't regret having gone
(c) to miss; **je regrette mon ancienne école** I miss my old school

régulier, régulière *adjective*
(a) regular
(b) steady

régulièrement *adverb* regularly

LE rein *noun*
(a) kidney; **une greffe du rein** a kidney transplant
(b) lower back; **j'ai mal aux reins** I have a pain in my lower back

LA reine *noun* queen

rejoindre *verb*
(a) to join; **je suis allé les rejoindre en Bretagne** I joined them in Brittany
(b) to catch up with; **partez devant, je vous rejoins** you go on ahead, I'll catch you up
(c) to meet; **j'ai prévu de les rejoindre devant le cinéma** I planned to meet

them outside the cinema

See verb table p. 324.

relâcher *verb*
(a) to release *(hostages, prisoners)*
(b) to loosen

LE **relais** *noun* relay race; **prendre le relais** to take over

LA **relation** *noun*
(a) relationship
(b) link, connection; **je l'ai mis en relation avec un ami** I put him in touch
with a friend of mine
(c) **avoir des relations** to have con-
nections

se relayer *reflexive verb* to take turns

relever
1 *verb*
(a) to put up *(one's hair)*
(b) to roll up *(one's sleeves)*
(c) to pick up *(something that has fallen)*
(d) to notice; **j'ai relevé plusieurs erreurs dans son texte** I noticed several
mistakes in his text
(e) to collect; **le prof va relever les copies dans cinq minutes** the teacher
will collect the papers in five minutes
2 *reflexive verb* **se relever** to get up

relier *verb* to connect, to link

LA **religieuse**[1] *noun* nun

religieux, religieuse[2] *adjective* religious

relire *verb*
(a) to read over again; **relis bien le
contrat avant de le signer** read over
the contract again carefully before
you sign it
(b) to read again, to reread; **j'ai relu le
roman car je ne m'en souvenais plus** I
read the novel again because I couldn't
remember it

See verb table p. 322.

remarquable *adjective* outstanding,
remarkable

LA **remarque** *noun* remark, comment

remarquer
1 *verb*
(a) to notice; **j'ai remarqué qu'il avait
une cicatrice** I noticed he had a scar;
**elle m'a fait remarquer que j'étais
en retard** she pointed out to me that I
was late
(b) **remarque, il a peut-être raison**
mind you, he may be right
(c) **se faire remarquer** to draw attention to oneself
2 *reflexive verb* **se remarquer** to be
noticeable; **il a rangé sa chambre et
ça se remarque** he's tidied his room
and it shows

Note that the English verb *to remark*
is never a translation for the French
verb *remarquer*.

rembobiner *verb* to rewind *(a cassette)*

rembourser *verb*
(a) to pay back *(a person, a loan)*
(b) to refund

LES **remerciements** *masculine plural
noun* thanks

remercier *verb* to thank; **je te remercie de m'avoir aidé** thanks for helping
me

remettre
1 *verb*
(a) to put back; **remets la télécommande sur la télévision** put the remote control back on top of the
television
(b) to put back on; **il a remis son manteau car il faisait froid** he put his coat
back on because it was cold
(c) to add; **j'ai remis du sel dans ma
soupe** I put some salt in my soup
(d) to hand over, to give; **est-ce que tu
as remis ta copie au prof?** have you
given your paper to the teacher?
(e) to put off; **la visite est remise à demain** the visit has been put off until tomorrow
2 *reflexive verb* **se remettre**
(a) to recover; **elle a mis très long-**

temps à se remettre de sa maladie she took a long time to recover from her illness

(**b**) **se remettre à faire quelque chose** to start doing something again; **elle s'est remise à pleurer** she started crying again

> The past participle of *remettre* is *remis(e)*. See verb table p. 322.

LE **remonte-pente** *noun* ski tow

> The plural of *remonte-pente* is *remonte-pentes.*

remonter *verb*

(**a**) to go back up, to come back up; **il est remonté au grenier** he went back up to the attic

(**b**) to take back up, to bring back up; **il a remonté la valise au grenier** he took the suitcase back up to the attic

(**c**) to wind up *(a watch, a toy)*

(**d**) **cette tradition remonte au début du siècle dernier** this tradition dates back to the beginning of the last century

LA **remorque** *noun* trailer

LE **remplaçant**, LA **remplaçante** *noun*

(**a**) substitute

(**b**) supply teacher; **elle est remplaçante** she's a supply teacher

remplacer *verb*

(**a**) to replace; **remplacer une ampoule** to change a light bulb

(**b**) to stand in for; **c'est monsieur Godefroy qui remplacera monsieur Fève pendant son absence** Mr Godefroy will be standing in for Mr Fève while he's away

remplir

1 *verb*

(**a**) to fill, to fill up; **il a rempli mon verre de champagne** he filled my glass with champagne

(**b**) **remplir un formulaire** to fill in a form

2 *reflexive verb* **se remplir** to fill up

remporter *verb*

(**a**) to take away; **est-ce que tu as remporté tes outils?** did you take your tools away with you?

(**b**) to win; **c'est Paul qui a remporté la course** Paul won the race

remuer *verb*

(**a**) to move

(**b**) to stir *(coffee, sauce)*

LE **renard** *noun* fox

LA **rencontre** *noun* meeting; **faire des rencontres** to meet people; **aller à la rencontre de quelqu'un** to go to meet somebody

rencontrer

1 *verb* to meet

2 *reflexive verb* **se rencontrer** to meet; **ils se sont rencontrés au lycée** they met at school

LE **rendez-vous** *noun*

(**a**) appointment; **n'oublie pas ton rendez-vous chez le dentiste** don't forget your dentist's appointment

(**b**) date; **il s'est fait beau pour son rendez-vous avec Isabelle** he got all dressed up for his date with Isabelle

(**c**) **donner rendez-vous à quelqu'un** to arrange to meet somebody; **ils se sont donné rendez-vous devant le musée** they arranged to meet outside the museum

> The word *rendez-vous* does not change in the plural.

se rendormir *reflexive verb* to go back to sleep

rendre

1 *verb*

(**a**) to give back, to return; **quand est-ce que tu vas me rendre mon CD?** when are you going to give me my CD back?; **j'ai encore oublié de rendre le livre à la bibliothèque** I forgot to take the book back to the library again

(**b**) to hand in; **est-ce que tu as rendu ta dissertation au prof?** have you handed your essay in to the teacher?

(**c**) to make; **la sauce m'a rendu malade** the sauce made me ill; **la nouvelle m'a rendu triste** I was saddened by the news

2 *reflexive verb* **se rendre**
(**a**) to surrender
(**b**) to go; **je me rends à l'école à pied** I walk to school
(**c**) **se rendre compte de quelque chose** to realize something

LE **renfermé** *noun* **sentir le renfermé** to smell musty

renifler *verb* to sniff

LE **renne** *noun* reindeer

renoncer *verb* **j'ai renoncé à l'idée d'aller à New York** I've given up the idea of going to New York; **je renonce à comprendre** I've given up trying to understand it

rénover *verb* to renovate

LE **renseignement** *noun*
(**a**) piece of information; **des renseignements** information
(**b**) **les renseignements** directory enquiries; **téléphone aux renseignements si tu n'as pas le numéro** call directory enquiries if you don't have the number

renseigner
1 *verb* **renseigner quelqu'un** to give somebody some information; **pardon, pouvez-vous me renseigner?** excuse me, could you help me, please?; **on nous a mal renseignés** we were given the wrong information
2 *reflexive verb* **se renseigner** to find out; **je vais me renseigner sur les prix** I'll find out about the prices

LA **rentrée** *noun* **la rentrée** *or* **la rentrée des classes** the beginning of the school year

La Rentrée

La rentrée refers to the beginning of the new school year in September, which sees French children returning to school after the long summer break (*les grandes*

vacances) which lasts for the whole of July and August. It is the time when everyone goes back to work in earnest after the more relaxed summer months.

rentrer *verb*
(**a**) to go back, to come back; **il rentre demain de son voyage d'affaires** he gets back from his business trip tomorrow; **il rentre tard du travail** he gets home late from work
(**b**) to go home, to come home; **c'est bizarre que ta sœur ne soit pas encore rentrée** it's strange that your sister's not home yet; **il est temps que Pierre rentre chez lui** it's time Pierre went home
(**c**) to go back in, to come back in; **dis aux enfants de rentrer, il fait froid dehors** tell the children to come in, it's cold outside
(**d**) to take in, to bring in; **rentrer la voiture** to put the car away; **je vais rentrer le linge, il commence à pleuvoir** I'm going to bring the washing in, it's starting to rain

renverser *verb*
(**a**) to knock over *(a glass, a vase)*
(**b**) to knock down, to run over *(a pedestrian)*
(**c**) to spill *(a liquid)*

renvoyer *verb*
(**a**) to send back *(mail)*
(**b**) to throw back *(a ball)*
(**c**) to dismiss *(an employee)*
(**d**) to expel *(a pupil)*

See verb table p. 322.

répandu, répandue *adjective* widespread

LA **réparation** *noun*
(**a**) repair
(**b**) **la surface de réparation** the penalty area

réparer *verb* to repair

repartir *verb*
(**a**) to go back
(**b**) to set off again

(c) to start again

See verb table p. 322.

répartir *verb* to share out

LE repas *noun* meal

LE repassage *noun* ironing; **faire le repassage** to do the ironing

repasser *verb*
(**a**) to call again; **le docteur repassera ce soir** the doctor will call again this evening
(**b**) to go back, to come back; **il faut que je repasse à l'épicerie, j'ai oublié d'acheter du lait** I need to go back to the grocer's, I forgot to buy milk
(**c**) to go past again; **le voilà qui repasse sur sa moto** he's just gone past on his motorbike again
(**d**) to iron *(clothes)*
(**e**) to resit *(an exam)*
(**f**) to show again *(a film)*; **ils repassent Alien au cinéma du coin** they're showing *Alien* again at the local cinema

repérer *verb* to spot; **ils se sont fait repérer** they've been spotted

répéter
1 *verb*
(**a**) to repeat
(**b**) to rehearse
(**c**) to practise
2 *reflexive verb* **se répéter**
(**a**) to repeat oneself
(**b**) to happen again; **il m'a promis que ça ne se répèterait pas** he promised me that it wouldn't happen again

LA répétition *noun*
(**a**) repetition; **son texte est plein de répétitions** his text is full of repetitions
(**b**) rehearsal

LE répondeur *noun* answering machine

répondre *verb* to answer, to reply; **il ne veut pas répondre au professeur** he doesn't want to answer the teacher; **tu n'as pas répondu à ma question**

you haven't answered my question

LA réponse *noun* answer

LE reportage *noun* report

LE repos *noun* rest; **il a besoin de repos** he needs rest

reposer
1 *verb* to put back down
2 *reflexive verb* **se reposer** to rest, to have a rest

repousser *verb*
(**a**) to grow again
(**b**) to postpone, to put off *(an event)*; **le match a été repoussé à la semaine prochaine** the match has been postponed until next week
(**c**) to push back, to push away

reprendre *verb*
(**a**) to take back; **est-ce que je peux reprendre mon stylo?** can I take my pen back?
(**b**) to take up again *(an activity)*; **j'ai décidé de reprendre le judo** I've decided to take up judo again; **les grévistes ont décidé de reprendre le travail** the strikers decided to go back to work
(**c**) to start again; **la réunion reprendra dans cinq minutes** the meeting will start again in five minutes
(**d**) **reprends de la soupe** have some more soup; **est-ce que je peux reprendre un biscuit?** can I take another biscuit?

See verb table p. 322.

LE représentant, LA représentante *noun*
(**a**) representative; **les représentants du syndicat** the union representatives
(**b**) **un représentant de commerce** a sales representative, a rep

LA représentation *noun* performance

représenter *verb*
(**a**) to represent; **à l'époque, cent livres représentait une fortune** at the time a hundred pounds was a fortune

(**b**) to show
(**c**) to perform

LE **reproche** *noun* criticism; **il n'arrête pas de me faire des reproches** he's always criticizing me

reprocher *verb* **reprocher quelque chose à quelqu'un** to criticize somebody for something; **il m'a reproché d'être arrivé en retard** he criticized me for being late

se reproduire *reflexive verb*
(**a**) to happen again; **il ne faut pas que ce genre d'incident se reproduise** this type of incident must never happen again
(**b**) to breed; **les souris se reproduisent très rapidement** mice breed very quickly

See verb table p. 320.

LA **république** *noun* republic; **la France est une république** France is a republic

répugnant, répugnante *adjective* disgusting, revolting

LE **requin** *noun* shark

LE **RER** *noun* express rail network serving Paris and its suburbs

RER is the abbreviation of *Réseau express régional.*

LA **réservation** *noun* reservation, booking

LA **réserve** *noun*
(**a**) stock, store; **ils font des réserves de bois pour l'hiver** they're stocking up on wood for the winter
(**b**) **une réserve naturelle** a nature reserve
(**c**) **une réserve indienne** an Indian reservation

réservé, réservée *adjective* reserved

réserver *verb*
(**a**) to book; **vous avez réservé?** do you have a reservation?
(**b**) to save; **je t'ai réservé une part de gâteau** I saved you a slice of cake

LE **réservoir** *noun*
(**a**) tank
(**b**) reservoir

LA **résidence** *noun*
(**a**) block of flats
(**b**) **une résidence secondaire** a second home
(**c**) **une résidence universitaire** a hall of residence

résister *verb*
(**a**) to resist
(**b**) to withstand; **la plante n'a pas résisté au gel** the plant didn't withstand the frost

résolu, résolue *adjective*
(**a**) determined; **je suis résolu à trouver le coupable** I'm determined to find the culprit
(**b**) solved; **le problème n'est pas encore résolu** the problem still hasn't been solved

Résolu(e) is the past participle of the verb *résoudre.* See verb table p. 324.

résoudre *verb* to solve; **résoudre un problème** to solve a problem

See verb table p. 324.

LE **respect** *noun* respect; **j'ai beaucoup de respect pour elle** I have a lot of respect for her

The *c* and the *t* of *respect* are not pronounced in French.

respecter *verb*
(**a**) to respect; **respecter les limitations de vitesse** to respect the speed limits; **les élèves doivent respecter leurs professeurs** pupils must show respect to their teachers
(**b**) to follow; **respecter les instructions** to follow the instructions

LA **respiration** *noun* breathing; **retenir sa respiration** to hold one's breath

respirer *verb* to breathe

LA **responsabilité** *noun* responsibility; **tu dois prendre tes responsa-**

bilités you must face up to your responsibilities

Do not confuse the spellings of the French *responsabilité* and English *responsibility*.

---

responsable

1 *adjective* responsible; **être responsable de quelque chose** to be responsible for something; **c'est quelqu'un de très responsable, il s'occupera bien des enfants** he's very responsible, he'll be fine at looking after the children
2 *noun* **le/la responsable**
(a) the person in charge; **je veux parler au responsable** I want to speak to the person in charge
(b) the person responsible; **les responsables de l'attentat seront punis** the people responsible for the attack will be punished

ressembler

1 *verb* **ressembler à** to look like; **Paul ressemble à son frère** Paul looks like his brother; **par endroits l'Écosse ressemble un peu à l'Auvergne** Scotland is rather like the Auvergne in places
2 *reflexive verb* **se ressembler** to look alike

ressentir *verb* to feel

See verb table p. 322.

LE **ressort** *noun* spring *(made of metal)*

ressortir *verb* to go out again

LE **reste** *noun*
(a) **le reste** the rest; **je me souviens des deux premiers vers mais j'oublié le reste du poème** I remember the first two lines but I've forgotten the rest of the poem
(b) **les restes** the leftovers; **un reste de fromage** some leftover cheese

rester *verb*
(a) to stay; **tu peux partir si tu veux, moi je reste** you can leave if you like, but I'm staying
(b) to be left; **il reste une part de gâteau** there's one slice of cake left; **il te reste de l'argent?** have you got any money left?

LE **resto** *noun* restaurant

Resto is an informal word; it is the shortened form of *restaurant*.

LE **résultat** *noun* result

LE **résumé** *noun* summary

résumer *verb* to summarize

rétablir

1 *verb* to restore; **le courant a été rétabli dans l'après-midi** the power was restored in the afternoon
2 *reflexive verb* **se rétablir** to recover

LE **retard** *noun* delay; **le train a du retard** the train is late; **le train a deux heures de retard** the train is two hours late; **je suis arrivé en retard à l'école ce matin** I was late for school this morning; **tu es encore en retard!** you're late again!

The *d* in *retard* is not pronounced.

---

retarder *verb*
(a) to be slow; **cette pendule retarde de dix minutes** this clock is ten minutes slow
(b) to put back *(a watch, a clock)*; **quand on va de France en Angleterre il faut retarder sa montre d'une heure** when you go to England from France you have to put your watch back an hour
(c) to put off, to postpone; **nous avons retardé notre départ de deux jours** we postponed our departure by two days
(d) to delay; **le mauvais temps nous a retardés** we were delayed by the bad weather; **désolé, j'ai été retardé** sorry, I got delayed

retenir

1 *verb*
(a) to remember; **il n'arrive pas à retenir les tables de multiplication** he can't remember his times tables
(b) to book, to reserve; **j'ai retenu**

deux places pour la représentation de ce soir I've booked two seats for tonight's performance

(c) **retenir son souffle** to hold one's breath

(d) **retenir quelqu'un** to hold somebody up

2 *reflexive verb* **se retenir**

(a) to hold on

(b) **se retenir de faire quelque chose** to stop oneself from doing something; **elle n'a pas pu se retenir de rire** she couldn't help laughing

See verb table p. 324.

retirer *verb*

(a) to take off *(clothes)*; **retire tes chaussures** take off your shoes

(b) to take out; **retire tes mains de tes poches** take your hands out of your pockets

(c) to withdraw; **il faut que je retire de l'argent** I need to withdraw some money

LE retour *noun*

(a) return; **être de retour** to be back; **à son retour** when he gets back

(b) return journey

retourner

1 *verb*

(a) to go back, to return; **je ne retournerai jamais chez lui** I'm never going back to his house

(b) to turn over; **retourne cette carte à jouer** turn over this playing card

(c) to turn inside out

2 *reflexive verb* **se retourner**

(a) to turn round

(b) to turn over, to overturn

LE retrait *noun* withdrawal

LA retraite *noun*

(a) retirement; **prendre sa retraite** to retire; **être à la retraite** to be retired

(b) retirement pension

LE retraité, LA retraitée *noun* retired person

rétrécir *verb* to shrink

retrouver

1 *verb*

(a) to find *(something lost)*; **je n'ai toujours pas retrouvé mes clés** I still haven't found my keys

(b) to meet; **je dois retrouver Marie à sept heures pour aller au cinéma** I'm supposed to meet Marie at seven o'clock to go to the cinema

2 *reflexive verb* **se retrouver**

(a) to meet, to meet up; **on se retrouve chez toi?** shall we meet at yours?

(b) to find oneself; **il s'est retrouvé sans travail** he found himself without a job; **se retrouver en prison** to find oneself in prison; **se retrouver chez soi** to be back home

(c) **je me suis trompé de métro, et je me suis retrouvé à l'autre bout de la ville** I got on the wrong metro and ended up at the other end of town

(d) **je ne m'y retrouve plus** I'm completely lost

LE rétroviseur *noun* rear-view mirror

LA réunion *noun* meeting

réunir

1 *verb*

(a) to bring together

(b) to collect

2 *reflexive verb* **se réunir** to meet

réussir *verb*

(a) to be successful; **ses parents veulent qu'il réussisse dans la vie** his parents want him to succeed in life

(b) **réussir à faire quelque chose** to manage to do something

(c) **il a réussi (à) son examen** he passed his exam

LA réussite *noun*

(a) success

(b) patience *(card game)*; **j'ai fait une réussite** I had a game of patience

LA revanche *noun*

(a) revenge

(b) return game

(c) **en revanche** on the other hand

LE rêve *noun* dream; **faire un rêve** to

have a dream; **faites de beaux rêves!** sweet dreams!; **des vacances de rêve** a dream holiday

LE **réveil** *noun* alarm clock

réveiller
1 *verb* **réveiller quelqu'un** to wake somebody up; **être réveillé** to be awake
2 *reflexive verb* **se réveiller** to wake up

LE **réveillon** *noun* meal eaten on Christmas Eve or New Year's Eve

revenir *verb*
(a) to come back; **je suis revenu hier** I came back yesterday; **je ne souviens plus de la date, mais ça va me revenir** I can't remember the date but it'll come back to me; **je n'en reviens pas!** I can't get over it!
(b) to come to; **mon voyage m'est revenu à mille euros** my trip came to one thousand euros; **ça revient très cher** it works out very expensive
(c) **il est revenu sur sa promesse** he went back on his promise
(d) **ça revient au même** it amounts to the same thing

See verb table p. 324.

LE **revenu** *noun* income

rêver *verb* to dream; **j'ai rêvé de lui la nuit dernière** I had a dream about him last night; **il rêve d'aller en vacances en Australie** his dream is to go to Australia on holiday; **j'ai rêvé que j'avais gagné au loto** I dreamt that I'd won the lottery

LE **revers** *noun*
(a) backhand
(b) lapel

rêveur, rêveuse *adjective* dreamy

réviser *verb*
(a) to revise; **elle ne peut pas sortir ce soir, elle doit réviser** she can't go out tonight, she has to revise
(b) to service; **il faut que je donne la voiture à réviser au garage** I have to take the car to the garage for a service

revoir *verb*
(a) to see again; **j'aimerais bien le revoir** I'd like to see him again; **je ne l'ai jamais revue** I never saw her again
(b) **au revoir** goodbye

See verb table p. 324.

LA **révolution** *noun* revolution

LE **revolver** *noun* gun, revolver

LA **revue** *noun* magazine

LE **rez-de-chaussée** *noun* ground floor

The word *rez-de-chaussée* does not change in the plural.

LE **Rhin** *noun* the Rhine

LE **rhume** *noun* cold; **elle a un gros rhume** she has a bad cold; **le rhume des foins** hay fever

ri *see* **rire**
on a bien ri we had a good laugh

Ri is the past participle of the verb *rire*. See verb table p. 324.

ricaner *verb* to snigger

riche *adjective* rich, wealthy

LA **richesse** *noun* wealth

LA **ride** *noun* wrinkle

LE **rideau** *noun* curtain; **ferme les rideaux** draw the curtains

The plural of *rideau* is *rideaux*.

ridicule *adjective* ridiculous

rien *pronoun*
(a) nothing; **rien du tout** nothing at all
(b) anything; **je n'ai rien compris** I didn't understand anything
(b) **rien que** just; **elle a dit ça rien que pour m'embêter** she said that just to annoy me; **rien que son sac coûte une fortune** her handbag alone costs a fortune
(c) **ça ne fait rien** it doesn't matter
(d) **merci! – de rien!** thank you! – you're welcome!

rigoler *verb*
(**a**) to laugh
(**b**) to have fun; **on a bien rigolé à la soirée de Claire** we had a lot of fun at Claire's party
(**c**) to joke; **j'ai dit ça pour rigoler** I said it as a joke

This word is informal.

rigolo, rigolote *adjective* funny

rimer *verb* to rhyme; **"livre" rime avec "ivre"** "livre" rhymes with "ivre"

rincer *verb* to rinse

rire
1 *verb* to laugh; **j'ai beaucoup ri** I laughed a lot; **elle a dit ça pour rire** she said that as a joke

See verb table p. 324.

2 *masculine noun* **un rire** a laugh; **il a un rire idiot** he has a stupid laugh

LE **risque** *noun* risk; **prendre des risques** to take risks

risqué, risquée *adjective* risky

risquer *verb* to risk; **il a risqué sa vie pour elle** he risked his life for her; **tu ne risques rien** you'll be quite safe; **elle risque de tomber** she might fall; **tu risques d'avoir un accident** you could easily have an accident

LE **rivage** *noun* shore

LA **rive** *noun* bank *(of a river)*

LA **rivière** *noun* river

LE **riz** *noun* rice

The *z* in *riz* is not pronounced.

LA **robe** *noun* dress; **une robe de mariée** a wedding dress; **une robe de chambre** a dressing gown

LE **robinet** *noun* tap

LE **robot** *noun* robot

The *t* in *robot* is not pronounced.

robuste *adjective* strong, sturdy

LA **roche** *noun* rock *(substance)*

LE **rocher** *noun* rock *(large stone)*

rocheux, rocheuse *adjective* rocky

LE **roi** *noun* king; **la fête des Rois** Twelfth Night

LE **rôle** *noun*
(**a**) part *(in a film, a play)*
(**b**) role; **il n'a pas d'ordres à donner aux employés, ce n'est pas son rôle** he shouldn't give orders to the employees, it's not his job

LE **roller** *noun* rollerblade®; **je fais du roller tous les jeudis** I go rollerblading every Thursday

romain, romaine *adjective* Roman

LE **roman** *noun* novel; **un roman policier** a detective novel

Note that the English word *Roman* is never a translation for the French word *roman*.

rompre
1 *verb*
(**a**) to break; **rompre la glace** to break the ice
(**b**) to split up; **Sylvie et Alexandre ont rompu** Sylvie and Alexandre have split up
2 *reflexive verb* **se rompre** to break

See verb table p. 324.

LES **ronces** *feminine plural noun* brambles

rond, ronde
1 *adjective* round
2 *masculine noun* **le rond**
(**a**) circle; **on tourne en rond** we're going round in circles
(**b**) **je n'ai plus un rond** *(informal phrase)* I'm completely broke

LA **rondelle** *noun* slice

LE **rond-point** *noun* roundabout

The plural of *rond-point* is *ronds-points*.

ronfler *verb* to snore

ronger
1 *verb* to gnaw; **le chien ronge son os** the dog is gnawing its bone

2 *reflexive verb* **se ronger** se ronger les ongles to bite one's nails

LE **rosbif** *noun* roast beef

rose
1 *adjective* pink; **une robe rose** a pink dress
2 *masculine noun* **le rose** pink; **le rose est sa couleur préférée** pink is her favourite colour; **elle voit la vie en rose** she sees things through rose-tinted spectacles
3 *feminine noun* **une rose** a rose; **un bouquet de roses rouges** a bunch of red roses

roter *verb* to burp

LE **rôti** *noun* roast; **un rôti de porc** roast pork

LA **roue** *noun*
(**a**) wheel; **une roue de secours** a spare wheel
(**b**) **faire la roue** to do a cartwheel
(**c**) **le paon fait la roue** the peacock is fanning its tail

rouge
1 *adjective* red; **du vin rouge** red wine
2 *masculine noun*
(**a**) **le rouge** red; **le rouge est ma couleur préférée** red is my favourite colour; **le feu est au rouge** the traffic lights are at red
(**b**) red wine; **il ne boit que du rouge** he only drinks red wine
(**c**) **rouge à lèvres** lipstick

LE **rouge-gorge** *noun* robin

The plural of *rouge-gorge* is *rouges-gorges*.

LA **rougeole** *noun* measles; **avoir la rougeole** to have measles

rougir *verb* to blush; **il rougit très facilement** he blushes very easily

LA **rouille** *noun* rust

rouillé, rouillée *adjective* rusty

rouiller *verb* to go rusty, to rust

LE **rouleau** *noun*
(**a**) roll; **un rouleau de papier toilette** a toilet roll
(**b**) **un rouleau à pâtisserie** a rolling pin
(**c**) roller *(wave)*
(**d**) **un rouleau compresseur** a steamroller
(**e**) **être au bout du rouleau** to be at the end of one's tether

The plural of *rouleau* is *rouleaux*.

rouler *verb*
(**a**) to roll; **la balle a roulé jusqu'en bas de la colline** the ball rolled down the hill; **rouler une cigarette** to roll a cigarette
(**b**) to roll up; **rouler un tapis** to roll up a rug
(**c**) to go; **la voiture roulait très vite** the car was going very fast
(**d**) to drive; **ça faisait une heure qu'on roulait quand il s'est mis à neiger** we'd been driving for an hour when it started snowing

rouspéter *verb* to grumble, to complain

This word is informal.

LE **Roumain,** LA **Roumaine** *noun (person)* Romanian

roumain, roumaine
1 *adjective* Romanian; **la culture roumaine** Romanian culture
2 *noun* **le roumain** *(language)* Romanian; **elle parle roumain** she speaks Romanian

LA **Roumanie** *noun* Romania

rousse *see* **roux**

LA **route** *noun*
(**a**) road; **c'est une route dangereuse** it's a dangerous road; **il y a trois heures de route pour aller à Lille** it's a three-hour drive to Lille
(**b**) way; **tu connais la route pour aller à Versailles?** do you know the way to Versailles?
(**c**) **en route** on the way; **on s'arrêtera en route pour manger** we'll stop on the way to eat; **en route!** let's go!; **se**

mettre en route to set out

(**d**) **mettre en route** to start up; **il a mis la machine à laver en route** he started the washing machine

routier, routière

1 *adjective* **la circulation routière** road traffic; **une carte routière** a road map

2 *masculine noun* **un routier** a long-distance lorry driver

roux, rousse

1 *adjective*

(**a**) red-haired

(**b**) red; **des cheveux roux** red hair; **un écureuil roux** a red squirrel

2 *noun* **un roux** a red-haired man, a redhead; **une rousse** a red-haired woman, a redhead

royal, royale *adjective* royal

The masculine plural of *royal* is *royaux*.

LE **royaume** *noun* kingdom

LE **Royaume-Uni** *noun* the United Kingdom

LE **ruban** *noun*

(**a**) ribbon; **elle a des rubans dans les cheveux** she has ribbons in her hair

(**b**) **le ruban adhésif** sticky tape

LA **rubéole** *noun* German measles

LA **rubrique** *noun* column *(in a newspaper)*

LA **ruche** *noun* hive, beehive

rude *adjective*

(**a**) tough

(**b**) harsh

Note that the English word *rude* is never a translation for the French word *rude*.

LA **rue** *noun* street; **être à la rue** to be homeless

se ruer *reflexive verb*

(**a**) **se ruer sur quelqu'un** to rush at somebody; **les enfants se sont rués sur la nourriture** the children made a mad dash for the food

(**b**) **se ruer vers** to rush towards; **tout le monde s'est rué vers la sortie** everybody rushed towards the exit

LA **ruelle** *noun* lane, alleyway

rugir *verb* to roar

rugueux, rugueuse *adjective* rough, coarse

LA **ruine** *noun* ruin; **la maison est en ruine** the house is in ruins

ruiner

1 *verb* to ruin; **tu vas nous ruiner si tu continues à acheter tous ces jeux vidéo** you're going to bankrupt us if you keep buying these computer games

2 *reflexive verb* **se ruiner** to spend a fortune; **il s'est ruiné en cadeaux** he spent a fortune on presents

LE **ruisseau** *noun* stream

The plural of *ruisseau* is *ruisseaux*.

LA **rumeur** *noun*

(**a**) rumour

(**b**) rumbling

LA **ruse** *noun*

(**a**) trick; **fais attention, c'est une ruse!** be careful, it's a trick!

(**b**) cunning

(**c**) trickery

rusé, rusée *adjective* cunning

LE/LA **Russe** *noun (person)* Russian; **les Russes** the Russians

russe

1 *adjective* Russian; **l'économie russe** the Russian economy

2 *masculine noun* **le russe** *(language)* Russian; **elle parle russe** she speaks Russian

In French, only the noun for the inhabitants of a country takes a capital letter, never the adjective or the noun for the language.

LA **Russie** *noun* Russia

LE **rythme** *noun*

(**a**) beat, rhythm

(**b**) rate, pace

s'

1 *pronoun* **il s'est coupé en se rasant** he's cut himself shaving; **elle s'est cassé la jambe** she broke her leg; **ils s'aiment** they love each other

> When *s'* is used in front of a verb beginning with a vowel or a mute h, then it is the abbreviation of *se*. See also **se**.

2 *conjunction* if; **je ne sais pas s'il viendra** I don't know if he'll come; **je te préviendrai s'ils sont en retard** I'll let you know if they're late

> When *s'* is used in front of *il* or *ils*, then it is the abbreviation of *si*. See also **si**.

sa *adjective*
(a) his; **Pierre a perdu sa montre** Pierre has lost his watch
(b) her; **Nadia cherche sa tasse** Nadia is looking for her cup
(c) its; **on reconnaît la femelle de l'espèce à sa petite taille** you can recognize the female of the species by its small size

> *Sa* is used in front of feminine nouns. The plural of *sa* is *ses. Sa* becomes *son* before a feminine noun starting with a vowel or a mute h, as in *son école, son histoire.* See also **ses** and **son¹**.

LE **sable** *noun* sand

LE **sablé** *noun* shortbread biscuit

LE **sablier** *noun* hourglass

LE **sabot** *noun*
(a) hoof
(b) clog

LE **sac** *noun* bag; **un sac à dos** a rucksack, a backpack; **un sac de couchage** a sleeping bag; **un sac à main** a handbag; **un sac poubelle** a bin liner, a bin bag

saccager *verb* to ransack

sache *see* **savoir**
il faut que je sache à quelle heure il arrivera I need know what time he'll be here

> *Sache* is a form of the verb *savoir* in the subjunctive. See verb table p. 324.

LE **sachet** *noun* sachet; **un sachet de thé** a teabag

LA **sacoche** *noun* bag; **une sacoche de vélo** a saddlebag

sacré, sacrée *adjective*
(a) sacred, holy
(b) **c'est un sacré menteur!** he's a total liar!

> Sense (b) is an informal use of *sacré*.

sage *adjective*
(a) wise
(b) good, well-behaved

LA **sage-femme** *noun* midwife; **elle est sage-femme** she's a midwife

> The plural of *sage-femme* is *sages-femmes*.

LA **sagesse** *noun* wisdom

LE **Sagittaire** *noun* Sagittarius; **il est Sagittaire** he's a Sagittarius

saignant, saignante *adjective* rare; **il aime sa viande saignante** he likes rare meat

saigner *verb* to bleed; **saigner du nez** to have a nosebleed

sain, saine *adjective*
(a) healthy; **il ne mange que de la nourriture très saine** he only eats very healthy food
(b) **sain et sauf** unhurt; **revenir sain et sauf** to come back safe and sound

saint, sainte
1 *adjective* holy; **un lieu saint** a holy place
2 *noun* **un saint, une sainte** a saint

> The *t* in *saint* is not pronounced.

Les Saints

Most days in the French calendar are associated with the name of a saint. It is customary to wish people *bonne fête* or to send them a card on their saint day, that is the day of the saint they were named after. For instance people called Georges have their *fête* on the 23rd of April because it is St George's day.

sais *see* **savoir**
je ne sais pas I don't know; **je sais nager** I can swim

> *Sais* is a form of the verb *savoir* in the present tense. See verb table p. 324.

saisir *verb*
(a) to grab, to grab hold of
(b) to grasp, to get; **il n'a pas saisi l'allusion** he didn't get the hint
(b) **saisir l'occasion** to jump at the opportunity

LA **saison** *noun* season

sait *see* **savoir**
il ne sait pas he doesn't know; **elle sait nager** she can swim

> *Sait* is a form of the verb *savoir* in the present tense. See verb table p. 324.

LA **salade** *noun*
(a) lettuce; **les lapins aiment la salade** rabbits like lettuce
(b) salad; **une salade de fruits** a fruit salad

LE **saladier** *noun* salad bowl

LE **salaire** *noun* salary, wages

LE **salarié, LA salariée** *noun* employee

sale *adjective* dirty

salé, salée *adjective* salty

saler *verb* to put salt on/in; **la soupe est trop salée** the soup is too salty

LA **saleté** *noun*
(a) dirt; **la cuisine était d'une saleté incroyable** the kitchen was unbelievably dirty
(b) **il y a une saleté sur ton pull** there's a dirty mark on your jumper; **il y a plein de saletés sur le trottoir** the pavement is covered in rubbish; **faire des saletés** to make a mess

salir
1 *verb* **salir quelque chose** to make something dirty
2 *reflexive verb* **se salir** to get dirty

LA **salle** *noun*
(a) room; **une salle d'attente** a waiting room; **une salle de bain** a bathroom; **une salle de classe** a classroom; **une salle à manger** a dining room; **une salle de séjour** a living room
(b) hall; **une salle de concert** a concert hall
(c) **une salle de cinéma** a cinema; **ce cinéma comprend trois salles** this cinema has three screens

LE **salon** *noun*
(a) living room, sitting room
(b) exhibition; **le Salon de l'Auto** the Motor Show

LA **salopette** *noun* dungarees

saluer *verb*
(a) to greet, to say hello to; **saluer quelqu'un de la main** to wave to somebody; **saluer quelqu'un de la tête** to nod to somebody
(b) to say goodbye
(c) to salute

salut *exclamation*
(a) hi

(**b**) bye

This word is informal.

LE **samedi** *noun* Saturday; **elle est venue samedi** she came on Saturday; **il fait du tennis le samedi** he plays tennis on Saturdays; **tous les samedis** every Saturday

In French, the names of days are not written with a capital.

LE **sang** *noun* blood

The *g* of *sang* is not pronounced.

LE **sanglier** *noun* wild boar

LE **sanglot** *noun* **éclater en sanglots** to burst into tears

sangloter *verb* to sob

sanguin, sanguine *adjective* **un groupe sanguin** a blood group; **une transfusion sanguine** a blood transfusion

sans *preposition* without

LA **sanisette**® *noun* superloo

LE/LA **sans-abri** *noun* homeless person; **les sans-abri** the homeless

The word *sans-abri* does not change in the plural.

LA **santé** *noun* health; **être en bonne santé** to be in good health; **à votre santé!** cheers!

saoul, saoule *adjective* drunk

LE **sapin** *noun* fir tree; **un sapin de Noël** a Christmas tree

satisfaire *verb*
(**a**) to satisfy
(**b**) **satisfaire aux besoins de quelqu'un** to meet somebody's needs

See verb table p. 317.

satisfaisant, satisfaisante *adjective* satisfactory

satisfait, satisfaite *adjective* satisfied; **je ne suis pas satisfait du résultat** I'm not happy with the result

LA **sauce** *noun*
(**a**) sauce
(**b**) gravy

LA **saucisse** *noun* sausage

LE **saucisson** *noun* cold sausage, salami

sauf *preposition*
(**a**) except
(**b**) **sauf si** unless; **sauf s'il pleut** unless it rains

LE **saule** *noun* willow; **un saule pleureur** a weeping willow

LE **saumon** *noun* salmon; **du saumon fumé** smoked salmon

saupoudrer *verb* to sprinkle; **j'ai saupoudré le gâteau de sucre glace** I sprinkled the cake with icing sugar

saura, saurai, saurez *see* savoir
on ne saura jamais qui est le coupable we'll never know who did it; **je saurai demain si j'ai été reçu à l'examen** I'll know tomorrow if I've passed the exam

Saura, saurai etc are forms of the verb *savoir* in the future tense. See verb table p. 324.

LE **saut** *noun*
(**a**) jump; **faire un saut** to jump; **je vais faire un saut à l'épicerie** I'm just popping out to the grocer's
(**b**) **le saut en hauteur** the high jump; **le saut en longueur** the long jump; **le saut à la perche** pole vaulting; **le saut à l'élastique** bungee jumping

sauter *verb*
(**a**) to jump; **il a sauté par-dessus la clôture** he jumped over the fence
(**b**) to blow up; **faire sauter un pont** to blow up a bridge
(**c**) to skip; **sauter à la corde** to skip *(with a skipping rope)*; **sauter un repas** to skip a meal; **sauter une classe** to skip a (school) year

LA **sauterelle** *noun* grasshopper

sauvage *adjective*
(**a**) wild; **des bêtes sauvages** wild

animals; **faire du camping sauvage** to camp out in the open
(**b**) unsociable; **elle est gentille mais elle est un peu sauvage** she's nice but she's a bit unsociable

sauvegarder *verb* to save *(a computer file)*

sauver
1 *verb* to save, to rescue; **il m'a sauvé la vie** he saved my life
2 *reflexive verb* **se sauver**
(**a**) to run away; **bon, je me sauve!** *(informal phrase)* OK, I'm off!
(**b**) to escape

LE savant, LA savante *noun* scientist

savoir *verb*
(**a**) to know; **je ne sais pas** I don't know; **comment veux-tu que je le sache?** how am I supposed to know?; **je n'en sais rien** I have no idea
(**b**) **il sait nager** he can swim; **est-ce que tu sais faire la roue?** can you do a cartwheel?

See verb table p. 324.

LE savon *noun* soap; **passer un savon à quelqu'un** *(informal phrase)* to tell somebody off

LE scandale *noun* scandal; **son livre a provoqué un scandale** his book caused a scandal

scandaleux, scandaleuse *adjective* outrageous; **c'est scandaleux!** it's outrageous!

LE/LA Scandinave *noun* *(person)* Scandinavian

scandinave *adjective* Scandinavian

In French, only the noun for the inhabitants of a country takes a capital letter, never the adjective.

LA Scandinavie *noun* Scandinavia

LA scène *noun*
(**a**) stage; **l'acteur est entré sur scène** the actor came on stage
(**b**) scene; **le dernier acte comprend cinq scènes** the last act has five scenes;

sa femme lui a fait une scène his wife made a scene; **une scène de ménage** a domestic squabble

LE schéma *noun* diagram

LA scie *noun* saw

LA science *noun* science; **les sciences physiques** physics; **il est fort en science** he's good at science

scientifique
1 *adjective* scientific
2 *noun* **un/une scientifique** a scientist

scier *verb* to saw

scolaire *adjective* school; **une sortie scolaire** a school trip; **les vacances scolaires** the school holidays

LE Scorpion *noun* Scorpio; **elle est Scorpion** she's a Scorpio

LE scorpion *noun* scorpion

LE scotch® *noun* sellotape®

LE scrupule *noun* scruple

LE sculpteur *noun* sculptor; **il est sculpteur** he's a sculptor

LE/LA SDF *noun* homeless person

SDF is the abbreviation of *sans domicile fixe*, which means "of no fixed abode". It does not change in the plural.

se *pronoun*
(**a**) himself; **il s'est coupé** he cut himself
(**b**) herself; **elle s'est brûlée** she burnt herself
(**c**) itself; **le chat s'est fait mal** the cat hurt itself
(**d**) themselves; **ils se regardent dans la glace** they're looking at themselves in the mirror; **elles se sont bien amusées** they enjoyed themselves
(**e**) each other, to each other; **ils s'aiment** they love each other; **elles s'écrivent souvent** they write to each other often
(**f**) **se laver les mains** to wash one's hands; **il se lave les mains** he's wash-

ing his hands; **elle s'est cassé le bras**
she broke her arm; **ils se brossent les
dents** they're brushing their teeth

> *Se* becomes *s'* in front of a vowel or a
> mute h. Note that there are many
> cases when *se* is simply not translated
> in English, as in *elle se souvient* (she
> remembers), *il se rase* (he shaves)
> and *ils se lèvent* (they get up).

LA **séance** *noun*
(**a**) showing; **nous allons voir le film à
la séance de huit heures** we're going
to the eight o'clock showing of the film
(**b**) session; **une séance d'entraînement** a training session

LE **seau** *noun* bucket

> The plural of *seau* is *seaux*.

sec, sèche *adjective*
(**a**) dry; **j'ai la peau sèche** I have dry
skin
(**b**) dried; **des fruits secs** dried fruit

LE **sèche-cheveux** *noun* hairdryer

> The word *sèche-cheveux* does not
> change in the plural.

LE **sèche-linge** *noun* tumble dryer

> The word *sèche-linge* does not
> change in the plural.

sécher
1 *verb*
(**a**) to dry
(**b**) **sécher un cours** *(informal phrase)*
to skip a class
2 *reflexive verb* **se sécher** to dry oneself

LA **sécheresse** *noun* drought

LE **séchoir** *noun*
(**a**) clothes horse
(**b**) hairdryer

second, seconde¹ *number* second

> The *c* in *second* is pronounced like
> a *g*.

secondaire *adjective* secondary; **l'enseignement secondaire** secondary

education; **c'est une question tout à
fait secondaire** that's a matter of secondary importance

> The *c* in *secondaire* is pronounced li-
> ke a *g*.

LA **seconde²** *noun*
(**a**) second; **une seconde s'il vous
plaît!** just a moment, please!
(**b**) fifth year of secondary school (for
pupils aged 15); **il est en seconde** he's
in his fifth year of secondary school

> See also **lycée** and **filière**.

(**c**) second class *(in a train)*; **il était en
première avec un ticket de seconde**
he was sitting in first class with a
second-class ticket

> The *c* in *seconde* is pronounced like
> a *g*.

secouer *verb* to shake

secourir *verb* to rescue

LE/LA **secouriste** *noun* first-aid worker; **il est secouriste** he's a first-aid
worker

LE **secours** *noun* help; **appeler du secours** to call for help; **porter secours
à quelqu'un** to give somebody help;
**les secours ne sont pas encore ar-
rivés** help hasn't arrived yet; **les premiers secours** first aid; **au secours!**
help!

secret, secrète
1 *adjective* secret
2 *masculine noun* **un secret** a secret

> The *t* in *secret* is not pronounced.

LE/LA **secrétaire** *noun* secretary; **elle
est secrétaire** she's a secretary

LA **sécurité** *noun*
(**a**) safety; **je me sens en sécurité** I feel
safe; **une ceinture de sécurité** a safety
belt
(**b**) security; **la Sécurité sociale** Social
Security

séduisant, séduisante *adjective*
attractive

LE **seigle** *noun* rye; **du pain de seigle** rye bread

LE **seigneur** *noun* lord

LE **sein** *noun* breast

seize *number* sixteen; **le seize novembre** the sixteenth of November; **nous sommes le seize octobre** it's the sixteenth of October; **à seize heures** at four o'clock in the afternoon

seizième *number* sixteenth

LE **séjour** *noun*
(a) stay; **pendant mon séjour en Espagne** during my stay in Spain; **un séjour linguistique** a language-learning trip
(b) **un séjour** *or* **une salle de séjour** a living room

LE **sel** *noun* salt

sélectionner *verb* to select

LA **selle** *noun* saddle

selon *preposition* according to; **selon elle** according to her; **selon moi** in my opinion; **selon le temps qu'il fait** depending on the weather

LA **semaine** *noun* week; **dans une semaine** in a week's time

semblable *adjective* similar

semblant *masculine noun* **faire semblant de faire quelque chose** to pretend to do something; **elle fait semblant de pleurer** she's pretending to cry

sembler *verb* to seem; **il semblait inquiet** he seemed worried; **il me semble que ce n'est pas une bonne idée** it doesn't seem like a good idea to me

LA **semelle** *noun* sole *(of a shoe)*

semer *verb* to sow *(seeds)*

LE **sens** *noun*
(a) meaning, sense; **je ne comprends pas le sens de ce mot** I don't understand the meaning of this word; **ce qu'il dit n'a aucun sens** what he's saying doesn't make any sense; **dans un sens je préfèrerais qu'il ne vienne pas** in a

way I'd rather he didn't come
(b) **le bon sens** common sense; **elle manque de bon sens** she lacks common sense
(c) **il n'a pas le sens de l'humour** he has no sense of humour; **mon père a le sens des affaires** my dad has good business sense
(d) direction; **dans le sens inverse** in the opposite direction; **tourne la clé dans l'autre sens** turn the key the other way; **sens dessus dessous** upside down
(e) **un sens unique** a one-way street; **le conducteur a pris un sens interdit** the driver went the wrong way down a one-way street; **un sens giratoire** a roundabout

LA **sensation** *noun* feeling, sensation

sensationnel, sensationnelle *adjective*
(a) sensational
(b) great, fantastic

> Sense (b) is an informal use of *sensationnel*.

sensible *adjective*
(a) sensitive; **c'est un garçon très sensible** he's a very sensitive boy
(b) noticeable; **une amélioration sensible** a noticeable improvement

> Note that the English word *sensible* is never a translation for the French word *sensible*.

LE **sentier** *noun* path

LE **sentiment** *noun* feeling

sentir
1 *verb*
(a) to smell; **je sentais une odeur de brûlé** I could smell burning; **je ne peux pas le sentir** *(informal phrase)* I can't stand him
(b) to smell of; **ça sent le poisson** it smells of fish
(c) to feel; **je n'ai rien senti quand il m'a fait la piqûre** I didn't feel a thing when he gave me the injection; **je sens**

que ce ne sera pas facile I have a feeling that it won't be easy

2 *reflexive verb* **se sentir** to feel; **il ne se sent pas bien** he doesn't feel well; **je me sens fatigué** I feel tired

See verb table p. 322.

séparer
1 *verb*
(**a**) to separate; **il faut séparer Paul et Georges, ils n'arrêtent pas de bavarder** we have to separate Paul and Georges, they won't stop chatting
(**b**) to divide; **le prof a séparé les élèves en deux groupes** the teacher divided the pupils into two groups
2 *reflexive verb* **se séparer** to separate; **les parents de Claude se sont séparés l'an dernler** Claude's parents separated last year

sept *number* seven; **le sept juillet** the seventh of July; **nous sommes le sept octobre** it's the seventh of October

The *p* in *sept* is not pronounced.

septante *number* seventy; **dans les années septante** in the seventies

Septante is only used in Belgium and Switzerland. In France people say *soixante-dix*.

septembre *masculine noun* September; **le premier septembre** the first of September; **le 12 septembre** the 12th of September

In French, the names of months are not written with a capital.

septième *number* seventh

The *p* in *septième* is not pronounced.

sera, serai, serez *see* être
elle sera chez son père demain she'll be at her father's tomorrow; **je serai en vacances à partir de lundi** I'll be on holiday from Monday; **demain vous serez partis** tomorrow you'll be gone

Sera, serai etc are forms of the verb

être in the future tense. See verb table p. 316.

LA **série** *noun* series; **une série d'attentats** a series of attacks; **une série télévisée** a TV series

sérieux, sérieuse *adjective*
(**a**) serious
(**b**) reliable

LA **seringue** *noun* syringe

serons, seront *see* être
nous serons toujours là pour toi we will always be there for you; **ils seront contents de te voir** they'll be happy to see you

Serons and *seront* are forms of the verb *être* in the future tense. See verb table p. 316.

séropositif, séropositive *adjective* HIV positive

LE **serpent** *noun* snake

The *t* in *serpent* is not pronounced.

LA **serpillère** *noun* floorcloth

LA **serre** *noun* greenhouse; **l'effet de serre** the greenhouse effect

serré, serrée *adjective*
(**a**) tight
(**b**) packed together

serrer
1 *verb*
(**a**) to grip; **il serrait la corde** he was gripping the rope
(**b**) to hold, to hold tightly; **elle serrait l'enfant contre elle** she held the child tightly against her
(**c**) **serrer la main à quelqu'un** to shake somebody's hand; **il a refusé de me serrer la main** he refused to shake my hand
(**d**) to tighten *(a belt, a screw)*
(**e**) to be too tight; **ces chaussures me serrent** these shoes are too tight
(**f**) **serrer les dents** to clench one's teeth
2 *reflexive verb* **se serrer** to squeeze up; **serrez-vous un peu pour faire de**

la place squeeze up a bit to make some room

LE **serre-tête** *noun* headband

> The word *serre-tête* does not change in the plural.

LA **serrure** *noun* lock

LE **serveur**, LA **serveuse** *noun* waiter/waitress; **elle est serveuse** she's a waitress

LE **service** *noun*
(**a**) favour; **est-ce que tu pourrais me rendre un service?** could you do me a favour?; **rendre service à quelqu'un** to be of help to somebody
(**b**) service *(in a restaurant)*; **le service n'est pas compris** service is not included
(**c**) department; **le service commercial** the sales department
(**d**) serve *(in tennis)*
(**e**) **le service militaire** military service

Le Service Militaire

For a long time a one-year period of military service was compulsory for young Frenchmen, unless they were declared unfit for service. As an alternative to military service, some chose to work overseas, often in developing countries. However, the French government recently decided to have only professional armed forces and military service has now been abolished.

LA **serviette** *noun*
(**a**) towel
(**b**) napkin, serviette
(**c**) briefcase

servir
1 *verb*
(**a**) to serve *(a customer, a dish)*
(**b**) to be useful; **ton parapluie m'a bien servi** your umbrella came in very useful; **emporte une lampe de poche, ça peut toujours servir** take a torch, it might come in useful; **à quoi sert cet objet?** what's this thing for?; **ça ne sert à rien de courir, le train est déjà**

parti there's no point running, the train has already left
2 *reflexive verb* **se servir**
(**a**) to help oneself
(**b**) **se servir de quelque chose** to use something; **qui s'est servi de mon ordinateur?** who used my computer?

> See verb table p. 324.

ses *adjective*
(**a**) his; **Patrick cherche ses amis** Patrick is looking for his friends
(**b**) her; **Nathalie a perdu ses lunettes** Nathalie lost her glasses
(**c**) its; **l'oiseau perd ses plumes** the bird is losing its feathers

> *Ses* is used in front of plural nouns. It is the plural of *sa* and *son*. See also **sa** and **son**[1].

seul, seule
1 *adjective*
(**a**) alone; **il était seul dans sa chambre** he was alone in his room; **nous nous sommes retrouvées seules** we found ourselves alone with each other; **elle est venue toute seule** she came alone
(**b**) lonely; **je me sens très seul** I feel very lonely
(**c**) **tout seul** by oneself; **il s'est habillé tout seul** he got dressed by himself
(**d**) only; **Philippe est mon seul ami** Philippe is my only friend
2 *noun* **le seul, la seule** the only one; **ce ne sont pas les seuls** they're not the only ones

seulement *adverb* only

LA **sève** *noun* sap

sévère *adjective* strict

LE **sexe** *noun* sex

LE **shampooing** *noun* shampoo

LE **short** *noun* shorts; **il porte un short** he's wearing shorts

si
1 *conjunction* if; **si tu le vois, dis lui que je veux lui parler** if you see him, tell him I want to speak to him; **je me**

demande s'il va pleuvoir I wonder if it's going to rain; **si seulement je pouvais gagner au loto!** if only I could win the lottery!

In this sense, *si* becomes *s'* in front of *il* and *ils*.

2 *adverb*
(**a**) so; **ne mange pas si vite!** don't eat so fast!; **il était si fatigué qu'il s'est endormi devant la télé** he was so tired that he fell asleep in front of the TV
(**b**) as; **elle n'est pas si riche que ça** she's not as rich as all that
(**c**) yes; **tu ne viens pas avec nous? – si!** aren't you coming with us? – yes I am!; **tu ne la connais pas – mais si!** you don't know her – yes I do!

Si is the equivalent of *oui* but it is only used in response to negative phrases.

LE **Sida** *noun* AIDS; **il a le Sida** he's got AIDS

LE **siècle** *noun* century

LE **siège** *noun* seat

sien, sienne *pronoun* **le sien, la sienne, les siens, les siennes** *(when the owner is male)* his; *(when the owner is female)* hers; **ce crayon, c'est le sien** this pencil is his/hers; **ce n'est pas ma tasse, c'est la sienne** this is not my cup, it's his/hers; **mes enfants et les siens** my children and his/hers

In French, possessive pronouns have the same gender and the same number as the nouns they stand for, eg the corresponding pronoun for *ses enfants* is *les siens* because the word *enfants* is masculine plural.

LA **sieste** *noun* nap; **faire la sieste** to take a nap

siffler *verb*
(**a**) to whistle
(**b**) to blow one's whistle
(**c**) to boo; **le chanteur s'est fait siffler par le public** the singer was booed by the audience
(**d**) to hiss

LE **sifflet** *noun* whistle; **donner un coup de sifflet** to blow the whistle

LE **signal** *noun* signal

The plural of *signal* is *signaux*.

signaler *verb* **signaler quelque chose à quelqu'un** to point something out to somebody; **je vous signale qu'il est interdit de fumer** I wish to point out to you that smoking is forbidden

LE **signe** *noun* sign; **faire signe à quelqu'un** to wave to somebody; **faire un signe de tête à quelqu'un** to nod to somebody

signer
1 *verb* to sign
2 *reflexive verb* **se signer** to cross oneself

signifier *verb* to mean; **cela signifie qu'il va perdre son emploi** it means that he's going to lose his job

LE **silence** *noun* silence; **il a refermé la porte en silence** he shut the door quietly; **silence!** quiet!

silencieux, silencieuse *adjective* silent, quiet

LA **silhouette** *noun*
(**a**) figure; **elle a une jolie silhouette** she has a nice figure
(**b**) outline, silhouette; **on le reconnaît de loin à sa silhouette** you can recognize him from a distance by his silhouette

s'il te plaît *adverb* please; **tu me prêtes ton stylo s'il te plaît?** can you lend me your pen, please?

s'il vous plaît *adverb* please; **vous avez l'heure, s'il vous plaît?** have you got the time, please?

simple *adjective*
(**a**) simple; **une question simple** a simple question
(**b**) **c'est une simple question de politesse** it's simply a question of good manners; **un simple oubli** a simple oversight; **c'est bien simple, je ne veux plus jamais le revoir!** it's very

simple, I don't want to see him ever again!

(c) single; **un aller simple** a single ticket

simplement *adverb* simply; **il a simplement oublié de te prévenir, c'est tout** he simply forgot to let you know, that's all; **il est très riche mais il vit très simplement** he's very rich but he leads a very simple life

sincère *adjective* sincere, genuine

LE **singe** *noun* monkey; **les grands singes** the apes; **faire le singe** to clown around

LE **singulier** *noun* singular

sinistre *adjective*
(a) sinister
(b) grim, bleak

sinon *conjunction* otherwise, or else

LA **sirène** *noun*
(a) siren
(b) mermaid

LE **sirop** *noun* syrup; **du sirop pour la toux** cough syrup

> The *p* in *sirop* is not pronounced.

LE **site** *noun* site; **un site Web** a website

LA **situation** *noun*
(a) situation; **une situation embarrassante** an embarrassing situation
(b) job; **leur fils a une très bonne situation** their son has a very good job

situé, située *adjective* situated, located; **leur maison est très bien située** their house is very well situated

se situer *reflexive verb*
(a) to be located
(b) to be set; **l'action se situe au Mexique** the action takes place in Mexico

six *number* six; **le six mai** the sixth of May; **nous sommes le six mars** it's the sixth of March

> *Six* is pronounced "si" in front of a consonant, "siz" in front of a vowel or a mute h and "sis" on its own.

sixième
1 *number* sixth
2 *feminine noun* **la sixième** the first year of secondary school (for pupils aged 11); **il est en sixième** he's in his first year of secondary school

> See also **collège**.

LE **ski** *noun*
(a) ski; **on peut louer des skis sur place** you can hire skis when you're there
(b) **le ski** skiing; **le ski de fond** cross-country skiing; **le ski nautique** water-skiing; **faire du ski** to ski, to go skiing

skier *verb* to ski; **elle skie bien** she's a good skier

LE **slip** *noun*
(a) pants
(b) **un slip de bain** swimming trunks

LE/LA **Slovaque** *noun (person)* Slovakian

slovaque
1 *adjective* Slovakian; **l'économie slovaque** the Slovakian economy
2 *masculine noun* **le slovaque** *(language)* Slovak; **elle parle slovaque** she speaks Slovak

> In French, only the noun for the inhabitants of a country takes a capital letter, never the adjective or the noun for the language.

LA **Slovaquie** *noun* Slovakia

LE/LA **Slovène** *noun (person)* Slovenian

slovène
1 *adjective* Slovenian; **l'économie slovène** the Slovenian economy
2 *masculine noun* **le slovène** *(language)* Slovene; **il parle slovène** she speaks Slovene

LA **Slovénie** *noun* Slovenia

LE **smoking** *noun* dinner jacket

social, sociale *adjective* social

> The masculine plural of *social* is *sociaux*.

LA **société** *noun*
(a) company; **ça fait dix ans qu'il travaille pour la même société** he's been working for the same company for ten years
(b) society; **nous vivons dans une société multiculturelle** we live in a multicultural society

LA **sœur** *noun* sister

soi *pronoun* oneself; **ce n'est pas bien de ne penser qu'à soi** it's wrong to think only of yourself; **ça va de soi** it goes without saying

soi-disant
1 *adjective* so-called; **un soi-disant écrivain** a so-called writer
2 *adverb* supposedly; **elle est sortie, soi-disant pour acheter du lait** she went out, supposedly to get some milk

LA **soie** *noun* silk; **une cravate en soie** a silk tie

LA **soif** *noun* thirst; **avoir soif** to be thirsty

soigner
1 *verb*
(a) to look after, to take care of
(b) to treat *(a sick person)*
2 *reflexive verb* **se soigner** to look after oneself

soigneux, soigneuse *adjective*
(a) careful; **il n'est pas soigneux avec ses affaires** he's careless with his things
(b) tidy

soi-même *pronoun* oneself; **c'est facile, on peut le faire soi-même** it's easy, you can do it yourself

LE **soin** *noun*
(a) care; **prendre soin de quelque chose** to take care of something; **il ne prend pas soin de ses affaires** he doesn't take care of his things; **prends soin d'elle!** take care of her!; **avec soin** carefully
(b) **des soins** treatment; **les premiers soins** first aid

LE **soir** *noun* evening; **ce soir** this evening, tonight; **hier soir** last night

LA **soirée** *noun*
(a) evening; **passe me voir dans la soirée** come and see me in the evening
(b) party

sois, soit¹ *see* être
(a) **il faut que je sois chez le dentiste à trois heures** I need to be at the dentist's at three; **nous irons en vacances en Bretagne, qu'il soit d'accord ou non** we're going to on holiday to Brittany whether he likes it or not
(b) **sois gentil avec ta sœur!** be nice to your sister!

Sois and *soit* are forms of the verb *être* in the subjunctive. *Sois* is also a form of the verb *être* in the imperative. See verb table p. 316.

soit² *conjunction* **soit... soit...** either... or...; **soit du thé, soit du café** either tea or coffee; **nous viendrons soit lundi soit mardi** we'll come on either Monday or Tuesday

LA **soixantaine** *noun* about sixty; **une soixantaine de personnes** about sixty people; **il a la soixantaine** he's about sixty years old

soixante *number* sixty; **les années soixante** the sixties; **soixante et un** sixty-one; **soixante-deux** sixty-two; **soixante-dix** seventy; **soixante et onze** seventy-one; **soixante-douze** seventy-two; **les années soixante-dix** the seventies

Soixante is pronounced "soissante".

LE **soja** *noun* soya; **de la sauce de soja** soy sauce

LE **sol** *noun*
(a) ground
(b) floor
(c) soil

solaire *adjective*
(a) solar; **l'énergie solaire** solar energy
(b) **de la crème solaire** sun cream

LE **soldat** *noun* soldier; **il est soldat** he's a soldier

The *t* of *soldat* is not pronounced. The word *soldat* does not have a feminine but it can also refer to a woman.

LES **soldes** *masculine plural noun* **les soldes** the sales; **faire les soldes** to go to the sales

LE **soleil** *noun* sun; **il y a du soleil** it's sunny

solide *adjective*
(**a**) solid
(**b**) strong

solitaire *adjective* solitary; **c'est quelqu'un de très solitaire** he's a very solitary person

LA **solitude** *noun* loneliness

sombre *adjective* dark

sombrer *verb* to sink

somme
1 *masculine noun* **un somme** a nap; **faire un somme** to take a nap
2 *feminine noun* **une somme** an amount; **c'est une très grosse somme d'argent** it's a very large sum of money

LE **sommeil** *noun* sleep; **avoir sommeil** to be sleepy

sommes *see* **être**
nous sommes contents we are happy; **nous sommes allés au cinéma** we went to the cinema

Sommes is a form of the verb *être* in the present tense. See verb table p. 316.

LE **sommet** *noun* summit

LE/LA **somnambule** *noun* sleepwalker

LE **somnifère** *nun* sleeping pill

son¹ *adjective*
(**a**) his; **Paul a pris son parapluie** Paul took his umbrella; **Claude a écrit à son amie** Claude wrote to his girlfriend
(**b**) her; **Marie a perdu son stylo** Marie lost her pen; **Claire cherche son agrafeuse** Claire is looking for her stapler

(**c**) its; **on reconnaît cet oiseau à son gros bec** you can recognize this bird by its large beak

Son is used in front of masculine nouns, as well as before feminine nouns starting with a vowel or a mute h, as in *son école, son histoire*. The plural of *son* is *ses* and the feminine is *sa*. See also **sa** and **ses**.

LE **son²** *noun*
(**a**) sound; **baisse le son** turn the sound down
(**b**) bran; **du pain au son** wholemeal bread

LE **sondage** *noun* survey; **un sondage d'opinion** an opinion poll

songer *verb* **songer à** to think of; **il n'a jamais songé à se marier** he's never considered getting married

sonner *verb*
(**a**) to ring; **le téléphone sonne** the phone's ringing
(**b**) to go off; **mon réveil n'a pas sonné ce matin** my alarm clock didn't go off this morning

LA **sonnerie** *noun*
(**a**) ringing
(**b**) bell
(**c**) alarm

LA **sonnette** *noun* bell

sont *see* **être**
ils sont contents they are happy; **ils sont allés en France** they went to France

Sont is a form of the verb *être* in the present tense. See verb table p. 316.

LA **sorcière** *noun* witch

LE **sort** *noun*
(**a**) fate; **tirer au sort** to draw lots; **il est content de son sort** he's happy with his lot
(**b**) spell; **jeter un sort à quelqu'un** to cast a spell on somebody

Note that the English word *sort* is never a translation for the French

word *sort*.
The *t* in *sort* is not pronounced.

LA **sorte** *noun* sort, kind; **en quelque sorte** so to speak

LA **sortie** *noun*
(a) exit, way out; **une sortie de secours** an emergency exit
(b) **ils se sont donné rendez-vous à la sortie de l'école** they arranged to meet after school
(c) outing; **une sortie scolaire** a school trip

sortir
1 *verb*
(a) to go out, to leave; **il vient juste de sortir** he's just left; **elle est sortie de la maison en courant** she ran out of the house
(b) to come out; **elle est tombée en sortant de l'église** she fell as she was coming out of the church; **le film sort demain** the film comes out tomorrow
(c) to go out; **mon frère sort souvent avec ses copains** my brother often goes out with his friends; **Julien sort avec la sœur de Luc** Julien is going out with Luc's sister
(d) to take out; **elle a sorti une enveloppe de son sac** she took an envelope out of her bag
2 *reflexive verb* **s'en sortir**
(a) to manage
(b) to pull through; **il a été très malade mais il s'en est sorti** he was very ill but he pulled through

LE **sosie** *noun* lookalike; **un sosie de Brad Pitt** a Brad Pitt lookalike

LA **sottise** *noun* stupidity; **il n'arrête pas de dire des sottises** he's always saying stupid things; **elle a fait une sottise** she did a stupid thing

LE **sou** *noun* **des sous** money; **je n'ai plus de sous** I've no money left

LE **souci** *noun* worry; **se faire du souci** to worry

soucieux, soucieuse *adjective* worried

LA **soucoupe** *noun*
(a) saucer
(b) **une soucoupe volante** a flying saucer

soudain, soudaine
1 *adjective* sudden; **mon arrivée soudaine les a surpris** my sudden arrival surprised them
2 *adverb* **soudain** suddenly

LE **souffle** *noun* breath; **je suis à bout de souffle** I'm out of breath; **reprendre son souffle** to get one's breath back

souffler *verb*
(a) to blow
(b) to blow out; **il a soufflé la bougie** he blew out the candle
(c) to get one's breath back; **laisse-moi souffler un peu** let me get my breath back
(d) to whisper; **quelqu'un lui a soufflé la bonne réponse** somebody whispered the answer to him

souffrant, souffrante *adjective* unwell, poorly

souffrir *verb*
(a) to be in pain, to suffer
(b) **je ne peux pas le souffrir** *(informal phrase)* I can't stand him

See verb table p. 320.

LE **souhait** *noun*
(a) wish; **faire un souhait** to make a wish
(b) **à tes souhaits!** *(when somebody sneezes)* bless you!

souhaiter *verb*
(a) to wish; **je te souhaite une bonne année** I wish you a happy new year
(b) to hope; **je lui souhaite de bien s'amuser** I hope he enjoys himself; **je souhaite qu'il vienne le plus vite possible** I hope he comes as quickly as possible; **je souhaite faire des études de médecine** I'd like to study medicine

soûl, soûle *adjective* drunk

soulager *verb* to relieve; **l'aspirine soulage la douleur** aspirin relieves pain

soulever *verb* to lift, to lift up

LE **soulier** *noun* shoe

souligner *verb* to underline

LE **soupçon** *noun* suspicion

soupçonner *verb* to suspect; **je le soupçonne de m'avoir volé de l'argent** I suspect him of stealing money from me

LA **soupe** *noun* soup

LA **soupière** *noun* soup tureen

LE **soupir** *noun* sigh; **pousser un soupir** to sigh

soupirer *verb* to sigh

souple *adjective*
(a) supple
(b) flexible

LA **source** *noun*
(a) spring; **une source d'eau chaude** a hot spring
(b) source; **une source d'énergie** an energy source; **le chômage est à la source de nombreux problèmes** unemployment is the source of many problems

LE **sourcil** *noun* eyebrow

sourd, sourde *adjective* deaf; **faire la sourde oreille** to turn a deaf ear

sourire
1 *verb* to smile; **sourire à quelqu'un** to smile at somebody
2 *masculine noun* **un sourire** a smile

See verb table p. 324.

LA **souris** *noun* mouse

sournois, sournoise *adjective* sly

sous *preposition* under; **sous l'eau** underwater; **sous terre** underground

sous-développé, sous-développée *adjective* underdeveloped

sous-entendu, sous-entendue
1 *adjective* implied

2 *masculine noun* **un sous-entendu** an insinuation

The plural of *sous-entendu* is *sous-entendus.*

sous-estimer *verb* to underestimate

sous-marin, sous-marine
1 *adjective* underwater; **des photos sous-marines** underwater photos; **la plongée sous-marine** scuba diving
2 *masculine noun* **un sous-marin** a submarine

The plural of *sous-marin* is *sous-marins.*

LE **sous-sol** *noun* basement

The plural of *sous-sol* is *sous-sols.*

LE **sous-titre** *noun* subtitle; **le film est en anglais avec des sous-titres français** the film is in English with French subtitles

The plural of *sous-titre* is *sous-titres.*

LA **soustraction** *noun* subtraction

LES **sous-vêtements** *masculine plural noun* underwear

soutenir *verb* to support

See verb table p. 324.

souterrain, souterraine
1 *adjective* underground; **un passage souterrain** an underground passage
2 *masculine noun* **un souterrain** an underground passage

LE **soutien-gorge** *noun* bra

The plural of *soutien-gorge* is *soutiens-gorge.*

souvenir
1 *masculine noun*
(a) memory; **des souvenirs d'enfance** childhood memories
(b) souvenir; **elle m'a rapporté un souvenir de son voyage à Venise** she brought me back a souvenir from Venice
2 *reflexive verb* **se souvenir** to remember; **je ne me souviens pas de**

son nom I can't remember his name

See verb table p. 324.

souvent *adverb* often

soyons, soyez *see* être
(a) **je ne crois pas que nous soyons en retard** I don't think we're late; **il faut que vous soyez à la gare avant midi** you need to be at the station by noon
(b) **soyons optimistes!** let's be optimistic!; **soyez sages!** be good!

Soyons and *soyez* are forms of the verb *être* in the subjunctive. They are also forms of the verb *être* in the imperative. See verb table p. 316.

LE **spaghetti** *noun* piece of spaghetti; **les spaghettis** spaghetti

LE **sparadrap** *noun* sticking plaster

spatial, spatiale *adjective* space; **la navette spatiale** the space shuttle; **l'exploration spatiale** space exploration

The masculine plural of *spatial* is *spatiaux*.

spécial, spéciale *adjective*
(a) special; **une offre spéciale** a special offer
(b) peculiar, odd; **ton frère est un peu spécial** your brother is a bit odd

The masculine plural of *spécial* is *spéciaux*.

spécialement *adverb*
(a) specially
(b) especially

LE **spectacle** *noun*
(a) show; **le spectacle commence à sept heures** the show starts at seven o'clock
(b) sight; **un spectacle attendrissant** a moving sight

Note that the English word *glasses* is never a translation for the French word *spectacles*.

LE **spectacteur,** LA **spectatrice** *noun*
(a) member of the audience; **les spectateurs** the audience
(b) spectator

LA **spéléologie** *noun* potholing

spirituel, spirituelle *adjective*
(a) spiritual
(b) witty

LE **sport** *noun* sport; **faire du sport** to do sport; **les sports d'hiver** winter sports; **aller aux sports d'hiver** to go skiing

The *t* in *sport* is not pronounced.

sportif, sportive
1 *adjective*
(a) sporty
(b) sports; **un club sportif** a sports club; **des équlpements sportifs** sports equipment
2 *noun* **un sportif** a sportsman; **une sportive** a sportswoman

LE **square** *noun* small public garden

Note that the English word *square* is never a translation for the French word *square*.

LE **squelette** *noun* skeleton

LE **stade** *noun*
(a) stadium
(b) stage; **à ce stade de l'enquête** at this stage of the investigation

LE **stage** *noun*
(a) training course; **faire un stage** to be on a training course
(b) placement; **je dois faire un stage en entreprise à la fin de l'année** I have to do a work placement at the end of the year
(c) course; **je fais un stage de voile cet été** I'm taking sailing lessons this summer

Note that the English word *stage* is never a translation for the French word *stage*.

LA **station** *noun*
(a) station; **une station de métro** a

metro station; **une station de radio** a radio station

(**b**) **une station de taxis** a taxi rank

(**c**) resort; **une station de ski** a ski resort; **une station balnéaire** a seaside resort

LE **stationnement** *noun* parking; **il est en stationnement interdit** he's parked illegally

stationner *verb* to park

LA **station-service** *noun* service station

The plural of *station-service* is *stations-service*.

LA **statue** *noun* statue

LE **steak** *noun* steak; **du steak haché** minced beef, mince

LE **stop** *noun*
(**a**) hitchhiking; **faire du stop** to hitchhike
(**b**) stop sign; **il n'a pas vu le stop** he didn't see the stop sign

LE **store** *noun* blind; **tu peux baisser le store?** can you lower the blind?

Note that the English word *store* is never a translation for the French word *store*.

strictement *adverb* strictly

LA **strophe** *noun* stanza

LE **studio** *noun*
(**a**) studio
(**b**) studio flat

stupéfait, stupéfaite *adjective* astonished

LE **stylo** *noun* pen; **un stylo bille** *or* **un stylo à bille** a ballpoint pen; **un stylo plume** *or* **un stylo à plume** a fountain pen

LE **stylo-feutre** *noun* felt-tip pen

The plural of *stylo-feutre* is *stylos-feutres*.

su, sue *see* **savoir**
je n'ai jamais su la fin de l'histoire I never found out the end of the story

Su(e) is the past participle of the verb *savoir*. See verb table p. 324.

subir *verb* to undergo; **subir des dégâts** to suffer damage

subitement *adverb* suddenly

subtil, subtile *adjective* subtle

The *b* in *subtil* is pronounced.

LA **subvention** *noun* subsidy

LE **succès** *noun* success; **avoir du succès** to be successful

The final *s* in *succès* is not pronounced.

LA **succursale** *noun* branch *(of a company)*

sucer *verb* to suck

LA **sucette** *noun* lollipop

LE **sucre** *noun* sugar; **du sucre en poudre** caster sugar; **du sucre roux** brown sugar; **un morceau de sucre** a sugar lump

sucré, sucrée *adjective*
(**a**) sweet
(**b**) sweetened

sucrer *verb*
(**a**) to put sugar in
(**b**) to sweeten

LES **sucreries** *feminine plural noun* sweet things

sud
1 *masculine noun* **le sud** the south; **c'est une ville située dans le sud du pays** it's a town in the south of the country; **Lyon est au sud de Paris** Lyon is to the south of Paris; **un vent du sud** a southerly wind; **l'Amérique du Sud** South America
2 *adjective* south, southern; **la côte sud** the south coast; **il habite dans la banlieue sud de la ville** he lives in the southern suburbs of the city

LE **Sud-Africain**, LA **Sud-Africaine** *noun (person)* South African

sud-africain, sud-africaine *adjective* South African

LE **Sud-Américain,** LA **Sud-Américaine** *noun (person)* South American

sud-américain, sud-américaine *adjective* South American

LE **sud-est** *noun* south-east

LE **sud-ouest** *noun* south-west

LA **Suède** *noun* Sweden

LE **Suédois,** LA **Suédoise** *noun (person)* Swede

suédois, suédoise
1 *adjective* Swedish; **l'économie suédoise** the Swedish economy
2 *masculine noun* **le suédois** *(language)* Swedish; **elle parle suédois** she speaks Swedish

In French, only the noun for the inhabitants of a country takes a capital letter, never the adjective or the noun for the language.

suer *verb*
(a) to sweat
(b) **faire suer quelqu'un** *(informal phrase)* to bug somebody

LA **sueur** *noun* sweat

suffire *verb* to be enough; **ça suffit!** that's enough!

See verb table p. 324.

suffisamment *adverb* enough; **est-ce qu'il y a suffisamment à manger?** is there enough to eat?

suffisant, suffisante *adjective* sufficient; **être suffisant** to be enough

suggérer *verb* to suggest

se suicider *reflexive verb* to commit suicide

suis *see* **être, suivre**
(a) **je suis content** I'm happy; **je suis allé au cinéma hier soir** I went to the cinema last night
(b) **je suis le règlement** I follow the rules

Suis is a form of the verb *être* in the present tense. It is also a form of the verb *suivre* in the present tense. See verb tables p. 316 and p. 324.

Suisse
1 *noun* **un Suisse** a Swiss man; **une Suisse** a Swiss woman; **les Suisses** the Swiss
2 *feminine noun* **la Suisse** Switzerland

suisse *adjective* Swiss; **l'économie suisse** the Swiss economy

LA **suite** *noun*
(a) **la suite** the rest; **je ferai la suite demain** I'll do the rest tomorrow
(b) sequel; **le film aura une suite** there will be a sequel to the film
(c) **tout de suite** straight away, immediately; **il a tout de suite compris** he understood immediately
(d) **de suite** in a row; **on a fait trois parties de suite** we played three games in a row
(e) **par la suite** afterwards

suivant, suivante
1 *adjective* following; **la semaine suivante** the following week
2 *noun* **le suivant, la suivante** the next one; **au suivant!** next!

suivre *verb*
(a) to follow; **à suivre** to be continued
(b) to keep up; **il a du mal à suivre à l'école** he has trouble keeping up at school
(c) to forward; **faire suivre du courrier** to forward mail
(d) **suivre des cours** to take lessons

See verb table p. 324.

LE **sujet** *noun*
(a) subject; **le sujet du verbe** the subject of the verb
(b) subject, topic; **un sujet de conversation** a topic of conversation
(c) **au sujet de** about; **c'est à quel sujet?** what's it about?

super
1 *adjective* great; **le film était super**

the film was great

> This word is informal. Note that it does not change in the plural.

2 *masculine noun* **le super** four-star petrol

LA **superficie** *noun* surface area

supérieur, supérieure *adjective*
(**a**) upper
(**b**) higher
(**c**) advanced
(**d**) superior; **supérieur à** superior to

LE **supermarché** *noun* supermarket

superposé *adjective* **des lits superposés** bunk beds

superstitieux, superstitieuse *adjective* superstitious

supplémentaire *adjective* extra, additional; **faire des heures supplémentaires** to work overtime

supplier *verb* to beg; **je t'en supplie** I beg you

> Note that the English word *supplier* is never a translation for the French verb *supplier*.

supporter *verb*
(**a**) to bear, to stand; **elle ne supporte pas la chaleur** she can't take the heat; **je ne peux pas le supporter** I can't stand him
(**b**) to bear the weight of, to support

supposer *verb* to suppose, to assume

supprimer *verb*
(**a**) to get rid of
(**b**) to delete
(**c**) to cancel
(**d**) to do away with

sur *preposition*
(**a**) on; **ton stylo est sur la table** your pen is on the table
(**b**) on, about; **il lit un livre sur les baleines** he's reading a book on whales
(**c**) out of; **quatre élèves sur dix** four out of ten pupils; **il a eu 16 sur 20 à sa rédaction** he got 16 out of 20 for his essay; **un jour sur deux** every other day

(**d**) by; **sa chambre fait trois mètres sur quatre** his room measures three metres by four

sûr, sûre *adjective*
(**a**) sure, certain; **je suis sûr qu'elle viendra** I'm sure she'll come; **j'en étais sûr!** I knew it!
(**b**) safe; **c'est plus sûr s'il t'accompagne** it's safer if he goes with you
(**c**) reliable; **tu peux lui faire confiance, c'est quelqu'un de très sûr** you can trust him, he's very reliable
(**d**) **bien sûr!** of course!

sûrement *adverb* probably; **il a sûrement oublié de faire sonner son réveil** he's probably forgotten to set his alarm clock; **sûrement pas!** certainly not!

LE **surf** *noun* surf; **faire du surf** to go surfing, to surf

LA **surface** *noun* surface area, area; **une grande surface** a hypermarket

surgelé, surgelée
1 *adjective* frozen
2 *masculine plural noun* **les surgelés** frozen food

LE **surligneur** *verb* highlighter

surmener *verb* to overwork; **il se sent surmené** he feels overworked

surnaturel, surnaturelle *adjective* supernatural

LE **surnom** *noun* nickname

surpeuplé, surpeuplée *adjective*
(**a**) overpopulated
(**b**) overcrowded

surprenant, surprenante *adjective* surprising

surprendre *verb*
(**a**) to surprise; **ça m'a surpris d'apprendre qu'il avait démissionné** I was surprised to hear that he'd resigned
(**b**) **surprendre quelqu'un en train de faire quelque chose** to catch somebody doing something; **le patron l'a surpris en train de voler dans la**

caisse the boss caught him stealing from the till

See verb table p. 322.

surpris, surprise[1] *adjective* surprised

Surpris(e) is the past participle of the verb *surprendre*.

LA **surprise**[2] *noun* surprise; **j'ai une surprise pour toi** I've got a surprise for you

LE **sursaut** *noun* start, jump; **se réveiller en sursaut** to wake up with a start

sursauter *verb* to jump, to start

surtout *adverb*
(**a**) especially
(**b**) above all

surveiller *verb*
(**a**) to watch, to keep an eye on
(**b**) to supervise

LE **survêtement** *noun* tracksuit

LE **survivant**, LA **survivante** *noun* survivor

survivre *verb* to survive

See verb table p. 324.

survoler *verb* to fly over

susceptible *adjective* touchy

suspendre *verb*
(**a**) to hang; **ils l'ont suspendu par les pieds** they hung him up by his feet
(**b**) to suspend

SVP *adverb* please

SVP is the written abbreviation of *s'il vous plaît*.

LA **syllabe** *noun* syllable

sympa *adjective* nice

Sympa is an informal word; it is the shortened form of *sympathique*.

LA **sympathie** *noun* **avoir de la sympathie pour quelqu'un** to be fond of somebody

Note that the English word *sympathy* is never a translation for the French word *sympathie*.

sympathique *adjective* nice

Note that the English word *sympathetic* is never a translation for the French word *sympathique*.

LE **syndicat** *noun* trade union; **le syndicat d'initiative** the tourist office

synthétique *adjective* man-made, synthetic

LA **Syrie** *noun* Syria

systématiquement *adverb* systematically

LE **système** *noun* system

t' *pronoun* **il t'aime** he loves you; **tu t'es coupé en te rasant** you've cut yourself shaving; **tu t'es cassé la jambe** you broke your leg

T' is the contracted form of *te* which is used in front of a vowel or a mute h. See also **te**.

ta *adjective* your; **ta mère** your mother; **ta valise** your suitcase

Ta is used in front of feminine nouns. The plural of *ta* is *tes*. *Ta* becomes *ton* before a feminine noun starting with a vowel or a mute h, as in *ton école*, *ton histoire*. See also **tes** and **ton**¹.

LE **tabac** *noun*
(**a**) tobacco; **il a acheté du tabac pour sa pipe** he bought some tobacco for his pipe
(**b**) smoking; **le tabac est mauvais pour la santé** smoking is bad for you

The *c* in *tabac* is not pronounced.

LA **table** *noun* table; **se mettre à table** to sit down at the table; **mettre la table** to lay the table; **à table!** food's ready!; **une table des matières** a table of contents; **une table de nuit** a bedside table; **les tables de multiplication** multiplication tables

LE **tableau** *noun*
(**a**) picture, painting
(**b**) blackboard, board; **Victor, au tableau!** Victor, come to the blackboard!
(**c**) **un tableau d'affichage** a notice board
(**d**) **un tableau de bord** a dashboard

The plural of *tableau* is *tableaux*.

LA **tablette** *noun* **une tablette de chocolat** a bar of chocolate

LE **tablier** *noun* apron

LE **tabouret** *noun* stool

LA **tache** *noun* stain

taché, tachée *adjective* stained

LA **tâche** *noun* task

tacher *verb* to stain

tâcher *verb* **tâcher de faire quelque chose** to try to do something; **je tâcherai de ne pas oublier** I'll try not to forget

LA **taie** *noun* **une taie d'oreiller** a pillow case

LA **taille** *noun*
(**a**) waist; **elle a la taille fine** she has a slim waist
(**b**) height
(**c**) size

LE **taille-crayon** *noun* pencil sharpener

The plural of *taille-crayon* is *taille-crayons*.

tailler *verb*
(**a**) to cut
(**b**) to trim
(**c**) to prune
(**d**) to sharpen

LE **tailleur** *noun*
(**a**) tailor; **il est tailleur** he's a tailor
(**b**) suit *(for women)*
(**c**) **s'asseoir en tailleur** to sit cross-legged

se taire *reflexive verb*
(**a**) to stop talking; **taisez-vous!** be quiet!
(**b**) to keep quiet

See verb table p. 324.

LE **talent** *noun* talent; **il a beaucoup de talent** he's very talented

The *t* in *talent* is not pronounced.

LE **talon** *noun* heel

LE **tambour** *noun* drum

LA **Tamise** *noun* the Thames, the River Thames

tandis que *conjunction*
(**a**) while; **je débarrassais la table tandis qu'il faisait la vaisselle** I was clearing the table while he was doing the dishes
(**b**) whereas, while; **il a très peu d'argent tandis que son frère est très riche** he has very little money while his brother's very rich

Tandis que becomes *tandis qu'* in front of a vowel or a mute h.

tant *adverb*
(**a**) so much; **je l'aime tant** I love him so much; **ne fume pas tant!** don't smoke so much!; **j'ai tant crié que j'ai perdu ma voix** I shouted so much that I lost my voice
(**b**) **tant de** so much; **tu fais tant de bruit que je ne peux pas dormir** you're making so much noise I can't sleep
(**c**) **tant de** so many; **il a tant de livres qu'il ne sait plus où les mettre** he has so many books he doesn't know where to put them all
(**d**) **tant que** as long as; **nous garderons cette voiture tant qu'elle roulera** we'll keep this car as long as it's still going; **sortons nous promener tant qu'il fait beau** let's go out for a walk while it's still nice
(**e**) **tant que** as much as, as many as; **mange tant que tu veux** eat as much as you want

(**f**) **tant mieux!** so much the better!; **tant pis!** too bad!
(**g**) **en tant que** as; **il a travaillé pour eux en tant que cuisinier** he worked for them as a cook

LA **tante** *noun* aunt

tantôt *adverb* sometimes; **je vais à la piscine tantôt le mardi, tantôt le jeudi** I sometimes go swimming on Tuesdays and sometimes on Thursdays

LE **tapage** *noun* din, racket

LA **tape** *noun* slap

taper *verb*
(**a**) to hit; **il m'a tapé** he hit me
(**b**) **les enfants s'amusaient à taper sur des casseroles** the children were amusing themselves by banging on saucepans
(**c**) **taper du pied** to stamp one's foot; **taper des mains** to clap one's hands
(**d**) **taper à la machine** to type; **taper une lettre** to type a letter
(**e**) **le soleil tape** the sun is beating down

LE **tapis** *noun*
(**a**) rug
(**b**) mat; **un tapis de souris** a mouse pad

LA **tapisserie** *noun* tapestry

taquiner *verb* to tease; **arrête de taquiner ta sœur** stop teasing your sister

tard *adverb* late; **je le ferai plus tard** I'll do it later; **il faut que je rentre à minuit au plus tard** I need to be home by midnight at the latest

tarder *verb* to be a long time coming; **sans tarder** without delay; **elle ne devrait plus tarder** she should be here any minute now

LE **tarif** *noun*
(**a**) price list
(**b**) price; **vous faites des tarifs réduits pour les étudiants?** do you do student discounts?

LA tarte *noun*
(a) tart; **une tarte aux pommes** an apple tart
(b) **ce n'est pas de la tarte** *(informal phrase)* it's no easy matter

LA tartine *noun* slice of bread

LE tas *noun*
(a) pile, heap; **un tas de sable** a pile of sand
(b) **un tas de** *(informal phrase)* lots of, a ton of; **il a eu un tas de problèmes** he's had a ton of problems

LA tasse *noun*
(a) cup
(b) **boire la tasse** *(informal phrase)* to get a mouthful of water

tâter *verb* to feel; **le docteur m'a tâté l'abdomen** the doctor felt my stomach

LE tatouage *noun* tattoo

tatouer *verb* to tattoo; **se faire tatouer** to get a tattoo

LE taudis *noun* slum

LA taupe *noun* mole *(animal)*; **il est myope comme une taupe** he's as blind as a bat

LE Taureau *noun* Taurus; **elle est Taureau** she's a Taurus

LE taureau *noun* bull

> The plural of *taureau* is *taureaux*.

LE taux *noun*
(a) rate
(b) level

LE/LA Tchèque *noun (person)* Czech

tchèque
1 *adjective* Czech; **la République tchèque** the Czech Republic; **l'économie tchèque** the Czech economy
2 *masculine noun* **le tchèque** *(language)* Czech; **elle parle Czech** she speaks Czech

> In French, only the noun for the inhabitants of a country takes a capital letter, never the adjective or the noun for the language.

LA Tchéquie *noun* the Czech Republic

te *pronoun*
(a) you; **il te connaît** he knows you; **je t'aime** I love you
(b) to you; **je te l'ai donné** I gave it to you
(c) yourself; **tu t'es brûlé** you burned yourself
(d) **tu te laveras les mains avant de manger** wash your hands before eating; **tu t'es cassé le bras** you broke your arm

> *Te* becomes *t'* in front of a vowel or a mute h. Note that there are many cases when *te* is simply not translated in English, as in *tu te souviens* (you remember), *tu te rases* (you shave) and *tu te lèves* (you get up).

LE technicien, LA technicienne *noun* technician; **il est technicien** he's a technician

technique
1 *adjective* technical; **des problèmes techniques** technical problems
2 *noun* **la technique** technique

teindre *verb* to dye

> See verb table p. 320.

teint, teinte
1 *adjective* dyed
2 *masculine noun* **le teint** complexion
3 *feminine noun* **la teinte** colour

LA teinturerie *noun* dry cleaner's

tel, telle *adjective*
(a) such; **des compositeurs tels que Bach et Mozart** composers such as Bach and Mozart; **la maison telle qu'il me l'a décrite a l'air très belle** the house sounds really beautiful the way he described it to me; **il n'y a rien que tel qu'un bon bain chaud pour se détendre** there's nothing like a nice hot bath to relax you
(b) **tel quel, telle quelle** just as it is; **il a tout laissé tel quel** he left everything just as it was

LA **télé** *noun* TV; **il passe sa vie devant la télé** he spends his life in front of the TV

This word is informal.

télécharger *verb* to download

LA **télécommande** *noun* remote control

LE **téléfilm** *noun* TV movie

LE **téléphérique** *noun* cable car

LE **téléphone** *noun* phone, telephone; **être au téléphone** to be on the phone

téléphoner *verb* to phone

LE **télésiège** *noun* chairlift

LE **téléski** *noun* ski tow

LE **téléspectateur,** LA **téléspectatrice** *noun* (television) viewer

LE **téléviseur** *noun* TV set

LA **télévision** *noun* television, TV; **j'ai vu ce film à la télévision** I saw this film on TV

telle *see* **tel**

tellement *adverb*
(**a**) so; **il est tellement gentil que je n'ose pas lui dire non** he's so nice that I can't refuse
(**b**) so much; **elle a tellement pleuré qu'elle a les yeux tout rouges** she's cried so much that her eyes are all red
(**c**) **tellement de** so much; **il y avait tellement de fumée qu'on ne voyait plus rien** there was so much smoke that you couldn't see a thing
(**d**) **tellement de** so many; **il a tellement de livres qu'il ne sait plus où les mettre** he has so many books that he doesn't know where to put them all
(**e**) **pas tellement** not particularly

LE **témoignage** *noun*
(**a**) testimony
(**b**) account

témoigner *verb* to testify

LE **témoin** *noun*
(**a**) witness; **elle a été témoin d'un accident** she witnessed an accident

(**b**) baton *(in a relay race)*

LA **température** *noun* temperature; **avoir de la température** to have a temperature

LA **tempête** *noun* storm; **une tempête de neige** a blizzard

LE **temps** *noun*
(**a**) time; **à temps** in time; **dans le temps** in the old days; **de temps en temps** from time to time; **il est grand temps de le prévenir** it's high time we told him
(**b**) weather; **quel temps fait-il?** what's the weather like?
(**c**) tense *(of a verb)*

LA **tendance** *noun*
(**a**) trend
(**b**) **avoir tendance à faire quelque chose** to tend to do something

tendre[1] *verb*
(**a**) to stretch
(**b**) to tighten
(**c**) **tendre quelque chose à quelqu'un** to hold something out to somebody; **il m'a tendu le marteau** he held out the hammer to me; **je lui ai tendu la main** I held out my hand to him
(**d**) **tendre un piège à quelqu'un** to set a trap for somebody

tendre[2] *adjective*
(**a**) tender
(**b**) loving

LA **tendresse** *noun* affection, tenderness

tendu, tendue *adjective*
(**a**) tight *(of rope, string)*
(**b**) tense *(of person, atmosphere)*

Tendu(e) is the past participle of *tendre*.

tenir
1 *verb*
(**a**) to hold; **il tenait un verre à la main** he was holding a glass in his hand
(**b**) to fit; **la valise ne tient pas dans le coffre de la voiture** the suitcase won't fit in the car boot

(c) to run; **ses parents tiennent une boulangerie** his parents run a bakery

(d) **tenir une promesse** to keep a promise

(e) **tenir à quelqu'un** to be fond of somebody; **il tient à elle** he's fond of her; **je tiens beaucoup à cette photo** I'm very fond of that picture

(f) **tenir à faire quelque chose** to insist on doing something; **il tient à le faire lui-même** he insists on doing it himself; **je ne tiens pas à ce qu'il vienne** I don't particularly want him to come

(g) **cela ne tient qu'à toi** it's entirely up to you; **si cela ne tenait qu'à moi** if I had my way

(h) **tenir de quelqu'un** to take after somebody; **il tient de son père, il a le même caractère** he takes after his father, he has the same character

(i) **tiens!** oh!, hey!; **tiens, voilà Pierre!** hey, there's Pierre!

(j) **tiens, tiens!** well, well!; **tiens, tiens! il m'avait caché ça** well, well, he hid that from me!

2 *reflexive verb* **se tenir**

(a) to stand; **il se tenait près de l'entrée** he was standing near the entrance; **se tenir droit** to stand up straight; **tiens-toi droit** straighten up; **tiens-toi bien sur ta chaise** sit properly on your chair; **tu as mal au dos parce que tu te tiens mal** you get backaches because of bad posture

(b) to hold on; **tiens-toi à la rampe** hold on to the banister

(c) to take place; **la réunion se tiendra dans son bureau** the meeting will take place in his office

(d) **bien se tenir** to behave; **se tenir tranquille** to keep quiet

(e) **se tenir par la main** to hold hands

> The past participle of *tenir* is *tenu(e)*. See verb table p. 324.

LE **tennis** *noun*

(a) tennis; **jouer au tennis** to play tennis

(b) **des tennis** trainers

LA **tension** *noun*

(a) tension

(b) blood pressure; **avoir de la tension** to have high blood pressure

LA **tentation** *noun* temptation

LA **tentative** *noun* attempt

LA **tente** *noun* tent

tenter *verb*

(a) to tempt; **ça ne te tente pas?** are you not tempted?

(b) **tenter de faire quelque chose** to attempt to do something

tenu¹, tenue *see* **tenir**

il n'a pas tenu sa promesse he didn't keep his promise

> *Tenu(e)* is the past participle of the verb *tenir*. See verb table p. 324.

LA **tenue²** *noun* outfit, clothes; **tenue de soirée** evening dress

LA **terminale** *noun* the last year of secondary school (for pupils aged 17); **elle est en terminale** she's in her last year of secondary school

> See also **lycée** and **filière**.

terminer

1 *verb* to finish; **je n'ai pas terminé mon travail** I haven't finished my work

2 *reflexive verb* **se terminer** to end; **la soirée s'est terminée par une discussion** the evening ended with a talk

terne *adjective* dull

LE **terrain** *noun*

(a) piece of land

(b) pitch; **un terrain de football** a football pitch; **un terrain de rugby** a rugby pitch

(c) **un terrain de camping** a campsite; **un terrain de jeux** a playground; **un terrain de sport** a sports ground; **un terrain vague** a waste ground

LA **terrasse** *noun*

(a) terrace

(b) **nous étions assis à la terrasse** *(in a café)* we were sitting outside

LA **terre** *noun*
(**a**) earth; **laTerre** the Earth
(**b**) soil; **la terre est bonne par ici** the soil is good around here
(**c**) land; **il interdit qu'on chasse sur ses terres** he doesn't allow hunting on his land
(**d**) ground; **sous terre** underground; **par terre** on the ground; **Lucie est tombée par terre** Lucie fell down; **son verre est tombé par terre** his glass fell on the floor

LA **terreur** *noun* terror

terrible *adjective*
(**a**) terrible, awful
(**b**) **pas terrible** nothing special, not terribly good

> Sense (b) is an informal use of the word *terrible*.

LE **territoire** *noun* territory

tes *adjective* your; **tes lunettes** your glasses; **tes gants** your gloves; **tes valises** your suitcases

> *Tes* is used in front of plural nouns. It is the plural of *ta* and *ton*. See also **ta** and **ton**[1].

LA **tête** *noun*
(**a**) head; **avoir la grosse tête** *(informal phrase)* to be big-headed; **tenir tête à quelqu'un** to stand up to somebody
(**b**) face; **il a une drôle de tête** he has a strange face
(**c**) **faire la tête** to sulk
(**d**) **être en tête** *(in a race)* to be in the lead; **être en tête de train** to be at the front of the train

LE **testament** *noun* will

LE **têtard** *noun* tadpole

LA **tétine** *noun*
(**a**) teat
(**b**) dummy

têtu, têtue *adjective* stubborn, obstinate

LE **texto** *noun* text message

LE **TGV** *noun* high-speed train

> *TGV* is the abbreviation of *train à grande vitesse*. It does not change in the plural.

Le TGV
France has a network of high-speed trains that reach speeds of over 200 mph. TGVs have considerably reduced the travel times between many French cities.

LE **thé** *noun* tea

LE **théâtre** *noun* theatre; **elle veut faire du théâtre** she wants to be an actress

LA **théière** *noun* teapot

LE **thème** *noun*
(**a**) theme
(**b**) translation into a foreign language

LE **thermomètre** *noun* thermometer

LE **thon** *noun* tuna

LE **tibia** *noun* shin

LE **ticket** *noun*
(**a**) ticket
(**b**) **ticket de caisse** till receipt

> The final *t* in *ticket* is not pronounced.

tiède *adjective*
(**a**) warm
(**b**) lukewarm

tien, tienne *pronoun* **le tien, la tienne, les tiens, les tiennes** yours; **ce crayon, c'est le tien** this pencil is yours; **ce n'est pas ma tasse, c'est la tienne** this cup is not mine, it's yours; **ces livres, ce sont les tiens** these books are yours

> In French, possessive pronouns have the same gender and the same number as the nouns they stand for, eg the corresponding pronoun for *tes livres* is *les tiens* because the word *livres* is masculine plural.

tiens, tient *see* **tenir**
je tiens un stylo dans la main I'm

holding a pen in my hand; **tiens! voilà Claude qui arrive** oh look, here comes Claude; **il tient son chat dans ses bras** he's holding his cat in his arms

Tiens and *tient* are forms of the verb *tenir* in the present tense. It is also a form of the verb *tenir* in the imperative. See verb table p. 324.

LE **tiers** *noun* third

LE **Tiers-Monde** *noun* Third World

LA **tige** *noun*
(**a**) stem, stalk
(**b**) rod

LE **tigre** *noun* tiger

LE **timbre** *noun* stamp

timide *adjective* shy

LE **tir** *noun*
(**a**) firing
(**b**) shooting
(**c**) **le tir à l'arc** archery

LE **tire-bouchon** *noun* corkscrew

The plural of *tire-bouchon* is *tire-bouchons*.

LA **tirelire** *noun* piggybank, moneybox

tirer *verb*
(**a**) to pull; **il m'a tiré les cheveux** he pulled my hair
(**b**) to draw; **tirer les rideaux** to draw the curtains; **tirer au sort** to draw lots
(**c**) **tirer la langue** to stick out one's tongue
(**d**) to fire; **ils ont tiré sur la foule** they opened fire on the crowd
(**e**) to shoot; **ne tirez pas!** don't shoot!

LE **tiroir** *noun* drawer

LA **tisane** *noun* herbal tea

tisser *verb* to weave

LE **tissu** *noun* material, cloth; **une casquette en tissu** a cloth cap

LE **titre** *noun*
(**a**) title
(**b**) headline; **les gros titres** the main headlines; **faire les gros titres** to hit the headlines

tituber *verb* to stagger

LE **toboggan** *noun* slide

toi *pronoun*
(**a**) you; **et toi, qu'en penses-tu?** what about you, what do you think?; **c'est à toi de jouer** it's your turn; **est-ce que ces lunettes sont à toi?** are these glasses yours?
(**b**) yourself; **ne pense pas qu'à toi** don't just think of yourself
(**c**) **assieds-toi** sit down; **dépêche-toi** hurry up

LA **toile** *noun*
(**a**) cloth, canvas; **une toile cirée** a waxed tablecloth
(**b**) painting, canvas
(**c**) **une toile d'araignée** a spider's web

LA **toilette** *noun*
(**a**) wash; **faire sa toilette** to wash, to get washed
(**b**) outfit; **de belles toilettes** nice outfits
(**c**) **les toilettes** the toilet; **il est aux toilettes** he's in the toilet

toi-même *pronoun* yourself; **fais-le toi-même** do it yourself; **imbécile! – toi-même!** idiot! – idiot yourself!

LE **toit** *noun* roof; **un toit ouvrant** a sunroof

LA **tôle** *noun* sheet metal; **tôle ondulée** corrugated iron

tolérer *verb* to tolerate

LA **tomate** *noun* tomato

LA **tombe** *noun* grave

tomber *verb*
(**a**) to fall; **les feuilles tombent** the leaves are falling; **tomber malade** to fall ill; **tomber amoureux** to fall in love; **Noël tombe un mercredi** Christmas falls on a Wednesday; **il est tombé de sa chaise** he fell off his chair
(**b**) **tu as fait tomber tes clés** you dropped your keys; **il a fait tomber la bouteille avec son coude** he knocked the bottle over with his elbow
(**c**) **tomber sur quelqu'un** to run into

somebody; **tomber sur quelque chose** to come across something; **je suis tombé sur ce livre par hasard** I came across this book by chance

(d) **je suis bien tombé** I was lucky; **je suis mal tombé** I was unlucky

(e) **tu tombes bien, il faut que je te parle** you've come just at the right time, I need to talk to you

(f) **ça tombe bien, je serai à Paris aussi ce jour-là** that's good timing, I'll be in Paris that day too

ton¹ *adjective* your; **ton père** your father; **ton livre** your book; **ton enfance** your childhood

---

Ton is used in front of masculine nouns, as well as before feminine nouns starting with a vowel or a mute h, as in *ton école, ton histoire*. The plural of *ton* is *tes* and the feminine is *ta*. See also **ta** and **tes**.

LE **ton²** *noun*

(a) tone of voice; **parle-moi sur un autre ton!** don't use that tone of voice with me!

(b) shade *(of a colour)*

LA **tondeuse** *noun*

(a) lawnmower

(b) clippers

(c) shears

tondre *verb*   **tondre la pelouse** to mow the lawn; **tondre un mouton** to shear a sheep; **il a tondu la pelouse** he mowed the lawn

LE **tonneau** *noun*

(a) barrel

(b) **la voiture a fait plusieurs tonneaux** the car rolled over several times

---

The plural of *tonneau* is *tonneaux*.

LE **tonnerre** *noun* thunder; **un coup de tonnerre** a thunderclap

LE **torchon** *noun*

(a) tea towel

(b) mess; **son cahier est un vrai torchon** his exercise book is a real mess

---

Sense (b) is an informal use of the word *torchon*.

---

tordre

1 *verb* to twist, to bend

2 *reflexive verb* **se tordre**

(a) **se tordre la cheville** to twist one's ankle; **elle s'est tordu le doigt** she bent her finger

(b) **se tordre de rire** *(informal phrase)* to be doubled up with laughter

LE **torrent** *noun*   torrent, mountain stream

The final *t* in *torrent* is not pronounced.

LE **torse** *noun* chest *(torso)*; **être torse nu** to be bare-chested

tort *masculine noun*   **avoir tort** to be wrong; **faire du tort à quelqu'un** to harm somebody; **à tort** wrongly

LE **torticolis** *noun* stiff neck

LA **tortue** *noun*

(a) tortoise

(b) turtle

tôt *adverb* early; **tôt ou tard** sooner or later; **ce n'est pas trop tôt!** it's about time!

total, totale

1 *adjective* total

2 *masculine noun* **le total** the total

The plural of the masculine adjective and the noun *total* is *totaux*.

---

totalement *adverb* totally, completely

touchant, touchante *adjective* touching

LA **touche** *noun*

(a) key *(of a keyboard, a piano)*

(b) button

(c) throw-in *(in football)*; line-out *(in rugby)*

toucher *verb*

(a) to touch; **qui a touché à mon ordinateur?** who's touched my computer?

(b) to feel; **ce tissu est très doux, touche-le** this material is really soft, feel it

(**c**) to hit *(a person, a target)*; **la balle l'a touché à la jambe** the bullet hit him in the leg

(**d**) to get, to receive *(money, salary)*

(**e**) to move, to touch; **leur gentillesse m'a beaucoup touché** I was very touched by their kindness

(**f**) to affect; **ces mesures touchent toutes les classes** these measures affect all classes

toujours *adverb*

(**a**) always; **il est toujours en train de se plaindre** he's always complaining; **pour toujours** forever

(**b**) still; **tu es toujours là?** are you still here?

LA tour¹ *noun*

(**a**) tower; **la tour Eiffel** the Eiffel Tower

(**b**) tower block, high-rise

(**c**) rook, castle *(in chess)*

La Tour Eiffel

The Eiffel Tower is France's best known monument and has become a symbol for France itself. It is 324 metres high and was built in 1889 for the Universal Exhibition in Paris. At first it was supposed to be dismantled after the exhibition but the decision was taken to keep it and it has since become the most distinctive feature of the Paris landscape.

LE tour² *noun*

(**a**) turn; **c'est ton tour** it's your turn; **faire quelque chose à tour de rôle** to take turns to do something

(**b**) **faire un tour** to go for a walk; **faire un tour en voiture** to go for a drive; **faire un tour en vélo** to go for a bike ride

(**c**) **faire le tour de quelque chose** to go round something; **il a fait le tour du monde** he went round the world; **le Tour de France** the Tour de France

(**d**) trick; **jouer un tour à quelqu'un** to play a trick on somebody

(**e**) **tour de taille** waist measurement

Le Tour de France

Cycling is a popular sport in France. The most famous cycling event in the world is *le Tour de France*, which was first held in 1903. The race is about 2000 miles long, is divided into stages and takes place over three weeks in July. It starts in a different town each year, but the home stretch is always the Champs-Élysées in Paris. The overall leader of each stage of the Tour de France wears a yellow jersey, *le maillot jaune*.

LE tourbillon *noun* whirlpool

LE tourisme *noun* tourism; **faire du tourisme** to go sightseeing

LE/LA touriste *noun* tourist

touristique *adjective* tourist; **un guide touristique** a guidebook; **cette région est très touristique** this region is very popular with tourists

LE tournant *noun*

(**a**) bend *(in a road)*

(**b**) turning point; **un tournant dans ma vie** a turning point in my life

tourner

1 *verb*

(**a**) to turn; **tourne à gauche** turn left

(**b**) **tourner autour de quelque chose** to go round something; **tourner autour du pot** to beat about the bush

(**c**) to shoot *(a film)*

(**d**) to go off

2 *reflexive verb* **se tourner** to turn round

LE tournesol *noun* sunflower

LE tournevis *noun* screwdriver

LE tournoi *noun* tournament

tous, toutes

1 *adjective*

(**a**) all; **tous les livres** all the books; **toutes les filles** all the girls; **tous/toutes les deux** both; **je les aime toutes les deux** I love both of them; **tous les trois** all three

(**b**) every; **tous les ans** every year; **toutes les semaines** every week; **tous**

les six mois every six months
2 *pronoun* all; **ils sont tous là** they're all there; **je les connais toutes** I know all of them; **il les a tous vendus** he sold them all

> *Tous* is the plural of *tout* and *toutes* is the plural of *toute*. See also **tout**.

LA **Toussaint** *noun* All Saints' day

tousser *verb* to cough

tout, toute
1 *adjective*
(**a**) all; **tout le travail** all the work; **il a mangé toute la soupe** he ate all the soup; **tout le temps** all the time; **tout la journée** all day long; **tout le monde** everyone
(**b**) the whole; **toute la classe** the whole class; **elle a mangé tout le gâteau** she ate the whole cake
(**c**) any; **tout candidat surpris en train de tricher sera éliminé** any candidate caught cheating will be disqualified; **de toute façon** in any case; **à tout moment** at any time

> The plural of *tout* is *tous* and the plural of *toute* is *toutes*. See also **tous**.

2 *adverb*
(**a**) very; **il est tout petit** he's very small; **elle est toute petite** she's very small; **des vêtements tout neufs** brand new clothes; **une voiture toute neuve** a brand new car; **c'est tout près** it's very near; **tout droit** straight ahead; **tout en haut** right at the top; **tout en bas** right at the bottom
(**b**) **tout à coup** suddenly; **tout de même** even so; **tout de même!** really!; **tout à fait** completely, exactly; **tout à l'heure** in a moment; **à tout à l'heure!** see you later!; **tout de suite** at once; **à tout de suite!** see you in a minute!
(**c**) **tout en** while; **tout en chantant** while singing
3 *pronoun* **tout**
(**a**) everything; **il a tout vendu** he sold everything; **j'ai tout vu** I saw every-

thing
(**b**) anything; **tout peut arriver** anything can happen
(**c**) all; **c'est tout** that's all; **en tout** in all
4 *masculine noun* **le tout**
(**a**) everything, the lot
(**b**) the most important thing; **le tout c'est de ne pas bafouiller** the most important thing is not to stutter
(**c**) **pas du tout** not at all; **rien du tout** nothing at all

toute *see* tout

toutefois *adverb* however

toutes *see* tous

LA **toux** *noun* cough

> The *x* in *toux* is not pronounced.

LE **trac** *noun* **avoir le trac** to be feeling nervous

LA **trace** *noun*
(**a**) trace; **des traces de sang** traces of blood
(**b**) mark; **des traces de doigt** finger marks; **des traces de pneus** tyre marks
(**c**) trail, track; **les chasseurs suivent les traces du sanglier** the hunters are following the trail left by the wild boar
(**d**) **des traces de pas** footprints

tracer *verb* to draw (*a circle, a line*)

LE **tracteur** *noun* tractor

LE **traducteur,** LA **traductrice** *noun* translator; **elle est traductrice** she's a translator

LA **traduction** *noun* translation

traduire *verb* to translate; **il a traduit le texte en anglais** he translated the text into English

> See verb table p. 320.

LE **trafic** *noun*
(**a**) trafficking
(**b**) traffic

LE **trafiquant,** LA **trafiquante** *noun* trafficker

trahir *verb* to betray

LA **trahison** *noun* betrayal

LE **train** *noun*
(a) train
(b) **être en train de faire quelque chose** to be doing something; **j'étais en train de travailler** I was working

LE **traîneau** *noun* sledge *(pulled by animals)*

> The plural of *traîneau* is *traîneaux*.

traîner *verb*
(a) to lie around; **il laisse ses affaires traîner partout** he leaves his things lying around everywhere
(b) to hang around; **elle traîne dans la rue avec ses copains** she hangs around the streets with her friends
(c) to drag; **il a traîné la boîte à travers la pièce** he dragged the box across the room
(d) to drag on; **les choses commencent à traîner en longueur!** things are beginning to drag on!; **ça n'a pas traîné!** it didn't take long!
(e) to dawdle; **tu vas être en retard si tu continues à traîner** you'll be late if you keep dawdling

LE **trait** *noun*
(a) line; **tirer un trait** to draw a line
(b) **un trait d'union** a hyphen
(c) feature; **les traits du visage** the facial features

> The final *t* in *trait* is not pronounced.

LE **traitement** *noun*
(a) treatment
(b) **traitement de texte** word processing

traiter *verb*
(a) to treat; **le patron traite mal ses employés** the boss treats his employees badly
(b) to call; **elle m'a traité d'idiot** she called me an idiot
(c) **traiter de** to be about; **de quoi traite l'exposé?** what's the talk about?

LE **traître** *noun* traitor

LE **trajet** *noun*
(a) trip, journey
(b) route

LE **tramway** *noun* tram

LA **tranche** *noun* slice

tranquille *adjective*
(a) quiet
(b) **laisse ta sœur tranquille** leave your sister alone; **laisse ça tranquille** leave that alone
(c) **sois tranquille!** don't worry!

LA **tranquillité** *noun* peace and quiet

transformer
1 *verb*
(a) to change, to transform
(b) to convert; **ils ont transformé cette pièce en bureau** they converted this room into an office
2 *reflexive verb* **se transformer elle s'est transformée en cygne** she turned into a swan

transgénique *adjective* genetically modified

transmettre *verb* **transmettre quelque chose à quelqu'un** to pass something on to somebody; **est-ce que tu lui as transmis le message?** did you pass on the message to him?

> See verb table p. 322.

transpercer *verb* to go through, to pierce

LA **transpiration** *noun* sweat, perspiration

transpirer *verb* to sweat, to perspire

LE **transport** *noun* transport; **les transports en commun** public transport

> The final *t* in *transport* is not pronounced.

transporter *verb* to carry, to transport

trapu, trapue *adjective* stocky

LE **travail** *noun*
(a) work

(**b**) job

> The plural of *travail* is *travaux*.

travailler *verb*
(**a**) to work
(**b**) to work on

travailleur, travailleuse
1 *adjective* hard-working
2 *noun* un travailleur, une travailleuse a worker

LES **travaux** *masculine plural noun*
(**a**) work; **ils font des travaux dans leur maison** they're doing work on their house
(**b**) roadworks; **il y a des travaux au bout de la rue** there are roadworks at the end of the street

> The plural of *travail* is *travaux*.

travers
1 *preposition* à travers through; **à travers le rideau** through the curtain; **je ne vois rien à travers** I can't see anything through it; **en travers de** across; **il y a un arbre en travers de la route** there is a tree lying across the road
2 *adjective* de travers crooked; **ton chapeau est de travers** your hat is crooked; **le tableau est de travers** the painting is crooked
3 *adverb* de travers the wrong way; **il prend tout de travers** he takes everything the wrong way; **j'ai avalé de travers** it went down the wrong way; **tout va de travers en ce moment** everything's going wrong at the moment; **comprendre de travers** to misunderstand

LA **traversée** *noun* crossing

traverser *verb*
(**a**) to cross
(**b**) to go through

trébucher *verb* to trip; **faire trébucher quelqu'un** to trip somebody up

LE **trèfle** *noun*
(**a**) clover; **un trèfle à quatre feuilles** a four-leaf clover

(**b**) clubs *(in cards)*; **le sept de trèfle** the seven of clubs

treize *number* thirteen; **le treize juillet** the thirteenth of July; **nous sommes le treize mars** it's the thirteenth of March; **à treize heures** at one o'clock in the afternoon

LE **tremblement** *noun*
(**a**) shaking
(**b**) **un tremblement de terre** an earthquake

trembler *verb* to shake, to tremble; **trembler de froid** to shiver with cold

trempé, trempée *adjective* soaking wet

tremper *verb*
(**a**) to soak; **se faire tremper** to get soaked
(**b**) to dip, to dunk; **il a trempé un biscuit dans son café** he dunked a biscuit in his coffee

LE **tremplin** *noun* springboard

LA **trentaine** *noun* about thirty; **une trentaine de personnes** about thirty people; **il a la trentaine** he's about thirty years old

trente *number* thirty; **il a trente ans** he's thirty; **le trente juillet** the thirtieth of July; **nous sommes le trente mars** it's the thirtieth of March; **trente et un** thirty-one; **trente-deux** thirty-two

trentième *number* thirtieth

très *adverb* very

LE **trésor** *noun* treasure

LA **tresse** *noun* plait; **elle porte des tresses** she wears her hair in plaits

LA **tribu** *noun* tribe

LE **tribunal** *noun* court

> The plural of *tribunal* is *tribunaux*.

LES **tribunes** *feminine plural noun* stand *(of a stadium)*

tricher *verb* to cheat

LE **tricheur,** LA **tricheuse** *noun* cheat, cheater

LE **tricot** *noun*
(a) knitting
(b) sweater

tricoter *verb* to knit

trier *verb*
(a) to sort *(mail)*; **trier par ordre alphabétique** to sort in alphabetical order
(b) to sort out

LE **trimestre** *noun* term

trimestriel, trimestrielle *adjective* quarterly

trinquer *verb* to clink glasses; **trinquer à quelque chose** to drink to something

LE **triomphe** *noun* triumph

triple
1 *adjective* treble, triple
2 *masculine noun* **le triple** three times as much

LES **triplés,** LES **triplées** *plural noun* triplets

triste *adjective* sad

LA **tristesse** *noun* sadness

LE **trognon** *noun* core; **un trognon de pomme** an apple core

trois *number* three; **le trois septembre** the third of September; **nous sommes le trois février** it's the third of February

troisième
1 *number* third
2 *feminine noun* **la troisième** the fourth year of secondary school (for pupils aged 14); **elle est en troisième** she's in her fourth year of secondary school

See also **collège**.

LE **trombone** *noun*
(a) trombone
(b) paper clip

LA **trompe** *noun* trunk *(of an elephant)*

tromper
1 *verb*

(a) to mislead, to deceive
(b) to be unfaithful to; **il trompe sa femme** he's unfaithful to his wife
2 *reflexive verb* **se tromper** to make a mistake; **se tromper de route** to take the wrong road; **je me suis trompé de numéro** I got the wrong number; **je me suis trompé de date** I got the date wrong

LA **trompette** *noun* trumpet

LE **tronc** *noun* trunk *(of a tree)*

The *c* in *tronc* is not pronounced.

trop *adverb*
(a) too; **il est trop tôt** it's too early
(b) too much; **tu parles trop** you talk too much; **il a trop bu** he had too much to drink
(c) **trop de** too much; **trop de sel** too much salt
(d) **trop de** too many; **trop de gens** too many people; **trois verres de trop** three glasses too many

LA **trottinette** *noun* scooter *(for children)*

LE **trottoir** *noun* pavement

LE **trou** *noun* hole; **un trou de mémoire** a memory lapse; **il habite un trou paumé en pleine campagne** he lives in the countryside in the middle of nowhere

trouer *verb* to make a hole in

LE **troupeau** *noun*
(a) herd
(b) flock

The plural of *troupeau* is *troupeaux*.

LA **trousse** *noun*
(a) pencil case
(b) **une trousse à outils** a tool kit; **une trousse de toilette** a toilet bag

trouver
1 *verb*
(a) to find; **je ne trouve pas mes clés** I can't find my keys
(b) to think; **je trouve ça idiot** I think it's stupid

2 *reflexive verb* **se trouver**
(**a**) **se trouver** to be; **ils se trouvent à Madrid** they're in Madrid
(**b**) to find; **elle s'est trouvé un copain** she's found herself a boyfriend
(**c**) **il se trouve petit** he thinks he's small
(**d**) **se trouver mal** to faint

LE **truc** *noun*
(**a**) thing; **j'ai un truc à te dire** I've got something to tell you
(**b**) trick; **ce n'est pas magique, il y a un truc** it's not magic, there's a trick to it

This word is informal.

LE **trucage** *noun* special effect

LA **truite** *noun* trout

LE **truquage** *noun* special effect

tu[1] *pronoun* you; **tu veux venir à la piscine avec moi?** do you want to come to the swimming pool with me?

Tu is used when speaking to one person you know well (a friend, a relative etc) or to someone your own age or younger. When speaking to one person you do not know well or to somebody to whom you want to show more respect (a teacher, a boss etc), you should use the polite form *vous* instead of *tu*. *Vous* is also used when speaking to more than one person, whether they are friends or people you don't know well. See also **vous**.

tu[2]**, tue** *see* **se taire**
je me suis tu I remained silent

Tu(e) is the past participle of the verb *se taire*. See verb table p. 324.

LE **tuba** *noun*
(**a**) tuba; **elle joue du tuba** she plays the tuba
(**b**) snorkel

LE **tube** *noun*
(**a**) tube; **un tube de dentifrice** a tube of toothpaste

(**b**) hit; **le tube de l'été** this summer's hit

Sense (b) is an informal use of *tube*.

tuer
1 *verb* to kill
2 *reflexive verb* **se tuer**
(**a**) to get killed; **il s'est tué en voiture** he got killed in a car accident
(**b**) to kill oneself

LE **tueur,** LA **tueuse** *noun* killer

LA **tuile** *noun* tile

LA **Tunisie** *noun* Tunisia

LE **tunnel** *noun* tunnel; **le tunnel sous la Manche** the Channel Tunnel

LE **Turc,** LA **Turque** *noun* (*person*) Turk

turc, turque
1 *adjective* Turkish; **l'économie turque** the Turkish economy
2 *masculine noun* **le turc** (*language*) Turkish; **il parle turc** he speaks Turkish

In French, only the noun for the inhabitants of a country takes a capital letter, never the adjective or the noun for the language.

LA **Turquie** *noun* Turkey

tutoyer *verb* to call somebody "tu"

See also **tu**[1].

LE **tuyau** *noun*
(**a**) pipe; **un tuyau d'échappement** an exhaust pipe
(**b**) hose

The plural of *tuyau* is *tuyaux*.

LE **tympan** *noun* eardrum

LE **type** *noun*
(**a**) type, kind
(**b**) looks; **il a le type méditerranéen** he has Mediterranean looks
(**c**) guy; **c'est un type formidable** he's a great guy

Sense (c) is an informal use of *type*.

typique *adjective* typical

U

L'UE *feminine noun* EU; **la Pologne fait maintenant partie de l'UE** Poland is now part of the EU

UE is the abbreviation of *Union européenne*.

un, une
1 *number* one; **ça coûte un euro** it costs one euro; **pendant une journée** for one day
2 *article* a, an; **un beau pays** a beautiful country; **un animal** an animal; **une grande ville** a big city
3 *pronoun* one; **un de ces jours** one of these days; **l'un d'entre eux** one of them; **l'une de mes amies** one of my friends; **les uns et les autres** everybody

uni, unie *adjective*
(**a**) united
(**b**) close; **c'est une famille très unie** they're a very close family
(**c**) plain; **une robe unie** a plain dress

UNE **union** *noun*
(**a**) union; **l'Union européenne** the European Union
(**b**) marriage

Note that the English word *trade union* is never a translation for the French word *union*.

unique *adjective*
(**a**) only; **tu es mon unique espoir** you are my only hope; **un enfant unique** an only child
(**b**) unique; **une occasion unique** a unique opportunity

uniquement *adverb* only

unir *verb*
(**a**) to unite
(**b**) to combine

L'unité *feminine noun*
(**a**) unity
(**b**) unit

L'univers *masculine noun* universe

The *s* in *univers* is not pronounced.

universitaire *adjective* university; **des études universitaires** university studies; **une ville universitaire** a university town

L'urgence *feminine noun*
(**a**) urgency; **il y a urgence** it's a matter of urgency; **d'urgence** urgently; **il a fallu l'opérer d'urgence** they had to perform emergency surgery on him
(**b**) emergency; **les urgences** *(in hospital)* casualty, accident and emergency

UNE **urne** *noun*
(**a**) urn
(**b**) ballot box; **aller aux urnes** to go to the polls

L'usage *masculine noun* use; **hors d'usage** out of order

UN **usager** *noun* user

usé, usée *adjective* worn

user
1 *verb* to wear out
2 *reflexive verb* **s'user** to wear out; **ces piles s'usent très vite** these batteries wear out very quickly

UNE **usine** *noun* factory

UN **ustensile** *noun* utensil

utile *adjective* useful; **il n'est pas utile d'avertir la police** there's no need to notify the police; **ton guide touristique m'a été très utile** your guidebook came in very useful

utiliser *verb* to use

ʟ**'utilité** *feminine noun* use, usefulness; **ce n'est pas d'une grande utilité** it isn't very useful

va *see* **aller**
  (**a**) **il va à l'école** he's going to school
  (**b**) **allez, va, c'est l'heure** come on, it's time to go

> *Va* is a form of the verb *aller* in the present tense. It is also a form of the verb *aller* in the imperative. See verb table p. 312.

LES vacances *feminine plural noun* holidays; **partir en vacances** to go on holiday; **les grandes vacances** the summer holidays

LA vacancier, LA vacancière *noun* holidaymaker

LE vaccin *noun* vaccine

vacciner *verb* to vaccinate

vache
  1 *feminine noun* **une vache** a cow
  2 *adjective* mean, rotten; **allez, ne sois pas vache** come on, don't be rotten

> This adjective is an informal use of *vache*.

vachement *adverb* really; **il fait vachement chaud aujourd'hui** it's really hot today

> This word is informal.

vagabonder *verb* to wander

vague
  1 *adjective* vague; **une vague idée** a vague idea
  2 *feminine noun* **une vague** a wave *(in the sea)*; **une vague de chaleur** a heatwave; **une vague de froid** a cold spell; **une vague d'attentats** a wave of bombings

vaincre *verb*
  (**a**) to defeat, to beat
  (**b**) to overcome; **il a vaincu sa peur de l'eau** he overcame his fear of water

> See verb table p. 324.

LE vaincu, LA vaincue *noun* loser

> *Vaincu(e)* is also the past participle of *vaincre*. See verb table p. 324.

LE vainqueur *noun* winner

vais *see* **aller**
  je vais à l'école I'm going to school; **je vais y réfléchir** I'll think about it

> *Vais* is a form of the verb *aller* in the present tense. See verb table p. 312.

LE vaisseau *noun*
  (**a**) vessel; **un vaisseau sanguin** a blood vessel
  (**b**) **un vaisseau spatial** a spaceship

> The plural of *vaisseau* is *vaisseaux*.

LA vaisselle *noun*
  (**a**) **faire la vaisselle** to do the washing-up, to wash the dishes
  (**b**) crockery, dishes

valable *adjective* valid

LE valet *noun*
  (**a**) manservant
  (**b**) jack *(in cards)*; **le valet de pique** the jack of spades

LA valeur *noun* value; **des objets de valeur** valuables; **une maison d'une valeur de deux millions de livres** a house worth two million pounds; **sans valeur** worthless

LA valise *noun* case, suitcase

LA **vallée** *noun* valley

valoir *verb*
(**a**) to be worth; **cela vaut une fortune** it's worth a fortune; **ce pantalon vaut cher** these trousers are expensive
(**b**) **ça vaut la peine** it's worth it; **ça vaut la peine d'y aller** it's worth going
(**c**) **valoir mieux** to be better; **il vaut mieux rester** it would be better to stay

See verb table p. 324.

LA **valse** *noun* waltz

valu, value *see* valoir
il aurait mieux valu rester à la maison we should have stayed at home

Valu(e) is the past participle of the verb *valoir*. See verb table p. 324.

LA **vanille** *noun* vanilla

se vanter *reflexive verb* to boast

LA **vapeur** *noun* steam; **un bateau à vapeur** a steamboat; **cuit à la vapeur** steamed

vaporiser *verb* to spray

LA **varappe** *noun* rock climbing

LA **varicelle** *noun* chickenpox; **il a la varicelle** he's got chickenpox

varié, variée *adjective* varied; **le travail de mon père n'est pas très varié** my dad's job isn't very varied

varier *verb* to vary; **la température varie selon les saisons** the temperature varies with the seasons

LA **variété** *noun*
(**a**) variety
(**b**) easy listening music, light music

Varsovie *noun* Warsaw

vas *see* aller
tu vas à la piscine demain? are you going swimming tomorrow?

Vas is a form of the verb *aller* in the present tense. See verb table p. 312.

vase
1 *masculine noun* **un vase** a vase
2 *feminine noun* **la vase** mud

vaste *adjective* huge, vast

vaudrait *see* valoir
cela vaudrait le coup d'essayer! it would be worth a try!

Vaudrait is a form of the verb *valoir* in the conditional. See verb table p. 324.

vaut *see* valoir
ce collier vaut une fortune this necklace is worth a fortune

Vaut is a form of the verb *valoir* in the present tense. See verb table p. 324.

LE **vautour** *noun* vulture

LE **veau** *noun*
(**a**) calf *(animal)*
(**b**) veal

The plural of *veau* is *veaux*.

vécu, vécue *see* vivre
il a vécu en Écosse pendant trente ans he lived in Scotland for thirty years

Vécu(e) is the past participle of the verb *vivre*. See verb table p. 324.

LA **vedette** *noun* star *(celebrity)*; **une vedette du cinema** a film star

végétal, végétale *adjective* vegetable; **de l'huile végétale** vegetable oil

The plural of *végétal* is *végétaux*.

LE **végétarien,** LA **végétarienne** *noun* vegetarian

LE **véhicule** *noun* vehicle

LA **veille** *noun* **la veille** the day before; **la veille de l'examen** the day before the exam; **la veille de Noël** Christmas Eve

veiller *verb* to stay up; **veiller à quelque chose** to see to something; **veille à ce qu'il ne soit pas en retard** make sure that he isn't late

LA **veine** *noun*
(**a**) vein
(**b**) **avoir de la veine** *(informal phrase)* to be lucky

LE **vélo** *noun* bike, bicycle; **faire du vélo** to cycle

LE **vélomoteur** *noun* moped

LE **velours** *noun* velvet; **le velours côtelé** corduroy, cord

LES **vendanges** *noun* grape harvest; **faire les vendanges** to harvest the grapes

LE **vendeur,** LA **vendeuse** *noun* shop assistant; **elle est vendeuse** she's a shop assistant

vendre
1 *verb* to sell; **à vendre** for sale; **il a vendu sa voiture** he sold his car
2 *reflexive verb* **se vendre** se vendre to sell; **ça se vend bien** it sells well

LE **vendredi** *noun* Friday; **elle est venue vendredi** she came on Friday; **il fait du tennis le vendredi** he plays tennis on Fridays; **tous les vendredis** every Friday

> In French, the names of days are not written with a capital.

vendu, vendue *see* **vendre**
il a vendu sa voiture he sold his car

> *Vendu(e)* is the past participle of the verb *vendre*.

vénéneux, vénéneuse *adjective* poisonous; **un champignon vénéneux** a poisonous mushroom

LA **vengeance** *noun* revenge

se venger *reflexive verb* to get one's revenge

venimeux, venimeuse *adjective* poisonous; **un serpent venimeux** a poisonous snake

LE **venin** *noun* venom

venir *verb*
(a) to come; **il faut faire venir le docteur** we need to send for the doctor; **il n'est pas venu hier** he didn't come yesterday
(b) **venir de faire quelque chose** to have just done something; **il vient de partir** he has just left

> See verb table p. 324.

Venise *noun* Venice

LE **vent** *noun* wind; **il y a beaucoup de vent aujourd'hui** it's very windy today

LA **vente** *noun* sale; **une vente aux enchères** an auction

LE **ventilateur** *noun* (electric) fan

LE **ventre** *noun* stomach

LE **ver** *noun* worm; **un ver de terre** an earthworm; **un ver luisant** a glow-worm

LE **verger** *noun* orchard

LE **verglas** *noun* black ice

véridique *adjective* true; **cette histoire est véridique** this is a true story

vérifier *verb* to check; **vérifie que la porte est bien fermée** check that the door is properly closed

véritable *adjective* real

LA **vérité** *noun* truth

LE **verlan** *noun* back slang

> **Le Verlan**
> This form of slang, which is very popular among young French people, involves inverting the syllables of words. The word *verlan* is itself the back-to-front version of *l'envers* meaning "the other way round". Some verlan terms are used or understood by a great many speakers, eg *laisse béton!* (*laisse tomber!* forget it!).

LE **vernis** *noun* varnish; **le vernis à ongles** nail varnish

verra, verrai, verras *see* **voir**
on pourra aller au cinéma demain? – on verra... can we go to the cinema tomorrow? – we'll see; **tu verras, c'est un très bon film** it's a very good film, you'll see

> *Verra, verrai* etc are forms of the verb *voir* in the future tense. See verb table p. 324.

LE **verre** *noun*
(**a**) glass; **un bol en verre** a glass bowl; **donne-moi un verre propre** give me a clean glass
(**b**) **boire un verre** *or* **prendre un verre** to have a drink
(**c**) lens *(of spectacles)*; **des verres de contact** contact lenses

verrez, verrons, verront *see* **voir**
vous verrez, c'est un très beau pays it's a very beautiful country, you'll see; **nous verrons ça demain** we'll see about that tomorrow

Verrez, verrons etc are forms of the verb *voir* in the future tense. See verb table p. 324.

LE **verrou** *noun* bolt *(on a door)*; **fermer une porte au verrou** to bolt a door

verrouiller *verb* to bolt; **il a oublié de verrouiller la porte** he forgot to bolt the door

LA **verrue** *noun* wart; **une verrue plantaire** a verruca

vers¹ *preposition*
(**a**) towards; **il s'est dirigé vers la rivière** he headed towards the river
(**b**) about, around; **on s'est donné rendez-vous vers sept heures** we decided to meet around seven o'clock

LE **vers²** *noun* line *(of a poem)*

verse *noun* **il pleut à verse** it's pouring with rain

LE **Verseau** *noun* Aquarius; **il est Verseau** he's an Aquarius

verser *verb*
(**a**) to pour
(**b**) to pay; **il a versé l'argent sur son compte en banque** he paid the money into his bank account

LA **version** *noun*
(**a**) version; **sa version des événements est différente** his version of events is different
(**b**) translation from a foreign language
(**c**) **un film en version originale** a film in the original language; **un film amér-**icain en version française an American film dubbed into French

LE **verso** *noun* back *(of a page)*; **voir au verso** see overleaf

vert, verte
1 *adjective* green; **une robe verte** a green dress
2 *masculine noun* **le vert** green; **le vert est ma couleur préférée** green is my favourite colour

vertical, verticale *adjective* vertical, upright

LE **vertige** *noun*
(**a**) **je redescends, j'ai le vertige** I'm going back down, I feel dizzy; **il ne peut pas faire d'alpinisme, il a le vertige** he can't go climbing, he suffers from vertigo
(**b**) **un vertige** a dizzy spell

LA **veste** *noun* jacket

Note that the English word *vest* is never a translation for the French *veste*.

LE **vestiaire** *noun*
(**a**) changing room
(**b**) cloakroom

LE **vêtement** *noun* garment, piece of clothing; **des vêtements** clothes, clothing

LE/LA **vétérinaire** *noun* vet; **elle est vétérinaire** she's a vet

LE **veuf** *noun* widower

veuille *see* **vouloir**
nous irons, qu'il le veuille ou non we're going whether he likes it or not

Veuille is a form of the verb *vouloir* in the subjunctive. See verb table p. 319.

veulent, veut *see* **vouloir**
ils veulent toujours être les meilleurs they always want to be the best; **elle veut venir avec nous** she wants to come with us

Veulent and *veut* are forms of the verb *vouloir* in the present tense. See verb table p. 319.

LA **veuve** *noun* widow

veux *see* **vouloir**

je ne veux pas aller au musée I don't want to go to the museum; **tu veux du gâteau?** do you want some cake?

> *Veux* is a form of the verb *vouloir* in the present tense. See verb table p. 319.

vexer

1 *verb* **vexer quelqu'un** to hurt somebody's feelings

2 *reflexive verb* **se vexer** to take offence

LA **viande** *noun* meat; **la viande rouge** red meat

vibrer *verb* to vibrate

LA **victime** *noun*

(a) victim

(b) casualty

LA **victoire** *noun* victory

vide

1 *adjective* empty; **mon verre est vide** my glass is empty

2 *masculine noun*

(a) **il était suspendu dans le vide** he was hanging in mid-air; **il a peur du vide** he's afraid of heights

(b) **emballé sous vide** vacuum-packed

vider

1 *verb* to empty

2 *reflexive verb* **se vider** to empty

LA **vie** *noun* life; **être en vie** to be alive

vieil *see* **vieux**

LE **vieillard** *noun* old man

vieille *see* **vieux**

LA **vieillesse** *noun* old age; **il est mort de vieillesse** he died of old age

vieillir *verb*

(a) to get old

(b) to age

viendra, viendrai, viendras *see* **venir**

est-ce que Claire viendra à ta fête? will Claire come to your party?; **je**

viendrai si j'en ai envie I will come if I want to; **tu viendras demain?** will you come tomorrow?

> *Viendra, viendrai* etc are forms of the verb *venir* in the future tense. See verb table p. 324.

viens, vient *see* **venir**

tu viens? are you coming?; **viens!** come!; **il vient le mercredi** he comes on Wednesdays; **je viens de le voir** I've just seen him

> *Viens* and *vient* are forms of the verb *venir* in the present tense. *Viens* is also a form of the verb *venir* in the imperative. See verb table p. 324.

LA **Vierge** *noun*

(a) Virgo; **je suis Vierge** I'm a Virgo

(b) **la Vierge** the Virgin Mary

vierge *adjective*

(a) virgin; **elle est vierge** she's a virgin

(b) blank; **une cassette vierge** a blank tape

LE **Viêt Nam** *noun* Vietnam

LE **Vietnamien**, LA **Vietnamienne** *noun (person)* Vietnamese

vietnamien, vietnamienne

1 *adjective* Vietnamese; **un restaurant vietnamien** a Vietnamese restaurant

2 *masculine noun* **le vietnamien** *(language)* Vietnamese; **elle parle vietnamien** she speaks Vietnamese

> In French, only the noun for the inhabitants of a country takes a capital letter, never the adjective or the noun for the language.

vieux, vieille

1 *adjective* old; **un vieux livre** an old book; **une vieille maison** an old house; **des vieux vêtements** old clothes; **un vieil homme** an old man; **un vieil arbre** an old tree

2 *noun* **un vieux** an old man; **une vieille** an old woman; **les vieux** old people; **mon vieux** *(informal phrase)* mate, pal; **comment ça va mon vieux?**

how are you, mate?

Vieil is used instead of *vieux* before masculine singular nouns beginning with a vowel or a mute h. The plural of *vieil* is still *vieux*: *de vieux arbres*.

vif, vive *adjective*
  (**a**) lively; **c'est un enfant très vif** he's a very lively child
  (**b**) sharp; **une douleur vive** a sharp pain
  (**c**) bright; **une couleur vive** a bright colour

LA **vigne** *noun*
  (**a**) vine
  (**b**) vineyard

LE **vignoble** *noun* vineyard

vilain, vilaine *adjective*
  (**a**) ugly
  (**b**) naughty
  (**c**) nasty

LA **villa** *noun*
  (**a**) detached house
  (**b**) villa

LE **village** *noun* village

LA **ville** *noun* town, city

LE **vin** *noun* wine

LE **vinaigre** *noun* vinegar

LA **vinaigrette** *noun* vinaigrette, French dressing

vingt *number* twenty; **il a vingt ans** he's twenty; **le vingt juillet** the twentieth of July; **nous sommes le vingt mai** it's the twentieth of May; **à vingt heures** at eight o'clock in the evening; **vingt et un** twenty-one; **à vingt et une heures** at nine o'clock in the evening; **vingt-deux** twenty-two; **à vingt-deux heures** at ten o'clock at night; **à vingt-trois heures** at eleven o'clock at night

The *g* in *vingt* is not pronounced. The *t* in *vingt* is pronounced in front of a vowel or a mute h. Otherwise the word is pronounced like *vin*.

LA **vingtaine** *noun* about twenty; **une vingtaine de personnes** about twenty people

The *g* in *vingtaine* is not pronounced.

vingtième *number* twentieth; **au vingtième siècle** in the twentieth century

The *g* in *vingtième* is not pronounced.

violent, violente *adjective* violent

The *t* in *violent* is not pronounced.

violet, violette
  1 *adjective* purple; **une robe violette** a purple dress
  2 *masculine noun* **le violet** purple; **le violet est ma couleur préférée** purple is my favourite colour
  3 *feminine noun* **une violette** a violet

LE **violon** *noun* violin; **jouer du violon** to play the violin

LE **violoncelle** *noun* cello; **jouer du violoncelle** to play the cello

LA **vipère** *noun* adder, viper

LE **virage** *noun* bend *(in a road)*

virer *verb* to fire; **se faire virer** to get fired; **il s'est fait virer du collège** he got expelled from school

This word is informal.

LA **virgule** *noun*
  (**a**) comma
  (**b**) decimal point; **trois virgule cinq** three point five

Note that in French commas are used in numbers instead of decimal points: *3,5* (= 3.5).

LE **virus** *noun* virus; **un virus informatique** a computer virus

LA **vis** *noun* screw

vis *see* **vivre**
je vis en Grande-Bretagne I live in Britain; **tu vis ici depuis longtemps?** have you lived here long?

Vis is a form of the verb *vivre* in the present tense. See verb table p. 324.

LE **visage** *noun* face

viser *verb* to aim at

LA **visière** *noun*
(a) peak *(of a cap)*
(b) visor *(of a helmet)*
(c) eyeshade

LA **vision** *noun*
(a) eyesight, vision
(b) **avoir des visions** to be seeing things

LA **visite** *noun* visit; **rendre visite à quelqu'un** to visit somebody; **avoir de la visite** to have visitors; **passer une visite médicale** to have a medical; **une visite guidée** a guided tour

visiter *verb* to visit; **visiter un appartement** to view a flat

LE **visiteur**, LA **visiteuse** *noun* visitor

LE **vison** *noun* mink; **un manteau en vison** a mink coat

visser *verb* to screw on

vit *see* **vivre**
il vit en France he lives in France; **elle vit ici depuis longtemps?** has she lived here long?

> *Vit* is a form of the verb *vivre* in the present tense. See verb table p. 324.

vite *adverb*
(a) quickly, fast; **il mange trop vite** he eats too quickly
(b) quick; **allez, vite!** come on, quick!; **faire vite** to be quick
(c) soon; **il sera vite guéri** he'll soon be better

LA **vitesse** *noun*
(a) speed; **à quelle vitesse est-ce que tu roulais?** how fast were you driving?; **en vitesse** quickly; **à toute vitesse** at top speed
(b) gear; **une voiture à cinq vitesses** a car with a five-speed gearbox; **changer de vitesse** to change gear

LE **viticulteur**, LA **viticultrice** *noun* wine grower; **elle est viticultrice** she's a wine grower

LE **vitrail** *noun* stained-glass window

> The plural of *vitrail* is *vitraux*.

LA **vitre** *noun* window, window pane; **remonte ta vitre, il fait froid dans la voiture** roll your window back up, it's cold in the car

LA **vitrine** *noun* shop window

vivant, vivante *adjective*
(a) alive
(b) living; **un organisme vivant** a living organism
(c) lively; **c'est un quartier très vivant** it's a very lively area

vive *exclamation* **vive la France!** long live France; **vive les vacances!** hurray for the holidays!

vivement *adverb* **vivement qu'il s'en aille!** I can't wait till he goes; **je suis vraiment fatigué, vivement les vacances!** I'm really tired, roll on the holidays!

vivre *verb* to live; **je vis en Écosse** I live in Scotland; **elle a vécu cent ans** she lived for a hundred years

> The past participle of *vivre* is *vécu(e)*. See verb table p. 324.

LE **vocabulaire** *noun* vocabulary

LE **vœu** *noun* wish; **meilleurs vœux** best wishes

> The plural of *vœu* is *vœux*.

voici *preposition*
(a) here is, this is; **voici ma maison** this is my house; **me voici!** here I am!
(b) here are, these are; **voici les résultats** here are the results

LA **voie** *noun*
(a) lane; **une autoroute à quatre voies** a four-lane motorway; **une voie sans issue** a dead end
(b) railway track; **le train part de la voie 3** the train leaves from platform 3
(c) **tu es sur la bonne voie** you're on the right track; **il est en voie de guérison** he's on the road to recovery; **un**

pays en voie de développement a developing country

voilà *preposition*
(a) here is, this is; **voilà le train** there's the train
(b) here are, these are; **voilà les documents que tu m'as demandés** here are the documents you asked me for

voile
1 *masculine noun* **un voile** a veil
2 *feminine noun*
(a) **une voile** a sail
(b) **la voile** sailing; **il fait de la voile** he goes sailing; **un stage de voile** sailing lessons

LE **voilier** *noun* sailing boat

voir
1 *verb*
(a) to see; **je n'ai pas vu ce film** I haven't seen that film; **voyons! un peu de bon sens!** come on! use a bit of common sense!; **je ne peux vraiment pas le voir!** *(informal phrase)* I really can't stand him!
(b) **faire voir quelque chose à quelqu'un** to show somebody something; **fais voir!** let me see!
(c) **ça n'a rien à voir avec moi** it's got nothing to do with me
2 *reflexive verb* **se voir**
(a) to see each other; **on se voit demain?** can we see each other tomorrow?
(b) to be visible; **la tache se voit encore** you can still see the stain
(c) **ça se voit qu'il est allé en Angleterre, il a fait de gros progrès en anglais** you can tell he's been to England, he's made huge progress in English
(d) to see oneself; **je ne me vois pas marié avec des enfants** I can't see myself married with children

The past participle of *voir* is *vu(e)*. See verb table p. 324.

voisin, voisine
1 *adjective* neighbouring; **le village voisin** the neighbouring village

2 *noun* **un voisin, une voisine** a neighbour

LA **voiture** *noun*
(a) car
(b) carriage

LA **voix** *noun*
(a) voice; **parler à voix basse** to whisper; **à voix haute** aloud
(b) vote

LE **vol** *noun*
(a) flight; **c'est un vol direct** it's a direct flight; **c'est à dix kilomètres à vol d'oiseau** it's ten kilometres away as the crow flies; **attraper quelque chose au vol** to catch something in mid-air
(b) theft; **un vol à main armée** an armed robbery

LA **volaille** *noun* **de la volaille** poultry

volant¹, volante *adjective* flying; **une soucoupe volante** a flying saucer

LE **volant²** *noun*
(a) steering wheel
(b) shuttlecock *(in badminton)*

LE **volcan** *noun* volcano

voler *verb*
(a) to fly
(b) to steal; **je me suis fait voler mon portefeuille** I've had my wallet stolen
(c) to rob *(a person)*; **ils volent les touristes** they rob tourists

LE **volet** *noun* shutter *(of a window)*

LE **voleur,** LA **voleuse** *noun* thief; **au voleur!** stop thief!

volontaire
1 *adjective* deliberate
2 *noun* **un/une volontaire** a volunteer

LA **volonté** *noun*
(a) willpower; **il a beaucoup de volonté** he has lots of willpower
(b) **bonne volonté** goodwill; **elle est pleine de bonne volonté** she's full of goodwill

volontiers *adverb*
(a) gladly; **j'irais volontiers avec lui** I'd gladly go with him

(**b**) with pleasure; **vous prendrez du café? – volontiers!** would you like some coffee? – I'd love some!

vomir *verb* to be sick, to vomit; **j'ai envie de vomir** I feel sick

vont *see* **aller**
elles **vont à l'école** they're going to school; **ils vont y réfléchir** they're going to think about it

Vont is a form of the verb *aller* in the present tense. See verb table p. 312.

vos *adjective* your; **n'oubliez pas vos gants** don't forget your gloves; **Madame, vous avez fait tomber vos clés** excuse me, you've dropped your keys

Vos is used in front of plural nouns. It is the plural of *votre*. See also **votre**.

voter *verb* to vote

votre *adjective* your; **votre professeur** your teacher; **votre école** your school; **Madame, vous oubliez votre sac!** excuse me, you've left your bag!

vôtre *pronoun* yours; **le vôtre, la vôtre, les vôtres** yours; **c'est le vôtre** it's yours; **mes enfants et les vôtres** my children and yours; **j'ai pris mon parapluie, vous avez pris le vôtre?** I've got my umbrella, did you take yours?

In French, possessive pronouns have the same gender and the same number as the nouns they stand for, eg the corresponding pronoun for *vos enfants* is *les vôtres* because the word *enfants* is plural.

voudra, voudras, voudrais *see* **vouloir**
(**a**) **je ne sais pas s'il voudra venir** I don't know if he'll want to come; **je sais que tu ne voudras pas venir avec moi** I know you won't want to come with me
(**b**) **je voudrais un verre d'eau** I would like a glass of water

Voudra and *voudras* are forms of the verb *vouloir* in the future tense. *Vou-*

drais is a form of the verb *vouloir* in the conditional. See verb table p. 319.

vouloir *verb*
(**a**) to want; **je veux rentrer à la maison** I want to go home; **je veux qu'elle vienne** I want her to come; **comme tu veux** as you wish
(**b**) **je voudrais** I would like; **je voudrais un café** I'd like a coffee; **elle voudrait vous voir** she'd like to see you
(**c**) **je veux bien** I don't mind; **je veux bien attendre** I don't mind waiting; **elle veut bien qu'on aille au théâtre** she doesn't mind going to the theatre
(**d**) **vouloir dire** to mean; **que veut dire ce mot?** what does this word mean?
(**e**) **je lui en veux de m'avoir menti** I'm angry with him for lying to me
(**f**) **veuillez entrer!** please come in!

See verb table p. 319.

voulu, voulue *adjective* deliberate; **ce n'est pas un hasard, c'est voulu** it wasn't an accident, it was deliberate

Voulu(e) is the past participle of the verb *vouloir*.

vous *pronoun*
(**a**) you; **vous êtes gentil** you're kind; **vous êtes nombreux** there are many of you
(**b**) you, to you; **il vous connaît** he knows you; **elle vous en a parlé** she spoke to you about it; **c'est pour vous** it's for you; **un ami à vous** a friend of yours; **ces livres ne sont pas à vous** these books aren't yours
(**c**) yourself; **vous êtes content de vous, Monsieur?** are you pleased with yourself?
(**d**) yourselves; **vous ne pensez qu'à vous** you only think about yourselves
(**e**) each other, to each other; **est-ce que vous vous connaissez?** do you know each other?; **est-ce que vous vous parlez?** do you speak to each other?
(**f**) **asseyez-vous** sit down; **arrêtez de**

vous battre! stop fighting!; **est-ce que vous vous rasez souvent?** do you shave often?; **allez-vous en!** go away!

Vous is used when speaking to more than one person, whether or not you know them well. It can also be the polite form of *tu*, in which case it refers to only one person: someone you do not know very well or somebody to whom you want to show more respect. In both cases, the translation will be *you*. See also **tu¹**.

As shown in (f), note that there are many cases when *vous* is simply not translated in English, as in *vous vous souvenez* (you remember), *vous vous rasez* (you shave) and *vous vous levez* (you get up).

vous-même *pronoun* yourself; **Monsieur, faites-le vous-même!** do it yourself!

vous-mêmes *pronoun* yourselves; **vous pouvez le faire vous-mêmes, vous êtes assez nombreux** you can do it yourselves, there are enough of you

vouvoyer *verb* to call somebody "vous"

See also note at **vous**.

LE voyage *noun* trip, journey; **il est en voyage** he's away on a trip; **bon voyage!** have a good trip!; **un voyage d'affaires** a business trip; **un voyage de noces** a honeymoon; **un voyage organisé** a package tour

voyager *verb* to travel

LE voyageur, LA voyageuse *noun*
(a) passenger
(b) traveller

LA voyelle *noun* vowel

voyez, voyons *see* **voir**
vous voyez le bâtiment, là-bas? can

you see the building over there?; **nous nous voyons toutes les semaines** we see each other every week

Voyez and *voyons* are forms of the verb *voir* in the present tense. See verb table p. 324.

LE voyou *noun* thug

vrai, vraie *adjective*
(a) true; **une histoire vraie** a true story
(b) real; **ce n'est pas son vrai nom** it isn't his real name

vraiment *adverb* really

vraisemblable *adjective*
(a) likely
(b) believable; **son excuse n'est pas vraisemblable du tout** his excuse isn't remotely believable

LE VTT *noun* mountain bike

VTT is the abbreviation of *vélo tout-terrain*. It does not change in the plural.

vu¹, vue *see* **voir**
(a) **je n'ai rien vu** I didn't see anything; **je cherche ma sœur, tu ne l'a pas vue?** I'm looking for my sister, have you seen her?
(b) **Catherine est bien vue par le prof** Catherine is well thought of by the teacher; **n'arrive pas en retard sinon tu vas te faire mal voir** don't be late or you won't make a good impression

Vu(e) is the past participle of the verb *voir*. See verb table p. 324.

LA vue² *noun*
(a) eyesight; **elle a une très bonne vue** she has very good eyesight
(b) view; **il y a une belle vue d'ici** there's a nice view from here
(c) **à vue d'œil** before one's eyes; **le niveau de la rivière monte à vue d'œil** the river is rising before our eyes

vulgaire *adjective* vulgar

W Y Z

LE **wagon** *noun* carriage

> The *w* of *wagon* is pronounced as a *v* in French.

LE **wagon-lit** *noun* sleeper, sleeping-car

> The plural of *wagon-lit* is *wagons-lits*. The *w* of *wagon* is pronounced as a *v* in French.

LE **wagon-restaurant** *noun* buffet car

> The plural of *wagon-restaurant* is *wagons-restaurants*. The *w* of *wagon* is pronounced as a *v* in French.

LES **W.-C.** *masculine plural noun* toilet

> *W.-C.* is pronounced "véssé" in French.

y *pronoun*
(**a**) there; **tu y es déjà allé?** have you ever been there?
(**b**) it; **j'y pense** I'm thinking about it; **je m'y attendais** I was expecting it; **ça y est!** that's it!
(**c**) **il y a** there is; *(in plural)* there are; **il y a un problème** there's a problem; **il y a vingt enfants** there are twenty children
(**d**) **il y a** *(indicating time)* ago; **il y a trois ans** three years ago; **il y a une heure qu'il travaille** he's been working for an hour

LE **yaourt** *noun* yoghurt

LES **yeux** *masculine plural noun* eyes; **elle a de beaux yeux** she has beautiful eyes

> *Yeux* is the plural of *œil*.

LE **zèbre** *noun* zebra

zéro *number* zero; **ils ont gagné deux-zéro** they won two-nil

LA **zone** *noun* area; **une zone industrielle** an industrial estate

zut *exclamation* oh no; **zut! j'ai oublié mes clés!** oh no, I've forgotten my keys!

French Verb Tables

Tenses	304
Regular Verbs	306
Spelling Changes in -er Verbs	310
Irregular Verbs	311

The following pages present tables of regular and irregular verbs, divided into the following sections:

- ► Regular -er verbs
- ► Regular -ir verbs
- ► Regular -re verbs
- ► Reflexive verbs
- ► Some common irregular verbs
- ► Other irregular verbs

Tenses

The tables on the following pages show you how to form six different tenses:

THE PRESENT TENSE

Je joue   I play/I am playing

The present tense tells us about something that is happening now or usually happens. (There are two forms in English but only one in French.)

To form the present tense of regular verbs, take the stem of the infinitive and add the endings. The stem is the infinitive minus the last two letters.

- donn**er**   donn**e**, donn**es**, donn**e**, donn**ons**, donn**ez**, donn**ent**
- fin**ir**   fin**is**, fin**is**, fin**it**, fin**issons**, fin**issez**, fin**issent**
- répond**re**   répond**s**, répond**s**, répond, répond**ons**, répond**ez**, répond**ent**

THE PERFECT TENSE

J'ai joué   I have played/I played
Je suis allé(e)   I have gone/I went

The perfect tense tells us about something that has happened or happened once in the past, ie a completed action.

The perfect tense of regular verbs is formed with the present tense of an auxiliary verb (**avoir** or **être**) and the past participle. To form the past participle of regular verbs, take off the last two letters to find the stem of the verb and add the appropriate ending:

- ► -er verbs: stem   + **é**   eg jouer   joué
- ► -ir verbs: stem   + **i**   eg finir   fini
- ► -re verbs: stem   + **u**   eg répondre   répondu

Most verbs form the perfect tense with **avoir**. There are a few irregular verbs which form the perfect tense with **être** (aller, venir, arriver, partir, entrer, sortir, monter, descendre, naître, mourir, rester, tomber, retourner).

THE IMPERFECT TENSE

Je jouais   I was playing / I used to play

The imperfect tense tells us about something that used to happen, happened for a long time or was happening, ie a regular, long-term or interrupted action.

To form the imperfect tense of regular verbs, take the stem of the infinitive and add the endings (-**ais**, -**ais**, -**ait**, -**ions**, -**iez**, -**aient**).

THE FUTURE TENSE

Je donnerai   I will give   Je prendrai   I will take

The future tense tells us about something that will happen in the future. To form the future tense of regular verbs, take the whole of the infinitive for -er and -ir verbs, and the infinitive minus the final **e** for -re verbs, and add the endings (-**ai**, -**as**, -**a**, -**ons**, -**ez**, -**ont**).

(The near future is used to talk about things that will happen soon. To form the near future you use the present tense of the verb **aller** plus the infinitive, eg Je vais aller au cinéma.)

THE CONDITIONAL

J'aimerais   I would like   Je prendrais   I would take

The conditional tells us about something that would happen. To form the conditional, take the whole of the infinitive for -er and -ir verbs, and the infinitive minus the final **e** for -re verbs, and add the endings (-**ais**, -**ais**, -**ait**, -**ions**, -**iez**, -**aient**).

THE PRESENT SUBJUNCTIVE

Je joue   I play

The subjunctive is used after certain expressions. These are indicated in the dictionary.

To form the present subjunctive of regular verbs, take the first person plural of the present tense, take off the -**ons** and add the endings (-**e**, -**es**, -**e**, -**ions**, -**iez**, -**ent**).

donner to give

Present
je donne
tu donnes
il donne
nous donnons
vous donnez
ils donnent

Perfect
j'ai donné
tu as donné
il a donné
nous avons donné
vous avez donné
ils ont donné

Imperfect
je donnais
tu donnais
il donnait
nous donnions
vous donniez
ils donnaient

Future
je donnerai
tu donneras
il donnera
nous donnerons
vous donnerez
ils donneront

Conditional
je donnerais
tu donnerais
il donnerait
nous donnerions
vous donneriez
ils donneraient

**Present
Subjunctive**
je donne
tu donnes
il donne
nous donnions
vous donniez
ils donnent

Imperative
donne
donnons
donnez

Present Participle
donnant

Past Participle
donné/donnée

finir to finish

Present	**Perfect**	**Imperfect**
je fin**is**	j'ai fini	je finiss**ais**
tu fin**is**	tu as fini	tu finiss**ais**
il fin**it**	il a fini	il finiss**ait**
nous fin**issons**	nous avons fini	nous finiss**ions**
vous fin**issez**	vous avez fini	vous finiss**iez**
ils fin**issent**	ils ont fini	ils finiss**aient**

Future	**Conditional**	**Present Subjunctive**
je finir**ai**	je finir**ais**	je finiss**e**
tu finir**as**	tu finir**ais**	tu finiss**es**
il finir**a**	il finir**ait**	il finiss**e**
nous finir**ons**	nous finir**ions**	nous finiss**ions**
vous finir**ez**	vous finir**iez**	vous finiss**iez**
ils finir**ont**	ils finir**aient**	ils finiss**ent**

Imperative
finis
finissons
finissez

Present Participle	**Past Participle**
finissant	fini / finie

vendre to sell

Present
je vend**s**
tu vend**s**
il vend
nous vend**ons**
vous vend**ez**
ils vend**ent**

Perfect
j'ai vendu
tu as vendu
il a vendu
nous avons vendu
vous avez vendu
ils ont vendu

Imperfect
je vend**ais**
tu vend**ais**
il vend**ait**
nous vend**ions**
vous vend**iez**
ils vend**aient**

Future
je vendr**ai**
tu vendr**as**
il vendr**a**
nous vendr**ons**
vous vendr**ez**
ils vendr**ont**

Conditional
je vendr**ais**
tu vendr**ais**
il vendr**ait**
nous vendr**ions**
vous vendr**iez**
ils vendr**aient**

Present Subjunctive
je vend**e**
tu vend**es**
il vend**e**
nous vend**ions**
vous vend**iez**
ils vend**ent**

Imperative
vends
vendons
vendez

Present Participle
vendant

Past Participle
vendu / vendue

se lever to get up

Present	**Perfect**	**Imperfect**
je me lève	je me suis levé	je me levais
tu te lèves	tu t'es levé	tu te levais
il se lève	il/elle s'est levé(e)	il se levait
nous nous levons	nous nous sommes levés	nous nous levions
vous vous levez	vous vous êtes levé(s)	vous vous leviez
ils se lèvent	ils/elles se sont levé(e)s	ils se levaient

Future	**Conditional**	**Present Subjunctive**
je me lèverai	je me lèverais	je me lève
tu te lèveras	tu te lèverais	tu te lèves
il se lèvera	il se lèverait	il se lève
nous nous lèverons	nous nous lèverions	nous nous levions
vous vous lèverez	vous vous lèveriez	vous vous leviez
ils se lèveront	ils se lèveraient	ils se lèvent

Imperative
lève-toi
levons-nous
levez-vous

Present Participle
se levant

Past Participle
levé/levée

Spelling Changes in -er Verbs

Verbs ending in **-ger** (eg **manger**) take an extra **e** before **a** or **o**: *Present* je mange, nous mangeons; *Imperfect* je mangeais, nous mangions; *Present participle* mangeant.

Verbs ending in **-cer** (eg **commencer**) change **c** to **ç** before **a** or **o**: *Present* je commence, nous commençons; *Imperfect* je commençais, nous commencions; *Present participle* commençant.

Verbs in **e** + consonant + **er** fall into two groups. In the first (eg **mener, peser, lever**), **e** becomes **è** before a silent **e** (in other words before the endings **-e, -es, -ent** in the present and subjunctive, and in the future and conditional tenses, eg **je mène, ils mèneront**).

The second group contains most verbs ending in **-eler** and **-eter** (eg **appeler, jeter**). These verbs change **l** to **ll** and **t** to **tt** before silent **e** (eg **j'appelle, ils appelleront; je jette, ils jetteront**). However, the verbs **geler, dégeler** and **acheter** fall into the above-mentioned first group.

Verbs containing **é** in their second from last syllable change **é** to **è** before the endings **-e, -es, -ent** in the present and subjunctive only (eg **je cède** but **je céderai**).

Verbs ending in **-yer** (eg **essuyer**) change **y** to **i** before silent **e** in the present and subjunctive, and in the future and conditional tenses (eg **j'essuie, ils essuieront**). However, in verbs ending in **-ayer** (eg **balayer**), this change is optional (eg **je balaie** or **balaye, ils balaieront** or **balayeront**).

Irregular Verbs

Many verbs in French are irregular. In the French-English side of the dictionary, notes in blue boxes tell you where to find out how these verbs are conjugated.

In the following pages we show eight of the most common French irregular verbs with all their forms (**aller**, **avoir**, **devoir**, **dire**, **être**, **faire**, **pouvoir**, **vouloir**). Other irregular verbs are then listed in a table which gives the **je**, **il** and **nous** forms, from which all their other forms can be derived. Verbs following a similar pattern are grouped together in this table, eg **abattre**, **combattre** are shown under **battre**.

aller to go

Present
je vais
tu vas
il va
nous allons
vous allez
ils vont

Perfect
je suis allé
tu es allé
il/elle est allé(e)
nous sommes allés
vous êtes allé(s)
ils/elles sont allé(e)s

Imperfect
j'allais
tu allais
il allait
nous allions
vous alliez
ils allaient

Future
j'irai
tu iras
il ira
nous irons
vous irez
ils iront

Conditional
j'irais
tu irais
il irait
nous irions
vous iriez
ils iraient

Present Subjunctive
j'aille
tu ailles
il aille
nous allions
vous alliez
ils aillent

Imperative
va (Note the exception: *vas-y*)
allons
allez

Present Participle
allant

Past Participle
allé/allée

Present

j'ai
tu as
il a
nous avons
vous avez
ils ont

Perfect

j'ai eu
tu as eu
il a eu
nous avons eu
vous avez eu
ils ont eu

Imperfect

j'avais
tu avais
il avait
nous avions
vous aviez
ils avaient

Future

j'aurai
tu auras
il aura
nous aurons
vous aurez
ils auront

Conditional

j'aurais
tu aurais
il aurait
nous aurions
vous auriez
ils auraient

Present Subjunctive

j'aie
tu aies
il ait
nous ayons
vous ayez
ils aient

Imperative

aie
ayons
ayez

Present Participle

ayant

Past Participle

eu/eue

devoir to have to, must

Present
je dois
tu dois
il doit
nous devons
vous devez
ils doivent

Perfect
j'ai dû
tu as dû
il a dû
nous avons dû
vous avez dû
ils ont dû

Imperfect
je devais
tu devais
il devait
nous devions
vous deviez
ils devaient

Future

je devrai
tu devras
il devra
nous devrons
vous devrez
ils devront

Conditional

je devrais
tu devrais
il devrait
nous devrions
vous devriez
ils devraient

**Present
Subjunctive**
je doive
tu doives
il doive
nous devions
vous deviez
ils doivent

Imperative
not used

Present Participle
devant

Past Participle
dû, due
(*plural* dus, dues)

dire to say

Present	**Perfect**	**Imperfect**
je dis	j'ai dit	je disais
tu dis	tu as dit	tu disais
il dit	il a dit	il disait
nous disons	nous avons dit	nous disions
vous dites	vous avez dit	vous disiez
ils disent	ils ont dit	ils disaient

Future	**Conditional**	**Present Subjunctive**
je dirai	je dirais	je dise
tu diras	tu dirais	tu dises
il dira	il dirait	il dise
nous dirons	nous dirions	nous disions
vous direz	vous diriez	vous disiez
ils diront	ils diraient	ils disent

Imperative
dis
disons
dites

Present Participle
disant

Past Participle
dit/dite

315

être to be

Present
je suis
tu es
il est
nous sommes
vous êtes
ils sont

Perfect
j'ai été
tu as été
il a été
nous avons été
vous avez été
ils ont été

Imperfect
j'étais
tu étais
il était
nous étions
vous étiez
ils étaient

Future

je serai
tu seras
il sera
nous serons
vous serez
ils seront

Conditional

je serais
tu serais
il serait
nous serions
vous seriez
ils seraient

Present Subjunctive
je sois
tu sois
il soit
nous soyons
vous soyez
ils soient

Imperative
sois
soyons
soyez

Present Participle
étant

Past Participle
été

faire to do, to make

défaire
refaire
satisfaire

Present
je fais
tu fais
il fait
nous faisons
vous faites
ils font

Perfect
j'ai fait
tu as fait
il a fait
nous avons fait
vous avez fait
ils ont fait

Imperfect
je faisais
tu faisais
il faisait
nous faisions
vous faisiez
ils faisaient

Future
je ferai
tu feras
il fera
nous ferons
vous ferez
ils feront

Conditional
je ferais
tu ferais
il ferait
nous ferions
vous feriez
ils feraient

Present Subjunctive
je fasse
tu fasses
il fasse
nous fassions
vous fassiez
ils fassent

Imperative
fais
faisons
faites

Present Participle
faisant

Past Participle
fait / faite

pouvoir to be able, can

Present
je peux
tu peux
il peut
nous pouvons
vous pouvez
ils peuvent

Perfect
j'ai pu
tu as pu
il a pu
nous avons pu
vous avez pu
ils ont pu

Imperfect
je pouvais
tu pouvais
il pouvait
nous pouvions
vous pouviez
ils pouvaient

Future

je pourrai
tu pourras
il pourra
nous pourrons
vous pourrez
ils pourront

Conditional

je pourrais
tu pourrais
il pourrait
nous pourrions
vous pourriez
ils pourraient

Present Subjunctive

je puisse
tu puisses
il puisse
nous puissions
vous puissiez
ils puissent

Imperative
not used

Present Participle
pouvant

Past Participle
pu

vouloir to want

Present

je veux
tu veux
il veut
nous voulons
vous voulez
ils veulent

Perfect

j'ai voulu
tu as voulu
il a voulu
nous avons voulu
vous avez voulu
ils ont voulu

Imperfect

je voulais
tu voulais
il voulait
nous voulions
vous vouliez
ils voulaient

Future

je voudrai
tu voudras
il voudra
nous voudrons
vous voudrez
ils voudront

Conditional

je voudrais
tu voudrais
il voudrait
nous voudrions
vous voudriez
ils voudraient

Present Subjunctive

je veuille
tu veuilles
il veuille
nous voulions
vous vouliez
ils veuillent

Imperative

veux / veuille
voulons / veuillons
voulez / veuillez

Present Participle

voulant

Past Participle

voulu / voulue

Infinitive	Present	Perfect	Imperfect
s'asseoir	je m'assieds il s'assied nous nous asseyons	je me suis assis	je m'asseyais
atteindre *déteindre, éteindre,* *peindre, teindre*	j'atteins il atteint nous atteignons	j'ai atteint	j'atteignais
battre *abattre, combattre,* *se débattre*	je bats il bat nous battons	j'ai battu	je battais
boire	je bois il boit nous buvons	j'ai bu	je buvais
bouillir	je bous il bout nous bouillons	j'ai bouilli	je bouillais
conclure *exclure, inclure*	je conclus il conclut nous concluons	j'ai conclu	je concluais
conduire *construire, déduire,* *détruire, introduire,* *produire, réduire,* *reproduire, traduire*	je conduis il conduit nous conduisons	j'ai conduit	je conduisais
connaître *apparaître,* *disparaître, paraître,* *reconnaître*	je connais il connaît nous connaissons	j'ai connu	je connaissais
coudre	je couds il coud nous cousons	j'ai cousu	je cousais
courir *parcourir*	je cours il court nous courons	j'ai couru	je courais
couvrir *découvrir, offrir,* *ouvrir, recouvrir,* *souffrir*	je couvre il couvre nous couvrons	j'ai couvert	je couvrais
craindre *plaindre*	je crains il craint nous craignons	j'ai craint	je craignais
croire	je crois il croit nous croyons	j'ai cru	je croyais
cueillir *accueillir*	je cueille il cueille nous cueillons	j'ai cueilli	je cueillais
cuire *nuire*	je cuis il cuit nous cuisons	j'ai cuit	je cuisais
dormir *endormir*	je dors il dort nous dormons	j'ai dormi	je dormais

Future	Conditional	Present Subjunctive	Present Participle	Past Participle
je m'assiérai	je m'assiérais	je m'asseye	asseyant	assis/assise
j'atteindrai	j'atteindrais	j'atteigne	atteignant	atteint/atteinte
je battrai	je battrais	je batte	battant	battu/battue
je boirai	je boirais	je boive	buvant	bu/bue
je bouillirai	je bouillirais	je bouille	bouillant	bouilli/bouillie
je conclurai	je conclurais	je conclue	concluant	conclu/conclue
je conduirai	je conduirais	je conduise	conduisant	conduit/conduite
je connaîtrai	je connaîtrais	je connaisse	connaissant	connu/connue
je coudrai	je coudrais	je couse	cousant	cousu/cousue
je courrai	je courrais	je coure	courant	couru/courue
je couvrirai	je couvrirais	je couvre	couvrant	couvert/couverte
je craindrai	je craindrais	je craigne	craignant	craint/crainte
je croirai	je croirais	je croie	croyant	cru/crue
je cueillerai	je cueillerais	je cueille	cueillant	cueilli/cueillie
je cuirai	je cuirais	je cuise	cuisant	cui/cuite
je dormirai	je dormirais	je dorme	dormant	dormi

Infinitive	Present	Perfect	Imperfect
écrire *décrire, inscrire*	j'écris il écrit nous écrivons	j'ai écrit	j'écrivais
envoyer *renvoyer*	j'envoie il envoie nous envoyons	j'ai envoyé	j'envoyais
faillir		j'ai failli	je faillissais
falloir	il faut	il a fallu	il fallait
fuir *s'enfuir*	je fuis il fuit nous fuyons	j'ai fui	je fuyais
haïr	je hais il hait nous haïssons	j'ai haï	je haïssais
interdire	j'interdis il interdit nous interdisons vous interdisez	j'ai interdit	j'interdisais
lire *élire, relire*	je lis il lit nous lisons	j'ai lu	je lisais
mentir *consentir, ressentir,* *sentir*	je mens il ment nous mentons	j'ai menti	je mentais
mettre *admettre, commettre* *permettre, promettre,* *remettre, transmettre*	je mets il met nous mettons	j'ai mis	je mettais
moudre	je mouds il moud nous moulons	j'ai moulu	je moulais
mourir	je meurs il meurt nous mourons	je suis mort	je mourais
naître	je nais il naît nous naissons	je suis né	je naissais
partir *repartir*	je pars il part nous partons	je suis parti	je partais
plaire *déplaire*	je plais il plaît nous plaisons	j'ai plu	je plaisais
pleuvoir	il pleut	il a plu	il pleuvait
prendre *apprendre,* *comprendre, reprendre,* *surprendre*	je prends il prend nous prenons	j'ai pris	je prenais
recevoir *apercevoir, décevoir*	je reçois il reçoit nous recevons	j'ai reçu	je recevais

Future	Conditional	Present Subjunctive	Present Participle	Past Participle
j'écrirai	j'écrirais	j'écrive	écrivant	écrit/écrite
j'enverrai	j'enverrais	j'envoie	envoyant	envoyé/envoyée
je faillirai	je faillirais	je faillisse	faillissant	failli
il faudra	il faudrait	il faille		fallu
je fuirai	je fuirais	je fuie	fuyant	fui/fuie
je haïrai	je haïrais	je haïsse	haïssant	haï/haïe
j'interdirai	j'interdirais	j'interdise	interdisant	interdit/interdite
je lirai	je lirais	je lise	lisant	lu/lue
je mentirai	je mentirais	je mente	mentant	menti
je mettrai	je mettrais	je mette	mettant	mis/mise
je moudrai	je moudrais	je moule	moulant	moulu/moulue
je mourrai	je mourrais	je meure	mourant	mort/morte
je naîtrai	je naîtrais	je naisse	naissant	né/née
je partirai	je partirais	je parte	partant	parti/partie
je plairai	je plairais	je plaise	plaisant	plu
il pleuvra	il pleuvrait	il pleuve	pleuvant	plu
je prendrai	je prendrais	je prenne	prenant	pris/prise
je recevrai	je recevrais	je reçoive	recevant	reçu/reçue

Infinitive	Present	Perfect	Imperfect
rejoindre *joindre*	je rejoins il rejoint nous rejoignons	j'ai rejoint	je rejoignais
résoudre	je résous il résout nous résolvons	j'ai résolu	je résolvais
rire *frire, sourire*	je ris il rit nous rions	j'ai ri	je riais
rompre *interrompre*	je romps il rompt nous rompons	j'ai rompu	je rompais
savoir	je sais il sait nous savons	j'ai su	je savais
servir	je sers il sert nous servons	j'ai servi	je servais
sortir	je sors il sort nous sortons	je suis sorti	je sortais
suffire	je suffis il suffit nous suffisons	j'ai suffi	je suffisais
suivre *poursuivre*	je suis il suit nous suivons	j'ai suivi	je suivais
se taire	je me tais il se tait nous nous taisons	je me suis tu	je me taisais
tenir *appartenir, contenir, entretenir, maintenir, obtenir, retenir, soutenir*	je tiens il tient nous tenons	j'ai tenu	je tenais
vaincre *convaincre*	je vaincs il vainc nous vainquons	j'ai vaincu	je vainquais
valoir	je vaux il vaut nous valons	j'ai valu	je valais
venir *convenir, devenir, intervenir, prévenir, provenir, revenir, se souvenir*	je viens il vient nous venons	je suis venu	je venais
vivre *survivre*	je vis il vit nous vivons	j'ai vécu	je vivais
voir *prévoir, revoir*	je vois il voit nous voyons	j'ai vu	je voyais

Future	Conditional	Present Subjunctive	Present Participle	Past Participle
je rejoindrai	je rejoindrais	je rejoigne	rejoignant	rejoint/rejointe
je résoudrai	je résoudrais	je résolve	résolvant	résolu/résolue
je rirai	je rirais	je rie	riant	ri
je romprai	je romprais	je rompe	rompant	rompu/rompue
je saurai	je saurais	je sache	sachant	su/sue
je servirai	je servirais	je serve	servant	servi/servie
je sortirai	je sortirais	je sorte	sortant	sorti/sortie
je suffirai	je suffirais	je suffise	suffisant	suffi
je suivrai	je suivrais	je suive	suivant	suivi/suivie
je me tairai	je me tairais	je me taise	taisant	tu/tue
je tiendrai	je tiendrais	je tienne	tenant	tenu/tenue
je vaincrai	je vaincrais	je vainque	vainquant	vaincu/vaincue
je vaudrai	je vaudrais	je vaille	valant	valu
je viendrai	je viendrais	je vienne	venant	venu/venue
je vivrai	je vivrais	je vive	vivant	vécu/vécue
je verrai	je verrais	je voie	voyant	vu/vue

English-French

a, an *article*
(a) un/une; **I have a brother** j'ai un frère; **I have a sister** j'ai une sœur

Un is used with masculine nouns and *une* is used with feminine nouns.

(b) *(with jobs or situations)* **he's a doctor** il est médecin; **she's a widow** elle est veuve

Note that when describing people's jobs or situations, French does not use an article (*un* or *une*).

(c) *(with parts of the body)* le/la; **he has a red nose** il a le nez rouge; **I have a sore throat** j'ai mal à la gorge

Le is used with masculine nouns and *la* is used with feminine nouns. *Le* and *la* become *l'* before a vowel or mute h.

(d) *(with prices, weights and speeds)* le/la; **30 pence a kilo** 30 pence le kilo; **one pound a dozen** une livre la douzaine; **20 pence a hundred grammes** 20 pence les cent grammes; **50 kilometres an hour** 50 kilomètres à l'heure

Les is the plural of *le* and *la*.

(e) *(with numbers of times, amounts)* par; **twice a month** deux fois par mois; **she earns £250 a week** elle gagne 250 livres par semaine

abandon *verb* abandonner

abbreviation *noun* une abréviation; **Dr is the abbreviation for "doctor"** Dr est l'abréviation de "docteur"

ability *noun* la capacité

able *adjective* **to be able to do some-**thing pouvoir faire quelque chose; **I won't be able to come** je ne pourrai pas venir

abortion *noun* un avortement; **to have an abortion** se faire avorter

about
1 *preposition*
(a) *(on the subject of)* sur; **it's a programme about animals** c'est une émission sur les animaux; **what's the film about?** de quoi parle le film?; **I'm worried about you** je m'inquiète pour toi; **to talk about something** parler de quelque chose; **we talked about school** nous avons parlé de l'école; **I don't want to talk about it** je ne veux pas en parler
(b) *(all around)* dans; **they run about the streets** ils courent dans les rues; **we walked about the town** nous nous sommes promenés dans la ville
2 *adverb*
(a) *(more or less)* environ; **there are about twenty children in the class** il y a environ vingt élèves dans la classe
(b) *(in the area)* **is Jack about?** est-ce que Jack est dans le coin?; **there was nobody about** il n'y avait personne
(c) *(all over the place)* partout; **the children like to run about** les enfants aiment bien courir partout; **he leaves his things lying about** il laisse traîner ses affaires partout
(d) *(on the point of)* sur le point de; **I was about to phone you** j'étais sur le point de t'appeler

above
1 *preposition*
(a) *(higher than)* au-dessus de; **birds**

were flying above my head des oiseaux volaient au-dessus de ma tête;
the water reached above their knees
l'eau leur montait jusqu'au-dessus des
genoux
(**b**) *(a higher number than)* plus de; **he
earns above £20,000 a year** il gagne
plus de 20 000 livres par an; **the temperature didn't rise above 10°C** la
température n'a pas dépassé 10°C
(**c**) **above all** surtout; **above all, don't
talk to any strangers** ne parle surtout
pas aux inconnus
2 *adverb*
(**a**) *(in a higher place)* **the tenants of
the flat above** les locataires du dessus; **in the example above** dans
l'exemple ci-dessus
(**b**) *(a higher number)* plus; **I want to
sell my bike for £50 or above** je veux
vendre mon vélo 50 livres ou plus

abroad *adverb* à l'étranger; **are you
going abroad this summer?** est-ce
que vous allez à l'étranger cet été?

absence *noun* l'absence *(feminine)*

absent *adjective* absent/absente; **he
was absent from school yesterday** il
était absent de l'école hier

absent-minded *adjective* distrait/
distraite

absolutely *adverb*
(**a**) *(completely)* tout à fait; **you're absolutely right** vous avez tout à fait raison
(**b**) *(used for emphasis)* vraiment; **she's
absolutely adorable!** elle est vraiment adorable!
(**c**) **absolutely not!** absolument pas!

abuse
1 *noun*
(**a**) *(cruelty)* les mauvais traitements
(masculine plural); **this is a case of
child abuse** cet enfant subit des mauvais traitements
(**b**) *(insults)* les injures *(feminine plural)*
2 *verb*
(**a**) *(treat cruelly)* maltraiter

(**b**) *(insult)* injurier

Note that the French verb *abuser* is
never a translation for the English
verb *to abuse*. It means *to take advantage.*

accelerate *verb* accélérer

accelerator *noun* un accélérateur

accent *noun*
(**a**) *(when speaking)* un accent; **he has
a northern accent** il a l'accent du
nord; **she speaks French with no accent** elle parle français sans aucun accent
(**b**) *(on a letter)* un accent

accept *verb*
(**a**) *(a gift, an offer, an apology)* accepter; **it's a beautiful ring, but I can't accept it** c'est une très belle bague, mais
je ne peux pas l'accepter
(**b**) *(admit)* reconnaître; **I accept that
it must be difficult for you** je reconnais que cela doit être difficile pour
vous
(**c**) *(into a school, a university)* admettre; **he's been accepted to study medicine** il a été admis en médecine

acceptable *adjective* acceptable; **this
kind of behaviour is not acceptable**
ce genre de comportement est inac-
ceptable

accident *noun*
(**a**) un accident; **she had an accident**
elle a eu un accident; **sorry, it was an
accident!** je suis désolé, je ne l'ai pas
fait exprès!
(**b**) **by accident** *(without meaning to)*
sans le faire exprès; *(by chance)* par
hasard; **I broke the window by accident** j'ai brisé la fenêtre sans le faire exprès; **we met by accident** nous nous
sommes rencontrés par hasard

accidentally *adverb (without meaning to)* sans le faire exprès; **I accidentally deleted the file** j'ai effacé le fichier sans le faire exprès

accommodation *noun* le logement;
it's hard to find accommodation in

this city il est difficile de trouver un logement dans cette ville

accompany *verb* accompagner; **she was accompanied by her brother** elle était accompagnée de son frère

according to *preposition*
(a) *(in somebody else's opinion)* selon, d'après; **according to him, French is easy** selon lui, le français c'est facile
(b) *(following)* selon, suivant; **we must play according to the rules** il faut jouer selon les règles; **everything went according to plan** tout s'est passé comme prévu

accordion *noun* un accordéon; **my dad plays the accordion** mon père joue de l'accordéon

> Note that when talking about playing musical instruments, French uses the expression *jouer de*.

account *noun*
(a) *(at a bank)* le compte; **I opened an account** j'ai ouvert un compte
(b) **on account of** à cause de; **the road was closed on account of the accident** la route était barrée à cause de l'accident
(c) **to take something into account** tenir compte de quelque chose *or* prendre quelque chose en compte

accountant *noun* le/la comptable; **my uncle is an accountant** mon oncle est comptable

> Note that when describing people's jobs or situations, French does not use an article (*un* or *une*).

accurate *adjective* précis/précise; **he gave a very accurate description of the thief** il a donné un signalement très précis du voleur

accurately *adverb* avec précision

accuse *verb* accuser; **he accused me of stealing his new CD** il m'a accusé d'avoir volé son nouveau CD

ace *noun* *(in cards)* un as; **the ace of hearts** l'as de cœur

ache
1 *noun* la douleur; **I have a stomach ache** j'ai mal au ventre
2 *verb* **my head aches** j'ai mal à la tête; **I ache all over** j'ai mal partout

achieve *verb*
(a) *(a result)* obtenir; **she achieved excellent results in her exams** elle a obtenu d'excellents résultats à ses examens
(b) *(a dream, an ambition)* réaliser; **she has achieved her ambition of becoming a singer** elle a réalisé ses ambitions en devenant chanteuse
(c) *(a goal, a level)* atteindre; **we achieved our objectives** nous avons atteint nos objectifs

> Note that the French verb *achever* is never a translation for the English verb *to achieve*. It means *to complete*.

achievement *noun* un exploit; **convincing her to come was quite an achievement** c'est un véritable exploit d'avoir réussi à la convaincre de venir

> Note that the French word *achèvement* is never a translation for the English word *achievement*. It means *completion*.

acrobat *noun* un/une acrobate

across
1 *preposition*
(a) *(from one side to the other of)* **he walked across the room** il a traversé la pièce; **she ran across the road** elle a traversé la route en courant; **we swam across the lake** nous avons traversé le lac à la nage; **he threw the plate across the room** il a lancé l'assiette à travers la pièce
(b) *(on the other side of)* **he lives across the road** il habite en face; **he sat across the table from me** il s'est assis à table en face de moi
2 *adverb* **to go across** traverser; **to run across** traverser en courant; **to swim across** traverser à la nage

act

1 *noun*

(**a**) *(action)* un acte; **she was caught in the act of taking the money** on l'a surprise en train de voler l'argent

(**b**) *(part of a play)* un acte

(**c**) *(in a circus, a show)* le numéro; **the children enjoyed the juggling act** les enfants ont bien aimé le numéro de jonglage

2 *verb*

(**a**) *(do something)* agir; **we must act now to prevent disaster** il faut agir maintenant pour éviter la catastrophe

(**b**) *(in a play, a film)* jouer; **I acted in the school play** j'ai joué dans la pièce de théâtre de l'école

action *noun*

(**a**) *(act)* une action, un acte; **he's not responsible for his actions** il n'est pas responsable de ses actes; **we need to take action** nous devons prendre des mesures

(**b**) **an action film** un film d'action

active *adjective*

(**a**) *(lively)* **it's important to keep active** il est important de rester actif; **she has a very active imagination** elle a une imagination débordante

(**b**) *(involved)* **he always plays an active part in discussions** il prend toujours une part active aux débats

activity *noun* une activité; **I do lots of after-school activities** j'ai plein d'activités extrascolaires

actor *noun* un acteur; **I want to be an actor** je veux être acteur

Note that when describing people's jobs or situations, French does not use an article (*un* or *une*).

actress *noun* une actrice; **she's an actress** elle est actrice

Note that when describing people's jobs or situations, French does not use an article (*un* or *une*).

actual *adjective*

(**a**) *(real)* réel/réelle; **did they use actual bullets in the film?** est-ce qu'ils ont utilisé des balles réelles dans le film?

(**b**) *(exact)* exact/exacte; **her actual words** ses paroles exactes

(**c**) *(used for emphasis)* **this is the actual dress she wore on stage** c'est cette robe-là qu'elle portait sur scène

Note that the French word *actuel* is never a translation for the English word *actual*. It means *current*.

actually *adverb*

(**a**) *(really)* vraiment; **what did he actually say?** qu'est-ce qu'il a dit exactement?; **did you actually say that?** tu as vraiment dit ça?

(**b**) *(in fact)* en fait; **actually, I will come with you** en fait, je vais venir avec vous

Note that the French word *actuellement* is never a translation for the English word *actually*. It means *currently*.

ad *noun*

(**a**) *(in the media)* la pub; **I'll make a cup of tea while the ads are on** je vais me faire un thé pendant la pub

(**b**) *(private)* une annonce; **there's an ad in the paper for a second-hand computer** il y a une annonce dans le journal pour un ordinateur d'occasion

add

1 *verb*

(**a**) *(something extra)* ajouter; **add her name to the list** ajoute son nom à la liste; **"and don't be late!" he added** "et sois à l'heure!" ajouta-t-il

(**b**) *(numbers)* additionner; **add seven and twelve** additionnez sept et douze

2 add up additionner; **make sure you add the numbers up correctly** faites attention à bien additionner les nombres; **they haven't learned to add up yet** ils n'ont pas encore appris à faire les additions

addict *noun* he became a drug addict il est devenu toxicomane; **I'm a coffee addict** je suis accro au café

addicted *adjective* **he's addicted to drugs** il est toxicomane; **I'm addicted to chocolate** je suis accro au chocolat

addition *noun*
(a) une addition; **the children are learning addition** les élèves sont en train d'apprendre à faire les additions; **he's the latest addition to the team** c'est le nouveau venu de l'équipe
(b) **in addition** de plus
(c) **in addition to** en plus de; **in addition to the written exam, there will also be an oral** en plus d'une épreuve écrite, il y aura un oral

address *noun* une adresse; **do you know Claire's address?** est-ce que tu connais l'adresse de Claire?; **my address is 5 Greenwood Lane** j'habite au 5 Greenwood Lane; **an address book** un carnet d'adresses

Do not confuse the spellings of the French *adresse* and English *address.*

adjust *verb*
(a) *(an object)* régler; **she adjusted her seat belt** elle a réglé sa ceinture de sécurité
(b) *(to a situation)* s'adapter; **he adjusted easily to his new school** il s'est facilement adapté à sa nouvelle école

administration *noun* *(in a company)* l'administration *(feminine)*; **she works in the administration department** elle travaille dans le service administratif

admire *verb* admirer

admit *verb*
(a) *(let in)* admettre; **he was admitted to hospital** il a été admis à l'hôpital
(b) *(agree)* reconnaître; **I admit that I was wrong** je reconnais que j'ai eu tort
(c) *(confess)* avouer; **he admitted taking the money** il a avoué avoir pris l'argent

adopt *verb* adopter; **my parents want to adopt a child** mes parents veulent adopter un enfant

adopted *adjective* adopté/adoptée; **David is adopted** David a été adopté; **my adopted son** mon fils adoptif

adult *noun* un/une adulte

advance
1 *noun*
(a) *(progress)* le progrès; **there have been great advances in medicine** il y a eu des progrès importants dans le domaine de la médecine
(b) *(of money)* une avance; **I asked my parents for an advance on my pocket money** j'ai demandé à mes parents une avance sur mon argent de poche
(c) **in advance** à l'avance; **you need to book in advance** il faut réserver à l'avance
2 *verb (make progress)* avancer

advanced *adjective*
(a) *(person)* avancé/avancée; **she's very advanced for her age** elle est vraiment en avance pour son âge
(b) *(course)* **he's taking an advanced French course** il prend des cours de perfectionnement en français

advantage *noun*
(a) un avantage; **what are the advantages of speaking a foreign language?** quels sont les avantages de pouvoir parler une langue étrangère?
(b) *(in tennis)* **advantage Henman** avantage Henman
(c) **to take advantage of** profiter de; **don't offer to help him, he'll only take advantage of you** ne lui propose pas de l'aider sinon il va profiter de toi

adventure *noun*
(a) une aventure; **he told me about his adventures** il m'a raconté ses aventures
(b) **an adventure story** une histoire d'aventure

adverb *noun* un adverbe

advert *noun*
(a) *(in the media)* la pub; **I'll make a**

cup of tea while the adverts are on je vais me faire un thé pendant la pub
(**b**) *(private)* une annonce; **she put an advert in the paper for a babysitter** elle a passé une annonce dans le journal pour trouver une baby-sitter

advertise *verb*
(**a**) *(in the media)* faire de la publicité; **they advertise on the radio** ils font de la publicité à la radio; **that actress advertises make-up** cette actrice fait de la publicité pour du maquillage
(**b**) *(privately)* passer une annonce; **she advertised for a babysitter** elle a passé une annonce pour trouver une baby-sitter

> Note that the French verb *avertir* is never a translation for the English verb *to advertise*. It means *to warn*.

advertisement *noun*
(**a**) *(in the media)* la publicité; **there are too many advertisements on television** il y a trop de publicités à la télévision
(**b**) *(private)* une annonce; **he put an advertisement in the paper** il a passé une annonce dans le journal

> Note that the French word *avertissement* is never a translation for the English word *advertisement*. It means *warning*.

advertising *noun* la publicité; **my sister works in advertising** ma sœur travaille dans la publicité

advice *noun*
(**a**) les conseils *(masculine plural)*; **she always takes her father's advice** elle suit toujours les conseils de son père
(**b**) **a piece of advice** un conseil; **he gave me a piece of advice** il m'a donné un conseil

advise *verb* conseiller; **I advise you to listen to your teachers** je te conseille d'écouter tes professeurs

aerial
1 *noun (for a radio, a TV)* une antenne

2 *adjective* aérien/aérienne; **an aerial photograph** une photographie aérienne

aerobics *noun* l'aérobic *(masculine)*; **I do aerobics on Tuesdays** je fais de l'aérobic le mardi

aeroplane *noun* un avion

affair *noun*
(**a**) *(matter, concern)* une affaire
(**b**) **current affairs** les questions d'actualité *(feminine plural)*
(**c**) *(relationship)* la liaison; **he had an affair with his secretary** il a eu une liaison avec sa secrétaire

affect *verb*
(**a**) *(have an effect on)* avoir une influence sur; **it affected his marks** cela a eu une influence sur ses résultats scolaires
(**b**) *(concern)* toucher, concerner; **the new rules affect all of us** le nouveau règlement nous concerne tous

afford *verb*
(**a**) *(have enough money for)* avoir les moyens d'acheter; **I can't afford a DVD player** je n'ai pas les moyens d'acheter un lecteur DVD; **they can't afford to go on holiday** ils n'ont pas les moyens de partir en vacances
(**b**) *(allow oneself)* se permettre; **I can't afford to be late** je ne peux pas me permettre d'arriver en retard

affordable *adjective* abordable

afraid *adjective*
(**a**) *(scared)* **to be afraid** avoir peur; **he's afraid of the dark** il a peur du noir; **I'm afraid to talk to him** j'ai peur de lui parler
(**b**) *(worried)* **I'm afraid he might be ill** j'ai peur qu'il soit malade

> The construction *avoir peur que* is always followed by the subjunctive.

(**c**) *(sorry)* **I'm afraid she's out** je suis désolé, mais elle n'est pas là; **I'm afraid so!** j'en ai bien peur!

Africa *noun* l'Afrique *(feminine)*; **have you ever been to Africa?** est-ce que tu es déjà allé en Afrique?; **Kenya is in Africa** le Kenya est en Afrique; **these animals come from Africa** ces animaux viennent d'Afrique

African
1 *adjective* africain/africaine
2 *noun (person)* un Africain/une Africaine

> In French, only the noun for the inhabitants of a country takes a capital letter, never the adjective.

after
1 *preposition*
(a) *(later than)* après; **I'll finish my work after lunch** je terminerai mon travail après manger; **it's after midnight** il est minuit passé
(b) *(behind)* **the dog was running after me** le chien me courait après; **close the door after you** ferme la porte derrière toi
(c) **after all** *(all things considered)* après tout; *(in spite of everything)* finalement; **she's only a child, after all** ce n'est qu'une enfant, après tout; **so you went to the party after all?** alors, tu es allé à la soirée finalement?
2 *conjunction* **I went out after having a shower** je suis sorti après m'être douché; **after we had washed up we watched a video** après avoir fait la vaisselle, nous avons regardé une cassette vidéo; **we left after she'd finished her homework** on est partis après qu'elle a fini ses devoirs
3 *adverb* après; **he left the day after** il est parti le jour d'après; **he died soon after** il est mort peu après

afternoon *noun*
(a) un/une après-midi; **every afternoon** tous les après-midi; **yesterday afternoon** hier après-midi; **tomorrow afternoon** demain après-midi; **I went to the beach in the afternoons** j'allais à la plage l'après-midi; **it's two o'clock in the afternoon** il est deux heures de l'après-midi; **good afternoon!** bonjour!

(b) **an afternoon nap** une sieste; **an afternoon snack** un goûter

> The word *après-midi* can be either masculine or feminine. It does not change in the plural.

aftershave *noun* l'après-rasage *(masculine)*

> The plural of *après-rasage* is *après-rasages*.

afterwards *adverb* après; **we'll have some cake afterwards** on mangera du gâteau après

again *adverb*
(a) *(once more)* encore; **they won again** ils ont encore gagné; **ask her again** demande-lui encore une fois; **to begin again** recommencer; **to come again** revenir; **to do again** refaire; **to see again** revoir
(b) *(with negative sentences)* plus; **I didn't see them again** je ne les ai plus jamais revus; **don't do it again!** ne recommence plus!; **not spaghetti again!** oh non, encore des spaghettis!

> When it occurs with a verb, *plus* is always used with *ne* (or *n'* before a vowel or mute h), which is placed in front of the verb, eg *je ne joue plus.*

against *preposition*
(a) *(in opposition to)* contre; **I'm against the death penalty** je suis contre la peine de mort; **the final will be England against Germany** la finale opposera l'Angleterre à l'Allemagne
(b) *(in contact with)* contre; **he leant his bike against the wall** il a appuyé son vélo contre le mur

age *noun*
(a) *(of a person)* l'âge *(masculine)*; **what age are you?** tu as quel âge?; **she's fifteen years of age** elle a quinze ans; **she's the same age as me** elle a le même âge que moi; **at the age of thirteen** à l'âge de treize ans
(b) *(period of time)* une époque; **the Stone Age** l'âge de pierre; **the Ice Age**

la période glaciaire
(c) **ages** une éternité; **I've been waiting ages** ça fait une éternité que j'attends

aged *adjective* âgé/âgée de; **I have a brother aged twenty-one** j'ai un frère âgé de vingt et un ans

agenda *noun* le programme

> Note that the French word *agenda* is never a translation for the English word *agenda*. It means *diary*.

aggressive *adjective* agressif/agressive

ago *adverb* il y a; **ten years ago** il y a dix ans; **he arrived an hour ago** il est arrivé il y a une heure; **it happened a long time ago** ça s'est passé il y a longtemps

agony *noun*
(a) la douleur atroce; **I was in agony** je souffrais horriblement
(b) **an agony aunt** une responsable du courrier du cœur

> Note that the French word *agonie* is never a translation for the English word *agony*. It means *death throes*.

agree *verb*
(a) *(be in agreement)* être d'accord; **I agree with you** je suis d'accord avec toi; **I don't agree with you** je ne suis pas d'accord avec toi; **she agrees with the government's decision** elle approuve la décision du gouvernement
(b) *(come to an agreement)* **they didn't manage to agree** ils n'ont pas réussi à se mettre d'accord; **to agree on a date** convenir d'une date; **they agreed to meet at seven o'clock** ils ont convenu de se retrouver à sept heures
(c) *(be willing to)* accepter; **I agreed to help him** j'ai accepté de l'aider

agreement *noun* un accord; **we are all in agreement** tout le monde est d'accord

ahead *adverb*
(a) *(in front)* devant; **he was walking**

ahead of us il marchait devant nous; **go straight ahead** continue tout droit; **I'll go on ahead** je pars devant
(b) *(in the lead)* **he is ahead of his class** il est en avance sur sa classe; **my team are five points ahead** mon équipe a cinq points d'avance
(c) *(in the future)* à l'avance; **you have to book ahead** il faut réserver les places à l'avance

aid
1 *noun* l'aide *(feminine)*
2 *verb* aider, venir en aide à; **the government must aid the flood victims** le gouvernement doit venir en aide aux victimes des inondations

AIDS *noun* le sida; **she has AIDS** elle a le sida; **he died of AIDS** il est mort du sida

aim
1 *noun* le but; **what's the aim of the game?** quel est le but du jeu?
2 *verb*
(a) viser; **he aimed at the target** il a visé la cible
(b) *(a gun)* braquer; **he aimed the gun at his enemy** il a braqué le pistolet sur son ennemi
(c) *(a product, a show)* destiner; **the programme is aimed at teenagers** l'émission est destinée aux adolescents
(d) **to aim to do something** avoir l'intention de faire quelque chose; **we aim to arrive before midnight** nous avons l'intention d'arriver avant minuit

air *noun*
(a) l'air *(masculine)*; **he threw his hat up into the air** il a lancé son chapeau en l'air; **I need some fresh air** j'ai besoin de prendre l'air; **the concert is in the open air** le concert est en plein air
(b) **an air hostess** une hôtesse de l'air; **my sister's an air hostess** ma sœur est hôtesse de l'air

> Note that when describing people's jobs or situations, French does not use an article (*un* or *une*).

air-conditioned *adjective* climatisé/climatisée

air-conditioning *noun* la climatisation; **our new car has air-conditioning** notre voiture est climatisée

aircraft *noun* un avion

airfare *noun* le prix du billet d'avion

airline *noun* la compagnie aérienne; **an airline ticket** un billet d'avion

airmail *noun* **I'd like to send this letter by airmail** je voudrais envoyer cette lettre par avion

airport *noun* un aéroport

aisle *noun*
(**a**) *(in a cinema, a supermarket)* une allée
(**b**) *(on a plane)* le couloir; **an aisle seat** une place côté couloir

alarm *noun*
(**a**) une alarme; **a burglar alarm** une alarme antivol; **a fire alarm** une alarme incendie
(**b**) **an alarm clock** un réveil; **he set his alarm clock for seven o'clock** il a mis son réveil à sonner à sept heures

album *noun* un album

alcohol *noun* l'alcool *(masculine)*; **they don't drink alcohol** ils ne boivent pas d'alcool

Note that the word *alcool* is pronounced "al-coll", not "al-cool".

alcoholic
1 *adjective (drink)* alcoolisé/alcoolisée
2 *noun (person)* un/une alcoolique

A levels *plural noun* le baccalauréat; **she's taking her A levels this year** elle passe son bac cette année

The equivalent of A levels in France is *le baccalauréat*, commonly known as *le bac*. Pupils may study for a "bac L" (arts subjects), "bac ES" (economics and social studies) or "bac S" (sciences). Although students choose one of these categories, the *bac* is not

as specific as *A levels* and includes many more subjects (around 10).

Algeria *noun* l'Algérie *(feminine)*; **she was born in Algeria** elle est née en Algérie; **have you ever been to Algeria?** est-ce que tu es déjà allé en Algérie?; **they come from Algeria** ils viennent d'Algérie

Algerian
1 *adjective* algérien/algérienne
2 *noun (person)* un Algérien/une Algérienne; **the Algerians** les Algériens *(masculine plural)*

In French, only the noun for the inhabitants of a country takes a capital letter, never the adjective.

alien *noun (extra-terrestrial)* un/une extraterrestre

alight *adjective* en feu; **to set something alight** mettre le feu à quelque chose; **to catch alight** prendre feu

alike *adverb*
(**a**) *(similar)* **to look alike** se ressembler; **the two brothers look alike** les deux frères se ressemblent
(**b**) *(in the same way)* de la même manière; **the twins are always dressed alike** les jumeaux sont toujours habillés de la même manière

alive *adjective* vivant/vivante, en vie; **are your great-grandparents still alive?** est-ce que tes arrière-grands-parents sont encore en vie?

all
1 *adjective*
(**a**) *(the whole of)* tout/toute; **all the cake** tout le gâteau; **all night** toute la nuit

Tout is used before masculine singular nouns and *toute* is used before feminine singular nouns.

(**b**) *(every one of)* tous/toutes; **all the boys** tous les garçons; **all the girls** toutes les filles; **all the children** tous les enfants

Tous is used before masculine plural nouns (*les garçons, les livres*) or mixed-gender groups (*les étudiants*). *Toutes* is used before feminine plural nouns only (*les filles, les fleurs*).

2 *pronoun*
(a) *(everything)* tout; **I did all I could** j'ai fait tout ce que j'ai pu; **take it all** prenez tout; **I want all of it** je le veux en entier

In this sense of *all*, *tout* is always used in the masculine singular form.

(b) *(everyone)* tous/toutes; **we all love him** nous l'aimons tous; **the girls all like dancing** les filles aiment toutes danser
3 *adverb*
(a) *(entirely)* tout/toute; **she's dressed all in black** elle est habillée tout en noir; **he's gone all red** il est devenu tout rouge; **she's gone all red** elle est devenue toute rouge; **they're all wet** ils sont tout mouillés

The adverb *tout* does not change before all masculine adjectives (even in the plural, hence *ils sont tout mouillés*) or before feminine adjectives beginning with a vowel or mute h: *elle est tout émue* (*émue* begins with a vowel), but it does change before other feminine adjectives, hence *elle est toute seule* (*seule* begins with a consonant).

(b) **not at all** pas du tout; **I don't like it at all** ça ne me plaît pas du tout; **I ate nothing at all** je n'ai rien mangé du tout
(c) *(in games)* **the score is two all** le score est de deux partout

allergy *noun* une allergie; **he has a peanut allergy** il est allergique aux cacahuètes

allergic *adjective* allergique; **I'm allergic to penicillin** je suis allergique à la pénicilline

alligator *noun* un alligator

all-night *adjective* **I went to an all-night party** je suis allé à une soirée qui a duré toute la nuit

allow *verb*
(a) **to allow somebody to do something** autoriser quelqu'un à faire quelque chose; **her parents don't allow her to go out at night** ses parents ne l'autorisent pas à sortir le soir; **they only allow her an hour of TV a day** ils ne lui autorisent qu'une heure de télévision par jour
(b) **to be allowed to do something** avoir le droit de faire quelque chose; **I'm allowed to do what I want** j'ai le droit de faire ce que je veux; **I'm not allowed sweets** je n'ai pas le droit de manger des bonbons
(c) **to be allowed** *(permissible)* être autorisé; **dictionaries are allowed in the exam** les dictionnaires ne sont pas autorisés à l'examen; **smoking is not allowed** il est interdit de fumer

all right
1 *adjective*
(a) *(not bad)* pas mal; **the film was all right** le film n'était pas mal
(b) *(in good health)* **are you all right?** ça va?; **I'm all right** ça va
(c) **is everything all right?** est-ce que tout va bien?; **is it all right if I watch TV?** est-ce que je peux regarder la télé?; **it's all right** *(it doesn't matter)* ça ne fait rien
2 *adverb*
(a) *(well)* bien; **the radio works all right** la radio marche bien
(b) *(in agreement)* d'accord; **all right, we'll meet at the station** d'accord, on se retrouve devant la gare

almond *noun* une amande

almost *adverb*
(a) presque; **it's almost six o'clock** il est presque six heures; **we're almost there** nous sommes presque arrivés
(b) **he almost missed his train** il a failli rater son train

alone *adjective*
(a) seul/seule; **he lives alone** il vit

seul; **she's travelling alone** elle voyage toute seule

(b) **to leave somebody alone** *(in peace)* laisser quelqu'un tranquille; **leave me alone** laisse-moi tranquille; **to leave something alone** ne pas toucher à quelque chose; **leave the computer alone!** ne touche pas à l'ordinateur!

along
1 *preposition* le long de; **they walked along the shore** ils se sont promenés le long de la plage
2 *adverb*
(a) **I was walking along** je me promenais; **he was driving along** il roulait; **move along!** avancez!; **can I bring a friend along?** est-ce que je peux amener un ami?
(b) **all along** *(right from the start)* depuis le début; **I knew it all along** je le savais depuis le début

aloud *adverb* à haute voix; **the teacher was reading aloud** le professeur lisait à haute voix

alphabet *noun* l'alphabet *(masculine)*

Alps *plural noun* **the Alps** les Alpes *(feminine plural)*

already *adverb* déjà; **he's already there** il est déjà là

alright *see* **all right**

also *adverb* aussi; **he also plays football** il joue aussi au football; **not only is she beautiful, she's also very clever** non seulement elle est belle, mais en plus elle est intelligente

alter *verb* *(change)* changer; **we're going to have to alter our plans** nous allons devoir changer nos projets

alternative
1 *adjective* autre; **we have to find an alternative solution** il faut trouver une autre solution
2 *noun* **there is no alternative** il n'y a pas d'autre solution

alternatively *adverb* ou bien, sinon; **alternatively, we could go to the**

beach ou bien on pourrait aller à la plage

although *conjunction* bien que; **although the book is long, it's very interesting** bien que le livre soit long, il est très intéressant

> The expression *bien que* is always followed by the subjunctive.

altogether *adverb* en tout; **how much is that altogether?** ça fait combien en tout?

always *adverb* toujours; **she always wears jeans** elle est toujours en jean; **he's always complaining** il n'arrête pas de se plaindre

a.m. *adverb* du matin; **we start school at nine a.m.** on commence les cours à neuf heures (du matin)

> Note that French does not use the terms *a.m.* and *p.m.* Instead, French people often use the 24-hour clock, so 6 *a.m.* would be *six heures (6h)*, but 6 *p.m.* would be *dix-huit heures (18h)*.

amaze *verb*
(a) *(surprise)* stupéfier; **his decision amazed his family** sa décision a stupéfié sa famille
(b) *(impress)* impressionner; **his courage amazes me** son courage m'impressionne

amazed *adjective* stupéfait/stupéfaite; **he was amazed when I told him the news** il était stupéfait quand je lui ai annoncé la nouvelle

amazing *adjective*
(a) *(surprising)* incroyable; **it's amazing that no one was hurt** c'est incroyable que personne n'ait été blessé
(b) *(impressive)* impressionnant/impressionnante; **the view from up here is amazing** on a une vue impressionnante d'ici

ambition *noun* une ambition; **his ambition is to go to university** il a pour ambition d'aller à l'université

ambitious *adjective* ambitieux/ambitieuse

ambulance *noun* une ambulance

America *noun*
(a) l'Amérique *(feminine)*; **she lives in America** elle habite en Amérique; **I've never been to America** je ne suis jamais allé en Amérique; **a map of America** une carte de l'Amérique
(b) **North America** l'Amérique du Nord; **South America** l'Amérique du Sud

American
1 *adjective* américain/américaine
2 *noun (person)* un Américain/une Américaine; **the Americans** les Américains *(masculine plural)*

In French, only the noun for the inhabitants of a country takes a capital letter, never the adjective.

among, amongst *preposition*
(a) *(in the midst of)* parmi; **among the crowd** parmi la foule
(b) *(one of)* **he's among the best students in the class** c'est un des meilleurs élèves de la classe; **among other things, he said we need to study harder** il a dit, entre autres, que nous devons travailler davantage
(c) *(between)* entre; **share out the sweets among the children** partagez les bonbons entre les enfants; **among friends** entre amis

amount *noun*
(a) *(quantity)* la quantité; **he has a large amount of luggage** il a beaucoup de bagages; **it takes a huge amount of time** ça prend énormément de temps
(b) *(of money)* la somme, le montant; **what is the total amount?** quel est le montant total?

amplifier *noun* un amplificateur

amuse *verb*
(a) *(make laugh)* faire rire; **he amuses me** il me fait rire
(b) *(occupy)* amuser; **he amused himself building sandcastles** il s'est amusé à faire des châteaux de sable; **she kept the children amused all afternoon** elle a occupé les enfants pendant toute l'après-midi

amusement *noun*
(a) l'amusement *(masculine)*; **much to everyone's amusement, I got soaking wet** au grand amusement de tous, j'ai été trempé jusqu'aux os
(b) **an amusement arcade** une salle de jeux électroniques

amusing *adjective* amusant/amusante

an *see* **a**

analyse *verb* analyser

ancestor *noun* un/une ancêtre

anchor *noun* une ancre

anchovy *noun* un anchois

ancient *adjective* **Ancient Greece** la Grèce antique; **we visited an ancient monument** nous avons visité un monument historique; **my grandpa's ancient!** mon grand-père est vraiment très vieux!

and *conjunction*
(a) et; **she can speak French and Spanish** elle parle français et espagnol; **get your hat and coat** va chercher ton bonnet et ton manteau
(b) *(to)* **go and look for it** va le chercher; **come and see me** viens me voir; **try and help me** essaie de m'aider
(c) *(in numbers)* **two hundred and two** deux cent deux; **an hour and twenty minutes** une heure vingt

angel *noun* un ange

anger
1 *noun* la colère
2 *verb* mettre en colère; **it angers me to see people drop litter in the street** ça me met en colère de voir des gens qui jettent des détritus par terre

angle *noun* un angle; **let's look at the problem from a different angle** considérons le problème sous un autre angle

angry *adjective* fâché/fâchée, en colère; **the teacher is angry with him** le prof est fâché contre lui; **he gets angry if you disagree with him** il se met en colère si quelqu'un n'est pas d'accord avec lui

animal *noun* un animal

> The plural of *animal* is *animaux*.

ankle *noun* la cheville

anniversary *noun* un anniversaire; **it's their 20th wedding anniversary** c'est leur vingtième anniversaire de mariage

announce *verb* annoncer; **the teacher announced that he was leaving** le professeur a annoncé son départ

announcement *noun* une annonce; **I have an important announcement to make** j'ai une annonce importante à faire

annoy *verb* énerver; **his stupid questions really annoy me** il m'énerve vraiment avec ses questions idiotes

annoyed *adjective* énervé/énervée; **she gets annoyed when I ask questions** elle s'énerve quand je pose des questions; **I'm annoyed with him for being late** il m'énerve parce qu'il est en retard

annoying *adjective* énervant/énervante; **my little sister's really annoying** ma petite sœur est vraiment énervante

annual *adjective* annuel/annuelle

anorak *noun* un anorak

another
1 *adjective* un/une autre; **I read it in another book** je l'ai lu dans un autre livre; **bring me another cup, this one's dirty** apportez-moi une autre tasse, celle-ci est sale; **would you like another sweet?** est-ce que tu veux un autre bonbon?; **can I have another drink?** est-ce que je peux reprendre à boire?

2 *pronoun*
(a) un/une autre; **she finished her drink and asked for another** elle a fini son verre et elle en a redemandé un autre; **another of the boys came forward** un autre garçon s'est avancé
(b) **one another** *(two people)* l'un l'autre/l'une l'autre; *(more than two people)* les uns les autres/les unes les autres; **they love one another** ils s'aiment; **the girls help one another** les filles s'aident les unes les autres

answer
1 *noun* la réponse; **do you know the answer to the question?** est-ce que tu connais la réponse à cette question?; **I phoned but there was no answer** j'ai téléphoné mais ça ne répondait pas
2 *verb* répondre à; **answer the question!** réponds à la question!
3 **answer back** répondre; **don't answer back!** et ne réponds pas!

answering machine *noun* le répondeur; **I left a message on her answering machine** j'ai laissé un message sur son répondeur

ant *noun* la fourmi

antenna *noun* une antenne

anthem *noun* **a national anthem** un hymne national

antibiotic *noun* un antibiotique; **he's on antibiotics** il est sous antibiotiques

anticlockwise *adverb* dans le sens inverse des aiguilles d'une montre

antiperspirant *noun* le déodorant

anxious *adjective* inquiet/inquiète; **I'm anxious about the operation** je m'inquiète à propos de l'opération

any
1 *adjective*
(a) *(some)* du/de la; **would you like any coffee?** est-ce que vous voulez du café?; **have you got any money?** est-ce que tu as de l'argent?; **do they want any sweets?** est-ce qu'ils veulent des bonbons?

Du is the contraction of *de* + *le* and is used before masculine nouns. *Du* and *de la* become *de l'* before a vowel or mute h. *Des* is the contraction of *de + les*, and does not change.

(b) *(in negative sentences)* **not any** *(none)* pas de; *(not one)* aucun/aucune; **there isn't any bread** il n'y a pas de pain; **I didn't have any beer** je n'ai pas bu de bière; **there weren't any children there** il n'y avait aucun enfant

When they occur with a verb, *pas de* and *aucun* are always used with *ne* (or *n'* before a vowel or a mute h), which is placed in front of the verb, eg *il n'a pas d'argent*.

(c) *(no matter which)* n'importe quel/quelle; **come any day you like** venez n'importe quel jour; **ask any woman** demande à n'importe quelle femme
(d) *(all)* tout/toute; **any pupil who forgets his books will be punished** tout élève qui oubliera ses livres sera puni; **give me any money you have** donne-moi tout l'argent que tu as
2 *pronoun*
(a) *(some of it, one of them)* en; **have you got any?** est-ce que tu en as?; **I haven't got any** je n'en ai pas; **did any of them go?** est-ce que certains d'entre eux y sont allés?

The pronoun *en* is used to replace *de* + *noun*.

(b) *(not one)* aucun/aucune; **he didn't vote for any of the candidates** il n'a voté pour aucun des candidats; **I don't like any of those colours** je n'aime aucune de ces couleurs

When it occurs with a verb, *aucun* is used with *ne* (or *n'* before a vowel or a mute h), which is placed in front of the verb, eg *je n'aime aucun des deux*.

(c) *(no matter which one)* n'importe lequel/laquelle; **we can watch any of these films** on peut regarder n'importe lequel de ces films

3 *adverb*
(a) *(some)* **any more** encore de; **do you want any more?** est-ce que tu en veux encore?; **do you want any more cake?** est-ce que vous voulez reprendre du gâteau?

The pronoun *en* is used to replace *de* + *noun*.

(b) *(none)* **any more** plus de; **I don't want any more cake** je ne veux plus de gâteau; **I don't want any more** je n'en veux plus
(c) **I can't go any further** je ne peux pas aller plus loin; **can't you walk any faster than that?** tu ne peux pas marcher plus vite que ça?

Note that when *plus* is used to mean *no more*, the final *s* is not pronounced.

anybody *pronoun*
(a) *(somebody)* quelqu'un; **would anybody like some more cake?** est-ce que quelqu'un veut reprendre du gâteau?; **is anybody home?** il y a quelqu'un?
(b) **not anybody** *(nobody)* personne; **there isn't anybody here** il n'y a personne ici; **she didn't speak to anybody** elle n'a parlé à personne

When it occurs with a verb, *personne* is used with *ne* (or *n'* before a vowel or a mute h), which is placed in front of the verb, eg *il ne parle à personne*.

(c) *(no matter who)* n'importe qui; **it could happen to anybody** ça pourrait arriver à n'importe qui; **invite anybody you want** invitez qui vous voulez

anyhow *adverb*
(a) *(in any case)* de toute façon; **it's too late now anyhow** de toute façon, il est trop tard maintenant
(b) *(carelessly)* n'importe comment; **she threw her things down just anyhow** elle a jeté ses affaires n'importe comment

anyone *see* **anybody**

anything *pronoun*
(a) *(something)* quelque chose; **can**

you see anything? est-ce que tu vois quelque chose?; **is there anything to eat?** est-ce qu'il y a quelque chose à manger?

(**b**) **not anything** *(nothing)* rien; **I can't see anything** je ne vois rien

> When it occurs with a verb, *rien* is always used with *ne* (or *n'* before a vowel or a mute h), which is placed in front of the verb, eg *il ne sait rien*.

(**c**) *(no matter what)* n'importe quoi; **she'd do anything for her children** elle ferait n'importe quoi pour ses enfants

(**d**) *(everything)* tout; **you can do anything you want** tu peux faire tout ce que tu veux; **I like anything with chocolate in it** j'aime tout ce qui est au chocolat

anyway *adverb*
(**a**) *(in any case)* de toute façon; **it's too late now anyway** de toute façon, il est trop tard maintenant
(**b**) *(nevertheless)* quand même; **I'm afraid I can't come, but thanks anyway** je suis désolé, je ne peux pas venir, mais merci quand même

anywhere *adverb*
(**a**) *(somewhere)* quelque part; **have you seen my keys anywhere?** est-ce que tu as vu mes clés quelque part?; **are you going anywhere tonight?** est-ce que tu sors ce soir?
(**b**) **not anywhere** *(nowhere)* nulle part; **I can't find my keys anywhere** je ne trouve mes clés nulle part

> When it occurs with a verb, *nulle part* is always used with *ne* (or *n'* before a vowel or a mute h), which is placed in front of the verb, eg *je ne les trouve nulle part*.

(**c**) *(no matter where)* n'importe où; **just put your bag down anywhere** pose ton sac n'importe où
(**d**) *(everywhere)* partout; **you can buy that book anywhere** on trouve ce livre partout

apart *adverb*
(**a**) *(separated)* **the cars were a metre apart** les deux voitures étaient à un mètre l'une de l'autre; **we have to keep them apart** il faut les séparer
(**b**) *(in pieces)* **to take a machine apart** démonter une machine; **this book's coming apart** ce livre perd ses pages
(**c**) **apart from** *(except for)* à part; **I don't know anyone apart from you** je ne connais personne à part toi

apartment *noun* un appartement

> Do not confuse the spellings of the French *appartement* and English *apartment*.

ape *noun* le singe

apologize *verb* s'excuser; **I was wrong, I apologize** j'ai eu tort, je m'excuse; **I apologize for having kept you waiting** excusez-moi de vous avoir fait attendre; **she apologized for the noise** elle s'est excusée pour le bruit

apology *noun* les excuses *(feminine plural)*; **I owe you an apology** je vous dois des excuses

apostrophe *noun* une apostrophe

apparently *adverb* apparemment; **they're getting married, apparently** apparemment, ils vont se marier; **apparently they've moved house** il paraît qu'ils ont déménagé

appeal *verb*
(**a**) *(please)* **to appeal to somebody** plaire à quelqu'un; **the idea appealed to me** l'idée m'a plu; **the film doesn't appeal to me** ce film ne me dit rien
(**b**) *(request)* lancer un appel; **the police are appealing for witnesses** la police a lancé un appel à témoins

appear *verb*
(**a**) *(come into view)* apparaître; **the ghost appeared at the window** le fantôme est apparu à la fenêtre
(**b**) *(seem)* sembler; **it appears that they're on holiday** il semblerait qu'ils soient en vacances; **she appears to**

have a lot of friends elle semble avoir beaucoup d'amis

appearance *noun*
(a) *(arrival)* une arrivée; **they were startled by the appearance of the teacher** ils ont été surpris par l'arrivée du professeur
(b) *(look)* l'apparence *(feminine)*; **she's always thinking about her appearance** elle ne pense qu'à son apparence

appetite *noun* l'appétit *(masculine)*; **to have a good appetite** avoir bon appétit; **she hasn't got a very big appetite** elle a un petit appétit

applaud *verb* applaudir

applause *noun* les applaudissements *(masculine plural)*; **we could hear applause** on entendait des applaudissements

apple *noun* la pomme; **apple juice** le jus de pommes; **an apple pie** une tarte aux pommes; **an apple tree** un pommier

appliance *noun* un appareil; **an electrical appliance** un appareil électrique

application *noun*
(a) *(for help, funding)* la demande
(b) **a job application** une candidature
(c) **an application form** *(requesting something)* un formulaire de demande; *(for a job)* un dossier de candidature

apply
1 *verb*
(a) *(a rule, a law)* s'appliquer; **the rules apply to all pupils** le règlement s'applique à tous les élèves
(b) *(put on)* appliquer; **he applied the paint with a roller** il a appliqué la peinture à l'aide d'un rouleau
2 apply for faire une demande de; **to apply for a grant** faire une demande de bourse; **to apply for a job** poser sa candidature à un poste

appointment *noun* le rendez-vous; **to make an appointment** prendre rendez-vous; **I have a doctor's appointment** j'ai rendez-vous chez le médecin

appreciate *verb*
(a) *(value)* apprécier; **they appreciate good food** ils apprécient la bonne cuisine
(b) *(be grateful for)* **I appreciate your help** je vous remercie de votre aide

approach *verb*
(a) *(get nearer)* approcher; **Christmas is approaching** Noël approche
(b) *(get nearer to)* approcher de; **we're approaching the castle** nous approchons du château
(c) *(go up to)* aborder; **a man approached me in the street** un homme m'a abordé dans la rue

appropriate *adjective* approprié/approprié; **those clothes are not appropriate for school** ce ne sont pas des vêtements appropriés pour l'école

approve *verb* **to approve of something** approuver quelque chose; **do you approve of the government's decision?** est-ce que vous approuvez la décision du gouvernement?; **they don't approve of my friends** mes amis ne leur plaisent pas

apricot *noun* un abricot; **apricot jam** la confiture d'abricots; **an apricot tree** un abricotier

April *noun* avril *(masculine)*; **the first of April** le premier avril; **the second of April** le deux avril; **the third of April** le trois avril; **in April** en avril

Names of months are not capitalized in French.

apron *noun* le tablier

aquarium *noun* un aquarium

Aquarius *noun* le Verseau; **he's (an) Aquarius** il est Verseau

Arab
1 *adjective* arabe
2 *noun (person)* un/une Arabe

In French, only the noun for the inhabitants of a country takes a capital letter, never the adjective.

Arabic
1 *adjective* arabe
2 *noun (language)* l'arabe *(masculine)*;
he speaks Arabic il parle arabe

> In French, only the noun for the inhabitants of a country takes a capital letter, never the adjective or the noun for the language.

arcade *noun*
(a) *(for shopping)* la galerie marchande
(b) *(for amusements)* la salle de jeux électroniques

arch *noun* un arc

architect *noun* un/une architecte; **his father's an architect** son père est architecte

> Note that when describing people's jobs or situations, French does not use an article (*un* or *une*).

architecture *noun* l'architecture *(feminine)*

area *noun*
(a) *(of a country)* la région; **this is a beautiful area** c'est une très belle région
(b) *(of a town)* le quartier; **I live in a nice area of town** j'habite dans un quartier agréable
(c) *(size)* la superficie; **the room has an area of 24 square metres** la pièce a une superficie de 24 mètres carrés

argue *verb* se disputer; **I often argue with my brother** je me dispute souvent avec mon frère; **they're arguing about money** ils se disputent pour une question d'argent

argument *noun* la dispute; **she's had an argument with her boyfriend** elle s'est disputée avec son copain; **they had an argument about money** ils se sont disputés pour une question d'argent

Aries *noun* le Bélier; **she's (an) Aries** elle est Bélier

arithmetic *noun* le calcul; **I'm no good at arithmetic** je suis nul en calcul

arm *noun* le bras

armchair *noun* le fauteuil

armpit *noun* une aisselle

army *noun* une armée

around
1 *preposition*
(a) *(surrounding)* autour de; **the guests were sitting around the table** les invités étaient assis autour de la table; **he's been around the world** il a fait le tour du monde
(b) *(in the area)* **is there a bank around here?** est-ce qu'il y a une banque par ici?; **we walked around the park** nous nous sommes promenés dans le parc
(c) *(more or less)* environ; **he's around your age** il a environ ton âge; **I'll be there around five** je serai là vers cinq heures
2 *adverb*
(a) *(surrounding)* autour; **the garden has trees all around** le jardin est entouré d'arbres
(b) *(all over the place)* partout; **the children were running around** les enfants couraient partout; **she leaves her things lying around** elle laisse traîner ses affaires partout
(c) *(in the area)* **is Jack around?** est-ce que Jack est dans le coin?; **are you around this weekend?** tu es là ce week-end?

arrange *verb*
(a) *(organize, plan)* organiser; **we've arranged a party** nous avons organisé une fête
(b) *(lay out)* disposer; **the chairs are arranged in a circle** les chaises sont disposées en cercle
(c) **to arrange to do something** *(with somebody else)* convenir de faire quelque chose; **they arranged to meet at the station** ils ont convenu de se retrouver à la gare

arrangement *noun*
(**a**) *(layout)* la disposition
(**b**) **to make arrangements to do something** prendre des dispositions pour faire quelque chose; **I've made all the arrangements** j'ai tout organisé

arrest
1 *verb* arrêter
2 *noun* une arrestation

arrival *noun* une arrivée

arrive *verb* arriver

arrogant *adjective* arrogant/arrogante

arrow *noun* la flèche

art *noun* l'art *(masculine)*; **I'm interested in art** je m'intéresse à l'art; **an art gallery** un musée d'art

artichoke *noun* un artichaut

article *noun* un article

artificial *adjective* artificiel/artificielle

artist *noun* un/une artiste

artistic *adjective* artistique

as
1 *conjunction*
(**a**) *(like)* comme; **she's a doctor, as is her sister** elle est médecin, comme sa sœur; **as I told you, it's a very small house** comme je vous l'ai dit, c'est une toute petite maison; **do as you like** fais ce que tu veux
(**b**) *(at the same time)* au moment où; **the phone rang as I was coming in** le téléphone a sonné au moment où j'entrais
(**c**) *(because)* puisque; **as it's raining, we'll catch the bus** puisqu'il pleut, on va prendre le bus
2 *preposition (in the role of)* **he's dressed as a clown** il est habillé en clown; **with Pierce Brosnan as James Bond** avec Pierce Brosnan dans le rôle de James Bond
3 *adverb*
(**a**) **as... as** aussi... que; **I'm as tall as you** je suis aussi grand que toi; **come**

as quickly as possible viens aussi vite que possible; **twice as... as** deux fois plus... que
(**b**) **as much as** autant que; **she works as much as me** elle travaille autant que moi; **I make as much money as him** je gagne autant d'argent que lui
(**c**) *(in set phrases)* **as white as a sheet** blanc comme un linge

ash *noun* la cendre

ashamed *adjective* **to be ashamed** avoir honte; **I'm ashamed of myself** j'ai honte

ashtray *noun* le cendrier

Asia *noun* l'Asie *(feminine)*; **China is in Asia** la Chine est en Asie; **have you ever been to Asia?** est-ce que tu es déjà allé en Asie?; **this dish is from Asia** ce plat vient d'Asie

Asian
1 *adjective (from Asia in general)* asiatique; *(from India)* indien/indienne; *(from Pakistan)* pakistanais/pakistanaise
2 *noun (person) (from India)* un Indien/une Indienne; *(from Pakistan)* un Pakistanais/une Pakistanaise

> In French, only the noun for the inhabitants of a country takes a capital letter, never the adjective.

> Note that the French word *Asiatique* is not a translation for *Asian* as it is used in Britain, meaning somebody from the Indian subcontinent. It usually refers to Oriental people (ie from countries such as China, Japan, Vietnam etc).

ask *verb*
(**a**) demander; **to ask a question** poser une question; **to ask somebody** demander à quelqu'un; **I asked him the time** je lui ai demandé l'heure; **ask your mother** demande à ta mère
(**b**) **to ask for something** demander quelque chose; **he asked for a drink** il a demandé à boire; **she asked me for a**

cigarette elle m'a demandé une cigarette

(c) **she asked to come with me** elle a demandé à venir avec moi; **I asked them to be quiet** je leur ai demandé de ne pas faire de bruit

(d) **I asked about the train fare** je me suis renseigné sur le prix du billet de train; **my mother was asking about you** ma mère a demandé de tes nouvelles

asleep *adjective*
(a) **to be asleep** dormir; **she's asleep** elle dort
(b) **to fall asleep** s'endormir; **he fell asleep** il s'est endormi

asparagus *noun* les asperges *(feminine plural)*; **I don't like asparagus** je n'aime pas les asperges

aspirin *noun* l'aspirine *(feminine)*; **an aspirin, an aspirin tablet** un cachet d'aspirine

assassinate *verb* assassiner

assassination *noun* un assassinat

assault
1 *noun*
(a) *(attack)* une agression
(b) **an assault course** un parcours du combattant
2 *verb* *(attack)* agresser; **he was assaulted in the street** il s'est fait agresser dans la rue

assemble *verb*
(a) *(come together)* se rassembler; **the pupils assembled in the classroom** les élèves se sont rassemblés dans la classe
(b) *(put together)* monter, assembler

assembly *noun* *(at school)* la réunion des élèves avant d'entrer en classe

assessment *noun*
(a) *(judgment)* une évaluation
(b) *(at school)* le contrôle des connaissances; **continuous assessment** le contrôle continu

assignment *noun* *(at school)* le devoir

assist *verb* aider

assistant *noun*
(a) *(helper)* un assistant/une assistante; **she's a French assistant** elle est assistante de français

Note that when describing people's jobs or situations, French does not use an article (*un* or *une*).

(b) *(in a shop)* le vendeur/la vendeuse

association *noun* une association

assorted *adjective*
(a) *(objects)* assortis/assorties; **a box of assorted chocolates** une boîte de chocolats assortis
(b) *(colours)* variés/variées

assume *verb*
(a) *(believe)* supposer; **I assume he's coming** je suppose qu'il vient; **let's assume that it's true** supposons que ce soit vrai
(b) **to assume responsibility for something** se charger de quelque chose

asthma *noun* l'asthme *(masculine)*; **I have asthma** je suis asthmatique; **an asthma attack** une crise d'asthme

astrology *noun* l'astrologie *(feminine)*

astronaut *noun* un/une astronaute; **she wants to be an astronaut** elle veut être astronaute

Note that when describing people's jobs or situations, French does not use an article (*un* or *une*).

astronomy *noun* l'astronomie *(feminine)*

at *preposition*
(a) *(in a particular place)* à; **I'm at the airport** je suis à l'aéroport; **we're at school** nous sommes à l'école
(b) *(giving a time)* à; **at six o'clock** à six heures; **at midnight** à minuit
(c) *(somebody's home or work)* chez; **he's at Martin's house** il est chez Martin; **I was at the doctor's** j'étais chez le médecin

(d) *(with periods of time)* **at night** la nuit; **at the weekend** le week-end

(e) *(with speeds and prices)* à; **she drives at 30 miles an hour** elle roule à 50 kilomètres à l'heure; **he sells them at £2 a kilo** il les vend 2 livres le kilo

(f) *(in the direction of)* **to look at somebody** regarder quelqu'un; **to shout at somebody** crier après quelqu'un; **to throw something at somebody** jeter quelque chose sur quelqu'un

(g) *(in an e-mail address)* **at sign** une arobase; **"gwilson at transex, dot, co, dot, uk"** "gwilson, arobase, transex, point, co, point, uk"

> Note that *à* + *le* becomes *au*, and *à* + *les* becomes *aux*.

athlete *noun* un/une athlète

athletic *adjective* sportif/sportive; **she's very athletic** elle est très sportive

athletics *noun* l'athlétisme *(masculine)*; **I like watching athletics** j'aime bien regarder l'athlétisme

Atlantic
1 *noun* **the Atlantic** l'Atlantique *(masculine)*
2 *adjective* atlantique; **the Atlantic coast** la côte atlantique

atlas *noun* un atlas

atmosphere *noun*
(a) *(of the earth)* l'atmosphère *(feminine)*
(b) *(of a place, an event)* l'ambiance *(feminine)*; **that bar has a really nice atmosphere** il y a une ambiance très sympa dans ce bar

attach *verb*
(a) *(fasten together)* attacher, accrocher; **I attached the badge to my jacket** j'ai accroché le badge à ma veste
(b) *(to a letter, an e-mail)* joindre; **please find attached my report** veuillez trouver ci-joint mon rapport

attack
1 *verb* attaquer; **the dog attacked me** le chien m'a attaqué

2 *noun* une attaque

attempt
1 *verb* essayer; **he attempted to stand up** il a essayé de se lever
2 *noun* un essai; **they made no attempt to help us** ils n'ont pas essayé de nous aider; **at the first attempt** du premier coup

attend *verb*
(a) *(a school, a church)* aller à; **he attends a private school** il va dans une école privée
(b) *(an event)* assister à; **everyone must attend the meeting** tout le monde doit assister à la réunion

> Note that the French verb *attendre* is never a translation for the English verb *to attend*. It means *to wait*.

attendant *noun* *(in a car park, a museum)* le gardien/la gardienne

attention *noun* l'attention *(feminine)*; **he waved to attract our attention** il a fait un geste de la main pour attirer notre attention; **pay attention to what the teacher says** écoute ce que dit le professeur

attic *noun* le grenier; **in the attic** au grenier

attitude *noun* l'attitude *(feminine)*; **a positive attitude** une attitude positive

attract *verb*
(a) *(draw)* attirer; **the programme attracted a lot of attention** l'émission a attiré l'attention de beaucoup de gens
(b) *(with people)* **to be attracted to somebody** être attiré par quelqu'un

attractive *adjective*
(a) *(object, place)* beau/belle
(b) *(person)* séduisant/séduisante; **there are lots of attractive girls here** il y a beaucoup de filles séduisantes ici

aubergine *noun* une aubergine

auburn *adjective* auburn; **she has auburn hair** elle a les cheveux auburn

> Note that *auburn* does not change in the feminine or in the plural.

auction *noun* la vente aux enchères

audience *noun (at the theatre, the cinema)* le public, les spectateurs *(masculine plural)*; *(for TV)* les téléspectateurs *(masculine plural)*

August *noun* août *(masculine)*; **the first of August** le premier août; **the second of August** le deux août; **the third of August** le trois août; **in August** en août

Names of months are not capitalized in French.

aunt *noun* la tante; **Aunt Julia** tante Julia

auntie *noun* la tata; **Auntie Julia** tata Julia

au pair *noun* la jeune fille au pair; **she's an au pair** elle est jeune fille au pair

Note that when describing people's jobs or situations, French does not use an article *(un* or *une)*.

Australia *noun* l'Australie *(feminine)*; **they live in Australia** ils habitent en Australie; **I'm going to Australia** je vais en Australie; **koalas come from Australia** les koalas viennent d'Australie

Australian
1 *adjective* australien/australienne
2 *noun (person)* un Australien/une Australienne; **the Australians** les Australiens *(masculine plural)*

In French, only the noun for the inhabitants of a country takes a capital letter, never the adjective.

Austria *noun* l'Autriche *(feminine)*; **he was born in Austria** il est né en Autriche; **have you ever been to Austria?** est-ce que tu es déjà allé en Autriche?; **these biscuits are from Austria** ces biscuits viennent d'Autriche

Austrian
1 *adjective* autrichien/autrichienne

2 *noun (person)* un Autrichien/une Autrichienne; **the Austrians** les Autrichiens *(masculine plural)*

In French, only the noun for the inhabitants of a country takes a capital letter, never the adjective.

authentic *adjective* authentique

author *noun* un auteur, un écrivain; **who is the author of this book?** quel est l'auteur de ce livre?; **she's an author** elle est écrivain

Note that when describing people's jobs or situations, French does not use an article *(un* or *une)*.

automatic *adjective* automatique

authority *noun* l'autorité *(feminine)*

autumn *noun* l'automne *(masculine)*; **in the autumn** en automne; **an autumn evening** une soirée d'automne

The *m* in *automne* is not pronounced.

available *adjective*
(a) *(accessible)* disponible; **the T-shirts are available in three sizes** les tee-shirts sont disponibles en trois tailles
(b) *(free)* libre, disponible; **are you available this weekend?** est-ce que tu es libre ce week-end?

avalanche *noun* une avalanche

avenue *noun* une avenue

average
1 *noun* la moyenne; **her score was above (the) average** elle a eu une note au-dessus de la moyenne; **on average** en moyenne; **they spend an average of £85 per week** ils dépensent en moyenne 85 livres par semaine
2 *adjective* moyen/moyenne; **the film was just average** le film était moyen; **she's of average height** elle est de taille moyenne

avocado *noun* un avocat

avoid *verb* éviter; **I think he's avoiding me** je crois qu'il m'évite; **to avoid**

doing something éviter de faire quelque chose

awake *adjective* **to be awake** *(not asleep yet)* être éveillé/éveillée; *(having just woken up)* être réveillé/réveillée; **he's still awake** il ne dort toujours pas; **to stay awake** rester éveillé; **to keep somebody awake** empêcher quelqu'un de dormir

award *noun* le prix

away *adverb*
(a) *(in distance)* **it's five kilometres away** c'est à cinq kilomètres d'ici; **it's ten minutes walk away** c'est à dix minutes à pied; **she lives far away** elle habite loin
(b) *(in time)* **a few days away** dans quelques jours
(c) *(absent)* absent/absente; **he's away** *(from the office, school)* il est absent
(d) **to go away** partir; **to run away**

s'enfuir; **to drive away** partir en voiture

awful *adjective* affreux/affreuse

awfully *adverb* très, extrêmement; **it's awfully hard** c'est extrêmement difficile; **I'm awfully sorry** je suis vraiment désolé

awkward *adjective*
(a) *(clumsy)* maladroit/maladroite
(b) *(difficult)* difficile; **their house is awkward to get to** leur maison est difficile d'accès
(c) *(embarrassing)* gênant/gênante; **it would be awkward if he met her** ce serait gênant s'il la rencontrait
(d) *(embarrassed)* gêné/gênée; **she felt awkward about going** ça la gênait d'y aller

axe *noun* la hache

baby *noun* le bébé; **when she was a baby** quand elle était bébé

baby-sit *verb* faire du baby-sitting

baby-sitter *noun* le/la baby-sitter

bachelor *noun* le célibataire

back

1 *noun*
(**a**) *(of a person, an animal, a book)* le dos; **she sat with her back to the window** elle était assise le dos tourné à la fenêtre
(**b**) *(of a house, a car)* l'arrière *(masculine)*; **I sat in the back of the car** je suis monté à l'arrière de la voiture
(**c**) *(of a room)* le fond; **they sat at the back of the class** ils se sont assis au fond de la classe
(**d**) *(of a chair)* le dossier

2 *adjective* arrière; **I've got a puncture in my back tyre** mon pneu arrière est crevé; **we'll use the back door** on va passer par la porte de derrière

> The adjective *arrière* does not change in the plural.

3 *adverb*
(**a**) *(towards the rear)* en arrière; **take a step back** fais un pas en arrière
(**b**) *(in return)* **I want my money back** je veux qu'on me rembourse; **to write back to somebody** répondre à quelqu'un; **to call somebody back** rappeler quelqu'un
(**c**) *(returning to starting point)* **to come back** revenir; **to go back** retourner; **to arrive back** rentrer; **I'll be back on Friday** je reviens vendredi; **they've gone back home** ils sont rentrés chez eux

4 *verb* **back up**
(**a**) *(support)* soutenir
(**b**) *(on a computer)* sauvegarder

backache *noun* le mal de dos; **I've got backache** j'ai mal au dos

background *noun*
(**a**) le fond; **on a green background** sur fond vert; **the painting has a blue background** le fond du tableau est bleu; **there's a lot of noise in the background** il y a beaucoup de bruit de fond
(**b**) *(social class)* le milieu; **he comes from a working-class background** il vient d'un milieu ouvrier
(**c**) *(education)* la formation
(**d**) *(of a situation)* le contexte; **the political background** le contexte politique

backpack

1 *noun* le sac à dos
2 *verb* voyager sac au dos; **he went backpacking around Europe** il est parti avec son sac à dos faire le tour de l'Europe

backstroke *noun* le dos crawlé; **I can do the backstroke** je sais nager le dos crawlé

backwards *adverb*
(**a**) *(towards the rear)* en arrière; **I fell backwards** je suis tombé en arrière; **he looked backwards** il a jeté un coup d'œil en arrière
(**b**) *(facing the wrong way)* **to walk backwards** marcher à reculons

backyard *noun* la cour de derrière

bacon *noun* le bacon; **bacon and eggs** des œufs au bacon

bacteria *plural noun* les bactéries *(feminine plural)*

bad *adjective*
(**a**) *(unpleasant)* mauvais/mauvaise; **there was a bad smell in the house** il y avait une mauvaise odeur dans la maison; **we've had bad weather this week** on a eu mauvais temps cette semaine; **that's too bad!** *(what a shame)* quel dommage!; *(tough luck)* tant pis!
(**b**) *(unhealthy)* mauvais/mauvaise; **smoking is bad for your health** le tabac est mauvais pour la santé; **to have bad teeth** avoir de mauvaises dents; **to have a bad back** avoir des problèmes de dos
(**c**) *(poor)* mauvais/mauvaise; **she's very bad at maths** elle est très mauvaise en maths; **they speak bad French** ils parlent mal français
(**d**) *(serious)* grave; **it was a bad accident** c'était un accident grave; **I have a bad cold** j'ai un gros rhume
(**e**) *(naughty)* vilain/vilaine; **the children were very bad** les enfants n'ont pas été sages du tout
(**f**) *(wicked)* méchant/méchante
(**g**) *(rotten)* pourri/pourrie; **this meat has gone bad** cette viande est pourrie
(**h**) **to feel bad** s'en vouloir; **I feel bad about what I said to him** je m'en veux de lui avoir dit ça

badge *noun* le badge

badger *noun* le blaireau

> The plural of *blaireau* is *blaireaux.*

badly *adverb*
(**a**) *(poorly)* mal; **he speaks English badly** il parle mal anglais; **these toys are badly made** ces jouets sont mal faits
(**b**) *(seriously)* gravement; **he was badly injured in the accident** il a été gravement blessé dans l'accident
(**c**) *(very much)* **we badly want to see her** nous avons très envie de la voir

badminton *noun* le badminton; **do you want to play badminton?** est-ce que tu veux jouer au badminton?

> Note that when talking about playing sports and games, French uses the expression *jouer à.*

bad-tempered *adjective* **he's bad-tempered today** il est de mauvaise humeur aujourd'hui; **he's always bad-tempered** il a mauvais caractère

bag *noun*
(**a**) le sac; **a plastic bag** un sac en plastique
(**b**) *(handbag)* le sac à main
(**c**) *(suitcase)* la valise; **have you packed your bags?** est-ce que tu as fait tes valises?

baggage *noun* les bagages *(masculine plural)*; **do you have a lot of baggage?** est-ce que vous avez beaucoup de bagages?; **I only have one piece of baggage** je n'ai qu'un bagage

> Do not confuse the spellings of the French *bagage* and English *baggage.*

baggy *adjective* large

bagpipes *noun* la cornemuse; **he plays the bagpipes** il joue de la cornemuse

> Note that when talking about musical instruments, French uses the expression *jouer de.*

bake *verb* **to bake something** faire cuire quelque chose au four; **to bake a cake** faire un gâteau; **I like baking** *(making cakes)* j'aime bien faire de la pâtisserie

baked *adjective* cuit/cuite au four; **baked beans** des haricots blancs à la sauce tomate; **a baked potato** une pomme de terre au four

baker *noun* le boulanger/la boulangère; **she's a baker** elle est boulangère; **I'm going to the baker's** je vais à la boulangerie

> Note that when describing people's jobs or situations, French does not use an article (*un* or *une*).

bakery *noun* la boulangerie

baking *noun* **I'll do some baking to-morrow** *(make cakes)* demain, je ferai de la pâtisserie

balance
1 *noun* l'équilibre *(masculine)*; **she tried to keep her balance** elle a essayé de garder l'équilibre; **I lost my balance** j'ai perdu l'équilibre
2 *verb (be in stable position)* être en équilibre; *(remain in stable position)* se tenir en équilibre; **the books were balanced on the desk** les livres étaient en équilibre sur le bureau

balcony *noun* le balcon

bald *adjective* chauve; **my dad's going bald** mon père devient chauve

ball *noun*
(a) *(for tennis, cricket, golf)* la balle
(b) *(for football, rugby, basketball)* le ballon
(c) *(for bowls, bowling)* la boule
(d) *(any round shape)* la boule; **to roll something into a ball** mettre quelque chose en boule
(e) *(dance)* le bal

> The plural of *bal* is *bals*.

ballet *noun* le ballet; **I'm going to the ballet this evening** je vais voir un ballet ce soir; **I go to ballet lessons** je fais de la danse classique; **a ballet dancer** un danseur/une danseuse de ballet; **a ballet shoe** un chausson de danse

balloon *noun*
(a) *(for children)* le ballon
(b) **a balloon, a hot-air balloon** une montgolfière

ballpoint *noun* **a ballpoint, a ball-point pen** un stylo à bille

ban *verb* interdire; **they banned me from seeing him** ils m'ont interdit de le voir

banana *noun* la banane

band *noun*
(a) *(pop, jazz or rock group)* le groupe; **he's in a band** il fait partie d'un groupe

(b) *(brass band)* la fanfare
(c) **an elastic band** un élastique

bandage
1 *noun* le bandage; **she has a bandage on her arm** elle a le bras bandé
2 *verb* bander; **the doctor bandaged my leg** le docteur m'a bandé la jambe

bang
1 *noun*
(a) *(explosion)* la détonation
(b) *(slam)* le claquement; **the door shut with a bang** la porte s'est refermée en claquant
2 *verb*
(a) *(knock)* cogner; **I banged my head on the shelf** je me suis cogné la tête contre l'étagère; **I banged on the door but nobody came** j'ai frappé à la porte mais personne n'est venu
(b) *(slam)* claquer; **the door banged shut** la porte s'est refermée en claquant; **she banged the door shut** elle a claqué la porte

bangle *noun* le bracelet

banister, banisters *noun* la rampe d'escalier

banjo *noun* le banjo; **he plays the banjo** il joue du banjo

> Note that when talking about playing musical instruments, French uses the expression *jouer de*.

bank *noun*
(a) *(for money)* la banque; **she has £10,000 in the bank** elle a 10 000 livres à la banque
(b) *(of a river)* le bord; **we had a picnic on the bank of the river** on a pique-niqué au bord de la rivière

banker *noun* le banquier/la banquière; **my father's a banker** mon père est banquier

> Note that when describing people's jobs or situations, French does not use an article (*un* or *une*).

banknote *noun* le billet de banque

banner *noun* la bannière

baptize *verb* baptiser

> The *p* in *baptiser* is not pronounced.

bar *noun*
(**a**) *(piece of metal)* la barre; *(on a window)* le barreau

> The plural of *barreau* is *barreaux*.

(**b**) *(pub)* le bar; **we went for a drink in the bar** on est allé prendre un verre au bar
(**c**) *(counter)* le bar
(**d**) **a bar of chocolate** une tablette de chocolat; **a bar of soap** un savon

barbecue
1 *noun* le barbecue
2 *verb* faire cuire au barbecue

barber *noun* le coiffeur pour hommes; **he went to the barber's** il est allé chez le coiffeur

bare *adjective* nu/nue; **she's got bare feet** elle est pieds nus; **the walls were bare** il n'y avait rien d'accroché aux murs

barefoot
1 *adjective* aux pieds nus; **a barefoot child** un enfant aux pieds nus
2 *adverb* pieds nus; **she goes barefoot** elle marche pieds nus

bargain *noun* une affaire; **to get a bargain** faire une bonne affaire

barely *adverb* à peine; **I barely know her** je la connais à peine

barge *noun* la péniche; **they live on a barge** ils vivent sur une péniche

bark
1 *noun*
(**a**) *(of a tree)* l'écorce *(feminine)*
(**b**) *(of a dog)* un aboiement
2 *verb* *(of a dog)* aboyer

barmaid *noun* la serveuse; **she's a barmaid here** elle est serveuse ici

barman *noun* le barman; **I'm a barman** je suis barman

barn *noun* la grange

barrel *noun* le tonneau

> The plural of *tonneau* is *tonneaux*.

barrier *noun* la barrière; **the language barrier** la barrière de la langue

barrister *noun* un avocat/une avocate; **she's a barrister** elle est avocate

> Note that when describing people's jobs or situations, French does not use an article (*un* or *une*).

base
1 *noun* la base
2 *verb* baser; **the film is based on a true story** ce film est tiré d'une histoire vraie

baseball *noun* le base-ball; **a baseball cap** une casquette de base-ball; **they're playing baseball** ils jouent au base-ball

> Note that when talking about playing sports and games, French uses the expression *jouer à*.

basement *noun* le sous-sol; **the study is in the basement** le bureau est au sous-sol

> The plural of *sous-sol* is *sous-sols*.

bash *verb* **I bashed him on the head** je lui ai donné un coup sur la tête; **I bashed my knee on the desk** je me suis cogné le genou contre le bureau

basic *adjective*
(**a**) *(elementary)* de base; **learn the basic vocabulary** apprenez le vocabulaire de base
(**b**) *(primitive)* rudimentaire; **their flat is really basic** leur appartement est très rudimentaire

basically *adverb* au fond; **they are both basically the same** au fond, ils sont tous les deux pareils; **basically, I agree with you** en gros, je suis d'accord avec vous

basil *noun* le basilic

basin *noun*
(**a**) *(sink)* le lavabo

(**b**) *(bowl)* la cuvette

basket *noun*
(**a**) *(for carrying shopping)* le panier
(**b**) *(for paper, bread)* la corbeille; **a wastepaper basket** une corbeille à papier

basketball *noun* le basket; **do you want to play basketball?** est-ce que tu veux jouer au basket?

Note that when talking about playing sports and games, French uses the expression *jouer à.*

bass *noun*
(**a**) *(guitar)* la (guitare) basse; *(double bass)* la contrebasse; **she plays bass in the band** elle joue de la basse dans le groupe
(**b**) *(on a stereo)* les basses *(feminine plural)*

bat *noun*
(**a**) *(animal)* la chauve-souris

The plural of *chauve-souris* is *chauves-souris.*

(**b**) *(for cricket, baseball)* la batte; *(for table tennis)* la raquette

bath *noun*
(**a**) *(bathtub)* la baignoire
(**b**) *(activity)* le bain; **she's having a bath** elle prend un bain

bathe *verb*
(**a**) *(have a bath)* prendre un bain
(**b**) *(go swimming)* se baigner
(**c**) *(soak)* tremper; **she bathed her feet** elle s'est trempé les pieds

bathing costume *noun* le maillot de bain

bathrobe *noun* la robe de chambre

bathroom *noun* la salle de bains

bathtub *noun* la baignoire

battery *noun*
(**a**) *(for an appliance)* la pile
(**b**) *(of a vehicle, a mobile phone)* la batterie; **the battery's dead** *(of a car)* la batterie est à plat; *(of a mobile phone)* il n'y a plus de batterie

battle *noun*
(**a**) *(in a war)* la bataille
(**b**) *(struggle)* la lutte

bay *noun*
(**a**) *(of sea)* la baie
(**b**) *(plant)* **a bay tree** un laurier; **a bay leaf** une feuille de laurier

be
1 *verb*
(**a**) *(describing things and people)* être; **Mary is pretty** Mary est jolie; **they are English** ils sont anglais; **he is a teacher** il est professeur; **the sky is blue** le ciel est bleu
(**b**) *(times and places)* être; **it is late** il est tard; **it's four o'clock** il est quatre heures; **tomorrow is Friday** demain, c'est vendredi; **it's the tenth of March** nous sommes le dix mars; **the books are on the table** les livres sont sur la table; **she's in York** elle est à York
(**c**) *(ages and sensations)* avoir; **I am twelve** j'ai douze ans; **we are cold** nous avons froid; **are you hungry?** est-ce que tu as faim?; **I'm thirsty** j'ai soif
(**d**) *(health)* aller; **how are you?** comment vas-tu?; **I'm well** je vais bien
(**e**) *(weather)* faire; **it's hot** il fait chaud; **it was a lovely day** il faisait très beau
(**f**) *(calculations)* faire; **two and two are four** deux et deux font quatre; **how much is it?** *(what is the total)* ça fait combien?; *(how much does it cost)* ça coûte combien?
(**g**) **have you been to Italy?** est-ce que tu es déjà allé en Italie?; **I've been here before** je suis déjà venu ici
(**h**) **there is, there are** *(in existence)* il y a; *(pointing out)* voilà; **there's a problem** il y a un problème; **there are no more glasses** il n'y a plus de verres; **there's my sister!** voilà ma sœur! **there they are!** les voilà!
(**i**) **here is, here are** voici; **here is your book** voici ton livre; **here they are!** les voici!
2 *auxiliary verb (continuous tenses)* **I**

am working je travaille; **she is sleeping** elle dort; **they were laughing** ils riaient

> The present continuous tense (*to be doing something*) is usually just translated by the present tense in French. The past continuous tense is translated by the imperfect.

beach *noun* la plage; **I want to go to the beach** je veux aller à la plage

bead *noun* la perle; **a string of beads** un collier de perles

beak *noun* le bec

beam
1 *noun*
(a) *(in a building, for gymnastics)* la poutre
(b) *(ray of light)* le rayon
2 *verb (smile)* faire un grand sourire

bean *noun* le haricot

bear
1 *noun (animal)* un ours
2 *verb*
(a) *(put up with)* supporter; **she can't bear the sight of blood** elle ne supporte pas la vue du sang
(b) **to bear something in mind** ne pas oublier quelque chose; **bear in mind that we have only two weeks left** n'oublie pas qu'il ne nous reste que deux semaines
(c) **to bear with somebody** patienter; **if you'll bear with me a minute, I'll explain** si vous voulez bien patienter un instant, je vais vous expliquer

beard *noun* la barbe

beast *noun* la bête

beat
1 *noun (in music)* le rythme
2 *verb*
(a) *(hit)* battre; **it's illegal to beat children** on n'a pas le droit de battre les enfants
(b) *(win)* battre; **she beat him at poker** elle l'a battu au poker
(c) *(in cooking)* battre; **first, beat the**

eggs commencez par battre les œufs
(d) *(heart)* battre; **my heart's beating very fast** mon cœur bat très vite
3 **beat up** tabasser; **he got beaten up** il s'est fait tabasser

beautician *noun* une esthéticienne; **her sister's a beautician** sa sœur est esthéticienne

beautiful *adjective* beau/belle; **a beautiful baby** un beau bébé; **a beautiful woman** une belle femme; **a beautiful tree** un bel arbre; **beautiful children** de beaux enfants

> Note that *beau* becomes *bel* before a vowel or mute h. The plural of *beau* or *bel* is *beaux* and the plural of *belle* is *belles*.

beauty *noun* la beauté; **a beauty salon** un institut de beauté; **a beauty spot** un grain de beauté; **a beauty therapist** une esthéticienne

beaver *noun* le castor

because *conjunction*
(a) parce que; **she's happy because it's sunny** elle est contente parce qu'il fait beau

> Note that *parce que* becomes *parce qu'* before a vowel.

(b) **because of** à cause de; **the road was closed because of the accident** la route était barrée à cause de l'accident; **because of her** à cause d'elle

> Note that *à cause de* becomes *à cause d'* before a vowel.

become *verb* devenir; **he became a doctor** il est devenu médecin

bed *noun* le lit; **to be in bed** être au lit; **to go to bed** aller au lit *or* aller se coucher; **to get out of bed** se lever

bedclothes *plural noun* les draps et couvertures *(masculine plural)*

bedroom *noun* la chambre

bedside *noun* le chevet; **a bedside lamp** une lampe de chevet; **a bedside table** une table de chevet

bedtime *noun* **it's bedtime** c'est l'heure d'aller se coucher; **it's past my bedtime** je devrais déjà être couché; **she told him a bedtime story** elle lui a raconté une histoire au lit

bee *noun* une abeille

beef *noun* le bœuf

beehive *noun* la ruche

beer *noun* la bière; **would you like a beer?** est-ce que tu veux une bière?

beetle *noun* le scarabée; *(any beetle-like insect)* la bestiole

beetroot *noun* la betterave

before
1 *adverb*
(**a**) avant; **why didn't you say so before?** pourquoi est-ce que tu ne l'as pas dit avant?; **the year before** l'année d'avant; **the day before** la veille
(**b**) *(already)* déjà; **I've been here before** je suis déjà venu ici
(**c**) **never before** jamais; **I have never seen him before** je ne l'ai jamais vu
2 *preposition* avant; **before Easter** avant Pâques; **I got here before you** je suis arrivé avant vous; **before that, she was a teacher** avant ça, elle était prof; **the day before yesterday** avant-hier
3 *conjunction* avant de, avant que; **I thanked him before leaving** je l'ai remercié avant de partir; **you should go before he gets back** tu devrais t'en aller avant qu'il revienne

Note that *avant que* is followed by the subjunctive.

beg *verb*
(**a**) *(in the street)* mendier
(**b**) **to beg somebody to do something** supplier quelqu'un de faire quelque chose; **he begged me to help him** il m'a supplié de l'aider; **she begged me for a cigarette** elle m'a supplié pour que je lui donne une cigarette

beggar *noun* le mendiant/la mendiante

begin *verb* commencer; **the concert is about to begin** le concert va commencer; **it began to rain** il a commencé à pleuvoir

beginner *noun* le débutant/la débutante; **a beginners' French class** un cours de français pour débutants

beginning *noun* le début; **at the beginning, in the beginning** au début

behalf *noun* **I'm calling on behalf of the manager** j'appelle de la part du directeur; **on my behalf** de ma part; **he's here on behalf of the president** il représente le président; **she accepted the award on his behalf** elle a reçu le prix pour lui

behave *verb*
(**a**) se comporter; **he behaves like an idiot** il se comporte comme un imbécile
(**b**) **to behave oneself** être sage; **behave (yourself)!** sois sage!

behaviour *noun* le comportement; **the children were on their best behaviour** les enfants se sont très bien comportés

behind
1 *preposition*
(**a**) derrière; **he hid behind a tree** il s'est caché derrière un arbre; **look behind you** regarde derrière toi
(**b**) *(in one's work or studies)* en retard; **she's behind the other pupils** elle est en retard sur les autres élèves
2 *adverb*
(**a**) derrière; **he cycled and I ran behind** il était en vélo et moi je courais derrière; **I left my umbrella behind** j'ai oublié mon parapluie
(**b**) *(in one's work or studies)* en retard; **I'm behind with my work** je suis en retard dans mon travail; **he's falling behind** il prend du retard

beige *adjective* beige; **she's wearing a beige skirt** elle porte une jupe beige

being *noun* **a human being** un être humain

Belgian
1 *adjective* belge
2 *noun* *(person)* le/la Belge; **the Belgians** les Belges *(masculine plural)*

> In French, only the noun for the inhabitants of a country takes a capital letter, never the adjective.

Belgium *noun* la Belgique; **he lives in Belgium** il habite en Belgique; **have you ever been to Belgium?** est-ce que tu es déjà allé en Belgique?; **these chocolates are from Belgium** ces chocolats viennent de Belgique

belief *noun*
(a) *(certainty)* la croyance; **this is beyond belief** c'est incroyable
(b) *(opinion)* la conviction; **it's my belief he's lying** je suis convaincu qu'il ment

believable *adjective* crédible; **his story was quite believable** son histoire était tout à fait crédible

believe *verb*
(a) croire; **I don't believe you** je ne te crois pas
(b) to believe in something croire à quelque chose; **he still believes in Father Christmas** il croit encore au père Noël; **to believe in God** croire en Dieu

bell *noun*
(a) *(in a church)* la cloche; *(hand-held)* la clochette
(b) *(on a door, a bicycle)* la sonnette; *(electric, at school)* la sonnerie; **I rang the bell** *(on a door)* j'ai sonné; **their teacher arrived after the bell had rung** leur prof est arrivé après la sonnerie; **the pupils ran out when the bell rang** les élèves sont sortis en courant quand la cloche a sonné

belly *noun* le ventre

belong *verb*
(a) *(property)* **to belong to** appartenir à; **that book belongs to me** ce livre m'appartient *or* ce livre est à moi
(b) *(in the right place)* **put the books back where they belong** remettez les livres à leur place; **the dishes belong in that cupboard** les assiettes vont dans ce placard

belongings *plural noun* les affaires *(feminine plural)*

below
1 *preposition* en dessous de; **they live in the flat below ours** ils habitent dans l'appartement en dessous du nôtre; **his marks are below average** ses notes sont en dessous de la moyenne
2 *adverb*
(a) *(underneath)* en dessous; **her name comes immediately below** son nom apparaît juste en dessous; **they live in the flat below** ils habitent dans l'appartement du dessous
(b) *(lower down)* en bas; **he could hear two men talking below** il entendait deux hommes parler en bas

belt *noun* la ceinture

bench *noun* le banc

bend
1 *noun*
(a) *(in the road)* le virage
(b) you're driving me round the bend! tu me rends dingue!
2 *verb*
(a) *(a part of the body)* plier; **bend your knees** pliez les genoux
(b) *(a piece of metal)* tordre; **the key is bent (out of shape)** la clé est tordue
3 bend down se baisser
4 bend over se pencher

beneath
1 *preposition*
(a) *(under)* sous; **the ground beneath my feet** le sol sous mes pieds
(b) *(unworthy of)* indigne de; **she thinks the work is beneath her** elle croit que ce travail est indigne d'elle
(c) *(inferior to)* inférieur/inférieure; **she thinks everybody's beneath her** elle croit que tout le monde lui est inférieur
2 *adverb* en dessous

beret *noun* le béret

berry *noun* la baie

beside *preposition* à côté de

besides
1 *preposition*
(a) *(in addition to)* en plus de; **besides playing squash, she plays tennis** en plus du squash, elle fait du tennis
(b) *(apart from)* à part; **what other skills do you have besides languages?** quelles compétences avez-vous à part les langues?
2 *adverb (anyway)* en plus; **besides, I don't even like funfairs** en plus, je n'aime même pas les fêtes foraines

best
1 *adjective* meilleur/meilleure; **she's my best friend** c'est ma meilleure amie; **it's one of the best films I've ever seen** c'est un des meilleurs films que j'aie jamais vu
2 *noun* **the best** le meilleur/la meilleure; **she's the best in the class** c'est la meilleure de la classe; **I did my best** j'ai fait de mon mieux
3 *adverb* le mieux; **he does it best** c'est lui qui le fait le mieux; **which one do you like best?** tu préfères lequel?; **they are the best paid** ce sont les mieux payés

bestseller *noun (book)* le best-seller; **this CD is the year's bestseller** ce CD est le plus gros succès de l'année

bet
1 *noun* le pari; **to make a bet** faire un pari
2 *verb* parier; **I bet she's lying** je parie qu'elle ment; **I bet her £5 he wouldn't come** j'ai parié 5 livres avec elle qu'il ne viendrait pas; **I bet on this horse** j'ai misé sur ce cheval

betray *verb* trahir; **you've betrayed my trust** tu as trahi ma confiance

better
1 *adjective*
(a) meilleur/meilleure; **I'm better at languages than he is** je suis meilleur en langues que lui; **it could be better** ça pourrait être mieux; **the weather is better** il fait meilleur
(b) *(in health)* mieux; **I'm feeling much better** je me sens beaucoup mieux
2 *adverb*
(a) mieux; **they speak French better than they used to** ils parlent mieux français qu'avant; **I liked his last book better** j'ai préféré son dernier livre
(b) **to get better** *(after an illness)* se remettre; *(improve)* s'améliorer; **get better soon!** remets-toi vite!; **the weather is getting better** le temps s'améliore
(c) **I'd better not wake him** il vaut mieux que je ne le réveille pas; **we'd better go** il vaut mieux que nous partions; **you'd better be on time!** tu as intérêt à être à l'heure!

between
1 *preposition*
(a) *(in space or in time)* entre; **don't eat between meals** ne mange pas entre les repas
(b) *(range)* entre; **it will cost between five and ten million** ça coûtera entre cinq et dix millions; **children aged between five and ten** les enfants de cinq à dix ans
(c) *(alternatives)* **you must choose between the two** il faut que tu choisisses l'un des deux
(d) *(division)* **he shared the cake between the children** il a partagé le gâteau entre les enfants
2 *adverb* **in between** entre les deux, au milieu; **there are two chairs with a table in between** il y a deux chaises, et une table au milieu

beyond
1 *preposition*
(a) *(further than)* après; **the house is beyond the church** la maison est située après l'église
(b) *(outside of)* **his stupidity is beyond belief** il est d'une bêtise incroyable; **it's beyond me** ça me dépasse

2 *adverb* au-delà; **you can see the beach and the mountains beyond** on peut voir la plage et au-delà les montagnes

bib *noun* le bavoir

Bible *noun* **the Bible** la Bible

bicycle *noun* la bicyclette, le vélo; **he was riding his bicycle** il faisait du vélo; **can you ride a bicycle?** est-ce que tu sais faire du vélo?

big *adjective*
(**a**) grand/grande; **they've got a big house** ils ont une grande maison
(**b**) *(dog, piece, package)* gros/grosse

bike *noun* le vélo; **he was riding his bike** il faisait du vélo; **can you ride a bike?** est-ce que tu sais faire du vélo?

bikini *noun* le bikini

bilingual *adjective* bilingue

bill *noun*
(**a**) *(sent to home)* la facture; **an electricity bill** une facture d'électricité
(**b**) *(in a restaurant)* l'addition *(feminine)*; **can we have the bill, please?** l'addition, s'il vous plaît

billboard *noun* le panneau d'affichage

The plural of *panneau d'affichage* is *panneaux d'affichage*.

billion *noun (one thousand million)* un milliard; **two billion** deux milliards; **it cost a billion dollars** ça a coûté un milliard de dollars

bin *noun* la poubelle; **to throw something in the bin** mettre quelque chose à la poubelle

bind *verb*
(**a**) *(tie)* attacher, lier
(**b**) *(link)* lier
(**c**) *(a book)* relier; **the book is bound in leather** le livre est relié en cuir

bingo
1 *noun* le bingo, le loto
2 *exclamation* **bingo! I found it** ça y est! je l'ai trouvé

binoculars *plural noun* les jumelles *(feminine plural)*

biography *noun* la biographie

biology *noun* la biologie; **he's very good at biology** il est fort en biologie

bird *noun* un oiseau

The plural of *oiseau* is *oiseaux*.

biro® *noun* le stylo à bille, le bic®

birth *noun* la naissance; **to give birth** accoucher; **she gave birth to a boy** elle a accouché d'un garçon; **a birth certificate** un acte de naissance

birthday *noun* un anniversaire; **it's my birthday today** c'est mon anniversaire aujourd'hui; **it's her 21st birthday** elle fête ses 21 ans; **happy birthday!** bon anniversaire!; **they're giving him a birthday party** ils organisent une fête pour son anniversaire; **a birthday cake** un gâteau d'anniversaire; **a birthday present** un cadeau d'anniversaire

biscuit *noun* le biscuit

bishop *noun*
(**a**) *(person)* un évêque
(**b**) *(in chess)* le fou

bit *noun*
(**a**) *(piece)* le morceau; **can I have a bit of cake?** est-ce que je peux avoir un morceau de gâteau?; **to come to bits** tomber en morceaux; **to take something to bits** démonter quelque chose

The plural of *morceau* is *morceaux*.

(**b**) **a bit of** *(small amount of)* un peu de; **do you want a bit of cheese?** est-ce que tu veux un peu de fromage?; **can I try a bit?** est-ce que je peux en goûter un peu?
(**c**) **a bit** *(a little)* un peu; **you're a bit late** tu es un peu en retard; **it's a bit too expensive** c'est un peu trop cher; **can he speak English? – a bit** qu'il parle anglais? – un peu
(**d**) **wait a bit** attends un peu; **I'll be there in a bit** j'arrive dans quelques minutes; **we sat down for a bit** on s'est assis un instant

(e) **not a bit** pas du tout; **she wasn't a bit angry** elle n'était pas du tout en colère

bite
1 *noun*
(a) *(from a person, an animal)* la morsure
(b) *(from an insect)* la piqûre; **I've got a mosquito bite** je me suis fait piquer par un moustique
(c) *(mouthful)* **I took a bite of the apple** j'ai mordu dans la pomme
(d) **to have a bite to eat** manger un morceau
2 *verb*
(a) *(person, animal)* mordre; **the horse bit him** le cheval l'a mordu
(b) *(insect)* piquer

bitter *adjective*
(a) *(taste)* amer/amère
(b) *(person)* amer/amère; **he's bitter about not being picked for the team** il est amer parce qu'il n'a pas été pris dans l'équipe
(c) *(cold, wind)* glacial/glaciale

> The masculine plural of *glacial* is *glacials* or *glaciaux*.

bizarre *adjective* bizarre

black *adjective* noir/noire; **she's wearing black trousers** elle porte un pantalon noir; **they drink black coffee** ils boivent du café noir; **she's black** elle est noire

blackberry *noun* la mûre; **blackberry jam** la confiture de mûres

blackbird *noun* le merle

blackboard *noun* le tableau; **I wrote it on the blackboard** je l'ai écrit au tableau

> The plural of *tableau* is *tableaux*.

blackcurrant *noun* le cassis; **blackcurrant jam** la confiture de cassis

blackmail
1 *verb* **to blackmail somebody** faire chanter quelqu'un; **he blackmailed me into helping him** il m'a forcé à l'aider en faisant du chantage
2 *noun* le chantage; **that's blackmail!** c'est du chantage!

blackout *noun*
(a) *(power cut)* la panne d'électricité
(b) *(during a war)* le black-out

blade *noun* la lame

blame
1 *verb* **she blamed me for breaking the vase** elle m'a reproché d'avoir cassé le vase; **they blamed the fire on him** ils l'ont accusé d'être à l'origine de l'incendie; **I blame you!** c'est de ta faute!; **don't blame me!** ce n'est pas de ma faute!
2 *noun* la responsabilité; **I got the blame for breaking the window** c'est moi qu'on a accusé d'avoir cassé la vitre

blank *adjective*
(a) *(paper)* blanc/blanche; **fill in the blank spaces** remplissez les blancs; **leave this line blank** n'écrivez rien sur cette ligne
(b) *(disk, tape, CD)* vierge
(c) *(screen)* **the screen went blank** il n'y avait plus rien sur l'écran
(d) *(mind)* **my mind went blank** j'ai eu un trou de mémoire

blanket *noun*
(a) *(on a bed)* la couverture
(b) **a blanket of snow** une couche de neige

blast *noun*
(a) *(from a bomb)* une explosion; **a lot of people were killed by the blast** l'explosion a entraîné la mort de nombreuses personnes
(b) *(of air)* une bouffée; **a blast of heat** une bouffée de chaleur; **a blast of wind** un coup de vent
(c) **(at) full blast** *(very loudly)* à fond; **she had the radio on (at) full blast** elle avait la radio à fond

blaze
1 *noun* *(large fire)* un incendie; **five people died in the blaze** l'incendie a fait cinq morts

2 *verb*
(**a**) *(fire)* être en flammes; **the house was blazing** la maison était en flammes
(**b**) *(lights)* **they left all the lights blazing** ils ont laissé toutes les lumières allumées

blazer *noun* le blazer

bleach
1 *noun*
(**a**) *(for cleaning)* l'eau de Javel *(feminine)*
(**b**) *(for lightening hair)* le décolorant
2 *verb*
(**a**) *(when doing washing)* **she bleached the sheets** elle a passé les draps à l'eau de Javel
(**b**) *(hair)* décolorer; **to bleach one's hair** se décolorer les cheveux

bleed *verb* saigner; **my finger's bleeding** je saigne du doigt

blender *noun* le mixeur

blind
1 *adjective* aveugle; **a blind man** un aveugle; **a blind woman** une aveugle; **she's been blind from birth** elle est aveugle de naissance; **blind people** les non-voyants *(masculine plural)*
2 *noun (on a window)* le store; **close the blinds** baisse les stores

blindfold
1 *noun* le bandeau; **he put a blindfold on me** il m'a mis un bandeau sur les yeux

The plural of *bandeau* is *bandeaux*.

2 *verb* **they blindfolded him** ils lui ont bandé les yeux
3 *adverb* **I could do it blindfold** je pourrais le faire les yeux fermés

blink *verb* cligner des yeux

blister *noun* une ampoule

blizzard *noun* la tempête de neige

block
1 *noun*
(**a**) *(building)* **a block of flats, a block** un immeuble

(**b**) *(buildings between two streets)* le pâté de maisons; **we live on the same block** nous habitons dans le même pâté de maisons
(**c**) *(lump of stone, wood)* le bloc
(**d**) **a mental block** un blocage psychologique; **I have a mental block about computers** je fais un blocage sur les ordinateurs
2 *verb*
(**a**) *(road, traffic)* bloquer
(**b**) *(pipe, hole)* boucher; **the toilet's blocked** les toilettes sont bouchées; **my nose is blocked** j'ai le nez bouché
(**c**) **to block somebody's way** barrer le passage à quelqu'un
3 block up *(pipe, hole)* boucher

bloke *noun* le type; **he's a nice bloke** c'est un type sympa

blond
1 *adjective* blond/blonde; **he's blond** il est blond; **he's got blond hair** il a les cheveux blonds
2 *noun* le blond; **she prefers blonds** elle préfère les blonds

blonde
1 *adjective* blond/blonde; **she's blonde** elle est blonde; **she's got blonde hair** elle a les cheveux blonds
2 *noun* la blonde; **he prefers blondes** il préfère les blondes

blood *noun* le sang; **to give blood** donner son sang; **blood pressure** la tension; **a blood test** une analyse de sang

bloom
1 *noun* **in bloom** *(tree, garden)* en fleurs; *(single flower)* éclos/éclose
2 *verb* fleurir

blossom *noun* la fleur; **a tree in blossom** un arbre en fleurs

blouse *noun* le chemisier

Note that the French word *blouse* is never a translation for the English word *blouse*. Its most common meaning is *overall*.

blow
1 *noun*
(**a**) *(with the fist, a hammer)* le coup; **she dealt him a blow** elle lui a donné un coup
(**b**) *(shock, disaster)* le choc; **her death came as a terrible blow** sa mort a été un choc terrible
2 *verb*
(**a**) *(of the wind, a person)* souffler; **the wind's blowing from the west** le vent souffle de l'ouest; **the door blew open** le vent a ouvert la porte
(**b**) **to blow one's nose** se moucher; **to blow somebody a kiss** envoyer un baiser à quelqu'un
3 blow away
(**a**) s'envoler; **my hat blew away** mon chapeau s'est envolé
(**b**) *(of the wind)* emporter; **the wind blew my papers away** le vent a emporté mes papiers
4 blow down
(**a**) tomber; **the chimney blew down** la cheminée est tombée
(**b**) *(of the wind)* faire tomber; **the wind blew the chimney down** le vent a fait tomber la cheminée
5 blow out **to blow out a candle** souffler une bougie
6 blow up
(**a**) *(explode)* exploser; **the car blew up** la voiture a explosé
(**b**) *(make explode)* faire sauter; **the terrorists blew up his car** les terroristes ont fait sauter sa voiture
(**c**) *(inflate)* gonfler; **she blew up some balloons** elle a gonflé des ballons

blow-dry
1 *noun* le brushing®; **a cut and blow-dry** une coupe-brushing
2 *verb* **to blow-dry one's hair** se sécher les cheveux; **to blow-dry somebody's hair** faire un brushing® à quelqu'un

blue *adjective* bleu/bleue; **a blue book** un livre bleu; **a blue car** une voiture bleue; **blue flowers** des fleurs bleues

blueberry *noun* la myrtille; **blue-**

berry jam la confiture de myrtilles

blunt *adjective* **a blunt knife** un couteau qui coupe mal; **a blunt pencil** un crayon mal taillé

blur *noun* *(vague shape)* **without my glasses, everything is a blur** sans mes lunettes, je vois tout flou

blurred *adjective* flou/floue

blush *verb* rougir

board
1 *noun*
(**a**) *(piece of wood)* la planche
(**b**) *(for notices)* le panneau d'affichage; **he stuck a notice on the board** il a mis une annonce au panneau d'affichage

> The plural of *panneau d'affichage* is *panneaux d'affichage*.

(**c**) *(for writing on)* le tableau; **the teacher is writing on the board** le professeur écrit au tableau

> The plural of *tableau* is *tableaux*.

(**d**) **a board game** un jeu de société
(**e**) **on board** à bord; **on board a ship** à bord d'un bateau; **to go on board** monter à bord
2 *verb* **to board a ship** monter à bord d'un bateau; **to board a plane** monter à bord d'un avion; **to board a train** monter dans un train; **flight 123 is now boarding** embarquement immédiat du vol 123

boarding school *noun* l'internat *(masculine)*; **they go to boarding school** ils sont internes

boast *verb* se vanter; **he boasted that he could beat me** il s'est vanté de pouvoir me battre

boat *noun* le bateau

> The plural of *bateau* is *bateaux*.

body *noun*
(**a**) le corps
(**b**) *(corpse)* le cadavre

bodyguard *noun* le garde du corps

boil
1 *noun (spot)* le furoncle
2 *verb*
(**a**) *(get hot)* bouillir; **the water's boiling** l'eau bout
(**b**) *(heat something up)* faire bouillir; **I boiled some water** j'ai fait bouillir de l'eau; **to boil vegetables** faire cuire des légumes à l'eau; **to boil an egg** faire cuire un œuf à la coque; **to boil the kettle** mettre la bouilloire en marche
3 **boil over** *(of a pan, liquid)* déborder

boiled *adjective* **a boiled egg** un œuf à la coque; **a boiled potato** une pomme de terre à l'eau

boiling *adjective*
(**a**) *(water)* bouillant/bouillante
(**b**) *(weather, temperature)* **it's boiling in here** on crève de chaud ici; **I'm boiling (hot)** je crève de chaud

bold *adjective*
(**a**) *(brave)* audacieux/audacieuse
(**b**) *(not shy)* sûr/sûre de soi
(**c**) **in bold type** en caractères gras; **it's written in bold** c'est écrit en gras

bolt
1 *noun*
(**a**) *(on a door)* le verrou
(**b**) *(for a nut)* le boulon; **nuts and bolts** les écrous et les boulons
(**c**) **a bolt of lightning** un éclair
2 *verb*
(**a**) *(lock)* verrouiller
(**b**) *(fasten)* boulonner; **the chairs were bolted to the floor** les chaises étaient fixées au sol par des boulons
(**c**) *(food)* engloutir

bomb
1 *noun* la bombe
2 *verb (blow up)* faire sauter; *(from the air)* bombarder; **terrorists bombed the building** les terroristes ont fait sauter le bâtiment; **they bombed the city** ils ont bombardé la ville

bond
1 *noun (tie)* le lien; **we have a very**

close bond nous sommes très proches
2 *verb* **we didn't really bond** on n'a pas vraiment accroché

bone *noun*
(**a**) *(of a person, an animal)* un os

> The word *os* does not change in the plural, but the *s* is not pronounced.

(**b**) *(of a fish)* une arête

bonfire *noun*
(**a**) *(for dead leaves)* le feu; **to build a bonfire** faire un feu
(**b**) *(for a celebration)* le feu de joie

> The plural of *feu* is *feux*.

bonus *noun*
(**a**) *(money)* la prime; **she got a Christmas bonus of £200** elle a reçu 200 livres de prime de fin d'année
(**b**) *(advantage)* **it's a real bonus having the station close by** c'est vraiment un plus d'avoir la gare tout près

book
1 *noun*
(**a**) *(for reading)* le livre; **a book club** un club de livres; **a book review** une critique littéraire; **a book token** un bon d'achat de livres
(**b**) *(for writing in)* le cahier
(**c**) *(of tickets, stamps)* le carnet
2 *verb* réserver; **I've booked a table for tonight** j'ai réservé une table pour ce soir; **have you booked?** est-ce que vous avez réservé?; **it's fully booked** c'est complet

bookcase *noun* la bibliothèque

booking *noun* la réservation; **to make a booking** faire une réservation

bookmark
1 *noun*
(**a**) *(for a book)* le marque-page

> The plural of *marque-page* is *marque-pages*.

(**b**) *(on the Internet)* le signet
2 *verb* **to bookmark a page** *(on the Internet)* créer un signet sur une page

bookshelf *noun* une étagère

bookshop *noun* la librairie

> Note that the French word *librairie* is never a translation for the English word *library*, which is translated as *bibliothèque*.

boost
1 *noun* **to give a boost to** *(the economy)* relancer; *(numbers)* augmenter; *(morale)* remonter; **the results gave her confidence a boost** les résultats lui ont redonné confiance
2 *verb (the economy)* relancer; *(numbers)* augmenter; *(morale)* remonter; **the results boosted her confidence** les résultats lui ont redonné confiance

boot *noun*
(**a**) *(long)* la botte; *(short)* la bottine; *(for sports)* la chaussure; **football boots** des chaussures de foot
(**b**) *(of a car)* le coffre

booth *noun* la cabine; **a phone booth** une cabine téléphonique

booze *noun* l'alcool *(masculine)*; **there's no more booze** il n'y a plus rien à boire

> Note that the word *alcool* is pronounced "al-coll", not "al-cool".

border
1 *noun*
(**a**) *(between countries)* la frontière; **to cross the border** passer la frontière; **on the border between Norway and Sweden** à la frontière entre la Norvège et la Suède
(**b**) *(edge)* le bord; **there were flowers along the border of the path** il y avait des fleurs au bord du chemin
(**c**) *(of a picture)* la bordure
2 *verb (be next to)* border; **the garden is bordered with flowers** le jardin est bordé de fleurs; **the countries that border the Mediterranean** les pays qui sont en bordure de la Méditerranée

bore
1 *verb* ennuyer; **politics bores me** la politique m'ennuie

2 *noun*
(**a**) *(person)* **he's such a bore!** ce qu'il est rasoir!
(**b**) *(thing, event)* **the film was a bit of a bore** le film était un peu ennuyeux; **what a bore!** quelle barbe!

bored *adjective* **to be bored, to get bored** s'ennuyer; **I'm bored stiff** je m'ennuie à mourir

boredom *noun* l'ennui *(masculine)*

boring *adjective* ennuyeux/ennuyeuse

born *adjective* né/née; **I was born in Scotland** je suis né en Écosse; **she was born in 1992** elle est née en 1992

borrow *verb* emprunter; **to borrow something from somebody** emprunter quelque chose à quelqu'un; **can I borrow your umbrella?** est-ce que je peux emprunter ton parapluie?

Bosnia *noun* la Bosnie; **he was born in Bosnia** il est né en Bosnie; **I've never been to Bosnia** je ne suis jamais allé en Bosnie; **they're from Bosnia** ils viennent de Bosnie

Bosnian
1 *adjective* bosniaque
2 *noun (person)* le/la Bosniaque; **the Bosnians** les Bosniaques *(masculine plural)*

> In French, only the noun for the inhabitants of a country takes a capital letter, never the adjective.

boss
1 *noun* le patron/la patronne
2 *verb* **boss about** donner des ordres à; **stop bossing me about!** arrête de me donner des ordres!

both
1 *adjective* les deux; **both dresses are pretty** les deux robes sont jolies; **she kissed him on both cheeks** elle l'a embrassé sur les deux joues
2 *pronoun* tous/toutes les deux; **we both said yes** nous avons dit oui tous les deux; **both of them are dead** ils sont morts tous les deux; **Claire and I**

both went Claire et moi y sommes allées toutes les deux
3 *adverb (at the same time)* à la fois; **she is both intelligent and beautiful** elle est à la fois belle et intelligente; **he speaks both French and Spanish** il parle français et espagnol

bother
1 *verb*
(**a**) *(annoy, disturb)* déranger; **I'm sorry to bother you** excusez-moi de vous déranger; **would it bother you if I opened the window?** ça vous dérange si j'ouvre la fenêtre?; **don't bother me!** laisse-moi tranquille!
(**b**) *(worry)* inquiéter; **don't bother yourself about me** ne vous inquiétez pas pour moi
(**c**) *(take the trouble)* se donner la peine; **please don't bother getting up!** ne vous donnez pas la peine de vous lever!; **I can't be bothered!** je n'ai pas le courage!
(**d**) **I'm not bothered** ça m'est égal
2 *noun (difficulties)* les ennuis *(masculine plural)*; **he's having a bit of bother with the car** il a quelques ennuis avec la voiture; **the trip isn't worth the bother** le voyage ne vaut pas la peine; **it's no bother at all** ça ne m'ennuie pas du tout

bottle *noun*
(**a**) *(for drinks)* la bouteille; **a bottle opener** un décapsuleur
(**b**) *(for perfume, medicine)* le flacon
(**c**) *(for a baby)* le biberon

bottom
1 *noun*
(**a**) *(part of the body)* le derrière
(**b**) *(lowest point)* le bas; **at the bottom of the page** en bas de la page; **at the bottom of the staircase** au bas de l'escalier
(**c**) *(deepest point)* le fond; **the ship touched the bottom** le navire a touché le fond; **at the bottom of my bag** au fond de mon sac
2 *adjective*
(**a**) *(lowest)* du bas; **it's on the bottom shelf** il est sur l'étagère du bas; **the bottom book in the pile** le livre qui est en bas de la pile; **the bottom floor** *(ground floor)* le rez-de-chaussée; *(basement)* le sous-sol
(**b**) *(lower)* inférieur/inférieure; **the bottom half of the screen** la partie inférieure de l'écran

bounce *verb*
(**a**) rebondir; **the ball bounced down the steps** la balle a rebondi de marche en marche
(**b**) *(intentionally)* faire rebondir; **he was bouncing the ball** il faisait rebondir le ballon
(**c**) *(jump)* sauter; **she's bouncing on the bed** elle saute sur le lit

bouquet *noun* le bouquet

bow[1] *noun*
(**a**) *(knot)* le nœud; **tie it in a bow** faites un nœud; **a bow tie** un nœud papillon
(**b**) *(weapon)* un arc; **a bow and arrow** un arc et des flèches
(**c**) *(in music)* un archet

bow[2]
1 *verb (as a greeting)* saluer de la tête; **the servants bowed to him** les domestiques l'ont salué; **he bowed his head** *(in shame)* il a baissé la tête
2 *noun* le salut; **the actors took a bow** les acteurs ont salué

bowl *noun*
(**a**) *(to eat out of)* le bol
(**b**) *(for washing-up)* la cuvette, la bassine

bowling *noun* le bowling; **we're going bowling** on va au bowling; **a bowling alley** un bowling

box[1] *noun (small)* la boîte; *(large)* la caisse; **a box of chocolates** une boîte de chocolats; **a cardboard box** un carton

box[2] *verb (as sport)* boxer

boxer *noun*
(**a**) le boxeur
(**b**) **boxer shorts** un caleçon; **he's**

wearing boxer shorts il porte un caleçon

boxing *noun* la boxe

Boxing Day *noun* le lendemain de Noël

boy *noun* le garçon; **a little boy** un petit garçon; **a boy band** un boys band

boyfriend *noun* le copain

bra *noun* le soutien-gorge

> The plural of *soutien-gorge* is *soutiens-gorge*.

bracelet *noun* le bracelet

braces *plural noun*
(a) *(on trousers)* les bretelles *(feminine plural)*
(b) *(for teeth)* un appareil dentaire

bracket *noun* la parenthèse; **in brackets** entre parenthèses

brag *verb* se vanter

braid
1 *noun* la tresse; **she wears her hair in braids** elle porte des tresses
2 *verb* tresser; **she braided my hair** elle m'a fait des tresses

brain *noun* le cerveau

> The plural of *cerveau* is *cerveaux*.

brake
1 *noun* le frein; **to put on the brakes** freiner
2 *verb* freiner

branch *noun*
(a) *(of a tree)* la branche
(b) *(of a bank)* une agence
(c) *(of a shop, a company)* la succursale

brand *noun* la marque; **he always buys the same brand of jeans** il achète toujours la même marque de jean

brand-new *adjective* tout neuf/toute neuve; **he's got a brand new car** il a une voiture toute neuve; **she's wearing brand new shoes** elle porte des chaussures toutes neuves

brandy *noun* le cognac

brave *adjective* courageux/courageuse

> Note that the French word *brave* is rarely a translation for the English word *brave*. Its most common meaning is *kind*.

bravery *noun* le courage

bread *noun* le pain; **a loaf of bread** un pain; **a slice of bread** une tranche de pain

breadcrumb *noun*
(a) la miette de pain
(b) **breadcrumbs** *(for coating)* la chapelure; **fish fried in breadcrumbs** du poisson pané

breadth *noun* la largeur

break
1 *noun*
(a) *(in an activity)* la pause; **I took a break** j'ai fait une pause; **we get an hour's break for lunch** on a une heure de pause pour le déjeuner
(b) *(between classes)* la récréation
(c) *(holiday)* les vacances *(feminine plural)*; **the Christmas break** les vacances de Noël; **the Easter break** les vacances de Pâques
2 *verb*
(a) casser; **I broke the window** j'ai cassé la vitre
(b) *(of an object)* se casser; **the glass broke** le verre s'est cassé
(c) *(of a machine)* tomber en panne; **the dishwasher broke last week** le lave-vaisselle est tombé en panne la semaine dernière
(d) *(a bone)* se casser; **she's broken her arm** elle s'est cassé le bras
(e) *(other phrases)* **he broke the news** il a annoncé la nouvelle; **to break somebody's heart** briser le cœur à quelqu'un; **to break a habit** se débarrasser d'une habitude; **to break the law** enfreindre la loi; **to break one's promise** ne pas tenir sa promesse; **to break a record** battre un record
3 **break down**

(**a**) *(of a car, a machine)* tomber en panne
(**b**) *(separate into parts)* décomposer
(**c**) *(of a person)* faire une dépression nerveuse
(**d**) **to break down a door** enfoncer une porte
(**e**) **to break down in tears** fondre en larmes
4 break in *(to a house)* entrer par effraction
5 break into *(a house)* entrer par effraction dans; **they've been broken into three times** *(burgled)* ils se sont fait cambrioler trois fois
6 break off
(**a**) **to break something off** détacher quelque chose; **a bit broke off** un morceau s'est détaché
(**b**) *(pause)* faire une pause; *(stop)* s'arrêter
(**c**) *(a relationship)* **to break it off** rompre; **they've broken off their engagement** ils ont rompu leurs fiançailles
7 break out
(**a**) *(of a war, a riot)* éclater
(**b**) *(of a fire, a disease)* se déclarer
8 break up
(**a**) *(of a crowd)* se disperser
(**b**) *(of a couple)* se séparer; **they're breaking up** ils se séparent; **to break up with somebody** se séparer de quelqu'un
(**c**) *(at school)* **the schools break up for summer soon** les écoles vont bientôt fermer pour l'été; **when do we break up?** quand est-ce qu'on est en vacances?

breakable
1 *adjective* cassable
2 *plural noun* **breakables** des objets fragiles

breakdown *noun*
(**a**) *(of a car)* la panne; **we've had a breakdown** nous sommes tombés en panne; **breakdown service** le service de dépannage; **a breakdown van, a breakdown truck** une dépanneuse

(**b**) **a nervous breakdown** une dépression nerveuse; **to have a nervous breakdown** faire une dépression nerveuse

breakfast *noun* le petit déjeuner; **to have breakfast** prendre le petit déjeuner; **I have cereal for breakfast** je prends des céréales au petit déjeuner

break-in *noun* *(burglary)* le cambriolage

breast *noun*
(**a**) *(of a woman)* le sein
(**b**) *(of chicken)* le blanc

breaststroke *noun* la brasse; **I can do the breaststroke** je sais nager la brasse

breath *noun*
(**a**) *(air)* le souffle; **to take a breath** respirer; **to be out of breath** être à bout de souffle; **to hold one's breath** retenir son souffle; **to go out for a breath of fresh air** sortir prendre l'air
(**b**) *(smell)* l'haleine *(feminine)*; **he has bad breath** il a mauvaise haleine

breathe *verb* respirer; **you can't breathe in here** *(it's too hot)* on étouffe ici

breathless *adjective* à bout de souffle, essoufflé/essouflée

breeze *noun* la brise

breezy *adjective* **it's breezy today** il y a un peu de vent aujourd'hui

bribe
1 *noun* le pot-de-vin; **he takes bribes** il touche des pots-de-vin

> The plural of *pot-de-vin* is *pots-de-vin*.

2 *verb* acheter; **I bribed him with sweets** je l'ai acheté en lui donnant des bonbons

brick *noun* la brique; **a brick wall** un mur de briques

bride *noun* la mariée; **the bride and groom** *(before the wedding)* les futurs époux; *(after the wedding)* les jeunes mariés

bridegroom *noun* le marié

bridesmaid *noun* la demoiselle d'honneur

bridge *noun*
(a) *(over water)* le pont
(b) *(card game)* le bridge; **do you want to play bridge?** est-ce que vous voulez faire une partie de bridge?

brief *adjective (discussion, report)* bref/brève; **to be brief, the results aren't good** en bref, les résultats ne sont pas bons

briefcase *noun* la mallette

briefly *adverb* brièvement

briefs *plural noun* le slip

bright *adjective*
(a) *(shiny)* brillant/brillante
(b) *(light, colour)* vif/vive; **it's bright red** c'est rouge vif
(c) *(weather, room)* clair/claire
(d) *(person)* intelligent/intelligente; **these pupils are very bright** ces élèves sont très intelligents
(e) *(idea)* génial/géniale; **that's a bright idea** c'est une idée géniale

> The masculine plural of *génial* is *géniaux*.

brighten
1 *verb*
(a) *(of a person)* s'animer
(b) *(of a face)* s'éclairer
(c) *(decorate)* égayer; **I put up new curtains to brighten the room** j'ai mis des nouveaux rideaux pour égayer la pièce
2 **brighten up**
(a) *(of the weather)* s'améliorer; **the weather's brightening up** le temps s'améliore
(b) *(of a person)* s'animer
(c) *(of a face)* s'éclairer

brightly *adverb* **the sun is shining brightly** il y a un soleil éclatant; **the street is brightly lit** la rue est bien éclairée

brilliant *adjective*
(a) *(person)* brillant/brillante, fort/forte; **he's brilliant at maths** il est très fort en maths
(b) *(idea, plan)* génial/géniale; **that's a brilliant idea** c'est une idée géniale

> The masculine plural of *génial* is *géniaux*.

bring
1 *verb*
(a) *(object)* apporter; **I brought my books** j'ai apporté mes livres
(b) *(person)* amener; **bring your friends** amenez vos amis; **her father's bringing her home today** son père la ramène à la maison aujourd'hui
2 **bring about** *(cause)* entraîner; **what brought about these changes?** qu'est-ce qui a entraîné ces changements?
3 **bring along** *(object)* apporter; *(person)* amener
4 **bring back** *(object)* rapporter; *(person)* ramener
5 **bring down**
(a) *(carry down)* descendre; **I'll bring the books down for you** je te descends les livres
(b) *(reduce)* faire baisser; **this will bring prices down** ça va faire baisser les prix
6 **bring in** *(object)* rentrer; *(person)* faire entrer; **bring her in** faites-la entrer
7 **bring round** *(object)* apporter; *(person)* amener
8 **bring up**
(a) *(carry up)* monter; **I'll bring the books up for you** je te monte les livres
(b) **to bring up a child** élever un enfant

Britain *noun* la Grande-Bretagne; **we live in Britain** nous habitons en Grande-Bretagne; **she wants to come to Britain** elle veut venir en Grande-Bretagne; **I'm from Britain** je viens de Grande-Bretagne

> Note that the French word *la Bretagne* is not a translation for the

English word *Britain.* It refers to Brittany in France.

British

1 *adjective* britannique
2 *noun (people)* **the British** les Britanniques *(masculine plural)*

In French, only the noun for the inhabitants of a country takes a capital letter, never the adjective.

Briton *noun (person)* le/la Britannique

Brittany *noun* la Bretagne; **they live in Brittany** ils habitent en Bretagne; **we're going to Brittany** nous allons en Bretagne; **he's from Brittany** il est breton

Note that the French word *la Bretagne* only refers to Brittany in France. The translation of *Britain* is *la Grande-Bretagne.*

broad *adjective* large

broadcast
1 *verb* diffuser; **the match will be broadcast live** le match sera diffusé en direct
2 *noun* une émission; **a live broadcast** une émission en direct

broccoli *noun* les brocolis *(masculine plural)*; **they don't like broccoli** ils n'aiment pas les brocolis

brochure *noun* la brochure

broke *adjective* fauché/fauchée; **I'm broke** je suis fauché *or* je n'ai plus un rond

broken *adjective* cassé/cassée; **my leg is broken** j'ai la jambe cassée

brooch *noun* la broche

broom *noun* le balai

brother *noun* le frère; **my big brother** mon grand frère; **my little brother** mon petit frère

brother-in-law *noun* le beau-frère

The plural of *beau-frère* is *beaux-frères.*

brow *noun*
(a) *(forehead)* le front
(b) *(eyebrow)* le sourcil

brown *adjective* marron; *(hair)* brun/brune, châtain; *(eyes)* marron; *(tanned)* bronzé/bronzée; **she has brown hair** elle a les cheveux bruns; **I have brown eyes** j'ai les yeux marron; **he's very brown after his holiday** il est rentré de vacances très bronzé

The adjective *marron* does not change in the plural or in the feminine. *Châtain* does not change in the feminine.

Brownie *noun (Guide)* la jeannette

brownie *noun (cake)* le brownie

bruise
1 *noun* le bleu; **I've got a bruise on my leg** j'ai un bleu à la jambe

The plural of *bleu* is *bleus.*

2 *verb* se faire un bleu à; **I've bruised my knee** je me suis fait un bleu au genou; **he bruises easily** il se fait des bleus très facilement

bruised *adjective (person)* couvert/couverte de bleus; **I've got a bruised knee** j'ai un bleu au genou

brunch *noun* le brunch

brush
1 *noun*
(a) *(for hair, clothes, teeth)* la brosse
(b) *(for sweeping)* le balai
(c) *(for painting)* le pinceau

The plural of *pinceau* is *pinceaux.*

2 *verb (clothes, shoes)* brosser; **to brush one's hair** se brosser les cheveux; **to brush one's teeth** se brosser les dents
3 **brush away** enlever d'un coup de brosse

Brussels *noun* Bruxelles; **a Brussels sprout** un chou de Bruxelles

The plural of *chou de Bruxelles* is *choux de Bruxelles.*

bubble

1 *noun* la bulle; **to blow bubbles** faire des bulles de savon
2 *verb (of a boiling liquid)* bouillonner

bucket *noun* le seau; **a bucket of water** un seau d'eau; **a bucket and spade** un seau et une pelle

> The plural of *seau* is *seaux*.

buckle

1 *noun* la boucle
2 *verb* boucler; **she buckled her belt** elle a bouclé sa ceinture

bud *noun*
(**a**) *(on a flower)* le bouton
(**b**) *(on a tree)* le bourgeon

Buddhist

1 *adjective* bouddhiste
2 *noun* le/la bouddhiste; **she's a Buddhist** elle est bouddhiste

> The names of religions and their followers are never capitalized in French.

budgerigar *noun* la perruche

budget

1 *noun* le budget; **I'm on a budget this month** mon budget est serré ce mois-ci
2 *verb* **she doesn't know how to budget** elle ne sait pas tenir un budget

budgie *noun* la perruche

buffalo *noun* le buffle

buffet *noun* le buffet; **a buffet lunch** un buffet; **a buffet car** un wagon-restaurant

> The plural of *wagon-restaurant* is *wagons-restaurants*.

bug

1 *noun*
(**a**) *(insect)* un insecte
(**b**) *(germ)* le virus
(**c**) *(in a computer program)* le bogue
2 *verb*
(**a**) *(annoy)* embêter; **it really bugs me** ça m'embête vraiment
(**b**) *(spy on)* **to bug a room** cacher des micros dans une pièce

buggy *noun (for baby)* la poussette

build

1 *verb (a house, a wall)* construire
2 build up
(**a**) *(develop)* développer; **they're building up their business** ils développent leur société
(**b**) **you need to build your strength up** tu as besoin de prendre des forces

builder *noun* un ouvrier du bâtiment; **he's a builder** il est ouvrier du bâtiment

> Note that when describing people's jobs or situations, French does not use an article (*un* or *une*).

building *noun*
(**a**) *(structure)* le bâtiment; **that's a beautiful building** c'est un beau bâtiment; **in my building** dans mon immeuble
(**b**) *(work)* la construction; **building will start on Monday** les travaux de construction commencent lundi; **a building site** un chantier

bulb *noun*
(**a**) *(for a lamp)* une ampoule
(**b**) *(of a plant)* le bulbe

bull *noun* le taureau

> The plural of *taureau* is *taureaux*.

bulldog *noun* le bouledogue

bulldozer *noun* le bulldozer

bullet *noun* la balle

bulletin board *noun (on a wall)* le panneau d'affichage

> The plural of *panneau d'affichage* is *panneaux d'affichage*.

bully

1 *noun (child)* la petite brute; *(adult)* le tyran; **his brother is a real bully** son frère est une vraie petite brute
2 *verb* persécuter; **he gets bullied by the other children at school** il se fait persécuter par les autres enfants de l'école

bump
1 *noun*
(**a**) *(on one's head, in a road)* la bosse
(**b**) *(collision)* le choc
2 *verb (hit)* cogner; **I bumped my head** je me suis cogné la tête
3 **bump into**
(**a**) *(collide with)* rentrer dans; **he bumped into a lamppost** il est rentré dans un réverbère
(**b**) *(meet by chance)* **to bump into somebody** tomber sur quelqu'un; **I bumped into an old friend** je suis tombé sur un ancien ami

bumpy *adjective (road)* cahoteux/cahoteuse; **we had a bumpy flight** nous avons été secoués dans l'avion

bun *noun*
(**a**) *(bread roll)* le pain au lait
(**b**) *(in hair)* le chignon

bunch *noun*
(**a**) *(of objects)* **a bunch of flowers** un bouquet de fleurs; **a bunch of grapes** une grappe de raisin; **a bunch of keys** un trousseau de clés
(**b**) *(of people)* le groupe; **his friends are a nice bunch** ses amis sont très sympas; **he was with a bunch of friends** il était avec un groupe d'amis
(**c**) **bunches** *(in one's hair)* les couettes *(feminine plural)*; **she wears her hair in bunches** elle porte des couettes

bundle
1 *noun*
(**a**) *(of clothes, washing)* la pile
(**b**) *(of papers, banknotes)* la liasse
2 *verb* **she bundled up the clothes** elle a mis les vêtements en paquet; **she bundled the baby up in a warm blanket** elle a emmitouflé le bébé dans une grosse couverture

bungalow *noun* la maison de plain-pied

burger *noun* le hamburger

burglar *noun* le cambrioleur/la cambrioleuse

burglary *noun* le cambriolage

burgle *verb* cambrioler; **we've been burgled** on s'est fait cambrioler

burn
1 *noun* la brûlure
2 *verb*
(**a**) brûler; **did you burn yourself?** est-ce que tu t'es brûlé?; **I burnt my fingers** je me suis brûlé les doigts; **I've burnt the potatoes** j'ai laissé brûler les pommes de terre; **the toast is burning** le pain est en train de brûler
(**b**) *(a CD)* graver
3 **burn down**
(**a**) brûler; **their house burnt down** leur maison a brûlé
(**b**) *(intentionally)* faire brûler; **they burnt down the school** ils ont fait brûler l'école

burning
1 *adjective*
(**a**) *(on fire)* en flammes; **the house is burning** la maison est en flammes
(**b**) *(very hot)* brûlant/brûlante
2 *noun (smell)* le brûlé; **there's a smell of burning** ça sent le brûlé

burst
1 *verb*
(**a**) *(explode)* éclater; **the balloon burst** le ballon a éclaté
(**b**) *(cause to explode)* faire éclater; **the dog burst the balloon** le chien a fait éclater le ballon
2 **burst into**
(**a**) *(enter)* **to burst into a room** entrer brusquement dans une pièce
(**b**) **to burst into flames** prendre feu; **to burst into tears** fondre en larmes

bury *verb*
(**a**) *(a dead person, a bone, a treasure)* enterrer
(**b**) *(a town, a house)* ensevelir; **the town was buried by the avalanche** la ville a été ensevelie sous l'avalanche
(**c**) *(put out of sight)* enfouir; **the letter was buried under my papers** la lettre était enfouie sous mes papiers

bus *noun* le bus; *(long-distance)* le car;

to catch the bus prendre le bus; **I come to school by bus** je viens à l'école en bus; **a bus shelter** un abribus®; **a bus stop** un arrêt de bus

bush *noun*
(a) *(plant)* le buisson
(b) **the bush** *(in Africa, Australia)* la brousse

business *noun*
(a) *(activity)* les affaires *(feminine plural)*; **business is good** les affaires vont bien; **she's in the fashion business** elle travaille dans la mode; **he's gone to London on business** il est allé à Londres pour affaires; **she's studying business** elle fait des études de commerce
(b) *(company)* une entreprise; **he runs a successful business** il a une entreprise qui marche bien
(c) *(matter)* **that's my business** ça me regarde; **that's none of your business!** ça ne te regarde pas!; **mind your own business!** occupe-toi de tes affaires!

businessman *noun* un homme d'affaires

businesswoman *noun* la femme d'affaires

busy *adjective*
(a) *(person)* occupé/occupée; **not now, I'm busy** pas maintenant, je suis occupé; **she was busy painting the kitchen** elle était occupée à peindre la cuisine; **it kept me busy all morning** ça m'a occupé toute la matinée
(b) *(day, schedule)* chargé/chargée; **I've had a busy day** j'ai eu une journée chargée; **he has a busy schedule** il a un emploi du temps chargé
(c) *(place)* **a busy street** une rue animée; **a busy road** une route à grande circulation; **the train was very busy** il y avait beaucoup de monde dans le train

but
1 *conjunction* mais; **he's small but strong** il est petit mais costaud; **my**

friends smoke, but I don't** mes amis fument, mais moi non; **I'll do it, but not right now** je vais le faire, mais pas tout de suite
2 *preposition* sauf; **any day but tomorrow** n'importe quel jour sauf demain; **nobody but me knew about it** personne d'autre que moi n'était au courant

butcher *noun* le boucher/la bouchère; **he's a butcher** il est boucher; **I'm going to the butcher's** je vais chez le boucher; **the butcher's shop** la boucherie

> Note that when describing people's jobs or situations, French does not use an article (*un* or *une*).

butter
1 *noun* le beurre
2 *verb* beurrer; **she buttered some bread** elle a beurré des tartines

butterfly *noun*
(a) *(insect)* le papillon
(b) *(in swimming)* le papillon; **can you do the butterfly?** est-ce que tu sais nager le papillon?
(c) **to have butterflies (in one's stomach)** avoir le trac

button
1 *noun*
(a) *(on clothes)* le bouton
(b) *(on a machine)* le bouton; **press the button** appuyez sur le bouton
(c) *(on a phone)* la touche
2 *verb* boutonner; **button your coat up** boutonne ton manteau

buy *verb* acheter; **he bought a CD** il a acheté un CD

buzz *verb* bourdonner

by
1 *preposition*
(a) par; **I'll send it by e-mail** je vais l'envoyer par e-mail; **it was built by the Romans** ça a été construit par les Romains
(b) *(created by)* de; **a book by Toni Morrison** un livre de Toni Morrison; **a film by Spielberg** un film de Spielberg

(c) *(as a result of)* en; **he learned to cook by watching his mother** il a appris à faire la cuisine en regardant sa mère; **we met by chance** nous nous sommes rencontrés par hasard
(d) *(with transport)* en; **to travel by train** voyager en train; **to come by car** venir en voiture
(e) *(next to)* à côté de; *(near)* près de; **he's sitting by the fire** il est assis près du feu; **a house by the sea** une maison au bord de la mer
(f) *(before)* avant; *(in time for)* pour; **by Friday** avant vendredi; **by 10 o'clock** avant 10 heures; **it must be done by tomorrow** ça doit être fait pour demain; **he should be here by now** il devrait déjà être arrivé
(g) *(according to)* **to call somebody by his name** appeler quelqu'un par son nom; **to know somebody by**

sight connaître quelqu'un de vue
(h) *(with numbers and quantities)* **to divide by three** diviser par trois; **to sell something by the kilo** vendre quelque chose au kilo; **one by one** un par un; **little by little** petit à petit
(i) **to be by oneself** être tout seul/toute seule; **I did it all by myself** je l'ai fait tout seul
(j) **by the way** à propos
2 *adverb*
(a) *(nearby)* **close by** tout près; **is there a bank close by?** est-ce qu'il y a une banque près d'ici?
(b) *(past)* **to go by** passer; **she drove by without stopping** elle est passée en voiture sans s'arrêter; **time goes by** le temps passe

bye, bye-bye *exclamation* salut, au revoir

cab *noun* le taxi; **a cab driver** un chauffeur de taxi

cabbage *noun* le chou

The plural of *chou* is *choux*.

cabin *noun*
(**a**) *(on a ship, a plane)* la cabine; **cabin baggage** les bagages à main; **the cabin crew** le personnel de cabine
(**b**) *(hut)* la cabane

cable *noun*
(**a**) *(wire)* le câble; **an electric cable** un câble électrique; **a cable car** un téléphérique
(**b**) **cable TV, cable** le câble; **it's only available on cable** ça n'existe que sur le câble

cactus *noun* le cactus

café *noun* le café

caffeine *noun* la caféine

Do not confuse the spellings of the French word *caféine* and the English *caffeine*.

cage *noun* la cage

cake *noun* *(large)* le gâteau; *(small)* la pâtisserie; **would you like some cake?** est-ce que vous voulez du gâteau?; **a cake shop** une pâtisserie

The plural of *gâteau* is *gâteaux*.

calculate *verb* calculer; **he calculated how much it would cost** il a calculé combien ça coûterait

calculation *noun* le calcul; **by my calculations, we should arrive about 4 o'clock** selon mes calculs, nous devrions arriver vers 16 heures

calculator *noun* la calculatrice

calendar *noun* le calendrier

calf *noun*
(**a**) *(animal)* le veau

The plural of *veau* is *veaux*.

(**b**) *(lower leg)* le mollet

call
1 *noun*
(**a**) *(shout)* un appel; **a call for help** un appel au secours; **I'll give you a call when dinner's ready** je t'appellerai quand le dîner sera prêt
(**b**) *(on the telephone)* le coup de téléphone; **I need to make a call** je dois passer un coup de téléphone; **I'll give you a call** je t'appelle
2 *verb*
(**a**) *(shout)* appeler; **"come quickly!" he called** "venez vite!" cria-t-il; **he called my name** il m'a appelé; **I'll call you when dinner's ready** je t'appellerai quand le dîner sera prêt
(**b**) *(on the telephone)* appeler; **I'll call you tonight** je t'appelle ce soir; **who's calling?** qui est à l'appareil?; **call the police** appelez la police; **call a taxi** appelle un taxi
(**c**) *(summon)* **somebody's calling you** on t'appelle
(**d**) *(name)* appeler; **call me Ruth** appelez-moi Ruth; **he's called David** il s'appelle David; **what's that animal called?** comment s'appelle cet animal?
(**e**) *(insult)* traiter de; **she called me a thief** elle m'a traité de voleur; **to call somebody names** injurier quelqu'un

3 call back *(on the telephone)* rappeler; **I'll call back later** je rappellerai plus tard
4 call for
(a) *(summon)* appeler; **she's calling for help** elle est en train d'appeler au secours; **the child called for his mother** l'enfant a appelé sa mère
(b) *(collect)* passer prendre; **I'll call for you at 6** je passerai te prendre à 18 heures
5 call in *(visit)* **to call in on somebody** passer chez quelqu'un; **I'll call in at the bakery on my way home** je passerai à la boulangerie en rentrant à la maison
6 call off *(cancel)* annuler; **they've called off the wedding** ils ont annulé le mariage; **the police called off their search** la police a arrêté ses recherches
7 call on *(visit)* **I'll call on her this evening** je passerai chez elle ce soir
8 call out *(shout)* crier; **he called out in pain** il a crié de douleur

calm
1 *adjective* calme; **the sea is calm today** la mer est calme aujourd'hui; **keep calm!** du calme!
2 *verb* **calm down** se calmer; **calm down!** calmez-vous!; **she managed to calm the children down** elle a réussi à calmer les enfants

calorie *noun* la calorie

camcorder *noun* le caméscope®

camel *noun* le chameau

> The plural of *chameau* is *chameaux*.

camera *noun* un appareil photo

> Note that the French word *caméra* only refers to a TV or film camera.

camp
1 *noun* le camp; **a holiday camp** *(for families)* un camp de vacances; *(for children)* une colonie de vacances
2 *verb* camper

campaign
1 *noun* la campagne; **she's leading a campaign against drugs** elle mène une campagne contre la drogue
2 *verb* mener une campagne; **to campaign for something** mener une campagne en faveur de quelque chose

camper *noun*
(a) *(person)* le campeur/la campeuse
(b) *(vehicle)* le camping-car

> The plural of *camping-car* is *camping-cars*.

camping *noun* le camping; **to go camping** faire du camping

campsite *noun* le camping

campus *noun* le campus

can
1 *noun*
(a) *(for food)* la boîte de conserve; **a can of tuna** une boîte de thon
(b) *(for drinks)* la canette; **a can of beer** une canette de bière
2 *verb*
(a) *(be able to)* pouvoir; **I can do it** je peux le faire; **can you come to the party?** est-ce que tu peux venir à la fête?; **he can be very stubborn** il peut être très têtu; **I'll come as soon as I can** je viendrai aussitôt que possible
(b) *(be allowed to)* pouvoir; **can I ask you something?** est-ce que je peux vous demander quelque chose?; **I've already said you can't go** je t'ai déjà dit que tu ne peux pas y aller
(c) *(know how to)* savoir; **I can swim** je sais nager; **can you drive?** est-ce que vous savez conduire?
(d) *(with verbs of perception)* **I can see her** je la vois; **I can't hear** je n'entends pas; **can you feel it?** tu le sens?
(e) *(expressing amazement or disbelief)* **how can you say that?** comment peux-tu dire une chose pareille?; **what can it be?** qu'est-ce que cela peut bien être?; **you can't be serious!** vous ne parlez pas sérieusement!

Canada *noun* le Canada; **he lives in Canada** il habite au Canada; **we're going to Canada** nous allons au

Canada; **they come from Canada** ils viennent du Canada

Canadian
1 *adjective* canadien/canadienne
2 *noun (person)* le Canadien/la Canadienne

In French, only the noun for the inhabitants of a country takes a capital letter, never the adjective.

canal *noun* le canal

The plural of *canal* is *canaux*.

canary *noun* le canari

cancel *verb* annuler; **the flight has been cancelled** le vol a été annulé

Cancer *noun* le Cancer; **she's (a) Cancer** elle est Cancer

cancer *noun* le cancer; **to have cancer** avoir le cancer; **breast cancer** le cancer du sein

candidate *noun* le candidat/la candidate

candle *noun* la bougie; **I lit a candle** j'ai allumé une bougie

candlestick *noun* le bougeoir

candyfloss *noun* la barbe à papa

cane *noun* *(for walking)* la canne

canned *adjective* en conserve; **canned tomatoes** des tomates en conserve

canoe
1 *noun* le canoë
2 *verb* faire du canoë; **we canoed down the river** nous avons descendu le fleuve en canoë

The French word *canoë* is pronounced "cano-é".

canoeing *noun* le canoë; **to go canoeing** faire du canoë

can-opener *noun* un ouvre-boîte

The plural of *ouvre-boîte* is *ouvre-boîtes*. The singular can also be found with an *s*: *un ouvre-boîtes*.

canteen *noun* la cantine

canvas *noun* la toile; **canvas shoes** des chaussures en toile

cap *noun*
(**a**) *(hat)* la casquette; **a swimming cap** un bonnet de bain
(**b**) *(of a pen)* le capuchon
(**c**) *(of a bottle)* la capsule

capable *adjective* capable; **she's not capable of lying** elle est incapable de mentir

capital
1 *noun*
(**a**) *(city)* la capitale; **what's the capital of Poland?** quelle est la capitale de la Pologne?
(**b**) *(letter)* la majuscule; **write in capitals** écrivez en majuscules
2 *adjective* majuscule; **capital letters** les lettres majuscules; **a capital A** un A majuscule

Capricorn *noun* le Capricorne; **I'm (a) Capricorn** je suis Capricorne

captain
1 *noun* le capitaine; **the ship's captain** le capitaine du navire
2 *verb* *(a sports team)* être capitaine de

capture *verb* *(a person, an animal)* capturer, prendre; **the police captured the thief** la police a capturé le voleur

car *noun* la voiture; **we can go by car** on peut y aller en voiture; **a car ferry** un ferry; **a car park** un parking

Note that the French word *car* is never a translation for the English word *car*. It means *coach*.

caramel *noun* le caramel

caravan *noun* la caravane; **we're going on a caravan holiday** on part en vacances en caravane

card *noun*
(**a**) *(with a message)* la carte; **a birthday card** une carte d'anniversaire; **a credit card** une carte de crédit; **a membership card** une carte de membre

(b) *(for playing)* la carte; **do you want to play cards?** est-ce que vous voulez jouer aux cartes?

(c) *(cardboard)* le carton

cardboard *noun* le carton; **a cardboard box** un carton

cardigan *noun* le cardigan, le gilet

cardphone *noun* le téléphone à carte

care
1 *noun*
(a) *(worry)* le souci
(b) *(attention)* le soin, l'attention *(feminine)*; **take care when you cross the road** fais attention en traversant la rue; **take care not to spill the paint** fais attention à ne pas renverser la peinture
(c) **to take care of somebody** s'occuper de quelqu'un; **who will take care of the baby?** qui va s'occuper du bébé?; **I'll take care of the reservations** je vais m'occuper des réservations; **I can take care of myself** je peux me débrouiller; **take care!** *(when leaving)* salut!
2 *verb*
(a) **to care about something** *(be interested in it)* s'intéresser à quelque chose; *(worry about it)* se soucier de quelque chose; **I don't care what people think** je me moque de ce que les gens pensent; **I don't care!** ça m'est égal!
(b) *(feel affection)* **to care about somebody** aimer quelqu'un
3 care for
(a) *(look after)* **to care for somebody** *(be responsible for)* s'occuper de quelqu'un; *(treat)* soigner; **the au pair cares for the children** c'est la jeune fille au pair qui s'occupe des enfants; **nurses care for the sick** les infirmières soignent les malades
(b) *(want)* **would you care for a drink?** est-ce que vous voulez boire quelque chose?; **would you care to come with me?** est-ce que vous aimeriez m'accompagner?

career *noun* la carrière; **a career in banking** une carrière dans la banque; **a careers advisor** un conseiller/une conseillère d'orientation; **careers guidance** l'orientation professionnelle; **careers centre** le centre d'orientation professionnelle

careful *adjective*
(a) *(person)* prudent/prudente; **be careful!** fais attention!; **be careful not to fall** fais attention de ne pas tomber; **she's careful with her money** elle surveille ses dépenses; **he's a careful driver** c'est un conducteur prudent
(b) *(work)* soigné/soignée; **this is a very careful piece of work** c'est un travail très soigné

carefully *adverb*
(a) *(cautiously)* prudemment; **drive carefully** roulez prudemment
(b) *(thoroughly)* soigneusement, avec soin; **listen carefully** écoutez attentivement

careless *noun*
(a) *(person)* négligent/négligente; **he's a very careless child** c'est un enfant peu soigneux
(b) *(work)* peu soigné/soignée; **it was a careless mistake** c'était une faute d'inattention

caretaker *noun* le/la concierge, le gardien/la gardienne; **my dad's a school caretaker** mon père est gardien d'école

Note that when describing people's jobs or situations, French does not use an article *(un* or *une).*

cargo *noun* la cargaison; **a cargo plane** un avion-cargo; **a cargo ship** un cargo

The plural of *avion-cargo* is *avions-cargos.*

Note that the French word *cargo* is never a translation for the English word *cargo.* It only means *cargo ship.*

Caribbean
1 *noun* **the Caribbean** *(islands)* les Antilles *(feminine plural)*; *(sea)* la mer des Antilles; **he's from the Caribbean** il vient des Antilles; **they live in the Caribbean** ils habitent aux Antilles; **I'm going to the Caribbean** je vais aux Antilles
2 *adjective* antillais/antillaise; **the Caribbean Islands** les Antilles *(feminine plural)*; **the Caribbean Sea** la mer des Antilles *or* la mer des Caraïbes; **she's Caribbean** elle est antillaise

carnival *noun* le carnaval

> The plural of *carnaval* is *carnavals*.

carol *noun* **a Christmas carol** un chant de Noël

carpenter *noun* *(for furniture)* le menuisier; *(for houses)* le charpentier; **he's a carpenter** il est charpentier

> Note that when describing people's jobs or situations, French does not use an article (*un* or *une*).

carpet *noun* *(rug)* le tapis; *(wall-to-wall)* la moquette

> Note that the French word *carpette* is never a translation for the English word *carpet*. It means *small rug*.

carpeting *noun* la moquette

carriage *noun* *(of a train)* le wagon

carrier bag *noun* le sac en plastique

carrot *noun* la carotte; **a carrot cake** un gâteau aux carottes

carry
1 *verb* porter; **she was carrying her baby in her arms** elle portait son enfant dans les bras
2 carry on continuer; **I carried on eating** j'ai continué à manger; **carry on!** continue!
3 carry out *(work, a programme)* effectuer; *(instructions)* exécuter; *(idea, plan)* réaliser

cart *noun* *(pulled by a horse)* la charrette

carton *noun* *(cardboard box)* le carton; *(of milk, juice)* la brique

cartoon *noun* *(film)* le dessin animé; *(comic strip)* la bande dessinée; *(picture)* le dessin humoristique

cartridge *noun* la cartouche; **an ink cartridge** une cartouche d'encre

carve *verb*
(a) *(sculpt)* sculpter; **the statue is carved out of marble** la statue est sculptée dans le marbre
(b) *(scratch)* graver; **she carved their names on the tree trunk** elle a gravé leurs noms sur le tronc d'arbre
(c) *(beef, chicken)* découper

case *noun*
(a) *(suitcase)* la valise; **I'm packing my case** je fais ma valise
(b) *(for glasses, a camera)* un étui; **a pencil case** une trousse
(c) *(situation)* le cas; **in that case, I'll wait** dans ce cas, je vais attendre; **that is not the case in Great Britain** ce n'est pas le cas en Grande-Bretagne; **it's a case of not having enough money** c'est une question d'argent
(d) **in case** au cas où; **in case you fall** au cas où tu tomberais; **in case of an emergency** en cas d'urgence; **take an umbrella just in case** prends un parapluie au cas où
(e) *(investigation)* une affaire; **the police are working on the case** la police enquête sur cette affaire; **a murder case** une affaire de meurtre
(f) *(trial)* le procès; **her case comes up next week** son procès a lieu la semaine prochaine

cash *noun*
(a) *(money)* l'argent *(masculine)*; **I've run out of cash** je n'ai plus d'argent
(b) *(as opposed to a cheque or a card)* les espèces *(feminine plural)*, le liquide; **I'd like to pay cash** je voudrais payer en espèces
(c) **a cash desk** une caisse; **a cash machine** un distributeur automatique; **a cash register** une caisse enregistreuse

cashew nut *noun* la noix de cajou

cashier *noun* le caissier/la caissière; **she's a cashier at the supermarket** elle est caissière au supermarché

casino *noun* le casino

casserole *noun*
(**a**) *(stew)* le ragoût; **a beef casserole** un ragoût de bœuf
(**b**) *(dish, pan)* la cocotte

> Note that the French word *casserole* is never a translation for the English word *casserole*. It means *saucepan*.

cassette *noun* la cassette; **a cassette player** un lecteur de cassettes; **a cassette recorder** un magnétophone à cassettes

cast
1 *noun*
(**a**) *(actors)* les acteurs *(masculine plural)*; **the cast is American** tous les acteurs sont américains
(**b**) *(for a broken limb)* le plâtre; **she has her arm in a cast** elle a le bras dans le plâtre
2 *verb*
(**a**) *(an actor)* **the director cast her in the role of the mother** le metteur en scène lui a attribué le rôle de la mère
(**b**) *(throw)* jeter; **it cast doubt on his ability** ça a jeté un doute sur ses capacités; **to cast a spell on somebody** jeter un sort à quelqu'un

castle *noun* le château

> The plural of *château* is *châteaux*.

casual *adjective*
(**a**) *(informal)* décontracté/décontractée; **I prefer casual clothes** je préfère les vêtements décontractés
(**b**) *(unimportant)* **it was just a casual remark** j'ai dit ça en passant

casualty *noun*
(**a**) *(victim)* la victime; *(injured)* le blessé/la blessée; *(dead)* le mort/la morte; **there were no casualties** il n'y a pas eu de victimes
(**b**) *(in hospital)* **casualty depart-**ment, casualty le service des urgences; **she was taken to casualty** on l'a emmenée aux urgences

cat *noun* le chat

catalogue *noun* le catalogue

catapult
1 *noun* le lance-pierres

> The word *lance-pierres* does not change in the plural.

2 *verb* catapulter; **he catapulted the stone over the wall** il a lancé la pierre par-dessus le mur

catch
1 *verb*
(**a**) *(get hold of)* attraper; **he caught the ball** il a attrapé la balle; **catch!** attrape!
(**b**) *(find)* attraper, prendre; **he got caught by the police** il s'est fait attraper par la police; **to catch somebody doing something** surprendre quelqu'un en train de faire quelque chose; **they were caught trying to escape** on les a surpris en train d'essayer de s'évader
(**c**) *(get stuck)* **to catch one's finger in something** se prendre le doigt dans quelque chose; **her skirt got caught in the door** sa jupe s'est prise dans la porte; **we got caught in the storm** nous avons été surpris par l'orage
(**d**) *(public transport)* prendre; **I caught the train** j'ai pris le train
(**e**) **to catch fire** prendre feu
2 catch up rattraper; **I'll catch up with you** je te rattraperai; **you must try and catch up** tu dois essayer de rattraper ton retard

catching *adjective* *(disease)* contagieux/contagieuse

category *noun* la catégorie

caterpillar *noun* la chenille

cathedral *noun* la cathédrale

Catholic
1 *adjective* catholique; **the Catholic Church** l'église catholique

2 *noun* le/la catholique; **she's a Catholic** elle est catholique

The names of religions and their followers are never capitalized in French.

cauliflower *noun* le chou-fleur

The plural of *chou-fleur* is *choux-fleurs*.

cause
1 *noun* la cause; **what was the cause of the accident?** quelle était la cause de l'accident?
2 *verb (problem, emotion)* causer; *(accident, illness)* provoquer; **the candle caused the fire** la bougie est à l'origine de l'incendie; **smoking causes cancer** fumer provoque le cancer

caution *noun*
(**a**) *(care)* la prudence; **we must proceed with caution** il faut agir avec prudence
(**b**) *(warning sign)* **caution!** attention!

Note that the French word *caution* is never a translation for the English word *caution*. Its most common meaning is *deposit* (eg paid when renting property).

cautious *adjective* prudent/prudente; **she's a cautious driver** c'est une conductrice prudente

cave *noun* la grotte, la caverne

Note that the French word *cave* is never a translation for the English word *cave*. It means *cellar*.

CD *noun* le CD; **a CD player** un lecteur de CD; **a CD burner, a CD writer** un graveur de CD

The word *CD* does not change in the plural.

CD-ROM *noun* le CD-ROM; **the CD-ROM drive** le lecteur de CD-ROM

The word *CD-ROM* does not change in the plural.

ceiling *noun* le plafond

celebrate *verb* fêter; **we're celebrating his birthday** nous fêtons son anniversaire; **let's celebrate!** *(have a party)* on va fêter ça!; *(have a drink)* on va arroser ça!

celebration *noun* la fête; **this calls for a celebration!** *(party)* il faut fêter ça!; *(drink)* ça s'arrose!

celebrity *noun* la célébrité

celery *noun* le céleri; **a stick of celery** une branche de céleri

cell *noun* la cellule

cellar *noun* la cave

Note that the French word *cellier* is not usually a translation for the English word *cellar*. It means *storeroom*.

cello *noun* le violoncelle; **my sister plays the cello** ma sœur joue du violoncelle

Note that when talking about playing musical instruments, French uses the expression *jouer de*.

cement *noun* le ciment; **the wall is made of cement** le mur est en ciment; **a cement mixer** une bétonnière

cemetery *noun* le cimetière

cent *noun* le cent; **it only costs 50 cents** ça ne coûte que 50 cents

centimetre *noun* le centimètre

centre *noun*
(**a**) *(middle)* le centre, le milieu; **he stood in the centre of the room** il se tenait au milieu de la pièce; **she lives in the town centre** elle habite au centre-ville
(**b**) *(building)* le centre; **a health centre** un centre médical; **a shopping centre** un centre commercial; **a sports centre** un centre sportif

century *noun* le siècle; **in the 20th century** au XXème siècle

cereal *noun*

(a) *(plant)* la céréale; **wheat is a cereal** le blé est une céréale
(b) *(for breakfast)* les céréales *(feminine plural)*; **do you want some cereal?** est-ce que tu veux des céréales?

ceremony *noun* la cérémonie

certain *adjective*
(a) *(sure)* certain/certaine, sûr/sûre; **I am certain that he will come** je suis certain qu'il viendra; **it's certain that she will get the job** il est sûr qu'elle aura le poste; **I know that for certain** j'en suis certain
(b) *(particular)* certain/certaine; **certain people disagree** certains ne sont pas d'accord
(c) **to make certain of something** s'assurer de quelque chose

certainly *adverb* bien sûr; **I will certainly come** je viendrai, c'est sûr; **can you help me? – certainly!** est-ce que vous pouvez m'aider? – mais bien sûr!; **did you tell him? – certainly not!** tu le lui as dit? – bien sûr que non!

Note that the most common meaning of the French word *certainement* is *probably*.

certificate *noun*
(a) le certificat; **a birth certificate** un certificat de naissance
(b) *(academic)* le diplôme; **a degree certificate** un diplôme (universitaire)

chain
1 *noun* la chaîne; **the dog is on a chain** le chien est attaché à une chaîne; **she had a gold chain round her neck** elle portait une chaîne en or autour du cou; **a bicycle chain** une chaîne de vélo
2 *verb* enchaîner; **the dog was chained to the post** le chien était attaché au poteau par une chaîne

chair *noun* la chaise; *(armchair)* le fauteuil

chairman *noun* le président/la présidente

chalet *noun* le chalet

chalk *noun* la craie; **a piece of chalk** une craie

challenge
1 *noun* le défi; **to throw down a challenge** lancer un défi; **to accept a challenge** relever un défi
2 *verb*
(a) **to challenge somebody to do something** défier quelqu'un de faire quelque chose; **he challenged me to a game of chess** il m'a proposé une partie d'échecs
(b) *(stimulate)* **you need a job that will challenge you** il te faut un travail stimulant

champagne *noun* le champagne

champion *noun* le champion/la championne; **she's the world champion** c'est la championne du monde

championship *noun* le championnat; **the world championship** le championnat du monde

chance *noun*
(a) *(possibility)* la chance, les chances *(feminine plural)*; **she stands a good chance of being chosen** elle a de bonnes chances d'être choisie; **he hasn't the slightest chance of winning** il n'a pas la moindre chance de gagner
(b) *(opportunity)* une occasion, une chance; **I haven't had a chance to write to him** je n'ai pas trouvé l'occasion de lui écrire; **it's your last chance** c'est ta dernière chance; **give me another chance** donne-moi une autre chance
(c) *(luck)* le hasard; **I met him by chance** je l'ai rencontré par hasard; **do you by any chance know his address?** est-ce que par hasard tu connaîtrais son adresse?

change
1 *noun*
(a) *(alteration)* le changement; **there's been a change in the weather** le temps a changé; **this trip will be a change for you** ce voyage te changera les idées; **he was early, for a change**

pour une fois, il était en avance
(**b**) *(money)* la monnaie; **here's your change** tenez, votre monnaie; **have you got change for a £10 note?** est-ce que tu as de la monnaie sur un billet de 10 livres?

2 *verb*
(**a**) changer; **you need to change this word** il faut que tu changes ce mot; **she's changed since I last saw her** elle a changé depuis la dernière fois que je l'ai vue
(**b**) *(become something else)* se transformer; **to change into something** se transformer en quelque chose; **the witch changed him into a frog** la sorcière l'a transformé en grenouille
(**c**) *(from one thing to another)* passer; **the lights changed from green to amber** les feux sont passés du vert à l'orange
(**d**) *(exchange for another one)* **can you change the CD?** est-ce que tu peux échanger le CD?; **to change places with somebody** changer de place avec quelqu'un; **to change one's mind** changer d'avis; **to change the subject** changer de sujet; **to change colour** changer de couleur
(**e**) *(change clothes)* se changer; **she's gone upstairs to change** elle est montée se changer; **I'll change into trousers** je vais me mettre en pantalon
(**f**) *(money)* changer; **to change pounds into euros** changer des livres en euros

3 change over passer; **France changed over to the euro in 2002** la France est passée à l'euro en 2002

changing room *noun*
(**a**) *(for sport)* le vestiaire
(**b**) *(in a shop)* la cabine d'essayage

Channel *noun* **the Channel** la Manche; **the Channel Tunnel** le tunnel sous la Manche

channel *noun* *(on television)* la chaîne; **can I change channels?** est-ce que je peux changer de chaîne?

chapter *noun* le chapitre

character *noun*
(**a**) *(personality)* le caractère; **the experience changed his character** cette expérience l'a transformé
(**b**) *(in a book, a film, a play)* le personnage; **the main character** le personnage principal

charge
1 *noun*
(**a**) *(cost)* le prix; **it's free of charge** c'est gratuit
(**b**) **in charge** responsable; **the person in charge** le/la responsable; **who's in charge here?** qui est le responsable ici?
2 *verb* *(ask for money)* **he charged me £15** il m'a fait payer 15 livres; **they didn't charge us for the coffee** ils ne nous ont pas fait payer le café

charm *noun*
(**a**) *(attractiveness)* le charme
(**b**) **a lucky charm** un porte-bonheur

The word *porte-bonheur* does not change in the plural.

charming *adjective* charmant/charmante

chart *noun*
(**a**) *(table)* le tableau

The plural of *tableau* is *tableaux*.

(**b**) **the charts** le hit-parade; **it's top of the charts** c'est le numéro un au hit-parade

chase
1 *noun* la poursuite
2 *verb* poursuivre; **the dog chased the postman** le chien a poursuivi le facteur
3 chase after **to chase after somebody** courir après quelqu'un
4 chase away **to chase somebody away** chasser quelqu'un

chat
1 *noun* **to have a chat with somebody** bavarder avec quelqu'un
2 *verb* bavarder; **he was chatting**

with his sister il bavardait avec sa sœur

cheap *adjective* bon marché, pas cher/chère; **the wine was cheap** le vin n'était pas cher

> The translation *bon marché* does not change in the plural or in the feminine.

cheaply *adverb* pour pas cher; **you can eat out cheaply** on peut manger au restaurant pour pas cher

cheat
1 *verb* tricher; **he always cheats at cards** il triche toujours aux cartes
2 *noun* le tricheur/la tricheuse

check
1 *noun* le contrôle, la vérification
2 *verb*
(a) *(verify)* vérifier; **I have to check the figures** je dois vérifier les chiffres; **check that everyone is here** vérifie que tout le monde est là
(b) *(examine)* contrôler; **the inspector checked our tickets** le contrôleur a contrôlé nos billets
3 check in
(a) *(at an airport)* se présenter à l'enregistrement; **I checked in my bags** j'ai enregistré mes bagages
(b) *(at a hotel)* signer le registre
4 check off *(on a list)* marquer, cocher
5 check out
(a) *(at a hotel)* régler sa note
(b) *(have a look at)* **check this out!** regarde-moi ça!
(c) *(try)* **there's a new club we could check out** il y a une nouvelle boîte que nous pourrions essayer

checked *adjective* *(material)* à carreaux; **a checked tablecloth** une nappe à carreaux

check-in *noun* *(at an airport)* l'enregistrement *(masculine)*; **a check-in desk** un comptoir d'enregistrement

checkout *noun* *(in a supermarket)* la caisse

checkup *noun* *(at the doctor's)* le bilan de santé; **to have a checkup** se faire faire un bilan de santé

cheek *noun*
(a) *(part of face)* la joue
(b) *(rudeness)* le culot; **what a cheek!** quel culot!

cheeky *adjective* impertinent/impertinente; **don't be cheeky!** pas d'impertinence!

cheer
1 *noun*
(a) les acclamations *(feminine plural)*; **I heard a cheer** j'ai entendu des acclamations; **three cheers for the winner!** hourra pour le gagnant!
(b) **cheers!** *(when drinking)* santé!
2 *verb* acclamer; **everyone cheered at the end** à la fin, tout le monde a poussé des acclamations
3 cheer up to cheer somebody up remonter le moral à quelqu'un; **cheer up!** courage!

cheerful *adjective* *(person)* de bonne humeur; *(atmosphere, room, music)* gai/gaie

cheese *noun* le fromage; **a cheese omelette** une omelette au fromage

cheeseburger *noun* le cheeseburger

cheesecake *noun* le gâteau au fromage

chef *noun* le chef cuisinier; **she wants to be a chef** elle veut être chef cuisinier

> Note that when describing people's jobs or situations, French does not use an article (*un* or *une*).

chemical
1 *noun* le produit chimique
2 *adjective* chimique; **a chemical reaction** une réaction chimique

chemist *noun* *(person)* le pharmacien/la pharmacienne; *(shop)* la pharmacie; **you can buy it at the chemist** on peut en acheter à la pharmacie; **my mother's a chemist** ma mère est pharmacienne

Note that when describing people's jobs or situations, French does not use an article (*un* or *une*).

chemistry *noun* la chimie

cheque *noun* le chèque; **I'd like to pay by cheque** je voudrais payer par chèque; **here is a cheque for £20** voici un chèque de 20 livres

cherry *noun* la cerise; **a cherry tart** une tarte aux cerises; **a cherry tree** un cerisier

chess *noun* les échecs *(masculine plural)*; **do you want to play chess?** tu veux jouer aux échecs?; **we had a game of chess** on a fait une partie d'échecs

chessboard *noun* un échiquier

chest *noun*
(a) *(part of body)* la poitrine
(b) *(box)* le coffre
(c) **a chest of drawers** une commode

chestnut *noun* la châtaigne; **a roast chestnut** une châtaigne grillée

chew *verb* mâcher

chewing gum *noun* le chewing-gum; **would you like a piece of chewing gum?** tu veux un chewing-gum?

The plural of the French word *chewing-gum* is *chewing-gums*.

chick *noun* le poussin

chicken *noun* le poulet; **a chicken sandwich** un sandwich au poulet

chickenpox *noun* la varicelle; **she has chickenpox** elle a la varicelle

chief
1 *noun* le chef
2 *adjective* principal/principale; **he's my chief assistant** c'est mon principal collaborateur

The masculine plural of *principal* is *principaux*.

child *noun* un/une enfant

childhood *noun* l'enfance *(feminine)*

childminder *noun* la gardienne d'enfants, la nourrice

chill
1 *noun* **to catch a chill** prendre froid
2 *verb*
(a) *(food, drink)* mettre au frais; **chill the wine before you drink it** mets le vin au frais avant de le boire
(b) *(relax)* se détendre; **I'm just going to chill this weekend** je vais me détendre ce week-end

chilli *noun* *(pepper)* le piment; *(meal)* le chili; **chilli con carne** le chili con carne

chilly *adjective* frais/fraîche; **it's chilly this morning** il fait frais ce matin; **I'm a bit chilly** j'ai un peu froid

chimney *noun* la cheminée

chimpanzee *noun* le chimpanzé

chin *noun* le menton

China *noun* la Chine; **Beijing is in China** Pékin se trouve en Chine; **we're going to China** nous allons en Chine; **this dress is from China** cette robe vient de Chine

china *noun* la porcelaine; **it's made of china** c'est en porcelaine; **a china plate** une assiette en porcelaine

Chinese
1 *adjective* chinois/chinoise
2 *noun*
(a) *(language)* le chinois; **he speaks Chinese** il parle chinois
(b) *(people)* **the Chinese** les Chinois *(masculine plural)*

In French, only the noun for the inhabitants of a country takes a capital letter, never the adjective or the noun for the language.

chip *noun*
(a) *(French fry)* la frite
(b) *(in a computer)* la puce

Note that the French word *chips* is never a translation for the British English word *chips*. It means *crisps*.

chipped *adjective*
(a) *(cup, plate)* ébréché/ébréchée
(b) *(tooth)* cassé/cassée

choc-ice *noun* un esquimau®

The plural of *esquimau*® is *esquimaux*.

chocolate *noun* le chocolat; **would you like a chocolate?** tu veux un chocolat?; **a bar of chocolate** une tablette de chocolat; **a chocolate cake** un gâteau au chocolat; **a hot chocolate** un chocolat chaud

choice *noun* le choix; **you have to make a choice** tu dois faire un choix; **I have no choice** je n'ai pas le choix

choir *noun* la chorale; **I sing in a choir** je fais partie d'une chorale

choke *verb* s'étouffer

choose *verb* choisir; **I chose the blue shirt** j'ai choisi la chemise bleue; **you must choose between three answers** il faut que tu choisisses entre trois réponses

chop
1 *verb* *(wood)* couper; *(food)* couper en morceaux; **chop the vegetables** coupez les légumes en morceaux
2 chop down *(a tree)* abattre

chopsticks *plural noun* les baguettes *(feminine plural)*

chord *noun* un accord

chorus *noun* le refrain

christening *noun* le baptême

The *p* in *baptême* is not pronounced.

Christian
1 *adjective* chrétien/chrétienne; **a Christian name** un prénom
2 *noun* le chrétien/la chrétienne; **she's a Christian** elle est chrétienne

The names of religions and their followers are never capitalized in French.

Christmas *noun* Noël *(masculine)*; **Merry Christmas!** joyeux Noël!;

Father Christmas le père Noël; **a Christmas present** un cadeau de Noël; **a Christmas tree** un sapin de Noël

chubby *adjective* *(person)* potelé/potelée; *(face)* joufflu/joufflue; **he's got chubby cheeks** il est joufflu

chuck
1 *verb*
(a) *(throw)* lancer, jeter; **I chucked the stone in the lake** j'ai lancé la pierre dans le lac
(b) *(a girlfriend, a boyfriend)* plaquer; **his girlfriend chucked him** sa copine l'a plaqué
2 chuck out balancer; **I chucked my old sweater out** j'ai balancé mon vieux pull

church *noun* une église; **they go to church** ils vont à l'église

cider *noun* le cidre

cigar *noun* le cigare

cigarette *noun* la cigarette; **a cigarette lighter** un briquet

cinema *noun* le cinéma; **shall we go to the cinema?** et si on allait au cinéma?

cinnamon *noun* la cannelle

circle *noun* le cercle

circus *noun* le cirque

citizen *noun* le citoyen/la citoyenne

city *noun* la ville; **the city centre** le centre-ville

civilization *noun* la civilisation

claim *verb*
(a) *(assert)* prétendre; **he claims to know all about it** il prétend être au courant
(b) *(demand)* réclamer; **I've come to claim my reward** je viens chercher ma récompense

clap *verb* applaudir

clapping *noun* les applaudissements *(masculine plural)*

clarinet *noun* la clarinette; **I play the clarinet** je joue de la clarinette

> Note that when talking about playing musical instruments, French uses the expression *jouer de*.

class *noun*
(**a**) *(of pupils)* la classe; **we're in the same class** nous sommes dans la même classe
(**b**) *(lesson)* le cours; **the French class** le cours de français; **they never stop talking in class** ils n'arrêtent pas de parler en classe
(**c**) *(transport)* **he travels first class** il voyage en première classe

classic
1 *adjective* classique; **that's a classic example** c'est un exemple classique
2 *noun* le classique; **this book is a classic** ce livre est un classique

classical *adjective* classique; **classical music** la musique classique

classmate *noun* le/la camarade de classe

classroom *noun* la classe, la salle de classe

claw *noun*
(**a**) *(of a cat, a dog)* la griffe
(**b**) *(of a crab, a lobster)* la pince

clay *noun* l'argile *(feminine)*; **a clay pot** un pot en argile

clean
1 *adjective* propre; **my hands are clean** j'ai les mains propres
2 *verb*
(**a**) nettoyer; **I cleaned the kitchen** j'ai nettoyé la cuisine
(**b**) **to clean one's teeth** se laver les dents; **to clean one's nails** se nettoyer les ongles

cleaner *noun*
(**a**) *(cleaning lady)* la femme de ménage; *(man)* un agent de service; *(in the street)* le balayeur/la balayeuse; **my mum's a cleaner** ma mère est femme de ménage

> Note that when describing people's jobs or situations, French does not use an article *(un or une)*.

(**b**) *(dry cleaner)* **the cleaner's** le pressing; **I took the clothes to the cleaner's** j'ai emporté les vêtements au pressing

cleaning *noun* **to do the cleaning** faire le ménage

clear
1 *adjective*
(**a**) *(water, sound, day)* clair/claire; **on a clear day** par temps clair; **she has a clear voice** elle a la voix claire
(**b**) *(obvious, understandable)* clair/claire; **it's clear that he's lying** il est clair qu'il ment; **is that clear?** c'est clair?
(**c**) *(unobstructed)* dégagé/dégagée; **a clear sky** un ciel dégagé
(**d**) *(distinct)* net/nette; **the picture is very clear** l'image est très nette
2 *verb*
(**a**) *(free of obstacles)* dégager; **to clear the road** dégager la route; **to clear the table** débarrasser la table
(**b**) **the sky is clearing** le ciel se dégage; **the fog is clearing** le brouillard se dissipe
3 clear out
(**a**) *(empty)* vider; **I cleared out the cupboard** j'ai vidé le placard
(**b**) *(throw out)* jeter; **help me clear out these old papers** aide-moi à jeter ces vieux papiers
4 clear up
(**a**) *(tidy up)* ranger; **clear up your stuff** range tes affaires
(**b**) *(become clearer)* **the weather is clearing up** ça s'éclaircit

clearly *adverb*
(**a**) *(write, explain)* clairement
(**b**) *(speak, hear)* distinctement
(**c**) *(see, understand)* bien
(**d**) *(obviously)* évidemment; **he is clearly wrong** il est évident qu'il a tort

clerk *noun* un employé/une employée; **she's a bank clerk** elle est employée de banque

Note that when describing people's jobs or situations, French does not use an article (*un* or *une*).

clever *adjective*
(**a**) *(bright)* intelligent/intelligente; **she's a very clever girl** c'est une fille très intelligente
(**b**) *(ingenious)* astucieux/astucieuse; **what a clever idea!** quelle bonne idée!
(**c**) *(skilful)* habile; **he's clever with his hands** il est habile de ses mains

click
1 *noun*
(**a**) *(sound)* le bruit sec, le déclic; **the door shut with a click** la porte s'est refermée avec un bruit sec
(**b**) *(with a mouse)* le clic; **a double-click** un double-clic
2 *verb*
(**a**) *(make a sound)* faire un bruit sec; **the door clicked shut** la porte s'est refermée avec un bruit sec; **to click one's fingers** claquer des doigts
(**b**) *(with a mouse)* cliquer; **to click on something** cliquer sur quelque chose; **double-click on the icon** cliquer deux fois sur l'icône

client *noun* le client/la cliente

cliff *noun* la falaise

climate *noun* le climat

climb
1 *verb* **to climb the stairs** monter l'escalier; **to climb a hill** grimper une colline; **to climb a mountain** faire l'ascension d'une montagne; **to climb a tree** grimper à un arbre; **to climb a wall** escalader un mur
2 climb down descendre; **he climbed down from the tree** il est descendu de l'arbre
3 climb up **to climb up the stairs** monter l'escalier; **to climb up a hill** grimper une colline; **to climb up a mountain** faire l'ascension d'une montagne; **to climb up a wall** escalader un mur

climber *noun* *(rock climber)* le varap-

peur/la varappeuse; *(mountaineer)* un/une alpiniste

climbing *noun* *(rock climbing)* l'escalade *(feminine)*; *(mountaineering)* l'alpinisme *(masculine)*; **she goes climbing** elle fait de l'escalade; **a climbing frame** une cage à poules; **a climbing wall** un mur d'escalade

clinic *noun* le centre médical

The plural of *centre médical* is *centres médicaux*.

clip
1 *noun* **a hair clip** une barrette; **a paper clip** un trombone
2 *verb* *(fasten)* attacher

cloakroom *noun*
(**a**) *(for coats)* le vestiaire; **I left my coat in the cloakroom** j'ai laissé mon manteau au vestiaire
(**b**) *(toilet)* les toilettes *(feminine plural)*; **where is the ladies' cloakroom?** où sont les toilettes des dames?

clock *noun* *(large)* une horloge; *(small)* la pendule

clockwise *adverb* dans le sens des aiguilles d'une montre

close¹
1 *adjective*
(**a**) *(nearby)* proche; **the school is close to the town hall** l'école est près de la mairie
(**b**) *(relative, friend)* proche; **he's a very close friend of mine** c'est un ami très proche
(**c**) *(weather)* **it's close today** il fait lourd aujourd'hui
2 *adverb* près; **she lives close by** elle habite tout près; **they walked close behind us** ils nous suivaient de près; **don't come too close** ne t'approche pas trop

close²
1 *verb*
(**a**) *(of a person)* fermer; **close your eyes** ferme les yeux; **they closed the road** ils ont fermé la route
(**b**) *(of a shop)* fermer; **the shops close**

at 6pm les magasins ferment à 18h; **the door closed behind them** la porte s'est fermée derrière eux
2 close down fermer; **the shop had to close down** le magasin a dû fermer

closed *adjective* fermé/fermée; **the shops are closed** les magasins sont fermés

closely *adverb* de près; **look at it closely** regarde-le de près

close-up *noun* le gros plan; **in close-up** en gros plan

closing *noun* la fermeture; **closing time** l'heure de fermeture

cloth *noun*
(a) *(material)* le tissu, l'étoffe *(feminine)*; **the cap is made of cloth** la casquette est en tissu
(b) *(for cleaning)* le chiffon

clothes *plural noun* les vêtements *(masculine plural)*; **to put one's clothes on** s'habiller; **to take one's clothes off** se déshabiller; **a clothes line** une corde à linge; **a clothes peg** une pince à linge

clothing *noun* les vêtements *(masculine plural)*

cloud
1 *noun* le nuage; **a cloud of smoke** un nuage de fumée
2 *verb* **cloud over** *(of the sky)* se couvrir

cloudy *adjective* *(weather, sky, day)* couvert/couverte; **it's cloudy today** le temps est couvert aujourd'hui

clown *noun* le clown

Clown is pronounced "cloon" in French.

club *noun*
(a) *(group)* le club; **I'm in a tennis club** je fais partie d'un club de tennis
(b) *(nightclub)* la boîte; **we could go to a club** on pourrait aller en boîte
(c) **a golf club** un club de golf
(d) *(in cards)* **clubs** trèfle *(masculine)*;

the ace of clubs l'as de trèfle

clue *noun*
(a) *(information)* un indice; **I'll give you a clue** je te donne un indice; **I haven't a clue!** je n'en ai aucune idée!
(b) *(in a crossword)* la définition; **what's the clue to 13 down?** quelle est la définition du 13 vertical?

clumsy *adjective* maladroit/maladroite

coach *noun*
(a) *(bus)* le car; **we're going by coach** nous y allons en car
(b) *(on a train)* le wagon
(c) *(trainer)* un entraîneur/une entraîneuse; **he's our basketball coach** c'est notre entraîneur de basket

coal *noun* le charbon; **a coal mine** une mine de charbon

coast *noun* la côte; **the town is on the south coast** la ville est sur la côte sud

coat *noun*
(a) le manteau; **I put my coat on** j'ai mis mon manteau

The plural of *manteau* is *manteaux*.

(b) **a coat of paint** une couche de peinture

coathanger *noun* le cintre

cobweb *noun* la toile d'araignée

cockerel *noun* le coq

cocktail *noun* le cocktail; **a cocktail bar** un bar; **a cocktail stick** une pique à apéritif

cocoa *noun* le cacao; **a cup of cocoa** un chocolat chaud

coconut *noun* la noix de coco; **a coconut cake** un gâteau à la noix de coco

cod *noun* la morue

code *noun* le code

coffee *noun* le café; **a cup of coffee** une tasse de café; **black coffee** le café noir; **white coffee** le café crème; **coffee ice-cream** la glace au café; **a coffee shop** un café

coffin *noun* le cercueil

coin *noun* la pièce de monnaie; **a 10p coin** une pièce de 10 pence

coincidence *noun* la coïncidence

coke® *noun* le coca-cola®, le coca®; **two cokes®, please** deux cocas, s'il vous plaît

cold
1 *adjective* froid/froide; **it's cold** *(weather)* il fait froid; *(food, object)* c'est froid; **I'm cold** j'ai froid; **my feet are cold** j'ai froid aux pieds; **a cold drink** une boisson fraîche
2 *noun*
(a) *(coldness)* le froid; **I don't like the cold** je n'aime pas le froid
(b) *(illness)* le rhume; **to catch a cold** attraper un rhume; **to have a cold** être enrhumé/enrhumée

coleslaw *noun* la salade de chou blanc à la mayonnaise

collapse *verb*
(a) *(fall down)* s'effondrer; **the building collapsed** le bâtiment s'est effondré
(b) *(faint)* s'évanouir

collar *noun*
(a) *(on clothes)* le col
(b) *(for a dog)* le collier

colleague *noun* le/la collègue

collect *verb*
(a) *(gather)* ramasser; **they collected their belongings** ils ont ramassé leurs affaires
(b) *(call for)* passer prendre; **I'll collect you at midday** je passerai vous prendre à midi
(c) *(as a hobby)* collectionner; **she collects teddy bears** elle collectionne les ours en peluche

collection *noun* la collection; **he has a huge stamp collection** il a une grande collection de timbres

college *noun*
(a) *(university)* une université
(b) *(sixth-form college)* le lycée

Note that the most common meaning of the French word *collège* is *secondary school* (for 11-15 year olds).

collide *verb* entrer en collision; **the two cars collided** les deux voitures sont entrées en collision; **the bus collided with the lorry** le bus est entré en collision avec le camion

colon *noun* les deux-points *(masculine plural)*

colour
1 *noun* la couleur; **what colour is her dress?** sa robe est de quelle couleur?
2 *verb* *(a picture)* colorier; **he coloured it blue** il l'a colorié en bleu
3 **colour in** *(a picture)* colorier

coloured *adjective* coloré/colorée; **she wears brightly coloured clothing** elle porte des vêtements aux couleurs vives; **a coloured pencil** un crayon de couleur

colourful *adjective* coloré/colorée

colouring *noun*
(a) *(of pictures)* le coloriage; **the children are doing some colouring** les enfants font du coloriage; **a colouring book** un album à colorier
(b) *(complexion)* le teint; **to have fair colouring** avoir le teint clair; **to have dark colouring** avoir le teint mat

column *noun*
(a) *(of a building)* la colonne
(b) *(newspaper section)* la rubrique; **he writes the sports column** il tient la rubrique des sports

comb
1 *noun* la peigne
2 *verb* **to comb one's hair** se peigner

come
1 *verb*
(a) venir; **he comes from France** il vient de France *or* il est français; **can you come to my party?** est-ce que tu peux venir à ma soirée?; **come here!** viens ici!; **come and see me tomorrow** venez me voir demain; **come and**

look viens voir
(**b**) *(arrive)* arriver; **I'm coming!** j'arrive!; **here come the children** voilà les enfants
2 come across
(**a**) *(find)* tomber sur; **I came across an interesting article yesterday** je suis tombé sur un article intéressant hier
(**b**) *(create an impression)* **they come across as nice people** ils ont l'air gentils
3 come along
(**a**) *(accompany)* venir; **would you like to come along?** est-ce que tu veux venir?
(**b**) *(hurry)* se dépêcher; **come along, we're late!** dépêche-toi, nous sommes en retard!
(**c**) *(arrive)* arriver; **everything was peaceful until you came along** tout était calme avant que tu arrives
4 come apart *(of a toy, shelves)* se démonter; **the book is coming apart** le livre perd ses pages
5 come back revenir; **I'll come back one day** je reviendrai un jour; **to come back home** rentrer
6 come down
(**a**) *(get down)* descendre; **come down from that tree!** descends de cet arbre!
(**b**) *(fall)* tomber; **the rain was coming down** la pluie tombait
7 come down with attraper; **I think I'm coming down with flu** je crois que j'ai attrapé la grippe
8 come for venir chercher; **I'll come for you at midday** je viendrai te chercher à midi; **he's come for his money** il est venu chercher son argent
9 come in entrer; **come in!** entrez!; **they came in through the window** ils sont entrés par la fenêtre
10 come into entrer dans; **come into the house** entrez dans la maison
11 come off se détacher; **a button came off my shirt** un bouton s'est détaché de ma chemise
12 come on come on! allez!
13 come out sortir; **he came out of**

the bedroom il est sorti de la chambre
14 come round
(**a**) *(visit)* **come round and see me one day** venez me voir un de ces jours
(**b**) *(regain consciousness)* reprendre connaissance
15 come to
(**a**) *(cost)* s'élever à; **the bill came to £50** la note s'est élevée à 50 livres
(**b**) *(regain consciousness)* reprendre connaissance
16 come up monter; **would you like to come up for a cup of tea?** vous voulez monter prendre un thé?
17 come up to *(reach)* arriver jusqu'à; **the water came up to my knees** l'eau m'arrivait jusqu'aux genoux
18 come up with I've come up with a solution j'ai trouvé une solution; **they came up with a wonderful idea** ils ont eu une idée géniale

comedian *noun* *(stand-up comic)* le/la comique; *(comic actor)* le comédien/la comédienne

comedy *noun* la comédie

comet *noun* la comète

comfort
1 *noun* le confort
2 *verb* consoler; **I comforted the children** j'ai consolé les enfants

comfortable *adjective*
(**a**) *(place)* confortable; **this bed is comfortable** ce lit est confortable
(**b**) *(person)* à l'aise; **make yourself comfortable** mettez-vous à l'aise

> Do not confuse the spellings of the French *confortable* and English *comfortable*.

comic *noun* la bande dessinée; **a comic book** une bande dessinée; **a comic strip** une bande dessinée

comma *noun* la virgule

command
1 *noun* un ordre; **to give a command** donner un ordre
2 *verb* ordonner

comment
1 *noun* une observation, un commentaire; **he made a comment about it** il a fait un commentaire à ce sujet
2 *verb* **she commented on his age** elle a fait des commentaires sur son âge

> Note that the French word *comment* is never a translation for the English word *comment*. It means *how*.

commercial
1 *noun* la publicité; **there are too many commercials on TV** il y a trop de publicités à la télé
2 *adjective* commercial/commericale

> The masculine plural of *commercial* is *commerciaux*.

commission *noun*
(**a**) *(committee, organization)* la commission
(**b**) *(fee)* la commission; **I get 5% commission** je reçois une commission de 5%

commit *verb (a crime)* commettre; **he committed a murder** il a commis un meurtre; **to commit suicide** se suicider

common
1 *adjective*
(**a**) *(frequent)* courant/courante; **it's a common name** c'est un nom courant
(**b**) *(ordinary)* ordinaire; **common sense** le bon sens
(**c**) *(shared)* commun/commune; **we have common interests** nous avons des intérêts communs
2 *noun* **in common** en commun; **they have nothing in common** ils n'ont rien en commun

communicate *verb* communiquer

communication *noun* la communication

communist
1 *adjective* communiste
2 *noun* le/la communiste

community *noun* la communauté; **the French community in London** la communauté française de Londres

commute *verb* **he commutes by train** il va au travail en train; **I commute to Bradford every day** je fais la navette tous les jours pour aller travailler à Bradford

compact *adjective* compact/compacte; **a compact disc** un disque compact

companion *noun* le compagnon/la compagne

company *noun*
(**a**) *(being with other people)* la compagnie; **she's good company** elle est d'agréable compagnie; **you can keep me company** tu peux me tenir compagnie
(**b**) *(business)* la société, l'entreprise *(feminine)*
(**c**) *(guests)* les invités *(masculine plural)*; **we've got company for dinner** nous avons des invités pour le dîner

compare *verb* comparer; **everyone compares me to my sister** tout le monde me compare à ma sœur; **compared with the others she's brilliant** elle est très douée par rapport aux autres

comparison *noun* la comparaison; **you can't make a comparison between the two** on ne peut pas faire la comparaison entre les deux; **she's very clever in comparison with the others** elle est très intelligente par rapport aux autres

compartment *noun* le compartiment; **this is the smoking compartment** c'est le compartiment fumeur

compass *noun* la boussole

compasses *plural noun* le compas

compete *verb*
(**a**) *(take part)* participer; **ten women are competing in the race** dix femmes participent à la course
(**b**) **to compete against somebody** être en compétition avec quelqu'un; **we're competing against Spain** nous sommes en compétition avec l'Espagne

(c) seven candidates are competing for the position sept candidats se disputent le poste

competent *adjective* compétent/compétente

competently *adverb* avec compétence

competition *noun*
(a) *(contest)* le concours; **she entered a poetry competition** elle s'est présentée à un concours de poésie
(b) *(in sport)* la compétition; **she takes part in competitions** elle fait de la compétition

competitive *adjective*
(a) *(person)* **he's so competitive** il a vraiment l'esprit de compétition
(b) *(activity)* **I don't like competitive sports** je n'aime pas les sports de compétition

competitor *noun* le concurrent/la concurrente

complain *verb* se plaindre; **she's complaining about the noise** elle se plaint du bruit

complaint *noun* la plainte, la réclamation; **I'd like to make a complaint** je voudrais faire une réclamation

complete
1 *adjective*
(a) *(whole)* complet/complète; **I have the complete set** j'ai la collection complète
(b) *(finished)* terminé/terminée; **the project is complete** le projet est terminé
(c) *(total)* total/totale; **a complete disaster** un désastre total; **he's a complete stranger** c'est un parfait inconnu; **she is a complete fool** elle est complètement idiote
2 *verb*
(a) *(add what is missing)* compléter; **I just need one more card to complete my collection** il me manque une seule carte pour compléter ma collection
(b) *(finish)* terminer; **they have com-**

pleted the project ils ont terminé le projet

completely *adverb* complètement; **it's completely finished** c'est complètement terminé

complex
1 *adjective* complexe
2 *noun*
(a) *(centre)* le complexe; **a shopping complex** un complexe commercial; **a sports complex** un complexe sportif; **a holiday complex** un centre de vacances
(b) *(insecurity)* le complexe; **she has a complex about her weight** elle fait un complexe à cause de son poids

complicate *verb* compliquer

complicated *adjective* compliqué/compliquée

complication *noun* la complication

compliment
1 *noun* le compliment; **to pay somebody a compliment** faire un compliment à quelqu'un
2 *verb* **to compliment somebody** faire un compliment à quelqu'un; **they complimented me on my French** ils m'ont fait des compliments pour mon français

composer *noun* le compositeur/la compositrice; **she's a composer** elle est compositrice

composition *noun*
(a) *(piece of music or literature)* la composition
(b) *(school essay)* la rédaction

comprehensive school *noun* le collège, l'école secondaire *(feminine)*

Note that the distinction between comprehensive schools and grammar schools does not exist in France.

compromise
1 *noun* le compromis
2 *verb* faire un compromis

compulsory *adjective* obligatoire

computer *noun* un ordinateur; **computer science** l'informatique *(feminine)*; **a computer game** un jeu électronique

computerized *adjective* informatisé/informatisée

computing *noun* l'informatique *(feminine)*; **she works in computing** elle travaille dans l'informatique

concentrate *verb* *(pay attention)* se concentrer; **I'm concentrating on my homework** je me concentre sur mes devoirs

concentration *noun* la concentration; **the work requires great concentration** le travail demande beaucoup de concentration

concern
1 *noun*
(**a**) *(interest)* **it's none of my concern** ça ne me regarde pas
(**b**) *(worry)* l'inquiétude *(feminine)*
2 *verb*
(**a**) *(affect)* concerner; **as far as I am concerned** en ce qui me concerne; **it doesn't concern you** ça ne vous regarde pas
(**b**) *(worry)* inquiéter

concerned *noun* *(worried)* inquiet/inquiète; **we are concerned about his health** nous sommes inquiets pour sa santé

concert *noun* le concert

conclusion *noun* la conclusion; **I came to the conclusion that he was lying** j'en ai conclu qu'il mentait

concrete *noun* le béton; **the building is made of concrete** le bâtiment est en béton

condition *noun*
(**a**) *(term)* la condition; **you can borrow the book, on one condition** tu peux emprunter le livre, à une condition
(**b**) *(state)* l'état *(masculine)*; **in good condition** en bon état; **in bad condition** en mauvais état

conditional *noun* le conditionnel; **the verb is in the conditional** le verbe est au conditionnel

conditioner *noun* l'après-shampooing *(masculine)*

condom *noun* le préservatif

conduct *verb* *(an orchestra)* diriger

conductor *noun* *(of an orchestra)* le chef d'orchestre; **she's a conductor** elle est chef d'orchestre

> Note that the French word *conducteur* is not a translation for the English word *conductor*. It means *driver*.

cone *noun* le cône; **an ice-cream cone** un cornet de glace

conference *noun* la conférence

confess *verb* avouer; **he confessed to the crime** il a avoué que c'était lui le coupable

confetti *noun* les confettis *(masculine plural)*

confidence *noun*
(**a**) *(faith)* la confiance; **we have confidence in her ability** nous avons confiance en ses capacités
(**b**) *(self-assurance)* l'assurance *(feminine)*; **he spoke with confidence** il a parlé avec assurance

> Note that the French word *confidence* is not always a translation for the English word *confidence*. It means *secret*.

confident *adjective*
(**a**) *(certain)* sûr/sûre; **we are confident that it will work** nous sommes sûrs que ça marchera
(**b**) *(self-assured)* sûr/sûre de soi; **she's very confident** elle est très sûre d'elle

confidential *adjective* confidentiel/confidentielle

conflict *noun* le conflit

confuse *verb*
(**a**) *(bewilder)* embrouiller; **don't confuse me!** ne m'embrouille pas!

(b) *(mix up)* confondre; **I always confuse Sweden with Switzerland** je confonds toujours la Suède avec la Suisse

confused *adjective* embrouillé/embrouillée; **I'm getting confused** je m'embrouille; **I'm a little confused as to why he did it** je ne comprends pas très bien pourquoi il a fait ça

Note that the French word *confus* is not usually a translation for the English word *confused*. Its most common meaning is *embarrassed*.

confusing *adjective* pas clair/claire; **her explanation was very confusing** ses explications n'étaient pas claires du tout

confusion *noun* la confusion

congratulate *verb* féliciter; **the teacher congratulated me on my results** le professeur m'a félicité pour mes résultats

congratulations *plural noun* les félicitations *(feminine plural)*; **congratulations!** félicitations!; **congratulations on passing your exams** félicitations pour tes examens

connect *verb*
(a) *(join together)* relier, **a road connects the two cities** une route relie les deux villes
(b) *(wires)* connecter; **connect this wire to the computer** connectez ce fil à l'ordinateur; **I'm trying to connect to the Internet** j'essaye de me connecter à Internet
(c) *(on a telephone)* **will you connect me with reservations, please?** est-ce que vous pouvez me passer les réservations?

connection *noun*
(a) *(link)* le rapport; **does this have a connection with what happened yesterday?** est-ce que ceci a un rapport avec ce qui s'est passé hier?
(b) *(on a telephone, a computer)* la connexion

(c) *(on a journey)* la correspondance; **I missed my connection** j'ai raté ma correspondance

conscience *noun* la conscience; **I have a clear conscience** j'ai la conscience tranquille; **he has a guilty conscience** il a mauvaise conscience

conscious *adjective* conscient/consciente; **he's not conscious yet** il n'a pas encore repris connaissance

consciousness *noun* la connaissance; **to lose consciousness** perdre connaissance; **to regain consciousness** reprendre connaissance

consequence *noun* la conséquence; **as a consequence, he lost his job** à cause de ça, il a perdu son travail

conservative *adjective* conservateur/conservatrice

consider *verb*
(a) *(think about)* réfléchir à; **I'll consider it** j'y réfléchirai; **have you considered buying a larger model?** est-ce que vous avez envisagé d'acheter un modèle plus grand?
(b) *(believe)* considérer; **I consider him a friend** je le considère comme un ami
(c) *(show regard for)* tenir compte de, penser à; **I have to consider my family** il faut que je tienne compte de ma famille

considerate *adjective* attentionné/attentionnée; **she's very considerate towards the children** elle est très attentionnée envers les enfants

considering
1 *preposition* pour; **he plays the piano very well, considering his age** il joue très bien du piano pour son âge
2 *conjunction* **considering she's only studied French for a year, she speaks it very well** elle parle très bien français pour quelqu'un qui ne l'étudie que depuis un an

consist *verb* **to consist of something** se composer de quelque chose; **the**

meal consists of soup and bread le repas se compose de soupe et de pain

consonant *noun* la consonne

constant *adjective*
(**a**) *(noise, pain, worry)* continuel/continuelle
(**b**) *(doubts, questions, complaining)* incessant/incessante

constantly *adverb* constamment, sans arrêt; **he's constantly asking questions** il n'arrête pas de poser des questions

contact
1 *verb* contacter; **you can contact me at this address** vous pouvez me contacter à cette adresse
2 *noun*
(**a**) *(communication)* le contact; **are you still in contact?** est-ce que vous êtes toujours en contact?
(**b**) **a contact lens** une lentille de contact; **she wears contact lenses** elle porte des lentilles de contact

contain *verb* contenir

container *noun* le récipient; **the soup is in a plastic container** la soupe est dans un récipient en plastique

contest *noun* le concours

contestant *noun* le concurrent/la concurrente

context *noun* le contexte

continent *noun*
(**a**) le continent
(**b**) **the Continent** l'Europe continentale *(feminine)*; **on the Continent** en Europe (continentale)

continual *adjective* continuel/continuelle

continue *verb*
(**a**) *(carry on)* continuer; **to continue doing something** continuer à faire quelque chose *or* continuer de faire quelque chose; **he continued speaking** il a continué à parler; **you must continue your studies** il faut que tu continues tes études

(**b**) *(after an interruption)* reprendre; **after lunch we continued working** après le déjeuner nous avons repris notre travail

continuous *adjective* continu/continue

contraception *noun* la contraception

contraceptive *noun* le contraceptif

contract *noun* le contrat; **I signed the contract** j'ai signé le contrat

contradict *verb* contredire; **you're contradicting yourself** tu te contredis

control
1 *noun*
(**a**) *(command, authority)* le contrôle; **the airport is under their control** ils contrôlent l'aéroport; **she has no control over the children** elle n'a aucune autorité sur les enfants; **the situation is under control** nous maîtrisons la situation; **the situation is out of control** la situation est incontrôlable; **he lost control (of himself)** il n'était plus maître de soi
(**b**) **the controls** *(of a car, a plane)* les commandes *(feminine plural)*
2 *verb*
(**a**) *(be in charge of)* diriger; **he controls the whole organization** il dirige l'ensemble de l'organisation
(**b**) *(regulate)* régler; **this button controls the volume** ce bouton règle le volume
(**c**) *(keep under control)* maîtriser; **control yourself!** maîtrise-toi!; **he can't control his pupils** il manque d'autorité sur ses élèves

convenient *adjective*
(**a**) *(suitable)* commode; **this is a convenient place to stop** c'est un endroit commode pour s'arrêter
(**b**) *(well-situated)* bien situé/située; **the flat is very convenient for the shops** l'appartement est bien situé pour les commerces

conversation *noun* la conversation;

I had a conversation with my brother j'ai eu une conversation avec mon frère

convince *verb* convaincre, persuader; **he convinced me** il m'a convaincu

cook
1 *verb*
(**a**) *(food)* faire cuire; *(meal)* préparer; **cook the chicken in the oven** faites cuire le poulet au four; **I'm cooking spaghetti bolognaise** je fais des spaghettis bolognaise
(**b**) *(of a person)* faire la cuisine; *(of food)* cuire; **can you cook?** est-ce que tu sais faire la cuisine?; **pasta cooks in 10 minutes** les pâtes cuisent en 10 minutes
2 *noun* le cuisinier/la cuisinière; **he's a good cook** il est bon cuisinier

cookbook *noun* le livre de cuisine

cooked *adjective* cuit/cuite

cooker *noun* la cuisinière

cookery *noun* la cuisine; **a cookery book** un livre de cuisine

cookie *noun* le biscuit

cooking *noun* la cuisine; **she likes cooking** elle aime faire la cuisine

cool
1 *adjective*
(**a**) *(temperature)* frais/fraîche; **it's cool in the evenings** il fait frais le soir
(**b**) *(calm)* calme; **keep cool!** du calme!
(**c**) *(great)* cool, super; **we had a really cool weekend** on a passé un super week-end; **it's not cool to smoke** ce n'est pas cool de fumer; **I'll be there at eight – cool!** je serai là à huit heures – super!
2 *verb* **cool down**
(**a**) *(of the weather)* se rafraîchir
(**b**) *(of a liquid)* se refroidir
(**c**) *(of a person)* se rafraîchir; **let's have a drink to cool down** prenons un verre pour nous rafraîchir

cop *noun* *(police officer)* le flic

cope *verb* *(manage)* s'en sortir; **she's coping very well on her own** elle s'en

sort très bien toute seule; **I can't cope any more** je ne m'en sors plus

copier *noun* *(photocopier)* la photocopieuse

copy
1 *noun*
(**a**) *(of a letter, a cassette)* la copie; **I need to make a copy of this letter** je dois faire une copie de cette lettre
(**b**) *(of a book, a magazine)* un exemplaire; **the book sold a million copies** le livre s'est vendu à un million d'exemplaires
2 *verb* copier; **he always copies his brother** il copie toujours son frère; **she copies from the other pupils** elle copie sur les autres élèves

cordless *adjective* sans fil; **a cordless telephone** un téléphone sans fil

corduroy *noun* le velours côtelé; **a corduroy jacket** une veste en velours côtelé

core *noun* *(of an apple)* le trognon

cork *noun*
(**a**) *(material)* le liège; **the board is made of cork** le panneau est en liège
(**b**) *(of a bottle)* le bouchon

corkscrew *noun* le tire-bouchon

> The plural of *tire-bouchon* is *tire-bouchons.*

corn *noun*
(**a**) *(cereal)* le blé
(**b**) *(sweetcorn)* le maïs; **corn on the cob** le maïs en épi

corner *noun*
(**a**) *(angle)* le coin, l'angle *(masculine)*; **the house on the corner** la maison qui fait l'angle; **the shop's just round the corner** le magasin est au coin de la rue
(**b**) *(bend in a road)* le virage
(**c**) *(in football)* le corner; **to take a corner** tirer un corner

cornflakes *plural noun* les corn flakes *(masculine plural)*

Cornwall *noun* la Cornouailles; **they**

live in Cornwall ils habitent en Cornouailles; **we're going to Cornwall** nous allons en Cornouailles; **I'm from Cornwall** je viens de Cornouailles

correct
1 *adjective* bon/bonne; **a correct answer** une bonne réponse; **if my memory is correct** si j'ai bonne mémoire **yes, that's correct** oui, c'est exact; **are these figures correct?** est-ce que ces chiffres sont exacts?; **you're correct** tu as raison
2 *verb* corriger; **the teacher corrected my grammar** le professeur a corrigé ma grammaire

correction *noun* la correction

correspond *verb*
(a) correspondre; **the pictures don't correspond to the text** les images ne correspondent pas au texte
(b) *(by letter)* correspondre; **they corresponded for many years** ils ont correspondu pendant des années

correspondence *noun* la correspondance

Do not confuse the spellings of the French *correspondance* and English *correspondence*.

corridor *noun* le couloir

Corsica *noun* la Corse; **he was born in Corsica** il est né en Corse; **have you ever been to Corsica?** est-ce que tu es déjà allé en Corse?

cost
1 *verb* coûter; **how much does it cost?** combien ça coûte?; **it costs £25** ça coûte 25 livres
2 *noun* le prix

costume *noun*
(a) *(on stage)* le costume; **the dancers wore beautiful costumes** les danseurs portaient de beaux costumes
(b) *(fancy dress)* le déguisement

cosy *adjective* confortable; **this is a cosy bed** c'est un lit confortable; **it's nice and cosy in here** on est bien ici

cot *noun* le lit d'enfant

cottage *noun*
(a) la petite maison; **a thatched cottage** une chaumière
(b) **cottage cheese** le fromage blanc

cotton *noun*
(a) le coton; **cotton socks** des chaussettes en coton
(b) **cotton wool** la ouate, le coton

couch *noun* le canapé

cough
1 *noun* la toux; **I've got a cough** je tousse
2 *verb* tousser; **she coughed loudly** elle a toussé fort

could *verb*
(a) *(indicating possibility)* **I'd come if I could** je viendrais si je pouvais; **you could be right** tu as peut-être raison; **you could have warned me!** tu aurais pu me prévenir!
(b) *(indicating ability)* **she couldn't walk** elle ne pouvait pas marcher; **she could read and write** elle savait lire et écrire
(c) *(making requests)* **could I borrow your sweater?** est-ce que je pourrais t'emprunter ton pull?; **could you help me, please?** est-ce que vous pourriez m'aider, s'il vous plaît?
(d) *(making suggestions)* **we could always telephone** nous pourrions toujours téléphoner; **couldn't you just apologize?** tu ne pourrais pas simplement t'excuser?
(e) *(with verbs of perception)* **I could hear them talking** je les entendais parler; **she couldn't see anything** elle ne voyait rien
(f) *(expressing amazement or disbelief)* **how could you say that?** comment est-ce que tu as pu dire ça?; **who on earth could that be?** qui diable cela peut-il bien être?

council *noun*
(a) *(elected body)* le conseil; **he's on the council** il est au conseil
(b) *(local government)* la municipalité

count *verb*
(**a**) *(number)* compter; **I counted ten people in the room** j'ai compté dix personnes dans la pièce; **count to 100** compte jusqu'à 100; **there were four of us, counting the baby** nous étions quatre en comptant le bébé
(**b**) *(be important)* compter; **it's the thought that counts** c'est l'intention qui compte; **he's under five so he doesn't count** il a moins de cinq ans, donc il ne compte pas
(**c**) **to count on somebody** compter sur quelqu'un; **you can count on me** vous pouvez compter sur moi

The *p* in *compter* is not pronounced.

countdown *noun* le compte à rebours

counter *noun*
(**a**) *(in a shop, a bar)* le comptoir

The *p* in *comptoir* is not pronounced.

(**b**) *(in a bank)* le guichet
(**c**) *(in a game)* le jeton

country *noun*
(**a**) *(nation)* le pays; **France is a beautiful country** la France est un beau pays
(**b**) *(countryside)* la campagne; **we live in the country** nous vivons à la campagne

countryside *noun*
(**a**) *(area)* la campagne
(**b**) *(scenery)* le paysage

county *noun* le comté

couple *noun*
(**a**) *(two people)* le couple
(**b**) **a couple of** *(a few)* quelques; *(two)* deux; **I had a couple of biscuits** j'ai mangé quelques biscuits; **it happened a couple of years ago** cela s'est passé il y a environ deux ans; **I'll be back in a couple of minutes** je reviens dans deux minutes

courage *noun* le courage

courgette *noun* la courgette

course *noun*
(**a**) *(lessons)* les cours *(masculine*

plural); **I'm doing a computer course** je suis des cours d'informatique
(**b**) *(of a meal)* le plat; **the first course** l'entrée *(feminine)*; **the main course** le plat principal
(**c**) **of course** bien sûr; **of course not** bien sûr que non; **of course she was angry!** bien sûr qu'elle était fâchée!
(**d**) **a golf course** un terrain de golf

court *noun*
(**a**) *(for judging criminals)* le tribunal; **to go to court** aller en justice; **to appear in court** comparaître devant le tribunal

The plural of *tribunal* is *tribunaux*.

(**b**) **a tennis court** un court de tennis; **a squash court** un court de squash

cousin *noun* le cousin/la cousine

cover
1 *noun*
(**a**) *(of a pan)* le couvercle
(**b**) *(for furniture)* la housse; **covers** *(on a bed)* les couvertures *(feminine plural)*
(**c**) *(of a book, a magazine)* la couverture
(**d**) *(shelter)* un abri; **to take cover** se mettre à l'abri
(**e**) **a cover version** *(of a song)* une reprise
2 *verb*
(**a**) couvrir; **to cover one's eyes** se couvrir les yeux; **to cover one's ears** se boucher les oreilles; **he's covered in mud** il est couvert de boue
(**b**) *(protect)* recouvrir; **she covered the child with a blanket** elle a recouvert l'enfant d'une couverture
3 cover up
(**a**) *(in order to hide)* recouvrir; **they covered up the bodies** ils ont recouvert les corps
(**b**) *(in order to keep warm)* couvrir; **keep the baby covered up** couvre bien le bébé

cow *noun* la vache

coward *noun* le/la lâche; **don't be**

such a coward ne sois pas aussi lâche

cowboy *noun* le cow-boy; **he came dressed as a cowboy** il est venu déguisé en cow-boy; **cowboy boots** des bottes de cow-boy

The plural of the French word *cowboy* is *cow-boys*.

crab *noun* le crabe

crack
1 *noun*
(a) *(in a glass, a bone, china)* la fêlure; **there's a crack in this glass** ce verre est fêlé
(b) *(in a wall)* la fissure; **there were some cracks in the wall** le mur était fissuré
2 *verb*
(a) *(break)* fêler; **you've cracked my cup** tu as fêlé ma tasse
(b) *(get broken)* se fêler; **the glass cracked** le verre s'est fêlé
(c) *(of a wall)* se fissurer
(d) *(a nut, an egg)* casser

cracked *adjective*
(a) *(glass, bone, china)* fêlé/fêlée
(b) *(wall)* fissuré/fissurée

cradle *noun* le berceau

The plural of *berceau* is *berceaux*.

crane *noun* la grue

crash
1 *noun*
(a) *(loud noise)* le fracas
(b) *(accident)* un accident; **we were in a crash** nous avons eu un accident de voiture; **a car crash** un accident de voiture; **a plane crash** un accident d'avion; **a crash helmet** un casque
2 *verb*
(a) *(of a car, a driver, a train)* avoir un accident; **to crash into something** rentrer dans quelque chose; **he crashed into a tree** il est rentré dans un arbre
(b) *(of a plane, a pilot)* s'écraser
(c) *(of a falling object)* **the vase crashed to the ground** le vase s'est fracassé par terre; **the bookcase came crashing down** la bibliothèque s'est écroulée
(d) *(of a computer)* tomber en panne

crawl
1 *verb*
(a) *(of a baby)* marcher à quatre pattes
(b) *(of an animal)* ramper
2 *noun* *(swimming stroke)* le crawl; **I can do the crawl** je sais nager le crawl

crayon *noun* le pastel

crazy *adjective* fou/folle; **those kids are driving me crazy** ces enfants me rendent fou; **I'm crazy about him** je suis folle de lui

cream *noun* la crème; **strawberries and cream** des fraises à la crème

create *verb* créer; **this will create problems** ça va créer des problèmes

creature *noun* *(living thing)* la créature

credit *noun*
(a) *(money)* le crédit; **to be in credit** avoir de l'argent sur son compte; **a credit card** une carte de crédit
(b) *(merit)* le mérite; **to take the credit for something** s'attribuer le mérite de quelque chose; **give him credit for his work** reconnais qu'il a bien travaillé

creep *verb* se glisser; **he crept into the room** il s'est glissé dans la pièce

creepy *adjective* qui donne la chair de poule; **it's a creepy story** c'est une histoire à vous donner la chair de poule

crew *noun*
(a) *(of a ship, a plane)* un équipage
(b) *(team)* une équipe; **a camera crew** une équipe de tournage

crib *noun* le berceau d'enfant

cricket *noun*
(a) *(game)* le cricket; **I play cricket** je joue au cricket
(b) *(insect)* le grillon

crime *noun* le crime; *(less serious)* le délit

criminal *noun* le criminel/la criminelle

crisis *noun* la crise

crisp
1 *adjective (biscuit, pastry)* croustillant/croustillante; *(apple, salad)* croquant/croquante
2 *noun (potato crisp)* la chips; **I like crisps** j'aime les chips

critical *adjective*
(a) *(negative)* critique; **he's always critical of my work** il n'arrête pas de critiquer mon travail
(b) *(serious, important)* critique; **she is in a critical condition** elle est dans un état critique

criticism *noun* la critique

criticize *verb* critiquer; **they criticized my pronunciation** ils ont critiqué ma prononciation

Croat
1 *adjective* croate
2 *noun*
(a) *(language)* le croate; **he speaks Croat** il parle croate
(b) *(person)* le/la Croate; **the Croats** les Croates *(masculine plural)*

> In French, only the noun for the inhabitants of a country takes a capital letter, never the adjective or the noun for the language.

Croatia *noun* la Croatie; **she was born in Croatia** elle est née en Croatie; **we're going to Croatia** nous allons en Croatie; **he's from Croatia** il vient de Croatie

Croatian
1 *adjective* croate
2 *noun*
(a) *(language)* le croate; **he speaks Croatian** il parle croate
(b) *(person)* le/la Croate; **the Croatians** les Croates *(masculine plural)*

crocodile *noun* le crocodile

crooked *adjective*
(a) *(badly positioned)* de travers; **the painting is crooked** le tableau est de travers

(b) *(stick)* recourbé/recourbée
(c) *(nose)* crochu/crochue

cross
1 *noun* la croix
2 *adjective* fâché/fâchée; **she's cross with me** elle est fâchée contre moi
3 *verb*
(a) *(go across)* traverser; **be careful when you cross the road** fais attention quand tu traverses la rue
(b) **to cross one's legs** croiser les jambes
4 **cross out** rayer, barrer
5 **cross over** traverser

crossing *noun*
(a) *(by boat)* la traversée; **we had a good crossing** la traversée s'est bien passée
(b) *(for pedestrians)* le passage pour piétons

crossroads *noun* le carrefour

crossword *noun* les mots croisés *(masculine plural)*; **I'm doing the crossword** je fais les mots croisés

crouch *verb* s'accroupir

crow *noun* le corbeau

> The plural of *corbeau* is *corbeaux*.

crowd *noun* la foule; **he got lost in the crowd** il s'est perdu dans la foule

crowded *adjective*
(a) *(room, train)* bondé/bondée; **the hall was crowded with people** la salle était bondée; **it's too crowded in here** il y a trop de monde ici
(b) *(street)* plein/pleine de monde

crown *noun* la couronne

cruel *adjective* cruel/cruelle

cruelty *noun* la cruauté

cruise *noun* la croisière; **they're going on a cruise** ils partent en croisière

crumb *noun* la miette

crumpet *noun* la petite galette ronde

crunchy *adjective*
(a) *(bread)* croustillant/croustillante

(b) *(apple, salad)* croquant/croquante

crush
1 *verb* écraser; **we were nearly crushed to death** on a failli être écrasés
2 *noun* **he's got a crush on you** il craque pour toi

crust *noun* la croûte; **a crust of bread** une croûte

crusty *adjective (bread)* croustillant/croustillante

crutch *noun* la béquille; **to walk on crutches** marcher avec des béquilles

cry
1 *noun (shout)* le cri; **he gave a cry of pain** il a poussé un cri de douleur
2 *verb*
(a) pleurer; **the baby is crying** le bébé pleure
(b) *(shout)* crier; **she cried for help** elle a crié à l'aide
3 **cry out** pousser un cri; **he cried out in pain** il a poussé un cri de douleur

Cub *noun* le louveteau; **he goes to Cubs on Fridays** il va aux louveteaux le vendredi

The plural of *louveteau* is *louveteaux*.

cub *noun (baby animal)* le petit/la petite

cube *noun (shape)* le cube; **a cube of sugar** un morceau de sucre

cuckoo *noun* le coucou

cucumber *noun* le concombre

cuddle
1 *verb* câliner
2 *noun* le câlin; **to give somebody a cuddle** faire un câlin à quelqu'un

cultural *adjective* culturel/culturelle

culture *noun* la culture

cunning *adjective*
(a) *(smart)* astucieux/astucieuse
(b) *(sly)* rusé/rusée; **he's as cunning as a fox** il est rusé comme un renard

cup *noun*
(a) *(for drinking)* la tasse; **a cup of coffee** une tasse de café
(b) *(prize)* la coupe; **they won the cup** ils ont gagné la coupe

cupboard *noun* le placard; **the biscuits are in the cupboard** les biscuits sont dans le placard

cure
1 *verb* guérir; **those tablets cured my headache** ces comprimés m'ont fait passer mon mal de tête
2 *noun* le remède; **there is no known cure for this disease** on ne connaît pas encore de remède pour cette maladie

curious *adjective* curieux/curieuse; **I'm curious to know what happened next** je suis curieux de savoir ce qui s'est passé après; **this is a very curious thing** c'est quelque chose de très curieux

curl
1 *noun (of hair)* la boucle
2 *verb (hair)* boucler; **she's curling her hair** elle se boucle les cheveux

curly *adjective (hair)* bouclé/bouclée; **very curly** frisé/frisée; **she has very curly hair** elle a les cheveux frisés

currency *noun* la devise; **I bought some foreign currency** j'ai acheté des devises étrangères

current
1 *adjective* actuel/actuelle; **the current exhibition at the Louvre** l'exposition qui a lieu en ce moment au Louvre
2 *noun*
(a) *(of water)* le courant; **he was swept away by the current** il a été emporté par le courant
(b) *(electric)* le courant

curry *noun* le curry; **chicken curry** le poulet au curry

curtain *noun* le rideau; **to draw the curtains** tirer les rideaux

The plural of *rideau* is *rideaux*.

curve *noun*
(a) *(shape)* la courbe
(b) *(in a road)* le virage
curved *adjective* courbe
cushion *noun* le coussin
custom *noun* la coutume
customer *noun* le client/la cliente
customs *noun* la douane; **to go through customs** passer la douane
cut *noun*
(a) *(injury)* la coupure; **she has a cut on her hand** elle a une coupure à la main
(b) *(reduction)* la réduction; **she took a cut in her wages** elle a accepté une réduction de salaire
2 *verb*
(a) *(slice)* couper; **these scissors don't cut very well** ces ciseaux ne coupent pas très bien; **he cut a slice of cake** il a coupé une tranche de gâteau; **to cut oneself** se couper; **to cut one's finger** se couper le doigt; **to cut somebody's hair** couper les cheveux à quelqu'un; **to cut the grass** tondre la pelouse
(b) *(reduce)* réduire; **prices have been cut** les prix ont été réduits
3 cut down *(a tree)* abattre
4 cut off
(a) *(remove)* couper
(b) *(the electricity, the telephone)* couper; **we got cut off** *(during a conversation)* nous avons été coupés; *(disconnected)* on nous a coupé le téléphone
5 cut out *(an article, a picture)* découper
6 cut up *(into pieces)* couper en morceaux; **cut the meat up into small pieces** coupe la viande en petits morceaux

cute *adjective* mignon/mignonne
cutlery *noun* les couverts *(masculine plural)*
CV *noun* le CV
cybercafé *noun* le cybercafé
cyberspace *noun* le cyberspace
cycle
1 *verb* faire du vélo; **I like cycling** j'aime faire du vélo; **I cycle to school** je vais à l'école en vélo
2 *noun* *(pattern)* le cycle
cyclist *noun* le/la cycliste
Cypriot
1 *adjective* chypriote
2 *noun* *(person)* le/la Chypriote; **the Cypriots** les Chypriotes *(masculine plural)*
Cyprus *noun* Chypre; **Cyprus is an island** Chypre est une île; **they live in Cyprus** ils habitent à Chypre; **have you ever been to Cyprus?** est-ce que tu es déjà allé à Chypre?; **she's from Cyprus** elle vient de Chypre
Czech
1 *adjective* tchèque
2 *noun*
(a) *(language)* le tchèque; **she speaks Czech** elle parle tchèque
(b) *(person)* le/la Tchèque; **the Czechs** les Tchèques *(masculine plural)*

> In French, only the noun for the inhabitants of a country takes a capital letter, never the adjective or the noun for the language.

dad *noun*
(**a**) *(term of address)* le papa; **hi, Dad!** bonjour papa!
(**b**) *(father)* le père; **my dad's French** mon père est français

daddy *noun*
(**a**) *(term of address)* le papa; **hi, Daddy!** bonjour papa!
(**b**) *(father)* le père; **my daddy's a mechanic** mon père est mécanicien

daffodil *noun* la jonquille

daily
1 *adjective* quotidien/quotidienne; **a daily newspaper** un quotidien
2 *adverb* tous les jours; **take the medicine twice daily** prenez les médicaments deux fois par jour

daisy *noun* la pâquerette

dam *noun* le barrage

damage
1 *noun* les dégâts *(masculine plural)*; **the storm did a lot of damage** l'orage a fait beaucoup de dégâts
2 *verb*
(**a**) *(a place, a building, a machine)* endommager; **the storm damaged a lot of trees** de nombreux arbres ont été endommagés par la tempête
(**b**) *(an object)* abîmer; **I damaged my mobile phone when I dropped it** j'ai abîmé mon téléphone portable en le faisant tomber
(**c**) *(health, reputation)* nuire à; **smoking can seriously damage your health** le tabac nuit gravement à la santé

damp *adjective* humide

dance
1 *noun*
(**a**) la danse; **she goes to dance classes** elle prend des cours de danse
(**b**) *(social event)* le bal

> The plural of *bal* is *bals*.

2 *verb* danser; **would you like to dance?** tu veux danser?

dancer *noun* le danseur/la danseuse; **she wants to be a dancer** elle veut être danseuse

dancing *noun* la danse; **we're going dancing** nous allons danser; **dancing shoes** les chaussures de danse

Dane *noun* *(person)* le Danois/la Danoise

danger *noun* le danger; **to be in danger** être en danger; **to be out of danger** être hors de danger; **he's in danger of failing his exams** il risque de rater ses examens

dangerous *adjective* dangereux/dangereuse

Danish
1 *adjective* danois/danoise
2 *noun*
(**a**) *(language)* le danois; **he speaks Danish** il parle danois
(**b**) *(people)* **the Danish** les Danois *(masculine plural)*

> In French, only the noun for the inhabitants of a country takes a capital letter, never the adjective or the noun for the language.

dare
1 *verb*

(**a**) *(risk)* oser; **I daren't speak to him** je n'ose pas lui parler
(**b**) *(challenge)* **I dare you to ask her!** je te défie de lui demander!; **I dare you!** chiche!
2 *noun* le défi; **I did it for a dare** je l'ai fait pour relever un défi

daring *adjective* audacieux/audacieuse

dark
1 *adjective*
(**a**) *(inside)* sombre; **it's dark in here** il fait sombre ici
(**b**) *(outside)* **it's dark** il fait nuit; **it's getting dark** il commence à faire nuit
(**c**) *(colour)* foncé/foncée; **she has dark eyes** elle a les yeux foncés; **dark blue** bleu foncé
2 *noun*
(**a**) *(darkness)* **the dark** le noir; **she's afraid of the dark** elle a peur du noir; **in the dark** dans le noir
(**b**) *(night-time)* **we must be home before dark** nous devons rentrer avant la nuit

dark-haired *adjective* aux cheveux foncés; **a dark-haired girl** une fille aux cheveux foncés; **I'm dark-haired** j'ai les cheveux foncés

darkness *noun* l'obscurité *(feminine)*; **the house was in darkness** la maison était dans l'obscurité

darling *noun* le chéri/la chérie; **yes, darling?** oui, chéri?

dart *noun* la fléchette; **they're playing darts** ils jouent aux fléchettes

dartboard *noun* la cible

dash
1 *verb* se précipiter; **I dashed towards him** je me suis précipité vers lui; **he dashed into the room** il est entré précipitamment dans la pièce; **I must dash** je dois filer
2 dash off partir en vitesse

data *noun*
(**a**) *(information)* les informations *(feminine plural)*; **they're collecting data on dolphins** ils recueillent des informations sur les dauphins
(**b**) *(on a computer)* les données *(feminine plural)*; **a piece of data** une donnée

date
1 *noun*
(**a**) *(day)* la date; **what's your date of birth?** quelle est ta date de naissance?; **what's the date today?** quel jour sommes-nous?
(**b**) *(meeting)* le rendez-vous; **I have a date tonight** j'ai un rendez-vous ce soir; **I went out on a date with him once** je suis sortie avec lui une fois
(**c**) *(person)* un ami/une amie; **can I bring a date?** je peux amener un ami?
(**d**) **to be up to date** *(work, list)* être à jour; *(person)* être au courant; **I'm not up to date with what's been happening** je ne suis pas au courant de ce qui s'est passé dernièrement
(**e**) **to be out of date** *(ticket, passport)* être périmé/périmée; *(idea, style)* être démodé/démodée
(**f**) *(fruit)* la datte
2 *verb* *(go out with)* sortir avec; **I'm dating him** je sors avec lui; **they've started dating** ils ont commencé à sortir ensemble

daughter *noun* la fille

daughter-in-law *noun* la belle-fille

> The plural of *belle-fille* is *belles-filles.*

dawn *noun* l'aube *(feminine)*; **he gets up at dawn** il se lève à l'aube

day *noun*
(**a**) le jour; **what day is it today?** quel jour sommes-nous?; **the day before** la veille; **the day before the party** la veille de la fête; **the day after** le lendemain; **the day after the party** le lendemain de la fête; **the other day** l'autre jour; **twice a day** deux fois par jour
(**b**) *(the whole day)* la journée; **it was a sunny day** c'était une journée ensoleillée; **he sleeps all day** il dort toute la journée

daylight *noun* le jour; **it was still daylight** il faisait encore jour

daytime *noun* la journée; **it happened in the daytime** ça s'est passé pendant la journée

dead *adjective* mort/morte; **a dead man** un mort; **a dead woman** une morte

deadline *noun* la date limite; **the deadline for returning your essays is next Monday** la date limite pour rendre vos dissertations est lundi prochain; **to meet a deadline** respecter un délai

deaf *adjective* sourd/sourde; **to go deaf** devenir sourd; **deaf and dumb** sourd-muet/sourde-muette

deal
1 *noun*
(a) *(arrangement)* le marché; **I made a deal with her** j'ai passé un marché avec elle; **it's a deal!** d'accord!; **to get a good deal** faire une bonne affaire
(b) **a great deal** beaucoup; **I have a great deal of work to do** j'ai beaucoup de travail à faire
2 *verb*
(a) *(in cards)* distribuer; **it's your turn to deal** c'est à toi de distribuer
(b) *(sell)* **the company deals in furniture** l'entreprise vend des meubles
(c) **to deal drugs** revendre de la drogue
3 **deal with** s'occuper de; **I'll deal with this** je m'en occupe

dear
1 *adjective*
(a) *(loved)* cher/chère; **he's a dear friend of mine** c'est un ami très cher
(b) *(in a letter)* **Dear Alice** Chère Alice; **Dear Mum and Dad** Chers Maman et Papa; **Dear Mr Thomas** Cher Monsieur; **Dear Sir or Madam** Monsieur, Madame
(c) *(expensive)* cher/chère
(d) **oh dear!** oh là là!
2 *noun (darling)* chéri/chérie; **thank you, dear** merci, chéri

death *noun* la mort; **to freeze to death** mourir de froid; **to be bored to death** s'ennuyer à mourir

debate
1 *noun* le débat
2 *verb* débattre; **the government are debating the issue** le gouvernement est en train de débattre de la question

debt *noun* la dette; **to be in debt** avoir des dettes

deceive *noun* tromper

Note that the French word *décevoir* is never a translation for the English word *deceive*. It means *to disappoint*.

December *noun* décembre *(masculine)*; **the first of December** le premier décembre; **the second of December** le deux décembre; **the third of December** le trois décembre; **in December** en décembre

Names of months are not capitalized in French.

decide *verb*
(a) *(make a decision)* décider; **I decided to phone her** j'ai décidé de lui téléphoner; **what have you decided?** qu'est-ce que vous avez décidé?
(b) *(make up one's mind)* se décider; **I can't decide** je n'arrive pas à me décider

decision *noun* la décision; **to make a decision** prendre une décision

deck *noun*
(a) *(of a ship)* le pont; **she's on deck** elle est sur le pont
(b) *(of a bus)* un étage; **the top deck** l'impériale *(feminine)*
(c) *(of cards)* le jeu

The plural of *jeu* is *jeux*.

deckchair *noun* la chaise longue

decorate *verb*
(a) *(a cake, a tree, a room)* décorer; **we decorated the Christmas tree** nous avons décoré le sapin de Noël

(**b**) *(paint)* peindre; *(wallpaper)* tapisser; **we've decorated the living room** *(painted it)* nous avons repeint le salon; *(wallpapered it)* nous avons retapissé le salon

decoration *noun* la décoration

deduct *verb* déduire; **they deducted £10 from the price** ils ont déduit 10 livres du prix

deep *adjective*
(**a**) profond/profonde; **we dug a deep hole** nous avons creusé un trou profond; **the lake is ten metres deep** le lac fait dix mètres de profondeur; **take a deep breath** respirez profondément
(**b**) *(sound)* grave; **a deep voice** une voix grave

deeply *adverb* profondément

deer *noun* le cerf

defeat
1 *verb* battre; **they were defeated by one goal to nil** ils ont été battus par un but à zéro
2 *noun* la défaite

defence *noun*
(**a**) *(protection)* la défense; **he came to her defence** il l'a défendue
(**b**) *(in sport)* la défense; **I play in defence** je joue en défense

defend *verb* défendre; **they defended their country** ils ont défendu leur pays; **I know how to defend myself** je sais me défendre

definite *adjective*
(**a**) *(exact)* précis/précise; **we have to set a definite date** nous devons fixer une date précise
(**b**) *(clear)* net/nette; **there has been a definite improvement in her work** son travail s'est nettement amélioré
(**c**) *(certain)* sûr/sûre; **it's not definite yet** ce n'est pas encore sûr

definitely *adverb* sans aucun doute; **I'll definitely be there** j'y serai, c'est sûr; **definitely not!** certainement pas!

definition *noun* la définition

defrost *verb*
(**a**) *(freezer)* dégivrer
(**b**) *(food)* décongeler

degree *noun*
(**a**) *(measurement)* le degré; **it's 25 degrees** il fait 25 degrés; **it was ten degrees below zero** il faisait dix degrés au-dessous de zéro; **a 45-degree angle** un angle de 45 degrés
(**b**) *(extent)* **you're right to a degree** tu as raison jusqu'à un certain point
(**c**) *(from a university)* le diplôme universitaire; **she has a master's degree in French** elle a une maîtrise de français

delay
1 *verb* retarder; **the flight was delayed for three hours** le vol a été retardé de trois heures
2 *noun* le retard; **we had an hour's delay** nous avons eu une heure de retard

delete *verb* effacer; **I've deleted the file** j'ai effacé le fichier; **the delete key** la touche d'effacement

deli *noun* le traiteur; **at the deli** chez le traiteur

deliberate *adjective* voulu/voulue

deliberately *adverb* exprès; **I didn't hurt him deliberately** je n'ai pas fait exprès de le blesser; **he didn't do it deliberately** il ne l'a pas fait exprès

delicate *adjective* délicat/délicate

delicatessen *noun* le traiteur; **at the delicatessen** chez le traiteur

delicious *adjective* délicieux/délicieuse

delighted *adjective* ravi/ravie; **I'm delighted to see you again** je suis ravi de vous revoir; **they're delighted with their new house** ils sont très contents de leur nouvelle maison

delightful *adjective* charmant/charmante

deliver *verb* livrer; **he delivers newspapers** il livre des journaux

delivery *noun* la livraison; **there is a charge for delivery** il y a des frais de livraison

demand
1 *verb* exiger; **she demanded to know the truth** elle a exigé de connaître la vérité

Note that the French verb *demander* is not usually a translation for the English verb *to demand*. Its most common meaning is *to ask*.

2 *noun*
(**a**) *(request)* la demande; **there's a huge demand for these trainers** ces baskets sont très demandées
(**b**) *(obligation)* une exigence; **her boss makes great demands on her** son chef exige beaucoup d'elle

Note that the French word *demande* is not usually a translation for the English word *demand*. Its most common meaning is *request*.

demanding *adjective* exigeant/exigeante; **the teacher is very demanding** le professeur est très exigeant

democracy *noun* la démocratie

democratic *adjective* démocratique

demonstrate *verb*
(**a**) *(show)* montrer; **he demonstrated how to use the DVD player** il nous a montré comment se servir du lecteur DVD
(**b**) *(protest)* manifester; **the students are demonstrating against higher fees** les étudiants manifestent contre l'augmentation des frais de scolarité

demonstration *noun*
(**a**) *(explanation)* la démonstration
(**b**) *(protest)* la manifestation

Note that the French word *démonstration* never means *protest*.

denim *noun* le jean; **a denim skirt** une jupe en jean

Denmark *noun* le Danemark; **he was born in Denmark** il est né au Dane-mark; **I'm going to Denmark** je vais au Danemark; **this cheese is from Denmark** ce fromage vient du Danemark

dent
1 *noun* la bosse; **there's a dent in the car** la voiture a une bosse
2 *verb* cabosser; **he dented his car** il a cabossé sa voiture

dentist *noun* le/la dentiste; **I'm going to the dentist** je vais chez le dentiste; **her mother's a dentist** sa mère est dentiste

Note that when describing people's jobs or situations, French does not use an article (*un* or *une*).

deny *verb* nier; **she denied having spoken to him** elle a nié lui avoir parlé

deodorant *noun* le déodorant

depart *verb* partir; **the train is about to depart** le train va partir

department *noun*
(**a**) *(in an organization)* le service; **she works in the accounts department** elle travaille au service de la comptabilité
(**b**) *(in a government)* le ministère; **the Department of Health** le ministère de la Santé
(**c**) *(in a shop)* le rayon; **the toy department** le rayon des jouets; **a department store** un grand magasin
(**d**) *(in a school)* le département; **the French department** le département de français

departure *noun* le départ; **our departure was delayed for three hours** notre départ a été retardé de trois heures; **the departure lounge** la salle d'embarquement

depend *verb*
(**a**) dépendre; **it depends** ça dépend; **it depends on the weather** ça dépend du temps
(**b**) **to depend on somebody** compter sur quelqu'un

depressed *adjective* déprimé/déprimée; **the winter makes me feel depressed** l'hiver me déprime

depth *noun* la profondeur; **the canal is about 12 metres in depth** le canal fait environ 12 mètres de profondeur; **we studied the book in depth** nous avons étudié le livre en profondeur

describe *verb* décrire; **can you describe the man?** est-ce que vous pouvez décrire cet homme?; **the book describes how they escaped** le livre décrit la façon dont ils se sont évadés

description *noun* la description; **write a description of the scene** décrivez la scène

desert
1 *noun* le désert
2 *verb* abandonner; **his friends have deserted him** ses amis l'ont abandonné

deserted *adjective* désert/déserte; **the streets were deserted** les rues étaient désertes

deserve *verb* mériter; **he deserves to be punished** il mérite qu'on le punisse *or* il mérite d'être puni

design
1 *verb*
(a) *(draw)* dessiner; **she designs jewellery** elle dessine des bijoux
(b) *(plan)* concevoir; **it's specially designed for low temperatures** c'est spécialement conçu pour les basses températures
2 *noun*
(a) *(pattern)* le motif; **the sweater has a geometric design** le pull a un motif géométrique
(b) *(layout)* le plan; **the design for the new museum** les plans du nouveau musée
(c) *(type)* le modèle; **this is our latest design** c'est notre dernier modèle

designer *noun*
(a) *(artist)* le dessinateur/la dessinatrice

(b) *(of clothes)* le/la styliste; **she wants to be a fashion designer** elle veut être styliste; **designer clothes** les vêtements de marque

desk *noun*
(a) *(for schoolchildren)* la table
(b) *(in an office)* le bureau

> The plural of *bureau* is *bureaux*.

desperate *adjective* désespéré/désespérée; **I'm desperate for a cup of tea** je meurs d'envie de boire une tasse de thé

despite *preposition* malgré; **he went out despite having homework to do** il est sorti malgré le fait qu'il avait des devoirs à faire

dessert *noun* le dessert; **what do you want for dessert?** qu'est-ce que tu veux comme dessert?

destination *noun* la destination; **we've reached our destination** nous sommes arrivés à destination

destroy *verb* détruire; **an explosion destroyed the railway station** une explosion a détruit la gare

destruction *noun* la destruction

detail *noun* le détail; **pay attention to detail** faites attention aux détails; **we discussed the problem in detail** nous avons discuté du problème en détail

detective *noun* un inspecteur/une inspectrice de police; **he's a detective** il est inspecteur de police; **a detective story** un roman policier

detention *noun* la retenue; **he's in detention** il est en retenue

determined *adjective* déterminé/déterminée; **I'm determined to lose weight this year** je suis déterminé à perdre du poids cette année

develop
1 *verb*
(a) *(a story, an idea, a camera film)* développer; **I got my photos developed** j'ai fait développer mes photos

(**b**) *(evolve)* se développer; **the country is developing fast** le pays se développe rapidement
2 develop into devenir; **she has developed into a talented pianist** elle est devenue une pianiste très douée

development *noun* le développement

device *noun* un appareil; **that's a useful device** c'est un appareil utile

devil *noun* le diable

dew *noun* la rosée

diabetes *noun* le diabète; **she has diabetes** elle a du diabète

diagonal *adjective* diagonal/diagonale

diagram *noun* le schéma

dial *verb* **to dial a number** composer un numéro *or* faire un numéro

diamond *noun*
(**a**) *(gem)* le diamant; **a diamond necklace** un collier de diamants
(**b**) *(in cards)* **diamonds** carreau *(masculine)*; **the ace of diamonds** l'as de carreau

diarrhoea *noun* la diarrhée; **to have diarrhoea** avoir la diarrhée

diary *noun*
(**a**) *(for appointments)* un agenda; **write it down in your diary** note-le dans ton agenda
(**b**) *(private)* le journal intime; **I keep a diary** j'ai un journal intime

The plural of *journal* is *journaux*.

dice *noun* le dé; **throw the dice** lance le dé

dictation *noun* la dictée; **we're doing dictation today** nous allons faire une dictée aujourd'hui

dictionary *noun* le dictionnaire; **look it up in the dictionary** cherche dans le dictionnaire

die
1 *verb* mourir; **she's dying** elle est en train de mourir; **he died** il est mort; **I'm dying for a drink** je meurs de soif; **I'm dying to meet him** je meurs d'envie de le rencontrer
2 die down *(of a storm, noise, excitement)* se calmer
3 die out *(of a species, a language)* disparaître

diet
1 *noun*
(**a**) *(for losing weight)* le régime; **to be on a diet** être au régime; **to go on a diet** se mettre au régime
(**b**) *(regular food)* l'alimentation *(feminine)*; **he has a healthy diet** il a une alimentation saine
2 *verb* être au régime; **he needs to diet** il faut qu'il se mette au régime

difference *noun* la différence; **it doesn't make any difference** ça ne fait aucune différence

different *adjective*
(**a**) *(changed)* différent/différente; **this book is very different from her last one** ce livre est très différent de son dernier
(**b**) *(various)* divers/diverses, plusieurs; **it comes in different colours** il existe en plusieurs couleurs

difficult *adjective* difficile; **French grammar is difficult** la grammaire française est difficile

difficulty *noun* la difficulté; **to have difficulty doing something** avoir du mal à faire quelque chose; **he has difficulty climbing the stairs** il a du mal à monter les escaliers

dig
1 *verb* creuser; **I dug a hole** j'ai creusé un trou; **to dig the garden** bêcher le jardin
2 dig up déterrer; **they dug up the treasure** ils ont déterré le trésor

digital *adjective* numérique; **a digital camera** un appareil photo numérique; **a digital clock** une horloge à affichage numérique; **digital television**

la télévision numérique

dim *adjective*
(**a**) *(light)* faible
(**b**) *(room)* sombre

dimple *noun* la fossette; **he has a dimple in his chin** il a une fossette au menton

din *noun* le vacarme; **stop making such a din** arrête ton vacarme

dinghy *noun* le bateau pneumatique

dining room *noun* la salle à manger

dinner *noun*
(**a**) *(evening meal)* le dîner; **what's for dinner?** qu'est-ce qu'on mange ce soir?; **a dinner party** un dîner; **dinner time** l'heure du dîner
(**b**) *(midday meal)* le déjeuner; **a dinner lady** une cantinière; **dinner time** l'heure du déjeuner

dinosaur *noun* le dinosaure

diploma *noun* le diplôme; **she has a diploma in computing** elle est diplômée en informatique

direct
1 *verb*
(**a**) *(give directions)* **to direct somebody** indiquer le chemin à quelqu'un; **can you direct me to the station?** pouvez-vous m'indiquer le chemin de la gare?
(**b**) *(a company)* diriger
(**c**) *(a film)* réaliser; *(a play)* mettre en scène; **the film was directed by Quentin Tarantino** c'est Quentin Tarantino qui a réalisé ce film
2 *adjective* direct/directe; **this is a direct flight** c'est un vol direct
3 *adverb* **you can fly direct from Edinburgh to Paris** il y a des vols directs d'Édimbourg à Paris

direction *noun*
(**a**) la direction; **are we going in the right direction?** est-ce que nous allons dans la bonne direction?; **he set off in the opposite direction** il est parti en sens inverse
(**b**) **to ask for directions** demander

son chemin; **to give somebody directions** indiquer le chemin à quelqu'un

directly *adverb* directement; **it's directly opposite the church** c'est juste en face de l'église

director *noun*
(**a**) *(of a company)* le directeur/la directrice
(**b**) *(of a film)* le réalisateur/la réalisatrice; *(of a play)* le metteur en scène; **his dad is a film director** son père est réalisateur

dirt *noun* la saleté; *(mud)* la boue; **he's covered in dirt** il est tout sale

dirty *adjective* sale; **this t-shirt is dirty** ce tee-shirt est sale; **to get dirty** se salir

disabled *adjective* handicapé/handicapée; **disabled people** les handicapés *(masculine plural)*

disadvantage *noun*
(**a**) *(bad point)* un inconvénient; **the disadvantage of going by train is that it takes longer** l'inconvénient du train, c'est que ça met plus de temps
(**b**) le désavantage; **her age puts her at a disadvantage** elle est désavantagée par son âge

disagree *verb* ne pas être d'accord; **I disagree** je ne suis pas d'accord; **I disagree with their decision** je n'approuve pas leur décision

disagreement *noun* le désaccord; **we are in disagreement** nous ne sommes pas d'accord; **we've had a disagreement** nous nous sommes disputés

disappear *verb* disparaître

disappoint *verb* décevoir

disappointed *adjective* déçu/déçue; **he was disappointed about not being invited** il a été déçu de ne pas avoir été invité; **I was disappointed with the hotel** l'hôtel m'a déçu

disappointing *adjective* décevant/

décevante; **the film was disappointing** le film était décevant

disapprove *verb* **to disapprove of something** désapprouver quelque chose; **she disapproves of drinking** elle est contre l'alcool; **my parents disapprove of my friends** mes parents n'aiment pas mes amis

disaster *noun* la catastrophe; **a natural disaster** une catastrophe naturelle

disc *noun* le disque

discipline *noun* la discipline

disco *noun*
(a) *(club)* la boîte de nuit
(b) *(party)* la soirée disco; **there's a disco on Friday** il y a une soirée disco vendredi

disconnect *verb*
(a) *(unplug)* débrancher; **you've disconnected my computer** tu as débranché mon ordinateur
(b) *(cut off)* couper; **our phone's been disconnected** on nous a coupé le téléphone

discount *noun* la réduction; **we got a discount** nous avons eu une réduction; **they offer a 10% discount for students** ils font une réduction de 10% aux étudiants

discover *verb*
(a) *(find)* découvrir; **they discovered an old painting in the attic** ils ont découvert un vieux tableau au grenier
(b) *(realize)* se rendre compte; **I discovered that he had been lying** je me suis rendu compte qu'il avait menti

discovery *noun* la découverte

discrimination *noun* la discrimination

discuss *verb* discuter de; **they're discussing the football match** ils discutent du match de foot

discussion *noun* la discussion; **we had a long discussion about money** nous avons eu une longue discussion à propos d'argent

disease *noun* la maladie

disguise
1 *verb* déguiser; **he escaped disguised as a policeman** il s'est échappé déguisé en policier
2 *noun* le déguisement; **in disguise** déguisé/déguisée

disgust *noun* le dégoût

disgusted *adjective* écœuré/écœurée; **I am disgusted with him** il m'écœure

disgusting *adjective* dégoûtant/dégoûtante; **how disgusting!** c'est dégoûtant!

dish
1 *noun*
(a) *(plate)* le plat; **I'll wash the dishes** je vais faire la vaisselle
(b) *(food)* le plat; **it's his favourite dish** c'est son plat préféré
2 *verb* **dish up** servir; **she dished up the potatoes** elle a servi les pommes de terre

dishonest *adjective* malhonnête

dishwasher *noun* le lave-vaisselle

The word *lave-vaisselle* does not change in the plural.

disk *noun* le disque; **a hard disk** un disque dur; **a floppy disk** une disquette

dislike *verb* ne pas aimer; **I dislike flying** je n'aime pas prendre l'avion

dismiss *verb* *(sack)* renvoyer

disobey *verb* désobéir à; **he disobeyed the teacher** il a désobéi au professeur

disorganized *adjective* *(person)* mal organisé/organisée

display
1 *verb*
(a) *(objects)* exposer; **he displayed his paintings** il a exposé ses tableaux
(b) *(information)* afficher; **the exam results are displayed on the noticeboard** les résultats des examens sont sur le panneau d'affichage

2 *noun* une exposition; **on display** exposé/exposée

disposable *adjective* jetable; **a disposable camera** un appareil photo jetable

disqualify *verb* *(from an exam)* exclure; *(from a competition)* disqualifier; **she was disqualified for cheating** elle a été exclue des examens pour avoir triché

disrupt *verb* perturber; **he disrupts the class** il perturbe la classe

distance *noun* la distance; **the house is some distance from the village** la maison est assez loin du village; **it's only a short distance away** c'est tout près

distant *adjective* lointain/lointaine; **in the distant future** dans un avenir lointain

distract *verb* distraire

distribute *verb*
(a) *(give out)* distribuer; **they're distributing leaflets** ils distribuent des prospectus
(b) *(share out)* répartir; **she distributed the sweets among the children** elle a réparti les bonbons entre les enfants

district *noun*
(a) *(part of a country)* la région
(b) *(part of a town)* le quartier

disturb *verb* déranger; **don't disturb him while he's working** ne le dérange pas quand il travaille

disturbing *adjective*
(a) *(worrying)* inquiétant/inquiétante; **this is disturbing news** c'est une nouvelle inquiétante
(b) *(upsetting)* perturbant/perturbante; **it's quite a disturbing film** c'est un film assez perturbant

ditch *noun* le fossé

dive *verb* plonger; **she dived into the swimming pool** elle a plongé dans la piscine

diver *noun* le plongeur/la plongeuse

divide *verb*
(a) *(split)* diviser; **they divided it into four parts** ils l'ont divisé en quatre; **divide the figure by two** divise ce chiffre par deux; **ten divided by two equals five** dix divisé par deux égale cinq
(b) *(share out)* partager; **we divide the work among us** nous nous partageons le travail
(c) *(separate)* séparer; **the Pyrenees divide France from Spain** la France et l'Espagne sont séparées par les Pyrénées

diving *noun*
(a) *(scuba diving)* la plongée; **I like diving** j'aime la plongée
(b) *(from a diving board)* le plongeon; **I like diving** j'aime plonger; **a diving board** un plongeoir

division *noun* la division

divorce
1 *noun* le divorce; **they're getting a divorce** ils divorcent
2 *verb* divorcer; **she divorced her husband** elle a divorcé d'avec son mari; **they're getting divorced** ils divorcent

divorced *adjective* divorcé/divorcée; **my parents are divorced** mes parents sont divorcés

DIY *noun* le bricolage; **my dad's a DIY expert** mon père est spécialiste du bricolage

dizzy *adjective* **to feel dizzy** avoir la tête qui tourne; **it made me dizzy** ça m'a donné le vertige

DJ
1 *noun* le/la DJ; **she's a DJ** elle est DJ
2 *verb* travailler comme DJ

do
1 *verb*
(a) faire; **what do you do for a living?** qu'est-ce que vous faites dans la vie?; **what are they doing?** qu'est-ce qu'ils font?; **what are you going to do?**

qu'est-ce que tu vas faire?; **what did you do with my umbrella?** qu'est-ce que tu as fait de mon parapluie?; **all she does is sleep** elle ne fait que dormir
(**b**) *(study)* étudier; **they do French** ils étudient le français; **she's doing medicine** elle fait des études de médecine
(**c**) *(perform)* s'en sortir; **I did well in the exam** je m'en suis bien sorti à l'examen; **well done!** bravo!
(**d**) *(be suitable)* faire l'affaire; **this one will do** celui-ci fera l'affaire
2 *auxiliary verb*
(**a**) *(used in questions and negative sentences)* **do you know her?** est-ce que tu la connais?; **did you see him?** est-ce que vous l'avez vu?; **do you like chocolate?** est-ce que tu aimes le chocolat?; **don't worry** ne t'inquiète pas
(**b**) *(used for emphasis)* **I don't like coffee, but I** *do* **like tea** je n'aime pas le café, mais j'aime bien le thé; **why don't you work?** – **I** *do* **work!** pourquoi tu ne travailles pas? – mais si, je travaille!

Note that the word *si* is used in place of *oui* when contradicting a negative statement.

(**c**) *(used to replace a verb)* **he sings better than I do** il chante mieux que moi; **I like chocolate – so do I** j'aime le chocolat – moi aussi; **he doesn't like carrots and neither do I** il n'aime pas les carottes et moi non plus; **do you like her?** – **no, I don't** tu l'aimes bien? – non; **do you like her?** – **yes, I do** tu l'aimes bien? – oui; **you don't like her** – **yes I do!** tu ne l'aimes pas – mais si!
(**d**) *(used after questions)* **you like him, don't you?** tu l'aimes bien, n'est-ce pas? *or* tu l'aimes bien, non?; **she lives here, doesn't she?** elle habite ici, n'est-ce pas?
3 do up
(**a**) *(clothes)* fermer; *(shoelaces)* faire; **do up your coat** ferme ton manteau
(**b**) *(house)* refaire; **we're doing up**

the living room on est en train de refaire le salon
4 do with
(**a**) *(be connected to)* **it has something to do with the meeting yesterday** c'est au sujet de la réunion d'hier; **it's nothing to do with me** ça n'a rien à voir avec moi; **this is nothing to do with you** tu n'as rien à voir là-dedans
(**b**) *(need)* **I could do with a cup of tea** je prendrai bien une tasse de thé; **the kitchen could do with a clean** la cuisine a besoin d'être nettoyée
5 do without se passer de; **they had to do without food** ils ont dû se passer de nourriture

doctor *noun* le médecin; **she's a doctor** elle est médecin; **I'm going to the doctor's** je vais chez le médecin; **she has a doctor's appointment** elle a un rendez-vous chez le médecin

Note that when describing people's jobs or situations, French does not use an article *(un* or *une)*.

document *noun* le document
dodge *verb*
(**a**) *(a ball, a falling rock)* éviter; **I dodged the ball** j'ai évité le ballon
(**b**) *(a blow)* esquiver
dodgems® *plural noun* les autos tamponneuses *(feminine plural)*
dodgy *adjective*
(**a**) *(person)* louche
(**b**) *(object)* **the brakes are a bit dodgy** les freins n'ont pas l'air de bien marcher; **this chair is a bit dodgy** cette chaise n'est pas très solide
(**c**) *(place)* **he lives in a dodgy area** il habite dans un quartier mal fréquenté
dog *noun* le chien
doll *noun* la poupée
dollar *noun* le dollar
dolphin *noun* le dauphin
domino *noun* le domino; **do you want to play dominoes?** est-ce que tu veux jouer aux dominos?

donate *verb* faire un don de; **I donated £10** j'ai fait un don de 10 livres

done *adjective*
(**a**) *(finished)* fini/finie; **are you done yet?** est-ce que tu as fini?; **I have to get this work done** je dois finir ce travail
(**b**) *(cooked)* cuit/cuite; **I think the pasta's done** je crois que les pâtes sont cuites

donkey *noun* un âne

door *noun*
(**a**) *(of a house, a room)* la porte
(**b**) *(of a car)* la portière

doorbell *noun* la sonnette; **to ring the doorbell** sonner à la porte

doorman *noun*
(**a**) *(at a hotel)* le portier; **his dad is a doorman in a luxury hotel** son père est portier dans un hôtel de luxe
(**b**) *(at a nightclub)* le videur; **his brother is a doorman in a club** son frère est videur dans une boîte de nuit

doormat *noun* le paillasson

doorstep *noun* le pas de la porte

doorway *noun* la porte; **the piano got stuck in the doorway** le piano est resté coincé dans la porte

dormitory *noun* le dortoir

dot *noun*
(**a**) *(small round mark)* le point
(**b**) *(in e-mail addresses)* **"dot, co, dot, uk"** "point, co, point, uk"
(**c**) *(on material)* le pois; **the skirt is black with white dots** la jupe est noire à pois blancs
(**d**) **at three o'clock on the dot** à trois heures pile

double
1 *adjective*
(**a**) double
(**b**) *(repeated)* **a double click** un double-clic; **"all" is spelt "a, double l"** "all" s'écrit "a, deux l"; **double two double three** *(when giving telephone numbers)* vingt-deux trente-trois

(**c**) **a double bed** un lit de deux personnes; **a double room** une chambre pour deux personnes
2 *adverb*
(**a**) *(twice as much)* le double; **she earns double my salary** elle gagne le double de moi
(**b**) **to see double** voir double
3 *verb* doubler; **they doubled her salary** ils ont doublé son salaire
4 *noun*
(**a**) *(identical person)* le sosie; **she's your double!** c'est ton sosie!
(**b**) *(in sport)* **doubles** un double; **mixed doubles** un double mixte; **to play doubles** faire un double

double bass *noun* la contrebasse; **he plays the double bass** il joue de la contrebasse

> Note that when talking about playing musical instruments, French uses the expression *jouer de*.

double-decker bus *noun* un autobus à impériale

doubt
1 *noun* le doute; **without a doubt** sans aucun doute; **no doubt he'll come** il viendra, c'est sûr
2 *verb* **to doubt something** douter de quelque chose; **I doubt it** j'en doute; **I doubt she'll come tonight** je doute qu'elle vienne ce soir

> Note that the subjunctive is used when expressing doubt or uncertainty.

doubtful *adjective* **to be doubtful about something** avoir des doutes sur quelque chose; **I'm doubtful about going** j'hésite à y aller; **it's doubtful that she'll come** ce n'est pas certain qu'elle vienne

dough *noun* la pâte

doughnut *noun* le beignet

dove *noun* la colombe

Dover *noun* Douvres

down
1 *preposition* en bas; **they live down**

the street ils habitent plus bas dans la rue; **to go down the stairs** descendre les escaliers; **to fall down the stairs** tomber en bas de l'escalier
2 *adverb* par terre; **I put my bags down** j'ai posé mes sacs par terre; **I fell down** je suis tombé par terre

downhill
1 *adjective* **the downhill journey** la descente; **downhill skiing** le ski alpin
2 *adverb* **to go downhill** descendre

download *verb* télécharger; **I downloaded the photos** j'ai téléchargé les photos

downstairs
1 *adverb* en bas; **my bag's downstairs** mon sac est en bas; **I went downstairs** je suis descendu
2 *adjective* d'en bas; **the downstairs phone** le téléphone d'en bas

downwards *adverb* vers le bas; **the road slopes downwards** la route descend

doze
1 *verb* sommeiller
2 doze off s'assoupir

dozen *noun* douzaine; **a dozen eggs** une douzaine d'œufs; **two dozen** deux douzaines; **half a dozen** une demi-douzaine; **I have dozens of things to do** j'ai des tas de choses à faire

drag
1 *verb* traîner; **I dragged my suitcase along the ground** j'ai traîné ma valise par terre
2 *noun* **what a drag!** quelle barbe!

dragon *noun* le dragon

dragonfly *noun* la libellule

drain
1 *noun*
(**a**) *(in the street)* un égout
(**b**) *(in the house)* **pour it down the drain** verse-le dans l'évier
2 *verb*
(**a**) *(pour water off)* égoutter; **drain the spaghetti** égouttez les spaghettis
(**b**) *(empty)* vider; **they've drained**

the lake ils ont vidé le lac

drama *noun*
(**a**) *(acting)* le théâtre; **she goes to drama lessons** elle fait du théâtre; **a drama school** une école de théâtre
(**b**) *(film, play)* le drame
(**c**) *(excitement)* **her life is full of drama** sa vie est pleine de rebondissements

dramatic *adjective*
(**a**) *(theatrical)* théâtral/théâtrale; **don't be so dramatic about it** n'en fais pas un drame
(**b**) *(spectacular)* spectaculaire; **the landscape here is dramatic** le paysage ici est spectaculaire

draught *noun* le courant d'air

draughts *noun* les dames *(feminine plural)*; **we played draughts** nous avons joué aux dames

draw
1 *verb*
(**a**) dessiner; **I'm drawing my house** je dessine ma maison
(**b**) **to draw the curtains** tirer les rideaux
(**c**) **he drew my attention to the mistake** il m'a fait remarquer la faute
(**d**) *(in sport)* faire match nul; **Italy drew against Spain** l'Italie et l'Espagne ont fait match nul
2 *noun* le match nul

drawer *noun* le tiroir; **a chest of drawers** une commode

drawing *noun*
(**a**) *(picture)* le dessin; **I did a drawing of the house** j'ai dessiné la maison
(**b**) *(activity)* **I like drawing** j'aime bien dessiner; **he's good at drawing** il dessine bien
(**c**) **a drawing pin** une punaise

dread *verb* appréhender; **I'm dreading the exam** j'appréhende l'examen

dreadful *adjective* affreux/affreuse

dream
1 *verb* rêver; **I dreamt I could fly** j'ai rêvé que je volais

2 *noun* le rêve; **I had a bad dream** j'ai fait un mauvais rêve; **I had a dream about her** j'ai rêvé d'elle; **sweet dreams!** fais de beaux rêves!

dress
1 *noun* la robe; **she's wearing a dress** elle porte une robe
2 *verb*
(**a**) *(put one's clothes on)* s'habiller; **she dresses well** elle s'habille bien
(**b**) *(put somebody else's clothes on)* habiller; **she dressed the child in pink** elle a habillé l'enfant en rose
3 dress up
(**a**) *(disguise oneself)* se déguiser; **he dressed up as Superman** il s'est déguisé en Superman
(**b**) *(put on smart clothes)* bien s'habiller; **she's getting dressed up to go clubbing** elle s'habille pour aller en boîte

dressed *adjective* habillé/habillée; **to get dressed** s'habiller; **he's badly dressed** il est mal habillé; **she's dressed in black** elle est habillée en noir

dresser *noun* le buffet

dressing *noun*
(**a**) *(for salad)* la sauce; **French dressing** la vinaigrette
(**b**) *(for a wound)* le pansement
(**c**) **a dressing gown** une robe de chambre
(**d**) **a dressing table** une coiffeuse

dried *adjective*
(**a**) *(fruit)* sec/sèche; **dried fruit** les fruits secs
(**b**) *(meat, flowers)* séché/séchée; **dried flowers** les fleurs séchées

drill
1 *noun* la perceuse
2 *verb* percer; **he drilled a hole in the wall** il a percé un trou dans le mur

drink
1 *noun*
(**a**) la boisson; **a hot drink** une boisson chaude; **a cold drink** une boisson fraîche; **may I have a drink?** est-ce que je peux boire quelque chose?; **a drink of water** un verre d'eau
(**b**) *(alcoholic)* le verre; **we're going for a drink tonight** nous allons prendre un verre ce soir
2 *verb* boire; **would you like something to drink?** voulez-vous boire quelque chose?; **I don't drink** *(alcohol)* je ne bois pas

drinking water *noun* l'eau potable *(feminine)*

drip
1 *noun* la goutte
2 *verb* goutter; **the tap is dripping** le robinet goutte

drive
1 *noun*
(**a**) *(outing)* **let's go for a drive** allons faire un tour en voiture
(**b**) *(distance)* **it's a 50-km drive** c'est un trajet de 50 km; **it's an hour's drive away** c'est à une heure en voiture
(**c**) *(in front of a house)* une allée
2 *verb*
(**a**) conduire; **can you drive?** est-ce que tu sais conduire?; **he drove me into town** il m'a conduit en ville
(**b**) *(go in one's car)* rouler; **he drives too fast** il roule trop vite
(**c**) *(travel by car)* aller en voiture; **are we walking or driving?** on y va à pied ou en voiture?
(**d**) **to drive somebody mad** rendre quelqu'un fou; **he drives me mad** il me rend fou
3 drive away partir en voiture
4 drive off partir en voiture

driver *noun*
(**a**) *(of a car)* le conducteur/la conductrice; **she's a good driver** elle conduit bien
(**b**) *(of a bus, a taxi, a lorry)* le chauffeur; **he's a taxi driver** il est chauffeur de taxi

driving *noun*
(**a**) **his driving is awful** il conduit très mal

(**b**) **a driving licence** un permis de conduire
(**c**) **she's just passed her driving test** elle vient d'avoir son permis; **I failed my driving test** j'ai raté mon permis

drop
1 *noun*
(**a**) *(of liquid)* la goutte; **a drop of blood** une goutte de sang
(**b**) *(lowering)* la baisse; **there's been a drop in prices** il y a eu une baisse des prix
2 *verb*
(**a**) laisser tomber; **she dropped the book** elle a laissé tomber le livre
(**b**) *(lower)* baisser; **prices have dropped** les prix ont baissé
(**c**) *(from a vehicle)* déposer; **I'll drop you at the corner** je vais te déposer au coin de la rue
3 **drop off** déposer; **they dropped me off at school** ils m'ont déposé à l'école

drought *noun* la sécheresse

drown *verb* se noyer

drug *noun*
(**a**) *(medicine)* le médicament
(**b**) *(illegal substance)* la drogue; **he takes drugs** il se drogue; **a drug addict** un drogué/une droguée

drum
1 *noun* le tambour; **the drums** *(in a band)* la batterie; **he plays the drums** il joue de la batterie
2 *verb* jouer de la batterie

drummer *noun* *(playing one drum)* le joueur/la joueuse de tambour; *(playing drums in a band)* le batteur/la batteuse; **she's a drummer** elle joue de la batterie

drumsticks *plural noun* les baguettes *(feminine plural)*

drunk *adjective* ivre; **to get drunk** se soûler

dry
1 *adjective*

(**a**) sec/sèche; **the washing is dry** le linge est sec
(**b**) *(weather)* **a dry day** une journée sans pluie; **tomorrow will be dry** il ne pleuvra pas demain
2 *verb* sécher; **the washing is drying** le linge sèche; **to dry oneself** se sécher; **to dry one's hair** se sécher les cheveux; **to dry the dishes** essuyer la vaisselle

dry-cleaner's *noun* le pressing; **take your coat to the dry-cleaner's** emporte ton manteau au pressing

dryer *noun* *(for clothes)* le séchoir; **a hair dryer** un sèche-cheveux; **a tumble dryer** un sèche-linge

The words *sèche-cheveux* and *sèche-linge* do not change in the plural.

duck¹ *noun* le canard

duck² *verb* se baisser; **he ducked to avoid the ball** il s'est baissé pour éviter le ballon

due *adjective*
(**a**) **there's a bus due now** un bus doit arriver d'un moment à l'autre; **we're due there at seven o'clock** nous devons y être à sept heures; **when is the baby due?** quand est-ce que le bébé doit naître?
(**b**) **due to** *(caused by)* dû/due à; **this problem is due to the economic crisis** ce problème est dû à la crise économique
(**c**) **due to** *(because of)* à cause de; **the boat arrived late due to fog** le bateau est arrivé en retard à cause du brouillard

dull *adjective*
(**a**) *(boring)* ennuyeux/ennuyeuse
(**b**) *(weather)* maussade
(**c**) *(colour)* terne

dumb *adjective*
(**a**) *(unable to speak)* muet/muette
(**b**) *(stupid)* bête; **that was a dumb thing to do** c'est bête d'avoir fait ça

dummy *noun* *(for baby)* la tétine

dump

1 *noun* **a rubbish dump** un dépôt d'ordures

2 *verb*

(a) déposer; **they dump the rubbish here** on dépose les ordures ici; **dump your bags in the corner** posez vos sacs dans le coin

(b) *(a girlfriend, a boyfriend)* plaquer; **she dumped him** elle l'a plaqué

during *preposition* pendant; **the baby sleeps during the day** le bébé dort pendant la journée

dusk *noun* le crépuscule; **at dusk** au crépuscule

dust

1 *noun* la poussière; **theTV's covered in dust** la télé est pleine de poussière

2 *verb* **I dusted my room** j'ai fait les poussières dans ma chambre

dustbin *noun* la poubelle; **throw it in the dustbin** jette-le à la poubelle

duster *noun* le chiffon à poussière

dustman *noun* un éboueur; **he's a dustman** il est éboueur

dusty *adjective* poussiéreux/poussiéreuse

Dutch

1 *adjective* hollandais/hollandaise

2 *noun*

(a) *(language)* le hollandais; **she speaks Dutch** elle parle hollandais

(b) *(people)* **the Dutch** les Hollandais *(masculine plural)*

In French, only the noun for the inhabitants of a country takes a capital letter, never the adjective or the noun for the language.

Dutchman *noun* un Hollandais

Dutchwoman *noun* une Hollandaise

duty *noun*

(a) le devoir; **it's your duty to help her** c'est ton devoir de l'aider

(b) **to be on duty** être de service; **to be off duty** ne pas être de service

duvet *noun* la couette; **a duvet cover** une housse de couette

---

Note that the French word *duvet* is never a translation for the English word *duvet*. It means *sleeping bag*.

DVD *noun* le DVD; **the film is on DVD** le film est sorti en DVD; **a DVD player** un lecteur de DVD

dwarf *noun* le nain/la naine

dye

1 *noun* la teinture

2 *verb* teindre; **she dyed the skirt black** elle a teint la jupe en noir; **to dye one's hair** se teindre les cheveux

each
1 *adjective* chaque; **each one** chacun/chacune
2 *pronoun*
(a) chacun/chacune; **each of us** chacun/chacune d'entre nous; **my brothers have a car each** mes frères ont chacun une voiture; **the peaches cost 59p each** les pêches coûtent 59 pence pièce
(b) **they hate each other** ils se détestent; **they love each other** ils s'aiment; **do you know each other?** est-ce que vous vous connaissez?; **we write to each other** nous nous écrivons

Note that French often uses the plural reflexive pronouns (*se*, *nous* and *vous*) to translate *each other*.

eager *adjective* **to be eager to do something** avoir vraiment envie de faire quelque chose; **she's always eager to please** elle veut toujours faire plaisir

eagle *noun* un aigle

ear *noun* une oreille; **he's scratching his ear** il se gratte l'oreille

earache *noun* **I have earache** *(one ear)* j'ai mal à l'oreille; *(both ears)* j'ai mal aux oreilles

early
1 *adverb*
(a) *(in the day)* tôt; **I always get up early** je me lève toujours tôt
(b) *(ahead of time)* en avance; **we got there early** nous sommes arrivés en avance

2 *adjective* **to have an early night** se coucher tôt; **in early summer** au début de l'été; **in the early 90s** au début des années 90

earn *verb* gagner; **to earn a living** gagner sa vie; **I earn £10 an hour** je gagne 10 livres de l'heure

earphones *noun* le casque

earring *noun* la boucle d'oreille; **I like your earrings** j'aime bien tes boucles d'oreille

earth *noun* la terre; **what on earth are you doing?** mais qu'est-ce que tu fais?; **pictures of the earth** des photos de la Terre

The word *terre* takes a capital letter when it refers to the planet.

earthquake *noun* le tremblement de terre

ease *noun*
(a) *(comfort)* l'aise *(feminine)*; **to be at ease** être à l'aise
(b) *(easiness)* la facilité; **to do something with ease** faire quelque chose sans difficultés

easily *adverb* facilement; **you'll easily pass the exam** tu n'auras aucun problème à réussir l'examen; **that's easily my favourite book** c'est de loin mon livre préféré

east
1 *noun* l'est *(masculine)*; **to the east of** à l'est de; **Manchester is to the east of Liverpool** Manchester est à l'est de Liverpool; **in the east of** dans l'est de; **Aberdeen is in the east of Scotland**

Aberdeen est dans l'est de l'Écosse
2 *adjective* est; **the east coast** la côte est; **an east wind** un vent d'est
3 *adverb* vers l'est; **they're heading east** ils se dirigent vers l'est

Easter *noun* Pâques *(masculine)*; **an Easter egg** un œuf de Pâques; **Easter Sunday** le dimanche de Pâques

eastern *adjective* **eastern France** l'est de la France; **Eastern Europe** l'Europe de l'Est

easy *adjective* facile; **French is easy** le français, c'est facile

eat
1 *verb* manger; **would you like something to eat?** est-ce que tu veux manger quelque chose?; **she's eating lunch** elle déjeune; **there's nothing to eat** il n'y a rien à manger
2 eat out aller au restaurant; **we eat out every Saturday night** nous allons au restaurant tous les samedis soirs

echo *noun* un écho

eclipse *noun* une éclipse; **an eclipse of the sun** une éclipse de soleil

economical *adjective* économique; **central heating is more economical** le chauffage central est plus économique

economics *noun* l'économie *(feminine)*; **she's studying economics** elle fait des études d'économie

economy *noun* l'économie *(feminine)*

edge *noun*
(**a**) *(of a table, a road)* le bord; **at the water's edge** au bord de l'eau
(**b**) *(of a knife)* le tranchant

edition *noun* une édition

editor *noun*
(**a**) *(of a book, a newspaper)* le rédacteur/la rédactrice; **she's an editor** elle est rédactrice
(**b**) *(of a film)* le monteur/la monteuse

Note that the French word *éditeur/éditrice* is never a translation for the English word *editor*. It means *publisher*.

Edinburgh *noun* Édimbourg

educate *verb* instruire; **she was educated abroad** elle a fait ses études à l'étranger

educated *adjective* instruit/instruite

education *noun*
(**a**) *(learning)* l'éducation *(feminine)*; **a good education is important** il est important de recevoir une bonne éducation
(**b**) *(teaching)* l'enseignement *(masculine)*

educational *adjective*
(**a**) *(system, film)* éducatif/éducative
(**b**) *(method, visit)* pédagogique
(**c**) *(book)* scolaire

eel *noun* une anguille

effect *noun* un effet; **special effects** des effets spéciaux

efficient *adjective* efficace; **she's a very efficient worker** elle travaille avec efficacité

effort *noun* un effort; **to make an effort** faire un effort

egg *noun* un œuf; **an egg white** un blanc d'œuf; **an egg yolk** un jaune d'œuf

Egypt *noun* l'Égypte *(feminine)*; **she lives in Egypt** elle habite en Égypte; **I'm going to Egypt** je vais en Égypte; **he comes from Egypt** il vient d'Égypte

eight *number* huit

The final *t* in *huit* is not pronounced in front of a consonant.

eighteen *number* dix-huit

The final *t* in *dix-huit* is not pronounced in front of a consonant.

eighteenth *number* dix-huitième; **the eighteenth car** la dix-huitième voiture; **the eighteenth of May** le dix-huit mai

eighth *number* huitième; **one eighth** *(fraction)* un huitième; **the eighth day** le huitième jour; **the eighth car**

la huitième voiture; **the eighth of May** le huit mai

eighty *number* quatre-vingts; **eighty pages** quatre-vingts pages; **eighty-one boys** quatre-vingt-un garçons; **eighty-one girls** quatre-vingt-une filles; **eighty-two** quatre-vingt-deux; **eighty-first** quatre-vingt-unième; **eighty-second** quatre-vingt-deuxième; **the eighties** les années quatre-vingt

> *Quatre-vingts* takes an *s* when it is used on its own or when it is followed by a noun, eg *quatre-vingts ans*. When it is followed by another number it is spelled without an *s*, eg *quatre-vingt-deux*.

either
1 *adjective*
(a) *(one or the other)* l'un ou l'autre/ l'une ou l'autre; *(with 'not')* ni l'un ni l'autre/ni l'une ni l'autre; **you can take either road** vous pouvez prendre l'une ou l'autre de ces routes; **I didn't like either book** je n'ai aimé ni l'un ni l'autre de ces livres
(b) *(each)* chaque; **on either side** de chaque côté *or* des deux côtés
2 *adverb* non plus; **I can't do it either** je n'y arrive pas non plus; **I don't like him – I don't either** je ne l'aime pas – moi non plus
3 *pronoun* l'un ou l'autre/l'une ou l'autre; *(with 'not')* ni l'un ni l'autre/ni l'une ni l'autre; **which of the two buses should I take? – you can take either** lequel de ces deux bus dois-je prendre? – vous pouvez prendre l'un ou l'autre; **what do you think of these skirts? – I don't like either of them** que penses-tu de ces jupes? – je n'aime ni l'une ni l'autre; **which would you like? – either** lequel est-ce que tu voudrais? – n'importe lequel *or* l'un ou l'autre
4 *conjunction* **either... or...** soit... soit...; *(with 'not')* ni... ni...; **either today or tomorrow** soit aujourd'hui, soit demain; **I don't know either him**

or his brother je ne connais ni lui ni son frère

elastic *noun* l'élastique *(masculine)*; **an elastic band** un élastique

elbow *noun* le coude; **he hurt his elbow** il s'est fait mal au coude

elder
1 *noun* un aîné/une aînée; **he's the elder of the two** c'est lui l'aîné
2 *adjective* aîné/aînée; **his elder sister** sa sœur aînée

eldest
1 *noun* un aîné/une aînée; **she's the eldest of the three** c'est elle l'aînée des trois
2 *adjective* aîné/aînée; **my eldest brother** mon frère aîné

elderly *adjective* âgé/âgée; **an elderly man** un homme âgé

election *noun* une élection

electric *adjective* électrique; **an electric blanket** une couverture chauffante; **an electric cooker** une cuisinière électrique

electrician *noun* un électricien/une électricienne; **my father is an electrician** mon père est électricien

> Note that when describing people's jobs or situations, French does not use an article (*un* or *une*).

electricity *noun* l'électricité *(feminine)*

electronic *adjective* électronique

element *noun*
(a) *(of nature, a problem)* un élément
(b) *(small amount)* la part; **an element of chance** une part de chance; **an element of danger** une part de danger

elephant *noun* un éléphant

eleven *number* onze

eleventh *number* onzième; **one eleventh** *(fraction)* un onzième; **the eleventh day** le onzième jour; **the eleventh car** la onzième voiture; **the eleventh**

of March le onze mars

else *adverb* **something else** autre chose; **nothing else** rien d'autre; **somewhere else** ailleurs; **who else?** qui d'autre?; **what else?** quoi d'autre?

elsewhere *adverb* ailleurs

e-mail
1 *noun* un e-mail; **she sent him an e-mail** elle lui a envoyé un e-mail; **an e-mail address** une adresse e-mail
2 *verb* **you can e-mail him** tu peux lui envoyer un e-mail; **I e-mailed the document to all the students** j'ai envoyé le document par e-mail à tous les élèves

embarrass *verb* gêner

embarrassed *adjective* gêné/gênée

embarrassing *adjective* gênant/gênante; **how embarrassing!** c'était vraiment gênant!

embassy *noun* une ambassade; **the British Embassy** l'ambassade de Grande-Bretagne

> Do not confuse the spellings of the French *ambassade* and English *embassy*.

emerald *noun* une émeraude; **an emerald ring** une bague en émeraude

emergency *noun* une urgence; **in an emergency** en cas d'urgence; **an emergency exit** une sortie de secours

emotion *noun* une émotion

emotional *adjective*
(**a**) *(person, reaction)* émotif/émotive
(**b**) *(problem)* émotionnel/émotionnelle

emphasize *verb*
(**a**) *(a point, a fact)* insister sur; **this point needs to be emphasized** il faut insister sur ce point; **he emphasized how important it was** il a souligné à quel point c'était important
(**b**) *(a word, a syllable)* appuyer sur

employ *verb* **to employ somebody** employer quelqu'un; **he's employed**

as a chef il est employé comme chef cuisinier

employee *noun* un employé/une employée; **we have 30 employees** nous avons 30 employés

employment *noun* l'emploi *(masculine)*

empty
1 *adjective* vide; **an empty bottle** une bouteille vide
2 *verb* vider; **he emptied the bin** il a vidé la poubelle

encourage *verb* encourager; **he encouraged me to study more** il m'a encouragé à étudier davantage

encouragement *noun* l'encouragement *(masculine)*; **I got lots of encouragement from my teacher** j'ai reçu beaucoup d'encouragements de la part de mon professeur

encyclopedia *noun* une encyclopédie

end
1 *noun*
(**a**) *(of a street, a box, a table)* le bout; **he lives at the end of the street** il habite au bout de la rue
(**b**) *(of a meeting, a month, a book)* la fin; **I'm going on holiday at the end of the month** je pars en vacances à la fin du mois
2 *verb*
(**a**) finir; **the film ends at 10 o'clock** le film finit à 10 heures
(**b**) *(a war, a meeting)* mettre fin à; **this put an end to their argument** cela a mis fin à leur dispute
3 end up finir; **he ended up in prison** il a fini en prison; **they ended up in York** ils se sont retrouvés à York

ending *noun*
(**a**) *(of a story)* la fin; **the film has a happy ending** le film se finit bien
(**b**) *(of a word)* la terminaison

endless *adjective*
(**a**) *(number, possibilities)* infini/infinie

(**b**) *(list, wait, task)* interminable

enemy *noun* un ennemi/une ennemie

Do not confuse the spellings of the French *ennemi* and English *enemy*.

energetic *adjective* énergique; **she's always very energetic** elle est toujours très énergique

energy *noun* l'énergie *(feminine)*; **she's full of energy** elle est pleine d'énergie

engaged *adjective*
(**a**) *(to be married)* fiancé/fiancée; **they got engaged** ils se sont fiancés; **they're engaged** ils sont fiancés; **he's engaged to my sister** il est fiancé à ma sœur
(**b**) *(phone, toilet)* occupé/occupée

Note that the French word *engagé* is not a translation for the English word *engaged*. It is used for artists and writers and means *politically active*.

engagement *noun*
(**a**) *(to marry)* les fiançailles *(feminine plural)*; **an engagement ring** une bague de fiançailles
(**b**) *(meeting)* le rendez-vous

engine *noun*
(**a**) *(of a vehicle)* le moteur
(**b**) *(of a train)* la locomotive

Note that the French word *engin* is not a translation for the English word *engine*. It usually means *machine*.

engineer *noun*
(**a**) un ingénieur; **my mother's a chemical engineer** ma mère est ingénieur chimiste
(**b**) *(mechanic)* le réparateur/la réparatrice

Note that the French word *ingénieur* is never used to mean *repairman*.

engineering *noun* l'ingénierie *(feminine)*; **she's studying engineering** elle fait des études d'ingénieur

England *noun* l'Angleterre *(feminine)*;
I live in England j'habite en Angleterre; **I'm going to England** je vais en Angleterre; **his father comes from England** son père est anglais

English
1 *adjective* anglais/anglaise
2 *noun*
(**a**) *(language)* l'anglais *(masculine)*; **he speaks English** il parle anglais
(**b**) *(people)* **the English** les Anglais *(masculine plural)*

In French, only the noun for the inhabitants of a country takes a capital letter, never the adjective or the noun for the language.

Englishman *noun* un Anglais

English-speaking *adjective* anglophone; **English-speaking countries** les pays anglophones

Englishwoman *noun* une Anglaise

enjoy *verb*
(**a**) *(a film, a book)* aimer; **I enjoy swimming** j'aime la natation
(**b**) **to enjoy oneself** s'amuser; **enjoy yourselves!** amusez-vous bien!

enjoyable *adjective* agréable; **an enjoyable evening** une soirée agréable

enjoyment *noun* le plaisir; **she gets enjoyment from gardening** elle prend plaisir à jardiner

enormous *adjective* énorme; **an enormous house** une maison énorme

enough
1 *adjective* assez de; **enough money** assez d'argent; **there isn't enough milk** il n'y a pas assez de lait
2 *adverb* assez; **are you warm enough?** est-ce que tu as assez chaud?
3 *pronoun* assez; **there's enough for everybody** il y en a assez pour tout le monde; **no thanks, I've had enough** non merci, j'ai assez mangé; **that's enough!** ça suffit!; **I've had enough!** j'en ai assez!; **I've had enough of his remarks** j'en ai assez de ses remarques

enquire *verb*
(a) *(seek information)* se renseigner; **he enquired about the price** il s'est renseigné sur le prix
(b) *(ask)* demander; **he enquired what time the shop closed** il a demandé à quelle heure fermait le magasin

enquiry *noun*
(a) *(official investigation)* une enquête
(b) *(request for information)* la demande de renseignements; **I'll make enquiries** je vais me renseigner

enter *verb*
(a) *(a room)* entrer dans; **she entered the building** elle est entrée dans le bâtiment
(b) *(a competition)* participer à; **she enters lots of competitions** elle participe à beaucoup de concours
(c) *(information)* **enter your password** tapez votre mot de passe

entertain *verb*
(a) *(amuse)* divertir, amuser; **I'm not here to entertain her** je ne suis pas là pour la divertir
(b) *(invite)* **we're entertaining guests this weekend** nous avons des invités ce week-end

entertainment *noun*
(a) *(amusement)* le divertissement
(b) *(performances)* le spectacle

enthusiasm *noun* l'enthousiasme *(masculine)*

enthusiastic *adjective* enthousiaste; **she's not very enthusiastic about her new boyfriend** elle n'est pas très enthousiaste quand elle parle de son nouveau copain

entire *adjective* entier/entière; **the entire world** le monde entier; **the entire day** toute la journée; **did you eat the entire cake?** est-ce que tu as mangé tout le gâteau?

entirely *adverb* tout à fait, entièrement; **I entirely agree** je suis tout à fait d'accord

entrance *noun* une entrée; **the entrance to the school** l'entrée de l'école

entry *noun* l'entrée *(feminine)*; **no entry** entrée interdite

envelope *noun* une enveloppe; **put the letter in an envelope** mets la lettre sous enveloppe

> Do not confuse the spellings of the French *enveloppe* and English *envelope*.

envious *adjective* envieux/envieuse; **to be envious of somebody** envier quelqu'un

environment *noun* l'environnement *(masculine)*; **to harm the environment** nuire à l'environnement

episode *noun*
(a) *(part of a story)* un épisode
(b) *(incident)* un incident

equal
1 *adjective* égal/égale; **equal quantities** des quantités égales
2 *noun* un égal/une égale; **I consider him my equal** je le considère comme mon égal

> The masculine plural of *égal* is *égaux*.

3 *verb* égaler; **two times five equals ten** deux fois cinq égale dix

equality *noun* l'égalité *(feminine)*

equator *noun* l'équateur *(masculine)*; **on the equator** à l'équateur

equipment *noun* l'équipement *(masculine)*; *(in an office, a school)* le matériel; **sports equipment** l'équipement sportif

equivalent
1 *noun* un équivalent; **the French equivalent of the Chancellor of the Exchequer** l'équivalent français du "Chancellor of the Exchequer"
2 *adjective* équivalent/équivalente; **a litre is equivalent to almost two pints** un litre équivaut à presque deux pintes

erase *verb* effacer

eraser *noun* la gomme

error *noun* une erreur; **I've made an error** j'ai fait une erreur

escalator *noun* un escalier roulant

escape *verb*
(**a**) *(from a place)* s'échapper; **the lion escaped from the zoo** le lion s'est échappé du zoo
(**b**) *(from prison)* s'évader; **he escaped from prison** il s'est évadé de prison
(**c**) *(from somebody, from danger)* échapper à; **he escaped from the police** il a échappé à la police
(**d**) *(avoid)* échapper à; **they escaped punishment** ils ont échappé à la punition

especially *adverb*
(**a**) *(in particular)* surtout; **I like sport, especially tennis** j'aime le sport, surtout le tennis
(**b**) *(more than normally)* particulièrement; **her new book is especially good** son dernier livre est particulièrement bien

essay *noun*
(**a**) *(at school)* la rédaction
(**b**) *(at university)* la dissertation; **an essay on Churchill** une dissertation sur Churchill

> Note that the French word *essai* is almost never a translation for the English word *essay*. Its most common meaning is *attempt*.

essential *adjective* essentiel/essentielle; **it is essential to wear proper hiking boots** il est essentiel de porter de bonnes chaussures de marche

estate *noun*
(**a**) *(land)* la propriété, le domaine; **an estate agent** un agent immobilier
(**b**) **the (housing) estate** *(of privately-owned houses)* le lotissement; *(of council houses)* la cité HLM
(**c**) **an estate car** un break
(**d**) **an industrial estate** une zone industrielle

estimate
1 *noun*
(**a**) *(calculation)* une évaluation
(**b**) *(for work, repairs)* un devis
2 *verb* estimer

Estonia *noun* l'Estonie *(feminine)*; **she lives in Estonia** elle habite en Estonie; **I'm going to Estonia** je vais en Estonie; **he comes from Estonia** il vient d'Estonie

Estonian
1 *adjective* estonien/estonienne
2 *noun*
(**a**) *(language)* l'estonien *(masculine)*; **she speaks Estonian** elle parle estonien
(**b**) *(person)* un Estonien/une Estonienne; **the Estonians** les Estoniens *(masculine plural)*

> In French, only the noun for the inhabitants of a country takes a capital letter, never the adjective or the noun for the language.

EU *noun* l'UE *(feminine)*

> UE is the abbreviation of *Union européenne*.

euro *noun* un euro

Europe *noun* l'Europe *(feminine)*; **I live in Europe** j'habite en Europe; **I'm going to Europe** je vais en Europe; **I come from Europe** je viens d'Europe

European
1 *adjective* européen/européenne; **the European Union** l'Union européenne *(feminine)*
2 *noun* un Européen/une Européenne

eve *noun* la veille; **Christmas Eve** la veille de Noël; **New Year's Eve** la Saint-Sylvestre

even¹ *adverb*
(**a**) même; **he even works on Sundays** il travaille même le dimanche; **even if he apologizes, I won't forgive him** même s'il s'excuse, je ne le lui pardonnerai pas
(**b**) **even better** encore mieux; **even**

more tired encore plus fatigué/fatiguée

(c) even though bien que; he forgot, even though I must have told him at least ten times il a oublié, bien que j'aie dû le lui dire au moins dix fois; he can't speak French even though he lived in Paris for five years il ne parle pas français bien qu'il ait vécu à Paris pendant cinq ans

The construction *bien que* is always followed by the subjunctive.

even² *adjective*
(a) *(flat)* égal/égale; *(smooth)* uni/unie; an even surface une surface plane
(b) *(equal)* égal/égale; at half-time the scores were even à la mi-temps les équipes étaient à égalité
(c) an even number un nombre pair

evening *noun*
(a) *(as opposed to the morning or the afternoon)* le soir; every evening tous les soirs; yesterday evening hier soir; tomorrow evening demain soir; I see my friends in the evenings je vois mes amis le soir; it's 10 o'clock in the evening il est 10 heures du soir; good evening! bonsoir!
(b) *(the whole evening)* la soirée; we had a nice evening nous avons passé une bonne soirée

event *noun* un événement; a sporting event une épreuve sportive

eventually *adverb* finalement; they will get married eventually ils finiront par se marier

Note that the French word *éventuellement* is never a translation for the English word *eventually*. It means *possibly*.

ever *adverb*
(a) *(at any time)* have you ever met him? tu l'as déjà rencontré?; nothing ever happens il n'arrive jamais rien; it's the best book I've ever read c'est le meilleur livre que j'aie jamais lu

(b) ever since the accident depuis l'accident; ever since then depuis ce moment-là; ever since I saw her depuis que je l'ai vue
(c) as ever comme d'habitude; she was late, as ever elle était en retard, comme d'habitude; he seemed as happy as ever il avait l'air toujours aussi heureux

every *adjective* chaque; every pupil chaque élève; every time I go out chaque fois que je sors; every day tous les jours; every other day tous les deux jours; every ten years tous les dix ans

everybody, everyone *pronoun* tout le monde; everybody should read the last chapter for homework tout le monde doit lire le dernier chapitre à la maison; everybody else tous les autres

everything *pronoun* tout; they sell everything ils vendent de tout; have you got everything? est-ce que tu as tout?; everything he says tout ce qu'il dit

everywhere *adverb* partout; I've looked everywhere for my keys j'ai cherché mes clés partout

evidence *noun* la preuve; *(testimony)* le témoignage; there's no evidence that he's guilty il n'existe aucune preuve de sa culpabilité

evil
1 *adjective*
(a) *(person)* méchant/méchante
(b) *(temper)* mauvais/mauvaise
2 *noun* le mal; good and evil le bien et le mal

exact *adjective* exact/exacte; what's the exact time? quelle est l'heure exacte?; the exact opposite exactement le contraire; I don't have the exact money je n'ai pas l'appoint

exactly *adverb* exactement; that's not exactly what I said ce n'est pas exactement ce que j'ai dit; it's 5 o'clock

exactly il est 5 heures pile

exaggerate *verb* exagérer; **stop exaggerating!** arrête d'exagérer!

exam *noun* un examen; **a French exam** un examen de français; **he passed his exams** il a réussi ses examens; **he failed his biology exam** il a raté son examen de biologie; **I'm sitting my history exam this morning** je passe mon examen d'histoire ce matin

examination *noun* un examen

examine *verb* examiner

example *noun* un exemple; **for example** par exemple

excellent *adjective* excellent/excellente; **she's an excellent cook** c'est une excellente cuisinière

except *preposition* sauf; **everybody except him** tout le monde sauf lui; **we're all going except for Susan** nous y allons tous, sauf Susan

exception *noun* une exception; **I'll make an exception for her** je ferai une exception pour elle

exchange
1 *noun* un échange; **in exchange for** en échange de; **an exchange visit** un échange
2 *verb* échanger; **he exchanged the CD for a video game** il a échangé le CD contre un jeu vidéo

excited *adjective* excité/excitée; **he's excited about his holidays** il est tout excité à l'idée de partir en vacances

excitement *noun* l'agitation *(feminine)*; *(enthusiasm)* l'enthousiasme *(masculine)*

exciting *adjective* passionnant/passionnante; **it's an exciting book** c'est un livre passionnant

exclamation mark *noun* le point d'exclamation

excuse
1 *noun* une excuse; **a good excuse** une bonne excuse

2 *verb* excuser; **excuse me!** pardon!, excusez-moi!

exercise
1 *noun* l'exercice *(masculine)*; **to take exercise** faire de l'exercice; **a grammar exercise** un exercice de grammaire; **an exercise book** un cahier
2 *verb* faire de l'exercice; **I exercise three times a week** je fais de l'exercice trois fois par semaine

Do not confuse the spellings of the French *exercice* and English *exercise*.

exhaust pipe *noun* le tuyau d'échappement

The plural of *tuyau* is *tuyaux*.

exhausted *adjective* épuisé/épuisée

exhausting *adjective* épuisant/épuisante; **this work is exhausting!** ce travail est épuisant!

exhibition *noun* une exposition; **a Picasso exhibition** une exposition de Picasso

Note that the French word *exhibition* is never a translation for the English word *exhibition*.

exist *verb* exister

exit *noun* la sortie; **I'll wait for you at the exit** je t'attends à la sortie

exotic *adjective* exotique

expect *verb*
(**a**) *(anticipate)* attendre; **I'm expecting a phone call** j'attends un coup de téléphone; **she's expecting a baby** elle attend un bébé
(**b**) *(want)* **I expect you to come** je compte sur ta présence
(**c**) *(suppose)* penser, supposer; **I expect he'll be late** je suppose qu'il sera en retard

expel *verb* expulser; *(from school)* renvoyer; **he's been expelled from school** il s'est fait renvoyer de l'école

expenses *plural noun* les frais *(masculine plural)*

expensive *adjective* cher/chère; **an expensive watch** une montre qui coûte cher

experience *noun* une expérience; **it was an interesting experience** c'était une expérience intéressante

experienced *adjective* expérimenté/expérimentée

experiment
1 *noun* une expérience
2 *verb* faire une expérience; **they experiment on animals** ils font des expériences sur les animaux

expert *noun* un expert/une experte; **an expert in astronomy** un expert en astronomie

expired *adjective (ticket, passport)* périmé/périmée

explain *verb* expliquer; **can you explain why you're late?** est-ce que tu peux m'expliquer pourquoi tu es en retard?

explanation *noun* une explication

explode *verb* exploser; **the bomb exploded** la bombe a explosé

explore *verb* explorer; **they explored the town** ils ont exploré la ville

explosion *noun* une explosion

export
1 *noun* l'exportation *(feminine)*
2 *verb* exporter

express
1 *adjective* **an express train** un train express
2 *verb* exprimer; **to express oneself** s'exprimer

expression *noun*
(a) *(phrase)* une expression
(b) *(look)* un air; **a puzzled expression** un air perplexe

extinct *adjective*
(a) *(animal, species)* disparu/disparue
(b) **an extinct volcano** un volcan éteint

extra
1 *adjective (train, hours)* supplémentaire; **there are some extra questions overleaf** il y a des questions supplémentaires au dos
2 *adverb* **to be extra careful** être extrêmement prudent/prudente; **to pay extra** payer un supplément; **extra large** très grand

extraordinary *adjective* extraordinaire

extreme
1 *adjective* extrême
2 *noun* un extrême; **he goes from one extreme to the other** il passe d'un extrême à l'autre

extremely *adverb* extrêmement; **I'm extremely angry** je suis extrêmement fâché

eye *noun* un œil; **I have blue eyes** j'ai les yeux bleus; **can you keep an eye on my bag?** est-ce que tu peux surveiller mon sac?

> The plural of *œil* is *yeux*.

eyebrow *noun* le sourcil

eyelash *noun* le cil

eyelid *noun* la paupière

eyesight *noun* la vue; **he has good eyesight** il a une bonne vue

fabric *noun* le tissu

> Note that the French word *fabrique* is never a translation for the English word *fabric*. It means *factory*.

face
1 *noun* le visage; **he's washing his face** il se lave le visage; **he pulled a face** il a fait une grimace
2 *verb* *(be opposite)* être en face de; **they were sitting facing each other** ils étaient assis l'un en face de l'autre; **the room faces the sea** la pièce donne sur la mer; **I can't face going** je n'ai pas le courage d'y aller

facilities *plural noun* *(for doing sport)* les équipements *(masculine plural)*, les installations *(feminine plural)*; **are there cooking facilities?** est-ce qu'il y a de quoi faire la cuisine?

fact *noun* le fait; **fact and fiction** la réalité et la fiction; **in fact** en fait

factory *noun* une usine; **a car factory** une usine d'automobiles

fade
1 *verb*
(a) *(of a colour)* passer; *(of a carpet, a curtain)* se décolorer
(b) *(of the light)* baisser
2 fade away *(of a noise)* diminuer

fail *verb*
(a) *(not succeed)* rater; **four pupils failed the exam** quatre élèves ont raté l'examen; **she passed but her sister failed** elle a réussi mais sa sœur a échoué
(b) *(malfunction)* **the brakes failed** les freins ont lâché

(c) *(used with a verb)* ne pas réussir à; **I failed to persuade him to come** je n'ai pas réussi à le convaincre de venir; **he failed to tell me** il ne me l'a pas dit; **she failed to answer his letter** elle n'a pas répondu à sa lettre; **I fail to understand why he said that** je ne comprends pas pourquoi il a dit ça

failure *noun*
(a) un échec; **the party was a failure** la fête était ratée
(b) **a failure** *(person)* un raté/une ratée

faint
1 *adjective*
(a) *(voice, hope, light)* faible
(b) **I feel faint** je me sens mal
2 *verb* s'évanouir; **she fainted yesterday** elle s'est évanouie hier

fair¹ *noun*
(a) *(funfair)* la fête foraine
(b) *(trade fair)* la foire

fair² *adjective*
(a) *(just)* juste; **that's not fair!** ce n'est pas juste!; **£50 is a fair price** 50 livres est un prix raisonnable
(b) *(quite good)* assez bon/assez bonne; **the festival attracted a fair amount of people** le festival a attiré pas mal de monde; **his marks are fair** ses notes sont assez bonnes
(c) *(weather)* beau/belle
(d) *(hair, person)* blond/blonde; *(skin)* clair/claire; **she has fair hair** elle a les cheveux blonds *or* elle est blonde; **a fair-haired girl** une fille blonde

fair-haired *adjective* aux cheveux blonds; **a fair-haired girl** une fille aux cheveux blonds; **I'm fair-haired** j'ai les cheveux blonds

fairly *adverb*
(a) *(justly)* équitablement; **they divided the inheritance fairly** ils ont partagé l'héritage équitablement; **to treat somebody fairly** traiter quelqu'un de manière équitable
(b) *(quite)* assez; **he's fairly tall** il est assez grand; **a fairly good book** un assez bon livre

fairy *noun* la fée

fairytale *noun* le conte de fées

faith *noun* la foi; **I have faith in him** je lui fais confiance

faithful *adjective* fidèle

fake
1 *adjective* faux/fausse; **a fake £10 note** un faux billet de 10 livres; **a fake beard** une fausse barbe
2 *verb* *(signature)* contrefaire

fall
1 *noun* la chute; **his mum has had a fall** sa mère a fait une chute
2 *verb*
(a) *(of a person)* tomber; **I fell down the stairs** je suis tombé dans l'escalier; **he's fallen in love with her** il est tombé amoureux d'elle; **I fell asleep** je me suis endormi
(b) *(of a price, a temperature)* baisser; **the temperature has fallen today** la température a baissé aujourd'hui
3 **fall down**
(a) *(of a person)* tomber
(b) *(of a building, a wall)* s'effondrer
4 **fall off** tomber; **I fell off my bike** je suis tombé de mon vélo
5 **fall out**
(a) *(of hair, a page)* tomber
(b) *(quarrel)* se brouiller; **Alison and Laura have fallen out** Alison et Laura se sont brouillées
6 **fall over** *(of a person, a thing)* tomber; **he fell over** il est tombé; **Claire fell over her bag** Claire a trébuché sur son sac et elle est tombée

false *adjective* faux/fausse; **a false friend** un faux ami

fame *noun* la renommée, la célébrité

familiar *adjective* familier/familière

family *noun* la famille; **she's on holiday with her family** elle est en vacances avec sa famille

famous *adjective* célèbre; **she's a famous singer** c'est une chanteuse célèbre

fan *noun*
(a) *(held in hand)* un éventail; *(electric)* le ventilateur
(b) *(of a pop star, a film star)* le/la fan; *(of a team)* le supporter; **a football fan** un supporter de football

fancy
1 *adjective* **fancy dress** le déguisement; **a fancy dress party** une soirée déguisée
2 *verb* avoir envie de; **do you fancy a cup of coffee?** tu as envie d'une tasse de café?; **I fancy going to the cinema tonight** j'ai envie d'aller au cinema ce soir; **he fancies her** elle lui plaît

fantastic *adjective* formidable; **that was a fantastic meal!** c'était un repas délicieux!

fantasy *noun* *(imagination)* la fantaisie; *(fanciful idea)* le fantasme; **he lives in a fantasy world** il vit dans un monde à lui

far
1 *adverb*
(a) *(in the distance)* loin; **is it far?** est-ce que c'est loin?; **it's not far** ce n'est pas loin; **the hotel isn't far from the station** l'hôtel n'est pas loin de la gare; **how far is it from London?** c'est à quelle distance de Londres?
(b) *(much)* beaucoup; **I ate far too much** j'ai beaucoup trop mangé; **his house is far bigger** sa maison est beaucoup plus grande
(c) **as far as I know** pour autant que je sache
(d) **so far** jusqu'ici; **I'm enjoying the**

book so far jusqu'ici le livre me plaît
2 *adjective* **the far end of the room**
l'autre bout de la pièce; **the Far East**
l'Extrême-Orient *(masculine)*

faraway *adjective* lointain/lointaine;
a faraway country un pays lointain

fare *noun* le prix du billet; **he pays half
fare** il paie demi-tarif

farm *noun* la ferme; **he lives on a farm**
il habite dans une ferme

farmer *noun* le fermier/la fermière;
he's a farmer il est fermier

> Note that when describing people's
> jobs or situations, French does not
> use an article (*un* or *une*).

farmhouse *noun* la ferme

farming *noun* l'agriculture *(feminine)*

fascinating *adjective* fascinant/fas-
cinante; **it's a fascinating story** c'est
une histoire fascinante

fashion *noun* la mode; **in fashion** à la
mode; **out of fashion** démodé/demo-
dée; **long skirts have gone out of
fashion** les jupes longues ne sont plus
à la mode

fashionable *adjective* à la mode; **a
fashionable dress** une robe à la mode

fast
1 *adjective* rapide; **a fast car** une voiture rapide; **my watch is fast** ma
montre avance; **fast food** la restaura-
tion rapide; **a fast food restaurant** un
fast food
2 *adverb*
(a) *(quickly)* vite; **she runs fast** elle
court vite
(b) **she is fast asleep** elle dort
profondément

fasten *verb*
(a) *(a window)* fermer
(b) *(a belt, buttons)* attacher; **fasten
your seatbelt** attachez votre ceinture

fat
1 *adjective*
(a) *(person, animal)* gros/grosse; **she's**

getting fat elle devient grosse
(b) *(food)* gras/grasse
2 *noun (on a person)* la graisse; *(on
meat)* le gras; **there's too much fat in
pizza** il y a a trop de graisse dans les
pizzas

fatal *adjective* mortel/mortelle; **a fatal
accident** un accident mortel

fate *noun* le destin

father *noun* le père; **Father's Day** la
fête des pères

father-in-law *noun* le beau-père

> The plural of *beau-père* is *beaux-
> pères*.

fault *noun*
(a) *(guilt)* la faute; **it's my fault** c'est de
ma faute; **it's not your fault** ce n'est
pas de ta faute; **whose fault is it?** à
qui la faute?
(b) *(in a person, a machine)* le défaut;
his worst fault is his impatience son
pire défaut, c'est qu'il manque de
patience

faulty *adjective* défectueux/défec-
tueuse; **this machine is faulty** cette
machine est défectueuse

favour *noun*
(a) *(kind action)* le service; **can you
do me a favour?** est-ce que tu peux
me rendre un service?
(b) **to be in favour of something** être
pour quelque chose; **he's in favour of
the war** il est pour la guerre

favourite *adjective* préféré/préférée;
what's your favourite colour? quelle
est ta couleur préférée?; **this is my favourite book** c'est mon livre préféré

fax
1 *noun (message, machine)* le fax; **she
sent me a fax** elle m'a envoyé un fax
2 *verb* faxer; **can you fax me the
document?** est-ce que vous pouvez
me faxer le document?

fear
1 *noun* la peur, la crainte
2 *verb* craindre; **you have nothing to**

fear tu n'as rien à craindre

feast *noun*
> (**a**) *(large meal)* le festin
> (**b**) *(celebration)* le banquet

feather *noun* la plume

feature *noun*
> (**a**) *(of a face)* le trait; **she has nice features** elle a de jolis traits
> (**b**) *(of a place, a machine)* la caractéristique; **the car has many safety features** la voiture a de nombreux dispositifs de sécurité

February *noun* février *(masculine)*; **the first of February** le premier février; **the second of February** le deux février; **the third of February** le trois février; **in February** en février

> Names of months are not capitalized in French.

fed up *adjective* **to be fed up** en avoir marre; **I'm fed up with him** j'en ai marre de lui; **I'm fed up doing homework, let's go out** j'en ai marre de faire mes devoirs, sortons

fee *noun*
> (**a**) *(for entry)* le droit d'entrée
> (**b**) *(of a doctor, a lawyer)* les honoraires *(masculine plural)*
> (**c**) *(for a university)* les frais de scolarité *(masculine plural)*

feed *verb* donner à manger à; **he feeds the dog twice a day** il donne à manger au chien deux fois par jour; **they haven't got enough money to feed their children** ils n'ont pas assez d'argent pour nourrir leurs enfants

feel *verb*
> (**a**) *(physically)* se sentir; **I don't feel well** je ne me sens pas bien; **I feel tired** je me sens fatigué; **I feel cold** j'ai froid; **I feel hungry** j'ai faim
> (**b**) *(emotionally)* **I feel very happy** je suis très heureux; **she feels sad** elle est triste; **I felt betrayed** je me suis senti trahi; **I feel I made the right decision** je crois que j'ai pris la bonne décision
> (**c**) *(be aware of)* sentir; **I didn't feel a**

thing je n'ai rien senti; **I felt the floor tremble** j'ai senti le sol trembler; **I felt her hand on mine** j'ai senti sa main sur la mienne
> (**d**) *(seem)* **the room felt hot** il faisait chaud dans la pièce; **it felt like a very long time** ça m'a semblé très long
> (**e**) *(with one's hands)* toucher; **feel how soft it is** touche comme c'est doux; **he felt for the light switch** il cherchait l'interrupteur à tâtons
> (**f**) **to feel like something** avoir envie de quelque chose; **to feel like doing something** avoir envie de faire quelque chose; **I feel like something to eat** j'ai envie de manger quelque chose; **do you feel like going out?** est-ce que tu as envie de sortir?

feeling *noun* *(emotion)* le sentiment; *(physical)* la sensation; **a feeling of anger** un sentiment de colère; **I had a feeling you'd call** j'avais le pressentiment que tu appellerais; **you hurt my feelings** tu m'as vexé

felt-tip *noun* **a felt-tip (pen)** un feutre

female
> **1** *adjective*
> (**a**) *(referring to animals)* femelle; **the female giraffe** la girafe femelle
> (**b**) *(referring to women)* féminin/féminine; **a female team** une équipe féminine; **the female sex** le sexe féminin; **a female teacher** une femme professeur
> **2** *noun*
> (**a**) *(animal)* la femelle
> (**b**) *(person)* la femme

feminine
> **1** *adjective* féminin/féminine
> **2** *noun* *(in grammar)* le féminin; **in the feminine** au féminin

fence *noun* la clôture

fencing *noun* l'escrime *(feminine)*; **he does fencing** il fait de l'escrime

fern *noun* la fougère

ferry *noun* le ferry; **we took the ferry to Caen** nous avons pris le ferry pour Caen

fertile *adjective* fertile

festival *noun* le festival; **the Edinburgh festival** le festival d'Édimbourg

The plural of *festival* is *festivals*.

fetch *verb* aller chercher; **go and fetch my keys** va me chercher mes clés

fever *noun* la fièvre; **she has a fever** elle a de la fièvre

few
1 *adjective*
(**a**) *(not many)* peu de; **few people** peu de gens
(**b**) **a few** *(some)* quelques; **a few teachers** quelques professeurs; **quite a few books** un bon nombre de livres
2 *pronoun*
(**a**) *(not many)* peu; **few of them** peu d'entre eux
(**b**) **a few** *(some)* quelques-uns/quelques-unes; **a few of us** quelques-uns d'entre nous

fewer
1 *adjective* moins de; **fewer people came this time** moins de gens sont venus cette fois-ci
2 *pronoun* moins; **she has fewer than I do** elle en a moins que moi

fewest
1 *adjective* le moins de; **I made the fewest mistakes** c'est moi qui ai fait le moins de fautes
2 *pronoun* le moins; **she has the fewest** c'est elle qui en a le moins

fiction *noun*
(**a**) *(opposite of fact)* la fiction; **she can't tell fact from fiction** elle ne fait pas la différence entre la réalité et la fiction
(**b**) *(books)* les romans *(masculine plural)*; **he reads a lot of fiction** il lit beaucoup de romans

field *noun*
(**a**) *(land)* le champ; **we had a picnic in a field** nous avons pique-niqué dans un champ
(**b**) *(for sport)* le terrain; **a football field** un terrain de football

(**c**) *(area of activity or knowledge)* le domaine; **biology isn't my field** la biologie n'est pas mon domaine

fierce *adjective*
(**a**) *(animal)* féroce
(**b**) *(attack, storm)* violent/violente

fifteen *number* quinze

fifteenth *number* quinzième; **the fifteenth day** le quinzième jour; **the fifteenth car** la quinzième voiture; **the fifteenth of March** le quinze mars

fifth *number* cinquième; **one fifth** *(fraction)* un cinquième; **the fifth film** le cinquième film; **the fifth car** la cinquième voiture; **the fifth of October** le cinq octobre

fiftieth *number* cinquantième

fifty *number* cinquante; **fifty-one** cinquante et un; **fifty-two** cinquante-deux; **fifty-first** cinquante et unième; **fifty-second** cinquante-deuxième; **the fifties** les années cinquante

fig *noun* la figue

fight
1 *noun*
(**a**) *(physical)* la bagarre
(**b**) *(argument)* la dispute; **she's had a fight with her boyfriend** elle s'est disputée avec son copain
(**c**) *(struggle)* la lutte; **the fight against unemployment** la lutte contre le chômage
2 *verb*
(**a**) *(physically)* se battre
(**b**) *(argue)* se disputer; **she's always fighting with her parents** elle est toujours en train de se disputer avec ses parents
(**c**) *(struggle)* lutter; **we must fight the spread of AIDS** nous devons lutter contre la propagation du sida

fighter *noun* le combattant/la combattante

figure *noun*
(**a**) *(number)* le chiffre
(**b**) *(body shape)* la silhouette; **she has**

a nice figure elle a une jolie silhouette
(c) *(person)* le personnage; an important figure in politics un personnage
important du monde politique

> Note that the French word *figure* is
> rarely a translation for the English
> word *figure*. Its most common mean-
> ing is *face*.

file¹ *noun*
(a) *(information, papers)* le dossier; I
have his name on file j'ai son nom
dans le dossier
(b) *(folder)* la chemise; *(with loose
leaves)* le classeur
(c) *(on a computer)* le fichier; I saved
the file j'ai sauvegardé le fichier

file²
1 *noun (for nails, metal)* la lime
2 *verb* limer; I'm filing my nails je me
lime les ongles

fill
1 *verb* remplir; fill that vase with
water remplis ce vase d'eau
2 fill in
(a) to fill in a hole boucher un trou
(b) to fill in a form remplir un formulaire
3 fill out to fill out a form remplir
un formulaire

filling
1 *adjective (food)* consistant/consis-
tante; that pizza was very filling
cette pizza m'a rassasié
2 *noun*
(a) *(in a tooth)* le plombage; I have
two fillings j'ai deux plombages
(b) *(for a sandwich, a pie)* la garniture

film *noun*
(a) *(movie)* le film; have you seen this
film? est-ce que tu as vu ce film?; a
film star une vedette de cinéma
(b) *(for a camera)* la pellicule

filthy *adjective*
(a) très sale; his house is filthy cette
maison est très sale
(b) filthy language des grossièretés
(feminine plural)

fin *noun*
(a) *(of a fish)* la nageoire
(b) *(of a shark)* un aileron

final
1 *adjective (last)* dernier/dernière;
the final time la dernière fois
2 *noun (in sport)* la finale

finally *adverb*
(a) *(lastly)* finalement; finally, I
would like to say... pour finir, je voudrais dire que...
(b) *(at last)* enfin; when he finally arrived all the guests had left finalement, quand il est arrivé tous les
invités étaient partis

finance
1 *noun* la finance; he works in finance il travaille dans la finance
2 *verb* financer

financial *adjective* financier/finan-
cière

find
1 *verb* trouver; have you found your
book? est-ce que tu as trouvé ton livre?; I can't find my glasses je ne
trouve pas mes lunettes
2 find out
(a) *(discover)* découvrir; she found
out the truth elle a découvert la vérité
(b) *(by asking questions)* se renseigner; I've found out what time they
close je me suis renseigné sur l'horaire
de fermeture

fine¹ *noun (as a punishment)* une
amende; a £500 fine une amende de
500 livres

fine²
1 *adjective*
(a) *(good)* excellent/excellente; I'm
fine, thanks, how are you? ça va bien,
merci, et toi?
(b) *(weather)* beau/belle; it will be
fine all day il fera beau toute la journée
(c) *(line, hair)* fin/fine
2 *adverb*
(a) *(well)* bien; I'm doing fine je vais

bien; **they get on fine** ils s'entendent bien
(**b**) *(OK)* d'accord; **fine, I'll be there** d'accord, j'y serai

finger *noun* le doigt

fingernail *noun* un ongle

fingerprint *noun* une empreinte digitale

finish
1 *noun (end)* la fin; *(of a race)* l'arrivée *(feminine)*; **from start to finish** du début à la fin
2 *verb (end)* finir; **have you finished your homework?** est-ce que tu as fini tes devoirs?; **I've finished writing to him** j'ai fini de lui écrire

Finland *noun* la Finlande; **I've never been to Finland** je ne suis jamais allé en Finlande; **they live in Finland** ils habitent en Finlande; **she comes from Finland** elle vient de Finlande

Finn *noun (person)* le Finlandais/la Finlandaise

Finnish
1 *adjective* finlandais/finlandaise
2 *noun*
(**a**) *(language)* le finnois, le finlandais; **she speaks Finnish** elle parle finnois *or* finlandais
(**b**) *(people)* **the Finnish** les Finlandais *(masculine plural)*

> In French, only the noun for the inhabitants of a country takes a capital letter, never the adjective or the noun for the language.

fir *noun* le sapin

fire
1 *noun*
(**a**) *(in a fireplace, at a campsite)* le feu; *(big blaze)* un incendie; **the house caught fire** la maison a pris feu; **the house is on fire** la maison est en feu *or* la maison brûle; **he set fire to the house** il a mis le feu à la maison; **a fire alarm** une alarme d'incendie; **the fire brigade** les pompiers *(masculine*

plural); **a fire engine** un camion de pompiers; **a fire escape** un escalier de secours; **a fire fighter** un pompier; **a fire station** une caserne de pompiers
(**b**) *(heater)* le radiateur; **a gas fire** un radiateur à gaz

> The plural of *feu* is *feux*.

2 *verb*
(**a**) *(shoot)* tirer; **to fire at somebody** tirer sur quelqu'un
(**b**) *(from a job)* renvoyer; **he fired her** il l'a renvoyée; **she got fired** elle a été renvoyée

fireman *noun* le pompier; **he's a fireman** il est pompier

> Note that when describing people's jobs or situations, French does not use an article (*un* or *une*).

fireplace *noun* la cheminée

firework *noun* la fusée; **fireworks** le feu d'artifice; **a firework display** un feu d'artifice

firm¹ *noun (company)* une entreprise; **he works for a small firm** il travaille pour une petite entreprise

firm² *adjective* ferme; **she's a firm teacher** elle est ferme avec ses élèves

first
1 *adjective* premier/première; **the first floor** le premier étage; **it's the first time I've seen this film** c'est la première fois que je vois ce film; **first aid** les premiers secours *(masculine plural)*; **a first name** un prénom
2 *adverb*
(**a**) *(firstly)* d'abord; **wash your hands first** lave-toi les mains d'abord; **first of all** tout d'abord; **at first** au début
(**b**) *(for the first time)* pour la première fois; **I first met her in London** je l'ai rencontrée pour la première fois à Londres
(**c**) *(before the others)* premier/première; **Tim arrived first** Tim est arrivé le premier
3 *pronoun* **the first** le premier/la

première; **he starts work on the first** il commence à travailler le premier du mois; **Anna was the first to arrive** Anna est arrivée la première

firstly *adverb* premièrement

fish
1 *noun* le poisson; **I love fish** j'adore le poisson; **a fish shop** une poissonnerie
2 *verb* pêcher; **he was fishing in the lake** il pêchait dans le lac

fisherman *noun* le pêcheur; **he's a fisherman** il est pêcheur

fishing *noun* la pêche; **I go fishing every Sunday** je vais à la pêche tous les dimanches; **a fishing rod** une canne à pêche

fishmonger *noun* le poissonnier/la poissonnière; **I went to the fishmonger's** je suis allé à la poissonnerie; **her father's a fishmonger** son père est poissonnier

Note that when describing people's jobs or situations, French does not use an article (*un* or *une*).

fist *noun* le poing

fit¹ *adjective* *(healthy)* en bonne santé; *(in good shape)* en forme; **to keep fit** se maintenir en forme; **she's very fit** elle est très en forme

fit² *verb*
(a) *(of clothes)* **that jacket doesn't fit you** cette veste ne te va pas; **this shirt fits, I'll buy it** cette chemise me va, je l'achète
(b) *(install)* poser; **to fit a carpet** poser de la moquette

fitness *noun* la forme physique; **fitness training** l'entraînement physique *(masculine)*

fitting room *noun* une cabine d'essayage

five *number* cinq

fix *verb*
(a) *(repair)* réparer; **he fixed the kettle** il a réparé la bouilloire

(b) *(decide)* fixer; **let's fix a time to meet** fixons une heure de rendez-vous
(c) *(attach)* fixer; **can you fix the painting to the wall?** est-ce que tu peux fixer le tableau au mur?

fixed *adjective* *(price)* fixe

fizzy *adjective* *(wine)* mousseux/mousseuse; *(soft drink)* gazeux/gazeuse; **a fizzy drink** une boisson gazeuse

flag *noun* le drapeau; **the American flag** le drapeau américain

The plural of *drapeau* is *drapeaux*.

flame *noun* la flamme; **the house went up in flames** la maison a pris feu

flamingo *noun* le flamant; **a pink flamingo** un flamant rose

flap *verb* **the bird is flapping its wings** l'oiseau bat des ailes

flash
1 *noun* *(light)* un éclair; **a flash of lightning** un éclair; **in a flash** en un clin d'œil
2 *verb* *(of a police car light, a sign)* clignoter

flask *noun* la (bouteille) thermos®

flat¹ *adjective*
(a) *(surface, roof)* plat/plate
(b) *(tyre)* à plat; **I've got a flat tyre** j'ai un pneu à plat

flat² *noun* un appartement; **I live in a flat** j'habite dans un appartement

flatmate *noun* le/la colocataire; **she has two flatmates** elle a deux colocataires

flatter *verb* flatter

flattering *adjective* flatteur/flatteuse

flavour *noun* *(taste)* le goût; *(of an ice cream, a yoghurt)* le parfum

flea *noun* la puce

fleece *noun* *(of a sheep)* la toison; *(fabric)* la laine polaire; *(garment)* la polaire

flesh *noun* la chair

flexible *adjective* flexible

flick *verb (press down on)* appuyer sur; **flick the TV on** allume la télé

flight *noun*
(**a**) *(of a plane, a bird)* le vol; **a flight to Paris** un vol pour Paris; **I'm getting the two o'clock flight** je prends l'avion de deux heures
(**b**) **a flight of stairs** un escalier; **two flights up from me** deux étages au-dessus de chez moi

flip-flops *plural noun* les tongs *(feminine plural)*

flippers *plural noun (for swimming)* les palmes *(feminine plural)*; *(of a seal)* les nageoires *(feminine plural)*

flirt
1 *noun (person)* le charmeur/la charmeuse
2 *verb* flirter; **to flirt with somebody** flirter avec quelqu'un

float *verb* flotter

flock *noun*
(**a**) *(of sheep)* le troupeau

The plural of *troupeau* is *troupeaux*.

(**b**) *(of birds)* le vol

flood *noun* une inondation; **there was a bad flood last night** il y a eu une grosse inondation hier soir

flooded *adjective* inondé/inondée; **the area is completely flooded** cette zone est complètement inondée

flooding *noun* une inondation

floor *noun*
(**a**) *(ground)* le sol; *(made of wood)* le plancher; **on the floor** par terre
(**b**) *(one level of a building)* un étage; **on the second floor** au deuxième étage

floppy disk *noun* la disquette

florist *noun* le/la fleuriste; **she's a florist** elle est fleuriste

floss
1 *noun* (**dental**) **floss** le fil dentaire
2 *verb* nettoyer avec du fil dentaire

flour *noun* la farine

flow *verb* couler

flower *noun* la fleur

flowerpot *noun* le pot de fleurs

flu *noun* la grippe; **he has the flu** il a la grippe

fluent *adjective* **he's fluent in French** il parle couramment le français

fluently *adverb* couramment; **he speaks French fluently** il parle couramment le français

flush
1 *noun (in the toilet)* la chasse (d'eau)
2 *verb*
(**a**) *(blush)* rougir
(**b**) **to flush the toilet** tirer la chasse d'eau

flute *noun* la flûte; **she plays the flute** elle joue de la flûte

Note that when talking about playing musical instruments, French uses the expression *jouer de*.

fly¹ *noun (insect)* la mouche

fly²
1 *verb*
(**a**) *(of a bird, a plane)* voler; **the birds were flying overhead** les oiseaux volaient au-dessus de nos têtes
(**b**) *(of a passenger)* prendre l'avion; **we flew to New York** nous sommes allés à New York en avion
(**c**) **to fly a kite** faire voler un cerf-volant
2 fly away s'envoler

flying
1 *adjective* **a flying saucer** une soucoupe volante
2 *noun (air travel)* l'avion *(masculine)*; **she loves flying** elle adore prendre l'avion; **I'm scared of flying** j'ai peur de prendre l'avion

flyover *noun* le pont routier

foal *noun* le poulain

foam *noun*
(**a**) *(on the sea)* l'écume *(feminine)*; *(in*

a bath) la mousse
(**b**) *(rubber)* la mousse; **a foam mattress** un matelas en mousse

focus
1 *noun*
(**a**) *(of a lens)* le foyer
(**b**) *(of attention, interest)* le centre
2 *verb*
(**a**) *(a lens, a camera)* mettre au point
(**b**) *(attention, energy)* concentrer
(**c**) **to focus on something** *(with a camera)* faire la mise au point sur quelque chose; **focus on the monument** fais la mise au point sur le monument
(**d**) *(of a debate, a speech, a speaker)* se concentrer sur quelque chose; **you need to focus on maths next term** il faut te concentrer sur les maths le trimestre prochain

fog *noun* le brouillard

foggy *adjective* **it's foggy** il y a du brouillard; **foggy weather** un temps brumeux

foil *noun* *(for cooking)* le papier d'aluminium

fold
1 *noun (in paper, cloth)* le pli
2 *verb* plier; **to fold one's arms** croiser les bras; **fold the letter in half** pliez la lettre en deux

folder *noun*
(**a**) *(for papers)* la chemise
(**b**) *(on a computer)* le dossier

follow *verb* suivre; **follow me** suivez-moi; **he followed me home** il m'a suivi jusqu'à chez moi

following *adjective (next)* suivant/suivante; **the following week** la semaine suivante

fond *adjective* **to be fond of somebody** aimer beaucoup quelqu'un; **to be fond of something** aimer beaucoup quelque chose

food *noun* la nourriture; **they've run out of food** ils n'ont plus de nourriture *or* ils n'ont plus rien à manger; **my**

favourite food is roast chicken mon plat préféré est le poulet rôti; **do you prefer Chinese food or Mexican food?** tu préfères la cuisine chinoise ou la cuisine mexicaine?

fool *noun* un/une imbécile; **you fool!** espèce d'imbécile!

foolish *adjective* bête

foot *noun*
(**a**) *(of a person)* le pied; **I have a sore foot** j'ai mal au pied
(**b**) *(of an animal)* la patte
(**c**) *(measurement)* le pied; **she's five feet tall** elle mesure 1 mètre 50

Note that people in France do not use feet as a unit of measurement, they use metres and centimetres (1 foot = 30.48 centimetres).

football *noun*
(**a**) *(game)* le football; **he likes playing football** il aime jouer au football
(**b**) *(ball)* le ballon (de football)

footballer *noun* le footballeur/la footballeuse

footstep *noun* le pas; **I heard footsteps** j'ai entendu des pas

for *preposition*
(**a**) *(with a purpose, a destination)* pour; **what's it for?** ça sert à quoi?; **who's that parcel for?** pour qui est ce colis?; **it's for my sister** c'est pour ma sœur; **the train for Glasgow** le train pour Glasgow
(**b**) *(for a period of)* pendant; **I will be here for a month** je serai ici pendant un mois; **we're going on holiday for a week** nous partons en vacances pendant une semaine; **I was in France for a month last year** j'ai passé un mois en France l'année dernière
(**c**) *(for a period of, in the past, up to the present moment)* depuis; **I've been here for a month** je suis ici depuis un mois; **he had been living in France for a year when he met her** il vivait en France depuis un an quand il l'a rencontrée

(d) *(with cost, amount)* **I bought it for £10** je l'ai acheté 10 livres; **a cheque for £100** un chèque de 100 livres
(e) *(representing)* **A is for Anne** A comme Anne; **what's the French for "book"?** comment dit-on "book" en français?

forbid *verb* interdire; **I forbid you to go out** je t'interdis de sortir

forbidden *adjective* interdit/interdite, défendu/défendue; **smoking is forbidden** il est interdit de fumer

force
1 *noun* la force
2 *verb*
(a) to force somebody to do something obliger quelqu'un à faire quelque chose; **to be forced to do something** être obligé de faire quelque chose; **he forced me to say yes** il m'a obligé à accepter
(b) to force something into something faire entrer quelque chose de force dans quelque chose; **to force a door open** forcer une porte; **he forced his way into the house** il a forcé la porte de la maison pour entrer

forehead *noun* le front

foreign *adjective* étranger/étrangère; **a foreign language** une langue étrangère

foreigner *noun* un étranger/une étrangère

forest *noun* la forêt; **there is a forest near the town** il y a une forêt près de la ville

forever *adverb*
(a) *(eternally)* pour toujours; **I could stay here forever** je pourrais rester ici pour toujours
(b) *(continually)* sans cesse; **he's forever forgetting things** il oublie toujours tout

forget *verb* oublier; **I forgot to tell you** j'ai oublié de te le dire; **don't forget to call me** n'oublie pas de m'appeler; **I forgot my purse** j'ai oublié mon

porte-monnaie; **I've forgotten your name** j'ai oublié votre nom

forgive *verb* *(person)* pardonner à; *(act, crime)* pardonner; **he never forgave me for that** il ne me l'a jamais pardonné

fork *noun*
(a) *(for eating)* la fourchette; **a knife and fork** un couteau et une fourchette
(b) *(for gardening)* la fourche

form
1 *noun*
(a) *(in a school)* la classe; **he's in the fourth form** il est en troisième
(b) *(paper to fill in)* le formulaire; **can you fill in this form?** veuillez remplir ce formulaire
(c) *(type)* le genre; **it's a form of insect** c'est un genre d'insecte
(d) *(shape)* la forme
2 *verb* *(organize, make)* former; **to form part of something** faire partie de quelque chose

formal *adjective*
(a) *(announcement, offer, dinner, invitation)* officiel/officielle; **formal dress** la tenue de soirée
(b) *(language)* soutenu/soutenue
(c) *(person, tone)* cérémonieux/cérémonieuse

former
1 *adjective* *(previous)* ancien/ancienne; **my former teacher** mon ancien professeur
2 *pronoun* **the former** celui-là/celle-là; *(plural)* ceux-là/celles-là

fortieth *number* quarantième

fortnight *noun* **a fortnight** quinze jours *(masculine plural)*; **a fortnight today** aujourd'hui en quinze; **she spent a fortnight in Spain** elle a passé quinze jours en Espagne; **once a fortnight** tous les quinze jours

fortunate *adjective* **to be fortunate** *(of a person)* avoir de la chance; **it's fortunate that he didn't see us** nous avons eu de la chance qu'il ne nous voie pas

fortunately *adverb* heureusement; **fortunately, I remembered to call him** heureusement, j'ai pensé à l'appeler

fortune *noun* la fortune; **she earns a fortune** elle gagne une fortune

forty *number* quarante; **forty-one** quarante et un; **forty-two** quarante-deux; **forty-first** quarante et unième; **forty-second** quarante-deuxième; **the forties** les années quarante

forward
1 *adverb* en avant; **to move forward** avancer
2 *adjective* avant

forwards *adverb* en avant

fossil *noun* le fossile

foul
1 *adjective*
(**a**) *(smell, taste)* infect/infecte
(**b**) *(language)* grossier/grossière
(**c**) **she's in a foul mood** elle est d'une humeur massacrante
(**d**) **foul play** *(in sport)* le jeu irrégulier; *(crime)* un acte criminel
2 *noun* *(in sport)* la faute

fountain *noun* la fontaine

four *number* quatre

fourteen *number* quatorze

fourteenth *number* quatorzième; **the fourteenth day** le quatorzième jour; **the fourteenth car** la quatorzième voiture; **the fourteenth of March** le quatorze mars

fourth *number* quatrième; **the fourth film** le quatrième film; **the fourth car** la quatrième voiture; **the fourth of October** le quatre octobre

fox *noun* le renard

fracture
1 *noun* la fracture
2 *verb* fracturer; **he's fractured his leg** il s'est fracturé la jambe

fragile *adjective* fragile; **a fragile parcel** un colis fragile

frame *noun*
(**a**) *(of a picture, a bicycle)* le cadre
(**b**) *(of a door, a window)* l'encadrement *(masculine)*
(**c**) *(of glasses)* la monture
(**d**) **she has a small frame** *(build)* elle est menue

France *noun* la France; **I live in France** j'habite en France; **I'm going to France** je vais en France; **my mother comes from France** ma mère est française

fraud *noun*
(**a**) *(person)* un imposteur
(**b**) *(crime)* la fraude
(**c**) *(deception)* la supercherie

freak
1 *noun* *(abnormal person)* le phénomène, le monstre; **a freak accident** un accident imprévisible
2 *verb*
(**a**) *(panic)* paniquer
(**b**) *(become angry)* piquer une crise; **my mum freaked when she saw my hair** ma mère a piqué une crise quand elle a vu mes cheveux
3 **freak out**
(**a**) *(panic)* paniquer
(**b**) *(become angry)* piquer une crise; **she'll freak out if you tell her** elle va piquer une crise si tu lui dis
(**c**) **to freak somebody out** faire flipper quelqu'un

freckle *noun* la tache de rousseur; **she has freckles on her nose** elle a des taches de rousseur sur le nez

free
1 *adjective*
(**a**) *(at liberty)* libre; **they set him free** ils l'ont libéré
(**b**) *(unoccupied)* libre; **is this seat free?** est-ce que cette place est libre?; **are you free this evening?** est-ce que tu es libre ce soir?
(**c**) *(without charge)* gratuit/gratuite; **a free gift** un cadeau
2 *verb* libérer

freedom *noun* la liberté

free-range *adjective* **free-range eggs** des œufs de poules élevées en plein air *(masculine plural)*; **free-range chicken** le poulet fermier

freeze
1 *verb*
(a) *(of water, a pipe)* geler; **the water has frozen** l'eau a gelé
(b) *(in a freezer)* congeler
2 **freeze up** *(of a lock, a pipe)* geler

freezer *noun* le congélateur; *(ice box)* le freezer

freezing *adjective*
(a) *(weather, room)* glacial/glaciale; **it's freezing today** il fait un froid glacial aujourd'hui

> The masculine plural of *glacial* is *glacials* or *glaciaux*.

(b) *(hands, fingers)* gelé/gelée; **I'm freezing** je suis gelé; **my feet are freezing** j'ai les pieds gelés

French
1 *adjective* français/française; **the French economy** l'économie française; **French fries** les frites *(feminine plural)*
2 *noun*
(a) *(language)* le français; **he speaks French** il parle français
(b) *(people)* **the French** les Français *(masculine plural)*

> In French, only the noun for the inhabitants of a country takes a capital letter, never the adjective or the noun for the language.

Frenchman *noun* le Français

French-speaking *adjective* francophone; **French-speaking countries** les pays francophones

Frenchwoman *noun* la Française

frequent *adjective* fréquent/fréquente

frequently *adverb* fréquemment

> The middle *e* of *fréquemment* is pronounced like the *a* in *cat*.

fresh *adjective*
(a) *(egg, fish, fruit)* frais/fraîche; **I'm going out to get some fresh air** je sors prendre l'air
(b) *(page, attempt, drink)* nouveau/nouvelle

> The masculine plural of *nouveau* is *nouveaux*. *Nouvel* is used instead of *nouveau* before masculine singular nouns beginning with a vowel or a mute h.

Friday *noun* le vendredi; **on Friday** vendredi; **I'm leaving on Friday** je m'en vais vendredi; **on Fridays** le vendredi; **he goes swimming on Fridays** il va à la piscine le vendredi; **every Friday** tous les vendredis; **next Friday** vendredi prochain; **last Friday** vendredi dernier

> In French, the names of days are not written with a capital.

fridge *noun* le frigo; **there's some orange juice in the fridge** il y a du jus d'orange dans le frigo

fried *adjective* frit/frite; **a fried egg** un œuf sur le plat

friend *noun* un ami/une amie; **Alison is my best friend** Alison est ma meilleure amie; **we're friends** nous sommes amis; **to make friends** se faire des amis; **he's friend with Paul** il est ami avec Paul

friendly *adjective* gentil/gentille; **his parents are very friendly** ses parents sont très gentils; **a friendly welcome** un accueil chaleureux; **they're very friendly in that shop** ils sont très aimables dans ce magasin

friendship *noun* l'amitié *(feminine)*

fright *noun* la peur; **you gave me a fright** tu m'as fait peur; **she got a fright** elle a eu peur

frighten *noun* faire peur à; **you frightened him** tu lui as fait peur

frightened *adjective* **to be frightened** avoir peur; **she's frightened of**

dogs elle a peur des chiens; **to be frightened of doing something** avoir peur de faire quelque chose

frightening *adjective* effrayant/effrayante; **a frightening film** un film effrayant

fringe *noun* la frange; **she has a fringe** elle a une frange

frizzy *adjective* crépu/crépue; **she has frizzy hair** elle a les cheveux crépus

frog *noun* la grenouille

from *preposition*
(**a**) *(expressing an origin)* de; **where are you from?** d'où êtes-vous?; **she's from Australia** elle est australienne; **I come from Leeds** je viens de Leeds
(**b**) *(expressing a time)* à partir de; **from tomorrow** à partir de demain; **from six o'clock to seven o'clock** de six heures à sept heures
(**c**) *(expressing a source)* de; **I got a letter from my cousin** j'ai reçu une lettre de mon cousin; **to borrow something from somebody** emprunter quelque chose à quelqu'un
(**d**) *(expressing removal)* de; **she drew a gun from her pocket** elle a sorti un revolver de sa poche; **he took a beer from the fridge** il a pris une bière dans le frigo; **to take something from somebody** prendre quelque chose à quelqu'un
(**e**) *(expressing a range)* **from... to...** de... à...; **children from seven to nine years** les enfants de sept à neuf ans

front
1 *adjective* **a front door** une porte d'entrée; **the front page** la première page
2 *noun*
(**a**) *(of a house, a shirt)* le devant; *(of a car)* l'avant *(masculine)*; **sit in the front of the car** assieds-toi à l'avant de la voiture
(**b**) **in front of** devant; **he's in front of the door** il est devant la porte
(**c**) **in front** devant; **to go in front** passer devant; **to be in front** *(in a race)* être en tête

frost *noun* le gel

frosty *adjective* **it's frosty** il gèle

frown *verb* froncer les sourcils; **she was frowning at me** elle me regardait en fronçant les sourcils

frozen *adjective* *(food)* surgelé/surgelée; **a frozen pizza** une pizza surgelée

fruit *noun* les fruits *(masculine plural)*; **I like fruit** j'aime les fruits; **a piece of fruit** un fruit; **some fruit** *(one piece)* un fruit; *(several pieces)* des fruits; **fruit juice** le jus de fruits; **fruit salad** la salade de fruits

frustrating *adjective* frustrant/frustrante

fry *verb* **to fry something** faire frire quelque chose; **she fried some bacon** elle a fait frire du bacon; **the sausages are frying** les saucisses sont en train de frire

frying pan *noun* la poêle

fudge *noun* le caramel mou

fuel *noun* le combustible; *(for a vehicle, an aircraft)* le carburant

full *adjective* plein/pleine; **the room was full of people** la salle était pleine de monde; **the sink is full of water** l'évier est rempli d'eau; **the hotel is full** l'hôtel est complet; **what is your full name?** quels sont vos nom et prénom?; **I'm full** *(after eating)* je n'ai plus faim; **it's a full moon tonight** c'est la pleine lune ce soir; **a full stop** un point

full-time
1 *adjective* à plein temps; **she has a full-time job** elle a un travail à plein temps
2 *adverb* à plein temps; **my mum works full-time** ma mère travaille à plein temps

fully *adverb* *(completely)* entièrement, complètement; **the house has been fully renovated** la maison a été entièrement rénovée; **I fully understand** je comprends parfaitement

fumes *plural noun* les fumées *(femi-*

nine plural); *(of a gas, a liquid)* les vapeurs *(feminine plural)*; **car fumes** les gaz d'échappement *(masculine plural)*

fun *noun* **that was fun** c'était amusant; **to have fun** s'amuser; **have fun!** amuse-toi bien!; **to do something for fun** faire quelque chose pour s'amuser; **to make fun of somebody** se moquer de quelqu'un; **he's always making fun of me** il se moque toujours de moi

function
1 *noun*
(**a**) *(role)* la fonction
(**b**) *(party)* la réception
2 *verb* fonctionner; **to function as something** faire fonction de quelque chose; **the sofa also functions as a bed** le canapé fait aussi lit

funeral *noun* un enterrement

funfair *noun* la fête foraine

funny *adjective*
(**a**) *(amusing)* drôle; **a funny story** une histoire drôle; **it's a funny programme** c'est une émission comique
(**b**) *(strange)* bizarre; **that fish tastes funny** ce poisson a un goût bizarre

fur *noun* la fourrure; **a fur coat** un manteau de fourrure

furious *adjective* furieux/furieuse; **she's furious with me** elle est furieuse contre moi

furnish *verb* meubler; **the flat isn't furnished** l'appartement n'est pas meublé

furniture *noun* les meubles *(masculine plural)*; **a piece of furniture** un meuble; **the furniture is nice** les meubles sont beaux

further
1 *adjective* plus loin; **further information** d'autres renseignements; **let me know if you need further information** dites-moi si vous avez besoin d'autres renseignements
2 *adverb* plus loin; **I can't walk any further** je ne peux pas faire un pas de plus; **it's not much further** ce n'est plus très loin

furthest
1 *adjective* le plus éloigné/la plus éloignée; **the furthest house** la maison la plus éloignée
2 *adverb* le plus loin; **Jane walked the furthest** c'est Jane qui est allée le plus loin

fuse
1 *noun* le fusible
2 *verb* **the lights have fused** les plombs ont sauté

fuss *noun* **to make a fuss** faire des histoires; **she always makes a fuss** elle fait toujours des histoires

fussy *adjective* difficile; **stop being so fussy!** arrête de faire le difficile!

future
1 *adjective* futur/future; **future generations** les générations futures; **the future tense** le futur
2 *noun*
(**a**) *(in time)* l'avenir *(masculine)*; **in future** à l'avenir; **in future, try to be on time** à l'avenir, essaie d'être à l'heure; **in the distant future** dans un avenir lointain
(**b**) *(in grammar)* le futur

gadget *noun* le gadget

gain
1 *noun*
(a) *(profit)* le gain
(b) *(increase)* une augmentation
2 *verb*
(a) *(experience, reputation)* acquérir
(b) *(sympathy, respect)* gagner
(c) **to gain speed** prendre de la vitesse; **to gain weight** prendre du poids; **have you gained weight?** est-ce que tu as pris du poids?

galaxy *noun* la galaxie

gale *noun* le grand vent

gallery *noun*
(a) *(for selling works of art)* la galerie
(b) *(for exhibiting works of art)* le musée
(c) *(for the public, the press)* la tribune

gallon *noun* le gallon

> Note that people in France don't use gallons as a unit of measurement for liquids, they use litres (1 gallon = 4.54 litres).

gallop *verb* galoper; **the horse galloped across the field** le cheval a traversé le champ au galop

gamble
1 *noun* le risque; **to take a gamble** prendre un risque
2 *verb* jouer; **he likes to gamble** il aime les jeux d'argent

gambler *noun* le joueur/la joueuse

gambling *noun* le jeu; **he likes gambling** il aime les jeux d'argent

game *noun*
(a) *(in general)* le jeu

> The plural of *jeu* is *jeux*.

(b) *(of football, cricket)* le match
(c) *(of cards, chess)* la partie; **what about a game of cards?** si on jouait aux cartes?
(d) **games** *(school subject)* le sport

gang *noun* la bande

gangster *noun* le gangster

gap *noun*
(a) *(empty space in a wall, a fence)* le trou; **the mouse got in through a gap in the floor** la souris est entrée par un trou dans le plancher
(b) *(in time)* un intervalle; **after a gap of two years** après un intervalle de deux ans
(c) *(difference)* un écart; **the gap between rich and poor** l'écart entre les riches et les pauvres
(d) *(in knowledge, education)* la lacune; **there are gaps in his education** il a des lacunes

garage *noun* le garage; **a garage mechanic** un garagiste; **he is a garage mechanic** il est garagiste

garden *noun* le jardin; **they're in the garden** ils sont dans le jardin

gardener *noun* le jardinier/la jardinière

gardening *noun* le jardinage; **I like gardening** j'aime jardiner; **to do some gardening** faire du jardinage

garlic *noun* l'ail *(masculine)*

gas *noun* le gaz; **a gas cooker** une cuisinière à gaz; **a gas fire** un radiateur à gaz

gate *noun*
(**a**) *(into a driveway, a field)* la barrière; *(into a garden)* la porte; **she left the garden gate open** elle a laissé la porte du jardin ouverte
(**b**) *(in an airport)* la porte

gather *verb*
(**a**) *(wood, papers, belongings)* ramasser; *(fruit, flowers)* cueillir; *(information)* recueillir; **they're gathering mushrooms** ils ramassent des champignons
(**b**) **to gather speed** prendre de la vitesse
(**c**) **they gathered round the fire** ils se sont rassemblés autour du feu

gathering *noun* le rassemblement

gay
1 *adjective* homosexuel/homosexuelle
2 *noun* un homosexuel/une homosexuelle

gaze *verb* **to gaze at somebody/something** regarder fixement quelqu'un/quelque chose; **to gaze out of the window** regarder par la fenêtre

gear *noun*
(**a**) *(on a car, a bicycle)* la vitesse; **to change gear** changer de vitesse
(**b**) *(equipment)* le matériel; **he brought all his camping gear** il a apporté tout son matériel de camping
(**c**) *(belongings)* les affaires *(feminine plural)*
(**d**) *(clothes)* les fringues *(feminine plural)*

gel *noun* le gel

Gemini *noun* les Gémeaux *(masculine plural)*; **I'm (a) Gemini** je suis Gémeaux

gender *noun*
(**a**) *(in grammar)* le genre
(**b**) *(of a person)* le sexe

gene *noun* le gène

general
1 *adjective* général/générale; **general knowledge** la culture générale; **the general public** le grand public
2 *noun*
(**a**) le général
(**b**) **in general** en général

> The plural of the noun *général* is *généraux*.

generally *adverb* généralement; **generally speaking** d'une manière générale

generation *noun* la génération; **the generation gap** le conflit des générations

generous *adjective* généreux/généreuse; **she's a very generous person** elle est très généreuse

genius *noun* le génie; **she's a genius** c'est un génie

gentle *adjective*
(**a**) *(person, voice, slope)* doux/douce
(**b**) *(exercise, speed)* modéré/modérée
(**c**) *(breeze, push)* léger/légère

gentleman *noun* le monsieur; **good morning, gentlemen** bonjour messieurs

gently *adverb* doucement

gents *plural noun* **the gents** les toilettes pour hommes *(feminine plural)*; **where's the gents, please?** où sont les toilettes, s'il vous plaît?

genuine *adjective*
(**a**) *(diamond)* véritable
(**b**) *(signature, work of art)* authentique
(**c**) *(sincere)* sincère

genuinely *adverb* sincèrement; **he's genuinely sorry** il est sincèrement désolé

geography *noun* la géographie

germ *noun* le microbe

German
1 *adjective* allemand/allemande; **German measles** la rubéole; **he's got German measles** il a la rubéole
2 *noun*
(**a**) *(language)* l'allemand *(masculine)*; **he speaks German** il parle allemand

(b) *(person)* un Allemand/une Allemande; **the Germans** les Allemands *(masculine plural)*

In French, only the noun for the inhabitants of a country takes a capital letter, never the adjective or the noun for the language.

Germany *noun* l'Allemagne *(feminine)*; **he lives in Germany** il habite en Allemagne; **I'm going to Germany** je vais en Allemagne; **her mother comes from Germany** sa mère est allemande

gesture
1 *noun* le geste
2 *verb* faire un geste; **to gesture to somebody** faire signe à quelqu'un

get
1 *verb*
(a) *(possess)* avoir; **they've got two dogs** ils ont deux chiens; **I haven't got a car** je n'ai pas de voiture
(b) *(receive)* recevoir; **I got a letter from my aunt** j'ai reçu une lettre de ma tante; **she's getting a computer for Christmas** elle va avoir un ordinateur pour Noël
(c) *(obtain)* obtenir; **the workers got what they wanted** les travailleurs ont obtenu ce qu'ils voulaient; **she got a job in a bank** elle a obtenu un poste dans une banque
(d) *(buy)* acheter; **can you get some milk when you're at the shop?** est-ce que tu pourras acheter du lait quand tu iras au magasin?; **did you get the paper?** est-ce que tu as acheté le journal?
(e) *(find)* trouver; **I got the idea from a book** j'ai trouvé l'idée dans un livre
(f) *(catch)* attraper; **she got the flu** elle a attrapé la grippe; **did you manage to get the train?** est-ce que tu as réussi à avoir ton train?
(g) *(fetch)* aller chercher; **can you go and get my glasses for me?** peux-tu aller me chercher mes lunettes?
(h) *(understand)* comprendre; **I don't get it** je ne comprends pas

(i) *(make)* **to get somebody to do something** faire faire quelque chose à quelqu'un; **we're getting the house repainted** nous faisons repeindre la maison; **get him to help you** demande-lui de t'aider
(j) *(go)* aller; **how are you getting to the airport?** comment est-ce que tu vas à l'aéroport?
(k) *(arrive)* arriver; **she's getting here this evening** elle arrive ce soir
(l) *(become)* devenir; **it's getting difficult** ça devient difficile; **she got angry** elle s'est mise en colère; **he's getting old** il vieillit; **she's getting thin** elle maigrit; **it's getting cold** ça se rafraîchit
(m) *(must)* **I've got to leave** je dois partir
2 get along with s'entendre avec; **she gets along with her family** elle s'entend bien avec sa famille
3 get away
(a) *(leave)* partir; *(escape)* s'enfuir; **the burglar got away** le voleur s'est enfui
(b) *(go on holiday)* partir en vacances; **I really need to get away** il faut vraiment que je parte en vacances
(c) **he won't get away with it this time** il ne s'en sortira pas comme ça cette fois
4 get back
(a) *(recover)* récupérer; **I didn't get my money back** je n'ai pas récupéré mon argent
(b) *(return)* revenir; **we got back on Saturday** nous sommes revenus samedi
5 get down descendre; **he got down from the ladder** il est descendu de l'échelle
6 get in
(a) *(enter)* entrer; **the burglars got in through the window** les voleurs sont entrés par la fenêtre
(b) *(come home)* rentrer; **he got in at midnight** il est rentré à minuit
(c) *(go into a car or train)* monter; **come on, get in!** allez, monte!

(**d**) *(of a plane, a train)* arriver; **the train gets in at six o'clock** le train arrive à six heures

7 get into *(a car, a train)* monter dans; **come on, get into the car** allez, monte dans la voiture

8 get off *(a bus, a train)* descendre de; **we get off at the next stop** nous descendons au prochain arrêt

9 get on
(**a**) *(a train, a bus)* monter dans; **he got on the bus** il est monté dans le bus
(**b**) *(fare)* **how are you getting on?** ça va?; **how did she get on at the interview?** comment s'est passé son entretien?
(**c**) **she gets on well with her sister** elle s'entend bien avec sa sœur; **we don't get on** on ne s'entend pas

10 get out sortir; **she doesn't get out much** elle ne sort pas beaucoup; **get out!** dehors!

11 get over *(an illness)* se remettre de; **Mary hasn't got over her flu yet** Mary ne s'est pas encore remise de sa grippe

12 get through *(squeeze through)* passer par; **he got through a hole in the fence** il est passé par un trou dans la clôture; **he was too big to get through** il était trop gros pour passer

13 get up *(from a bed, a chair)* se lever; **I get up at eight o'clock** je me lève à huit heures

ghost *noun* le fantôme

giant *noun* le géant/la géante

gift *noun* le cadeau; **a gift shop** une boutique de cadeaux; **a gift token** un chèque-cadeau; **gift wrap** du papier-cadeau

> The plural of *cadeau* is *cadeaux*. The plural of *chèque-cadeau* is *chèques-cadeaux*.

gigantic *adjective* gigantesque; **they've got a gigantic garden** ils ont un jardin gigantesque

giggle *verb* rire bêtement

ginger
1 *noun* le gingembre
2 *adj* **she has ginger hair** elle a les cheveux roux

giraffe *noun* la girafe

girl *noun*
(**a**) *(child)* la fille, la petite fille
(**b**) *(teenager)* la jeune fille

girlfriend *noun* *(of a boy)* la petite amie; *(of a girl)* une amie; **his girlfriend is called Laura** sa petite amie s'appelle Laura

give
1 *verb*
(**a**) *(in general)* donner; **give me that cup** donne-moi cette tasse; **give it to me** donne-le-moi; **give it to them** donne-le-leur
(**b**) *(as a present)* offrir; **she gave me a book for my birthday** elle m'a offert un livre pour mon anniversaire

2 give away donner; **he gave all his money away** il a donné tout son argent

3 give back rendre; **can you give me back my pen?** peux-tu me rendre mon stylo?

4 give in
(**a**) *(under pressure)* céder; **you shouldn't give in to her so easily** tu ne devrais pas lui céder aussi facilement
(**b**) *(give up)* abandonner; **I give in, what's the answer?** j'abandonne, quelle est la réponse?

5 give out distribuer; **the teacher gave out the exam papers** le professeur a distribué les sujets d'examen

6 give up abandonner; **he gave up smoking** il a arrêté de fumer; **he gave up the piano** il a abandonné le piano

glad *adjective* content/contente; **I'm glad you're coming with me** je suis content que tu viennes avec moi; **I'm glad he's here** je suis content qu'il soit là

glamorous *adjective* *(person)* élégant/élégante; *(job, image)* prestigieux/prestigieuse; *(restaurant)* chic

glance *verb* to glance at somebody jeter un coup d'œil à quelqu'un; **he glanced at the clock** il a jeté un coup d'œil à la pendule

glass *noun* le verre; **a glass of wine** un verre de vin; **a wine glass** un verre à vin; **would you like a glass of milk?** est-ce que tu voudrais un verre de lait?

glasses *plural noun (for eyes)* les lunettes *(feminine plural)*; **she wears glasses** elle porte des lunettes

glide *verb* planer

glider *noun* le planeur

glitter *verb* scintiller

global *adjective* global/globale; **global warming** le réchauffement de la planète

The masculine plural of *global* is *globaux*.

gloomy *adjective (person)* triste; *(room)* lugubre

glove *noun* le gant; **a pair of gloves** une paire de gants

glow *verb* rougeoyer

glue
1 *noun* la colle
2 *verb* coller; **glue the paper onto the box** colle le papier sur la boîte

go
1 *verb*
(**a**) aller; **we're going to France** nous allons en France; **Jenny went to the cinema** Jenny est allée au cinéma; **I'm going home** je rentre chez moi
(**b**) *(leave)* partir; **the bus has already gone** le bus est déjà parti; **I've got to go** je dois partir
(**c**) *(work)* marcher, fonctionner; **the car won't go** la voiture ne marche pas
(**d**) *(progress)* aller; **the interview went well** l'entretien s'est bien passé
(**e**) *(become)* devenir; **he went mad** il est devenu fou; **she went red** elle a rougi
(**f**) *(with the future tense)* aller; **I'm going to call him** je vais l'appeler; **it's**

going to rain il va pleuvoir
2 go away partir; **she went away** elle est partie; **go away!** va-t'en!
3 go back retourner; **she went back home** elle est rentrée à la maison; **she went back to sleep** elle s'est rendormie
4 go down
(**a**) *(descend)* descendre; **she went down the stairs** elle a descendu l'escalier
(**b**) *(decrease)* baisser; **prices have gone down** les prix ont baissé
(**c**) *(of a balloon, a tyre)* se dégonfler
5 go in entrer; **she knocked on the door and went in** elle a frappé à la porte avant d'entrer
6 go into entrer dans; **she went into the bedroom** elle est entrée dans la chambre
7 go off
(**a**) *(of a bomb)* exploser
(**b**) *(of an alarm)* se déclencher; *(of an alarm clock)* sonner; **my alarm clock goes off at seven** mon réveil sonne à sept heures
(**c**) *(of milk, meat)* tourner; **that milk has gone off** le lait a tourné
8 go on
(**a**) *(continue)* continuer; **they went on laughing** ils ont continué à rire
(**b**) *(happen)* se passer; **what's going on?** qu'est-ce qui se passe?
9 go out
(**a**) *(leave the house)* sortir; **are you going out tonight?** est-ce que tu sors ce soir?
(**b**) *(date)* **Jessica is going out with Mark** Jessica sort avec Mark
(**c**) **the fire has gone out** le feu s'est éteint
10 go round
(**a**) *(visit)* **to go round the shops** aller faire les magasins
(**b**) **she's gone round to Emily's** elle est allée chez Emily
11 go up
(**a**) *(climb)* monter; **she went up the stairs** elle a monté l'escalier
(**b**) *(increase)* monter; **prices have**

gone up les prix ont monté

goal *noun* le but; **he scored a goal** il a marqué un but; **you need to set yourself a goal** il faut te fixer un but

goalkeeper *noun* le gardien de but

goat *noun* la chèvre; **do you like goat's cheese?** tu aimes le fromage de chèvre?

god *noun* le dieu; **God** Dieu; **do you believe in God?** est-ce que tu crois en Dieu?; **for God's sake!** pour l'amour de Dieu!

> The plural of *dieu* is *dieux*.

goddaughter *noun* la filleule

godfather *noun* le parrain

godmother *noun* la marraine

godson *noun* le filleul

goggles *plural noun*
(**a**) *(for swimming)* les lunettes de plongée *(feminine plural)*
(**b**) *(for skiing)* les lunettes de ski *(feminine plural)*
(**c**) *(for a worker)* les lunettes protectrices *(feminine plural)*

go-kart *noun* le kart

gold *noun* l'or *(masculine)*; **a gold bracelet** un bracelet en or; **a gold medal** une médaille d'or

golden *adjective* doré/dorée

goldfish *noun* le poisson rouge

golf *noun* le golf; **they play golf** ils jouent au golf; **a golf ball** une balle de golf; **a golf club** un club de golf; **a golf course** un terrain de golf

good
1 *adjective*
(**a**) bon/bonne; **it's a good film** c'est un bon film; **she's very good at maths** elle est très forte en maths; **that tastes good** c'est bon; **broccoli is good for you** les brocolis sont bons pour la santé; **have a good time!** amuse-toi bien!
(**b**) *(well-behaved)* sage; **be good!** sois sage!

(**c**) *(kind)* gentil/gentille; **he's very good to me** il est très gentil avec moi
(**d**) *(fortunate)* **it's a good thing he didn't see you** heureusement qu'il ne t'a pas vu
(**e**) *(in greetings)* **good morning** bonjour; **good afternoon** bonjour; **good evening** bonsoir; **good night** bonsoir; *(before going to bed)* bonne nuit
2 *noun*
(**a**) **this book is no good** ce livre est nul; **it's no good crying** ça ne sert à rien de pleurer
(**b**) **it will do you good** ça te fera du bien
(**c**) **for good** pour toujours; **she's gone for good** elle est partie pour toujours

goodbye *exclamation* au revoir

good-looking *adjective* beau/belle; **Connor is very good-looking** Connor est très beau

goods *plural noun* les marchandises *(feminine plural)*

goose *noun* une oie

gooseberry *noun* la groseille à maquereau

gorgeous *adjective* magnifique; *(meal)* excellent/excellente; **his girlfriend is gorgeous** sa petite amie est magnifique

gorilla *noun* le gorille

gossip
1 *noun*
(**a**) *(talk)* les bavardages *(masculine plural)*; *(ill-natured)* les commérages *(masculine plural)*
(**b**) *(person)* la commère
2 *verb* bavarder; *(ill-naturedly)* faire des commérages

government *noun* le gouvernement

gown *noun* la robe

grab *verb* **to grab somebody** *or* **to grab hold of somebody** attraper quelqu'un; **to grab something** *or* **to grab hold of something** attraper quelque chose; **he grabbed hold of my arm** il m'a attrapé par le bras

graceful *adjective* gracieux/gracieuse; **the dancer is very graceful** la danseuse est très gracieuse

grade *noun*
(**a**) *(rank)* le grade
(**b**) *(in profession)* un échelon

gradually *adverb* peu à peu; **her French has gradually improved** son français s'est amélioré peu à peu

grain *noun* le grain; **a grain of rice** un grain de riz

gram, gramme *noun* le gramme; **100 grams of butter** 100 grammes de beurre

grammar *noun* la grammaire; **grammar school** le collège, le lycée

Note that the distinction between comprehensive schools and grammar schools does not exist in France.

grand *adjective* somptueux/somptueuse; **the palace is very grand** le palais est vraiment somptueux

grandad *noun* le papi

grandchild *noun* *(boy)* le petit-fils; *(girl)* la petite-fille

The plural of *petit-fils* is *petits-fils.* The plural of *petite-fille* is *petites-filles.*

granddad *noun* le papi, le pépé

granddaughter *noun* la petite-fille

The plural of *petite-fille* is *petites-filles.*

grandfather *noun* le grand-père

The plural of *grand-père* is *grands-pères.*

grandma *noun* la mamie

grandmother *noun* la grand-mère

The plural of *grand-mère* is *grands-mères.*

grandpa *noun* le papi, le pépé

grandparents *plural noun* les grands-parents *(masculine plural)*

grandson *noun* le petit-fils

The plural of *petit-fils* is *petits-fils.*

granny *noun* la mamie, la mémé

grant
1 *noun*
(**a**) *(financial aid)* la subvention
(**b**) *(for a student)* la bourse; **she'll get a grant when she goes to university** elle bénéficiera d'une bourse lorsqu'elle ira à l'université
2 *verb*
(**a**) *(permission)* donner
(**b**) *(an interview, a request)* accorder
(**c**) **he takes her for granted** il n'a aucun égard pour elle

grape *noun* le grain de raisin; **some grapes** du raisin; **a bunch of grapes** une grappe de raisin

grapefruit *noun* le pamplemousse; **grapefruit juice** le jus de pamplemousse

graph *noun* le graphique

grass *noun* l'herbe *(feminine)*; *(lawn)* la pelouse; **the grass is wet** l'herbe est mouillée; **to cut the grass** tondre la pelouse; **don't walk on the grass** ne marche pas sur la pelouse

grasshopper *noun* la sauterelle

grate *verb* râper; **grated cheese** du fromage râpé

grateful *adjective* reconnaissant/reconnaissante; **I'm grateful for your help** je te suis reconnaissante pour ton aide

grater *noun* la râpe

grave *noun* la tombe

gravestone *noun* la pierre tombale

gravy *noun* le jus de viande

graze *verb* écorcher; **he grazed his knee** il s'est écorché le genou

grease *noun* la graisse

greasy *adjective* gras/grasse; **she has**

greasy hair elle a les cheveux gras; **the meat was very greasy** la viande était très grasse

great *adjective*
(**a**) *(large, important)* grand/grande; **a great many people** un très grand nombre de personnes; **the party was a great success** la fête était vraiment réussie
(**b**) *(excellent)* génial/géniale; **it's a great film** c'est un film génial; **you look great!** tu es magnifique!

The masculine plural of *génial* is *géniaux*.

Great Britain *noun* la Grande-Bretagne; **I live in Great Britain** j'habite en Grande-Bretagne; **I'm going to Great Britain** je vais en Grande-Bretagne; **his father is from Great Britain** son père est britannique

great-grandfather *noun* l'arrière-grand-père *(masculine)*

The plural of *arrière-grand-père* is *arrière-grands-pères*.

great-grandmother *noun* l'arrière-grand-mère *(feminine)*

The plural of *arrière-grand-mère* is *arrière-grands-mères*.

Greece *noun* la Grèce; **she lives in Greece** elle habite en Grèce; **he's going to Greece** il va en Grèce; **her father is from Greece** son père est grec

greed *noun*
(**a**) *(for food)* la gourmandise
(**b**) *(for money)* l'avidité *(feminine)*

greedy *adjective*
(**a**) *(for food)* gourmand/gourmande
(**b**) *(for money)* avide

Greek
1 *adjective* grec/grecque
2 *noun*
(**a**) *(language)* le grec; **they speak Greek** ils parlent grec
(**b**) *(person)* le Grec/la Grecque; **the**

Greeks les Grecs *(masculine plural)*

green *adjective* vert/verte; **a green coat** un manteau vert; **a green car** une voiture verte; **I have green eyes** j'ai les yeux verts

greengrocer *noun* le marchand/la marchande de fruits et légumes

greenhouse *noun* la serre

greet *verb*
(**a**) *(say hello to)* saluer
(**b**) *(welcome)* accueillir

greetings *plural noun* les vœux *(masculine plural)*

grey *adjective* gris/grise; **a grey dog** un chien gris; **a grey skirt** une jupe grise; **I have grey eyes** j'ai les yeux gris

grill
1 *noun* le gril; **put the chicken under the grill** mets le poulet sous le gril
2 *verb* faire griller; **she's grilling some chicken** elle fait griller du poulet

grin
1 *noun* le large sourire
2 *verb* avoir un large sourire; **she was grinning at him** elle lui faisait un large sourire

grind *verb* *(coffee, pepper)* moudre; **I've ground some coffee** j'ai moulu du café

grip *verb*
(**a**) *(grab)* saisir; **he suddenly gripped my arm** il m'a saisi le bras
(**b**) *(hold)* serrer; **she was gripping my arm** elle me serrait le bras

groan *verb* gémir; **he groaned in pain** il a gémi de douleur

grocer *noun* un épicier/une épicière; **a grocer's (shop)** une épicerie; **he's a grocer** il est épicier; **I'm going to the grocer's** je vais chez l'épicier

groceries *plural noun* *(food)* les provisions *(feminine plural)*

ground *noun*
(**a**) le sol; **on the ground** par terre; **the ground floor** le rez-de-chaussée

(b) *(for camping, football)* le terrain

group *noun* le groupe; **a nice group of people** un groupe de gens sympathiques

grow
1 *verb*
(a) *(of a person, an animal)* grandir; *(of a plant, hair)* pousser; **he's grown another two centimetres** il a encore grandi de deux centimètres; **I'm letting my hair grow** je me laisse pousser les cheveux
(b) *(become)* **to grow old** vieillir; **to grow angry** se fâcher
2 **grow up** devenir adulte; **oh, grow up!** oh, arrête de faire l'enfant!

growl *verb* grogner

grown-up *noun* la grande personne

growth *noun* la croissance; **the growth in the population** la croissance de la population

grumpy *adjective* grognon/grognonne

grunt *verb* grogner

guarantee
1 *noun* la garantie; **the TV is under guarantee** le téléviseur est sous garantie
2 *verb* garantir; **I guarantee that she'll come** je garantis qu'elle viendra

guard
1 *noun*
(a) *(soldier, security guard)* le garde; **a guard dog** un chien de garde
(b) *(in a prison)* le gardien/la gardienne
(c) *(on a train)* le chef de train
2 *verb* garder

guess *verb* deviner; **guess what!** devine quoi!; **guess who I saw yesterday** devine qui j'ai croisé hier?; **I guess (so)** je crois

guest *noun* un invité/une invitée; *(in a hotel)* le client/la cliente; **we're having dinner guests tomorrow** nous avons des invités pour le dîner demain

Guide *noun (scout)* une éclaireuse

guide
1 *noun* *(person, book)* le guide; **a guide to France** un guide de la France; **a guide dog** un chien d'aveugle
2 *verb* guider

guidebook *noun* le guide

guilt *noun* la culpabilité

guilty *adjective* coupable; **I feel guilty** je me sens coupable

guinea pig *noun* le cobaye

guitar *noun* la guitare; **he plays the guitar** il joue de la guitare

gum *noun*
(a) *(for chewing)* le chewing-gum; **a piece of gum** un chewing-gum
(b) *(in the mouth)* la gencive

gun *noun* le pistolet; *(rifle)* le fusil; *(firing shells)* le canon

gunshot *noun* le coup de feu

gutter *noun*
(a) *(in the street)* le caniveau

The plural of *caniveau* is *caniveaux*.

(b) *(on the roof)* la gouttière

guy *noun (man)* le type; **her brother is a nice guy** son frère est un type sympathique

gym *noun*
(a) *(in a school)* le gymnase
(b) *(fitness centre)* le club de gym; **I go to the gym twice a week** je vais au club de gym deux fois par semaine
(c) *(gymnastics)* la gym; **gym shoes** les chaussures de gym *(feminine plural)*

gymnastics *noun* la gymnastique; **he does gymnastics** il fait de la gymnastique

H

habit *noun* une habitude; **to get into the habit of doing something** prendre l'habitude de faire quelque chose; **to be in the habit of doing something** avoir l'habitude de faire quelque chose

hacker *noun* le pirate informatique

haddock *noun* un églefin

hail[1]
1 *noun* la grêle
2 *verb* **it's hailing** il grêle

hail[2] *verb* *(a taxi)* héler

hair *noun*
(a) *(on the head)* les cheveux *(masculine plural)*; **a hair** un cheveu; **I have brown hair** j'ai les cheveux châtains; **to brush one's hair** se brosser les cheveux; **to get one's hair cut** se faire couper les cheveux
(b) *(on the body, of an animal)* les poils *(masculine plural)*

hairbrush *noun* la brosse à cheveux

haircut *noun* la coupe de cheveux; **to have a haircut** se faire couper les cheveux

hairdresser *noun* le coiffeur/la coiffeuse; **my aunt is a hairdresser** ma tante est coiffeuse; **I'm going to the hairdresser's** je vais chez le coiffeur

hairdryer *noun* le sèche-cheveux

The word *sèche-cheveux* does not change in the plural.

hairspray *noun* la laque

hairstyle *noun* la coiffure

hairy *adjective* poilu/poilue

half
1 *noun*
(a) la moitié; **to cut something in half** couper quelque chose en deux; **half an apple** une demi-pomme
(b) *(with expressions of time)* **half an hour** une demi-heure; **half past ten** dix heures et demie
(c) *(fraction)* le demi, la moitié; **four and a half** quatre et demi
2 *adjective* **a half day** une demi-journée; **a half hour** une demi-heure; **are you going anywhere for half term?** est-ce que tu pars pour les vacances?; **half time** la mi-temps; **at half time** à la mi-temps

halfway *adverb* à mi-chemin; **halfway between the school and the post office** à mi-chemin entre l'école et la poste

hall *noun*
(a) *(big room)* la salle
(b) *(entrance to a house)* une entrée

hallway *noun*
(a) *(entrance room)* une entrée
(b) *(corridor)* le couloir

halve *verb*
(a) *(cake, fruit)* couper en deux
(b) *(number)* réduire de moitié

ham *noun* le jambon; **a ham sandwich** un sandwich au jambon

hamburger *noun* le hamburger

hammer
1 *noun* le marteau

The plural of *marteau* is *marteaux*.

2 *verb* **to hammer a nail into something** enfoncer un clou dans quelque

chose; **he was hammering on the door** il tambourinait à la porte

hamster *noun* le hamster

hand
1 *noun*
(**a**) *(of a person)* la main; **they were holding hands** ils se tenaient par la main; **hand in hand** la main dans la main; **hand luggage** les bagages à main *(masculine plural)*
(**b**) *(of a watch, a clock)* une aiguille
2 *verb* passer; **can you hand me that book?** peux-tu me passer ce livre?
3 hand in remettre; **has anybody handed in an umbrella?** est-ce que quelqu'un vous a remis un parapluie?
4 hand out distribuer; **the teacher handed out the exam papers** le professeur a distribué les sujets d'examen
5 hand over *(pass)* passer; *(transfer)* remettre; **can you hand me over that torch?** est-ce que tu peux me passer la lampe de poche?; **the weapons were handed over to the police** les armes ont été remises à la police

handbag *noun* le sac à main

handbrake *noun* le frein à main

handicapped *adjective* handicapé/handicapée

handkerchief *noun* le mouchoir

handle
1 *noun*
(**a**) *(of a door, a suitcase)* la poignée
(**b**) *(of a knife, a broom, a saucepan)* le manche
(**c**) *(of a cup, a bucket)* une anse
2 *verb*
(**a**) *(touch, hold)* manipuler, toucher
(**b**) *(cope with)* faire face à; **can he handle the situation?** est-ce qu'il arrive à faire face à la situation?

handlebars *noun* le guidon

handmade *adjective* fait/faite à la main; **a handmade blanket** une couverture faite à la main

handsome *adjective* beau/belle; **he's a handsome man** c'est un bel homme

Note that *beau* becomes *bel* before a vowel or mute h. The plural of *beau* or *bel* is *beaux*.

handwriting *noun* l'écriture *(feminine)*; **she has nice handwriting** elle a une jolie écriture

handy *adjective*
(**a**) *(useful)* pratique; **my new bag is very handy** mon nouveau sac est très pratique
(**b**) *(within reach)* à portée de main; **have you got a pen handy?** est-ce que tu as un stylo à portée de main?
(**c**) *(convenient)* commode; **the flat's handy for the shops** l'appartement est tout près des commerces

hang
1 *verb*
(**a**) *(from the ceiling)* suspendre; **he hung the light from the ceiling** il a supendu la lampe au plafond; **the light is hanging from the ceiling** la lampe est suspendue au plafond
(**b**) *(on the wall)* accrocher; **he hung the picture on the wall** il a accroché le tableau au mur; **the picture is hanging on the bedroom wall** le tableau est accroché au mur de la chambre
(**c**) *(criminal)* pendre; **they hanged him** ils l'ont pendu
2 hang about, hang around traîner; **he's hanging about with his friends** il traîne avec ses amis
3 hang on *(wait)* patienter, attendre; **hang on a minute!** attends une minute!
4 hang out
(**a**) *(of a tongue, a shirt)* pendre
(**b**) **to hang out the washing** étendre le linge dehors
5 hang up
(**a**) *(picture, coat)* accrocher; **I'll hang up your coat** je vais accrocher ton manteau
(**b**) *(on the phone)* raccrocher; **don't hang up!** ne raccroche pas!
(**c**) **to hang up the washing** étendre le linge

hangar *noun* le hangar

hanger *noun* le cintre

hang-glider *noun* le deltaplane

hangover *noun* la gueule de bois; **to have a hangover** avoir la gueule de bois

happen *verb* arriver; **what's happening?** qu'est-ce qui se passe?; **something bad has happened** quelque chose de grave est arrivé; **it happened last summer** ça s'est passé l'été dernier; **what happened to her?** qu'est-ce qu'il lui est arrivé?

happiness *noun* le bonheur

happy *adjective* heureux/heureuse; **the teacher is happy with her work** le professeur est content de son travail; **happy Christmas!** joyeux Noël!; **happy New Year!** bonne année!; **happy birthday!** joyeux anniversaire!

harbour *noun* le port

hard
1 *adjective*
(a) *(solid)* dur/dure; **this chair is too hard** cette chaise est trop dure; **a hard disk** un disque dur
(b) *(difficult)* dur/dure, difficile; **the exam was very hard** l'examen était très difficile
2 *adverb* **to work hard** travailler dur; **I tried hard** j'ai fait beaucoup d'efforts

hardback *noun* le livre relié; **she only buys hardbacks** elle n'achète que des livres reliés

hard-boiled *noun* **a hard-boiled egg** un œuf dur

hardly *adverb* à peine; **I'd hardly arrived when...** j'étais à peine arrivé quand...; **you've hardly eaten anything** tu n'as presque rien mangé; **hardly anyone** presque personne

hardware *noun* *(of a computer)* le matériel

hard-working *adjective* travailleur/travailleuse

hare *noun* le lièvre

harm
1 *noun* le mal; **to do somebody harm** faire du mal à quelqu'un; **there's no harm in trying** ça ne coûte rien d'essayer
2 *verb* **to harm somebody** faire du mal à quelqu'un

harmful *adjective*
(a) *(chemical)* nocif/nocive
(b) *(medicine)* dangereux/dangereuse
(c) *(insect)* nuisible

harmless *adjective* inoffensif/inoffensive

harmonica *noun* un harmonica; **to play the harmonica** jouer de l'harmonica

harp *noun* la harpe; **to play the harp** jouer de la harpe

harsh *adjective*
(a) *(person, tone, treatment)* dur/dure
(b) *(climate)* rude
(c) *(rules)* sévère

harvest
1 *noun*
(a) *(of crops)* la moisson
(b) *(of fruit)* la récolte
(c) *(of grapes)* la vendange
2 *verb*
(a) *(crops)* moissonner
(b) *(fruit)* récolter
(c) *(grapes)* vendanger

hat *noun* le chapeau; *(woolly)* le bonnet

The plural of *chapeau* is *chapeaux*.

hatch *verb* *(of a chick, an egg)* éclore

hate *verb* détester; **I hate cheese** je déteste le fromage; **she hates getting up early** elle déteste se lever de bonne heure

haunted *adjective* hanté/hantée; **a haunted house** une maison hantée

have
1 *verb*
(a) *(own)* avoir; **I have two brothers**

j'ai deux frères; **they have a big house** ils ont une grande maison; **we don't have a car** nous n'avons pas de voiture; **do you have a computer?** est-ce que tu as un ordinateur?

(**b**) *(with illnesses)* **I have a cold** je suis enrhumé/enrhumée; **she has the flu** elle a la grippe; **she has measles** elle a la rougeole

(**c**) *(with an activity)* **she's having a shower** elle prend une douche; **we have lunch at one o'clock** nous déjeunons à une heure; **I'll have a glass of wine** je vais prendre un verre de vin; **she had a nice time** elle s'est bien amusée

(**d**) *(with an obligation)* **to have to do something** devoir faire quelque chose; **I have to go** je dois partir; **you don't have to come with me** tu n'es pas obligé de m'accompagner

(**e**) **to have something done** faire faire quelque chose; **I had the cable installed** j'ai fait installer le câble; **I had my hair cut** je me suis fait couper les cheveux

2 *auxiliary verb*

(**a**) *(with the perfect or pluperfect tense)* **I've read that book** j'ai lu ce livre; **she's left already** elle est déjà partie; **I had forgotten** j'avais oublié; **have you seen him today?** est-ce que tu l'as vu aujourd'hui?; **I've been studying French for two years** j'étudie le français depuis deux ans; **I had been living in York for two years** j'habitais York depuis deux ans; **we've seen this film already – no we haven't!** nous avons déjà vu ce film – mais non!

(**b**) *(in questions and answers)* **he's finished, hasn't he?** il a terminé, n'est-ce pas? *or* il a terminé, non?; **he hasn't phoned, has he?** est-ce qu'il a téléphoné?

hawk *noun* le faucon

hay *noun* le foin; **hay fever** le rhume des foins; **I have hay fever** j'ai le rhume des foins

hazelnut *noun* la noisette

he *pronoun* il; **he's very nice** il est très sympa; **he's a teacher** il est professeur; **he and I** lui et moi; **he and I are both Scottish** lui et moi sommes écossais

head *noun*

(**a**) *(of a person, an animal)* la tête; **I have a sore head** j'ai mal à la tête

(**b**) *(leader)* le chef; **he's the head of the department** c'est le chef du service

(**c**) *(of a school)* le directeur/la directrice

headache *noun* **I have a headache** j'ai mal à la tête

headlight *noun* le phare

headline *noun* le titre

headmaster *noun* le directeur d'école; **he's a headmaster** il est directeur d'école; **he was sent to the headmaster** il a été envoyé chez le directeur

headmistress *noun* la directrice; **she's a headmistress** elle est directrice d'école; **he was sent to the headmistress** il a été envoyé chez la directrice

headphones *plural noun* les écouteurs *(masculine plural)*

headscarf *noun* le foulard

heal *verb*
(**a**) *(of a wound)* cicatriser
(**b**) *(of a bruise, a scratch)* disparaître

health *noun* la santé; **I'm in good health** je suis en bonne santé

healthy *adjective*
(**a**) *(person)* en bonne santé
(**b**) *(food, body, life)* sain/saine

heap *noun* le tas; **a heap of clothes** un tas de vêtements; **the papers were in a heap** les papiers formaient un tas

hear *verb* entendre; **I can't hear you** je ne t'entends pas; **did you hear a noise?** est-ce que tu as entendu un bruit?; **I heard him come in** je l'ai entendu entrer; **have you heard the news?**

est-ce que tu as appris la nouvelle?; **I've never heard of him** je n'ai jamais entendu parler de lui; **I heard from him last week** j'ai eu de ses nouvelles la semaine dernière

heart *noun*
(a) le cœur; **a heart attack** une crise cardiaque; **to learn something by heart** apprendre quelque chose par cœur; **I know the words by heart** je connais les paroles par cœur
(b) *(in cards)* **hearts** cœur *(masculine)*; **the ace of hearts** l'as de cœur

heartbeat *noun* *(rhythm)* le pouls; *(single beat)* le battement de cœur

heartbroken *adjective* **she's heartbroken** elle a le cœur brisé

heat
1 *noun* la chaleur; **a heat wave** une vague de chaleur
2 *verb* chauffer; **heat the milk in a saucepan** faites chauffer le lait dans une casserole
3 **heat up** faire chauffer; **heat it up in the microwave** fais-le chauffer au micro-ondes

heater *noun* le radiateur; **can you turn the heater on?** est-ce que tu peux allumer le radiateur?

heating *noun* le chauffage; **he turned the heating off** il a éteint le chauffage

heaven *noun* le paradis

heavy *adjective*
(a) *(in weight)* lourd/lourde; **my suitcase is heavy** ma valise est lourde
(b) *(coat, shoes)* gros/grosse; **it's cold outside, wear your heavy coat** il fait froid dehors, mets ton gros manteau
(c) *(rain)* fort/forte

Hebrew *noun* *(language)* l'hébreu *(masculine)*; **he speaks Hebrew** il parle hébreu

hedge *noun* la haie

hedgehog *noun* le hérisson

heel *noun* le talon; **she wears high heels** elle porte des talons hauts

height *noun*
(a) *(of a wall, a tree, a building)* la hauteur
(b) *(of a person)* la taille; **what height are you?** combien mesures-tu?
(c) *(of a plane, a mountain)* l'altitude *(feminine)*

heir *noun* un héritier/une héritière

helicopter *noun* l'hélicoptère *(masculine)*

hell *noun* l'enfer *(masculine)*

hello *exclamation* bonjour; *(when answering the phone)* allô; **he said hello to me** il m'a dit bonjour

helmet *noun* le casque

help
1 *noun* l'aide *(feminine)*; **do you need some help?** est-ce que tu as besoin d'aide?
2 *verb*
(a) aider; **he helped me with my homework** il m'a aidé à faire mes devoirs; **I'll help you wash the windows** je t'aiderai à laver les carreaux; **help yourself!** sers-toi!; **help yourself to chips** sers-toi des frites
(b) **I couldn't help laughing** je ne pouvais pas m'empêcher de rire; **I can't help it** je n'y peux rien

helpful *adjective*
(a) *(person)* serviable; **she's always very helpful** elle est toujours très serviable
(b) *(object)* utile

helping *noun* la portion; **have another helping of pasta** reprends des pâtes; **can I have a second helping?** est-ce que je peux en reprendre?

helpless *adjective* impuissant/impuissante

hen *noun* la poule

her
1 *pronoun*
(a) la; **I see her** je la vois; **I saw her** je l'ai vue

In French *la* becomes *l'* in front of a vowel or a mute h.

(**b**) *(after a preposition or the verb "to be")* elle; **it's her** c'est elle; **in front of her** devant elle

(**c**) *(indirect)* lui; **give her the newspaper** donne-lui le journal; **I'll give it to her** je le lui donnerai

2 *adjective*

(**a**) *(when the thing possessed is masculine singular in French)* son; **this is her pen** c'est son stylo

(**b**) *(when the thing possessed is feminine singular in French)* sa; **this is her cup** c'est sa tasse; **her school** son école; **her story** son histoire

Note that *sa* becomes *son* before a vowel or mute h.

(**c**) *(when the thing possessed is plural in French)* ses; **these are her books** ce sont ses livres; **these are her glasses** ce sont ses lunettes

(**d**) *(when used with parts of the body)* **she's brushing her teeth** elle se brosse les dents; **she broke her leg** elle s'est cassé la jambe

The form used in French is determined by the gender and number of the noun that follows.

herb *noun* une herbe aromatique

herbal *adjective* à base de plantes; **herbal tea** la tisane

herd *noun* le troupeau; **a herd of cattle** un troupeau de bovins

The plural of *troupeau* is *troupeaux*.

here *adverb*

(**a**) ici; **come here** viens ici; **over here** par ici; **she's not here** elle n'est pas là

(**b**) **here's my house** voici ma maison; **here are my pencils** voici mes crayons; **here I am** me voici

hero *noun* le héros

heroine *noun* l'héroïne *(feminine)*

hers *pronoun*

(**a**) *(when the thing possessed is mascu-*

line singular in French) le sien; **it's not your pen, it's hers** ce n'est pas ton stylo, c'est le sien; **this pen is hers** ce stylo est à elle

(**b**) *(when the thing possessed is feminine singular in French)* la sienne; **it's not my cup, it's hers** ce n'est pas ma tasse, c'est la sienne; **this cup is hers** cette tasse est à elle

(**c**) *(when the thing possessed is masculine plural in French)* les siens; **these are not your books, they're hers** ce ne sont pas tes livres, ce sont les siens; **these books are hers** ces livres sont à elle

(**d**) *(when the thing possessed is feminine plural in French)* les siennes; **these are not your glasses, they're hers** ce ne sont pas tes lunettes, ce sont les siennes; **these glasses are hers** ces lunettes sont à elle

The form used in French is determined by the gender and number of the noun it stands for.

herself *pronoun*

(**a**) elle-même; **she did it herself** elle l'a fait elle-même

(**b**) *(with a reflexive verb)* se; **she spoils herself** elle se gâte; **she hurt herself** elle s'est blessée

In French *se* becomes *s'* in front of a vowel or a mute h.

(**c**) *(after a preposition)* elle; **she thinks only of herself** elle ne pense qu'à elle

hesitate *verb* hésiter; **don't hesitate to ask me** n'hésite pas à me demander

hesitation *noun* l'hésitation *(feminine)*

hi *exclamation* salut

hiccup *noun* le hoquet; **I have (the) hiccups** j'ai le hoquet

hide *verb*

(**a**) *(somebody, something)* cacher; **he's hidden my keys** il a caché mes clés

(b) *(oneself)* se cacher; **he was hiding in the wardrobe** il se cachait dans l'armoire

hide-and-seek *noun* le jeu de cache-cache; **the children are playing hide-and-seek** les enfants jouent à cache-cache

hiding place *noun* la cachette

hi-fi *noun* la chaîne hi-fi

high *adjective*
(a) *(tree, mountain, building)* haut/haute; **the building is 20 metres high** le bâtiment fait 20 mètres de haut; **how high is the Eiffel Tower?** combien mesure la tour Eiffel?; **the high jump** le saut en hauteur
(b) *(price, level, number)* élevé/élevée; **at high speed** à grande vitesse
(c) *(voice, tone)* aigu/aiguë
(d) **to have a high temperature** avoir beaucoup de température

higher *adjective*
(a) *(number, quality)* supérieur/supérieure; **higher education** l'enseignement supérieur *(masculine)*
(b) plus haut/haute; **it's higher than the Eiffel Tower** c'est plus haut que la tour Eiffel

highlight
1 *noun*
(a) *(best part)* le meilleur moment; **the highlight of the holiday was when we went jet-skiing** le meilleur moment des vacances, c'est quand on est allé faire du scooter des mers
(b) *(in hair)* **highlights** les mèches *(feminine plural)*; **she has blonde highlights** elle a des mèches blondes
2 *verb (with a highlighter pen)* surligner; *(on a computer)* sélectionner

highlighter *noun (pen)* le surligneur

high-tech *adjective* de pointe; **a high-tech industry** une industrie de pointe

hijack *verb* détourner; **a plane was hijacked yesterday** un avion a été détourné hier

hike
1 *noun* la randonnée; **we went on a hike** nous avons fait une randonnée
2 *verb* faire de la randonnée

hiking *noun* la randonnée; **to go hiking** faire de la randonnée

hilarious *adjective* hilarant/hilarante; **theTV programme is hilarious** l'émission est hilarante

hill *noun* la colline; **we live at the top of the hill** nous habitons en haut de la colline; **I climbed the hill** j'ai grimpé la colline

him *pronoun*
(a) le; **I see him** je le vois; **I saw him** je l'ai vu

> In French *le* becomes *l'* in front of a vowel or a mute h.

(b) *(after a preposition or the verb "to be")* lui; **it's him** c'est lui; **in front of him** devant lui
(c) *(indirect)* lui; **give him the newspaper** donne-lui le journal; **I'll give it to him** je le lui donnerai

himself *pronoun*
(a) lui-même; **he did it himself** il l'a fait lui-même
(b) *(with a reflexive verb)* se; **he spoils himself** il se gâte; **he hurt himself** il s'est blessé

> In French *se* becomes *s'* in front of a vowel or a mute h.

(c) *(after a preposition)* lui; **he thinks only of himself** il ne pense qu'à lui

Hindu
1 *noun (person)* un Hindou/une Hindoue
2 *adjective* hindou/hindoue

hip *noun* la hanche

hippopotamus *noun* l'hippopotame *(masculine)*

hire
1 *noun* la location; **for hire** à louer
2 *verb* louer; **we hired a car** nous avons loué une voiture

his

1 *adjective*

(**a**) *(when the thing possessed is masculine singular in French)* son; **this is his pen** c'est son stylo

(**b**) *(when the thing possessed is feminine singular in French)* sa; **this is his cup** c'est sa tasse; **his school** son école; **his story** son histoire

> Note that *sa* becomes *son* before a vowel or mute h.

(**c**) *(when the thing possessed is plural in French)* ses; **these are his books** ce sont ses livres; **these are his glasses** ce sont ses lunettes

(**d**) *(when used with parts of the body)* **he's brushing his teeth** il se brosse les dents; **he broke his leg** il s'est cassé la jambe

> The form used in French is determined by the gender and number of the noun that follows.

2 *pronoun*

(**a**) *(when the thing possessed is masculine singular in French)* le sien; **it's not your pen, it's his** ce n'est pas ton stylo, c'est le sien; **this pen is his** ce stylo est à lui

(**b**) *(when the thing possessed is feminine singular in French)* la sienne; **it's not my cup, it's his** ce n'est pas ma tasse, c'est la sienne; **this cup is his** cette tasse est à lui

(**c**) *(when the thing possessed is masculine plural in French)* les siens; **these are not your books, they're his** ce ne sont pas tes livres, ce sont les siens; **these books are his** ces livres sont à lui

(**d**) *(when the thing possessed is feminine plural in French)* les siennes; **these are not your glasses, they're his** ce ne sont pas tes lunettes, ce sont les siennes; **these glasses are his** ces lunettes sont à lui

> The form used in French is determined by the gender and number of the noun it stands for.

historical *adjective* historique

history *noun* l'histoire *(feminine)*; **English history** l'histoire de l'Angleterre; **a history book** un livre d'histoire; **my history teacher** mon professeur d'histoire

hit *verb* frapper; **he's always hitting his brother** il est toujours en train de frapper son frère; **the car hit the wall** la voiture a heurté le mur; **I hit my head on the door** je me suis cogné la tête contre la porte; **the bullet hit him in the leg** la balle l'a atteint à la jambe

hitchhike *verb* faire de l'auto-stop; **she hitchhiked to Paris** elle est allée à Paris en auto-stop

hitchhiker *noun* un auto-stoppeur/ une auto-stoppeuse

hive *noun* la ruche

hoarse *adjective* enroué/enrouée

hobby *noun* le passe-temps; **my hobbies are swimming and playing football** mes passe-temps sont la natation et le football; **what's your favourite hobby?** quel est ton passe-temps préféré?

> The word *passe-temps* does not change in the plural.

hockey *noun* le hockey sur gazon; **to play hockey** jouer au hockey sur gazon; **a hockey stick** une crosse de hockey sur gazon

hold

1 *noun* **to get hold of somebody** *(grab)* saisir quelqu'un; *(find)* trouver quelqu'un; **she got hold of my arm** elle m'a saisi le bras; **this book is difficult to get hold of** ce livre est difficile à trouver

2 *verb*

(**a**) *(grip)* tenir; **she held my hand** elle me tenait la main; **I was holding my keys** je tenais mes clés; **they were holding hands** ils se donnaient la main; **she was holding the child by the hand** elle tenait l'enfant par la main (**b**) *(contain)* contenir; **the bottle holds two litres** la bouteille contient deux litres

(**c**) *(a party, an exhibition)* organiser; **we hold a weekly meeting** nous nous réunissons une fois par semaine

(**d**) **to hold one's breath** retenir son souffle

3 hold on

(**a**) *(wait)* attendre; **hold on a minute!** attends une minute!

(**b**) *(grip tightly)* **to hold on to something** se tenir à quelque chose; **hold on to the railing and you won't fall** tiens-toi à la rampe pour ne pas tomber; **hold on!** tenez bon!

(**c**) *(keep)* **to hold on to something** garder quelque chose; **can you hold on to my ticket?** est-ce que tu peux garder mon ticket?

4 hold out tendre; **he held out his hand** il a tendu la main

5 hold up

(**a**) *(raise)* lever; **he held up his hand** il a levé la main

(**b**) *(make late)* retarder; **sorry, I got held up** excusez-moi, j'ai été retardé

(**c**) *(support)* soutenir; **the beam holds the ceiling up** la poutre soutient le plafond

(**d**) *(rob)* attaquer; **they held up a bank** ils ont attaqué une banque

hold-up *noun*

(**a**) *(delay)* le retard

(**b**) *(traffic jam)* le bouchon, l'embouteillage *(masculine)*; **there was a hold-up on the motorway** il y avait un bouchon sur l'autoroute

(**c**) *(attack)* le hold-up; **there was a hold-up at the post office** il y a eu un hold-up au bureau de poste

In French the word *hold-up* does not change in the plural.

hole *noun* le trou; **my jumper has a hole in it** mon pull a un trou

holiday *noun*

(**a**) **holiday** or **holidays** les vacances *(feminine plural)*; **I'm on holiday** je

suis en vacances; **we go on holiday tomorrow** nous partons en vacances demain; **the school holidays** les vacances scolaires

(**b**) *(day off work)* le congé; **I've only got five days' holiday left this year** il me reste que cinq jours de congé cette année

(**c**) *(public holiday)* le jour férié; **Easter Monday is a holiday** le lundi de Pâques est férié

Holland *noun* la Hollande; **she lives in Holland** elle habite en Hollande; **we're going to Holland** nous allons en Hollande; **he's from Holland** il est hollandais

hollow *adjective* creux/creuse

holly *noun* le houx

Note that the *x* in *houx* is not pronounced.

holy *adjective* saint/sainte

home

1 *noun*

(**a**) *(house)* la maison; **she left home when she was 17** elle a quitté la maison à 17 ans; **my home town** ma ville natale

(**b**) *(country)* la patrie; **France will always be my home** la France sera toujours ma patrie

2 *adverb* à la maison; **I'm going home** je rentre (à la maison); **she's at home** elle est à la maison; **it's good to be home** c'est bon d'être chez soi

homeless *adjective* **to be homeless** être sans abri; **a homeless man** un sans-abri; **the homeless** les sans-abri *(masculine plural)*

home-made *adjective* fait maison/ faite maison; **a home-made cake** un gâteau fait maison

homesick *adjective* **to be homesick** avoir le mal du pays

homework *noun* les devoirs *(masculine plural)*; **she's doing her homework** elle fait ses devoirs

homosexual
1 *adjective* homosexuel/homosexuelle
2 *noun* un homosexuel/une homosexuelle

honest *adjective* honnête; **to be honest, I wasn't expecting this** pour être honnête, je ne m'attendais pas à ça; **are you being honest?** est-ce que tu es sincère?

honestly *adverb* honnêtement; **honestly, it wasn't me!** je te le jure, ce n'était pas moi!

honesty *noun* l'honnêteté *(feminine)*

honey *noun* le miel

honeymoon *noun* le voyage de noces; **they're on honeymoon** ils sont en voyage de noces

honk *verb (in car)* klaxonner

honour *noun* l'honneur *(masculine)*

hood *noun (of coat)* la capuche

hoof *noun* le sabot

hook *noun*
(a) *(in general)* le crochet
(b) *(on clothes)* une agrafe
(c) *(to catch fish)* un hameçon
(d) **she left the phone off the hook** elle a laissé le téléphone décroché

hooligan *noun* le hooligan

hoover®
1 *noun* un aspirateur
2 *verb* passer l'aspirateur; **can you hoover your bedroom?** est-ce que tu peux passer l'aspirateur dans ta chambre?

hop *verb* sauter à cloche-pied

hope
1 *noun* l'espoir *(masculine)*
2 *verb* espérer; **I hope he calls me** j'espère qu'il va m'appeler; **I hope to go to France next year** j'espère aller en France l'année prochaine; **I hope I'll see her at the party** j'espère que je la verrai à la fête; **I hope so** j'espère que oui; **I hope not** j'espère que non

hopeful *adjective*
(a) *(person)* optimiste

(b) *(situation, news)* encourageant/encourageante

hopefully *adverb*
(a) **I'll hopefully see him tonight** j'espère le voir ce soir
(b) *(in a state of hope)* plein d'espoir/pleine d'espoir; **he was waiting hopefully at the door** il attendait à la porte, plein d'espoir

hopeless *adjective*
(a) *(without hope)* désespéré/désespérée; **a hopeless situation** une situation désespérée
(b) *(very bad)* nul/nulle; **I'm hopeless at maths** je suis nul en maths

horizon *noun* l'horizon *(masculine)*; **on the horizon** à l'horizon

horizontal *adjective* horizontal/horizontale

> The masculine plural of *horizontal* is *horizontaux*.

horn *noun*
(a) *(on an animal)* la corne
(b) *(in a car)* le klaxon®

horoscope *noun* un horoscope

horrible *adjective* horrible; **a horrible jumper** un pull horrible; **to be horrible to somebody** être horrible avec quelqu'un; **it's a horrible day** il fait un temps épouvantable

horror *noun* l'horreur *(feminine)*; **a horror film** un film d'horreur

horse *noun* le cheval

> The plural of *cheval* is *chevaux*.

horseback *noun* **on horseback** à cheval

horseracing *noun* les courses de chevaux *(feminine plural)*

horseriding *noun* l'équitation *(feminine)*; **I go horseriding** je fais de l'équitation

hose
1 *noun*
(a) *(of a fireman)* le tuyau

(**b**) *(for watering)* le tuyau d'arrosage

> The plural of *tuyau* is *tuyaux*.

2 *verb (a garden, plants)* arroser

hosepipe *noun* le tuyau d'arrosage

hospital *noun* un hôpital; **he's in hospital** il est à l'hôpital

> The plural of *hôpital* is *hôpitaux*.

host *noun* un hôte

hostage *noun* un otage; **he was taken hostage** on l'a pris en otage

hostess *noun* une hôtesse

hot *adjective*
(**a**) *(weather, water, food)* chaud/ chaude; **I'm hot** j'ai chaud; **it's hot today** il fait chaud aujourd'hui; **a hot dog** un hot dog
(**b**) *(pepper, curry)* épicé/épicée; **I like hot food** j'aime manger épicé *or* j'aime la nourriture épicée

hotel *noun* un hôtel; **we stayed in a hotel** nous avons dormi à l'hôtel; **a hotel room** une chambre d'hôtel

hour *noun* une heure; **an hour and a half** une heure et demie; **I spent two hours on my homework** j'ai passé deux heures sur mes devoirs; **£15 an hour** 15 livres de l'heure

house *noun* la maison; **she's coming to my house** elle vient chez moi; **they live in a big house** ils habitent une grande maison

household *noun* le ménage; **95 per cent of households have a television set** 95 pour cent des ménages possèdent un poste de télévision

housewife *noun* la femme au foyer; **my mum's a housewife** ma mère est femme au foyer

housework *noun* le ménage; **he's doing the housework** il fait le ménage

housing estate *noun* le lotissement; *(council-owned)* la cité HLM

hovercraft *noun* un aéroglisseur

how *adverb*
(**a**) comment; **how are you?** comment vas-tu?; **how was your holiday?** comment se sont passées tes vacances?; **how do you get to the station from here?** comment est-ce qu'on va à la gare à partir d'ici?; **how about pizza for dinner?** ça te dirait une pizza pour le dîner?; **I don't know how to do it** je ne sais pas comment faire; **how old are you?** quel âge as-tu?; **how tall are you?** combien est-ce que tu mesures?; **how long does it take to drive to London?** ça prend combien de temps pour aller à Londres en voiture?
(**b**) **how much?** combien?; **how much time have we got?** on a combien de temps?; **how much does it cost?** ça coûte combien?
(**c**) **how many?** combien?; **how many students?** combien d'étudiants?
(**d**) **how kind of you!** comme c'est gentil de ta part!; **how incredible!** c'est incroyable!

however *conjunction* cependant; **however, I don't entirely agree with him** cependant, je ne suis pas entièrement d'accord avec lui

howl *verb* hurler

hug
1 *noun* **to give somebody a hug** serrer quelqu'un dans ses bras
2 *verb* serrer dans ses bras; **he hugged me** il m'a serré dans ses bras

huge *adjective* énorme, immense; **they live in a huge house** ils habitent dans une maison immense

hum *verb*
(**a**) *(of a person)* fredonner; **she was humming a tune** elle fredonnait un air
(**b**) *(of an engine, a fridge)* ronronner

human
1 *noun* un humain
2 *adjective* humain/humaine; **a human being** un être humain

humid *adjective* humide; **it's very humid outside** c'est très humide dehors

humour *noun* l'humour *(masculine)*; **he has a good sense of humour** il a le sens de l'humour

hump *noun* la bosse

hundred *number* a hundred cent; **a hundred and one** cent un; **a hundred metres** cent mètres; **two hundred metres** deux cents mètres; **two hundred and fifty metres** deux cent cinquante mètres; **hundreds of books** des centaines de livres; **a hundred percent** cent pour cent; **about a hundred** une centaine; **about a hundred pounds** une centaine de livres

hundredth *number* centième; **one hundredth** un centième

Hungarian
1 *adjective* hongrois/hongroise
2 *noun*
(a) *(language)* le hongrois; **she speaks Hungarian** elle parle hongrois
(b) *(person)* le Hongrois/la Hongroise; **the Hungarians** les Hongrois *(masculine plural)*

In French, only the noun for the inhabitants of a country takes a capital letter, never the adjective or the noun for the language.

Hungary *noun* la Hongrie; **he lives in Hungary** il habite en Hongrie; **we're going to Hungary** nous allons en Hongrie; **her mother comes from Hungary** sa mère est hongroise

hunger *noun* la faim

hungry *adjective* **to be hungry** avoir faim; **I'm very hungry** j'ai très faim

hunt *verb*
(a) *(an animal)* chasser; **to go hunting** aller à la chasse
(b) *(look for)* **to hunt for something** chercher quelque chose; **I hunted everywhere for my keys** j'ai cherché mes clés partout

hunter *noun* le chasseur/la chasseuse

hurricane *noun* un ouragan

hurry
1 *noun* **to be in a hurry** être pressé/pressée; **she's in a hurry** elle est pressée; **to do something in a hurry** faire quelque chose en vitesse; **I did my homework in a hurry** j'ai fait mes devoirs en vitesse; **there's no hurry** rien ne presse
2 *verb* se dépêcher; **hurry, we're going to be late!** dépêche-toi, on va être en retard!; **she hurried out** elle s'est dépêchée de sortir
3 hurry up se dépêcher; **hurry up!** dépêche-toi!

hurt
1 *verb*
(a) *(causing pain)* **my foot hurts** j'ai mal au pied; **her head hurts** elle a mal à la tête
(b) *(injure)* **no one got hurt in the accident** personne n'a été blessé dans l'accident; **did you hurt yourself?** tu t'es fait mal?; **I hurt myself when I fell** je me suis fait mal en tombant; **I hurt my elbow on the door** je me suis fait mal au coude contre la porte
(c) *(of words)* blesser; **you really hurt her when you said that** tu l'as vraiment blessée en lui disant ça
2 *adjective* blessé/blessée; **are you hurt?** est-ce que tu es blessé?; **she's badly hurt** elle est grièvement blessée; **she's hurt that you didn't tell her** elle est blessée parce que tu ne le lui as pas dit

husband *noun* le mari

hut *noun* la cabane

hygiene *noun* l'hygiène *(feminine)*

hygienic *adjective* hygiénique

hypermarket *noun* un hypermarché

hyphen *noun* le trait d'union

hypocrite *noun* un/une hypocrite

I *pronoun* je; **I'm called Ellen** je m'appelle Ellen; **I'm English** je suis anglais/anglaise; **I'm 13 years old** j'ai 13 ans; **he and I** lui et moi; **he and I went shopping** lui et moi sommes allés faire des courses

ice *noun* la glace; *(on the road)* le verglas; **an orange juice with ice** un jus d'orange avec des glaçons; **an ice cube** un glaçon; **ice hockey** le hockey sur glace; **an ice rink** une patinoire; **an ice skate** un patin à glace

iceberg *noun* un iceberg

ice-cold *adjective* glacé/glacée

ice-cream *noun* la glace; **I like chocolate ice-cream** j'aime la glace au chocolat

Iceland *noun* l'Islande *(feminine)* ; **she lives in Iceland** elle habite en Islande; **we're going to Iceland** nous allons en Islande; **her grandmother comes from Iceland** sa grand-mère est islandaise

Icelander *noun* un Islandais/une Islandaise

Icelandic
1 *adjective* islandais/islandaise
2 *noun (language)* l'islandais *(masculine)*; **she speaks Icelandic** elle parle islandais

In French, only the noun for the inhabitants of a country takes a capital letter, never the adjective or the noun for the language.

ice-skate *verb* faire du patin à glace

ice-skating *noun* le patin à glace; **I'm** going **ice-skating tomorrow** je vais faire du patin à glace demain

icicle *noun* le glaçon

icing *noun* le glaçage; **icing sugar** le sucre glace

icon *noun* une icône; **double-click on the icon** cliquez deux fois sur l'icône

icy *adjective (ice-cold)* glacé/glacée; *(weather)* glacial/glaciale; **the roads are icy** il y a du verglas sur les routes

ID *noun* la pièce d'identité; **do you have any ID?** est-ce que vous avez une pièce d'identité?; **an ID card** une carte d'identité

idea *noun* une idée; **that's a good idea** c'est une bonne idée; **I've got an idea** j'ai une idée; **(I've) no idea!** (je n'en ai) aucune idée!

ideal *adjective* idéal/idéale; **that scarf would be an ideal present** cette écharpe serait un cadeau idéal

identical *adjective* identique; **his car is almost identical to mine** sa voiture est presque identique à la mienne; **they're identical twins** *(boys)* ce sont de vrais jumeaux; *(girls)* ce sont de vraies jumelles

identification *noun* la pièce d'identité; **do you have any identification?** est-ce que vous avez une pièce d'identité?

identify *verb* identifier

identity *noun* l'identité *(feminine)*; **his identity hasn't been confirmed** son identité n'a pas été confirmée; **an identity card** une carte d'identité

idiot *noun* un idiot/une idiote; **you idiot!** espèce d'idiot/d'idiote!

if *conjunction* si; **if he's late** s'il est en retard; **if I were rich** si j'étais riche; **if I had any money I'd lend you some** si j'avais de l'argent je t'en prêterais; **if not** sinon; **I'll be there at five, if not before** j'y serai à cinq heures, si ce n'est avant; **if only I'd stayed at home!** si seulement j'étais resté chez moi!; **if I were you I wouldn't go** à ta place je n'irais pas

ignore *verb* **to ignore somebody** ignorer quelqu'un; **she ignored me but I know she saw me** elle m'a ignoré mais je sais qu'elle m'a vu; **to ignore something** ne tenir aucun compte de quelque chose; **he ignored my warning** il n'a pas tenu compte de mon avertissement *or* il a ignoré mon avertissement

ill *adjective*
(a) *(sick)* malade; **I feel ill** je me sens malade; **to be taken ill** tomber malade; **he's seriously ill** il est gravement malade
(b) *(bad)* **his comments caused some ill feeling among the staff** ses commentaires ont provoqué des ressentiments parmi le personnel

illegal *adjective* illégal/illégale; **it's illegal to park there** c'est illégal de se garer à cet endroit

illness *noun* la maladie; **he has a serious illness** il a une maladie grave

illustration *noun* une illustration

image *noun* une image; **she's changed her image** elle a changé d'image

imagination *noun* l'imagination *(feminine)*; **it's all in your imagination!** tu te fais des idées!

imagine *verb* imaginer; **I imagine he'll be at the meeting** j'imagine qu'il sera à la réunion; **I can't imagine why he said that** je n'arrive pas à comprendre pourquoi il a dit ça; **you're imagining things!** tu te fais des idées!

imitate *verb* imiter

imitation *noun* une imitation

immediate *adjective* immédiat/immédiate

immediately *adverb* tout de suite, immédiatement; **I want to see him immediately** je veux le voir tout de suite

immigrant *noun* un immigré/une immigrée

impatient *adjective* impatient/impatiente; **I'm getting impatient** je m'impatiente

import
1 *noun* une importation
2 *verb* importer

importance *noun* l'importance *(feminine)*

important *adjective* important/importante; **it's not important** ce n'est pas important; **it's important to her** c'est important pour elle

impossible *adjective* impossible; **it's impossible for me to come** il m'est impossible de venir

impression *noun* une impression; **she made a good impression** elle a fait bonne impression; **he made a bad impression on me** il m'a fait mauvaise impression

impressive *adjective* impressionnant/impressionnante; **her exam results are impressive** ses résultats aux examens sont vraiment impressionnants

improve *verb* améliorer; **I want to improve my French** je veux améliorer mon français; **her French has improved** elle a fait des progrès en français; **the weather has improved** le temps s'est amélioré

improvement *noun* une amélioration; **there's been no improvement** il n'y a pas eu d'amélioration; **they made an improvement to the system** ils ont amélioré le système

in *preposition*
(**a**) *(with a place)* **in the garden** dans le jardin; **in the book** dans le livre; **in London** à Londres; **in France** en France; **in Japan** au Japon; **in the USA** aux États-Unis; **in hospital** à l'hôpital; **in bed** au lit; **in here** ici; **in there** là-dedans
(**b**) *(with time)* en; **in 1985** en 1985; **in April** en avril; **in the 1990s** dans les années 90; **I'll see you in an hour** je te vois dans une heure; **I did it in an hour** je l'ai fait en une heure; **in the morning** le matin; **in the evening** le soir
(**c**) *(indicating how something is done)* **in French** en français; **in pencil** au crayon
(**d**) *(with numbers, quantities)* **one in ten** un sur dix; **in tens** dix par dix

inch *noun* le pouce; **she is five feet eight inches tall** elle mesure 1 mètre 73

Note that people in France don't use inches as a unit of measurement, they use centimetres (1 inch = 2.54 centimetres).

include *verb* comprendre; **the price includes accommodation** le logement est compris dans le prix; **service is included** le service est compris

including *preposition* y compris; **seven including the children** sept y compris les enfants; **four not including me** quatre sans me compter

income *noun* le revenu; **income tax** l'impôt sur le revenu *(masculine)*

inconvenient *adjective* **to be inconvenient for somebody** déranger quelqu'un; **if it's inconvenient** si ça vous dérange

incorrect *adjective (number, result, answer)* faux/fausse; **you're incorrect** *(you're mistaken)* tu te trompes; *(you've given the wrong answer)* tu as faux

increase
1 *noun* l'augmentation *(feminine)*; **an**

increase in crime une augmentation de la criminalité
2 *verb* augmenter; **to increase in price** augmenter; **petrol has increased in price** l'essence a augmenté

incredible *adjective* incroyable

indeed *adverb*
(**a**) *(certainly)* en effet; **it's getting late – it is indeed** il se fait tard – en effet; **are you going to the party? – I am indeed** est-ce que tu vas à la fête? – oui, j'y vais
(**b**) *(used for emphasis)* vraiment; **very big indeed** vraiment très grand; **thank you very much indeed** merci infiniment

independence *noun* l'indépendance *(feminine)*

Do not confuse the spellings of the French *indépendance* and English *independence*.

independent *adjective* indépendant/indépendante

Do not confuse the spellings of the French *indépendant* and English *independent*.

index *noun* l'index *(masculine)*; **the index finger** l'index

India *noun* l'Inde *(feminine)*; **they live in India** ils habitent en Inde; **I'm going to India next year** je vais en Inde l'année prochaine; **her grandfather comes from India** son grand-père est indien

Indian
1 *adjective* indien/indienne
2 *noun (person)* un Indien/une Indienne; **the Indians** les Indiens *(masculine plural)*

In French, only the noun for the inhabitants of a country takes a capital letter, never the adjective.

indicate *verb* indiquer; *(in a car)* mettre son clignotant; **indicate before you turn left** mets ton clignotant avant de tourner à gauche

indigestion *noun* l'indigestion *(feminine)*; **to have indigestion** avoir une indigestion

individual
1 *noun* un individu
2 *adjective*
(a) *(personal)* individuel/individuelle; **an individual portion** une portion individuelle
(b) *(particular)* particulier/particulière; **each individual case is different** chaque cas est différent

individually *adverb* individuellement; **I'll talk to you individually** je vous parlerai individuellement; **you can't buy them individually** ils ne se vendent pas à la pièce

indoor *adjective* **indoor games** les jeux d'intérieur *(masculine plural)*; **an indoor pool** une piscine couverte

indoors *adverb* à l'intérieur; **to go indoors** rentrer

industrial *adjective* industriel/industrielle; **an industrial estate** une zone industrielle

industry *noun* l'industrie *(feminine)*

infant *noun* *(baby)* le bébé; *(small child)* le petit/la petite enfant; **an infant school** une école pour les enfants de cinq à huit ans

infect *verb* infecter; **the wound became infected** la plaie s'est infectée

infection *noun* une infection; **a throat infection** une angine

infectious *adjective*
(a) *(disease)* infectieux/infectieuse
(b) *(person)* contagieux/contagieuse

infinitive *noun* l'infinitif *(masculine)*

infirmary *noun* un hôpital

The plural of *hôpital* is *hôpitaux*.

inflatable *adjective* gonflable; **an inflatable mattress** un matelas gonflable

influence
1 *noun* l'influence *(feminine)*; **he's a good influence on her** il a une bonne influence sur elle
2 *verb* influencer; **don't try to influence her** n'essaie pas de l'influencer

inform *verb* informer; **they informed us that they would be late** ils nous ont informés qu'ils seraient en retard

informal *adjective*
(a) *(relaxed)* décontracté/décontractée; **an informal chat** une conversation décontractée
(b) *(word, expression)* familier/familière

information *noun* les renseignements *(masculine plural)*; **a piece of information** un renseignement; **I need information on university courses** j'ai besoin de renseignements sur les cours de l'université

ingredient *noun* un ingrédient

inhabitant *noun* un habitant/une habitante

initials *plural noun* les initiales *(feminine plural)*

injection *noun* la piqûre; **to give somebody an injection** faire une piqûre à quelqu'un; **a tetanus injection** un vaccin contre le ténanos

injure *verb* blesser; **he's injured his leg** il s'est blessé à la jambe

Note that the French verb *injurier* is never a translation for the English verb *to injure*. It means *to insult, to abuse*.

injured
1 *adjective* blessé/blessée; **he's badly injured** il est grièvement blessé
2 *plural noun* **the injured** les blessés *(masculine plural)*

injury *noun* la blessure; **a head injury** une blessure à la tête

Note that the French word *injure* is never a translation for the English word *injury*. It means *insult*.

ink *noun* l'encre *(feminine)*; **an ink pen** un stylo à encre; **an ink stain** une tache d'encre

inn *noun* une auberge

innocent *adjective* innocent/innocente

inquire *verb*
(**a**) *(seek information)* se renseigner; **he inquired about the price** il s'est renseigné sur le prix
(**b**) *(ask)* demander; **he inquired what time the shop closed** il a demandé à quelle heure fermait le magasin

inquiry *noun*
(**a**) *(official investigation)* une enquête
(**b**) *(request for information)* la demande de renseignements; **I'll make inquiries** je vais me renseigner

insane *adjective* fou/folle

insect *noun* un insecte

inside
1 *adverb* à l'intérieur; **the children are playing inside** les enfants sont en train de jouer à l'intérieur; **come inside!** entrez!
2 *adjective* intérieur/intérieure; **the inside pocket** la poche intérieure
3 *noun* l'intérieur *(masculine)*; **on the inside** à l'intérieur; **the inside of the church is more interesting than the outside** l'intérieur de l'église est plus intéressant que l'extérieur; **inside out** à l'envers; **he put on his jacket inside out** il a mis sa veste à l'envers
4 *preposition* à l'intérieur de; **inside the car** à l'intérieur de la voiture

insist *verb* insister; **to insist on something** exiger quelque chose; **she's insisting on coming with us** elle insiste pour venir avec nous; **I insist that you come** je tiens à ce que tu viennes

inspect *verb* examiner; **they inspected our luggage** ils ont examiné nos bagages

inspector *noun* un inspecteur/une inspectrice; *(on a train)* le contrôleur/la contrôleuse

inspire *verb* inspirer

install *verb* installer

instant
1 *noun* un instant; **do it this instant!** fais-le tout de suite!
2 *adjective* immédiat/immédiate; **instant coffee** le café soluble

instantly *adverb* instantanément

instead *adverb*
(**a**) *(in place of something)* à la place; **I'll wear the black shoes instead of the brown ones** je mettrai les chaussures noires à la place des marron; **I don't want a sandwich, I'll have a salad instead** je ne veux pas de sandwich, je vais prendre une salade à la place
(**b**) *(in place of somebody)* **her son came instead of her** son fils est venu à sa place; **I'll be away so Julie will come instead** je ne serai pas là, Julie viendra donc à ma place
(**c**) **instead of going to the cinema, we went for a drink** au lieu d'aller au cinéma, nous sommes allés boire un verre; **we're going to Spain instead of Greece this year** cette année nous allons en Espagne au lieu d'aller en Grèce

instinct *noun* un instinct

In French, the *c* and *t* in *instinct* are not pronounced.

institution *noun* *(organization)* une institution; *(public, financial)* un établissement

instruct *verb* **to instruct somebody to do something** charger quelqu'un de faire quelque chose; **we have been instructed to accompany you** nous sommes chargés de vous accompagner; **we were instructed to wait outside** on nous a demandé d'attendre dehors

instructions *plural noun* *(orders)* les instructions *(feminine plural)*; *(for use)* le mode d'emploi; **read the instructions first** lisez le mode d'emploi d'abord

instructor *noun* le moniteur/la monitrice; **a ski instructor** un moniteur/une monitrice de ski; **he's a driving instructor** il est moniteur d'auto-école

Note that when describing people's jobs or situations, French does not use an article (*un* or *une*).

instrument *noun* un instrument; **do you play an instrument?** est-ce que tu joues d'un instrument?

Note that when talking about playing musical instruments, French uses the expression *jouer de*.

insult
1 *noun* une insulte
2 *verb* insulter

insurance *noun* l'assurance *(feminine)*; **to take out insurance** prendre une assurance; **an insurance policy** une police d'assurance

insure *verb* assurer; **her house isn't insured** sa maison n'est pas assurée

intellectual
1 *adjective* intellectuel/intellectuelle
2 *noun* un intellectuel/une intellectuelle

intelligence *noun*
(a) *(cleverness)* l'intelligence *(feminine)*
(b) *(secret information)* les renseignements *(masculine plural)*

intelligent *adjective* intelligent/intelligente; **she's a very intelligent girl** c'est une fille très intelligente

intend *verb* **to intend to do something** avoir l'intention de faire quelque chose; **I intend to go to university** j'ai l'intention d'aller à l'université

intensive *adjective* intensif/intensive; **intensive care** les soins intensifs *(masculine plural)*

intention *noun* l'intention *(feminine)*; **she has no intention of coming** elle n'a aucune intention de venir

intentional *noun* intentionnel/intentionnelle; **it wasn't intentional** ce n'était pas intentionnel

intentionally *adverb* exprès; **I didn't do it intentionally** je ne l'ai pas fait exprès

interest
1 *noun* l'intérêt *(masculine)*; **my interests are reading and music** mes centres d'intérêt sont la lecture et la musique; **she has an interest in astronomy** elle s'intéresse à l'astronomie; **he takes a great interest in politics** il s'intéresse beaucoup à la politique
2 *verb* intéresser; **it doesn't interest me** cela ne m'intéresse pas

interested *adjective* intéressé/intéressée; **to be interested in something** s'intéresser à quelque chose; **I'm interested in music** je m'intéresse à la musique; **I'm not interested** cela ne m'intéresse pas

interesting *adjective* intéressant/intéressante; **the book was very interesting** le livre était très intéressant

interfere *verb* se mêler; **she's always interfering in my life** elle se mêle toujours de mes affaires; **don't interfere with my computer** ne touche pas à mon ordinateur; **stop interfering!** arrête de te mêler de ce qui ne te regarde pas!

international *adjective* international/internationale

The masculine plural of *international* is *internationaux*.

Internet *noun* Internet *(masculine)*; **to surf the Internet** naviguer sur Internet; **I'm on the Internet** je suis sur Internet; **an Internet café** un cybercafé

interpreter *noun* un/une interprète

interrupt *verb* interrompre; **I'm sorry to interrupt you** je suis désolé de vous interrompre; **don't interrupt, I'm talking to your sister** ne m'interromps pas, je parle à ta sœur

interruption *noun* une interruption

interval *noun* un intervalle; *(at the theatre, the cinema)* un entracte; **at regular intervals** à intervalles réguliers; **a 15-minute interval** un entracte de 15 minutes; **at 15-minute intervals** toutes les 15 minutes

interview
1 *noun*
(**a**) *(for a job)* un entretien; **a job interview** un entretien d'embauche
(**b**) *(on TV, in a newspaper, a magazine)* une interview; **an interview with Tom Cruise** une interview de Tom Cruise
2 *verb*
(**a**) *(for a job)* faire passer un entretien à; **who interviewed you for the job?** qui vous a fait passer l'entretien d'embauche?
(**b**) *(on TV, in a newspaper, a magazine)* interviewer; **she interviewed David Beckham** elle a interviewé David Beckham

into *preposition*
(**a**) dans; **go into the bedroom** va dans la chambre; **to get into bed** se mettre au lit *or* se coucher
(**b**) en; **to translate something into French** traduire quelque chose en français; **cut the pizza into six** coupe la pizza en six

introduce *verb* **to introduce somebody to somebody** présenter quelqu'un à quelqu'un; **to introduce oneself** se présenter; **he introduced me to his brother** il m'a présenté à son frère; **let me introduce you to my sister** je te présente ma sœur

introduction *noun* une introduction

invade *verb* envahir; **when Germany invaded Poland** quand l'Allemagne a envahi la Pologne

invalid *noun (ill person)* le/la malade; *(disabled person)* un/une infirme

invent *verb* inventer

invention *noun* une invention

inventor *noun* un inventeur/une inventrice

inverted commas *plural noun* les guillemets *(masculine plural)*; **in inverted commas** entre guillemets

investigate *verb* examiner; *(crime)* enquêter sur

investigation *noun* un examen; *(of crime)* une enquête

invisible *adjective* invisible

invitation *noun* une invitation; **did you get an invitation to the party?** tu as reçu une invitation pour la fête?

invite *verb* inviter; **Lindsay has invited Chloe to her party** Lindsay a invité Chloe à sa fête

involve *noun*
(**a**) *(entail)* nécessiter; **it involves a lot of work** ça nécessite beaucoup de travail; **his job involves travelling a lot** son travail l'amène à beaucoup voyager
(**b**) *(concern)* concerner; **this involves all of you** cela vous concerne tous
(**c**) *(bring in)* impliquer; **several ministers were involved in the scandal** plusieurs ministres ont été impliqués dans le scandale; **the whole school got involved in the show** toute l'école a participé au spectacle

involved *adjective* **15 pupils are involved in the project** 15 élèves participent au projet; **there's a lot of work involved** cela nécessite beaucoup de travail

Iran *noun* l'Iran *(masculine)*; **he lives in Iran** il habite en Iran; **he's going to Iran** il va en Iran; **his father comes from Iran** son père est iranien

Iranian
1 *adjective* iranien/iranienne
2 *noun (person)* un Iranien/une Iranienne; **the Iranians** les Iraniens *(masculine plural)*

Iraq *noun* l'Irak *(masculine)*; **he lives**

in Iraq il habite en Irak; **he's going to Iraq** il va en Irak; **his mother comes from Iraq** sa mère est irakienne

Iraqi
1 *adjective* irakien/irakienne
2 *noun* *(person)* un Irakien/une Irakienne; **the Iraqis** les Irakiens *(masculine plural)*

Ireland *noun* l'Irlande *(feminine)*; **he lives in Ireland** il habite en Irlande; **he's going to Ireland** il va en Irlande; **her parents come from Ireland** ses parents sont irlandais

Irish
1 *adjective* irlandais/irlandaise
2 *noun*
(**a**) *(language)* l'irlandais *(masculine)*; **he speaks Irish** il parle irlandais
(**b**) *(people)* **the Irish** les Irlandais *(masculine plural)*

> In French, only the noun for the inhabitants of a country takes a capital letter, never the adjective or the noun for the language.

Irishman *noun* un Irlandais

Irishwoman *noun* une Irlandaise

iron
1 *noun*
(**a**) *(metal)* le fer; **an iron bar** une barre de fer
(**b**) *(for clothes)* le fer à repasser
2 *verb* *(clothes)* repasser; **can you iron my trousers?** est-ce que tu peux repasser mon pantalon?

ironic *adjective* ironique

ironing *noun* le repassage; **she's doing the ironing** elle fait le repassage

irrelevant *adjective* *(remark)* hors de propos; **that's irrelevant!** cela n'a rien à voir!

irresponsible *adjective* irresponsable

> Do not confuse the spellings of the French *irresponsable* and English *irresponsible*.

irritating *adjective* irritant/irritante

Islamic *adjective* islamique

island *noun* une île

isolated *adjective* isolé/isolée

Israel *noun* Israël *(masculine)*; **they live in Israel** ils habitent en Israël; **have you ever been to Israel?** est-ce que tu es déjà allé en Israël?; **she comes from Israel** elle est israélienne

Israeli
1 *adjective* israélien/israélienne
2 *noun* *(person)* un Israélien/une Israélienne; **the Israelis** les Israéliens *(masculine plural)*

issue *noun*
(**a**) *(question)* la question; **it's a very important issue** c'est une question très importante
(**b**) *(of a magazine)* le numéro; **this month's issue** le numéro du mois

it *pronoun*
(**a**) *(masculine subject in French)* il; *(feminine subject in French)* elle; **where's the book? – it's on the shelf** où est le livre? – il est sur l'étagère; **turn the TV on – it's not working** allume la télé – elle ne marche pas
(**b**) *(masculine or impersonal object in French)* le; *(feminine object in French)* la; **I've lost my purse, have you seen it?** j'ai perdu mon porte-monnaie, est-ce que tu l'as vu?; **take this plate and put it on the table** prends cette assiette et mets-la sur la table
(**c**) *(impersonal subject)* il; **it's raining** il pleut; **it's hot** il fait chaud; **it's four o'clock** il est quatre heures
(**d**) *(non-specific subject)* ce; **it's good** c'est bon; **who is it?** qui est-ce?; **it was Kirsty who told me** c'est Kirsty qui me l'a dit; **it's impossible to study with the TV on** c'est impossible de travailler avec la télé allumée
(**e**) *(after a preposition)* **he stepped on it** il a marché dessus; **he walked under it** il est passé en-dessous; **the bank is on the corner and there's a café**

beside it la banque est au coin de la rue et il y a un café à côté (**f**) **of it, from it, about it** en; **what do you think of it?** qu'est-ce que tu en penses?

Italian
1 *adjective* italien/italienne
2 *noun*
(**a**) *(language)* l'italien *(masculine)*; **they speak Italian** ils parlent italien (**b**) *(person)* un Italien/une Italienne; **the Italians** les Italiens *(masculine plural)*

In French, only the noun for the inhabitants of a country takes a capital letter, never the adjective or the noun for the language.

Italy *noun* l'Italie *(feminine)*; **they live in Italy** ils habitent en Italie; **have you ever been to Italy?** est-ce que tu es déjà allé en Italie?; **she comes from Italy** elle est italienne

itch
1 *noun* la démangeaison
2 *verb* démanger; **my leg itches** ma jambe me démange

itchy *adjective* **I have an itchy hand** ma main me démange

item *noun* un article; **an item of clothing** un vêtement

its *adjective*
(**a**) *(when the thing possessed is masculine in French)* son; **its bone** son os
(**b**) *(when the thing possessed is feminine in French)* sa; **its tail** sa queue; **its ear** son oreille

Note that *sa* becomes *son* before a vowel or mute h.

(**c**) *(when the thing possessed is plural in French)* ses; **its puppies** ses chiots
(**d**) **the dog hurt its paw** le chien s'est blessé à la patte

The form used is determined by the gender and number of the noun that follows and not by the possessor.

itself *pronoun*
(**a**) *(with a reflexive verb)* se; **the dog hurt itself** le chien s'est blessé

Note that *se* becomes *s'* before a vowel or mute h.

(**b**) *(after a preposition)* tout seul/toute seule; **don't leave the dog by itself** ne laisse pas le chien tout seul; **your room won't tidy itself** ta chambre ne va pas se ranger toute seule

ivory *noun* l'ivoire *(masculine)*; **an ivory ornament** un bibelot en ivoire

ivy *noun* le lierre

jab
1 *noun*
(**a**) *(with the elbow, the finger)* le coup
(**b**) *(injection)* la piqûre; **to give somebody a jab** faire une piqûre à quelqu'un
2 *verb* **he jabbed her in the leg with a pencil** il lui a donné un coup de crayon dans la jambe

jacket *noun* la veste; **a jacket potato** une pomme de terre au four

jail
1 *noun* la prison; **he's in jail** il est en prison
2 *verb* emprisonner; **he was jailed for three years** il a été condamné à trois ans de prison

jam
1 *noun*
(**a**) *(fruit preserve)* la confiture; **a slice of bread and jam** une tartine à la confiture
(**b**) **a (traffic) jam** un embouteillage
2 *verb* entasser; **I jammed my clothes in the suitcase** j'ai entassé mes vêtements dans la valise

Jamaica *noun* la Jamaïque; **they live in Jamaica** ils habitent en Jamaïque; **have you ever been to Jamaica?** est-ce que tu es déjà allé en Jamaïque?; **his parents come from Jamaica** ses parents viennent de la Jamaïque

Jamaican
1 *adjective* jamaïcain/jamaïcaine
2 *noun (person)* le Jamaïcain/la Jamaïcaine; **the Jamaicans** les Jamaïcains *(masculine plural)*

jammed *adjective (stuck)* coincé/

coincée; **the cupboard door's jammed** la porte du placard est coincée

January *noun* janvier *(masculine)*; **the first of January** le premier janvier; **the second of January** le deux janvier; **the third of January** le trois janvier; **in January** en janvier

Names of months are not capitalized in French.

Japan *noun* le Japon; **they live in Japan** ils habitent au Japon; **have you ever been to Japan?** est-ce que tu es déjà allé au Japon?; **his father comes from Japan** son père est japonais

Japanese
1 *adjective* japonais/japonaise
2 *noun*
(**a**) *(language)* le japonais; **he speaks Japanese** il parle japonais
(**b**) *(person)* le Japonais/la Japonaise; **the Japanese** les Japonais *(masculine plural)*

In French, only the noun for the inhabitants of a country takes a capital letter, never the adjective or the noun for the language.

jar *noun* le pot; **a jar of jam** un pot de confiture

jaw *noun* la mâchoire; **my jaw aches** j'ai mal à la mâchoire

jazz *noun* le jazz; **I like jazz** j'aime le jazz

jealous *adjective* jaloux/jalouse; **she's jealous of you** elle est jalouse de toi

jealousy *noun* la jalousie

jeans *plural noun* le jean; **a pair of jeans** un jean

jeep® *noun* la jeep®

jelly *noun* la gelée; **strawberry jelly** la gelée de fraise

jellyfish *noun* la méduse

jersey *noun* le pull

jet *noun*
(a) *(plane)* un avion à réaction
(b) *(of a liquid, steam)* le jet

jetty *noun* la jetée

Jew *noun (person)* le Juif/la Juive; **the Jews** les Juifs *(masculine plural)*

jewel *noun* le bijou

> The plural of *bijou* is *bijoux*.

jeweller *noun* le bijoutier/la bijoutière; **a jeweller's** *(shop)* une bijouterie; **he's a jeweller** il est bijoutier

> Note that when describing people's jobs or situations, French does not use an article (*un* or *une*).

jewellery *noun* les bijoux *(masculine plural)*

Jewish *adjective* juif/juive

> The names of religions and their followers are never capitalized in French.

jigsaw *noun* le puzzle

job *noun*
(a) *(employment)* le travail; **he's looking for a job** il cherche du travail; **what's her job?** qu'est-ce qu'elle fait comme travail?; **she has a good job** elle a un bon travail
(b) *(task)* la tâche; **I only give him simple jobs to do** je ne lui donne que des tâches faciles; **he did a good job** il a fait du bon travail; **it's my job to water the plants** c'est moi qui arrose les plantes

jobless *adjective* sans emploi

jockey *noun* le jockey

jog *verb*
(a) *(shake)* secouer; *(push)* pousser

(b) *(run)* faire du jogging; **she jogs to work every morning** tous les matins, elle fait son jogging en allant au travail

jogging *noun* le jogging; **to go jogging** faire du jogging

join
1 *verb*
(a) **to join somebody** *(meet up with)* rejoindre quelqu'un; **can I join you?** puis-je me joindre à vous?
(b) *(club)* adhérer à; *(army)* s'engager dans; *(discussion, game)* se joindre à; **he's joined a gym** il a adhéré à un club de gym; **to join the queue** se mettre à la queue
(c) *(put together)* joindre; *(wires, pipes)* raccorder; **the railway joins the two towns** la voie ferrée raccorde les deux villes
2 **join in** **to join in something** participer à quelque chose; **she never joins in** elle ne participe jamais

joint
1 *adjective* commun/commune; **it was a joint decision** c'était une décision commune
2 *noun (in the body)* une articulation; **my joints ache** j'ai mal aux articulations
(b) *(of meat)* le rôti; **a joint of beef** un rôti de bœuf

joke
1 *noun* la plaisanterie, la blague; **to tell a joke** raconter une blague; **a practical joke** une farce; **we played a practical joke on him** on lui a fait une farce
2 *verb* plaisanter; **I was only joking!** je plaisantais!

jolly *adjective* gai/gaie

Jordan *noun* la Jordanie; **he lives in Jordan** il habite en Jordanie; **we're going to Jordan** nous allons en Jordanie; **he's from Jordan** il vient de Jordanie

journalism *noun* le journalisme

journalist *noun* le/la journaliste; **she's a journalist** elle est journaliste

Note that when describing people's jobs or situations, French does not use an article (*un* or *une*).

journey *noun* le voyage; *(short)* le trajet; **have a good journey!** bon voyage!; **to go on a journey** partir en voyage

joy *noun* la joie

judge
1 *noun* le/la juge
2 *verb* juger

judo *noun* le judo; **he does judo** il fait du judo

jug *noun* le pichet

juggle *verb* jongler

juggler *noun* le jongleur/la jongleuse

juice *noun* le jus; **orange juice** le jus d'orange

juicy *adjective* juteux/juteuse; **a juicy pear** une poire juteuse

July *noun* juillet *(masculine)*; **the first of July** le premier juillet; **the second of July** le deux juillet; **the third of July** le trois juillet; **in July** en juillet

Names of months are not capitalized in French.

jump
1 *noun* le saut
2 *verb*
(**a**) *(in the air)* sauter; **he jumped over the wall** il a sauté par-dessus le mur
(**b**) *(in fear)* sursauter; **you made me jump** tu m'as fait sursauter

jumper *noun* le pull

June *noun* juin *(masculine)*; **the first of June** le premier juin; **the second of June** le deux juin; **the third of June**

le trois juin; **in June** en juin

Names of months are not capitalized in French.

jungle *noun* la jungle; **in the jungle** dans la jungle

junior
1 *adjective (younger)* plus jeune; *(in rank, status)* subalterne; **a junior doctor** un/une interne; **a junior school** une école primaire pour les enfants de sept à onze ans
2 *noun (in a school)* un écolier/une écolière

junk *noun (unwanted things)* le bric-à-brac; *(rubbish)* la camelote; **junk food** les cochonneries *(feminine plural)*; **a junk shop** un magasin de brocante

jury *noun* le jury

just *adverb*
(**a**) *(barely)* **I just missed the train** j'ai raté le train de peu; **just before seven o'clock** juste avant sept heures; **just in time** juste à temps; **the bank is just after the roundabout** la banque est juste après le rond-point
(**b**) *(exactly)* exactement; **that's just what I told her** c'est exactement ce que je lui ai dit; **the phone rang just as I was leaving** le téléphone a sonné au moment précis où je partais; **he's just as clever as his brother** il est aussi intelligent que son frère
(**c**) *(only)* **she's just a baby** ce n'est qu'un bébé
(**d**) **she has just left** elle vient de partir; **she had just left** elle venait de partir

justice *noun* la justice

kangaroo *noun* le kangourou

karate *noun* le karaté; **she does karate** elle fait du karaté

kebab *noun* la brochette; **a shish kebab** un chiche-kébab; **a doner kebab** un sandwich grec

keen *adjective* enthousiaste; **I asked her to come with us but she's not very keen** je lui ai demandé de venir avec nous mais elle n'est pas très enthousiaste; **he's keen on golf** il aime beaucoup le golf; **I'm keen to try windsurfing** j'ai vraiment envie d'essayer la planche à voile; **she's a keen gardener** c'est une passionnée de jardinage

keep
1 *verb*
(**a**) *(retain)* garder; **keep the change!** gardez la monnaie!; **you can keep the jumper I lent you** tu peux garder le pull que je t'ai prêté; **can you keep a secret?** tu sais garder un secret?
(**b**) **to keep a diary** tenir un journal; **to keep a promise** tenir une promesse
(**c**) *(maintain in a certain condition)* **to keep something secret** garder quelque chose secret; **he kept me waiting** il m'a fait attendre; **keep your room tidy** ne mets pas de désordre dans ta chambre; **he keeps fit** il se maintient en forme
(**d**) *(remain)* **keep calm!** restez calmes!; **will everyone please keep quiet** un peu de silence, s'il vous plaît
(**e**) *(continue)* **to keep doing something** continuer à faire quelque chose; **she keeps interrupting me** elle n'ar-

rête pas de m'interrompre
2 keep away ne pas s'approcher; **keep away from me!** n'approche pas!; **keep away from those people** évitez ces gens-là
3 keep down **you should keep your voice down** tu devrais parler moins fort; **keep the noise down!** faites moins de bruit!
4 keep out **keep out** *(on a sign)* défense d'entrer; **keep out of my business** ne te mêle pas de mes affaires
5 keep up **to keep up with somebody** suivre quelqu'un; **he has trouble keeping up with the rest of the class** il a du mal à suivre le reste de la classe

keep-fit *noun* la gymnastique; **she enjoys keep-fit** elle aime bien la gymnastique

kennel *noun* la niche; **the dog is in the kennel** le chien est dans la niche

kerb *noun* le bord du trottoir

ketchup *noun* le ketchup

kettle *noun* la bouilloire; **can you put the kettle on, please?** tu peux mettre de l'eau à chauffer dans la bouilloire, s'il te plaît?

key *noun*
(**a**) *(for a door)* la clé; **the key to the back door** la clé de la porte de derrière
(**b**) *(of a piano, a computer)* la touche

keyboard *noun* le clavier

keyhole *noun* le trou de serrure

keyring *noun* le porte-clés

The word *porte-clés* does not change in the plural.

kick
1 *noun* le coup de pied; **he gave me a kick** il m'a donné un coup de pied
2 *verb*
(**a**) *(a person)* donner un coup de pied à; **stop kicking me!** arrête de me donner des coups de pied!
(**b**) *(a ball)* donner un coup de pied dans; **he kicked the ball over the wall** il a envoyé le ballon par-dessus le mur d'un coup de pied

kid *noun* *(child)* le/la gosse; **where are the kids?** où sont les gosses?; **his kid brother** son petit frère

kidnap *verb* enlever

kidney *noun*
(**a**) *(part of the body)* le rein
(**b**) *(meat)* le rognon
(**c**) **a kidney bean** un haricot rouge

kill *verb* tuer; **she was killed instantly** elle a été tuée sur le coup; **he killed himself** il s'est suicidé

killer *noun* *(murderer)* le meutrier/la meurtrière; *(professional)* le tueur/la tueuse

kilo *noun* le kilo

kilogram, kilogramme *noun* le kilogramme

kilometre *noun* le kilomètre; **it's ten kilometres away** c'est à dix kilomètres

kind¹ *noun* la sorte, le genre; **what kind of books do you like?** quel genre de livres aimes-tu?; **all kinds of things** toutes sortes de choses; **it's a kind of plant** c'est une sorte de plante; **what kind of insect is that?** quel genre d'insecte est-ce que c'est?

kind² *adjective* gentil/gentille; **that was kind of you** c'était gentil de ta part; **she's always been kind to me** elle a toujours été gentille avec moi

kindness *noun* la gentillesse

king *noun* le roi; **King Charles** le roi Charles

kingdom *noun* le royaume; **the ani-** mal kingdom le règne animal

kiosk *noun* le kiosque; **a newspaper kiosk** un kiosque à journaux

kiss
1 *noun* le baiser; **he gave me a kiss** il m'a donné un baiser
2 *verb*
(**a**) *(somebody)* embrasser; **she kissed me** elle m'a embrassé
(**b**) *(mutually)* s'embrasser; **they were kissing** ils s'embrassaient

kit *noun* *(equipment)* le matériel; **I've forgotten my PE kit** j'ai oublié mes affaires de sport; **a first-aid kit** une trousse de secours

kitchen *noun* la cuisine; **kitchen roll** l'essuie-tout *(masculine)*; **a kitchen sink** un évier

kite *noun* le cerf-volant

The plural of *cerf-volant* is *cerfs-volants*.

kitten *noun* le chaton

kiwi fruit *noun* le kiwi

knee *noun* le genou; **he hurt his knee** il s'est fait mal au genou

The plural of *genou* is *genoux*.

kneel *verb* s'agenouiller; **I knelt down** je me suis agenouillé; **I was kneeling** j'étais à genoux

knickers *plural noun* la culotte; **a pair of knickers** une culotte

knife *noun* le couteau

The plural of *couteau* is *couteaux*.

knight *noun* le chevalier; *(in chess)* le cavalier

knit *verb* tricoter; **she's knitting a jumper** elle tricote un pull

knitting *noun* le tricot; **she goes to knitting classes** elle prend des cours de tricot; **she's very good at knitting** elle tricote très bien; **a knitting needle** une aiguille à tricoter

knob *noun* *(on door)* le bouton

knock
1 *noun* le coup; **there was a knock at the door** on a frappé à la porte
2 *verb* frapper; **he knocked on the door** il a frappé à la porte; **I knocked my head on the car door** je me suis cogné la tête contre la portière de la voiture
3 **knock down** *(a person)* renverser; *(a wall, a building)* abattre; **he was knocked down yesterday** il s'est fait renverser hier; **they're knocking down the old church** ils sont en train de démolir la vieille église
4 **knock in** *(a nail)* enfoncer
5 **knock out**
(a) *(make unconscious)* **to knock somebody out** assommer quelqu'un; *(in boxing)* mettre quelqu'un K.-O.
(b) *(eliminate)* **England were knocked out of the World Cup** l'Angleterre a été éliminée de la Coupe du Monde
6 **knock over** renverser; **she knocked over the vase** elle a renversé le vase

knot *noun* le nœud; **tie a knot in the rope** fais un nœud à la corde

know *verb*
(a) connaître; **I know her brother** je connais son frère; **I don't know France very well** je ne connais pas bien la France; **I'm getting to know people** je commence à connaître du monde
(b) savoir; **I don't know** je ne sais pas; **you're late – I know** tu es en retard – je sais; **I don't know how to get to Brighton** je ne sais pas comment aller à Brighton; **do you know any German?** sais-tu parler allemand?; **she knows a lot about nature** elle sait beaucoup de choses sur la nature

knowledge *noun* la connaissance; **her knowledge of Spanish is very good** elle a une très bonne connaissance de l'espagnol

knuckle *noun* la jointure du doigt; **I grazed my knuckles on the wall** je me suis écorché les doigts contre le mur

Kuwait *noun* le Koweït; **he lives in Kuwait** il habite au Koweït; **we're going to Kuwait** nous allons au Koweït; **he's from Kuwait** il vient du Koweït

label *noun* une étiquette

laboratory *noun* le laboratoire

labour *noun* la main-d'œuvre; **the labour costs £500** la main-d'œuvre coûte 500 livres

labourer *noun* un ouvrier/une ouvrière; **he's a labourer** il est ouvrier

Note that when describing people's jobs or situations, French does not use an article (*un* or *une*).

lace *noun*
(a) *(decorative)* la dentelle; **a lace tablecloth** une nappe en dentelle
(b) *(for shoes)* le lacet; **tie your laces** attache tes lacets

lack
1 *noun* le manque; **he didn't get the job because of his lack of experience** il n'a pas eu le poste à cause de son manque d'expérience
2 *verb* manquer de; **he lacks experience** il manque d'expérience; **she doesn't lack confidence** elle ne manque pas d'assurance

ladder *noun* une échelle

lady *noun* la dame; **the ladies** *(toilet)* les toilettes pour dames; **where's the ladies, please?** où sont les toilettes, s'il vous plaît?

ladybird *noun* la coccinelle

lager *noun* la bière blonde

laid-back *adjective* décontracté/décontractée; **our teacher is very laid-back** notre professeur est très décontracté

lake *noun* le lac; **Lake Geneva** le lac Léman

lamb *noun* un agneau; **roast lamb** l'agneau rôti

The plural of *agneau* is *agneaux*.

lame *adjective* boiteux/boiteuse; **she's lame** elle boite

lamp *noun* la lampe

lamppost *noun* le réverbère, le lampadaire

lampshade *noun* un abat-jour

The word *abat-jour* does not change in the plural.

land
1 *noun*
(a) *(ground)* la terre; *(piece of ground)* le terrain; **they own all the land behind their house** tout le terrain derrière leur maison leur appartient
(b) *(country)* le pays
2 *verb*
(a) *(of a person, a ball)* tomber; **she landed on her back when she fell** elle est tombée sur le dos
(b) *(of a plane)* atterrir; **the plane is due to land in 40 minutes** l'avion doit atterrir dans 40 minutes; **what time do we land?** à quelle heure atterrissons-nous?

landing *noun*
(a) *(of a plane)* un atterrissage; **an emergency landing** un atterrissage d'urgence
(b) *(at the top of stairs)* le palier

landlady *noun* la propriétaire

landlord *noun* le propriétaire

landscape *noun* le paysage

lane *noun*
(a) *(in the country)* le chemin; **a country lane** un chemin de campagne
(b) *(part of the road)* la voie; **you're in the wrong lane** tu n'es pas sur la bonne voie

language *noun*
(a) *(of a country)* la langue; **she speaks four languages** elle parle quatre langues; **a language laboratory** *or* **a language lab** un laboratoire de langues; **a language teacher** un professeur de langues
(b) *(way of expressing oneself)* le langage; **medical language** le langage médical

lap *noun (knees)* les genoux *(masculine plural)*; **she was sitting on his lap** elle était assise sur ses genoux

laptop *noun* l'ordinateur portable *(masculine)*

large *adjective (big)* grand/grande; *(fat, bulky)* gros/grosse; **France is a large country** la France est un grand pays; **he took a large helping of pasta** il a pris une grosse portion de pâtes; **a large number of people were there** il y avait beaucoup de monde

lark *noun* une alouette

laser *noun* le laser

last¹
1 *adjective* dernier/dernière; **last week** la semaine dernière; **last Sunday** dimanche dernier; **last night** *(evening)* hier soir; *(night)* la nuit dernière; **the last time I saw him** la dernière fois que je l'ai vu; **at the last minute** à la dernière minute; **what's your last name?** quel est votre nom de famille?
2 *adverb*
(a) pour la dernière fois; **I last saw her in the summer** je l'ai vue pour la dernière fois en été
(b) **to do something last** faire

quelque chose en dernier; **she arrived last** elle est arrivée en dernier
3 *noun*
(a) le dernier/la dernière; **he's always the last to arrive** il est toujours le dernier arrivé
(b) **at last** enfin; **here you are at last!** te voilà enfin!

last² *verb* durer; **the ceremony will last for one hour** la cérémonie durera une heure; **the food should last us a week** la nourriture devrait nous durer une semaine

late
1 *adjective*
(a) *(not on time)* en retard; **sorry I'm late** désolé d'être en retard; **he's always late** il est toujours en retard; **I was an hour late** j'avais une heure de retard; **it's too late** c'est trop tard
(b) *(far on in time)* tard; **it's getting late** il se fait tard; **in the late afternoon** en fin d'après-midi; **in late summer** à la fin de l'été
2 *adverb* tard; **he's working late tonight** il travaille tard ce soir

lately *adverb* ces derniers temps; **have you spoken to her lately?** est-ce que tu lui as parlé ces derniers temps?

Latin
1 *noun* le latin; **my Latin teacher** mon professeur de latin
2 *adjective* latin/latine; **Latin America** l'Amérique latine *(feminine)*

Latvia *noun* la Lettonie; **she lives in Latvia** elle habite en Lettonie; **I'm going to Latvia** je vais en Lettonie; **he comes from Latvia** il vient de Lettonie

Latvian
1 *adjective* letton/lettonne
2 *noun*
(a) *(language)* le letton; **she speaks Latvian** elle parle letton
(b) *(person)* le Letton/la Lettonne; **the Latvians** les Lettons *(masculine plural)*

In French, only the noun for the inhabitants of a country takes a capital letter, never the adjective or the noun for the language.

laugh
1 *noun* le rire; **I did it for a laugh** je l'ai fait pour rire; **we had a good laugh** nous avons bien rigolé
2 *verb* rire; **I laughed at the joke** la blague m'a fait rire; **stop laughing at me!** arrête de te moquer de moi!; **she burst out laughing** elle a éclaté de rire

laughter *noun* les rires *(masculine plural)*; **we heard laughter** nous avons entendu des rires

launderette *noun* la laverie automatique

laundry *noun*
(a) *(clothes)* le linge; **she's doing the laundry** elle fait la lessive
(b) *(place)* la blanchisserie; **can you take the clothes to the laundry?** est-ce que tu peux apporter les vêtements à la blanchisserie?

lavatory *noun* les toilettes *(feminine plural)*

lavender *noun* la lavande

law *noun*
(a) *(rule, set of rules)* la loi; **he broke the law** il a enfreint la loi; **that's against the law** c'est illégal
(b) *(study, system, profession)* le droit; **I want to study law** je veux faire des études de droit

lawn *noun* la pelouse; **he's mowing the lawn** il tond la pelouse

lawnmower *noun* la tondeuse à gazon

lawyer *noun* un avocat/une avocate; **her mum's a lawyer** sa mère est avocate

Note that when describing people's jobs or situations, French does not use an article (*un* or *une*).

lay *verb*
(a) *(put)* poser; **lay it flat on the table** pose-le à plat sur la table; **to lay a carpet** poser une moquette
(b) **to lay the table** mettre la table; **have you laid the table?** est-ce que tu as mis la table?
(c) **to lay an egg** pondre un œuf; **the hen laid an egg** la poule a pondu un œuf

layer *noun* la couche; **a thick layer of cream** une épaisse couche de crème

lazy *adjective* paresseux/paresseuse; **don't be so lazy!** ne sois pas si paresseux!

lead¹ *noun*
(a) *(metal)* le plomb; **a lead pipe** un tuyau en plomb
(b) *(in a pencil)* la mine

lead²
1 *noun*
(a) **to be in the lead** *(of a runner, a cyclist)* être en tête; *(of a team)* mener; **at half-time England was in the lead** à la mi-temps l'Angleterre menait
(b) *(for dog)* la laisse
2 *verb*
(a) mener; **the road leads to the village** la route mène au village; **the stairs lead up to the attic** l'escalier mène au grenier
(b) *(guide)* conduire; **to lead the way** montrer le chemin; **he led her down the stairs** il l'a conduite au bas des escaliers
(c) *(persuade)* amener; **what led you to apply for this job?** qu'est-ce qui vous a amené à vous présenter pour ce poste?; **this leads me to believe he lied** cela m'amène à penser qu'il a menti
(d) *(of a runner)* être en tête; *(of a team)* mener; **Scotland are leading by one goal** l'Écosse mène d'un but

leader *noun*
(a) *(of a team, a group)* le chef; **she's the group leader** c'est le chef du groupe
(b) *(of a country, a party)* le dirigeant/la dirigeante

leaf *noun* la feuille; **the trees are losing their leaves** les arbres perdent leurs feuilles

leaflet *noun* le prospectus

leak
1 *noun* la fuite; **there's a leak in the roof** il y a une fuite dans le toit; **a gas leak** une fuite de gaz
2 *verb* fuir; **the tap is leaking** le robinet fuit; **the roof's leaking** il y a une fuite dans le toit

lean¹
1 *verb*
(a) *(prop)* appuyer; **lean your bike against that wall** pose ton vélo contre le mur; **he was leaning his elbows on the table** il était accoudé à la table
(b) *(of a building, a tree)* pencher; **my bike's leaning against the wall** mon vélo est appuyé contre le mur; **she was leaning against the wall** elle était appuyée contre le mur
2 **lean back**
(a) **he leaned his head back** il a penché la tête en arrière
(b) *(of a person)* se pencher en arrière; **he leaned back against the wall** il s'est adossé au mur
3 **lean forward** *(of a person)* se pencher en avant; **she leaned forward** elle s'est penchée en avant
4 **lean out**
(a) **he leaned his head out of the window** il a passé la tête par la fenêtre
(b) *(of a person)* se pencher au dehors; **he was leaning out of the window** il se penchait par la fenêtre

lean² *adjective (meat)* maigre

leap
1 *noun* le bond; **a leap year** une année bissextile
2 *verb* bondir; **he leapt out of his chair** il a bondi hors de son fauteuil

learn *verb* apprendre; **I'm learning French** j'apprends le français; **he's learning the violin** il apprend à jouer du violon; **he's learning to drive next year** il apprend à conduire l'année prochaine

learner *noun* le débutant/la débutante

leash *noun* la laisse; **to keep a dog on a leash** tenir un chien en laisse

least
1 *adjective* **the least** *(the smallest amount of)* le moins de; **she has the least money** c'est elle qui a le moins d'argent; **she makes the least effort** c'est elle qui fait le moins d'efforts
2 *adverb*
(a) *(work, pay)* le moins; **this job pays the least** c'est ce travail qui rapporte le moins
(b) **the least difficult** le/la moins difficile; **the least interesting film** le film le moins intéressant
3 *pronoun*
(a) **the least** le moins; **I have the least** c'est moi qui en ai le moins
(b) **at least** *(not less than)* au moins; *(anyway)* du moins; **there were at least a hundred people there** il y avait au moins une centaine de personnes; **at least you passed** au moins tu as réussi; **she'll be there, at least that's what she told me** elle sera là, du moins c'est ce qu'elle m'a dit
(c) **not in the least** pas du tout; **I'm not in the least angry** je ne suis pas du tout fâché

leather *noun* le cuir; **a leather jacket** un blouson en cuir

leave
1 *noun* le congé; **she's on leave** elle est en congé
2 *verb*
(a) *(allow to remain)* laisser; **leave her alone!** laisse-la tranquille!; **can you leave the window open?** est-ce que tu peux laisser la fenêtre ouverte?; **she left half her pasta** elle a laissé la moitié de ses pâtes
(b) *(forget)* oublier; **I left my umbrella on the bus** j'ai oublié mon parapluie dans le bus
(c) *(go away from)* quitter; **she left home three years ago** elle a quitté la

maison il y a trois ans; **when did she leave Paris?** quand est-ce qu'elle a quitté Paris?

(**d**) *(go away)* partir; **she left yesterday** elle est partie hier; **my flight leaves at ten o'clock** mon avion part à dix heures

3 leave behind *(on purpose)* laisser; *(accidentally)* oublier; **somebody left their watch behind** quelqu'un a oublié sa montre

4 leave out

(**a**) *(omit)* oublier; **you've left out the comma** tu as oublié la virgule

(**b**) *(exclude)* exclure; **he feels left out** il se sent exclu

Lebanon *noun* **the Lebanon** le Liban; **he lives in the Lebanon** il habite au Liban; **we're going to the Lebanon** nous allons au Liban; **his parents come from the Lebanon** ses parents viennent du Liban

lecture

1 *noun*

(**a**) *(talk)* la conférence; **a lecture on astronomy** une conférence sur l'astronomie

(**b**) *(at university)* le cours magistral; **I have a French lecture this afternoon** j'ai un cours de français cet après-midi

> The plural of *cours magistral* is *cours magistraux.*

2 *verb*

(**a**) *(give a talk)* donner une conférence; **he lectures on astronomy** il donne des conférences sur l'astronomie

(**b**) *(at university)* donner un cours magistral; **he lectures at the University of Edinburgh** il enseigne à l'Université d'Édimbourg

(**c**) *(reprimand)* **to lecture somebody** faire la morale à quelqu'un; **my mum's always lecturing me!** ma mère est toujours en train de me faire la morale!

> Note that the French word *lecture* is never a translation for the English word *lecture*. It means *reading*.

lecturer *noun* un enseignant/une enseignante; **my German lecturer** mon professeur d'allemand; **he's a lecturer** il est enseignant

leek *noun* le poireau

> The plural of *poireau* is *poireaux*.

left[1] *adjective* *(remaining)* **to be left** rester; **there's no milk left** il ne reste plus de lait; **are there any cakes left?** est-ce qu'il reste des gâteaux?; **we have ten minutes left** il nous reste dix minutes

left[2]

1 *adjective* gauche; **my left hand** ma main gauche

2 *adverb* à gauche; **turn left at the traffic lights** tourne à gauche au feu

3 *noun* **the left** la gauche; **on the left** à gauche; **it's to the left of the armchair** c'est à gauche du fauteuil

left-hand *adjective* de gauche; **it's on the left-hand shelf** c'est sur l'étagère de gauche; **on the left-hand side** à gauche

left-handed *adjective* gaucher/gauchère; **she's left-handed** elle est gauchère

leftover *adjective* **the leftover chicken** le restant de poulet; **she made soup with the leftover vegetables** elle a fait de la soupe avec le restant de légumes

leftovers *plural noun* les restes *(masculine plural)*; **the leftovers are in the fridge** les restes sont dans le frigo

leg *noun* *(of a person)* la jambe; *(of an animal)* la patte; **she hurt her leg** elle s'est fait mal à la jambe; **a table leg** un pied de table; **a chicken leg** une cuisse de poulet; **a leg of lamb** un gigot d'agneau

legal *adjective* légal/légale

> The masculine plural of *légal* is *légaux.*

legally *adverb* légalement

leisure *noun* les loisirs *(masculine plural)*; **a leisure centre** un centre de loisirs; **what do you do in your leisure time?** que fais-tu pendant ton temps libre?

lemon *noun* le citron; **lemon juice** le jus de citron

lemonade *noun* la limonade

lend *verb* prêter; **he lent me his bike** il m'a prêté son vélo; **could you lend me 50p?** est-ce que tu pourrais me prêter 50 pence?

length *noun* la longueur; **what length is it?** ça fait combien de long?; **what length is the room?** quelle est la longueur de la pièce?; **it's five metres in length** ça fait cinq mètres de long; **he swam ten lengths** il a fait dix longueurs

lens *noun*
(**a**) *(of a camera)* un objectif
(**b**) *(of glasses)* le verre; (**contact**) **lenses** les lentilles de contact *(feminine plural)*

lentil *noun* la lentille; **lentil soup** la soupe aux lentilles

Leo *noun* le Lion; **she's (a) Leo** elle est Lion

leopard *noun* le léopard

less
1 *adjective* moins de; **he has less money than you** il a moins d'argent que toi
2 *adverb*
(**a**) *(work, pay, cost)* moins; **this one costs less** celui-ci coûte moins cher
(**b**) *(used with an adjective)* moins; **less interesting** moins intéressant; **this book is less interesting than the other one** ce livre est moins intéressant que l'autre; **she's less intelligent than her sister** elle est moins intelligente que sa sœur
3 *pronoun* **less than a kilo** moins d'un kilo; **it took me less than five minutes** ça m'a pris moins de cinq minutes; **I see him less than I used to** je le vois moins qu'avant

lesson *noun* la leçon; **a geography lesson** une leçon de geographie; **she's taking driving lessons** elle prend des leçons de conduite

let
1 *verb*
(**a**) *(allow)* laisser; **my mum won't let me go to the party** ma mère ne veut pas me laisser aller à la fête
(**b**) *(when making suggestions)* **let's stay here** restons ici; **let's go for a walk** allons nous promener; **let's go!** allons-y!
(**c**) **to let go of something** lâcher quelque chose; **don't let go of the dog's lead** ne lâche pas la laisse du chien; **let me go!** lâche-moi!
2 let down we can't go out, the babysitter's let us down on ne peux pas sortir, la babysitter nous a fait faux bond; **I expected better, you've really let me down** j'attendais mieux de toi, tu m'as vraiment déçu
3 let in laisser entrer; **don't let him in!** ne le laisse pas entrer!; **I'll let myself in** je me servirai de ma clé
4 let off
(**a**) *(a bomb)* lâcher; *(fireworks)* tirer; **they were letting off fireworks** ils tiraient un feu d'artifice
(**b**) *(excuse)* ne pas punir; **I'll let you off this time but don't do it again** je ne te punirai pas cette fois-ci mais ne recommence pas
5 let out laisser sortir; **the teacher let us out early** le professeur nous a laissé sortir plus tôt

letter *noun* la lettre; **the first letter of the alphabet** la première lettre de l'alphabet; **I got a letter from my brother** j'ai reçu une lettre de mon frère

letterbox *noun* la boîte à lettres

lettuce *noun* la salade

level
1 *noun* le niveau; **on the same level** au même niveau

The plural of *niveau* is *niveaux*.

2 *adjective*
(**a**) *(flat)* plat/plate; *(not sloping)* horizontal/horizontale; **a level surface** une surface plane

The masculine plural of *horizontal* is *horizontaux*.

(**b**) *(equal in score)* à égalité; **the teams are level at half-time** les équipes sont à égalité à la mi-temps

liar *noun* le menteur/la menteuse

liberty *noun* la liberté

Libra *noun* la Balance; **he's (a) Libra** il est Balance

librarian *noun* le/la bibliothécaire; **she's a librarian** elle est bibliothécaire

Note that the French word *libraire* is never a translation for the English word *librarian*. It means *bookseller*.

library *noun* la bibliothèque; **a library book** un livre de bibliothèque

Note that the French word *librairie* is never a translation for the English word *library*. It means *bookshop*.

licence *noun* le permis; **a licence plate** une plaque d'immatriculation

lick *verb* lécher; **the dog licked her hand** le chien lui a léché la main

lid *noun*
(**a**) *(of a pot, a jar)* le couvercle; **where's the lid for the saucepan?** où se trouve le couvercle de la casserole?
(**b**) *(of a bottle)* le bouchon

lie¹
1 *noun* le mensonge; **he's telling a lie** il ment; **you shouldn't tell lies** tu ne devrais pas dire de mensonges; **I tell a lie** je me trompe
2 *verb* mentir; **don't lie to me!** ne me mens pas!; **I know he's lying** je sais qu'il ment

lie²
1 *verb*
(**a**) *(go into a lying position)* s'allonger; *(be in a lying position)* être allongé/allongée; **go and lie on the bed** va t'allonger sur le lit; **she was lying on the sofa** elle était allongée sur le canapé; **she lay on the beach all day** elle est restée allongée sur la plage toute la journée
(**b**) *(of thing)* être; **the papers were lying on the table** les papiers étaient sur la table; **your watch is lying on the floor** ta montre traîne par terre
2 lie down s'allonger; **I'm going to lie down** je vais m'allonger; **he was lying down on the bed** il était allongé sur le lit
3 lie in faire la grasse matinée

lie-in *noun* **to have a lie-in** faire la grasse matinée

life *noun* la vie; **I've lived in London all my life** j'ai habité à Londres toute ma vie; **he saved her life** il lui a sauvé la vie; **a life jacket** un gilet de sauvetage

lifebelt *noun* la bouée de sauvetage

lifeboat *noun* le canot de sauvetage

lifeguard *noun* le maître nageur

lifestyle *noun* le style de vie

lift
1 *noun*
(**a**) *(elevator)* un ascenseur; **we took the lift** nous avons pris l'ascenseur
(**b**) *(in a car)* **to give somebody a lift** emmener quelqu'un en voiture; **he gave me a lift home** il m'a ramené en voiture; **do you need a lift?** tu as besoin que je t'emmène?
2 *verb*
(**a**) *(an object)* soulever; **can you lift that box for me?** tu peux soulever cette caisse?; **I lifted the books out of the crate** j'ai sorti les livres de la caisse
(**b**) *(one's head, arm, leg)* lever; **he lifted his head** il a levé la tête

light¹
1 *noun*
(**a**) *(illumination)* la lumière; **there's not enough light to read by** il n'y a

pas assez de lumière pour lire (**b**) *(light source)* la lumière; *(lamp)* la lampe; *(headlight)* le phare; **can you turn the light on?** est-ce que tu peux allumer la lumière?; **a light bulb** une ampoule (**c**) *(fire)* le feu; **do you have a light?** est-ce que tu as du feu?; **he set light to the wood** il a mis le feu au bois (**d**) **(traffic) lights** les feux de circulation *(masculine plural)*; **turn left at the lights** tournez à gauche au feu **2** *verb (a cigarette, a fire, gas)* allumer **3** *adjective (not dark, bright)* clair/claire; **light blue** bleu clair; **a light blue dress** une robe bleu clair

light² *adjective (not heavy)* léger/légère; **my suitcase is light, I'll be able to carry it** ma valise est légère, je serai capable de la porter; **we ate a light meal** nous avons pris un repas léger; **I'm a light sleeper** j'ai le sommeil léger

lighter *noun* le briquet

lighthouse *noun* le phare

lightning *noun* les éclairs *(masculine plural)*; **a flash of lightning** un éclair; **he was struck by lightning** il a été frappé par la foudre; **thunder and lightning** le tonnerre et la foudre

like¹ *preposition* (**a**) *(similar to)* comme; **a car like mine** une voiture comme la mienne; **she looks like her mother** elle ressemble à sa mère; **it tastes like chicken** ça a le goût de poulet (**b**) *(asking for a description)* **what's he like?** comment est-il?; **what's the weather like?** quel temps fait-il?; **what was it like?** comment c'était? (**c**) *(such as)* comme; **people like you** des gens comme vous

like² *verb* (**a**) *(enjoy)* aimer; **he likes school** il aime l'école; **I like reading** j'aime lire; **I don't like getting up early** je n'aime pas me lever tôt (**b**) *(a person)* aimer bien; **I like him** je l'aime bien; **I like Lauren better than**

Mandy j'aime mieux Lauren que Mandy (**c**) **I would like** je voudrais; **I'd like a coffee** je voudrais un café; **I'd like to leave** je voudrais partir; **would you like another glass of wine?** est-ce que tu voudrais un autre verre de vin?; **would you like me to leave?** est-ce que tu voudrais que je parte?; **if you like** si tu veux

likely *adjective* probable; **it's likely to rain** il va probablement pleuvoir; **it's more than likely** c'est plus que probable

lilac *adjective* lilas; **a lilac dress** une robe lilas

limb *noun* le membre

lime *noun* le citron vert; **lime juice** le jus de citron vert

limit
1 *noun* la limite
2 *verb* limiter; **I'm limiting myself to one cigarette a day** je me limite à une cigarette par jour

limited *adjective* limité/limitée; **there was a very limited choice** il y avait un choix très limité

limp
1 *noun* **to have a limp** *or* **to walk with a limp** boiter
2 *verb* boiter

line
1 *noun*
(**a**) *(mark)* la ligne; *(drawn)* le trait; **to draw a line** tracer un trait; **a straight line** une ligne droite
(**b**) *(of a poem)* le vers; *(of a piece of writing)* la ligne; **he got 100 lines** on lui a donné 100 lignes à copier; **I'll drop her a line** je lui enverrai un mot
(**c**) *(of people, cars)* la file
(**d**) *(track)* la voie; *(route of public transport)* la ligne
(**e**) *(for telephone)* la ligne; **the line's engaged** la ligne est occupée
2 *verb* **the road is lined with trees** la route est bordée d'arbres

3 line up se mettre en file; **line up outside the classroom** mettez-vous en file devant la classe

linen *noun*
(a) *(fabric)* le lin; **a linen sheet** un drap en lin
(b) *(sheets)* le linge

link
1 *noun*
(a) *(of a chain)* le maillon; **the weak link** le maillon faible
(b) *(connection)* le lien; **there's no link between the two events** il n'y aucun lien entre les deux événements
2 *verb*
(a) *(physically)* relier; **the towns are linked by a bridge** les villes sont reliées par un pont
(b) *(by a connection)* lier; **the two crimes are linked** les deux crimes sont liés

lino *noun* le lino

lion *noun* le lion; **a lion cub** un lionceau

The plural of *lionceau* is *lionceaux*.

lip *noun* la lèvre; **I bit my lip** je me suis mordu la lèvre; **lip gloss** le brillant à lèvres

lip-read *verb* lire sur les lèvres; **can you lip-read?** est-ce que vous savez lire sur les lèvres?

lipstick *noun* le rouge à lèvres

liquid *noun* le liquide

liquorice *noun* le/la réglisse

list
1 *noun* la liste; **your name's not on the list** ton nom n'est pas sur la liste; **I made a list of things to do** j'ai fait une liste de choses à faire
2 *verb* faire la liste de; **list everything you have to do for your exam** fais une liste de tout ce que tu as à faire pour tes examens

listen *noun* écouter; **I'm listening to the radio** j'écoute la radio; **listen to me** écoute-moi; **he wouldn't listen** il

n'a rien voulu savoir

literally *adverb* littéralement

literature *noun* la littérature; **French literature** la littérature française

Do not confuse the spellings of the French *littérature* and English *literature*.

Lithuania *noun* la Lituanie; **she lives in Lithuania** elle habite en Lituanie; **I'm going to Lithuania** je vais en Lituanie; **he comes from Lithuania** il est Lituanien.

Lithuanian
1 *adjective* lituanien/lituanienne
2 *noun*
(a) *(language)* le lituanien; **she speaks Lithuanian** elle parle lituanien
(b) *(person)* le Lituanien/la Lituanienne; **the Lithuanians** les Lituaniens *(masculine plural)*

In French, only the noun for the inhabitants of a country takes a capital letter, never the adjective or the noun for the language.

litre *noun* le litre; **a litre of milk** un litre de lait

litter *noun* *(in the street)* les détritus *(masculine plural)*; **to drop litter** jeter des détritus par terre; **a litter bin** une poubelle

little
1 *adjective*
(a) *(small)* petit/petite; **when I was little** quand j'étais petit; **a little girl** une petite fille; **my little finger** mon petit doigt; **in a little while** dans un petit moment
(b) *(not much)* peu de; **they have little money** ils ont peu d'argent; **we have very little time** nous avons très peu de temps
(c) **a little** un peu de; **a little money** un peu d'argent; **he speaks a little French** il parle un peu français
2 *adverb* *(not much)* peu; **I see him very little** je le vois très peu

3 *pronoun* **a little** un peu; **do you want some water? – yes, a little** tu veux de l'eau? – oui, un peu; **would you like a little more?** est-ce que tu en voudrais encore un peu?; **little by little** peu à peu

live¹ *verb* vivre; *(reside)* habiter, vivre; **she lives with her dad** elle vit avec son père; **they live in a big house** ils habitent dans une grande maison; **he lives in Newcastle** il habite Newcastle *or* il habite à Newcastle; **I live in Clark Street** j'habite Clark Street; **they live in the same street** il habitent dans la même rue; **they live together** ils vivent ensemble; **she's still living** elle est toujours en vie

live² *adjective*
(**a**) *(living)* vivant/vivante; **a live animal** un animal vivant
(**b**) *(not recorded)* en direct; **a live broadcast** une émission en direct

lively *adjective* *(person)* vivant/vivante; *(street, place)* animé/animée

liver *noun* le foie

living
1 *adjective* *(animal, being)* vivant/vivante
2 *noun* la vie; **to earn a living** gagner sa vie; **what does he do for a living?** qu'est-ce qu'il fait dans la vie?; **a living room** un salon

lizard *noun* le lézard

load
1 *noun*
(**a**) *(something carried)* la charge
(**b**) **loads of money, a load of money** beaucoup d'argent; **we've got loads of time** nous avons largement le temps
2 *verb* charger; **he's loading the bags into the car** il est en train de charger les sacs dans la voiture; **is the gun loaded?** est-ce que le pistolet est chargé?

loaf *noun* le pain; **a loaf of bread** un pain

loan
1 *noun*
(**a**) *(when borrowing)* un emprunt; **I got a loan from the bank** j'ai fait un emprunt à la banque
(**b**) *(when lending)* le prêt; **the bank gave me a loan** la banque m'a accordé un prêt
2 *verb* prêter; **he loaned me his car** il m'a prêté sa voiture

lobster *noun* le homard

local *adjective* local/locale; *(of the neighbourhood)* du quartier; **a local newspaper** un journal local; **the local bakery** la boulangerie du quartier

> The masculine plural of *local* is *locaux*.

locally *adverb* **he lives locally** il habite dans le quartier

location *noun* un emplacement; **the hotel is in a nice location** l'hôtel est bien situé

> Note that the French word *location* is never a translation for the English word *location*. It means *renting*.

lock
1 *noun* la serrure
2 *verb* fermer à clé; **did you lock the door?** est-ce que tu as fermé la porte à clé?
3 lock in **he locked me in** il m'a enfermé; **he locked himself in** il s'est enfermé; **they locked her in her room** ils l'ont enfermée dans sa chambre
4 lock out **he locked me out** il m'a enfermé dehors; **he locked himself out** il s'est enfermé dehors; **she locked me out of the house** elle m'a enfermé à l'extérieur de la maison
5 lock up fermer à clé; **don't forget to lock up** n'oublie pas de fermer à clé

locker *noun* le casier

loft *noun* le grenier; **there's plenty of space in the loft** il y a plein de place dans le grenier

log *noun* la bûche; **a log cabin** une cabane en rondins

logical *adjective* logique

lollipop *noun* la sucette

London *noun* Londres; **I live in London** j'habite à Londres; **I'm going to London on Monday** je vais à Londres lundi; **he comes from London** il vient de Londres

lonely *adjective* *(person)* seul/seule; *(place)* isolé/isolée; **to feel lonely** se sentir seul

long¹
1 *adjective*
(**a**) *(in size)* long/longue; **a long dress** une robe longue; **how long is the table?** quelle est la longueur de la table?; **the room is four metres long** la pièce fait quatre mètres de long; **it's a long way** c'est loin; **the long jump** le saut en longueur
(**b**) *(in time)* long/longue; **the film is three hours long** le film dure trois heures; **a long time ago** il y a longtemps; **I've known her a long time** je la connais depuis longtemps
2 *adverb*
(**a**) longtemps; **we didn't stay long** nous ne sommes pas restés longtemps; **he won't be long** il n'en a pas pour longtemps; **how long have you known her?** depuis combien de temps est-ce que tu la connais?; **how long will it take?** combien de temps est-ce que ça va prendre?
(**b**) **as long as** *(during the time that)* tant que; *(provided that)* à condition que; **I will stay as long as you need me** je resterai tant que tu auras besoin de moi; **you can go out as long as you're back before midnight** tu peux sortir à condition que tu rentres avant minuit

long² *verb* **I'm longing to see her again** j'ai hâte de la revoir; **I'm longing for the holidays** j'ai hâte d'être en vacances

longer *adverb* **five minutes longer** cinq minutes de plus; **I couldn't wait any longer** je ne pouvais plus attendre; **I no longer see him** je ne le vois plus

long-sighted *adjective* presbyte; **she's long-sighted** elle est presbyte

loo *noun* les toilettes *(feminine plural)*; **where's the loo?** où sont les toilettes?

look
1 *noun*
(**a**) *(act of looking)* **to have a look at something** regarder quelque chose; **let me have a look** fais voir; **I must have a look for that book** il faut que je cherche ce livre
(**b**) *(glance)* le regard; **she gave me a dirty look** elle m'a jeté un regard noir
2 *verb*
(**a**) regarder; **come and look!** viens voir!; **I'm just looking, thanks** je ne fais que regarder, merci
(**b**) *(seem)* avoir l'air; **she looks tired** elle a l'air fatigué; **you look cold** tu as l'air d'avoir froid; **the food didn't look very good** la nourriture n'avait pas l'air très appétissante; **what does she look like?** comment est-elle?; **she looks like her mum** elle ressemble à sa mère; **they look alike** ils se ressemblent
3 look after
(**a**) *(take care of)* s'occuper de; **can you look after the children tomorrow?** est-ce que tu peux garder les enfants demain?
(**b**) *(keep safely)* garder; **can you look after my bag for me?** est-ce que tu peux surveiller mon sac?
4 look at regarder; **he's looking at you** il te regarde; **can I look at your book?** est-ce que je peux regarder ton livre?
5 look for chercher; **I'm looking for my bag** je cherche mon sac
6 look forward to attendre avec impatience; **I'm really looking forward to the holidays** j'attends les vacances avec beaucoup d'impatience

7 look out faire attention; **look out! fais attention!**

8 look round
(**a**) *(turn one's head)* se retourner; **he looked round to see who it was** il s'est retourné pour voir qui c'était
(**b**) **we looked round the shops** nous avons fait les magasins

9 look up
(**a**) *(with the eyes)* lever les yeux
(**b**) **to look up a word in the dictionary** chercher un mot dans le dictionnaire

loose *adjective*
(**a**) *(knot, belt, screw)* desserré/desserrée; **the screw is loose** la vis est desserrée; **she has a loose tooth** elle a une dent qui bouge
(**b**) *(page)* détaché/détachée; **some pages have come loose** certaines pages se sont détachées
(**c**) *(clothes)* ample; **my skirt is too loose at the waist** ma jupe est trop ample au niveau de la taille

loosen *verb (a knot, a belt, a screw)* desserrer

lord *noun* le seigneur; **Lord Clyde** lord Clyde

lorry *noun* le camion; **a lorry driver** un camionneur/une camionneuse

lose *verb* perdre; **I've lost my umbrella** j'ai perdu mon parapluie; **she's lost weight** elle a perdu du poids; **I've lost my appetite** j'ai perdu l'appétit; **England lost last night** l'Angleterre a perdu hier soir

loser *noun* le perdant/la perdante; **don't be such a bad loser!** ne sois pas si mauvais perdant!

loss *noun* la perte; **the company has made a loss** la société a perdu de l'argent

lost *adjective* perdu/perdue; **can you help me, I'm lost** pouvez-vous m'aider, je suis perdu; **I got lost** je me suis perdu

lost-property office *noun* le bureau des objets trouvés

lot *noun*
(**a**) **a lot of, lots of** beaucoup de; **a lot of money, lots of money** beaucoup d'argent; **quite a lot of books** pas mal de livres; **I have quite a lot of friends** j'ai pas mal d'amis
(**b**) **a lot** beaucoup; **I read a lot** je lis beaucoup; **thanks a lot!** merci beaucoup!; **I have a lot to do** j'ai beaucoup de choses à faire
(**c**) **lots** beaucoup; **I have lots** j'en ai beaucoup; **I miss him lots** il me manque beaucoup
(**d**) **the lot** *(everything)* le tout; **he drank the lot** il a tout bu

lottery *noun* la loterie; **he won the lottery** il a gagné à la loterie

loud
1 *adjective* fort/forte; **the music's too loud** la musique est trop forte; **a loud noise** un grand bruit
2 *adverb* fort; **he speaks too loud** il parle trop fort; **he read out loud to her** il lui a lu à haute voix

loudly *adverb* fort; **she was singing loudly** elle chantait fort; **don't speak so loudly!** ne parle pas si fort!

loudspeaker *noun* un haut-parleur

> The plural of *haut-parleur* is *haut-parleurs*.

lounge *noun* le salon

love
1 *noun* l'amour *(masculine)*; **to be in love** être amoureux/amoureuse; **she's in love with him** elle est amoureuse de lui; **to fall in love** tomber amoureux/amoureuse; **he fell in love with her** il est tombé amoureux d'elle; **give my love to your parents** embrasse tes parents pour moi
2 *verb (a person)* aimer; *(a thing, an activity)* adorer; **I love you** je t'aime; **I love chocolate cake** j'adore le gâteau au chocolat; **I love playing football** j'adore jouer au football

lovely *adjective*
(**a**) *(beautiful)* beau/belle; **their**

house is lovely leur maison est belle; **the weather was lovely** il a fait beau

The masculine plural of *beau* is *beaux*.

(**b**) *(very good)* excellent/excellente; **I had a lovely holiday** j'ai passé des vacances excellentes; **this cake is lovely** ce gâteau est excellent
(**c**) *(charming)* charmant/charmante; **her mum's a lovely woman** sa mère est une femme charmante

low
1 *adjective* bas/basse; **a low wall** un mur bas; **he spoke in a low voice** il a parlé à voix basse
2 *adverb* bas; **turn the music down low** baisse la musique

low-fat *adjective* allégé/allegée; **low-fat mayonnaise** la mayonnaise allégée

luck *noun* la chance; **to have good luck** avoir de la chance; **good luck!** bonne chance!; **bad luck!** pas de chance!; **you're in luck** tu as de la chance; **you're out of luck** tu n'as pas de chance; **he wished her luck** il lui a souhaité bonne chance

luckily *adverb* heureusement; **luckily he didn't see me** heureusement, il ne m'a pas vu

lucky *adjective* **to be lucky** avoir de la chance; **it's lucky I was there** heureusement que j'étais là

luggage *noun* les bagages *(masculine plural)*; **my luggage is over there** mes bagages sont là-bas; **one piece of luggage** un bagage; **a luggage rack** un porte-bagages

The word *porte-bagages* does not change in the plural.

lump *noun*
(**a**) *(piece)* le morceau; **a lump of cheese** un morceau de fromage; **a lump of sugar, a sugar lump** un morceau de sucre

The plural of *morceau* is *morceaux*.

(**b**) *(bump)* la bosse; **I have a lump on my head** j'ai une bosse à la tête

lunch *noun* le déjeuner; **what's for lunch?** qu'est-ce qu'il y a pour le déjeuner?; **I had soup for lunch** j'ai pris de la soupe pour le déjeuner; **I'm having lunch** je suis en train de déjeuner; **the lunch hour** la pause de midi

lunchbox *noun* la boîte à sandwichs

lung *noun* le poumon; **lung cancer** le cancer du poumon

Luxembourg *noun* le Luxembourg; **she lives in Luxembourg** elle habite au Luxembourg; **they're going to Luxembourg** ils vont au Luxembourg; **his mum comes from Luxembourg** sa mère est luxembourgeoise

luxury *noun* le luxe; **a luxury car** une voiture de luxe

M m

mac *noun (raincoat)* un imperméable

macaroni *noun* les macaronis *(masculine plural)*; **I love macaroni** j'adore les macaronis

machine *noun*
(**a**) la machine; **a sewing machine** une machine à coudre
(**b**) **a machine gun** une mitrailleuse

mad *adjective*
(**a**) *(insane)* fou/folle; **are you mad?** mais tu es fou!; **she went mad** elle est devenue folle
(**b**) *(angry)* en colère; **my mother is mad at me for breaking the vase** ma mère est en colère contre moi parce que j'ai cassé le vase; **he went mad** il s'est mis en colère
(**c**) **he's mad about tennis** il adore le tennis; **she's mad about him** elle est folle de lui

madam *noun* madame *(feminine)*; **would you like some coffee, madam?** est-ce que vous prendrez du café, madame?; **Dear Madam** *(in a letter)* Madame

madly *adverb* **she was screaming madly** elle criait comme une folle; **he's madly in love with her** il est fou amoureux d'elle

madman *noun* le fou; **he drives like a madman** il conduit comme un fou

madness *noun* la folie; **this is madness!** c'est de la folie!

magazine *noun* le magazine, la revue; **a sports magazine** un magazine de sport

magic
1 *noun* la magie
2 *adjective* magique; **a magic wand** une baguette magique

magician *noun* le magicien/la magicienne

magnet *noun* un aimant

magnifying glass *noun* la loupe

maid *noun* la domestique, la bonne

maiden name *noun* le nom de jeune fille

mail
1 *noun*
(**a**) *(letters)* le courrier; **is there any mail today?** est-ce qu'il y a du courrier aujourd'hui?
(**b**) *(postal service)* la poste; **by mail** par la poste
2 *verb* poster; **can you mail this letter for me, please?** est-ce que tu peux poster cette lettre pour moi, s'il te plaît?

mailbox *noun* la boîte aux lettres

main *adjective* principal/principale; **the main actors** les acteurs principaux; **the main course** le plat principal

The masculine plural of *principal* is *principaux*.

mainly *adverb* surtout

maintenance *noun* l'entretien *(masculine)*

maize *noun* le maïs

The word *maïs* is pronounced almost like the English word *mice*.

major *adjective* majeur/majeure; **it's a major problem** c'est un problème majeur; **a major road** une grande route

majority *noun* la majorité

make
1 *noun* la marque; **what make of washing machine do you have?** quelle est la marque de votre machine à laver?
2 *verb*
(**a**) faire; **she wants to make a cake** elle veut faire un gâteau; **stop making a noise!** arrête de faire du bruit!; **he made lots of mistakes** il a fait plein de fautes; **have you made your bed?** est-ce que tu as fait ton lit?; **six and six make twelve** six et six font douze
(**b**) *(produce)* fabriquer; **these toys are made in China** ces jouets sont fabriqués en Chine; **he made this table himself** il a fabriqué cette table lui-même; **it's made of plastic** c'est en plastique
(**c**) *(earn)* gagner; **she makes over £50,000 a year** elle gagne plus de 50 000 livres par an
(**d**) *(prepare)* préparer, faire; **I'll go and make the dinner** je vais préparer le repas; **he's making coffee** il est en train de faire du café
(**e**) *(cause to be)* rendre; **to make somebody happy** rendre quelqu'un heureux; **it made him ill** ça l'a rendu malade; **it made me thirsty** ça m'a donné soif
(**f**) **to make somebody do something** faire faire quelque chose à quelqu'un; **my mum made me tidy my room** ma mère m'a fait ranger ma chambre; **he made me laugh** il m'a fait rire
3 make out
(**a**) *(see)* distinguer; **I could barely make out the house in the fog** j'arrivais à peine à distinguer la maison dans le brouillard
(**b**) *(understand)* comprendre; **I can't make her out at all** je ne la comprends pas du tout
(**c**) *(write)* faire; **to make out a list** faire une liste

4 make up
(**a**) *(invent)* inventer; **he made up an excuse** il a inventé une excuse
(**b**) *(end a quarrel)* se réconcilier; **they never made up after their argument** ils ne se sont jamais réconciliés après leur dispute

make-up *noun* le maquillage; **to put on one's make-up** se maquiller

male
1 *adjective*
(**a**) *(referring to animals)* mâle; **a male butterfly** un papillon mâle
(**b**) *(referring to men)* masculin/masculine; **male fashion** la mode masculine; **the male sex** le sexe masculin; **a male nurse** un infirmier
2 *noun* le mâle

mall *noun* **a mall, a shopping mall** un centre commercial

> The plural of *centre commercial* is *centres commerciaux.*

Malta *noun* Malte *(feminine)*; **Malta is part of the EU** Malte fait partie de l'Union européenne; **he lives in Malta** il habite à Malte; **she's going to Malta** elle va à Malte; **she's from Malta** elle vient de Malte

Maltese
1 *adjective* maltais/maltaise
2 *noun*
(**a**) *(language)* le maltais; **he speaks Maltese** il parle maltais
(**b**) *(person)* le Maltais/la Maltaise; **the Maltese** les Maltais *(masculine plural)*

> In French, only the noun for the inhabitants of a country takes a capital letter, never the adjective or the noun for the language.

mammal *noun* le mammifère

man *noun* un homme

manage *verb*
(**a**) *(run)* diriger; **he manages a shoe factory** il dirige une usine de chaussures

(**b**) *(deal with a situation, get by)* se débrouiller, y arriver; **I can manage on my own** je peux me débrouiller tout seul; **are you managing?** tu y arrives?
(**c**) **to manage to do something** réussir à faire quelque chose; **he managed to get a pay rise** il a réussi à avoir une augmentation

management *noun*
(**a**) *(organizing)* la gestion; **he's studying management** il étudie la gestion
(**b**) *(people in charge)* la direction

manager *noun*
(**a**) *(of a company)* le directeur/la directrice; **my dad is a manager** mon père est directeur
(**b**) *(of a shop, a café)* le gérant/la gérante

mango *noun* la mangue

maniac *noun* le fou/la folle; **she drives like a maniac** elle conduit comme une folle

mankind *noun* l'humanité *(feminine)*

man-made *adjective*
(**a**) *(lake, hill)* artificiel/artificielle
(**b**) *(fibre, material)* synthétique

manner *noun*
(**a**) *(way)* la manière, la façon; **the manner in which he said it** la manière dont il l'a dit
(**b**) *(behaviour)* **manners** les manières; **to teach somebody manners** apprendre les bonnes manières à quelqu'un; **it's bad manners not to say hello** ce n'est pas poli de ne pas dire bonjour

mansion *noun* le manoir

mantelpiece *noun* la cheminée; **the clock is on the mantelpiece** la pendule est sur la cheminée

many
1 *adjective*
(**a**) beaucoup de; **there were many cars in the car park** il y avait beaucoup de voitures dans le parking; **there are many people in town** il y a beaucoup de monde en ville

(**b**) **too many** trop de; **there are too many people on the beach** il y a trop de monde sur la plage
(**c**) **as many… as** autant de… que; **have as many biscuits as you want** prends autant de biscuits que tu veux; **I don't have as many friends as she does** je n'ai pas autant d'amis qu'elle
(**d**) **so many** tellement de; **there were so many people** il y avait tellement de monde
(**e**) **how many** combien de; **how many CDs have you got?** combien de CD est-ce que tu as?
2 *pronoun*
(**a**) beaucoup; **I can only give you one biscuit because I haven't got many** je ne peux te donner qu'un biscuit car je n'en ai pas beaucoup; **there are many** il y en a beaucoup *or* il y en a plein
(**b**) **I have too many** j'en ai trop; **I have so many** j'en ai tellement
(**c**) **how many** combien; **how many have you got?** combien est-ce que tu en as?

map *noun*
(**a**) *(of a country, a region)* la carte; **a map of France** une carte de France
(**b**) *(of a town)* le plan; **a map of Paris** un plan de Paris

maple *noun* un érable; **maple syrup** le sirop d'érable

marble *noun*
(**a**) *(stone)* le marbre; **a marble table** une table en marbre
(**b**) *(toy)* la bille; **to play marbles** jouer aux billes

March *noun* mars *(masculine)*; **the first of March** le premier mars; **the second of March** le deux mars; **the third of March** le trois mars; **in March** en mars

---

Names of months are not capitalized in French.

---

march
1 *verb*
(**a**) *(of soldiers)* défiler

(**b**) *(of protesters)* manifester
2 *noun (protest)* la manifestation

mare *noun* la jument

margarine *noun* la margarine

margin *noun* la marge; **in the margin** dans la marge

mark
1 *noun*
(**a**) *(stain)* la tache; **there's a mark on your jumper** il y a une tache sur ton pull
(**b**) *(trace)* la trace, la marque; **the cup left a mark on the table** la tasse a laissé une trace sur la table
(**c**) *(at school)* la note; **he gets good marks** il a de bonnes notes
2 *verb*
(**a**) *(stain)* tacher
(**b**) *(indicate)* indiquer; **he marked the place on the map** il a indiqué le lieu sur la carte
(**c**) *(of a teacher)* corriger; **the teacher hasn't marked my essay yet** le prof n'a pas encore corrigé ma rédaction

market *noun* le marché; **I bought some strawberries at the market** j'ai acheté des fraises au marché; **there's no market for these products** il n'y a pas de marché pour ces produits

marketing *noun* le marketing

marmalade *noun* la confiture d'oranges

marriage *noun* le mariage

Do not confuse the spellings of the French *mariage* and English *marriage*.

married *adjective* marié/mariée; **a married woman** une femme mariée

marry *verb*
(**a**) se marier; **she married very young** elle s'est mariée très jeune
(**b**) *(somebody)* épouser; **he married an American** il a épousé une Américaine
(**c**) **to get married to somebody** se marier avec quelqu'un

marvellous *adjective* merveilleux/merveilleuse

marzipan *noun* la pâte d'amandes

masculine
1 *adjective* masculin/masculine
2 *noun* le masculin; **in the masculine** au masculin

mashed potatoes *noun* la purée (de pommes de terre); **he doesn't like mashed potatoes** il n'aime pas la purée

mask *noun* le masque

mass *noun*
(**a**) **masses of** plein de; **he has masses of books** il a plein de livres
(**b**) *(church service)* la messe; **to go to mass** aller à la messe

massage *noun* le massage; **she gave me a massage** elle m'a fait un massage

massive *noun* énorme

mast *noun* le mât

master *noun* le maître

masterpiece *noun* le chef-d'œuvre

The *f* in *chef-d'œuvre* is not pronounced. The plural of *chef-d'œuvre* is *chefs-d'œuvre*.

mat *noun*
(**a**) *(on the floor)* le petit tapis
(**b**) *(on a doorstep)* le paillasson
(**c**) **a table mat** un set de table

match
1 *noun*
(**a**) *(for lighting things)* une allumette; **a box of matches** une boîte d'allumettes
(**b**) *(in sport)* le match; **a tennis match** un match de tennis
2 *verb* **her handbag matches her shoes** son sac est assorti à ses chaussures

matchbox *noun* la boîte d'allumettes

matching *adjective* assorti/assortie; **a matching handbag and shoes** un sac à main et des chaussures assortis

mate *noun*
(a) *(friend)* le copain/la copine
(b) *(term of address)* **watch where you're going, mate!** regarde où tu vas!

material
1 *adjective* matériel/matérielle; **material possessions** les biens matériels
2 *noun*
(a) *(cloth)* le tissu
(b) *(substance)* la matière; **raw materials** les matières premières

mathematics *noun* les mathématiques *(feminine plural)*

maths *noun* les maths *(feminine plural)*; **he loves maths** il adore les maths

matter
1 *noun*
(a) *(issue, question)* une question, une affaire; **it's a matter of taste** c'est une question de goût
(b) *(problem)* **what's the matter?** qu'est-ce qu'il y a?; **what's the matter with you?** qu'est-ce que tu as?; **there's something the matter** il y a quelque chose qui ne va pas
2 *verb* avoir de l'importance; **it doesn't matter** ça n'a pas d'importance *or* ça ne fait rien

mattress *noun* le matelas

maximum
1 *adjective* maximum; **the maximum temperature** la température maximum
2 *noun* le maximum; **we'll stay for a maximum of three days** nous resterons trois jours au maximum

May *noun* mai *(masculine)*; **the first of May** le premier mai; **the second of May** le deux mai; **the third of May** le trois mai; **in May** en mai

Names of months are not capitalized in French.

may *verb*
(a) *(possibility)* pouvoir; **she may come tonight** il se peut qu'elle vienne ce soir; **I may be wrong** je me trompe

peut-être; **we may as well leave** on ferait aussi bien de partir
(b) *(permission)* pouvoir; **may I leave the table?** est-ce que je peux quitter la table?

maybe *adverb* peut-être; **maybe she'll come** peut-être qu'elle viendra *or* elle viendra peut-être

mayor *noun* le maire

me *pronoun*
(a) me; **she sees me** elle me voit; **she saw me** elle m'a vu

In French *me* becomes *m'* in front of a vowel or a mute h.

(b) *(after a preposition or the verb "to be")* moi; **it's me** c'est moi; **in front of me** devant moi; **answer me** réponds-moi
(c) *(indirect)* moi; **give me the newspaper** donne-moi le journal; **give it to me** donne-le-moi; **he gave it to me** il me l'a donné

meadow *noun* le pré

meal *noun* le repas

mean¹ *verb*
(a) *(signify)* vouloir dire; **what does it mean?** qu'est-ce que ça veut dire?; **that's not what I meant** ce n'est pas ce que je voulais dire
(b) *(intend)* **to mean to do something** avoir l'intention de faire quelque chose *or* vouloir faire quelque chose; **I meant to tell her but I forgot** je voulais le lui dire mais j'ai oublié; **I didn't mean to!** je ne l'ai pas fait exprès; **I mean it!** je suis sérieux! *or* je ne plaisante pas!; **these flowers are meant for you** ces fleurs sont pour toi; **you were meant to write your essay by Friday** tu étais censé écrire ta rédaction pour vendredi

mean² *adjective*
(a) *(with money)* avare; **he's so mean that he didn't give me a birthday present** il est tellement avare qu'il ne m'a pas offert de cadeau d'anniversaire
(b) *(nasty)* méchant/méchante; **don't**

be mean to your little sister ne sois pas méchant avec ta petite sœur

meaning *noun* le sens, la signification

means *noun* le moyen; **a means of transport** un moyen de transport; **there are other means of doing it** il y a d'autres moyens de le faire

meanwhile *adverb*
(**a**) *(while something else is happening)* en attendant; **the dinner will soon be ready, meanwhile you can lay the table** le repas sera bientôt prêt, en attendant tu peux mettre la table
(**b**) *(during this time)* pendant ce temps; **meanwhile I was stuck in the lift** pendant ce temps j'étais coincé dans l'ascenseur

measles *noun* la rougeole; **I've got measles** j'ai la rougeole

measure *verb* mesurer; **the garden measures 25 metres by 20** le jardin mesure 25 mètres sur 20; **you need to measure the table before you buy it** il faut que tu mesures la table avant de l'acheter

measurement *noun* la dimension; **what are the measurements of the room?** quelles sont les dimensions de la pièce?

meat *noun* la viande

mechanic *noun* le mécanicien/la mécanicienne; **my brother is a mechanic** mon frère est mécanicien

Note that the French word *mécanique* is never a translation for the English word *mechanic*. It means *mechanics*.

mechanism *noun* le mécanisme

medal *noun* la médaille

media *noun* **the media** les médias *(masculine plural)*

medical *adjective* médical/médicale; **a medical student** un étudiant en médecine

The masculine plural of *médical* is *médicaux*.

medicine *noun*
(**a**) *(drug)* le médicament; **take your medicine** prends ton médicament
(**b**) *(science)* la médecine; **she's studying medicine** elle fait des études de médecine

Do not confuse the spellings of the French *médecine* and English *medicine*.

Mediterranean
1 *adjective (country, climate)* méditerranéen/méditerranéenne; **the Mediterranean Sea** la mer Méditerranée
2 *noun* **the Mediterranean** la Méditerranée

medium *adjective* moyen/moyenne

meet *verb*
(**a**) *(see for the first time)* rencontrer; **I met her at a party** je l'ai rencontrée à une soirée; **we met in school** nous nous sommes rencontrés au lycée
(**b**) *(bump into)* rencontrer; **guess who I met in the street yesterday?** devine qui j'ai rencontré dans la rue hier?
(**c**) *(be introduced to)* faire la connaissance de; **have you met Paul's parents?** est-ce que tu as fait la connaissance des parents de Paul?; **pleased to meet you** enchanté de faire votre connaissance
(**d**) *(arrange to see)* retrouver; **I'm meeting him tonight at nine** je le retrouve ce soir à neuf heures; **shall we meet outside the cinema?** on se retrouve devant le cinéma?
(**e**) *(collect)* aller/venir chercher; **I told her that I'd meet her at the station** je lui ai dit que j'irais la chercher à la gare; **can you meet me at the airport?** tu peux venir me chercher à l'aéroport?

meeting *noun*
(**a**) *(for work)* la réunion
(**b**) *(between two people)* la rencontre

melody *noun* la mélodie

melon *noun* le melon

melt *verb* fondre; **the ice has melted** la glace a fondu; **put the butter in the fridge or it'll melt** mets le beurre au frigidaire sinon il va fondre

member *noun* le membre

memorize *verb* apprendre par cœur, mémoriser; **he memorized the words to the song** il a appris les paroles de la chanson par cœur

memory *noun*
(**a**) *(faculty)* la mémoire; **he has a good memory** il a une bonne mémoire; **he has a bad memory** il a une mauvaise mémoire; **he's losing his memory** il perd la mémoire
(**b**) *(something remembered)* le souvenir; **childhood memories** les souvenirs d'enfance

mend *verb*
(**a**) *(a car, a piece of furniture)* réparer
(**b**) *(a piece of clothing)* raccommoder

mental *adjective* mental/mentale; **a mental illness** une maladie mentale; **mental arithmetic** le calcul mental

> The masculine plural of *mental* is *mentaux*.

mention *verb* parler de, mentionner; **she never mentions her past** elle ne parle jamais de son passé; **he mentioned her name in his speech** il a mentionné son nom dans son discours

menu *noun* le menu

mercy *noun* la pitié

merry *adjective* joyeux/joyeuse; **Merry Christmas!** joyeux Noël!

merry-go-round *noun* le manège

mess
1 *noun*
(**a**) *(untidy state)* le désordre, le fouillis; **his room is in a mess** sa chambre est en désordre
(**b**) *(dirt)* les saletés *(feminine plural)*; **you'll have to clean up the mess**

you've made il va falloir que tu nettoies tes saletés
2 mess about, mess around
(**a**) *(play the fool)* faire l'imbécile; **stop messing about and listen to me!** arrête de faire l'imbécile et écoute-moi!
(**b**) *(have fun)* s'amuser; **the children are messing about in their room** les enfants s'amusent dans leur chambre
(**c**) *(fiddle with)* toucher à; **don't mess about with my computer** ne touche pas à mon ordinateur

message *noun* le message

messenger *noun* le messager/la messagère

messy *adjective*
(**a**) *(untidy)* en désordre; **his room is messy** sa chambre est en désordre
(**b**) *(dirty)* sale; **don't get all messy** ne te salis pas

metal *noun* le métal; **it's made of metal** c'est en métal

> The plural of *metal* is *métaux*.

meter *noun*
(**a**) *(parking meter)* le parcmètre; **don't forget to put money in the meter** n'oublie pas de mettre de l'argent dans le parcmètre
(**b**) *(for gas, electricity, in a taxi)* le compteur; **to read the meter** relever le compteur

> The *p* in *compteur* is not pronounced.

method *noun* la méthode

metre *noun* le mètre

Mexican
1 *adjective* mexicain/mexicaine
2 *noun* *(person)* le Mexicain/la Mexicaine; **the Mexicans** les Mexicains *(masculine plural)*

> In French, only the noun for the inhabitants of a country takes a capital letter, never the adjective.

Mexico *noun*
(**a**) le Mexique; **he lives in Mexico** il

habite au Mexique; **have you ever been to Mexico?** est-ce que tu es déjà allé au Mexique?; **it comes from Mexico** ça vient du Mexique (b) **Mexico City** Mexico; **he lives in Mexico City** il habite à Mexico

microchip *noun* la puce (électronique)

microphone *noun* le micro

microscope *noun* le microscope

microwave *noun (oven)* le four à micro-ondes, le micro-ondes

The word *micro-ondes* does not change in the plural.

midday *noun* midi *(masculine)*; **we'll leave at midday** nous partirons à midi

middle *noun* le milieu; **in the middle of the room** au milieu de la pièce; **in the middle of the night** au milieu de la nuit

The plural of *milieu* is *milieux*.

middle-aged *adjective* d'une cinquantaine d'années; **his parents are middle-aged** ses parents ont une cinquantaine d'années

middle-class *adjective* bourgeois/bourgeoise; **she comes from a very middle-class family** elle vient d'une famille très bourgeoise

midnight *noun* minuit *(masculine)*; **it's midnight** il est minuit; **at midnight** à minuit

midwife *noun* la sage-femme

The plural of *sage-femme* is *sages-femmes*.

might *verb* **it might rain** il va peut-être pleuvoir *or* il se pourrait qu'il pleuve; **I might come** je viendrai peut-être

mild *adjective* doux/douce; **a mild climate** un climat doux

mile *noun* le mile; **he lives miles away from here** il habite à des kilomètres d'ici

Note that people in France do not use miles as a unit of distance, they use kilometres (1 mile = 1.609 kilometres).

military
1 *adjective* militaire
2 *noun* **the military** l'armée *(feminine)*

milk *noun* le lait

milkman *noun* le laitier

mill *noun* le moulin

millimetre *noun* le millimètre

million *noun* **a million** un million; **a million people** un million de personnes; **two million** deux millions

millionaire *noun* le/la millionnaire

Do not confuse the spellings of the French *millionnaire* and English *millionaire*.

mince *noun (meat)* la viande hachée

mind
1 *noun*
(a) l'esprit *(masculine)*; **it went clean out of my mind** ça m'est complètement sorti de l'esprit
(b) **to change one's mind** changer d'avis; **he changed his mind again** il a encore changé d'avis; **to make up one's mind** se décider; **make up your mind!** décide-toi!; **he has a lot on his mind** il a beaucoup de soucis; **I have something on my mind** il y a quelque chose qui me préoccupe
2 *verb*
(a) *(look after)* garder, surveiller; **can you mind my suitcase, I'll be right back** tu peux garder ma valise, je reviens tout de suite; **he agreed to mind the children while I went shopping** il a bien voulu garder les enfants pendant que j'allais faire des courses; **mind your own business!** occupe-toi de tes affaires!
(b) *(be bothered about)* **do you mind if I smoke?** ça vous dérange si je fume?; **I don't mind walking there** ça ne me

dérange pas d'y aller à pied; **one or the other, I don't mind!** l'un ou l'autre, ça m'est égal!; **never mind!** *(it doesn't matter)* ça ne fait rien!; *(don't worry)* ne vous en faites pas!; **I wouldn't mind a cup of tea** je prendrais bien une tasse de thé (c) *(be careful of)* **mind the step!** attention à la marche!; **mind the cat!** attention au chat!

(d) **mind you, I'm not surprised** remarque, cela ne m'étonne pas

mine¹ *pronoun*
(a) *(when the thing possessed is masculine in French)* le mien; **it's not your pen, it's mine** ce n'est pas ton stylo, c'est le mien; **this pen is mine** ce stylo est à moi
(b) *(when the thing possessed is feminine in French)* la mienne; **it's not Paul's cup, it's mine** ce n'est pas la tasse de Paul, c'est la mienne; **this cup is mine** cette tasse est à moi
(c) *(when the thing possessed is masculine plural in French)* les miens; **these are not Claire's books, they're mine** ce ne sont pas les livres de Claire, ce sont les miens; **these books are mine** ces livres sont à moi
(d) *(when the thing possessed is feminine plural in French)* les miennes; **these are not your glasses, they're mine** ce ne sont pas tes lunettes, ce sont les miennes; **these glasses are mine** ces lunettes sont à moi

The form used in French is determined by the gender and number of the noun it stands for.

mine² *noun* la mine; **a coal mine** une mine de charbon; **a gold mine** une mine d'or

miner *noun* le mineur; **a coal miner** un mineur de charbon; **my grandfather was a miner** mon grand-père était mineur

mineral water *noun* l'eau minérale *(feminine)*

minimum
1 *adjective* minimum; **the minimum temperature** la température minimum
2 *noun* le minimum; **we'll stay for a minimum of three days** nous resterons trois jours au minimum

miniskirt *noun* la minijupe

minister *noun*
(a) *(in a government)* le/la ministre; **his father was a minister** son père était ministre
(b) *(religious)* le pasteur

minor *adjective* mineur/mineure; **a minor problem** un problème mineur

minority *noun* la minorité; **an ethnic minority** une minorité ethnique

mint *noun* la menthe; **mint tea** le thé à la menthe

minus *preposition* moins; **seven minus two equals five** sept moins deux font cinq; **it's minus five outside** il fait moins cinq dehors

minute *noun* la minute; **just a minute, please** une minute, s'il vous plaît

miracle *noun* le miracle

mirror *noun*
(a) *(looking glass)* la glace, le miroir
(b) *(in a car)* le rétroviseur

misbehave *noun* se conduire mal; **did he misbehave?** est-ce qu'il s'est mal conduit?; **she misbehaved** elle s'est mal conduite

mischief *noun* les bêtises *(feminine plural)*; **he's been up to mischief again** il a encore fait des bêtises

mischievous *adjective*
(a) *(playful)* malicieux/malicieuse
(b) *(naughty)* vilain/vilaine

miserable *adjective*
(a) *(person)* malheureux/malheureuse; **you look really miserable** tu as l'air vraiment malheureux
(b) *(weather)* épouvantable

Note that the French word *misérable* is never a translation for the English word *miserable*. It means *very poor*.

misery *noun* le malheur

Note that the French word *misère* is not a translation for the English word *misery*. It means *extreme poverty*.

mishap *noun* un incident

Miss *noun* Mademoiselle *(feminine)*; **Miss Jenkins** Mademoiselle Jenkins

In French, the abbreviation of *Mademoiselle* is *Mlle*.

miss
1 *verb*
(**a**) *(fail to catch or to reach)* rater; **she missed the train** elle a raté le train; **he missed the target** il a raté la cible
(**b**) **I miss her** elle me manque; **I missed you** tu m'as manqué; **they miss their friends** leurs amis leur manquent
2 miss out
(**a**) *(leave out)* sauter; **you missed out a paragraph** tu as sauté un paragraphe
(**b**) *(be deprived of)* rater quelque chose; **I feel like I'm missing out** j'ai l'impression de rater quelque chose

missile *noun* le missile

missing *adjective*
(**a**) *(lost)* **to be missing** avoir disparu; **my pen is missing** mon stylo a disparu; **their son is missing** leur fils a disparu; **to go missing** disparaître; **she went missing yesterday** elle a disparu hier
(**b**) *(short)* **to be missing** manquer; **there are some pages missing** il manque quelques pages; **the missing pages** les pages qui manquent

mission *noun* la mission

mist *noun* la brume

mistake
1 *noun*
(**a**) *(in spelling, grammar)* la faute; **a spelling mistake** une faute d'orthographe
(**b**) *(in a calculation, one's judgment)* une erreur; **by mistake** par erreur; **to make a mistake** se tromper *or* faire une erreur; **anybody can make a mistake** tout le monde peut se tromper; **he made a big mistake when he resigned** il a fait une grave erreur en démissionnant
2 *verb* **to mistake somebody for somebody else** prendre quelqu'un pour quelqu'un d'autre; **I mistook him for his brother** je l'ai pris pour son frère

mistaken *adjective* **to be mistaken** se tromper; **if he thinks that I'm going to lend him money he's mistaken** s'il s'imagine que je vais lui prêter de l'argent il se trompe

mistletoe *noun* le gui

misty *adjective* brumeux/brumeuse

misunderstand *verb* mal comprendre; **I misunderstood you** je t'ai mal compris

misunderstanding *noun* le malentendu

mix
1 *verb*
(**a**) *(blend together)* mélanger; **mix the eggs and the flour** mélangez les œufs et la farine
(**b**) **to mix with somebody** fréquenter quelqu'un; **I don't like the people he mixes with** je n'aime pas les gens qu'il fréquente
2 mix up
(**a**) *(people, dates)* confondre; **I always mix her up with her sister** je la confonds toujours avec sa sœur; **I'm getting mixed up** je ne m'y retrouve plus
(**b**) *(ingredients, papers)* mélanger; **mix up all the ingredients** mélangez tous les ingrédients; **who mixed up my papers?** qui a mis le désordre dans mes papiers?

mixture *noun* le mélange

moan *verb*
(a) *(groan)* gémir; **he moaned in pain** il a gémi de douleur
(b) *(complain)* râler; **he's always moaning** il n'arrête pas de râler

mobile
1 *noun (phone)* le portable
2 *adjective* **a mobile phone** un téléphone portable

model *noun*
(a) *(of a particular product)* le modèle; **it's their latest model** c'est leur dernier modèle
(b) *(of something bigger)* la maquette, le modèle réduit; **he loves building models** il adore faire des maquettes
(c) *(person)* le mannequin; **she's a model** elle est mannequin

Note that the word *mannequin* is masculine but it can refer to both men and women.

modem *noun* le modem

modern *adjective* moderne; **modern art** l'art moderne; **modern languages** les langues vivantes

modest *adjective* modeste

mole *noun*
(a) *(animal)* la taupe
(b) *(on the skin)* le grain de beauté

moment *noun*
(a) un instant; **in a moment** dans un instant; **he should be here any moment** il devrait arriver d'un instant à l'autre; **just a moment, please!** un instant, s'il vous plaît!
(b) le moment; **at the moment** en ce moment; **at the last moment** au dernier moment

Monday *noun* le lundi; **on Monday** lundi; **I'm leaving on Monday** je m'en vais lundi; **on Mondays** le lundi; **he goes swimming on Mondays** il va à la piscine le lundi; **every Monday** tous les lundis; **next Monday** lundi prochain; **last Monday** lundi dernier

In French, the names of days are not written with a capital.

money *noun* l'argent *(masculine)*

Note that the French word *monnaie* is never a translation for the English word *money.* It either means *currency* or *small change.*

monk *noun* le moine

monkey *noun* le singe

monster *noun* le monstre

month *noun* le mois; **this month** ce mois-ci; **next month** le mois prochain; **last month** le mois dernier; **twice a month** deux fois par mois; **every month** tous les mois

monthly
1 *adjective* mensuel/mensuelle; **a monthly magazine** un magazine mensuel *or* un mensuel
2 *adverb* tous les mois; **I visit him monthly** je lui rend visite tous les mois; **twice monthly** deux fois par mois

monument *noun* le monument

mood *noun* l'humeur *(feminine)*; **I'm in a bad mood** je suis de mauvaise humeur; **he's in a good mood** il est de bonne humeur

moody *adverb*
(a) *(bad-tempered)* de mauvaise humeur; **he's moody today** il est de mauvaise humeur aujourd'hui
(b) *(changeable)* d'humeur changeante

moon *noun* la lune

moonlight *noun* le clair de lune; **in the moonlight** au clair de lune

mop
1 *noun (for the floor)* le balai-éponge

The plural of *balai-éponge* is *balais-éponges.*

2 *verb* **to mop the floor** laver par terre
3 **mop up** éponger; **I mopped up the milk I'd spilled on the floor** j'ai

épongé le lait que j'avais renversé par terre

moped *noun* le vélomoteur

moral
1 *adjective* moral/morale; **to give somebody moral support** soutenir quelqu'un moralement

The masculine plural of *moral* is *moraux*.

2 *noun* la morale; **the moral of the story** la morale de l'histoire

more
1 *adjective*
(a) plus de; **he has more books than you** il a plus de livres que toi; **there are more than ten** il y en a plus de dix; **she lived in more than ten countries** elle a vécu dans plus de dix pays; **he has many more CDs than me** il a beaucoup plus de CD que moi; **they have much more money than us** ils ont beaucoup plus d'argent que nous
(b) *(in questions)* encore de; **would you like more soup?** est-ce que tu veux encore de la soupe?; **can I have some more tea?** est-ce que je peux avoir encore du thé?
(c) *(additional)* de plus; **we need three more people to form a team** on a besoin de trois personnes de plus pour former une équipe
(d) **no more** ne... plus de; **I have no more money, I don't have any more money** je n'ai plus d'argent
(e) **more and more** de plus en plus de; **he has more and more problems** il a de plus en plus de problèmes
2 *adverb*
(a) plus; **do it more slowly** fais-le plus lentement; **you need to work more if you want to succeed** il faut que tu travailles plus si tu veux réussir; **I like her more than I used to** je l'aime plus qu'avant
(b) **more or less** plus ou moins
(c) **more and more** de plus en plus; **he's more and more unhappy** il est de plus en plus malheureux

(d) **once more** une fois de plus
(e) **any more** plus; **he doesn't drink any more** il ne boit plus; **she doesn't want to see him any more** elle ne veut plus le voir
3 *pronoun* plus; **there's no more** il n'y en a plus; **she doesn't have any more** elle n'en a plus; **can I have some more?** je peux en reprendre?

morning *noun*
(a) *(as opposed to the afternoon or the evening)* le matin; **every morning** tous les matins; **yesterday morning** hier matin; **tomorrow morning** demain matin; **I went to the beach in the mornings** j'allais à la plage le matin; **it's two o'clock in the morning** il est deux heures du matin; **good morning!** bonjour!
(b) *(the whole morning)* la matinée; **he stayed here all morning** il est resté ici toute la matinée

Morocco *noun* le Maroc; **he lives in Morocco** il habite au Maroc; **we're going to Morocco** nous allons au Maroc; **they come from Morocco** ils viennent du Maroc

Moroccan
1 *adjective* marocain/marocaine
2 *noun* *(person)* le Marocain/la Marocaine; **the Moroccans** les Marocains *(masculine plural)*

In French, only the noun for the inhabitants of a country takes a capital letter, never the adjective.

Moscow *noun* Moscou

mosque *noun* la mosquée

mosquito *noun* le moustique; **a mosquito bite** une piqûre de moustique

moss *noun* la mousse

most
1 *adjective*
(a) *(the majority of)* la plupart des; **most women** la plupart des femmes
(b) *(the greatest amount of)* **the most** le plus de; **I have the most books** c'est moi qui ai le plus de livres; **he has the**

most money c'est lui qui a le plus d'argent
2 *adverb*
(**a**) *(in comparisons)* plus; **she's the most beautiful** c'est la plus belle; **he's the most talkative of all** c'est le plus bavard de tous; **they're the most experienced** ce sont les plus expérimentés
(**b**) *(very)* extrêmement; **this is most annoying** c'est extrêmement ennuyeux
(**c**) **most of all** *(especially)* surtout; **and most of all, I'd like to thank my parents** et surtout, je voudrais remercier mes parents
3 *pronoun*
(**a**) *(the majority)* la plupart; **most of the people** la plupart des gens; **most of the time** la plupart du temps; **he ate most of the cake** il a mangé la plus grande partie du gâteau; **I know most of them** je connais la plupart d'entre eux
(**b**) *(the greatest amount)* le plus; **he earns the most** c'est lui qui gagne le plus; **of all of us, he's the one who eats the most** de nous tous, c'est lui qui mange le plus; **he made the most of the situation** il a tiré le meilleur parti de la situation; **she made the most of her holiday** elle a profité au maximum de ses vacances; **we'll stay for a week at the very most** on restera une semaine tout au plus

mostly *adverb*
(**a**) *(mainly)* surtout, principalement
(**b**) *(usually)* le plus souvent; **mostly I get home quite early** le plus souvent, je rentre à la maison assez tôt

moth *noun*
(**a**) *(that comes out at night)* le papillon de nuit
(**b**) *(in clothes)* la mite

mother *noun* la mère

mother-in-law *noun* la belle-mère

The plural of *belle-mère* is *belles-mères*.

motivation *noun* la motivation

motor *noun* le moteur

motorbike, motorcycle *noun* la moto

motorist *noun* un/une automobiliste

motorway *noun* une autoroute

motto *noun* la devise

mountain *noun*
(**a**) la montagne; **we spent a week in the mountains** on a passé une semaine à la montagne
(**b**) **a mountain bike** un VTT

VTT is the abbreviation of *vélo tout-terrain*. It does not change in the plural.

mountaineer *noun* un/une alpiniste

mountaineering *noun* l'alpinisme *(masculine)*

mouse *noun* *(animal, computer device)* la souris

mousse *noun* la mousse; **chocolate mousse** la mousse au chocolat

moustache *noun* la moustache

mouth *noun*
(**a**) *(of a person)* la bouche
(**b**) *(of an animal)* la gueule

move
1 *noun*
(**a**) *(action)* le mouvement; **he was making a move towards the door when the phone rang** il s'apprêtait à aller ouvrir quand le téléphone a sonné; **we should make a move** *(leave)* on devrait y aller
(**b**) *(turn in a game)* le tour; **it's my move** c'est mon tour *or* c'est à moi de jouer
(**c**) *(change of home)* le déménagement; **the vase got broken during the move** le vase s'est cassé pendant le déménagement
(**d**) **to get a move on** *(hurry)* se dépêcher; **get a move on!** dépêche-toi!
2 *verb*
(**a**) bouger; **stop moving if you want**

me to take your picture arrête de bouger si tu veux que je te prenne en photo; **stop moving your legs like that!** arrête de remuer les jambes comme ça!
(**b**) *(change the place of)* bouger, déplacer; **can you help me move this table?** est-ce que tu peux m'aider à bouger cette table?; **I'll move the car** je vais déplacer la voiture
(**c**) *(in order to make room for others)* se pousser; **would you mind moving a bit, please?** est-ce que vous pourriez vous pousser un peu, s'il vous plaît?
(**d**) **to move, to move house** déménager; **we're moving to Edinburgh next month** nous déménageons à Édimbourg le mois prochain; **when are you moving house?** quand est-ce que vous déménagez?
(**e**) *(emotionally)* émouvoir; **the film really moved me** le film m'a vraiment ému
3 move about, move around se déplacer
4 move away partir
5 move back reculer
6 move down descendre
7 move forward avancer
8 move in emménager; **the new tenants are moving in tomorrow** les nouveaux locataires emménagent demain
9 move off
(**a**) *(of a person)* s'éloigner
(**b**) *(of a vehicle)* démarrer
10 move out déménager; **when are you moving out?** quand est-ce que vous déménagez?
11 move over se pousser; **move over a bit, please** pousse-toi un peu, s'il te plaît

movement *noun* le mouvement

movie *noun* le film; **they went to the movies** ils sont allés au cinéma; **a movie star** une vedette de cinéma

moving *adjective*
(**a**) *(not still)* en marche; **he jumped out of the moving train** il a sauté du

train en marche
(**b**) *(touching)* émouvant/émouvante; **it was a very moving speech** c'était un discours très émouvant

mow *verb* tondre; **he mowed the lawn** il a tondu la pelouse

mower *noun* la tondeuse à gazon

Mr *noun* M.; **Mr Jones** M. Jones

M. is the abbreviation of Monsieur.

Mrs *noun* Mme; **Mrs Smith** Mme Smith

Mme is the abbreviation of Madame.

Ms *noun* Mme; **Ms Martin** Mme Martin

Mme is the abbreviation of Madame. In French, when you don't know if a woman is married or not you call her Madame.

much
1 *adjective*
(**a**) beaucoup de; **we haven't got much time** nous n'avons pas beaucoup de temps; **they haven't got much money** ils n'ont pas beaucoup d'argent
(**b**) **too much** trop de; **I have too much work to do** j'ai trop de travail
(**c**) **as much... as...** autant de... que...; **take as much lemonade as you want** prends autant de limonade que tu veux; **there's twice as much traffic as yesterday** il y a deux fois plus de circulation qu'hier
(**d**) **so much** tellement de; **it takes up so much time** ça prend tellement de temps; **I didn't know it would make so much noise** je ne savais pas que ça ferait autant de bruit
(**e**) **how much** combien de; **how much money?** combien d'argent?; **how much milk do you want in your tea?** quelle quantité de lait est-ce que tu veux dans ton thé?
2 *adverb*
(**a**) beaucoup; **very much** beaucoup; **thank you very much** merci beaucoup; **I've seen that film but I didn't**

like it much j'ai vu ce film mais je n'ai l'ai pas beaucoup aimé; **they don't go out much** ils ne sortent pas beaucoup; **this wine is much better than the one I had yesterday** ce vin est bien meilleur que celui que j'ai bu hier
(**b**) **too much** trop; **he talks too much** il parle trop
(**c**) **so much** tellement; **I love him so much** je l'aime tellement
3 *pronoun*
(**a**) beaucoup; **there isn't much left** il n'en reste pas beaucoup; **have as much as you like** prends-en autant que tu veux; **that's a bit much!** c'est un peu fort!
(**b**) **how much** combien; **how much does it cost?** combien ça coûte?

mud *noun* la boue; **there's mud on the carpet** il y a de la boue sur la moquette

muddy *adjective* boueux/boueuse; **muddy water** de l'eau boueuse; **his hands are muddy** il a les mains couvertes de boue

mug¹ *noun* (*for coffee, tea*) la grande tasse

mug² *verb* (*in the street*) agresser; **he was mugged on his way home yesterday** il s'est fait agresser hier en rentrant chez lui

multiply *verb* multiplier; **divide by eight and multiply by five** divise par huit et multiplie par cinq

mum *noun*
(**a**) (*term of address*) la maman; **thanks, Mum!** merci, maman!
(**b**) (*mother*) la mère; **I'll ask my mum** je vais demander à ma mère

mumble *verb* marmonner

mummy¹ *noun*
(**a**) (*term of address*) la maman; **thanks, Mummy!** merci, maman!
(**b**) (*mother*) la mère; **my mummy's a nurse** ma mère est infirmière

mummy² *noun* (*Egyptian*) la momie

mumps *noun* les oreillons (*masculine plural*); **he's got mumps** il a les oreillons

murder
1 *noun* le meurtre
2 *verb* assassiner; **she was murdered** elle a été assassinée

murderer *noun* le meurtrier/la meurtrière, l'assassin (*masculine*)

muscle *noun* le muscle

muscular *adjective* musclé/musclée

museum *noun* le musée

mushroom *noun* le champignon

music *noun* la musique

musical
1 *adjective* **a musical instrument** un instrument de musique; **she's very musical** elle est très musicienne
2 *noun* (*show*) la comédie musicale

musician *noun* le musicien/la musicienne; **his dad is a musician** son père est musicien

Muslim
1 *adjective* musulman/musulmane
2 *noun* le musulman/la musulmane; **she's a Muslim** elle est musulmane

The names of religions and their followers are never capitalized in French.

mussel *noun* la moule

must *verb*
(**a**) (*obligation*) devoir; **I must go to the bank** je dois aller à la banque *or* il faut que j'aille à la banque; **you must warn him** tu dois le prévenir *or* il faut que tu le préviennes
(**b**) (*probability*) devoir; **he must have forgotten** il a dû oublier; **she must be delighted** elle doit être ravie
(**c**) (*suggestion*) **we must go out for a drink one day** il faut que nous allions boire un verre un de ces jours

mustard *noun* la moutarde

mutton *noun* le mouton

my *adjective*
(**a**) (*when the thing possessed is masculine singular in French*) mon; **this is my pen** c'est mon stylo

(**b**) *(when the thing possessed is feminine singular in French)* ma; **this is my cup** c'est ma tasse; **my school** mon école; **my story** mon histoire

> Note that *ma* becomes *mon* before a vowel or mute h.

(**c**) *(when the thing possessed is plural in French)* mes; **these are my books** ce sont mes livres; **these are my glasses** ce sont mes lunettes
(**d**) *(when used with parts of the body)* **I'm brushing my teeth** je me brosse les dents; **I broke my leg** je me suis cassé la jambe

> The form used in French is determined by the gender and number of the noun that follows.

myself *pronoun*
(**a**) moi-même; **I did it myself** je l'ai fait moi-même
(**b**) *(with a reflexive verb)* me; **I spoil myself** je me gâte; **I hurt myself** je me suis blessé

> Note that *me* becomes *m'* before a vowel or mute h.

(**c**) *(after a preposition)* moi; **I'll keep it for myself** je le garderai pour moi

mysterious *adjective* mystérieux/ mystérieuse

mystery *noun* le mystère

myth *noun* le mythe

nag *verb* **to nag somebody** harceler quelqu'un; **stop nagging me!** arrête de me harceler!

nail
1 *noun*
(**a**) *(of a finger, a toe)* un ongle; **a nail file** une lime à ongles; **nail polish, nail varnish** le vernis à ongles
(**b**) *(made of metal)* le clou
2 *verb* clouer; **he nailed the lid down** il a cloué le couvercle

naive *adjective* naïf/naïve

naked *adjective* nu/nue

name
1 *noun* le nom; **I don't know the name of the street** je ne connais pas le nom de la rue; **my name is Joe** je m'appelle Joe; **her name is Sally** elle s'appelle Sally; **what's her first name?** quel est son prénom?
2 *verb* nommer; **name the capital of Sweden** nommez la capitale de la Suède

namely *adverb* à savoir; **the largest city in Britain, namely London** la plus grande ville de Grande-Bretagne, à savoir Londres

nanny *noun*
(**a**) *(who looks after children)* la nourrice
(**b**) *(grandmother)* la mamie

nap
1 *noun* **to have a nap** faire un somme
2 *verb* faire un somme

napkin *noun* la serviette de table

nappy *noun* la couche

narrate *verb* raconter

narrative *noun* une histoire

narrator *noun* le narrateur/la narratrice

narrow *adjective* étroit/étroite

narrowly *adverb* de peu; **he was narrowly defeated** il a été battu de peu

narrow-minded *adjective* borné/bornée; **don't be so narrow-minded!** ne sois pas si borné!

nasty *adjective*
(**a**) *(bad)* mauvais/mauvaise; **a nasty smell** une mauvaise odeur
(**b**) *(spiteful)* méchant/méchante; **stop being nasty to your sister** ne sois pas méchant avec ta sœur
(**c**) *(serious)* grave; **a nasty injury** une blessure grave

nation *noun* la nation

national *adjective* national/nationale; **a national anthem** un hymne national

The masculine plural of *national* is *nationaux*.

nationality *noun* la nationalité; **what nationality is he?** de quelle nationalité est-il?

native *adjective*
(**a**) *(region)* natal/natale; **my native city** ma ville natale; **his native country** son pays natal
(**b**) *(language)* maternel/maternelle; **his native language** sa langue maternelle; **he's an English native speaker** il est de langue maternelle anglaise

NATO *noun* l'OTAN *(feminine)*

OTAN is the abbreviation of *Organisation du traité de l'Atlantique Nord.*

natter *verb* bavarder

natural *adjective* naturel/naturelle; **it's only natural!** c'est tout à fait naturel!

naturally *adverb* naturellement; **naturally, I was very pleased** naturellement, j'étais très content; **apples are naturally sweet** les pommes sont naturellement sucrées

nature *noun* la nature; **he's interested in nature** il s'intéresse à la nature; **a nature reserve** une réserve naturelle

naughty *adjective* vilain/vilaine; **he's been naughty today** il a été vilain aujourd'hui

nausea *noun* la nausée

nauseous *adjective* **to feel nauseous** avoir envie de vomir

navel *noun* le nombril

navigate *verb* naviguer

navy
1 *noun*
(**a**) *(military)* la marine; **he's in the navy** il est dans la marine
(**b**) *(colour)* bleu marine
2 *adjective* **navy blue** bleu marine; **his gloves are navy blue** ses gants sont bleu marine

Note that *bleu marine* does not change in the plural.

near
1 *preposition* près de, à côté de; **the bank is near the post office** la banque est à côté de la poste; **near the end** vers la fin
2 *adverb* près; **near to something** près de quelque chose; **stand a little nearer** approche-toi un peu
3 *adjective* proche; **in the near future** dans un avenir proche; **he calculated to the nearest pound** il a calculé à une livre près; **where is the nearest**

supermarket? où est le supermarché le plus proche?
4 *verb* approcher de; **we're nearing our destination** nous approchons de notre destination

nearby
1 *adverb* tout près; **we live nearby** nous habitons tout près
2 *adjective* proche, pas loin; **we went to a nearby restaurant** nous sommes allés dans un restaurant non loin de là

nearly *adverb* presque; **we're nearly there** on est presque arrivés; **it's nearly midnight** il est presque minuit; **she nearly fell** elle a failli tomber

neat *adjective*
(**a**) *(clothes, work)* soigné/soignée
(**b**) *(office, desk, room)* bien rangé/bien rangée

neatly *adverb* soigneusement; **he always folds his clothes neatly before going to bed** il plie toujours ses affaires soigneusement avant de se coucher

necessarily *adverb* nécessairement; **not necessarily** pas forcément

necessary *adjective* nécessaire; **have you got the necessary equipment?** est-ce que tu as le matériel nécessaire?

necessity *noun* la nécessité; **to do something out of necessity** faire quelque chose par nécessité

neck *noun*
(**a**) *(of a person)* le cou; **he hurt his neck** il s'est fait mal au cou
(**b**) *(of a dress, a T-shirt)* le col, une encolure
(**c**) *(of a bottle)* le goulot

necklace *noun* le collier

nectarine *noun* la nectarine, le brugnon

need
1 *noun* le besoin; **to be in need of something** avoir besoin de quelque chose
2 *verb* **to need something** avoir besoin de quelque chose; **I need new**

shoes j'ai besoin d'une nouvelle paire de chaussures; **you need it** tu en as besoin; **I need to go** il faut que je parte *or* je dois partir; **you need to learn your lesson** il faut que tu apprennes ta leçon *or* tu dois apprendre ta leçon; **her hair needs cutting** il faut qu'elle se fasse couper les cheveux; **you don't need to come if you don't want to** tu n'es pas obligé de venir si tu n'en as pas envie; **you needn't knock before you come in** ce n'est pas la peine de frapper avant d'entrer

needle *noun* une aiguille

needlessly *adverb* inutilement

needy *adjective* nécessiteux/nécessiteuse

negative
1 *adjective* négatif/négative
2 *noun* (of a photo) le négatif

neglect *verb* négliger

negotiate *verb* négocier

Do not confuse the spellings of the French *négocier* and English *negotiate*.

negotiation *noun* la négociation

Do not confuse the spellings of the French *négociation* and English *negotiation*.

neigh *verb* hennir

neighbour *noun* le voisin/la voisine

neighbourhood *noun* le quartier; **we live in the same neighbourhood** nous habitons dans le même quartier

neighbouring *adjective* voisin/voisine; **the neighbouring countries** les pays voisins

neither
1 *conjunction* **neither... nor...** ni... ni...; **it's neither good nor bad** ce n'est ni bien ni mal; **he's neither handsome nor ugly** il n'est ni beau ni laid; **he neither drinks nor smokes** il ne boit pas et ne fume pas non plus
2 *adverb* non plus; **neither do I** moi

non plus; **she can't read and neither can he** elle ne sait pas lire, et lui non plus
3 *adjective* aucun/aucune des deux; **neither boy came** aucun des deux garçons n'est venu
4 *pronoun* aucun/aucune des deux, ni l'un ni l'autre/ni l'une ni l'autre; **I was shown two dresses but I liked neither of them** on m'a montré deux robes mais aucune des deux ne me plaisait

When they occur with a verb, *ni... ni*, *non plus* and *aucun* are always used with *ne* (or *n'* before a vowel or a mute h), which is placed in front of the verb, eg *il ne fume pas non plus, aucun des deux garçons n'est venu.*

neon *noun* le néon; **a neon light** un néon

nephew *noun* le neveu

The plural of *neveu* is *neveux*.

nerve *noun*
(a) (in the body) le nerf; **he gets on my nerves** il me tape sur les nerfs *or* il m'énerve

The *f* in *nerf* is not pronounced.

(b) (courage) le courage; **he didn't have the nerve to ask her out for dinner** il n'a pas eu le courage de l'inviter à dîner au restaurant
(c) (cheek) le culot; **he's got a nerve!** il a un sacré culot!

nerve-racking *adjective* éprouvant/éprouvante

nervous *adjective* nerveux/nerveuse; **the nervous system** le système nerveux; **a nervous breakdown** une dépression nerveuse; **he's nervous about his visit to the dentist** il appréhende sa visite chez le dentiste; **I'm nervous about flying** j'ai peur de voyager en avion

nest *noun* le nid

The *d* in *nid* is not pronounced.

Net *noun* *(Internet)* **the Net** le Net

net¹ *noun* le filet; **a fishing net** un filet de pêche

net² *adjective* *(profit, weight, salary)* net/nette

Netherlands *noun* **the Netherlands** les Pays-Bas *(masculine plural)*; **they're going to the Netherlands** ils vont aux Pays-Bas; **he lives in the Netherlands** il vit aux Pays-Bas; **it comes from the Netherlands** ça vient des Pays-Bas

nettle *noun* une ortie

network *noun* le réseau

The plural of *réseau* is *réseaux*.

neutral *adjective* neutre; **a neutral country** un pays neutre

never *adverb* ne... jamais; **she never lies** elle ne ment jamais; **I'll never forgive you** je ne te pardonnerai jamais; **never!** jamais!; **never mind!** *(it doesn't matter)* ça ne fait rien!; *(don't worry)* ne vous en faites pas!

When it occurs with a verb, *jamais* is always used with *ne* (or *n'* before a vowel or a mute h), which is placed in front of the verb, eg *elle ne vient jamais*.

never-ending *adjective* interminable

nevertheless *adverb* néanmoins

new *adjective*
(**a**) *(most recent)* nouveau/nouvelle; **I haven't got his new telephone number** je n'ai pas son nouveau numéro de téléphone; **a new friend** un nouvel ami

Nouveau becomes *nouvel* in front of a vowel or a mute h. The masculine plural of *nouveau* is *nouveaux*.

(**b**) *(brand new)* neuf/neuve; **I've got new shoes** j'ai des chaussures neuves; **she's got a brand new watch** elle a une montre toute neuve
(**c**) *(different)* autre; **bring me a new glass, this one is dirty** apporte-moi un autre verre, celui-ci est sale

newborn *adjective* **a newborn baby** un nouveau-né/une nouveau-née

The masculine plural of *nouveau-né* is *nouveau-nés*, the feminine plural is *nouveau-nées*.

newcomer *noun* le nouveau venu/la nouvelle venue

newly *adverb* récemment

The middle *e* in *récemment* is pronounced like the *a* in *cat*.

newlyweds *plural noun* les jeunes mariés *(masculine plural)*

news *noun*
(**a**) *(in general)* **the news** les nouvelles *(feminine plural)*; **a piece of news** une nouvelle; **have you had any news from her?** est-ce que tu as eu de ses nouvelles?; **that's good news!** c'est une bonne nouvelle!
(**b**) *(in the media)* **the news** les informations *(feminine plural)*; **he's watching the news** il regarde les informations; **this case has been in the news lately** on a parlé de cette affaire récemment aux informations; **a news item** une information

newsagent *noun* le marchand/la marchande de journaux

newsflash *noun* le flash d'informations

newsletter *noun* le bulletin

newspaper *noun* le journal

The plural of *journal* is *journaux*

newsreader *noun* le présentateur/la présentatrice du journal

New Zealand *noun* la Nouvelle-Zélande; **they live in New Zealand** ils habitent en Nouvelle-Zélande; **they went to New Zealand** ils sont allés en Nouvelle-Zélande; **he's from New Zealand** il vient de Nouvelle-Zélande

next
1 *adjective*
(**a**) *(immediately after)* prochain/

prochaine; **next Wednesday** mercredi prochain; **next week** la semaine prochaine; **next month** le mois prochain (**b**) *(in a series)* suivant/suivante; **the next page** la page suivante; **next! au suivant!; the next day** le lendemain; **you're next** c'est ton tour ensuite; **the next size up** la taille au-dessus (**c**) *(next door)* d'à côté; **he works in the next office** il travaille dans le bureau d'à côté; **they live next door** ils habitent à côté
2 *adverb*
(**a**) *(afterwards)* ensuite; **what happened next?** que s'est-il passé ensuite? (**b**) *(next time)* la prochaine fois; **when you see him next** la prochaine fois que tu le verras (**c**) **next to** à côté de; **the museum is next to the town hall** le musée est à côté de la mairie

next-door *adjective* d'à côté; **the next-door neighbour** le voisin d'à côté

nibble *verb* grignoter

nice *adjective*
(**a**) *(kind)* gentil/gentille; **she's always been nice to me** elle a toujours été gentille avec moi (**b**) *(pleasant)* bon/bonne; **we had a nice holiday** nous avons passé de bonnes vacances; **this is very nice wine** ce vin est très bon; **have a nice day!** bonne journée! (**c**) *(beautiful)* beau/belle; **they have a nice house** ils ont une belle maison; **it's a nice day** il fait beau; **you look nice in that dress** cette robe te va très bien (**d**) **nice and warm** bien chaud/chaude; **nice and cool** bien frais/fraîche; **nice and early** de bonne heure

The masculine plural of *beau* is *beaux*.

nicely *adverb*
(**a**) *(well)* bien; **she always dresses nicely** elle s'habille toujours bien (**b**) *(politely)* gentiment; **maybe he'll say yes if you ask him nicely** il dira

peut-être oui si tu le lui demandes gentiment

nickname *noun* le surnom

niece *noun* la nièce

night *noun*
(**a**) *(when it's dark)* la nuit; **this animal hunts at night** cet animal chasse la nuit; **I couldn't sleep last night** je n'ai pas réussi à dormir la nuit dernière; **good night!** bonne nuit!; **to have an early night** se coucher tôt; **to have a late night** se coucher tard (**b**) *(evening)* le soir; **she rang me last night** elle m'a téléphoné hier soir; **they don't go out much at night** ils ne sortent pas beaucoup le soir

nightcap *noun* **do you fancy a nightcap?** tu veux boire un petit verre avant d'aller te coucher?

nightclub *noun* la boîte de nuit

nightdress, nightie *noun* la chemise de nuit

nightingale *noun* le rossignol

nightlife *noun* la vie nocturne; **there's not much nightlife** il n'y a pas grand-chose à faire le soir

nightmare *noun* le cauchemar; **he had a nightmare last night** il a fait un cauchemar la nuit dernière

nightly *adverb*
(**a**) *(every evening)* tous les soirs (**b**) *(every night)* toutes les nuits

nil *number* zéro; **two nil** deux à zéro

nimble *adjective* agile

nine *number* neuf

Neuf is pronounced "neuve" in front of *heures* and *ans*.

nineteen *number* dix-neuf

Dix-neuf is pronounced "diz-neuve" in front of *heures* and *ans*.

ninety *number* quatre-vingt-dix; **the nineties** les années quatre-vingt-dix; **ninety-one** quatre-vingt-onze; **ninety-two** quatre-vingt-douze

ninth *number* le neuvième/la neuvième; **a ninth** *(fraction)* un neuvième; **the ninth of November** le neuf novembre

nipple *noun* le mamelon

nitrogen *noun* l'azote *(masculine)*

no
1 *adverb*
(**a**) *(opposite of "yes")* non; **no thanks** non merci
(**b**) *(not)* ne... pas; **he's no stronger than me** il n'est pas plus fort que moi
2 *adjective* ne... pas de, ne... aucun/ aucune; **there's no bread** il n'y a pas de pain; **they have no money** ils n'ont pas d'argent; **I have no idea** je n'en ai aucune idée; **no smoking** *(on a sign)* défense de fumer

> When they occur with a verb, *pas de* and *aucun* are always used with *ne* (or *n'* before a vowel or a mute h), which is placed in front of the verb, eg *il n'a pas d'argent.*

nobody *pronoun* personne; **nobody came** personne n'est venu; **nobody knows** personne ne sait; **he knows nobody** il ne connaît personne

> When it occurs with a verb, *personne* is used with *ne* (or *n'* before a vowel or a mute h), which is placed in front of the verb, eg *personne n'est venu.*

nod
1 *noun* un signe de tête
2 *verb*
(**a**) *(to say yes)* faire oui de la tête
(**b**) *(to say hello)* faire un signe de tête; **he nodded at me** il m'a fait un signe de la tête

noise *noun* le bruit

noisily *adverb* bruyamment

noisy *adjective* bruyant/bruyante

nominate *verb*
(**a**) *(appoint)* nommer
(**b**) *(propose)* proposer

none *pronoun* aucun/aucune; **none of**

us aucun d'entre nous; **I invited several friends but none came** j'ai invité plusieurs amis mais aucun n'est venu; **she wanted more soup but there was none left** elle voulait reprendre de la soupe mais il n'y en avait plus; **I've read none of the books** je n'ai lu aucun des livres

> When it occurs with a verb, *aucun* is used with *ne* (or *n'* before a vowel or a mute h), which is placed in front of the verb, eg *aucun n'est venu.*

nonetheless *adverb* néanmoins

nonexistent *adjective* inexistant/ inexistante

nonsense *noun* les absurdités *(feminine plural)*; **that's nonsense** c'est absurde; **nonsense!** n'importe quoi!

non-smoker *noun*
(**a**) *(personne)* le non-fumeur/la non-fumeuse; **non-smokers** les non-fumeurs
(**b**) *(train compartment)* un compartiment non-fumeurs

noodles *noun* les nouilles *(feminine plural)*

noon *noun* le midi *(masculine)*; **at noon** à midi

no-one *see* **nobody**

nor
1 *conjunction* **neither... nor...** ni... ni...; **neither you nor me** ni toi ni moi; **he's neither handsome nor ugly** il n'est ni beau ni laid; **he neither drinks nor smokes** il ne boit pas et ne fume pas non plus
2 *adverb* non plus; **nor do I** moi non plus; **if you don't go, nor shall I** si tu n'y vas pas, je n'irai pas non plus

> When they occur with a verb, *ni... ni* and *non plus* are always used with *ne* (or *n'* before a vowel or a mute h), which is placed in front of the verb, eg *il ne fume pas non plus.*

normal *adjective* normal/normale

The masculine plural of *normal* is *normaux*.

normally *adverb* normalement, habituellement

north
1 *noun* le nord; **north of, to the north of** au nord de; **Leeds is north of Sheffield** Leeds est au nord de Sheffield; **in the north of** dans le nord de; **Inverness is in the north of Scotland** Inverness est dans le nord de l'Écosse
2 *adjective* nord; **the north coast** la côte nord; **North America** l'Amérique du Nord; **the North Pole** le pôle Nord; **the North Sea** la mer du Nord
3 *adverb* vers le nord; **they're heading north** ils se dirigent vers le nord

northeast
1 *noun* le nord-est; **he lives in the northeast of England** il habite dans le nord-est de l'Angleterre
2 *adjective* nord-est

northern *adjective* du nord; **Northern Europe** l'Europe du Nord; **Northern Ireland** l'Irlande du Nord; **northern France** le nord de la France; **northern England** le nord de l'Angleterre

northwest
1 *noun* le nord-ouest; **the Lake District in the northwest of England** le Lake District est dans le nord-ouest de l'Angleterre
2 *adjective* nord-est

Norway *noun* la Norvège; **they live in Norway** ils habitent en Norvège; **she's never been to Norway** elle n'est jamais allée en Norvège; **she's from Norway** elle est norvégienne

Norwegian
1 *adjective* norvégien/norvégienne
2 *noun*
(**a**) *(language)* le norvégien; **he speaks Norwegian** il parle norvégien
(**b**) *(person)* le Norvégien/la Norvégienne; **the Norwegians** les Norvégiens *(masculine plural)*

In French, only the noun for the inhabitants of a country take a capital letter, never the adjective or the noun for the language.

nose *noun* le nez; **she's scratching her nose** elle se gratte le nez

nosebleed *noun* **to have a nosebleed** saigner du nez; **she had a nosebleed** elle a saigné du nez

nosey *adjective* indiscret/indiscrète

no-smoking *adjective* non-fumeurs

nostril *noun* la narine

nosy *see* **nosey**

not *adverb*
(**a**) *(used with a verb)* ne... pas; **he's not there** il n'est pas là; **he doesn't smoke** il ne fume pas; **he didn't come** il n'est pas venu

When it is used with a verb, *not* is translated by *ne* in front of the verb (or *n'* before a vowel or mute h) and by *pas* after the verb, eg *il ne fume pas*. In compound tenses *pas* goes between the auxiliary and the past participle as in *il n'est pas venu*.

(**b**) *(used with an adverb)* pas; **not yet** pas encore; **not at all** pas du tout; **thank you so much! – not at all!** merci infiniment! – je vous en prie!
(**c**) non; **I think not** je pense que non; **I hope not** j'espère que non; **not guilty** non coupable

notch *noun*
(**a**) *(in wood)* une encoche
(**b**) *(in a belt)* un cran

note
1 *noun*
(**a**) *(written information)* la note; **to take notes** prendre des notes; **to make a note of something** prendre quelque chose en note
(**b**) *(in music)* la note; **the violinist played a wrong note** le violoniste a fait une fausse note
(**c**) *(letter)* le message, le mot; **he left a note for you** il a laissé un mot pour toi

(d) *(paper money)* le billet de banque; **a five-pound note** un billet de cinq livres

2 *verb (notice)* remarquer, constater

3 note down noter; **she noted down my phone number** elle a noté mon numéro de téléphone

notebook *noun*
(a) *(for school)* le cahier
(b) *(smaller)* le carnet

noted *adjective (famous)* éminent/ éminente

notepad *noun* le bloc-notes

The plural of *bloc-notes* is *blocsnotes*.

notepaper *noun* le papier à lettres

nothing *pronoun*
(a) rien; **nothing at all** rien du tout; **nothing much** pas grand-chose; **he gave it to me for nothing** il me l'a donné pour rien; **nothing has been decided yet** rien n'a encore été décidé
(b) ne... rien; **he knows nothing** il ne sait rien; **she heard nothing** elle n'a rien entendu; **I've got nothing to do with it** je n'y suis pour rien

When it occurs with a verb, *rien* is always used with *ne* (or *n'* before a vowel or a mute h), which is placed in front of the verb, eg *rien n'a changé, il ne sait rien*.

notice
1 *noun*
(a) *(written sign)* une pancarte, un écriteau

The plural of *écriteau* is *écriteaux*.

(b) *(warning)* le préavis; **they gave him a week's notice** ils lui ont donné un préavis d'une semaine; **at short notice** au dernier moment; **until further notice** jusqu'à nouvel ordre; **he handed in his notice** il a donné sa démission
(c) *(attention)* **to take notice of something** faire attention à quelque chose; **he took no notice of what I told him**

il n'a pas fait attention à ce que je lui ai dit; **don't take any notice!** ne fais pas attention!

Note that the French word *notice* is never a translation for the English word *notice*. It means *instructions* (for an appliance).

2 *verb* remarquer; **did you notice that he was wearing glasses?** est-ce que tu as remarqué qu'il portait des lunettes?

noticeable *adjective* perceptible

noticeboard *noun* le tableau d'affichage

The plural of *tableau d'affichage* is *tableaux d'affichage*.

notorious *adjective* tristement célèbre

nought *number* le zéro

noun *noun* le nom

novel *noun* le roman

novelist *noun* le romancier/la romancière; **his dad is a novelist** son père est romancier

November *noun* novembre *(masculine)*; **the first of November** le premier novembre; **the second of November** le deux novembre; **the third of November** le trois novembre; **in November** en novembre

Names of months are not capitalized in French.

now *adverb*
(a) *(at this moment in time)* maintenant; **until now, up to now** jusqu'ici *or* jusqu'à maintenant; **from now on** désormais; **now and then, now and again** de temps en temps; **for now** pour le moment; **she ought to be here by now** elle devrait déjà être arrivée
(b) *(used before a sentence)* bon, bien; **now, where was I?** bon, où est-ce que j'en étais?

nowadays *adverb* de nos jours; **nowadays most people know how**

to use a computer de nos jours la plupart des gens savent se servir d'un ordinateur

nowhere *adverb* nulle part; **nowhere else** nulle part ailleurs

nuclear *adjective* nucléaire; **nuclear power** l'énergie nucléaire; **a nuclear power station** une centrale nucléaire

nude
1 *adjective* nu/nue
2 *noun* **in the nude** tout nu/toute nue

nudge
1 *noun* le coup de coude; **to give somebody a nudge** donner un coup de coude à quelqu'un
2 *verb* **to nudge somebody** donner un coup de coude à quelqu'un

nuisance *noun*
(a) *(annoying thing)* **to be a nuisance** être pénible; **it's a nuisance having to get up so early** c'est pénible de devoir se lever si tôt
(b) *(annoying person)* **stop being a nuisance!** arrête de m'embêter!; **he's such a nuisance!** qu'est-ce qu'il est pénible! *or* qu'est-ce qu'il est casse-pieds!

numb *adjective* engourdi/engourdie; **my hands are numb with cold** j'ai les mains engourdies par le froid

number
1 *noun*
(a) le nombre; **a number of** un certain nombre de; **we had a number of problems** on a eu un certain nombre de problèmes
(b) *(single digit)* le chiffre
(c) *(on a passport, a page, a card, a bus)* le numéro; **a telephone number** un numéro de téléphone; **I dialled the wrong number** j'ai fait un faux numéro; **a number plate** une plaque d'immatriculation
2 *verb* numéroter

nun *noun* la religieuse

nurse
1 *noun* un infirmier/une infirmière; **my sister is a nurse** ma sœur est infirmière

> Note that when describing people's jobs or situations, French does not use an article (*un* or *une*).

2 *verb* *(look after)* **to nurse somebody** soigner quelqu'un

nursery *noun*
(a) *(children's room)* la chambre d'enfants
(b) *(for children)* la crèche; **a nursery school** une école maternelle; **a nursery rhyme** une comptine

> The *p* in *comptine* is not pronounced.

(c) *(for plants, trees)* la pépinière

nursing home *noun* la maison de retraite

nut *noun*
(a) *(walnut)* la noix; *(hazelnut)* la noisette; **a Brazil nut** une noix du Brésil; **a cashew nut** une noix de cajou

> French doesn't have a general term for nuts as a type of food. You need to specify what kind of nut you are talking about.

(b) *(for a bolt)* un écrou

nutcracker *noun* le casse-noix

> The word *casse-noix* does not change in the plural.

nutmeg *noun* la noix de muscade

nutritious *adjective* nourrissant/nourrissante

nuts *adjective* *(crazy)* cinglé/cinglée

nutshell *noun* **in a nutshell** en un mot

nylon *noun* le nylon®; **a nylon shirt** une chemise en nylon®

oak *noun* le chêne; **an oak table** une table en chêne

oar *noun* la rame, l'aviron *(masculine)*

oats *noun* l'avoine *(feminine)*

obedient *adjective* obéissant/obéissante

obey *verb* obéir; **he didn't obey my orders** il n'a pas obéi à mes ordres; **you must obey your parents** tu dois obéir à tes parents

object *noun* un objet

oblige *verb* obliger; **to be obliged to do something** être obligé de faire quelque chose

oblong *adjective* rectangulaire

oboe *noun* le hautbois; **I play the oboe** je joue du hautbois

> Note that when talking about playing musical instruments, French uses the expression *jouer de.*

obscene *adjective* obscène

observant *adjective* observateur/observatrice

observe *verb* observer

obsessed *adjective* **she's obsessed with the idea of becoming an actress** elle n'a qu'une idée en tête, devenir actrice; **she's obsessed with cleanliness** c'est une maniaque de la propreté

obsession *noun* une obsession

obstacle *noun* un obstacle

obtain *adjective* obtenir

obvious *adjective* évident/évidente

obviously *adverb* de toute évidence; **he obviously got the wrong number** de toute évidence, il s'est trompé de numéro; **she's obviously lying** il est évident qu'elle ment

occasion *noun* une occasion; **on special occasions** pour les grandes occasions; **on several occasions** à plusieurs reprises; **on this occasion** cette fois-ci

occasionally *adverb* de temps en temps; **he visits me occasionally** il vient me voir de temps en temps

occupation *noun*
(**a**) *(job)* le métier; **what's her occupation?** qu'est-ce qu'elle fait comme métier?
(**b**) *(of a country)* l'occupation *(feminine)*; **the country is under British occupation** le pays est sous occupation britannique

occupied *adjective* occupé/occupée; **she kept the children occupied** elle a occupé les enfants

ocean *noun* un océan

o'clock *adverb* **it's five o'clock** il est cinq heures; **at five o'clock** à cinq heures

October *noun* octobre *(masculine)*; **the first of October** le premier octobre; **the second of October** le deux octobre; **the third of Octobre** le trois octobre; **in October** en octobre

> Names of months are not capitalized in French.

octopus *noun* la pieuvre

odd *adjective*

(a) *(strange)* bizarre, étrange
(b) *(opposite of even)* impair; **an odd number** un nombre impair
(c) *(not matching)* dépareillé/dépareillée; **he was wearing odd socks** il portait des chaussettes dépareillées

of *preposition*
(a) *(with an amount, a quantity)* de; **a litre of milk** un litre de lait; **a bottle of wine** une bouteille de vin; **a bunch of flowers** un bouquet de fleurs; **a girl of ten** une fille de dix ans; **hundreds of people** des centaines de personnes; **a lot of money** beaucoup d'argent; **five of you** cinq d'entre vous; **there are five of us** nous sommes cinq
(b) *(belonging to)* de; **the centre of London** le centre de Londres; **a friend of mine** un de mes amis
(c) *(with material)* **it's made of wood** c'est en bois
(d) *(with dates)* **the 4th of October** le 4 octobre
(e) **of it, of them** en; **she loves his paintings, she has six of them** elle adore ses tableaux, elle en a six; **I have a lot of it/of them** j'en ai beaucoup

> Note that *de* becomes *d'* in front of a vowel or a mute h and that *de + le* is contracted to *du* (as in *la porte du garage*) and *de + les* to *des* (as in *le professeur des élèves*). However, *de + la* and *de + l'* do not change.

of course *see* **course**

off
1 *adjective*
(a) *(light, radio)* éteint/éteinte; *(gas, tap)* fermé/fermée
(b) *(milk)* tourné; *(food)* avarié/avariée
(c) *(cancelled)* annulé/annulée; **the show is off** le spectacle a été annulé
(d) *(absent from work or school)* absent/absente
2 *adverb*
(a) **right, I'm off** bon, je m'en vais; **I'm off to the swimming pool** je vais à la piscine

(b) *(not at work)* **to take a day off** prendre un jour de congé; **Monday is his day off** il ne travaille pas le lundi; **I need to take some time off** j'ai besoin de prendre des vacances
3 *preposition*
(a) *(away from)* de; **the ship sank a few miles off the coast** le bateau a coulé à quelques kilomètres de la côte; **he fell off his bicycle** il est tombé de vélo; **he jumped off the bridge** il a sauté du pont; **to get off the bus** descendre du bus; **the handle has come off the saucepan** le manche s'est détaché de la casserole
(b) *(absent from)* **he's off work today** il ne travaille pas aujourd'hui; **she was off school yesterday** elle n'est pas allée à l'école hier
(c) *(with prices)* **ten pounds off the normal price** dix livres de réduction sur le prix normal

offence *noun* le délit; **to commit an offence** commettre un délit; **to take offence** se vexer

offend *verb* offenser, blesser; **I didn't mean to offend you** je ne voulais pas t'offenser

offer
1 *noun* une offre, la proposition; **a job offer** une offre d'emploi; **on special offer** en promotion
2 *verb* proposer; **he offered me a job** il m'a proposé un emploi; **he offered to drive me to the airport** il m'a proposé de m'emmener à l'aéroport

office *noun* le bureau; **his father works in an office** son père travaille dans un bureau

> The plural of *bureau* is *bureaux*.

officer *noun*
(a) *(in the police)* **an officer, a police officer** un agent de police; **his dad is a police officer** son père est agent de police
(b) *(in the army)* un officier

official *adjective* officiel/officielle;

the country has two official languages le pays a deux langues officielles

off-licence *noun* le marchand de vins et spiritueux

offline *adjective* *(computer)* non connecté/non connectée; **to go offline** se déconnecter

often *adverb* souvent; **I don't often see her** je ne la vois pas souvent; **how often does he write to you?** est-ce qu'il t'écrit souvent?

oil *noun*
(a) *(in cooking, for machines)* l'huile *(feminine)*
(b) *(for fuel)* le pétrole; **an oil slick** une marée noire; **an oil well** un puits de pétrole

oily *adjective*
(a) *(hands, rags)* graisseux/graisseuse
(b) *(skin, hair)* gras/grasse

ointment *noun* la pommade

OK, okay
1 *adverb* d'accord; **OK, I'll phone him** d'accord, je vais lui téléphoner
2 *adjective*
(a) *(acceptable)* **is it OK if I give him your address?** est-ce que tu es d'accord pour que je lui donne ton adresse?; **is it OK with you?** ça te va?; **the play was OK but not great** la pièce n'était pas mal mais elle n'était pas géniale
(b) *(well)* **are you OK?** ça va?; **don't worry, I'm OK** ne t'inquiète pas, ça va

old *adjective*
(a) *(not young)* vieux/vieille; **an old book** un vieux livre; **an old woman** une vieille femme; **an old man** un vieil homme; **old people** les personnes âgées

Note that *vieux* becomes *vieil* before a vowel or mute h.

(b) *(former)* ancien/ancienne; **this is my old school** c'est mon ancienne école

When it means *former*, the word *ancien* is always placed in front of the noun it is describing.

(c) **how old is she?** quel âge a-t-elle?; **she's ten years old** elle a dix ans; **her older brother** son frère aîné; **the oldest daughter** la fille aînée

old-fashioned *adjective*
(a) *(clothes, style)* démodé/démodée
(b) *(person)* vieux jeu

Note that *vieux jeu* does not change in the feminine or in the plural.

olive *noun* une olive; **olive oil** l'huile d'olive

omelette *noun* une omelette; **a mushroom omelette** une omelette aux champignons

on
1 *adjective (light, radio)* allumé/allumée; *(gas, tap)* ouvert/ouverte; *(machine)* en marche
2 *adverb*
(a) **what's on at the cinema?** qu'est-ce qu'ils passent au cinéma?; **did he have his hat on?** est-ce qu'il avait son chapeau sur la tête?; **turn the light on** allume la lumière; **put your helmet on** mets ton casque
(b) **he was talking on and on** il n'arrêtait pas de parler
3 *preposition*
(a) sur; **the bottle is on the table** la bouteille est sur la table; **have you got any books on architecture?** est-ce que vous avez des livres sur l'architecture?
(b) à; **what's on TV?** qu'est-ce qu'il y a à la télé?; **it's on page 10** c'est à la page 10; **on the right** à droite; **on the left** à gauche
(c) dans; **I'm on the train** je suis dans le train; **on a plane** dans un avion; **you're not allowed to smoke on the bus** il est interdit de fumer dans le bus
(d) en; **he's on holiday** il est en vacances; **they're on strike** ils sont en grève
(e) *(with expressions of time)* **I'll come**

on Monday je viendrai lundi; **he comes on Mondays** il vient le lundi; **it happened on the 4th of July** ça s'est passé le 4 juillet; **on my arrival** à mon arrivée; **from now on** à partir de maintenant

once
1 *adverb*
(a) *(on one occasion)* une fois; **I did it only once** je ne l'ai fait qu'une fois; **once a month** une fois par mois; **once again, once more** encore une fois; **once in a while** de temps en temps; **we go to a restaurant every once in a while** nous allons au restaurant de temps en temps
(b) *(in the past)* autrefois; **people once believed that the world was flat** autrefois, les gens croyaient que la Terre était plate
(c) **at once** *(straight away)* tout de suite; *(at the same time)* à la fois; **you must do it at once** il faut que tu le fasses tout de suite; **everything happened at once** tout est arrivé en même temps
2 *conjunction* une fois que; **return the book to the library once you've read it** rapporte le livre à la bibliothèque une fois que tu l'auras lu

one
1 *number* un/une; **one, two, three** un, deux, trois; **on page one** à la page un; **one glass** un verre; **one table** une table
2 *adjective (only)* seul/seule; **the one person who can help us is John** John est la seule personne qui puisse nous aider
3 *pronoun*
(a) un/une; **I've got plenty of sweets, do you want one?** j'ai plein de bonbons, tu en veux un?; **this one** celui-ci/celle-ci; **that one** celui-là/celle-là; **which car do you prefer? – I prefer the red one** quelle voiture préfères-tu? – je préfère la rouge
(b) *(somebody)* on; **one never knows** on ne sait jamais

oneself *pronoun*
(a) soi-même; **it's simpler to do it oneself** c'est plus simple de le faire soi-même
(b) se; **to cut oneself** se couper

> In French, *se* becomes *s'* in front of a vowel or a mute.

(c) soi; **one shouldn't think only about oneself** il ne faut pas penser qu'à soi

one-way *adjective* **a one-way ticket** un aller simple; **a one-way street** une rue à sens unique

onion *noun* un oignon; **onion soup** la soupe à l'oignon

> The *oi* of *oignon* is pronounced *o*.

online *adjective (computer)* en ligne; **to be online** être connecté; **I bought my ticket online** j'ai acheté mon billet sur Internet

only
1 *adjective*
(a) seul/seule; **he's the only boy in the class** c'est le seul garçon de la classe
(b) unique; **he's an only child** il est fils unique; **she's an only child** elle est fille unique
2 *adverb*
(a) seulement; **I'd like to go, but only if you come with me** j'aimerais bien y aller, mais seulement si tu viens avec moi
(b) ne ... que, seulement; **she only drinks water** elle ne boit que de l'eau *or* elle boit seulement de l'eau; **I only have ten pounds** je n'ai que dix livres *or* j'ai seulement dix livres; **it's only a scratch** ce n'est qu'une égratignure *or* c'est seulement une égratignure

> In this sense, *only* can be translated by placing *ne* (or *n'* before a vowel or mute h) in front of the verb and *que* immediately after the verb, eg *je n'ai que dix livres*.

3 *conjunction* mais; **it's the same**

model, only smaller c'est le même modèle, mais en plus petit

onto, on to *preposition* sur

onwards *adverb*
(**a**) *(forwards)* en avant; **to go onwards** avancer
(**b**) **from... onwards** à partir de...; **from tomorrow onwards** à partir de demain

open
1 *adjective* ouvert/ouverte; **in the open air** en plein air; **the door is wide open** la porte est grande ouverte
2 *verb*
(**a**) ouvrir; **he opened the door** il a ouvert la porte; **the shop opens at 10 o'clock** le magasin ouvre à 10 heures
(**b**) s'ouvrir; **the door opens automatically** la porte s'ouvre automatiquement

open-air *adjective* en plein air; **an open-air concert** un concert en plein air

opening *noun* une ouverture

opera *noun* un opéra; **an opera house** un opéra

> Note that the French word *opéra* means both *opera* and *opera house*.

operate *verb* **to operate on somebody** opérer quelqu'un; **they had to operate on him** ils ont dû l'opérer

operation *noun* une opération; **she has to have an operation** elle doit se faire opérer; **he had an operation on his knee** il s'est fait opérer du genou

operator *noun* un opérateur/une opératrice

opinion *noun* un avis, une opinion; **in my opinion** à mon avis; **an opinion poll** un sondage d'opinion; **what's your opinion?** qu'en penses-tu?; **public opinion** l'opinion publique

opportunity *noun* une occasion; **it'll be an opportunity to meet him** ce sera une occasion de faire sa connaissance

opposite
1 *preposition* en face de; **the post office is opposite the school** la poste est en face de l'école
2 *adverb* en face; **the house opposite** la maison en face; **he lives opposite** il habite en face
3 *adjective* opposé/opposée; **they went in opposite directions** ils ont pris des directions opposées; **cars coming from the opposite direction** les voitures qui viennent en sens inverse
4 *noun* le contraire; **it's the opposite of what I've been told** c'est le contraire de ce qu'on m'a dit

optician *noun* un opticien/une opticienne; **she's an optician** elle est opticienne

optional *adjective* facultatif/facultative

optimistic *adjective* optimiste

or *conjunction*
(**a**) ou; **Paul or his brother** Paul ou son frère
(**b**) **he can't drive or ride a bike** il ne sait ni conduire ni faire du vélo; **he doesn't drink or smoke** il ne boit pas et ne fume pas non plus
(**c**) sinon; **don't hit it too hard or it'll break** ne tape pas trop fort dessus sinon ça va casser

oral *adjective* oral/orale; **an oral exam** un oral

> The masculine plural of *oral* is *oraux*.

orange
1 *adjective* orange; **orange shoes** des chaussures orange

> In French the adjective *orange* does not change in the plural.

2 *noun (fruit)* une orange; **I like oranges** j'aime les oranges; **orange juice** le jus d'orange; **an orange tree** un oranger

orchard *noun* le verger

orchestra *noun* un orchestre

order

1 *noun*
(**a**) *(instruction)* un ordre; **to give somebody an order** donner un ordre à quelqu'un
(**b**) *(sequence)* l'ordre *(masculine)*; **in alphabetical order** par ordre alphabétique
(**c**) *(in a restaurant, for goods)* la commande; **to place an order** passer une commande
(**d**) *(peace)* l'ordre *(masculine)*; **to restore order** rétablir l'ordre
(**e**) **out of order** *(machine)* en panne; **the lift is out of order** l'ascenseur est en panne; **in working order** en état de marche
(**f**) **in order to** pour; **in order to simplify things** pour simplifier les choses
2 *verb*
(**a**) *(instruct)* ordonner à; **he ordered me to leave the room** il m'a ordonné de quitter la pièce
(**b**) *(in a restaurant)* commander; **we'd like to order, please** nous voudrions commander, s'il vous plaît

ordinary *adjective* ordinaire; **you can wear your ordinary clothes** tu peux porter tes vêtements de tous les jours; **they're an ordinary family** c'est une famille comme une autre

organ *noun*
(**a**) *(part of the body)* un organe
(**b**) *(musical instrument)* un orgue; **he plays the organ** il joue de l'orgue

organic *adjective* biologique, bio; **organic products** les produits biologiques

organization *noun* une organisation

organize *verb* organiser; **you need to get organized** il faut t'organiser

oriental *adjective* oriental/orientale

> The masculine plural of *oriental* is *orientaux.*

original *adjective*
(**a**) *(innovative)* original/originale; **an original idea** une idée originale

> The masculine plural of *original* is *originaux.*

(**b**) *(first)* originel/originelle; **the original inhabitants of the country** les habitants originels du pays

originally *adverb* au départ

orphan *noun* un orphelin/une orpheline

ostrich *noun* une autruche

other

1 *adjective* autre; **the other car** l'autre voiture; **I went to her place the other day** je suis allé chez elle l'autre jour; **I don't like this skirt, I'll take the other one** je n'aime pas cette jupe, je vais prendre l'autre; **there are other things to do** il y a d'autres choses à faire
2 *pronoun* autre; **the others** les autres; **some do, others don't** les uns le font, les autres pas

otherwise

1 *adverb* *(differently)* autrement; **we couldn't do otherwise** nous n'avons pas pu faire autrement
2 *conjunction* *(or else)* sinon; **put a jumper on, otherwise you'll catch a cold** mets un pull, sinon tu vas attraper froid

ouch *exclamation* aïe

ought *verb*
(**a**) *(to express obligation)* devoir; **you ought to leave** tu devrais partir; **I ought to have done it** j'aurais dû le faire
(**b**) *(to express probability)* devoir; **he ought to win** il devrait gagner; **it ought to be ready** ça devrait être prêt

our *adjective*
(**a**) *(when the thing possessed is singular in French)* notre; **our country** notre pays; **our house** notre maison
(**b**) *(when the thing possessed is plural in French)* nos; **these are our books** ce sont nos livres; **these are our suitcases** ce sont nos valises
(**c**) *(when used with parts of the body)*

we washed our hands nous nous sommes lavé les mains

ours *pronoun*
(a) *(when the thing possessed is masculine singular in French)* le nôtre; **it's not your turn, it's ours** ce n'est pas votre tour, c'est le nôtre
(b) *(when the thing possessed is feminine singular in French)* la nôtre; **this is not your table, it's ours** ce n'est pas votre table, c'est la nôtre; **this land is ours** cette terre est à nous
(c) *(when the thing possessed is plural in French)* les nôtres; **these are not Claire's books, they're ours** ce ne sont pas les livres de Claire, ce sont les nôtres; **these bottles are ours** ces bouteilles sont à nous

The form used in French is determined by the gender and number of the noun it stands for.

ourselves *pronoun*
(a) nous-mêmes; **we did it ourselves** nous l'avons fait nous-mêmes
(b) *(with a reflexive verb)* nous; **we spoil ourselves** nous nous gâtons; **we hurt ourselves** nous nous sommes blessés
(c) *(after a preposition)* nous; **we'll keep it for ourselves** nous le garderons pour nous

out
1 *adverb*
(a) *(outside)* dehors; **it's cold out** il fait froid dehors; **I was out in the garden** j'étais dans le jardin; **where's the way out?** où est la sortie?
(b) *(not at home)* **he's out** il n'est pas là *or* il est sorti
(c) *(light, fire)* éteint/éteinte
2 *preposition* **out of**
(a) *(to indicate a place or a direction)* **she walked out of the house** elle est sortie de la maison; **he ran out of the garden** il est sorti du jardin en courant; **she was out of the room when it happened** elle n'était pas dans la pièce quand ça s'est passé; **out of the**

country à l'étranger; **she's out of town** elle n'est pas en ville
(b) *(through)* par; **he fell out of the window** il est tombé par la fenêtre
(c) *(from)* dans; **he was drinking out of a wine glass** il buvait dans un verre à vin; **he copied the article out of a book** il a copié l'article dans un livre; **he took a gun out of his pocket** il a sorti un pistolet de sa poche
(d) *(of)* **it's made out of wood** c'est en bois
(e) *(in)* sur; **one out of three people** une personne sur trois
(f) *(because of)* par; **he did it out of jealousy** il l'a fait par jalousie; **out of curiosity** par curiosité
(g) *(without)* **we're out of sugar** nous n'avons plus de sucre
(h) **out of date** *(passport, permit, food)* périmé/périmée; *(clothes)* démodé/démodée; *(ideas)* dépassé/dépassée

outdoor *adjective*
(a) *(pool, market)* en plein air
(b) *(sports)* de plein air

outdoors *adverb (outside)* dehors

outer space *noun* le cosmos, l'espace *(masculine)*

outfit *noun*
(a) *(clothes)* la tenue
(b) *(disguise)* la panoplie; **a pirate's outfit** une panoplie de pirate

outing *noun* une excursion, la sortie; **an outing to the zoo** une sortie au zoo

outline *noun* la silhouette; **we could see the outline of the ship in the fog** on voyait la silhouette du bateau dans le brouillard

outside
1 *adverb* dehors; **the children are playing outside** les enfants sont en train de jouer dehors
2 *adjective* extérieur/extérieure; **the outside wall** le mur extérieur
3 *noun* l'extérieur *(masculine)*; **the**

outside of the church is more interesting than the inside l'extérieur de l'église est plus intéressant que l'intérieur
4 *preposition*
(a) devant; **there was a car outside the house** il y avait une voiture devant la maison; **let's meet outside the cinema** retrouvons-nous devant le cinéma
(b) à l'extérieur de; **there is a nice castle outside the city** il y a un beau château à l'extérieur de la ville

outskirts *noun* la banlieue; **we live on the outskirts of Dublin** nous habitons la banlieue de Dublin

oval *adjective* ovale

oven *noun* le four

over
1 *preposition*
(a) *(on)* sur; **he had his jacket over his arm** il avait sa veste sur le bras; **he spilled wine over his shirt** il a renversé du vin sur sa chemise
(b) *(above)* au-dessus de; **the plane flew over the city** l'avion est passé au-dessus de la ville; **there's a painting hanging over the piano** il y a un tableau au-dessus du piano
(c) *(to get to the other side)* par-dessus; **he jumped over the gate** il a sauté par-dessus la barrière
(d) *(more than)* plus de; **people over 60** les gens de plus de 60 ans
(e) *(during)* pendant; **I saw them over the weekend** je les ai vus pendant le week-end
(f) *(on the other side of)* de l'autre côté de; **he lives over the road** il habite de l'autre côté de la rue
(g) **all over Italy** dans toute l'Italie; **all over the carpet** partout sur le tapis; **I've looked all over the house for my wallet** j'ai cherché mon portefeuille dans toute la maison
(h) **over here** ici; **over there** là-bas
2 *adjective (finished)* fini/finie, terminé/terminée; **we'll go as soon as**

the film is over nous irons dès que le film sera terminé; **it's all over** c'est fini
3 *adverb*
(a) *(to somebody's house)* **to ask somebody over** inviter quelqu'un; **have you ever been over to his house?** est-ce que tu es déjà allé chez lui?
(b) *(repeating something)* **to do something all over again** refaire quelque chose; **over and over again** encore et encore

overalls *plural noun* le bleu de travail

overcharge *verb* faire payer trop cher; **he overcharged me** il m'a fait payer trop cher

overcoat *noun* le pardessus

overcome *verb* surmonter

overcrowded *adjective* *(country, city)* surpeuplé/surpeuplée; *(train, bus, pub)* bondé/bondée

overflow *verb* déborder

overhead
1 *adverb* au-dessus; **there was an eagle circling overhead** un aigle planait au-dessus de nos têtes
2 *adjective (cable)* aérien/aérienne

overlook *verb*
(a) *(of a window, a hotel)* donner sur; **our room overlooked the car park** notre chambre donnait sur le parking
(b) *(fail to notice)* négliger; **we've overlooked that problem** nous avons négligé ce problème

overnight
1 *adverb*
(a) *(during the night)* pendant la nuit; **she stayed overnight** elle est restée la nuit
(b) *(suddenly)* du jour au lendemain; **it won't happen overnight** ça n'arrivera pas du jour au lendemain
2 *adjective* de nuit; **an overnight flight** un vol de nuit

overseas *adverb* à l'étranger; **they live overseas** ils habitent à l'étranger

oversleep *verb* ne pas se réveiller (à

temps); **I'm sorry I'm late, I overslept** je suis désolé d'arriver en retard, je ne me suis pas réveillé

overtake *verb* dépasser, doubler

overweight *adjective* trop gros/ grosse

owe *verb* devoir; **I owe him a lot of money** je lui dois beaucoup d'argent

owl *noun* le hibou, la chouette

The plural of *hibou* is *hiboux*.

own

1 *adjective* propre; **her own money** son propre argent; **how could he do that to his own brother?** comment a-t-il pu faire ça à son propre frère?; **use your own computer** sers-toi de ton propre ordinateur

2 *pronoun* **no need to lend me your telephone, I'll use my own** inutile de me prêter ton téléphone, je me servirai du mien; **the house is my own** la mai-

son est à moi; **she has money of her own** elle a de l'argent à elle; **I'll do it on my own** je le ferai tout seul; **she built the house on her own** elle a construit la maison toute seule; **he got his own back** il s'est vengé

3 *verb* avoir, posséder; **she owns three cars** elle a trois voitures; **he owns several factories** il possède plusieurs usines

4 own up avouer; **he owned up to stealing the money** il a avoué avoir volé l'argent

owner *noun* le/la propriétaire

ox *noun* le bœuf

The plural of *bœuf* is pronounced "beu".

oxygen *noun* l'oxygène *(masculine)*

oyster *noun* une huître

ozone *noun* l'ozone *(masculine)*; **the ozone layer** la couche d'ozone

pace
1 *noun* une allure; **at a brisk pace** à vive allure
2 *verb* **to pace up and down** faire les cent pas

Pacific *noun* **the Pacific** le Pacifique

pack
1 *noun*
(**a**) *(packet)* le paquet; **a pack of cigarettes** un paquet de cigarettes
(**b**) *(to be carried on one's back)* le sac à dos
(**c**) *(of beer, milk)* le pack
(**d**) **a pack of cards** un jeu de cartes
(**e**) **a pack of wolves** une meute de loups
2 *verb* faire ses bagages; **I need to pack my suitcase** je dois faire ma valise; **I only packed one jumper** je n'ai mis qu'un pull dans ma valise
3 **pack up** ranger; **pack up your things, it's time to go** rangez vos affaires, c'est l'heure de partir; **pack everything up in boxes** mettez tout dans des cartons

package *noun* le paquet

packed *adjective*
(**a**) *(room, train)* bondé/bondée; **the pub was packed** le pub était bondé
(**b**) **a packed lunch** un panier-repas

The plural of *panier-repas* is *paniers-repas*.

packaging *noun* l'emballage *(masculine)*

packet *noun* le paquet

paddle
1 *noun*

(**a**) *(oar)* la pagaie
(**b**) **to go for a paddle** patauger
2 *verb*
(**a**) *(walk in the water)* patauger
(**b**) **to paddle a boat** pagayer

padlock *noun* le cadenas

page *noun* la page; **on page 6** à la page 6

pail *noun* le seau

The plural of *seau* is *seaux*.

pain *noun*
(**a**) la douleur; **he's in pain** il souffre; **I have a pain in my foot** j'ai mal au pied
(**b**) **he's a pain** il est pénible

painful *adjective* douloureux/douloureuse

painkiller *noun* un analgésique

paint
1 *noun* la peinture
2 *verb* peindre; **he's painting a tree** il peint un arbre; **we're painting the kitchen** nous peignons la cuisine

paintbrush *noun* le pinceau

The plural of *pinceau* is *pinceaux*.

painter *noun* le peintre; **he's a painter** il est peintre

Note that when talking about people's jobs or situations, French does not use an article (*un* or *une*).

painting *noun*
(**a**) *(activity)* la peinture; **he likes painting** il aime faire de la peinture
(**b**) *(picture)* le tableau; **it's a painting by Gauguin** c'est un tableau de Gauguin

The plural of *tableau* is *tableaux*.

pair *noun (of shoes, scissors)* une paire; **a pair of trousers** un pantalon

Pakistan *noun* le Pakistan; **he lives in Pakistan** il habite au Pakistan; **have you ever been to Pakistan?** est-ce que tu es déjà allé au Pakistan?; **it comes from Pakistan** ça vient du Pakistan

Pakistani
1 *adjective* pakistanais/pakistanaise
2 *noun (person)* le Pakistanais/la Pakistanaise; **the Pakistanis** les Pakistanais *(masculine plural)*

In French, only the noun for the inhabitants of a country takes a capital letter, never the adjective.

pal *noun* le copain/la copine

palace *noun* le palais

Note that the French word *palace* is never a translation for the English word *palace*. It means *luxury hotel*.

pale *adjective* pâle

palm *noun*
(a) *(of the hand)* la paume; **he was holding the key in the palm of his hand** il tenait la clé dans la paume de sa main
(b) **a palm tree** un palmier

pan *noun*
(a) *(saucepan)* la casserole
(b) *(frying pan)* la poêle

The word *poêle* is pronounced "pwal".

pancake *noun* la crêpe

panda *noun* le panda

pane *noun* la vitre; **a pane of glass** une vitre

panic
1 *noun* la panique
2 *verb* s'affoler; **he panicked when he saw smoke** il s'est affolé quand il a vu de la fumée

pant *verb* haleter; **the dog was panting** le chien haletait

pants *plural noun (underwear)* le slip; *(boxer shorts)* le caleçon

paper *noun*
(a) *(for writing on)* le papier
(b) *(newspaper)* le journal

The plural of *journal* is *journaux*.

paperback *noun* le livre de poche

parachute *noun* le parachute

paradise *noun* le paradis

paragraph *noun* le paragraphe

parallel *adjective* parallèle

parasol *noun* le parasol

parcel *noun* le paquet, le colis

pardon
1 *noun* **pardon?** *(what did you say?)* pardon?, comment?; **I beg your pardon** je vous prie de m'excuser
2 *verb* **pardon me!** *(sorry)* pardon!

parent *noun (father)* le père; *(mother)* la mère; **a single-parent family** une famille monoparentale; **parents** les parents *(masculine plural)*; **his parents are Spanish** ses parents sont espagnols

Note that the French word *parent* cannot be used in the singular to mean "one of the two parents". When used in the singular, the French word *parent* means *a relative*.

parents-in-law *plural noun* les beaux-parents *(masculine plural)*

Paris *noun* Paris; **he lives in Paris** il habite à Paris; **she's going to Paris on Monday** elle va à Paris lundi; **she comes from Paris** elle vient de Paris

park
1 *noun*
(a) *(garden)* le parc
(b) **a car park** un parking
2 *verb*
(a) se garer; **where did you park?** où est-ce que tu t'es garé?

(**b**) garer; **I need to park the car** il faut que je gare la voiture

parking *noun* le stationnement; **parking is not allowed in the city centre** le stationnement est interdit au centre-ville; **a parking meter** un parcmètre

> Note that the French word *parking* is never a translation for the English word *parking*. It means *car park*.

parliament *noun* le parlement

parrot *noun* le perroquet

parsley *noun* le persil

part
1 *noun*
(**a**) *(section)* la partie; **I preferred the first part of the film** j'ai préféré la première partie du film; **he sold part of the company** il a vendu une partie de l'entreprise
(**b**) *(in a film or a play)* le rôle; **he plays the part of the husband** il joue le rôle du mari
(**c**) *(component)* la pièce; **spare parts** des pièces de rechange
(**d**) **to take part in something** participer à quelque chose; **he took part in the show** il a participé au spectacle
2 *verb* se séparer; **they parted on good terms** ils se sont quittés bons amis

particular
1 *adjective* particulier/particulière
2 *noun* **in particular** en particulier

particularly *adverb* particulièrement

parting *noun* *(in hair)* la raie

partly *adverb* en partie; **he's partly to blame** il est en partie responsable

partner *noun*
(**a**) *(in sport, dancing)* le/la partenaire
(**b**) *(boyfriend, husband)* le compagnon; *(girlfriend, wife)* la compagne

part-time
1 *adjective* **a part-time job** un travail à temps partiel

2 *adverb* **she works part-time** elle travaille à temps partiel

party *noun*
(**a**) *(with friends)* la fête; **a birthday party** une fête d'anniversaire
(**b**) *(formal occasion)* la soirée
(**c**) *(political)* le parti; **a political party** un parti politique

parsnip *noun* le panais

pass
1 *noun*
(**a**) *(to gain admission)* un laissez-passer

> The word *laissez-passer* does not change in the plural.

(**b**) *(in ball games)* la passe
(**c**) *(for unlimited access)* la carte d'abonnement; **a bus pass** une carte d'abonnement de bus
(**d**) *(in an exam)* **to get a pass** être reçu/reçue; **he got a pass in maths** il a été reçu en maths
(**e**) *(in a mountain range)* le col
2 *verb*
(**a**) *(give)* passer; **can you pass the salt, please?** tu peux me passer le sel, s'il te plaît?
(**b**) *(go past)* passer devant; **it's the second time we've passed this church** ça fait deux fois qu'on passe devant cette église; **I passed him on the street yesterday** je l'ai croisé dans la rue hier
(**c**) *(in an exam)* être reçu/reçue, réussir; **he passed his exam** il a été reçu à son examen

> Note that when talking about exams the French verb *passer* is never a translation for the English word *to pass*. It means *to take, to sit*.

3 **pass on** transmettre; **I passed on the message** j'ai transmis le message
4 **pass out** s'évanouir; **he passed out** il s'est évanoui
5 **pass round** faire passer; **pass the peanuts round, please** fais passer les cacahuètes, s'il te plaît

passage *noun*
(**a**) *(in a book, a speech)* le passage
(**b**) *(in a building)* le couloir

passenger *noun* le passager/la passagère

passer-by *noun* le passant/la passante

passion *noun* la passion; **he's got a passion for chess** il a la passion des échecs

passive *adjective* passif/passive

passport *noun* le passeport

password *noun* le mot de passe

past
1 *noun* le passé; **stop thinking about the past** arrête de penser au passé; **in the past** autrefois; **in the past not many people went on foreign holidays** autrefois, peu de gens allaient en vacances à l'étranger
2 *preposition*
(**a**) *(in front of)* devant; **we went past the station** nous sommes passés devant la gare
(**b**) *(beyond)* après; **it's past the post office** c'est après la poste
(**c**) *(later than)* **it's past four o'clock** il est quatre heures passées; **it's five past three** il est trois heures cinq; **it's half past two** il est deux heures et demie
3 *adjective*
(**a**) *(in grammar)* **the past tense** le passé
(**b**) *(just gone by)* dernier/dernière; **these past months** ces derniers mois

pasta *noun* les pâtes *(feminine plural)*; **would you like some pasta?** est-ce que tu veux des pâtes?

paste
1 *noun (glue)* la colle
2 *verb (stick)* coller

pastime *noun* le passe-temps

The word *passe-temps* does not change in the plural.

pastry *noun*
(**a**) *(dough)* la pâte

(**b**) *(cake)* la pâtisserie

pat *verb*
(**a**) *(tap lightly)* tapoter; **he patted me on the head** il m'a donné une petite tape sur la tête
(**b**) *(a cat, a dog)* caresser

patch *noun*
(**a**) *(on clothing)* la pièce
(**b**) *(over an eye)* le bandeau

The plural of *bandeau* is *bandeaux*.

(**c**) *(on a tyre)* la rustine

path *noun*
(**a**) *(in a garden, a park)* une allée
(**b**) *(in the countryside)* le chemin; *(narrower)* le sentier

pathetic *adjective* lamentable; **you're pathetic!** tu es lamentable!

patience *noun* la patience; **he hasn't got much patience** il n'a pas beaucoup de patience

patient
1 *adjective* patient/patiente
2 *noun (sick person)* le patient/la patiente

patiently *adverb* avec patience

pattern *noun* le motif, le dessin

pause
1 *noun* la pause
2 *verb* faire une pause

pavement *noun* le trottoir

paw *noun* la patte

pay
1 *noun* le salaire; **the pay isn't that good** le salaire n'est pas formidable
2 *verb*
(**a**) payer; **I paid the bill** j'ai payé l'addition; **I haven't been paid yet** je n'ai pas encore été payé; **who paid for the coffees?** qui a payé les cafés?
(**b**) **to pay attention** faire attention; **pay attention!** fais attention! *or* écoute!; **I wasn't paying attention to what he was saying** je ne faisais pas attention à ce qu'il disait *or* je n'écoutais pas ce qu'il disait; **don't pay any**

attention to them ne fais pas attention à eux
(c) to pay somebody a visit rendre visite à quelqu'un; I paid him a visit je lui ai rendu visite
3 pay back rembourser

payment *noun* le paiement

payphone *noun* le téléphone public

PC *noun* *(personal computer)* le PC

PE *noun* l'EPS *(feminine)*

EPS is the abbreviation of *éducation physique et sportive.*

pea *noun* le petit pois

peace *noun*
(a) la paix
(b) peace and quiet la tranquillité; leave him in peace laisse-le tranquille

peaceful *adjective*
(a) *(quiet)* calme, paisible; a peaceful village un village paisible
(b) *(not violent)* pacifique; a peaceful demonstration une manifestation pacifique

peach *noun* la pêche

peacock *noun* le paon

The word *paon* is pronounced like the first syllable of *pantalon.*

peak *noun*
(a) *(of a mountain)* le sommet
(b) *(of a cap)* la visière
(c) peak season la haute saison

peanut *noun* la cacahuète; peanut butter le beurre de cacahuète; a peanut butter sandwich un sandwich au beurre de cacahuète

pear *noun* la poire

pearl *noun* la perle

pebble *noun* *(in general)* le caillou; *(on the beach)* le galet

The plural of *caillou* is *cailloux.*

peculiar *adjective* bizarre; he's a bit peculiar il est un peu bizarre

pedal
1 *noun* la pédale
2 *verb* pédaler

pedestrian *noun* le piéton; a pedestrian crossing un passage pour piétons *or* un passage piéton

pee *noun* le pipi; to have a pee faire pipi

peek *verb* to peek at something jeter un coup d'œil à quelque chose; no peeking! défense de regarder!

peel
1 *noun* *(of an orange, a lemon)* l'écorce *(feminine)*; *(of a potato, an apple)* la peau
2 *verb*
(a) *(fruit, vegetables)* éplucher
(b) *(of somebody's skin)* peler; my nose is peeling mon nez pèle
3 peel off
(a) enlever, décoller; you can peel off the label tu peux enlever l'étiquette
(b) s'enlever, se décoller; the label peels off easily l'étiquette s'enlève facilement

peep *verb* to peep at something jeter un coup d'œil à quelque chose; no peeping! défense de regarder!

peg *noun*
(a) *(for a tent)* le piquet
(b) *(for a coat, a hat)* le portemanteau

The plural of *portemanteau* is *portemanteaux.*

(c) a peg, a clothes peg une pince à linge

pen *noun* le stylo

penalty *noun*
(a) *(fine)* une amende; he had to pay a penalty il a dû payer une amende
(b) *(in football)* le penalty; *(in rugby)* la pénalité

pence *plural noun* les pence *(masculine plural)*; it costs fifty pence ça coûte cinquante pence

pencil *noun* le crayon; a pencil case une trousse; a pencil sharpener un taille-crayon

The word *taille-crayon* does not change in the plural.

penguin *noun* le pingouin, le manchot

penknife *noun* le canif

penny *noun* le penny; **I found a penny on the ground** j'ai trouvé un penny par terre

pension *noun* la retraite; **he's on a pension** il est à la retraite

pensioner *noun* le retraité/la retraitée

people *noun*
(a) les gens *(masculine plural)*; **a lot of people don't know this** beaucoup de gens ne le savent pas; **I don't like those people** je n'aime pas ces gens-là; **there were lots of people in the street** il y avait beaucoup de monde dans la rue; **people say it's impossible** on dit que c'est impossible
(b) *(individuals)* les personnes *(feminine plural)*; **there were six people in the waiting room** il y avait six personnes dans la salle d'attente
(c) **English people** les Anglais; **French people** les Français; **blind people** les aveugles; **young people** les jeunes

pepper *noun*
(a) *(spice)* le poivre
(b) *(vegetable)* le poivron; **a red pepper** un poivron rouge

peppermint *noun (sweet)* le bonbon à la menthe; **peppermint tea** le thé à la menthe

per *preposition* par; **one drink per person** une boisson par personne; **a hundred kilometres per hour** cent kilomètres à l'heure

percent *adverb* pour cent

perfect *adjective* parfait/parfaite; **nobody's perfect** personne n'est parfait; **the perfect tense** le passé composé

perfectly *adverb* parfaitement

perform *verb*
(a) *(a play, a role, a piece of music)* jouer
(b) *(a job, a task)* exécuter

performance *noun*
(a) *(show)* le spectacle
(b) *(of an actor)* une interprétation; **he gave an excellent performance as Othello** son interprétation du rôle d'Othello était remarquable
(c) **the team gave a great performance** l'équipe a très bien joué; **the team gave a poor performance** l'équipe n'a pas bien joué

perfume *noun* le parfum; **I never wear perfume** je ne mets jamais de parfum

perhaps *adverb* peut-être; **perhaps he's forgotten** il a peut-être oublié *or* peut-être qu'il a oublié; **perhaps not** peut-être que non

period *noun*
(a) *(time)* la période; **he's going through a difficult period** il traverse une période difficile
(b) *(in school)* une heure de cours; **a maths period** un cours de maths; **a double French period** deux heures de français
(c) *(historical)* une époque; **the Elizabethan period** l'époque élisabéthaine
(d) *(of a woman)* les règles *(feminine plural)*; **I've got my period** j'ai mes règles

permanent *adjective* permanent/permanente

permission *noun* la permission; **have you got permission to do that?** est-ce que tu as la permission de faire ça?; **you need to ask for permission first** il faut d'abord demander la permission

permit
1 *verb* permettre; **is smoking permitted?** est-ce qu'il est permis de fumer?; **smoking is not permitted** il est interdit de fumer

2 *noun* le permis; **a fishing permit** un permis de pêche

person *noun* la personne

> Note that the word *personne* is always feminine, even when it refers to a man.

personal *adjective*
(a) personnel/personnelle; **don't ask personal questions** ne posez pas de questions personnelles; **he's a personal friend of mine** c'est un ami intime
(b) **a personal stereo** un baladeur, un walkman®

personality *noun* la personnalité

personally *adverb* personnellement

persuade *verb* persuader, convaincre; **he persuaded me to go with him** il m'a convaincu de venir avec lui

pessimistic *adjective* pessimiste

pest *noun*
(a) *(animal)* un animal nuisible; *(insect)* un insecte nuisible
(b) *(annoying person)* **stop being a pest!** arrête de m'embêter!; **he's such a pest!** ce qu'il est pénible! *or* ce qu'il est casse-pieds!

pet *noun* un animal domestique; **he has several pets** il a plusieurs animaux domestiques

petal *noun* le pétale

petrol *noun* l'essence *(feminine)*; **we need to get some petrol** il faut que l'on prenne de l'essence; **a petrol station** une station-service

> The plural of *station-service* is *stations-service*. Note that in that sense the French word *pétrole* is never a translation for the English word *petrol*. It means *oil, petroleum*.

pharmacy *noun* la pharmacie

philosophy *noun* la philosophie

phone
1 *noun* le téléphone; **to be on the phone** être au téléphone; **a mobile phone** un téléphone portable; **a phone book** un annuaire; **a phone box** une cabine téléphonique; **a phone call** un coup de téléphone; **to make a phone call** téléphoner, passer un coup de téléphone; **he made several phone calls** il a passé plusieurs coups de téléphone; **a phone number** un numéro de téléphone

2 *verb*
(a) téléphoner; **did Heather phone?** est-ce que Heather a téléphoné?
(b) téléphoner à; **I phoned Jessica yesterday** j'ai téléphoné à Jessica hier; **I need to phone her** il faut que je lui téléphone

3 phone back rappeler; **can you phone her back?** est-ce que tu peux la rappeler?

phonecard *noun* la carte téléphonique

photo *noun* la photo; **to take a photo** prendre une photo; **he took a photo of us** il nous a pris en photo

photocopier *noun* la photocopieuse

photocopy
1 *noun* la photocopie; **to make a photocopy of something** faire une photocopie de quelque chose
2 *verb* photocopier

photograph *noun* la photo; **he took a photograph of us** il nous a pris en photo

> Note that the French word *photographe* is never a translation for the English word *photograph*. It means *photographer*.

photographer *noun* le/la photographe; **my uncle is a photographer** mon oncle est photographe

photography *noun* la photographie, la photo; **he's interested in photography** il s'intéresse à la photo

phrase *noun* une expression; **a phrase book** un guide de conversation

physical *adjective* physique

physics *noun* la physique; **he's good at physics** il est bon en physique

pianist *noun* le/la pianiste

piano *noun* le piano; **he plays the piano** il joue du piano

> Note that when talking about playing musical instruments, French uses the expression *jouer de*.

pick
1 *noun*
(**a**) **take your pick** fais ton choix
(**b**) *(tool)* le pic; **an ice pick** un pic à glace
2 *verb*
(**a**) *(choose)* choisir; **pick a card** choisis une carte; **he always picks the most expensive dish** il choisit toujours le plat le plus cher; **he wasn't picked for the team** il n'a pas été sélectionné pour l'équipe
(**b**) *(gather)* cueillir; **she picked some flowers** elle a cueilli des fleurs
(**c**) **to pick one's nose** se mettre les doigts dans le nez
(**d**) **to pick a fight** chercher la bagarre
3 pick on **to pick on somebody** s'en prendre à quelqu'un; **stop picking on me!** arrête de t'en prendre à moi!
4 pick out choisir
5 pick up
(**a**) *(from the ground)* ramasser; **pick up your socks** ramasse tes chaussettes
(**b**) *(fetch, collect)* aller chercher; **I've got to go and pick up the children** il faut que j'aille chercher les enfants; **she picked me up at the airport** elle est venue me chercher à l'aéroport
(**c**) *(learn)* apprendre; **he picked up a little French during his stay there** il a appris un peu de français pendant son séjour

picnic *noun* le pique-nique; **to go for a picnic** faire un pique-nique

> The plural of *pique-nique* is *pique-niques*.

picture *noun*
(**a**) *(painting)* le tableau; **a picture by**

Monet un tableau de Monet

> The plural of *tableau* is *tableaux*.

(**b**) *(drawing)* le dessin; **to draw a picture** faire un dessin; **she drew a picture of her house** elle a dessiné sa maison
(**c**) *(photo)* la photo; **to take a picture of somebody** prendre quelqu'un en photo
(**d**) *(on TV, in a children's book)* une image; *(illustrating text)* une illustration

pie *noun (open)* la tarte; *(with pastry on top)* la tourte; **an apple pie** une tarte aux pommes

piece *noun*
(**a**) *(bit)* le morceau; **a piece of bread** un morceau de pain

> The plural of *morceau* is *morceaux*.

(**b**) *(coin)* la pièce; **a fifty-pence piece** une pièce de cinquante pence
(**c**) *(of a machine, a jigsaw)* la pièce; **there's one piece missing** il manque une pièce
(**d**) **a piece of news** une nouvelle; **a piece of advice** un conseil; **a piece of furniture** un meuble; **a piece of fruit** un fruit; **a piece of work** un travail

pier *noun* la jetée

pierce *verb* percer; **she had her ears pierced** elle s'est fait percer les oreilles

pig *noun* le cochon, le porc

> The *c* in *porc* is not pronounced.

piggyback *noun* **to give somebody a piggyback** prendre quelqu'un sur son dos

piggybank *noun* la tirelire

pigeon *noun* le pigeon

pigtail *noun* la natte; **she has pigtails** elle porte des nattes

pile
1 *noun*
(**a**) *(heap)* le tas; **I've got piles of work to do** j'ai beaucoup de travail à faire

(**b**) *(stack)* la pile; **a pile of CDs** une pile de CD; **a pile of clothes** une pile de vêtements
2 *verb*
(**a**) *(in a heap)* entasser
(**b**) *(in a stack)* empiler
3 pile up s'accumuler; **debts are starting to pile up** les dettes commencent à s'accumuler

pill *noun* la pilule; **the pill** *(contraceptive)* la pilule

pillow *noun* un oreiller

pillowcase *noun* la taie d'oreiller

pilot *noun* le pilote (d'avion); **she's a pilot** elle est pilote

pimple *noun* le bouton

pin
1 *noun*
(**a**) une épingle
(**b**) *(drawing pin)* la punaise
(**c**) **to have pins and needles** avoir des fourmis; **I've got pins and needles in my foot** j'ai des fourmis dans le pied

Note that the French word *pin* is never a translation for the English word *pin*. It means *pine tree*.

2 *verb*
(**a**) épingler; **she pinned the brooch to her jacket** elle a épinglé la broche à sa veste
(**b**) punaiser; **I pinned a notice on the door** j'ai punaisé une affiche sur la porte
3 pin up they pinned up a sign ils ont accroché un écriteau au mur

pinball *noun (machine)* le flipper; **to play pinball** jouer au flipper

pinch *verb*
(**a**) *(with fingers)* pincer
(**b**) *(steal)* piquer

The French word *piquer* is informal, like the English verb *to pinch*.

pine tree *noun* le pin

pineapple *noun* un ananas

pink *adjective* rose; **a pink jumper** un

pull rose; **pink flowers** des fleurs roses

pint *noun*
(**a**) *(unit)* le demi-litre; **he gave a pint of blood** il a donné un demi-litre de sang

Note that people in France do not use pints as a unit of measurement for liquids, they use litres (1 pint = 0.57 litre).

(**b**) *(beer)* **they went for a pint** ils sont allés boire une bière

pip *noun (in fruit)* le pépin

pipe *noun*
(**a**) *(for smoking)* la pipe
(**b**) *(for water, gas)* le tuyau

The plural of *tuyau* is *tuyaux*.

pirate *noun* le pirate

Pisces *noun* les Poissons *(masculine plural)*; **she's (a) Pisces** elle est Poissons

pistachio *noun* la pistache

pistol *noun* le pistolet

pitch *noun* le terrain; **a football pitch** un terrain de football

pity
1 *noun*
(**a**) *(compassion)* la pitié
(**b**) *(to express regret)* **what a pity!** quel dommage!; **it's a pity!** c'est dommage!; **it's a pity you didn't come** c'est dommage que tu ne sois pas venu
2 *verb* plaindre

pizza *noun* la pizza

place
1 *noun*
(**a**) *(spot)* un endroit, le lieu; **it's an ideal place for a picnic** c'est un endroit idéal pour pique-niquer; **what's your place of birth?** quel est votre lieu de naissance?
(**b**) *(seat, space, position)* la place; **put it back in the right place** remets-le à sa place; **I lost my place in the queue** j'ai perdu ma place dans la queue; **I swapped places with Paul** j'ai changé

de place avec Paul

(**c**) *(house)* la maison; *(flat)* un appartement; **have you ever been to his place?** tu es déjà allé chez lui?; **would you like to come to my place?** est-ce que tu veux venir chez moi?

(**d**) **to take place** se passer, avoir lieu; **it took place two years ago** ça s'est passé il y a deux ans; **the festival takes place every year** le festival a lieu tous les ans

(**e**) **all over the place** partout; **I looked all over the place** j'ai cherché partout

(**f**) **in the first place** d'abord; **you shouldn't have said it in the first place** d'abord, tu n'aurais pas dû le dire
2 *verb* mettre, placer; **he placed it in a drawer** il l'a mis dans un tiroir

plain

1 *adjective*
(**a**) *(clear, obvious)* clair/claire; **it's plain that he's lying** il est clair qu'il ment; **I made it quite plain to him that he had no choice** je lui ai bien fait comprendre qu'il n'avait pas le choix
(**b**) *(simple)* simple; **I like good plain cooking** j'aime la cuisine simple
(**c**) *(not patterned)* uni/unie; **plain blue wallpaper** du papier peint bleu uni
(**d**) *(unflavoured)* nature; **a plain yoghurt** un yaourt nature; **a plain omelette** une omelette nature; **plain chocolate** le chocolat noir
(**e**) *(not very attractive)* quelconque; **his sister is rather plain** sa sœur est plutôt quelconque
2 *noun* la plaine

plait *noun (in hair)* la natte; **she has plaits** elle porte des nattes

plan

1 *noun*
(**a**) *(for the future)* le projet; **what are your plans for the summer?** quels sont vos projets pour cet été?; **I'm sorry, I already have plans for tonight** je suis désolé, je suis déjà pris ce soir
(**b**) *(course of action)* le plan; **I have a**

plan j'ai un plan; **everything went according to plan** tout s'est passé comme prévu
(**c**) *(map)* le plan; **I'll draw you a plan of the office** je vais vous dessiner un plan du bureau
2 *verb*
(**a**) *(organize)* préparer, organiser; **you need to plan your holidays** il faut que tu prépares tes vacances; **have you got anything planned for tonight?** est-ce que tu as quelque chose de prévu pour ce soir?
(**b**) *(intend)* avoir l'intention de; **to plan to do something** avoir l'intention de faire quelque chose; **I plan to visit him this summer** j'ai l'intention de lui rendre visite cet été

plane *noun* un avion; **they travelled by plane** ils ont voyagé en avion

planet *noun* la planète

plank *noun* la planche

plant

1 *noun* la plante
2 *verb* planter

plaster *noun*
(**a**) *(for a wall, a broken limb)* le plâtre
(**b**) **a sticking plaster** un pansement

plastic *noun* le plastique; **a plastic cup** un gobelet en plastique

plate *noun* une assiette

platform *noun*
(**a**) *(at a train station)* le quai
(**b**) *(for a speaker, an actor)* une estrade

play

1 *noun (drama)* la pièce de théâtre
2 *verb*
(**a**) *(have fun)* jouer; **the children are playing in the garden** les enfants jouent dans le jardin
(**b**) *(a sport, a game)* jouer à; **he likes playing football** il aime jouer au football; **he plays tennis very well** il joue très bien au tennis; **would you like to play cards?** est-ce que tu veux jouer aux cartes?
(**c**) *(a musical instrument)* jouer de;

can he play the piano? est-ce qu'il sait jouer du piano?; **he plays the guitar very well** il joue très bien de la guitare (**d**) *(put on)* mettre; **can I play one of your CDs?** est-ce que je peux mettre un de tes CD?; **we watched a video and played some music** on a regardé une cassette vidéo et on a écouté de la musique

player *noun*
(**a**) *(person)* le joueur/la joueuse; **a football player** un footballeur
(**b**) **a CD player** un lecteur de CD; **a DVD player** un lecteur de DVD

playful *adjective* joueur/joueuse

playground *noun*
(**a**) *(in a school)* la cour de récréation
(**b**) *(in a park, a town)* le terrain de jeux

playgroup *noun* la garderie

playtime *noun* la récréation; **they had a game of football at playtime** ils ont joué au football pendant la récréation

playwright *noun* le/la dramaturge

pleasant *adjective* agréable

please
1 *adverb (polite form)* s'il vous plaît; *(familiar form)* s'il te plaît; **can you lend me your bike, please?** est-ce que tu peux me prêter ton vélo, s'il te plaît?
2 *verb* **to please somebody** faire plaisir à quelqu'un; **do as you please** fais comme tu veux

pleased *adjective* content/contente; **he's very pleased with his new computer** il est très content de son nouvel ordinateur

pleasure *noun* le plaisir

plenty *pronoun* beaucoup; **plenty of** beaucoup de; **she has plenty of courage** elle a beaucoup de courage; **we've got plenty of books at home** nous avons beaucoup de livres à la maison; **I have plenty** j'en ai beaucoup; **thank**

you, that's plenty merci, c'est suffisant

pliers *plural noun* la pince; **can you pass me the pliers, please?** est-ce que tu peux me passer la pince, s'il te plaît?

plot
1 *noun*
(**a**) *(conspiracy)* le complot
(**b**) *(of a story)* une intrigue; **the plot is too complicated** l'intrigue est trop compliquée
(**c**) *(of land)* la parcelle de terrain
2 *verb* comploter

plough
1 *noun* la charrue
2 *verb* labourer; **he's ploughing the field** il laboure le champ

plug
1 *noun*
(**a**) *(electrical)* la prise de courant
(**b**) *(for a bath, a sink)* le bouchon
2 *verb* **plug in** brancher

plum *noun* la prune; **a plum tree** un prunier

plumber *noun* le plombier; **my dad is a plumber** mon père est plombier

Note that when describing people's jobs or situations, French does not use an article (*un* or *une*).

plural *noun* le pluriel; **in the plural** au pluriel

plus *preposition* plus; **five plus five is ten** cinq plus cinq font dix; **a plus sign** un signe plus

p.m. *adverb (afternoon)* de l'après-midi; *(evening)* du soir; **it's three p.m.** il est trois heures de l'après-midi; **it's eleven p.m.** il est onze heures du soir

Note that French does not use the terms *a.m.* and *p.m.* Instead, French people often use the 24-hour clock, so *six a.m.* would be *six heures* (6h), but *six p.m.* would be *dix-huit heures* (18h).

pocket *noun* la poche; **pocket money** l'argent de poche

poem *noun* le poème

poet *noun* le poète

poetry *noun* la poésie

point
1 *noun*
(**a**) *(moment)* le moment; **at that point** à ce moment-là; **at that point he walked into the room** à ce moment-là il est entré dans la pièce; **I was on the point of leaving** j'étais sur le point de partir
(**b**) *(use)* **what's the point of going there?** à quoi ça sert d'aller là-bas?; **there's no point in crying like that** ça ne sert à rien de pleurer comme ça; **there's no point in staying here** ça ne sert à rien de rester ici
(**c**) *(important thing)* **that's not the point!** ce n'est pas la question!; **get to the point!** viens-en au fait!; **the point is that she lied to me** le fait est qu'elle m'a menti
(**d**) *(in scores)* le point; **the other team is three points ahead of us** l'autre équipe a trois points d'avance sur nous
(**e**) *(decimal point)* la virgule; **three point two** trois virgule deux

In French, decimals are written with a comma, not a decimal point. For instance 3.2 is written *3,2*.

(**f**) *(of a needle, a pencil)* la pointe
(**g**) *(observation)* la remarque; **he made a good point** il a fait une remarque intéressante
(**h**) **a point of view** un point de vue
2 *verb*
(**a**) **to point one's finger at somebody** montrer quelqu'un du doigt; **don't point!** ne montre pas du doigt!; **the sign was pointing in the direction of the castle** le panneau indiquait la direction du château
(**b**) **to point a gun at somebody** braquer un revolver sur quelqu'un
3 point out

(**a**) *(show)* montrer, indiquer; **il pointed out the house to me** il m'a montré la maison du doigt
(**b**) *(mention)* signaler; **she pointed out several mistakes** elle a signalé plusieurs erreurs

pointed *adjective* pointu/pointue

pointless *adjective* inutile

poison
1 *noun* le poison
2 *verb* empoisonner; **she tried to poison me** elle a essayé de m'empoisonner

poisonous *adjective* *(fumes, chemicals)* toxique; *(plant, mushroom)* vénéneux/vénéneuse; *(snake, spider)* venimeux/venimeuse

poker *noun*
(**a**) *(card game)* le poker; **to play poker** jouer au poker
(**b**) *(for a fire)* le tisonnier

Poland *noun* la Pologne; **he lives in Poland** il habite en Pologne; **have you ever been to Poland?** est-ce que tu es déjà allé en Pologne?; **it comes from Poland** ça vient de Pologne

polar *adjective*
(**a**) polaire
(**b**) **a polar bear** un ours blanc *or* un ours polaire

Pole *noun* le Polonais/la Polonaise

pole *noun*
(**a**) *(stick)* le poteau

The plural of *poteau* is *poteaux*.

(**b**) **the North Pole** le pôle Nord; **the South Pole** le pôle Sud

police *noun* la police; **a police car** une voiture de police; **a police station** un commissariat de police

policeman *noun* un agent de police, le policier; **his brother is a policeman** son frère est agent de police

policewoman *noun* la femme policier, la policière

Polish
1 *adjective* polonais/polonaise

2 *noun*
(**a**) *(language)* le polonais; **she speaks Polish** elle parle polonais
(**b**) *(people)* **the Polish** les Polonais *(masculine plural)*

In French, only the noun for the inhabitants of a country takes a capital letter, never the adjective or the noun for the language.

polish
1 *noun* *(for furniture)* la cire; *(for shoes)* le cirage
2 *verb* cirer

polite *adjective* poli/polie; **be polite to her** sois poli avec elle

politely *noun* poliment

political *adjective* politique

politician *noun* le politicien/la politicienne

politics *noun* la politique; **he's interested in politics** il s'intéresse à la politique

pollute *verb* polluer

pollution *noun* la pollution

pond *noun*
(**a**) *(large)* un étang; *(smaller)* une mare
(**b**) *(man-made, in a garden or a park)* un bassin

pony *noun* le poney

ponytail *noun* la queue de cheval; **she's got a ponytail** elle a une queue de cheval

poodle *noun* le caniche

pool *noun*
(**a**) *(for swimming)* la piscine
(**b**) *(puddle)* la flaque; **a pool of blood** une flaque de sang
(**c**) *(small pond)* la mare
(**d**) *(game)* le billard; **to play pool** jouer au billard

poor *adjective*
(**a**) *(not rich, deserving pity)* pauvre; **it's a very poor country** c'est un pays très pauvre; **poor Paul!** pauvre Paul!;

poor me! pauvre de moi!; **poor people** les pauvres
(**b**) *(bad)* mauvais/mauvaise

poorly
1 *adjective* souffrant/souffrante
2 *adverb* mal; **the book was poorly translated** le livre a été mal traduit

pop
1 *adjective* pop; **pop music** la musique pop; **pop songs** les chansons pop

The adjective *pop* does not change in the feminine or plural.

2 *verb*
(**a**) *(put)* mettre; **I popped it in a bag** je l'ai mis dans un sac; **she popped her head out of the window** elle a passé la tête par la fenêtre
(**b**) *(go)* **to pop out** sortir un instant; **would you like to pop in for a minute?** est-ce que tu veux entrer une minute?; **I'll pop in and see you this evening** je passerai te voir ce soir; **could you pop round to the baker's?** est-ce que tu pourrais faire un saut chez le boulanger?

popcorn *noun* le pop-corn

pope *noun* le pape

poppy *noun* le coquelicot

popular *adjective* populaire; **this singer is very popular with young people** ce chanteur a beaucoup de succès auprès des jeunes

population *noun* la population

porch *noun* le porche

pork *noun* le porc; **a pork chop** une côtelette de porc

The *c* in *porc* is not pronounced.

port *noun* *(harbour)* le port

portable *adjective* portable; **a portable TV** un téléviseur portable

porter *noun* *(who carries luggage)* le porteur

portion *noun*
(**a**) *(of food)* la portion

(b) *(part)* la partie

portrait *noun* le portrait

Portugal *noun* le Portugal; **he lives in Portugal** il habite au Portugal; **have you ever been to Portugal?** est-ce que tu es déjà allé au Portugal?; **he's from Portugal** il est portugais

Portuguese
1 *adjective* portugais/portugaise
2 *noun*
(a) *(language)* le portugais; **he speaks Portuguese** il parle portugais
(b) *(person)* le Portugais/la Portugaise; **the Portuguese** les Portugais *(masculine plural)*

In French, only the noun for the inhabitants of a country takes a capital letter, never the adjective or the noun for the language.

posh *adjective* chic; **we ate in a posh restaurant** nous avons mangé dans un restaurant chic; **he's got a posh accent** il a un accent snob

The word *chic* does not change in the feminine or in the plural.

position *noun* la position

positive *adjective*
(a) *(tone, message)* positif/positive; **the test is positive** le test est positif; **it's important to have a positive attitude** il est important d'avoir une attitude positive
(b) *(sure)* certain/certaine; **I'm positive** j'en suis certain

possibility *noun* la possibilité; **it's a possibility** c'est une possibilité

possible *adjective* possible; **it's possible that he'll come** il est possible qu'il vienne; **as soon as possible** dès que possible; **as quickly as possible** le plus rapidement possible; **try to give as many details as possible** essaie de donner le plus de détails possible; **he works as little as possible** il travaille le moins possible; **as far as possible** autant que possible

possibly *adverb*
(a) *(perhaps)* peut-être
(b) *(used for emphasis)* **I can't possibly accept** je ne peux vraiment pas accepter; **I'll do all I possibly can** je ferai tout mon possible

post
1 *adjective*
(a) *(letters)* le courrier; *(service)* la poste; **is there any post for me?** est-ce qu'il y a du courrier pour moi?; **I'll put the letter in the post** je mettrai la lettre à la poste; **a post office** un bureau de poste
(b) *(pole)* le poteau

The plural of *poteau* is *poteaux*.

2 *verb* poster; **have you posted the letter?** est-ce que tu as posté la lettre?

postage *noun* *(cost)* le tarif postal

postbox *noun* la boîte aux lettres

postcard *noun* la carte postale

postcode *noun* le code postal

poster *noun* *(for advertising)* une affiche; *(decorative)* le poster

postman *noun* le facteur; **he's a postman** il est facteur

postpone *verb* reporter; **the meeting was postponed** la réunion a été reportée

pot *noun*
(a) *(for a plant, a paint)* le pot; **to make a pot of tea** faire du thé; **a pot of jam** un pot de confiture
(b) *(for cooking)* la casserole

potato *noun* la pomme de terre

poultry *noun* la volaille

pound *noun* *(weight, money)* la livre

pour *verb*
(a) verser; **he poured some milk onto his cereal** il a versé du lait dans ses céréales; **can I pour you a drink?** je te sers un verre?
(b) **it's pouring, it's pouring with rain** il pleut à verse; **in the pouring rain** sous une pluie battante

(**c**) **water was pouring into the cellar** l'eau entrait à flots dans la cave; **blood poured from the wound** la blessure saignait abondamment

poverty *noun* la pauvreté

powder *noun* la poudre

power *noun*
(**a**) *(authority)* le pouvoir; **to be in power** être au pouvoir
(**b**) *(strength)* la puissance; **military power** la puissance militaire
(**c**) *(energy)* l'énergie *(feminine)*; **nuclear power** l'énergie nucléaire
(**d**) *(electricity)* le courant électrique; **a power cut** une coupure de courant; **a power station** une centrale électrique

powerful *adjective* puissant/puissante

practical *adjective*
(**a**) *(tool, clothes)* pratique
(**b**) **a practical joke** une farce; **to play a practical joke on somebody** faire une farce à quelqu'un

practically *adverb (almost)* pratiquement, presque

practice *noun*
(**a**) *(training)* l'entraînement *(masculine)*; **I haven't had much practice** je ne me suis pas beaucoup entraîné; **are you going to football practice tomorrow?** tu vas à l'entraînement de football demain?
(**b**) *(exercises)* les exercices *(masculine plural)*; **have you done your piano practice?** est-ce que tu as fait tes exercices de piano?
(**c**) **in practice** dans la pratique

practise *verb*
(**a**) *(of a musician)* s'exercer; **how do you expect to become a great pianist if you don't practise?** comment veux-tu devenir un grand pianiste si tu ne t'exerces pas?; **have you been practising the guitar this week?** est-ce que tu as travaillé ta guitare cette semaine?; **he's practising with his band**

il est en train de répéter avec son groupe
(**b**) *(of a sportsperson)* s'entraîner; **I practise every Sunday with the team** je m'entraîne tous les dimanches avec l'équipe
(**c**) **to practise a language** pratiquer une langue

praise
1 *noun* les éloges *(masculine plural)*
2 *verb* faire l'éloge de; **he praised the book** il a fait l'éloge du livre; **he praised his colleague** il a fait l'éloge de son collègue; **he praised me for my courage** il m'a félicité pour mon courage

pram *noun* le landau

The plural of *landau* is *landaus*.

prawn *noun* la crevette

pray *verb* prier; **I prayed that they wouldn't hear me** j'ai prié pour qu'ils ne m'entendent pas

prayer *noun* la prière

precious *adjective* précieux/précieuse

precise *adjective* précis/précise

precisely *adverb* précisément

predictable *adjective* prévisible

prefer *verb* préférer; **I prefer Paris to London** je préfère Paris à Londres; **he prefers to walk rather than take the bus** il préfère marcher plutôt que de prendre le bus

pregnant *noun* enceinte; **she's three months pregnant** elle est enceinte de trois mois

prejudice *noun* le préjugé

prejudiced *adjective* **to be prejudiced** avoir des préjugés; **he's prejudiced against French people** il a des préjugés contre les Français

prepare *verb*
(**a**) *(get something ready)* préparer; **I need to prepare my speech for tomorrow** il faut que je prépare mon discours pour demain

(b) *(get ready)* se préparer; **the country is preparing for war** le pays se prépare à la guerre

prepared *adjective* **to be prepared to do something** être prêt à faire quelque chose; **is she prepared to go and live there?** est-ce qu'elle est prête à aller vivre là-bas?; **I'm prepared for anything** je suis prêt à tout

prescription *noun* une ordonnance

presence *noun* la présence; **in the presence of** en présence de

present
1 *adjective*
(a) *(not absent)* présent/présente; **they were all present at the meeting** ils étaient tous présents à la réunion
(b) *(current)* actuel/actuelle; **the present situation is worrying** la situation actuelle est préoccupante
(c) **the present tense** le présent
2 *noun*
(a) *(gift)* le cadeau; **to give somebody a present** faire un cadeau à quelqu'un

The plural of *cadeau* is *cadeaux*.

(b) *(time)* **the present** le présent; **for the present** pour le moment; **at present** à présent
3 *verb*
(a) *(a TV programme)* présenter
(b) *(a prize, a diploma)* remettre; **they presented him with an award** ils lui ont remis un prix

presentation *noun* la présentation

presenter *noun* le présentateur/la présentatrice; **she's a TV presenter** elle est présentatrice de télévision

president *noun* le président/la présidente

press
1 *noun* **the press** *(newspapers)* la press; **a press conference** une conférence de presse
2 *verb*
(a) *(button, switch)* appuyer sur; **press the button** appuie sur le bouton
(b) *(clothes)* repasser

press-up *noun* la pompe; **he did 50 press-ups** il a fait 50 pompes

pressure *noun* la pression; **to be under pressure** être sous pression

pretend *verb* faire semblant; **to pretend to do something** faire semblant de faire quelque chose; **he pretended that he hadn't heard** il a fait semblant de ne pas entendre

Note that the French word *prétendre* is not a translation for the English word *pretend*. It means *to claim*.

pretty
1 *adjective* joli/jolie
2 *adverb* assez; **I was pretty pleased with myself** j'étais assez content de moi

prevent *verb* empêcher; **his injury has prevented him from playing** sa blessure l'a empêché de jouer

previous *adjective* précédent/précédente

previously *adverb* auparavant

prey *noun* la proie

price *noun* le prix; **petrol has gone up in price** le prix de l'essence a augmenté; **a price tag** une étiquette

prick *verb* piquer; **she pricked her finger when she was sewing** elle s'est piqué le doigt en cousant

pride *noun*
(a) *(satisfaction)* la fierté; **to take pride in something** être fier de quelque chose
(b) *(self-esteem)* l'amour-propre *(masculine)*

priest *noun* le prêtre

primary school *noun* une école primaire

Prime Minister *noun* le Premier ministre

prince *noun* le prince

princess *noun* la princesse

principal *adjective* *(main)* principal/principale

The masculine plural of *principal* is *principaux*.

print
1 *noun*
(**a**) *(of a photograph)* une épreuve, un tirage
(**b**) *(mark)* une empreinte
2 *verb*
(**a**) *(a newspaper, a book)* imprimer
(**b**) *(write)* écrire en caractères d'imprimerie; **print your name, please** écrivez votre nom en caractères d'imprimerie, s'il vous plaît
3 print out imprimer

printer *noun* *(of a computer)* une imprimante

priority *noun* la priorité

prison *noun* la prison; **to put somebody in prison** mettre quelqu'un en prison

prisoner *noun* le prisonnier/la prisonnière; **a prisoner of war** un prisonnier de guerre

privacy *noun* l'intimité *(feminine)*

private *adjective* privé/privée; **a private school** une école privée; **my private life** ma vie privée; **he takes private lessons** il prend des cours particuliers

privately *adverb* en privé

prize *noun* le prix; **he won first prize** il a gagné le premier prix

probable *adjective* probable

probably *adverb* probablement

problem *noun* le problème; **no problem!** pas de problème!; **I had problems opening the door** j'ai eu du mal à ouvrir la porte

produce *verb*
(**a**) *(make)* produire, fabriquer; **Denmark produces dairy products** le Danemark est un pays producteur de produits laitiers; **they produce washing machines** ils fabriquent des machines à laver

(**b**) *(a film)* produire; *(a play)* mettre en scène; **they produced a play** ils ont mis en scène une pièce de théâtre

product *noun* le produit

production *noun* la production

profession *noun* la profession

professional *adjective* professionnel/professionnelle

profit *noun* le bénéfice

professor *noun* le professeur d'université; **she's a professor** elle est professeur d'université

program *noun* *(for a computer)* le programme

programme *noun*
(**a**) *(on the radio, TV)* une émission; **a TV programme** une émission de télévision

Note that in French *le programme de télévision* means *the TV guide*.

(**b**) *(planned activities)* le programme; **what's on the programme for this afternoon?** qu'est-ce qu'il y a au programme cet après-midi?

progress *noun* le progrès; **to make progress** progresser; **the investigation is making progress** l'enquête progresse; **he's making progress in French** il fait des progrès en français

project *noun*
(**a**) *(plan)* le projet; **they're working on a new building project** ils travaillent sur un nouveau projet de construction
(**b**) *(at school)* le dossier; **David is doing a project on pollution** David fait un dossier sur la pollution

promise
1 *noun* la promesse; **to make a promise** faire une promesse; **he never keeps his promises** il ne tient jamais ses promesses
2 *verb* promettre; **I promised him that we'd go to the cinema** je lui ai promis qu'on irait au cinéma

pronounce *verb* prononcer; **how do you pronounce it?** comment est-ce que ça se prononce?

pronunciation *noun* la prononciation

> Do not confuse the spellings of the French *prononciation* and English *pronunciation*.

proof *noun* la preuve; **have you got any proof?** est-ce que tu as des preuves?

proper *adjective*
(a) *(suitable)* approprié/appropriée; **have you got the proper equipment?** est-ce que tu as le matériel approprié?
(b) *(real)* vrai/vraie; **I haven't had a proper holiday for ages** ça fait très longtemps que je n'ai pas pris de vraies vacances

> Note that the French word *propre* is never a translation for the English word *proper*. It means *clean* when it's placed after a noun (*une maison propre*) or *own* when it's placed in front of a noun (*mon propre frère*).

properly *adverb* correctement

property *noun* la propriété; **private property** *(on a sign)* propriété privée

proposal *noun* la proposition

propose *verb*
(a) *(suggest)* proposer; **I propose that we go home** je propose qu'on rentre
(b) **to propose to somebody** demander quelqu'un en mariage

prospects *plural noun* les perspectives *(feminine plural)*; **this job has no prospects** ce travail n'offre aucune perspective

protect *verb* protéger

protection *noun* la protection

protest
1 *noun* la protestation; *(demonstration)* la manifestation
2 *verb* protester; **they're protesting against the war** ils protestent contre la guerre

Protestant
1 *adjective* protestant/protestante
2 *noun* le protestant/la protestante

> The names of religions and their followers are never capitalized in French.

protester *noun* le manifestant/la manifestante

proud *adjective* fier/fière; **he's very proud of his children** il est très fier de ses enfants

prove *verb* prouver

proverb *noun* le proverbe

provide *verb* fournir; **they don't provide the meals** ils ne fournissent pas les repas; **to provide somebody with something** fournir quelque chose à quelqu'un; **this provided me with an excuse** ça m'a fourni une excuse

prune *noun* le pruneau

> The plural of *pruneau* is *pruneaux*. Note that the French word *prune* is never a translation for the English word *prune*. It means *plum*.

psychiatrist *noun* le/la psychiatre

> Note that the *p* is pronounced in all French words beginning with *psy*.

psychologist *noun* le/la psychologue

psychology *noun* la psychologie

pub *noun* le pub

> Do not confuse *le pub* and *la pub*. The latter is short for *la publicité*.

public
1 *adjective*
(a) public/publique; **public opinion** l'opinion publique; **public transport** les transports en commun
(b) **a public school** une école privée
(c) **a public holiday** un jour férié
2 *noun* **the public** le public; **open to the public** ouvert au public; **in public** en public

publish *verb* publier

publisher *noun* un éditeur/une éditrice

pudding *noun*
(a) *(dessert)* le dessert
(b) **black pudding** le boudin noir

puddle *noun* la flaque d'eau

pull
1 *verb* tirer; **she pulled my hair** elle m'a tiré les cheveux; **he pulled the trigger** il a appuyé sur la gâchette; **I've pulled a muscle** je me suis fait un claquage
2 pull down
(a) *(lower)* baisser; **pull the blind down** baisse le store; **he pulled his trousers down** il a baissé son pantalon
(b) *(knock down)* démolir; **they pulled down the old railway station** ils ont démoli l'ancienne gare
3 pull in *(of a vehicle)* s'arrêter; **the train pulled in at the station** le train est entré en gare
4 pull off *(remove)* enlever; **pull off the label** enlève l'étiquette
5 pull out
(a) *(tear out)* arracher; **he had two teeth pulled out** il s'est fait arracher deux dents
(b) *(remove)* enlever; **she pulled the cork out of the bottle** elle a enlevé le bouchon de la bouteille
(c) *(take out)* sortir, prendre; **he pulled a gun out of his pocket** il a sorti un pistolet de sa poche
6 pull over *(in a car)* se rabattre; **he pulled over to let the fire engine past** il s'est rabattu pour laisser passer le camion de pompiers
7 pull through s'en sortir; **he had a serious accident but he pulled through** il a eu un accident grave mais il s'en est sorti
8 pull up
(a) *(draw upwards)* remonter; **he pulled up his socks** il a remonté ses chaussettes
(b) *(tear out)* arracher; **she was pulling up weeds** elle arrachait des mauvaises herbes
(c) *(in a car)* s'arrêter; **my dad pulled up because he heard a strange noise** mon père s'est arrêté parce qu'il a entendu un bruit bizarre

pulse *noun* le pouls; **he took my pulse** il m'a pris le pouls

The word *pouls* is pronounced "pou".

pump
1 *noun* la pompe; **a bicycle pump** une pompe à vélo
2 *verb* **pump up** gonfler

pumpkin *noun* la citrouille

punch
1 *noun* *(blow)* le coup de poing
2 *verb* donner un coup de poing à; **he punched me in the stomach** il m'a donné un coup de poing dans le ventre

punctual *adjective* ponctuel/ponctuelle

puncture *noun* la crevaison; **we had a puncture** on a crevé

punish *verb* punir; **he was punished for telling lies** il a été puni pour avoir menti

punishment *noun* la punition; **I had to dig the garden as a punishment** comme punition, j'ai dû bêcher le jardin

pup *noun* le chiot

The *t* in *chiot* is not pronounced.

pupil *noun*
(a) *(in a school)* un/une élève
(b) *(of the eye)* la pupille

puppet *noun* la marionnette

puppy *noun* le chiot

The *t* in *chiot* is not pronounced.

purchase *verb* acheter

pure *adjective* pur/pure

purple *adjective* violet/violette; **a purple jumper** un pull violet; **a purple**

skirt une jupe violette; **purple flowers** des fleurs violettes

purpose *noun*
(a) *(aim)* le but; **what is the purpose of your visit?** quel est le but de votre visite?
(b) **on purpose** exprès; **she did it on purpose** elle l'a fait exprès

purr *verb* ronronner; **the cat was purring** le chat ronronnait

purse *noun* le porte-monnaie

> The word *porte-monnaie* does not change in the plural.

push
1 *noun* **to give somebody a push** pousser quelqu'un; **give the door a big push** pousse la porte bien fort
2 *verb*
(a) *(move)* pousser; **can you help me push the car?** est-ce que tu peux m'aider à pousser la voiture?
(b) *(press)* appuyer sur; **she pushed the button** elle a appuyé sur le bouton
3 **push in** resquiller

pushchair *noun* la poussette

put
1 *verb* mettre; **I put the keys on the table** j'ai mis les clés sur la table; **it put me in a really good mood** ça m'a mis de très bonne humeur
2 **put away** ranger; **he needs to put his toys away** il faut qu'il range ses jouets
3 **put back**
(a) *(in a specific place)* remettre; **put it back where you found it** remets-le où tu l'as trouvé
(b) **to put back the clocks by an hour** retarder les pendules d'une heure
4 **put down**
(a) *(on the ground, a table)* poser; **he put his fork down** il a posé sa fourchette; **you can put your bag down** tu peux poser ton sac
(b) *(write)* noter; **he put his name down for the course** il s'est inscrit au cours

(c) **to put the phone down** raccrocher
5 **put in** installer; **we're having central heating put in** nous faisons installer le chauffage central
6 **put off**
(a) *(delay)* reporter; **they decided to put off the match** ils ont décidé de reporter le match
(b) *(repel)* **to put somebody off something** dégoûter quelqu'un de quelque chose; **it put me off skiing for good** ça m'a définitivement dégoûté du ski
7 **put on**
(a) *(wear)* mettre; **I put on my coat** j'ai mis mon manteau
(b) *(switch on)* mettre, allumer; **I put the heating on** j'ai mis le chauffage; **put the TV on** allume la télé
(c) *(play)* mettre; **can I put on a CD?** est-ce que je peux mettre un CD?
(d) *(produce)* monter; **we're putting on a show at school** on monte un spectacle à l'école
(e) **to put on weight** grossir; **she's put on a lot of weight** elle a beaucoup grossi
(f) *(pretend)* faire semblant; **he isn't really in pain, he's putting it on** il n'a pas vraiment mal, il fait semblant
8 **put out**
(a) *(extinguish)* éteindre; **he put out his cigarette** il a éteint sa cigarette
(b) **to put out one's hand** tendre la main
9 **put through** passer; **can you put me through to the sales department?** est-ce que vous pouvez me passer le service des ventes?
10 **put up**
(a) *(raise)* lever; **he put his hand up** il a levé la main
(b) *(on the wall)* mettre; **he put the poster up on his wall** il a mis le poster sur son mur
(c) *(erect)* **to put up a tent** monter une tente; **to put up shelves** installer des étagères
(d) *(increase)* augmenter; **they've put**

up the price of petrol ils ont augmenté le prix de l'essence
11 put up with *(accept)* supporter; **I can't put up with the noise** je ne supporte pas ce bruit

puzzle *noun*
(a) *(game)* **a puzzle, a jigsaw puzzle** un puzzle; **a crossword puzzle** des mots croisés
(b) *(mystery)* le mystère

puzzled *adjective* perplexe; **she looked puzzled** elle avait l'air perplexe

pyjamas *plural noun* le pyjama; **where are your pyjamas?** où est ton pyjama?

qualified *adjective*
(**a**) *(holding a diploma)* diplômé/diplômée; **a qualified nurse** une infirmière diplômée
(**b**) *(competent)* qualifié/qualifiée; **our staff are highly qualified** notre personnel est hautement qualifié

quality *noun* la qualité; **it's good quality leather** c'est du cuir de bonne qualité; **this coat is of very poor quality** ce manteau est de très mauvaise qualité

quantity *noun* la quantité

quarrel
1 *noun* la dispute; **she had a quarrel with her best friend** elle s'est disputée avec sa meilleure amie
2 *verb* se disputer; **they quarrel a lot** ils se disputent souvent

quarter *noun*
(**a**) le quart; **he lost a quarter of his fortune** il a perdu un quart de sa fortune
(**b**) **a quarter of an hour** un quart d'heure; **two and a quarter hours** deux heures et quart; **it's a quarter past two** il est deux heures et quart; **it's a quarter to two** il est deux heures moins le quart

quay *noun* le quai

queen *noun*
(**a**) *(monarch)* la reine; **the Queen of Belgium** la reine de Belgique
(**b**) *(in cards)* la dame; **the queen of clubs** la dame de trèfle

question
1 *noun*
(**a**) la question; **it's out of the ques-**tion c'est hors de question; **it's a question of trust** c'est une question de confiance
(**b**) **a question mark** un point d'interrogation
2 *verb* interroger; **the police want to question him about the robbery** la police veut l'interroger à propos du cambriolage

questionnaire *noun* le questionnaire

queue
1 *noun* la queue; **there was a long queue outside the shop** il y avait une longue queue devant le magasin
2 *verb* faire la queue

quick
1 *adjective* rapide; **that was quick!** ça a été rapide!; **he had a quick look** il a jeté un coup d'œil rapide; **I'll have a quick shower** je vais prendre une douche en vitesse; **try and be quick** essaie de faire vite; **he's a quick worker** il travaille vite
2 *adverb* vite; **quick, come in!** vite, entre!

quickly *adverb* vite

quiet *adjective*
(**a**) *(peaceful)* tranquille; **it's a very quiet village** c'est un village très tranquille
(**b**) *(not noisy)* silencieux/silencieuse; **the house was very quiet** il n'y avait aucun bruit dans la maison; **be quiet!** tais-toi!
(**c**) *(reserved)* réservé/réservée; **he's a very quiet child** c'est un enfant très réservé

quietly *adverb*
(a) *(gently, not loudly)* doucement; **I can't hear you, you're speaking too quietly** je ne t'entends pas, tu parles trop doucement; **shut the door quietly** ferme la porte doucement *or* sans faire de bruit
(b) *(silently)* sans bruit; **he came in quietly** il est entré sans bruit

quilt *noun* un édredon

quit *verb*
(a) *(give up)* abandonner; **this game is too hard, I quit** ce jeu est trop dur, j'abandonne
(b) *(resign)* démissionner; **I've had enough of this job, I want to quit** j'en ai assez de ce travail, j'ai envie de démissionner

quite *adverb*
(a) *(rather)* assez, plutôt; **the flat is quite big** l'appartement est assez grand; **I quite liked that film** j'ai plutôt aimé ce film
(b) *(entirely)* tout à fait; **I'm quite sure that he'll come** je suis tout à fait certain qu'il viendra; **you're quite right** tu as tout à fait raison
(c) *(used for emphasis)* **it was quite a surprise** ça a été une véritable surprise
(d) **quite a lot** beaucoup; **he has quite a lot of books** il a beaucoup de livres; **I travel quite a lot** je voyage beaucoup; **she goes there quite a lot** elle y va souvent

quiz *noun*
(a) *(in a magazine)* le questionnaire
(b) **a quiz, a quiz show** *(on TV)* un jeu télévisé; *(on the radio)* un jeu radiophonique
(c) *(at school)* le contrôle; **we had a maths quiz** on a eu un contrôle de maths

quotation *noun*
(a) la citation; **it's a quotation from Shakespeare** c'est une citation de Shakespeare
(b) **quotation marks** les guillemets *(masculine plural)*; **in quotation marks** entre guillemets

quote
1 *noun*
(a) la citation; **it's a quote from Orwell** c'est une citation d'Orwell
(b) **quotes** *(quotation marks)* les guillemets *(masculine plural)*; **in quotes** entre guillemets
2 *verb* citer; **he's always quoting Churchill** il n'arrête pas de citer Churchill

rabbit *noun* le lapin

rabies *noun* la rage; **the dog's got rabies** le chien a la rage

race
1 *noun*
(**a**) *(competition)* la course
(**b**) *(group of people)* la race; **the human race** la race humaine
(**c**) **the races** *(horseracing)* les courses
2 *verb*
(**a**) *(compete)* faire la course; **I'll race you!** on fait la course?
(**b**) *(rush)* courir; **we had to race to the station** il a fallu courir jusqu'à la gare; **he raced out** il est sorti en courant

racecourse *noun* le champ de courses

racehorse *noun* le cheval de course

> The plural of *cheval* is *chevaux*.

racetrack *noun* la piste; *(for horses)* le champ de courses

racing *noun* **a racing car** une voiture de course; **a racing driver** un pilote de course

racism *noun* le racisme

racist
1 *adjective* raciste
2 *noun* le/la raciste

rack *noun*
(**a**) *(set of shelves)* une étagère
(**b**) *(on a bike, for luggage)* le porte-bagages

> The word *porte-bagages* does not change in the plural.

(**c**) *(for bottles)* le casier

racket *noun*
(**a**) *(for tennis)* la raquette
(**b**) *(noise)* le vacarme

radar *noun* le radar

radiator *noun* le radiateur

radio *noun* la radio; **on the radio** à la radio; **a radio station** une station de radio

radish *noun* le radis

raffle *noun* la tombola; **a raffle ticket** un billet de tombola

raft *noun* le radeau

> The plural of *radeau* is *radeaux*.

rag *noun* *(piece of cloth)* le chiffon; **to be dressed in rags** être en haillons

rage *noun* la rage; **to be in a rage** être furieux/furieuse

raid
1 *noun*
(**a**) *(by the police)* la descente; **a police raid** une descente de police
(**b**) *(by the army)* le raid
(**c**) *(by thieves)* le hold-up

> The word *hold-up* does not change in the plural.

2 *verb*
(**a**) *(of the police)* faire une descente dans; **the police raided the nightclub** la police a fait une descente dans la boîte de nuit
(**b**) *(of the army)* faire un raid dans; **the army raided the village** l'armée a fait un raid dans le village
(**c**) *(of thieves)* faire un hold-up dans;

they raided the jeweller's ils ont fait un hold-up dans la bijouterie

rail *noun*
(**a**) *(on stairs)* la rampe; *(on a balcony)* la balustrade
(**b**) *(for trains)* le rail; **he went there by rail** il y est allé en train

railings *plural noun* la grille; **he chained his bicycle to the railings** il a attaché son vélo à la grille

railway *noun*
(**a**) le chemin de fer; **he works for the railways** il travaille pour les chemins de fer; **a railway line** une ligne de chemin de fer; **a railway track** une voie ferrée
(**b**) **a railway station** une gare

rain
1 *noun* la pluie
2 *verb* pleuvoir; **it's raining** il pleut

rainbow *noun* un arc-en-ciel

The plural of *arc-en-ciel* is *arcs-en-ciel*.

raincoat *noun* un imperméable

rainforest *noun* la forêt tropicale humide

rainy *noun* pluvieux/pluvieuse

raise *verb*
(**a**) *(lift)* lever; **she raised her hand** elle a levé la main
(**b**) *(increase)* augmenter; **they raised the price of petrol** ils ont augmenté le prix de l'essence
(**c**) *(improve)* améliorer; **we need to raise standards if we don't want to lose customers** il faut améliorer le niveau si on ne veut pas perdre de clients
(**d**) *(bring up)* élever; **they were raised by their father** ils ont été élevés par leur père
(**e**) *(mention)* soulever; **nobody raised the problem** personne n'a soulevé le problème
(**f**) **to raise one's voice** *(in anger)* élever la voix *or* hausser le ton
(**g**) **to raise funds** réunir des fonds

raisin *noun* le raisin sec

Note that when used on its own, the French word *raisin* means *grapes*.

rake *noun* le râteau

The plural of *râteau* is *râteaux*.

ranch *noun* le ranch

random *noun* **at random** au hasard; **to do something at random** faire quelque chose au hasard; **I just made a random guess** j'ai deviné tout à fait par hasard

range *noun*
(**a**) *(of sizes, colours)* le choix; *(of prices)* la gamme; **they offer a wide range of activities** ils proposent un grand choix d'activités
(**b**) **a mountain range** une chaîne de montagnes

ransom *noun* la rançon

rare *adjective*
(**a**) *(not common)* rare; **a rare species** une espèce rare
(**b**) *(meat)* saignant/saignante

rarely *adverb* rarement

rash *noun* une éruption cutanée

raspberry *noun* la framboise; **raspberry jam** la confiture de framboises; **a raspberry tart** une tarte aux framboises

rat *noun* le rat

Note that the *t* in *rat* is not pronounced.

rate *noun*
(**a**) *(figure)* le taux; **the interest rate** le taux d'intérêt; **the divorce rate** le taux de divorce
(**b**) *(price)* le tarif; **we have special rates for families** on fait des tarifs spéciaux pour les familles
(**c**) *(speed)* le rythme; **at this rate we'll never be finished tomorrow** à ce rythme on n'aura jamais fini demain

rather *adverb*
(**a**) *(quite)* plutôt; **he's rather tall** il est

plutôt grand

(b) *(preferably)* **I'd rather stay here** j'aimerais mieux rester ici; **I'd rather he came some other day** je préférerais qu'il vienne un autre jour

(c) **rather than** plutôt que; **we should go to the museum rather than stay at home** on devrait aller au musée plutôt que de rester à la maison

rattle

1 *noun*

(a) *(noise)* le bruit, le cliquetis

(b) *(baby's toy)* le hochet

2 *verb*

(a) *(keys)* agiter; **he was rattling his keys** il agitait ses clés

(b) *(of keys)* faire du bruit; **his keys were rattling in his pocket** on entendait ses clés dans sa poche

(c) *(of a door, a window)* vibrer

rattlesnake *noun* le serpent à sonnette

raw *adjective*

(a) *(food)* cru/crue; **raw fish** le poisson cru

(b) **raw materials** les matières premières

ray *noun*

(a) le rayon; **the sun's rays** les rayons du soleil

(b) **a ray of hope** une lueur d'espoir

razor *noun* le rasoir; **a razor blade** une lame de rasoir

reach

1 *noun* **to be out of reach** être hors de portée; **the flat is within easy reach of the city centre** l'appartement est à proximité du centre-ville

2 *verb*

(a) *(arrive at)* atteindre; **we reached London before nightfall** nous avons atteint Londres avant la tombée de la nuit; **the missile didn't reach its target** le missile n'a pas atteint sa cible

(b) *(by stretching one's arm)* **to reach for something, to reach out for something** étendre le bras pour attra-

per quelque chose; **the book fell behind the piano and I can't reach it** le livre est tombé derrière le piano et je n'arrive pas à l'attraper; **the box is too high, I can't reach** la boîte est trop haute, je n'arrive pas à l'attraper; **he reached for his camera** il a pris son appareil photo

(c) *(touch)* toucher; **he can reach the ceiling** il arrive à toucher le plafond

(d) *(agree on)* parvenir à; **they couldn't reach a decision** ils ne sont pas parvenus à une décision

(d) *(get in touch with)* joindre; **you can reach him on his mobile** tu peux le joindre sur son portable

(e) *(be delivered to)* parvenir à; **the letter never reached him** la lettre ne lui est jamais parvenue

react *verb* réagir

reaction *noun* la réaction; **what was her reaction?** quelle a été sa réaction?; **he had a bad reaction to the drugs** il a mal réagi aux médicaments

read

1 *verb*

(a) *(a book, a newspaper, a letter)* lire; **she reads a lot** elle lit beaucoup

(b) *(a meter)* relever; **somebody came to read the meter** quelqu'un est venu relever le compteur

2 read out **to read something out** lire quelque chose à haute voix

reader *noun* le lecteur/la lectrice

reading *noun* la lecture; **I have a lot of reading to do** j'ai beaucoup de lecture à faire

ready *adjective* prêt/prête; **are you ready to go?** est-ce que tu es prêt?; **to get ready** se préparer; **to get ready to do something** se préparer à faire quelque chose; **to get something ready** préparer quelque chose; **he's getting the dinner ready** il est en train de préparer le repas

ready-made *adjective* tout prêt/toute prête

real *adjective*
(**a**) *(true)* vrai/vraie; **it isn't his real name** ce n'est pas son vrai nom
(**b**) *(authentic, not fake)* véritable; **it isn't real leather** ce n'est pas du cuir véritable
(**c**) *(actual)* réel/réelle; **the real world** le monde réel; **in real life** dans la réalité

realistic *adjective* réaliste

reality *noun* la réalité; **in reality** en réalité

realize *verb* se rendre compte de; **I don't think you realize the work involved** je ne crois pas que tu te rendes compte de tout le travail que ça représente; **I soon realized that something was wrong** je me suis vite rendu compte que quelque chose n'allait pas

really *adverb* vraiment; **this cake is really delicious** ce gâteau est vraiment délicieux; **really?** c'est vrai?

rear
1 *adjective* arrière; **the rear wheels** les roues arrière

> The adjective *arrière* does not change in the plural.

2 *noun* l'arrière *(masculine)*; **we were sitting at the rear of the bus** nous étions assis à l'arrière du bus

reason *noun* la raison; **he refused to tell me the reason why** il a refusé de me dire pourquoi; **what's his reason for not accepting?** pourquoi est-ce qu'il n'a pas accepté?

reasonable *adjective*
(**a**) *(sensible)* raisonnable
(**b**) *(moderate)* raisonnable; **£10 is very reasonable** 10 livres, c'est tout à fait raisonnable
(**c**) *(acceptable)* passable; **the meal was reasonable** le repas était passable

reasonably *adverb* assez; **he played reasonably well** il a assez bien joué; **it's reasonably well paid** c'est assez bien payé

reassure *verb* rassurer

rebel
1 *noun* le/la rebelle
2 *verb* se rebeller

receipt *noun* le reçu

receive *verb* recevoir; **I received a letter** j'ai reçu une lettre

recent *adjective* récent/récente

recently *adverb* récemment

> The middle *e* in *récemment* is pronounced like the *a* in *cat*.

reception *noun*
(**a**) *(in a hotel)* la réception; **leave the keys at reception** laisse les clés à la réception
(**b**) *(party)* la réception; **a wedding reception** une réception de mariage

receptionist *noun* le/la réceptionniste

recharge *verb* recharger

rechargeable *adjective* rechargeable

recipe *noun* la recette de cuisine

reckon *verb* penser; **I reckon he must have forgotten** je pense qu'il a dû oublier; **what do you reckon?** qu'est-ce que tu en penses?

recognize *verb* reconnaître; **at first I didn't recognize him** au début je ne l'ai pas reconnu

recommend *verb* recommander; **he recommended the film to me** il m'a recommandé ce film

> Do not confuse the spellings of the French *recommander* and English *recommend*.

record
1 *noun*
(**a**) *(for playing music)* le disque; **it's my favourite record** c'est mon disque préféré; **a record player** un tourne-disque

> The plural of *tourne-disque* is *tourne-disques*.

(b) *(in sport)* le record; **she hopes to beat the world record** elle espère battre le record du monde
(c) *(file)* le dossier; **the letter isn't in your records** la lettre n'est pas dans votre dossier
(d) *(note)* **you should keep a record of how much you spend** tu devrais noter ce que tu dépenses; **we have no record of this** nous n'en avons aucune trace
2 *verb* enregistrer

recorder *noun* la flûte à bec; **I play the recorder** je joue de la flûte à bec

recording *noun* un enregistrement

recover *verb* se remettre; **he never recovered from his accident** il ne s'est jamais remis de son accident

rectangle *noun* le rectangle

recycle *verb* recycler

red *adjective*
(a) *(in general)* rouge; **a red skirt** une jupe rouge; **a red light** un feu rouge; **a red card** *(in football)* un carton rouge; **he went red when he heard her name** il est devenu tout rouge quand il a entendu son nom
(b) *(hair)* roux/rousse; **she has red hair** elle a les cheveux roux

red-haired *adjective* aux cheveux roux; **a red-haired girl** une fille aux cheveux roux; **I'm red-haired** j'ai les cheveux roux

redhead *noun* le roux/la rousse

redo *verb* refaire; **he made me redo the work** il m'a fait refaire le travail

reduce *verb* réduire; **they've reduced my salary by 20 per cent** ils ont réduit mon salaire de 20 pour cent

reduction *noun* la réduction; **they refused to give me a reduction** ils ont refusé de me faire une réduction; **a ten percent reduction** une réduction de dix pour cent

reef *noun* le récif; **a coral reef** un récif de corail

refer *verb* **to refer to something** faire allusion à quelque chose

referee *noun* un/une arbitre

reference *noun*
(a) une allusion; **he made no reference to the incident** il n'a pas fait allusion à l'incident
(b) *(when applying for a job)* les références *(feminine plural)*; **she refused to give me a reference** elle a refusé de me fournir des références

reflect *verb* refléter

reflection *noun* *(in a mirror)* le reflet, l'image *(feminine)*

reflex *noun* le réflexe

refresh *verb* rafraîchir

refreshing *adjective* rafraîchissant/rafraîchissante

refreshments *plural noun* les rafraîchissements *(masculine plural)*

refrigerator *noun* le réfrigérateur

refugee *noun* le réfugié/la réfugiée

refund
1 *noun* le remboursement; **he managed to get a refund** il a réussi à se faire rembourser
2 *verb* rembourser; **they refunded her** ils l'ont remboursée

refuse
1 *noun* les ordures *(feminine plural)*
2 *verb* refuser; **he refused to do his homework** il a refusé de faire ses devoirs

region *noun*
(a) *(part of a country)* la région; **it's a beautiful region** c'est une région magnifique
(b) **in the region of** environ; **it costs in the region of £200** ça coûte environ 200 livres

register
1 *noun* le registre; *(at school)* le cahier d'appel; **to take the register** faire l'appel
2 *verb* s'inscrire; **she registered for**

the **evening class** elle s'est inscrite aux cours du soir

registration *noun* une inscription; **a registration number** un numéro d'immatriculation

regret
1 *noun* le regret
2 *verb* regretter; **do you regret going there?** est-ce que tu regrettes d'y être allé?

regular *adjective*
(**a**) *(steady, even)* régulier/régulière; **at regular intervals** à intervalles réguliers; **on a regular basis** régulièrement; **she's a regular visitor to New York** elle va régulièrement à New York
(**b**) *(usual)* habituel/habituelle; **at the regular place** à l'endroit habituel
(**c**) *(price, size, portion)* normal/normale; **a regular portion of fries** une portion de frites normale

The masculine plural of *normal* is *normaux.*

regularly *adverb* régulièrement

rehearsal *noun* la répétition

rehearse *verb* répéter

reign
1 *noun* le règne
2 *verb* régner

reindeer *noun* le renne

reject *verb* rejeter

relapse *noun* la rechute

related *adjective*
(**a**) *(connected)* lié/liée; **the two incidents are not related** les deux incidents ne sont pas liés
(**b**) *(belonging to the same family)* apparenté/apparentée; **they have the same name but they're not related** ils ont le même nom mais ils ne sont pas apparentés

relation *noun*
(**a**) *(link)* le rapport
(**b**) *(relative)* le parent/la parente; **he's a very distant relation** c'est un parent

très éloigné; **is she a relation of yours?** est-ce qu'elle est de votre famille?; **he has relations in France** il a de la famille en France

relationship *noun* les relations *(feminine plural)*; **we have a good relationship** nous nous entendons bien

relative
1 *adjective* relatif/relative
2 *noun* le parent/la parente; **she's the only relative I've got left** c'est la seule parente qui me reste; **he has relatives in Canada** il a de la famille au Canada

relatively *adverb* relativement

relax *verb* se détendre; **he finds it hard to relax** il a du mal à se détendre

relaxed *adjective* décontracté/décontractée

relaxing *adjective* reposant/reposante

release *verb*
(**a**) *(set free)* libérer; **the hostages have been released** les otages ont été libérés
(**b**) *(make available)* sortir; **the film will be released next month** le film sort le mois prochain; **they've just released their second album** ils viennent de sortir leur deuxième album

relevant *adjective* pertinent/pertinente; **this is a relevant question** c'est une question pertinente; **this is not relevant to our discussion** ça n'a aucun rapport avec notre discussion

reliable *adjective* fiable

relief *noun* le soulagement; **what a relief!** quel soulagement!

relieved *adjective* soulagé/soulagée

religion *noun* la religion

religious *adjective*
(**a**) *(linked to religion)* religieux/religieuse
(**b**) *(believing in God)* croyant/croyante

reluctant *adjective* **he was reluctant**

to tell me what happened il hésitait à me dire ce qui s'était passé; **I was reluctant to leave him alone** j'hésitais à le laisser tout seul

rely on *verb* compter sur; **you can't rely on him** on ne peut pas compter sur lui

remain *verb* rester

remaining *adjective* **he spent the remaining three days in Paris** il a passé les trois jours qui restaient à Paris

remains *plural noun* les restes *(masculine plural)*

remark *noun* la remarque

remember *verb* se souvenir de; **I don't remember** je ne m'en souviens pas; **do you remember your grandmother?** est-ce que tu te souviens de ta grand-mère?; **I remember him** je me souviens de lui; **I remember locking the door** je me souviens d'avoir fermé la porte à clé; **remember you've got your guitar lesson tonight** souviens-toi que tu as ta leçon de guitare ce soir; **remember to water the plants** pense à arroser les plantes *or* n'oublie pas d'arroser les plantes

remind *verb* rappeler; **remind me to phone her** rappelle-moi de lui téléphoner *or* fais-moi penser à lui téléphoner; **he reminds me of my brother** il me rappelle mon frère; **let me remind you that smoking is not permitted** je vous rappelle qu'il est interdit de fumer; **that reminds me** à propos

remote *adjective*
(**a**) isolé/isolée; **they live in a remote village** ils habitent dans un village isolé
(**b**) **a remote control** une télécommande

remove *verb* enlever, retirer; **can you remove your things from my desk, please?** est-ce que tu peux enlever tes affaires de mon bureau, s'il te plaît?

renew *verb* renouveler

rent
1 *noun* le loyer
2 *verb* louer; **they rented a house in the countryside** ils ont loué une maison à la campagne
3 **rent out** louer; **they're renting out their flat to students** ils louent leur appartement à des étudiants

repair
1 *noun* la réparation; **he's doing some repairs to his bike** il fait des réparations sur son vélo
2 *verb* réparer; **they haven't repaired the lift yet** ils n'ont pas encore réparé l'ascenseur; **to have something repaired** faire réparer quelque chose

repay *verb* rembourser

repeat *verb* répéter; **to repeat a year** redoubler une classe

replace *verb* remplacer; **they're trying to find somebody to replace him** ils essaient de trouver quelqu'un pour le remplacer

replica *noun* une imitation, une copie

reply
1 *noun* la réponse; **I didn't get a reply to my question** je n'ai pas eu de réponse à ma question
2 *verb* répondre; **he didn't reply to my letter** il n'a pas répondu à ma lettre

report
1 *noun*
(**a**) *(summary)* le rapport, le compte-rendu; **a book report** un compte-rendu de lecture

The plural of *compte-rendu* is *comptes-rendus*.

(**b**) *(in the news)* le reportage
(**c**) *(at school)* le bulletin scolaire
2 *verb*
(**a**) *(mention)* signaler; **nobody reported the burglary** personne n'a signalé le cambriolage
(**c**) *(go)* se présenter; **report to my office tomorrow morning** présentez-vous à mon bureau demain matin

reporter *noun* le/la journaliste, le/la reporter

represent *verb* représenter

representative
1 *adjective* représentatif/représentative
2 *noun* le représentant/la réprésentante

reptile *noun* le reptile

republic *noun* la république

reputation *noun* la réputation; **he has a reputation for being difficult** il a la réputation d'être difficile

request
1 *noun* la demande; **he came at his grandmother's request** il est venu à la demande de sa grand-mère
2 *verb* demander; **he was requested to leave** on lui a demandé de partir

require *verb*
(a) *(necessitate)* demander; **it requires a lot of patience** ça demande beaucoup de patience
(b) *(need)* avoir besoin de; **just let me know if you require anything** dites-moi si vous avez besoin de quoi que ce soit

rescue
1 *noun* le secours; **I went to her rescue** je suis allé à son secours; **a rescue operation** une opération de sauvetage; **a rescue team** une équipe de sauvetage
2 *verb* sauver

research *noun* la recherche; **she does research on fossils** elle fait de la recherche sur les fossiles; **he's doing some research for his project** il fait des recherches pour son dossier

researcher *noun* le chercheur/la chercheuse; **he's a researcher** il est chercheur

reservation *noun* la réservation

reserve *verb* réserver; **I've reserved a table for two** j'ai réservé une table pour deux

resident *noun*
(a) *(of a country, a city, a street)* un habitant/une habitante
(b) *(of a hotel)* le client/la cliente
(c) *(foreigner in a country)* le résident/la résidente

resign *verb* démissionner

resist *verb* résister à; **I couldn't resist temptation** je n'ai pas pu résister à la tentation

resort
1 *noun*
(a) *(place)* la station balnéaire; **a ski resort** une station de ski
(b) **as a last resort** en dernier recours
2 *verb* **to resort to something** avoir recours à quelque chose; **there's no need to resort to violence** inutile d'avoir recours à la violence

resource *noun* la ressource; **they lack resources** ils manquent de ressources; **natural resources** les ressources naturelles

respect
1 *noun* le respect; **to have respect for somebody** avoir du respect pour quelqu'un
2 *verb* respecter

In French, the *c* and *t* in *respect* are not pronounced; however they are pronounced in the word *respecter*.

responsibility *noun* la responsabilité; **feeding the cat is your responsibility** c'est à toi de donner à manger au chat

responsible *adjective* responsable; **he claims that he isn't responsible for the accident** il dit qu'il n'est pas responsable de l'accident

Do not confuse the spellings of the French *responsable* and English *responsible*.

rest
1 *noun*
(a) *(break, pause)* le repos; **to have a rest** se reposer

(**b**) *(remainder)* **the rest** le reste; **he ate the rest of the cake** il a mangé le reste du gâteau; **the rest of them** les autres; **the rest of the pupils** les autres élèves

2 *verb*

(**a**) *(have a break)* se reposer; **you need to rest** il faut que tu te reposes

(**b**) *(lean)* appuyer; **he rested the ladder against the wall** il a appuyé l'échelle contre le mur

restaurant *noun* le restaurant

result *noun* le résultat

retire *verb (from work)* prendre sa retraite; **he retired last year** il a pris sa retraite l'année dernière

return

1 *noun*

(**a**) le retour; **on his return to France** à son retour en France

(**b**) **a return, a return ticket** un aller-retour; **one return ticket to Glasgow, please** un aller-retour pour Glasgow, s'il vous plaît

The plural of *aller-retour* is *allers-retours*.

(**c**) **a return match** un match retour

(**d**) **in return** en échange; **they never asked for anything in return** ils n'ont jamais rien demandé en échange; **I gave her a bottle of wine in return for her help** je lui ai offert une bouteille de vin pour la remercier de son aide

2 *verb*

(**a**) *(come back)* revenir; **I'll tell him when he returns** je le lui dirai quand il reviendra

(**b**) *(go back)* retourner; **they didn't like it here so they returned to Australia** ils ne se plaisaient pas ici alors ils sont retournés en Australie

(**c**) *(come or go back home)* rentrer à la maison

(**d**) *(give back)* rendre, rapporter; **I haven't returned the book to the library** je n'ai pas rapporté le livre à la bibliothèque

(**e**) *(send back)* renvoyer; **I need to return the form by the end of the week** il faut que je renvoie le formulaire d'ici la fin de la semaine

(**f**) **to return somebody's call** rappeler quelqu'un; **can you return her call?** est-ce que tu peux la rappeler?

reunion *noun* les retrouvailles *(feminine plural)*, la réunion; **a family reunion** une réunion de famille

Note that the most common meaning of the French word *réunion* is *meeting*.

reveal *verb* révéler

revenge *noun* la vengeance; **to get one's revenge** se venger; **Andy swore he'd get his revenge on Simon** Andy a juré qu'il se vengerait de Simon

reverse *verb (in a vehicle)* faire marche arrière; **I reversed into a lamppost** je suis rentré dans un lampadaire en faisant marche arrière

review *noun* la critique; **his latest album got good reviews** son dernier album a eu de bonnes critiques

revise *verb* réviser; **did you revise for the test?** est-ce que tu as révisé avant l'interrogation?

revision *noun* les révisions *(feminine plural)*; **to do some revision** faire des révisions

revolting *adjective* dégoûtant/dégoûtante; **the food was revolting** la nourriture était dégoûtante

revolution *noun* la révolution; **the French Revolution** la Révolution française

reward

1 *noun* la récompense

2 *verb* récompenser; **he was rewarded for his courage** il a été récompensé pour son courage

rewind *verb* rembobiner; **rewind the tape before returning it** rembobine la cassette avant de la rendre

rhinoceros *noun* le rhinocéros

rhubarb *noun* la rhubarbe

rhyme *verb* rimer; **"head" doesn't rhyme with "bead"** "head" ne rime pas avec "bead"

rhythm *noun* le rythme

> Do not confuse the spellings of the French *rythme* and English *rhythm*.

rib *noun* la côte; **he broke a rib** il s'est cassé une côte

ribbon *noun* le ruban

rice *noun* le riz; **rice pudding** le riz au lait

> Note that the *z* in *riz* is not pronounced.

rich *adjective* riche; **rich people** les riches

rid *adjective* **to get rid of something** se débarrasser de quelque chose; **they got rid of him** ils se sont débarrassés de lui

riddle *noun* la devinette; **to ask somebody a riddle** poser une devinette à quelqu'un

ride
1 *noun (on a bicycle, by car, on horseback)* la promenade, le tour; **to go for a ride** aller faire une promenade *or* aller faire un tour; **he gave me a ride to the airport** il m'a emmené à l'aéroport en voiture
2 *verb*
(a) **to ride a horse** monter à cheval; **can he ride a horse?** est-ce qu'il sait faire du cheval?
(b) **to ride a bicycle** faire du vélo; **he rides his bicycle to work every day** il va au travail en vélo tous les jours

rider *noun*
(a) *(on horseback)* le cavalier/la cavalière
(b) *(on a bicycle)* le/la cycliste
(c) *(on a motorcycle)* le/la motocycliste

ridiculous *adjective* ridicule

rifle *noun* le fusil

> Note that the *l* in *fusil* is not pronounced.

right
1 *adjective*
(a) *(opposite of left)* droit/droite; **my right hand** ma main droite
(b) *(opposite of wrong)* bon/bonne; **that's not the right answer** ce n'est pas la bonne réponse; **you're right!** tu as raison!; **that's right!** c'est vrai!; **he was right to stand up for her** il a eu raison de la défendre
(c) *(exact)* juste; **have you got the right time?** est-ce que tu as l'heure juste?
(d) *(what should be done)* bien; **it isn't right to make fun of others** ce n'est pas bien de se moquer des autres
(e) *(fair)* juste; **this isn't right!** ce n'est pas juste!
2 *adverb*
(a) *(not left)* à droite; **turn right** tourne à droite
(b) *(correctly)* correctement; **try to do it right this time** essaie de le faire correctement cette fois-ci
(c) *(used for emphasis)* **he was sitting right next to me** il était assis juste à côté de moi; **right until the last minute** jusqu'à la toute dernière minute; **I'll do it right away** je vais le faire tout de suite; **I need to go right now** il faut que je parte tout de suite
(d) bon; **right, where were we?** bon, où en étions-nous?
3 *noun*
(a) *(opposite of left)* **the right** la droite; **on the right** à droite; **it's to the right of the table** c'est à droite de la table
(b) *(opposite of wrong)* le bien; **he's old enough to know right from wrong** il est assez grand pour faire la différence entre le bien et le mal
(c) *(permission)* le droit; **you've got the right to choose** tu as le droit de choisir; **he's got no right to treat her like this** il n'a pas le droit de la traiter

comme ça; **human rights** les droits de l'homme

right-hand *adjective* de droite; **it's on the right-hand shelf** c'est sur l'étagère de droite; **on the right-hand side** à droite

right-handed *adjective* droitier/droitière; **she's right-handed** elle est droitière

ring
1 *noun*
(a) *(on a finger, on curtains)* un anneau; **a wedding ring** une alliance; **a ring binder** un classeur à anneaux

The plural of *anneau* is *anneaux*.

(b) *(with a stone)* la bague
(c) *(circle)* le cercle; **they were sitting in a ring** ils étaient assis en cercle
(d) *(sound of a doorbell)* le coup de sonnette; *(sound of a telephone, of an alarm clock)* la sonnerie; **to give somebody a ring** téléphoner à quelqu'un
(e) *(in boxing)* le ring; *(in a circus)* la piste
2 *verb*
(a) *(phone)* téléphoner; **don't forget to ring me** n'oublie pas de me téléphoner
(b) *(make a ringing sound)* sonner; **the phone is ringing** le téléphone sonne; **have you rung the bell?** est-ce que tu as sonné?; **somebody rang the doorbell** on a sonné à la porte
3 **ring back** rappeler; **can you ring me back later?** est-ce que tu peux me rappeler plus tard?
4 **ring up** téléphoner à; **to ring somebody up** téléphoner à quelqu'un; **I rang her up last night** je lui ai téléphoné hier soir

rinse *verb* rincer

riot *noun* une émeute

rip
1 *verb*
(a) *(tear)* déchirer; **he ripped his trousers on the barbed wire** il a déchiré

son pantalon sur le fil de fer barbelé
(b) *(get torn)* se déchirer; **the plastic bag ripped** le sac en plastique s'est déchiré
2 **rip up** déchirer; **he ripped up the letter** il a déchiré la lettre

ripe *adjective* mûr/mûre

rise
1 *noun* une hausse, une augmentation; **the rise in the price of petrol** la hausse du prix de l'essence; **he asked for a pay rise** il a demandé une augmentation
2 *verb*
(a) *(of the temperature, prices)* augmenter; **the price of petrol has risen sharply** le prix de l'essence a nettement augmenté
(b) *(of the sun)* se lever; **the sun is rising** le soleil se lève
(c) *(of a ballon, smoke)* monter, s'élever; **the water is rising** l'eau monte

risk *noun* le risque; **to take risks** prendre des risques; **do it at your own risk** faites-le à vos risques et périls

risky *adjective* risqué/risquée

rival *noun* le rival/la rivale

The plural of *rival* is *rivaux*.

river *noun* *(that flows into another river)* la rivière; *(that flows into the sea)* le fleuve

road *noun*
(a) *(large)* la route; **the road to Edinburgh** la route d'Édimbourg
(b) *(street)* la rue; **he lives just down the road** il habite un peu plus loin dans la même rue

roadworks *plural noun* les travaux *(masculine plural)*

roam *verb* errer; **I was roaming around town all afternoon** j'ai erré dans la ville tout l'après-midi

roar *verb* rugir

roast *verb*
(a) *(cook)* faire rôtir; **I'm roasting a chicken for dinner** je vais faire un

poulet rôti pour ce soir
(**b**) *(be cooking)* rôtir; **the chicken is roasting** le poulet est en train de rôtir

rob *verb*
(**a**) *(a person)* **to rob somebody** voler quelqu'un; **to rob somebody of something** voler quelque chose à quelqu'un
(**b**) *(a bank)* dévaliser; *(a house)* cambrioler

robber *noun* le voleur/la voleuse

robbery *noun* le vol; **an armed robbery** un vol à main armée

robin *noun* le rouge-gorge

> The plural of *rouge-gorge* is *rouges-gorges*.

robot *noun* le robot

> Note that the *t* in *robot* is not pronounced.

rock¹ *noun*
(**a**) *(block of stone)* le rocher; *(substance)* la roche; **rock climbing** la varappe
(**b**) *(music)* le rock

rock² *verb*
(**a**) *(move backwards and forwards)* se balancer; **he was rocking in his chair** il se balançait sur sa chaise
(**b**) **to rock a baby** bercer un enfant

rocket *noun* la fusée

rod *noun* une barre; **a fishing rod** une canne à pêche

roll
1 *noun*
(**a**) *(of paper)* le rouleau

> The plural of *rouleau* is *rouleaux*.

(**b**) *(bread)* le petit pain
2 *verb* rouler
3 roll over se retourner
4 roll up rouler; **to roll up one's sleeves** se retrousser les manches

rollerblades® *plural noun* les rollers *(masculine plural)*

rollercoaster *noun* les montagnes russes *(feminine plural)*

roller-skate *noun* le patin à roulettes

rolling pin *noun* le rouleau à pâtisserie

Roman
1 *adjective* romain/romaine
2 *noun* *(person)* le Romain/la Romaine; **the Romans** les Romains *(masculine plural)*

Romania *noun* la Roumanie; **he lives in Romania** il habite en Roumanie; **have you ever been to Romania?** est-ce que tu es déjà allé en Roumanie?; **she's from Romania** elle vient de Roumanie

Romanian
1 *adjective* roumain/roumaine
2 *noun*
(**a**) *(language)* le roumain; **he speaks Romanian** il parle roumain
(**b**) *(person)* le Roumain/la Roumaine; **the Romanians** les Roumains *(masculine plural)*

> In French, only the noun for the inhabitants of a country takes a capital letter, never the adjective or the noun for the language.

romantic *adjective* romantique

roof *noun* le toit

room *noun*
(**a**) *(in a house)* la pièce
(**b**) *(bedroom)* la chambre; **Claire is in her room** Claire est dans sa chambre
(**c**) *(in a school, for public events)* la salle; **they found a room to practise in** ils ont trouvé une salle pour répéter
(**d**) *(space)* la place; **there isn't enough room for the piano here** il n'y a pas assez de place pour le piano ici

root *noun* la racine

rope *noun* la corde

rose *noun* la rose

rot *verb* pourrir; **the bananas are rotting** les bananes sont en train de pourrir

rotten *adjective* *(fruit, egg, wood)* pourri/pourrie; **rotten weather** un temps pourri; **we had a rotten time at the party** on s'est vraiment embêtés à la soirée

rough *adjective*
(**a**) *(not smooth)* rugueux/rugueuse; **she's got rough skin** elle a la peau rugueuse; **the sea is rough** la mer est agitée
(**b**) *(harsh)* brutal/brutale; **James is rough with his little brother** James est brutal avec son petit frère; **a rough area** un quartier difficile
(**c**) *(difficult)* rude; **life was rough in those days** la vie était rude en ce temps-là
(**d**) *(not precise)* approximatif/approximative; **a rough figure** un chiffre approximatif

roughly *adverb*
(**a**) *(more or less)* à peu près, environ; **it'll cost you roughly £200** ça te coûtera environ 200 livres
(**b**) *(harshly)* brutalement

round
1 *adjective* *(in shape)* rond/ronde; **the Earth is round** la Terre est ronde
2 *preposition*
(**a**) autour de; **they were sitting round the table** ils étaient assis autour de la table; **she travelled round the world** elle a fait le tour du monde; **we went round the shops** on a fait les magasins; **round here** par ici; **it's just round the corner** c'est juste au coin de la rue
(**b**) **round about** environ; **round about £500** environ 500 livres
3 *adverb*
(**a**) autour; **there's a wall all round** il y a un mur tout autour
(**b**) **to go round to somebody's house** passer chez quelqu'un; **she's never asked me round** elle ne m'a jamais invité chez elle
(**c**) **all year round** toute l'année; **it's open all year round** c'est ouvert toute l'année

4 *noun*
(**a**) *(in a contest)* la manche
(**b**) *(in boxing)* la reprise
(**c**) *(in an election)* le tour
(**d**) **a round of drinks** une tournée; **he never buys a round** il ne paye jamais une tournée

roundabout *noun*
(**a**) *(at a fairground)* le manège
(**b**) *(for traffic)* le rond-point

The plural of *rond-point* is *ronds-points*.

route *noun* un itinéraire; **what's the quickest route?** quel est l'itinéraire le plus rapide?

row¹
1 *noun*
(**a**) *(of people)* le rang; *(of houses, trees)* la rangée
(**b**) *(one behind the other)* la file; **a row of cars** une file de voitures
(**c**) **in a row** *(without interruption)* de suite; **four days in a row** quatre jours de suite
2 *verb* *(in a boat)* ramer; **they rowed across the Channel** ils ont traversé la Manche à la rame

row²
1 *noun*
(**a**) *(quarrel)* la dispute; **they had a row** ils se sont disputés
(**b**) *(noise)* le vacarme; **you're making a terrible row** vous faites un vacarme épouvantable
2 *verb* *(quarrel)* se disputer; **his parents are constantly rowing** ses parents se disputent sans arrêt

rowing *noun* *(sport)* l'aviron *(masculine)*; **he loves rowing** il adore l'aviron

royal *adjective* royal/royale

The masculine plural of *royal* is *royaux*.

rub
1 *verb* frotter
2 rub out effacer; **he rubbed out his name** il a effacé son nom

rubber *noun*
(a) *(substance)* le caoutchouc
(b) *(eraser)* la gomme
(c) a rubber band un élastique

rubbish *noun*
(a) *(waste)* les ordures *(feminine plural)*; to collect the rubbish ramasser les ordures; a rubbish bin une poubelle; a rubbish dump une décharge
(b) *(bad quality products)* la camelote; that shop sells a load of rubbish ils vendent de la camelote dans ce magasin
(c) *(nonsense)* les bêtises *(feminine plural)*; you're talking rubbish tu dis des bêtises; rubbish! n'importe quoi!; this book is rubbish ce livre est nul; this TV programme is rubbish cette émission est nulle

rucksack *noun* le sac à dos

rude *adjective*
(a) *(not polite)* impoli/impolie; it's rude not to say thank you ce n'est pas poli de ne pas dire merci
(b) *(coarse)* grossier/grossière; a rude word un gros mot

rug *noun* le petit tapis

rugby *noun* le rugby; he plays rugby il joue au rugby

ruin *verb*
(a) *(spoil)* gâcher; he ruined the evening il a gâché la soirée; the new building ruins the landscape la nouvelle construction gâche le paysage
(b) *(damage)* abîmer; he ruined his new trousers il a abîmé son nouveau pantalon
(c) *(destroy)* ruiner; he ruined his health il s'est ruiné la santé
(d) *(leave without any money)* ruiner; the stock market collapse ruined him l'effondrement de la bourse l'a ruiné

ruins *plural noun* les ruines *(feminine plural)*; the house is in ruins la maison est en ruine *or* la maison est en ruines

rule
1 *noun* la règle; the rules of the game les règles du jeu; the rules and regulations le règlement; it's against the school rules c'est contraire au règlement de l'école
2 *verb* *(of a king)* régner; *(of a leader)* diriger; the king ruled over the country for thirty years le roi a régné sur le pays pendant trente ans

ruler *noun*
(a) *(for measuring)* la règle
(b) *(person)* le dirigeant/la dirigeante

rumour *noun* la rumeur

run
1 *noun*
(a) la course à pied; a 20-kilometre run une course de 20 kilomètres; to go for a run aller courir
(b) in the long run à long terme
(c) on the run en fuite; the murderer is still on the run le tueur est toujours en fuite
2 *verb*
(a) courir; he ran 20 kilometres today il a couru 20 kilomètres aujourd'hui; he ran across the road il a traversé la route en courant; he ran up the stairs il a monté les escaliers en courant
(b) *(of a tap, somebody's nose, tears)* couler; my nose is running j'ai le nez qui coule; to run a bath faire couler un bain; tears were running down her cheeks des larmes coulaient le long de ses joues
(c) *(of buses, trains)* circuler; this train doesn't run on Sundays ce train ne circule pas le dimanche
(d) *(drive)* conduire; I can run you to the station je peux te conduire à la gare; he ran her home il l'a reconduite chez elle
(e) *(of an engine, a machine)* fonctionner; the engine runs on diesel le moteur fonctionne au diesel; the machine is running la machine est en marche
(f) *(manage)* diriger; her dad runs a

chain of restaurants son père dirige une chaîne de restaurants

(**g**) *(organize)* organiser; **they run courses for adults** ils organisent des cours pour adultes

(**h**) *(in the wash)* déteindre; **your jeans have run onto my white shirt** ton jean a déteint sur ma chemise blanche

(**i**) **he's running a temperature** il a de la température

(**j**) **we're running late** nous sommes en retard

3 run away s'enfuir; **the thief ran away** le voleur s'est enfui; **he ran away from home** il a fait une fugue

4 run into

(**a**) *(meet)* **to run into somebody** tomber sur quelqu'un *or* rencontrer quelqu'un; **I ran into Colin on the street yesterday** je suis tombé sur Colin dans la rue hier

(**b**) *(encounter)* rencontrer; **we ran into problems** on a rencontré des problèmes

(**c**) *(crash into)* rentrer dans; **I ran into a lamppost** je suis rentrée dans un réverbère; **be more careful, you nearly ran into me!** fais attention, tu as failli me rentrer dedans!

5 run out we've run out of coffee nous n'avons plus de café; **I'm running out of money** je n'ai presque plus d'argent; **time is running out** il ne reste presque plus de temps; **I'm running out of patience** je perds patience

6 run over écraser; **the cat was run over by a car** le chat s'est fait écraser par une voiture

rung *noun (of a ladder)* le barreau

The plural of *barreau* is *barreaux*.

runner *noun* le coureur à pied/la coureuse à pied

runner-up *noun* le second/la seconde

running

1 *adjective* consécutif/consécutive; **he won the race for the fifth year running** il a gagné la course pour la cinquième année consécutive

2 *noun* la course à pied

runway *noun* la piste

rush

1 *noun* la hâte; **to do something in a rush** faire quelque chose à la hâte; **I'm in a rush** je suis très pressé; **the rush hour** l'heure de pointe

2 *verb*

(**a**) *(hurry)* se dépêcher; **I have to rush or I'll miss my plane** il faut que je me dépêche sinon je vais rater mon avion

(**b**) *(move forward)* se précipiter; **I rushed home after work** je me suis précipité chez moi après le travail; **he rushed to help her** il s'est précipité pour lui venir en aide

Russia *noun* la Russie; **he lives in Russia** il habite en Russie; **have you ever been to Russia?** est-ce que tu es déjà allé en Russie?; **I brought it back from Russia** je l'ai ramené de Russie

Russian

1 *adjective* russe

2 *noun*

(**a**) *(language)* le russe; **he speaks Russian** il parle russe

(**b**) *(person)* le/la Russe; **the Russians** les Russes *(masculine plural)*

In French, only the noun for the inhabitants of a country takes a capital letter, never the adjective or the noun for the language.

rust *noun* la rouille

rusty *adjective* rouillé/rouillée; **his Spanish is a bit rusty** son espagnol est un peu rouillé

sack *noun*
(a) *(bag)* le sac
(b) *(dismissal)* **my boss gave me the sack** mon patron m'a viré; **he got the sack** il s'est fait virer

sacrifice
1 *noun* le sacrifice
2 *verb* sacrifier

sad *adjective* triste

saddle *noun* la selle

sadly *adverb*
(a) *(unhappily)* tristement; **she looked at me sadly** elle m'a regardé tristement
(b) *(unfortunately)* malheureusement; **sadly, I won't be able to come** malheureusement, je ne pourrai pas venir

safe
1 *adjective*
(a) *(not in danger)* en sécurité; **the money's safe in the bank** l'argent est en sécurité à la banque; **I don't feel safe** je ne me sens pas en sécurité
(b) *(not dangerous)* sûr/sûre; **this isn't a very safe area** ce quartier n'est pas très sûr; **a safe driver** un conducteur prudent; **is this ladder safe?** est-ce que cette échelle est solide?; **have a safe journey!** bon voyage!
(c) *(unharmed)* sain et sauf/saine et sauve
2 *noun (for money)* le coffre-fort

The plural of *coffre-fort* is *coffres-forts*.

safely *adverb*
(a) *(work, play)* en toute sécurité

(b) *(drive)* prudemment

The first *e* in *prudemment* is pronounced like the *a* in *cat*.

(c) **she arrived safely** elle est bien arrivée; **the parcel arrived safely** le colis est bien arrivé

safety *noun* la sécurité; **a safety belt** une ceinture de sécurité; **a safety helmet** un casque; **a safety pin** une épingle à nourrice

Sagittarius *noun* le Sagittaire; **he's (a) Sagittarius** il est Sagittaire

sail
1 *noun (on a boat)* la voile
2 *verb*
(a) *(of a boat, a person)* naviguer; **they sailed around the Mediterranean** ils ont fait le tour de la Méditerranée en bateau
(b) *(leave)* prendre la mer
(c) *(go sailing)* faire de la voile

sailing *noun (sport)* la voile; **he goes sailing** il fait de la voile; **a sailing boat** un voilier

sailor *noun* le marin; **he's a sailor** il est marin

saint *noun* le saint/la sainte

salad *noun* la salade; **a cheese salad** une salade au fromage; **a fruit salad** une salade de fruits; **a salad bowl** un saladier

salary *noun* le salaire

sale *noun*
(a) la vente; **on sale** en vente; **for sale** à vendre; **our house is up for sale** nous avons mis notre maison en vente

(**b**) *(at reduced prices)* **the sales** les soldes *(masculine plural)*; **I went to the sales** j'ai fait les soldes; **I got it in a sale** je l'ai acheté en solde

sales assistant *noun* le vendeur/la vendeuse; **she's a sales assistant** elle est vendeuse

> Note that when describing people's jobs or situations, French does not use an article (*un* or *une*).

salesman *noun*
(**a**) *(who travels)* le représentant; **he's a salesman** il est représentant
(**b**) *(in a shop)* le vendeur

saleswoman *noun*
(**a**) *(who travels)* la représentante; **she's a saleswoman** elle est représentante
(**b**) *(in a shop)* la vendeuse

salmon *noun* le saumon

salt *noun* le sel

salty *adjective* salé/salée

same

1 *adjective* même; **we're going the same way** nous allons dans la même direction; **their son is the same age as ours** leur fils a le même âge que le nôtre; **she's wearing the same glasses as you** elle porte les mêmes lunettes que toi
2 *pronoun*
(**a**) *(same one)* **the same** le même, la même, les mêmes

> The pronoun *le même* has the same gender and the same number as the noun it stands for, hence the use of *la même* for *la robe* and *les mêmes* for *les livres* in the examples above.

(**b**) *(same thing)* **the same** la même chose *or* pareil; **I'll have the same, please** je vais prendre la même chose, s'il vous plaît; **it's always the same** c'est toujours pareil; **it's the same in Italy** c'est pareil en Italie; **it's not the same** ce n'est pas pareil
3 *adverb*
(**a**) **the same** de la même façon; **it's**

not spelt the same ça ne s'écrit pas de la même façon; **they all taste the same** ils ont tous le même goût; **all these houses look the same** ces maisons se ressemblent toutes
(**b**) **all the same** quand même; **all the same, I still like her** je l'aime bien quand même; **thanks all the same** merci quand même

sand *noun* le sable

sandal *noun* la sandale

sandcastle *noun* le château de sable

> The plural of *château de sable* is *châteaux de sable*.

sandwich *noun* le sandwich; **a ham sandwich** un sandwich au jambon

sane *adjective*
(**a**) *(person)* sain/saine d'esprit
(**b**) *(action, behaviour, idea)* sensé/sensée

Santa Claus *noun* le père Noël

sarcastic *adjective* sarcastique

sardine *noun* la sardine

satellite *noun* le satellite; **satellite TV** la télévision par satellite; **a satellite dish** une antenne parabolique

satisfactory *adjective* satisfaisant/satisfaisante

satisfied *adjective* satisfait/satisfaite; **the teacher isn't satisfied with their work** le professeur n'est pas satisfait de leur travail

satisfy *verb* satisfaire

satsuma *noun* la mandarine

Saturday *noun* le samedi; **on Saturday** samedi; **she came on Saturday** elle est venue samedi; **on Saturdays** le samedi; **he plays golf on Saturdays** il joue au golf le samedi; **every Saturday** tous les samedis; **next Saturday** samedi prochain; **last Saturday** samedi dernier

> In French, the names of days are not written with a capital.

sauce *noun* la sauce; **tomato sauce** la sauce tomate

saucepan *noun* la casserole

saucer *noun* la soucoupe

Saudi Arabia *noun* l'Arabie saoudite *(feminine)*; **have you ever been to Saudi Arabia?** est-ce que tu es déjà allé en Arabie saoudite?; **he lives in Saudi Arabia** il vit en Arabie saoudite; **he comes from Saudi Arabia** il vient d'Arabie saoudite

sauna *noun* le sauna; **to have a sauna** aller au sauna

sausage *noun*
(a) *(for cooking with)* la saucisse; **a sausage roll** un friand à la saucisse
(b) *(cold, for slicing)* le saucisson

save
1 *verb*
(a) *(rescue)* sauver; **he saved me from the fire** il m'a sauvé de l'incendie
(b) *(keep)* garder; **I'll save you a place** je te garderai une place
(c) *(money)* économiser; **how much money have you saved?** combien est-ce que tu as économisé?; **I'm saving to buy a car** je fais des économies pour acheter une voiture
(d) *(time)* gagner; **I could save a lot of time** je pourrais gagner beaucoup de temps
(e) *(a computer file)* sauvegarder
(f) *(spare)* **that will save you the bother of going** ça t'évitera d'y aller; **it'll save you getting up early** ça t'évitera de te lever tôt
2 **save up** faire des économies; **I'm saving up to buy a computer** je fais des économies pour acheter un ordinateur

savings *plural noun* les économies *(feminine plural)*; **I don't have any savings** je n'ai pas d'économies; **a savings account** un compte d'épargne; **a savings bank** une caisse d'épargne

savoury *adjective* salé/salée; **a savoury biscuit** un biscuit salé

saxophone *noun* le saxophone; **I play the saxophone** je joue du saxophone

saw
1 *noun* la scie
2 *verb* scier; **he sawed the table in half** il a scié la table en deux

say *verb*
(a) dire; **she said hello to them** elle leur a dit bonjour; **he said he was sorry** il a dit qu'il était désolé; **say what you think** dites ce que vous pensez; **"not at all," she said** "pas du tout," dit-elle; **they say he's rich** on dit qu'il est riche; **if I had, say, £1,000** si j'avais, disons, 1000 livres
(b) *(suppose)* supposer; **say your plan doesn't work?** supposons que votre plan ne marche pas?
(c) *(indicate)* indiquer; **the clock says 10.40** la pendule indique 10h40; **the sign says 50 km** le panneau indique 50 km
(d) **that is to say** c'est-à-dire

saying *noun* le dicton

scale *noun*
(a) *(of musical notes)* la gamme
(b) *(of a map)* une échelle
(c) *(of a fish)* une écaille

scales *plural noun* *(for weighing)* la balance; **bathroom scales** le pèse-personne

The plural of *pèse-personne* is *pèse-personnes*.

scandal *noun* le scandale; **she caused a scandal** elle a provoqué un scandale

Scandinavia *noun* la Scandinavie; **Norway is in Scandinavia** la Norvège est en Scandinavie; **I've never been to Scandinavia** je ne suis jamais allé en Scandinavie

Scandinavian
1 *adjective* scandinave
2 *noun (person)* le/la Scandinave; **the Scandinavians** les Scandinaves *(masculine plural)*

scar *noun* la cicatrice; **he has acne scars** il a des cicatrices d'acné

scare *verb* faire peur à; **thunder really scares me** le tonnerre me fait vraiment très peur

scared *adjective* **to be scared** avoir peur; **I'm scared of snakes** j'ai peur des serpents; **he's scared to ask her** il a peur de lui demander

scary *adjective* **a scary story** une histoire qui fait peur; **this film is very scary** ce film fait très peur

scarf *noun*
(**a**) *(long)* une écharpe
(**b**) *(square)* le foulard

scatter *verb*
(**a**) *(toys, papers)* éparpiller; **toys were scattered all over the room** il y avait des jouets éparpillés partout dans la pièce
(**b**) *(crumbs, seeds)* **she scattered crumbs for the birds** elle a jeté des miettes de pain aux oiseaux
(**c**) *(of a crowd)* se disperser; **the crowd scattered** la foule s'est dispersée

scene *noun*
(**a**) *(part of a play, a film, a story)* la scène; **the murder scene** la scène du meurtre; **the scene is set in Paris** la scène se passe à Paris
(**b**) *(where something takes place)* le lieu; **the police soon arrived on the scene** la police est rapidement arrivée sur les lieux
(**c**) *(fuss)* le scandale; **she made a scene** elle a fait un scandale

scenery *noun*
(**a**) *(landscape)* le paysage
(**b**) *(in a play)* le décor

scent *noun* *(smell)* une odeur; *(perfume)* le parfum

schedule *noun*
(**a**) *(for work)* le planning; **our work is ahead of schedule** nous sommes en avance dans notre travail; **we're behind schedule** nous sommes en retard dans notre travail
(**b**) *(for activities)* le programme; **we have a busy schedule** nous avons un programme chargé

scholarship *noun* la bourse; **a scholarship student** un boursier/une boursière

school *noun*
(**a**) une école; **he's going to school** il va à l'école; **he's at school** il est à l'école
(**b**) **a school book** un livre de classe; **a school bus** un car de ramassage scolaire; **school dinners** les repas à la cantine; **a school friend** un/une camarade de classe; **a school report** un bulletin scolaire; **a school trip** un voyage scolaire; **a school uniform** un uniforme scolaire; **a school year** une année scolaire

École is a very general term in French and a more precise term is normally used. Depending on the context, the word *school* can be translated by *l'école primaire* (from age 6 to 11), *le collège* (from age 11 to 14) or *le lycée* (from age 15 to 18). For example, if you are talking about somebody who is 13 years old, you will often translate *he's going to school* by *il va au collège*.

schoolbag *noun* le cartable

schoolboy *noun* un élève

schoolgirl *noun* une élève

schoolteacher *noun*
(**a**) *(at primary school)* un instituteur/une institutrice; **she's a schoolteacher** elle est institutrice
(**b**) *(at secondary school)* le professeur, le/la prof

Note that the word *professeur* is always masculine (*le professeur*) but it can also refer to a woman (*elle est professeur*). In informal language, *professeur* is often shortened to *prof*, which can be either masculine or feminine (*le prof* or *la prof*).

schoolwork *noun* le travail scolaire

science *noun*
(**a**) la science; **she studies science** elle fait des études scientifiques; **I've always been interested in science** j'ai toujours été intéressé par les sciences
(**b**) **science fiction** la science-fiction

scientific *adjective* scientifique

scientist *noun* le/la scientifique

scissors *plural noun* les ciseaux *(masculine plural)*; **a pair of scissors** une paire de ciseaux

scooter *noun*
(**a**) *(child's)* la trottinette
(**b**) *(small motorbike)* le scooter

score
1 *noun*
(**a**) *(in sport, a quiz)* le score
(**b**) *(in an exam, a test)* la note; **I got a high score** j'ai eu une bonne note
(**c**) *(in music)* la partition
2 *verb* **Beckham scored a goal** Beckham a marqué un but; **I scored a point** j'ai marqué un point

Scorpio *noun* le Scorpion; **he's (a) Scorpio** il est Scorpion

Scot *noun* un Écossais/une Écossaise

Scotland *noun* l'Écosse *(feminine)*; **I live in Scotland** j'habite en Écosse; **I'm going to Scotland** je vais en Écosse; **he comes from Scotland** il est écossais

Scottish
1 *adjective* écossais/écossaise
2 *noun (people)* **the Scottish** les Écossais

> In French, only the noun for the inhabitants of a country takes a capital letter, never the adjective.

scout *noun* le scout/la scoute

scrape
1 *verb*
(**a**) *(graze)* écorcher; **I scraped my knee** je me suis écorché le genou
(**b**) *(damage)* rayer; **he's scraped the**

car il a rayé la voiture
(**c**) *(vegetables, dishes, boots)* gratter
2 scrape through **I scraped through the exam** j'ai réussi l'examen de justesse

scratch
1 *noun*
(**a**) *(injury)* une écorchure; **it's just a scratch** ce n'est qu'une écorchure
(**b**) *(mark on furniture, a record)* la rayure
(**c**) **to be up to scratch** être à la hauteur; **his work is not always up to scratch** son travail n'est pas toujours à la hauteur
(**d**) **to start something from scratch** commencer quelque chose en partant de zéro
2 *verb*
(**a**) *(rub)* gratter; **can you scratch my back?** est-ce que tu peux me gratter le dos?; **she scratched her head** elle s'est gratté la tête; **stop scratching** arrête de te gratter
(**b**) *(injure)* griffer; **the cat scratched my hand** le chat m'a griffé la main; **he's badly scratched because he fell in the brambles** il est tout écorché parce qu'il est tombé dans les ronces
(**c**) *(damage)* rayer; **he's scratched the car** il a rayé la voiture

scratchcard *noun* la carte à gratter

scream
1 *verb* hurler; **the teacher screamed at me** le professeur m'a hurlé dessus; **she screamed with pain** elle a hurlé de douleur; **she screamed with laughter** elle riait aux éclats
2 *noun* le hurlement; **she gave a loud scream** elle a poussé un hurlement; **screams of laughter** des éclats de rire

screen *noun*
(**a**) *(of a TV, a computer, a cinema)* un écran
(**b**) *(for privacy)* le paravent; **she got changed behind the screen** elle s'est changée derrière le paravent

screenplay *noun* le scénario

screw
1 *noun* *(for fixing something)* la vis; **a screw top** un couvercle qui se visse
2 *verb* *(a bolt, a lid on a bottle)* visser; **screw the lid on** visse le bouchon

screwdriver *noun* le tournevis

scribble *verb* griffonner; **I scribbled them a note** je leur ai griffonné un mot

scrub *verb*
(**a**) *(a floor)* nettoyer à la brosse
(**b**) *(a saucepan, a sink)* récurer
(**c**) *(one's face, clothes)* frotter

scuba diving *noun* la plongée sous-marine; **I go scuba diving** je fais de la plongée sous-marine

sculpture *noun* la sculpture

sea *noun* la mer; **by the sea** au bord de la mer; **they spent six months at sea** ils ont passé six mois en mer; **the sea air** l'air marin; **a sea lion** une otarie; **a sea urchin** un oursin

seafood *noun* les fruits de mer *(masculine plural)*

seafront *noun* le bord de mer; **a seafront hotel** un hôtel au bord de la mer

seagull *noun* la mouette

seal
1 *noun*
(**a**) *(animal)* le phoque
(**b**) *(on a letter)* le cachet
2 *verb* *(an envelope, a jar)* fermer

search *verb*
(**a**) **to search for something** chercher quelque chose; **I'm searching for my keys** je cherche mes clés
(**b**) *(a person, a room, a bag)* fouiller; **the police searched the flat for drugs** la police a fouillé l'appartement à la recherche de drogue; **the spectators were searched before they were let in** les spectateurs ont été fouillés à l'entrée

seashell *noun* le coquillage; **we collected seashells on the beach** nous avons ramassé des coquillages sur la plage

seashore *noun* le rivage

seasick *adjective* **to be seasick** avoir le mal de mer

seaside *noun* le bord de la mer; **we live at the seaside, we live by the seaside** nous habitons au bord de la mer; **they went to the seaside** ils sont allés à la mer; **a seaside resort** une station balnéaire

season *noun*
(**a**) la saison; **the tourist season** la saison touristique
(**b**) **a season ticket** un abonnement; **a season ticket holder** un abonné/une abonnée

seat *noun*
(**a**) *(chair, stool)* le siège; **take a seat** asseyez-vous
(**b**) *(on a bus, in a theatre)* la place; **keep me a seat** garde-moi une place
(**c**) *(bench-like)* la banquette; **put it on the back seat of the car** mets-le sur la banquette arrière

seatbelt *noun* la ceinture de sécurité

seaweed *noun* les algues *(feminine plural)*

second
1 *noun* la seconde; **15 minutes and 28 seconds** 15 minutes et 28 secondes; **the ambulance arrived within seconds** l'ambulance est arrivée en quelques secondes
2 *adjective* deuxième; **on the second floor** au deuxième étage; **it's the second time he's phoned** c'est la deuxième fois qu'il appelle
3 *adverb*
(**a**) *(after the first)* deuxième; **I arrived second** je suis arrivé deuxième; **it's the second largest city in France** c'est la deuxième ville de France
(**b**) *(secondly)* deuxièmement; **first, it's very difficult, and second, it's too expensive** premièrement, c'est très difficile, et deuxièmement, c'est trop cher
4 *pronoun* **the second** le/la deuxième;

she was the second to arrive elle est arrivée la deuxième; **he starts work on the second** il commence à travailler le deux

secondary *adjective* secondaire; **a secondary school** un collège; **a secondary school teacher** un professeur du secondaire

> Depending on the context, the term *secondary school* can be translated by *collège* (from age 11 to 14) or *lycée* (from age 15 to 18). For example, if you are talking about somebody who is 16 years old, you will often translate *he's at secondary school* by *il est au lycée.*

second-hand *adjective* d'occasion; **a second-hand car** une voiture d'occasion

secret
1 *noun* le secret; **I'll tell you a secret** je vais te dire un secret; **he did it in secret** il l'a fait en secret
2 *adjective* secret/secrète; **a secret agent** un agent secret; **keep it secret!** ne le dis à personne!

secretary *noun*
(**a**) *(in a company)* le/la secrétaire; **she's a secretary** elle est secrétaire
(**b**) *(in a government)* le/la ministre; **the Foreign Secretary** le ministre des Affaires étrangères

section *noun*
(**a**) *(of a book, an exam)* la partie
(**b**) *(of a machine, furniture)* un élément
(**c**) *(of a newspaper)* la rubrique; **the sports section** la rubrique sportive
(**d**) *(of a road)* le tronçon
(**e**) *(cross-section)* la coupe

see
1 *verb*
(**a**) voir; **I can see the sea** je vois la mer; **I can't see without my glasses** je ne vois rien sans mes lunettes; **let me see your hands** fais-moi voir tes mains; **go and see her** va la voir; **I**

saw what happened j'ai vu ce qui s'est passé; **I can see why you were worried** je comprends pourquoi vous étiez inquiet; **I see what you mean** je vois ce que tu veux dire
(**b**) *(accompany)* accompagner; **I'll see you to the bus stop** je t'accompagne jusqu'à l'arrêt du bus; **I'll see you home** je te raccompagne chez toi
(**c**) *(make sure)* s'assurer; **see that all the lights are off before you leave** assurez-vous que toutes les lumières sont éteintes avant de partir
(**d**) **see you!** salut!; **see you later!** *(soon)* à tout à l'heure!; *(later)* à plus tard!; **see you soon!** à bientôt!; **see you tomorrow!** à demain!
2 **see about**
(**a**) *(deal with)* s'occuper de; **I'll see about making the reservations** je m'occuperai des réservations
(**b**) *(think about)* **we'll have to see about that** on verra
3 **see off** **to see somebody off** dire au revoir à quelqu'un; **she came to see me off at the station** elle est venue à la gare me dire au revoir
4 **see to**
(**a**) **to see to something** s'occuper de quelque chose; **I'll see to the dinner** je m'occuperai du dîner
(**b**) **I need to get my car seen to** il faut que je fasse réparer ma voiture; **you need to get this wound seen to** il faut que tu ailles faire soigner cette plaie

seed *noun*
(**a**) *(of a plant)* la graine
(**b**) *(of a fruit)* le pépin

seek *verb* chercher; **to seek shelter** chercher refuge; **they sought his advice** ils lui ont demandé conseil

seem *verb*
(**a**) avoir l'air; **she seems very nice** elle a l'air très gentille; **he didn't seem to know** il n'avait pas l'air de savoir
(**b**) *(impersonal)* sembler; **it seems like an excellent idea** cela me semble être une excellente idée; **there seems**

to be some mistake il semble qu'il y ait une erreur; **it would seem that he already knew** il semblerait qu'il était déjà au courant

seesaw *noun* le tapecul

see-through *adjective* transparent/ transparente

seize *verb*
(a) *(an object, a person)* saisir
(b) *(a city, a territory)* s'emparer de

seldom *adverb* rarement; **I seldom see her** je la vois rarement

select *verb* choisir

self-confidence *noun* la confiance en soi; **she lacks self-confidence** elle manque de confiance en elle; **he's full of self-confidence** il a une grande confiance en lui

self-confident *adjective* sûr/sûre de soi; **she's not very self-confident** elle n'est pas très sûre d'elle

self-conscious *adjective* gêné/gênée

self-control *noun*
(a) *(in general)* la maîtrise de soi; **he has no self-control** il ne sait pas se maîtriser
(b) *(when angry)* le sang-froid; **he lost his self-control** il a perdu son sang-froid

self-defence *noun*
(a) *(physical)* l'autodéfense *(feminine)*; **a self-defence class** un cours d'auto-défense
(b) *(motive)* la légitime défense; **she killed him in self-defence** elle l'a tué en légitime défense

selfish *adjective* égoïste

self-service *noun*
(a) *(shop)* le libre-service
(b) *(restaurant)* le self-service

> The plural of *libre-service* is *libres-services* and the plural of *self-service* is *self-services*.

sell
1 *verb* vendre; **he sells cars** il vend des voitures; **he sold me his video games** il m'a vendu ses jeux vidéo; **the book is selling well** le livre se vend bien
2 **sell out** all the tickets are sold out tous les billets ont été vendus; **it's sold out** *(for a product in a shop)* nous n'en avons plus; *(for a show)* c'est complet

sell-by date *noun* la date limite de vente

sellotape® *noun* le scotch®

semester *noun* le semestre

semicolon *noun* le point-virgule

> The plural of *point-virgule* is *points-virgules.*

semi-detached house *noun* la maison jumelée

semifinal *noun* la demi-finale

> The plural of *demi-finale* is *demi-finales.*

semi-skimmed milk *noun* le lait demi-écrémé

send
1 *verb* envoyer; **he sent a postcard to his grandparents** il a envoyé une carte postale à ses grands-parents; **send him an e-mail** envoie-lui un e-mail; **the teacher sent him home** le professeur l'a renvoyé chez lui
2 **send back** renvoyer
3 **send for** *(a doctor, a taxi)* appeler
4 **send off**
(a) *(a letter, a person)* envoyer; **they sent us off to bed** ils nous ont envoyés nous coucher; **I've sent off for a catalogue** j'ai demandé à me faire envoyer un catalogue
(b) *(a player)* expulser; **he was sent off the field** il a été expulsé du terrain
5 **send out** envoyer; **we sent him out for coffee** nous l'avons envoyé chercher du café

senior
1 *adjective*
(a) *(older)* plus âgé/âgée; **a senior citizen** une personne âgée

(**b**) *(higher ranked)* supérieur/supérieure; **a senior officer** un officier supérieur
(**c**) **a senior school** un lycée
2 *noun*
(**a**) *(an older person)* un aîné/une aînée; **he is six months my senior** il est de six mois mon aîné
(**b**) *(a person with a higher rank)* un supérieur/une supérieure
(**c**) **the seniors** *(at school)* les élèves des grandes classes

sense *noun*
(**a**) *(faculty)* le sens; **the sense of hearing** l'ouïe *(feminine)*; **the sense of sight** la vue; **the sense of smell** l'odorat *(masculine)*; **the sense of taste** le goût; **the sense of touch** le toucher; **he's got a good sense of humour** il a le sens de l'humour
(**b**) *(meaning)* le sens; **it doesn't make sense** ça n'a aucun sens; **she tried to make sense of the text** elle a essayé de comprendre le texte
(**c**) *(feeling)* le sentiment; **a sense of injustice** un sentiment d'injustice
(**d**) *(notion)* la notion; **I lost all sense of time** j'ai perdu toute notion de l'heure
(**e**) *(wisdom)* **common sense** le bon sens; **she had the good sense to check the brakes** elle a eu la bonne idée de vérifier les freins; **there's no sense in staying** ça ne sert à rien de rester

sensible *adjective*
(**a**) *(person)* raisonnable
(**b**) *(choice)* judicieux/judicieuse
(**c**) *(clothes, shoes)* pratique

Note that the French word *sensible* is never a translation for the English word *sensible*. It means *sensitive*.

sensitive *adjective*
(**a**) *(skin, person)* sensible; **sensitive to the cold** frileux/frileuse; **she's very sensitive about her accent** elle n'aime pas qu'on lui parle de son accent
(**b**) *(issue, situation)* délicat/délicate

sentence *noun*
(**a**) *(group of words)* la phrase
(**b**) *(punishment)* la condamnation; **the death sentence** la condamnation à mort; **a prison sentence** une peine de prison

sentimental *adjective* sentimental/sentimentale

The masculine plural of *sentimental* is *sentimentaux*.

separate
1 *adjective*
(**a**) *(not joined)* à part; **a separate room** une pièce à part; **my brother and I have separate bedrooms** mon frère et moi avons chacun notre chambre; **we have to keep the cat and the dog separate** il faut séparer le chat et le chien
(**b**) *(different)* différent/différente; **this word has two separate meanings** ce mot a deux sens différents; **that's quite a separate matter** c'est une autre histoire
2 *verb*
(**a**) séparer; **separate the whites from the yolks** séparez les blancs des jaunes
(**b**) *(of a couple)* se séparer; **my parents separated two years ago** mes parents se sont séparés il y a deux ans

separately *adverb* séparément

September *noun* septembre *(masculine)*; **the first of September** le premier septembre; **the second of September** le deux septembre; **the third of September** le trois septembre; **in September** en septembre

Names of months are not capitalized in French.

Serb
1 *adjective* serbe
2 *noun* *(person)* le/la Serbe; **the Serbs** les Serbes *(masculine plural)*

Serbia *noun* la Serbie; **she lives in Serbia** elle habite en Serbie; **I'm going**

to **Serbia** je vais en Serbie; **he comes from Serbia** il vient de Serbie

Serbian
1 *adjective* serbe
2 *noun*
(**a**) *(language)* le serbe; **he speaks Serbian** il parle serbe
(**b**) *(person)* le/la Serbe; **the Serbians** les Serbes *(masculine plural)*

> In French, only the noun for the inhabitants of a country takes a capital letter, never the adjective or the noun for the language.

serial
1 *noun* le feuilleton; **a TV serial** un feuilleton télévisé
2 *adjective* en série; **a serial killer** un tueur en série

series *noun* la série; **a series of disasters** une série de catastrophes; **a TV series** une série télévisée

serious *adjective*
(**a**) *(student, book)* sérieux/sérieuse
(**b**) *(illness, mistake, accident)* grave

seriously *adverb*
(**a**) *(in earnest)* sérieusement; **I'm seriously thinking of resigning** je pense sérieusement à démissionner; **I didn't take it seriously** je ne l'ai pas pris au sérieux; **she takes herself too seriously** elle se prend trop au sérieux
(**b**) **seriously ill** gravement malade; **seriously injured** gravement blessé/blessée

servant *noun* le/la domestique

serve *verb*
(**a**) *(in a restaurant, in tennis, in the army)* servir; **dinner is served** le dîner est servi; **this dish is often served with rice** on sert souvent ce plat avec du riz
(**b**) **it serves you right!** c'est bien fait pour toi!

service *noun*
(**a**) *(in a restaurant, in tennis, in the army)* le service; **the service was very slow** ils ont mis du temps à nous servir; **service included** service compris; **military service** le service militaire
(**b**) *(in a church)* un office
(**c**) *(on the road)* **a service station** une station-service; **let's stop at the next services** arrêtons-nous à la prochaine aire de service

> The plural of *station-service* is *stations-service*.

serviette *noun* la serviette de table

session *noun* la séance; **we've got a training session tonight** on a une séance d'entraînement ce soir

set
1 *noun*
(**a**) *(of keys)* le jeu

> The plural of *jeu* is *jeux*.

(**b**) *(of stamps)* la série
(**c**) *(of books)* la collection
(**d**) *(game)* **a chess set** un jeu d'échecs
(**e**) *(in theatre)* le décor; *(in cinema, TV)* le plateau; **a set designer** un décorateur/une décoratrice
(**f**) *(in cinema)* le plateau; **the actors are waiting on the set** les acteurs attendent sur le plateau

> The plural of *plateau* is *plateaux*.

(**g**) *(in tennis)* le set; **a set point** une balle de set
2 *adjective*
(**a**) *(fixed)* fixe; **a set price** un prix fixe; **a set menu** un menu; **a set phrase** une expression figée
(**b**) *(resolute)* déterminé/déterminée; **I'm set on finishing it today** je suis déterminé à le finir ce soir
(**c**) *(ready)* prêt/prête; **we are all set to go** nous sommes prêts à partir
(**d**) *(school book, subject)* au programme
3 *verb*
(**a**) *(put)* mettre; **to set something down** poser quelque chose; **he set his cases down on the platform** il a posé ses valises sur le quai
(**b**) *(adjust)* **I've set the alarm for six**

o'clock j'ai mis le réveil à six heures; **could you set the video?** est-ce que tu peux programmer le magnétoscope?

(**c**) *(decide on)* fixer; **we need to set a date** nous devons fixer une date; **I've set myself a target** je me suis fixé un objectif

(**d**) *(at school)* donner; **she set us some homework** elle nous a donné des devoirs; **who sets the exam questions?** qui choisit les questions de l'examen?

(**e**) **to set the table** mettre le couvert; **to set something on fire** mettre le feu à quelque chose; **to set a record** établir un record; **to set a good example** montrer le bon exemple

(**f**) **to set somebody free** libérer quelqu'un

(**g**) **the film is set in Montreal** le film se passe à Montréal; **the story is set in the 18th century** l'histoire se passe au XVIIIᵉ siècle

(**h**) **he set to work** il s'est mis au travail

(**i**) **the sun is setting** le soleil se couche

4 set off

(**a**) *(leave)* partir; **we're setting off tomorrow** nous partons demain; **I set off to explore the town** je suis parti explorer la ville

(**b**) *(an alarm)* déclencher

(**c**) *(a bomb)* faire exploser

5 set out

(**a**) *(leave)* partir; **they set out for school** ils sont partis à l'école

(**b**) *(arrange)* disposer; **I set out the chess pieces** j'ai disposé les pièces sur l'échiquier

(**c**) *(undertake)* entreprendre; **he never finishes what he sets out to do** il ne termine jamais ce qu'il entreprend

6 set up

(**a**) *(a tent, a company)* monter; **to set up home** s'installer

(**b**) *(a piece of equipment)* installer

(**c**) *(a meeting)* organiser

(**d**) *(a person)* monter un coup contre; **I've been set up** j'ai été victime d'un coup monté

settee *noun* le canapé

settle

1 *verb*

(**a**) *(in a country)* s'installer

(**b**) *(a problem)* régler

(**c**) **that's settled, that settles it** c'est décidé

2 settle down

(**a**) *(in a chair)* s'installer

(**b**) *(calm down)* se calmer

(**c**) *(in a new home)* s'installer

(**d**) *(in a new school)* s'habituer

3 settle in

(**a**) *(in a new home)* s'installer

(**b**) *(in a new school)* s'habituer

seven *number* sept

seventeen *number* dix-sept

seventeenth *number* dix-septième; **the seventeenth day** le dix-septième jour; **the seventeenth car** la dix-septième voiture; **the seventeenth of March** le dix-sept mars

seventh *number* septième; **two-sevenths** *(fraction)* deux septièmes; **the seventh film** le septième film; **the seventh car** la septième voiture; **the seventh of October** le sept octobre

seventy *number* soixante-dix; **seventy-one** soixante et onze; **seventy-two** soixante-douze; **seventy-first** soixante et onzième; **seventy-second** soixante-douzième; **the seventies** les années soixante-dix

several

1 *adjective* plusieurs

2 *pronoun* plusieurs; **several of them** plusieurs d'entre eux

sew *verb* coudre; **she sewed a button on my shirt** elle a cousu un bouton à ma chemise

sewer *noun* *(drain)* un égout

sewing *noun*

(**a**) la couture; **she likes sewing** elle aime la couture

(**b**) **a sewing machine** une machine à coudre

sex *noun*
(**a**) *(gender)* le sexe; **sex discrimination** la discrimination sexuelle
(**b**) *(sexual intercourse)* les rapports sexuels *(masculine plural)*; **to have sex with somebody** avoir des rapports sexuels avec quelqu'un *or* faire l'amour avec quelqu'un; **sex education** l'éducation sexuelle *(feminine)*

shabby *adjective* miteux/miteuse

shade *noun*
(**a**) *(cool place)* l'ombre *(feminine)*; **in the shade** à l'ombre
(**b**) *(of colour)* la nuance; **it's a lovely shade of blue** c'est un joli bleu
(**c**) *(for a lamp)* un abat-jour

The word *abat-jour* does not change in the plural.

shadow *noun* une ombre

shady *adjective*
(**a**) *(place)* ombragé/ombragée
(**b**) *(tree)* qui donne de l'ombre
(**c**) *(person)* louche

shake *verb*
(**a**) *(a rug, a person, a box)* secouer
(**b**) *(a bottle)* agiter
(**c**) **to shake hands with somebody** serrer la main à quelqu'un; **we shook hands** nous nous sommes serré la main
(**d**) **to shake one's head** faire non de la tête
(**e**) *(tremble)* trembler; **to shake with fear** trembler de peur; **the explosion shook the whole building** l'explosion a fait trembler tout l'immeuble

shall *auxiliary verb*
(**a**) *(future tense)* **I shall come tomorrow** je viendrai demain; **we shall see** nous verrons
(**b**) *(in questions, suggestions)* **shall I open the window?** voulez-vous que j'ouvre la fenêtre?; **shall I leave?** veux-tu que je parte?; **shall we go?** on y va?; **let's go for a swim, shall we?** et si on allait nager?

shallow *adjective*
(**a**) *(water, hole)* peu profond/pro-

fonde; **the river is shallow** la rivière n'est pas profonde; **the shallow end** *(of a swimming pool)* le petit bain
(**b**) *(person, conversation)* superficiel/superficielle

shame *noun*
(**a**) *(feeling)* la honte
(**b**) *(pity)* **what a shame!** quel dommage!; **it's a shame!** c'est dommage!; **it's a shame you didn't come** c'est dommage que tu ne sois pas venu

shampoo *noun* le shampooing

shandy *noun* le panaché

shape *noun*
(**a**) la forme; **in the shape of a triangle** en forme de triangle; **to take shape** prendre forme
(**b**) **he's in good shape** il est en forme; **he's in bad shape** il n'est pas en forme; **I'm rather out of shape** je ne suis pas très en forme

shaped *adjective* **shaped like a triangle** en forme de triangle

share
1 *noun* *(portion)* la part
2 *verb* partager
3 share out they shared out the cakes *(between themselves)* ils se sont partagé les gâteaux; *(among others)* ils ont distribué les gâteaux

shark *noun* le requin

sharp
1 *adjective*
(**a**) *(knife, blade)* tranchant/tranchante; **these scissors are sharp** ces ciseaux coupent bien
(**b**) *(pencil, needle)* pointu/pointue
(**c**) *(bend, movement)* brusque
(**d**) *(mind, pain)* vif/vive
(**e**) *(person)* intelligent/intelligente
(**f**) *(criticism, tone)* acerbe
2 *adverb* **at six o'clock sharp** à six heures pile

sharpen *verb*
(**a**) *(a pencil)* tailler
(**b**) *(a knife)* aiguiser

shave *verb* se raser; **he needs to shave**

il a besoin de se raser; **to shave one's legs** se raser les jambes

shaving *noun* le rasage; **shaving cream** la crème à raser

she *pronoun* elle; **she's very intelligent** elle est très intelligente; **she's an actress** elle est actrice; **she's a very nice girl** c'est une fille très gentille; **she and I** elle et moi

shed *noun*
(**a**) *(in a garden)* la remise; **a bicycle shed** une remise à vélos
(**b**) *(for goods, for an aircraft)* le hangar

sheep *noun* le mouton

sheet *noun*
(**a**) *(on a bed)* le drap
(**b**) **a sheet of paper** une feuille de papier; **a sheet of metal** une plaque; **a sheet of ice** une plaque de verglas

shelf *noun*
(**a**) une étagère; **a set of shelves** une étagère
(**b**) *(in a shop, a library)* le rayon

shell *noun*
(**a**) *(on a beach)* le coquillage
(**b**) *(of an egg, a nut, a snail)* la coquille
(**c**) *(of a lobster, a tortoise)* la carapace

shellfish *noun*
(**a**) *(crustacean)* le crustacé
(**b**) *(mollusc)* le coquillage
(**c**) *(as food)* les fruits de mer *(masculine plural)*

shelter
1 *noun*
(**a**) un abri; **to take shelter** se mettre à l'abri
(**b**) *(for homeless people)* un refuge; **an animal shelter** un refuge pour animaux
2 *verb*
(**a**) *(take shelter)* s'abriter; **he sheltered from the rain in a shop doorway** il s'est abrité de la pluie dans l'entrée d'un magasin
(**b**) *(give shelter)* héberger

shepherd *noun*
(**a**) le berger

(**b**) **shepherd's pie** le hachis Parmentier

shield
1 *noun (of a soldier)* le bouclier
2 *verb* protéger; **to shield one's eyes from the sun** se protéger les yeux du soleil

shift
1 *noun*
(**a**) *(change)* le changement
(**b**) *(computer key)* la touche majuscule
(**c**) **she works shifts** elle fait les trois-huit
2 *verb (an object)* bouger

shin *noun* le tibia

shine *verb*
(**a**) briller; **the sun's shining** le soleil brille *or* il y a du soleil
(**b**) **to shine a light on something** éclairer quelque chose

shiny *adjective* brillant/brillante

ship *noun* le bateau; *(larger)* le navire; **a sailing ship** un voilier; **a passenger ship** un paquebot

The plural of *bateau* is *bateaux*.

shipwreck *noun* le naufrage

shirt *noun*
(**a**) la chemise
(**b**) *(worn by sportsmen)* le maillot

shiver
1 *verb* trembler; **to shiver with fear** trembler de peur
2 *noun* le frisson; **it gives me the shivers** ça me donne des frissons

shock
1 *noun*
(**a**) *(emotional blow)* le choc; **it came as a shock to me** ça m'a fait un choc; **to be in shock** être en état de choc
(**b**) *(electric)* la décharge; **to get a shock, to get an electric shock** recevoir une décharge
2 *verb*
(**a**) *(upset)* bouleverser
(**b**) *(surprise)* stupéfier
(**c**) *(scandalize)* choquer

shocked *adjective*
(a) *(upset)* bouleversé/bouleversée
(b) *(surprised)* stupéfait/stupéfaite
(c) *(scandalized)* choqué/choquée

shocking *adjective*
(a) *(scandalous)* scandaleux/scandaleuse
(b) *(very bad)* affreux/affreuse

shoe *noun*
(a) la chaussure; **a pair of shoes** une paire de chaussures; **my shoe size** ma pointure; **what's your shoe size?** tu chausses du combien?; **shoe polish** le cirage; **a shoe repairer** un cordonnier; **a shoe shop** un magasin de chaussures
(b) **a horse shoe** un fer à cheval

shoelace *noun* le lacet; **your shoelace is undone** ton lacet est défait

shoot *verb*
(a) *(fire)* tirer; **I shot at the target** j'ai tiré sur la cible
(b) *(kill)* tuer par balle, abattre; **he was shot dead** il a été abattu
(c) *(injure)* blesser par balle; **she was shot in the stomach** elle a reçu une balle dans le ventre
(d) *(hunt)* chasser
(e) *(in football)* tirer
(f) **to shoot in** entrer en trombe; **to shoot past** passer en trombe
(g) **to shoot a film** tourner un film

shooting *noun*
(a) *(firing)* la fusillade, les coups de feu *(masculine plural)*
(b) *(in sport, at targets)* le tir; **a shooting match** un concours de tir; **a shooting range** un champ de tir
(c) *(hunting)* la chasse
(d) *(of a film)* le tournage
(e) **a shooting star** une étoile filante

shop
1 *noun* le magasin; **a toy shop** un magasin de jouets; **a sports shop** un magasin de sport; **a shop assistant** un vendeur/une vendeuse; **a shop window** une vitrine

2 *verb*
(a) *(for food)* faire ses courses; **I always shop at the local supermarket** je fais toujours mes courses au supermarché du coin
(b) *(for everything else)* faire des courses; **do you want to go shopping on Saturday?** tu veux aller faire des courses samedi?; **I went shopping for a new dress** je suis allée faire les magasins pour m'acheter une nouvelle robe

shopkeeper *noun* le commerçant/la commerçante; **she's a shopkeeper** elle est commerçante

shopper *noun* **the streets were crowded with shoppers** les rues étaient bondées de gens qui faisaient leurs courses

shopping *noun*
(a) les courses *(feminine plural)*; **I do all the shopping** c'est moi qui fais toutes les courses; **she went to do some shopping** elle est partie faire les magasins; **a shopping bag** un sac à provisions; **a shopping basket** un panier; **a shopping centre** un centre commercial; **a shopping list** une liste de courses; **a shopping trolley** un caddie®
(b) *(goods bought)* les achats *(masculine plural)*; **he helped me carry my shopping** il m'a aidé à porter mes achats

shore *noun*
(a) *(of the sea)* le rivage
(b) *(of a lake, a river)* la rive
(c) *(dry land)* la terre; **to be on shore** être à terre; **to go on shore** débarquer

short
1 *adjective*
(a) *(in length)* court/courte; **she has short hair** elle a les cheveux courts; **you have a short memory** tu as la mémoire courte; **the days are getting shorter** les jours raccourcissent; **a short story** une nouvelle; **in short** en bref
(b) *(person, walk)* petit/petite; **she's really short** elle est vraiment petite;

it's only a short distance from here ce n'est pas très loin d'ici

(c) **Bill is short for William** Bill est le diminutif de William; **EU is short for European Union** UE est l'abréviation de Union européenne

(d) **to be short of something** manquer de quelque chose; **we're short of milk** on n'a plus beaucoup de lait; **I'm 50p short** il me manque 50 pence

2 *adverb*

(a) **to stop short** s'arrêter net

(b) **we're running short of time** nous n'avons plus beaucoup de temps

shorten *verb*

(a) *(a dress, a speech, a trip)* raccourcir

(b) *(a word, a name)* abréger

shortly *adverb*

(a) *(soon)* bientôt; **I'll join you shortly** je vous rejoins bientôt

(b) *(not long)* peu de temps; **shortly before he arrived** peu de temps avant son arrivée; **shortly afterwards** peu de temps après

shorts *plural noun* le short; **a pair of football shorts** un short de foot

short-sighted *adjective* myope

shot *noun*

(a) *(from a gun)* le coup de feu; **he fired four shots** il a tiré quatre coups de feu; **he fired a shot at the policeman** il a tiré sur le policier

(b) *(at goal)* le tir; *(in tennis)* le coup; **good shot!** bien joué!; **the shot put** le lancer du poids

(c) *(photo)* la photo

(d) *(injection)* la piqûre

should *auxiliary verb*

(a) *(expressing duty, probability, regret)* devoir; **I should work** je devrais travailler; **I should be working** je devrais être en train de travailler; **I should have worked** j'aurais dû travailler; **they should arrive soon** ils devraient bientôt arriver; **I should never have gone** je n'aurais jamais dû y aller; **you shouldn't laugh at him** vous ne devriez pas vous moquer de lui

(b) *(conditional tense)* **I shouldn't be surprised if they got married** cela ne m'étonnerait pas qu'ils se marient; **I should think it costs about £50** je dirais que ça coûte dans les 50 livres

shoulder *noun* une épaule; **he's got broad shoulders** il est large d'épaules; **a shoulder bag** un sac à bandoulière; **a shoulder strap** *(on a dress, a top)* une bretelle; *(on a bag)* une bandoulière

shout

1 *noun* le cri; **a shout of joy** un cri de joie; **give me a shout if you need help** appelle-moi si tu as besoin d'aide

2 *verb* crier; **the teacher shouted at me for being late** le professeur m'a crié dessus parce que j'étais en retard; **she shouted for help** elle a appelé au secours

shovel *noun* la pelle

show

1 *noun*

(a) *(concert, play)* le spectacle

(b) *(TV programme)* une émission

(c) *(exhibition)* une exposition; **to be on show** être exposé/exposée

(d) *(trade fair)* le salon; **the motor show** le salon de l'automobile

2 *verb*

(a) montrer; **show me your presents** montre-moi tes cadeaux; **he showed the letter to his mum** il a montré la lettre à sa mère; **I'll show you how it works** je vais vous montrer comment ça marche; **it just goes to show that nothing's impossible** ça montre bien que rien n'est impossible

(b) *(escort)* **I'll show you the way** je vais vous montrer le chemin; **let me show you to your room** je vais vous montrer votre chambre

(c) *(be visible)* se voir; **she doesn't like him and it shows** elle ne l'aime pas, et ça se voit

(d) *(a film, a TV programme)* passer; **the programme will be shown tomorrow** cette émission passera demain

3 show in faire entrer; **his secretary showed me in** sa secrétaire m'a fait entrer
4 show off
(a) frimer; **it's just to show off in front of his friends** c'est simplement pour frimer devant ses copains; **stop showing off!** arrête de faire ton intéressant!
(b) *(one's knowledge)* étaler
5 show round faire visiter; **I'll show you round the house** je vais vous faire visiter la maison
6 show up *(turn up)* arriver; **only two of our guests have shown up** seuls deux de nos invités sont arrivés; **he didn't show up** il ne s'est pas présenté

shower *noun*
(a) la douche; **he's having a shower** il prend une douche; **he's in the shower** il est sous la douche; **shower gel** le gel douche
(b) *(of rain)* une averse

show-off *noun* le frimeur/la frimeuse; **stop being such a show-off!** arrête de frimer!

shrimp *noun* la crevette

shrink *verb*
(a) *(of clothes)* rétrécir; **it shrank in the wash** ça a rétréci au lavage
(b) *(of a number)* diminuer; **the number of candidates has shrunk** le nombre de candidats a diminué

shut
1 *adjective* fermé/fermée
2 *verb* fermer; **shut your eyes** ferme les yeux; **the post office shuts at six o'clock** la poste ferme à six heures; **the door won't shut** la porte ne ferme pas
3 shut off
(a) *(gas, electricity)* couper
(b) *(road)* fermer
4 shut out
(a) *(the light)* bloquer
(b) **to shut somebody out** enfermer quelqu'un dehors

5 shut up
(a) *(close)* fermer
(b) *(be quiet)* se taire; **shut up!** tais-toi! *or* la ferme! *or* ferme-la!

shuttle *noun* la navette; **a space shuttle** une navette spatiale

shy *adjective* timide

sick *adjective*
(a) *(ill)* malade; **to get sick** tomber malade; **to be off sick** être en congé maladie; **sick leave** le congé maladie; **a sick note** un mot d'absence
(b) **to be sick** *(vomit)* vomir; **to feel sick** *(nauseous)* avoir envie de vomir
(c) *(fed up, disgusted)* **to be sick of something** en avoir marre de quelque chose; **I'm sick of telling you!** j'en ai marre de te le répéter!; **I'm sick and tired of your stories** j'en ai marre de tes histoires; **you make me sick!** tu me dégoûtes!

sickness *noun*
(a) *(illness)* la maladie
(b) *(nausea)* la nausée

side
1 *noun*
(a) *(of a person, an object etc)* le côté; **on my mother's side** du côté de ma mère; **to lean to one side** se pencher sur le côté; **to put something to one side** mettre quelque chose de côté; **he took me to one side** il m'a pris à part; **on the left-hand side** à gauche; **on the right-hand side** à droite; **side by side** côte à côte
(b) *(of a road, a river)* le bord
(c) *(of a hill)* le flanc
(d) *(in a game)* une équipe
(e) **to take sides** prendre parti; **I'm on your side** je suis de ton côté
2 *adjective*
(a) *(door, window)* latéral/latérale

The masculine plural of *latéral* is *latéraux*.

(b) **side effects** les effets secondaires *(masculine plural)*

sideboard *noun* le buffet

sideburns *plural noun* les pattes *(feminine plural)*

sideways *adverb*
(**a**) *(glance, turn, fall, lean)* sur le côté
(**b**) *(move)* latéralement; **to step sideways** faire un pas de côté

sieve *noun* la passoire

sigh
1 *noun* le soupir; **to heave a sigh** pousser un soupir
2 *verb* soupirer; **to sigh with relief** pousser un soupir de soulagement

sight *noun*
(**a**) *(faculty, act of seeing)* la vue; **he lost his sight** il a perdu la vue; **I can't stand the sight of blood** je ne supporte pas la vue du sang; **to catch sight of something** apercevoir quelque chose; **I know her by sight** je la connais de vue
(**b**) *(range of vision)* **in sight** en vue; **to come into sight** apparaître; **to be out of sight** être caché/cachée
(**c**) *(thing seen)* **it was a sad sight** c'était triste à voir; **the cliffs were an impressive sight** les falaises étaient impressionnantes à voir
(**d**) **at first sight** à première vue; **it was love at first sight** ça a été le coup de foudre

sightseeing *noun* le tourisme; **I did some sightseeing in Rome** j'ai visité Rome

sign
1 *noun*
(**a**) *(gesture, symbol, indication)* le signe; **to make a sign to somebody** faire signe à quelqu'un; **as a sign of respect** en signe de respect; **a star sign** un signe astrologique; **sign language** le langage des signes
(**b**) *(notice)* la pancarte; **a for sale sign** une pancarte "à vendre"
(**c**) *(on a road)* le panneau; **traffic signs** les panneaux de signalisation

The plural of *panneau* is *panneaux*.

(**d**) *(over a shop, a pub)* une enseigne

2 *verb*
(**a**) *(a document)* signer; **to sign one's name** signer
(**b**) *(a sportsperson)* engager; **he signed for Manchester United** il a signé un contrat avec Manchester United

signal
1 *noun* le signal

The plural of *signal* is *signaux*.

2 *verb*
(**a**) *(in a car)* mettre son clignotant
(**b**) *(make gesture)* faire des signes; **she was signalling for us to stop** elle nous faisait signe de nous arrêter

signature *noun* la signature

significant *adjective* important/importante; **a significant role** un rôle important

signpost *noun* le panneau indicateur

The plural of *panneau indicateur* is *panneaux indicateurs*.

silence *noun* le silence

silent *adjective*
(**a**) silencieux/silencieuse
(**b**) **a silent film** un film muet

silently *adverb* silencieusement

silk *noun* la soie; **a silk blouse** une chemise en soie

silly *adjective* bête; **it was silly of me to ask** c'était bête de ma part de demander ça

silver *noun* l'argent *(masculine)*; **a silver bracelet** un bracelet en argent; **a silver medal** une médaille d'argent

similar *adjective* semblable; **your problem is similar to mine** votre problème est semblable au mien; **her dress is similar to mine** sa robe ressemble à la mienne; **they're very similar** ils se ressemblent beaucoup

simple *adjective* simple

simply *adverb*
(**a**) *(in a simple way)* simplement
(**b**) *(just)* **it's not simply a matter of**

money ce n'est pas une simple question d'argent

sin *noun* le péché

since

1 *preposition* depuis; **he has been talking about it since yesterday** il en parle depuis hier; **since when?** depuis quand?; **ever since that day** depuis ce jour-là

> Note that when the present perfect is used with *since* in English, the French use the present tense, as in the first example above.

2 *conjunction*
(**a**) depuis que; **I've worn glasses since I was six** je porte des lunettes depuis l'âge de six ans; **it's ages since we went to the cinema** ça fait une éternité que nous ne sommes pas allés au cinéma; **ever since she got married** depuis qu'elle s'est mariée
(**b**) *(because)* puisque, comme; **since you don't want to go, I'll go by myself** puisque tu ne veux pas y aller, j'irai tout seul
3 *adverb* depuis; **I've never seen him since** je ne l'ai jamais revu depuis

sincere *adjective* sincère

sincerely *adverb*
(**a**) sincèrement; **I sincerely hope we can be friends** j'espère sincèrement que nous serons amis
(**b**) **Yours sincerely** *(in a letter)* je vous prie d'agréer mes sentiments les meilleurs

sing *verb* chanter

singer *noun* le chanteur/la chanteuse; **she's a jazz singer** elle est chanteuse de jazz

single
1 *adjective*
(**a**) *(only one)* seul/seule; **the room was lit by a single lamp** la pièce était éclairée par une seule lampe; **don't say a single word** ne dites pas un mot; **in single file** en file indienne
(**b**) *(for one person)* **a single bed** un lit

à une place; **a single room** une chambre pour une personne
(**c**) *(without a partner)* célibataire; **a single man** un célibataire; **a single woman** une célibataire; **she's a single parent** c'est une mère célibataire
(**d**) *(one way)* **a single ticket** un aller simple
(**e**) **every single day** tous les jours; **every single time** à chaque fois
2 *noun*
(**a**) *(ticket)* un aller simple; **a single to London** un aller simple pour Londres
(**b**) *(CD)* le single

singular *noun* le singulier; **in the singular** au singulier

sink
1 *noun*
(**a**) *(in a kitchen)* un évier
(**b**) *(in a bathroom)* le lavabo
2 *verb*
(**a**) *(of a boat)* couler
(**b**) *(of a person)* se laisser tomber; **I sank into the armchair** je me suis laissé tomber dans le fauteuil
(**c**) *(in mud, snow, sand)* s'enfoncer; **the wheels sank into the mud** les roues s'enfonçaient dans la boue

sip
1 *noun* la petite gorgée; **she took a sip of wine** elle a bu une petite gorgée de vin
2 *verb* boire à petites gorgées

sir *noun* monsieur *(masculine)*; **would you like some coffee, sir?** est-ce que vous prendrez du café, monsieur?; **Dear Sir** *(in a letter)* Monsieur

siren *noun* la sirène

sister *noun* la sœur; **my big sister** ma grande sœur; **my little sister** ma petite sœur

sister-in-law *noun* la belle-sœur

> The plural of *belle-sœur* is *belles-sœurs*.

sit
1 *verb*
(**a**) *(take a seat)* s'asseoir; **she came**

and sat next to me elle est venue s'asseoir à côté de moi
(**b**) *(be seated)* être assis/assise; **she sat beside me all evening** elle était assise à côté de moi toute la soirée; **they were sitting at the table** ils étaient assis à table; **he was sitting on the floor** il était assis par terre
(**c**) *(be situated)* être; **your keys are sitting right in front of you** tes clés sont là, juste devant toi
(**d**) *(an exam)* passer; **she didn't pass the exam she sat last week** elle n'a pas réussi l'examen qu'elle a passé la semaine dernière

Note that the French *passer un examen* means *to sit an exam* and not *to pass an exam,* which is translated by *réussir un examen.*

2 sit down s'asseoir; **please sit down** asseyez-vous
3 sit up se redresser; **sit up straight!** redresse-toi!

sitting room *noun* le salon

situated *adjective* situé/située

situation *noun* la situation

six *number* six

The word *six* is pronounced "si" in front of a consonant, "siz" in front of a vowel or mute h and "sis" on its own.

sixteen *number* seize

sixteenth *number* seizième; **the sixteenth card** la seizième carte; **the sixteenth of March** le seize mars

sixth *number* sixième; **two sixths** *(fraction)* deux sixièmes; **the sixth day** le sixième jour; **the sixth door** la sixième porte; **the sixth of March** le six mars

sixty *number* soixante; **sixty-one boys** soixante et un garçons; **sixty-one girls** soixante et une filles; **sixty-two** soixante-deux; **sixty-first** soixante et unième; **sixty-second** soixante-deuxième; **the sixties** les années soixante

Soixante is pronounced "soissante".

size *noun*
(**a**) *(of a person, of clothes)* la taille; **what size are you?** quelle taille fais-tu?
(**b**) *(of shoes)* la pointure; **what size are you?** tu chausses du combien?
(**c**) *(of a room, of furniture)* la taille, les dimensions *(feminine plural)*; **the rooms are the same size** les pièces sont de la même taille *or* les pièces ont les mêmes dimensions
(**d**) *(of a country)* l'étendue *(feminine),* la superficie

skate
1 *noun*
(**a**) *(for ice-skating)* le patin à glace
(**b**) *(for roller-skating)* le patin à roulettes
2 *verb*
(**a**) *(ice-skate)* faire du patin à glace, patiner; **to go skating** faire du patin à glace *or* faire du patinage
(**b**) *(roller-skating)* faire du patin à roulettes; **to go skating** faire du patin à roulettes

skateboard *noun* le skateboard

skater *noun* le patineur/la patineuse

skating *noun*
(**a**) *(ice-skating)* le patin à glace, le patinage; **a skating rink** une patinoire
(**b**) *(roller-skating)* le patin à roulettes; **a skating rink** une piste de patin à roulettes

skeleton *noun* le squelette

sketch *noun*
(**a**) *(drawing)* le croquis
(**b**) *(in theatre)* le sketch

ski
1 *noun* le ski; **a pair of skis** une paire de skis; **a ski instructor** un moniteur/une monitrice de ski; **a ski lift** un télésiège; **a ski slope** une piste de ski; **a ski suit** une combinaison de ski; **a ski tow** un téléski
2 *verb* faire du ski, skier; **we didn't ski because of the weather** on n'a pas fait de ski à cause du temps; **to go skiing** aller faire du ski

skid *verb*
(**a**) *(of a car)* déraper
(**b**) *(of a person, an object)* glisser

skier *noun* le skieur/la skieuse

skiing *noun* le ski; **I went on a skiing holiday** je suis parti au ski *or* je suis parti aux sports d'hiver

skilful *adjective* habile, adroit/adroite

skill *noun*
(**a**) *(quality)* l'habileté *(feminine)*; **it takes a lot of skill** ça demande beaucoup d'habileté
(**b**) *(knowledge)* la compétence, l'aptitude *(feminine)*; **language skills** les aptitudes linguistiques

skimmed milk *noun* le lait écrémé

skin *noun* la peau; **he has dark skin** il a la peau brune; **he has fair skin** il a la peau claire; **she has good skin** elle a une belle peau; **I was soaked to the skin** j'étais trempé jusqu'aux os

The plural of *peau* is *peaux*.

skinny *adjective* maigre

skip *verb*
(**a**) *(hop about)* sautiller
(**b**) *(with a skipping rope)* sauter à la corde
(**c**) **to skip a meal** sauter un repas; **to skip a chapter** sauter un chapitre
(**d**) **to skip a class** sécher un cours

skipping rope *noun* la corde à sauter

skirt *noun* la jupe; **she's wearing a skirt** elle porte une jupe

skull *noun* le crâne

sky *noun* le ciel

skydiving *noun* le saut en chute libre

skyscraper *noun* le gratte-ciel

The word *gratte-ciel* does not change in the plural.

slam *verb* *(a door)* claquer

slang *noun* l'argot *(masculine)*

slap
1 *noun*
(**a**) *(on the face)* la gifle; **I got a slap in the face** j'ai reçu une gifle
(**b**) *(on the back, the wrist)* la tape
2 *verb*
(**a**) *(on the face)* **she slapped his face** elle l'a giflé
(**b**) *(on the back, the wrist)* **he slapped me on the back** il m'a donné une tape dans le dos

slave *noun* un/une esclave

sledge
1 *noun*
(**a**) *(for fun or sport)* la luge
(**b**) *(pulled by animals)* le traîneau

The plural of *traîneau* is *traîneaux*.

2 *verb* faire de la luge; **the children have gone sledging** les enfants sont partis faire de la luge

sleep
1 *noun* le sommeil; **I need a good night's sleep** j'ai besoin d'une bonne nuit de sommeil; **I only had three hours' sleep** je n'ai dormi que trois heures; **to go to sleep** s'endormir; **to get back to sleep** se rendormir; **they had to put my dog to sleep** ils ont dû piquer mon chien
2 *verb* dormir; **he's sleeping** il dort; **can I sleep at your place?** est-ce que je peux dormir chez toi?; **did you sleep well?** est-ce que tu as bien dormi?; **sleep well!** bonne nuit!
3 sleep in
(**a**) *(involuntarily)* ne pas se réveiller; **I'm sorry, I slept in** je suis désolé, je ne me suis pas réveillé
(**b**) *(voluntarily)* faire la grasse matinée; **you'll be able to sleep in on Saturday** tu pourras faire la grasse matinée samedi

sleepy *adjective* **to be sleepy** avoir sommeil *or* avoir envie de dormir

sleet
1 *noun* la neige fondue

2 *verb* **it's sleeting** il tombe de la neige fondue

sleeve *noun* la manche

slice
1 *noun*
(**a**) *(of bread, meat)* la tranche; **she cut the meat into slices** elle a coupé la viande en tranches
(**b**) *(of lemon, salami, carrot)* la rondelle
(**c**) *(of pizza)* la part; **she cut the pizza into eight slices** elle a coupé la pizza en huit
2 *verb*
(**a**) *(bread, meat)* couper en tranches
(**b**) *(lemon, salami, carrot)* couper en rondelles
(**c**) **to slice something in half** couper quelque chose en deux

slide
1 *noun*
(**a**) *(for children)* le toboggan
(**b**) *(photo)* la diapositive
(**c**) *(for hair)* la barrette
2 *verb*
(**a**) *(on a slippery surface)* glisser; **he slid on the ice** il a glissé sur la glace; **the dish slid off the table** le plat a glissé de la table
(**b**) *(move quietly)* se glisser; **the snake slid through the grass** le serpent s'est glissé entre les herbes

slight *adjective*
(**a**) *(mistake, problem, difference)* léger/légère, petit/petite
(**b**) **the slightest** le/la moindre; **I haven't the slightest idea** je n'en ai pas la moindre idée; **they haven't the slightest chance of winning** ils n'ont pas la moindre chance de gagner

slightly *adverb* un peu, légèrement

slim *adjective* mince

slip
1 *noun*
(**a**) *(of paper)* le bout
(**b**) *(mistake)* une erreur; **a slip of the tongue** un lapsus

(**c**) *(woman's underwear) (full-length)* la combinaison; *(waist-length)* le jupon

> Note that the French word *slip* is never a translation for the English word *slip*. It means *pants*.

2 *verb*
(**a**) *(slide)* glisser; **he slipped on the ice** il a glissé sur la glace; **it slipped out of my hands** ça m'a glissé des mains
(**b**) *(move quickly or quietly)* se glisser; **she slipped quietly into the room** elle s'est glissée discrètement dans la pièce

slipper *noun* le chausson; **a pair of slippers** une paire de chaussons

slippery *adjective* glissant/glissante; **it's slippery** ça glisse

slope
1 *noun* la pente; **a steep slope** une pente raide
2 *verb* **to slope, to be sloping** être en pente

slot *noun*
(**a**) *(in a box, a machine)* la fente
(**b**) **a slot machine** *(vending machine)* un distributeur automatique; *(for gambling)* une machine à sous

Slovakia *noun* la Slovaquie; **I've never been to Slovakia** je ne suis jamais allé en Slovaquie; **they live in Slovakia** ils habitent en Slovaquie; **she comes from Slovakia** elle vient de Slovaquie

Slovakian
1 *adjective* slovaque
2 *noun*
(**a**) *(language)* le slovaque; **he speaks Slovakian** il parle slovaque
(**b**) *(person)* le/la Slovaque; **the Slovakians** les Slovaques *(masculine plural)*

Slovenia *noun* la Slovénie; **I've never been to Slovenia** je ne suis jamais allé en Slovénie; **they live in Slovenia** ils habitent en Slovénie; **she comes from Slovenia** elle vient de Slovénie

Slovenian

1 *adjective* slovène
2 *noun*
(a) *(language)* le slovène; **he speaks Slovenian** il parle slovène
(b) *(person)* le/la Slovène; **the Slovenians** les Slovènes *(masculine plural)*

slow

1 *adjective*
(a) lent/lente; **she's a slow worker** elle travaille lentement; **I'm a slow reader** je lis lentement; **they're making slow progress** ils avancent lentement; **in slow motion** au ralenti
(b) **my watch is slow** ma montre retarde; **the clock's three minutes slow** la pendule retarde de trois minutes
2 *adverb* lentement
3 *verb* **slow down** ralentir

slowly *adverb* lentement

slug *noun* la limace

slum *noun*

(a) *(district)* le quartier pauvre
(b) *(house)* le taudis

smack

1 *noun*
(a) *(on the bottom)* la fessée
(b) *(on the face)* la gifle; **I got a smack in the face** j'ai reçu une gifle
2 *verb*
(a) *(on the face)* **she smacked his face** elle l'a giflé
(b) *(on the bottom)* **my mum smacked my bottom** ma mère m'a donné une fessée

small *adjective*

(a) *(in size)* petit/petite; **a small garden** un petit jardin; **a small ad** une petite annonce; **small change** la petite monnaie; **in small letters** en lettres minuscules
(b) *(in number)* **a small family** une famille peu nombreuse

smart *adjective*

(a) *(clever)* malin/maligne; **it wasn't very smart of him** ce n'était pas très malin de sa part

(b) *(elegant)* chic; **this is a smart restaurant** c'est un restaurant chic

> Note that the adjective *chic* does not change in the plural or in the feminine: *des vêtements chic.*

smash *verb*

(a) *(break)* casser; **I've smashed my glasses** j'ai cassé mes lunettes; **to smash something to pieces** casser quelque chose en mille morceaux
(b) *(get broken)* se casser; **the vase smashed into pieces** le vase s'est cassé en mille morceaux
(c) **he smashed the door open** il a enfoncé la porte
(d) **the car smashed into the wall** la voiture est rentrée dans le mur

smell

1 *noun*
(a) *(odour)* une odeur; **there was a smell of burning** il y avait une odeur de brûlé; **there's a bad smell** ça sent mauvais
(b) *(sense)* l'odorat *(masculine)*; **he has no sense of smell** il n'a pas d'odorat
2 *verb* sentir; **I can smell burning** ça sent le brûlé; **it smells good** ça sent bon; **it smells of lavender** ça sent la lavande

smelly *adjective* qui sent mauvais; **it's smelly in here** ça sent mauvais ici

smile

1 *noun* le sourire; **he has a nice smile** il a un joli sourire
2 *verb* sourire; **she smiled at me** elle m'a souri

smoke

1 *noun* la fumée
2 *verb* fumer; **he's smoking a cigarette** il fume une cigarette; **do you smoke?** est-ce que vous fumez?; **no smoking** défense de fumer

smoky *adjective (room)* enfumé/enfumée

smooth *adjective*

(a) *(surface)* lisse

(**b**) *(skin)* doux/douce
(**c**) *(sea)* calme

snack *noun* *(meal)* le casse-croûte

The word *casse-croûte* does not change in the plural.

snail *noun* un escargot

snake *noun* le serpent

snap
1 *verb*
(**a**) *(break)* casser; **he snapped the branch in half** il a cassé la branche en deux
(**b**) *(get broken)* se casser net; **the branch snapped in two** la branche s'est cassée net
(**c**) *(speak sharply)* **to snap at somebody** parler sèchement à quelqu'un
(**d**) *(make a noise)* claquer; **he snapped his fingers** il a claqué des doigts
2 *noun* *(noise)* le bruit sec; **the branch broke with a snap** la branche a cassé avec un bruit sec

snapshot *noun* la photo

snatch *verb* *(grab)* arracher; **a boy on a motorbike snatched her bag** un garçon en moto lui a arraché son sac

sneak *verb* se glisser; **to sneak into a room** se glisser dans une pièce; **to sneak out of a room** sortir d'une pièce sans se faire remarquer; **we sneaked in at the back** nous nous sommes glissés dans le fond discrètement; **he sneaked up on me** il s'est approché de moi sans faire de bruit

sneeze
1 *noun* un éternuement
2 *verb* éternuer

sniff *verb*
(**a**) *(from cold, crying)* renifler
(**b**) *(of a dog)* flairer

snob *noun* le/la snob

snooker *noun* le billard; **to play snooker** jouer au billard

snore *verb* ronfler

snorkel *noun* le tuba

snow
1 *noun* la neige; **covered with snow** enneigé/enneigée
2 *verb* neiger; **it's snowing** il neige

snowball *noun* la boule de neige

snowflake *noun* le flocon de neige

snowman *noun* le bonhomme de neige

snowplough *noun* le chasse-neige

The word *chasse-neige* does not change in the plural.

snowstorm *noun* la tempête de neige

so
1 *adverb*
(**a**) *(to such a degree)* si, tellement; **it's so easy** c'est si facile *or* c'est tellement facile; **I was so angry I almost hit him** j'étais tellement en colère que j'ai failli le frapper; **I'm not so sure of that** je n'en suis pas si sûr
(**b**) *(yes)* **if so** si oui; **I think so** je pense *or* je pense que oui; **I don't think so** je ne crois pas; **I hope so** j'espère que oui; **I suppose so** je suppose; **I told you so!** je te l'avais bien dit!; **is that so?** c'est vrai?; **you're late – so I am** tu es en retard – ah oui, tu as raison
(**c**) *(also)* aussi; **so am I** moi aussi; **so do we** nous aussi; **so can they** eux aussi
(**d**) *(about)* **or so** environ; **there were ten or so people** il y avait environ dix personnes
(**e**) **so much** *(after a verb)* tellement; **I miss you so much** tu me manques tellement; **it's never rained so much** il n'a jamais plu autant
(**f**) **so much, so many** *(before a noun)* tellement de, autant de; **so much work** tellement de travail; **so many people** tellement de gens; **they've never seen so much money** ils n'ont jamais vu autant d'argent
2 *conjunction*
(**a**) *(therefore)* donc, alors; **she has a bad temper, so be careful** elle a mauvais caractère, donc fais attention

(**b**) *(introducing a remark)* alors; **so then she left** alors elle est partie; **so that's why!** alors c'est pour ça!; **so what?** et alors?

(**c**) **so as to** pour; **she went to bed early so as not to be tired the next day** elle s'est couchée tôt pour ne pas être fatiguée le lendemain

(**d**) **so that** pour que; **they tied him up so that he couldn't escape** ils l'ont attaché pour qu'il ne s'échappe pas; **he sat down so that I could see better** il s'est assis pour que je puisse mieux voir

> Note that *pour que* is always followed by the subjunctive.

soak *verb*
(**a**) *(person)* tremper; **I'm soaked to the skin** je suis trempé jusqu'aux os
(**b**) *(washing, food)* faire tremper

soap *noun*
(**a**) *(for washing)* le savon
(**b**) *(on TV)* **a soap, a soap opera** un feuilleton

sob
1 *noun* le sanglot
2 *verb* sangloter

soccer *noun* le football, le foot

social *adjective* social/sociale; **a social club** un club; **social life** la vie sociale; **he doesn't have much of a social life** il ne sort pas beaucoup; **a social worker** un assistant social/une assistante sociale

> The masculine plural of *social* is *sociaux*.

society *noun*
(**a**) *(community)* la société; **in society** dans la société
(**b**) *(association)* une association

sock *noun* la chaussette; **a pair of socks** une paire de chaussettes

socket *noun* *(for a plug)* la prise de courant

soda *noun* l'eau gazeuse *(feminine)*

sofa *noun* le canapé

soft *adjective*
(**a**) *(to touch)* doux/douce; **she has soft skin** elle a la peau douce; **a soft toy** une peluche
(**b**) *(yielding, not firm)* mou/molle; **this bed is too soft** ce lit est trop mou
(**c**) *(not strict)* indulgent/indulgente; **you're too soft on him** vous êtes trop indulgent avec lui; **she has a soft spot for him** elle a un faible pour lui
(**d**) *(voice, colour, weather)* doux/douce
(**e**) *(job, life)* facile; **the soft option** la solution de facilité
(**f**) **a soft drink** une boisson non alcoolisée

softly *adverb* *(quietly, gently)* doucement

software *noun* le logiciel; **a software package** un logiciel

soil *noun* la terre

soldier *noun* le soldat; **he's a soldier** il est soldat

sole *noun*
(**a**) *(of a shoe)* la semelle
(**b**) **the soles of the feet** la plante des pieds

solicitor *noun*
(**a**) *(for drawing up documents)* le notaire; **she's a solicitor** elle est notaire
(**b**) *(for court work)* un avocat/une avocate; **my dad's a solicitor** mon père est avocat

> Note that when describing people's jobs or situations, French does not use an article (*un* or *une*).

solid *adjective*
(**a**) *(car, bridge)* solide
(**b**) *(gold, oak)* massif/massive
(**c**) *(line)* continu/continue
(**d**) **I worked for eight solid hours** j'ai travaillé huit heures d'affilée

solution *noun* la solution

solve *verb* résoudre; **they have solved the problem** ils ont résolu le problème

some

1 *adjective*

(**a**) *(a certain quantity of)* du/de la; **some cheese** du fromage; **some beer** de la bière; **some garlic** de l'ail; **some water** de l'eau

> *Du* is the contraction of *de* + *le* and is used before masculine nouns. *Du* and *de la* become *de l'* before a vowel or mute h.

(**b**) *(a certain number of)* des; **some red flowers** des fleurs rouges; **some pretty flowers** des jolies fleurs *or* de jolies fleurs

> *Des* is the contraction of *de* + *les*. It often becomes *de* in front of an adjective.

(**c**) *(a little)* un peu de; **I need some peace and quiet** j'ai besoin d'un peu de tranquillité

(**d**) *(a few)* quelques; **I have some apples** j'ai quelques pommes

(**e**) *(a considerable amount of)* un certain/une certaine; **after some time** après un certain temps; **it's some distance away** c'est assez loin

(**f**) *(a considerable number of)* quelques, plusieurs; **it happened some months ago** ça s'est passé il y a quelques mois; **some miles away** à plusieurs kilomètres

(**g**) *(as opposed to others)* certains/certaines; **some pupils don't like school** certains élèves n'aiment pas l'école; **some people say he'll never come back** certains disent qu'il ne reviendra jamais

(**h**) *(unspecified)* **in some book or other** dans un livre quelconque; **for some reason or other** pour une raison ou pour une autre; **some day** un jour ou l'autre; **some fool left the door open** un imbécile a laissé la porte ouverte

2 *pronoun*

(**a**) *(a certain quantity of it)* en; **I bought a bottle of wine, do you want some?** j'ai acheté une bouteille de vin, tu en veux?; **there's some left** il en reste un peu; **some of my wine** un peu de mon vin

> The pronoun *en* is used to replace *de* + *noun*.

(**b**) *(a certain number of them)* quelques-uns/quelques-unes; **some of my sweets** quelques-uns de mes bonbons; **I saw some of them** j'en ai vu quelques-uns

(**c**) *(as opposed to others)* certains/certaines; **some say it wasn't an accident** certains disent que ce n'était pas un accident; **some of the guests** certains invités

3 *adverb* environ; **it's some fifty kilometres from London** c'est à environ cinquante kilomètres de Londres

somebody *pronoun* quelqu'un; **somebody else** quelqu'un d'autre; **somebody important** quelqu'un d'important

somehow *adverb*

(**a**) *(in some way)* d'une manière ou d'une autre; **I'll manage somehow** j'y arriverai d'une manière ou d'une autre

(**b**) *(for some reason)* d'une certaine manière; **somehow I'm not surprised he didn't come** d'une certaine manière, cela ne m'étonne pas qu'il ne soit pas venu

someone *see* **somebody**

something *pronoun* quelque chose; **something else** quelque chose d'autre *or* autre chose; **something interesting** quelque chose d'intéressant; **would you like something to eat?** est-ce que vous voulez manger quelque chose?

sometime *adverb*

(**a**) *(in the future)* **come and see us sometime** venez nous voir un de ces jours; **sometime soon** bientôt; **sometime before next April** avant le mois d'avril

(**b**) *(in the past)* **she phoned sometime last week** elle a téléphoné la semaine dernière; **the last time I saw** him was sometime in August la dernière fois que je l'ai vu, c'était en août

sometimes *adverb* quelquefois, parfois

somewhere *adverb*
(a) quelque part; **somewhere in the house** quelque part dans la maison; **somewhere in France** quelque part en France; **she's somewhere around** elle est quelque part par là
(b) **somewhere else** ailleurs

son *noun* le fils

> The word *fils* is pronounced "fis".

song *noun*
(a) la chanson
(b) *(of birds)* le chant

son-in-law *noun* le gendre

soon *adverb*
(a) *(in a short time)* bientôt; **see you soon!** à bientôt!; **I'll be back soon** je reviens bientôt; **soon after** peu après
(b) *(early)* tôt; **it's too soon to know** il est trop tôt pour savoir; **sooner or later** tôt ou tard; **the sooner the better** le plus tôt sera le mieux
(c) *(quickly)* vite; **I spoke too soon!** j'ai parlé trop vite!
(d) **as soon as** aussitôt que, dès que; **as soon as possible** aussitôt que possible *or* dès que possible; **as soon as she leaves** aussitôt qu'elle partira *or* dès qu'elle partira

> Unlike in English where the present tense is used, French uses the future tense after *aussitôt que* or *dès que* when the action described will take place in the future.

(e) *(preferring something)* **I'd just as soon stay** j'aimerais autant rester; **I'd sooner do it alone** je préférerais le faire seul

sore *adjective* **I've got a sore throat** j'ai mal à la gorge; **I've got sore eyes** j'ai les yeux irrités; **my legs are sore** j'ai mal aux jambes *or* mes jambes me font mal; **it's sore** ça fait mal

sorrow *noun* le chagrin

sorry *adjective*
(a) *(apologetic)* désolé/désolée; **I'm sorry I'm late** je suis désolé d'être en retard; **sorry to interrupt you** excusez-moi de vous interrompre; **sorry I forgot your birthday** désolé d'avoir oublié ton anniversaire; **sorry about the delay!** excusez-moi pour ce retard!; **to say sorry to somebody** s'excuser auprès de quelqu'un; **sorry!** *(excuse me)* désolé! *or* excusez-moi!; **sorry?** *(not hearing properly)* pardon?
(b) *(regretful)* **to be sorry** regretter; **she'll be sorry!** elle le regrettera!; **I'm sorry she can't come** c'est dommage qu'elle ne puisse pas venir
(c) *(sympathetic)* **to feel sorry for somebody** plaindre quelqu'un; **I feel sorry for her** je la plains; **to feel sorry for oneself** s'apitoyer sur son sort

sort
1 *noun*
(a) *(kind, type)* la sorte; **a sort of** une sorte de; **it's a sort of gun** c'est une sorte de fusil; **all sorts of** toutes sortes de; **what sort of tree is it?** qu'est-ce que c'est comme arbre?; **that sort of thing** ce genre de chose; **she's not that sort of a person** ce n'est pas son genre
(b) **he's out of sorts** *(a little unwell)* il n'est pas dans son assiette; *(in a bad mood)* il est de mauvaise humeur
(c) **this is sort of embarrassing** c'est plutôt gênant; **I sort of expected it** je m'y attendais un peu
2 *verb* trier; **to sort the mail** trier le courrier
3 sort out
(a) *(tidy up)* ranger
(b) *(separate)* séparer; **I'm sorting out the dirty laundry** je trie le linge sale
(c) *(arrange)* s'occuper de; **I'll go and sort out the tickets** je vais m'occuper des billets; **we have to sort out a date for the meeting** nous devons choisir une date pour la réunion
(d) *(settle, solve)* régler; **it's sorted out** c'est réglé; **she needs time to sort**

herself out il lui faut du temps pour régler ses problèmes

soul *noun (spirit)* l'âme *(feminine)*

sound
1 *adjective*
(**a**) *(person)* sain/saine, en bonne santé; **to be of sound mind** être sain d'esprit
(**b**) *(building, structure)* solide
(**c**) *(advice, argument, basis, investment)* bon/bonne
2 *noun*
(**a**) *(of a voice, an instrument, a television)* le son
(**b**) *(of footsteps, wind, cars)* le bruit
3 *verb*
(**a**) **to sound the alarm** sonner l'alarme; **to sound one's horn** klaxonner; **it sounds hollow** ça sonne creux
(**b**) *(seem)* sembler, avoir l'air; **he sounded sad** il semblait triste *or* il avait l'air triste; **that sounds like a good idea** ça me semble être une bonne idée; **it doesn't sound very interesting** ça n'a pas l'air très intéressant; **it sounds like Mozart** on dirait du Mozart

soundtrack *noun* la bande originale

soup *noun* la soupe; **tomato soup** la soupe de tomates

sour *adjective* aigre

south
1 *noun* le sud; **south of, to the south of** au sud de; **Sheffield is south of Leeds** Sheffield est au sud de Leeds; **in the south of** dans le sud de; **London is in the south of England** Londres est dans le sud de l'Angleterre
2 *adjective* sud; **the south coast** la côte sud; **South America** l'Amérique du Sud; **the South Pole** le pôle Sud
3 *adverb* vers le sud; **they're heading south** ils se dirigent vers le sud

South Africa *noun* l'Afrique du Sud *(feminine)*; **he lives in South Africa** il habite en Afrique du Sud; **have you ever been to South Africa?** est-ce

que tu es déjà allé en Afrique du Sud?

South African
1 *adjective* sud-africain/sud-africaine, d'Afrique du Sud
2 *noun (person)* le Sud-Africain/la Sud-Africaine; **the South Africans** les Sud-Africains *(masculine plural)*

In French, only the noun for the inhabitants of a country takes a capital letter, never the adjective.

southeast
1 *noun* le sud-est; **London is in the southeast of England** Londres est dans le sud-est de l'Angleterre
2 *adjective* sud-est

southern *adjective* du sud; **Southern Europe** l'Europe du Sud; **southern France** le sud de la France; **southern England** le sud de l'Angleterre

southwest
1 *noun* le sud-ouest; **Cornwall is in the southwest of England** Cornwall est dans le sud-ouest de l'Angleterre
2 *adjective* sud-ouest

souvenir *noun* le souvenir

sow *verb (seeds)* semer

soy sauce *noun* la sauce de soja

soya *noun* le soja; **a soya bean** une graine de soja; **soya milk** le lait de soja

space *noun*
(**a**) *(outer space)* l'espace *(masculine)*; **a space shuttle** une navette spatiale
(**b**) *(between two words, two things)* un espace
(**c**) *(room)* la place; **there's not a lot of space** il n'y a pas beaucoup de place; **it takes up space** ça prend de la place

spaceship *noun* le vaisseau spatial

The plural of *vaisseau spatial* is *vaisseaux spatiaux*.

spacesuit *noun* la combinaison spatiale

spade *noun*
(**a**) *(for gardening)* la bêche
(**b**) *(for children)* la pelle

(c) *(in cards)* **spades** pique *(masculine)*; **the ace of spades** l'as de pique

spaghetti *noun* les spaghettis *(masculine plural)*

Spain *noun* l'Espagne *(feminine)*; **I've never been to Spain** je ne suis jamais allé en Espagne; **they live in Spain** ils habitent en Espagne; **her family comes from Spain** sa famille vient d'Espagne

Spaniard *noun* un Espagnol/une Espagnole

Spanish
1 *adjective* espagnol/espagnole
2 *noun*
(a) *(language)* l'espagnol *(masculine)*; **he speaks Spanish** il parle espagnol
(b) *(people)* **the Spanish** les Espagnols *(masculine plural)*

In French, only the noun for the inhabitants of a country takes a capital letter, never the adjective or the noun for the language.

spare
1 *adjective*
(a) *(extra)* en plus; **I've got two spare tickets** j'ai deux billets en plus; **do you have a spare pen?** est-ce que tu peux me prêter un stylo?
(b) *(available)* disponible, libre; **a spare seat** une place de libre; **the spare room** la chambre d'amis; **spare time** le temps libre, les loisirs
(c) *(kept in reserve)* de rechange; **a spare part** une pièce de rechange; **a spare wheel** une roue de secours
2 *verb*
(a) *(give away)* **I don't have time to spare** je n'ai pas le temps; **can you spare me five minutes** pouvez-vous m'accorder cinq minutes?; **could you spare me some milk?** est-ce que tu peux me donner un peu de lait?
(b) *(details)* épargner; **spare me the details!** épargne-moi les détails!

spark *noun* *(from a flame, electricity)* une étincelle

sparkle *verb*
(a) *(shine)* étinceler, briller
(b) *(fizz)* pétiller

sparkling *adjective*
(a) *(shining)* étincelant/étincelante, brillant/brillante; **she's got sparkling eyes** elle a les yeux qui brillent
(b) **sparkling water** l'eau gazeuse; **sparkling wine** le vin mousseux

sparrow *noun* le moineau

The plural of *moineau* is *moineaux*.

speak
1 *verb*
(a) *(talk)* parler; **she spoke to the teacher** elle a parlé au professeur; **we spoke about the film** nous avons parlé du film; **I speak French** je parle français; **she doesn't speak Spanish** elle ne parle pas espagnol; **can you speak more slowly, please?** est-ce que vous pouvez parler plus lentement, s'il vous plaît?
(b) *(say)* dire; **she has never spoken a word to me** elle ne m'a jamais dit un mot
(c) *(on the phone)* **who's speaking?** qui est à l'appareil?
2 speak up *(louder)* parler plus fort; **can you speak up, please?** est-ce que vous pouvez parler plus fort, s'il vous plaît?

speaker *noun*
(a) *(in a meeting, a conference)* un intervenant/une intervenante; **she's a good speaker** elle s'exprime bien en public
(b) **an English speaker** un/une anglophone; **a French speaker** un/une francophone
(c) *(of a stereo)* une enceinte

special
1 *adjective*
(a) spécial/spéciale; **a special offer** une offre spéciale; **special effects** les effets spéciaux

The masculine plural of *spécial* is *spéciaux*.

(b) *(care, attention, reason)* particulier/particulière; **children with special needs** les enfants qui ont des difficultés d'apprentissage
2 *noun* **today's special** *(in a restaurant)* le plat du jour

specialist *noun* le/la spécialiste

speciality *noun* la spécialité; **a local speciality** une spécialité de la région

specially *adverb*
(a) *(chosen, designed)* spécialement; **the coat was specially made for him** le manteau a été fait tout spécialement pour lui
(b) *(in particular)* particulièrement; **he's specially interested in old cars** il s'intéresse tout particulièrement aux vieilles voitures

species *noun* une espèce; **a rare species of butterfly** une espèce rare de papillon

spectator *noun* le spectateur/la spectatrice

speech *noun*
(a) *(talk)* le discours; **to give a speech** faire un discours
(b) *(ability to speak)* la parole; **he lost the power of speech** il a perdu la parole; **freedom of speech** la liberté d'expression

speed
1 *noun* la vitesse; **at high speed** à toute vitesse; **a speed camera** un radar; **the speed limit** la limitation de vitesse
2 *verb* aller à toute vitesse; **he sped down the street** il a descendu la rue à toute vitesse
3 **speed up** aller plus vite, accélérer

spell
1 *noun (magic trick)* le sort; **to cast a spell on somebody** jeter un sort à quelqu'un
2 *verb*
(a) *(write)* écrire; **they've spelt my name wrong** ils ont mal écrit mon nom

(b) *(say aloud)* épeler; **could you spell your name for me?** est-ce que vous pouvez épeler votre nom?

spellchecker *noun* le correcteur orthographique

spelling *noun* l'orthographe *(feminine)*; **his spelling is awful** il est nul en orthographe; **a spelling mistake** une faute d'orthographe

spend *verb*
(a) *(money)* dépenser; **I spent a lot of money on clothes** j'ai dépensé beaucoup d'argent en vêtements
(b) *(time)* passer; **I spent the whole afternoon reading** j'ai passé toute l'après-midi à lire

spending *noun* les dépenses *(feminine plural)*; **spending money** l'argent de poche

spice *noun* une épice

spicy *adjective* épicé/épicée

spider *noun* une araignée; **a spider's web** une toile d'araignée

spill *verb*
(a) *(cause to fall)* renverser; **I spilt orange juice down my dress** j'ai renversé du jus d'orange sur ma robe
(b) *(fall)* se répandre; **the wine spilt on the carpet** le vin s'est répandu sur la moquette
(c) **to spill the beans** vendre la mèche

spin
1 *verb*
(a) *(cause to rotate)* faire tourner; **it's your turn to spin the wheel** c'est à toi de faire tourner la roue
(b) *(rotate)* tourner
(c) **my head's spinning** j'ai la tête qui tourne
2 **spin round** *(face opposite direction)* se retourner; **he suddenly spun round** il s'est retourné brusquement

spinach *noun* les épinards *(masculine plural)*; **I don't like spinach** je n'aime pas les épinards

spine *noun* *(of a person)* la colonne vertébrale

spire *noun* la flèche

spirit *noun*
(**a**) *(soul, being)* l'esprit *(masculine)*
(**b**) *(attitude, mood)* **I'm in good spirits** je suis de bonne humeur; **she's in low spirits** elle est déprimée
(**c**) **spirits** *(alcohol)* les spiritueux *(masculine plural)*

spit *verb* cracher; **she spat at him** elle lui a craché dessus

spite *noun*
(**a**) *(nastiness)* la méchanceté; **to do something out of spite** faire quelque chose par méchanceté
(**b**) **in spite of** malgré; **in spite of myself** malgré moi

splash *verb* *(with water, mud, drink)* éclabousser

splendid *adjective*
(**a**) *(beautiful)* magnifique, splendide
(**b**) *(very good)* excellent/excellente; **that's a splendid idea** c'est une idée excellente

splinter *noun* *(of wood, glass)* un éclat; *(in one's finger)* une écharde

split
1 *verb*
(**a**) *(cut)* fendre; **he split the log in half** il a fendu la bûche en deux
(**b**) *(break)* se fendre; **the slate split in two** l'ardoise s'est fendue en deux
(**c**) *(tear)* déchirer; **I've split my trousers** j'ai déchiré mon pantalon
(**d**) *(get torn)* se déchirer; **the bag split open** le sac s'est déchiré
(**e**) *(divide)* diviser; **we were split into two groups** on nous a divisés en deux groupes
(**f**) *(share)* partager; **let's split the profits** partageons les bénéfices
2 split up
(**a**) *(share out)* se partager; **we should split up the work between us** nous devrions nous partager le travail
(**b**) *(separate)* séparer; **the teacher**

split the boys up le professeur a séparé les garçons
(**c**) *(of a couple)* se séparer; **they've split up** ils se sont séparés

spoil *verb*
(**a**) *(an event, a holiday)* gâcher
(**b**) *(an object)* abîmer
(**c**) *(a child)* gâter

sponge *noun*
(**a**) une éponge
(**b**) **a sponge cake** une génoise

spooky *adjective*
(**a**) *(frightening)* sinistre
(**b**) *(odd)* bizarre

spoon *noun* la cuillère; **a soup spoon** une cuillère à soupe; **a wooden spoon** une cuillère en bois

spoonful *noun* la cuillerée

sport *noun* le sport; **I do a lot of sport** je fais beaucoup de sport; **a sports centre** un complexe sportif

sportsman *noun* le sportif

sportswoman *noun* la sportive

spot
1 *noun*
(**a**) *(stain, mark)* la tache
(**b**) *(dot)* le pois; **a tie with red spots** une cravate à pois rouges
(**c**) *(on an animal)* la tache
(**d**) *(pimple)* le bouton
(**e**) *(place)* un endroit
(**f**) **on the spot** *(at once)* sur-le-champ; *(at the scene)* sur place
2 *verb* *(notice)* repérer; **I spotted her in the crowd** je l'ai repérée dans la foule

spotless *adjective* impeccable

sprain *verb* **I sprained my ankle** je me suis foulé la cheville; *(more seriously)* je me suis fait une entorse à la cheville

spray
1 *noun* *(can)* la bombe; **spray paint** la peinture en bombe
2 *verb*
(**a**) *(perfume)* vaporiser
(**b**) *(crops, paint)* pulvériser

(**c**) *(graffiti)* écrire à la bombe
(**d**) **he sprayed me with water** il m'a
aspergé d'eau

spread

1 *verb*
(**a**) *(butter, ointment)* étaler; **he spread
his papers on the desk** il a étalé ses
papiers sur le bureau
(**b**) *(one's arms, legs)* écarter
(**c**) *(news)* répandre
(**d**) *(a rumour, a disease, germs)* propager
(**e**) *(of a fire, a rumour, a disease,
germs)* se propager
2 spread out
(**a**) *(a map, a newspaper)* étaler
(**b**) *(of people)* se disperser

spring

1 *noun*
(**a**) *(season)* le printemps; **in the
spring** au printemps
(**b**) *(piece of metal)* le ressort
(**c**) *(of water)* la source; **spring water**
l'eau de source
(**d**) **a spring onion** une ciboule; **a
spring roll** un rouleau de printemps
2 *verb*
(**a**) *(leap)* bondir, sauter; **he sprang to
his feet** il s'est levé d'un bond
(**b**) **the door sprang open** la porte
s'est ouverte brusquement

springtime *noun* le printemps; **in
the springtime** au printemps

sprouts *noun* **(Brussels) sprouts** les
choux de Bruxelles *(masculine plural)*

spy

1 *noun* un espion/une espionne; **a spy
novel** un roman d'espionnage
2 *verb* faire de l'espionnage
3 spy on espionner; **are you spying
on me?** tu m'espionnes?

spying *noun* l'espionnage *(masculine)*

square

1 *adjective* *(in shape)* carré/carrée; **a
square metre** un mètre carré
2 *noun*
(**a**) *(shape)* le carré; **cut it into squares**

coupe-le en carrés
(**b**) *(place)* la place; **the market square**
la place du marché

squash

1 *noun* le squash; **my parents play
squash** mes parents jouent au squash
2 *verb (crush)* écraser

squat *verb* s'accroupir; **he was squatting** il était accroupi

squeak *verb*
(**a**) *(of a mouse)* pousser un petit cri
(**b**) *(of a floorboard, a door)* grincer
(**c**) *(of shoes)* crisser

squeeze

1 *verb*
(**a**) *(a fruit, a sponge)* presser
(**b**) *(somebody's hand)* serrer; **she
squeezed my hand tightly** elle m'a
serré fermement la main
(**c**) *(force)* faire entrer; **I can't squeeze
another thing into my suitcase** je ne
peux plus rien faire entrer dans ma valise
2 squeeze in se glisser
3 squeeze up se serrer

squirrel *noun* un écureuil

stab *verb* poignarder; **he was stabbed
in the back** il a été poignardé dans le
dos; **to stab to death** tuer à coups de
couteau

stable

1 *adjective* stable
2 *noun* une écurie; **a riding stable** un
centre équestre

stack

1 *noun*
(**a**) *(pile)* la pile; **a stack of books** une
pile de livres
(**b**) *(large quantity)* le tas; **I've written
stacks of postcards** j'ai écrit un tas de
cartes postales
2 *verb (chairs, glasses, books)* empiler

stadium *noun* le stade

staff *noun*
(**a**) *(of a company)* le personnel
(**b**) *(of a school)* les professeurs *(masculine plural)*

stag *noun* le cerf

> The *f* in *cerf* is not pronounced.

stage *noun*
(**a**) *(in a theatre)* la scène; **to go on stage** monter sur scène
(**b**) *(phase)* le stade, la phase; **the first stage of the project** la première phase du projet; **at this stage of the investigation** à ce stade de l'enquête; **to do something in stages** faire quelque chose par étapes

> Note that the French word *stage* is never a translation for the English word *stage*. It means *training course* or *work placement*.

stain
1 *noun* la tache; **an ink stain** une tache d'encre
2 *verb* tacher; **his shirt was stained with blood** sa chemise était tachée de sang

staircase *noun* un escalier

stairs *plural noun* un escalier, les escaliers; **I fell down the stairs** je suis tombé dans l'escalier *or* je suis tombé dans les escaliers

stale *adjective (bread, cake)* rassis/rassise

stalk *noun (of a flower)* la tige

stall
1 *noun*
(**a**) *(in a market)* un étal

> The plural of *étal* is *étals*.

(**b**) *(at a fair, an exhibition)* le stand
(**c**) *(for newspapers, flowers)* le kiosque
2 *verb (of a vehicle)* caler

stammer
1 *noun* le bégaiement; **he has a stammer** il bégaie
2 *verb* bégayer

stamp
1 *noun*
(**a**) *(on a letter)* le timbre
(**b**) **a rubber stamp** un tampon

2 *verb*
(**a**) *(a passport, a document)* tamponner
(**b**) **to stamp one's foot** taper du pied

stand
1 *noun*
(**a**) *(for newspapers)* le kiosque
(**b**) *(at an exhibition, a fair)* le stand
(**c**) *(at sports ground)* la tribune
(**d**) *(of a lamp)* le pied
(**e**) *(for postcards, sunglasses)* le présentoir
2 *verb*
(**a**) *(be on one's feet)* être debout, se tenir debout; **to remain standing** rester debout; **I could hardly stand** je tenais à peine debout; **I don't mind standing** ça ne me gêne pas de rester debout; **he stood on my toe** il m'a marché sur le pied; **stand still!** ne bougez pas!
(**b**) *(rise to one's feet)* se lever
(**c**) *(be located)* se trouver; **the fort stands on a hill** la forteresse se trouve en haut d'une colline
(**d**) *(set, place)* mettre; **she stood her umbrella in the corner** elle a mis son parapluie dans le coin
(**e**) *(bear, endure)* supporter; **I can't stand him** je ne peux pas le supporter; **I can't stand it any longer!** je n'en peux plus!; **I can't stand football** je déteste le foot
(**f**) **he stands a chance of winning** il a de bonnes chances de gagner; **you don't stand a chance!** tu n'as pas la moindre chance
3 stand back reculer
4 stand for
(**a**) *(mean)* vouloir dire; **what does DNA stand for?** que veut dire ADN?
(**b**) *(tolerate)* tolérer; **I won't stand for it** je ne le tolérerai pas
5 stand out ressortir; **these colours stand out** ces couleurs ressortent bien; **he stands out in a crowd** on le remarque dans la foule
6 stand up
(**a**) *(rise to one's feet)* se lever; **stand up!** levez-vous!

(**b**) *(be on one's feet)* être debout

(**c**) **to stand something up** mettre quelque chose debout

7 stand up for défendre; **he's always stood up for the oppressed** il a toujours défendu les opprimés

8 stand up to to stand up to somebody tenir tête à quelqu'un; **to stand up to something** résister à quelque chose

standard

1 *noun*

(**a**) *(level)* le niveau; **he's up to standard** il a le niveau requis; **he's below standard** il est en dessous du niveau requis; **the standard of living** le niveau de vie

> The plural of *niveau* is *niveaux*.

(**b**) *(set requirement)* la norme; **to comply with European standards** être conforme aux normes européennes

(**c**) *(moral principle)* **she has high standards** elle est très exigeante

2 *adjective*

(**a**) *(model, size)* standard

> Note that the French adjective *standard* does not change in the plural or in the feminine.

(**b**) *(usual, ordinary)* normal/normale

> The masculine plural of *normal* is *normaux*.

staple

1 *noun (for paper)* une agrafe

2 *verb (paper)* agrafer

stapler *noun* une agrafeuse

star

1 *noun*

(**a**) *(in the sky)* une étoile; **she's reading her stars** *(horoscope)* elle lit son horoscope

(**b**) *(famous person)* la vedette, la star; **a film star** une vedette de cinéma *or* une star de cinéma

2 *verb* **the film stars Keanu Reeves** le film a pour vedette Keanu Reeves;

who's starring in this film? qui joue dans ce film?

stare *verb* **to stare at something** regarder quelque chose fixement *or* fixer quelque chose des yeux; **she was staring at me** elle me regardait fixement; **it's rude to stare!** ça ne se fait pas de fixer les gens comme ça!

start

1 *noun*

(**a**) *(beginning)* le début; **at the start of the book** au début du livre; **at the very start** au tout début; **for a start** pour commencer

(**b**) *(starting place)* le départ; **where's the start of the race?** où est le départ de la course?

(**c**) *(jump)* le sursaut; **she woke up with a start** elle s'est réveillée en sursaut; **to give somebody a start** faire sursauter quelqu'un

2 *verb*

(**a**) *(begin)* commencer; **it's starting to rain** il commence à pleuvoir; **she started by reading the text** elle a commencé par lire le texte; **to start again** recommencer; **I started laughing** je me suis mis à rire

(**b**) *(a business)* créer

(**c**) *(a rumour, a fashion)* lancer

(**d**) *(a fire, a war)* déclencher

(**e**) *(a machine, an engine)* mettre en marche

(**f**) *(a car)* démarrer

(**g**) *(a computer)* allumer

(**h**) *(jump involuntarily)* sursauter

3 start off

(**a**) *(begin)* commencer; **start off by beating the eggs** commencez par battre les œufs

(**b**) *(an argument, a debate)* commencer

4 start out

(**a**) *(begin)* commencer; **he started out as a teacher** il a commencé comme professeur

(**b**) *(leave)* partir

5 start up

(**a**) *(a business, a political party)* créer

(**b**) *(a restaurant, a shop)* ouvrir
(**c**) *(a machine, an engine)* mettre en marche
(**d**) *(a car)* démarrer
(**e**) *(a computer)* allumer

starve *verb* mourir de faim; **I'm starving!** je meurs de faim!

state
1 *noun*
(**a**) *(condition)* l'état *(masculine)*; **his car is in a bad state** sa voiture est en mauvais état; **she's in a bad state** elle va mal; **a state of mind** un état d'esprit; **in a state of shock** en état de choc
(**b**) *(political body, nation)* un État; **a head of state** un chef d'État; **a state school** une école publique

Unlike English, *État* always has a capital letter in French when it refers to a country or part of a country.

2 *verb*
(**a**) *(say)* déclarer; **he stated that he was not responsible** il a déclaré qu'il n'était pas responsable
(**b**) *(one's name, address)* donner, indiquer; **please state your full name** veuillez indiquer vos nom et prénom

statement *noun*
(**a**) la déclaration
(**b**) *(made to the police)* la déposition; **she made a statement** elle a fait une déposition
(**c**) **a bank statement** un relevé de compte

station *noun*
(**a**) *(for trains)* la gare; **a bus station** une gare routière; **a tube station** une station de métro
(**b**) **a police station** un commissariat de police
(**c**) **a radio station** une station de radio

stationery *noun*
(**a**) *(writing paper)* le papier à lettres
(**b**) **office stationery** les fournitures de bureau *(feminine plural)*

statue *noun* la statue

stay
1 *noun (visit)* le séjour; **enjoy your stay!** bon séjour!
2 *verb*
(**a**) *(remain)* rester; **stay still** reste tranquille; **I stayed at home** je suis resté chez moi; **I stayed in bed** je suis resté au lit; **let's stay calm** restons calmes; **I stayed there for two weeks** j'y suis resté deux semaines
(**b**) *(live temporarily)* loger; **I'm staying with friends** je loge chez des amis; **to stay in a hotel** loger à l'hôtel
(**c**) *(spend)* passer; **I'm staying the night in London** je passe la nuit à Londres
3 stay away
(**a**) *(not go near)* ne pas s'approcher; **stay away from me!** ne t'approche pas de moi!
(**b**) *(not go)* ne pas aller; **she stayed away from school last week** elle n'est pas allée à l'école la semaine dernière
4 stay in *(stay at home)* rester chez soi; **I'd rather stay in tonight** je préfère rester chez moi ce soir
5 stay out
(**a**) *(not go home)* ne pas rentrer; **she stayed out all night** elle n'est pas rentrée de la nuit; **to stay out late** rentrer tard
(**b**) *(not get involved)* **stay out of this!** ne te mêle pas de ça!
6 stay up *(not go to bed)* ne pas se coucher; **he stayed up all night** il est resté debout toute la nuit; **to stay up late** se coucher tard

steady *adjective*
(**a**) *(stable)* stable; **the boat is not very steady** le bateau n'est pas très stable; **a steady job** un emploi stable
(**b**) *(regular, constant)* régulier/régulière

steak *noun* le steak

steal *verb* voler; **he stole it from me** il me l'a volé

steam *noun*
(a) *(in the air)* la vapeur; **a steam engine** une locomotive à vapeur
(b) *(on a window)* la buée

steel *noun* l'acier *(masculine)*; **a steel door** une porte en acier

steep *adjective* *(stairs, slope, climb)* raide

steering wheel *noun* le volant

stem *noun* *(of a plant)* la tige

step
1 *noun*
(a) *(of stairs)* la marche
(b) *(pace)* le pas; **to take two steps forward** faire deux pas en avant; **watch your step!** fais attention où tu mets les pieds!
(c) *(action, measure)* la mesure; **to take steps** prendre des mesures
(d) *(stage)* une étape; **step by step** petit à petit
2 *verb (walk)* marcher; **I stepped on his foot** je lui ai marché sur le pied; **I stepped off the train** je suis descendu du train
3 step aside s'écarter
4 step back reculer
5 step forward
(a) *(move forward)* avancer
(b) *(volunteer)* se porter volontaire
6 step in
(a) *(come in)* entrer
(b) *(intervene)* intervenir

stepdaughter *noun* la belle-fille

The plural of *belle-fille* is *belles-filles*.

stepfather *noun* le beau-père

The plural of *beau-père* is *beaux-pères*.

stepladder *noun* un escabeau

The plural of *escabeau* is *escabeaux*.

stepmother *noun* la belle-mère

The plural of *belle-mère* is *belles-mères*.

stepson *noun* le beau-fils

The plural of *beau-fils* is *beaux-fils*.

stereo *noun* la chaîne stéréo

stew *noun* le ragoût

stewardess *noun* une hôtesse de l'air; **my sister is a stewardess** ma sœur est hôtesse de l'air

stick
1 *noun*
(a) *(of wood, a lollipop, for skiing)* le bâton
(b) *(for walking)* la canne
2 *verb*
(a) *(attach)* coller; **to stick a stamp on an envelope** coller un timbre sur une enveloppe; **the dough stuck to my fingers** la pâte collait à mes doigts
(b) *(become jammed)* se coincer; **this drawer keeps sticking** ce tiroir n'arrête pas de se coincer
(c) *(jab, stab)* planter; **he stuck his fork into the meat** il a planté sa fourchette dans la viande
(d) *(put)* mettre; **stick it in your pocket** mets-le dans ta poche
3 stick out
(a) *(protrude)* **your ticket is sticking out of your pocket** ton billet dépasse de ta poche; **her ears stick out** elle a les oreilles décollées; **her teeth stick out** elle a les dents qui avancent
(b) **to stick one's tongue out** tirer la langue; **he stuck his tongue out at me** il m'a tiré la langue
4 stick up *(a sign, a poster)* mettre

sticker *noun* un autocollant

sticky *adjective*
(a) *(hands, fingers)* collant/collante
(b) *(label)* adhésif/adhésive; **sticky tape** le ruban adhésif *or* le scotch®
(c) *(weather, skin)* moite

stiff
1 *adjective*
(a) *(rigid)* rigide, raide; **stiff cardboard** du carton rigide
(b) *(difficult)* dur/dure
(c) *(handle, hinge, drawer)* dur/dure

(d) *(fine, punishment)* sévère
(e) *(strong)* fort/forte; **a stiff drink** une boisson forte
(f) **to be stiff** *(after exercise)* avoir des courbatures; **to have a stiff neck** avoir un torticolis
2 *adverb* **to be bored stiff** s'ennuyer à mourir; **to be scared stiff** être mort/ morte de peur

still
1 *adverb*
(a) *(up to a given point in time)* encore, toujours; **he's still here** il est encore là *or* il est toujours là; **he's still not here** il n'est toujours pas là; **is it still raining?** est-ce qu'il pleut encore? *or* est-ce qu'il pleut toujours?; **I still have £20** il me reste 20 livres *or* j'ai encore 20 livres
(b) *(all the same)* quand même; **it's difficult, but it's still better than my last job** c'est difficile mais c'est quand même mieux que mon dernier emploi; **still, it could have been worse** enfin, ça aurait pu être pire
(c) *(even)* encore; **still more to do** encore plus de choses à faire
2 *adjective*
(a) *(person)* immobile; **stand still!** ne bouge pas!
(b) *(calm)* calme
(c) **still water** de l'eau plate *or* de l'eau non gazeuse

sting
1 *verb* piquer; **the bee might sting you** l'abeille pourrait te piquer; **my eyes are stinging** j'ai les yeux qui piquent
2 *noun* la piqûre

stink *verb* puer; **it stinks in here** ça pue ici

stir *verb* remuer

stitch
1 *noun*
(a) *(in sewing)* le point
(b) *(in knitting)* la maille
(c) *(in a wound)* le point de suture; **she had to have ten stitches** ils ont dû lui

faire dix points de suture
(d) *(pain in the side)* le point de côté
2 *verb*
(a) *(material)* coudre; **she stitched the hem** elle a cousu l'ourlet; **to stitch a button back on** recoudre un bouton
(b) *(a wound)* suturer

stocking *noun* le bas

stomach *noun*
(a) *(organ)* l'estomac *(masculine)*; **to have an upset stomach** avoir l'estomac barbouillé
(b) *(front part of the body)* le ventre; **lie on your stomach** couchez-vous sur le ventre; **to have stomach ache** avoir mal au ventre

stone *noun*
(a) *(material)* la pierre; **the houses are made of stone** les maisons sont en pierre
(b) *(pebble)* le caillou; *(bigger)* la pierre

> The plural of *caillou* is *cailloux*.

(c) *(in a fruit)* le noyau

> The plural of *noyau* is *noyaux*.

(d) *(unit of weight)* **she weighs about eight stone** elle pèse environ cinquante kilos

> Note that people in France do not use stones as a unit of weight, they use kilos (1 stone = 6.348 kilos).

stool *noun* *(seat)* le tabouret

stop
1 *noun* *(stopping place, halt)* un arrêt; **a bus stop** un arrêt de bus; **this is my stop** je descends ici; **a ten-minute stop** dix minutes d'arrêt; **to come to a stop** s'arrêter; **to put a stop to something** mettre fin à quelque chose
2 *verb*
(a) *(cease, cause to halt)* arrêter; **stop shouting** arrête de crier; **stop it!** arrête!; **he managed to stop the car** il a réussi à arrêter la voiture
(b) *(come to a halt, to an end)* s'arrêter; **the train stopped** le train s'est arrêté;

the clock has stopped l'horloge s'est arrêtée; **the rain should stop soon** la pluie devrait bientôt s'arrêter
(**c**) *(prevent)* empêcher; **to stop somebody from doing something** empêcher quelqu'un de faire quelque chose; **I couldn't stop myself** je n'ai pas pu m'en empêcher

stopwatch *noun* le chronomètre

store
1 *noun*
(**a**) *(large shop)* le grand magasin; **a department store** un grand magasin
(**b**) *(supply of food)* la provision
(**c**) *(warehouse)* un entrepôt
2 *verb*
(**a**) *(put in storage)* entreposer
(**b**) *(keep)* conserver; **store in a cool place** à conserver au frais
(**c**) *(on a computer)* stocker

storey *noun* un étage; **a four-storey building** un immeuble de quatre étages

stork *noun* la cigogne

storm *noun*
(**a**) *(with wind, rain, snow)* la tempête
(**b**) *(with thunder)* un orage

stormy *adjective* orageux/orageuse

story *noun* une histoire; **he told the children a story** il a raconté une histoire aux enfants; **a ghost story** une histoire de fantômes; **a fairy story** un conte de fées; **a true story** une histoire vraie

stove *noun* la cuisinière

straight
1 *adjective*
(**a**) *(not curved, level)* droit/droite; **a straight line** une ligne droite; **the picture isn't straight** le tableau n'est pas droit
(**b**) *(not curly)* raide; **she's got straight hair** elle a les cheveux raides
(**c**) *(honest)* honnête
(**d**) *(frank)* franc/franche; **a straight answer** une réponse franche
(**e**) *(in a row)* de suite; **I had three**

straight wins j'ai gagné trois fois de suite
(**f**) **to put things straight** arranger les choses; **to set the record straight** mettre les choses au clair
2 *adverb*
(**a**) *(in a straight line, upright)* droit; **try and walk straight** essaie de marcher droit; **straight ahead** tout droit; **sit up straight!** tiens-toi droit!
(**b**) *(immediately)* tout de suite; **I'll be straight back** je reviens tout de suite; **straight away, straight off** tout de suite

straightaway *adverb* tout de suite

strange *adjective*
(**a**) *(odd)* bizarre, étrange; **she has some strange ideas** elle a des idées bizarres; **it was strange to see her in a dress** ça faisait bizarre de la voir en robe
(**b**) *(not known)* inconnu/inconnue

stranger *noun*
(**a**) *(unknown person)* un inconnu/une inconnue; **don't talk to strangers** ne parle pas aux inconnus
(**b**) *(person from elsewhere)* **I'm a stranger here** je ne suis pas d'ici

strangle *verb* étrangler

strap *noun*
(**a**) *(for a shoulder bag)* la bandoulière
(**b**) *(for a watch)* le bracelet
(**c**) *(for a dress, a bra)* la bretelle
(**d**) *(for a sandal)* la lanière
(**e**) *(for a suitcase, a camera)* la courroie

strategy *noun* la stratégie

straw *noun*
(**a**) *(material)* la paille; **a straw hat** un chapeau de paille; **a straw mat** un paillasson
(**b**) *(for drinking)* la paille; **to drink through a straw** boire avec une paille

strawberry *noun* la fraise; **strawberry jam** la confiture de fraises; **strawberry ice cream** la glace à la fraise

stream *noun* le ruisseau

The plural of *ruisseau* is *ruisseaux*.

street *noun* la rue; **in the street** dans la rue; **a street map** un plan de la ville; **a street sweeper** *(person)* un balayeur/une balayeuse

streetlamp *noun* le lampadaire

strength *noun* la force; **to get one's strength back** reprendre des forces; **to lose strength** s'affaiblir

stress
1 *noun*
(**a**) *(nervous tension)* le stress; **she's under a lot of stress** elle est très stressée
(**b**) *(on a word, a syllable)* un accent
2 *verb (a fact, a detail, qualities)* insister sur; **I would like to stress the following point** j'aimerais insister sur le point suivant

stressed *adjective*
(**a**) *(person)* stressé/stressée
(**b**) *(relationship)* tendu/tendue
(**c**) *(word, syllable)* accentué/accentuée

stressful *adjective* stressant/stressante

stretch
1 *verb*
(**a**) *(a rope, an elastic band)* tendre
(**b**) *(when waking up)* s'étirer
(**c**) **to go and stretch one's legs** aller se dégourdir les jambes
2 **stretch out**
(**a**) *(on a bed, on the grass)* s'allonger
(**b**) **he stretched his legs out** il a allongé les jambes; **I stretched out my hand** j'ai tendu la main

stretcher *noun* le brancard

strict *adjective* strict/stricte

strike
1 *noun*
(**a**) *(industrial)* la grève; **to go on strike** faire grève; **to be on strike** être en grève; **a postal strike** une grève des postes
(**b**) *(military)* une attaque; **an air strike** une attaque aérienne *or* un raid aérien
2 *verb*
(**a**) *(hit)* frapper; **he struck him** il l'a frappé; **he struck him with his fist** il lui a donné un coup de poing
(**b**) *(collide with)* heurter; **the car struck the wall** la voiture a heurté le mur
(**c**) *(a match)* allumer
(**d**) *(impress)* frapper; **it was the first thing that struck me** c'est la première chose qui m'a frappé
(**e**) **to strike a bargain** conclure un marché
(**f**) **the clock struck ten** l'horloge a sonné dix heures

striker *noun*
(**a**) *(person on strike)* le/la gréviste
(**b**) *(in football)* le buteur/la buteuse

striking *adjective (noticeable)* frappant/frappante

string *noun*
(**a**) *(for a parcel)* la ficelle; **a piece of string** un bout de ficelle
(**b**) *(of an apron)* le cordon
(**c**) *(of a guitar, a racket)* la corde

strip
1 *noun*
(**a**) *(of paper)* la bande
(**b**) **a cartoon strip** une bande dessinée
2 *verb (get undressed)* se déshabiller

stripe *noun* la rayure

striped *adjective* rayé/rayée, à rayures

stroke
1 *noun*
(**a**) *(blow)* le coup
(**b**) *(swimming style)* la nage
(**c**) *(caress)* la caresse; **she gave the cat a stroke** elle a caressé le chat
(**d**) *(illness)* **to have a stroke** avoir une attaque
(**e**) **a stroke of luck** un coup de chance
(**f**) **on the stroke of midnight** sur le coup de minuit
2 *verb (caress)* caresser; **she's stroking**

the cat elle caresse le chat; **he stroked my hand** il m'a caressé la main

stroll
1 *verb* se promener
2 *noun* le petit tour; **I'm going for a stroll** je vais faire un petit tour

strong *adjective*
(**a**) *(person, drink, wind)* fort/forte; **he's strong** il est fort *or* il a de la force; **a strong personality** une forte personnalité; **he's got a strong accent** il a un fort accent; **there was a strong smell of gas** il y avait une forte odeur de gaz
(**b**) *(shoes, chair, building)* solide
(**c**) *(colour)* vif/vive
(**d**) *(language, words)* grossier/grossière

struggle
1 *noun* la lutte
2 *verb*
(**a**) *(fight)* se battre; **he struggled with him** il s'est battu avec lui; **the child struggled to get free** l'enfant se débattait
(**b**) *(have trouble)* **to struggle to do something** avoir du mal à faire quelque chose; **I struggled to open the door** j'ai eu du mal à ouvrir la porte

stubborn *adjective (person)* têtu/têtue

stuck *adjective*
(**a**) *(unable to move)* coincé/coincée; **the door's stuck** la porte est coincée; **he got his head stuck** sa tête est restée coincée
(**b**) *(unable to leave)* bloqué/bloquée; **we got stuck in traffic** nous étions bloqués dans les embouteillages; **I was stuck at the airport for six hours** j'ai été bloqué à l'aéroport pendant six heures
(**c**) *(unable to answer)* **I got stuck on the last question** j'ai séché sur la dernière question

student *noun*
(**a**) *(at school)* un/une élève
(**b**) *(at university)* un étudiant/une étudiante

studio *noun*
(**a**) *(of an artist)* un atelier
(**b**) **a television studio** un studio de télévision
(**c**) **a studio flat** un studio

study
1 *verb*
(**a**) *(at university)* faire des études; **she's studying medicine** elle fait des études de médecine; **she's studying to be an architect** elle fait des études d'architecture
(**b**) *(a lesson, a subject)* étudier; **I can't study with that music on!** je n'arrive pas à étudier avec cette musique!; **to study for an exam** réviser pour un examen
2 *noun*
(**a**) *(room)* le bureau
(**b**) *(research)* une étude
3 *plural noun* **studies** les études *(feminine plural)*; **how are your studies going?** comment vont tes études?

stuff
1 *noun*
(**a**) *(thing)* le truc, les trucs; **what's that stuff?** c'est quoi ce truc?; **there's all kinds of stuff in this drawer** il y a des tas de trucs dans ce tiroir
(**b**) *(belongings)* les affaires *(feminine plural)*; **clear your stuff off the table** enlève tes affaires de la table
2 *verb*
(**a**) *(fill)* bourrer; **his pockets are stuffed with sweets** ses poches sont bourrées de bonbons
(**b**) *(shove)* fourrer; **just stuff everything under the bed** tu n'as qu'à tout fourrer sous le lit
(**c**) *(eat)* **to stuff oneself** s'empiffrer; **the children are stuffing themselves with cake** les enfants s'empiffrent de gâteau

stuffed *adjective*
(**a**) *(tomatoes, turkey)* farci/farcie
(**b**) *(chair, cushion)* rembourré/rembourrée
(**c**) *(animal)* empaillé/empaillée

stunt *noun (in a film)* la cascade; **a stunt man** un cascadeur; **a stunt woman** une cascadeuse

stupid *adjective* bête; **stop saying stupid things** arrête de dire des bêtises; **I've done something stupid** j'ai fait une bêtise

stutter
1 *noun* le bégaiement; **he has a stutter** il bégaie
2 *verb* bégayer

style *noun*
(a) *(manner, design)* le style; **the house is decorated in a modern style** l'intérieur de la maison est moderne; **I don't like this writer's style** je n'aime pas le style de cet écrivain
(b) *(fashion)* la mode; **she's dressed in the latest style** elle est habillée à la dernière mode
(c) *(elegance)* la classe; **she has great style** elle a beaucoup de classe

stylish *adjective* chic

> Note that the adjective *chic* does not change in the plural or in the feminine: *des vêtements chic.*

subject *noun*
(a) *(of a conversation, a book, a sentence)* le sujet; **let's change the subject** parlons d'autre chose; **what's the subject of your essay?** quel est le sujet de ta dissertation?
(b) *(at school)* la matière; **what's your favourite subject?** quelle est ta matière préférée?

submarine *noun* le sous-marin

> The plural of *sous-marin* is *sous-marins.*

subscription *noun* un abonnement; **I took out a subscription to a science magazine** je me suis abonné à un magazine scientifique

subtitle *noun* le sous-titre

> The plural of *sous-titre* is *sous-titres.*

subtle *adjective* subtil/subtile

subtract *verb* ôter, retrancher; **subtract 52 from 110** ôtez 52 de 110 *or* retranchez 52 de 110

suburb *noun* la banlieue; **the London suburbs** la banlieue de Londres; **I live in the suburbs** j'habite en banlieue

subway *noun (underpass)* le passage souterrain

succeed *verb* réussir

success *noun* le succès, la réussite; **his success in the exam** son succès à l'examen; **this film is a success** ce film a du succès; **the party was a success** la fête était réussie

successful *adjective*
(a) *(attempt, evening)* réussi/réussie; **I was successful in convincing them** j'ai réussi à les convaincre
(b) *(writer, singer)* à succès; **this book was very successful** ce livre a eu un succès fou
(c) *(company)* qui marche bien; **he runs a successful restaurant** il a un restaurant qui marche bien
(d) *(businessperson)* qui a réussi; **he's a successful lawyer** c'est un avocat qui a réussi

such
1 *adjective*
(a) *(of the same kind)* tel/telle, pareil/pareille; **such a question** une telle question *or* une question pareille; **how could you say such a thing?** comment est-ce que tu as pu dire une chose pareille?; **I did no such thing!** je n'ai rien fait de tel!; **there's no such thing as aliens** les extraterrestres n'existent pas
(b) **such as** tel/telle que; **countries such as Spain or Portugal** des pays tels que l'Espagne ou le Portugal; **such as?** comme quoi par exemple?
(c) *(so much)* **he is such a liar** il est tellement menteur; **such noise** tellement de bruit *or* tant de bruit
2 *adverb*
(a) *(so very)* si, tellement; **we had such a good time** on s'est tellement bien

amusés; **he's such a nice man** c'est un homme si gentil; **she has such a nice voice** elle a une si jolie voix; **it was such a long time ago** ça fait tellement longtemps; **such a lot of books** tellement de livres *or* tant de livres
(**b**) *(in comparisons)* aussi; **I've never seen such a beautiful house as this** je n'ai jamais vu une maison aussi belle que celle-ci

suck *verb*
(**a**) *(one's thumb, a lollipop)* sucer
(**b**) *(dust)* aspirer; **the dust is sucked into the bag** la poussière est aspirée dans le sac

sudden *adjective*
(**a**) *(pain, change)* soudain/soudaine; **this is all very sudden!** c'est plutôt inattendu!
(**b**) *(movement)* brusque
(**c**) **sudden death** la mort subite
(**d**) **all of a sudden** tout à coup

suddenly *adverb*
(**a**) tout à coup; **suddenly, it started to rain** tout à coup il s'est mis à pleuvoir
(**b**) *(stop, brake)* brusquement
(**c**) *(die)* subitement

suede *noun* le daim; **a suede jacket** une veste en daim

suffer *verb*
(**a**) souffrir; **she suffered a lot** elle a beaucoup souffert
(**b**) **she's suffering from a cold** elle a un rhume; **he suffers from diabetes** il est diabétique

sugar *noun* le sucre; **a sugar lump** un morceau de sucre; **a sugar bowl** un sucrier

suggest *verb* suggérer; **I suggest we go and see him** je suggère qu'on aille le voir

> The expression *suggérer que* is always followed by the subjunctive.

suggestion *noun* la suggestion; **to make a suggestion** suggérer quelque chose

suicide *noun* le suicide; **to commit suicide** se suicider

suit
1 *noun*
(**a**) *(for men)* le costume
(**b**) *(for women)* le tailleur
(**c**) *(for a particular activity)* la combinaison
2 *verb*
(**a**) *(of clothes, colour)* aller à; **that jacket suits you** cette veste te va bien
(**b**) *(of date, time, job, food)* convenir à; **if that suits you** si ça vous convient; **Tuesday suits me best** c'est mardi qui me convient le mieux

suitable *adjective* *(appropriate)* approprié/appopriée, convenable; **a suitable gift** un cadeau approprié; **it's not suitable for children** ça ne convient pas aux enfants

suitcase *noun* la valise

sum
1 *noun*
(**a**) *(amount of money, total)* la somme; **a large sum of money** une importante somme d'argent
(**b**) *(calculation)* le calcul; **I'm bad at sums** je suis nul en calcul
2 *verb* **sum up** résumer

summary *noun* le résumé

summer *noun* l'été *(masculine)*; **in the summer** en été; **a summer's day** un jour d'été

summertime *noun* l'été *(masculine)*; **in the summertime** en été

sun *noun* le soleil; **the sun is shining** le soleil brille *or* il y a du soleil; **the sun is rising** le soleil se lève; **the sun is setting** le soleil se couche; **in the sun** au soleil; **sun cream** la crème solaire

sunbathe *verb* se faire bronzer; **I was sunbathing in the garden** je me faisais bronzer dans le jardin

sunblock *noun* l'écran total *(masculine)*

sunburn *noun* le coup de soleil

sunburnt *adjective* **I got sunburnt** j'ai attrapé un coup de soleil

Sunday *noun* le dimanche; **on Sunday** dimanche; **he came on Sunday** il est venu dimanche; **on Sundays** le dimanche; **she plays tennis on Sundays** elle joue au tennis le dimanche; **every Sunday** tous les dimanches; **next Sunday** dimanche prochain; **last Sunday** dimanche dernier

> In French, the names of days are not written with a capital.

sunflower *noun* le tournesol; **sunflower oil** l'huile de tournesol

sunglasses *plural noun* les lunettes de soleil *(feminine plural)*

sunlight *noun* le soleil; **in the sunlight** au soleil

sunny *adjective (day, place)* ensoleillé/ensoleillée; **a sunny day** une journée ensoleillée; **it's sunny** il y a du soleil

sunrise *noun* le lever du soleil

sunset *noun* le coucher du soleil

sunshine *noun* le soleil; **in the sunshine** au soleil

suntan *noun* le bronzage; **to have a suntan** être bronzé/bronzée; **to get a suntan** bronzer; **suntan lotion** le lait solaire

suntanned *adjective* bronzé/bronzée

superior *adjective* supérieur/supérieure; **superior to** supérieur à

supermarket *noun* le supermarché

supernatural *adjective* surnaturel/surnaturelle

superstitious *adjective* superstitieux/superstitieuse

supper *noun*
(**a**) *(evening meal)* le dîner; **what's for supper?** qu'est-ce qu'on mange ce soir?; **I had steak for supper** j'ai mangé du steak au dîner; **supper time** l'heure du dîner

(**b**) *(late at night)* le souper

supply
1 *noun*
(**a**) *(stock)* la provision; **water is in short supply** on manque d'eau; **office supplies** les fournitures de bureau
(**b**) *(act of supplying)* l'approvisionnement *(masculine)*; **supply and demand** l'offre et la demande
2 *adjective* **a supply teacher** un remplaçant/une remplaçante
3 *verb* fournir; **they supply bread to all the local shops** ils fournissent le pain à tous les magasins du coin

> Note that the French verb *supplier* is never a translation for the English word *to supply*. It means *to beg*.

support
1 *noun* *(backing, help)* le soutien
2 *verb*
(**a**) *(help)* soutenir; **she supports the Labour Party** elle soutient le parti travailliste
(**b**) *(financially)* subvenir aux besoins de; **he has three children to support** il doit subvenir aux besoins de trois enfants
(**c**) *(a team)* être un supporter/une supportrice de; **I support Liverpool** je suis un supporter de Liverpool

> Note that that the French verb *supporter* is not a translation for the English verb *to support*. Its most common meaning is *to bear*.

supporter *noun*
(**a**) *(of a team)* le supporter/la supportrice
(**b**) *(of a cause, a party)* le sympathisant/la sympathisante

suppose *verb*
(**a**) *(assume)* supposer; **I suppose so** je suppose que oui; **suppose he comes back** supposons qu'il revienne
(**b**) *(think)* penser; **do you suppose he'll do it?** est-ce que tu penses qu'il va le faire?
(**c**) *(making a suggestion)* **suppose we**

go? et si nous partions?

supposed *adjective*
(a) *(meant)* **to be supposed to do something** être censé/censée faire quelque chose; **she's supposed to be in London** elle est censée être à Londres
(b) *(reputed)* **the film is supposed to be good** il paraît que c'est un bon film

sure *adjective*
(a) sûr/sûre; **I'm sure of it** j'en suis sûr; **I don't know for sure** je n'en suis pas absolument sûr; **she's sure of herself** elle est sûre d'elle; **that's for sure** ça, c'est sûr; **they're sure to get caught** ils vont sûrement se faire prendre
(b) **be sure to phone him** n'oublie pas de l'appeler
(c) **to make sure** s'assurer; **make sure you don't leave anything on the train** assure-toi de rien laisser dans le train

surf *verb*
(a) *(in the sea)* faire du surf; **he goes surfing every weekend** il fait du surf tous les week-ends
(b) **to surf the Net** naviguer sur Internet

surface
1 *noun* la surface
2 *verb* *(of a submarine, a diver)* remonter à la surface

surfboard *noun* la planche de surf

surfer *noun*
(a) *(in the sea)* le surfeur/la surfeuse
(b) *(on the Internet)* un/une internaute

surgeon *noun* le chirurgien/la chirurgienne; **he's a surgeon** il est chirurgien

surgery *noun*
(a) *(field of medicine)* la chirurgie; **cosmetic surgery** la chirurgie esthétique
(b) *(surgical treatment)* une intervention chirurgicale; **he's going to have surgery** il va se faire opérer
(c) *(place)* le cabinet médical

surname *noun* le nom de famille

Note that the French word *surnom* is never a translation for the English word *surname*. It means *nickname*.

surprise
1 *noun* la surprise; **what a surprise!** quelle surprise!; **to take somebody by surprise** prendre quelqu'un par surprise
2 *verb* surprendre; **it surprises me that she didn't get a good mark** ça me surprend qu'elle n'ait pas eu une bonne note

suprised *adjective* surpris/surprise; **I was really surprised** j'ai été très surpris; **I'm not surprised** ça ne me m'étonne pas

surprising *adjective* surprenant/surprenante; **it's not at all surprising** cela n'a rien de surprenant

surrender *verb* se rendre; **he surrendered to the police** il s'est rendu à la police

surround *verb*
(a) entourer; **the garden is surrounded by a wall** le jardin est entouré d'un mur
(b) *(of the police, the enemy)* cerner; **they were surrounded by the police** ils étaient cernés par la police

surroundings *plural noun*
(a) *(environment)* le milieu; **the animal is in its natural surroundings** l'animal est dans son milieu naturel

The plural of *milieu* is *milieux*.

(b) *(setting)* le cadre; **the house is set in beautiful surroundings** la maison est située dans un cadre magnifique
(c) *(of a town)* les environs *(masculine plural)*

survive *verb* survivre; **nobody thought she'd survive** personne ne pensait qu'elle survivrait; **he survived the accident** il a survécu à l'accident

suspect
1 *noun* le suspect/la suspecte

2 *verb* soupçonner; **the police suspect him of murder** la police le soupçonne de meurtre

suspicion *noun* le soupçon; **to be under suspicion** être soupçonné/soupçonnée

suspicious *adjective*
(**a**) *(person)* méfiant/méfiante
(**b**) *(object, death)* suspect/suspecte

swallow *verb* avaler

swamp
1 *noun* le marais
2 *verb* **she was swamped with calls** elle a été submergée d'appels; **I'm swamped with work** je suis débordé de travail

swan *noun* le cygne

swap
1 *noun* **to do a swap** faire un échange
2 *verb* échanger; **I'll swap you this CD for that one** je t'échange ce CD contre celui-là; **to swap places with somebody** changer de place avec quelqu'un

swarm *noun* *(of bees)* un essaim

swear *verb*
(**a**) *(promise)* jurer; **he swore that it was true** il a juré que c'était vrai; **it wasn't me, I swear!** ce n'était pas moi, je le jure!
(**b**) *(curse)* dire des gros mots; **don't swear!** ne dis pas de gros mots!; **to swear at somebody** injurier quelqu'un

swearword *noun* le gros mot

sweat
1 *noun* la transpiration, la sueur
2 *verb* transpirer; **he's sweating** il transpire *or* il est en sueur

sweater *noun* le pull

sweatshirt *noun* le sweat-shirt

> The plural of the French *sweat-shirt* is *sweat-shirts*.

sweaty *adjective*
(**a**) *(person)* en sueur
(**b**) *(hands)* moite

Swede *noun* le Suédois/la Suédoise

swede *noun* *(vegetable)* le navet

Sweden *noun* la Suède; **I've never been to Sweden** je ne suis jamais allé en Suède; **she lives in Sweden** elle habite en Suède; **he comes from Sweden** il est suédois

Swedish
1 *adjective* suédois/suédoise
2 *noun*
(**a**) *(language)* le suédois; **he speaks Swedish** il parle suédois
(**b**) *(people)* **the Swedish** les Suédois *(masculine plural)*

> In French, only the noun for the inhabitants of a country takes a capital letter, never the adjective or the noun for the language.

sweep *verb*
(**a**) *(the floor, a room, a street)* balayer
(**b**) *(a chimney)* ramoner

sweet
1 *adjective*
(**a**) *(sugary)* sucré/sucrée; **I don't have a sweet tooth** je n'aime pas trop tout ce qui est sucré
(**b**) *(kind)* gentil/gentille; **it was very sweet of you** c'était très gentil de votre part
(**c**) *(cute)* mignon/mignonne, adorable; **what a sweet little baby!** quel adorable bébé!
(**d**) *(wine, honey, air, voice)* doux/douce
(**e**) *(smell)* agréable
2 *noun*
(**a**) *(confectionery)* le bonbon; **a sweet shop** une confiserie
(**b**) *(dessert)* le dessert

sweetcorn *noun* le maïs

swell, swell up *verb* enfler; **his leg swelled up** sa jambe a enflé

swim
1 *noun* **to go for a swim** aller se baigner
2 *verb* nager; **I can't swim** je ne sais pas nager; **he swam across the river**

il a traversé la rivière à la nage; **to go swimming** *(for fun)* aller se baigner; *(for sport)* faire de la natation; **I went swimming in the lake** je suis allé me baigner dans le lac

swimmer *noun* le nageur/la nageuse; **he's a very good swimmer** il nage très bien

swimming *noun* la natation; **a swimming lesson** un cours de natation; **a swimming pool** une piscine; **a swimming cap** un bonnet de bain; **a swimming costume** un maillot de bain; **swimming trunks** un slip de bain

swimsuit *noun* le maillot de bain

swing
1 *noun (for children)* la balançoire
2 *verb*
(a) balancer; **he was swinging his arms** il balançait les bras
(b) se balancer; **the monkey swang from branch to branch** le singe se balançait d'une branche à une autre

Swiss
1 *adjective* suisse
2 *noun (people)* **the Swiss** les Suisses *(masculine plural)*

> In French, only the noun for the inhabitants of a country takes a capital letter, never the adjective.

switch
1 *noun*
(a) *(for a light)* un interrupteur
(b) *(for a television)* le bouton
(c) *(change)* le changement; **the switch to the euro** le passage à l'euro
2 *verb (change)* changer de; **I'd like to switch to another subject** j'aimerais changer de sujet; **to switch channels** changer de chaîne; **she switched**

places with me elle a changé de place avec moi
3 **switch off** éteindre; **switch the TV off** éteins la télé
4 **switch on**
(a) *(the light, the heating, a kettle)* allumer
(b) *(the engine, a vacuum cleaner)* mettre en marche; **she switched on the washing machine** elle a mis en marche la machine à laver
5 **switch over** *(change TV channels)* changer de chaîne

Switzerland *noun* la Suisse; **I've never been to Switzerland** je ne suis jamais allé en Suisse; **she lives in Switzerland** elle habite en Suisse; **it comes from Switzerland** ça vient de Suisse

swollen *adjective* enflé/enflée

sword *noun* une épée

syllable *noun* la syllabe

syllabus *noun* le programme; **on the syllabus** au programme

symbol *noun* le symbole

sympathetic *adjective* compatissant/compatissante

> Note that the French word *sympathique* is not a translation for the English word *sympathetic*. It means *nice*.

synagogue *noun* la synagogue

syrup *noun* le sirop; **strawberry syrup** le sirop de fraise; **cough syrup** le sirop contre la toux

system *noun* le système; **the educational system** le système éducatif

Tt

table *noun*
(**a**) *(furniture)* la table; **to lay the table** mettre la table *or* mettre le couvert; **to clear the table** débarrasser la table
(**b**) *(of facts, figures)* le tableau, la table; **a table of contents** une table des matières

> The plural of *tableau* is *tableaux*.

(**c**) **table tennis** le ping-pong; **to play table tennis** jouer au ping-pong

tablecloth *noun* la nappe

tablespoon *noun* la cuillère à soupe; **two tablespoons of sugar** deux cuillères à soupe de sucre

tablet *noun* *(pill)* le comprimé

tag *noun* *(label)* une étiquette

tail *noun* *(of an animal)* la queue

tailor *noun* le tailleur; **he's a tailor** il est tailleur

take
1 *verb*
(**a**) *(get hold of)* prendre; **I took the book that was on the table** j'ai pris le livre qui était sur la table; **she took me by the arm** elle m'a pris par le bras
(**b**) *(lead)* emmener; **her father takes her to school** son père l'emmène à l'école; **he took me to see a film** il m'a emmené voir un film; **he took me home** il m'a raccompagné; **he took the dog for a walk** il est allé promener le chien
(**c**) *(carry along)* emporter; **he took his binoculars with him** il a emporté ses jumelles
(**d**) *(give)* apporter; **she took her mum a cup of tea** elle a apporté une tasse de thé à sa mère
(**e**) *(go by)* prendre; **I take the bus to school** je prends le bus pour aller à l'école
(**f**) *(require)* **how long does it take?** ça prend combien de temps?; **I took an hour to do it** j'ai mis une heure à le faire; **it takes time to learn a language** il faut du temps pour apprendre une langue; **it takes courage to do it** il faut du courage pour le faire
(**g**) *(bear)* supporter; **my parents can't take the heat** mes parents ne supportent pas la chaleur; **I can't take it any more** je n'en peux plus
(**h**) *(react to)* **he took it very badly** il l'a très mal pris
(**i**) *(with sizes)* faire; **what size do you take?** *(for clothes)* quelle taille faites-vous?; *(for shoes)* vous chaussez du combien?; **I take a size 8** *(in clothes)* je fais du 36; **I take a size 5** *(in shoes)* je chausse du 38
(**j**) *(other phrases)* **to take an exam** passer un examen; **to take a shower** prendre une douche; **to take a photo** prendre une photo; **to take a look at something** jeter un coup d'œil à quelque chose; **to take an interest in something** s'intéresser à quelque chose
(**k**) **to take place** avoir lieu; **the meeting is taking place in the staffroom** la réunion a lieu dans la salle des professeurs
2 take apart démonter
3 take away
(**a**) *(an object)* emporter; **sandwiches to take away** sandwichs à emporter
(**b**) *(a person)* emmener
(**c**) *(remove)* enlever; **take that knife**

away from him enlève-lui ce couteau
(**d**) *(subtract)* ôter, retrancher; **take
away four from nine and you get
five** ôtez quatre de neuf et vous obte-
nez cinq

4 take back
(**a**) *(get back)* reprendre; **she took
back the present she had given him**
elle a repris le cadeau qu'elle lui avait
offert
(**b**) *(return to a shop, a person)* rapporter; **I took it back to the shop** je l'ai
rapporté au magasin
(**c**) *(withdraw)* retirer; **I take back
everything I said** je retire tout ce que
j'ai dit

5 take down
(**a**) *(write down)* noter; **I took down
the number** j'ai noté le numéro; **to
take down notes** prendre des notes
(**b**) *(carry down)* descendre; **I forgot
to take the rubbish down** j'ai oublié
de descendre les poubelles
(**c**) *(from a shelf)* prendre
(**d**) *(a poster)* enlever
(**e**) *(a painting, a curtain)* décrocher
(**f**) *(a tent, scaffolding)* démonter
(**g**) *(a wall)* démolir
(**h**) *(trousers)* baisser; **he took his
trousers down** il a baissé son pantalon

6 take off
(**a**) *(remove)* enlever; **take your shoes
off** enlève tes chaussures; **to take
one's clothes off** se déshabiller
(**b**) *(of a plane)* décoller
(**c**) *(lead away)* emmener

7 take out
(**a**) *(from a box, one's pocket)* sortir
(**b**) *(money)* retirer
(**c**) *(a tooth)* arracher
(**d**) *(a stain)* enlever
(**e**) *(a subscription, insurance)* prendre
(**f**) *(a person, an animal)* **he took her
out to the cinema** il l'a emmenée au
cinéma; **I took the dog out** je suis allé
promener le chien

8 take over *(a job, a business)* reprendre

9 take up

(**a**) *(carry up)* monter; **can you take
these boxes up to the attic?** est-ce
que tu peux monter ces cartons au grenier?
(**b**) *(pick up)* prendre
(**c**) *(a hobby)* se mettre à; **he's taken up
badminton** il s'est mis au badminton
(**d**) *(room, space)* prendre; **this table
takes up too much room** cette table
prend trop de place

takeaway *noun*
(**a**) *(food)* le plat à emporter; **we're
having a Chinese takeaway for dinner** on va commander un repas chinois à emporter pour le dîner
(**b**) *(restaurant)* un restaurant qui fait
des plats à emporter

take-off *noun (of a plane)* le décollage

tale *noun*
(**a**) *(story)* une histoire; **to tell a tale**
raconter une histoire
(**b**) *(legend)* le conte; **a fairy tale** un
conte de fées
(**c**) **to tell tales** *(tell on somebody)* rapporter; **she's been telling tales to the
teacher again** elle est encore allée
rapporter à la maîtresse

talent *noun* le talent; **she has great
musical talent** elle est très douée pour
la musique

talented *adjective* doué/douée

talk
1 *noun*
(**a**) *(conversation)* la conversation; **I'll
have a talk with him about it** je lui
en parlerai
(**b**) *(speech, lecture)* un exposé; **to give
a talk on something** faire un exposé
sur quelque chose
(**c**) *(gossip)* **there is talk of him resigning** le bruit court qu'il va démissionner
2 *verb* parler; **we talked about her
problems** nous avons parlé de ses problèmes; **I'll talk to my mother** j'en parlerai à ma mère; **they're talking in
Spanish** ils parlent en espagnol; **he's
talking to himself** il parle tout seul;

you're talking nonsense! tu dis n'importe quoi!

talkative *adjective* bavard/bavarde

tall *adjective*
(a) *(person)* grand/grande; **how tall are you?** combien est-ce que tu mesures?; **I'm five feet tall** je mesure un mètre cinquante
(b) *(building, object)* haut/haute; **how tall is that tree?** quelle est la hauteur de cet arbre?; **it's at least thirty feet tall** il fait au moins neuf mètres de haut

tame
1 *adjective (animal)* apprivoisé/apprivoisée
2 *verb (a small animal)* apprivoiser; *(a lion, a tiger)* dompter

tampon *noun* le tampon

tan *noun* le bronzage; **to have a tan** être bronzé/bronzée; **to get a tan** se faire bronzer

tangerine *noun* la mandarine

tank *noun*
(a) *(for a liquid, petrol)* le réservoir
(b) *(for fish)* un aquarium
(c) *(army vehicle)* le tank, le char

tap
1 *noun*
(a) *(for water)* le robinet; **tap water** l'eau du robinet
(b) *(light knock)* la petite tape
(c) *(dancing)* les claquettes *(feminine plural)*; **she does tap dancing** elle fait des claquettes
2 *verb (strike)* taper légèrement

tape
1 *noun*
(a) *(for music)* la cassette; **a tape recorder** un magnétophone
(b) *(for films)* la cassette vidéo

> The plural of *cassette vidéo* is *cassettes vidéo*.

(c) *(sticky tape)* le ruban adhésif, le scotch®
(d) **a tape measure** un mètre

2 *verb*
(a) *(a film, a song)* enregistrer
(b) *(with sticky tape)* scotcher

target *noun* la cible

tart *noun* la tarte; **an apple tart** une tarte aux pommes

task *noun* la tâche

taste
1 *noun*
(a) *(sense, flavour, liking)* le goût
(b) *(sample)* **can I have a taste of the chocolate cake?** est-ce que je peux goûter le gâteau au chocolat?
2 *verb* **to taste something** goûter quelque chose; **do you want to taste?** tu veux goûter?; **it tastes like fish** ça a le goût de poisson; **it tastes funny** ça a un drôle de goût

tasty *adjective* délicieux/délicieuse

tattoo *noun* le tatouage; **to get a tattoo** se faire tatouer

Taurus *noun* le Taureau; **he's (a) Taurus** il est Taureau

tax *noun*
(a) *(on income)* un impôt
(b) *(on goods)* la taxe

taxi *noun* le taxi

tea *noun*
(a) *(drink)* le thé; **a cup of tea** une tasse de thé
(b) *(afternoon snack)* le goûter
(c) *(evening meal)* le dîner
(d) **a tea towel** un torchon

teabag *noun* le sachet de thé

teach *verb*
(a) *(a person)* apprendre; **he taught me to play the piano** il m'a appris à jouer du piano
(b) *(a school subject)* enseigner; **she teaches French** elle enseigne le français

teacher *noun*
(a) *(at primary school)* un instituteur/une institutrice; **she's a teacher** elle est institutrice
(b) *(at secondary school)* le professeur;

she's a French teacher elle est professeur de français

Note that the word *professeur* is always masculine (*le professeur*) but it can also refer to a woman (*elle est professeur*). In informal language, *professeur* is often shortened to *prof*, which can be either masculine or feminine (*le prof* or *la prof*).

team *noun* une équipe; **a football team** une équipe de foot

teapot *noun* la théière

tear¹
1 *noun* (*rip*) la déchirure
2 *verb* (*clothes, a page*) déchirer; **I tore my trousers** j'ai déchiré mon pantalon
3 tear out (*a page*) arracher
4 tear up (*a letter*) déchirer

tear² *noun* (*in the eye*) la larme; **she's in tears** elle est en larmes; **she burst into tears** elle a fondu en larmes

tease *verb* taquiner; **she's always teasing her brother** elle est toujours en train de taquiner son frère; **I'm only teasing** c'est pour rire

teaspoon *noun* la petite cuillère, la cuillère à café; **two teaspoons of sugar** deux cuillères à café de sucre

technical *adjective* technique; **technical drawing** le dessin industriel

technique *noun* la technique

technology *noun* la technologie

teddy bear *noun* un ours en peluche

teenage *adjective*
(**a**) (*boy, girl*) adolescent/adolescente; **during my teenage years** pendant mon adolescence
(**b**) (*fashion, magazine*) pour les jeunes

teenager *noun* un adolescent/une adolescente

teens *plural noun* l'adolescence (*feminine*); **she's in her teens** c'est une adolescente

telephone *noun* le téléphone; **a tele-**

phone box une cabine téléphonique; **a telephone call** un coup de téléphone; **a telephone number** un numéro de téléphone

telescope *noun* le télescope

television *noun* la télévision; **to watch television** regarder la télévision; **on television** à la télévision; **a television programme** une émission de télévision

tell
1 *verb*
(**a**) (*say to*) dire à; **I told my friends what I thought** j'ai dit à mes amis ce que je pensais; **she told me to tidy my room** elle m'a dit de ranger ma chambre
(**b**) **to tell somebody about something** parler à quelqu'un de quelque chose; **I told him about my plans** je lui ai parlé de mes projets
(**c**) (*a story, a joke*) raconter
(**d**) (*the truth, a lie, a secret*) dire
(**e**) (*distinguish*) distinguer; **how can you tell one from the other?** comment les distinguez-vous l'un de l'autre?
(**f**) (*see*) voir; **you can tell he's disappointed** on voit bien qu'il est déçu
2 tell off **to tell somebody off** gronder quelqu'un; **I got told off** je me suis fait gronder

telly *noun* la télé; **to watch telly** regarder la télé; **on telly** à la télé

temper *noun* **to keep one's temper** rester calme; **to lose one's temper** se mettre en colère; **to be in a bad temper** être de mauvaise humeur

temperature *noun* la température; **I had a temperature** j'avais de la température

temple *noun*
(**a**) (*church*) le temple
(**b**) (*side of the head*) la tempe

temporary *adjective*
(**a**) (*accommodation, solution*) provisoire

(**b**) *(job)* temporaire

tempt *verb* tenter; **I'm tempted to accept** je suis tenté d'accepter

tempting *adjective* tentant/tentante

ten *number* dix

> *Dix* is pronounced "di" in front of a consonant, "diz" in front of a vowel or a mute h and "dis" on its own.

tennis *noun* le tennis; **I played tennis yesterday** j'ai joué au tennis hier

tense
1 *adjective (person, situation)* tendu/tendue
2 *noun (in grammar)* le temps; **in the present tense** au présent

tent *noun* la tente

tenth *number* dixième; **three tenths** *(fraction)* trois dixièmes; **the tenth film** le dixième film; **the tenth car** la dixième voiture; **the tenth of June** le dix juin

term *noun (part of the school year)* le trimestre

terrace *noun (patio)* la terrasse

terraced house *noun* **I live in a terraced house** j'habite dans une rue où toutes les maisons se touchent

terrible *adjective*
(**a**) *(accident, shock)* terrible
(**b**) *(weather, dream, conditions)* affreux/affreuse, épouvantable
(**c**) *(at doing something)* nul/nulle; **I'm terrible at French** je suis nul en français
(**d**) **to feel terrible about something** *(guilty)* s'en vouloir au sujet de quelque chose; **I feel terrible about what I said to him** je m'en veux de ce que je lui ai dit

terrific *adjective*
(**a**) *(excellent)* génial/géniale; **it's a terrific film** c'est un film génial

> The masculine plural of *génial* is *géniaux*.

(**b**) *(huge, intense)* **terrific heat** une

chaleur terrible; **a terrific noise** un bruit épouvantable

terrified *adjective* terrifié/terrifiée; **I'm terrified of spiders** j'ai très peur des araignées

terrify *verb* terrifier

terrifying *adjective* terrifiant/terrifiante

terrorism *noun* le terrorisme

terrorist *noun* le/la terroriste; **a terrorist attack** un attentat terroriste

test
1 *noun*
(**a**) *(in school)* un contrôle, une interrogation; **a written test** une interrogation écrite; **a French test** un contrôle de français
(**b**) *(scientific, technical)* le test; **to carry out tests** faire des tests; **a test tube** une éprouvette; **a nuclear test** un essai nucléaire
(**c**) *(medical)* un examen; **they're running tests on her** ils lui font passer des examens
(**d**) **a blood test** une analyse de sang
(**e**) **I passed my driving test** j'ai eu mon permis de conduire
2 *verb*
(**a**) *(try out)* essayer
(**b**) *(a pupil)* interroger
(**c**) *(a machine, a vaccine)* tester
(**d**) *(sight, hearing)* examiner; **I'm getting my eyes tested** je vais me faire examiner la vue
(**e**) *(blood, water)* analyser

text
1 *noun*
(**a**) *(document)* le texte
(**b**) *(text message)* le texto
2 *verb* **to text somebody** envoyer un texto à quelqu'un; **text me tonight** envoie-moi un texto ce soir

textbook *noun* le manuel; **a history textbook** un manuel d'histoire

Thames *noun* **the Thames** la Tamise

than *conjunction*
(**a**) que; **he plays tennis better than I**

do il joue mieux au tennis que moi
(b) *(with numbers)* de; **more than ten people** plus de dix personnes; **more than once** plus d'une fois

thank *verb*
(a) remercier; **I thanked him for the present** je l'ai remercié pour le cadeau; **she thanked us for coming** elle nous a remerciés d'être venus
(b) **thank you!** merci!; **thank you very much!** merci beaucoup!; **thank you for your help** merci pour ton aide; **thank you for coming** merci d'être venu; **no, thank you!** non, merci!

thanks
1 *exclamation* merci; **thanks a lot!** merci beaucoup!; **thanks for your postcard** merci pour ta carte
2 *plural noun*
(a) les remerciements *(masculine plural)*; **give her my thanks** remercie-la pour moi
(b) **thanks to** grâce à; **thanks to you, I saved money** grâce à toi, j'ai économisé de l'argent

that
1 *conjunction* que; **I hope that she will come** j'espère qu'elle viendra

> *Que* becomes *qu'* before a vowel or mute h.

2 *adjective*
(a) ce/cette; **that book** ce livre; **that question** cette question

> *Ce* is used with masculine nouns and *cette* is used with feminine nouns. *Ce* becomes *cet* in front of a vowel or a mute h, eg *cet appareil*, *cet homme*.

(b) *(opposed to "this")* ce...-là/cette...-là; **I prefer that film** je préfère ce film-là; **take that cup** prends cette tasse-là
(c) **that one** celui-là/celle-là; **I don't want this book, I want that one** je ne veux pas ce livre, je veux celui-là
3 *pronoun*
(a) ça, cela; **I don't like that** je n'aime pas ça

> *Cela* is more formal and less common than *ça*.

(b) *(when "that" is the subject of the sentence)* ce; **that's strange** c'est bizarre; **that's what she told me** c'est ce qu'elle m'a dit; **who's that?** qui est-ce?; **what's that?** qu'est-ce que c'est?

> *Ce* becomes *c'* in front of *e* and *é*, eg *c'est amusant*.

4 *relative pronoun*
(a) *(when "that" is the subject of the verb)* qui; **the letter that came yesterday** la lettre qui est arrivée hier
(b) *(when "that" is the object of the verb)* que; **the woman that I saw** la femme que j'ai vue
(c) *(with a preposition)* lequel/laquelle; **the box that I put it in** le carton dans lequel je l'ai mis; **the girl that he's talking to** la fille avec laquelle il parle; **the film that we're talking about** le film dont nous parlons; **the songs that I was thinking of** les chansons auxquelles je pensais; **the building that I walked past** le bâtiment à côté duquel je suis passé

> The plural of *lequel* is *lesquels* and the plural of *laquelle* is *lesquelles*. When used with the preposition *à*, *lequel/laquelle* become *auquel/à laquelle* (*auxquels/auxquelles* in plural). When used with the preposition *de*, *lequel/laquelle* become *duquel/de laquelle* (*desquels/desquelles* in plural).

(d) *(when)* où; **the day that you arrived** le jour où tu es arrivé
5 *adverb* **that high** haut comme ça; **he's not that good-looking** il n'est pas si beau que ça; **it's not that cold** il ne fait pas si froid que ça

thaw *verb*
(a) *(of snow, ice)* fondre
(b) *(of frozen food)* se décongeler

the *article*
(a) le/la, *(plural)* les; **the pen** le stylo; **the house** la maison; **the airport**

l'aéroport; **the children** les enfants

Le is used with masculine nouns and la is used with feminine nouns. Le and la become l' before a vowel or mute h. The plural of le and la is les.

(**b**) **of the** du/de la, (plural) des; **a page of the book** une page du livre; **the mother of the child** la mère de l'enfant

Note that de + le is contracted to du and de + les to des. However, de + la and de + l' do not change.

(**c**) **from the** du/de la, (plural) des; **a passage from the book** un extrait du livre

(**d**) **to the** au/à la, (plural) aux; **I gave it to the teacher** je l'ai donné au professeur

Note that à + le is contracted to au and à + les to aux. However, à + la and à + l' do not change.

(**e**) **at the** au/à la, (plural) aux; **she's at the station** elle est à la gare

(**f**) (in comparisons) **the more I see him, the less I like him** plus je le vois, moins je l'apprécie

theatre noun le théâtre

theft noun le vol

their adjective
(**a**) (when the thing possessed is maculine or feminine singular in French) leur; **this is their ball** c'est leur ballon; **this is their car** c'est leur voiture
(**b**) (when the thing possessed is plural in French) leurs; **these are their shoes** ce sont leurs chaussures
(**c**) (when used with parts of the body) **the children are brushing their teeth** les enfants se brossent les dents; **they each broke their leg** ils se sont tous les deux cassé la jambe

The form used in French is determined by the number of the noun it stands for.

theirs pronoun
(**a**) (when the thing possessed is maculine singular in French) le leur; **it's not our ball, it's theirs** ce n'est pas notre ballon, c'est le leur; **this ball is theirs** ce ballon est à eux
(**b**) (when the thing possessed is feminine singular in French) la leur; **it's not the Smiths' car, it's theirs** ce n'est pas la voiture des Smith, c'est la leur; **this car is theirs** cette voiture est à eux
(**c**) (when the thing possessed is plural in French) les leurs; **these are not our books, they're theirs** ce ne sont pas nos livres, ce sont les leurs; **these shoes are theirs** ces chaussures sont à eux

The form used in French is determined by the gender and number of the noun it stands for.

them pronoun
(**a**) (direct object) les; **I hate them** je les déteste; **I met them yesterday** je les ai rencontrés hier
(**b**) (indirect object) leur; **give the money to them, give them the money** donne-leur l'argent; **I'll give it to them** je le leur donnerai
(**c**) (after prepositions and after "to be") eux/elles; **I bought it for the boys, it's for them** je l'ai acheté pour les garçons, c'est pour eux; **my sisters live abroad; I often think of them** mes sœurs vivent à l'étranger; je pense souvent à elles; **it's them!** ce sont eux/elles!

theme noun
(**a**) le thème; **a theme park** un parc à thème
(**b**) **theme music** (of a TV programme) la chanson du générique

themselves pronoun
(**a**) eux-mêmes/elles-mêmes; **my parents painted the house themselves** mes parents ont peint la maison eux-mêmes
(**b**) (reflexive use) se; **the boys hurt themselves** les garçons se sont blessés; **the girls are enjoying themselves** les filles s'amusent bien

Se becomes *s'* before a vowel or mute h.

(**c**) *(after a preposition)* eux/elles; **my brothers only think about themselves** mes frères ne pensent qu'à eux; **my sisters are by themselves** mes sœurs sont toutes seules

then *adverb*
(**a**) *(at that time)* alors, à cette époque; **we were very young then** on était très jeunes à cette époque; **since then** depuis
(**b**) *(next)* ensuite, puis; **I watched TV then I went to bed** j'ai regardé la télé, puis je suis allé me coucher; **and then?** et puis?
(**c**) *(in that case)* alors; **it's raining – take an umbrella then** il pleut – alors prends un parapluie; **what do you suggest, then?** qu'est-ce que vous suggérez alors?

theory *noun* la théorie; **in theory** en théorie *or* en principe

therapy *noun* la thérapie

there
1 *pronoun* **there is, there are** il y a; **there was, there were** il y avait; **there has been** il y a eu; **there will be** il y aura; **there's no room** il n'y a pas de place; **there are no more glasses** il n'y a plus de verres; **there isn't any** il n'y en a pas; **there weren't many people** il n'y avait pas beaucoup de monde
2 *adverb*
(**a**) *(in that place)* là; **he isn't there** il n'est pas là
(**b**) *(to that place)* y; **they're going there tomorrow** ils y vont demain
(**c**) *(over there)* là-bas; **the weather's nice there** il fait beau là-bas
(**d**) **there it is!** le voilà!; **there they are!** les voilà!; **there's my sister!** voilà ma sœur!; **there you are!** *(when giving something)* voilà!

therefore *adverb* donc

thermometer *noun* le thermomètre

these
1 *adjective*
(**a**) ces; **these books** ces livres

Ces is the plural of *ce* and *cette*.

(**b**) *(opposed to "those")* ces...-ci; **I prefer these shoes to those ones** je préfère ces chaussures-ci à celles-là
(**c**) **these ones** ceux-ci/celles-ci
2 *pronoun (these ones)* ceux-ci/celles-ci; **I've picked the shoes I want; I want these** j'ai choisi les chaussures que je veux; je veux celles-ci

they *pronoun*
(**a**) ils/elles; **I've read these books, they're really interesting** j'ai lu ces livres, ils sont très intéressants; **I know these girls, they're really nice** je connais ces filles, elles sont très sympas; **they're strange people** ce sont des gens bizarres

The pronouns *ils* is used to replace a masculine plural noun (*les enfants = ils*) and *elles* is used to replace a feminine plural noun (*les maisons = elles*).

(**b**) *(people in general)* on; **in Spain they eat later** en Espagne, on mange plus tard; **they say it's easy** on dit que c'est facile

thick *adjective*
(**a**) épais/épaisse; **I've got thick hair** j'ai les cheveux épais; **the wall is a metre thick** le mur fait un mètre d'épaisseur
(**b**) *(stupid)* bête

thief *noun* le voleur/la voleuse

thigh *noun* la cuisse

thin *adjective*
(**a**) *(wall, book, lips)* mince
(**b**) *(person, leg)* maigre; **she got thinner** elle a maigri
(**c**) *(clothing, slice, paper)* fin/fine

thing *noun*
(**a**) la chose; **what's that thing?** c'est quoi ça?; **I can't, I've got things to do** je ne peux pas, j'ai des choses à faire; **she's taking things too seriously** elle

prend les choses trop au sérieux; **the important thing is to tell the truth** l'important, c'est de dire la vérité; **the thing is, I can't really afford it** le problème, c'est que je n'ai pas vraiment les moyens
(**b**) **I don't know a thing about algebra** je n'y connais rien en algèbre; **I can't see a thing** je n'y vois rien
(**c**) **my things** *(belongings)* mes affaires *(feminine plural)*; **my school things** mes affaires d'école

think
1 *verb*
(**a**) *(have in mind, believe)* penser; **what do you think?** qu'en penses-tu?; **I think she's right** je pense qu'elle a raison; **I think so** je pense que oui; **I don't think so** je ne pense pas
(**b**) *(imagine)* imaginer; **just think what we could do with all that money!** imagine ce qu'on pourrait faire avec tout cet argent!
(**c**) *(use one's mind, ponder)* réfléchir; **think before you speak** réfléchis avant de parler; **think carefully** réfléchis bien
2 think about *(have in mind, consider)* penser à, réfléchir à; **what are you thinking about?** à quoi penses-tu?; **I'm thinking about the exams** je pense aux examens; **I'll think about your offer** je vais réfléchir à ta proposition
3 think of
(**a**) *(have in mind)* penser à; **I often think of you** je pense souvent à toi; **I'm thinking of moving out** j'envisage de déménager
(**b**) *(have an opinion about)* penser de; **what did you think of the book?** qu'est-ce que tu as pensé du livre?

third *number*
(**a**) troisième; **the third day** le troisième jour; **the third girl** la troisième fille; **the third of July** le trois juillet
(**b**) *(fraction)* le tiers; **one third of the population** un tiers de la population; **two thirds** deux tiers

thirst *noun* la soif

thirsty *adjective* **to be thirsty** avoir soif; **I'm very thirsty** j'ai très soif

thirteen *number* treize

thirteenth *number* treizième; **the thirteenth lorry** le treizième camion; **the thirteenth time** la treizième fois; **the thirteenth of August** le treize août

thirtieth *number* trentième; **the thirtieth pupil** le trentième élève; **the thirtieth time** la treizième fois; **the thirtieth of September** le trente septembre

thirty *number* trente; **thirty-one boys** trente et un garçons; **thirty-one girls** trente et une filles; **thirty-two** trente-deux; **thirty-first** trente et unième; **thirty-second** trente-deuxième; **in the thirties** dans les années trente

this
1 *adjective*
(**a**) ce/cette; **this book** ce livre; **this question** cette question

Ce is used with masculine nouns and *cette* is used with feminine nouns. *Ce* becomes *cet* in front of a vowel or a mute h, eg *cet appareil, cet homme.*

(**b**) *(opposed to "that")* ce...-ci/cette...-ci; **I prefer this film** je préfère ce film-ci; **take this cup** prends cette tasse-ci
(**c**) **this one** celui-ci/celle-ci; **I don't want that book, I want this one** je ne veux pas ce livre, je veux celui-ci
2 *pronoun*
(**a**) ça, ceci; **I don't like this** je n'aime pas ça; **I do it like this** je le fais comme ça

Ceci is more formal and less common than *ça.*

(**b**) *(when "that" is the subject of the sentence)* ce; **this is strange** c'est bizarre; **this is what she told me** c'est ce qu'elle m'a dit; **who's this?** qui est-ce?; **what's this?** qu'est-ce que c'est?; **this is Sarah**

Jervis *(on the phone)* c'est Sarah Jervis à l'appareil

> *Ce* becomes *c'* in front of *e* and *é*, eg *c'est amusant*.

3 *adverb* **this high** haut comme ça; **I've never read a book this good** je n'ai jamais lu de livre aussi bien

thistle *noun* le chardon

thorn *noun* une épine

thorough *adjective (research, worker)* minutieux/minutieuse

thoroughly *adverb*
(**a**) *(in detail)* à fond; **the carpet has been thoroughly cleaned** le tapis a été nettoyé à fond; **read the questions thoroughly** lisez attentivement les questions
(**b**) *(totally)* tout à fait; **I thoroughly agree** je suis tout à fait d'accord

those
1 *adjective*
(**a**) ces; **those books** ces livres

> *Ces* is the plural of *ce* and *cette*.

(**b**) *(opposed to "these")* ces...-là; **I prefer those shoes** je préfère ces chaussures-là
(**c**) **those ones** ceux-là/celles-là; **I don't want these biscuits, I want those ones** je ne veux pas ces biscuits, je veux ceux-là
2 *pronoun (those ones)* ceux-là/celles-là; **I don't want these shoes, I want those** je ne veux pas ces chaussures, je veux celles-là

though
1 *conjunction* **though, even though** bien que; **he wants to go to school even though he's ill** il veut aller à l'école bien qu'il soit malade; **as though** comme si; **it was as though he couldn't see me** c'était comme s'il ne me voyait pas

> The expression *bien que* is always followed by the subjunctive.

2 *adverb* pourtant, mais; **he's a strange man, I like him though** il est

bizarre, pourtant je l'aime bien

thought *noun*
(**a**) *(idea)* une idée; **I've had a thought** j'ai eu une idée
(**b**) *(thinking)* la pensée; **I'll give it some thought** j'y réfléchirai

thousand *noun* **a thousand** mille; **a thousand metres** mille mètres; **two thousand metres** deux mille mètres; **two thousand and fifty metres** deux mille cinquante mètres; **thousands of people** des milliers de gens

thread *noun* le fil

threat *noun* la menace

threaten *verb* menacer

three *number* trois

thrilled *adjective* ravi/ravie; **I was thrilled with my birthday present** j'étais ravi de mon cadeau d'anniversaire

thriller *noun* le thriller

throat *noun* la gorge; **I have a sore throat** j'ai mal à la gorge

throne *noun* le trône

through
1 *preposition*
(**a**) *(with a place)* à travers, par; **I could hear them through the wall** je les entendais à travers le mur; **I went through their garden** je suis passé par leur jardin *or* j'ai traversé leur jardin; **I was looking through the window** je regardais par la fenêtre; **to go through a red light** brûler un feu rouge
(**b**) *(in the course of)* **all through his life** pendant toute sa vie; **I'm halfway through the book** j'ai lu la moitié du livre
(**c**) *(by means of)* par; **I sent it through the post** je l'ai envoyé par la poste; **I found out through my brother** je l'ai appris par mon frère
2 *adverb*
(**a**) **to get through to somebody** *(on the phone)* joindre quelqu'un; **I'll put**

you **through to him** je vous le passe
(**b**) **to get through to the final** se qualifier pour la finale
(**c**) **to let somebody through** laisser passer quelqu'un

throw
1 *verb*
(**a**) *(any other object)* jeter, lancer; **can you throw me my keys?** est-ce tu peux me lancer mes clés?; **she threw stones at him** elle lui a jeté des pierres; **he threw himself at him** il s'est jeté sur lui
(**b**) *(in sport)* lancer
2 **throw away** jeter
3 **throw out**
(**a**) *(object)* jeter
(**b**) **to throw somebody out** mettre quelqu'un à la porte; **he was thrown out of school** il a été renvoyé de l'école
4 **throw up** *(vomit)* vomir

thug *noun* le voyou

thumb *noun* le pouce

thunder *noun* le tonnerre; **a clap of thunder** un coup de tonnerre

thunderstorm *noun* un orage

Thursday *noun* le jeudi; **on Thursday** jeudi; **he arrived on Thursday** il est arrivé jeudi; **on Thursdays** le jeudi; **she plays badminton on Thursdays** elle joue au badminton le jeudi; **every Thursday** tous les jeudis; **next Thursday** jeudi prochain; **last Thursday** jeudi dernier

In French, the names of days are not written with a capital.

tick
1 *noun (mark)* **to put a tick against something** cocher quelque chose
2 *verb* cocher

ticket *noun*
(**a**) *(for a train, a plane, the cinema, a concert)* le billet
(**b**) *(for the bus, the underground)* le ticket
(**c**) **a ticket inspector** un contrôleur/ une contrôleuse; **a ticket office** un

guichet
(**d**) **a parking ticket** un PV; **a speeding ticket** un PV

PV is the abbreviation of *procès-verbal*. It does not change in the plural.

tickle *verb* chatouiller

ticklish *adjective* chatouilleux/cha-touilleuse

tide *noun* la marée; **at high tide** à ma-rée haute; **at low tide** à marée basse

tidy
1 *adjective*
(**a**) *(room)* bien rangé/rangée
(**b**) *(hair)* bien coiffé/coiffée
(**c**) *(work, handwriting, appearance)* soigné/soignée
(**d**) *(person)* ordonné/ordonnée
2 *verb* ranger
3 **tidy up** ranger

tie
1 *noun*
(**a**) *(around the neck)* la cravate
(**b**) *(in a match)* le match nul; **the match ended in a tie** les deux équipes ont fait match nul
(**c**) *(in a race, a contest)* **there was a tie for second place** il y a eu égalité pour la deuxième place
2 *verb*
(**a**) *(fasten)* attacher; **they tied him to a tree** il l'ont attaché à un arbre; **to tie a knot in something** faire un nœud à quelque chose
(**b**) *(in a match)* faire match nul
(**c**) *(in a race, a contest)* être à égalité
3 **tie up**
(**a**) *(an animal, a person)* attacher
(**b**) *(a parcel)* ficeler

tiger *noun* le tigre

tight *adjective*
(**a**) *(screw, knot, clothes)* serré/serrée; **these trousers are too tight for me** ce pantalon me serre trop
(**b**) *(close-fitting)* moulant/moulante; **tight jeans** un jean moulant

tighten *verb* serrer

tightly *adverb*
(a) *(hold, squeeze)* fortement
(b) *(shut, seal)* bien; **make sure the lid's on tightly** vérifie que le couvercle est bien fermé

tights *plural noun* le collant; **a pair of tights** un collant

tile *noun*
(a) *(on a roof)* la tuile
(b) *(on a wall, a floor)* le carreau

The plural of *carreau* is *carreaux*.

till¹ *see* **until**

till² *noun* *(for money)* la caisse

time
1 *noun*
(a) le temps; **there's no time to lose** il n'y a pas de temps à perdre; **she spends all her time reading** elle passe son temps à lire; **you have plenty of time to finish it** vous avez largement le temps de le finir; **most of the time** la plupart du temps; **in time** à temps; **I arrived just in time** je suis arrivé juste à temps
(b) *(on the clock)* l'heure *(feminine)*; **what time is it?** quelle heure est-il?; **this time tomorrow** demain à la même heure; **on time** à l'heure; **the time difference is two hours** il y a un décalage horaire de deux heures
(c) *(point in time)* le moment; **for the time being** pour le moment; **in three weeks' time** dans trois semaines; **a long time ago** il y a longtemps; **this time next year** l'année prochaine à la même époque
(d) *(occasion)* la fois; **she succeeds every time** elle réussit à chaque fois; **the last time he came he was in a bad mood** la dernière fois qu'il est venu il était de mauvaise humeur; **several times** plusieurs fois; **five times** cinq fois
(e) *(period in history)* l'époque *(feminine)*; **in Victorian times** à l'époque victorienne
(f) **to have a good time** bien s'amuser;

we had a really good time last night on s'est vraiment bien amusé hier soir
(g) **four times two is eight** quatre fois deux égale huit
2 *verb* *(a runner)* chronométrer

timetable *noun*
(a) *(for transport)* un horaire; **do you have a bus timetable?** est-ce que tu as les horaires des bus?
(b) *(schedule)* un emploi du temps; **we've been given our timetable for this term** on nous a donné notre emploi du temps pour ce trimestre

timid *adjective* timide

tin *noun*
(a) *(metal)* l'étain *(masculine)*
(b) *(container)* la boîte; **a biscuit tin** une boîte de biscuits
(c) *(can)* la boîte de conserve; **a tin of beans** une boîte de haricots; **a tin opener** un ouvre-boîte

The plural of *ouvre-boîte* is *ouvre-boîtes*. The singular can also be found with an *s*: *un ouvre-boîtes*.

tinfoil *noun* le papier d'aluminium

tinned *adjective* en boîte; **tinned tomatoes** les tomates en boîte; **tinned food** les conserves *(feminine plural)*

tinsel *noun* les guirlandes de Noël *(feminine plural)*

tiny *adjective* tout petit/toute petite; **a tiny bit** un tout petit peu

tip
1 *noun*
(a) *(end)* le bout; **the tips of one's fingers** le bout des doigts; **his name is on the tip of my tongue** j'ai son nom sur le bout de la langue
(b) *(money)* le pourboire
(c) *(piece of advice)* le conseil
2 *verb*
(a) *(pour)* verser; **she tipped the sugar into the bowl** elle a versé le sucre dans le bol
(b) *(give money to)* donner un pourboire à

tiptoe *noun* **on tiptoe** sur la pointe des pieds

tired *adjective*
(a) *(exhausted)* fatigué/fatiguée
(b) *(fed up)* **to be tired of something** en avoir assez de quelque chose; **I'm tired of their excuses** j'en ai assez de leurs excuses

tiring *adjective* fatigant/fatigante

tissue *noun* *(handkerchief)* le mouchoir en papier; **tissue paper** le papier de soie

> Note that the French word *tissu* is never a translation for the English word *tissue*. It means *cloth* or *fabric*.

title *noun* le titre

to *preposition*
(a) *(direction)* à; **I walk to school** je vais à l'école à pied; **to go to France** aller en France; **to go to Canada** aller au Canada; **to go to New York** aller à New York; **to the left** à gauche

> Note that *à* + *le* is contracted to *au* (as in *il va au cinéma*, *il va au Canada*) and *à* + *les* to *aux* (as in *aux États-Unis*). However, *à* + *la* and *à* + *l'* do not change. Note also that with feminine countries, the preposition *en* is used instead of saying *à la* : *en France*, *en Angleterre* etc.

(b) *(time)* à; **from four o'clock to five o'clock** de quatre heures à cinq heures; **it's ten to six** il est six heures moins dix
(c) *(somebody's house, shop)* chez; **I'm invited to Fiona's** je suis invité chez Fiona; **I'm going to the doctor's** je vais chez le médecin
(d) *(up as far as)* jusqu'à; **to count to ten** compter jusqu'à dix
(e) *(with indirect objects)* à; **he gave it to his mother** il l'a donné à sa mère; **give it to me** donne-le-moi; **he spoke to his teacher about it** il en a parlé à son professeur
(f) *(towards)* envers; **he's very kind to me** il est très gentil avec moi

(g) *(with infinitives)* à, de; **to go** aller; **my sister is learning to drive** ma sœur apprend à conduire; **it's easy to say** c'est facile à dire; **I've got a lot to do** j'ai beaucoup de choses à faire; **I decided to do it** j'ai décidé de le faire; **she told me to stay** elle m'a dit de rester; **I want him to know the truth** je veux qu'il sache la vérité
(h) *(in order to)* pour; **I came here to please you** je suis venu ici pour te faire plaisir

toad *noun* le crapaud

toast
1 *noun*
(a) *(bread)* le pain grillé; **a piece of toast** une tartine grillée
(b) *(drink)* le toast; **to propose a toast** porter un toast; **to drink a toast to somebody** boire à la santé de quelqu'un
2 *verb* faire griller

toasted *adjective* grillé/grillée; **a toasted sandwich** un sandwich grillé

toaster *noun* le grille-pain

> The word *grille-pain* does not change in the plural.

tobacco *noun* le tabac

today *adverb* aujourd'hui; **a week ago today** il y a exactement une semaine aujourd'hui; **a week from today** aujourd'hui en huit; **what's today's date?** quelle est la date d'aujourd'hui?; **today is 17th March** nous sommes le 17 mars

toddler *noun* le tout petit/la toute petite; **he's just a toddler** il est encore tout petit

toe *noun* un orteil; **the big toe** le gros orteil; **you stepped on my toes** tu m'as marché sur les pieds

toffee *noun* le caramel; **a toffee apple** une pomme d'amour

together *adverb*
(a) ensemble; **we went to school together** on est allé à l'école ensemble;

those colours go well together ces couleurs vont bien ensemble; **we get on well together** on s'entend bien
(**b**) **together with** avec; **I took it back together with the receipt** je l'ai rapporté avec le ticket de caisse

toilet *noun* les toilettes *(feminine plural)*; **to go to the toilet** aller aux toilettes; **toilet paper** le papier toilette

tomato *noun* la tomate; **tomato juice** le jus de tomates

tomorrow *adverb* demain; **tomorrow morning** demain matin; **see you tomorrow!** à demain!; **tomorrow is Monday** demain, c'est lundi

ton *noun*
(**a**) *(weight)* la tonne
(**b**) **tons of people** des tas de gens

tone *noun*
(**a**) *(of the voice)* le ton; **don't speak to me in that tone!** ne me parle pas sur ce ton!
(**b**) *(dialling tone)* la tonalité
(**c**) **please speak after the tone** veuillez parler après le signal sonore

tongue *noun* la langue; **he stuck his tongue out at me** il m'a tiré la langue

tonight *adverb*
(**a**) *(this evening)* ce soir; **we're going to the cinema tonight** on va au cinéma ce soir
(**b**) *(during the night)* cette nuit; **I hope I sleep well tonight** j'espère que je vais bien dormir cette nuit

tonsillitis *noun* une angine; **I have tonsillitis** j'ai une angine

tonsils *plural noun* les amygdales *(feminine plural)*

The *g* in *amygdales* is not pronounced.

too *adverb*
(**a**) *(also)* aussi; **me too** moi aussi
(**b**) *(excessively)* trop; **it's too difficult** c'est trop difficile
(**c**) **too much, too many** *(after a noun or a verb)* trop; **you drink too much** tu

bois trop; **you've eaten too many** tu en as mangé trop; **two glasses too many** deux verres de trop
(**d**) **too much, too many** *(followed by a noun)* trop de; **too much sugar** trop de sucre; **too many newspapers** trop de journaux

tool *noun* un outil

The *l* in *outil* is not pronounced.

tooth *noun* la dent

toothache *noun* **I have toothache** j'ai mal aux dents

toothbrush *noun* la brosse à dents

toothpaste *noun* le dentifrice

top
1 *noun*
(**a**) *(of a mountain, a tree)* le sommet
(**b**) *(of a ladder, a page)* le haut; **at the top of the stairs** en haut des escaliers
(**c**) *(piece of clothing)* le haut; **my pyjama top** mon haut de pyjama; **I bought a new top** je me suis acheté un nouveau haut
(**d**) *(of a cake)* le dessus; **on top** dessus; **on top of the wardrobe** sur l'armoire
(**e**) *(of a box, a pan)* le couvercle
(**f**) *(of a pen)* le capuchon
(**g**) *(of a wine bottle)* le bouchon; *(of a beer bottle)* la capsule
(**h**) **he's at the top of the class** il est premier de la classe
2 *adjective*
(**a**) *(highest)* **the top shelf** l'étagère du haut; **the top floor** le dernier étage
(**b**) *(best)* **she got the top mark in history** elle a eu la meilleure note en histoire

topic *noun* le sujet

torch *noun* *(electric)* la lampe de poche

tortoise *noun* la tortue

torture
1 *noun* la torture
2 *verb* torturer

toss *verb* lancer; **she tossed him the ball** elle lui a lancé la balle; **to toss a**

coin jouer à pile ou face

total

1 *adjective* total/totale

> The masculine plural of *total* is *totaux*.

2 *noun* le total; **in total** au total

totally *adverb* totalement; **I'm totally exhausted** je suis complètement épuisé

touch

1 *noun*

(**a**) *(sense, act of touching)* le toucher

(**b**) *(communication)* **to be in touch** être en contact; **to get in touch with somebody** contacter quelqu'un; **to lose touch with somebody** perdre quelqu'un de vue; **keep in touch!** donne de tes nouvelles!

2 *verb*

(**a**) *(physically, emotionally)* toucher; **he touched my arm** il m'a touché le bras; **I was touched by her speech** son discours m'a touché

(**b**) *(interfere with)* toucher à; **don't touch my things** ne touche pas à mes affaires

touchy *adjective*

(**a**) *(person)* susceptible

(**b**) *(question, situation)* délicat/délicate

tough *adjective*

(**a**) *(person, shoes)* solide, robuste

(**b**) *(meat, life)* dur/dure

(**c**) *(area, criminal)* dangereux/dangereuse

(**d**) *(problem, work)* dur/dure, difficile

tour *noun*

(**a**) *(trip)* le voyage; **he went on a tour of China** il est allé faire un voyage en Chine

(**b**) *(of a museum, a town)* la visite; **we went on a tour of the factory** nous avons visité l'usine; **a guided tour** une visite guidée; **a tour guide** un/une guide

(**c**) *(by a singer, a band)* la tournée; **the band is on tour in Europe** le groupe est en tournée en Europe

tourism *noun* le tourisme

tourist *noun* le/la touriste

towards *preposition*

(**a**) *(in the direction of, near)* vers; **he turned towards her** il s'est tourné vers elle; **towards the end of his life** vers la fin de sa vie

(**b**) *(directed at)* envers, avec; **she's cruel towards me** elle est cruelle envers moi *or* elle est cruelle avec moi

towel *noun* la serviette

tower *noun* la tour; **a tower block** une tour d'habitation

town *noun* la ville; **I live in a small town** j'habite dans une petite ville; **I'm going into town** je vais en ville; **the town centre** le centre-ville; **the town council** le conseil municipal; **the town hall** la mairie

toy *noun* le jouet

trace *noun* la trace

track *noun*

(**a**) *(path)* le chemin

(**b**) *(for running)* la piste

(**c**) *(for trains)* la voie ferrée

(**d**) *(on a CD)* le morceau

(**e**) *(of an animal)* la trace

(**f**) **I've lost track of how much money I've spent** je ne sais plus combien d'argent j'ai dépensé; **I can't keep track of current affairs** je n'arrive pas à suivre les actualités

tracksuit *noun* le survêtement

tractor *noun* le tracteur

trade

1 *noun*

(**a**) *(buying and selling)* le commerce; **the tea trade** le commerce du thé

(**b**) *(profession)* **he's a plumber by trade** il est plombier de son métier; **a trade union** un syndicat

2 *verb* *(swap)* échanger; **he traded a CD for a video game** il a échangé un CD contre un jeu vidéo

tradition *noun* la tradition

traffic *noun*
(a) *(on roads)* la circulation; **a traffic jam** un embouteillage; **traffic lights** les feux *(masculine plural)*; **a traffic warden** un contractuel/une contractuelle
(b) *(in drugs, arms)* le trafic

tragedy *noun* la tragédie

tragic *adjective* tragique

trailer *noun*
(a) *(for a car)* la remorque
(b) *(for a film)* la bande-annonce

> The plural of *bande-annonce* is *bandes-annonces*.

train
1 *noun*
(a) *(railway)* le train; **I went there by train** j'y suis allé en train; **on the train** dans le train
(b) *(underground)* le métro
2 *verb*
(a) *(an employee)* former;
(b) *(a sportsperson)* entraîner; **who's training him?** qui est son entraîneur?
(c) *(an animal)* dresser
(d) **to train for a race** s'entraîner pour une course; **they train three times a week** ils s'entraînent trois fois par semaine
(e) **to train as a doctor** suivre une formation de médecin

trained *adjective*
(a) *(nurse, teacher)* diplômé/diplômée
(b) *(animal)* dressé/dressée

trainee *noun* le/la stagiaire; **a trainee journalist** un/une journaliste stagiaire

trainer *noun*
(a) *(of sportspeople)* un entraîneur/une entraîneuse
(b) *(of animals)* la dresseur/la dresseuse
(c) *(shoe)* la basket; **a pair of trainers** une paire de baskets

training *noun*
(a) *(of an employee)* la formation; **a training course** un stage de formation
(b) *(of a sportsperson)* l'entraînement

(masculine); **to be in training** s'entraîner; **to be out of training** manquer d'entraînement; **a training session** un entraînement
(c) *(of an animal)* le dressage

tram *noun* le tramway

tramp
1 *noun (down-and-out)* le clochard/la clocharde
2 *verb (walk heavily)* marcher d'un pas lourd

trampoline *noun* le trampoline

transfer *verb*
(a) *(person)* transférer; *(employee)* muter
(b) *(money)* virer

transform *verb* transformer

translate *verb* traduire; **to translate from French into English** traduire du français vers l'anglais

translation *noun* la traduction

translator *noun* le traducteur/la traductrice; **she's a translator** elle est traductrice

transparent *adjective* transparent/transparente

transport
1 *noun* le transport; **public transport** les transports en commun
2 *verb* transporter

trap
1 *noun* le piège; **to set a trap** tendre un piège
2 *verb*
(a) *(an animal)* prendre au piège
(b) *(trick)* piéger
(c) *(immobilize)* coincer; **I was trapped in the lift** j'étais coincé dans l'ascenseur

travel
1 *noun* les voyages *(masculine plural)*; **a travel agency** une agence de voyages
2 *verb*
(a) *(to a country)* voyager; **to travel by train** voyager en train; **to travel round the world** faire le tour du monde

(**b**) *(a distance)* faire; **I travelled 50 miles to get here** j'ai fait 80 kilomètres pour venir ici

traveller *noun* le voyageur/la voyageuse; **a traveller's cheque** un chèque de voyage

tray *noun* le plateau

> The plural of *plateau* is *plateaux*.

tread *verb* marcher; **he trod on my foot** il m'a marché sur le pied

treasure *noun* le trésor; **a treasure hunt** une chasse au trésor

treat
1 *verb*
(**a**) *(a person, a problem)* traiter; **he treats her well** il la traite bien
(**b**) *(a patient, an illness)* soigner
(**c**) **to treat somebody to something** payer quelque chose à quelqu'un; **I treated myself to a new coat** je me suis payé un nouveau manteau
2 *noun*
(**a**) *(pleasure)* le plaisir
(**b**) *(present)* le cadeau; **it's my treat** c'est moi qui offre
(**c**) *(food)* **these chocolates are a real treat** ces chocolats sont un vrai régal

treatment *noun* le traitement

treaty *noun* le traité

tree *noun* un arbre; **a fruit tree** un arbre fruitier

tremble *verb* trembler

trial *noun*
(**a**) *(in court)* le procès; **to go on trial** passer en jugement
(**b**) *(test)* un essai; **a trial period** une période d'essai

triangle *noun* le triangle

trick
1 *noun*
(**a**) *(joke)* la farce, le tour; **to play a trick on somebody** faire une farce à quelqu'un
(**b**) *(by a magician)* le tour
2 *verb* tromper

tricky *adjective* difficile

trip
1 *noun*
(**a**) *(journey)* le voyage; **to go on a trip** partir en voyage; **a school trip** un voyage scolaire
(**b**) *(outing)* une excursion
2 *verb* *(stumble)* trébucher
3 trip up
(**a**) *(make somebody stumble)* faire trébucher; *(intentionally)* faire un croche-pied à
(**b**) *(stumble)* trébucher

trolley *noun* le chariot

trombone *noun* le trombone; **he plays the trombone** il joue du trombone

trophy *noun* le trophée

> Although it ends in *-ée*, this word is masculine.

tropical *adjective* tropical/tropicale

> The masculine plural of *tropical* is *tropicaux*.

trot *verb* trotter

trouble
1 *noun*
(**a**) *(difficulty)* les ennuis *(masculine plural)*; **to be in trouble** avoir des ennuis; **to get into trouble** s'attirer des ennuis
(**b**) *(inconvenience)* la peine; **to go to the trouble of doing something** se donner la peine de faire quelque chose; **it's not worth the trouble** ça n'en vaut pas la peine; **if it's no trouble** si ça ne vous dérange pas
(**c**) **to have trouble doing something** avoir du mal à faire quelque chose; **I had trouble falling asleep** j'ai eu du mal à m'endormir
2 *verb* *(disturb)* déranger; **I'm sorry to trouble you** excusez-moi de vous déranger

trousers *plural noun* le pantalon; **a pair of trousers** un pantalon; **I bought some new trousers** j'ai acheté un nouveau pantalon

trout *noun* la truite

truant *noun* **to play truant** sécher les cours

> Note that the French word *truand* is never a translation for the English word *truant*. It means *crook*.

truck *noun* le camion; **a truck driver** un camionneur/une camionneuse

true *adjective* vrai/vraie; **is it true?** c'est vrai?; **to come true** se réaliser

trumpet *noun* la trompette; **he plays the trumpet** il joue de la trompette

trunk *noun*
(**a**) *(of a tree)* le tronc
(**b**) *(of an elephant)* la trompe
(**c**) *(luggage)* la malle

trunks *plural noun* *(for swimming)* le slip de bain

trust
1 *noun* la confiance
2 *verb* **to trust somebody** faire confiance à quelqu'un; **she's not to be trusted** on ne peut pas lui faire confiance

truth *noun* la vérité; **to tell the truth about something** dire la vérité sur quelque chose

try
1 *noun*
(**a**) *(attempt, test)* un essai; **we can give it a try** on peut essayer; **it's worth a try** ça vaut le coup d'essayer
(**b**) *(in rugby)* un essai; **to score a try** marquer un essai
2 *verb*
(**a**) essayer; **try again** recommence *or* réessaie
(**b**) *(food)* goûter
3 try on *(clothes)* essayer
4 try out *(a new car, a recipe)* essayer

T-shirt *noun* le tee-shirt

> The plural of *tee-shirt* is *tee-shirts*.

tube *noun*
(**a**) *(of toothpaste, paint)* le tube
(**b**) *(underground)* **the tube** le métro;

a tube station une station de métro

Tuesday *noun* le mardi; **on Tuesday** mardi; **I saw him on Tuesday** je l'ai vu mardi; **on Tuesdays** le mardi; **he plays golf on Tuesdays** il joue au golf le mardi; **every Tuesday** tous les mardis; **next Tuesday** mardi prochain; **last Tuesday** mardi dernier

> In French, the names of days are not written with a capital.

tulip *noun* la tulipe

tumble dryer *noun* le sèche-linge

> The word *sèche-linge* does not change in the plural.

tummy *noun* le ventre; **I have tummy ache** j'ai mal au ventre

tuna *noun* le thon; **a tuna sandwich** un sandwich au thon

tune
1 *noun*
(**a**) *(music)* un air
(**b**) **to sing in tune** chanter juste; **to sing out of tune** chanter faux
2 *verb*
(**a**) *(a musical instrument)* accorder
(**b**) *(an engine, a radio)* régler

Tunisia *noun* la Tunisie; **I've never been to Tunisia** je ne suis jamais allé en Tunisie; **they live in Tunisia** ils habitent en Tunisie; **she comes from Tunisia** elle vient de Tunisie

Tunisian
1 *adjective* tunisien/tunisienne
2 *noun* *(person)* le Tunisien/la Tunisienne; **the Tunisians** les Tunisiens *(masculine plural)*

> In French, only the noun for the inhabitants of a country takes a capital letter, never the adjective.

tunnel *noun* le tunnel

Turk *noun* le Turc/la Turque

Turkey *noun* la Turquie; **I've never been to Turkey** je ne suis jamais allé en Turquie; **they live in Turkey** ils habitent en Turquie; **it comes from Turkey** ça vient de Turquie

turkey *noun* la dinde

Turkish
1 *adjective* turc/turque
2 *noun* *(language)* le turc; **he speaks Turkish** il parle turc

In French, only the noun for the inhabitants of a country takes a capital letter, never the adjective or the noun for the language.

turn
1 *noun*
(**a**) *(in a game, a queue)* le tour; **it's my turn to play** c'est mon tour de jouer *or* c'est à moi de jouer; **whose turn is it to play?** c'est à qui de jouer?; **to take it in turns to do the dishes** faire la vaisselle à tour de rôle
(**b**) *(curve in the road)* le virage
(**c**) *(change of direction)* **we took a right turn** nous avons tourné à droite
2 *verb*
(**a**) *(cause to move)* tourner; **turn the knob to the right** tournez le bouton vers la droite; **turn the page** tournez la page
(**b**) *(go round, move)* tourner; **he turned the corner** il a tourné au coin de la rue; **turn right** tournez à droite
(**c**) *(look round)* se retourner; **I turned to ask him a question** je me suis retourné pour lui poser une question; **she turned towards him** elle s'est tournée vers lui
(**d**) *(become)* devenir; **he turned nasty** il est devenu méchant; **it turned blue** c'est devenu bleu; **he's just turned forty** il vient d'avoir quarante ans
(**e**) **to turn into something** se transformer en quelque chose; **to turn something into something** transformer quelque chose en quelque chose; **the theatre has been turned into a library** le théâtre a été transformé en bibliothèque
3 **turn around** *(look round)* se retourner

4 turn down
(**a**) *(an oven, the heating, music)* baisser; **turn the radio down** baisse la radio
(**b**) *(an offer, an invitation)* refuser
5 turn off
(**a**) *(a TV, a light, the heating)* éteindre
(**b**) *(a tap)* fermer
(**c**) *(an engine, a washing machine)* arrêter
6 turn on
(**a**) *(a TV, a light, the heating)* allumer
(**b**) *(a tap)* ouvrir
(**c**) *(an engine, a washing machine)* mettre en marche
7 turn out
(**a**) *(the light)* éteindre
(**b**) *(result, end up)* s'avérer; **his answer turned out to be false** sa réponse s'est avérée fausse; **the evening turned out badly** la soirée a mal tourné; **everything will turn out fine** tout va s'arranger
8 turn over
(**a**) *(a page)* tourner
(**b**) *(a box, a bucket)* retourner
(**c**) *(in one's bed)* se retourner
(**d**) *(change channels)* changer de chaîne
9 turn round *(look round)* se retourner
10 turn up
(**a**) *(arrive)* arriver
(**b**) *(be found)* **your keys will turn up** tu finiras par retrouver tes clés
(**c**) *(an oven, the heating, music)* mettre plus fort; **turn the volume up** monte le son

turning *noun* le virage

turnip *noun* le navet

turquoise *adjective* turquoise

The word *turquoise* does not change in the plural.

turtle *noun* la tortue de mer

TV *noun* la télé; **to watch TV** regarder la télé; **on TV** à la télé; **a TV programme** une émission de télé

tweezers *plural noun* la pince à épiler

twelfth *number* douzième; **the twelfth film** le douzième film; **the twelfth car** la douzième voiture; **the twelfth of October** le douze octobre

twelve *number* douze

twentieth *number* vingtième; **the twentieth century** le vingtième siècle; **the twentieth car** la vingtième voiture; **the twentieth of November** le vingt novembre

twenty *number* vingt; **twenty-one boys** vingt et un garçons; **twenty-one girls** vingt et une filles; **twenty-two** vingt-deux; **twenty-first** vingt et unième; **twenty-second** vingt-deuxième; **in the twenties** dans les années vingt

> In front of a vowel or mute h, the *t* of *vingt* is pronounced. Otherwise the word is pronounced like *vin*.

twice *adverb* deux fois; **I've already told you twice** je te l'ai déjà dit deux fois; **twice a month** deux fois par mois; **she can run twice as fast as me** elle court deux fois plus vite que moi; **it's twice as good** c'est deux fois mieux; **twice as many CDs** deux fois plus de CD

twig *noun* la brindille

twin *noun* le jumeau/la jumelle; **my twin brother** mon frère jumeau; **my twin sister** ma sœur jumelle

> The plural of *jumeau* is *jumeaux*.

twist *verb*
(**a**) *(bend)* tordre
(**b**) *(turn)* tourner
(**c**) *(wind)* enrouler; **to twist something around something** enrouler quelque chose autour de quelque chose; **the wires got twisted** les fils se sont entortillés
(**d**) *(injure)* se tordre; **I twisted my ankle** je me suis tordu la cheville
(**e**) **to twist somebody's arm** *(physically)* tordre le bras de quelqu'un; *(persuade)* forcer la main à quelqu'un

two *number* deux

type
1 *noun* le genre; **a type of hat** un genre de chapeau; **he's the type of person I admire** c'est le genre de personne que j'admire; **the sporty type** le genre sportif
2 *verb (on a computer)* taper

typewriter *noun* la machine à écrire

typical *adjective* typique

tyre *noun* le pneu

ugly *adjective* laid/laide

UK *noun* le Royaume-Uni; **she's coming to the UK** elle vient au Royaume-Uni; **we live in the UK** nous habitons au Royaume-Uni

umbrella *noun* le parapluie

unable *adjective*
(a) **to be unable to do something** *(in general)* ne pas pouvoir faire quelque chose; **I'm unable to help you** je ne peux pas t'aider
(b) *(incapable)* incapable; **he seems unable to understand** il semble incapable de comprendre; **he's unable to walk** il ne peut pas marcher

unattractive *adjective* peu attrayant/peu attrayante; *(person)* peu attirant/peu attirante

unbearable *adjective* insupportable

unbelievable *adjective* incroyable

uncertain *adjective*
(a) *(date, future)* incertain/incertaine
(b) **to be uncertain of something** ne pas être sûr/sûre de quelque chose

uncle *noun* un oncle

uncomfortable *adjective*
(a) *(chair, clothes, shoes)* pas confortable; **these shoes are really uncomfortable** ces chaussures ne sont pas du tout confortables
(b) *(uneasy)* mal à l'aise
(c) *(embarassed)* gêné/gênée; **I feel uncomfortable asking my parents for money** ça me gêne de demander de l'argent à mes parents

unconscious *adjective* sans connaissance; **to fall unconscious** perdre connaissance

under *preposition*
(a) *(underneath)* sous; **the dog is under the table** le chien est sous la table
(b) *(less than)* moins de; **children under nine** les enfants de moins de neuf ans

underground
1 *adjective* souterrain/souterraine; **an underground car park** un parking souterrain
2 *noun* **the underground** le métro

underline *verb* souligner

underneath
1 *preposition* sous; **she's wearing a jumper underneath her coat** elle porte un pull sous son manteau
2 *adverb* dessous; **he picked up the book and found the ticket underneath** il a soulevé le livre et a trouvé le billet dessous
3 *noun* le dessous; **the underneath of the box is black** le dessous de la boîte est noir

underpaid *adjective* sous-payé/sous-payée

underpants *noun* *(briefs)* le slip; *(boxer shorts)* le caleçon

understand *verb* comprendre; **he doesn't understand French** il ne comprend pas le français; **I didn't understand** je n'ai pas compris

understandable *adjective* compréhensible

understanding
1 *adjective* *(sensitive)* compréhensif/compréhensive

2 *noun*
(**a**) *(comprehension)* la compréhension; **you have no understanding of the problem** tu ne comprends pas le problème
(**b**) *(agreement)* un accord; **we've reached an understanding** nous sommes parvenus à un accord

underwater
1 *adjective* sous-marin/sous-marine; **an underwater camera** une caméra sous-marine
2 *adverb* sous l'eau; **to swim underwater** nager sous l'eau

underwear *noun* les sous-vêtements *(masculine plural)*

undo *verb*
(**a**) *(a knot, a button)* défaire
(**b**) *(shoes)* délacer
(**c**) *(damage)* réparer

undone *adjective*
(**a**) *(knot, button)* défait/défaite; **your button has come undone** ton bouton s'est défait
(**b**) *(shoes)* délacé/délacée

undress *verb*
(**a**) *(get undressed)* se déshabiller
(**b**) **to undress somebody** déshabiller quelqu'un; **to get undressed** se déshabiller

uneasy *adjective*
(**a**) *(uncomfortable)* mal à l'aise
(**b**) *(worried)* inquiet/inquiète; **I feel uneasy about this trip** je suis inquiet au sujet de ce voyage

unemployed
1 *adjective* au chômage; **she was unemployed for months** elle est restée au chômage pendant des mois
2 *plural noun* **the unemployed** les chômeurs *(masculine plural)*

unemployment *noun* le chômage

unexpected *adjective* inattendu/inattendue; **it was completely unexpected** on ne s'y attendait pas du tout

unexpectedly *adverb* **to arrive unexpectedly** arriver à l'improviste

unfair *adjective* injuste; **the teacher was unfair to him** le professeur s'est montré injuste envers lui; **that's unfair!** ce n'est pas juste! *or* c'est injuste!

unfairly *adverb* injustement

unfasten *verb* défaire

unfit *adjective*
(**a**) *(unsuitable)* **she's unfit for this type of job** elle n'est pas faite pour ce genre de travail
(**b**) *(in bad shape)* **I'm unfit** je ne suis pas en forme

unfold *verb* *(a newspaper, a map)* déplier

unforgivable *adjective* impardonnable

unfortunate *adjective*
(**a**) *(unlucky)* malheureux/malheureuse; **the unfortunate people whose houses were flooded** les malheureux dont les maisons ont été inondées; **he's been very unfortunate** il n'a vraiment pas eu de chance
(**b**) *(difficult, awkward)* fâcheux/fâcheuse; **an unfortunate situation** une situation fâcheuse

unfortunately *adverb* malheureusement

unfriendly *adjective*
(**a**) *(personne)* peu aimable
(**b**) *(place)* inhospitalier/inhospitalière

unhappy *adjective*
(**a**) *(miserable)* malheureux/malheureuse
(**b**) *(not pleased)* **I'm unhappy with my results** je ne suis pas content de mes résultats

unhealthy *adjective*
(**a**) *(person)* en mauvaise santé
(**b**) *(food, climate)* malsain/malsaine

uniform *noun* un uniforme; **in uniform** en uniforme; **the school uniform** l'uniforme de l'école

unimportant *adjective* sans importance

union *noun*
(**a**) *(between countries, people)* l'union *(feminine)*
(**b**) *(trade union)* le syndicat
(**c**) **the Union Jack** le drapeau britannique

unit *noun*
(**a**) *(of measurement)* une unité
(**b**) *(of furniture)* un élément
(**c**) *(of a hospital)* le service

united *adjective* *(family, country)* uni/unie

United Kingdom *noun* le Royaume-Uni; **she's coming to the United Kingdom** elle vient au Royaume-Uni; **we live in the United Kingdom** nous habitons au Royaume-Uni

United States *noun* les États-Unis *(masculine plural)*; **we're going to the United States** nous allons aux États-Unis; **she lives in the United States** elle habite aux États-Unis

universe *noun* l'univers *(masculine)*

university *noun* une université; **he's at university** il est à l'université

unkind *adjective* pas gentil/gentille; **he's unkind to his sister** il n'est pas gentil avec sa sœur; **to say unkind things to somebody** dire des méchancetés à quelqu'un

unknown *adjective* inconnu/inconnue; **an unknown person** un inconnu

unleaded *adjective* *(petrol)* sans plomb

unless *conjunction* à moins que; **unless she comes** à moins qu'elle ne vienne; **you won't win unless you practise** tu ne gagneras pas si tu ne t'entraînes pas; **will you do it? – not unless you pay me** tu vas le faire? – seulement si tu me paies

Note that *à moins que* is always followed by the subjunctive.

unlike *preposition* **he's unlike his brother** il n'est pas comme son frère;

unlike me, she's very slim contrairement à moi, elle est très mince; **it's unlike him to be late** cela ne lui ressemble pas d'arriver en retard

unlikely *adjective* peu probable; **it's unlikely to rain** il est peu probable qu'il pleuve

Note that the subjunctive is used when expressing doubt or uncertainty.

unload *verb* *(a car, goods)* décharger

unlock *verb* ouvrir

unluckily *adverb* malheureusement

unlucky *adjective*
(**a**) **he's unlucky** il n'a pas de chance
(**b**) **it's unlucky to break a mirror** ça porte malheur de casser un miroir

unmarried *adjective* célibataire

unnecessary *adjective* inutile

unpack *verb*
(**a**) *(a suitcase)* défaire; **I need to unpack my suitcase, I need to unpack** il faut que je défasse ma valise
(**b**) *(shopping, belongings)* déballer

unpleasant *adjective* désagréable

unplug *verb* débrancher

unpopular *adjective* peu populaire; **this music is unpopular with young people** cette musique n'a pas beaucoup de succès auprès des jeunes; **she's unpopular at school** les autres élèves à l'école ne l'aiment pas beaucoup

unsafe *adjective*
(**a**) *(dangerous)* dangereux/dangereuse
(**b**) *(in danger)* en danger; **I feel unsafe here** je ne me sens pas en sécurité ici

unscrew *verb* dévisser

unsuccessful *adjective* **to be unsuccessful** *(of a person)* ne pas réussir; *(of an effort, an attempt)* échouer; **I was unsuccessful in my attempts to find her** je n'ai pas réussi à la trouver; **the**

festival was unsuccessful le festival a été un échec

unsure *adjective* **to be unsure of something** ne pas être sûr/sûre de quelque chose; **they were unsure what to do** ils ne savaient pas trop quoi faire; **she's unsure of herself** elle n'est pas sûre d'elle

untidy *adjective*
(**a**) *(room)* en désordre
(**b**) *(appearance)* négligé/négligée
(**c**) *(person)* désordonné/désordonnée

untie *verb*
(**a**) *(a parcel, a knot, shoelaces)* défaire
(**b**) *(a person, hands)* détacher

until
1 *preposition*
(**a**) *(up to)* jusqu'à; **until now** jusqu'à présent; **until then** jusque là; **until Friday** jusqu'à vendredi; **until 2006** jusqu'en 2006
(**b**) *(before)* avant; **not until tomorrow** pas avant demain
2 *conjunction* jusqu'à ce que; **I'll stay until she gets back** je vais rester jusqu'à ce qu'elle revienne

Note that the expression *jusqu'à ce que* is always followed by the subjunctive.

untrue *adjective* faux/fausse

unusual *adjective*
(**a**) *(uncommon)* inhabituel/inhabituelle; **it's not unusual** ce n'est pas rare
(**b**) *(strange)* bizarre

unwell *adjective* souffrant/souffrante

unwrap *verb*
(**a**) *(a parcel)* ouvrir
(**b**) *(food, goods)* déballer

up
1 *adverb*
(**a**) *(at the top, to the top)* en haut; **I went all the way up** je suis monté jusqu'en haut; **up here** ici; **up there** là-haut
(**b**) *(in the air)* en l'air; **to put one's**

hand up lever la main
(**c**) *(increased)* **prices have gone up** les prix ont augmenté
(**d**) *(and over)* **it's for children aged seven and up** c'est pour les enfants de sept ans et plus
(**e**) **up to** *(as far as)* jusqu'à; **right up to the door** jusqu'à la porte; **to go up to somebody** s'approcher de quelqu'un; **up to now** jusqu'ici; **up to then** jusque-là; **that's up to you** ça dépend de toi; **it's up to you to tell her** c'est à toi de le lui dire
2 *preposition* **he's up the ladder** il est sur l'échelle; **they're up the tree** ils sont dans l'arbre; **to go up the stairs** monter les escaliers; **they live up the street** ils habitent plus haut dans la rue
3 *adjective (out of bed)* levé/levée, debout; **I was up at seven** j'étais levé à sept heures *or* j'étais debout à sept heures

uphill *adverb* **to go uphill** monter; **to run uphill** monter une côte en courant

upright *adjective* *(straight)* droit/droite

upset
1 *adjective*
(**a**) *(unhappy)* triste
(**b**) *(distressed)* bouleversé/bouleversée; **she was really upset by the accident** l'accident l'a vraiment bouleversée
(**c**) **to have an upset stomach** avoir l'estomac dérangé
2 *verb*
(**a**) **to upset somebody** *(distress)* faire de la peine à quelqu'un; *(annoy)* contrarier quelqu'un
(**b**) *(plans, a routine)* déranger
(**c**) *(a drink, a container)* renverser

upsetting *adjective*
(**a**) *(saddening)* triste
(**b**) *(distressing)* bouleversant/bouleversante; **I found the experience upsetting** cette expérience m'a bouleversé

upside down
1 *adjective* à l'envers; **the map is upside down** la carte est à l'envers
2 *adverb* à l'envers; **you're holding it upside down** tu le tiens à l'envers

upstairs
1 *adverb* en haut; **the bedroom is upstairs** la chambre est en haut; **they live upstairs from us** ils habitent au-dessus de chez nous; **to go upstairs** monter
2 *adjective*
(a) **the upstairs bathroom** la salle de bain du haut
(b) **our upstairs neighbours** nos voisins du dessus

up-to-date *adjective*
(a) *(news)* récent/récente
(b) *(information, figures, diary)* à jour
(c) *(method, technology)* moderne
(d) *(clothes)* à la mode

upwards *adverb*
(a) vers le haut; **to look upwards** regarder en haut
(b) **from £100 upwards** à partir de 100 livres; **for children from ten upwards** pour les enfants à partir de dix ans

urgent *adjective* urgent/urgente

urgently *adverb* d'urgence; **a doctor is urgently needed** on demande un médecin d'urgence

US *noun* les États-Unis *(masculine plural)*; **we're going to the US** nous allons aux États-Unis; **she lives in the US** elle habite aux États-Unis

us *pronoun* nous; **it's us!** c'est nous!; **he'll give it to us** il nous le donnera; **come with us** viens avec nous

USA *noun* les États-Unis *(masculine plural)*; **we're going to the USA** nous allons aux États-Unis; **she lives in the USA** elle habite aux États-Unis

use
1 *noun*
(a) l'utilisation *(feminine)*, l'usage *(masculine)*; **to make use of something** faire usage de quelque chose; **it's a word in everyday use** c'est un mot d'usage courant; **directions for use** le mode d'emploi
(b) **to be of use to somebody** être utile à quelqu'un; **this dictionary might be of use to you** ce dictionnaire pourrait t'être utile
(c) **it's no use crying** ça ne sert à rien de pleurer; **what the use of worrying?** à quoi bon s'inquiéter?
2 *verb* **to use something** se servir de quelque chose *or* utiliser quelque chose; **are you using this knife?** est-ce que tu te sers de ce couteau?; **this computer is easy to use** cet ordinateur est facile à utiliser; **what's it used for?** à quoi est-ce que ça sert?; **it's used for measuring distances** ça sert à mesurer les distances

Note that the French word *user* is rarely a translation for the English word *to use*. It usually means *to wear out*.

3 **use up**
(a) *(food, fuel)* finir; **I used up all the milk** j'ai fini le lait; **the paper is all used up** il ne reste plus de papier
(b) *(ideas, energy, patience)* épuiser; **she used up all her strength** elle a épuisé toutes ses forces
(c) *(money)* dépenser

use-by date *noun* la date limite de consommation

used
1 *auxiliary verb* **used to** **I used to sing** avant, je chantais; **she used to jog every Sunday** avant, elle faisait du jogging tous les dimanches

Note that the expression *used to do something* is translated into French by putting the verb in the imperfect tense.

2 *adjective*
(a) *(book, car)* d'occasion
(b) **to be used to doing something** avoir l'habitude de faire quelque chose; **I'm used to working alone** j'ai

l'habitude de travailler seul; **I'm used to it now** j'ai l'habitude maintenant
(**c**) **to get used to doing something** s'habituer à faire quelque chose; **I can't get used to it** je n'arrive pas à m'y habituer

useful *adjective* utile; **this book was very useful to me** ce livre m'a été très utile; **that's useful to know** c'est bon à savoir

useless *adjective*
(**a**) *(not useful)* inutile
(**b**) *(incompetent)* nul/nulle; **I'm useless at geography** je suis nul en géographie
(**c**) **it's useless trying to convince him** ça ne sert à rien d'essayer de le convaincre

user *noun*
(**a**) *(of a computer, a product)* un utilisateur/une utilisatrice
(**b**) *(of a road, public transport)* un usager/une usagère

usual *adjective* habituel/habituelle; **I'll come at the usual time** je viendrai à l'heure habituelle; **I got up earlier than usual** je me suis levé plus tôt que d'habitude

usually *adverb* d'habitude; **I usually get up at seven** d'habitude je me lève à sept heures

vacant *adjective*
(**a**) *(room, seat)* libre
(**b**) *(position)* vacant/vacante

vacation *noun* les vacances *(feminine plural)*; **to be on vacation** être en vacances

vacuum
1 *noun* **a vacuum cleaner** un aspirateur
2 *verb* passer l'aspirateur; **to vacuum a room** passer l'aspirateur dans une pièce

vaguely *adverb* vaguement; **I vaguely remember it** je m'en souviens vaguement

Valentine *noun* **a Valentine's card** une carte de la Saint-Valentin; **Valentine's Day** la Saint-Valentin

valid *adjective* valable; **the ticket is valid for six months** le billet est valable six mois; **my passport is no longer valid** mon passeport est périmé

valley *noun* la vallée

valuable
1 *adjective*
(**a**) *(object)* de valeur; **nothing valuable was stolen** aucun objet de valeur n'a été volé
(**b**) *(advice, contribution)* précieux/précieuse
2 *plural noun* **valuables** les objets de valeur *(masculine plural)*

value *noun* la valeur; **it's of little value** ça n'a pas grande valeur

van *noun* la camionnette

vanilla *noun* la vanille; **vanilla ice cream** la glace à la vanille

vanish *verb* disparaître; **she vanished** elle a disparu

varied *adjective* varié/variée

variety *noun*
(**a**) *(diversity)* la variété; **the work lacks variety** le travail n'est pas très varié; **a variety show** un spectacle de variétés
(**b**) *(assortment)* **for a variety of reasons** pour des raisons diverses; **there is a wide variety of colours to choose from** il y a un grand choix de couleurs
(**c**) *(type)* le type; **different varieties of cheese** différents types de fromage

various *adjective*
(**a**) *(different)* divers/diverse; **we talked about various things** nous avons parlé de choses diverses
(**b**) *(several)* plusieurs; **various people saw it** plusieurs personnes l'ont vu

varnish
1 *noun* le vernis; **nail varnish** le vernis à ongles
2 *verb* vernir

vary *verb* varier; **you should vary your diet** tu devrais varier ton alimentation; **it varies** ça dépend

vase *noun* le vase

vast *adjective* immense; **a vast number of people** un grand nombre de gens; **the vast majority of people** la grande majorité des gens

vegetable *noun* le légume; **green vegetables** les légumes verts

vegetarian
1 *noun* le végétarien/la végétarienne; **he's a vegetarian** il est végétarien

2 *adjective* végétarien/végétarienne

vehicle *noun* le véhicule

veil *noun* le voile

vein *noun* la veine

velvet *noun* le velours; **a velvet jacket** une veste en velours

verb *noun* le verbe

vertical *adjective* vertical/verticale

> The masculine plural of *vertical* is *verticaux*.

very
1 *adverb*
(a) très; **very good** très bon; **very much** beaucoup
(b) *(used for emphasis)* **my very best friend** mon meilleur ami; **the very first** le tout premier; **the very same** exactement le même; **at the very latest** au plus tard
2 *adjective (used for emphasis)* même; **this very day** aujourd'hui même; **in this very house** dans cette maison même; **at that very moment** juste à ce moment-là; **at the very top** tout en haut

vest *noun*
(a) *(for men)* le maillot de corps
(b) *(for women)* la chemise

> Note that the French word *veste* is never a translation for the English word *vest*. It means *jacket*.

vet *noun* le/la vétérinaire; **she's a vet** elle est vétérinaire

vicious *adjective*
(a) *(violent)* violent/violente; **a vicious blow** un coup violent
(b) *(nasty)* méchant/méchante; **a vicious dog** un chien méchant
(c) **a vicious circle** un cercle vicieux

> Note that the French word *vicieux* is rarely a translation for the English word *vicious*. Depending on the context, it can mean *perverted* or *sly*.

victim *noun* la victime

> Note that the word *victime* is always feminine, even when it refers to a man.

victory *noun* la victoire

video
1 *noun*
(a) *(film)* la vidéo; **a video of the World Cup** une vidéo de la Coupe du Monde; **a music video** un clip
(b) *(tape)* la cassette vidéo; **I have it on video** je l'ai en cassette vidéo; **a video shop** un vidéoclub

> The plural of *cassette vidéo* is *cassettes vidéo*.

(c) *(recorder)* le magnétoscope; **to set the video** programmer le magnétoscope
(d) **a video game** un jeu vidéo

> The plural of *jeu vidéo* is *jeux vidéo*.

2 *verb*
(a) *(record)* enregistrer
(b) *(film)* filmer

Vietnam *noun* le Viêt Nam; **we're going to Vietnam** nous allons au Viêt Nam; **she lives in Vietnam** elle habite au Viêt Nam

Vietnamese
1 *adjective* vietnamien/vietnamienne
2 *noun*
(a) *(language)* le vietnamien; **he speaks Vietnamese** il parle vietnamien
(b) *(person)* le Vietnamien/la Vietnamienne; **the Vietnamese** les Vietnamiens *(masculine plural)*

> In French, only the noun for the inhabitants of a country takes a capital letter, never the adjective or the noun for the language.

view *noun*
(a) *(sight)* la vue; **a room with a view** une chambre avec vue
(b) *(opinion)* une opinion, un avis; **what's your view on the matter?** quelle est votre opinion sur la question?; **in my view** à mon avis; **a point**

of view un point de vue

(**c**) *(intention)* **they bought the house with a view to letting it** ils ont acheté la maison dans le but de la louer

(**d**) **in view of** *(considering)* étant donné; **in view of what has happened** étant donné ce qui s'est passé

viewer *noun (of a TV programme)* le téléspectateur/la téléspectatrice

village *noun* le village; **the village hall** la salle des fêtes

vinegar *noun* le vinaigre

violence *noun* la violence

violent *adjective* violent/violente

violin *noun* le violon; **he plays the violin** il joue du violon

Virgo *noun* la Vierge; **he's (a) Virgo** il est Vierge

virus *noun* le virus

visible *adjective* visible

visit
1 *noun*
(**a**) *(of a person)* la visite; **to pay somebody a visit** rendre visite à quelqu'un
(**b**) *(to a place)* le séjour; **this is my first visit to France** c'est la première fois que je viens en France
2 *verb*
(**a**) *(a person)* rendre visite à; **she visited her grandma** elle a rendu visite à sa grand-mère; **to visit the doctor** aller chez le médecin
(**b**) *(a place)* visiter; **we visited the museum** nous avons visité le musée

visitor *noun*
(**a**) *(to a person)* un invité/une invitée; **we have visitors at the moment** nous avons des invités en ce moment; **the patient has visitors** le malade a de la visite
(**b**) *(to a place)* le visiteur/la visiteuse; **we get lots of American visitors to the town** nous avons beaucoup de visiteurs américains dans la ville

visual *adjective* visuel/visuelle; **visual arts** les arts plastiques

vital *adjective* vital/vitale

The masculine plural of *vital* is *vitaux*.

vitamin *noun* la vitamine

vocabulary *noun* le vocabulaire

vocal *adjective (music)* vocal/vocale; **vocal cords** les cordes vocales

The masculine plural of *vocal* is *vocaux*.

voice *noun* la voix; **to speak in a loud voice** parler à voix haute; **to speak in a low voice** à voix basse; **at the top of one's voice** à tue-tête

volcano *noun* le volcan

volleyball *noun* le volley-ball; **they're playing volleyball** ils jouent au volley-ball

volume *noun* le volume

voluntary *adjective*
(**a**) *(freely given)* volontaire; **a voluntary contribution** une contribution volontaire
(**b**) *(unpaid)* bénévole; **I do voluntary work** je fais du travail bénévole *or* je fais du bénévolat
(**c**) *(optional)* facultatif/facultative; **attendance is voluntary** la participation est facultative

volunteer
1 *noun*
(**a**) le/la volontaire; **are there any volunteers?** est-ce qu'il y a des volontaires?
(**b**) *(charity worker)* le/la bénévole
2 *verb*
(**a**) se porter volontaire; **I volunteered to help them** je me suis porté volontaire pour les aider
(**b**) **he volunteered his services as a guide** il s'est proposé comme guide

vomit
1 *noun* le vomi
2 *verb* vomir

vote
1 *noun*
(**a**) *(choice)* le vote; **to take a vote on**

something voter sur quelque chose
(**b**) *(paper)* la voix; **she got the majority of the votes** elle a obtenu la majorité des voix
(**c**) *(right)* le droit de vote; **British women got the vote in 1928** les femmes
britanniques ont obtenu le droit de
vote en 1928
2 *verb* voter; **to vote Labour** voter travailliste; **to vote in favour of something** voter pour quelque chose; **to**

vote against something voter contre
quelque chose

voucher *noun* le bon; **a gift voucher**
un chèque-cadeau

The plural of *chèque-cadeau* is *chè-
ques-cadeaux.*

vowel *noun* la voyelle

vulture *noun* le vautour

waffle *noun* la gaufre

wag *verb* remuer; **the dog's wagging its tail** le chien remue la queue; **to wag one's finger at somebody** menacer quelqu'un du doigt

wages *plural noun* le salaire; **he earns good wages** il est bien payé

waist *noun* la taille

waistcoat *noun* le gilet

wait
1 *noun* l'attente *(feminine)*; **we had a long wait** nous avons dû attendre longtemps
2 *verb*
(a) attendre; **wait a minute** attendez un instant; **wait and see!** attends voir!
(b) **to wait for somebody** attendre quelqu'un; **I was waiting for the rain to stop** j'attendais que la pluie s'arrête
(c) **to keep somebody waiting** faire attendre quelqu'un
(d) **I can't wait to see him** j'ai hâte de le voir

waiter *noun* le serveur

waiting *noun* l'attente *(feminine)*; **a waiting list** une liste d'attente; **a waiting room** une salle d'attente

waitress *noun* la serveuse

wake up *verb*
(a) se réveiller; **wake up!** réveille-toi!
(b) **to wake somebody up** réveiller quelqu'un

Wales *noun* le pays de Galles; **I live in Wales** j'habite au pays de Galles; **I'm going to Wales** je vais au pays de Galles; **I come from Wales** je viens du pays de Galles

walk
1 *noun*
(a) *(stroll)* la promenade; **to go for a walk** faire une promenade; **to take the dog for a walk** aller promener le chien
(b) *(distance)* **it's a long walk** c'est loin à pied; **it's only a short walk from here** c'est à deux pas d'ici
2 *verb*
(a) marcher; **he can't walk** il ne peut pas marcher
(b) *(for pleasure)* se promener; **we walked around the town** nous nous sommes promenés dans la ville
(c) *(go on foot)* aller à pied; **I missed the bus so I had to walk home** j'ai raté le bus donc j'ai dû rentrer à pied; **we walked down the street** nous avons descendu la rue à pied
(d) **to walk somebody home** raccompagner quelqu'un
(e) **to walk the dog** promener le chien
3 **walk away** partir
4 **walk in** entrer
5 **walk off** partir
6 **walk out**
(a) *(go out)* sortir
(b) **his wife walked out on him** sa femme l'a quitté

walking *noun* la marche; **I like walking** j'aime bien marcher; **walking shoes** des chaussures de marche; **a walking stick** une canne

walkman® *noun* le baladeur, le walkman®

wall *noun* le mur

wallet *noun* le portefeuille

wallpaper

1 *noun* le papier peint, la tapisserie
2 *verb* tapisser

walnut

noun la noix; **a walnut cake** un gâteau aux noix; **a walnut tree** un noyer

wand

noun la baguette; **a magic wand** une baguette magique

wander

1 *verb*
(a) *(move slowly)* flâner; **to wander the streets** flâner dans les rues
(b) *(move away)* s'éloigner; **don't wander too far** ne vous éloignez pas trop
(c) **my mind was wandering** j'avais l'esprit ailleurs
2 **wander about, wander around** errer; **to wander about aimlessly** errer sans but; **I was wandering about the house** j'errais dans la maison; **they wandered around the town** ils se sont promenés dans la ville
3 **wander off** s'éloigner; **don't wander off** ne vous éloignez pas trop

want

verb
(a) vouloir; **I want a cup of coffee** je veux une tasse de café; **she didn't want to go** elle n'a pas voulu y aller
(b) *(need)* avoir besoin de; **this coat wants cleaning** ce manteau a besoin d'être nettoyé
(c) *(ask for)* **the boss wants you** le patron veut te voir; **you're wanted on the phone** on te demande au téléphone
(d) **he's wanted by the police** il est recherché par la police

war

noun la guerre; **they're at war** ils sont en guerre; **a war film** un film de guerre

wardrobe

noun
(a) *(cupboard)* une armoire
(b) *(clothes)* la garde-robe

> The plural of *garde-robe* is *garde-robes*.

warehouse

noun un entrepôt

warm

1 *adjective*
(a) chaud/chaude; **I'm warm** j'ai chaud; **it's warm outside** il fait chaud dehors; **to get warm** se réchauffer
(b) *(friendly)* chaleureux/chaleureuse; **a warm welcome** un accueil chaleureux; **a warm smile** un sourire accueillant
2 *verb* **warm up**
(a) *(food)* faire chauffer
(b) *(get warmer)* se réchauffer
(c) *(before exercise)* s'échauffer

warmth

noun la chaleur

warn

verb avertir, prévenir; **she warned me about him** elle m'a mis en garde contre lui; **I warned them of the danger** je les ai avertis du danger; **she warned them that she would be late** elle les a prévenus qu'elle serait en retard; **we must warn the police** il faut prévenir la police; **he warned me not to do it** il m'a déconseillé de le faire

warning

noun
(a) *(caution)* un avertissement; **the police gave him a warning** la police lui a donné un avertissement; **a warning signal** un signal d'alerte
(b) *(advance notice)* **we only received a few days' warning** nous n'avons été prévenus que quelques jours à l'avance; **he left without any warning** il est parti sans prévenir

wash

1 *noun*
(a) **to have a wash** se laver; **to give something a wash** laver quelque chose
(b) *(for clothes)* **the stain came out in the wash** la tache est partie au lavage; **your jeans are in the wash** *(in the laundry basket)* ton jean est au sale; *(in the washing machine)* ton jean est dans la machine à laver
2 *verb*
(a) *(clean)* laver; **I washed the sheets** j'ai lavé les draps

(**b**) *(have a wash)* se laver
(**c**) **to wash one's hands** se laver les mains; **to wash one's hair** se laver les cheveux
3 wash up faire la vaisselle

washbasin *noun* le lavabo

washing *noun*
(**a**) *(cleaning)* le lavage
(**b**) *(of clothes)* **to do the washing** faire la lessive; **a washing machine** une machine à laver; **washing powder** la lessive
(**c**) *(dirty clothes)* le linge sale
(**d**) *(clean clothes)* le linge propre

washing-up *noun* la vaisselle; **to do the washing-up** faire la vaisselle; **washing-up liquid** le liquide vaisselle

wasp *noun* la guêpe

waste
1 *noun*
(**a**) *(of money, food)* le gaspillage
(**b**) **a waste of time** une perte de temps
2 *verb*
(**a**) *(money, food)* gaspiller
(**b**) *(time)* perdre

watch
1 *noun (on the wrist)* la montre
2 *verb* regarder; **to watch television** regarder la télévision; **I watched him working** je l'ai regardé travailler
3 watch out faire attention; **watch out for the cars!** fais attention aux voitures!; **watch out!** attention!

water
1 *noun* l'eau *(feminine)*; **a glass of water** un verre d'eau; **a water pistol** un pistolet à eau; **water skiing** le ski nautique
2 *verb*
(**a**) *(plants, garden)* arroser
(**b**) **my eyes are watering** j'ai les yeux qui pleurent; **it makes my mouth water** ça me met l'eau à la bouche

watercolour *noun*
(**a**) *(painting)* une aquarelle
(**b**) *(paint)* **he paints in watercolours** il peint à l'aquarelle

waterfall *noun* la cascade

watermelon *noun* la pastèque

wave
1 *noun*
(**a**) *(in the sea)* la vague
(**b**) *(with one's hand)* le signe de la main; **she gave us a wave** elle nous a fait un signe de la main
2 *verb*
(**a**) *(with one's hand)* faire un signe de la main; **I waved to them** je leur ai fait un signe de la main; **they waved goodbye to us** ils nous ont fait au revoir de la main
(**b**) *(shake)* agiter; **to wave a flag** agiter un drapeau; **to wave one's arms about** agiter les bras

wavelength *noun* la longueur d'onde; **we're on the same wavelength** nous sommes sur la même longueur d'onde

wavy *adjective* ondulé/ondulée; **she has wavy hair** elle a les cheveux ondulés

wax
1 *noun*
(**a**) la cire
(**b**) **a wax crayon** un pastel
2 *verb* **to wax one's legs** s'épiler les jambes

way *noun*
(**a**) *(path)* le chemin; **this is the way to the station** c'est le chemin de la gare; **to go the right way** prendre le bon chemin; **to go the wrong way** se tromper de chemin; **on the way** en chemin
(**b**) *(direction)* **which way?** par où?; **this way** par ici; **that way** par là; **the way in** l'entrée *(feminine)*; **the way out** la sortie
(**c**) *(distance)* **it's a long way** c'est loin; **it's only a short way** ce n'est pas très loin
(**d**) *(manner)* la manière; **the way you talk to her** la manière dont tu lui parles; **I do things in my own way** je fais

les choses à ma manière
(**e**) **to be in somebody's way** gêner quelqu'un; **you're in my way** tu me gênes; **get out of the way!** pousse-toi!; **this table is in the way** cette table est dans le passage
(**f**) **in a way** d'une certaine manière
(**g**) **no way!** pas question!

we *pronoun* nous, on; **we are English** nous sommes anglais; **we went to the cinema** nous sommes allés au cinéma *or* on est allé au cinéma

> *On* is less formal than *nous* but very common. Note that *on* is always conjugated as the third person singular (like *il* and *elle*) even when it means *nous*.

weak *adjective*
(**a**) *(person, character)* faible
(**b**) *(tea, coffee)* léger/légère

weakness *noun*
(**a**) *(physical)* la faiblesse
(**b**) *(moral)* **she has a weakness for chocolate** elle a un faible pour le chocolat

wealth *noun* la richesse

wealthy *adjective* riche

weapon *noun* une arme

wear
1 *verb* porter; **he wears glasses** il porte des lunettes; **she's wearing black** elle est habillée en noir; **does she wear make-up?** est-ce qu'elle se maquille?
2 wear out
(**a**) *(damage)* user; **he's worn out the soles of his shoes** il a usé les semelles de ses chaussures
(**b**) *(get damaged)* s'user; **his shoes have worn out** ses chaussures se sont usées
(**c**) *(exhaust)* épuiser; **you're wearing yourself out working so hard** tu t'épuises à tant travailler; **I'm worn out** je suis épuisé

weary *adjective* fatigué/fatiguée; **to grow weary of something** se lasser de quelque chose

weather *noun*
(**a**) le temps; **what's the weather like?** quel temps fait-il?
(**b**) **the weather forecast** la météo; **what's the weather forecast?** que dit la météo?

Web *noun* **the Web** le Web; **a Web page** une page Web

web *noun* *(of a spider)* la toile

website *noun* le site Web

wedding *noun* le mariage; **a wedding anniversary** un anniversaire de mariage; **a wedding ring** une alliance

Wednesday *noun* le mercredi; **on Wednesday** mercredi; **she left on Wednesday** elle est partie mercredi; **on Wednesdays** le mercredi; **she goes swimming on Wednesdays** elle va à la piscine le mercredi; **every Wednesday** tous les mercredis; **next Wednesday** mercredi prochain; **last Wednesday** mercredi dernier

> In French, the names of days are not written with a capital.

weed
1 *noun* la mauvaise herbe
2 *verb* désherber

week *noun* la semaine; **next week** la semaine prochaine; **last week** la semaine dernière; **twice a week** deux fois par semaine; **every week** toutes les semaines; **a week from now** dans une semaine; **we're leaving a week on Friday** nous partons vendredi de la semaine prochaine

weekend *noun* le week-end; **at the weekend** le week-end; **have a good weekend!** bon week-end!

> The plural of *week-end* is *week-ends*.

weekly
1 *adjective* hebdomadaire; **a weekly magazine** un magazine hebdomadaire *or* un hebdomadaire
2 *adverb* toutes les semaines; **I visit him weekly** je lui rend visite toutes les

semaines; **twice weekly** deux fois par semaine

weigh *noun* peser; **to weigh oneself** se peser; **how much do you weigh?** tu pèses combien?; **it weighs two kilos** ça pèse deux kilos

weight *noun* le poids; **to lose weight** perdre du poids; **to put on weight** prendre du poids

weightlifting *noun* l'haltérophilie *(feminine)*

weird *adjective* bizarre

welcome
1 *exclamation* bienvenue; **welcome home!** bienvenue à la maison!
2 *adjective*
(a) bienvenu/bienvenue; **he's always welcome** il est toujours le bienvenu; **he made me very welcome** il m'a fait bon accueil
(b) *(permitted)* **you're welcome to take my car** tu peux prendre ma voiture si tu veux
(c) *(when thanked)* **you're welcome!** je vous en prie!; *(less formal)* de rien!
3 *noun* un accueil; **to give somebody a warm welcome** faire un accueil chaleureux à quelqu'un
4 *verb* accueillir; **there's a party to welcome the new students** il y a une fête pour accueillir les nouveaux étudiants

well¹
1 *adjective (healthy)* **I'm well** je vais bien; **he's not very well** il ne va pas très bien; **to get well** se rétablir
2 *adverb*
(a) bien; **she speaks French very well** elle parle très bien français; **everything is going well** tout se passe bien; **to do well** bien réussir; **you did well in the exam** tu as bien réussi à l'examen; **well done!** bravo!
(b) *(used for emphasis)* **it's well worth trying** cela vaut la peine d'essayer; **she's well over 40** elle a bien plus de 40 ans
(c) **as well** aussi; **I'd like one as well**

j'en voudrais un aussi
(d) **as well as** ainsi que; **as well as two cats, he has a dog** il a deux chats ainsi qu'un chien
3 *exclamation* **well!** eh bien!; **well, as I was saying** eh bien, comme je vous le disais; **well, who was it?** alors, c'était qui?; **it was huge, well, quite big** c'était énorme, enfin, assez grand; **well, well, well!** tiens, tiens!

well² *noun* *(for water)* le puits; **an oil well** un puits de pétrole

well-behaved *adjective* sage

well-dressed *adjective* bien habillé/habillée

wellingtons *plural noun* les bottes en caoutchouc *(feminine plural)*

well-known *adjective* connu/connue

well-off *adjective* riche

well-paid *adjective* bien payé/payée

Welsh
1 *adjective* gallois/galloise
2 *noun*
(a) *(language)* le gallois
(b) *(people)* **the Welsh** les Gallois *(masculine plural)*

Welshman *noun* le Gallois

Welshwoman *noun* la Galloise

west
1 *noun* l'ouest *(masculine)*; **to the west of** à l'ouest de; **he lives to the west of Paris** il habite à l'ouest de Paris; **in the west of** dans l'est de; **Glasgow is in the west of Scotland** Glasgow est dans l'ouest de l'Écosse
2 *adjective* ouest; **the west coast** la côte ouest; **a west wind** un vent d'ouest
3 *adverb* vers l'ouest; **they're heading west** ils se dirigent vers l'ouest

western
1 *adjective* **western France** l'ouest de la France; **Western Europe** l'Europe de l'Ouest *or* l'Europe occidentale; **the western world** le monde occidental

2 *noun* *(film)* le western

West Indian
1 *adjective* antillais/antillaise
2 *noun* *(person)* un Antillais/une Antillaise; **the West Indians** les Antillais *(masculine plural)*

West Indies *plural noun* les Antilles *(feminine plural)*; **I've never been to the West Indies** je ne suis jamais allé aux Antilles; **they live in the West Indies** ils habitent aux Antilles; **she comes from the West Indies** elle vient des Antilles

wet *adjective*
(**a**) mouillé/mouillée; **to get wet** se mouiller; **to get one's feet wet** se mouiller les pieds
(**b**) *(weather)* pluvieux/pluvieuse

wetsuit *noun* la combinaison de plongée

whale *noun* la baleine

what
1 *adjective*
(**a**) quel/quelle; **what day is it?** quel jour sommes-nous?; **what time is it?** quelle heure est-il?; **show me what books you want** montre-moi quels livres tu veux; **what colours do you prefer?** quelles couleurs préfères-tu?

> *Quel* is used with masculine nouns and *quelle* is used with feminine nouns. The masculine plural is *quels* and the feminine plural is *quelles*.

(**b**) *(in exclamations)* **what a pity!** quel dommage!; **what a good idea!** quelle bonne idée!; **what lovely children!** quels charmants enfants!; **what beautiful flowers!** quelles jolies fleurs!
2 *pronoun*
(**a**) *(when "what" is the subject of the verb)* qu'est-ce qui; **what's happening?** qu'est-ce qui se passe?
(**b**) *(when "what" is the object of the verb)* qu'est-ce que; **what's that?** qu'est-ce que c'est?; **what did you do?** qu'est-ce que tu as fait?

> Note that *qu'est-ce que* becomes *qu'est-ce qu'* in front of a vowel or a mute h.

(**c**) *(with a preposition)* quoi; **what's that for?** à quoi ça sert?; **what are you thinking about?** à quoi penses-tu?; **what are you talking about?** de quoi parles-tu?
(**d**) *(in descriptions)* comment; **what's it like?** c'est comment?; **what's the French for "dog"?** comment dit-on "dog" en français?; **what's your name?** comment tu t'appelles?
(**e**) *(in suggestions)* **what about a game of tennis?** et si on faisait une partie de tennis?; **what if we went to the beach?** et si on allait à la plage?; **what about me?** et moi?
3 *exclamation* quoi; **what! another new dress?** quoi, encore une nouvelle robe?; **are you mad or what?** tu es fou ou quoi?
4 *relative pronoun*
(**a**) *(when "what" is the subject of the verb)* ce qui; **tell me what's going on** dis-moi ce qui se passe
(**b**) *(when "what" is the object of the verb)* ce que, quoi; **that's not what I said** ce n'est pas ce que j'ai dit; **I don't know what to say** je ne sais pas quoi dire; **it's what we talked about yesterday** c'est ce dont on a parlé hier

> As shown in the examples in (b), *what* is usually translated by *ce que* when it is followed by a conjugated verb and by *quoi* when it is followed by an infinitive verb.

whatever
1 *adjective* *(no matter what)* quel que soit/quelle que soit; **I'll buy it whatever price they ask** je l'achèterai quel que soit le prix qu'ils demandent; **I want that car whatever colour it is** je veux cette voiture quelle que soit la couleur

> The masculine plural is *quels que soient* and the feminine plural is *quelles que soient*.

2 *pronoun*
(**a**) *(no matter what)* quoi que; **whatever happens, keep calm** quoi qu'il arrive, restez calme
(**b**) *(everything that)* tout ce que; **you can eat whatever you like** tu peux manger tout ce que tu veux

wheat *noun* le blé

wheel *noun*
(**a**) *(on a vehicle)* la roue
(**b**) *(on a trolley, a suitcase)* la roulette

wheelbarrow *noun* la brouette

wheelchair *noun* le fauteuil roulant

when
1 *adverb* quand; **when are we leaving?** quand est-ce qu'on part?; **when did this happen?** quand est-ce que ça s'est passé?; **when does the shop shut?** à quelle heure ferme le magasin?
2 *conjunction* quand; **he was asleep when I came home** il dormait quand je suis rentré; **tell me when you've finished** dis-moi quand tu auras terminé; **phone me when you're there** appelle-moi quand tu seras là-bas

Note that French uses the future tense (and not the present as in English) when the action described will take place in the future.

whenever *conjunction*
(**a**) *(each time that)* chaque fois que; **whenever I hear that song I think of you** chaque fois que j'entends cette chanson je pense à toi
(**b**) *(at any time)* quand; **he can come whenever he likes** il peut venir quand il veut

where
1 *adverb* où; **where is it?** c'est où?; **where are you going?** où est-ce que tu vas?; **where are you from?** d'où viens-tu?
2 *conjunction* où; **go where you like** allez où vous voulez
3 *relative pronoun* où; **the town where I was born** la ville où je suis né

wherever *conjunction*
(**a**) *(in every place)* partout où; **I see him wherever I go** je le vois partout où je vais
(**b**) *(no matter where)* où; **we'll go wherever you want** nous irons où tu voudras; **sit wherever there's room** asseyez-vous là où il y a de la place

whether *conjunction*
(**a**) *(if)* si; **I don't know whether it's true** je ne sais pas si c'est vrai; **it depends on whether you're in a hurry or not** cela dépend si vous êtes pressé ou non
(**b**) **we're going whether he likes it or not** on y va que cela lui plaise ou non

Note that when *whether* is used in sense (b), the verb in French is in the subjunctive.

which
1 *adjective* quel/quelle; **tell me which book you want** dis-moi quel livre tu veux; **which colour do you prefer?** quelle couleur préfères-tu?; **which restaurants are the best?** quels sont les meilleurs restaurants?; **which towns did you visit?** quelles villes avez-vous visitées?
2 *pronoun* lequel/laquelle; **which of these books is yours?** lequel de ces livres est le tien?; **which of the two girls is prettiest?** laquelle des deux filles est la plus jolie?; **look at the car! – which one?** regarde la voiture! – laquelle?; **he broke one of my CDs – which one?** il a cassé un de mes CD – lequel?; **which ones?** lesquels/lesquelles?
3 *relative pronoun*
(**a**) *(when "which" is the subject of the verb)* qui; *(when "which" is the object of the verb)* que; **the house which is for sale** la maison qui est à vendre; **the film which we saw** le film que nous avons vu

Note that *qui* is used in the first example because *which* is the subject of the verb *to be* (the house is for sale). *Que* is used in the second example because *which* is the object of the verb *to see* (I saw the film).

(**b**) *(when referring back to a previous statement) (when "which" is the subject of the verb)* ce qui; *(when "which" is the object of the verb)* ce que; **he's getting married, which surprises me** il va se marier, ce qui m'étonne; **she was born in France, which I didn't know** elle est née en France, ce que je ne savais pas

Note that *ce qui* is used in the first example because *which* is the subject of the verb *to surprise* (it is the fact that he's getting married that surprises me). *Ce que* is used in the second example because *which* is the object of the verb *to know* (I didn't know that she was born in France).

(**c**) *(with a preposition)* **the countries which we're going to** les pays où nous allons; **the pen which I'm writing with** le stylo avec lequel j'écris

while
1 *conjunction*
(**a**) *(when)* pendant que; **you can lay the table while I'm cooking** tu peux mettre la table pendant que je fais la cuisine; **I fell asleep while reading** je me suis endormi en lisant; **he read the paper while he waited for the bus** il a lu le journal en attendant le bus

When *while* is directly followed by a verb ending in *-ing*, or when the subject of the two verbs in the sentence is the same (as in the last example), French often uses the gerund: *en* + verb ending in *-ant*.

(**b**) *(whereas)* alors que; **she likes Spain while I prefer Greece** elle aime bien l'Espagne alors que je préfère la Grèce
2 *noun* **a while** un moment; **this will take quite a while** ça va prendre un certain temps; **after a while** au bout d'un moment; **a little while ago** il y a peu de temps; **a long while** longtemps

whip
1 *noun* le fouet
2 *verb* fouetter; **whipped cream** de la crème fouettée

whiskers *noun (of a cat)* les moustaches *(feminine plural)*

whisper *verb* chuchoter; **stop whispering!** arrêtez de chuchoter!

whistle
1 *noun*
(**a**) *(noise)* le sifflement
(**b**) *(object)* le sifflet; **to blow a whistle** siffler *or* donner un coup de sifflet
2 *verb*
(**a**) *(using one's mouth)* siffler; **he was whistling his favourite tune** il sifflait son air préféré
(**b**) *(using a whistle)* donner un coup de sifflet

white
1 *adjective* blanc/blanche; **a white man** un Blanc; **a white woman** une Blanche; **white people** les Blancs
2 *noun* le blanc; **she's dressed in white** elle est habillé en blanc; **an egg white** un blanc d'œuf

who
1 *pronoun (in questions)* qui; **who is it?** qui est-ce?; **who's speaking?** *(on the phone)* qui est à l'appareil?; **who told you that?** qui vous a dit ça? **who did you see?** qui est-ce que tu as vu? *or* qui as-tu vu?
2 *relative pronoun* qui; **the people who came yesterday** les gens qui sont venus hier; **Jayne's father, who is a doctor, was there** le père de Jayne, qui est médecin, était là

whoever *pronoun*
(**a**) *(the person who)* celui/celle qui; **whoever wants it can have it** celui qui le veut peut le prendre

The masculine plural of *celui qui* is *ceux qui* and the feminine plural of *celle qui* is *celles qui*.

(**b**) *(no matter who)* qui que; **whoever you are** qui que vous soyez; **whoever** you vote for quelle que soit la personne pour qui vous votez

> Note that *qui que* is always followed by the subjunctive.

whole

1 *adjective* tout/toute, entier/entière; **the whole truth** toute la vérité; **the whole cake** tout le gâteau; **the whole world** le monde entier; **a whole week** toute une semaine *or* une semaine entière

2 *noun* l'ensemble *(masculine)*; **on the whole** dans l'ensemble; **I've lived here the whole of my life** j'ai habité ici toute ma vie

whom

1 *pronoun* *(in formal questions)* qui; **for whom was the book written?** pour qui le livre a-t-il été écrit?

2 *relative pronoun*
(**a**) *(when "whom" is the object of the verb)* que; **the man whom you saw** l'homme que vous avez vu
(**b**) *(with a preposition)* qui; **the person to whom I am writing** la personne à qui j'écris; **the man to whom you gave the money** l'homme à qui vous avez donné l'argent; **the person about whom we are speaking** la personne dont nous parlons

whose

1 *adjective*
(**a**) *(in questions)* à qui; **whose car is he driving?** à qui est la voiture qu'il conduit?; **whose fault is it?** à qui la faute?
(**b**) *(in sentences that are not questions)* dont; **he's the pupil whose work I showed you** c'est l'élève dont je t'ai montré le travail

2 *pronoun* à qui; **whose is it?** à qui est-ce?; **whose are these gloves?** à qui sont ces gants?

why

1 *adverb* pourquoi; **why did you tell him?** pourquoi est-ce que tu le lui as dit?; **why not sell the car?** pourquoi ne pas vendre la voiture?; **why**

not? pourquoi pas?

2 *conjunction* pourquoi; **I'll tell you why I don't like her** je vais vous dire pourquoi je ne l'aime pas; **I wonder why he left** je me demande pourquoi il est parti

3 *relative pronoun* **this is the reason why she didn't come** c'est la raison pour laquelle elle n'est pas venue

wicked *adjective*
(**a**) *(evil)* méchant/méchante
(**b**) *(great)* génial/géniale; **this song's wicked!** elle est géniale, cette chanson!

> The masculine plural of *génial* is *géniaux*.

wide

1 *adjective*
(**a**) *(broad)* large; **the room is three metres wide** la pièce fait trois mètres de large
(**b**) *(vast)* grand/grande; **a wide variety of colours** un grand choix de couleurs

2 *adverb* **the door is wide open** la porte est grande ouverte; **he's wide awake** il est bien réveillé

widespread *adjective* répandu/répandue

widow *noun* la veuve

widower *noun* le veuf

width *noun* la largeur

wife *noun* la femme

wig *noun* la perruque

wild *adjective*
(**a**) *(animal, plant)* sauvage
(**b**) *(crazy, out of control)* fou/folle; **it was a wild party** c'était une fête délirante
(**c**) *(weather)* très mauvais/mauvaise

wildlife *noun* la faune et la flore; **a wildlife park** une réserve naturelle

will

1 *auxiliary verb*
(**a**) *(future tense)* **he will come** il viendra; **you'll tell him** tu le lui diras; **they will not do it** ils ne le feront pas; **I**

won't go on holiday this year je n'irai pas en vacances cette année; **I will have finished by five o'clock** j'aurai fini avant cinq heures; **you will do it, won't you?** tu le feras, n'est-ce pas?
(**b**) *(in questions, requests)* **will you help me?** tu veux bien m'aider?; **won't you sit down?** vous ne voulez pas vous asseoir?; **will you be quiet!** vous voulez bien vous taire!
(**c**) *(with objects)* **the car won't start** la voiture ne démarre pas; **the door won't shut** la porte ne ferme pas
2 *noun (of a dead person)* le testament

willing *adjective* **I'm willing to try** je veux bien essayer; **he's always willing to help** il est toujours prêt à rendre service

win *verb* gagner; **she won first prize** elle a gagné le premier prix; **I think Spain will win** je crois que l'Espagne va gagner

wind¹ *noun* le vent; **there's a strong wind** il y a beaucoup de vent

wind²
1 *verb (roll)* enrouler; **I wound a scarf round my neck** j'ai enroulé une écharpe autour de mon cou
2 wind up
(**a**) *(a clock, a toy, a car window)* remonter
(**b**) *(tease)* faire marcher; **they're just winding you up** ils te font marcher

windmill *noun* le moulin à vent

window *noun*
(**a**) *(of a house)* la fenêtre
(**b**) *(of a car, a bus)* la vitre
(**c**) *(of a shop)* la vitrine

windscreen *noun*
(**a**) le pare-brise

> The word *pare-brise* does not change in the plural.

(**b**) **a windscreen wiper** un essuie-glace

> The plural of *essuie-glace* is *essuie-glaces*.

windsurfing *noun* la planche à voile; **they go windsurfing** ils font de la planche à voile

windy *adjective* **it's windy** il y a du vent

wine *noun* le vin; **a wine glass** un verre à vin

wing *noun* une aile

wink
1 *noun* le clin d'œil; **he gave me a wink** il m'a fait un clin d'œil
2 *verb* faire un clin d'œil; **I winked at them** je leur ai fait un clin d'œil

winner *noun* le gagnant/la gagnante

winter *noun* l'hiver *(masculine)*; **in winter** en hiver

wintertime *noun* l'hiver *(masculine)*; **in the wintertime** en hiver

wipe *verb* essuyer; **I wiped the table** j'ai essuyé la table; **he wiped his hands** il s'est essuyé les mains

wire *noun*
(**a**) *(made of metal)* le fil de fer
(**b**) *(electrical)* le fil électrique

wisdom *noun* la sagesse

wise *adjective*
(**a**) *(knowledgeable)* sage
(**b**) *(sensible)* prudent/prudente; **I don't think it's wise to invite him** je ne crois pas que ce soit prudent de l'inviter

wish
1 *verb*
(**a**) *(want)* souhaiter; **he doesn't wish to discuss it** il ne souhaite pas en parler; **I wish to be left alone** je souhaite qu'on me laisse tranquille; **she wished for a puppy** elle voulait avoir un chiot
(**b**) *(in expressions of goodwill)* souhaiter; **I wished him luck** je lui ai souhaité bonne chance; **he wished me a pleasant journey** il m'a souhaité un bon voyage
(**c**) *(want something unlikely or impossible)* **I wish you would come** j'aimerais bien que tu viennes; **I wish I**

could fly j'aimerais pouvoir voler; **I wish I had seen it!** si seulement j'avais pu le voir!; **I wish you had told me sooner** j'aurais aimé que tu me le dises avant

2 *noun* un vœu; **make a wish!** fais un vœu!

The plural of *vœu* is *vœux*.

witch *noun* la sorcière

with *preposition*
(**a**) avec; **come with me** viens avec moi; **I cut it with a knife** je l'ai coupé avec un couteau
(**b**) *(in a description)* à; **a knife with a silver handle** un couteau à manche d'argent; **the girl with the glasses** la fille aux lunettes
(**c**) *(at the home of)* chez; **he lives with his grandmother** il habite chez sa grand-mère
(**d**) *(because of)* de; **he was trembling with rage** il tremblait de rage; **she's sick with worry** elle est malade d'inquiétude; **I'm very pleased with him** je suis très content de lui

within *preposition*
(**a**) *(inside)* à l'intérieur de, au sein de; **there are problems within the company** il y a des problèmes au sein de l'entreprise
(**b**) *(in the space of)* **she had finished within the hour** elle avait fini en moins d'une heure; **I'll be back within a week** je serai de retour d'ici une semaine; **within minutes** en quelques minutes
(**c**) *(not beyond)* à moins de; **it's within ten kilometres of the city** c'est à moins de dix kilomètres de la ville

without *preposition* sans; **I'd like a pizza without onions** je voudrais une pizza sans oignons; **I did it without her knowing** je l'ai fait sans qu'elle le sache

witness
1 *noun* le témoin
2 *verb* être témoin de; **did you witness the accident?** avez-vous été témoin de l'accident?

wizard *noun* le sorcier

wolf *noun* le loup

woman *noun* la femme

wonder
1 *noun* la merveille; **the seven wonders of the world** les sept merveilles du monde; **no wonder they refused** ce n'est pas étonnant qu'ils aient refusé
2 *verb* se demander; **I wonder where my keys are** je me demande où sont mes clés; **no wonder!** ce n'est pas étonnant!; **I wonder why** je me demande pourquoi

wonderful *adjective* merveilleux/merveilleuse

wood *noun* le bois; **the table is made of wood** la table est en bois; **we went for a walk in the woods** nous sommes allés nous promener dans les bois

wooden *noun* en bois; **a wooden house** une maison en bois

wool *noun* la laine

woollen *adjective* en laine; **a woollen scarf** une écharpe en laine

woolly *adjective* en laine; **woolly socks** des chaussettes en laine

word *noun*
(**a**) le mot; **don't say a word!** pas un mot!; **what's the French word for "head"?** comment dit-on "head" en français?
(**b**) *(conversation, remarks)* **can I have a word with you?** est-ce que je peux te parler?; **let me give you a word of advice** je vais te donner un petit conseil
(**c**) *(news)* les nouvelles *(feminine plural)*; **have you had any word from him?** avez-vous eu de ses nouvelles?
(**d**) *(promise)* la parole; **I give you my word** je te donne ma parole; **he kept his word** il a tenu parole
(**e**) **words** *(of a song)* les paroles *(feminine plural)*

work

1 *noun*

(a) *(activity, place)* le travail; **I have a lot of work to do** j'ai beaucoup de travail à faire; **she's at work** elle est au travail

(b) **a work of art** une œuvre d'art

(c) **road works** les travaux *(masculine plural)*

2 *verb*

(a) *(of a person)* travailler; **they work hard** ils travaillent dur; **he's working on a novel** il travaille sur un roman

(b) *(of a machine, a method)* marcher, fonctionner; **do you think it will work?** tu crois que ça va marcher?; **how does this machine work?** comment fonctionne cette machine?; **the lift isn't working** l'ascenseur ne marche pas

3 work out

(a) *(calculate)* calculer; **can you work out how much it will cost?** est-ce que tu peux calculer combien ça va coûter?

(b) *(understand)* arriver à comprendre; **I can't work out why he did it** je n'arrive pas à comprendre pourquoi il a fait ça

(c) *(turn out)* **it worked out well for me** ça s'est bien passé pour moi; **it all worked out in the end** tout a fini par s'arranger

(d) *(exercise)* faire de l'exercice

worker *noun* *(in general)* le travailleur/la travailleuse; *(doing manual work)* un ouvrier/une ouvrière; **she's a good worker** elle travaille bien

working-class *adjective* ouvrier/ouvrière; **a working-class district** un quartier ouvrier

workman *noun* un ouvrier

workout *noun* la séance d'entraînement

workshop *noun* un atelier

world *noun* le monde; **he's the best footballer in the world** c'est le meilleur footballeur du monde; **I want to go round the world** je veux faire le tour du monde; **he's famous all over the world** il est connu partout dans le monde; **the world champion** le champion/la championne du monde; **a world record** un record du monde

worldwide

1 *adjective* mondial/mondiale; **it's a worldwide phenomenon** c'est un phénomène mondial

The masculine plural of *mondial* is *mondiaux*.

2 *adverb* dans le monde entier; **this product is sold worldwide** ce produit se vend dans le monde entier

worm *noun* le ver

worn *adjective* *(clothes, shoes)* usé/usée

worn-out *adjective*

(a) *(clothes, shoes)* complètement usé/usée

(b) *(battery)* usé/usée

(c) *(person)* épuisé/épuisée

worried *adjective* inquiet/inquiète; **I'm worried about you** je m'inquiète pour toi

worry

1 *noun* le souci; **she has money worries** elle a des soucis d'argent; **it's causing me a lot of worry** cela m'inquiète beaucoup

2 *verb*

(a) *(be anxious)* s'inquiéter; **she worries about her son** elle s'inquiète pour son fils; **there's nothing to worry about** il n'y a pas de quoi s'inquiéter; **don't worry!** ne t'inquiète pas!

(b) *(make anxious)* inquiéter; **the situation worries me** la situation m'inquiète

worrying *adjective* inquiétant/inquiétante

worse

1 *adjective*

(a) pire; **your problems are worse than ours** vos problèmes sont pires que les nôtres; **it could be worse** ça pourrait être pire; **there's nothing**

worse than arriving late il n'y a rien de pire que d'arriver en retard; **I'm bad at maths but she's even worse** je suis mauvais en maths mais elle est encore plus mauvaise que moi; **to get worse** empirer
(b) *(in health)* plus mal; **I feel even worse than yesterday** je me sens encore plus mal qu'hier
2 *adverb* plus mal; **you could do a lot worse** tu aurais pu tomber plus mal; **the team played worse than usual** l'équipe a joué plus mal que d'habitude

worst
1 *adjective*
(a) plus mauvais/mauvaise; **it's the worst book I've ever read** c'est le plus mauvais livre que j'aie jamais lu
(b) pire; **he's my worst enemy** c'est mon pire ennemi; **the worst thing about it was the heat** le pire c'était la chaleur
2 *noun*
(a) **the worst** le/la pire; **all the questions were difficult, but the last one was the worst** toutes les questions étaient difficiles, mais la dernière était la pire; **he's the worst in the class** c'est le plus mauvais de la classe
(b) **if the worst comes to the worst** au pire
3 *adverb* le plus mal; **out of all of us I played worst** c'est moi qui ai joué le plus mal de nous tous; **they are the worst paid** ce sont les plus mal payés

worth
1 *adjective*
(a) **to be worth** valoir; **how much is it worth?** ça vaut combien?
(b) **to be worth it** *(worth the trouble)* valoir la peine; **it's not worth it** ça n'en vaut pas la peine; **it's worth trying** ça vaut la peine d'essayer; **the film's worth seeing** le film vaut la peine d'être vu; **it's worth knowing** c'est bon à savoir
2 *noun (value)* la valeur; **I'd like £20 worth of petrol** je voudrais pour 20

livres d'essence; **I've got my money's worth** j'en ai eu pour mon argent

worthless *adjective* sans valeur

worthwhile *adjective* **it's worthwhile** ça vaut la peine *or* ça vaut le coup

would *auxiliary verb*
(a) *(conditional tense)* **I would stay** je resterais; **she would have done it** elle l'aurait fait; **I would help you if I could** je t'aiderais si je le pouvais
(b) *(in questions, requests)* vouloir; **would you like a drink?** est-ce que vous voulez boire quelque chose; **would you please be quiet!** voulez-vous vous taire, s'il vous plaît!
(c) *(expressing a desire)* **I would like to go** j'aimerais bien y aller; **I would rather go alone** je préférerais y aller seul
(d) *(in reported speech)* **she told me she would be there** elle m'a dit qu'elle serait là; **I said I would do it** j'ai dit que je le ferais
(e) *(in the past)* **she would come home exhausted** elle rentrait très fatiguée

When *would* is used in this way to describe something that used to happen regularly, the verb in French is in the imperfect.

(d) *(with objects)* **the car wouldn't start** la voiture ne démarrait pas; **the door wouldn't shut** la porte ne fermait pas

wound
1 *noun* la blessure
2 *verb* blesser; **he was badly wounded** il a été gravement blessé

wrap
1 *verb*
(a) *(a package, a present)* emballer; **he's wrapping his presents** il est en train d'emballer ses cadeaux
(b) *(a person)* envelopper; **the baby was wrapped in a blanket** le bébé était enveloppé dans une couverture

2 wrap up
(a) *(a package, a present)* emballer
(b) *(a person)* envelopper

wrapper *noun*
(a) *(packaging)* un emballage
(b) *(of a sweet)* le papier

wrapping *noun*
(a) *(packaging)* l'emballage *(masculine)*
(b) **wrapping paper** *(for a gift)* le papier cadeau

wreck
1 *noun (ship, car, person)* une épave;
I'm a nervous wreck je suis à bout
2 *verb*
(a) *(a car)* détruire; **the car was wrecked in the accident** la voiture a été détruite dans l'accident
(b) *(a ship)* **the ship was wrecked on these rocks** le bateau a fait naufrage sur ces rochers
(c) *(spoil)* gâcher; **you've wrecked my life!** tu as gâché ma vie!

wrestler *noun* le lutteur/la lutteuse

wrestling *noun* la lutte; *(freestyle)* le catch; **he does wrestling** il fait de la lutte *or* il fait du catch

wrinkle *noun (on the skin)* la ride; *(in fabric)* le faux pli

wrinkled *adjective (skin)* ridé/ridée; *(fabric, clothes)* froissé/froissée

wrist *noun* le poignet

write
1 *verb* écrire; **he's writing a letter** il écrit une lettre; **I wrote to my grandma** j'ai écrit à ma grand-mère
2 **write back** répondre; **please write back soon** réponds-moi vite, s'il te plaît
3 **write down** noter; **write the number down or you'll forget it** note le numéro, sinon tu vas l'oublier

writer *noun*
(a) *(of a book)* un écrivain; **I want to be a writer** je veux être écrivain
(b) *(of a letter, an article)* un auteur

> Note that the words *écrivain* and *auteur* are masculine but can refer to both men and women.

writing *noun* l'écriture *(feminine)*;
they learn reading and writing ils apprennent la lecture et l'écriture; **this is a good piece of writing** c'est bien écrit; **that's my writing** c'est mon écriture; **writing paper** le papier à lettres

wrong *adjective*
(a) *(incorrect)* **you've put them in the wrong order** tu ne les as pas mis dans le bon ordre; **that's the wrong answer** ce n'est pas la bonne réponse; **you've got the wrong number** vous vous êtes trompé de numéro; **my watch is wrong** ma montre n'est pas à l'heure; **to be wrong** *(of a person)* avoir tort; **you're wrong!** tu as tort!
(b) *(what should not be done)* mal; **it's wrong to tell lies** c'est mal de mentir
(c) *(not as it should be)* **something's wrong** quelque chose ne va pas; **something's wrong with her arm** elle a quelque chose au bras; **what's wrong with you?** qu'est-ce que tu as?
2 *adverb*
(a) *(incorrectly)* mal; **you've spelt my name wrong** vous avez mal écrit mon nom; **you've added it up wrong** vous avez mal calculé
(b) **to go wrong** *(of a plan)* mal tourner; *(of a machine)* tomber en panne
3 *noun* le mal; **he's old enough to know right from wrong** il est assez grand pour faire la différence entre le bien et le mal

wrongly *adverb*
(a) *(incorrectly)* mal; **this word is spelt wrongly** ce mot est mal écrit
(b) *(unfairly)* à tort; **I've been wrongly accused** on m'a accusé à tort

X-ray

1 *noun* la radio; **to have an X-ray** passer une radio
2 *verb* radiographer *or* faire une radio de; **they X-rayed her lungs** ils lui ont fait une radio des poumons

xylophone *noun* le xylophone; **he plays the xylophone** il joue du xylophone

Note that when talking about playing musical instruments, French uses the expression *jouer de*.

yacht *noun* le yacht

yard *noun*
(**a**) *(of a farm, a house)* la cour
(**b**) *(unit of measurement)* un mètre

> Note that in France people don't use yards as a unit of measurement, they use metres (a yard is very nearly equal to a metre).

yawn *verb* bâiller

year *noun*
(**a**) un an; **I'm twelve years old** j'ai douze ans; **I met him a year ago** je l'ai rencontré il y a un an; **twice a year** deux fois par an; **I lived in France for three years** j'ai vécu en France pendant trois ans
(**b**) *(the whole year)* une année; **I live here all year** j'habite ici toute l'année; **this year** cette année; **last year** l'année dernière; **next year** l'année prochaine; **happy New Year!** bonne année!
(**c**) *(at school)* une année; **I'm in the first year** je suis en première année

> *Année* is used with adjectives (eg *une bonne année*) and when duration is implied (eg *toute l'année*). *An* is mainly used to indicate a date or the age of a person.

yell *verb* hurler; **the teacher yelled at me** le prof m'a hurlé dessus

yellow *adjective* jaune

yes *adverb*
(**a**) oui; **he said yes** il a dit oui; **yes, please** oui, s'il vous plaît
(**b**) si; **he's not here – yes, he is!** il n'est pas là – mais si!; **don't you like coffee? – yes, I do!** tu n'aimes pas le café? – si!

> *Si* is used instead of *oui* when you answer a negative question or contradict a statement, as in these examples.

yesterday *adverb* hier; **the day before yesterday** avant-hier

yet *adverb*
(**a**) encore; **I haven't finished yet** je n'ai pas encore fini; **he's late yet again** il est en retard, encore une fois
(**b**) *(in questions)* déjà; **has he arrived yet?** est-ce qu'il est déjà arrivé?
(**c**) *(at the moment)* tout de suite; **we're not going just yet** nous ne partons pas tout de suite

yoga *noun* le yoga; **she does yoga** elle fait du yoga

yoghurt *noun* le yaourt

yolk *noun* le jaune d'œuf

you *pronoun*
(**a**) *(when "you" is the subject of the verb)* tu, *(formal or plural)* vous; **you should go and tidy your room** tu devrais aller ranger ta chambre; **would you like a drink?** voulez-vous boire quelque chose?; **did you all do your homework?** est-ce que vous avez tous fait vos devoirs?

> *Tu* (and *te* or *toi*) is used when speaking to one person you know well (a friend, a relative etc), or to somebody your own age or younger. When speaking to somebody you don't know very well or to somebody to whom you want to show more

respect (a teacher, a boss etc), you should use the polite form *vous* instead of *tu*. *Vous* is also used when speaking to more than one person, whether or not you know them well.

(**b**) *(when "you" is the object of the verb)* te, *(formal or plural)* vous; **I hate you** je te/vous déteste; **I'll give you the book tomorrow** je te/vous donnerai le livre demain; **can I ask you something?** est-ce que je peux te/vous demander quelque chose?

> Note that *te* becomes *t'* before a vowel or mute h.

(**c**) *(after a preposition or the verb "to be")* toi, *(formal or plural)* vous; **I did it for you** je l'ai fait pour toi/vous; **I often think of you** je pense souvent à toi/vous; **it's you** c'est toi/vous
(**d**) *(impersonal use)* on; **you never know** on ne sait jamais

young *adjective*
(**a**) jeune; **young people** les jeunes; **she's younger than me** elle est plus jeune que moi; **she's two years younger than me** elle a deux ans de moins que moi
(**b**) **my younger brother** mon petit frère; **my younger sister** ma petite sœur; **my youngest brother** le plus jeune de mes frères

your *adjective*
(**a**) *(when the thing possessed is masculine singular in French)* ton, *(formal or plural)* votre; **this is your pen** c'est ton/votre stylo
(**b**) *(when the thing possessed is feminine singular in French)* ta, *(formal or plural)* votre; **this is your cup** c'est ta/votre tasse; **your school** ton/votre école; **your story** ton/votre histoire

> Note that *ta* becomes *ton* before a vowel or mute h.

(**c**) *(when the thing possessed is plural in French)* tes, *(formal or plural)* vos; **these are your books** ce sont tes/vos crayons; **these are your glasses** ce

sont tes/vos lunettes
(**d**) *(when used with parts of the body)* **Elaine, you should wash your hands** Elaine, tu devrais te laver les mains; **you should all go and wash your hands** vous devriez tous aller vous laver les mains

> The form used in French is determined by the gender and number of the noun it stands for.

yours *pronoun*
(**a**) *(when the thing possessed is masculine singular in French)* le tien, *(formal or plural)* le vôtre; **it's not my pen, it's yours** ce n'est pas mon crayon, c'est le tien/le vôtre; **this pen is yours** ce crayon est à toi/à vous
(**b**) *(when the thing possessed is feminine singular in French)* la tienne, *(formal or plural)* la vôtre; **it's not my cup, it's yours** ce n'est pas ma tasse, c'est la tienne/la vôtre; **this cup is yours** cette tasse est à toi/à vous
(**c**) *(when the thing possessed is masculine plural in French)* les tiens, *(formal or plural)* les vôtres; **these are not my books, they're yours** ce ne sont pas mes livres, ce sont les tiens/les vôtres; **these books are yours** ces livres sont à toi/à vous
(**d**) *(when the thing possessed is feminine plural in French)* les tiennes, *(formal or plural)* les vôtres; **these are not my glasses, they're yours** ce ne sont . pas mes lunettes, ce sont les tiennes/ les vôtres; **these glasses are yours** ces lunettes sont à vous

> The form used in French is determined by the gender and number of the noun it stands for.

yourself *pronoun*
(**a**) toi-même, *(formal)* vous-même; **do it yourself** fais-le toi-même/faites-le vous-même
(**b**) *(with a reflexive verb)* te, *(formal)* vous; **you cut yourself** tu t'es coupé/vous vous êtes coupé; **are you enjoying yourself?** est-ce que tu t'amuses

bien/est-ce que vous vous amusez bien?

Note that _te_ becomes _t'_ before a vowel or mute h.

(**c**) _(after a preposition)_ toi, _(formal)_ vous; **keep it for yourself** garde-le pour toi/gardez-le pour vous

yourselves _pronoun_
(**a**) vous-mêmes; **do it yourselves** faites-le vous-mêmes
(**b**) _(with a reflexive verb)_ vous; **did you hurt yourselves?** est-ce que vous vous êtes blessés?; **are you enjoying yourselves?** est-ce que vous vous

amusez bien?
(**c**) _(after a preposition)_ vous; **keep it for yourselves** gardez-le pour vous

youth _noun_
(**a**) _(period)_ la jeunesse; **in my youth** dans ma jeunesse
(**b**) _(young man)_ un adolescent
(**c**) **a youth hostel** une auberge de jeunesse; **a youth worker** un éducateur/une éducatrice

yo-yo _noun_ le yo-yo®

The French word _yo-yo®_ does not change in the plural.

Zz

zebra *noun*
  (**a**) le zèbre
  (**b**) **a zebra crossing** un passage pour piétons

zero *number* zéro

zip
  1 *noun* *(fastener)* la fermeture éclair®

  2 *verb* **zip up** can you zip up my dress? est-ce que tu peux remonter la fermeture éclair de ma robe?; **zip your jacket up!** ferme ta veste!

zone *noun* la zone

zoo *noun* le zoo

Other School titles from Chambers

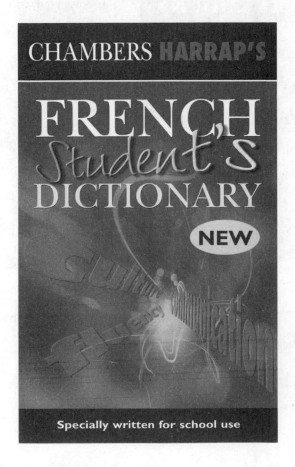

French Student's Dictionary
ISBN: 0550 10183 7
Hardback
832pp
Price: £8.99

Chambers School Dictionary
ISBN: 0550 10073 3
Hardback
704pp
Price: £7.99

Chambers School Thesaurus
ISBN: 0550 10074 1
Hardback
656pp
Price: £7.99